D0066598

The Law and Policy of the World Trade Organization

As the leading student text in the field, this title provides both a detailed examination of the law of the World Trade Organization and a clear introduction to the basic principles and underlying logic of the world trading system. It explores the institutional aspects of the WTO together with the substantive law. New to this edition are examinations of the WTO rules on the protection of intellectual property rights and the rules on technical barriers to trade and sanitary and phytosanitary measures. Assignments are integrated throughout to allow students to assess their understanding, while chapter summaries reinforce learning. In addition, exercises have been included to draw on primary sources and real-life trade scenarios, enabling students to hone their practical and analytical skills. The title is an essential tool for any student of the WTO, either at undergraduate or at postgraduate level. Practising lawyers and policy-makers who are looking for an introduction to WTO law will also find this title invaluable.

PETER VAN DEN BOSSCHE is Professor of International Economic Law, Head of the Department of International and European Law and Academic Director of the Institute for Globalisation and International Regulation at Maastricht University, the Netherlands. He studied law at the University of Antwerp (Lic. jur.), the University of Michigan (LLM) and the European University Institute, Florence (Dr jur.). From 1997 to 2001, Peter Van den Bossche was Counsellor to the Appellate Body of the WTO, Geneva. In 2001 he served as Acting Director of the Appellate Body Secretariat.

The Law and Policy of the World Trade Organization

Text, Cases and Materials

Second Edition

Peter Van den Bossche

Maastricht University

CAMBRIDGE
UNIVERSITY PRESS

CAMBRIDGE UNIVERSITY PRESS

Cambridge, New York, Melbourne, Madrid, Cape Town, Singapore, São Paulo, Delhi

Cambridge University Press
The Edinburgh Building, Cambridge CB2 8RU, UK

Published in the United States of America by Cambridge University Press, New York

www.cambridge.org
Information on this title: www.cambridge.org/9780521727594

© Peter Van den Bossche 2008

This publication is in copyright. Subject to statutory exception
and to the provisions of relevant collective licensing agreements,
no reproduction of any part may take place without
the written permission of Cambridge University Press.

First published 2008

Printed in the United Kingdom at the University Press, Cambridge

A catalogue record for this publication is available from the British Library

Library of Congress Cataloguing in Publication data

ISBN 978-0-521-89890-4 hardback
ISBN 978-0-521-72759-4 paperback

Cambridge University Press has no responsibility for
the persistence or accuracy of URLs for external or
third-party internet websites referred to in this book,
and does not guarantee that any content on such
websites is, or will remain, accurate or appropriate.

Contents

Figures

Preface to the first edition

S ince the entry into force of the *WTO Agreement* in January 1995, international trade law has developed from a technical backwater of international law to one of its most vibrant fields. Before 1995, international trade law was taught at few universities and was only of interest to a relatively small group of legal practitioners. Over the past decade, however, interest in this field of international law has increased dramatically. Students, academics, legal practitioners, advisers of businesses and NGOs, and officials of national governments and international organisations have woken up to its importance. Now, most universities give much attention to trade law in international law courses or offer specialised courses on WTO law.

Concrete plans for this book were first made on the eve of my departure from the WTO and return to academia at the end of 2001. For five years, I had the privilege to serve, during the seminal early days of the WTO and its law, as a senior legal advisor to the Appellate Body of the WTO.

This book is primarily a textbook for graduate and senior undergraduate students of law. However, it was also written with practising lawyers and policy-makers, looking for an introduction to WTO law, in mind. The book covers both the institutional and the substantive law of the WTO. Chapter 1 is an introduction on whether economic globalisation and international trade are a bane or a blessing, on the need for WTO law, and on the main principles and sources of this law. Chapter 2 discusses the WTO as the prime intergovernmental organisation for international trade, and deals with its origins, objectives, functions, membership, institutional structure and decision-making procedures. Chapter 3 concerns the WTO's all-important and unique dispute settlement system and explores the origins, principles, institutions and proceedings of WTO dispute settlement. Chapter 4 discusses the fundamental WTO principles of non-discrimination, the most-favoured-nation treatment obligation and the national treatment obligation as they apply to trade in goods and trade in services. Chapter 5 deals with market access for goods, services and service suppliers and discusses, *inter alia*, the WTO rules on tariff and non-tariff barriers to trade in goods and barriers to trade in services. Chapter 6 concerns the WTO rules on unfair trade and, in particular, the rules on dumping and subsidised trade. Chapter 7 deals with the inevitable conflict between trade liberalisation and other societal values and interests. It discusses the many situations in which WTO law allows Members to deviate from the basic rules and let other societal values and interests prevail over trade liberalisation. The concluding chapter 8 briefly sets out two major challenges for the future of the WTO, namely, the integration of developing countries in the multilateral trading system and the further expansion of the scope of WTO law. While the treatment of the law is often quite detailed, the prime aim of this textbook is to make clear the basic principles and underlying logic of WTO law and the world trading system.

Special attention was given to the focus, approach and structure of this book. Each section contains questions and assignments, to allow students to assess their understanding and to develop useful practical skills. At the end of each chapter, there is a helpful summary as well as an exercise on specific true-to-life international trade problems encountered by the Kingdom of Richland, a developed-country Member, and the Republic of Newland, a developing-country Member. These exercises are ideally intended to be dealt with in tutorials, but are equally suitable for individual study. While challenging, these exercises can be done on the basis of the knowledge acquired in the chapter they conclude. It was a deliberate choice to refer sparingly to the vast academic literature on many of the topics addressed in this book. The focus is clearly on the provisions of the WTO agreements themselves, the case law of panels and the Appellate Body and official policy documents. For advanced courses on WTO law, this book can be usefully supplemented by academic articles from the *Journal of International Economic Law*, the *Journal of World Trade*, the *World Trade Review* and other specialised or general law journals. The reader can find suggestions on recent academic articles and case law, organised according to the chapters of this book, at www.egeg.org.

In writing this book I owe much to many. I am particularly indebted to Gabrielle Marceau and Denise Prévost who supported and encouraged me from the beginning and commented on all chapters. I am similarly indebted to Edwin Vermulst and Folkert Graafsma who also read through the whole manuscript and made many useful comments, and to Julie Soloway, who made a very important contribution to the section on dumping and anti-dumping measures. I am grateful to Marco Bronckers, Stephanie Cartier, Bill Davey, Piet Eeckhout, Barbara Eggers, Lothar Ehring, Mary Footer, Susan Hainsworth, Valerie Hughes, Pieter-Jan Kuijper, Bernard Kuiten, Hoe Lim, Jim Mathis, Marielle Matthee, Elisabetta Montaguti, Joost Pauwelyn, Roberto Rios Herrera, Jochem Wiers, Jan Wouters and Werner Zdouc, who all read, and commented on, specific chapters, or contributed otherwise to this book. I would like to pay tribute to John Jackson, my first mentor and guide in the land of international trade. I would also like to acknowledge my profound and lasting debt towards the Members of the original Appellate Body, and, in particular, James Bacchus, Claus-Dieter Ehlermann, Florentino Feliciano and Julio Lacarte, whom I had the privilege to serve for five years and from whom I learned so much. I address a special word of thanks to Debra Steger, the first director of the Appellate Body Secretariat and 'sister-in-arms' during the fascinating but very demanding first years of the Appellate Body. I am grateful to Finola O'Sullivan, publisher at Cambridge University Press, and her staff, Jane O'Regan, Mary Leighton, Martin Gleeson, Eva Huehne and Jennie Rubio, for their confidence and excellent support. I am equally grateful to the Faculty of Law of Maastricht University, for facilitating the work on this book. My special thanks to Paul Adriaans, Sophie Janssen and Roger Snijder. Finally, this book would never have been finished without the untiring help and capable assistance of, in particular, Adeshola Odusanya, Katalin Fritz and Carol Ní Ghiollarnáth, my research assistants, and also Iveta Alexovičová, Natalya Bayurova, Kasper Hermans, Stelios Katevatis, Sergey Ripinsky, Eva Schöfer, Nikolaos Skoutaris, Damian Smith and Ruta Zarnauskaite, all graduate or undergraduate students at Maastricht University in the period 2002–4. Of course, none of those mentioned above bears any responsibility for any error or omission in this book. In recognition of the support I received from so many colleagues and students in the writing of this book, all royalties go to Maastricht University to set up a scholarship and research fund for students and scholars from developing countries.

Peter Van den Bossche
Maastricht, September 2004

Preface to the second edition

In the three years that have passed since I completed work on the first edition of this book, the interest in the world trading system has continued to grow. Ever more universities offer courses on international economic law in general and WTO law in particular. While unsubstantiated and misinformed criticism of the WTO is still the rave and *bon ton* in many circles, the WTO seems to be doing a better job at selling itself and slowly enlarging its base of support. This is all the more amazing since opposition to economic globalisation is not weakening and the Doha Development Round has thus far mainly produced disappointment. Perhaps there is a growing realisation, or in some circles reluctant acceptance, that the WTO and its law – while obviously wanting in many respects – make an effective contribution to managing economic globalisation and international trade. The WTO, and in particular its dispute settlement system applying and interpreting WTO law, have done a good job in balancing trade liberalisation with other societal values and interests, such as the protection of public health, the environment and economic development of developing countries. However, undoubtedly, the road is still long and the journey hazardous.

Braced by encouragement and inspired by comments of readers from Lesotho to India, many of them students but also many government officials and legal practitioners, I started in early 2007 on the second edition of *The Law and Policy of the World Trade Organization*. This second edition not only updates and revises the 2005 edition, it also considerably expands the text by including a new chapter, entitled 'Towards harmonisation of national regulation', discussing in some detail the rules of the *TRIPS Agreement* on the protection of intellectual property rights, the *TBT Agreement* on technical barriers to trade, and the *SPS Agreement* on sanitary and phytosanitary measures.

The writing of this second edition has been a much larger task than I had initially envisaged. Fortunately, as with the first edition, I had much help. To many of those I thanked in the Preface of the first edition, I owe once again my thanks for their support and advice. I appreciate the continued support of Gabrielle Marceau. Chapter 6 has greatly benefited from the comments of Edwin Vermulst and Katalin Fritz. The section on the *TRIPS Agreement* of chapter 8 owes much to the comments of Anselm Kamperman Sanders. I am particularly indebted to Denise Prévost, my senior research associate at Maastricht University. Without her commitment, knowledge of WTO law and eye for detail this second edition would not have been. She is the principal author of large parts of the new chapter 8. I am also indebted to Marieke van Overveld, a former Maastricht student and graduate of the World Trade Institute, who diligently and with great stamina selected and prepared materials for the second edition. My heartfelt thanks go Iveta Alexovičová, Nina Buttgen, Anke Dahrendorf, Ana Maria Daza Vargas, Lennard Duijvestijn, Vydyanathan Lakshmanan, Elissavet Malathouni, Angeliki Mavridou, Bas Megens, Lorin van Nuland, Gustavo Ferreira Ribeiro, Mark Seitter and Wen Shuying, my researchers and research assistants, at Maastricht University and elsewhere, whose untiring help and capable assistance made work on this second edition definitely lighter. Of course, none of those mentioned above bear any responsibility for any error or omission in this book. I am grateful to Finola O'Sullivan, Editorial Director, Law, at Cambridge University Press and her staff, in particular Sinéad Moloney, Richard Woodham and Diane Ilott, for their continued confidence and unfailing support. I am equally grateful to the Faculty of Law of Maastricht University for facilitating the work on the second edition of this book. My special thanks go to Marijn Blok, my secretary at the Maastricht Faculty of Law. With the royalties from the first edition of this book, the Maastricht University Fund for Education and Research in International Economic Law (MUFERIEL) was established. This Fund, which is now managed by the Institute for Globalisation and International Regulation at Maastricht University (www.igir.org), has been used to give financial assistance to students and scholars from developing countries. I intend to use the royalties of the second edition for the same purpose. Finally, I would like to dedicate this second edition to Patricia Murillo Montesdeoca, my wife, for her patience and unwavering support.

Peter Van den Bossche
Maastricht, December 2007

Table of cases

Decisions by the Arbitrators (Article 22.6 of the DSU)

Awards of the Arbitrators (Article 25 of the DSU)

Table of Agreements

1

Economic globalisation and the law of the WTO

Contents

1.1. INTRODUCTION

At the largest-ever gathering of Heads of State and Government, the Millennium Summit of the United Nations in September 2000, the UN General Assembly solemnly declared:

> We will spare no effort to free our fellow men, women, and children from the abject and dehumanizing conditions of extreme poverty, to which more than a billion of them are

currently subjected. We are committed to making the right to development a reality for everyone and to freeing the entire human race from want.[1]

It was decided to *halve* the proportion of the world's people living in extreme poverty by the year 2015.[2] While data of the World Bank show that the number of people living in extreme poverty[3] is declining, the enormity of the task ahead is obvious to all. According to the latest data available, 985 million people still live in extreme poverty.[4] Moreover, the income gap between the richest 20 per cent of the world's population and the poorest 20 per cent does not cease to grow. During the 1990s, this gap increased from 60:1 to 86:1.[5] In discussing the greatest challenges that the world faces, Jimmy Carter, the former US President, stated in his Nobel Peace Prize Lecture in December 2002:

> Among all the possible choices, I decided that the most serious and universal problem is the growing chasm between the richest and poorest people on earth. The results of this disparity are root causes of most of the world's unresolved problems, including starvation, illiteracy, environmental degradation, violent conflict, and unnecessary illnesses that range from guinea worm to HIV/Aids.[6]

Another Nobel Peace Prize winner, Muhammad Yunus, founder of the Garmeen Bank for the Poor, stated in his Nobel Lecture in December 2006:

> World's income distribution gives a very telling story. Ninety-four percent of the world income goes to 40 percent of the population while sixty percent of people live on only 6 percent of world income. Half of the world population lives on two dollars a day. Over one billion people live on less than a dollar a day. This is no formula for peace . . . Poverty is the absence of all human rights. The frustrations, hostility and anger generated by abject poverty cannot sustain peace in any society. For building stable peace we must find ways to provide opportunities for people to live decent lives.[7]

One of the defining features of today's world is the process of economic globalisation, a process characterised by high levels of international trade and foreign direct investment. This chapter examines this process and notes the broad consensus among economists and policy-makers that economic globalisation in general, and international trade and foreign direct investment in particular, offers an unprecedented *opportunity* to significantly reduce poverty worldwide.[8]

---

[1] United Nations General Assembly, *UN Millennium Declaration*, Resolution adopted on 8 September 2000, para. 11.   [2] *Ibid.*, para. 19.   [3] Extreme poverty is defined as living on less than $1 a day.

[4] Note that the number of people living in extreme poverty in developing countries fell by 260 million in the period 1990–2004. This is in large part due to massive poverty reduction in China. See World Bank, *World Development Indicators 2007*, www.worldbank.org/data/wdi2007/index.htm, visited on 30 October 2007. In contrast, the number of people in absolute poverty continued to increase in Sub-Saharan Africa, rising by almost 60 million.

[5] Note that the income gap between the richest 20 per cent of the world's population and the poorest 20 per cent stood at around 3:1 in 1820, 11:1 in 1913 and 30:1 in 1970. See http://hdr.undp.org/reports/global/1999/en, visited on 1 January 2004.

[6] President Jimmy Carter, Nobel Lecture, Oslo, 10 December 2002, available at http://nobelprize.org/nobel_prizes/peace/laureates/2002/carter-lecture.html, visited on 7 November 2007.

[7] Muhammad Yunus, Nobel Lecture, Oslo, 10 December 2006, available at http://nobelprize.org/nobel_prizes/peace/laureates/2006/yunus-lecture-en.html, visited on 7 November 2007.

[8] The World Bank, for instance, estimated that abolishing all trade barriers could increase global income by US$2.8 trillion and lift 320 million people out of poverty by 2015. See M. Bacchetta and M. Jansen, *Adjusting to Trade Liberalization: The Role of Policy, Institutions and WTO Disciplines*, Special Studies Series (WTO, 2003), 6.

However, to ensure that this opportunity is realised, economic globalisation has to be *managed* and *regulated* at the international level. If not, economic globalisation is likely to be a curse, rather than a blessing, to humankind, aggravating economic inequality, social injustice, environmental degradation and cultural dispossession. The law of the World Trade Organization is currently the most ambitious effort to manage and regulate international trade. By way of introduction to this book, this chapter discusses the need for international rules on international trade, and gives an overview of the basic rules and disciplines of WTO law. It also discusses the different sources of WTO law and examines the sometimes contentious relationship between WTO law and other international law as well as between WTO law and national law.

1.2. ECONOMIC GLOBALISATION AND INTERNATIONAL TRADE

1.2.1. The emergence of the global economy

1.2.1.1. The concept of 'economic globalisation'

'Economic globalisation' has been a popular buzzword for more than a decade now. Politicians, government officials, businesspeople, trade unionists, environmentalists, church leaders, public health experts, third-world activists, economists and lawyers all speak of 'economic globalisation'. The concepts of 'globalisation', and, in particular, 'economic globalisation' have been used by many to describe one of the defining features of the post-Cold War world in which we live. But what do these terms mean?

Joseph Stiglitz, former Chief Economist of the World Bank and winner of the Nobel Prize for Economics in 2001, described the concept of globalisation, in his 2002 book, *Globalization and Its Discontents*, as:

> the closer integration of the countries and peoples of the world which has been brought about by the enormous reduction of costs of transportation and communication, and the breaking down of artificial barriers to the flow of goods, services, capital, knowledge, and (to a lesser extent) people across borders.[9]

In *The Lexus and the Olive Tree: Understanding Globalisation*, Thomas Friedman, the award-winning journalist of the *New York Times*, defined 'globalisation' as follows:

> it is the inexorable integration of markets, nation-states and technologies to a degree never witnessed before – in a way that is enabling individuals, corporations and nation-states to reach around the world farther, faster, deeper and cheaper than ever before, and in a way that is enabling the world to reach into individuals, corporations and nation-states farther, faster, deeper and cheaper than ever before.[10]

[9] J. Stiglitz, *Globalization and Its Discontents* (Penguin, 2002), 9.
[10] T. Friedman, *The Lexus and the Olive Tree: Understanding Globalisation*, 2nd edition (First Anchor Books, 2000), 9.

Economic globalisation is a multifaceted phenomenon which undoubtedly is not yet fully understood. In essence, however, economic globalisation is the gradual integration of national economies into one borderless global economy. It encompasses both (free) international trade and (unrestricted) foreign direct investment. Economic globalisation affects people everywhere and in many aspects of their daily lives. It affects their jobs, their food, their health, their education and their leisure time.

While economic globalisation is often presented as a new phenomenon, it deserves to be mentioned that today's global economic integration is not unprecedented. During the fifty years before the First World War, there were also large cross-border flows of goods and capital and, more than now, of people. In that period, globalisation was driven by the lowering of trade barriers and by significant reductions in transport costs resulting from technological innovations such as railways and steamships. If one looks at the ratio of trade to output, Britain and France are only slightly more open to trade today than they were in 1913, while Japan is less open now than it was then.[11] However, that earlier attempt at globalisation ended with the First World War and was followed by one of the darkest periods in the history of humankind.

While the *trend* towards globalisation is clear, the extent of today's global economic integration can be, and frequently is, exaggerated. International trade should normally force high-cost domestic producers to lower their prices and bring the prices of products and services between different countries closer together. However, large divergences in prices persist. Even within the European Union, price differences from one country to another remain significant for a number of products and services. This is partly due to differences in transport costs, taxes and the efficiency of distribution networks. But it is also due, at least outside the European Union, to the continued existence of important barriers to trade. Further, while goods, services and capital move across borders with greater ease, restrictions on the free movement of workers, i.e. restrictions on economic migration, remain multiple and rigorous.

Questions and Assignments 1.1

How would you define 'economic globalisation'? Does economic globalisation also affect non-economic matters? Give three concrete examples of how *you* are affected by economic globalisation. Is economic globalisation a historically unique and all-pervasive phenomenon?

1.2.1.2. *Forces driving economic globalisation*

It is commonly argued that economic globalisation has been driven by two main forces. The first, *technology*, makes globalisation feasible; the second, the

---

[11] 'One World?', *The Economist*, 18 October 1997.

liberalisation of trade and foreign direct investment, makes it happen.[12] Due to technological innovations resulting in a dramatic fall in transport, communication and computing costs, the natural barriers of time and space that separate national markets have been coming down. Between 1920 and 1990, average ocean freight and port charges for US import and export cargo fell by almost 70 per cent. Between 1930 and 1990, average air-transport fares per passenger mile fell by 84 per cent.[13] The cost of a three-minute telephone call between New York and London has fallen from US$300 in 1930 to US$1 in 1997 (in 1996 dollars); the cost of computer processing power has been falling by an average of 30 per cent per year in real terms over recent decades.[14] As noted by Thomas Friedman in his 2005 book, *The World is Flat – A Brief History of the Globalised World in the Twenty-first Century*:

> Clearly, it is now possible for more people than ever to collaborate and compete in real time with more other people on more different kinds of work from more different corners of the planet and on more equal footing than at any previous time in the history of the world – using computers, e-mail, networks, teleconferencing, and dynamic new software.[15]

As a result of cheap and efficient communication, companies can locate different parts of their production process in different parts of the world while remaining in close contact. Activities such as writing software or accounting can be carried out anywhere in the world, far away from the customer or consumer. New technological developments are likely to further accelerate the process of economic globalisation.

The second driving force of economic globalisation has been the liberalisation of international trade and foreign direct investment. Over the last fifty years, most developed countries have gradually but significantly lowered barriers to foreign trade and allowed free movement of capital. In recent years, the liberalisation of trade and investment has become a worldwide trend, including in developing countries, although liberalisation still proceeds at different speeds in different parts of the world.

In his book, *Has Globalization Gone Too Far?*, Dani Rodrik, of the John F. Kennedy School of Government at Harvard University, highlighted an arguably less positive dimension of globalisation:

> Globalization is not occurring in a vacuum. It is part of a broader trend that we may call marketization. Receding government, deregulation, and the shrinking of social obligations are the domestic counterparts of the intertwining of national economies. Globalization could not have advanced this far without these complementary forces.[16]

While some politicians and opinion-makers claim otherwise, the process of economic globalisation is not irreversible. Lionel Barber, US Managing Editor of the *Financial Times*, noted in 2004:

---

[12] See also M. Wolf, 'Global Opportunities', *Financial Times*, 6 May 1997.
[13] R. Porter, 'The Global Trading System in the 21st Century', in R. Porter, P. Sauvé A, Subramanian and A. Beviglia Zampetti (eds.), *Efficiency, Equity and Legitimacy: The Multilateral Trading System at the Millennium* (Brookings Institution Press, 2001), 4.   [14] 'One World?', *The Economist*, 18 October 1997.
[15] T. Friedman, *The World is Flat – A Brief History of the Globalised World in the Twenty-first Century* (Farrar, Straus & Giroux, 2005), 8.
[16] D. Rodrik, *Has Globalization Gone Too Far?* (Institute for International Economics, 1997), 85.

> For all its merits, globalization must never be taken for granted. The continued integration of the world economy depends on support not only from rich beneficiaries in the west but increasingly from the still disadvantaged in Africa, India, and Latin America. Cultural barriers also pose increasingly powerful obstacles to globalization. The rise of Islamic fundamentalism offers an alternative vision of society, one which will appeal to all those left behind in countries with exploding populations and persistent high unemployment among young people.[17]

However, it would be very difficult, and foolhardy, for governments to reverse the current globalisation process. Three reasons come to mind. First, new technology has created distribution channels especially for services, such as satellite communications and the Internet, that governments with protectionist intentions will find very difficult to control. Secondly, liberal international trade policies now have a firm institutional basis in the multilateral trading system of the WTO, discussed in detail in this book. Thirdly, the price to be paid in terms of economic prosperity for withdrawing from the global economy would be very high. Autarkies, such as North Korea, do not flourish in today's world.

Questions and Assignments 1.2

What explains the process of economic globalisation? Could governments reverse the process of economic globalisation? Should they?

1.2.1.3. Facts and figures on world trade and investment

In 1948, world exports of goods amounted to US$58 billion per year. By 2006, world exports of goods had increased to US$11,783 billion, or almost US$12 trillion, per year.[18] World exports of commercial services, marginal in 1948, amounted in 2006 to US$2,755 billion.[19]

The ratio of global trade in goods and commercial services to world gross domestic product (GDP) is a reliable measurement of economic globalisation. In 1950, exports of goods and commercial services represented 8 per cent of GDP; in 2000, these exports represented 24.6 per cent of GDP.[20]

It is not only the volume and value of world trade in goods and the ratio of global trade to GDP that have changed significantly over the last fifty years. The share of world trade of various regions of the world also changed over this period. Most remarkable are the decline of the share of North America (the United States, Canada and Mexico) from 28.1 per cent in 1948 to 14.2 per cent in 2006, and the increase of the share of Western Europe (primarily the European

---

[17] L. Barber, 'A Symposium of Views: Is Continued Globalisation of the World Economy Inevitable?' *The International Economy*, Summer 2004, 70.
[18] See WTO, *International Trade Statistics 2007*, available at www.wto.org/english/res_e/statis_e/its2007_e/section1_e/i06.xls, visited on 30 November 2007.
[19] See WTO, *International Trade Statistics 2007*, available at www.wto.org/english/res_e/statis_e/its2007_e/section3_e/iii01.xls, visited on 30 November 2007.
[20] See World Bank, *World Data Profile*, available at http://devdata.worldbank.org/external/CPProfile.asp?PTYPE=CP&CCODE=WLD, visited on 1 December 2007.

Union) from 35.1 per cent in 1948 to 42.1 per cent in 2006 (down from 45.9 per cent in 2003).[21] Equally remarkable are the steep decline of the shares of both Latin America (down from 11.3 per cent to 3.6 per cent) and Africa (down from 7.3 per cent to 3.1 per cent), and the significant increase of Asia's share (up from 14 per cent to 27.8 per cent).[22] The share of developing countries, as a group, in world trade has increased over the last fifteen years. However, it must be noted that all fifty least-developed countries together still account for only 0.5 per cent of world trade. Their share has actually fallen over time – it stood at 1.7 per cent in 1970.

Developing countries have registered particularly rapid increases in their ratios of exports to GDP. Exports now account for more than one-quarter of their combined GDP, a proportion which is higher than that of many developed countries.[23] Also, the composition of exports from developing countries has changed in recent years. While many developing countries remain dependent on their exports of primary commodities, the share of manufactured goods has been growing. Since the early 1990s, there has been a boom in high-technology exports, with countries such as China, India and Mexico emerging as major suppliers of cutting-edge technologies, as well as labour-intensive goods.[24]

With respect to trade between developing countries, Supachai Panitchpakdi, the then WTO Director-General and current Secretary-General of UNCTAD, noted:

> Enhanced South–South activity offers a potentially great source of expanded trade opportunities in the coming decade. Between 1990 and 2001, South–South trade grew faster than world trade with the share of intra-developing country trade in world merchandise exports rising from 6.5% to 10.6%.[25]

Next to international trade, an important aspect of economic globalisation is foreign direct investment (FDI). FDI inflows have increased from US$59 billion in 1982 to US$1,306 billion in 2006.[26] Worldwide employment of personnel in foreign affiliates increased from 21.5 million in 1982 to 72.6 million in 2006.[27]

The *World Investment Report 2007* underlined the growing importance of FDI in developing countries. In 2006, FDI inflows attained their highest level ever for developing countries and transition economies, accounting for US$379 billion, representing an increase of 55.9 per cent as compared to 2001, when FDI inflows accounted for US$212 billion.[28] The UNCTAD data also show, however, that foreign investment remains very unequally distributed. In 2006, developed

---

[21] See WTO, *International Trade Statistics 2007*, available at. www.wto.org/english/res_e/statis_e/its2007_e/section1_e/i06.xls, visited on 30 November 2007.   [22] *Ibid.*

[23] Oxfam, *Rigged Rules and Double Standards: Trade, Globalization and the Fight Against Poverty*, 2002, Summary of chapter 1, available at www.maketradefair.org, visited on 11 August 2003.   [24] *Ibid.*

[25] Supachai Panitchpakdi, 'The Doha Development Agenda: What's at Stake for Business in the Developing World?', *International Trade Forum*, August 2003, available at www.tradeforum.org/news/fullstory.php/aid/557/The_Doha_Development_Agenda:_What%92s_at_Stake_for_Business_in_the_Developing_World_.html, visited on 15 May 2004.

[26] See UNCTAD Secretariat, *World Investment Report 2007: Transnational Corporations, Extractive Industries and Development, An Overview*, available at www.unctad.org/en/docs/wir2007overview_en.pdf, visited on 30 November 2007, 9.   [27] *Ibid.*, 10.   [28] *Ibid.*, 2.

economies had a share of 65.7 per cent in global FDI inflows and 84.1 per cent in global FDI outflows, compared to 29 per cent of global inflows and 14.3 per cent of global outflows for developing economies.[29] Least-developed countries accounted for less than 1 per cent of global inward FDI stock in 2006..[30]

The *Financial Times* reported this telling example of economic globalisation in February 2003:

> Dr Martens, boot-maker to generations of punks, skinheads and factory workers, will this month quietly end centuries of volume shoe manufacturing in Britain by moving its production to a dusty plain in southern China.
>
> . . . The Pearl river delta – an area the size of Belgium that winds inland from Hong Kong through a series of tightly packed islands – produces $10 billion worth of exports and attracts $1 billion of foreign investment a month. Already, 30m people work in manufacturing here; every day thousands more pour off trains from farms further north.
>
> . . . The catalyst for the delta's explosive export growth is globalisation. China joined the World Trade Organization last year. Increasing competition, falling transport costs and flagging consumer demand are forcing multi-national manufacturing companies to flock to the region with the lowest production costs.
>
> In Dr Martens' case, fierce price competition from rival US brands already produced in China forced the company's hand. 'It was absolutely obvious from the moment I arrived that we had to move to China like everyone else,' says David Suddens, managing director. Dr Martens will outsource production to factories owned by Pou Chen and Golden Chang, Taiwanese companies that moved to the mainland to take advantage of lower labour costs.
>
> Pou Chen's plants, one in Zhuhai and one in Dongguan, employ 110,000 people and churn out 100m pairs of shoes a year for Nike, Adidas, Caterpillar, Timberland, Hush Puppy, Reebok, Puma and others.
>
> . . . Dr Martens pays its 1,100 UK workers about $490 a week and has built a stadium for the local football club. Pou Chen pays about Rmn800 ($100) a month, or 36 cents an hour, for up to 69 hours a week and provides dormitories for migrant workers who must obey strict curfews. The light, well ventilated working conditions are far better than many visitors expect. Stung by complaints of exploitation, Nike and other buyers have full-time local offices monitoring most aspects of employee life.
>
> . . . Nevertheless, older shoe factories are beginning to find it hard to attract and retain workers tempted by better-paid jobs in other plants. Pou Chen is opening a factory further inland where labour is more plentiful.[31]

In August 2003, the *Financial Times* reported on the globalisation of the trade in services with the following story:

> Clutching her side in pain, the woman with suspected appendicitis who was rushed to a hospital on the outskirts of Philadelphia last week had little time to ponder how dependent her life had become on the relentless forces of globalisation. Within minutes of her arrival at the Crozer-Chester Medical Center, the recommendation on whether to operate was being made by a doctor reading her computer-aided tomography (CAT) scan from a computer screen 5,800 miles away in the Middle East.
>
> Jonathan Schlakman, a Harvard-trained radiologist based in Jerusalem, is one of a new breed of skilled professionals proving that geographic distance is no obstacle to outsourcing even the highest paid jobs to overseas locations. The migration of white-collar work has moved up the value chain from call centre operators and back-office clerks to occupations such as equity research, accounting, computer programming and chip design.

---

[29] *Ibid.*, 2.   [30] *Ibid.*, 17.
[31] D. Roberts and J. Kynge, 'The New Workshop of the World', *Financial Times*, 3 February 2003.

The trend – still only a trickle at present – may look to some like a temporary fad pursued by companies seeking to cut costs. For trade unions in the US and Europe, it heralds a fundamental restructuring of rich-world economies, akin to the globalisation of manufacturing in the 1980s and the outsourcing of unskilled service jobs in the 1990s.

At present, only 35 patients' scans are transmitted each day from US emergency rooms to Dr Schlakman's small team of doctors in Israel. But with senior radiologists costing up to $300,000 a year to hire in the US and many emergency cases arriving at night, the use of medical expertise based in a different time zone and earning less than half US rates is almost certain to rise. 'It's much more expensive to use night staff in the US because they need time off the following day,' says Dr Schlakman.[32]

Patients also travel around the world to find good and affordable medical care. An increasing number of foreigners are going to India for heart bypass operations. The average cost, including air fare, is about US$7,000 – roughly one-quarter of what it would be in the UK private sector – and there are no waiting lists. At the Escorts Heart Institute in New Delhi, almost 4,000 heart operations were performed in the year ending August 2006.[33] At 0.8 per cent, Escorts' mortality rate was comparable with international standards.[34]

Questions and Assignments 1.3

Discuss the trends in international trade and foreign direct investment over the last ten years. Do these trends reveal an ever-increasing degree of economic globalisation? Comment on the developing countries' share in world trade in goods and services.

1.2.2.　Economic globalisation: a blessing or a curse?

1.2.2.1.　*Backlash against economic globalisation*

Everyone around the world feels the effects of economic globalisation, but these effects are not felt by all in an even or equitable way. Over the last ten years, massive street protests in Seattle, Prague, Montreal, Washington, Geneva, Göteborg, Genoa and Zurich have shown that many people in developed countries are 'dissatisfied' with economic globalisation.[35] As Fred Bergsten, Director of the Institute for International Economics in Washington DC, noted at the 2000 Annual Meeting of the Trilateral Commission:

there is a big backlash against globalization. We see it in the financial world. We certainly see it in the trading world as well. It's much more fundamental than pure economics. We know that globalization does increase income and social disparities within countries. We know that globalization does leave some countries and certainly some groups of people behind. We do know that a lot of Europeans don't want to eat genetically modified American foods and that adds to their resistance to globalization. We know that a lot of Americans worry about races to the bottom, labor standards, environmental standards,

---

[32] D. Roberts, E. Luce and K. Merchant, 'Service Industries Go Global', *Financial Times*, 20 August 2003.
[33] See www.ehirc.com/individuals/statistics.htm, visited on 28 October 2007.　　[34] *Ibid.*
[35] See 'In the Shadow of Prosperity', *The Economist*, 18 January 2007.

and other perceived doubts about dealing with the rest of the world. We know that a lot of developing countries are raising doubts about the entire system, and such specifics as whether having agreed to the enshrinement of intellectual property rights is really in their national interest. . . . There is therefore a backlash against [globalization], which I think we have to take as an extremely serious economic, political, and social matter.[36]

According to opponents of the current economic globalisation process, there is excessive emphasis on the economic interests of transnational corporations. In their opinion, social, cultural and environmental interests and the interests of developing countries are not sufficiently taken into account. Often, they hold economic globalisation responsible for world poverty and hunger, environmental disasters, unemployment and many other wrongs of today's world. To many, global economic integration is a malignant force that is destroying the livelihood of millions of workers and exacerbates inequality, social injustice and environmental degradation.

A 2001 study by the Institute of International Economics in Washington DC concluded that numerous surveys indicated that a significant number of Americans opposed further liberalisation of trade, immigration and foreign direct investment, and that an absolute majority of Americans wanted liberalisation to go more slowly. According to the study, most Americans know the advantages of open markets but tend to view the costs – especially the supposedly negative impact on American jobs and wages – as more important.[37] In Europe, the popular backlash against economic globalisation is probably even more pronounced. In some European countries, in particular France, there is a widespread perception that globalisation is a product of a conspiracy of ruthless Anglo-Saxons.[38] Also, in leading developing countries such as India and Brazil, sections of the population appear equally fearful of, and hostile towards, further trade liberalisation and economic globalisation. WTO Director-General Pascal Lamy noted in 2007:

[P]ublic opinion has become considerably more anxious about the effects of globalization. We have thus seen concerns, for instance, about the impact on socioeconomic fabrics of increased competition or about outsourcing labour-intensive services. The issue of global trade imbalances has also been taken up in similar terms. Some people are no longer convinced that a rising tide of trade will lift all boats. Many countries today are at a crossroads, whether to continue to support more open trade or erect new walls to imported goods and services or foreign investments.[39]

Unfortunately, the discussion of globalisation and trade liberalisation is often emotionally charged and thus not always productive. Oxfam noted in its 2002 study, *Rigged Rules and Double Standards: Trade, Globalization, and the Fight Against Poverty*, the following:

---

[36] F. Bergsten, 'The Backlash Against Globalization', Remarks made to the 2000 Annual Meeting of the Trilateral Commission in Tokyo, available at www.trilateral.org/annmtgs/trialog/trlgtxts/t54/ber.htm, visited on 15 May 2004.

[37] As reported by R. Dale, 'Anti-Globalization Forces Gain Steam: Movement Brings Together Strange Bedfellows from Right and Left', *International Herald Tribune*, 16 March 2001.

[38] F. Bolkenstein, 'To the Enemies of Globalization', *Wall Street Journal*, 25 September 2000.

[39] See P. Lamy, 'Trends and Issues Facing Global Trade', Speech delivered in Kuala Lumpur, Malaysia on 17 August 2007, available at www.wto.org/english/news_e/sppl_e/sppl65_e.htm, visited on 29 October 2007.

Current debates about trade are dominated by ritualistic exchanges between two camps: the 'globaphiles' and the 'globaphobes'. 'Globaphiles' argue that trade is already making globalisation work for the poor. Their prescription for the future is 'more of the same'. 'Globaphobes' turn this world-view on its head. They argue that trade is inherently bad for the poor. Participation in trade, so the argument runs, inevitably leads to more poverty and inequality. The corollary of this view is 'the less trade the better'.

The anti-globalisation movement deserves credit. It has raised profoundly important questions about social justice – and it has forced the failures of globalisation on to the political agenda. However, the war of words between trade optimists and trade pessimists that accompanies virtually every international meeting is counter-productive. Both world views fly in the face of the evidence – and neither offers any hope for the future.[40]

1.2.2.2. Problems of current economic globalisation

Economic globalisation and international trade currently give rise to problems and tensions in developed as well as developing countries.

Bill Jordan, General Secretary of the International Confederation of Free Trade Unions, wrote in December 2000:

If you want to belittle a point of view, it is easiest to caricature that point of view as nothing more than a slogan daubed on a placard and paraded through the streets. Too often this has led to misrepresenting the views of labor unions in the face of globalization . . . The international labor movement is not against globalization; indeed we would agree that globalization can be a big part of the answer to the problems of the world's poor. But it also is a big part of the problem. In other words, globalization is neither entirely beneficial nor entirely harmful. It is not an unstoppable force of nature, but is shaped by those who set the rules. And while it has the potential to help lift more than 2 billion people out of poverty, it is not doing so now.[41]

War on Want, one of the more thought-provoking NGOs with close links to the international labour movement, summarises its position regarding economic globalisation as follows:

Jobs are always welcomed by those who live in the developing world. But many of these employees are paid next to nothing, and work in dangerous conditions facing physical and verbal abuse from their employers. Meanwhile, in the developed world, workers are being laid off at an alarming rate and made to feel that they need to compete with workers in the developing world. The globalisation of trade and investment affects labour standards, working conditions, the environment, human health and many other aspects of our lives. Currently, too little attention is being paid to these effects. We need to ensure there are global rules to govern the effects of a global economy.[42]

War on Want is not opposed to globalisation, but wants to see the benefits of globalisation more evenly spread across the world. According to this NGO, economic globalisation now primarily benefits transnational corporations (TNCs)

---

[40] Oxfam, *Rigged Rules and Double Standards: Trade, Globalization, and the Fight Against Poverty*, 2002, Summary of chapter 1, available at: www.maketradefair.org/en/index.php?file=03042002153411. htm&cat=3&subcat=3&select=4, visited on 15 May 2004.

[41] B. Jordan, 'Yes to Globalization, But Protect the Poor', *International Herald Tribune*, 21 December 2000.

[42] Excerpts from 'The Global Workplace', a project of War on Want, available at www.globalworkplace.org/?lid=74, visited on 15 May 2004.

and often spells disaster for industries in developing countries as well as for workers worldwide:

> TNCs can treat the world like their assembly line – manufacturing goods where labour is cheapest, basing operations where taxes are lowest and selling goods where the price is highest. If taxes or labour laws are imposed in one country, they can simply move to another.[43]

ATTAC, the Association for the Taxation of Financial Transactions for the Aid of Citizens, takes a similar position against 'corporate globalisation', which, it contends, results in:

> the concentration of wealth in the hands of the rich few, growing inequality within and between nations, increasing poverty for the majority of the world's peoples, displacement of farmers and workers especially in third world countries, and unsustainable patterns of production and consumption.[44]

ATTAC argues for the replacement of the current 'unfair and oppressive trade system' with a new, socially just and sustainable trading framework. This framework should be one that protects cultural, biological, economic and social diversity; introduces progressive policies to prioritise local economies and trade; secures internationally recognised economic, cultural, social and labour rights; and reclaims the sovereignty of peoples and national and subnational democratic decision-making processes.[45]

Daniel Mittler from Greenpeace International noted in 2004:

> Greenpeace opposes the current form of globalization that is increasing corporate power. Free trade at all costs is leading to the overuse of natural resources, more pollution as we produce and consume more, and greater inequities both among and within countries. This kind of globalization will and should be obstructed. If it were to continue unchecked, the global ecosystem will collapse. Business as usual is in real danger of undermining the ecological basis of our economic system.[46]

Developing countries' governments and third-world activists commonly argue: first, that developing countries are being forced to open their markets too far, too fast; secondly, that rich countries are conspiring to keep their markets closed to products from developing countries which compete with their products (in particular agricultural products, textiles and clothing); and, thirdly, that developing countries lack the resources and the information to negotiate effectively, to implement trade agreements and to exploit world trade rules to their advantage. Former UN Secretary-General Kofi Annan once noted:

> Try to imagine what globalization can possibly mean to the half of humanity that has never made or received a telephone call; or to the people of Sub-Saharan Africa, who have less Internet access than the inhabitants of the borough of Manhattan.[47]

---

[43] *Ibid.*
[44] Excerpts from ATTAC Quarterly Report, September 2001, *International Trade*, no. 2, vol. I, available at www.attac.org, visited on 11 August 2003.   [45] *Ibid.*
[46] L. Barber, 'A Symposium of Views: Is Continued Globalisation of the World Economy Inevitable?' *The International Economy*, Summer 2004, 74.
[47] From the Address by UN Secretary-General Kofi Annan in Davos, Switzerland, on 28 January 2001 to the World Economic Forum, available at www.unis.unvienna.org/unis/pressrels/2001/sg2772.html, visited on 13 August 2003.

While not sharing the extreme positions of anti-globalists and being careful 'not to make the mistake of attributing to globalization the blemishes of other faces',[48] many observers and scholars recognise the dangers of the economic globalisation process.

In his 2002 book, *Globalization and Its Discontents*, Joseph Stiglitz reflected on the bright side of globalisation as follows:

> Opening up to international trade has helped many countries grow far more quickly than they would otherwise have done. International trade helps economic development when a country's exports drive its economic growth. Export-led growth was the centrepiece of the industrial policy that enriched much of Asia and left millions of people there far better off. Because of globalization many people in the world now live longer than before and their standard of living is far better. People in the West may regard low-paying jobs at Nike as exploitation, but for many people in the developing world, working in a factory is a far better option than staying down on the farm and growing rice.
>
> Globalization has reduced the sense of isolation felt in much of the developing world and has given many people in the developing countries access to knowledge well beyond the reach of even the wealthiest in any country a century ago . . . Even when there are negative sides to globalization, there are often benefits. Opening up the Jamaican milk market to US imports in 1992 may have hurt local dairy farmers but it also meant poor children could get milk more cheaply. New foreign firms may hurt protected state-owned enterprises but they can also lead to the introduction of new technologies, access to new markets, and the creation of new industries.[49]

Stiglitz commented that those who vilify globalisation too often overlook its benefits.[50] However, Stiglitz pointed out:

> [T]he proponents of globalization have been, if anything, even more unbalanced. To them, globalization (which typically is associated with accepting triumphant capitalism, American style) *is* progress; developing countries must accept it, if they are to grow and to fight poverty effectively. But to many in the developing world, globalization has not brought the promised economic benefits.[51]

Elsewhere, Stiglitz wrote about the problems and dangers of current economic globalisation and trade liberalisation:

> We should be frank. Trade liberalization, conducted in the wrong way, too fast, in the absence of adequate safety nets, with insufficient reciprocity and assistance on the part of developed countries, can contribute to an increase in poverty . . .
>
> Complete openness can expose a country to greater risk from external shocks. Poor countries may find it particularly hard to buffer these shocks and to bear the costs they incur, and they typically have weak safety nets, or none at all, to protect the poor. These shocks, resulting essentially from contagion associated with globalization, integration and interdependence can affect workers and employers in the developed world. It must be said, however, that highly industrialized countries are able to deal with these shocks a lot better through re-employment and through other safety nets.[52]

In 2006, Stiglitz reflected on the dark side of globalisation as follows:

---

[48] J. Bhagwati, 'Globalization in Your Face', *Foreign Affairs*, July/August 2000, 137.
[49] J. Stiglitz, *Globalization and Its Discontents* (Penguin, 2002), 4–5.   [50] *Ibid.,* 5   [51] *Ibid.*
[52] J. Stiglitz, 'Addressing Developing Country Priorities and Needs in the Millennium Round', in R. Porter and P. Sauvé (eds.), *Seattle, the WTO and the Future of the Multilateral Trading System* (Harvard University Press, 2000), 53–5.

> There were once hopes that globalisation would benefit all, both in advanced industrial countries and the developing world. Today, the downside of globalisation is increasingly apparent. Not only do good things go more easily across borders, so do bad; including terrorism. We see an unfair global trade regime that impedes development and an unstable global financial system in which poor countries repeatedly find themselves with unmanageable debt burdens. Money should flow from the rich to the poor countries, but increasingly, it goes in the opposite direction.
>
> What is remarkable about globalisation is the disparity between the promise and the reality. Globalisation seems to have unified so much of the world against it, perhaps because there appear to be so many losers and so few winners . . . Growing inequality in the advanced industrial countries was a long predicted but seldom advertised consequence: full economic integration implies the equalisation of unskilled wages throughout the world. Although this has not (yet) happened, the downward pressure on those at the bottom is evident. Unfettered globalisation actually has the potential to make many people in advanced industrial countries worse off, even if economic growth increases.[53]

On the positive and negative aspects of economic globalisation, Pascal Lamy, the WTO Director-General, made the following remarks in August 2007:

> Globalization has enabled individuals, corporations and nation-states to influence actions and events around the world – faster, deeper and cheaper than ever before – and equally to derive benefits for them. Trade opening and the vanishing of many walls have the potential for expanding freedom, empowerment, democracy, innovation, social and cultural exchanges, while offering outstanding opportunities for dialogue and understanding. This is the good side of globalization.
>
> But the global nature of an increasing number of worrisome phenomena – the scarcity of energy resources, the deterioration of the environment, the migratory movements provoked by insecurity, poverty and political instability or even financial markets volatility, as we have seen in recent weeks – are also by-products of globalization. Indeed, it can be argued that in some instances, globalization has reinforced the strong economies and weakened those that were already weak.[54]

In a 2007 contribution to the *Financial Times*, Dani Rodrik asked whether the greatest threat to globalization is: the 'protesters on the streets every time the International Monetary Fund or the World Trade Organization meets', or 'globalisation's cheerleaders, who push for continued market opening while denying that the troubles surrounding globalisation are rooted in the policies they advocate'.[55] According to Rodrik:

> A good case can be made that the latter camp presents the greater menace. Anti-globalisers are marginalised. But cheerleaders in Washington, London and the elite universities of north America and Europe shape the intellectual climate. If they get their way, they are more likely to put globalisation at risk than the protesters they condemn for ignorance of sound economics. That is because the greatest obstacle to sustaining a healthy, globalised economy is no longer insufficient openness. Markets are freer from government interference than they have ever been. Import restrictions such as tariff and non-tariff barriers are lower than ever. Capital flows in huge magnitudes. Despite barriers, legal and illegal immigration approaches levels not seen since the 19th century . . . Closed markets may have been a fundamental problem during the 1950s and 1960s; it is hard to believe they still are.

---

[53] J. Stiglitz, 'We Have Become Rich Countries of Poor People', *Financial Times*, 7 September 2006.
[54] See P. Lamy, 'Trends and Issues Facing Global Trade', Speech delivered in Kuala Lumpur, Malaysia on 17 August 2007, available at www.wto.org/english/news_e/sppl_e/sppl65_e.htm, visited on 29 October 2007.
[55] D. Rodrik, 'The Cheerleaders' Threat to Global Trade', *Financial Times*, 26 March 2007.

> The greatest risk to globalisation is elsewhere. It lies in the prospect that national govern-
> ments' room for manoeuvre will shrink to such levels that they will be unable to
> deliver the policies that their electorates want and need in order to buy into the global
> economy.[56]

In Rodrik's opinion, developed and developing countries need flexibility – or
'breathing space – to interfere in trade:

> Rich countries need . . . flexibility to interfere in trade when trade conflicts with deeply
> held values at home – as, for example, with child labour or health and safety concerns –
> or severely weakens the bargaining power of workers. Poor nations need room to engage
> in exchange rate and industrial policies that will diversify and restructure their economies,
> without which their ability to benefit from globalisation is circumscribed.[57]

In reply to the question contained in the title of his 1997 book, *Has Globalization
Gone Too Far?*, Rodrik had already stated that, in his opinion, this is not the case if
'policymakers act wisely and imaginatively'.[58]

In *The Lexus and the Olive Tree*, Thomas Friedman also saw the need for government action when he noted:

> the more I observed the system of globalization at work, the more obvious it was that it
> had unleashed forest-crushing forces of development and Disney-round-the-clock homog-
> enization, which, if left unchecked, had the potential to destroy the environment and
> uproot cultures at a pace never before seen in human history.[59]

Questions and Assignments 1.4

What are the main dangers associated with the current process of
economic globalisation? Who stands to gain most from the current
process of economic globalisation? Who loses?

1.2.3. Trade liberalisation versus protectionism

1.2.3.1. *The case for international trade and liberalisation*

Economic globalisation in general and international trade in particular is
blamed by many for much that is wrong in today's world: from hunger and child
labour to environmental pollution and cultural impoverishment. Is international trade beneficial to anyone other than multinational corporations, the
well-educated in developed countries and the privileged elite in developing
countries? Can economic globalisation in general and international trade in particular benefit all humankind?

Most economists agree that countries can benefit from international trade. In
1776, Adam Smith wrote in his classic book, *The Wealth of Nations*:

[56] *Ibid.*   [57] *Ibid.*
[58] D. Rodrik, *Has Globalization Gone Too Far?* (Institute for International Economics, 1997), 9.
[59] T. Friedman, *The Lexus and the Olive Tree: Understanding Globalisation*, 2nd edition (First Anchor Books, 2000),
   23.

It is the maxim of every prudent master of a family, never to attempt to make at home what it will cost him more to make than to buy. The tailor does not attempt to make his own shoes, but he buys them from the shoemaker. The shoemaker does not attempt to make his own cloths, but employs a tailor. The farmer attempts to make neither the one nor the other, but employs those different artificers. All of them find it for their interest to employ their whole industry in a way in which they have some advantage over their neighbours, and to purchase with a part of its produce, or what is the same thing, with the price of a part of it, whatever else they have occasion for.

What is prudence in the conduct of every private family, can scarce be folly in that of a great kingdom. If a foreign country can supply us with a commodity cheaper than we ourselves can make it, better buy it of them with some part of the produce of our own industry, employed in a way in which we have some advantage. The general industry of the country . . . will not thereby be diminished, no more than the above-mentioned artificers; but only left to find out the way in which it can be employed with the greatest advantage. It is certainly not employed to the greatest advantage, when it is thus directed towards an object which it can buy cheaper than it can make.[60]

Smith's lucid and compelling argument for specialisation and international trade was further built upon by David Ricardo who, in his 1817 book, *The Principles of Political Economy and Taxation*, developed the theory of 'comparative advantage'. This theory is still the predominant explanation for why countries, even the poorest, can and do benefit from international trade.

What did the classical economist David Ricardo (1772–1823) mean when he coined the term *comparative advantage*? Suppose country A is better than country B at making automobiles, and country B is better than country A at making bread. It is obvious (the academics would say 'trivial') that both would benefit if A specialized in automobiles, B specialized in bread and they traded their products. That is a case of *absolute* advantage. But what if a country is bad at making everything? Will trade drive all producers out of business? The answer, according to Ricardo, is no. The reason is the principle of comparative advantage, arguably the single most powerful insight in economics. According to the principle of comparative advantage, countries A and B still stand to benefit from trading with each other even if A is better than B at making everything, both automobiles and bread. If A is much more superior at making automobiles and only slightly superior at making bread, then A should still invest resources in what it does best – producing automobiles – and export the product to B. B should still invest in what it does best – making bread – and export that product to A, even if it is not as efficient as A. Both would still benefit from the trade. A country does not have to be best at anything to gain from trade. That is *comparative* advantage. The theory is one of the most widely accepted among economists. It is also one of the most misunderstood among non-economists because it is confused with *absolute* advantage. It is often claimed, for example, that some countries have no comparative advantage in anything. That is virtually impossible. Think about it . . .[61]

The Ricardo model is of course a vast simplification, in that it is built on two products and two countries only and assumes constant costs and constant prices. Many of the complexities of the modern economy are not taken into account in this model. Economists in the twentieth century have endeavoured to refine and build on the classic Ricardo model. While pushing the analysis further, the refined models, such as the Hekscher–Ohlin model, have confirmed

---

[60] A. Smith, *An Inquiry into the Nature and Causes of the Wealth of Nations* (1776), edited by E. Cannan (University of Chicago Press, 1976), vol. 1, 478–9.
[61] WTO Secretariat, *Trading into the Future*, 2nd edition, revised (WTO, 2001), 9.

the basic conclusions drawn from the Ricardo model concerning the theory of comparative advantage and the gains from trade via specialisation.[62]

While the theory of comparative advantage has won approval from most economists since the early nineteenth century and continues to win approval,[63] Jagdish Bhagwati observed in *Free Trade Today* that it has only infrequently carried credibility with the populace at large. In search of an explanation, he noted that when asked which proposition in the social science was the most counterintuitive yet compelling, Paul Samuelson, the 1970 winner of the Nobel Prize for Economics, chose the theory of comparative advantage.[64]

According to Samuelson, there is essentially only one – but one very powerful – argument for freer trade:

> Free trade promotes a mutually profitable division of labor, greatly enhances the potential real national product for all nations, and makes possible higher standards of living all over the globe.[65]

On the question whether free trade, or rather freer international trade, indeed leads to greater economic growth, Jagdish Bhagwati observed:

> So those who assert that free trade will also lead necessarily to greater growth *either* are ignorant of the finer nuances of theory and the vast literature to the contrary on the subject at hand *or* are nonetheless basing their argument on a different premise: that is, that the preponderant evidence on the issue (in the postwar period) suggests that freer trade tends to lead to greater growth after all.[66]

A 2001 study by the World Bank showed that the developing countries that increased their integration into the world economy in the 1980s and 1990s achieved higher growth in incomes, longer life expectancy and better schooling. These countries, home to some 3 billion people, enjoyed an average 5 per cent growth rate in income per capita in the 1990s compared to 2 per cent in developed countries. Many of these countries, including China and India, have adopted domestic policies and institutions that have enabled people to take advantage of global markets and have thus sharply increased the share of trade in their GDP. These countries have been catching up with the rich ones – their annual growth rates increased from 1 per cent in the 1960s to 5 per cent in the 1990s. In 2006, India and China achieved an economic growth of 9.4 per cent and 11.1 per cent respectively.[67] However, not all countries have integrated successfully into the

---

[62] Note, however, as Jagdish Bhagwati does, that: 'The case of free trade rests on the extension to an open economy of the case for market-determined allocation of resources. If market prices reflect "true" or social costs, then clearly Adam Smith's invisible hand can be trusted to guide us to efficiency; and free trade can correspondingly be shown to be the optimal way to choose trade (and associated domestic production). But if markets do not work well, or are absent or incomplete, then the invisible hand may point in the wrong direction: free trade cannot then be asserted to be the best policy.' See J. Bhagwati, *Free Trade Today* (Princeton University Press, 2002), 12.

[63] For a dissenting, neo-Marxist view from legal scholars, see M. H. Davis and D. Neacsu, 'Legitimacy, Globally: The Incoherence of Free Trade Practice, Global Economics and Their Governing Principles of Political Economy', *Kansas City Law Review*, 2001, 733–90.

[64] See J. Bhagwati, *Free Trade Today* (Princeton University Press, 2002), 5.

[65] P. Samuelson, *Economics*, 10th edition (1976), 692.

[66] J. Bhagwati, *Free Trade Today* (Princeton University Press, 2002), 42.

[67] The *Economist* Intelligence Unit: Country Briefings: China, available at www.economist.com/countries/ China/profile.cfm?folder=Profile-Economic%20Structure, and India, available at www.economist.com/ countries/India/profile.cfm?folder=Profile-Economic%20Structure, visited on 29 October 2007.

global economy. The World Bank's 2001 report found that some 2 billion people – particularly in Sub-Saharan Africa, the Middle East and the former Soviet Union – live in countries that are being left behind. On average these economies have contracted, poverty has increased and education levels have risen less rapidly than in the more globalised countries.[68]

As a 2000 WTO study, *Trade, Income Disparity and Poverty*, on the relationship between international trade and poverty concluded, the evidence seems to indicate that trade liberalisation is *generally* a positive contributor to poverty alleviation. It allows people to exploit their productive potential, assists economic growth, curtails arbitrary policy interventions and helps to insulate against shocks in the domestic economy. The study warned, however, that most trade reforms will create some losers (some even in the long run). Poverty may be exacerbated temporarily, but the appropriate policy response in those cases is to alleviate the hardship and facilitate adjustments rather than abandon the reform process.[69] A 2003 WTO study, *Adjusting to Trade Liberalization*, concluded that adjustment costs are typically smaller, and sometimes much smaller, than the gains from trade.[70] Also, governments can identify individuals and groups that are likely to suffer from the adjustment process, and they can develop policies to alleviate the burden on those adversely affected.[71]

In its 2002 study, *Rigged Rules and Double Standards: Trade, Globalization, and the Fight Against Poverty*, Oxfam stated:

> History makes a mockery of the claim that trade cannot work for the poor. Participation in world trade has figured prominently in many of the most successful cases of poverty reduction – and, compared with aid, it has far more potential to benefit the poor.[72]

According to Oxfam, since the mid-1970s rapid growth in exports has contributed to a wider process of economic growth which has lifted more than 400 million people out of poverty.[73] Few will question that international trade has the *potential* to make a significant contribution to economic growth and poverty reduction. However, it is definitely not a 'magic bullet for achieving development'.[74] More is needed to achieve sustained economic growth and widespread poverty reduction.[75]

International trade not only has the potential for bringing economic benefits, there may also be considerable non-economic gains. International trade increases both the incentives for not making war and the costs of going to war.

[68] P. Collier and D. Dollar, *Globalization, Growth and Poverty: Building an Inclusive World Economy* (World Bank, 2001), available at http://econ.worldbank.org, visited on 15 May 2004. See also J. Sachs and A. Warner, 'Economic Reform and the Process of Global Integration', *Brookings Papers on Economic Activity*, 1 (1995), 1–95; and A. Krueger, 'Trade Policy and Economic Development: How We Learn', *NBER Working Paper Series* (Working Paper 5896) (1997).

[69] See D. Ben-David, H. Nordström and A. Winters, *Trade, Income Disparity and Poverty*, Special Studies Series (WTO, 2000), 6.

[70] See M. Bacchetta and M. Jansen, *Adjusting to Trade Liberalization: The Role of Policy, Institutions and WTO Disciplines*, Special Studies Series (WTO, 2003), 6.   [71] *Ibid.*

[72] Oxfam, *Rigged Rules and Double Standards: Trade, Globalization, and the Fight Against Poverty*, 2002, Summary of chapter 2, available at www.maketradefair.org, visited on 11 August 2003.   [73] *Ibid.*

[74] See Justice C. Nwobike, 'The Emerging Trade Regime under the Cotonou Partnership Agreement: Its Human Rights Implications', *Journal of World Trade*, 2006, 292   [75] See below, p. ##.

International trade intensifies cross-border contacts and exchange of ideas, which may contribute to better mutual understanding. In a free-trading world, other countries and their people are more readily seen as business partners, less as enemies. As Baron de Montesquieu wrote in 1748 in *De l'Esprit des Lois*:

> Peace is the natural effect of trade. Two nations who traffic with each other become recip-
> rocally dependent; for if one has an interest in buying, the other has an interest in selling;
> and thus their union is founded on their mutual necessities.[76]

A country taking trade-restrictive measures directly inflicts economic hardship upon exporting countries. Therefore, trade protectionism is a festering source of conflict. It is often stated that 'if goods do not cross frontiers, soldiers will'.[77] Likewise, international trade can make an important contribution to peaceful and constructive international relations. Just two weeks after the terrorist attacks of 11 September 2001 on the World Trade Center in New York and on the Pentagon in Washington DC, Robert Zoellick, the then US Trade Representative and current President of the World Bank, made the following simple but profound statement about the importance of continued openness in trade:

> Let me be clear where I stand: Erecting new barriers and closing old borders will not help
> the impoverished. It will not feed hundreds of millions struggling for subsistence. It will
> not liberate the persecuted. It will not improve the environment in developing countries or
> reverse the spread of AIDS. It will not help the railway orphans I visited in India. It will
> not improve the livelihoods of the union members I met in Latin America. It will not aid
> the committed Indonesians I visited who are trying to build a functioning, tolerant
> democracy in the largest Muslim nation in the world.[78]

Two months after the attacks of 11 September 2001, the WTO Members agreed to start the Doha Development Round, a new round of negotiations on the further liberalisation of international trade. According to WTO Director-General Pascal Lamy, the rationale behind this decision was, and in his view remains, simple: 'terrorism is about increasing instability; global trade rules are about promoting stability'.[79]

However, as Edward Alden wrote in the *Financial Times* in February 2003:

> US trade policy risks isolating the Muslim states that are on the front line in the war on
> terrorism, according to a study released on Tuesday. The report – from the Washington-
> based Progressive Policy Institute – warns that the Muslim world has been 'the blank spot
> on the map of the Bush administration's trade policy'. It adds: 'That policy risks under-
> mining, rather than supporting, the war on terrorism.' The failing economies of many

---

[76] C. de Montesquieu, *De l'Esprit des Lois*, original version available online at
http://classiques.uqac.ca/classiques/montesquieu/de_esprit_des_lois/de_esprit_des_lois_tdm.html. An
English translation by Thomas Nugent is available at www.constitution.org/cm/sol.htm, visited on 8
November 2007.

[77] P. Lamy, 'Managing Global Security: the Strategic Importance of Global Trade', Speech to the International
Institute for Strategic Studies, in Geneva on 8 September 2007, available at
www.wto.org/english/news_e/sppl_e/sppl66_e.htm, visited on 28 October 2007.

[78] As reported by the then WTO Director-General Mike Moore in a speech to the Foreign Affairs Commission
of the French Assemblée Nationale in October 2001, available at www.wto.org, visited on 6 February 2004.

[79] P. Lamy, 'Managing Global Security: the Strategic Importance of Global Trade', Speech to the International
Institute for Strategic Studies, in Geneva on 8 September 2007, available at www.wto.org/english/news_
e/sppl_e/sppl66_e.htm, visited on 28 October 2007.

> Muslim states have been repeatedly acknowledged by the White House as fertile recruit-
> ing grounds for terrorist groups. But critics say the US has done little to tackle the
> problem, and has been stingy with trade concessions to some of its closest allies in the
> war on terrorism. Kursheed Kasuri, Pakistan's foreign minister, said last week that 'eco-
> nomics is the key to fighting terrorism', and criticised Washington for failing to offer
> greater trade concessions. Pakistan had hoped for about $1 billion in additional sales of
> textiles and clothing to the US to offset the costs of the war on terrorism, but – under
> pressure from its own textile industry – the US granted just $143m.[80]

Apart from peaceful relations between nations, open international trade may
also promote democracy. In *Free Trade Today*, Jagdish Bhagwati observed:

> One could argue this proposition by a syllogism: openness to the benefits of trade brings
> prosperity that, in turn, creates or expands the middle class that then seeks the end of
> authoritarianism. This would fit well with the experience in South Korea, for instance. It
> was also the argument that changed a lot of minds when the issue of China's entry into
> the WTO came up in the US Congress recently. I guess there is something to it.[81]

It has been reported that international trade and investment have already had a
certain impact on the political system in China:

> Not only is the southern boom town of Shenzhen about to be designated a test-bed for the
> boldest political reform since the 1949 revolution but cities in coastal China are also
> embarking on experiments to introduce checks and balances to single party rule. Yu Youjun,
> mayor of Shenzhen, said in an interview that the wishes of multinational corporations were
> one motive for the city's experiment. Foreign companies, especially those establishing
> high-technology factories, are mindful of the need to protect intellectual property. For this,
> they need a fair local government. 'Every multinational company and investor is influenced
> by the investment environment created by governments', said Mr Yu, whose city was
> chosen 22 years ago as a laboratory for China's first capitalist reforms and now leads the
> country in per capita income. The 'hard environment' of roads, railways, ports and telecom-
> munications was important for multinationals, Mr Yu said. But more crucial was the 'soft
> environment', meaning a government that is 'democratic' and transparent. 'We have made
> achievements in building our economic structural reform', said Mr Yu. 'Now we need to
> make reforms to our political system to promote democratic politics.'[82]

1.2.3.2. Reasons and excuses for protectionist trade policies

While most economists advise that countries should – in their own interest and
that of the world at large – pursue policies aimed at promoting international
trade and exchange goods and services on the basis of their comparative advantage, political decision-makers do not necessarily heed this wise advice. In fact,
countries frequently intervene in international trade by adopting trade restrictive measures. Why do countries restrict international trade? Why do they adopt
protectionist trade policies? A prime reason is to protect a domestic industry,
and employment in that industry, from competition arising from imported
products, foreign services or service suppliers. As noted in the 2003 WTO study
on *Adjusting to Trade Liberalization*:

---

[80] E. Alden, 'US Trade Policy "Isolates Muslim States" ', *Financial Times*, 4 February 2003.
[81] J. Bhagwati, *Free Trade Today* (Princeton University Press, 2002), 43–4.
[82] D. Roberts and J. Kynge, 'The New Workshop of the World', *Financial Times*, 3 February 2003.

In the United States, for instance, 45,000 steelworkers have lost their jobs since 1997 and 30 per cent of the country's steel making capacity has filed for bankruptcy since 1998, while steel imports were on the rise. In Mozambique liberalization of trade in cashew nuts resulted in 8,500 of 10,000 cashew processing workers losing their jobs.[83]

When a domestic industry is in crisis and jobs are lost, the political decision-makers may well 'scramble for shelter' by adopting protectionist measures.[84] This may happen even when the decision-makers are well aware that such measures are by no means the best response to the crisis in the industry concerned. While the import competition would probably benefit most of their constituents (through lower prices, better quality and/or more choice), import competition is likely to hurt a small group of their constituents significantly (through lower salaries or job losses). If this small group is vocal and well organised, as it often is, it will put a great deal of pressure on the elected decision-makers to take protectionist measures for the benefit of the few and to the detriment of the many. In such a situation, protectionism can constitute 'good' politics.[85] The *public choice theory* explains that, when the majority of the voters are unconcerned with the (*per capita* small) losses they suffer, the vote-maximising political decision-makers will ignore the interests of the many, and support the interests of the vocal and well-organised few. WTO Director-General Pascal Lamy has called for recognition of the fact that the politics of trade suffer from an 'inbuilt asymmetry'. He noted:

[T]hose who benefit from gains in purchasing power stemming from trade opening are millions, but they are little aware of the source of their gains. Those who suffer from trade opening are thousands who can easily identify the source of their pain. For politicians, such an asymmetry is difficult to cope with and too often the easy way out is to treat foreigners as scapegoats, which we know is one of the safest old tricks of domestic politics.[86]

However, as discussed above, trade protectionist measures to protect the interests of some eventually leave everyone worse off. Joseph Stiglitz, reflecting on his own experience as Chairman of the Council of Economic Advisors in the Clinton Administration, observed in this respect:

One might have thought that each country would promote liberalization in those sectors where it had most to gain from a societal perspective; and similarly, that it would be most willing to give up protectionism in those sectors where protection was costing the most. But political logic prevails over economic logic: after all, if economic logic dominated, countries would engage in trade liberalization on their own. High levels of protection are usually indicative of strong political forces, and these higher barriers may be the last to give way . . . The political force behind the resistance to free trade is a simple one: Although the country as a whole may be better off under free trade, some special interests will actually be worse off. And although policy could in principle rectify this situation (by

---

[83] M. Bacchetta and M. Jansen, *Adjusting to Trade Liberalization: The Role of Policy, Institutions and WTO Disciplines*, Special Studies Series (WTO, 2003), 6.

[84] 'Survey World Trade', *The Economist*, 3 October 1998, 3.

[85] B. Hoekman and M. Kostecki, *The Political Economy of the World Trading System: The WTO and Beyond*, 2nd edition (Oxford University Press, 2001), 22.

[86] See P. Lamy, 'Trends and Issues Facing Global Trade', Speech delivered in Kuala Lumpur, Malaysia on 17 August 2007, available at www.wto.org/english/news_e/sppl_e/sppl65_e.htm, visited on 29 October 2007.

using redistribution to make everybody better off), in actuality, the required compensations are seldom paid.[87]

Another reason for national decision-makers to pursue a protectionist trade policy is *infant industry protection*.[88] The argument for infant industry protection was made by Alexander Hamilton in 1791, Friedrich List in 1841 and John Stuart Mill in 1848, and has been invoked many times since. In the nineteenth century, the infant manufacturing industries of the United States and Germany were protected against import competition on the basis of this argument. Today, this argument may be of particular relevance to developing countries, which may find that while they have a potential comparative advantage in certain industries, new producers in these countries cannot (yet) compete with established producers in the developed countries. By means of a customs duty or import restriction, temporary protection is then given to the national producers to allow them to become strong enough to compete with well-established producers. The infant industry argument for protectionist measures has definitely some appeal and validity. However, protecting the new producers from import competition does not necessarily remedy the problems that caused the new producers to be uncompetitive. Furthermore, the success of an infant industry policy crucially depends on a correct diagnosis of which industries could over time become competitive. It is often very difficult for governments to identify, in an objective manner and free from pressure from special interest groups, the new industries that merit protection. Moreover, in practice, the protection, which is by nature intended to be temporary, frequently becomes permanent. When it becomes clear that the protected national industry will never 'grow up' and will always be unable to face import competition, it is often politically difficult to remove the protection in place.[89]

When a country is in a position to lower the price it pays for imports by restricting its imports, national decision-makers of that country may also be tempted to adopt trade restrictive measures on the basis of the *optimal tariff* argument. If a country can reduce world demand for a product, by raising the tariff on that product, it may make economic sense to raise the tariff, and thus restrict trade, because this will lead to the cutting of the world price of the product concerned. In this way, a country can tilt the terms of trade in its favour. Alan Deardorff and Robert Stern noted in this respect:

> This argument is sometimes thought to require that the country in question be large and therefore to apply only to such large industrialized countries as the US. However, the argument applies to some extent to any country that is not insignificantly small. Furthermore the size that is important is not the size of the country as a whole but rather its share of world trade in markets in which it exports and imports.[90]

[87] J. Stiglitz, 'Addressing Developing Country Priorities and Needs in the Millennium Round', in R. Porter and P. Sauvé (eds.), *Seattle, the WTO and the Future of the Multilateral Trading System* (Harvard University Press, 2000), 51–3.   [88] See also below, pp. 725–6.
[89] A. Deardorff and R. Stern, 'Current Issues in US Trade Policies: An Overview', in R. Stern (ed.), *US Trade Policies in a Changing World Economy* (Massachusetts Institute of Technology, 1987), 39–40.
[90] *Ibid.*, 37–8.

However, as Deardorff and Stern observed, it is a key feature of the optimal tariff argument that it involves gains by one country at other countries' expense. It is thus referred to as an 'exploitative intervention' policy.

> Such policies are typically available to more than one country, each of which can have adverse effects on the others (and even many), and therefore require that strategic issues be considered. Like other forms of exploitative intervention the optimal tariff argument is likely to find countries in the classic position of the Prisoner's Dilemma; that is, each country has available a policy that will benefit itself at the expense of others, but if all countries simultaneously pursue that policy, all are likely to lose.[91]

A relatively new argument for national decision-makers to opt for trade restrictions is the *strategic trade policy* argument. In an industry with economies of scale, a country may, by imposing a tariff or quantitative restriction and thus reserving the domestic market for a domestic firm, allow that firm to cut its costs and undercut foreign competitors in other markets. This may work in an industry where economies of scale are sufficiently large that there is only room for very few profitable companies in the world market. Economists reckon that this might be the case for civil aircraft, semiconductors and cars.[92] The aim of government intervention is to ensure that the domestic rather than a foreign company establishes itself on the world market and thus contributes to the national economic welfare. However, as Paul Krugman noted:

> Strategic trade policy aimed at securing excess returns for domestic firms and support for industries that are believed to yield national benefits are both beggar-thy-neighbour policies and raise income at the expense of other countries. A country that attempts to use such policies will probably provoke retaliation. In many (though not all) cases, a trade war between two interventionist governments will leave both countries worse off than if a hands-off approach were adopted by both.[93]

This does not mean that such policies will not be pursued, because, as Krugman also pointed out:

> Governments do not necessarily act in the national interest, especially when making detailed microeconomic interventions. Instead, they are influenced by interest group pressures. The kinds of interventions that new trade theory suggests can raise national income will typically raise the welfare of small, fortunate groups by large amounts, while imposing costs on larger, more diffuse groups. The result, as with any microeconomic policy, can easily be that excessive or misguided intervention takes place because the beneficiaries have more knowledge and influence than the losers.[94]

Trade-restrictive measures, and, in particular, customs duties, have also been and still are imposed to *generate revenue for government*. Taxing trade is an easy method to collect revenue. While taxation of trade for revenue is no longer significant for developed countries, for many developing country governments customs duties remain a significant source of revenue.[95]

---

[91] *Ibid.*, 37–8.   [92] 'Survey World Trade', *The Economist*, 3 October 1998, 6.
[93] P. Krugman, 'Is Free Trade Passé?', *Journal of Economic Perspectives*, 1987, 141.   [94] *Ibid.*
[95] See below, pp. 404–5, 409–11.

Governments also adopt trade restrictive measures for reasons of *national secu-rity* and *self-sufficiency*. The steel industry, as well as farmers, can, for example, be heard to argue that their presence and prosperity is essential to the national security of the country. The basic argument is that a country should be able to rely on its domestic industries and farmers to meet its basic needs for vital mate-rial and food, because it will be impossible to rely – in times of crisis and conflict – on imports from other countries. Allan Sykes noted in this respect:

> The likelihood of imports becoming unavailable in wartime must then be carefully consid-ered. For a nation like the United States, serious interruption of seaborne commercial traffic seems unlikely to occur for most goods and commodities in any scenario short of global conventional conflict on the scale of World War II. The probability of such conflict seems small at best in the nuclear age. Further, in the event of an interruption in seaborne traffic, adjacent trading partners may be able to take up much of the slack on many items . . .
>
> Where interruption of necessary imports seems a serious risk, the next issue is whether domestic capacity can be restored with reasonable dispatch. Even if an industry has closed down certain productive facilities that might be needed in wartime, it does not follow that those facilities cannot be reopened or rebuilt quickly enough to satisfy essen-tial needs.
>
> Finally, stockpiling during peacetime may well be a superior alternative to the protec-tion of domestic capacity. Where the item in question is not perishable, a nation might be better off by buying up a supply of vital material at low prices in an open trading system than to burden itself over time with the high prices attendant on protectionism as a hedge against armed conflict. The funds tied up in a stockpile have some opportunity cost to be sure, but this cost can easily be smaller than the costs of excluding efficient foreign sup-pliers from the domestic market.[96]

Sykes concluded that arguments for protectionism from the national security perspective will rarely hold up to careful scrutiny.[97]

Finally, and to an ever more significant extent, governments adopt trade restrictive measures, or measures that have a trade restrictive effect, in pursuit of non-economic societal values such as public morals, public health, consumer safety, a clean environment and cultural identity. Trade in products or services that do not meet specific health, safety or environmental regulations or stan-dards or that may, more generally, threaten a fundamental societal value may be prohibited or significantly limited. Many of such trade restrictive measures are not only legitimate but also necessary. Other such measures, however, are mere fronts for protectionist measures intending to shield domestic producers from import competition. Protectionism can take on very sophisticated guises.[98]

Questions and Assignments 1.5

Why is it that according to most economists even the poorest countries can, at least in theory, benefit from international trade? Why do governments resort to trade restrictive measures?

---

[96] J. Jackson, W. Davey and A. Sykes, *Legal Problems of International Economic Relations*, 4th edition (Westgroup, 2002), 20–1.   [97] *Ibid.*   [98] See below, pp. 650–1.

1.2.4. Globalisation and trade to the benefit of all?

In presenting the *United Nations Millennium Report* to the UN General Assembly in April 2000, former UN Secretary General Kofi Annan spoke of addressing the inequities of globalisation as the 'overarching challenge' of our times. In this presentation to the General Assembly, he argued as follows:

> the benefits of globalization are obvious . . . faster growth; higher living standards; and new opportunities, not only for individuals, but also for better understanding between nations, and for common action. One problem is that, at present, these opportunities are far from equally distributed. How can we say that the half of the human race, which has yet to make or receive a telephone call, let alone use a computer, is taking part in global-ization? We cannot, without insulting their poverty. A second problem is that, even where the global market does reach, it is not yet underpinned, as national markets are, by rules based on shared social objectives. In the absence of such rules, globalization makes many people feel they are at the mercy of unpredictable forces.
> . . . the overarching challenge of our times is to make globalization mean more than bigger markets. To make a success of this great upheaval, we must learn how to govern better, and – above all – how to govern better together. We need to make our States stronger and more effective at the national level. And we need to get them working together on global issues, all pulling their weight and all having their say.[99]

In the *Millennium Declaration* adopted by the UN General Assembly on 8 September 2000, the Heads of State and Government of the Member States of the United Nations solemnly declared:

> We believe that the central challenge we face today is to ensure that globalization becomes a positive force for all the world's people. For while globalization offers great opportunities, at present its benefits are very unevenly shared, while its costs are unevenly distributed. We recognize that developing countries and countries with economies in tran-sition face special difficulties in responding to this central challenge. Thus, only through broad and sustained efforts to create a shared future, based upon our common humanity in all its diversity, can globalization be made fully inclusive and equitable. These efforts must include policies and measures, at the global level, which correspond to the needs of developing countries and economies in transition and are formulated and implemented with their effective participation.[100]

Three years later, at the Cancún Session of the WTO Ministerial Conference in September 2003, Kofi Annan noted, not without a certain measure of frustration:

> The reality of the international trading system today does not match the rhetoric (of improving the quality of life). Instead of open markets, there are too many barriers that stunt, stifle and starve. Instead of fair competition, there are subsidies by rich countries that tilt the playing field against the poor. And instead of global rules negotiated by all, in the interest of all, and adhered to by all, there is too much closed-door decision-making, too much protection of special interests, and too many broken promises.[101]

In its 2002 study, *Rigged Rules and Double Standards: Trade, Globalization, and the Fight Against Poverty*, Oxfam formulated recommendations and suggestions to

---

[99] United Nations General Assembly, *UN Millennium Declaration*, Resolution adopted on 8 September 2000, para. 11.   [100] *Ibid.*, para. 5.
[101] See www.wto.mvs.com/mino3_webcast_e.htm/archives, visited on 31 May 2004.

make economic globalisation and international trade work for the poor. According to Oxfam, international trade can realise its full potential only if rich and poor countries alike take action to *redistribute opportunities* in favour of the poor. This will require action at the national level, new forms of international cooperation and a new architecture of global governance at the WTO. With respect to action at the national level, Oxfam observed:

> The challenge of extending opportunity at the national level goes beyond the narrow confines of trade policy. Inequalities in health and education services, and in the ownership of assets, are a formidable barrier to making markets work for poor people. Lacking access to land, marketing infrastructure, and financial resources, the poor are often least equipped to take advantage of market opportunities, and the most vulnerable to competition from imports.
>
> In many countries, extensive corruption and excessive bureaucracy act as a tax on trade – and the tax falls most heavily on the poor.[102]

With respect to international cooperation, Oxfam noted:

> International cooperation must be strengthened in a range of areas. Developing countries need development assistance if they are to integrate into world markets on more favourable terms and to extend opportunities to the poor.
>
> Yet rich countries reduced their aid budgets by $13 billion between 1992 and 2000. Some of the heaviest cuts fell on the poorest countries and in areas – such as agriculture – where well-targeted aid can make a difference to levels of poverty.[103]

With respect to a new architecture of global governance at the WTO, Oxfam stated:

> The WTO is one of the youngest international institutions, but it is old before its time. Behind the facade of a 'membership-driven' organisation is a governance system based on a dictatorship of wealth. Rich countries have a disproportionate influence. This is partly because of a failure of representational democracy. Each WTO country may have one vote, but eleven of its members among the least-developed countries are not even represented at the WTO base in Geneva.[104]

Oxfam correctly stated that, just as in any national economy, economic integration in the global economy can be a source of shared prosperity and poverty reduction, or a source of increasing inequality and exclusion:

> Managed well, the international trading system can lift millions out of poverty. Managed badly, it will leave whole economies even more marginalised. The same is true at a national level. Good governance can make trade work in the interests of the poor. Bad governance can make it work against them.[105]

According to Oxfam, international trade is at present badly managed, both at the global level and, in many countries, at the national level.[106]

In a reaction to this study, the European Commission took issue with Oxfam's finding that the European Union is the most protectionist of the large trading

---

[102] Oxfam, *Rigged Rules and Double Standards: Trade, Globalization, and the Fight Against Poverty*, 2002, Summary of chapter 9, available at www.maketradefair.org/en/index.php?file=03042002174753. htm&cat=3&subcat=3&select=12, visited on 15 June 2004.   [103] *Ibid*.   [104] *Ibid*.   [105] *Ibid*.
[106] *Ibid*.

entities *but* fully supported Oxfam's analysis of how trade could help to fight poverty. Commenting on the report, the then EU Trade Commissioner Pascal Lamy said:

> The Oxfam report is a substantive and in general well-researched contribution to the debate on the link between trade and development. I fully share the basic philosophy underlying the report: trade has the potential to lift millions out of poverty (and this is borne out by past experience, for instance in East Asia), but the benefits of trade are not automatic – a lot depends on the domestic context.[107]

In a speech to the G-20 Finance Ministers and Central Bank Governors in November 2001, James Wolfensohn, then President of the World Bank, made the following analysis of the challenge of economic globalisation:

> In my view, with the improvements in both technology and policies that we have seen over recent decades, some form of globalization is with us to stay. But the kind of globalization is not yet certain: it can be either a *globalization of development and poverty reduction* – such as we have begun to see in recent decades, although this trend still cannot be taken for granted – or a *globalization of conflict, poverty, disease, and inequality.* What can we do to tip the scales decisively toward the right kind of globalization?[108]

To ensure that economic globalisation and trade liberalisation contribute to economic development, equity and the well-being of all people, Wolfensohn advocated the following four-point agenda for action: better governance, reduction of trade barriers, more development aid and better international cooperation:

> First, developing countries must continue the move toward *better policies, investment climate, and governance.* Despite progress in macroeconomic management and openness, there remain many domestic barriers to integration. Many countries have fallen short in creating an investment climate for productivity, growth, entrepreneurship, and jobs. These domestic barriers include inadequate transport infrastructure, poor governance, bureaucratic harassment of small businesses, a lack of electric power, an unskilled workforce . . . And countries also need to make possible the participation of poor people in growth, through support for targeted education, health, social protection, and their involvement in key decisions that shape their lives. Poor people need much greater voice.
>
> Second, all countries – developed and developing – must *reduce trade barriers* and give developing countries a better chance in world markets . . . Rich countries must increase market access for the exports of developing countries, through both multilateral negotiations and unilateral action, to increase the payoffs to developing-country policy and institutional reforms. Dismantling trade barriers, as our recent publication *Global Economic Prospects: Making Trade Work for the World's Poor* shows, could increase income in developing countries by an estimated $1.5 trillion over a decade and increase GDP growth in the developing countries by 0.5 per cent per year over the long run. This in turn would lift an additional 300 million people out of poverty by 2015 (even beyond the 600 million that will escape poverty with the growth we are currently anticipating) . . .
>
> Third, developed countries must *increase development aid*, but allocate it better and cut down the burden its implementation can impose . . . The evidence from the Bank's research is that well-directed aid, combined with strong reform efforts, can greatly reduce poverty. If

---

[107] European Commission, Memorandum, Brussels, 22 April 2002, available at www.europa.eu.int, visited on 15 July 2004.
[108] 'Responding to the Challenges of Globalization', Remarks to the G-20 Finance Ministers and Central Bank Governors by James D. Wolfensohn, President, World Bank Group, Ottawa, 17 November 2001, available at www.worldbank.org, visited on 15 November 2002.

we are serious about ensuring a beneficial globalization and meeting multilateral development goals we have all signed up to, we must double ODA [overseas development aid] from its current level of about $50 billion a year.

Fourth, we must *act as a global community* where it really matters. Effective globalization requires institutions of global governance, and multilateral action to confront global problems and provide global public goods. This means confronting terrorism, internationalized crime, and money laundering, as we are doing in response to September 11th. But it also means that as a community, we need to address longer-term needs, by: combating communicable diseases like AIDS and malaria; building an equitable global trading system; promoting financial stability to prevent deep and sudden crises; and safeguarding the natural resources and environment on which so many poor people depend for their livelihoods. As we do all this, we must bring poor countries into the decision-making of this global community.[109]

According to Wolfensohn, if the international community can act on these four priorities, it will have created the conditions to achieve true global integration and to reach the millennium goals of halving extreme poverty by 2015.[110]

In addressing the question of how to ensure that economic globalisation and international trade benefits all, WTO Director-General Pascal Lamy noted in 2007 that this question has two sides:

A first one is how to ensure trade benefits are shared more fairly among nations. The second side is how to ensure a better distribution of the benefits stemming from trade within a nation.

On the first side, I believe two elements are fundamental: fairer multilateral trade rules and building of trade capacity in developing countries. One primary objective of the ongoing WTO negotiations under the Doha Development Agenda is precisely to address the remaining imbalances in the WTO rules against developing countries, whether in agriculture or in areas such as textiles or footwear . . . But negotiating a fairer playing field, difficult as it is, will not be enough. New trade opportunities do not automatically convert into growth and development. The international community also has a responsibility to make sure poorer countries have the capacity to trade and make full use of the market access opportunities provided to them, through more and better focused Aid for Trade . . .

The second side, as I said, is how to ensure a better distribution of the benefits stemming from trade within a nation. Trade opening can and does translate into greater growth and poverty alleviation, but this is neither automatic [nor] immediate. Trade opening must be accompanied by a solid domestic agenda to spur on growth and cushion adjustment costs. Appropriate tax policies, competition policy, investment in quality education, social safety nets and innovation fostering healthy environments must all be part of the mix needed for trade to translate into real benefits for the people. In this respect, trade policy cannot be isolated from domestic macroeconomic, social or structural policies. The same trade policy will result in different outcomes depending on the quality of economic policies, and this is true across the board, whether you look at the US, Europe, Japan, or at Vietnam, Cambodia, Kenya or Paraguay.[111]

In remarks to the UNCTAD Trade and Development Board meeting in September 2006, Lamy stated:

Let me start by saying that I share the views expressed in the Report about the contribution that trade can make to development and to poverty alleviation. Trade is today a

---

[109] *Ibid.*   [110] See *ibid.*

[111] P. Lamy, 'Trends and Issues Facing Global Trade', Speech delivered in Kuala Lumpur, Malaysia on 17 August 2007, available at www.wto.org/english/news_e/sppl_e/sppl65_e.htm, visited on 29 October 2007.

> crucial ingredient in a policy mix which must nevertheless contain many other ingredients to achieve successfully this objective. This means, no blind adherence to free trade. But this also means no blind adherence to governments doing pretty much anything and certainly no blind adherence protectionism. If trade opening is not sufficient, it remains a necessary ingredient. This is the core of what I have called the '*Geneva Consensus*'.
> [Emphasis added][112]

It must be noted, however, that not all share the belief in this 'Geneva Consensus' and the 'conditional optimism' of Oxfam, the World Bank and the WTO. In a reaction to what some call the rhetoric of 'globalisation as opportunity', the President of Tanzania, Benjamin Mkapa, said in a statement made at the 2000 Annual Meeting of the World Economic Forum in Davos:

> Globalisation can deliver, just as Tanzania can play in the World Cup and win it.[113]

It is clear that economic openness is a necessary but not a sufficient condition for economic development and prosperity. The simple spread of markets will not eliminate poverty. A global economy and more international trade will not automatically lead to rising prosperity for all countries and for all people. Good governance is undoubtedly as important as international trade. Without functioning State institutions and without a legal system that protects fundamental rights and property and enforces contracts, globalisation will not bring prosperity but, on the contrary, poverty, corruption and exploitation.

Peter Sutherland, former GATT and WTO Director-General and EU Commissioner and currently Chairman of BP Amoco and Goldman Sachs International, emphasised that more than free markets is needed to eradicate poverty and inequality:

> There are those who oppose redistribution policies in principle, whether in the domestic or the international context. This is wrong. It is morally wrong, it is pragmatically wrong, and we ought not be ashamed to say so. I have been personally and deeply committed to promoting the market system through my entire career. Yet it is quite obvious to me that the market will never provide all of the answers to the problems of poverty and inequality. The fact is that there are those who will not be able to develop their economies simply because market access has been provided. I do not believe that we in the global community will adequately live up to our responsibility if we have done no more than provide the poorest people and the poorest countries with an opportunity to succeed. We must also provide them with a foundation from which they have a reasonable chance of seizing that opportunity – decent health care, primary education, basic infrastructure.[114]

It is worth noting that there is also a cultural dimension to the issue of globalisation which may make it harder for certain countries and people to make use

---

[112] P. Lamy, Opening Remarks, 53rd Session of the UNCTAD Trade and Development Board, 27 September 2006, available at www.wto.org/english/news_e/sppl_e/sppl40_e.htm, visited on 20 October 2007. On the 'Geneva Consensus', see also P. Lamy, 'Humanising Globalization', Speech delivered in Santiago de Chile, Chile on 30 January 2006, available at www.wto.org/english/news_e/sppl_e/sppl16_e.htm, visited on 25 October 2007; and P. Lamy, 'Towards Global Governance?', Master of Public Affairs inaugural lecture at the Institut d'Études Politiques de Paris on 21 October 2005, available at www.wto.org/english/news_e/sppl_e/sppl12_e.htm, visited on 25 October 2007.
[113] As reported by J. Harris, 'Globalisation and World's Poor', *Economic and Political Weekly*, 9 June 2001, 2034.
[114] P. Sutherland, 'Beyond the Market, a Different Kind of Equity', *International Herald Tribune*, 20 February 1997.

of the opportunity globalisation, and international trade, offers for economic development:

> Much of Latin America, for example, abandoned trade protectionism and favoritism for local companies. Between 1985 and 1996, average tariffs fell from 50 per cent to 10 per cent. The results have been modest. What explains the contrasts? Perhaps culture. The gospel of capitalism presumes that human nature is constant. Given the proper incentives – the ability to profit from hard work and risk taking – people will strive. Maybe not. In a recent book, 'Culture Matters: How Values Shape Human Progress', scholars from the United States, Africa and Latin America argue that strong social and moral values predispose some peoples for and against economic growth. As a result of history, tradition and religion, some societies cannot easily adopt capitalist attitudes and institutions. Even when they try, they often fail because it is so unnatural. 'Competition is central to the success of an enterprise, the politician, the intellectual and the professional', writes Mariano Grondona, an Argentine political scientist and columnist. 'In resistant societies, competition is condemned as a form of aggression.' Daniel Etounga-Manguelle of Cameroon contends that Africa suffers from a reverence for its history. 'In traditional African society, which exalts the glorious past of ancestors through tales and fables, nothing is done to prepare for the future', he writes. Once stated, culture's impact seems obvious.[115]

However, culture, though deep, is not immutable. Culture is changed by experience. There are multiple examples of cultures changing over time. One such example, India, has shifted since the late 1980s from protectionism and State control towards pro-market policies, thereby raising annual economic growth to more than 9.4 per cent in 2006.[116]

Reflecting on the 'acceptability' of economic globalisation and international trade in particular in developed countries, Dani Rodrik concluded his book, *Has Globalization Gone Too Far?*, as follows:

> The broader challenge for the 21st century is to engineer a new balance between market and society, one that will continue to unleash the creative energies of private entrepreneurship without eroding the social basis of cooperation. The tensions between globalization and social cohesion are real, and they are unlikely to disappear of their own accord.[117]

The General Secretary of the International Confederation of Free Trade Unions wrote in December 2000:

> [G]lobalization is neither entirely beneficial nor entirely harmful. It is not an unstoppable force of nature, but is shaped by those who set the rules . . . The labor movement's position is simply that the rules governing globalization should protect the interests of the poor and not just the rich, and that the benefits of increased trade and increased global output should be shared by all.[118]

Over the past ten years, the UN High Commissioner for Human Rights has argued repeatedly that fair and equitable economic globalisation and trade liberalisation can only be achieved by adopting a *human rights approach* to both processes. The UN Committee on Economic, Social and Cultural Rights adopted

---

[115] R. Samuelson, 'Persistent Poverty Defies the Wisdom on Globalization', *International Herald Tribune*, 21 September 2000.   [116] See above, p. 17.

[117] D. Rodrik, *Has Globalization Gone Too Far?* (Institute for International Economics, 1997), 85.

[118] B. Jordan, 'Yes to Globalization, But Protect the Poor', *International Herald Tribune*, 21 December 2000.

in 1999 a resolution stating that 'trade liberalization must be understood as a means, not an end' and that:

> The end which trade liberalization should serve is the objective of human well-being to which the international human rights instruments give legal expression. In this regard the Committee wishes to remind WTO Members of the central and fundamental nature of human rights obligations.[119]

Joseph Stiglitz described, in *Globalization and Its Discontents*, the experience of the United States during the nineteenth century with the formation of its national economy and the regulating and supporting role played by the federal government in that process.[120] According to Stiglitz, the experience of the United States makes a good parallel for today's globalisation. The contrast helps illustrate the successes of the past and the failures of the present:

> Today, with the continuing decline in transportation and communication costs, and the reduction of man-made barriers to the flow of goods, services, and capital (though there remain serious barriers to the free flow of labor), we have a process of 'globalization' analogous to the earlier processes in which national economies were formed. Unfortunately, we have no world government, accountable to the people in every country, to oversee the globalization process in a fashion comparable to the way national governments guided the nationalization process. Instead, we have a system that might be called *global governance without global government*, one in which a few institutions – the World Bank, the IMF, the WTO – and a few players – the finance, commerce, and trade ministries, closely linked to certain financial and commercial interests – dominate the scene, but in which those affected by their decisions are left almost voiceless.[121]

Criticising the current system of what he referred to as 'global governance without global government', Stiglitz called for a reform of the rules governing the international economic order. According to Stiglitz:

> Globalization can be reshaped, and when it is, when it is properly, fairly run, with all countries having a voice in policies affecting them, there is a possibility that it will help to create a new global economy in which growth is not only more sustainable and less volatile but the fruits of this growth are more equitably shared.[122]

Muhammad Yunus noted in his Nobel Peace Prize Lecture in December 2006:

> I support globalization and believe it can bring more benefits to the poor than its alternative. But it must be the right kind of globalization. To me, globalization is like a hundred-lane highway criss-crossing the world. If it is a free-for-all highway, its lanes will be taken over by the giant trucks from powerful economies. Bangladeshi rickshaw will be thrown off the highway. In order to have a win–win globalization we must have traffic rules, traffic police, and traffic authority for this global highway. Rule of "strongest takes it all" must be replaced by rules that ensure that the poorest have a place and piece of the action, without being elbowed out by the strong.[123]

---

[119] United Nations Economic and Social Council, 'Statement of the UN Committee on Economic, Social and Cultural Rights to the Third Ministerial Conference of the World Trade Organization (Seattle, 30 November to 3 December 1999)', adopted at the 47th meeting, twenty-first session, 26 November 1999, E/C.12/1999/9, 2.   [120] J. Stiglitz, *Globalization and Its Discontents* (Penguin, 2002), 21.
[121] *Ibid.*, 21–2.   [122] *Ibid.*, 22.
[123] Muhammad Yunus, Nobel Lecture, Oslo, 10 December 2006, available at http://nobelprize.org/nobel_prizes/peace/laureates/2006/yunus-lecture-en.html, visited on 27 October 2007.

Questions and Assignments 1.6

How can economic globalisation and international trade be made 'a positive force for all the world's people' as mandated in the *UN Millennium Declaration*? What is referred to as the 'Geneva Consensus'? What does Joseph Stiglitz mean when he refers to 'global governance without global government'? What is needed to ensure that there is room for a Bangladeshi rickshaw on Muhammad Yunus' hundred-lane highway?

1.3. INTERNATIONAL TRADE AND THE LAW OF THE WTO

As discussed above, economic globalisation and international trade need to be properly managed and regulated if they are to be of benefit to all humankind. This section discusses:

- the need for and existence of international rules for international trade; and
- the basic rules and disciplines of WTO law.

1.3.1. International rules for international trade

1.3.1.1. *Need for international rules*

Peter Sutherland wrote in 1997:

> The greatest economic challenge facing the world is the *need to create an international system* that not only maximizes global growth but also achieves a greater measure of equity, a system that both integrates emerging powers and assists currently marginalized countries in their efforts to participate in worldwide economic expansion . . . The most important means available to secure peace and prosperity into the future is to develop effective multilateral approaches and institutions.[124]
>
> [Emphasis added]

These multilateral approaches and institutions to which Sutherland referred embrace many structures and take many forms but, as John Jackson noted:

> it is very clear that law and legal norms play the most important part of the institutions which are essential to make markets work. The notion that 'rule of law' (ambiguous as that phrase is) or a *rule-based or rule-oriented system* of human institutions is essential to a beneficial operation of markets, is a constantly recurring theme in many writings.[125]
>
> [Emphasis added]

Ronald Coase wrote:

> It is evident that, for their operation, markets . . . require the establishment of legal rules governing the rights and duties of those carrying out transactions . . . *To realize all the gains of trade* . . . there has to be a legal system and political order.[126]
>
> [Emphasis added]

---

[124] P. Sutherland, 'Beyond the Market, a Different Kind of Equity', *International Herald Tribune*, 20 February 1997.

[125] J. Jackson, 'Global Economics and International Economic Law', *Journal of International Economic Law*, 1998, 5 (reproduced by permission of Oxford University Press).

[126] R. Coase, *The Firm, the Market and the Law* (reprint of 1960 article), chapter 5, as quoted by Jackson, *ibid.*, 4.

But what exactly is the role of legal rules and, in particular, international legal rules in international trade? How do international trade rules allow countries to realise the gains of international trade?

There are basically four related reasons why there is a need for international trade rules. First, countries must be restrained from adopting trade-restrictive measures both in their own interest and in that of the world economy. International trade rules *restrain* countries from taking trade-restrictive measures. As noted above, national policy-makers may come under considerable pressure from influential interest groups to adopt trade-restrictive measures in order to protect domestic industries from import competition. Such measures may benefit the specific, short-term interests of the groups advocating them but they very seldom benefit the general economic interests of the country adopting them.[127] As Ernst-Ulrich Petersmann observed:

> Governments know very well . . . that by 'tying their hands to the mast' (like Ulysses when he approached the island of the Sirenes), reciprocal international pre-commitments help them to resist the siren-like temptations from 'rent-seeking' interest groups at home.[128]

Countries also realise that, if they take trade-restrictive measures, other countries will do so too. This may lead to an escalation of trade-restrictive measures, a disastrous move for international trade and for global economic welfare. International trade rules help to avoid such escalation.

A second and closely related reason why international trade rules are necessary is the need of traders and investors for a degree of *security and predictability*. Traders and investors operating, or intending to operate, in a country that is bound by international legal rules will be able to predict better how that country will act in the future on matters affecting their operations in that country. The predictability and security resulting from international trade rules will encourage investments and trade and will thus contribute to global economic welfare. As John Jackson wrote:

> At least in the context of economic behaviour . . . and particularly when that behaviour is set in circumstances of decentralized decision-making, as in a market economy, rules can have important operational functions. They may provide the only predictability or stability to a potential investment or trade-development situation. Without such predictability or stability, trade or investment flows might be even more risky and therefore more inhibited than otherwise . . . To put it another way, the policies which tend to reduce some risks, lower the 'risk premium' required by entrepreneurs to enter into international transactions. This should result in a general increase in the efficiency of various economic activities, contributing to greater welfare for everyone.[129]

A third reason why international trade rules are necessary is that national governments alone simply cannot *cope with the challenges presented by economic*

---

[127] See above, p. 21. On the optimal tariff argument and the strategic trade policy argument, see above, pp. 22–3.
[128] E. U. Petersmann, *The GATT/WTO Dispute Settlement System: International Law, International Organizations and Dispute Settlement* (Kluwer Law International, 1997), 36–7.
[129] J. Jackson, 'Global Economics and International Economic Law', *Journal of International Economic Law*, 1998, 5–6.

globalisation. The protection of important societal values such as public health, a clean environment, consumer safety, cultural identity and minimum labour standards is, as a result of the greatly increased levels of trade in goods and services, no longer a purely national matter but ever more a matter with significant international ramifications. Attempts to ensure the protection of these values at the national level alone are doomed to be ineffective and futile. Further, domestic regulatory measures regarding, for example, product safety, health, environmental protection and labour conditions may constitute important barriers to trade. These measures are often not directly or expressly related to the regulation of trade but the fact that they differ from country to country acts as a significant constraint on trade. International trade rules serve to ensure that countries only maintain national regulatory measures that are *necessary* for the protection of the key societal values referred to above.[130] International trade rules may also introduce a degree of harmonisation of domestic regulatory measures and thus promote an effective, international protection of these societal values.[131]

A fourth and final reason why international trade rules are necessary is the need to achieve a *greater measure of equity* in international economic relations. As Father Lacordaire had stated in his renowned 1835 sermons at the Notre Dame in Paris:

> Entre le faible et le fort, entre le riche et le pauvre . . . c'est la liberté qui opprime et la loi qui affranchit.[132]

Without international trade rules, binding and enforceable on rich as well as poor countries, and rules recognising the special needs of developing countries, many of these countries would not be able to integrate fully in the world trading system and derive an equitable share of the gains of international trade.

However, for international legal rules to play these multiple roles, such rules have, of course, to be observed. It is clear that international trade rules are not always adhered to. Yet, while most attention, of both the media and academia, is inevitably paid to instances of breach, it should be stressed that international trade rules are generally well observed. Countries realise that they cannot expect other countries to observe the rules if they do not do so themselves. The desire to be able to depend on other countries' compliance with the rules leads many countries to observe the rules even though this might be politically inconvenient in a given situation.[133]

All countries and their people benefit from the existence of rules on international trade making the trading environment more predictable and stable.

---

[130] See below, pp. 621–9.   [131] See below, p. 616.

[132] Translation: 'Between the weak and the powerful, between the rich and the poor . . . it is freedom that oppresses and the law that sets free.' Abbé Jean-Baptiste Lacordaire (1802–61) was the greatest French pulpit orator of the nineteenth century.

[133] See L. Henkin, *How Nations Behave*, 2nd edition (1979); R. Fisher, *Improving Compliance with International Law* (1981); and A. Chayes, *The New Sovereignty: Compliance with International Regulatory Agreements* (1995), as referred to in J. Jackson, 'Global Economics and International Economic Law', *Journal of International Economic Law*, 1998, 5.

However, provided the rules take into account their specific interests and needs, developing countries, with generally limited economic, political and military power, should benefit even more from the existence of rules on international trade. The weaker countries are likely to suffer most where the law of the jungle reigns. They are more likely to thrive in a *rules-based*, rather than a power-based, international trading system.

While developing countries stand to benefit most from rules and disciplines on international trade, some developing countries frequently argue in favour of freedom from such rules and disciplines to allow them to pursue their domestic policy objectives. As reported in *BRIDGES Weekly Trade News Digest*, at the 2006 Annual Session of the Trade and Development Board of UNCTAD:

> ministers and top trade diplomats returned to the so-called 'policy space' debate. This hinges on the extent to which governments should have to constrain their ability to pursue particular policies by embracing international economic rules. The issue has been a contentious one, with several developing countries calling for more space to pursue development policy, while industrialised countries peddle the merits of tying governments' hands in order to avoid policy missteps. Nevertheless, member states managed to agree on language referring to the importance of policy space to developing countries. The report adopted at the end of the week of discussions stated that 'It is for each government to evaluate the trade-off between the benefits of accepting international rules and commitments and the constraints posed by the loss of policy space. It is particularly important for developing countries, bearing in mind development goals and objectives, that all countries take into account the need for appropriate balance between national policy space and international disciplines and commitments.'[134]

At the start of this Session, WTO Director-General Pascal Lamy had stated in his opening remarks:

> An important part of this year's report is devoted to the issues of policy autonomy or policy space. The basic argument which UNCTAD is making is that international commitments in the finance or trade fields are preventing developing countries from realizing their true development potential, in that governments are prevented from intervening in the economy in ways that are essential to progress. When using this argument, I believe it is important to make the case not just for policy space but for 'good policy' space. We need to make a convincing case as to why a particular policy is needed, basing ourselves on the facts.[135]

Questions and Assignments 1.7

Is there a need for international rules on trade? Who benefits from these rules and why? Do international rules on trade necessarily conflict with the 'policy space' that many governments of developing countries claim?

---

[134] 'UNCTAD governing body highlights need for "policy space"', *BRIDGES Weekly Trade News Digest*, 18 October 2006.
[135] P. Lamy, Opening Remarks, 53rd Session of the UNCTAD Trade and Development Board, 27 September 2006, available at www.wto.org/english/news_e/sppl_e/sppl40_e.htm, visited on 20 October 2007.

1.3.1.2. International economic law and WTO law

The legal rules, discussed above, governing trade relations between countries are part of international economic law. International economic law is a very broad field of international law. With regard to the concept of 'international economic law', John Jackson noted that:

> [it] is not by any means a new phenomenon although the phrase may be considered relatively new. International law has always had considerable 'economic content', as manifested by international economic institutions and by the international law jurisprudence throughout the centuries devoted to various economic subjects including trade, investment, commerce, and navigation (FCN treaties). In addition, activities of the League of Nations, as well as, more currently, the United Nations, have had a very substantial economic institutional dimension.[136]

Jackson once suggested that 90 per cent of international law work relates in fact to international economic law in some form or another. He also observed that international economic law does not enjoy as much glamour or media attention as work on armed conflicts and human rights do.[137]

International economic law can be defined, broadly, as covering all those international rules pertaining to economic transactions and relations, as well as those pertaining to governmental regulation of economic matters. As such, international economic law includes international rules on trade in goods and services, economic development, intellectual property rights, foreign direct investment, international finance and monetary matters, commodities, food, health, transport, communications, natural resources, private commercial transactions, nuclear energy, etc. International rules on international trade in goods and services, i.e. international trade law, constitute the 'hard core' of international economic law.

International trade law consists of, on the one hand, numerous bilateral or regional trade agreements and, on the other hand, multilateral trade agreements. Examples of bilateral and regional trade agreements are manifold. The *North American Free Trade Agreement* (NAFTA) and the *MERCOSUR Agreement* are typical examples of regional trade agreements. *The Trade Agreement between the United States and Israel* or the *Agreement on Trade in Wine between the European Community and Australia* are examples of bilateral trade agreements. The number of multilateral trade agreements is more limited. This group includes, for example, the 1983 *International Convention on the Harmonised Commodity Description and Coding System* (the '*Brussels Convention*') and the 1973 *International Convention on the Simplification and Harmonisation of Customs Procedures*, as revised in 2000 (the '*Kyoto Convention*'). The most important and broadest of all multilateral trade agreements is the *Marrakesh Agreement Establishing the World Trade Organization*,

---

[136] J. Jackson, 'International Economic Law: Complexity and Puzzles', *Journal of International Economic Law*, 2007, 3
[137] J. Jackson, 'International Economic Law: Reflections on the "Boilerroom" of International Relations', *American University Journal of International Law and Policy*, 1995, 596.

concluded on 15 April 1994. It is the law of this Agreement – the law of the WTO – which is the subject-matter of this book.

Questions and Assignments 1.8

What is international economic law and what does it cover? How does WTO law relate to international economic law?

1.3.2. Basic rules and principles of WTO law

The law of the WTO is a complex set of rules dealing with trade in goods and services and the protection of intellectual property rights. WTO law addresses a broad spectrum of issues, ranging from tariffs, import quotas and customs formalities to compulsory licensing, food safety regulations and national security measures. However, five groups of basic rules and principles can be distinguished:

- the principles of non-discrimination;
- the rules on market access;
- the rules on unfair trade;
- the rules on conflicts between trade liberalisation and other societal values and interests; including the rules on special and differential treatment for developing countries; and
- the rules promoting harmonisation of national regulation in specific fields.

In addition, WTO law contains institutional and procedural rules, including those relating to decision-making and dispute settlement.

These substantive and procedural rules and principles of WTO law make up what is commonly referred to as the *multilateral trading system*. Referring to this system, Peter Sutherland and others wrote in 2001:

> The multilateral trading system, with the World Trade Organization (WTO) at its centre, is the most important tool of global economic management and development we possess.[138]

Martin Wolf of the *Financial Times* noted in 2001:

> The multilateral trading system at the beginning of the twenty-first century is the most remarkable achievement in institutionalized global economic cooperation that there has ever been.[139]

The Economist noted the following in June 2005 with regard to the relevance of the rules of the multilateral trading system:

---

[138] P. Sutherland, J. Sewell and D. Weiner, 'Challenges Facing the WTO and Policies to Address Global Governance', in G. Sampson (ed.), *The Role of the World Trade Organization in Global Governance* (United Nations University Press, 2001), 81.
[139] M. Wolf, 'What the World Needs from the Multilateral Trading System', in G. Sampson (ed.), *The Role of the World Trade Organization in Global Governance* (United Nations University Press, 2001), 182.

Wherever you look, trade tensions are on the rise. America and the European Union are squealing about surging textile imports from China; both are slapping on 'safeguard' quotas to stem the flow. China is furious and has retaliated by scrapping voluntary export taxes on its textile exporters. Meanwhile Americans and Europeans are, once again, spitting at each other about subsidies to Boeing and Airbus. Both sides this week formally filed complaints at the World Trade Organization. Set against an increasingly protectionist backdrop – whether in America's Congress or among France's *non*-voters – this rash of disputes might suggest an ominous outlook for the global trading system.

There is one bright spot, however. The recent tensions show just how integral the rules of the global trading system, and the WTO that adjudicates those rules, have become to the way countries, rich and poor alike, think about trade policy. The safeguard quotas that America and Europe are using to staunch Chinese textiles may be of dubious economic merit, but they were agreed under the terms of China's entry into the WTO and therefore have limits (they must go by 2008). China can, and no doubt will, file a complaint if it reckons their application is unfair. Even on the aircraft dispute, the shift to an independent arbiter may be more constructive than endless acrimonious bilateral negotiations. And in America, the global rules are proving an important bulwark against protectionist backsliding. The Bush administration has been able to deter some of Congress's more extreme China-bashing plans by pointing out that they are illegal under world trade rules.[140]

The following sections of this chapter briefly review these basic rules and principles constituting the multilateral trading system. They will be discussed in greater detail in subsequent chapters of this book.

1.3.2.1. *Principles of non-discrimination*

There are two principles of non-discrimination in WTO law: the most-favoured-nation (MFN) treatment obligation and the national treatment obligation.

The *MFN treatment obligation* requires a WTO Member that grants certain favourable treatment to another country to grant that same favourable treatment to all other WTO Members. A WTO Member is not allowed to discriminate *between* its trading partners by, for example, giving the products imported from some countries more favourable treatment with respect to market access than the treatment it accords to the products of other Members.[141] In spite of many exceptions and deviations from this obligation, the MFN treatment obligation is the single most important rule in WTO law. Without this rule the multilateral trading system could and would not exist. Chapter 4 examines in detail this rule as it applies to trade in goods and trade in services.[142]

The *national treatment obligation* requires a WTO Member to treat foreign products, services and service suppliers no less favourably than it treats 'like' domestic products, services and service suppliers. Where the national treatment obligation applies, foreign products, for example, should, once they have crossed the border and entered the domestic market, not be subject to less favourable taxation or regulation than 'like' domestic products. Pursuant to the national treatment obligation, a WTO Member is not allowed to discriminate *against* foreign products, services and service suppliers. The national treatment obligation is an

---

[140] 'The Key to Trade and Aid', *The Economist*, 2 June 2005.
[141] See Article I of the GATT 1994 and Article II of the GATS.   [142] See below, pp. 322–43.

important rule in WTO law which has given rise to many trade disputes. For trade in goods, the national treatment obligation has *general* application to all trade.[143] By contrast, for trade in services, the national treatment obligation does not have such general application. It applies only to the extent a WTO Member has explicitly committed itself to grant 'national treatment' in respect of specific service sectors.[144] Such commitments to give 'national treatment' are made in a Member's Schedule of Specific Commitments on Services. Chapter 4 of this book discusses in detail the national treatment obligation as it applies to trade in goods and services.[145]

1.3.2.2. *Rules on market access*

WTO law contains four groups of rules regarding market access:

- rules on *customs duties* (i.e. tariffs);
- rules on *other duties and financial charges*;
- rules on *quantitative restrictions*; and
- rules on *other 'non-tariff barriers'*, such as rules on transparency of trade regulations; customs formalities; and government procurement practices.

Under WTO law, the imposition of customs duties is not prohibited and, in fact, WTO Members impose customs duties on many products. However, WTO law calls upon WTO Members to negotiate mutually beneficial reductions of customs duties.[146] These negotiations result in tariff concessions or bindings, set out in a Member's Schedule of Concessions. On products for which a tariff concession or binding exists, the customs duties imposed may no longer exceed the maximum level of duty agreed to.[147] Chapter 5 examines the rules applicable to customs duties.[148] It also discusses the rules on other duties and financial charges.[149]

While customs duties are, in principle, not prohibited, quantitative restrictions on trade in goods are, as a general rule, forbidden.[150] Unless one of many exceptions applies, WTO Members are not allowed to ban the importation or exportation of goods or to subject them to quotas. With respect to trade in services, quantitative restrictions are, in principle, prohibited in service sectors for which specific market-access commitments have been undertaken.[151] In those sectors, quantitative restrictions can only be imposed if such restrictions have been inscribed in a Member's Schedule of Specific Commitments. Chapter 5 examines the rules applicable to quantitative restrictions on trade in goods and services.[152]

Among 'other non-tariff barriers', the lack of transparency of national trade regulations definitely stands out as a major barrier to international trade. Uncertainty and confusion regarding the trade rules applicable in other countries

---

[143] See Article III of the GATT 1994.   [144] See Article XVII of the GATS.   [145] See below, pp. 344–95.
[146] See Article XXVIII *bis* of the GATT 1994.   [147] See Article II of the GATT 1994.
[148] See below, pp. 403–38.   [149] See below, pp. 438–44.   [150] See Article XI of the GATT 1994.
[151] Article XVI of the GATS. In fact, the prohibition of Article XVI of the GATS applies only to 'market access barriers' as defined in Article XVI:2. See below, pp. 477–81.   [152] See below, pp. 444–93.

has a chilling effect on trade. Likewise, the arbitrary application of these rules also discourages traders and hampers trade. Transparency and the fair application of trade regulations are therefore part of the basic rules on market access examined in Chapter 5.[153] Non-tariff barriers to trade, such as customs formalities and practices of government procurement, are, for many products and in many countries, more important barriers to trade than customs duties or quantitative restrictions. The rules on many of these non-tariff barriers are examined in chapter 5.[154]

1.3.2.3. Rules on unfair trade

WTO law, at present, does not provide for general rules on unfair trade practices, but it does have a number of detailed rules that relate to specific forms of 'unfair' trade. These rules deal with dumping and subsidised trade.

Dumping, i.e. bringing a product onto the market of another country at a price less than the normal value of that product, is condemned but not prohibited in WTO law. However, when the dumping causes or threatens to cause material injury to the domestic industry of a Member producing a 'like' product, WTO law allows that Member to impose anti-dumping duties on the dumped products in order to offset the dumping.[155] The rules on the imposition of these anti-dumping duties are examined in chapter 6.

Subsidies, i.e. financial contributions by governments or public bodies that confer a benefit, are subject to an intricate set of rules.[156] Some subsidies, such as export subsidies, are, as a rule, prohibited. Other subsidies are not prohibited but, when they cause adverse effects to the interests of other Members, the subsidising Member should withdraw the subsidy or take appropriate steps to remove the adverse effects. If the subsidising Member fails to do so, countermeasures commensurate with the degree and nature of the adverse effect may be authorised.[157] If a prohibited or other subsidy causes or threatens to cause material injury to the domestic industry of a Member producing a 'like' product, that Member is authorised to impose countervailing duties on the subsidised products to offset the subsidisation. Subsidies relating to agricultural products are subject to different (more lenient) rules.[158] The rules applicable to subsidies and countervailing duties are examined in chapter 6.

1.3.2.4. Trade liberalisation versus other societal values and interests

Apart from the basic rules and principles referred to above, WTO law also provides for rules that address the conflict between trade liberalisation and other

---

[153] See below, pp. 460–70.

[154] See below, pp. 470–6. Technical barriers to trade and the lack of protection of intellectual property rights can also be seen as forms of 'other non-tariff barriers', but since the rules on these barriers are quite specific in nature, they are discussed separately in chapter 8 of this book. See below, pp. 741–884.

[155] See Article VI of the GATT 1994 and the *Anti-Dumping Agreement*.

[156] See Articles VI and XVI of the GATT 1994 and the *Agreement on Subsidies and Countervailing Measures* (the 'SCM Agreement').   [157] See Article 7.9 of the *SCM Agreement*.

[158] Articles 6–11 of the *Agreement on Agriculture*.

societal values and interests. These rules, which are commonly referred to as 'exceptions', allow WTO Members to deviate – under specific conditions – from basic WTO rules and disciplines in order to take account of economic and non-economic values and interests that compete or conflict with free trade. The *non-economic* values and interests include the protection of the environment, public health, public morals, national treasures and national security. The relevant rules can be found in, for example, Articles XX and XXI of the GATT 1994 and Articles XIV and XIV *bis* of the GATS. The *economic* interests include the protection of a domestic industry from serious injury inflicted by an unexpected and sharp surge in imports, the safeguarding of the balance of payments and the pursuit of regional economic integration. The relevant rules can be found in, for example, Articles XII, XIX and XXIV of the GATT 1994, Articles V, X and XII of the GATS and the *Agreement on Safeguards*. The WTO rules allowing Members to take into account economic or non-economic values and interests that may conflict with free trade are examined in detail in chapter 7.[159]

Recognising the need for positive efforts designed to ensure that developing-country Members, and especially the least-developed countries among them, are integrated into the multilateral trading system,[160] WTO law includes many provisions granting a degree of special and differential treatment to developing-country Members.[161] These provisions attempt to take the special needs of developing countries into account. In many areas, they provide for fewer obligations or differing rules for developing countries as well as for technical assistance. The rules on the special and differential treatment of developing-country Members are examined in detail throughout this book, but particularly in chapter 7.[162]

1.3.2.5. *Rules promoting harmonisation of national regulation*

A final group of substantive rules of WTO law that deserves separate attention are the rules promoting harmonisation of national regulation contained in the *TBT Agreement*, the *SPS Agreement* and the *TRIPS Agreement*. The *TBT Agreement* sets out rules on technical regulations, standards and conformity assessment procedures. The *SPS Agreement* contains obligations applicable to sanitary and phytosanitary measures. The *TRIPS Agreement* lays down minimum requirements for the protection of intellectual property rights. The rules in these three agreements have in common that they go far beyond the usual trade liberalisation rules and venture into 'behind-the-border' regulatory areas to a greater extent than other WTO agreements dealing with 'other non-tariff barriers' to trade. In addition to the usual WTO disciplines, they promote regulatory harmonisation around international standards. These rules are discussed in chapter 8.[163]

---

[159] See below, pp. 615–95.   [160] See *WTO Agreement*, Preamble, second paragraph.
[161] For example, Article XVIII and Part IV of the GATT 1994 as well as the Enabling Clause. See below, pp. 723–31.   [162] See below, pp. 723–31.   [163] See below, pp. 741–884.

1.3.2.6. Institutional and procedural rules

All basic rules and principles referred to above are substantive rules and principles. However, the multilateral trading system also includes, and depends on, institutional and procedural rules relating to decision-making and dispute settlement. The rules regarding the institutions and procedures for the formulation and implementation of trade rules are discussed in detail in chapter 2. The rules and procedures regarding the settlement of trade disputes are dealt with in chapter 3.

Questions and Assignments 1.9

What are the basic rules and principles that make up the multilateral trading system? What is the most fundamental principle of WTO law? Does WTO law take into account the special situation of developing countries? Does WTO law address the conflict between trade liberalisation and other economic and non-economic societal values and interests?

1.4. SOURCES OF WTO LAW

WTO law is, by international law standards, a sprawling and complex body of law. This section reviews the sources of WTO law. Not all sources of WTO law reviewed below are of the same nature or are on the same legal footing. Some sources provide for specific legal rights and obligations for WTO Members that these Members can enforce through WTO dispute settlement.[164] Many other sources, reviewed below, do not in and by themselves provide for specific, enforceable rights and obligations. They are nevertheless sources of WTO law as they 'clarify' or 'define' the law that applies between WTO Members on WTO matters.[165]

The principal source of WTO law is the *Marrakesh Agreement Establishing the World Trade Organization*, concluded on 15 April 1994 and in force since 1 January 1995. Other sources of WTO law include WTO dispute settlement reports, acts of WTO bodies, agreements concluded in the context of the WTO, customary international law, general principles of law, other international agreements, subsequent practice of WTO Members, teachings of the most highly qualified publicists and, finally, the negotiating history.

1.4.1. The Marrakesh Agreement Establishing the World Trade Organization

The *Marrakesh Agreement Establishing the World Trade Organization* (the 'WTO Agreement') is the most ambitious and far-reaching international trade agree-

---

[164] I.e. Members can claim the violation of these rights and obligations before WTO dispute settlement bodies.
[165] Arguably, the respondent Member in a dispute could invoke rules 'generated' by these sources of WTO law in defence of a claim of violation. This is, however, controversial. See below, pp. 53–9.

ment ever concluded.[166] It consists of a short basic agreement (of sixteen articles) and numerous other agreements and understandings included in the annexes to this basic agreement.

Agreement Establishing the World Trade Organization
ANNEX 1
ANNEX 1A: Multilateral Agreements on Trade in Goods
        General Agreement on Tariffs and Trade 1994
        Agreement on Agriculture
        Agreement on the Application of Sanitary and Phytosanitary Measures
        Agreement on Textiles and Clothing
        Agreement on Technical Barriers to Trade
        Agreement on Trade-Related Investment Measures
        Agreement on Implementation of Article VI of the General Agreement on Tariffs and Trade 1994
        Agreement on Implementation of Article VII of the General Agreement on Tariffs and Trade 1994
        Agreement on Preshipment Inspection
        Agreement on Rules of Origin
        Agreement on Import Licensing Procedures
        Agreement on Subsidies and Countervailing Measures
        Agreement on Safeguards
ANNEX 1B: General Agreement on Trade in Services and Annexes
ANNEX 1C: Agreement on Trade-Related Aspects of Intellectual Property Rights
ANNEX 2: Understanding on Rules and Procedures Governing the Settlement of Disputes
ANNEX 3: Trade Policy Review Mechanism
ANNEX 4: Plurilateral Trade Agreements
        Agreement on Trade in Civil Aircraft
        Agreement on Government Procurement

On the relationship between the *WTO Agreement* and its Annexes as well as on the binding nature of the Annexes, Article II of the *WTO Agreement* states:

> 2. The agreements and associated legal instruments included in Annexes 1, 2 and 3 (hereinafter referred to as 'Multilateral Trade Agreements') are integral parts of this Agreement, binding on all Members.
>
> 3. The agreements and associated legal instruments included in Annex 4 (hereinafter referred to as 'Plurilateral Trade Agreements') are also part of this Agreement for those Members that have accepted them, and are binding on those Members. The Plurilateral Trade Agreements do not create either obligations or rights for Members that have not accepted them.

[166] The official version of the *WTO Agreement* and its Annexes is published by the WTO and Cambridge University Press as *The Results of the Uruguay Round of Multilateral Trade Negotiations: The Legal Texts*. The *Legal Texts* are an indispensable instrument for international trade law practitioners and scholars. The *WTO Agreement* and its Annexes are also available on the WTO website: www.wto.org.

While the *WTO Agreement* consists of many agreements, the WTO Appellate Body in one of the first cases before it, *Brazil – Desiccated Coconut*, stressed the 'single undertaking' nature of the *WTO Agreement*.[167] All multilateral WTO agreements apply equally and are equally binding on all WTO Members. The provisions of these agreements represent 'an *inseparable package* of rights and disciplines which have to be considered in conjunction'.[168]

Furthermore, Article XVI:3 of the *WTO Agreement* provides:

> In the event of a conflict between a provision of this Agreement and a provision of any of the Multilateral Trade Agreements, the provision of this Agreement shall prevail to the extent of the conflict.

Most of the substantive WTO law is found in the agreements contained in Annex 1. This Annex consists of three parts. Annex 1A contains thirteen multilateral agreements on trade in goods; Annex 1B contains the *General Agreement on Trade in Services* (the 'GATS'); and Annex 1C the *Agreement on Trade-Related Aspects of Intellectual Property Rights* (the '*TRIPS Agreement*'). The most important of the thirteen multilateral agreements on trade in goods, contained in Annex 1A, is the *General Agreement on Tariffs and Trade 1994* (the 'GATT 1994'). The plurilateral agreements in Annex 4 also contain provisions of substantive law but they are only binding upon those WTO Members that are a party to these agreements.

Annexes 2 and 3 cover, respectively, the *Understanding on Rules and Procedures for the Settlement of Disputes* (the 'DSU') and the *Trade Policy Review Mechanism* (the 'TPRM'), and contain procedural provisions.

1.4.1.1. General Agreement on Tariffs and Trade 1994

The GATT 1994 sets out the basic rules for trade in goods. This agreement is, however, somewhat unusual in its appearance and structure. Paragraph 1 of the introductory text of the GATT 1994 states:

> The General Agreement on Tariffs and Trade 1994 ('GATT 1994') shall consist of:
>
> a. the provisions in the General Agreement on Tariffs and Trade, dated 30 October 1947, annexed to the Final Act Adopted at the Conclusion of the Second Session of the Preparatory Committee of the United Nations Conference on Trade and Employment (excluding the Protocol of Provisional Application), as rectified, amended or modified by the terms of legal instruments which have entered into force before the date of entry into force of the WTO Agreement;
>
> b. the provisions of the legal instruments set forth below that have entered into force under the GATT 1947 before the date of entry into force of the WTO Agreement:
>
>   i.   protocols and certifications relating to tariff concessions;
>
>   ii. protocols of accession (excluding the provisions *(a)* concerning provisional application and withdrawal of provisional application and *(b)* providing that Part II of

---

[167] See Appellate Body Report, *Brazil – Desiccated Coconut*, 177.

[168] See e.g. Appellate Body Report, *Argentina – Footwear (EC)*, para. 81. In *Korea – Dairy*, the Appellate Body explicitly agreed with the statement of the Panel in that case that '[i]t is now well established that the *WTO Agreement* is a "Single Undertaking" and therefore all WTO obligations are generally cumulative and Members must comply with all of them simultaneously'. See Appellate Body Report, *Korea – Dairy*, para. 74.

GATT 1947 shall be applied provisionally to the fullest extent not inconsistent with legislation existing on the date of the Protocol);

iii. decisions on waivers granted under Article XXV of GATT 1947 and still in force on the date of entry into force of the WTO Agreement;

iv. other decisions of the CONTRACTING PARTIES to GATT 1947;

c. the Understandings set forth below:

i. Understanding on the Interpretation of Article II:1(b) of the General Agreement on Tariffs and Trade 1994;

ii. Understanding on the Interpretation of Article XVII of the General Agreement on Tariffs and Trade 1994;

iii. Understanding on Balance-of-Payments Provisions of the General Agreement on Tariffs and Trade 1994;

iv. Understanding on the Interpretation of Article XXIV of the General Agreement on Tariffs and Trade 1994;

v. Understanding in Respect of Waivers of Obligations under the General Agreement on Tariffs and Trade 1994;

vi. Understanding on the Interpretation of Article XXVIII of the General Agreement on Tariffs and Trade 1994; and

d. the Marrakesh Protocol to GATT 1994.

The GATT 1994 would obviously have been a less confusing and more user-friendly legal instrument if the negotiators had drafted a *new* text reflecting the basic rules on trade in goods as agreed during the Uruguay Round. However, as paragraph 1(a) of the introductory text of the GATT 1994, quoted above, shows, the Uruguay Round negotiators chose to *incorporate by reference* the provisions of the GATT 1947 into the GATT 1994.[169] By doing so, they were able to limit the debate on the provisions of the GATT 1994. If the negotiators had opted for a *new* text reflecting the basic rules on trade in goods, it would not have been possible to keep a lid on the many contentious issues relating to the interpretation and application of GATT provisions.[170]

The current arrangement obliges one to consult the provisions of the GATT 1947, the provisions of relevant GATT 1947 legal instruments and the Understandings agreed upon during the Uruguay Round in order to know what the GATT 1994 rules on trade in goods are. The negotiators were obviously aware that this arrangement might lead to some confusion, especially with regard to the continued relevance of the GATT 1947. They therefore felt the need to state explicitly in Article II:4 of the *WTO Agreement* that:

The General Agreement on Tariffs and Trade 1994 as specified in Annex 1A (hereinafter referred to as 'GATT 1994') is legally distinct from the General Agreement on Tariffs and Trade, dated 30 October 1947 . . . (hereinafter referred to as 'GATT 1947').

It should be stressed that the GATT 1947 is in fact no longer in force. It was terminated in 1996. Its provisions, however, have been incorporated in the GATT

---

[169] Together with the provisions of the GATT 1947, the provisions of the legal instruments that have entered into force under the GATT 1947, referred to in paragraph 1(b) of the introductory text of the GATT 1994, are incorporated into the GATT 1994.

[170] It was understood among the negotiators that these issues concerning the interpretation and application of GATT 1947 provisions could and would be addressed in the context of dispute settlement under the *WTO Agreement*. Only a few contentious GATT issues were addressed and resolved during the Uruguay Round negotiations. See the *Understandings* listed in paragraph 1(c) of the introductory text of the GATT 1994 and included in this instrument.

1994. To facilitate the necessary reference to the provisions of the GATT 1947 – and for that reason only – the official WTO *Legal Texts* include the complete text of the GATT 1947.

The GATT 1994 contains rules on most-favoured-nation treatment (Article I); tariff concessions (Article II); national treatment on internal taxation and regulation (Article III); anti-dumping and countervailing duties (Article VI); valuation for customs purposes (Article VII); customs fees and formalities (Article VIII); marks of origin (Article IX); the publication and administration of trade regulations (Article X); quantitative restrictions (Article XI); restrictions to safeguard the balance of payments (Article XII); administration of quantitative restrictions (Article XIII); exchange arrangements (Article XV); subsidies (Article XVI); State trading enterprises (Article XVII); governmental assistance to economic development (Article XVIII); safeguard measures (Article XIX); general exceptions (Article XX); security exceptions (Article XXI); dispute settlement (Articles XXII and XXIII); regional economic integration (Article XXIV); modification of tariff schedules (Article XXVIII), tariff negotiations (Article XXVIII *bis*); and trade and development (Articles XXXVI to XXXVIII of Part 4). A number of these provisions have been amended by one of the *Understandings* listed above. Finally, note the *Marrakesh Protocol*, which is an important part of the GATT 1994. This Protocol contains the national Schedules of Concessions of all WTO Members. In these national schedules, the commitments to eliminate or reduce customs duties applicable to trade in goods are recorded. The Protocol is over 25,000 pages long and is a key instrument for traders and trade officials.

The provisions of the GATT 1994 will be discussed in detail in chapters 3 to 7 of this book.

1.4.1.2. *Other multilateral agreements on trade in goods*

In addition to the GATT 1994, Annex 1A to the *WTO Agreement* contains a number of other multilateral agreements on trade in goods. These agreements include:

- the *Agreement on Agriculture*, which requires the use of tariffs instead of quotas or other quantitative restrictions, imposes minimum market access requirements and provides for specific rules on domestic support and export subsidies in the agricultural sector;
- the *Agreement on the Application of Sanitary and Phytosanitary Measures* (the 'SPS Agreement'), which regulates the use by WTO Members of measures adopted to ensure food safety and protect the life and health of humans, animals and plants from pests and diseases;
- the *Agreement on Textiles and Clothing*, which provided for the gradual elimination by 1 January 2005 of quotas on textiles and clothing (and is no longer in force);
- the *Agreement on Technical Barriers to Trade* (the 'TBT Agreement'), which regulates the use by WTO Members of technical regulations and standards and procedures to test conformity with these regulations and standards;

- the *Agreement on Trade-Related Investment Measures* (the '*TRIMS Agreement*'), which provides that WTO Members' regulations dealing with foreign investments must respect the obligations in Article III (national treatment obligation) and Article XI (prohibition on quantitative restrictions) of the GATT 1994;
- the *Agreement on Implementation of Article VI of the General Agreement on Tariffs and Trade 1994* (the '*Anti-dumping Agreement*'), which provides for detailed rules on the use of anti-dumping measures;
- the *Agreement on Implementation of Article VII of the General Agreement on Tariffs and Trade 1994* (the '*Customs Valuation Agreement*'), which sets out in detail the rules to be used by national customs authorities for valuing goods for customs purposes;
- the *Agreement on Preshipment Inspection*, which regulates activities relating to the verification of the quality, the quantity, the price and/or the customs classification of goods to be exported;
- the *Agreement on Rules of Origin*, which provides for negotiations aimed at the harmonisation of non-preferential rules of origin and sets out disciplines to govern the application of these rules of origin, both during and after the negotiations on harmonisation, and, in Annex II thereof, sets out disciplines applicable to preferential rules of origin;
- the *Agreement on Import Licensing Procedures*, which sets out rules on the use of import licensing procedures;
- the *Agreement on Subsidies and Countervailing Measures* (the '*SCM Agreement*'), which provides for detailed rules on subsidies and the use of countervailing measures; and
- the *Agreement on Safeguards*, which provides for detailed rules on the use of safeguard measures and prohibits the use of voluntary export restraints.

All of these agreements will be discussed in more detail in the following chapters.

Most of these multilateral agreements on trade in goods provide for rules that are more detailed than, and sometimes possibly in conflict with, the rules contained in the GATT 1994. The Interpretative Note to Annex 1A addresses the relationship between the GATT 1994 and the other multilateral agreements on trade in goods. It states:

> In the event of conflict between a provision of the *General Agreement on Tariffs and Trade 1994* and a provision of another agreement in Annex 1A to the *Agreement Establishing the World Trade Organization* (referred to in the agreements in Annex 1A as the '*WTO Agreement*'), the provision of the other agreement shall prevail to the extent of the conflict.
>
> [Emphasis added]

However, it is only where a provision of the GATT 1994 and a provision of another multilateral agreement on trade in goods are in *conflict* that the provision of the other multilateral agreement on trade in goods will prevail. Provisions are in conflict only where adherence to the one provision will necessarily lead to a violation of the other provision and the provisions can, therefore, not be read as complementing each other.[171] If there is no conflict, both the GATT 1994 and the relevant other multilateral agreement on trade in goods apply. In *Argentina – Footwear (EC)*, the Appellate Body ruled with regard to the relationship between, and the application of, the safeguard provision of the GATT 1994 (Article XIX) and the *Agreement on Safeguards* that:

> The GATT 1994 and the *Agreement on Safeguards* are *both* Multilateral Agreements on Trade in Goods contained in Annex 1A of the *WTO Agreement*, and, as such, are *both* 'integral parts' of the same treaty, the *WTO Agreement*, that are 'binding on all Members'. Therefore, the provisions of Article XIX of the GATT 1994 *and* the provisions of the *Agreement on Safeguards* are *all* provisions of one treaty, the *WTO Agreement*. They entered into force as part of that treaty at the same time. They apply equally and are equally binding on all WTO Members. And, as these provisions relate to the same thing, namely the application by Members of safeguard measures, the Panel was correct in saying that 'Article XIX of GATT and the Safeguards Agreement must *a fortiori* be read as representing an *inseparable package* of rights and disciplines which have to be considered in conjunction'.[172]

1.4.1.3. General Agreement on Trade in Services

Unlike the GATT 1994, the *General Agreement on Trade in Services* (the 'GATS') is a totally new agreement. It is the first ever multilateral agreement on trade in services. The GATS establishes a regulatory framework within which WTO Members can undertake and implement commitments for the liberalisation of trade in services.

The GATS covers all measures of Members affecting trade in services.[173] Trade in services is defined in Article I:2 of the GATS as the supply of a service:

- from the territory of one Member into the territory of any other Member (cross-border supply);
- in the territory of one Member to the service consumer of any other Member (consumption abroad);
- by a service supplier of one Member, through a commercial presence in the territory of any other Member (supply through a commercial presence); and
- by a service supplier of one Member, through the presence of natural persons of a Member in the territory of any other Member (supply through the presence of natural persons).

'Services' includes any service in any sector except services supplied in the exercise of governmental authority.[174] The supply of services includes the production, distribution, marketing, sale and delivery of a service.[175] It is clear from the third mode of supply, i.e. supply through a commercial presence, that the GATS also covers measures relating to foreign investment by suppliers of services.

---

[171] Note that in international law, there is a strong presumption against conflict as it can be assumed that countries will not undertake conflicting obligations.

[172] Appellate Body Report, *Argentina – Footwear (EC)*, para. 81.   [173] Article I:1 of the GATS.

[174] Article I:3(b) of the GATS.   [175] Article XXVIII(b) of the GATS.

The GATS contains provisions on most-favoured-nation treatment (Article II); transparency (Article III); increasing participation of developing countries (Article IV); economic integration (Article V); domestic regulation (Article VI); recognition (Article VII); emergency safeguard measures (Article X); payments and transfers (Article XI); restrictions to safeguard the balance of payments (Article XII); government procurement (Article XIII); general exceptions (Article XIV); security exceptions (Article XIV *bis*); subsidies (Article XV); market access (Article XVI); national treatment (Article XVII); negotiation and schedules of specific commitments (Articles XIX to XXI); dispute settlement (Articles XXII and XXIII); and institutional issues (Articles XXIV to XXVI). Attached to the GATS are a number of annexes, including the Annex on Article II Exemptions, the Annex on Movement of Natural Persons Supplying Services under the Agreement, and the Annexes on Financial Services. The Schedules of Specific Commitments of all WTO Members concerning their market access and national treatment commitments are also attached to the GATS and form an integral part thereof.[176]

On the relationship between the GATS and the GATT 1994, and in particular the question whether they are mutually exclusive agreements, the Appellate Body ruled in *EC – Bananas III*:

> The GATS was not intended to deal with the same subject matter as the GATT 1994. The GATS was intended to deal with a subject matter not covered by the GATT 1994, that is, with trade in services. Thus, the GATS applies to the supply of services . . . Given the respective scope of application of the two agreements, they may or may not overlap, depending on the nature of the measures at issue. Certain measures could be found to fall exclusively within the scope of the GATT 1994, when they affect trade in goods as goods. Certain measures could be found to fall exclusively within the scope of the GATS, when they affect the supply of services as services. There is yet a third category of measures that could be found to fall within the scope of both the GATT 1994 and the GATS. These are measures that involve a service relating to a particular good or a service supplied in conjunction with a particular good. In all such cases in this third category, the measure in question could be scrutinized under both the GATT 1994 and the GATS. However, while the same measure could be scrutinized under both agreements, the specific aspects of that measure examined under each agreement could be different. Under the GATT 1994, the focus is on how the measure affects the goods involved. Under the GATS, the focus is on how the measure affects the supply of the service or the service suppliers involved. Whether a certain measure affecting the supply of a service related to a particular good is scrutinized under the GATT 1994 or the GATS, or both, is a matter that can only be determined on a case-by-case basis.[177]

A measure restricting trade in bananas may thus be challenged both under the GATT 1994 (to the extent that it affects trade in goods) and under the GATS (to the extent that it affects the supply of services, such as, for example, wholesale trade services).

---

[176] See Article XX of the GATS. The Final Act also contains an Understanding on Commitments in Financial Services that is not part of the *WTO Agreement* but which was the basis for post-1995 negotiations on the liberalisation of financial services. See below, pp. 492–3.

[177] Appellate Body Report, *EC – Bananas III*, para. 221.

The GATS is examined in detail in chapters 4, 5 and 7.[178]

1.4.1.4. Agreement on Trade-Related Aspects of Intellectual Property Rights

The *Agreement on Trade-Related Aspects of Intellectual Property Rights* (the '*TRIPS Agreement*') is not an agreement concerning trade or trade measures. However, the value of many goods and services, particularly those traded by developed countries, is largely determined by the idea, the design or the invention they incorporate. If that value is not protected by protecting the intellectual property rights against the use of ideas, designs or inventions without compensating the intellectual property right holder, trade in these products or services will not thrive. For that reason, developed-country Members sought and obtained the inclusion in the *WTO Agreement* of an agreement specifying minimum standards of protection of intellectual property rights and requiring the effective enforcement of these rights. The *TRIPS Agreement* covers seven types of intellectual property:

* copyright and related rights (Articles 9–14);
* trademarks (Articles 15–21);
* geographical indications (Articles 22–4);
* industrial designs (Articles 25–6);
* patents (Articles 27–34);
* layout-designs (topographies) of integrated circuits (Articles 35–8); and
* undisclosed information, including trade secrets (Article 39).

With regard to these types of intellectual property, the *TRIPS Agreement* provides for minimum standards of protection. With regard to copyright, for example, Article 12 provides:

> Whenever the term of protection of a work, other than a photographic work or a work of applied art, is calculated on a basis other than the life of a natural person, such term shall be no less than 50 years from the end of the calendar year of authorized publication, or, failing such authorized publication within 50 years from the making of the work, 50 years from the end of the calendar year of making.

Furthermore, the *TRIPS Agreement* requires WTO Members to ensure that enforcement procedures and remedies are available to permit effective action against any act of infringement of the intellectual property rights referred to above, including civil and administrative procedures and remedies, provisional measures and criminal procedures (Articles 41–61). Pursuant to Articles 3 and 4 of the *TRIPS Agreement*, each WTO Member must accord other WTO Members national treatment and most-favoured-nation treatment, subject to a number of exceptions. The *TRIPS Agreement* frequently refers to other intellectual property agreements, such as the *Paris Convention for the Protection of Industrial Property (1967)*, the *Berne Convention for the Protection of Literary and Artistic Works (1971)*, the

---

[178] See below, pp. 334–43, 390–5, 476–99, 652–64, 669–70, 709–14, 722–3

Rome Convention for the Protection of Performers, Producers of Phonograms and Broadcasting Organizations (1961) and the *Washington Treaty on Intellectual Property in Respect of Integrated Circuits (1989)*, making provisions of these agreements applicable to all WTO Members.[179]

The *TRIPS Agreement* is examined in chapter 8 of this book.[180]

1.4.1.5. *Understanding on Rules and Procedures for the Settlement of Disputes*

The *Understanding on Rules and Procedures for the Settlement of Disputes*, commonly referred to as the *Dispute Settlement Understanding* or DSU, is arguably the single most important achievement of the Uruguay Round negotiations. The WTO dispute settlement system applies to all disputes between WTO Members arising under the WTO agreements. In 1997, Renato Ruggiero, then Director-General of the WTO, referred to the dispute settlement system provided for by the DSU as:

> in many ways the central pillar of the multilateral trading system and the WTO's most individual contribution to the stability of the global economy.[181]

Building on almost fifty years of experience with settling trade disputes in the context of the GATT 1947, the DSU provides for a dispute settlement system, characterised by compulsory jurisdiction, short timeframes, an appellate review process and an enforcement mechanism.

The DSU provides for rules on the coverage and scope of the dispute settlement system, its administration, its objectives and its operation (Articles 1–3); on mandatory pre-litigation consultations (Article 4); on good offices, conciliation and mediation (Article 5); on the panel process (Articles 6–16 and 18–20); on the appellate review process (Articles 17–20); on compliance and enforcement (Articles 21–2); on a ban on unilateral action (Article 23); on least-developed-country Members (Article 24); on arbitration as an alternative means of dispute settlement (Article 25); on non-violation and situation complaints (Article 26); and on the role of the WTO Secretariat (Article 27). Attached to the DSU are Appendices on the WTO agreements covered by the DSU (Appendix 1), on special or additional rules and procedures on dispute settlement contained in WTO agreements (Appendix 2); on the working procedures of panels (Appendix 3); and on expert review groups (Appendix 4).

The WTO dispute settlement system is discussed in detail in chapter 3 of this book.[182]

1.4.1.6. *Trade Policy Review Mechanism*

It is very important for WTO Members, their citizens and companies involved in trade to be informed as fully as possible about trade regulations and policies of

---

[179] E.g. Article 2.1 of the *TRIPS Agreement* (with regard to the *Paris Convention*); and Article 9 of the *TRIPS Agreement* (with regard to the *Berne Convention*). [180] See below, pp. 742–805.
[181] As reported in WTO, *Trading into the Future*, 2nd edition, revised (WTO, 2001), 38.
[182] See below, pp. 169–311.

other WTO Members. To that end, many of the WTO agreements referred to above provide for an obligation on WTO Members to inform or notify the WTO of new trade regulations, measures or policies or changes to existing ones. In addition, however, the WTO conducts regular reviews of individual Members' trade policies. The procedural rules for these reviews are set out in Annex 3 on the *Trade Policy Review Mechanism*. This mechanism is discussed in Chapter 2 of this book.[183]

1.4.1.7. Plurilateral agreements

All agreements in Annexes 1 to 3 are binding on all WTO Members. Membership of the WTO is conditional upon the acceptance of these 'multilateral agreements'. In contrast, Annex 4 contains two agreements, referred to as 'plurilateral agreements', which are only binding on those WTO Members that are a party to these agreements.[184]

The first plurilateral agreement is the *Agreement on Trade in Civil Aircraft*. This is, in fact, an agreement concluded during the 1979 Tokyo Round of trade negotiations. Attempts during the Uruguay Round to negotiate a new agreement failed. The *Agreement on Trade in Civil Aircraft*, which is of particular interest to the United States and the European Communities:

- provides for duty-free trade in civil aircraft and parts thereof;
- prohibits quotas and other trade restrictions on civil aircraft; and
- addresses the issue of government support to aircraft manufacturers.

Disputes relating to this agreement *cannot* be brought to the WTO dispute settlement system for resolution.

The second plurilateral agreement is the *Agreement on Government Procurement*. Under GATT 1994 and GATS rules, WTO Members are free to discriminate in favour of domestic products, services and service suppliers in the context of government procurement. This is an important exception to the national treatment obligations of Article III of the GATT 1994 and Article XVII of the GATS.[185] Under the terms of the *Agreement on Government Procurement*, the parties have agreed to accord national treatment in respect of government procurement by designated government entities.[186] The agreement also obliges parties to make procurement opportunities public, and to provide for a procedure allowing unsuccessful bidders to challenge a procurement award. Disputes under the *Agreement on Government Procurement* can be, and have already been, brought to the WTO dispute settlement system for resolution.[187]

---

[183] See below, pp. 93–5, 121–4.

[184] When the *WTO Agreement* entered into force on 1 January 1995, Annex 4 held four, and not two, plurilateral agreements. However, the *International Dairy Agreement* and the *International Bovine Meat Agreement* were terminated at the end of 1997.

[185] See Article III:8(a) of the GATT 1994 and Article XIII of the GATS. See also below, pp. 472–6, 497–8.

[186] See below, pp. 473–4.   [187] E.g. Panel Report, *Korea – Procurement*.

1.4.1.8. *Ministerial Decisions and Declarations*

Finally, note the twenty-seven Ministerial Decisions and Declarations, which together with the *WTO Agreement* form the Final Act adopted in Marrakesh in April 1994 at the end of the Uruguay Round negotiations. These Ministerial Decisions and Declarations include, for example, the Decision on Measures in Favour of Least-Developed Countries,[188] the Declaration on the Contribution of the World Trade Organization to Achieving Greater Coherence in Global Economic Policymaking[189] and the Decision on the Application and Review of the Understanding on Rules and Procedures Governing the Settlement of Disputes.[190] These Ministerial Decisions and Declarations do not generate specific rights and obligations for WTO Members which can be enforced through WTO dispute settlement.

Questions and Assignments 1.10

Look in the *Legal Texts* and skim through all the WTO agreements referred to above. Add tabs to your copy of the *Legal Texts* for easy reference to the various agreements. Explain briefly what each of these agreements deals with. What is the difference between multilateral and plurilateral agreements? What is the relationship between the GATT 1994 and other multilateral agreements on trade in goods? Which agreement prevails in case of conflict? When does a conflict exist? What is the relationship between the GATT 1994 and the GATS? Can these two agreements be applied to one and the same measure?

1.4.2. Other sources of WTO law

While the *WTO Agreement* with its multiple annexes is undisputedly the principal source of WTO law, it is not the only source of WTO law. This section examines:

- WTO dispute settlement reports;
- acts of WTO bodies;
- agreements concluded in the context of the WTO;
- customary international law;
- general principles of law;
- other international agreements;
- subsequent practice of WTO Members;
- teachings of the most highly qualified publicists; and
- the negotiating history.

All the above may, to varying degrees, *clarify* or *define* the law applicable between WTO Members on WTO matters.

---

[188] See below, pp. 802–3.　　[189] See below, p. 96.　　[190] See below, p. 308, footnote 718.

1.4.2.1. WTO dispute settlement reports

Reports of WTO panels and the Appellate Body are the most important 'other' source of WTO law. In addition, reports of old GATT panels are also a source of WTO law. In principle, adopted panel and Appellate Body reports are only binding on the parties to a particular dispute. However, in *Japan – Alcoholic Beverages II* the Appellate Body held with regard to prior GATT panel reports:

> Adopted panel reports are an important part of the GATT *acquis*. They are often considered by subsequent panels. They create legitimate expectations among WTO Members, and, therefore, should be taken into account where they are relevant to any dispute.[191]

In adopting this approach, the Appellate Body was clearly inspired by the practice of the International Court of Justice. Article 59 of the *Statute of the International Court of Justice* provides that the decisions of the Court have no binding force except between the parties and in respect of the particular case. The Appellate Body noted that:

> [t]his has not inhibited the development by that Court (and its predecessor) of a body of case law in which considerable reliance on the value of previous decisions is readily discernible.[192]

This Appellate Body ruling in *Japan – Alcoholic Beverages II* on prior GATT panel reports also applies *mutatis mutandis* to WTO panel reports and, even more so, to Appellate Body reports. In *US – Shrimp (Article 21.5 – Malaysia)*, the Appellate Body held with respect to its reasoning in *Japan – Alcoholic Beverages II*:

> This reasoning applies to adopted Appellate Body Reports as well. Thus, in taking into account the reasoning in an adopted Appellate Body Report – a Report, moreover, that was directly relevant to the Panel's disposition of the issues before it – the Panel did not err. The Panel was correct in using our findings as a tool for its own reasoning.[193]

Adopted reports are not 'binding precedent' for panels or the Appellate Body. However, as David Palmeter and Petros Mavroidis stated:

> Adopted reports have strong persuasive power and may be viewed as a form of nonbinding precedent.[194]

Following precedent makes sense for reasons of fairness and legitimacy, for reasons of efficiency and for reasons of legal clarity and certainty. In practice, Appellate Body rulings play a very important role in WTO law, and prior rulings are generally followed by panels and the Appellate Body itself. In *US – Oil Country Tubular Goods Sunset Reviews*, the Appellate Body found that:

---

[191] Appellate Body Report, *Japan – Alcoholic Beverages II*, 108. With regard to unadopted GATT panel reports, the Appellate Body agreed with the Panel in *Japan – Alcoholic Beverages II* that they 'have no legal status in the GATT or WTO system' but 'a panel could nevertheless find useful guidance in the reasoning of an unadopted panel report that it considered to be relevant'. See Panel Report, *Japan – Alcoholic Beverages II*, 6.10.   [192] *Ibid.*, footnote 30.
[193] Appellate Body Report, *US – Shrimp (Article 21.5 – Malaysia)*, para. 109.
[194] D. Palmeter and P. Mavroidis, 'The WTO Legal System: Sources of Law', *American Journal of International Law*, 1998, 401.

following the Appellate Body's conclusions in earlier disputes is not only appropriate, but is what would be expected from panels, especially where the issues are the same.[195]

As noted by Gregory Shaffer, panel and Appellate Body reports will not only be important in future disputes heard by panels and the Appellate Body, but will also play a significant role in 'settlements negotiated in the law's shadow'.[196]

1.4.2.2. *Acts of WTO bodies and agreements concluded in the context of the WTO*

Acts of WTO organs, such as authoritative interpretations and waivers,[197] are clearly a source of WTO law which give rise to rights and obligations for WTO Members that can be enforced through the dispute settlement system. Other acts of WTO organs, for example the Decision of the Ministerial Conference on Implementation-Related Issues and Concerns[198] or the Decision of the SPS Committee on Equivalence,[199] are definitely sources of WTO law and must be taken into account by panels and the Appellate Body. They are an integral part of WTO law. However, they do not provide for rights and obligations which can be enforced through the dispute settlement system. No claim of violation can be based on these acts.[200]

The same holds true for trade agreements which are concluded by WTO Members in the context of the WTO but which are neither attached to the *WTO Agreement* nor included in the list of covered agreements of Appendix 1 of the DSU.[201]

1.4.2.3. *Customary international law*

Article 3.2 of the DSU provides, in relevant part:

> The Members recognize that [the WTO dispute settlement system] serves to preserve the rights and obligations of Members under the covered agreements, and to clarify the existing provisions of those agreements *in accordance with customary rules of interpretation of public international law.*
>
> [Emphasis added]

The DSU thus explicitly refers to customary international law on treaty interpretation and makes this law applicable in the context of the WTO. It is debated whether other rules of customary international law are also part of WTO law.[202]

---

[195] Appellate Body Report, *US – Oil Country Tubular Goods Sunset Reviews*, para. 188. See also e.g. Panel Report, *US – Shrimp (Ecuador)*, para. 7.37.

[196] G. Shaffer, 'Recognizing Public Goods in WTO Dispute Settlement: Who Participates? Who Decides? The Case of TRIPS and Pharmaceutical Patent Protection', *Journal of International Economic Law*, 2004, 471.

[197] For a discussion of authoritative interpretations and waivers, see below, pp. 141–5.

[198] Ministerial Conference, Decision of 14 November 2001, WT/MIN(01)/17, dated 20 November 2001.

[199] Committee on Sanitary and Phytosanitary Measures, *Decision on the Implementation of Article 4 of the Agreement on the Application of Sanitary and Phytosanitary Measures*, G/SPS/19, dated 26 October 2001.

[200] For a discussion on the scope of the jurisdiction of the WTO dispute settlement system, see below, pp. 178–81.

[201] E.g. *Agreement on Trade in Information Technology Products (ITA)*, in *Annex to Ministerial Declaration on Trade in Information Technology Products*, adopted on 13 December 1996 at the Singapore Session of the Ministerial Conference.

[202] This debate is of particular relevance with respect to the available remedies for breach of WTO law. See below, pp. 218–31.

In *Korea – Procurement*, the Panel ruled that customary international law applies:

> to the extent that the WTO treaty agreements do not 'contract out' from it.[203]

Customary international law is part of general international law and the rules of general international law are, in principle, binding on all States. Each new State, as well as each new treaty, is automatically born into it. The rules of general international law, including the rules of customary international law, fill the gaps left by treaties. They are not applicable *only* when, and to the extent that, a treaty – *in casu*, the *WTO Agreement* – has 'contracted out' of certain rules of general international law.

As noted by Joost Pauwelyn, the Appellate Body and panels have frequently referred to and applied rules of general international law, including rules of customary international law.[204] They did so independently of giving meaning to specific words in a given WTO provision. The Appellate Body has made reference to and/or applied customary rules on dispute settlement and, in particular, on standing,[205] representation by private counsel,[206] the burden of proof,[207] and the treatment of municipal law.[208] In addition, panels have referred to and/or applied customary rules on State responsibility and, in particular, rules on countermeasures[209] and attribution.[210] The customary rules on State responsibility and, in particular, rules on compensation of damages caused by unlawful acts, are often referred to as rules the *WTO Agreement* has contracted out of.[211]

1.4.2.4. *General principles of law*

Like customary international law, general principles of law are part of general international law. As noted in the previous section, rules of general international law are, in principle, binding on all States. The rules of general international law, including the general principles of law, fill the gaps left by treaties. They are not applicable *only* when, and to the extent that, a treaty – *in casu*, the *WTO Agreement* – has 'contracted out' of certain rules of general international law. Both panels and the Appellate Body have referred to and used general principles of law as a basis for their rulings or in support of their reasoning. In *US – Shrimp*, the Appellate Body noted with regard to the principle of good faith:

> The chapeau of Article XX is, in fact, but one expression of the principle of good faith. This principle, at once a general principle of law and a general principle of international

---

[203] Panel Report, *Korea – Procurement*, para. 7.96. As the Panel Report was not appealed, the Appellate Body did not have the opportunity to review this finding.

[204] J. Pauwelyn, *Conflict of Norms in Public International Law: How WTO Law Relates to Other Norms of International Law* (Cambridge University Press, 2003), 210–11 and 470.

[205] See Appellate Body Report, *EC – Bananas III*, para. 133.   [206] *Ibid.*, para. 10.

[207] See generally, Appellate Body Report, *US – Wool Shirts and Blouses*, 14.

[208] See Appellate Body Report, *India – Patents (US)*, para. 65.

[209] See Decision by the Arbitrators, *EC – Bananas III (Article 22.6 – EC)*, para. 63; and Decision by the Arbitrators, *Brazil – Aircraft (Article 22.6 – Brazil)*, para. 3.44 and footnotes 46 and 48.

[210] See Panel Report, *Canada – Dairy*, para. 7.77 and footnote 427; and Panel Report, *Turkey – Textiles*, para. 9.33.   [211] See below, p. 230.

law, controls the exercise of rights by states. One application of this general principle, the application widely known as the doctrine of *abus de droit*, prohibits the abusive exercise of a state's rights and enjoins that whenever the assertion of a right 'impinges on the field covered by [a] treaty obligation, it must be exercised bona fide, that is to say, reasonably'. An abusive exercise by a Member of its own treaty right thus results in a breach of the treaty rights of the other Members and, as well, a violation of the treaty obligation of the Member so acting .[212]

The principle of due process,[213] the principle of proportionality,[214] the principle of judicial economy,[215] the principle of non-retroactivity[216] and the interpretative principle of effectiveness[217] have also been applied by panels and the Appellate Body in numerous reports. In at least one report, the Appellate Body applied the interpretative principle of *in dubio mitius*.[218]

1.4.2.5. *Other international agreements*

Other international agreements can also be a source of WTO law. This is definitely the case when these agreements are referred to specifically in a WTO agreement. As mentioned above, the *TRIPS Agreement* refers to a number of other intellectual property agreements, such as the *Paris Convention (1967)* and the *Berne Convention (1971)*, thus making provisions of these agreements part of WTO law, applicable to all WTO Members and enforceable through WTO dispute settlement. The *SCM Agreement* refers to the *OECD Arrangement on Guidelines for Officially Supported Export Credits*.[219]

Whether, and, if so, to what extent, other international agreements *not* referred to in a WTO agreement can be a source of WTO law, is a controversial issue. This issue is of particular relevance to multilateral environmental agreements (MEAs) and ILO Conventions on minimum labour standards. It is broadly accepted that these other international agreements may play a significant role in the interpretation of WTO legal provisions. Article 31 of the *Vienna Convention on the Law of Treaties* (the '*Vienna Convention*'), which applies in WTO dispute settlement,[220] states in paragraph 3(c) that, in the interpretation of a treaty provision, the interpreter must take into account together with the context:

any relevant rules of international law applicable in the relations between the parties.[221]

---

[212] See Appellate Body Report, *US – Shrimp*, para. 158. See also Appellate Body Report, *US – FSC*, para. 166.
[213] See Appellate Body Report, *US – Shrimp*, para. 182.
[214] *Ibid.*, para. 141. See also Appellate Body Report, *US – Cotton Yarn*, para. 120.
[215] See Appellate Body Report, *Australia – Salmon*, paras. 219–26.
[216] See Appellate Body Report, *Brazil – Desiccated Coconut*, 179; Appellate Body Report, *EC – Bananas III*, para. 235; and Appellate Body Report, *Canada – Patent Term*, paras. 71–4.
[217] See Appellate Body Report, *US – Gasoline*, 16; and Appellate Body Report, *Korea – Dairy*, para. 81.
[218] See Appellate Body Report, *EC – Hormones*, footnote 154.
[219] Annex I(k) to the *SCM Agreement*. Grants by governments of export credits that meet the requirements of this Arrangement are not considered an export subsidy prohibited under the *SCM Agreement*.
[220] See below, pp. 201–2.
[221] The Panel in *Argentina – Poultry Anti-Dumping Duties* stated that 'it is not entirely clear that Article 31.3(c) of the Vienna Convention would apply . . . [as] it is not clear to us that a rule applicable between only several WTO Members would constitute a relevant rule of international law applicable in the relations between the "parties" ' Panel Report, *Argentina – Poultry Anti-Dumping Duties*, footnote 64.

In *US – Shrimp*, the Appellate Body made use of principles laid down in multilateral environmental agreements such as the *United Nations Convention on the Law of the Sea*, the *Convention on Biological Diversity* and the *Convention on the Conservation of Migratory Species of Wild Animals* ('CITES') to *interpret* Article XX of the GATT 1994, although not all parties to this dispute were parties to these agreements.[222] As noted by Meinhard Hilf, the Appellate Body in that case imported from these environmental agreements the principle of cooperation into the chapeau of Article XX of the GATT 1994.[223]

However, it is controversial whether these other international agreements can be a source of WTO law in the sense that they provide rights and obligations for Members that can be invoked in WTO dispute settlement procedures. As discussed below, Joost Pauwelyn has argued in this respect that WTO Members cannot base a claim before a WTO panel on the violation of rights and obligations set out in a non-WTO agreement. However, in his opinion, WTO Members that are parties to a particular non-WTO agreement can invoke in a WTO dispute between them the rules of that agreement as a defence against a claim of violation of WTO rules.[224] This position is, however, quite controversial. Other WTO scholars do not agree that rules of non-WTO agreements can be invoked before a panel or the Appellate Body as a defence.[225]

1.4.2.6. *Subsequent practice of WTO Members*

Pursuant to Article 31.3(b) of the *Vienna Convention*, 'subsequent practice' is to be taken into account in the interpretation of the rights and obligations set out in the *WTO Agreement*. Therefore, 'subsequent practice' of the WTO, WTO organs or WTO Members must be considered to be a source of WTO law. In *Japan – Alcoholic Beverages II*, the Appellate Body stated:

> the essence of subsequent practice in interpreting a treaty has been recognized as a 'concordant, common and consistent' sequence of acts or pronouncements which is sufficient to establish a discernible pattern implying the agreement of the parties regarding its interpretation. An isolated act is generally not sufficient to establish subsequent practice; it is a sequence of acts establishing the agreement of the parties that is relevant.[226]

Footnote 221 *(cont.)*

In *EC – Approval and Marketing of Biotech Products*, the Panel held 'the parties' in Article 31.3(c) of the *Vienna Convention* to mean those States that have consented to be bound by the treaty being interpreted (i.e. *all* WTO Members). According to the Panel, a treaty interpreter is not *required* to have regard to treaties signed by only some WTO Members as context under Article 31.3(c) of the *Vienna Convention*, but would have the *discretion* to use such treaties as informative tools in establishing the ordinary meaning of the words used. Panel Report, *EC – Approval and Marketing of Biotech Products*, paras 7.68 and 7.92–7.93. See also below, pp. 204–5 and, in particular, the criticism of a study group of the UN International Law Commission on this finding of the Panel in *EC – Approval and Marketing of Biotech Products*.

[222] See below, pp. 204–5.

[223] See M. Hilf, 'Power, Rules and Principles in WTO/GATT Law', *Journal of International Economic Law*, 2001, 123.

[224] See J. Pauwelyn, *Conflict of Norms in Public International Law: How WTO Law Relates to Other Norms of International Law* (Cambridge University Press, 2003), 473 and 491.   [225] See below, pp. 62–3.

[226] See Appellate Body Report, *Japan – Alcoholic Beverages II*, 106–7.

1.4.2.7. Teachings of publicists and the negotiating history

Pursuant to Article 38(1) of the *Statute of the International Court of Justice*, the 'teachings of the most highly qualified publicists' are subsidiary means for the determination of rules of international law. WTO panels and the Appellate Body regularly cite the writings of scholars in support of their reasoning.[227]

Pursuant to Article 32 of the *Vienna Convention*, the negotiating history of an agreement may serve as a supplementary means of interpretation. However, there is no formally recorded negotiating history of the *WTO Agreement* and WTO panels and the Appellate Body give little importance to the personal recollections of negotiators.[228] Note that the negotiating history of the GATT 1947 has been and continues to be of relevance in the interpretation of the provisions of the GATT 1994.[229]

Questions and Assignments 1.11

Briefly discuss *all* sources of WTO law. Are panel and Appellate Body reports of relevance only to the parties to a dispute? Have the Appellate Body and panels referred to and applied rules of customary international law and general principles of law? Can multilateral environmental agreements concluded between WTO Members be in any way a source of WTO law? Do decisions of WTO organs provide for legal rights and obligations for Members?

1.5. WTO LAW IN CONTEXT

Earlier in this chapter, WTO law was described as a principal component of international economic law, which itself is an important part of public international law. However, the relationship between WTO law and *international law* deserves to be explored further. Likewise, the relationship between WTO law and *national law* also raises questions that need to be addressed.

1.5.1. WTO law and international law

1.5.1.1. WTO law as an integral part of international law

In the past, most handbooks on international law and general courses on this topic gave little or no attention to international trade law. International law commonly excluded the regulation of international trade from its purview.

---

[227] See e.g. Appellate Body Report, *US – Wool Shirts and Blouses*, footnotes 15 and 16 (on burden of proof).
[228] See below, p. 206. On the importance of the 'circumstances surrounding the conclusion' of the *WTO Agreement* for the interpretation of its provisions, see below, pp. 205–6. See also Panel Report, *Mexico – Telecoms*, para. 7.44; and Appellate Body Report, *US – Gambling*, paras. 158–213.
[229] The Panel in *EC – Tariff Preferences* referred to the 1971 Waiver Decision and the Enabling Clause as negotiating history/preparatory work within the meaning of Article 32 of the *Vienna Convention*. See Panel Report, *EC – Tariff Preferences*, para. 7.88. See also Appellate Body Report, *US – Gambling*, paras. 158–213; Panel Report, *Mexico – Telecoms*, para. 7.44.

In his 1996 Hague Lecture, Donald McRae noted:

> International trade law and international economic law were not of concern to international lawyers; trade and economic law were not central to the way international lawyers defined their discipline . . . Particular social traditions may have played some role in this. In some countries the idea of commerce, of buying and selling, or of economic matters generally, was not viewed with favour. The professions of medicine and law were respectable; those engaged in business did not have the same social status. This, no doubt, helped fashion the attitudes of international lawyers to international trade law and international economic law . . . The field of trade law, and that of economic matters generally, are seen as closely intertwined with the field of economics which is perceived as presenting a barrier to those without formal training in that discipline. In his extremely insightful work, *International Law in a Divided World*, Professor Cassese, who does recognize the significance of international economic relations to the study of international law, and devotes a full chapter to it, nevertheless states that 'international economic relations are usually the hunting ground of a few specialists, who often jealously hold for themselves the key to this abstruse admixture of law and economics'.[230]

However, in the current era of globalisation, economic issues and problems have moved to the frontlines of international relations and international law. In a later article, McRae described the work of the WTO as the 'new frontier' of international law.[231] This development is gradually gaining acceptance and recognition among international lawyers.[232]

In the past, international trade lawyers have also been quite ambivalent with regard to the relationship between international trade law and international law. Many considered international trade law to be a self-contained system of international law.[233] This position has now been discredited. International trade law, and in particular WTO law, is now generally considered to be an integral part of international law. WTO Director-General Pascal Lamy, in his address to the European Society of International Law in 2006, noted:

> The effectiveness and legitimacy of the WTO depend on how it relates to norms of other legal systems and on the nature and quality of its relationships with other international organizations . . . [T]he WTO, far from being hegemonic, as it is sometimes portrayed to be, recognizes its limited competence and the specialization of other international organizations. In this sense the WTO participates in the construction of international coherence and reinforces the international legal order.[234]

A genuine turning point in the relationship between international law and international trade law was the 1996 Appellate Body Report in *US – Gasoline*. In this report, its very first, the Appellate Body ruled that Article 3.2 of the DSU,

[230] D. McRae, *The Contribution of International Trade Law to the Development of International Law*, Academy of International Law, *Recueil des Cours*, vol. 260, 1996, 114–15.

[231] D. McRae, 'The WTO in International Law: Tradition Continued or New Frontier?', *Journal of International Economic Law*, 2000, 30 and 41 (reproduced by permission of Oxford University Press).

[232] See e.g. M. D. Evans, *International Law* (Oxford University Press, 2006); G. D. Triggs, *International Law: Contemporary Principles and Practices* (Butterworths, 2006); J. Klabbers, *An Introduction to International Institutional Law* (Cambridge University Press, 2002); and P. Sands and P. Klein, *Bowett's Law of International Institutions* (Sweet & Maxwell, 2001).

[233] See P. J. Kuijper, 'The Law of GATT as a Special Field of International Law: Ignorance, Further Refinement or Self-Contained System of International Law?', *Netherlands Yearbook of International Law*, 1994, 257.

[234] This address was published in P. Lamy, 'The Place of the WTO and Its Law in the International Legal Order', *European Journal of International Law*, 2007, 977.

which directs panels and the Appellate Body to interpret the WTO agreements according to the 'customary rules of interpretation of public international law', reflects:

> a measure of recognition that the *General Agreement* is not to be read in clinical isolation from public international law.[235]

The discussion above of the sources of WTO law shows that WTO law is *not* a closed, self-contained system, isolated from the rest of international law. General international law, composed of customary international law and general principles of law, is binding on WTO Members and is, in principle, part of the law applicable between WTO Members. Customary rules and general principles fill the gaps left by the *WTO Agreement*, unless the *WTO Agreement* has clearly 'contracted out' of these rules and principles.[236] Furthermore, WTO law must be interpreted taking into account other norms of international law.[237]

1.5.1.2. *Conflicts between WTO agreements and other agreements*

It may happen that the rights and obligations of WTO Members under the WTO agreements are in conflict with their rights and obligations under other international agreements. A classic example of such a conflict is the situation in which a multilateral environmental agreement (an 'MEA') obliges the parties to that agreement to impose quantitative restrictions on trade in certain products whereas Article XI of the GATT 1994 prohibits such restrictions. WTO Director-General Pascal Lamy has pointed out in this regard:

> The WTO, its treaty provisions and their interpretation, confirms the absence of any hierarchy between WTO norms and those norms developed in other forums: WTO norms do not supersede or trump other international norms.[238]

First, it should be noted that WTO rules should, if possible, be interpreted in such a way that they do not conflict with other rules of international law (i.e. the general principle against conflicting interpretation). As Gabrielle Marceau noted:

> Panels and the Appellate Body have the obligation to interpret the WTO provisions in taking into account all relevant rules of international law applicable to the relations between the WTO Members. One of those rules is the general principle against conflicting interpretation (Article 31.3(c) together with 30 of the Vienna Convention). Therefore, in most cases the proper interpretation of the relevant WTO provisions – themselves often drafted in terms of specific prohibitions leaving open a series of WTO compatible alternative measures – should lead to a reading of the WTO provisions so as to avoid conflict with other treaty provisions.[239]

---

[235] Appellate Body Report, *US – Gasoline*, 16.   [236] See above, p. 56.
[237] See Article 31.3(c) on the *Vienna Convention on the Law of Treaties*. See above, p. 57.
[238] P. Lamy, 'The Place of the WTO and Its Law in the International Legal Order', *European Journal of International Law*, 2007, 978.
[239] G. Marceau, 'Conflicts of Norms and Conflicts of Jurisdictions: The Relationship Between the WTO Agreement and MEAs and Other Treaties', *Journal of World Trade*, 2001, 1129.

While there will undoubtedly be instances in which conflicts between WTO rules and non-WTO rules can be avoided through clever interpretation, in many other instances this will not be possible. As already briefly mentioned above, Joost Pauwelyn has an innovative and well-thought-out view on the conflict of WTO rules with non-WTO rules.[240] Pauwelyn's view is controversial but is gradually receiving more support from fellow WTO scholars. Central to Pauwelyn's view is that most WTO obligations are essentially reciprocal in nature.[241] Reciprocal obligations are obligations from which parties to a multilateral treaty may deviate, as long as such deviation does not infringe the rights of third parties. Pauwelyn explains his view on the conflict between WTO rules and non-WTO rules as follows:

> In the event of conflict involving WTO provisions, WTO provisions may not always prevail, including before a WTO panel. The trade obligations in the WTO treaty are of the 'reciprocal type'. They are not of an 'integral nature'. Hence, WTO provisions can be deviated from as between a limited number of WTO members only, as long as this deviation does not breach third party rights. Affecting the economic interests of other WTO members does not amount to breaching their WTO rights. Recognizing that WTO obligations are of a reciprocal nature allows for the taking into account of the diversity of needs and interests of different WTO members. It shows that in most cases of conflict between, for example, human rights and environmental conventions (generally setting out obligations of an 'integral type'), on the one hand, and WTO obligations (of the 'reciprocal' type), on the other, the WTO provisions will have to give way.[242]

According to Pauwelyn, in case of conflict, rules of MEAs or other international agreements, such as human rights treaties, may thus often prevail over rules of WTO law. However, Pauwelyn added:

> the fact that non-WTO norms may . . . prevail over the WTO treaty, even as before a WTO panel, does not mean that WTO panels must judicially enforce compliance with these non-WTO rules. Non-WTO rules may be part of the applicable law before a WTO panel, and hence offer, in particular, a valid legal defence against claims of WTO breach. However, they cannot form the basis of legal claims, the jurisdiction of WTO panels being limited to claims under WTO covered agreements only.[243]

This particular view of the relationship between WTO rules and conflicting rules of other international agreements is not shared by all WTO scholars. On the contrary, Gabrielle Marceau has argued that WTO panels confronted with a conflict between a WTO rule and a non-WTO rule may perhaps have alternative courses of action to deal with the conflict, but that:

> any of these alternative courses of action would be possible only to the extent that the conclusions reached by the panels do not constitute an amendment of the WTO, or do not add to or diminish the rights and obligations of WTO Members or do not affect the rights of third WTO Members.[244]

---

[240] See above, p. 58.
[241] Pauwelyn regards reciprocal obligations as a 'promise . . . made towards each and every state individually' whereas he views integral obligations as a 'promise . . . towards the collectivity of all state parties taken together'. J. Pauwelyn, *Conflict of Norms in Public International Law: How WTO Law Relates to Other Norms of International Law* (Cambridge University Press, 2003), 476.   [242] *Ibid.*, 491.
[243] *Ibid.*, 491.
[244] G. Marceau, 'Conflicts of Norms and Conflicts of Jurisdictions: The Relationship Between the WTO Agreement and MEAs and Other Treaties', *Journal of World Trade*, 2001, 1130.

As Marceau noted, and as discussed in chapter 3,[245] it is prohibited for panels and the Appellate Body to 'add to or diminish the rights and obligations' of WTO Members, as provided for in the WTO agreements.[246] Should panels or the Appellate Body allow a respondent to invoke a non-WTO rule in defence of a claim of violation of WTO law, would they not, in fact, 'add to or diminish the rights and obligations' of WTO Members?

Questions and Assignments 1.12

Is WTO law a self-contained system of law or is it an integral part of international law? Do you agree with the analysis of Joost Pauwelyn on the relationship between WTO agreements and MEAs? In your opinion, what should a panel do when confronted with a WTO rule that is in conflict with a provision of an MEA concluded *after* the conclusion of the *WTO Agreement*?

1.5.2. WTO law and national law

There are two aspects of the relationship between WTO law and national law that need to be examined: first, the place of national law in WTO law; and, secondly, the place of WTO law in the domestic legal order.

1.5.2.1. *National law in WTO law*

With regard to the place of national law in WTO law, Article XVI:4 of the *WTO Agreement* states:

> Each Member shall ensure the conformity of its laws, regulations and administrative procedures with its obligations as provided in the annexed Agreements.

It is a general rule of international law, reflected in Article 27 of the *Vienna Convention*, that:

> A party may not invoke the provisions of its internal law as justification for its failure to perform a treaty.

In *Brazil – Aircraft (Article 21.5 – Canada)*, the Appellate Body had occasion to observe:

> We note Brazil's argument before the Article 21.5 Panel that Brazil has a contractual obligation under domestic law to issue PROEX bonds pursuant to commitments that have already been made, and that Brazil could be liable for damages for breach of contract under Brazilian law if it failed to respect its contractual obligations. In response to a question from us at the oral hearing, however, Brazil conceded that *a WTO Member's domestic law does not excuse that Member from fulfilling its international obligations.*[247]
>
> [Emphasis added]

---

[245] See below, pp. 174–5.   [246] See Articles 3.2 and 19.2 of the DSU.
[247] Appellate Body Report, *Brazil – Aircraft (Article 21.5 – Canada)*, para. 46.

Note, however, that with regard to measures and actions by regional and local governments and authorities, Article XXIV:12 of the GATT 1994 provides:

> Each Member shall take such reasonable measures as may be available to it to ensure observance of the provisions of this Agreement by the regional and local governments and authorities within its territories.[248]

It follows that WTO Members are obliged to enforce compliance with the obligations under the GATT 1994 by regional and local governments and authorities *only* to the extent that they – i.e. the Members – dispose of the necessary constitutional powers to do so.[249] Note that Article XXIV:12 has been interpreted narrowly.[250] The Panel in *Brazil – Retreaded Tyres* found that the measures of Rio Grande do Sul, a state of the Federative Republic of Brazil, are attributable to Brazil as a WTO Member.[251] The Panel also found in that case that the Brazilian government is ultimately responsible for ensuring that its constituent states respect Brazil's obligations under the WTO.[252] Further, note that where it is not possible to secure compliance with the obligations under the GATT 1994, the provisions relating to compensation and suspension of concessions, discussed in chapter 3, apply.[253]

With respect to the question of how panels and the Appellate Body should handle national law, the Appellate Body held in *India – Patents* that, in public international law, an international tribunal may treat municipal law in several ways. Municipal law may serve as evidence of facts and may provide evidence of State practice. Municipal law may also constitute evidence of compliance or non-compliance with international obligations. The Appellate Body found support for this position in the ruling of the Permanent Court of International Justice in *Certain German Interests in Polish Upper Silesia*, in which the Court had observed:

> It might be asked whether a difficulty does not arise from the fact that the Court would have to deal with the Polish law of July 14th, 1920. This, however, does not appear to be the case. From the standpoint of International Law and of the Court which is its organ, municipal laws are merely facts which express the will and constitute the activities of States, in the same manner as do legal decisions and administrative measures. The Court is certainly not *called upon to interpret* the Polish law as such; but there is nothing to prevent the Court's giving judgment on *the question whether or not*, in applying that law, *Poland is acting in conformity with its obligations* towards Germany under the Geneva Convention.[254]
>
> [Emphasis added]

In *India – Patents (US)*, the Appellate Body thus concluded:

> It is clear that an examination of the relevant aspects of Indian municipal law ... is essential to determining whether India has complied with its obligations under Article 70.8(a). There was simply no way for the Panel to make this determination without

---

[248] See also the *Understanding on the Interpretation of Article XXIV of the General Agreement on Tariffs and Trade 1994*, para. 13.
[249] T. Cottier and K. Schefer, 'The Relationship Between World Trade Organization Law, National Law and Regional Law', *Journal of International Economic Law*, 1998, 85–6.
[250] See GATT Panel Report, *Canada – Provincial Liquor Boards (US)*, BISD 39S/27.
[251] See Panel Report, *Brazil – Retreaded Tyres*, para. 7.400.   [252] See *ibid.*, para. 7.406.
[253] See *Understanding on the Interpretation of Article XXIV of the General Agreement on Tariffs and Trade 1994*, para. 14, last sentence.   [254] [1926] PCIJ Rep., Series A, No. 7, 19.

engaging in an examination of Indian law. But, as in the *Certain German Interests in Polish Upper Silesia* case . . . before the Permanent Court of International Justice, in this case, the Panel was not interpreting Indian law 'as such'; rather, the Panel was examining Indian law solely for the purpose of determining whether India had met its obligations under the *TRIPS Agreement*.[255]

Many WTO panels have in fact conducted a detailed examination of the domestic law of a Member in assessing the conformity of that domestic law with the relevant WTO obligations. Thomas Cottier and Krista Schefer noted in this respect:

Interpretation of national or regional rules by respective authorities should essentially be recognized as questions of fact and be treated with deference. Panels have no authority to construe rules of national or regional law *de novo* and to substitute their reading for what national or regional authorities, whether delegations, administrations or courts, have found to be the proper meaning of the law. Yet, a problem arises if it is apparent that the interpretation of national or regional law is manifestly incompatible with the text and/or context of national or regional rules. How should a panel and the Appellate Body react to this situation? . . . Panels are called upon to declare whether national or regional rules, *and the way they are applied*, are compatible with those set out in the WTO agreements.[256]

[Emphasis added]

Cottier and Schefer thus pleaded for panels and the Appellate Body to afford a degree of deference to the interpretation given by national authorities to provisions of their national law. However, Cottier and Schefer also stress that panels and the Appellate Body will look not only at whether these provisions are WTO-consistent, but also at whether the way in which these provisions are in fact applied is WTO-consistent.

1.5.2.2. *WTO law in national law*

With respect to the role of WTO law in the national legal order, it should first be observed that, where a provision of national law allows different interpretations, this provision should, whenever possible, be interpreted in a manner that avoids any conflict with WTO law. In the United States, the European Union and elsewhere, national courts have adopted this doctrine of *treaty-consistent interpretation*. The European Court of Justice (ECJ) stated in 1996 in *Commission v. Germany (International Dairy Arrangement)* with regard to the GATT 1947:

When the wording of secondary EC legislation is open to more than one interpretation, preference should be given as far as possible to the interpretation which renders the provision consistent with the Treaty . . . Similarly, the primacy of international agreements concluded by the Community over the provisions of secondary Community legislation means that such provisions must, so far as is possible, be interpreted in a manner consistent with those agreements.[257]

---

[255] Appellate Body Report, *India – Patents (US)*, para. 66. See also Appellate Body Report, *US – Section 211 Appropriations Act*, paras. 104–5.

[256] T. Cottier and K. Schefer, 'The Relationship Between World Trade Organization Law, National Law and Regional Law', *Journal of International Economic Law*, 1998, 86 (reproduced by permission of Oxford University Press).

[257] Judgment of the Court of 10 September 1996, *Commission of the European Communities v. Federal Republic of Germany (International Dairy Arrangement)*, Case C-61/94, [1996] ECR I-3989, para. 52.

The ECJ confirmed the doctrine of treaty-consistent interpretation of national/ EC law with regard to the *WTO Agreement* in its judgments in *Hermès* (1998) and *Schieving-Nijstad* (2001).[258]

If a conflict between a provision of national law and a WTO law provision cannot be avoided through treaty-consistent interpretation, the question arises as to whether the provision of WTO law can be invoked before the national court to challenge the legality and validity of the provision of national law. Can a German importer of bananas challenge the EC's import regime for bananas in court on the basis that this regime is inconsistent with, for example, Articles I, XI and XIII of the GATT 1994? Can a US beef exporter challenge the EC import ban on hormone-treated meat on the basis that this ban is inconsistent with the provisions of the *SPS Agreement*? Can a Brazilian steel exporter challenge an anti-dumping duty imposed by India on its hot-rolled steel before an Indian court on the basis that this duty is inconsistent with the provisions of the *Anti-Dumping Agreement*? This is the issue of the 'direct effect' of provisions of WTO law.[259]

It is clear that if provisions of WTO law were to have direct effect and could be invoked to challenge the legality of national measures, this would significantly increase the enforceability and effectiveness of these provisions for it would give Members much less flexibility in respect of compliance. Non-compliance with WTO obligations could and would then be sanctioned by domestic courts.

There is a fierce academic debate on whether provisions of WTO law should be granted direct effect. On that debate, Cottier and Schefer wrote:

> Among the scholars writing on the topic of direct effect of international trade agreements, there are three that stand out as the main proponents of the two schools of thought on the issue: Jan Tumlir and Ernst Ulrich Petersmann advocating direct effect and John H. Jackson for the critics of direct effect. A fourth author, Piet Eeckhout, has set out what we call an 'intermediate position' on the issue.[260]

With respect to the arguments of the advocates of the direct effect of WTO rules, Cottier and Schefer noted:

> The late Jan Tumlir, whose main thesis supporting direct effect is followed by Ernst Ulrich Petersmann, looks at the direct effect of trade treaties as a weapon against inherently protectionist tendencies in domestic law systems. Tumlir and Petersmann set forth the idea of 'constitutionalizing' international trade principles, elevating the rights of an individual to trade freely with foreigners to the level of a fundamental right. To prevent the erosion of a state's sovereignty, Tumlir suggests granting individuals the right to invoke treaty provisions in front of their domestic courts. Allowing for standing in this way would be available to those citizens harmed by protectionist national policies put into effect by other national interest groups. Thus, direct effect widely defined 'helps to

---

[258] See Judgment of the Court of 13 September 2001, *Schieving-Nijstad vof and Others* v. *Robert Groeneveld*, Case C-89/99, [2001] ECR I-5851; and Judgment of the Court of 15 June 1998, *Hermès International and FHT Marketing Choice BV*, Case 53/96, [1998] ECR I-3603.

[259] The issue of direct effect, i.e. the issue of direct invocability, is to be distinguished from the issue of direct applicability, i.e. the issue whether a national act of transformation is necessary for an international agreement to become part of national law. On the latter issue, it should be noted that WTO law is directly applicable in the EC legal order. It became part of EC law without any act of transformation.

[260] T. Cottier and K. Schefer, 'The Relationship Between World Trade Organization Law, National Law and Regional Law', *Journal of International Economic Law*, 1998, 93.

correct the asymmetries in the political process' . . . Pleading for keeping the possibility of judicial review open to individuals, Jacques Bourgeois put it quite bluntly: 'Quite simply, what is in the end the use of making law, also international law, designed to protect private parties, if these private parties cannot rely on it?'[261]

For the advocates of direct effect of WTO rules, direct effect is a necessary and effective 'weapon' against national governments which encroach on the right to trade freely with foreigners, a right these advocates of direct effect consider to be a fundamental right.

John Jackson, and with him many others, objects to the direct effect of WTO rules. Central to his position against the direct effect of WTO rules is that direct effect might be dangerous for democracy and that it conflicts with the legitimate wish of legislatures to adapt international treaty language to the domestic legal system. Cottier and Schefer noted:

John Jackson . . . basically supports US trade policies of denying direct effect due to the imbalances in the institutional balance of government it would cause domestically . . . He does . . . find the idea of granting standing and allowing for an international treaty to be superior to federal legislation (let alone the constitution) to be dangerous to the idea of democracy and democratic representation of individuals . . . While Jackson acknowledges that governments have an obligation to abide by international commitments they undertake, direct effect is not necessary to ensure this. The stronger reasons for denying direct effect are what Jackson calls 'functional arguments'. These arguments include the fact that '[s]ome constitutions provide for very little democratic participation in the treaty-making process; for example, by giving no formal role to Parliaments or structuring the government so that control over foreign relations is held by certain elites'. There are also legitimate desires of legislatures to adapt international treaty language to the domestic legal system (such as translating the obligations into the native language, using local terms for legal principles, or further explaining certain provisions). And, some governments may want the opportunity to implement the obligations in a national legislative process because 'the act of transformation sometimes becomes part of a purely *internal* power struggle, and may be used by certain governmental institutions to enhance their powers vis-à-vis other governmental entities' or 'even, perhaps, . . . the legislature desires to preserve the *option to breach* the treaty in its method of application'. Even such uses of the separate implementation process are legitimate in Professor Jackson's mind because 'some breaches may be "minor" and therefore *preferable to the alternative of refusing to join the treaty altogether*'. Finally, Jackson argues that if treaties are given direct effect automatically, the characteristic of direct effect itself will not necessarily guarantee that the national courts will apply the treaty rules.[262]

An intermediate position in this debate on the direct effect of WTO law has been taken by Piet Eeckhout. Eeckhout opposed direct effect of WTO law but conceded that if a case has been specifically decided by the WTO dispute settlement system, domestic effect should be given to this decision. According to Eeckhout:

the reasons for not granting direct effect – whether it is the agreement's flexibility, or the division of powers between the legislature and the judiciary, or the respect of appropriate dispute settlement forums – cease to be valid where a violation is established.[263]

---

[261] *Ibid.*, 93–5.   [262] *Ibid.*, 97–8.
[263] P. Eeckhout, 'The Domestic Legal Status of the WTO Agreements: Interconnecting Legal Systems', *Common Market Law Review*, 1997, 53.

The *WTO Agreement* could have specified what effect its provisions are to have in the domestic legal order of WTO Members. However, it did not do so. Therefore, although each Member must fully execute the commitments which it has undertaken, it is free to determine the legal means appropriate for attaining that end in its domestic legal system.

At present, most WTO Members, including the European Communities, the United States, China, India, Japan, South Africa and Canada, refuse to give 'direct effect' to WTO law.[264] Only a few WTO Members give 'direct effect' to WTO law.[265]

The European Court of Justice (ECJ) addressed the issue of whether it could review the legality of Community law in the light of WTO law in its judgment of 23 November 1999 in *Portugal* v. *Council*. As the ECJ did not want:

- to deprive the European Community of the possibility for temporary non-compliance with WTO law provided for in Article 22 of the DSU (the temporary non-compliance argument),[266] and
- to deprive the legislative or executive organs of the Community of the scope for manoeuvre with respect to compliance enjoyed by their counterparts in the Community's trading partners (the non-reciprocity argument),[267]

it concluded:

> having regard to their nature and structure, the WTO agreements are not in principle among the rules in the light of which the Court is to review the legality of measures adopted by the Community institutions.[268]

In support of the conclusion reached, the ECJ noted that this interpretation corresponded to what was stated in the preamble to the Council Decision of 22 December 1994 on the conclusion of the *WTO Agreement*. In this Decision, the Council of Ministers of the European Union stated that:

> [b]y its nature, the Agreement Establishing the World Trade Organization, including the Annexes thereto, is not susceptible to being directly invoked in Community or Member State courts.[269]

---

[264] For an overview of whether specific WTO Members give direct effect to WTO law in their domestic legal order, see C. George and S. Orava (eds.), *A WTO Guide for Global Business* (Cameron May, 2002), 398.

[265] See below, footnote 277.

[266] See Judgment of the Court of 23 November 1999, *Portuguese Republic* v. *Council of the European Union*, Case C-149/96, [1999] ECR I-8395, para. 40. With respect to this possibility for temporary non-compliance with WTO law, see below, pp. 225–9.   [267] See *ibid.*, para. 46.

[268] *Ibid.*, para. 47. These arguments were reiterated in Judgment of the Court of 1 March 2005, *Van Parys* v. *Belgisch Interventie- en Restitutiebureau*, Case C-377/02, [2005] ECR I-1465 and Judgment of the Court of First Instance of 3 February 2005, *Chiquita* v. *Commission* Case T-19/01. These arguments have recently been convincingly criticised by Advocate General Ruiz-Jarabo Colomer. See the Opinion of Advocate General Ruiz-Jarabo Colomer of 23 January 2007, in *Merck Genéricos-Produtos Farmacêuticos Ldª* v. *Merck & Co. Inc. and Merck Sharp & Dohme Ldª* , Case C-431/05, paras. 81–6.

[269] Council Decision 94/800/EC of 22 December 1994 concerning the conclusion on behalf of the European Community, as regards matters within its competence, of the agreements reached in the Uruguay Round multilateral negotiations, OJ 1994, L336, 1. Note that the European Commission and the Council of Ministers were in agreement on the issue of 'direct effect' of WTO law. The text adopted by the Council had been proposed by the Commission.

In its judgment of 14 December 2000 in *Dior* v. *TUK*, the ECJ confirmed its reasoning in *Portugal* v. *Council* and concluded that private persons cannot invoke WTO law before the courts by virtue of Community law.[270]

As an exception to the general rule, the ECJ does, however, grant direct effect to provisions of the *WTO Agreement* when the Community intended to implement a particular obligation assumed in the context of the WTO, *or* where the Community measure refers expressly to the precise provisions of the WTO agreements. In its judgment of 22 June 1989 in *Fediol* v. *Commission* and that of 7 May 1991 in *Nakajima* v. *Council*, the ECJ gave direct effect to provisions of the GATT 1947 in these circumstances.[271] With respect to provisions of the *WTO Agreement*, the ECJ ruled in its judgment of 9 January 2003 in *Petrotub* v. *Council*:

> where the Community intended to implement a particular obligation assumed in the context of the WTO, or where the Community measure refers expressly to precise provisions of the agreements and understandings contained in the annexes to the WTO Agreement, it is for the Court to review the legality of the Community measure in question in the light of the WTO rules (see, in particular, *Portugal* v. *Council*, paragraph 49).[272]

Note that in its judgments of 30 September 2003 in the *Biret* v. *Council* cases, the ECJ left the possibility open for an action for damages against the European Community. Such a judgment could be based on a Community measure that was found to be inconsistent with WTO law by the WTO Dispute Settlement Body *if* the damage occurred after the end of the reasonable period of time for implementation of the recommendations and rulings of the Dispute Settlement Body.[273] However, this possibility was recently excluded by the Court of First Instance (CFI) in the *Chiquita Brands* case. The CFI held that as a WTO Member has a choice of many different ways to implement a panel or Appellate Body ruling, and such implementation does not resemble the situation where the Community intends to implement a particular WTO obligation as under the *Nakajima* exception, an individual cannot rely on an infringement by the Community of WTO law to show unlawful conduct on the part of the Community.[274]

---

[270] See Judgment of the Court of 14 December 2000, *Parfums Christian Dior SA* v. *TUK Consultancy BV and Assco Gerüste GmbH* and *Rob van Dijk* v. *Wilhelm Layher GmbH & Co. KG and Layher BV*, Joined Cases C-300/98 and C-392/98, [2000] ECR I-11307, paras. 42–4.

[271] See Judgment of the Court of 22 June 1989, *Fédération de l'industrie de l'huilerie de la CEE (Fediol)* v. *Commission of the European Communities*, Case 70/87, [1989] ECR 1781; and Judgment of the Court of 7 May 1991, *Nakajima All Precision Co. Ltd* v. *Council of the European Communities*, Case 69/89, [1991] ECR I-2069.

[272] See Judgment of the Court of 9 January 2003, *Petrotub SA and Republica SA* v. *Council of the European Communities*, Case C-76/00 P, para. 54. That these are the only two exceptions even in situations where the WTO's Dispute Settlement Body has adopted a report finding the legislation at issue incompatible with WTO law, was confirmed in Judgment of the Court of 1 March 2005, *Van Parys* v. *Belgisch Interventie- en Restitutiebureau*, Case C-377/02, [2005] ECR I-1465, paras. 39–40 and 52.

[273] See Judgment of the Court of 30 September 2003, *Biret International SA* v. *Council of the European Union*, Case C-93/02 P; and Judgment of the Court of 30 September 2003, *Etablissements Biret et Cie SA* v. *Council of the European Union*, Case C-94/02 P.

[274] Judgment of the Court of First Instance of 3 February 2005, *Chiquita* v. *Commission*, Case T-19/01, paras. 156–70 See in this regard P. J. Kuijper, 'From Initiating Proceedings to Ensuring Implementation: The Links with the Community Legal Order', in G. Sacerdotti, A. Yanovich and J. Bohanes (eds.), *The WTO at Ten: The Contribution of the Dispute Settlement System* (Cambridge University Press, 2006), 277–8.

In the *Merck* case, the ECJ was faced with the question whether it was contrary to Community law for Article 33 of the *TRIPS Agreement* (providing a minimum term of patent protection of twenty years) to be applied directly by a national court of a Member State of the European Union in proceedings before it. Following its approach in *Dior* v. *TUK*,[275] and noting that Article 33 of the *TRIPS Agreement* falls within the sphere of patents, an area 'in which the Community has not yet legislated and which consequently falls within the competence of the Member States',[276] the ECJ held that 'it is not contrary to Community law for Article 33 of the *TRIPS Agreement* to be directly applied by a national court subject to the conditions provided for by national law'.[277]

With regard to the domestic law effect of WTO law in the United States, the Restatement (Third) of Foreign Relations Law of the United States provides:

> Since generally the United States is obligated to comply with a treaty as soon as it comes into force for the United States, compliance is facilitated and expedited if the treaty is self-executing . . . Therefore, if the Executive Branch has not requested implementing legislation and Congress has not enacted such legislation, there is a strong presumption that the treaty has been considered self-executing by the political branches, and should be considered self-executing by the courts.[278]

In the United States, trade treaties have historically been granted direct effect in court.[279] As has been the case with a number of other recent trade agreements,[280] the approval of the *WTO Agreement* was made conditional upon the inclusion of a provision in the implementing legislation, explicitly denying direct effect to the Agreement.[281] As David Leebron noted:

> Although Congress specifically approved the agreements, it simultaneously provided 'no provision of any of the Uruguay Round Agreements, nor the application of any such provision to any person or circumstances, that is inconsistent with any law of the United States shall have effect'. Furthermore, Congress mandated that no person other than the United States 'shall have any cause of action or defence under any of the Uruguay Round Agreements' or challenge "any action or inaction . . . of the United States, any state, or any political subdivision of a state on the ground that such action or inaction is inconsistent" with one of those agreements. In short, the Uruguay Agreements themselves are

---

[275] Judgment of the Court of 14 December 2000, *Parfums Christian Dior SA* v. *TUK Consultancy BV andAssco Gerüste GmbH* and *Rob van Dijk* v. *Wilhelm Layher GmbH & Co. KG and Layher BV*, Joined Cases C-300/98 and C-392/98, [2000] ECR I-11307, para. 48. In that case, the ECJ held that in fields not governed by Community law, that law 'neither requires not forbids that the legal order of a Member State should accord to individuals the right to rely directly on the rule laid down by Article 50(6) of TRIPs'.

[276] Judgment of the Court of 11 September 2007, *Merck Genéricos-Produtos Farmacêuticos Ldª* v. *Merck & Co. Inc. and Merck Sharp & Dohme Ldª*, Case C-431/05, para. 34.

[277] *Ibid.*, para. 48. It is interesting to note that the domestic courts of several Member States of the European Union have accepted the direct effect of provisions of the *TRIPS Agreement*. For Germany, see e.g. Bundesgerichtshof, Urteil vom 25.2.1999 –I ZR 118/96 – *Kopienversanddienst; OLG München* (with regard to the direct effect of Articles 9 and 13 of the *TRIPS Agreement*). For Ireland, see e.g. *Allen & Hanbury and another, Controller of Patents, Designs and Trademarks* (1997); for the Netherlands, see e.g. Rb. 's-Gravenhage 1 April 1998 (kortgeding), BIE 2001, pp. 119–22 Mistral/Tiki – 45(1).

[278] Restatement (Third) of Foreign Relations Law of the United States, para. 111, Reporters' Notes, reproduced in B. Carter and P. Trimble, *International Law* (Little, Brown and Co., 1991), 151.

[279] See T. Cottier and K. Schefer, 'The Relationship Between World Trade Organization Law, National Law and Regional Law', *Journal of International Economic Law*, 1998, 107.

[280] See e.g. the *North American Free Trade Agreement* (NAFTA), 17 December 1992.

[281] See Uruguay Round Agreements Act of 1994, 19 USC $ 3512, Pub. L No. 104–305 (1996), para. 102(c).

unlikely to be directly applied in any proceedings other than a proceeding brought by the United States for the purpose of enforcing obligations under the agreements.[282]

India likewise, denies direct effect to WTO law. Indian courts will not consider the consistency of any domestic statute vis-à-vis WTO law, as they are constitutionally barred from striking down domestic law on grounds of violation of international law. The Madras High Court in *Novartis* v. *Union of India*,[283] the only decision on this point to date, seems to have adopted a very strict approach. At issue in *Novartis* v. *Union of India* was the decision of the Indian authorities to deny – on the basis of Section 3(d) of the Indian Patent Act – the pharmaceutical multinational Novartis a patent on Glivec, a cancer medicine, thereby allowing the production of cheap generic copies. Before the Madras High Court, Novartis challenged *inter alia* the consistency of Section 3(d) of the Indian Patent Act with the relevant provisions of the *TRIPS Agreement*. The Madras High Court held that as the WTO provides a comprehensive mechanism for the settlement of dispute in the DSU any dispute under WTO law are properly litigated through this mechanism.[284]

Questions and Assignments 1.13

Can a WTO Member ever invoke national law as a justification for its failure to comply with WTO obligations? In your opinion, should WTO provisions have direct effect? Does any WTO Member give direct effect to WTO provisions in its internal legal order? Why does the ECJ deny direct effect to provisions of WTO law? Are there any exceptions?

1.6. SUMMARY

One of the defining features of today's world is the process of economic globalisation, with high levels of international trade and foreign direct investment. There is broad consensus among economists and policy-makers that economic globalisation in general and international trade in particular offer an unprecedented *opportunity* to reduce poverty worldwide significantly. However, to ensure that this opportunity is realised, economic globalisation and international trade have to be 'accompanied' by good governance in developing countries and more development assistance from developed countries *and* have to be *managed* and *regulated* at the international level. If not, economic globalisation and international trade are likely to be a curse, rather than a blessing to humankind, aggravating economic inequality, social injustice, environmental degradation and

---

[282] D. Leebron, 'Implementation of the Uruguay Round Results in the United States', in J. Jackson and A. Sykes (eds.), *Implementing the Uruguay Round* (Oxford University Press, 1997), 212.

[283] See Judgment of the Madras High Court, dated 6 August 2007, published in *Madras Law Journal*, 2007, 1153, also available at http://judis.nic.in/chennai/qrydisp.asp?tfnm=11121, visited on 23 August 2007.

[284] The Madras High Court also refused to exercise its discretion to grant declaratory relief as it would serve no useful purpose to the petitioner.

cultural dispossession. Managing and regulating economic globalisation and international trade so that they benefit all is one of the prime challenges of the international community in the twenty-first century.

International rules on trade are necessary for basically four related reasons:

- to restrain countries from taking trade-restrictive measures;
- to give traders and investors a degree of security and predictability regarding the trade policies of other countries;
- to cope with the challenges presented by economic globalisation with respect to the protection of important societal values such as public health, a clean environment, consumer safety, cultural identity and minimum labour standards; and
- to achieve a greater measure of equity in international economic relations.

WTO law, which is the core of international economic law, provides for such rules on international trade. There are six groups of basic rules and principles of WTO law:

- the principles of non-discrimination;
- the rules on market access;
- the rules on unfair trade;
- the rules on conflicts between trade liberalisation and other societal values and interests;
- the rules promoting harmonisation of national regulation; and
- the rules relating to institutional and procedural issues.

The principal source of WTO law is the *WTO agreement*, in force since 1 January 1995. The *WTO Agreement* is a short agreement (of sixteen articles) establishing the World Trade Organization but contains, in its annexes, a significant number of agreements with substantive and/or procedural provisions, such as the GATT 1994, the GATS, the *TRIPS Agreement* and the DSU. However, the *WTO Agreement* is not the only source of WTO law. WTO dispute settlement reports, acts of WTO bodies, agreements concluded in the context of the WTO, customary international law, general principles of law, other international agreements, subsequent practice of WTO Members, teachings of the most highly qualified publicists and the negotiating history may all, to varying degrees, be sources of WTO law. Note that not all these elements of WTO law are of the same nature or on the same legal footing. Some sources, such as the *WTO Agreement* and most of the agreements annexed to it, provide for specific legal rights and obligations for WTO Members that these Members can enforce through WTO dispute settlement. Other sources, such as the WTO dispute settlement reports, general principles of law, customary international law and non-WTO agreements, do not provide for specific, enforceable rights and obligations but they do 'clarify' and /or 'define' the law that applies between WTO Members on WTO matters.

While for many years international trade law was not part of the mainstream of international law, WTO law is now the 'new frontier' of international law. Nobody questions that WTO law is an integral part of public international law.

However, the relationship between WTO rules and other, conflicting rules of public international law, such as rules of MEAs, is controversial. A generally accepted view on this relationship is yet to emerge.

With regard to the relationship between WTO law and the national law of WTO Members, it is undisputed that WTO Members must ensure that their national law is consistent with WTO law. Note also that, while some WTO scholars forcefully plead for the granting of direct effect to WTO law in the domestic legal order of WTO Members, most WTO Members refuse to grant such effect to WTO law. In most WTO Members, a breach of WTO law obligations cannot be challenged or invoked in domestic courts.

1.7. EXERCISE: GLOBAPHILES VERSUS GLOBAPHOBES

Last Sunday, more than 50,000 people demonstrated in the streets of Nontes, the capital of Newland, against economic globalisation, free trade and the Government's plan to join the WTO. The Republic of Newland is a developing, lower-middle-income country with a population of 30 million people. It has a booming export-oriented toy manufacturing industry and an up-and-coming steel industry. However, many of its other industries and its farms are unable to compete with foreign goods and services.

The demonstration was organised by the Newland Coalition for a Better World (NCBW), representing Newland's labour unions and its main environmental, consumer and human rights organisations. When small groups of radicals, led by a moustached farmer, attacked and destroyed a McJohn's restaurant along the route, the police intervened to disperse the demonstrators with tear gas. Three hours of violent clashes between the police and a group of about 500 young demonstrators ensued, leaving several people wounded.

At an emergency cabinet meeting called on Sunday evening, the Prime Minister announced that he would invite the Chairman of the NCBW to a public debate on economic globalisation, international trade and the Government's plan to join the WTO. On Monday, the Chairman accepted the challenge. The debate is to be broadcast live on Wednesday evening.

You serve on the personal staff of the Prime Minister, and it is your job to prepare him for this important debate by briefing him as fully as possible on all the positive and negative aspects – economic, political and legal – of:

- economic globalisation;
- international trade; and
- WTO membership.

With regard to WTO membership, you expect the Chairman of the NCBW, a professor of constitutional law, to question, *inter alia*, why it would be in the interest of Newland to 'squander its sovereignty' and accept a host of new international obligations. You expect him to argue that the core WTO rules and disciplines are about opening foreign markets for the benefit of multinationals. From articles and speeches of the Chairman of the NCBW, you know that three issues are of particular concern to him, namely:

- whether the *WTO Agreement* encompasses all WTO law (or there is more to WTO law than the rights and obligations set out in the *WTO Agreement*);
- whether the *WTO Agreement* will prevail over Newland's Constitution and over other international agreements (such as MEAs and ILO Conventions); and
- whether WTO law will have, or should have, direct effect in Newland's courts.

To prepare the Prime Minister well, you and your colleagues decide to stage a trial debate in which one group, Group A, takes a 'globaphile' position and another group, Group B, a 'globaphobe' position.

Contents

2.1. INTRODUCTION

The World Trade Organization was established and became operational on 1 January 1995. It is the youngest of all the major international intergovernmental organisations and yet it is arguably one of the most influential in these times of economic globalisation. As Marco Bronckers stated, it has 'the potential to become a key pillar of global governance'.[1] The WTO is also one of the most controversial international organisations. It has been referred as '*un gouvernement mondial dans l'ombre*'.[2] Guy de Jonquières of the *Financial Times* observed that the emergence of the WTO as a prime target for protests of many kinds reflects:

> growing public awareness – but often imperfect understanding – of its role in promoting, and formulating rules for, global economic integration.[3]

Many critics of the WTO claim that the WTO is 'pathologically secretive, conspiratorial and unaccountable to sovereign States and their electorate'.[4] According to Joseph Nye of the Kennedy School of Government of Harvard University, these detractors may, to some extent, have a case. Nye wrote in November 2000:

> [Anti-globalisation protesters] assert that official transnational institutions like the World Bank and the International Monetary Fund are effectively accountable to no one. How true is their claim? Some defenders point out that the WTO, for example, is a weak organization with a small budget and staff, hardly the stuff of world government by fiat. Moreover, unlike unelected nongovernmental organizations, the WTO, the World Bank and the IMF tend to be highly responsive to national governments, which are the real source of legitimacy . . . Even though these organizations are inherently weak, their rules and resources can exert powerful effects. Moreover, the protesters are right that a lack of transparency often weakens accountability . . . Increased accountability for the WTO,

---

[1] M. Bronckers, 'More Power to the WTO?', *Journal of International Economic Law*, 2001, 41 (reproduced by permission of Oxford University Press).

[2] M. Khoh, 'Un gouvernement mondial dans l'ombre', *Le Monde Diplomatique*, May 1997. Translation: 'A lurking world government'.

[3] G. de Jonquières, 'The WTO's Capacity to Arouse Controversy Highlights a Growing Public Awareness of Its Role', *Financial Times*, 24 September 1999.

[4] G. de Jonquières, 'Prime Target for Protests: WTO Ministerial Conference', *Financial Times*, 24 September 1999.

World Bank and other official transnational organizations will address many of the legitimate concerns of anti-globalization protestors, while neutralizing their more dubious criticisms. International institutions are too important to be left to demagogues, no matter how well-meaning.[5]

Developing-country Members criticise the WTO and object to what they consider to be their 'marginalisation' within the WTO's negotiation and rule-making processes.

This chapter discusses the distinctive features of the WTO as the primary international organisation for international trade and trade-related matters. It first explores the origins of the WTO, a young institution with a long history. Subsequently, it examines:

- the mandate of the WTO, i.e. its objectives and functions;
- the membership of the WTO and the accession process;
- the institutional structure of the WTO; and
- the WTO's decision-making procedures, with particular attention to the role of developing-country Members and NGOs therein.

In general, this chapter seeks to address the issue of the legitimacy and effectiveness of the WTO as the main international organisation for managing and regulating international trade.

2.2. THE ORIGINS OF THE WTO

The origins of the WTO lie in the *General Agreement on Tariffs and Trade* of 1947, commonly referred to as the 'GATT 1947'. The study of these origins is relevant because the decisions, procedures and customary practices of the GATT 1947 still guide the WTO in its actions. Article XVI:1 of the *WTO Agreement* states:

Except as otherwise provided under this Agreement or the Multilateral Trade Agreements, the WTO shall be guided by the decisions, procedures and customary practices followed by the CONTRACTING PARTIES to GATT 1947 and the bodies established in the framework of GATT 1947.[6]

This section will discuss:

- the genesis of the GATT 1947 and its operation as the *de facto* international organisation for international trade until the end of 1994; and
- the GATT Uruguay Round of Multilateral Trade Negotiations (1986–94) and the emergence of the WTO, operational as of 1 January 1995.

---

[5] J. Nye, 'Take Globalization Protests Seriously', *International Herald Tribune*, 25 November 2000.
[6] Note that in June 2006 the WTO made public all official GATT documents (1947–95), adding 49,000 previously restricted documents to the 39,000 already in the public domain. See www.wto.org/english/docs_e/gattdocs_e.htm, visited on 15 September 2007.

2.2.1. The General Agreement on Tariffs and Trade of 1947

2.2.1.1. The GATT 1947 and the International Trade Organization

The history of the GATT begins in December 1945 when the United States invited its war-time allies to enter into negotiations to conclude a multilateral agreement for the reciprocal reduction of tariffs on trade in goods. These multilateral tariff negotiations took place in the context of a more ambitious project on international trade. At the proposal of the United States, the newly established United Nations Economic and Social Council adopted a resolution, in February 1946, calling for a conference to draft a charter for an 'International Trade Organization' (ITO).[7] At the 1944 Bretton Woods Conference, where the International Monetary Fund (IMF) and the International Bank for Reconstruction and Development (the 'World Bank') were established, the problems of trade had not been taken up as such, but the Conference did recognise the need for a comparable international institution for trade to complement the IMF and the World Bank.[8] A Preparatory Committee was established in February 1946 and met for the first time in London in October 1946 to work on the charter of an international organisation for trade.[9] The work was continued from April to November 1947 in Geneva. As John Jackson explained:

> The 1947 Geneva meeting was actually an elaborate conference in three major parts. One part was devoted to continuing the preparation of a charter for a major international trade institution, the ITO. A second part was devoted to the negotiation of a multilateral agreement to reduce tariffs reciprocally. A third part concentrated on drafting the 'general clauses' of obligations relating to the tariff obligations. These two latter parts together would constitute the General Agreement on Tariffs and Trade. The 'general clauses' of the draft GATT imposed obligations on nations to refrain from a variety of trade-impeding measures.[10]

The negotiations on the GATT advanced well in Geneva, and by October 1947 the negotiators had reached an agreement. The negotiations on the ITO, however, were more difficult and it was clear, towards the end of the 1947 Geneva meeting, that the *ITO Charter* would not be finished before 1948. Although the GATT was intended to be attached to the *ITO Charter*, many negotiators felt that it was not possible to wait until the *ITO Charter* was finished to bring the GATT into force. According to Jackson, there were two main reasons for this:

> First, although the tariff concessions were still secret, the negotiators knew that the content of the concessions would begin to be known. World trade patterns could thus be

---

[7] 1 UN ECOSOC Res. 13, UN Doc. E/22 (1946). For an overview of the negotiations of the GATT 1947 and the ITO with references to official documents, see *Analytical Index: Guide to GATT Law and Practice* (WTO, 1995), 3–6.

[8] See J. Jackson, *The World Trade Organization: Constitution and Jurisprudence* (Royal Institute of International Affairs, 1998), 15–16, who refers to United Nations Monetary and Financial Conference (Bretton Woods, NH, 1–22 July 1944), Proceedings and Documents 941 (US Department of State Publications No. 2866, 1948).

[9] The work in London proceeded on the basis of a proposal by the United States entitled 'Suggested Charter for an International Trade Organization'.

[10] J. Jackson, *The World Trade Organization: Constitution and Jurisprudence* (Royal Institute of International Affairs, 1998), 16.

> seriously disrupted if a prolonged delay occurred before the tariff concessions came into force. Second, the US negotiators were acting under the authority of the US trade legislation which had been renewed in 1945 . . . But the 1945 Act expired in mid-1948. Thus, there was a strong motivation on the part of the United States to bring the GATT into force before this Act expired.[11]

It was therefore decided to bring the provisions of the GATT into force immediately. However, this created a new problem. Under the provisions of their constitutional law, some countries could not agree to certain obligations of the GATT (and, in particular, those obligations that might require changes to national legislation) without submitting this agreement to their parliaments. Since they anticipated the need to submit the final draft of the *ITO Charter* to their parliaments in late 1948 or the following year, they feared that 'to spend the political effort required to get the GATT through the legislature might jeopardise the later effort to get the ITO passed'.[12] Therefore, they preferred to take the *ITO Charter* and the GATT to their legislatures as one package.

To resolve this problem, on 30 October 1947, eight of the twenty-three countries that had negotiated the GATT 1947 signed the 'Protocol of Provisional Application of the General Agreement on Tariffs and Trade' (PPA). Pursuant to this Protocol, these Contracting Parties undertook:

> *to apply provisionally on and after 1 January 1948*:
>
> a. Parts I and III of the General Agreement on Tariffs and Trade; and
> b. Part II of that Agreement to the fullest extent not inconsistent with existing legislation.[13]

The other fifteen of the original twenty-three Contracting Parties also soon agreed to the provisional application of the GATT 1947 through the PPA. Pursuant to the PPA, Part I (containing the MFN obligation and the tariff concessions) and Part III (containing procedural provisions) would apply in full, while Part II (containing most of the substantive provisions, the application of which could require the modification of national legislation and thus the involvement of the legislature) only applied to the extent that it was not inconsistent with existing legislation. According to the PPA, a GATT Contracting Party was entitled to retain any provision of its legislation which was inconsistent with a GATT Part II obligation.[14] The PPA thus provided for an 'existing legislation exception', also referred to as 'grandfather rights'. This was quite 'convenient' and explains why the GATT 1947 itself was never adopted by the Contracting Parties. Until 1995, the provisions of the GATT 1947 were applied through the PPA of 30 October 1947.

In March 1948, the negotiations on the *ITO Charter* were successfully completed in Havana. The Charter provided for the establishment of the ITO, and set out basic rules and disciplines for international trade and other international economic matters. However, the *ITO Charter* never entered into force. While the United

---

[11] *Ibid.*, 17–18.   [12] *Ibid.*, 18.   [13] GATT BISD, vol. IV, 77 (emphasis added).
[14] J. Jackson, *The World Trade Organization: Constitution and Jurisprudence* (Royal Institute of International Affairs, 1998), 18.

States had been the initiator of, and driving force behind, the negotiations on the *ITO Charter*, the United States Congress could not agree to approve it. In 1951, President Truman eventually decided that he would no longer seek Congressional approval of the *ITO Charter*. Since no country was interested in establishing an international organisation for trade of which the United States, the world's leading economy and trading nation, would not be a member, the ITO was 'still-born'. As the ITO was intended to complete the Bretton Woods structure of international economic institutions, its demise left a significant gap in that structure.

2.2.1.2. *The GATT as a de facto international organisation for trade*

In the absence of an international organisation for trade, countries turned, from the early fifties, to the only existing multilateral international 'institution' for trade, the GATT 1947, to handle problems concerning their trade relations.[15] Although the GATT was conceived as a multilateral *agreement* for the reduction of tariffs, and *not* an international *organisation*, it would over the years successfully 'transform' itself – in a pragmatic and incremental manner – into a *de facto* international organisation. The 'institutional' provisions in the GATT 1947 were scant. Article XXV of the GATT 1947, entitled 'Joint Action by the Contracting Parties', stated:

> 1. Representatives of the contracting parties shall meet from time to time for the purpose of giving effect to those provisions of this Agreement which involve joint action and, generally, with a view to facilitating the operation and furthering the objectives of this Agreement. Wherever reference is made in this Agreement to the contracting parties acting jointly they are designated as the CONTRACTING PARTIES.
> 2. The Secretary-General of the United Nations is requested to convene the first meeting of the CONTRACTING PARTIES, which shall take place not later than March 1, 1948.
> 3. Each contracting party shall be entitled to have one vote at all meetings of the CONTRACTING PARTIES.
> 4. Except as otherwise provided for in this Agreement, decisions of the CONTRACTING PARTIES shall be taken by a majority of the votes cast.
> 5. In exceptional circumstances not elsewhere provided for in this Agreement, the CONTRACTING PARTIES may waive an obligation imposed upon a contracting party by this Agreement; *Provided* that any such decision shall be approved by a two-thirds majority of the votes cast and that such majority shall comprise more than half of the contracting parties.

However, over the years, the GATT generated – through experimentation and trial and error – some fairly elaborate procedures for conducting its business. Some of these procedures were clearly 'contrary' to Article XXV quoted above. For example, in practice, under the GATT voting was very uncommon; decisions were taken by consensus.

In spite of its scanty institutional framework, the GATT was very successful in reducing tariffs on trade in goods, in particular on industrial goods from devel-

---

[15] A second and more modest attempt in 1955 to establish an 'Organization for Trade Cooperation' also failed because the US Congress was again unwilling to give its approval.

oped countries. In eight negotiating rounds between 1947 and 1994, the average level of tariffs of developed countries on industrial products was brought down from over 40 per cent to less than 4 per cent.[16] The first five negotiating rounds (Geneva (1947), Annecy (1949), Torquay (1951), Geneva (1956) and Dillon (1960–1)) focused on the reduction of tariffs. As from the Kennedy Round (1964–7) onwards, however, the negotiations would increasingly focus on non-tariff barriers (which were rapidly becoming a more serious barrier to trade than tariffs). With respect to the reduction of non-tariff barriers, the GATT was notably less successful than it was with the reduction of tariffs. Negotiations on the reduction of non-tariff barriers were much more complex and, therefore, required, *inter alia*, a more 'sophisticated' institutional framework than that of the GATT. The Kennedy Round produced very few results on non-tariff barriers. The Tokyo Round (1973–9) produced better results; however, a number of the agreements or codes decided upon clearly showed a lack of real consensus among the negotiators and proved to be difficult to implement. Moreover, the Tokyo Round agreements were plurilateral, rather than multilateral, in nature and did not bind many Contracting Parties.[17] In the early 1980s, it was clear that a new round of trade negotiations would be necessary. As Jackson noted:

> the world was becoming increasingly complex and interdependent, and it was becoming more and more obvious that the GATT rules were not satisfactorily providing the measure of discipline that was needed to prevent tensions and damaging national activity.[18]

The United States and a few other countries were in favour of a round with a very broad agenda including new subjects such as trade in services and the protection of intellectual property rights. Other countries objected to such a broad agenda or were opposed to the starting of a round altogether. However, in September 1986, at Punta del Este, Uruguay, the GATT Contracting Parties eventually agreed to the start of a new round.

Questions and Assignments 2.1

Briefly outline the historical origins of the GATT. Was the Bretton Woods system of international economic organisations already complete in 1946? If not, what was missing? Explain how the constitutional law of the United States and of other countries played a decisive role in the genesis of the GATT. Why and how did the GATT become the *de facto* international organisation for trade? Did the GATT 1947 ever enter into force? How did the PPA solve the problem faced by those countries that needed parliamentary approval of the GATT 1947? Has the GATT been a success?

---

[16] See also below, p. 86.
[17] On the distinction between multilateral and plurilateral agreements, see above, p. 52.
[18] J. Jackson, *The World Trade Organization: Constitution and Jurisprudence* (Royal Institute of International Affairs, 1998), 24.

2.2.2. Uruguay Round of Multilateral Trade Negotiations

2.2.2.1. Ministerial Declaration of Punta del Este

The 1986 Punta del Este Declaration contained a very broad and ambitious mandate for negotiations. According to this Declaration, the Uruguay Round negotiations would cover, *inter alia*, trade in goods (including trade in agricultural products and trade in textiles), as well as – for the first time in history – trade in services. The establishment of a new international organisation for trade was not, however, among the Uruguay Round's initial objectives. The Punta del Este Declaration explicitly recognised the need for institutional reforms in the GATT system but the ambitions were limited in this respect. The Declaration stated in pertinent part:

> Negotiations shall aim to develop understandings and arrangements:
>
> i.   to enhance the surveillance in the GATT to enable regular monitoring of trade policies and practices of contracting parties and their impact on the functioning of the multilateral system;
> ii. to improve the overall effectiveness and decision-making of the GATT as an institution, including *inter alia*, through involvement of Ministers;
> iii. to increase the contribution of the GATT to achieving greater coherence in global economic policy-making through strengthening its relationship with other international organizations responsible for monetary and financial matters.[19]

2.2.2.2. Negotiations on a new international organisation for trade

During the first years of the Uruguay Round negotiations, major progress was made with respect to all of the institutional issues identified in the Ministerial Declaration. In December 1988 at the Montreal Ministerial Mid-Term Review Conference it was decided in principle to implement, on a provisional basis, a Trade Policy Review Mechanism to improve adherence to GATT rules.[20] This Mid-Term Review also resulted in an agreement attempting to create greater cooperation between the GATT, the IMF and the World Bank as 'a first step to explore ways to achieve greater coherence in global economic policy making'.[21] In April 1989, it was agreed that in order to improve the functioning of the GATT, the Contracting Parties would meet at least once every two years at ministerial level.[22] At the time, however, the establishment of a new international trade organisation had not been discussed. It was the then Italian Trade Minister Renato Ruggiero (later the second Director-General of the WTO) who, in February 1990, first floated the idea of establishing a new international organisation for trade. A few months later, in April 1990, Canada formally proposed the establishment of what it called a 'World Trade Organization', a fully fledged

---

[19] *Ministerial Declaration on the Uruguay Round*, GATT MIN.DEC, dated 20 September 1986, Part I, Section D, part 4E, 'Functioning of the GATT System'.
[20] In April 1989, the CONTRACTING PARTIES formally established the Trade Policy Review Mechanism.
[21] T. Stewart, *The GATT Uruguay Round* (Kluwer Law and Taxation,1993), vol. III, 1927.   [22] See *ibid.*, 1928.

international organisation which was to administer the different multilateral instruments related to international trade. This included the GATT, the GATS and other instruments being developed in the context of the ongoing negotiations.[23] Along the same lines, the European Community submitted a proposal, in July 1990, calling for the establishment of a 'Multilateral Trade Organization'. The European Community argued that the GATT needed a sound institutional framework 'to ensure the effective implementation of the results of the Uruguay Round'.[24]

The reactions by the United States and most developing countries to these proposals were anything but enthusiastic.[25] In 1990 there was still little support for a major institutional overhaul.[26] Fear of supranationalism, the reluctance of major trading nations to give in to voting equality and the traditional worry of national leaders about 'tying their hands' were thought to inhibit the possibility of reconstructing the GATT into an international organisation for trade.[27] The December 1990 Brussels Draft Final Act, discussed at what was initially planned to be the closing conference of the Uruguay Round, did not contain an agreement with regard to a new international organisation for trade.[28] Albeit for very different reasons, this conference was a total failure, and the Uruguay Round was subsequently suspended.[29] In April 1991, however, the negotiations were taken up again, and, in November 1991, the European Community, Canada and Mexico drafted a joint proposal for an international trade organisation. This joint proposal served as the basis for further negotiations which resulted, in December 1991, in the draft *Agreement Establishing the Multilateral Trade Organization*. The latter agreement was part of the 1991 Draft Final Act, commonly referred to as the Dunkel Draft, after the then Director-General of the GATT.[30]

For the reasons already referred to above, the United States remained opposed to the establishment of a Multilateral Trade Organization and actively campaigned against the idea throughout 1992. Despite the United States' efforts, by early 1993 most participants in the Round were prepared to agree to the establishment of a Multilateral Trade Organization. This isolation of the United States

---

[23] See *ibid.*, 1942–3.

[24] See *Communication from the European Community*, GATT Doc. No. MTN.GNG/NG14/W/42, dated 9 July 1990, 2.

[25] Many developing countries were hostile to the idea of an international trade organisation, unless this organisation was instituted within the framework of the United Nations. UNCTAD tried to present itself as a possible multilateral trade organisation. See T. Stewart, *The GATT Uruguay Round* (Kluwer Law and Taxation, 1993), vol. III, 1944.

[26] J. Jackson, 'Strengthening the International Legal Framework of the GATT–MTN System: Reform Proposals for the New GATT Round 1991', in E. U. Petersmann and M. Hilf (eds.), *The New GATT Round of Multilateral Trade Negotiations: Legal and Economic Problems* (Kluwer, 1991), 17, 21 and 22. See also P. VerLoren van Themaat, in *ibid.*, 29: 'It is highly unlikely that the world's government leaders would be willing, at this point in history, to even start serious discussions about such a new institution.'

[27] See J. Jackson, 'Strengthening the International Legal Framework of the GATT–MTN System: Reform Proposals for the New GATT Round 1991', in *ibid.*, 21.

[28] *Draft Final Act Embodying the Results of the Uruguay Round of Multilateral Trade Negotiations*, GATT Doc. MTN.TNC/W/35/Rev.1, dated 3 December 1990.

[29] The negotiations broke down because of the fundamental disagreement between the European Community and the United States on the issue of agricultural subsidies.

[30] *Draft Final Act Embodying the Results of the Uruguay Round of Multilateral Trade Negotiations*, GATT Doc. MTN.TNC/W/FA, dated 20 December 1991.

perhaps explains the turnabout in its position during 1993 when the new Clinton Administration dropped its outspoken opposition to a new international trade organisation. Nevertheless, uncertainty about US support for such a new international organisation persisted until the last days of the Round.[31] The United States formally agreed to the establishment of the new organisation on 15 December 1993. To the surprise of many, however, the United States demanded a change of name as a condition for giving its consent. The United States suggested that the name of the new organisation should be the 'World Trade Organization' as had originally been proposed by Canada. The proponents of an international trade organisation had opted for 'Multilateral Trade Organization', as was proposed by the European Community, in the hope that this rather technical and therefore less menacing name would appease the United States and others opposed to an international organisation perceived as a threat to national sovereignty. Reportedly, the United States did not want to give the European Community the satisfaction of having given the new organisation its name, and further considered that an organisation with such a tongue-twisting and unappealing name as the 'Multilateral Trade Organization' would have a hard time winning the hearts and minds of the American people.[32] The *Agreement Establishing the World Trade Organization*, commonly referred to as the *WTO Agreement*, was signed in Marrakesh in April 1994, and entered into force on 1 January 1995.[33] A perceptive observer, Gary Sampson, noted:

> Those who constructed the WTO are proud of having created what has been described as the greatest ever achievement in institutionalized global economic cooperation.[34]

The Sutherland Report on *The Future of the WTO* noted:

> The creation of the World Trade Organization (WTO) in 1995 was the most dramatic advance in multilateralism since the inspired period of institution building of the late 1940s.[35]

Questions and Assignments 2.2

Did the Punta del Este Ministerial Declaration recognise the need for a new international organisation for trade? Briefly outline the events between 1990 and 1993 that led to an agreement on the establishment of a new international trade organisation in December 1993. Which countries were the driving forces behind the establishment of the WTO? Why were

---

[31] Withholding its consent to a new international trade organisation proved a useful bargaining chip in negotiations with the European Community. See *Financial Times*, 16 December 1993, 5.

[32] See *ibid*. Note that the World Trade Organization and the World Tourism Organization concluded an agreement on the use of the acronym 'WTO'. To avoid confusion, the World Trade Organization agreed to use a distinct logo and avoid using the acronym in the context of tourism. See GATT Doc. MTN.TNC/W/ 146, 4.

[33] Note that, after the entry into force of the *WTO Agreement* and the establishment of the WTO on 1 January 1995, the WTO and the GATT existed side by side for one year. The GATT 1947 was terminated only at the end of 1995.

[34] G. Sampson, 'Overview', in G. Sampson (ed.), *The Role of The World Trade Organization in Global Governance* (United Nations University Press, 2001), 5.

[35] Report by the Consultative Board to the Director-General Supachai Panitchpakdi, *The Future of the WTO: Addressing Institutional Challenges in the New Millennium* (the 'Sutherland Report') (WTO, 2004), paras. 1 and 7, available at www.wto.org/english/thewto_e/10anniv_e/future_wto_e.htm, visited on 20 September 2007.

other countries opposed to this idea? When were the negotiations on the *WTO Agreement* successfully concluded? When and where was the *WTO Agreement* signed? When did the *WTO Agreement* enter into force?

2.3. MANDATE OF THE WTO

The WTO was formally established and became operational on 1 January 1995 when the *WTO Agreement* entered into force. Pursuant to the *WTO Agreement*, the WTO has a broad and ambitious mandate. This section examines two main aspects of this mandate:

* the objectives of the WTO; and
* the functions of the WTO.

2.3.1. Objectives of the WTO

The reasons for establishing the WTO and the policy objectives of this international organisation are set out in the Preamble to the *WTO Agreement*. According to the Preamble, the Parties to the *WTO Agreement* agreed to the terms of this agreement and the establishment of the WTO:

> *Recognizing* that their relations in the field of trade and economic endeavour should be conducted with a view to raising standards of living, ensuring full employment and a large and steadily growing volume of real income and effective demand, and expanding the production of and trade in goods and services, while allowing for the optimal use of the world's resources in accordance with the objective of sustainable development, seeking both to protect and preserve the environment and to enhance the means for doing so in a manner consistent with their respective needs and concerns at different levels of economic development,
>
>   *Recognizing* further that there is need for positive efforts designed to ensure that developing countries, and especially the least developed among them, secure a share in the growth in international trade commensurate with the needs of their economic development . . .

The ultimate objectives of the WTO are thus:

* the increase of standards of living;
* the attainment of full employment;
* the growth of real income and effective demand; and
* the expansion of production of, and trade in, goods and services.

However, it is clear from the Preamble that in pursuing these objectives the WTO must take into account the need for preservation of the environment and the needs of developing countries. The Preamble stresses the importance of *sustainable* economic development, i.e. economic development taking account of environmental as well as social concerns. The Preamble also stresses the importance of the *integration* of developing countries, and in particular least-developed countries, in the world trading system. Both of these aspects were absent from the Preamble to the GATT 1947.

The statements in the Preamble on the objectives of the WTO are not without legal significance. In *US – Shrimp*, the Appellate Body stated:

> [The language of the Preamble to the *WTO Agreement*] demonstrates a recognition by WTO negotiators that optimal use of the world's resources should be made in accordance with the objective of sustainable development. As this preambular language reflects the intentions of negotiators of the *WTO Agreement*, we believe it must *add colour, texture and shading to our interpretation of the agreements* annexed to the *WTO Agreement*, in this case, the GATT 1994. We have already observed that Article XX(g) of the GATT 1994 is appropriately read with the perspective embodied in the above preamble.[36]
>
> [Emphasis added]

The preambular statements of the objectives of the WTO contradict the contention that the WTO is only about trade liberalisation without regard for environmental degradation and global poverty.

The Preamble also states how these objectives are to be achieved:

> *Being desirous* of contributing to these objectives by entering into reciprocal and mutually advantageous arrangements directed to the substantial reduction of tariffs and other barriers to trade and to the elimination of discriminatory treatment in international trade relations,
>
> *Resolved*, therefore, to develop an integrated, more viable and durable multilateral trading system encompassing the General Agreement on Tariffs and Trade, the results of past trade liberalization efforts, and all of the results of the Uruguay Round of Multilateral Trade Negotiations,
>
> *Determined* to preserve the basic principles and to further the objectives underlying this multilateral trading system,

According to the Preamble to the *WTO Agreement*, the two main instruments, or means, to achieve the objectives of the WTO are:

- the reduction of tariff barriers and other barriers to trade; and
- the elimination of discriminatory treatment in international trade relations.

The reduction of trade barriers and elimination of discrimination were also the two main instruments of the GATT 1947, but the *WTO Agreement* aims at constituting the basis of an integrated, *more* viable and *more* durable multilateral trading system.

In the Doha Ministerial Declaration of 14 November 2001, the WTO Members stated, with regard to the objectives of the WTO and its instruments for achieving these objectives:

> We ... strongly reaffirm the principles and objectives set out in the Marrakesh Agreement Establishing the World Trade Organization, and pledge to reject the use of protectionism.
>
> International trade can play a major role in the promotion of economic development and the alleviation of poverty. We recognize the need for all our peoples to benefit from the increased opportunities and welfare gains that the multilateral trading system generates. The majority of WTO Members are developing countries. We seek to place their needs and interests at the heart of the Work Programme adopted in this Declaration. Recalling the Preamble to the Marrakesh Agreement, we shall continue to make positive

---

[36] Appellate Body Report, *US – Shrimp*, para. 153.

efforts designed to *ensure that developing countries*, and especially the least-developed among them, *secure a share in the growth of world trade* commensurate with the needs of their economic development . . .

We strongly reaffirm our commitment to the objective of *sustainable development*, as stated in the Preamble to the Marrakesh Agreement. We are convinced that the aims of upholding and safeguarding an open and non-discriminatory multilateral trading system, and acting for the protection of the environment and the promotion of sustainable development, can and must be mutually supportive.[37]

[Emphasis added]

Questions and Assignments 2.3

What are the objectives of the WTO? Are the economic development of developing countries and environmental protection objectives of the WTO? Explain. What is the legal significance of the Preamble to the *WTO Agreement*? What are the main instruments, or means, of the WTO for achieving its objectives?

2.3.2. Functions of the WTO

In the broadest of terms, the primary function of the WTO is to:

provide the common institutional framework for the conduct of trade relations among its Members in matters related to the agreements and associated legal instruments included in the Annexes to [the WTO] Agreement.[38]

More specifically, the WTO has been assigned six widely defined functions. Article III of the *WTO Agreement* states:

1. The WTO shall *facilitate the implementation*, administration and operation, and further the objectives, of this Agreement and of the Multilateral Trade Agreements, and shall also provide the framework for the implementation, administration and operation of the Plurilateral Trade Agreements.
2. The WTO shall provide the *forum for negotiations* among its Members concerning their multilateral trade relations in matters dealt with under the agreements in the Annexes to this Agreement. The WTO may also provide a forum for further negotiations among its Members concerning their multilateral trade relations, and a framework for the implementation of the results of such negotiations, as may be decided by the Ministerial Conference.
3. The WTO shall administer the Understanding on Rules and Procedures Governing the *Settlement of Disputes* (hereinafter referred to as the 'Dispute Settlement Understanding' or 'DSU') in Annex 2 to this Agreement.
4. The WTO shall administer the *Trade Policy Review Mechanism* (hereinafter referred to as the 'TPRM') provided for in Annex 3 to this Agreement.
5. With a view to achieving greater coherence in global economic policy-making, the WTO shall *cooperate*, as appropriate, with the International Monetary Fund and with the International Bank for Reconstruction and Development and its affiliated agencies.

[Emphasis added]

---

[37] Ministerial Conference, *Doha Ministerial Declaration*, WT/MIN(01)/DEC/1, dated 20 November 2001, paras. 1, 2 and 6.   [38] Article II:1 of the *WTO Agreement*.

In addition to the functions of the WTO explicitly referred to in Article III of the *WTO Agreement*, technical assistance to developing-country Members, to allow the latter to integrate into the world trading system, is, undisputedly, also an important function of the WTO.

This section will examine the following functions of the WTO:

* the implementation of the WTO agreements;
* the negotiation of new agreements;
* the settlement of disputes;
* trade policy review;
* cooperation with other organisations; and
* technical assistance to developing countries.

2.3.2.1. *Implementation of the WTO agreements*

According to Article III of the *WTO Agreement*, the first function of the WTO is to facilitate the implementation, administration and operation of the *WTO Agreement* and the multilateral and plurilateral agreements annexed to it.[39] The WTO is also entrusted with the task of furthering the objectives of these agreements. For two concrete examples of what this function of 'facilitating' and 'furthering' entails, we refer to the work of the WTO Committee on Sanitary and Phytosanitary Measures (the 'SPS Committee') and the work of the WTO Committee on Safeguards. Article 12, paragraph 2, of the *SPS Agreement* states that the SPS Committee shall, *inter alia*:

> encourage and facilitate ad hoc consultations or negotiations among Members on specific sanitary or phytosanitary issues. The Committee shall encourage the use of international standards, guidelines or recommendations by all Members and, in this regard, shall sponsor technical consultation and study with the objective of increasing coordination and integration between international and national systems and approaches for approving the use of food additives or for establishing tolerances for contaminants in foods, beverages or feedstuffs.

Pursuant to Article 13 of the *Agreement on Safeguards*, the tasks of the Committee on Safeguards include:

> a. to monitor, and report annually to the Council for Trade in Goods on, the general implementation of this Agreement and make recommendations towards its improvement;
> b. to find, upon request of an affected Member, whether or not the procedural requirements of this Agreement have been complied with in connection with a safeguard measure, and report its findings to the Council for Trade in Goods;
> c. to assist Members, if they so request, in their consultations under the provisions of this Agreement;

This function of facilitating the implementation, administration and operation of the WTO agreements and furthering the objectives of these agreements is an

---

[39] For an overview of these agreements, see above, pp. 42–53.

essential function of the WTO. It involves most of its bodies and takes up much of their time.[40]

Questions and Assignments 2.4

Give two concrete examples of how the WTO facilitates the implementation, administration and operation of the *WTO Agreement* other than the examples given in this section.

2.3.2.2. *Negotiation of new agreements*

A second function of the WTO is to provide a permanent forum for negotiations amongst its Members. The WTO provides 'the' forum for negotiations on matters already covered by the WTO and the WTO is 'a' forum among others with regard to negotiations on matters not yet addressed. To date, WTO Members have negotiated and concluded five trade agreements, in the framework of the WTO, providing for:

* further market access commitments for specific services and service providers (on financial services in 1995 and 1997,[41] on basic telecommunications services in 1997[42] and on the movement of natural persons in 1995[43]); and
* the liberalisation of trade in information technology products in 1996.[44]

Since the conclusion of these specific agreements in the first years of the WTO, no further agreements have been negotiated and concluded in the framework of the WTO. While the WTO provides a *permanent* forum for negotiations, in practice Members seem to require the political momentum, and the opportunity for package deals, brought by an old GATT-type round of negotiations covering a wide range of matters.

After failing dismally to do so at the Seattle Session of the Ministerial Conference in November–December 1999, the WTO decided at the Doha Session of the Ministerial Conference in November 2001 to start a new round of multilateral trade negotiations, commonly referred to as the 'Doha Development Round'. In the Doha Ministerial Declaration, the WTO Members stressed their 'commitment to the WTO as the unique forum for global trade rule-making and

---

[40] For a list and a description of these WTO bodies, see below, pp. 117–38.
[41] *Second Protocol to the General Agreement on Trade in Services*, S/L/11, dated 24 July 1995; and *Fifth Protocol to the General Agreement on Trade in Services*, S/L/45, dated 3 December 1997.
[42] *Fourth Protocol to the General Agreement on Trade in Services*, S/L/20, dated 30 April 1996.
[43] *Third Protocol to the General Agreement on Trade in Services*, S/L/12, dated 24 July 1995.
[44] *Agreement on Trade in Information Technology Products (ITA)*, in *Ministerial Declaration on Trade in Information Technology Products*, adopted on 13 December 1996 and entered into force on 1 July 1997. The ITA was agreed at the close of the Singapore Session of the Ministerial Conference in December 1996. The ITA provides for the elimination of customs duties and other duties and charges on information technology products by the year 2000 on an MFN basis. The implementation of the ITA, however, was contingent on approximately 90 per cent of world trade in IT products being covered by the ITA. On 26 March 1997 that criterion was met. In 2007, Seventy Members were party to the ITA. See www.wto.org/english/tratop_e/inftec_e/insotec_e.htm, visited on 1 December 2007.

liberalization'.[45] Pursuant to the Doha Ministerial Declaration, the Doha Development Round negotiations should have been concluded no later than 1 January 2005. However, this and subsequent deadlines were not met and the negotiations are currently still ongoing.

The Ministerial Declaration provides for an ambitious agenda for negotiations. These negotiations include matters on which WTO Members had agreed in the *WTO Agreement* to continue negotiations, such as:

- trade in agricultural products;[46] and
- trade in services.[47]

In fact, negotiations on these matters had already started in early 2000. Furthermore, the Doha Development Round negotiations include negotiations on matters such as:

- problems of developing-country Members with the implementation of the existing WTO agreements (the so-called 'implementation issues');
- market access for non-agricultural products;
- TRIPS issues such as access for developing countries to essential medicines and the protection of geographical indications;
- rules on anti-dumping duties, subsidies and regional trade agreements;
- dispute settlement; and
- special and differential treatment for developing-country Members and least-developed-country Members.[48]

It is important to note that the Doha Ministerial Declaration stated with regard to the negotiations on these distinct matters that 'the conduct, conclusion and entry into force of the outcome of the negotiations shall be treated as parts of a single undertaking'.[49] Under this 'single undertaking' approach to the negotiations, there is no agreement on anything until there is an agreement on everything.

Some WTO Members, and in particular the European Communities, wanted a broader agenda for the Doha Development Round. They also wanted the WTO to start negotiations on, for example, the relationship between trade and investment, the relationship between trade and competition law and the relationship between trade and core labour standards. There was, however, strong opposition, especially among developing-country Members, to the inclusion of some or all of these matters on the agenda of negotiations. At the Doha Session of the Ministerial Conference, WTO Members decided that there will be no negotiations, within the context of the WTO, on the relationship between trade and core labour standards. However, with respect to what is commonly referred to as the 'Singapore issues',[50] namely:

---

[45] Ministerial Conference, *Doha Ministerial Declaration*, WT/MIN(01)/DEC/1, dated 20 November 2001, para. 4.
[46] See Article 20 of the *Agreement on Agriculture*.   [47] See Article XIX of the GATS.
[48] For a complete list of the matters on the agenda of the Doha Development Round, see Ministerial Conference, *Doha Ministerial Declaration*, WT/MIN(01)/DEC/1, dated 20 November 2001.
[49] *Ibid.*, para. 47. The only exception to the single undertaking approach relates to the negotiations on the improvements to and clarifications of the *Dispute Settlement Understanding*. See *ibid.*

- the relationship between trade and investment,
- the relationship between trade and competition law,
- transparency in government procurement, and
- trade facilitation,

the WTO Members decided in Doha that negotiations would start after they had agreed, by 'explicit consensus', on the modalities of these negotiations.[51] This agreement on the modalities of the negotiations on the Singapore issues was to be reached at the next session of the Ministerial Conference in Cancún in September 2003. However, at this session, no such agreement was reached. Developing-country Members were unwilling to consent to the request of the European Communities and others to start negotiations on the Singapore issues. Moreover, at the Cancún Session, it became clear that little progress had been achieved on most of the issues on which Members had been negotiating since the start of the negotiations in February 2002. As during the Uruguay Round negotiations, agricultural subsidies and market access for agricultural products were again the most contentious issues on the negotiating table.[52] The Cancún Session of the Ministerial Conference turned out to be a dismal failure, with nothing agreed upon.[53] In diplomatic language masking the deep sense of failure and disappointment, the Ministerial Statement adopted at the close of the Cancún Session on 14 September 2003 read:

> All participants have worked hard and constructively to make progress as required under the Doha mandates. We have, indeed, made considerable progress. However, more work needs to be done in some key areas to enable us to proceed towards the conclusion of the negotiations in fulfilment of the commitments we took at Doha.[54]

The deadlock in the negotiations after the Cancún Session was only overcome during the summer of 2004 when, following weeks of intense discussions, a new Doha Work Programme was adopted by the General Council on 1 August 2004.[55] In its Decision of 1 August, the General Council called on all Members 'to redouble their efforts towards the conclusion of a balanced overall outcome of the Doha Development Agenda'.[56] A key element of the Decision of the General Council was not to start negotiations on the Singapore issues with the exception of the issue of trade facilitation.[57] The 'redoubling of efforts' did not, however, have the results hoped for. At the Hong Kong Session of the Ministerial Conference in December 2005, agreement was reached on the elimination of agricultural export subsidies

---

[50] At the Singapore Session of the Ministerial Conference in December 1996, these issues were first identified as possible issues for further negotiations within the WTO.

[51] Note that the concept of 'explicit consensus' was a *novum* in WTO law. See below, p. 139.

[52] See below, pp. 416–17, 600–4.

[53] Note that in the run-up to the Cancún Session of the Ministerial Conference, the General Council of the WTO did reach an agreement on the waiver to the *TRIPS Agreement* enabling the import by developing countries of generic medicines produced under compulsory licences. See General Council, *Decision on the Implementation of paragraph 6 of the Doha Declaration on TRIPS and Public Health*, WT/L/540, dated 1 September 2003. See further below, p. 791.

[54] Ministerial Conference, *Ministerial Statement*, WT/MIN(03)/20, dated 23 September 2003, para. 3.

[55] See General Council, *Doha Work Programme Decision adopted by the General Council on 1 August 2001*, WT/L/579, dated 2 August 2001.   [56] *Ibid.*, para. 3.   [57] See below, pp. 471–2.

by 2013.[58] This was in itself a significant achievement but of little value if no agreement was also reached on all other major issues on the negotiating table, such as market access for agricultural products, domestic support for agricultural production, market access for non-agricultural products (NAMA), and the liberalisation of trade in services. With regard to these other issues, Members were unfortunately only able to agree to disagree and to put forward the summer of 2006 as a new deadline for agreement on the broad lines of an overall deal on market access for non-agricultural products.[59] When that deadline was missed, WTO Director-General Lamy decided at the end of July 2006 to suspend the negotiations.[60] In February 2007, the negotiations were resumed. While progress has been made since the resumption of the negotiations, to date Members have not been able to achieve a breakthrough allowing for the conclusion of an overall agreement. At the General Council meeting of 9 October 2007, Director-General Pascal Lamy reported on the progress in the negotiations as follows:

> We have regained a good level of momentum in our work, and the challenge now is to accelerate it in the days and weeks ahead, so that the necessary compromises can be found. However, now more than ever, time is running against us. As I have stated before, progress is now being made but we must increase the pace at which we move ahead in agriculture and NAMA, so that we can then bring all the elements of the Round together, as we have to do under the Single Undertaking. And let me recall that we must keep firmly in mind the need to reflect the Development Dimension of this Round, including Special and Differential Treatment, in all our work . . . Since the summer, all of you have put much effort into the negotiating process. We should enable it to achieve its full potential so we can conclude the Round successfully and ambitiously. I remain convinced that this deal is as doable as it is essential.[61]

Whether Lamy's guarded optimism was justified and his couched words of warning to Members were heard, the future will tell.

The role of the WTO Director-General, the Trade Negotiations Committee (TNC) and the various negotiating groups in the Doha Development Round negotiations is discussed later in this chapter.[62] It suffices to note here that all publicly available documents, reports and position papers relating to the Doha Development Round negotiations are available on the WTO website as WT/TN documents.[63]

Questions and Assignments 2.5

Has the WTO thus far been successful as a forum for the negotiation of new multilateral trade agreements? What is on the agenda of the Doha Development Round? What is not on the agenda? Find out exactly what the Doha Ministerial Declaration of November 2001 says about the

---

[58] See Ministerial Conference, *Hong Kong Ministerial Declaration*, WT/MIN(05)/DEC, dated 22 December 2005, para. 6 The elimination of export subsidies by 2013 was an important concession on the part of the European Communities.
[59] See Annex B to the *Hong Kong Ministerial Declaration*, WT/MIN(05)/DEC, dated 22 December 2005.
[60] See WTO News, 'Talks Suspended. "Today there are only losers" ', available at www.wto.org/english/news_e/news06_e/mod06_summary_24july_e.htm, visited on 28 November 2007.
[61] See WTO News, 'Lamy urges further acceleration of negotiations', available at www.wto.org/english/news_e/news07_e/tnc_chair_report_oct07_e.htm, visited on 10 October 2007.
[62] See below, pp. 105–6, 127–8, 134–6.
[63] See http://docsonline.wto.org/gen_home.asp?language=1&_=1, visited on 20 November 2007.

relationship between trade and core labour standards. What are the major issues in the Doha Development Round negotiations? Assess the likelihood of a successful completion of the Doha Development Round before the end of the decade.

2.3.2.3. Dispute settlement

A third and very important function of the WTO is the administration of the WTO dispute settlement system. As stated in Article 3.2 of the *Dispute Settlement Understanding*:

> The dispute settlement system of the WTO is a central element in providing security and predictability to the multilateral trading system.

The prompt settlement of disputes under the WTO agreements is essential for the effective functioning of the WTO and for maintaining a proper balance between the rights and obligations of Members.[64] The WTO dispute settlement system serves:

- to preserve the rights and obligations of Members under the WTO agreements; and
- to clarify the existing provisions of those agreements.[65]

The dispute settlement system is explicitly proscribed from adding to or diminishing the rights and obligations provided in the WTO agreements.[66]

The WTO dispute settlement system, referred to as the 'jewel in the crown' of the WTO, has been operational for thirteen years now, and has arguably been the most prolific of all intergovernmental dispute settlement systems in that period. Since 1 January 1995, 369 disputes have been brought to the WTO system for resolution.[67] Some of these disputes, involving, for example, national legislation on public health or environmental protection, were politically sensitive and have attracted considerable attention from the media. With its compulsory jurisdiction, its strict time-frames, its confidential and closed nature, the possibility of appellate review and the detailed mechanism to ensure compliance with recommendations and rulings, the WTO dispute settlement system is unique among international dispute settlement systems. Chapter 3 examines in detail the basic principles, institutions and proceedings of the WTO dispute settlement system.[68]

2.3.2.4. Trade policy review

A fourth function of the WTO is the administration of the trade policy review mechanism (TPRM).[69] The TPRM provides for the regular *collective* appreciation

---

[64] See Article 3.3 of the DSU.   [65] See Article 3.2, second sentence, of the DSU.
[66] See Article 3.2, last sentence, of the DSU.
[67] See www.wto.org/english/tratop_e/dispu_e/dispu_status_e.htm, visited on 15 November 2007.
[68] See below, pp. 169–311.   [69] See Annex 3 to the *WTO Agreement*, entitled 'Trade Policy Review Mechanism'.

and evaluation of the full range of *individual* Members' trade policies and practices and their impact on the functioning of the multilateral trading system.[70] The purpose of the TPRM is:

- to achieve greater transparency in, and understanding of, the trade policies and practices of Members; and
- to contribute, in this way, to improved adherence by all Members to rules, disciplines and commitments made under the WTO agreements.

Under the TPRM, the trade policies and practices of all Members are subject to *periodic review*. The frequency of review is determined by reference to each Member's share of world trade in a recent representative period.[71] The four largest trading entities, i.e., the European Communities,[72] the United States, Japan and China, are subject to review every two years. The next sixteen are reviewed every four years. Other Members are reviewed every six years, except that for least-developed-country Members a longer period may be fixed.[73]

The trade policy reviews are carried out by the Trade Policy Review Body (TPRB)[74] on the basis of two reports: a report supplied by the Member under review, in which the Member describes the trade policy and practices it pursues; and a report, drawn up by the WTO Secretariat, based on the information available to it and that provided by the Member under review.[75] These reports, together with the concluding remarks by the TPRB Chairperson and the minutes of the meeting of the TPRB, are published shortly after the review and are a valuable source of information on a WTO Member's trade policy. The TPR reports and the minutes of the TPRB are searchable by country and available on the WTO website as WT/TPR documents.[76]

Since 1 January 1995, the WTO has conducted 193 trade policy reviews. During 2007, the TPRB carried out 18 reviews.[77] Almost all Members have had their trade policy reviewed once or more.

It is important to note that the TPRM is not intended to serve as a basis for the enforcement of specific obligations under the WTO agreements or for dispute settlement procedures.[78] However, by *publicly* deploring inconsistencies with WTO law of a Member's trade policy or practices, the TPRM intends to 'shame' Members into compliance and to bolster domestic opposition to trade policy and practices inconsistent with WTO law. Likewise, by *publicly* praising WTO-consistent trade

---

[70] See *Trade Policy Review Mechanism*, para. A(i).   [71] See *ibid.*, para. C(ii).

[72] It is understood that the review of entities having a common external policy covering more than one Member shall cover all components of policy affecting trade, including relevant policies and practices of the individual Members. See *ibid.*

[73] Exceptionally, in the event of changes in a Member's trade policies or practices that may have a significant impact on its trading partners, the Member concerned may be requested by the TPRB, after consultation, to bring forward its next review. See *ibid.*   [74] See below, pp. 122–4.

[75] The two reports cover all aspects of the Member's trade policies, including its domestic laws and regulations, the institutional framework, bilateral, regional and other preferential agreements, the wider economic needs and the external environment.

[76] See www.wto.org/english/tratop_e/tpr_e/tpr_e.htm, visited on 15 November 2007.

[77] *Ibid.* The Members concerned were Chad; Japan; Argentina; the European Communities; Australia; Canada; Macau, China; Costa Rica; India; Central African Republic; Indonesia; Bahrain; Panama; Cameroon and Gabon; Peru; the organization of Eastern Caribbean States; Thailand; and Turkey.

[78] See Trade Policy Review Mechanism. para. A(i).

policies, the TPRM bolsters, both internationally and domestically, support for such policies. By way of example, note the remarks made by the TPRB Chairperson at the conclusion of the trade policy review of Bangladesh in 2006. In these concluding remarks, the TPRB Chairperson stated:

> Members commended Bangladesh's efforts to ensure steady growth of GDP through prudent macroeconomic policies and reforms in certain areas, despite endogenous and exogenous challenges. While noting efforts to improve governance, certain Members encouraged Bangladesh to increase its capacity for revenue collection and move away from dependence on tariffs and other border charges as a main source of revenue. Some Members considered that there was room for progress in implementing privatization plans. Members congratulated Bangladesh on its increased Foreign Direct Investment inflows during the period under review and encouraged further improvements in the foreign investment framework. Members noted that Bangladesh's comprehensive poverty reduction strategy had led to an improvement of certain social indicators, including the share of people living below the poverty line. Trade and trade policy measures were an integral part of these efforts.[79]

Trade policy reviews of developing-country Members also give an opportunity to identify the needs of these countries in terms of technical and other assistance. The remarks of the TPRB Chairperson at the conclusion of the trade policy review of Pakistan in 2002 are also noteworthy:

> Purely as an aside, and as much a comment on the review process as on this Review, I was struck by [Pakistan's] Secretary Beg's remarks that questions had given his delegation food for considerable thought and that sources of information had been found of which he was unaware. This goes to the heart of our work: not only do we learn a lot about the Member, but often the Member learns a lot about itself. Moreover, this is put into a multilateral setting, thus serving to strengthen our system. Increasingly our work highlights the value of the Trade Policy Review Body.[80]

Apart from carrying out individual trade policy reviews, the TPRB also undertakes an *annual overview* of developments in the international trading environment which have an impact on the multilateral trading system. To assist the TPRB with this review, the Director-General presents an *annual report* setting out the major activities of the WTO and highlighting significant policy issues affecting the trading system.[81]

Questions and Assignments 2.6

What is the objective of the Trade Policy Review Mechanism? Is trade policy review under the WTO comparable with WTO dispute settlement? Find the latest trade policy review reports concerning the European Communities and the United States on the WTO website. Find also the latest WTO Annual Report.

---

[79] Trade Policy Review Body – Review of Bangladesh – TPRB's Evaluation, PRESS/TPRB/269, dated 13 and 15 September 2006.
[80] Trade Policy Review Body – Review of Pakistan – TPRB's Evaluation, PRESS/TPRB/187, dated 25 January 2002.   [81] See e.g. WTO Secretariat, *WTO Annual Report 2007*, 6.

2.3.2.5. Cooperation with other organisations

Article III:5 of the *WTO Agreement* refers specifically to cooperation with the IMF and the World Bank. Such cooperation is mandated by the need for greater coherence in global economic policy-making. The 'linkages' between the different aspects of global economic policy (financial, monetary and trade) require that the international institutions with responsibilities in these areas follow coherent and mutually supportive policies. It is therefore stated in the Uruguay Round *Declaration on the Contribution of the World Trade Organization to Achieving Greater Coherence in Global Economic Policymaking*, commonly referred to as the *Declaration on Coherence*, that the WTO should:

> pursue and develop cooperation with the international organizations responsible for monetary and financial matters, while respecting the mandate, the confidentiality requirements and the necessary autonomy in decision-making procedures of each institution, and avoiding the imposition on governments of cross-conditionality or additional conditions. Ministers further invite the Director-General of the WTO to review with the Managing Director of the International Monetary Fund and the President of the World Bank, the implications of the WTO's responsibilities for its cooperation with the Bretton Woods institutions, as well as the forms such cooperation might take, with a view to achieving greater coherence in global economic policymaking.[82]

The WTO has concluded agreements with both the IMF and the World Bank to give form to the cooperation required by Article III:5 of the *WTO Agreement*.[83] These agreements provide for consultations and the exchange of information between the WTO Secretariat and the staff of the IMF and the World Bank. The WTO, the IMF and the World Bank now cooperate quite closely on a day-to-day basis, in particular in the area of technical assistance to developing countries. Along with three other international organisations,[84] the IMF and the World Bank participate actively in a WTO-led Integrated Framework for Trade-Related Technical Assistance (IF) to help the least-developed countries expand their exports.[85] Furthermore, the IMF and the World Bank have observer status in the WTO and the WTO attends the meetings of the IMF and the World Bank. Officials of the three organisations meet regularly to discuss issues of global economic policy coherence.

Pursuant to Article V:1 of the *WTO Agreement*, the WTO is also to cooperate with other international organisations. Article V, which is entitled 'Relations with Other Organizations', states in its first paragraph:

> The General Council shall make appropriate arrangements for effective cooperation with other intergovernmental organizations that have responsibilities related to those of the WTO.

---

[82] *Declaration on the Contribution of the World Trade Organization to Achieving Greater Coherence in Global Economic Policymaking*, Final Act Embodying the Results of the Uruguay Round of Multilateral Trade Negotiations, para. 5.

[83] *Agreement between the International Monetary Fund and the World Trade Organization*, contained in Annex I to WT/GC/W/43, dated 4 November 1996; and the *Agreement between the International Bank for Reconstruction and Development and the International Development Association and the World Trade Organization*, contained in Annex II to WT/GC/W/43, dated 4 November 1996.   [84] UNCTAD, the ITC and the UNDP.

[85] See below, p. 99.

The WTO has made cooperation arrangements with, *inter alia*, the World Intellectual Property Organization (WIPO) and the United Nations Conference on Trade and Development (UNCTAD). In these and other international organisations the WTO has observer status.[86] The WTO and UNCTAD also cooperate in a joint venture, the International Trade Centre (ITC). The ITC works with developing countries and economies in transition to set up effective trade promotion programmes to expand their exports and improve their import operations.

In addition, the WTO Secretariat has concluded a large number of so-called Memoranda of Understanding (MOUs) with other international secretariats. These MOUs provide mainly for technical assistance from the WTO to these other secretariats or the geographical regions in which they work. In September 2003, for example, the then WTO Director-General, Supachai Panitchpakdi, and the Secretary-General of the ACP Group, Jean-Robert Goulongana, signed an MOU committing both organisations to cooperate more closely to provide training, technical assistance and support to negotiators of the ACP Member States in the Doha Development Round.[87] Almost 100 international intergovernmental organisations have been granted formal or *ad hoc* observer status with WTO councils and committees.[88]

In addition to cooperating with international intergovernmental organisations, the WTO also cooperates with non-governmental organisations (NGOs). Article V:2 of the *WTO Agreement* states:

> The General Council may make appropriate arrangements for consultation and cooperation with non-governmental organizations concerned with matters related to those of the WTO.

On 18 July 1996, the General Council therefore adopted a set of guidelines clarifying the framework for relations with NGOs.[89] In these guidelines, the General Council explicitly 'recognize[s] the role NGOs can play to increase the awareness of the public in respect of WTO activities'.[90]

It is important for the WTO to maintain a positive dialogue with the various components of civil society. To date, 'cooperation' with NGOs has essentially focused on:

- the attendance by NGOs of sessions of the Ministerial Conference;
- symposia or public forums for NGOs;
- regular briefings for NGOs on the work of WTO councils, committees and working groups; and
- the frequent contact between the WTO Secretariat and NGOs.

The WTO Secretariat also regularly forwards a list to WTO Members of documents, position papers and newsletters submitted by NGOs. This list is made

---

[86] See WTO Secretariat, *WTO Annual Report 2007*, 61.
[87] The ACP (African, Caribbean and Pacific) Group comprises seventy-nine members, forty of which are least-developed countries, most of them from Africa. The objective of the ACP Group is to contribute to the economic development and social progress of its Member States. See also below, pp. 106, 114.
[88] See WTO Secretariat, *WTO Annual Report 2007*, 4.
[89] *Guidelines for Arrangements on Relations with Non-Governmental Organizations*, Decision adopted by the General Council on 18 July 1996, WT/L/162, dated 23 July 1996.   [90] *Ibid.*

available on a special section of the WTO's website, devoted to NGOs' issues and WTO activities organised for the benefit of NGOs.[91] In the Doha Ministerial Declaration, Members stated:

> we are committed to making the WTO's operations more transparent, including through more effective and prompt dissemination of information, and to improve dialogue with the public.[92]

The extent and focus of cooperation between the WTO and NGOs is discussed in more detail later in this chapter.[93]

Questions and Assignments 2.7

Why and how does the WTO cooperate with international intergovernmental organisations? Why and how does the WTO cooperate with NGOs? Find out about the next WTO/NGO event on the WTO website.

2.3.2.6. Technical assistance to developing countries

The functions of the WTO listed in Article III of the *WTO Agreement* do not explicitly include technical assistance to developing-country Members. Yet this is, in practice, an important function of the WTO. Of course, it could be argued that this function is implied in the other functions discussed above, in particular the function of facilitating the implementation, administration and operation, and of furthering the objectives, of the *WTO Agreement*. However, in view of its importance, it deserves to be mentioned separately.

In order to exercise their rights and obligations under the *WTO Agreement*, to reap the benefits of their membership of the WTO and to participate fully and effectively in trade negotiations, most developing-country Members need to have significantly more expertise and resources in the area of trade law and policy. This is recognised in many WTO agreements, including the *SPS Agreement*, the *TBT Agreement*, the *TRIPS Agreement*, the *Customs Valuation Agreement* and the DSU, which all specifically provide for technical assistance to developing-country Members. This technical assistance may take the form of bilateral assistance, given by developed-country Members, or multilateral assistance, given by the WTO Secretariat.[94]

At its Doha Session in November 2001, the Ministerial Conference declared that:

> technical cooperation and capacity building are core elements of the development dimension of the multilateral trading system.[95]

---

[91] See www.wto.org/english/forums_e/ngo_e/ngo_e.htm, visited on 15 September 2007.
[92] Ministerial Conference, *Doha Ministerial Declaration*, WT/MIN(01)/DEC/1, dated 20 November 2001, para. 10.
[93] See below, pp. 152–9.
[94] Note that Article 9 of the *SPS Agreement* also refers to assistance by other international organisations.
[95] Ministerial Conference, *Doha Ministerial Declaration*, WT/MIN(01)/DEC/1, dated 20 November 2001, para. 38.

As an essential element of the Doha Development Agenda, in 2002, the WTO embarked on a programme of greatly enhanced support for developing countries.[96]

In his 2003 report on technical cooperation and capacity-building at the Cancún Session of the Ministerial Conference, the then WTO Director-General, Supachai Panitchpakdi, stated:

> the challenges for the Secretariat in the area of technical cooperation and training were unprecedented. This was due to the high number of requests for assistance, the ever expanding priorities, increasing cooperation with all stakeholders, an ever growing interest in the WTO on the part of all layers of society, a rapidly evolving multilateral trading system, and the complexity of the subject matter of the negotiations and work programme.[97]

Since 2005, WTO Members have donated over 50 million Swiss francs to the Doha Development Agenda Global Trust Fund.[98] The Global Trust Fund has significantly complemented the regular budget as a source of funding for the WTO Secretariat's training and technical assistance activities.[99]

The WTO has also significantly improved coordination with other international organisations (World Bank, IMF, UNCTAD, etc.), with regional banks and regional organisations and with bilateral governmental donors. The coordination with the World Bank, the IMF and other international organisations takes place in the context of the Integrated Framework for Trade-Related Technical Assistance (IF). The IF has two objectives:

- to integrate trade priorities into the national development plans and poverty reduction strategies of least-developed countries; and
- to assist in the coordinated delivery of trade-related assistance to these countries.[100]

The WTO also takes a leading role in the Joint Integrated Technical Assistance Programme (JITAP) for Selected African and Least-Developed Countries. The JITAP is a major capacity-building programme put in place by the WTO, UNCTAD and the ITC to address trade-related capacity constraints of African countries.

The WTO Secretariat organises, mostly in response to a specific request from one or more developing-country Members:

- *general seminars* on the multilateral trading system and the WTO;
- *technical seminars and workshops* focusing on a particular area of trade law or policy; and

---

[96] *Ibid.*, para. 41.   [97] WT/MIN(03)/3, dated 14 August 2003, para. 7.
[98] See www.wto.org/english/tratop_e/devel_e/teccop_e/financing_trta_e.htm, visited on 15 September 2007.
[99] See below, pp. 101–2, 162–3.
[100] At the Hong Kong Session of the Ministerial Conference in December 2005, a Task Force was established to formulate recommendations for improving the operation of the IF. See *Hong Kong Ministerial Declaration*, adopted 18 December 2005, WT/MIN(05)/DEC, paras. 48–51. The Task Force's recommendations were adopted in June 2006 and efforts to apply the recommendations in practice are currently ongoing. In early 2007, the Programme Implementation Unit (PIU) became operational. The mandate of the PIU is 'to provide guidance and support in coordination and monitoring to all IF LDCs during every stage of the IF process, from the first application to join the IF-process through to the full implementation of the DTIS and the Action Matrix'. See the First IF Newsletter, published in May 2007, available at www.wto.org/english/tratop_e/devel_e/teccop_e/if_e.htm, visited on 21 July 2007.

- *technical missions* to assist developing-country Members on specific tasks related to the implementation of obligations under the WTO agreements (such as the adoption of trade legislation or notifications), to provide support to mainstream trade into national plans for economic development and to assist in their strategies for poverty reduction.

In 2006, the WTO Secretariat organised 486 technical cooperation activities.[101] These activities reached in total almost 30,000 government officials of developing-country Members.[102] The introductory, general or advanced courses offered by the WTO Secretariat run from a few days to three months and cover the full range of WTO issues. In view of the interest in the three-month-long, general WTO *Trade Policy Course*, the WTO decided in 2002 to organise this course not only in Geneva but also in developing countries in cooperation with local universities. The first of such trade policy courses took place in Africa: two in Nairobi for English-speaking African countries and one in Casablanca for French-speaking African countries.[103] While in general highly regarded, note that one African diplomat reportedly stated, with respect to the WTO training courses and seminars:

> the Secretariat attempts to put us through university in a period of three days; as a result I come out even more confused than when I started. These are complex issues that must be addressed in layers. We can't do the whole thing together.[104]

A 2007 addition to the WTO's offer of courses and other training activities is eTraining, the WTO distance-learning project.[105] The aim of eTraining is to provide online training on matters related to international trade and WTO agreements to government officials from developing countries and economies in transition which are WTO Members or Observers.[106]

The WTO also organises a programme known as 'Geneva Week', a special week-long event bringing together representatives of developing-country Members and Observers that do not have a permanent mission in Geneva.[107] The objectives of Geneva Week are to introduce participants to WTO issues and work processes, and to provide information about the range of technical assistance available. During their stay in Geneva, participants have an opportunity to be involved in the work of WTO bodies. They also have the opportunity to interact with officials from other Geneva-based agencies, and with Geneva-based delegations. Geneva Week was initiated in 1999, and has since been held at least once a year.

---

[101] See WTO Secretariat, *WTO Annual Report 2007*, 5. These activities involved over 4,000 mission days of WTO Secretariat staff. See *ibid*. Within the WTO Secretariat the divisions most involved in technical assistance and capacity-building are the Training and Technical Cooperation Institute, the Development Division and the Technical Cooperation Audit. However, other divisions of the WTO Secretariat also contribute to the WTO's technical assistance and capacity-building efforts.   [102] See *ibid*.
[103] See WT/MIN(03)/3, dated 14 August 2003, para. 13.
[104] Reported by Shefali Sharma, *WTO Decision Making: A Broken Process*, WTO Cancún Series Paper No. 4 (Institute for Agriculture and Trade Policy, 2003), 10.
[105] See https://etraining.wto.org, visited on 20 November 2007.
[106] It is unfortunate that to date eTraining courses are open *only* to government officials from developing countries and economies in transition.   [107] See below, p. 107.

Since 1997, the WTO Secretariat has set up 'Reference Centres' in developing countries.[108] These Reference Centres allow government officials, as well as the local business and academic communities, to access essential documents instantly via the WTO website. To date, 153 Reference Centres have been established in 107 countries all over the world.[109]

In November 2002, the OECD and the WTO established a database which gives details of the trade-related technical-assistance and capacity-building activities of all donors (bilateral, regional and multilateral). This database gives an overall picture of technical development activities, which helps the coordination of such activities and aims to avoid costly overlap.[110]

At the Hong Kong Session of the Ministerial Conference in December 2005, Members agreed that additional efforts should be made to help developing countries, and in particular least-developed countries:

> to build the supply-side capacity and trade-related infrastructure that they need to assist them to implement and benefit from WTO Agreements and more broadly to expand their trade.[111]

To that end Members agreed to expand 'Aid for Trade', i.e. aid that 'finances trade-related technical assistance, trade-related infrastructure and aid to develop productive capacity'.[112] Members requested the WTO Director-General to create a task force to provide recommendations on how to operationalise Aid for Trade *and* to consult with Members as well as with relevant international organisations, such as the IMF and World Bank, and the regional development banks on 'appropriate mechanisms to secure additional financial resources for Aid for Trade'.[113] The Task Force established after the Hong Kong Session of the Ministerial Conference submitted in July 2006 its recommendations to the WTO General Council, which endorsed these recommendations in October 2006.[114] Pursuant to the recommendations of the Task Force, Aid for Trade should aim at strengthening the identification of needs at the country level, donor response and the bridge between donor response and needs.[115] The recommendations of the Task Force also included the establishment of a monitoring body in the WTO which would undertake a periodic global review based on reports of stakeholders including Members, relevant international organisations and the regional development banks. In November 2007, the WTO and the stakeholders referred to above conducted the first global review of Aid for Trade. At this occasion, WTO Director-General Pascal Lamy noted optimistically:

> We are moving from making trade possible to making trade happen. With Aid for Trade, we have the tools to break the shackles that have been holding back the trade potential of many

---

[108] The WTO Secretariat provides governments with computers and other hardware, software and the training required for the operation of these Reference Centres.

[109] See www.wto.org/english/tratop_e/devel_e/train_e/ref_centres_e.htm, visited on 1 December 2007.

[110] See http://tcbdb.wto.org, visited on 15 September 2007.

[111] Ministerial Conference, *Hong Kong Ministerial Declaration*, adopted on 18 December 2005, WT/MIN(05)/DEC, dated 22 December 2005, para. 57.

[112] See www.wto.org/english/tratop_e/devel_e/a4t_e/aid4trade_e.htm, visited on 19 November 2007.

[113] Ministerial Conference, *Hong Kong Ministerial Declaration*, adopted on 18 December 2005, WT/MIN(05)/DEC, dated 22 December 2005, para. 57.

[114] See www.wto.org/english/tratop_e/devel_e/a4t_e/aid4trade_e.htm, visited on 19 November 2007.

[115] WTO Aid for Trade Task Force, *Recommendations of the Task Force on Aid for Trade*, WT/AFT/1, dated 27 July 2006.

poor countries, such as substandard infrastructure, lack of modern technology and inadequate financing. We want to ensure – from the very beginning – that developing countries can take advantage of the new trading opportunities that will emerge from the Doha Round.[116]

For an overview of the WTO's current efforts regarding trade-related technical assistance to developing countries, refer to the Technical Assistance and Training Plan 2007.[117]

Questions and Assignments 2.8

Give a brief overview of the technical assistance efforts of the WTO. How does the WTO coordinate its technical assistance efforts with the efforts of other organisations and donors? Look up how much of the WTO budget of the current year is earmarked for technical cooperation, trade policy courses and the WTO contribution to the ITC.

2.4. MEMBERSHIP OF THE WTO

2.4.1. Current membership

The membership of the WTO is quasi-universal. It includes all major trading powers and most developing countries. The Members of the WTO represent 92 per cent of the global population and 95 per cent of world trade. On 15 November 2007, the 151 Members of the WTO were:

Albania, 8 September 2000; **Angola**, 23 November 1996; **Antigua and Barbuda**, 1 January 1995; **Argentina**, 1 January 1995; **Armenia**, 5 February 2003; **Australia**, 1 January 1995; **Austria**, 1 January 1995; **Bahrain**, 1 January 1995; **Bangladesh**, 1 January 1995; **Barbados**, 1 January 1995; **Belgium**, 1 January 1995; **Belize**, 1 January 1995; **Benin**, 22 February 1996; **Bolivia**, 12 September 1995; **Botswana**, 31 May 1995; **Brazil**, 1 January 1995; **Brunei Darussalam**, 1 January 1995; **Bulgaria**, 1 December 1996; **Burkina Faso**, 3 June 1995; **Burundi**, 23 July 1995; **Cambodia**, 13 October 2004; **Cameroon**, 13 December 1995; **Canada**, 1 January 1995; **Central African Republic**, 31 May 1995; **Chad**, 19 October 1996; **Chile**, 1 January 1995; **China**, 11 December 2001; **Chinese Taipei**, 1 January 2002; **Colombia**, 30 April 1995; **Congo**, 27 March 1997; **Costa Rica**, 1 January 1995; **Côte d'Ivoire**, 1 January 1995; **Croatia**, 30 November 2000; **Cuba**, 20 April 1995; **Cyprus**, 30 July 1995; **Czech Republic**, 1 January 1995; **Democratic Republic of the Congo**, 1 January 1997; **Denmark**, 1 January 1995; **Djibouti**, 31 May 1995; **Dominica**, 1 January 1995; **Dominican Republic**, 9 March 1995; **Ecuador**, 21 January 1996; **Egypt**, 30 June 1995; **El Salvador**, 7 May 1995; **Estonia**,

---

[116] See www.wto.org/english/news_e/pres07_e/pr500_e.htm, visited on 19 November 2007.
[117] See WT/COMTD/W/151, dated 17 October 2006.

13 November 1999; **European Communities**, 1 January 1995; **Fiji**,
14 January 1996; **Finland**, 1 January 1995; **Former Yugoslav Republic of
Macedonia**, 4 April 2003; **France**, 1 January 1995; **Gabon**, 1 January 1995;
The Gambia, 23 October 1996; **Georgia**, 14 June 2000; **Germany**,
1 January 1995; **Ghana**, 1 January 1995; **Greece**, 1 January 1995;
Grenada, 22 February 1996; **Guatemala**, 21 July 1995; **Guinea**,
25 October 1995; **Guinea Bissau**, 31 May 1995; **Guyana**, 1 January 1995;
Haiti, 30 January 1996; **Honduras**, 1 January 1995; **Hong Kong, China**,
1 January 1995; **Hungary**, 1 January 1995; **Iceland**, 1 January 1995; **India**,
1 January 1995; **Indonesia**, 1 January 1995; **Ireland**, 1 January 1995;
Israel, 21 April 1995; **Italy**, 1 January 1995; **Jamaica**, 9 March 1995; **Japan**,
1 January 1995; **Jordan**, 11 April 2000; **Kenya**, 1 January 1995; **Korea,
Republic of**, 1 January 1995; **Kuwait**, 1 January 1995; **Kyrgyz Republic**,
20 December 1998; **Latvia**, 10 February 1999; **Lesotho**, 31 May 1995;
Liechtenstein, 1 September 1995; **Lithuania**, 31 May 2001; **Luxembourg**,
1 January 1995; **Macao, China**, 1 January 1995; **Madagascar**,
17 November 1995; **Malawi**, 31 May 1995; **Malaysia**, 1 January 1995;
Maldives, 31 May 1995; **Mali**, 31 May 1995; **Malta**, 1 January 1995;
Mauritania, 31 May 1995; **Mauritius**, 1 January 1995; **Mexico**, 1 January
1995; **Moldova**, 26 July 2001; **Mongolia**, 29 January 1997; **Morocco**,
1 January 1995; **Mozambique**, 26 August 1995; **Myanmar**, 1 January
1995; **Namibia**, 1 January 1995; **Nepal**, 23 April 2004, **Netherlands**
(including the Netherlands Antilles), 1 January 1995; **New Zealand**, 1
January 1995; **Nicaragua**, 3 September 1995; **Niger**, 13 December 1996;
Nigeria, 1 January 1995; **Norway**, 1 January 1995; **Oman**, 9 November
2000; **Pakistan**, 1 January 1995; **Panama**, 6 September 1997; **Papua New
Guinea**, 9 June 1996; **Paraguay**, 1 January 1995; **Peru**, 1 January 1995;
Philippines, 1 January 1995; **Poland**, 1 July 1995; **Portugal**, 1 January
1995; **Qatar**, 13 January 1996; **Romania**, 1 January 1995; **Rwanda**, 22 May
1996; **Saint Kitts and Nevis**, 21 February 1996; **Saint Lucia**, 1 January
1995; **Saint Vincent and the Grenadines**, 1 January 1995; **Saudi Arabia**,
11 December 2005; **Senegal**, 1 January 1995; **Sierra Leone**, 23 July 1995;
Singapore, 1 January 1995; **Slovak Republic**, 1 January 1995; **Slovenia**,
30 July 1995; **Solomon Islands**, 26 July 1996; **South Africa**, 1 January
1995; **Spain**, 1 January 1995; **Sri Lanka**, 1 January 1995; **Suriname**, 1
January 1995; **Swaziland**, 1 January 1995; **Sweden**, 1 January 1995;
Switzerland, 1 July 1995; **Tanzania**, 1 January 1995; **Thailand**, 1 January
1995; **Togo**, 31 May 1995; **Tonga**, 27 July 2007; **Trinidad and Tobago**,
1 March 1995; **Tunisia**, 29 March 1995; **Turkey**, 26 March 1995; **Uganda**,
1 January 1995; **United Arab Emirates**, 10 April 1996; **United Kingdom**,
1 January 1995; **United States of America**, 1 January 1995; **Uruguay**,
1 January 1995; **Venezuela**, 1 January 1995; **Viet Nam**, 11 January 2007;
Zambia, 1 January 1995; **Zimbabwe**, 5 March 1995.[118]

[118] See www.wto.org/english/thewto_e/whatis_e/tif_e/org6_e.htm, visited on 15 November 2007. The date after the name of the country or separate customs territory refers to the date on which the country or separate customs territory became a Member of the WTO. Since December 2005, three countries have joined the WTO. Saudi Arabia became the 149th Member on 11 December 2005. Viet Nam became the 150th Member on 11 January 2007 and Tonga became the 151st Member on 27 July 2007.

2.4.1.1. States and customs territories

The WTO membership does not include only States. Separate customs territories possessing full autonomy in the conduct of their external commercial relations and in the other matters covered by the *WTO Agreement* can also be WTO Members.[119] There are currently three WTO Members which are not States but separate customs territories: Hong Kong, China (commonly referred to as Hong Kong), Macau, China (commonly referred to as Macau) and Chinese Taipei (which joined the WTO as the Separate Customs Territory of Taiwan, Penghu, Kinmen and Matsu).

2.4.1.2. The European Communities

The European Communities is also a WTO Member but this is a case apart, specifically provided for in the *WTO Agreement*.[120] Both the European Communities and all the Member States of the European Union are Members of the WTO. This reflects the division of competence between the European Communities and the Member States in the various areas covered by the *WTO Agreement* (trade in goods; trade in services; and the protection of intellectual property rights). As is clear from Articles IX, XI and XIV of the *WTO Agreement*, it is the European Communities, and not the European Community or the European Union, which is a Member of the WTO. The reason for this also lies in EU constitutional law. The European Communities, and not the European Community, is a WTO Member because at the time of the negotiations it was unclear whether the European Community, one of the then three Communities, had the necessary competence to conclude the *WTO Agreement*. In *Opinion 1/94*, the European Court of Justice established that, of the then three European Communities (EC, ECSC and Euratom), only the European Community needed to be involved in the WTO. However, the ECJ's clarification of the legal situation came after the *WTO Agreement* had been signed. The European Communities, and not the European Union, is a WTO Member, because in 1994 – the time of the conclusion of the *WTO Agreement* – the European Union did not yet have *any* competence to conclude international agreements.

Note that both the European Communities and all Member States of the European Union are *full* Members of the WTO and that all obligations of the *WTO Agreement* apply equally to all of them. Irrespective of the internal division of competence between the European Communities and the Member States of the European Union, they can all be held responsible for compliance with all the obligations under the *WTO Agreement*.

---

[119] See Article XII of the *WTO Agreement*. The Explanatory Notes attached to the *WTO Agreement* stipulate that the 'terms "country" or "countries" as used in this Agreement and the Multilateral Trade Agreements are to be understood to include any separate customs territory Member of the WTO. In the case of a separate customs territory Member of the WTO, where an expression in this Agreement and the Multilateral Trade Agreements is qualified by the term "national", such expression shall be read as pertaining to that customs territory, unless otherwise specified.'   [120] See Article XI:1 of the *WTO Agreement*.

2.4.1.3. Developing-country Members

Three-quarters of the 151 Members of the WTO are developing countries. There is no WTO definition of a 'developing country'. The status of 'developing-country Member' is based, to a large extent, on self-selection. Members announce whether they are 'developed' or 'developing' countries. As discussed further in this book, developing-country Members benefit from special and differential treatment under many of the WTO agreements and receive WTO technical assistance.[121] Other Members can, and occasionally do, challenge the decision of a Member to make use of special and differential treatment provisions available to developing countries.[122]

On 15 November 2007, there were thirty-two least-developed countries among the developing-country Members. The WTO recognises as least-developed countries those countries which have been designated as such by the United Nations.[123] Least-developed countries benefit from additional special and differential treatment.[124] The least-developed countries among the WTO Members are: Angola, Bangladesh, Benin, Burkina Faso, Burundi, Cambodia, Central African Republic, Chad, Democratic Republic of the Congo, Djibouti, The Gambia, Guinea, Guinea Bissau, Haiti, Lesotho, Madagascar, Malawi, Maldives, Mali, Mauritania, Mozambique, Myanmar, Nepal, Niger, Rwanda, Senegal, Sierra Leone, Solomon Islands, Tanzania, Togo, Uganda and Zambia.[125]

In recent years, and in particular since the failure of the Seattle Session of the Ministerial Conference at the end of 1999, developing-country Members have played an increasingly important role in the WTO, not only because of their numbers but also because of their increasing importance in the global economy.[126] Because of the size of their economies and the fact that they often act as spokespersons for other developing countries, China, Brazil and India are today undoubtedly the most influential and 'activist' Members among the developing-country Members. While their interests do not always converge, these countries are formidable champions of the cause of the developing-country Members within the WTO.

2.4.1.4. Groups and alliances within the WTO

The developing-country Members and the least-developed-country Members are not the only distinguishable groups within the WTO membership. Other formal or informal groups and alliances exist in the WTO.

---

[121] See e.g. below, pp. 135, 162, 554–6, 604–5, 726–30.

[122] Note also that in the context of the national Generalised Systems of Preferences (GSP), adopted under the Enabling Clause of the GATT 1994 (see below, pp. 727–8), it is the preference-giving Member that decides which countries qualify for the preferential tariff treatment.

[123] Note that the share of world trade of the least-developed countries is around 0.5 per cent of the total and, therefore, marginal. See also above, pp. 6–9.   [124] See above, pp. 40–1.

[125] Ten other least-developed countries are in the process of accession to the WTO and therefore have Observer status. They are: Afghanistan, Bhutan, Cape Verde, Ethiopia, Laos, Saõ Tomé and Principe, Samoa, Sudan, Vanuatu and Yemen. Furthermore, Equatorial Guinea, also a least-developed country, is a WTO Observer. See www.wto.org/english/thewto_e/whatis_e/tif_e/org7_e.htm, visited on 23 August 2007.

[126] See above, pp. 7–8.

Some of these groups have been formed to defend common interests and advance common positions; they coordinate (or try to coordinate) positions and, when appropriate, speak in unison. This category of groups includes the *Association of South East Asian Nations* (ASEAN,[127] the *Caribbean Community* (CARICOM) and the *African, Caribbean and Pacific Group* (ACP). However, the *North American Free Trade Agreement* (NAFTA)[128] and the *Southern Common Market* (MERCOSUR),[129] while constituting significant efforts at regional economic integration, have not, or have hardly ever, spoken with one voice within the WTO. A well-known and quite effective alliance of a different kind is the Cairns group of nineteen agricultural-produce-exporting developed and developing countries.[130] This group was set up in the mid-1980s to campaign for agricultural trade liberalisation and was an important force in negotiations on trade in agricultural products. However, at the Cancún Session of the Ministerial Conference in September 2003, the Cairns group seemed to have all but disappeared. In the run-up to, and at, the Cancún Session, a new influential group of developing countries, including China, India, Indonesia, Brazil, Egypt, Argentina and South Africa, emerged. This group, commonly referred to as the 'G-20', forcefully demanded the dismantling of the trade-distorting and protectionist agricultural policies of the European Communities, the United States and other industrialised countries.[131] Also in Cancún, a new group known as the ACP/LDC/AU alliance (an alliance made up of the ACP countries, the least-developed countries and the countries of the African Union) emerged as the 'representative' of the interests of the poorest countries.[132]

Other groups have been formed to allow for discussion in small(er) groups of Members, to agree on new initiatives, to break deadlocks and to achieve compromises. The best-known example of such a group was the Quad, which during the Uruguay Round and in the early years of the WTO was the group of the then four largest trading entities, i.e. the European Communities, the United States, Japan and Canada. The Quad was at the core of all negotiations. However, the Quad has now been replaced by a new group of key WTO Members: the European Communities, the United States, India, Brazil and China (often referred to as the G-4 when excluding China and as the G-5 when including China). Without agreement among these key Members, progress within the WTO on the further liberalisation and/or regulation of trade is not feasible. This shift in political power

---

[127] I.e. Brunei Darussalam, Cambodia, Indonesia, Malaysia, Myanmar, the Philippines, Singapore, Thailand and Viet Nam. The remaining Member of ASEAN, namely Laos, is negotiating its accession to the WTO.
[128] I.e. Canada, Mexico and the US.
[129] I.e. Argentina, Brazil, Paraguay, Uruguay and Venezuela. Note that Bolivia, Chile, Colombia, Ecuador and Peru are associate members of MERCOSUR.
[130] I.e. Argentina, Australia, Bolivia, Brazil, Canada, Chile, Colombia, Costa Rica, Guatemala, Indonesia, Malaysia, New Zealand, Pakistan, Paraguay, Peru, the Philippines, South Africa, Thailand and Uruguay. See www.cairnsgroup.org/map/index.html, visited on 19 September 2007.
[131] The G-20 includes five countries from Africa: Egypt, Nigeria, South Africa, Tanzania and Zimbabwe; six countries from Asia: China, India, Indonesia, Pakistan, the Philippines and Thailand; and eight countries from Latin America: Argentina, Bolivia, Brazil, Chile, Cuba, Mexico, Paraguay and Venezuela. Contrary to what the term 'G-20' seems to imply, the *number* of countries that are members of the G-20 has in fact varied over time.   [132] This group is also referred to as the 'G-90'.

within the WTO reflects the growing importance of China, India and Brazil in the world economy.[133]

2.4.1.5. Observers

The WTO also has thirty-one Observer Governments.[134] With the exception of the Holy See, these Observer Governments must start accession negotiations within five years of becoming an Observer.[135] Occasionally, the decision on granting Observer status leads to controversy. For example, in January 2004, the European Communities agreed to back a US-sponsored request by Iraq's Governing Council for Observer status. However, the European Communities stressed that it also wanted to extend this status to Iran and Syria, an initiative opposed by the United States.[136] At its meeting on 11 February 2004, the General Council granted Iraq Observer status.[137] At the same meeting, the General Council also considered Iran's request to begin accession negotiations. The European Communities, China, India, Indonesia and other Members supported this request. However, as the United States was opposed, the General Council decided to postpone a decision on Iran's request.[138]

In 1997, the General Council granted permanent Observer status to the UN, UNCTAD, the FAO, WIPO and the OECD.[139] The IMF and the World Bank have permanent Observer status under their respective agreements with the WTO.[140] Other international organisations have Observer status in the WTO bodies that deal in particular with the matters within their mandate. As such, the Joint FAO/WHO Codex Alimentarius Commission has Observer status in the WTO SPS Committee; and the Convention on International Trade in Endangered Species (CITES) in the WTO Committee on Trade and Environment.[141]

2.4.1.6. Representation in Geneva

Most Members have a permanent diplomatic mission in Geneva.[142] This is often a mission to all Geneva-based international organisations; however, a growing number of Members have a separate mission to the WTO. This is the case, for example, for the United States, the European Communities, India, Honduras and Malaysia. The meetings of WTO bodies are usually attended by diplomats from the mission, but, increasingly, government officials specialising in a

---

[133] Note that in the summer of 2004, a group, referred to as the 'Five Interested Parties', consisting of Australia, Brazil, the European Communities, India and the United States, played a crucial role in breaking the deadlock in the Doha Development Round negotiations and reaching an agreement on the new Doha Work Programme. See above, p. 91.
[134] See www.wto.org/english/thewto_e/whatis_e/tif_e/org6_e.htm, visited on 15 November 2007.   [135] *Ibid.*
[136] See T. Buck and G. de Jonquières, 'EU Backs Iraqi Plea for WTO Status', *Financial Times*, 26 January 2004.
[137] See *BRIDGES Weekly Trade News Digest*, 12 February 2004.   [138] See *ibid.*
[139] See WT/GC/M/18. Also, the ITC, a joint subsidiary of the WTO and UNCTAD, was granted permanent Observer status. See General Council, *Minutes of Meeting*, WT/GC/M/25, dated 4 February 1998.
[140] See above, p. 96.
[141] For an exhaustive list of all international organisations having Observer status in the WTO or in one or more WTO bodies, see www.wto.org/english/thewto_e/igo_obs_e.htm, visited on 30 November 2007.
[142] There are, however, more than twenty WTO Members that do not have any form of representation in Geneva. See also above, p. 100.

specific matter are flown in to attend meetings in Geneva and present their governments' views.

Questions and Assignments 2.9

Can non-State entities become Members of the WTO? If so, give three examples of such Members. Explain why both the European Communities and all the Member States of the European Union are Members of the WTO. Why is the European Communities, and not the European Community or the European Union, a Member of the WTO? When will a country 'qualify' as a developing-country Member or as a least-developed-country Member? Discuss briefly the various groups and alliances that exist within the WTO membership. Comment on the demise of the Quad and the emergence of the G-4/G-5.

2.4.2. Accession

Becoming a Member of the WTO is not an easy matter. This section discusses the accession process and looks at some recent and future accessions.

2.4.2.1. *The accession process*

The *WTO Agreement* initially provided for two ways of becoming a WTO Member. The first, 'original membership', was provided for in Article XI of the *WTO Agreement*, and allowed Contracting Parties to the GATT 1947 (and the European Communities) to join the WTO by:

- accepting the terms of the *WTO Agreement* and the Multilateral Trade Agreements; and
- making concessions and commitments for both trade in goods and services (embodied in national schedules annexed to the GATT 1994 and the GATS respectively).[143]

This way of becoming a WTO Member was only available until March 1997.[144] All but one of the GATT Contracting Parties became WTO Members in this way.[145] Of the 151 WTO Members, 123 are 'original Members' in that they became Members pursuant to Article XI of the *WTO Agreement*.

---

[143] The term 'original membership' is an unfortunate misnomer. It suggests that there are two sorts of membership with different rights. This is not the case. In principle, all Members have the same membership rights (and obligations). The term 'original membership' is used merely to distinguish between the different ways of acquiring membership. It has been noted, however, that in the context of WTO accession, applicants have been denied transition periods provided for in WTO agreements on the grounds that these transition periods were only available to original Members. See e.g. WT/ACC/7/Rev.2 at p. 3 (the paragraph on transition periods), which specifically distinguishes between original Members and new Members.

[144] The General Council had initially set the deadline for becoming a WTO Member in this way at 1 January 1997 but later agreed on a short extension.

[145] Yugoslavia is the only GATT Contracting Party which did not become a WTO Member in this way.

The second way of becoming a WTO Member is through accession, and this way is open indefinitely. The procedure for accession is set out in Article XII of the *WTO Agreement*. This provision states:

1. Any State or separate customs territory possessing full autonomy in the conduct of its external commercial relations and of the other matters provided for in this Agreement and the Multilateral Trade Agreements may accede to this Agreement, on terms to be agreed between it and the WTO. Such accession shall apply to this Agreement and the Multilateral Trade Agreements annexed thereto.
2. Decisions on accession shall be taken by the Ministerial Conference. The Ministerial Conference shall approve the agreement on the terms of accession by a two-thirds majority of the Members of the WTO.
3. Accession to a Plurilateral Trade Agreement shall be governed by the provisions of that Agreement.

To become a WTO Member through accession, a State or customs territory has to negotiate the terms of accession with the current Members. The candidate for membership must always accept the terms of the *WTO Agreement* and all Multilateral Trade Agreements. This is not up for negotiation. The subjects of the accession negotiations are the market access commitments and concessions the candidate for membership has to make. A 'ticket of admission' is negotiated. When a State or customs territory accedes to the WTO, it instantly benefits from all the efforts that WTO Members have undertaken to date to reduce barriers to trade and increase market access. In return for the access to the markets of current Members that a new Member will obtain, that new Member will itself have to open up its market for the current Members. The extent of the market access commitments and concessions that a candidate for membership will be expected to make will depend to a large extent on its economic development.

Generally speaking, there are four phases in the accession process. In the first phase – the 'tell us about yourself' phase – the State or customs territory applying for membership has to report on all aspects of its trade and economic policies that are relevant to the obligations under the WTO agreements, and to submit a memorandum on these policies to the WTO. A WTO working party established especially to deal with the request for accession will examine this memorandum.[146]

When the working party has made satisfactory progress with its examination of the trade and economic policies, the second phase is initiated. In this phase – the 'work out with us individually what you have to offer' phase – parallel bilateral negotiations on market access begin between the candidate for membership and individual Members. These negotiations are bilateral because different Members have different trading interests, but it should be recalled that the new Member's market access commitments and concessions will eventually apply equally to all WTO Members as a result of the MFN treatment obligation.[147] These bilateral market access negotiations can be very difficult.

---

[146] See *Members and Accession: Becoming a Member of the WTO*, Cancún WTO Ministerial 2003 Briefing Notes, available at www.wto.org/english/thewto_e/minist_e/min03_e/brief_e/brief23_e.htm, visited on 19 September 2007.   [147] On the MFN treatment obligation, see above, pp. 38–9, and below, pp. 322–43.

Once the working party has fully completed its examination of the trade and economic policies of the candidate *and* individual Members and the candidate for membership have successfully concluded the parallel bilateral market access negotiations, the third phase of the accession process can start. In this phase – the 'let's draft membership terms' phase – the working party finalises the terms of accession which are set out in a report, a draft membership treaty ('protocol of accession') and lists ('Schedules') of the market access commitments and concessions of the candidate for membership. This package is submitted to the Ministerial Conference or the General Council.

In the fourth and final phase of the accession process – the 'decision' phase – the Ministerial Conference or the General Council decides by consensus or, if consensus cannot be achieved, by a two-thirds majority of WTO Members, on the application for membership.[148] In case of a positive decision, the candidate for membership accedes to the WTO thirty days after it has deposited its instrument of ratification of the membership treaty (i.e. the protocol of accession).

Even when no major problems are encountered, accession negotiations are typically long. The shortest accession negotiation to date was that of the Kyrgyz Republic, lasting two years and ten months.[149] The accession negotiations with Algeria have been going on since 1987.[150] The delays in completing accession negotiations have been severely criticised. However, this situation is not only the result of hard bargaining on the part of WTO Members or political factors. It is also a result of the tardy supply of information and making of the necessary policy adjustments on the part of the candidate for membership. Adapting to WTO rules usually requires significant changes in national legislation and practices. It can take years to draft, approve and apply the new legislation required for accession to the WTO. Least-developed countries, in particular, often lack the administrative capacity to conduct the complex negotiations and to develop and apply the necessary changes in national legislation and practices. In December 2002, the General Council agreed on guidelines to facilitate the accession of least-developed countries to the WTO, in accordance with a mandate given at the Doha Session of the Ministerial Conference in November 2001.[151] These guidelines concern, *inter alia*, technical assistance and capacity-building.

2.4.2.2. Past and future accessions

On 15 November 2007, there were twenty-nine States negotiating their accession to the WTO. The most important ongoing accession negotiations, in both economic and political terms, are those with Russia, the largest economy still outside the WTO. A major issue in the negotiations with Russia on WTO accession has been the low energy prices in Russia. The European Communities

---

[148] On decision-making within the WTO, see below, pp. 138–61.
[149] See 'WTO membership – in brief', dated 11 January 2007, available at www.wto.org/english/thewto_e/acc_e/acc_e.htm, visited on 15 September 2007.
[150] Before 1995, Algeria attempted to become a Contracting Party to the GATT 1947.
[151] See General Council, *Decision of the General Council*, WT/GC/W/485, dated 4 December 2002.

considered these prices to be the result of an unfair State subsidy which distorts global competition. The European Communities thus required Russia to raise its domestic energy prices. In October 2003, President Putin reportedly said on this divisive issue:

> EU bureaucrats either don't understand it or deliberately put unacceptable conditions for Russia to join the WTO. We cannot move to world energy prices in a single day. It will ruin the country's economy.[152]

In response, a spokesperson for then EU Trade Commissioner Lamy stated:

> the WTO's adhesion process is not political, it's a process that consists in fulfilling rules and regulations that exist already at the WTO . . . When a country doesn't meet them, it doesn't join.[153]

In May 2004, Russia reached a bilateral agreement on market access concessions with the European Communities, its biggest trade partner, thus clearing a major hurdle in the accession process. In November 2006, Russia reached a bilateral agreement on market access concessions with the United States, an agreement which seemed to be the last major hurdle on its road to WTO membership. However, in November 2007, Russia was still not a WTO Member. This state of affairs is partly due to the opposition of Georgia to Russian membership as long as the problem of the allegedly illegal customs checkpoints on the Russian border with the Russian-backed separatist regions of Abkhazia and South Ossetia has not been resolved. It is partly due to recent problems in Russia's trade relations with the United States and the European Communities as a result of its agricultural subsidies and food health regulations that have a negative impact on exports from the United States and Poland.[154] Frustrated with the lack of progress in the accession negotiations, President Putin declared in June 2007 that the WTO was 'archaic, undemocratic and inflexible'.[155]

Since 2000, Albania, Armenia, Cambodia, China, Chinese Taipei, Croatia, the Former Yugoslav Republic of Macedonia, Georgia, Jordan, Lithuania, Moldova, Nepal, Oman, Saudi Arabia, Tonga, and Viet Nam successfully completed their accession negotiations.[156] In 2003, Cambodia and Nepal became the first least-developed countries to successfully complete accession negotiations. Tonga joined the WTO on 27 July 2007 as its 151st Member. Note that on 6 December 2007 and on 25 January 2008 the General Council adopted the decision on the accession of Cape Verde and Ukraine respectively. The countries may thus be expected to become the 152nd and 153rd Members of the WTO.

The most difficult and most important accession negotiations ever conducted were those with the People's Republic of China. In 1947, China was one of the original signatories of the GATT but, after the revolution in 1949, the Chinese nationalist government in Chinese Taipei announced that China would leave

---

[152] See WTO Forum, *WTO Newsletter*, 10 October 2003.
[153] *BRIDGES Weekly Trade News Digest*, 12 February 2004, 8.
[154] See F. Williams, 'Ukraine Ahead of Russia in WTO Entry Bid', *Financial Times*, 26 July 2007.   [155] *Ibid.*
[156] See www.wto.org/english/thewto_e/acc_e/members_brief_e.doc, visited on 19 September 2007.

the GATT system. The government of the People's Republic of China in Beijing never recognised this withdrawal decision and, in 1986, it notified the GATT of its wish to resume its status as a GATT Contracting Party. The GATT Contracting Parties considered, however, that China would have to negotiate its re-accession. In 1987, a GATT Working Party on the Accession of China was established and in 1995 this Working Party was converted into a WTO Working Party. On 16 November 1999, Frances Williams and Neil Buckley of the *Financial Times* reported at a crucial moment of these protracted negotiations as follows:

> Completion of negotiations with Washington does not mean China can now join the WTO, though it is an essential step in the process. Beijing has to conclude market-opening negotiations on goods and services with each of its main trading partners and its terms of entry must then be approved by all WTO members. The first half of 2000 is the earliest realistic date for entry . . . China has now completed membership talks with 13 nations, including Japan, Australia, Chile and Hungary. However, it has yet to conclude negotiations with the European Union and 23 other trading partners, among them Canada, Brazil, India and Switzerland. Of those, the EU is the most crucial for China's hopes of entry. Officials suggested yesterday that senior European Commission negotiators might depart for China within days, followed later by Pascal Lamy, the EU's new trade commissioner. The deal with the US was broadly welcomed in Brussels yesterday, where officials said about 80 per cent of the package was in common with the EU's aims . . . In the 20 per cent of the package where the EU has differences, officials said there were three main areas of concern. First, there are differences on certain tariffs. The EU has specific requirements on between 300 and 400 lines where it exports more than the US, including some agricultural equipment, as well as ceramics and glassware, cosmetics, leather goods and shoes. In some areas where the EU and US have similar interests, Brussels has been pressing for bigger tariff reductions, such as on cars. Secondly, the EU has particular demands in services. In life insurance, seen as a big growth area, it wants to secure the same number of operating licences as the US, and a similar possibility to set-up wholly-owned operations in China – something Beijing has so far not been prepared to give. In telecoms, it wants to ensure the possibility of eventually owning more than 50 per cent of operators, not just in fixed-line services, but in mobile telephony, paging and satellite phones . . . The EU also has concerns on some 'horizontal' issues, such as export performance requirements – where foreign companies manufacturing in China are required to export as much as 70 per cent of turnover – and conditions on technology transfer. It is pressing for commitments to non-discrimination and transparency in government procurement. Under the WTO's Most Favoured Nation rule the best terms negotiated by any one member must be extended to all. So the US, which has wide-ranging trade interests in China, can set the pace for the rest. However, other countries may want to hold out for a better deal in certain sectors to which they attach more importance than the US.[157]

The accession negotiations with China eventually took almost fifteen years and resulted in a legal text of some 900 pages. At its Doha Session in November 2001, the Ministerial Conference approved by consensus the text of the agreement for China's entry into the WTO. On 11 December 2001, China formally became a Member of the WTO.[158]

In order to join the WTO, China has agreed to undertake a series of important market access commitments and concessions and to offer a more predictable environment for trade and foreign investment in accordance with WTO rules.

---

[157] F. Williams and N. Buckley, 'Europe the Next Stop on the Negotiation Trail', *Financial Times*, 16 November 1999.   [158] *China Accession Protocol*, WT/ACC/CHN/49, dated 1 October 2001.

While China reserves the right of exclusive State trading for products such as cereals, tobacco, fuels and minerals, and maintains some restrictions on transportation and distribution of goods inside the country, many of the restrictions on foreign companies were to be eliminated or considerably eased after a three-year phase-out period. During a twelve-year period starting from the date of accession, a special transitional safeguard mechanism applies. This mechanism allows other WTO Members to restrict – more easily than under the normal rules on safeguard measures – imports of products of Chinese origin that cause or threaten to cause market disruption to their domestic producers.[159] On the other hand, prohibitions, quantitative restrictions or other measures maintained against imports from China, in a manner inconsistent with the *WTO Agreement*, are phased out or otherwise dealt with in accordance with mutually agreed terms and timetables specified in an annex to the Protocol of Accession.[160]

Questions and Assignments 2.10

Is the country of which you are a national an 'original Member' of the WTO? Does it matter whether it is or not? Why does the WTO, as do other international organisations, not automatically allow any country willing to accept the obligations of membership to become a Member? Discuss the various steps in the process of accession to the WTO.

2.4.3. Obligations of membership

Article XVI:4 of the *WTO Agreement* provides that:

> Each Member shall ensure the conformity of its laws, regulations and administrative procedures with its obligations as provided in the annexed Agreements.

Article XVI:5 of the *WTO Agreement* provides that:

> No reservations may be made in respect of any provision of this Agreement. Reservations in respect of any of the provisions of the Multilateral Trade Agreements may only be made to the extent provided for in those Agreements. Reservations in respect of a provision of a Plurilateral Trade Agreement shall be governed by the provisions of that Agreement.[161]

One should note, however, the possibility of obtaining a waiver of obligations under the WTO agreements and the 'non-application' clause, both discussed below.

---

[159] For a discussion of this system, and the additional safeguard system for Chinese textiles, see below, pp. 694–5.

[160] See 'WTO Successfully Concludes Negotiations on China's Entry', WTO Press/243, dated 17 September 2001.

[161] Note that there are a number of exceptions to the general rule of Article XVI:5 of the *WTO Agreement* that no reservations can be made to the provisions of the Multilateral Trade Agreements. See e.g. Article 15.1 of the *TBT Agreement* and Article 32.2 of the *SCM Agreement*. To date, however, no reservation has been made under these exceptions.

2.4.3.1. *Waiver of WTO obligations*

When a Member finds it difficult, if not impossible, to meet an obligation under one of the WTO agreements, that Member can request the WTO to waive the 'problematic' obligation. Pursuant to Article IX:3 of the *WTO Agreement*, 'exceptional circumstances' may justify such a waiver.[162] The decision of the Ministerial Conference (or the General Council) granting the waiver shall state the exceptional circumstances, the terms and conditions governing the application of the waiver and the date on which the waiver shall be terminated.[163] The procedure for taking this decision is examined below.[164]

As is provided in Article IX:4 of the *WTO Agreement*, any waiver granted for a period of more than one year shall be reviewed annually. The General Council shall examine whether the exceptional circumstances justifying the waiver still exist and whether the terms and conditions attached to the waiver have been met. On the basis of this annual review, the waiver may be extended, modified or terminated. Until now, these annual reviews have, however, been largely *pro forma*. The Annual Report of the General Council gives an overview every year of all Article IX:3 decisions on new waivers and Article IX:4 reviews of existing waivers.[165]

One of the most important waivers currently in force is a waiver of the MFN treatment obligation under Article I:1 of the GATT 1994, granted to the European Communities, with respect to preferential tariff treatment given to products of African, Caribbean and Pacific countries under the terms of the Cotonou *ACP–EC Partnership Agreement*. This waiver, in force since 2001, expires on 31 December 2007.

Another waiver for preferential treatment is that granted to the European Communities for its trade preference scheme with regard to the Western Balkans to 'promote economic expansion and recovery'. The General Council agreed on 28 July 2006 to extend this waiver until 31 December 2011.[166]

Yet another waiver worth noting is the waiver granted to Australia, Brazil, Canada, Israel, Japan, Korea, the Philippines, Sierra Leone, Thailand, the United Arab Emirates and the United States to allow these Members to take domestic measures under the Kimberley Process aimed at banning trade in conflict diamonds, also referred to as 'blood diamonds'.[167] This WTO waiver, granted in 2003 and extended in 2006,[168] exempts trade measures taken under the Kimberley

---

[162] Note that, for waivers of GATT 1994 obligations, provisions of the *Understanding in Respect of Waivers of Obligations under the General Agreement on Tariffs and Trade 1994* also apply.

[163] Article IX:4 of the *WTO Agreement*.   [164] See below, pp. 142–3.

[165] See e.g. General Council, *Annual Report* (2003), WT/GC/76, dated 6 January 2004, 7.

[166] See General Council, *European Communities' Preferences for Albania, Bosnia and Herzegovina, Croatia, Serbia and Montenegro, and the Former Yugoslav Republic of Macedonia*, WT/L/564, dated 2 August 2006.

[167] In November 2002, the participants in the Kimberley Process issued the Interlaken Declaration expressing their intent to implement an international scheme of certification for rough diamonds to help break the link between armed conflict and the trade in rough diamonds. The Kimberley Process provides that each participant should 'ensure that no shipment of rough diamonds is imported or exported to a non-Participant'.

[168] Decision of the General Council of 15 May 2003, *Waiver concerning Kimberley Process Certification Scheme for Rough Diamonds*, WT/L/518, dated 27 May 2003. This waiver was extended by the Decision of the General Council of 15 December 2006, *Kimberley Process Certification Scheme for Rough Diamonds*, WT/L/676, dated 19 December 2006.

Process by these eleven Members (and other Members that join subsequently) from the MFN treatment obligation (Article I:1 of the GATT 1994), from the prohibition of quantitative restrictions (Article XI:1 of the GATT 1994) and from the obligation of non-discriminatory administration of quantitative restrictions (Article XIII:1 of the GATT 1994).[169]

With regard to essential medicines for HIV, malaria and other life-threatening diseases, note the Decision of the General Council of 30 August 2003, which waives obligations under Article 31(f) and (h) of the *TRIPS Agreement* to give developing countries access to these essential medicines.[170]

In *EC – Bananas III*, the European Communities argued that the Lomé Waiver, which waived the provisions of Article I:1 of the GATT 1994, should be interpreted to waive also the provisions of Article XIII of the GATT 1994. In that case, the Panel accepted this argument to the extent that 'the scope of Article XIII:1 is identical with that of Article I'.[171] The Appellate Body reversed this finding and noted, with regard to the nature and the interpretation of waivers, the following:

> Although the *WTO Agreement* does not provide any specific rules on the interpretation of waivers, Article IX of the *WTO Agreement* and the *Understanding in Respect of Waivers of Obligations under the General Agreement on Tariffs and Trade 1994*, which provide requirements for granting and renewing waivers, stress the exceptional nature of waivers and subject waivers to strict disciplines. Thus, waivers should be interpreted with great care.[172]

2.4.3.2. 'Non-application' clause

For political or other reasons (including economic reasons), a Member may not want the WTO rules to apply to its trade relations with another Member. Article XIII of the *WTO Agreement*, entitled 'Non-Application of Multilateral Trade Agreements between Particular Members', states:

> 1. This Agreement and the Multilateral Trade Agreements in Annexes 1 and 2 shall not apply as between any Member and any other Member if either of the Members, at the time either becomes a Member, does not consent to such application.
> 2. Paragraph 1 may be invoked between original Members of the WTO which were contracting parties to GATT 1947 only where Article XXXV of that Agreement had been invoked earlier and was effective as between those contracting parties at the time of entry into force for them of this Agreement.
> 3. Paragraph 1 shall apply between a Member and another Member which has acceded under Article XII only if the Member not consenting to the application has so notified the Ministerial Conference before the approval of the agreement on the terms of accession by the Ministerial Conference.
> 4. The Ministerial Conference may review the operation of this Article in particular cases at the request of any Member and make appropriate recommendations.
> 5. Non-application of a Plurilateral Trade Agreement between parties to that Agreement shall be governed by the provisions of that Agreement.

It is thus possible for a Member to prevent WTO rules from applying to its trade relations with another Member. However, the 'non-application' or 'opt-out'

---

[169] On these GATT 1994 obligations, see below, pp. 322–33, 444–54, 455.   [170] See below, pp. 789–92.
[171] Panel Report, *EC – Bananas III*, para. 7.107.   [172] Appellate Body Report, *EC – Bananas III*, para. 185.

clause has to be invoked at the time that this Member, or the other, joins the WTO. The 'opt-out' clause cannot be invoked at any later time. The decision to opt out must be notified to the Ministerial Conference (or the General Council) before the latter decides on the accession.[173]

In practice, the importance of the 'non-application' clause under the *WTO Agreement* has been limited. Only the United States has made use of this clause in respect of some former Communist countries.[174] Currently, no WTO Member invokes the 'non-application' clause.

Questions and Assignments 2.11

What is a 'waiver' of WTO obligations and under what conditions can it be granted? Find out how many and which waivers currently apply in favour of the European Communities. Can the European Communities invoke the 'non-application' clause against a WTO Member that is guilty of gross violations of human rights or acts of aggression against other countries?

2.4.4. Withdrawal and expulsion

Article XV of the *WTO Agreement* states:

> 1. Any Member may withdraw from this Agreement. Such withdrawal shall apply both to this Agreement and the Multilateral Trade Agreements and shall take effect upon the expiration of six months from the date on which written notice of withdrawal is received by the Director-General of the WTO.
> 2. Withdrawal from a Plurilateral Trade Agreement shall be governed by the provisions of that Agreement.

Any Member may, at any time, unilaterally withdraw from the WTO. A withdrawal only takes effect, however, upon the expiration of six months from the notification of the decision to withdraw.[175] It should be noted that, when a Member withdraws from the WTO, it cannot remain a party to the Multilateral Trade Agreements. To date, no Member has ever withdrawn from the WTO. A group of Caribbean banana-producing countries, very disappointed with the outcome of the *EC – Bananas III* dispute, reportedly 'threatened' at one point to withdraw from the WTO but did not do so.

The *WTO Agreement* does not provide for a general procedure for the expulsion of a Member. There is no procedure to exclude from the WTO States that systematically breach their obligations under the WTO agreements. There are also no rules or procedures for the expulsion of Members that are guilty of gross

---

[173] Between the Contracting Parties of the GATT 1947 which joined the WTO as original Members, an opt-out is only possible to the extent that such opt-out already existed under the GATT 1947.
[174] Between 1 January 1995 and 30 June 2001, the United States invoked the 'non-application' clause of Article XIII:1 of the *WTO Agreement* with respect to Georgia, Kyrgyz Republic, Moldova, Mongolia and Romania. See *WTO Analytical Index*, vol. 1, 97.
[175] The notification to withdraw is made to the WTO Director-General.

violations of human rights or acts of aggression.[176] The expulsion of a Member is, however, provided for as a possibility in the specific case of the non-acceptance of an amendment.[177]

Questions and Assignments 2.12

Can a Member withdraw from the WTO? If so, how? Has any Member ever withdrawn from the WTO? Can a WTO Member, guilty of gross violations of human rights or acts of aggression against other countries, be expelled from the WTO?

2.5. INSTITUTIONAL STRUCTURE OF THE WTO

To carry out the functions and tasks entrusted to the WTO, the *WTO Agreement* provides for manifold bodies. This section examines:

- the basic institutional structure;
- the Ministerial Conference;
- the General Council, the DSB and the TPRB;
- specialised councils, committees and working parties;
- the Trade Negotiations Committee;
- political bodies lacking in the WTO structure;
- quasi-judicial and other non-political bodies of the WTO; and
- the WTO Secretariat.

2.5.1. Basic structure

The basic institutional structure of the WTO is set out in Article IV of the *WTO Agreement*. Subordinate committees and working groups have been added to this structure by later decisions.

There are, at present, a total of seventy WTO bodies, of which thirty-four are standing bodies.[178] Many of these WTO bodies meet on a regular basis, making for a heavy workload for WTO diplomats. In 2001, WTO bodies held nearly 1,000 formal and informal meetings.[179] Sometimes as many as four or five formal meetings were convened at the same time.[180] For many developing-country

---

[176] Note, however, that the UN Security Council could impose trade sanctions or a trade embargo on such Members and that, pursuant to Article XXI of the GATT 1994 and Article XIV *bis* of the GATS, other Members would be able to apply those sanctions or that embargo. See below, pp. 664–70.

[177] See below, p. 144.

[178] See Statement by Miguel Rodriguez Mendoza, WTO Deputy Director-General, to the General Council on 13 February 2002, *Minutes of Meeting*, WT/GC/M/73, dated 11 March 2002. This number includes the TNC and the two negotiating groups established by the TNC. See below, pp. 127–8. The *ad hoc* bodies (i.e. the non-standing bodies) comprise the TNC, the two TNC negotiating groups, twenty-eight accession working groups and five plurilateral bodies.

[179] See *ibid*. In 2001, there were nearly 400 formal meetings, 500 informal meetings and some 90 other meetings such as symposia, workshops and seminars organised under the auspices of WTO bodies. The number of meetings is calculated on the basis of half-day units.   [180] See *ibid*.

Figure 2.1 WTO organisation chart[181]

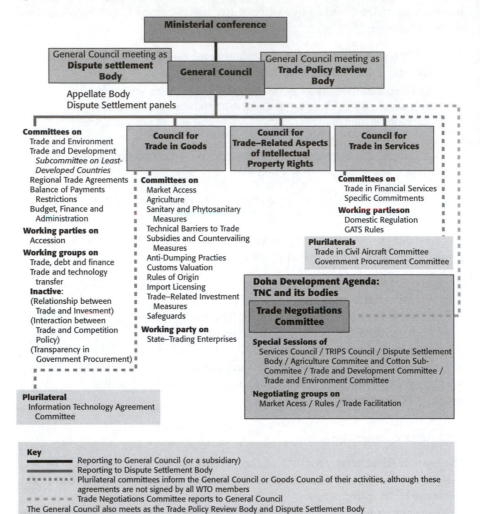

Members, with no delegation or only a small permanent delegation in Geneva, this is a serious problem.[182] The schedule of meetings at the WTO is posted on the WTO website.[183] Consider the schedule of meetings for November 2007, as shown in Figure 2.2.

The institutional structure of the WTO includes, at the highest level, the Ministerial Conference, at a second level, the General Council, the DSB and the TPRB and, at lower levels, specialised councils, committees and working parties. Furthermore, this structure includes quasi-judicial and other non-political bodies, as well as the WTO Secretariat. Note, however, that, unlike other interna-

---

[181] See www.wto.org/english/thewto_e/whatis_e/tif_e/org2_e.htm, visited on 24 November 2007.
[182] See below, pp. 148–51.   [183] See www.wto.org/english/news_e/news_e.htm, visited on 15 September 2007.

Figure 2.2 Programme of meetings in November 2007[184]

Date	Time	Meeting
5	09.30	Trade Policy Review Body – Organisation of Eastern Caribbean States
6		Committee on Trade and Development – Session on Aid for Trade
7	09.30	Trade Policy Review Body – Organisation of Eastern Caribbean States
7–9		Committee on Technical Barriers to Trade
7		Committee on Trade in Civil Aircraft
8		Committee on Budget, Finance and Administration
12	10.00	Committee on Trade in Financial Services Fax
14		Committee on Trade and Development – Dedicated Session
14		Committee on Balance-of-Payments Restrictions
16	10.00	Council for Trade in Services
19–23	09.30	Geneva Week (Non-resident Members and Observers)
19		Dispute Settlement Body
20		General Council – Coherence
21–22		Committee on Agriculture
23		Council for Trade in Goods
23		Committee on Budget, Finance and Administration
26 ∝ 28		Trade Policy Review Body – Thailand
29–30		Committee on Regional Trade Agreements

tional organisations, the WTO does not have any permanent body through which the 'dialogue' between the WTO and civil society can take place.[185] Furthermore, the WTO does not have an executive body, comprising only a core group of WTO Members, to facilitate the process of deliberation and decision-making.

Questions and Assignments 2.13

Briefly describe the basic institutional structure of the WTO. Is the list of WTO bodies prescribed in Article IV of the *WTO Agreement* an exhaustive list? Look up the programme of meetings at the WTO for this month. Which of these meetings would you definitely want to attend if you were a small, sugar-exporting, least-developed-country Member (with a diplomatic staff of two for all international organisations in Geneva)?

2.5.2. Ministerial Conference

Article IV:1 of the *WTO Agreement* states:

> There shall be a Ministerial Conference composed of representatives of all the Members, which shall meet at least once every two years. The Ministerial Conference shall carry out the functions of the WTO and take actions necessary to this effect. The Ministerial

[184] See www.wto.org/meets_public/meets_e.pdf, visited on 4 October 2007.
[185] On the involvement of NGOs and civil society in WTO decision-making, see below, pp. 152–9.

> Conference shall have the authority to take decisions on all matters under any of the Multilateral Trade Agreements, if so requested by a Member, in accordance with the specific requirements for decision-making in this Agreement and in the relevant Multilateral Trade Agreement.

The Ministerial Conference is the 'supreme' body of the WTO. It is composed of minister-level representatives from *all* Members and has decision-making powers on *all* matters under *any* of the multilateral WTO agreements.[186] However, it is not clear whether this very broad power to make decisions, in fact, enables the Ministerial Conference to take decisions which are *legally binding* on WTO Members.[187] With regard to the Decision of 15 December 2000 regarding Implementation-Related Issues and Concerns,[188] a decision based, *inter alia*, on Article IV:1 of the *WTO Agreement* and containing several clauses which begin with the words 'Members shall . . .', Pieter-Jan Kuijper, then Director of the WTO Legal Affairs Division, noted that:

> It is as yet unclear whether this is taken by Members as laying down a political or a legal commitment.[189]

In addition to this very broad decision-making power, the Ministerial Conference has been explicitly granted a number of specific powers, such as:

- adopting authoritative interpretations of the WTO agreements;[190]
- granting waivers;[191]
- adopting amendments;[192]
- making decisions on accession;[193] and
- appointing the Director-General and adopting staff regulations.[194]

The Ministerial Conference is not often in session. Since 1995, there have only been six sessions of the Ministerial Conference, each lasting only a few days: Singapore (1996),[195] Geneva (1998),[196] Seattle (1999),[197] Doha (2001),[198] Cancún

---

[186] For the Rules of Procedure for the Ministerial Conference, see WT/L/161, dated 25 July 1996.

[187] See, in this respect, P. J. Kuijper, 'Some Institutional Issues Presently Before the WTO', in D. Kennedy and J. Southwick (eds.), *The Political Economy of International Trade Law: Essays in Honor of Robert E. Hudec* (Cambridge University Press, 2002), 82.

[188] General Council, *Implementation-Related Issues and Concerns*, Decision of 15 December 2000, WT/L/384, dated 19 December 2000. This was a Decision by the General Council exercising the authority of the Ministerial Conference in between sessions of the Ministerial Conference. See below, pp. 121–2.

[189] P. J. Kuijper, 'Some Institutional Issues Presently Before the WTO', in D. Kennedy and J. Southwick (eds.), *The Political Economy of International Trade Law: Essays in Honor of Robert E. Hudec* (Cambridge University Press, 2002), 82, footnote 3.   [190] Article IX:2 of the *WTO Agreement*. See below, pp. 141–2.

[191] Article IX:3 of the *WTO Agreement*. See below, pp. 142–3.

[192] Article X of the *WTO Agreement*. See below, pp. 143–4.

[193] Article XII of the *WTO Agreement*. See below, p. 142.

[194] Article VI:2 and VI:3 of the *WTO Agreement*. See below, pp. 132–4. Note also that, pursuant to Article XII:5(b) and XII:6 of the GATS, the Ministerial Conference also has the power to establish certain procedures in connection with balance-of-payments restrictions (see below, p. 126). Pursuant to Article 64.3 of the *TRIPS Agreement*, the Ministerial Conference has the power to extend the non-application of non-violation complaints to the *TRIPS Agreement* (see below, pp. 800–1).

[195] For the Ministerial Declarations adopted at the Singapore Session of the Ministerial Conference in 1996, see WT/MIN(96)/DEC, dated 18 December 1996, and WT/MIN(96)/16, dated 13 December 1996.

[196] For the Ministerial Declarations adopted at the Geneva Session of the Ministerial Conference in 1998, see WT/MIN(98)/DEC/1, dated 25 may 1998, and WT/MIN(98)/DEC/2, dated 25 may 1998.

[197] No Ministerial Declaration was adopted at the Seattle Session of the Ministerial Conference in 1999.

[198] For the Ministerial Declarations and Decisions adopted at the Doha Session of the Ministerial Conference in 2001, see WT/MIN(01)/DEC/1, dated 20 November 2001, WT/MIN(01)/DEC/2, dated 20 November 2001,

(2003)[199] and Hong Kong (2005).[200] Sessions of the Ministerial Conference are major media events and focus the minds of the political leaders of WTO Members on the current challenges to, and the future of, the multilateral trading system. They offer a much-needed biennial opportunity to give political leadership and guidance to the WTO and its actions. The next session of the Ministerial Conference should normally have been held in December 2007. Due to the lack of progress in the Doha Development Round negotiations, however, no session was held at that time.

Questions and Assignments 2.14

Discuss the composition and the scope of the decision-making competence of the Ministerial Conference.

2.5.3. General Council, DSB and TPRB

2.5.3.1. *General Council*

Article IV:2 of the *WTO Agreement* states:

> There shall be a General Council composed of representatives of all the Members, which shall meet as appropriate. In the intervals between meetings of the Ministerial Conference, its functions shall be conducted by the General Council. The General Council shall also carry out the functions assigned to it by this Agreement. The General Council shall establish its rules of procedure and approve the rules of procedure for the Committees provided for in paragraph 7.

The General Council is composed of ambassador-level diplomats and normally meets once every two months.[201] All WTO Members are represented in the General Council. As with all other WTO bodies, except the Ministerial Conference, the General Council normally meets on the premises of the WTO Secretariat in Geneva. Each year, the General Council elects its Chairperson from among its members. The Chairperson of the General Council holds the highest elected office within the WTO. In February 2008, the General Council elected Bruce Gosper, Australia's Ambassador and Permanent Representative to the WTO, as its Chairperson for 2008.[202]

The General Council is responsible for the continuing, 'day-to-day' management of the WTO and its many activities. In between sessions of the Ministerial

---

WT/MIN(01)/15, dated 14 November 2001, WT/MIN(01)/16, dated 14 November 2001, and WT/MIN(01)/17, dated 20 November 2001.

[199] No Ministerial Declaration was adopted at the Cancún Session of the Ministerial Conference in 2003. However, the Ministerial Conference did issue a Ministerial Statement. See WT/MIN(03)/20, dated 23 September 2003.

[200] For the Ministerial Declaration adopted at the Hong Kong Session of the Ministerial Conference in 2005, see WT/MIN(05)/DEC, dated 22 December 2005.

[201] For the Rules of Procedure of the General Council, see WT/L/161, dated 25 July 1996.

[202] The list of the 2008 chairpersons of all WTO bodies can be found on the WTO's website, at www.wto.org/english/news_e/pres08_e/pr512_e.htm, visited on 10 February 2008.

Conference, the General Council exercises the full powers of the Ministerial Conference.[203]

In addition, the General Council also carries out some functions specifically assigned to it. The General Council is responsible for adopting the annual budget and the financial regulations[204] and making appropriate arrangements for effective cooperation with international organisations and NGOs.[205]

By way of example of the matters dealt with by the General Council, consider the list of matters discussed at the General Council meeting of 9 May 2007, set out in figure 2.3.

Rule 37 of the *Rules of Procedure for the Meetings of the General Council* states:

> The meeting of the General Council shall ordinarily be held in private. It may be decided that a particular meeting or meetings should be held in public.

In practice, the General Council always meets behind closed doors. After the meeting, the Chairperson may issue a *communiqué* to the press.[206] The Chairperson and/or the Director-General, assisted by the WTO spokesperson, usually hold a press conference after the meeting. The minutes of a meeting of the General Council (as are the minutes of meetings of all WTO bodies except the TPRB) are 'restricted' documents, i.e. not available to the public, until they are 'de-restricted' under the rules on the de-restriction of official documents.[207] Later in this chapter, the alleged lack of transparency and openness of the General Council and other WTO bodies is discussed in more detail.[208]

2.5.3.2. DSB and TPRB

The functions specifically assigned to the General Council also cover dispute settlement and trade policy review.

Article IV:3 and 4 of the *WTO Agreement* state respectively:

> 3. The General Council shall convene as appropriate to discharge the responsibilities of the Dispute Settlement Body provided for in the Dispute Settlement Understanding. The Dispute Settlement Body may have its own chairman and shall establish such rules of procedure as it deems necessary for the fulfilment of those responsibilities.
> 4. The General Council shall convene as appropriate to discharge the responsibilities of the Trade Policy Review Body provided for in the TPRM. The Trade Policy Review Body may have its own chairman and shall establish such rules of procedure as it deems necessary for the fulfilment of those responsibilities.

The General Council, the Dispute Settlement Body (DSB) and the Trade Policy Review Body (TPRB) are, in fact, the same body. The DSB and the TPRB are the

---

[203] Note that, when the Ministerial Conference is in session, it will typically focus on issues other than the exercise of the specific powers entrusted to it. See also P. J. Kuijper, 'Some Institutional Issues Presently Before the WTO', in D. Kennedy and J. Southwick (eds.), *The Political Economy of International Trade Law: Essays in Honor of Robert E. Hudec* (Cambridge University Press, 2002), 83.
[204] Article VII:3 of the *WTO Agreement*.   [205] Article V:1 of the *WTO Agreement*.
[206] See Rule 38 of the Rules of Procedure for the Meetings of the General Council, WT/L/161, dated 25 July 1996.
[207] General Council, *Decision on Procedures for the Circulation and Derestriction of WTO Documents*, WT/L/452, dated 16 May 2002. For a discussion on the rules of de-restriction, see below, p. 158.
[208] See below, pp. 149–51, 154–6.

Figure 2.3 Excerpt from the minutes of the meeting of the General Council of 9 May 2007[209]

WORLD TRADE Organization

RESTRICTED

WT/GC/M/108

26 June 2007

(07–2686)

General Council 9 May 2007

MINUTES OF MEETING

Held in the Centre William Rappard

on 9 May 2007

Chairman: Mr Muhamad Noor (Malaysia)

Prior to the close of the meeting, the Chairman bid farewell on behalf of all to the outgoing Administrative Assistant in the Council & TNC Division, Ms Margaret Kennedy, thanking her for her years of conscientious and dedicated service.

---

alter ego of the General Council; they are two emanations of the General Council. When the General Council administers the WTO dispute settlement system, it convenes and acts as the DSB. When the General Council administers the WTO trade policy review mechanism, it convenes and acts as the TPRB. To date, the DSB and the TPRB have always had a different Chairperson from the General

---

[209] See WT/GC/M/108, dated 26 June 2007.

Council,[210] and both the DSB and the TPRB have developed their own Rules of Procedure, which take account of the special features of their work.[211]

The DSB has a regular meeting once a month, but in between additional meetings called 'special meetings' may be requested by WTO Members in order to enable them to exercise their rights within specified timeframes as provided for in the DSU.[212] In 2006, for example, the DSB met in total twenty-two times.[213] The TPRB also meets at least once a month. In February 2008, Ambassadors Mario Matus of Chile and Yonov Frederick Agah of Nigeria were elected as Chairpersons for 2008 of the DSB and the TPRB respectively.[214]

Questions and Assignments 2.15

What is the relationship between the Ministerial Conference and the General Council? What is the relationship between the General Council and the DSB? Look up who serves this year as the Chairperson of the General Council, the DSB and the TPRB. Find the minutes of the last meeting of the General Council. What issues were on the agenda of this meeting?

2.5.4. Specialised councils, committees and working parties

2.5.4.1. Specialised councils

At the level below the General Council, the DSB and the TPRB, there are three so-called specialised councils: the Council for Trade in Goods (CTG),[215] the Council for Trade in Services (CTS)[216] and the Council for TRIPS.[217] Article IV:5 of the *WTO Agreement* states:

There shall be a Council for Trade in Goods, a Council for Trade in Services and a Council for Trade-Related Aspects of Intellectual Property Rights (hereinafter referred to as the 'Council for TRIPS'), which shall operate under the general guidance of the General Council. The Council for Trade in Goods shall oversee the functioning of the Multilateral Trade Agreements in Annex 1A. The Council for Trade in Services shall oversee the functioning of the General Agreement on Trade in Services (hereinafter referred to as 'GATS'). The Council for TRIPS shall oversee the functioning of the Agreement on Trade-Related Aspects of Intellectual Property Rights (hereinafter referred to as the 'Agreement on TRIPS'). These Councils shall carry out the functions assigned to them by their respective agreements and by the General Council. They shall establish their respective rules of procedure subject to the approval of the General Council. Membership in these Councils shall be open to representatives of all Members. These Councils shall meet as necessary to carry out their functions.

[210] Note, however, that traditionally the Chairperson of the DSB becomes the Chairperson of the General Council.
[211] For the Rules of Procedure for the TPRB, see Trade Policy Review Body, *Rules of Procedure for Meetings of the Trade Policy Review Body*, WT/TPR/6/Rev.1, dated 10 October 2005. For the Rules of Procedure for the DSB, see below, pp. 235–8. Note that the TPRB and the DSB follow, *mutatis mutandis* and with certain deviations, the Rules of Procedure for the General Council (WT/L/160).   [212] See below, pp. 237–8.
[213] See WTO Secretariat *WTO Annual Report 2007*, 36.   [214] See above, footnote 202.
[215] For the Rules of Procedure for the CTG, see WTL/79, dated 7 August 1995.
[216] For the Rules of Procedure for the CTS, see S/L/15, dated 19 October 1995.
[217] For the Rules of Procedure for the Council for TRIPS, see IP/C/1, dated 28 September 1995.

In 2006, for example, the CTG met four times in formal session and the CTS met five times.[218] Furthermore, these specialised councils also met informally. All WTO Members are represented in these specialised councils although some Members, in particular developing-country Members, may find it difficult to attend all meetings. Under the general guidance of the General Council, these specialised councils oversee the functioning of the multilateral agreements in Annex 1A, 1B and 1C of the *WTO Agreement* respectively. They assist the General Council and the Ministerial Conference in carrying out their functions. They carry out both the tasks which the General Council delegates to them, and the tasks which the *WTO Agreement*, the GATS or the *TRIPS Agreement* explicitly confer on them. For example, in May 2000, the General Council decided:

> to direct the Council on Trade in Goods to give positive consideration to individual requests presented in accordance with Article 5.3 by developing countries for extension to transition periods for implementation of the TRIMs Agreement.[219]

The *WTO Agreement* itself explicitly stipulates, for example, that the Ministerial Conference and the General Council may only exercise their authority to adopt authoritative interpretations of the multilateral trade agreements of Annex 1 on the basis of a recommendation from the specialised council overseeing the functioning of the agreement at issue.[220] The specialised councils also play a role in the procedure for the adoption of waivers and the amendment procedure.[221] The GATS explicitly empowers the CTS to develop disciplines on domestic regulation under Article VI:4 and to establish rules and procedures for the rectification and modification of schedules under Article XXI of the GATS. The *TRIPS Agreement* empowers the TRIPS Council to extend, upon a duly motivated request, the ten-year transition period for the implementation of the *TRIPS Agreement* granted to the least-developed-country Members.[222]

Overall, however, few specific powers have been entrusted to the specialised councils, and their general power to *oversee* the functioning of relevant agreements does not explicitly include the power to take any decision, political or legal.[223]

There are instances in which WTO bodies go beyond their powers. An often-cited example is the extension of the deadline for the entry into force of the result of negotiations on emergency safeguard measures in the field of services, adopted by the CTS. Article X:1 of the GATS sets this deadline explicitly at 'not later than three years from the date of entry into force of the *WTO Agreement*', i.e. on 1 January 1998. This treaty-mandated deadline was extended five times by three successive decisions by the CTS although the CTS clearly did not have any

---

[218] WTO Secretariat, *WTO Annual Report 2007*, 25 and 35.
[219] See WT/GC/M/55, dated 16 June 2000, Annex II, third bullet point.
[220] Article IX:2 of the *WTO Agreement*.   [221] Article IX:3(b) and Article X:1 of the *WTO Agreement*.
[222] Article 66.1 of the *TRIPS Agreement*. See e.g. the decision of the TRIPS Council of 29 November 2005 to further delay the date for the entry into force of the *TRIPS Agreement* for least-developed countries until 1 July 2013. See 'Poorest countries given more time to apply intellectual property rules', dated 29 November 2005, available at www.wto.org/english/news_e/pres05_e/pr424_e.htm, visited on 23 July 2007. See further below, p. 803.
[223] See also P. J. Kuijper, 'Some Institutional Issues Presently Before the WTO', in D. Kennedy and J. Southwick (eds.), *The Political Economy of International Trade Law: Essays in Honor of Robert E. Hudec* (Cambridge University Press, 2002), 84.

legal mandate to do so.[224] The political need to extend the deadline prevailed over any concern about the CTS acting *ultra vires*.

2.5.4.2. Committees and working parties

In addition to the three specialised councils, there are a number of committees and working parties that assist the Ministerial Conference and the General Council in carrying out their functions. The committees include the important Committee on Trade and Development. Article IV:7 of the *WTO Agreement* states in pertinent part:

> The Ministerial Conference shall establish a Committee on Trade and Development, a Committee on Balance-of-Payments Restrictions and a Committee on Budget, Finance and Administration, which shall carry out the functions assigned to them by this Agreement and by the Multilateral Trade Agreements, and any additional functions assigned to them by the General Council, and may establish such additional Committees with such functions as it may deem appropriate . . . Membership in these Committees shall be open to representatives of all Members.

In exercising the power conferred on it in Article IV:7, the General Council established:

- the Committee on Trade and Environment in 1995;[225] and
- the Committee on Regional Trade Agreements in 1996.[226]

Furthermore, all but one of the Multilateral Agreements on Trade in Goods provide for a committee to carry out certain functions relating to the implementation of the particular agreement.[227] All of these committees are under the authority of, and report to, the CTG. In practice, however, they tend to be relatively independent, arguably due to the technical nature of their work. Note, by way of example, the SCM Committee. Article 24.1 of the *SCM Agreement* states:

> There is hereby established a Committee on Subsidies and Countervailing Measures composed of representatives from each of the Members. The Committee shall elect its own Chairman and shall meet not less than twice a year and otherwise as envisaged by relevant provisions of this Agreement at the request of any Member. The Committee shall carry out responsibilities as assigned to it under this Agreement or by the Members and it shall afford Members the opportunity of consulting on any matter relating to the operation of the Agreement or the furtherance of its objectives. The WTO Secretariat shall act as the secretariat to the Committee.[228]

---

[224] See e.g. *Decision on Negotiations on Emergency Safeguard Measures*, S/L/43, dated 2 December 1997; *Second Decision on Negotiations on Emergency Safeguard Measures*, S/L/73, dated 5 July 1999; and *Third Decision on Negotiations on Emergency Safeguard Measures*, S/L/90, dated 8 December 2000. The most recent extension was decided on in March 2004.

[225] This Committee was established at the same meeting of the General Council on 31 January 1995, at which the Committee on Trade and Development, the Committee on Balance-of-Payment Restrictions and the Committee on the Budget, Finance and Administration were established (see WT/GC/M/1).

[226] See WT/GC/M/10, dated 6 March 1996, para. 11.

[227] The exception is the *Agreement on Preshipment Inspection*. However, the CTG established a Committee on Preshipment Inspection.

[228] The powers of the Committee on Anti-Dumping (AD) Practices, the Committee on Customs Valuation (CV) and the Committee on Technical Barriers to Trade (TBT) are worded in similar terms.

Note that under Article 27.4 of the *SCM Agreement*, the SCM Committee has the power to determine whether a request to extend the special transitional period, for the maintenance of export subsidies by developing countries, is justified.[229] Such specific decision-making powers to add to, or diminish, the obligations of certain Members are, however, quite exceptional.[230]

Furthermore, Article IV:6 of the *WTO Agreement* provides that the specialised councils may also establish subsidiary bodies as required. For example, the Council for Trade in Services created the Working Party on Professional Services. A number of committees also have this power to establish subordinate bodies where necessary.[231]

Temporary subsidiary bodies, set up to study and report on a particular issue, are usually referred to as 'working parties'. In November 2007, there were almost thirty working parties on the accession of candidate Members.

When a working party, a committee or a specialised council is called upon to take a decision but is unable to do so, the applicable Rules of Procedure commonly require the matter to be referred to a higher body if a Member so requests.

The Plurilateral Agreements, i.e. the *Agreement on Trade in Civil Aircraft* and the *Agreement on Government Procurement*, provide for a Committee on Trade in Civil Aircraft and a Committee on Government Procurement respectively. These bodies carry out the functions assigned to them under those agreements. They operate within the institutional framework of the WTO, keeping the General Council informed of their activities on a regular basis.[232]

2.5.5. Trade Negotiations Committee

The Doha Development Round negotiations are conducted in the Trade Negotiations Committee (TNC) and its subordinate negotiating bodies.[233] The TNC was established by the Ministerial Conference at its Doha Session in November 2001.[234] This body supervises the overall conduct of the negotiations under the authority of the General Council. The TNC reports on the progress of the negotiations to each regular meeting of the General Council. The 'detailed' negotiations take place either in special sessions of standing WTO bodies or in specially created negotiating groups. At its first meeting on 28 January and 1 February 2002, the TNC established two such new negotiating groups, one on market access and one on rules. Most of the negotiations, however, take place in special sessions of standing WTO bodies (such as the Dispute Settlement Body, the Council for Trade in Services and the Committee on Agriculture). The TNC

---

[229] Furthermore, Article 29.4 of the *SCM Agreement* gives the SCM Committee the power to allow Members in the process of transformation into a market economy to derogate from their notified programmes and measures and their timeframes.

[230] Another example is the power given to the TBT Committee under Article 12.8 of the *TBT Agreement* relating to granting exceptions from TBT obligations to developing-country Members.

[231] See e.g. Article 13.2 of the *TBT Agreement*.   [232] See Article IV:8 of the *WTO Agreement*.

[233] See above, pp. 89–92.

[234] Ministerial Conference, *Doha Ministerial Declaration*, WT/MIN(01)/DEC/1, dated 20 November 2001, para. 46.

and its negotiating bodies consist of all the WTO Members and all countries negotiating membership.[235]

On 1 February 2002, the TNC elected the WTO Director-General *ex officio* to chair the TNC. The TNC is the only political WTO body chaired by an international official, rather than a diplomat of a Member. Note that the choice of the WTO Director-General as Chairperson of the TNC was controversial among WTO Members.

2.5.6. Political bodies lacking in the WTO structure

Unlike other international organisations, such as the IMF and the World Bank, the WTO does not have an executive body or organ consisting of the most important Members and a selection of other Members. In other international organisations having such a large membership, an executive body facilitates decision-making by concentrating discussions in a smaller but representative group of members.[236] Also, unlike other international organisations such as the OECD and the ILO, the WTO does not have any permanent body in which entities other than governments are represented.

2.5.6.1. A WTO executive body?

As discussed above, all political WTO bodies are composed of the 151 WTO Members. However, it is clear that it is impossible to negotiate effectively with such a large number. Therefore, in the GATT 1947 and now the WTO, mechanisms have been developed to reduce the number of countries actively participating in the deliberations of WTO bodies. Hoekman and Kostecki noted in this respect:

> The first and most important device is to involve only 'principals', at least initially. To some extent this is a natural process – a country that has no agricultural sector is unlikely to be interested in discussions centering on the reduction of agricultural trade barriers. In general the quad – Canada, the EU, Japan and the US – are part of any group that forms to discuss any topic. They are supplemented by countries that have a principal supplying interest in a product, and the major (potential) importers whose policies are the subject of interest. Finally a number of countries that have established a reputation as spokespersons tend to be involved in most major meetings. Historically, such countries have included India . . . Egypt, and the former Yugoslavia.[237]

In the days of the GATT 1947, contentious issues were often hotly debated in 'green room meetings', named after a conference room next to the office of the Director-General. These green room meetings, bringing together about twenty or so delegations at the invitation of the Director-General,

---

[235] Note, however, that decisions on agreements that would result from the negotiations are taken by WTO Members only. See also above, p. 120.

[236] B. Hoekman and M. Kostecki, *The Political Economy of the World Trading System: The WTO and Beyond*, 2nd edition (Oxford University Press, 2001), 60.

[237] *Ibid.* For a discussion on the current importance of the Quad, see above, pp. 106–7.

> were part of a consultative process through which the major countries and a representative set of developing countries . . . tried to hammer out the outlines of acceptable proposals or negotiating agendas. Such meetings generally involved the active participation and input of the Director-General . . . Once a deal has emerged, it is submitted to the general . . . membership. Although amendments may be made, these are usually marginal.[238]

Green room meetings (i.e. inner circle meetings) comprised usually no more than twenty Members, including the Quad, Members deemed to have a vital interest in the issue under discussion and developing-country Members that play a leading role, such as Brazil, India and South Africa. The least-developed-country Members are frequently represented by Bangladesh.

After the establishment of the WTO, the practice of green room meetings continued. However, this practice was one of the reasons for the dismal failure of the Seattle Session of the Ministerial Conference in 1999. At Seattle, major trading powers and selected developing countries tried to agree on the agenda for a new round in green room meetings. Many developing-country Members, excluded from these meetings, revolted because they felt that they were not kept informed and that their views were not considered. The problem of full and effective participation of developing countries in the WTO decision-making process is discussed in more detail below.[239]

In this context, the Heads of Delegation Meetings (HODs) and the practice of 'Mini-Ministerials' should also be mentioned. HODs are informal meetings to which ambassadors alone (i.e. the heads of delegation) are invited to attend. However, as *all* ambassadors are invited, these meetings may still be too 'crowded' for effective deliberation.[240] By contrast, 'Mini-Ministerials' are informal meetings of trade ministers of key Members to forge consensus on particularly divisive matters. In the context of the Doha Development Round negotiations, a number of 'Mini-Ministerials' have been held in a fruitless attempt to break the deadlock.

There have been a number of proposals to create an executive body, or a 'Security Council for Trade' type of body, within the WTO institutional structure to facilitate decision-making. To date, however, such proposals have not received much support from WTO Members.[241] The 2004 Sutherland Report on *The Future of the WTO* recommended that the frequency of meetings between policy-makers should be increased and the informal 'Mini-Ministerials' should be replaced by the establishment of a 'senior level consultative body', similar to the one which operated in the GATT for many years.[242] The membership of this body, in order for it to be effective, should not exceed thirty Members. While most seats might be filled on a 'rotating basis – drawing', taking into account different criteria, such as 'geographical areas, regional trading arrangements or mixed constituencies', the permanent presence of certain Members would be a 'must' given the significance of their trade flows.[243]

---

[238] *Ibid.*, 60–1.   [239] See below, pp. 148–51.
[240] The 'HOD plus One' are meetings where the ambassador can also select another senior diplomat to attend the meeting with him or her.
[241] See General Council, *Minutes of Meeting*, WT/GC/M/91, dated 26 January 2005, 20.
[242] See Report by the Consultative Board to the Director-General Supachai Panitchpakdi, *The Future of the WTO: Addressing Institutional Challenges in the New Millennium* (the 'Sutherland Report') (WTO, 2004), para. 323.
[243] *Ibid.*, para. 325.

2.5.6.2. WTO consultative bodies

The WTO does not have any permanent consultative body in which representatives of national parliaments or NGOs are represented. As is the case in other international organisations, such a body could serve as a forum for 'dialogue' between the WTO and civil society.

The European Communities has proposed the establishment of a WTO Parliamentary Consultative Assembly. While there seems to be little support for the establishment of such an assembly, it should be noted that, in recent years, contacts with national parliamentarians have been greatly enhanced through regular visits to capitals by the WTO Director-General and through various seminars and briefings with the Inter-Parliamentary Union, the European Parliament and the US Congress.

While strongly supporting the principle that only WTO Members have the authority to make decisions in the WTO, Canada, for example, has argued that 'outside voices', such as expert NGOs, can provide valuable advice to Members.[244] To manage this process of obtaining specialised advice, the WTO could set up *ad hoc* advisory boards to provide non-binding advice on WTO-related issues. These boards could be composed of individuals and/or NGOs, and should reflect a broad range of views and interests. However, suggestions to establish such consultative bodies comprising representatives of NGOs have received little support from Members to date. In 2003, the WTO Director-General established on his *own initiative* two advisory bodies: the Informal NGO Advisory Body and the Informal Business Advisory Body. The Informal NGO Advisory Body, which is made up of eleven high-level representatives from NGOs, provides a platform for dialogue with NGOs from around the world. The Informal Business Advisory Body, which comprises fourteen captains of industry, provides a platform for dialogue with international business organisations and leading companies from developed as well as developing-country Members. Both bodies advise the WTO Director-General, channel the positions of civil society and global business on trade issues to the WTO and ultimately aim at facilitating mutual understanding. These advisory bodies are expected to meet twice a year.[245]

Questions and Assignments 2.16

In your opinion, should the WTO have an executive body and/or a consultative assembly?

2.5.7. Quasi-judicial and other non-political bodies

All the WTO bodies discussed above are political in nature. The WTO also has a number of quasi-judicial and other non-political bodies. The most

---

[244] See also below, pp. 153–4.
[245] Note that the WTO website does not include any information on these advisory bodies. See www.wto.org, visited on 17 September 2007.

prominent among the quasi-judicial bodies are the *ad hoc* dispute settlement panels and the standing Appellate Body, which are discussed in detail in chapter 3.[246]

The WTO also has other non-political bodies. An example of such a body is the Permanent Group of Experts (PGE) provided for under the *SCM Agreement*. Paragraphs 3 and 4 of Article 24 of the *SCM Agreement* state:

> 3. The [SCM] Committee shall establish a Permanent Group of Experts composed of five independent persons, highly qualified in the fields of subsidies and trade relations. The experts will be elected by the Committee and one of them will be replaced every year. The PGE may be requested to assist a panel, as provided for in paragraph 5 of Article 4. The Committee may also seek an advisory opinion on the existence and nature of any subsidy.
> 4. The PGE may be consulted by any Member and may give advisory opinions on the nature of any subsidy proposed to be introduced or currently maintained by that Member. Such advisory opinions will be confidential and may not be invoked in proceedings under Article 7.

Reportedly, to date no use has yet been made of the PGE.

Until 1 January 2005, a prime example of a non-political body was the Textile Monitoring Body (TMB). Article 8.1 of the *Agreement on Textiles and Clothing* stated:

> In order to supervise the implementation of this Agreement, to examine all measures taken under this Agreement and their conformity therewith, and to take the actions specifically required of it by this Agreement, the Textiles Monitoring Body ('TMB') is hereby established. The TMB shall consist of a Chairman and 10 members. Its membership shall be balanced and broadly representative of the Members and shall provide for rotation of its members at appropriate intervals. The members shall be appointed by Members designated by the Council for Trade in Goods to serve on the TMB, discharging their function on an *ad personam* basis.[247]

The TMB was a non-political body in view of its mandate and the fact that its members discharged their function independently and on an *ad personam* basis (not as the representative of a WTO Member). As discussed above, the *Agreement on Textiles and Clothing* ceased to be in force on 1 January 2005 and, as of that date, the TMB therefore also ceased to exist.[248]

Questions and Assignments 2.17

Find out who currently sits on the Permanent Group of Experts provided for in Article 24 of the *SCM Agreement*. What is the mandate of the PGE and has the PGE been successful in exercising this mandate?

---

[246] See below, pp. 238–69.
[247] Note that para. 1.4 of the *Working Procedures for the Textiles Monitoring Body* states: 'In discharging their functions in accordance with paragraph 1.1 above, TMB members and alternates undertake not to solicit, accept or act upon instructions from governments, nor to be influenced by any other organisations or undue extraneous factors. They shall disclose to the Chairman any information that they may consider likely to impede their capacity to discharge their functions on an *ad personam* basis.' See *Working Procedures for the Textiles Monitoring Body*, adopted on 26 July 1995, G/TMB/R/1. Note also para. V of the *Rules of Conduct for the Understanding on Rules and Procedures Governing the Settlement of Disputes*, WT/DSB/RC/1, dated 11 December 1996.   [248] See above, p. 46. See also below, pp. 452–3.

2.5.8. WTO Secretariat

The WTO Secretariat is based in Geneva,[249] and has a staff of 625 persons.[250] This makes it undoubtedly one of the smallest secretariats of any of the major international organisations.[251] However, as Hoekman and Kostecki observed:

> The small size of the secretariat is somewhat misleading . . . [T]he WTO is a network-based organization. The WTO secretariat and the national delegates in Geneva work in close cooperation with numerous civil servants in their respective capitals . . . The total size of the network is impossible to determine, but certainly spans at least 5,000 people.[252]

As discussed below, the Secretariat's prime function is to keep the 'WTO network' operating smoothly.

2.5.8.1. Appointment of the Director-General

The Secretariat is headed by a Director-General, who is appointed by the Ministerial Conference.[253] The Ministerial Conference adopts regulations setting out the powers, duties, conditions of service and the term of office of the Director-General.

In the brief history of the WTO, the appointment of the Director-General has often been a contentious matter.[254] In particular, the appointments of former Director-General Dr Supachai Panitchpakdi, and his predecessor, Mr Mike Moore, were divisive. In March 1999, Frances Williams of the *Financial Times* reported on the search for a replacement for Mr Renato Ruggiero, the WTO's second Director-General, as follows:

> The search for a new head of the World Trade Organization appeared to have reached an impasse yesterday, raising fears of an interregnum when Renato Ruggiero, the present director-general, steps aside at the end of April. After missing two deadlines for the selection of Mr Ruggiero's successor, the WTO members last week set March 12 as their new target date, but this, too, looks in danger of slipping. Consultations with members over the past months have not changed the rankings of the four candidates, according to a report yesterday to the WTO's general council. Among the 118 members which have now

---

[249] Article VI:1 of the *WTO Agreement*. The WTO Secretariat has its offices in Geneva at the Centre William Rappard (154, rue de Lausanne), by Lake Geneva. Note that the Secretariat of the WTO Appellate Body, which is independent of the WTO Secretariat, is also housed in the Centre William Rappard. See below, pp. 257–61.   [250] See www.wto.org/english/thewto_e/secre_e/intro_e.htm, visited on 15 November 2007.

[251] Note that in the mid-1990s the FAO cut staff at its headquarters in Rome by more jobs than there were at the time in the whole WTO Secretariat. See J. Madeley, 'UN Farm Aid Agency Wins Renewed Pledges of Funding', *Financial Times*, 25 February 1997.

[252] B. Hoekman and M. Kostecki, *The Political Economy of the World Trading System: The WTO and Beyond*, 2nd edition (Oxford University Press, 2001), 55.   [253] See Article VI:2 of the *WTO Agreement*.

[254] Only the appointment of Mr Peter Sutherland, the last Director-General of the GATT, to become the first Director-General of the WTO was not contentious. To date, the following persons have served as WTO Director-General:

Mr Peter Sutherland from Ireland (January 1995–April 1995);
Mr Renato Ruggiero from Italy (May 1995–April 1999);
Mr Mike Moore from New Zealand (September 1999–August 2002);
Dr Supachai Panitchpakdi from Thailand (September 2002–August 2005); and
Mr Pascal Lamy from France (September 2005–August 2009).

expressed a view, Supachai Panitchpakdi, Thailand's deputy premier, continues to lead the field with 39 first preferences, followed closely by Hassan Abuyoub, a former Moroccan trade minister, who has significantly improved his relative position at 35. Roy MacLaren, former Canadian trade minister, is third with 23 first preferences, just in front of Mike Moore, former New Zealand premier, with 21. However, Mr Moore had the most second preferences (32) compared with 23 for Mr Supachai, 11 for Mr Abuyoub and eight for Mr MacLaren. Several countries yesterday called for weaker candidates to drop out to make it easier to reach consensus, while some developing countries urged a vote if consensus is not achieved by the end of the month. A vote is opposed by many WTO members, however, because they argue that the next director-general should clearly be acceptable to all 134 member countries. On a purely arithmetic basis, Mr MacLaren would seem to be in the weakest position but he has some influential backers including the US which claims to be supporting him alongside Mike Moore. Sir Leon Brittan, the European Union trade commissioner, also favours Mr MacLaren though EU Members are split between all four candidates.[255]

After a year-long effort to appoint a successor to Renato Ruggiero, WTO Members finally agreed on 22 July 1999 to an unprecedented term-sharing arrangement under which Mike Moore, of New Zealand, was appointed as Director-General for a term of three years beginning on 1 September 1999, and Supachai Panitchpakdi, of Thailand, was appointed for a three-year term beginning on 1 September 2002.[256] Mike Moore, a former printer, social worker and trade union researcher, was the youngest Member of Parliament ever elected in New Zealand. In the 1980s, he served six years as New Zealand's Minister of Overseas Trade and Marketing, and was New Zealand's Prime Minister for a brief period in 1990. When he took office as Director-General of the WTO, a few weeks before the fated Seattle Session of the Ministerial Conference, Mr Moore, the first non-European to head the WTO (or the GATT), stated that he intended to defend the WTO as an organisation 'where the little guy not only has a say but where he can protect and defend his trading rights', and pledged to make the expansion of trading opportunities for the world's poorest countries a top priority during his three-year term.[257]

On 1 September 2002, Supachai Panitchpakdi took over from Mike Moore. Supachai held a range of senior government positions in Thailand and was directly in charge of Thailand's participation in the final stages of the Uruguay Round negotiations. At the time of his appointment to the post of WTO Director-General for the period 2002–5, Supachai served as Thailand's Deputy Prime Minister and Minister of Commerce.

The current Director-General, Pascal Lamy, of France, took office on 1 September 2005. Lamy served as the EU Trade Commissioner for five years before his appointment. Lamy began his career in the French civil service, served as Chief of Staff to Jacques Delors, President of the European Commission, and later was CEO of the bank Credit Lyonnais.

[255] F. Williams, 'Impasse in Search for World Trade Chief', *Financial Times*, 2 March 1999.
[256] In its decision on this 'double' appointment, the General Council stressed that this arrangement did not constitute a precedent for future appointments of the Director-General and agreed to work towards establishing 'a comprehensive set of rules and procedures for such appointments' by the end of September 2000.
[257] F. Williams, 'Moore Takes up WTO Post with Pledge on Poor', *Financial Times*, 2 September 1999.

At its meeting of 10 December 2002, the General Council adopted new procedures for the appointment of a Director-General.[258] Under these new procedures, the appointment process shall start nine months prior to the expiry of the term of an incumbent Director-General. The various steps of the process are carefully set out. The process shall be conducted by the Chair of the General Council, assisted by the Chairs of the Dispute Settlement Body and the Trade Policy Review Body acting as facilitators. Only WTO Members may nominate candidates. Candidates should have extensive experience in international relations, encompassing economic, trade and/or political experience; a firm commitment to the work and objectives of the WTO; proven leadership and managerial ability; and demonstrable communication skills. While the Sutherland Report on *The Future of the WTO* found these procedures to be steps in the right direction, it stated that it:

> would favour the abandonment of the agreement that permits WTO Members to make nominations only of their own nationals or that candidates must have the backing of their own governments. Indeed, there would be more logic in disallowing such national nominations completely. Any tendency towards alternating between developing and developed countries and any regional sequencing should be avoided. By the same token we would favour reducing the intensity of candidate 'campaigns'. A further option requiring that an initial independent search for appropriate candidates be carried out may be worth further examination.[259]

The overriding objective of Members is to reach a decision on the appointment of a Director-General by consensus. However, note that the new procedures explicitly state:

> If, after having carried out all the procedures set out above, it has not been possible for the General Council to take a decision by consensus by the deadline provided for the appointment, Members should consider the possibility of recourse to a vote as a last resort by a procedure to be determined at that time. Recourse to a vote for the appointment of a Director-General shall be understood to be an exceptional departure from the customary practice of decision-making by consensus, and shall not establish any precedent for such recourse in respect of any future decisions in the WTO.[260]

2.5.8.2. Role of the Director-General and the WTO Secretariat

The Members of the WTO set the agenda and make decisions. Neither the Director-General nor the WTO Secretariat has any autonomous decision-making powers. The Director-General and the WTO Secretariat act primarily as an 'honest broker' in, or a 'facilitator' of, the decision-making processes within the WTO. They are not expected to act as initiators of proposals for action or reform. In such a seemingly modest role, the Director-General and the WTO Secretariat can, however, make an important contribution to the building of consensus among Members on a specific agreement or decision. Note, in this respect, that

---

[258] See General Council, *Decision on the Procedures for the Appointment of Directors-General,* adopted 10 December 2002, WT/L/509, dated 20 January 2003.

[259] Report by the Consultative Board to the Director-General Supachai Panitchpakdi, *The Future of the WTO: Addressing Institutional Challenges in the New Millennium* (the 'Sutherland Report') (WTO, 2004), para. 352, available at www.wto.org/english/thewto_e/10anniv_e/future_wto_e.htm, visited on 20 September 2007.

[260] General Council, *Decision on the Procedures for the Appointment of Directors-General,* adopted 10 December 2002, WT/L/509, dated 20 January 2003, para. 21.

in February 2002 the Trade Negotiations Committee (TNC), the body overseeing the Doha Development Round negotiations, elected the Director-General *ex officio* to chair the TNC.

In a speech in January 2003, Supachai Panitchpakdi, speaking about his role and that of the WTO Secretariat, noted:

> As you know the WTO is, if I may use the cliché, a 'member-driven' organization. In the negotiations, Member governments negotiate directly with each other. As Chairman of the TNC, I shall be doing my utmost to keep all Members on board, facilitate their discussions, mediate in their problems and consult with all. And the WTO Secretariat, through its technical assistance work programme, is working hard to help developing and least-developed-country Members prepare effectively for the negotiations. But we cannot make any decisions on behalf of Members, we cannot unplug blockages when Members' positions are intractable and we cannot force consensus. It is Members who have the very difficult responsibility of developing policy positions, negotiating concessions and deciding how far they are able to go in any given area.[261]

Nevertheless, developing-country Members are reported to be apprehensive regarding the role of the Director-General and the WTO Secretariat. In a joint communication, addressing, *inter alia*, the issue of their role at sessions of the Ministerial Conference, fifteen developing-country Members, led by India, stated:

> The Secretariat and the Director-General of the WTO . . . should assume a neutral/ impartial and objective role. They shall not express views explicitly or otherwise on the specific issues being discussed in the Ministerial Conference.[262]

The Sutherland Report on *The Future of the WTO* recommended, however, that the Director-General and the WTO Secretariat take on a greater, more proactive role. The Report stated:

> The WTO needs a convincing and persistent institutional voice of its own. If Members are not prepared to defend and promote the principles they subscribe to, then the Secretariat must be free to do so . . . Further, a clearer – though always careful – lead on policy issues should be emerging from the Secretariat. Members should not be afraid of asking the Secretariat to provide policy analysis.[263]

The main duties of the WTO Secretariat are:

- to provide technical and professional support for the various WTO bodies;
- to provide technical assistance to developing-country Members;
- to monitor and analyse developments in world trade;
- to advise governments of countries wishing to become Members of the WTO; and
- to provide information to the public and the media.

---

[261] See Supachai Panitchpakdi, *Build Up: The Road to Mexico*, speech on 8 January 2003 at Plenary Session XI of the Partnership Summit 2003 in Hyderabad, available at www.wto.org/english/news_e/spsp_e/spsp09_e.htm, visited on 19 September 2007.

[262] Communication from Cuba, Dominican Republic, Egypt, Honduras, India, Indonesia, Jamaica, Kenya, Malaysia, Mauritius, Pakistan, Sri Lanka, Tanzania, Uganda and Zimbabwe, *Preparatory Process in Geneva and Negotiating Procedure at the Ministerial Conferences*, WT/GC/W/471, dated 24 April 2002, para. i.

[263] Report by the Consultative Board to the Director-General Supachai Panitchpakdi, *The Future of the WTO: Addressing Institutional Challenges in the New Millennium* (the 'Sutherland Report') (WTO, 2004), paras. 361 and 366, available at www.wto.org/english/thewto_e/10anniv_e/future_wto_e.htm, visited on 20 September 2007.

Furthermore, the Secretariat also provides administrative support and legal assistance for WTO dispute settlement panels.[264] The Appellate Body has its own Secretariat which is independent of the WTO Secretariat but which shares the same facilities and makes use of the general support services of the WTO Secretariat (translation, library, etc.).[265]

With regard to the status of the Director-General and WTO staff as independent and impartial international officials, Article VI:4 of the *WTO Agreement* states:

> The responsibilities of the Director-General and of the staff of the Secretariat shall be exclusively international in character. In the discharge of their duties, the Director-General and the staff of the Secretariat shall not seek or accept instructions from any government or any other authority external to the WTO. They shall refrain from any action which might adversely reflect on their position as international officials. The Members of the WTO shall respect the international character of the responsibilities of the Director-General and of the staff of the Secretariat and shall not seek to influence them in the discharge of their duties.

2.5.8.3. The structure and composition of the WTO Secretariat

As noted above, the WTO Secretariat is headed by the WTO Director-General. The Director-General is assisted by four Deputy Directors-General (DDGs), also political appointees, serving for a limited period of time. They are appointed by the Director-General – in consultation with WTO Members – and form, together with the Director-General, the senior management of the WTO Secretariat. Currently, Alejandro Jara (of Chile), Valentine Sendanyoye Rugwabiza (of Rwanda), Harsh V. Singh (of India) and Rufus H. Yerxa (of the United States) serve as DDGs under Pascal Lamy.[266] The number of DDGs has been the subject of discussions in the General Council.[267] While it is argued that there could be fewer than four, having four DDGs makes it possible for the main regions of the world to be represented in senior management.

The WTO Secretariat is organised into divisions with a functional role (e.g. the Rules Division, the Services Division and the Market Access Division), divisions with an information and liaison role (e.g. the Information and Media Relations Division) and divisions with a supporting role (e.g. the Administration and General Services Division and the Language Services and Documentation Division). Divisions are normally headed by a Director who reports to one of the WTO's four Deputy Directors-General or directly to the Director-General. In addition to divisions, the WTO Secretariat also includes the Institute for Training and Technical Cooperation (ITTC), which was established in 2003 to ensure a coherent and coordinated approach to capacity-building and technical assistance.[268]

---

[264] See below, pp. 256–7.   [265] See below, p. 261.
[266] See www.wto.org/english/thewto_e/dg_e/ddgs_e.htm, visited on 15 November 2007.
[267] See Statement by Ambassador Ali Mchumo, Chairman of the General Council, at the Meeting on 6 October 1999, WT/GC/27, dated 12 October 1999.
[268] Also note in this respect the Technical Assistance Management Committee (TAMC) in which all relevant WTO Divisions are represented.

Figure 2.4 WTO Secretariat organisation chart[269]

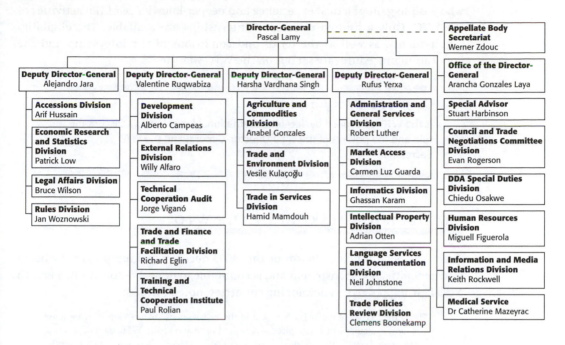

The Director-General appoints the staff and determines their duties and conditions of service in accordance with the *Staff Regulations* adopted by the Ministerial Conference.[270]

About sixty different nationalities are represented in the staff of the WTO Secretariat. Nationals of France, the United Kingdom, Spain, Switzerland and the United States (in numerical order) are best represented among the staff. The representation of developing-country nationals in the staff is growing but remains a matter of concern. Only nationals of WTO Members can be officials of the WTO Secretariat but there are no formal or informal national quotas.[271] Most of the professional staff are lawyers or economists. The working languages within the WTO Secretariat are English, French and Spanish, with English being the language most frequently used.

---

[269] See WTO Secretariat, *Annual Report 2007*, available at www.wto.org/english/res_e/booksp_e/anrep_e/anrep07_e.pdf, visited on 15 August 2007. Note that the *WTO Annual Report 2007* incorrectly identifies the Appellate Body Secretariat as part of the WTO Secretariat. See above, p. 132, and below, p. 261.

[270] See Article VI:3 of the *WTO Agreement*. According to the *Staff Regulations*, the paramount objective in the determination of conditions of service is to secure staff members of the highest standards of competence, efficiency and integrity and to meet the requirements of the WTO taking into account the needs and aspirations of the staff members. The Director-General has established and administers *Staff Rules*. The *Staff Rules* implement the provisions of the *Staff Regulations*. The Director-General furthermore issues staff administrative memoranda in elaboration of the *Staff Rules*.

[271] Vacancies are the subject of open competition. The final selection of professional staff is done on the basis of a written exam and an interview. The recruitment process is highly competitive. Vacancies are advertised by means of vacancy notices, the distribution of which is made to all WTO Members. They are also posted on the WTO's website (www.wto.org) and, where appropriate, advertised in the international press.

The WTO Secretariat has an internship programme for graduate students who wish to gain practical experience and deeper knowledge of the activities of the WTO. Only a limited number of internships are available. The eligibility requirements, as well as the terms and conditions of the internship and the application procedure, are set out on the WTO website.[272]

Questions and Assignments 2.18

Is the WTO controlled by 'faceless international bureaucrats'? Discuss the role and the powers of the WTO Director-General and the WTO Secretariat.

2.6. DECISION-MAKING IN THE WTO

There has been much criticism of the WTO decision-making process as being undemocratic, non-transparent and accountable to none. War on Want, a British NGO fighting poverty in developing countries, noted in 2003:

> The current crisis in the WTO is rooted in the undemocratic nature of the organisation and the negotiations that take place within it. The image of the WTO as a democratic organisation is without foundation. From formulating the agenda to reaching a decision, the process is dominated by the most powerful and richest countries. As such, negotiations at the WTO are fertile ground for horse-trading that inevitably favour those with greatest financial and political might. To keep on top of the massive agenda at the WTO, rich countries, such as US, EU, Japan and Canada, have large teams of well-resourced specialists in Geneva. Half of the poorest countries in the WTO cannot even afford one.[273]

This section examines:

- the normal decision-making procedure, which applies as the default procedure;
- a number of special procedures for specific decisions;
- WTO decision-making in practice;
- the participation of developing-country Members in WTO decision-making;
- the involvement of NGOs; and
- the form and legal basis of WTO decisions.

In brief, this section addresses the criticism of War on Want and others. There is rhyme and reason for the current WTO decision-making procedures.

2.6.1. Normal procedure

The normal decision-making procedure for WTO bodies is set out in Article IX:1 of the *WTO Agreement*, which states:

---

[272] See www.wto.org/english/thewto_e/vacan_e/intern_e.htm, visited on 20 November 2007.
[273] Excerpt from '5th Ministerial: Free Trade on Trial', available at www.waronwant.org/5th%20Ministerial%3A%20Free%20Trade%20on%20Trial%205543.twl, visited on 19 September 2007.

> The WTO shall continue the practice of decision-making by consensus followed under GATT 1947. Except as otherwise provided, where a decision cannot be arrived at by consensus, the matter at issue shall be decided by voting. At meetings of the Ministerial Conference and the General Council, each Member of the WTO shall have one vote . . . Decisions of the Ministerial Conference and the General Council shall be taken by a majority of the votes cast, unless otherwise provided in this Agreement or in the relevant Multilateral Trade Agreement.[274]

2.6.1.1. *Decision-making by consensus*

Pursuant to Article IX:1 of the *WTO Agreement*, Members first try to take decisions *by consensus*. Footnote 1 to Article IX defines consensus decision-making by WTO bodies as follows:

> The body concerned shall be deemed to have decided by consensus on a matter submitted for its consideration, if no Member, present at the meeting when the decision is taken, *formally* objects to the proposed decision.
>
>   [Emphasis added]

In other words, unless a Member *explicitly* objects to the proposed decision, that decision is taken.[275] No voting takes place.[276] Decision-making by consensus gives all Members *veto power*.[277] John Jackson noted, however, in this respect:

> the practice . . . is that some countries that have difficulty with a particular decision will nevertheless remain silent out of deference to countries with a substantially higher stake in the pragmatic economic consequences of a decision.[278]

Decision-making by consensus in practice involves a degree of deference to economic power. It is only when important national, economic or other interests are at stake that a WTO Member would consider blocking the consensus.[279]

As Hoekman and Kostecki noted, decision-making by consensus is a useful device to ensure that only decisions which have a good chance of being

---

[274] The Rules of Procedure of the various WTO bodies set out the quorum requirement. For example, Rule 16 of the *Rules of Procedure for the Meetings of the General Council* states: 'A simple majority of the Members shall constitute a quorum.' Most WTO bodies have the same quorum requirement. Currently, seventy-six of the WTO Members must be present at the meeting in order to take valid decisions. In practice, the quorum is not checked.

[275] Note that the Doha Ministerial Declaration of November 2001 introduced the concept of 'explicit consensus' (for decisions on the inclusion of 'Singapore issues' in the agenda of the Doha Development Round). See above, p. 91. It is not clear what is meant by 'explicit consensus'. The inclusion of this concept in the Doha Ministerial Declaration was, however, a condition of India and other developing-country Members for agreeing to adopt the Declaration. At the close of the Doha Session of the Ministerial Conference, the Conference Chair, the Qatari Finance, Economy and Trade Minister Youssef Hussain Kamal, stated that 'his understanding of the requirement of "explicit consensus" was that it would: give each member the right to take a position on modalities that would prevent negotiations from proceeding after the Fifth Session of the Ministerial Conference until that member is prepared to join in an explicit consensus'. See www.wto.org/english/thewto_e/minist_e/min01_e/mindecl_e.htm, visited on 16 September 2007. If this is indeed the meaning of the concept of 'explicit consensus', the question arises whether an 'explicit' consensus differs from a 'normal' consensus.

[276] In decision-making by consensus, unlike in decision-making by unanimity, no voting takes place.

[277] As noted in the Sutherland Report, however, the definition of consensus favours Members that can afford to be present at all meetings, since absence does not defeat a consensus. See Report by the Consultative Board to the Director-General Supachai Panitchpakdi, *The Future of the WTO: Addressing Institutional Challenges in the New Millennium* (the 'Sutherland Report') (WTO 2004), para. 282.

[278] J. Jackson, *The World Trade Organization: Constitution and Jurisprudence* (Royal Institute of International Affairs, 1998), 46.   [279] See *ibid.*

implemented are adopted because the decisions adopted are all decisions to which there was no major opposition. However, Hoekman and Kostecki also observed that decision-making by consensus:

> reinforces conservative tendencies in the system. Proposals for change can be adopted only if unopposed, creating the potential for paralysis.[280]

2.6.1.2. Decision-making by majority voting

If consensus cannot be achieved, Article IX:1 of the *WTO Agreement* provides for voting on a one-country/one-vote basis. Under the normal procedure, decisions are then taken by a majority of the votes cast. Whereas each WTO Member has one vote, Article IX:1 of the *WTO Agreement* provides in pertinent part:

> Where the European Communities exercise their right to vote, they shall have a number of votes equal to the number of their member States which are Members of the WTO.

In a footnote to this sentence, it is further explained that the number of votes of the European Communities and its Member States shall in no case exceed the number of the Member States of the European Union. It is thus clear that either the European Communities *or* the Member States of the European Union will participate in a vote. Who participates in a vote is not a matter of WTO law but of EU constitutional law. For reasons relating to the practice of WTO decision-making, discussed below, the fact that the European Communities currently has twenty-seven votes and the United States, China and India only one, does not have much, if any, impact on the political decision-making processes at the WTO.[281]

It should be pointed out that, as a rule, the European Commission speaks for the European Communities *and* the Member States of the European Union at meetings of WTO bodies, even if those bodies deal with matters that are not within the exclusive competence of the European Community. Delegates from the EU Member States attend the meetings but do not speak. The EU Member States speak (and vote, if a vote is called) only with regard to budgetary matters and organisational matters (e.g. the election of the Director-General). Furthermore, the Ministers of the EU Member States make short formal statements at the biennial sessions of the Ministerial Conference.

Questions and Assignments 2.19

What is decision-making by consensus? In practice, does it amount to a veto power for each WTO Member? Can WTO bodies take decisions by voting? Do all WTO Members have the same number of votes? How many votes do the United States, the European Communities, China, Belgium and Saint Lucia have? In your opinion, should the number of votes of Members be related to the size of their population or their share of world trade?

---

[280] B. Hoekman and M. Kostecki, *The Political Economy of the World Trading System: The WTO and Beyond*, 2nd edition (Oxford University Press, 2001), 57.   [281] See below, pp. 145–7.

2.6.2. Special procedures

The *WTO Agreement* sets out a number of decision-making procedures which deviate from the normal procedure discussed above. This section deals with:

- decision-making by the DSB;
- authoritative interpretations;
- accessions;
- waivers;
- amendments; and
- the annual budget and financial regulations.[282]

2.6.2.1. Decision-making by the DSB

Footnote 3 to Article IX of the *WTO Agreement* provides:

> Decisions by the General Council when convened as the Dispute Settlement Body shall be taken only in accordance with the provisions of paragraph 4 of Article 2 of the Dispute Settlement Understanding.

Article 2.4 of the DSU states:

> Where the rules and procedures of this Understanding provide for the DSB to take a decision, it shall do so by consensus.[283]

As discussed in detail in chapter 3, the DSB takes certain decisions, such as decisions on the establishment of a panel or decisions on the adoption of dispute settlement reports, by reverse consensus. Other decisions, such as the appointment of Members of the Appellate Body, are taken by a normal consensus.[284]

2.6.2.2. Authoritative interpretations

Article IX:2 of the *WTO Agreement* states:

> The Ministerial Conference and the General Council shall have the exclusive authority to adopt interpretations of this Agreement and of the Multilateral Trade Agreements. In the case of an interpretation of a Multilateral Trade Agreement in Annex 1, they shall exercise their authority on the basis of a recommendation by the Council overseeing the functioning of that Agreement. The decision to adopt an interpretation shall be taken by a three-fourths majority of the Members. This paragraph shall not be used in a manner that would undermine the amendment provisions in Article X.

Article IX:2 explicitly states that the Ministerial Conference and the General Council have the *exclusive* authority to adopt interpretations of provisions of the

---

[282] Note that this is not an exhaustive list of special decision-making procedures. See e.g. Article 12.1 of the *SPS Agreement*, which is not dealt with in this section. According to this provision, the SPS Committee always takes its decisions by consensus.

[283] Footnote 1 to Article 2.4 of the DSU stipulates: 'The DSB shall be deemed to have decided by consensus on a matter submitted for its consideration, if no Member, present at the meeting of the DSB when the decision is taken, formally objects to the proposed decision.'   [284] See below, p. 259.

WTO agreements. This may appear surprising since it was noted in chapter 1 that, pursuant to Article 3.2 of the DSU, the WTO dispute settlement system serves to 'clarify', i.e. interpret, the provisions of the WTO agreements. However, these interpretations by panels or the Appellate Body cannot and may not – also pursuant to Article 3.2 of the DSU – add to or diminish the rights and obligations of Members. Furthermore, these interpretations are, in principle, only binding on the parties to the dispute.[285] The interpretation referred to in Article IX:2 of the *WTO Agreement*, which is commonly referred to as 'authoritative interpretation', is of a different nature. This interpretation, by the highest political bodies of the WTO, is binding on all WTO Members and may affect their rights and obligations (although the right of interpretation should not be used so as to undermine the amendment provisions).

To date, the WTO has not made any *explicit* use of the possibility to adopt 'authoritative interpretations'. The Decision of the Ministerial Conference on *Implementation-Related Issues and Concerns*, taken at the Doha Session on 14 November 2001, contains a number of provisions which are obviously interpretations of provisions of the WTO agreements. However, in its preamble, the Decision does not explicitly refer to Article IX:2 of the *WTO Agreement*.

2.6.2.3. Accessions

As already discussed above and provided for in Article XII:2 of the *WTO Agreement*, decisions on the accession of new Members are taken by the Ministerial Conference or, in between sessions of the latter, by the General Council.[286] Pursuant to Article XII:2, decisions on accession are to be taken by a two-thirds majority of WTO Members. However, on 15 November 1995, the General Council agreed that for decisions on accession it will first seek to reach consensus. Only when a decision cannot be arrived at by consensus, shall the matter be decided by a two-thirds majority vote.[287] To date, only the 1995 decision on the accession of Ecuador was taken by majority vote.

2.6.2.4. Waivers

As discussed above, a Member unable to meet an obligation under one of the WTO agreements may request the WTO to waive that obligation.[288] With respect to the decision-making procedure to be followed, Article IX:3 of the *WTO Agreement* provides:

> In exceptional circumstances, the Ministerial Conference may decide to waive an obligation imposed on a Member by this Agreement or any of the Multilateral Trade Agreements, provided that any such decision shall be taken by three fourths of the Members unless otherwise provided for in this paragraph.

---

[285] See below, pp. 255–6.   [286] See above, pp. 108–10.

[287] Statement by the Chairman as agreed by the General Council on 15 November 1995, *Decision-Making Procedures under Articles IX and XII of the WTO Agreement*, WT/L/93, dated 24 November 1995.

[288] With respect to the conditions under which waivers of WTO obligations can be granted, see above, pp. 114–15.

a. A request for a waiver concerning this Agreement shall be submitted to the Ministerial Conference for consideration pursuant to the practice of decision-making by consensus. The Ministerial Conference shall establish a time-period, which shall not exceed 90 days, to consider the request. If consensus is not reached during the time-period, any decision to grant a waiver shall be taken by three fourths of the Members.

b. A request for a waiver concerning the Multilateral Trade Agreements in Annexes 1A or 1B or 1C and their annexes shall be submitted initially to the Council for Trade in Goods, the Council for Trade in Services or the Council for TRIPS, respectively, for consideration during a time-period which shall not exceed 90 days. At the end of the time-period, the relevant Council shall submit a report to the Ministerial Conference.

Although explicitly provided for, decisions on waivers are, in practice, not taken by a three-fourths majority of the Members. WTO Members decided, in 1995, not to apply the provisions allowing for a vote, but to continue to take decisions on waivers by consensus.[289]

2.6.2.5. Amendments

The most complex of all special decision-making procedures are the procedures for amending the WTO agreements. Article X:1 of the *WTO Agreement* states:

Any Member of the WTO may initiate a proposal to amend the provisions of this Agreement or the Multilateral Trade Agreements in Annex 1 by submitting such proposal to the Ministerial Conference. The Councils listed in paragraph 5 of Article IV may also submit to the Ministerial Conference proposals to amend the provisions of the corresponding Multilateral Trade Agreements in Annex 1 the functioning of which they oversee. Unless the Ministerial Conference decides on a longer period, for a period of 90 days after the proposal has been tabled formally at the Ministerial Conference any decision by the Ministerial Conference to submit the proposed amendment to the Members for acceptance shall be taken by consensus . . . If consensus is reached, the Ministerial Conference shall forthwith submit the proposed amendment to the Members for acceptance. If consensus is not reached at a meeting of the Ministerial Conference within the established period, the Ministerial Conference shall decide by a two-thirds majority of the Members whether to submit the proposed amendment to the Members for acceptance . . .

In general, the amendment procedure is as follows. Individual Members or one of the three specialised councils initiate the amendment procedure by submitting an amendment proposal to the Ministerial Conference or the General Council. In the first period of at least ninety days, the Ministerial Conference or the General Council tries to reach consensus on the proposal for amendment. If consensus cannot be reached, the Ministerial Conference or the General Council resorts to voting. To be adopted, the proposal for amendment requires a two-thirds majority of the Members. Once adopted by consensus or by a two-thirds majority, the proposal is forthwith submitted to the Members for acceptance in accordance with their national constitutional requirements and procedures. An amendment shall take effect for the Members that have accepted the amendment upon acceptance by two-thirds of the Members.[290] As a rule, the amendment is effective only in respect of those Members that have accepted it.[291] However, Article X:2 lists a

---

[289] See footnote 162.   [290] See Article X:3 of the *WTO Agreement*.   [291] See *ibid.*

number of fundamental provisions (concerning the MFN treatment obligation under the GATT 1994, the GATS and the *TRIPS Agreement*, the GATT 1994 tariff schedules and WTO decision-making and amendment) which have to be accepted by all Members before they can take effect. Moreover, a decision to amend the DSU must be made by consensus, and amendments to the DSU take effect for all Members upon approval by the Ministerial Conference. These amendments are not submitted to the Members for acceptance.[292] Article X:4 also provides that amendments that do not alter the rights and obligations of the Members take effect for *all* Members upon acceptance by *two-thirds* of the Members.

Finally, Article X:3 states in pertinent part:

> The Ministerial Conference may decide by a three-fourths majority of the Members that any amendment made effective under this paragraph is of such a nature that any Member which has not accepted it within a period specified by the Ministerial Conference in each case shall be free to withdraw from the WTO or to remain a Member with the consent of the Ministerial Conference.

While conveyed in very diplomatic language, this means, in effect, that a Member who refuses to accept certain amendments may be expelled from the WTO. The actual importance of this provision, however, seems limited. Note that this power also existed under the GATT 1947 but was never used.[293] It is likely that this will also be the case in the WTO.

The first and thus far only amendment to the WTO agreements was adopted by the General Council in December 2005 and concerned an amendment to the *TRIPS Agreement*.[294] Pursuant to the amendment decision, an Article 31 *bis* is inserted after Article 31 of the *TRIPS Agreement* and an Annex to the *TRIPS Agreement* is inserted after Article 73 thereof. As discussed in chapter 8, the amendment concerns changes to the *TRIPS Agreement* relating to the conditions under which compulsory licences may be granted for the production of essential medicines.[295] Pursuant to Article X:3 of the *WTO Agreement*, this amendment will take effect when two-thirds of the Members have accepted the amendment.[296]

2.6.2.6. *Annual budget and financial regulations*

Finally, the adoption of the annual budget and financial regulations also entails a special decision-making procedure. Pursuant to Article VII:3 of the *WTO Agreement*, the General Council adopts the annual budget and the financial regulations by a two-thirds majority comprising more than half of the Members of the WTO. For a more detailed discussion, refer to the last section of this chapter.[297]

---

[292] See Article X:8 of the *WTO Agreement*.
[293] See *Analytical Index: Guide to GATT Law and Practice*, 6th edition (GATT, 1994), 934.
[294] General Council, *Decision of 6 December 2005 on the Amendment of the TRIPS Agreement*, WT/L/641, dated 8 December 2005.   [295] See below, pp. 790–1.
[296] On 1 December 2007, merely 13 of the 151 Members had accepted the amendment. See www.wto. org/english/tratop_e/trips_e/amendment_e.htm, visited on 1 December 2007.   [297] See below, pp. 161–3.

Questions and Assignments 2.20

How does the WTO decide on waivers of WTO obligations? What is the difference between 'authoritative interpretations' under Article IX:2 of the *WTO Agreement* and interpretation by panels and the Appellate Body under Article 3.2 of the DSU? What is the difference between 'authoritative interpretations' under Article IX:2 of the *WTO Agreement* and 'amendments' under Article X thereof? Should Members want to amend Article III of the GATT 1994 or Article 5 of the DSU, what are the procedural requirements for such amendments? Has the *WTO Agreement* already been amended?

2.6.3. WTO decision-making in practice

2.6.3.1. *Decision-making by consensus versus voting*

Although the *WTO Agreement* provides for the possibility to take decisions by voting, it is exceptional for WTO bodies to vote. In 1999, when discussion on the selection of a new Director-General became deadlocked, some developing countries suggested that the decision on the new Director-General should be taken by vote (as provided for in Article IX:1 of the *WTO Agreement*). However, this suggestion was not well received, in particular by the developed countries, who argued that this was 'contrary to the way things were done in the WTO'.[298] Jackson wrote:

> the spirit and practice of the GATT has always been to try to accommodate through consensus negotiation procedures the views of as many countries as possible, but certainly to give weight to the views of countries that have power in the trading system. This is not likely to change.[299]

In a speech in February 2000 at UNCTAD X in Bangkok, a few weeks after the failure of the Seattle Session of the Ministerial Conference, Mike Moore, the then WTO Director-General, stated:

> the consensus principle which is at the heart of the WTO system – and which is a fundamental democratic guarantee – is not negotiable.[300]

It cannot be disputed that decisions taken by consensus, i.e. decisions taken collectively, have more 'democratic legitimacy' than decisions taken by

---

[298] Note, however, that the Decision on the Procedures for the Appointment of Directors-General, adopted in 2002, states that: 'Members should consider the possibility of recourse to a vote as a last resort by a procedure to be determined at that time.' See General Council, *Decision on the Procedures for the Appointment of Directors-General*, adopted 10 December 2002, WT/L/509, dated 20 January 2003, para. 21. See also above, pp. 132–4.

[299] J. Jackson, *The World Trade Organization: Constitution and Jurisprudence* (Royal Institute of International Affairs, 1998), 45.

[300] M. Moore, *Back on Track for Trade and Development*, keynote address at the UNCTAD X, Bangkok, on 16 February 2000, available at www.wto.org/english/news_e/spmm_e/spmm24_e.htm, visited on 15 September 2007.

majority vote. At the same time, it should be noted that the consensus requirement does, of course, make decision-making in the WTO difficult and susceptible to paralysis. After the failure of the Cancún Session of the Ministerial Conference in September 2003, the *Financial Times* reported on the frustration of the European Communities with the consensus requirement as follows:

> Mr Lamy [the EU's trade commissioner] also expanded on his calls for a sweeping overhaul of the way in which the 146-strong WTO operates, and promised that the EU would come up with a set of reform proposals. His comments made clear that he is primarily concerned with the body's consensus-driven approach. 'I think it's above dispute that the principle of the permanent sit-in of 146 trade ministers in order to take a number of very detailed decisions . . . is a theory that visibly does not work', he said. A Commission official said Mr Lamy was not yet in a position to come up with a set of rounded proposals but that they were likely to address the WTO's most obvious shortfalls. 'Everything needs to be done by consensus. Even the agenda needs to be decided by consensus. And the powers of the WTO director-general are very limited', the official said. 'All that is incredibly complicated with 146 members.'[301]

According to the 2004 Sutherland Report on *The Future of the WTO*, there is definitely 'a larger sense of legitimacy' for decisions adopted by consensus.[302] The Sutherland Report noted, however, that:

> As the number of Members grows larger and larger (now 148, perhaps going to 170 and more), it becomes harder and harder to implement needed measures that require decisions, even when there is a vast majority of the Members that desire a measure. The consensus requirement can result in the majority's will being blocked by even one country. If the measure involved a fundamental change, such difficulty would probably be worthwhile, as adding a measure of 'constitutional stability' to the organization. But often there are non-fundamental measures at stake, some of which are just fine-tuning to keep the rules abreast of changing economic and other circumstances.[303]

The Sutherland Report recommended that:

> WTO Members give serious further study to the problems associated with achieving consensus in light of possible distinctions that could be made for certain types of decisions, such as purely procedural issues.[304]

and that:

> WTO Members cause the General Council to adopt a Declaration that a Member considering blocking a measure which otherwise has very broad consensus support shall only block such consensus if it declares in writing, with reasons included, that the matter is one of vital national interest to it.[305]

[301] T. Buck, 'EU May Rethink Multilateral Trade Role', *Financial Times*, 16 September 2003.
[302] Report by the Consultative Board to the Director-General Supachai Panitchpakdi, *The Future of the WTO: Addressing Institutional Challenges in the New Millennium* (the 'Sutherland Report') (WTO, 2004), para. 282.
[303] *Ibid.*, para. 283. As noted by the Sutherland Report, observers of WTO decision-making sometimes contend that consensus decision-making is not a problem as they do not observe many instances in which consensus is blocked. However, it should be noted that 'almost all potential decisions are prepared informally in advance and usually do not move to a formal proposition in a decision-making body if they are not ripe for consensus'. See *ibid.*, para. 285.   [304] *Ibid.*, para. 288.   [305] *Ibid.*, para. 289.

Questions and Assignments 2.21

Why are WTO Members so hesitant to resort to decision-making by voting? Would decision-making by voting be to the advantage of the developing-country Members?

2.6.3.2. The process of WTO decision-making in practice

The process of decision-making at the WTO is well illustrated by the following example regarding the LDC Group's participation in the Hong Kong Session of the Ministerial Conference in 2005. The task of coordination of the LDC Group, the group of least-developed country Members, rotates every six months between LDC Members having permanent missions in Geneva. In the run-up to, and at, the Hong Kong Session of the Ministerial Conference, Zambia acted as the LDC Coordinator. The Zambian diplomats were assisted in this task by Mark Pearson, Director of the Regional Trade Facilitation Programme (RTFP), a UK-funded programme to promote and improve trade in southern Africa. The following are excerpts from a statement of Mark Pearson on his personal impressions of the WTO negotiation process at the Hong Kong Session of the Ministerial Conference in December 2005. This statement gives the reader a rare view behind the 'closed doors' of WTO negotiations and decision-making. Pearson wrote:

> A Briefing Book for Ministers was prepared, which was translated into French and 3 copies were given to each LDC Delegation which were well received and used extensively. The Zambian team also prepared a Briefing Book exclusively for Hon. Patel to use in the negotiations. This gave negotiating positions and possible positions of other Members as well as possible responses from the LDCs.
>
> Zambia, as LDC Coordinator, was invited to the Green Room consultation process. The Green Room process, which was renamed Chairman's Consultative Group (CCG), is meant to assist the WTO to broker deals in seemingly difficult situations. There do not seem to be any rules as to who is invited to the Green Room but all Group Coordinators are invited plus other influential countries. Some Groups or countries (including US, EU and South Africa) had two Ministers present, one Trade Minister and one Agricultural Minister). The rules are strict and each Minister is allowed to be accompanied by only one official (1+1). Only Ministers can sit at the table and only Ministers can speak. The meeting is done in English and, if necessary (such as for Japan and Senegal), personal interpretation is done.
>
> Prior to Hong Kong the information was that the conference centre was covered by WiFi so the team opted to use WiFi enabled PDAs to communicate between the CCG and the support team outside. As it turned out, there was WiFi throughout the Conference Centre except in the Green Room. Communication was done by SMS and Blackberry (USTR are issued with Blackberrys as standard) and by going out of the CCG, into an anteroom where other officials were allowed, to consult.
>
> The negotiating process in Hong Kong was tortuous in that there was a CCG meeting held for 5 consecutive nights (Tuesday to Saturday) and two other CCG meetings during the day. For two nights the CCG went throughout the night and for the other 3 nights the meetings went on to around 3.00am to 4.00am. On Saturday night the CCG started at 10.30pm and finished at 9.00am the next morning.
>
> The CCG process in HK started with Agriculture, then moved to NAMA then Services then Development. Special and Different Treatment (SDT) for LDCs, which was really

> the only development aspect discussed (apart from Cotton, which was discussed as part of Agriculture), was, therefore, always discussed in the early hours of the morning when Ministers were at their most tired, with lowest concentration levels and lowest tolerance levels. There was a need to take these external factors into account in the negotiations. The positions and the arguments had to be expressed in a simplified, quickfire manner as, by the time the LDC slot came up, Ministers were in no mood for long and detailed presentations and discussions.
>
> Although there is only one official inside the CCG there is a need for other officials to be available during the CCG consultations. These other officials waited in anterooms. So it was not only the Minister and his official who lacked sleep. In the case of the LDCs it was the whole of the core negotiating team who had to stay up most of the night and then function effectively the next day.
>
> After the final CCG process, which ended at 9.00am on Saturday, we went back to the full LDC Group to explain what the outcome of the CCG process had been. There were attempts by one or two LDCs to convince the LDC Group to walk away from the agreement reached in the CCG. On the one hand there was the opinion that what had been agreed was of no value to the LDCs as it did not offer any more than what was already offered by EBA and AGOA . The other view was that the CCG agreement was a platform from which further progress could be made, and that if the Group walked away from this deal it would be a long time before the Group could be as organised as it was then to launch a similar offensive. The Coordinator suggested that the text agreed in the CCG could be accepted by the LDCs if it was adopted as a 'framework' agreement, with the modalities to be worked out after HK. This compromise was acceptable to the LDC Group and this is how the text was accepted by the LDC Group.[306]

Pearson's comments clearly show the high demands on negotiators in negotiations and decision-making within the WTO. Note that in spite of all the hard work, the Hong Kong Session of the Ministerial Conference did not result in a breakthrough in the Doha Development Round negotiations.[307]

2.6.4. Participation of developing-country Members

As already discussed above, the WTO commonly takes decisions by consensus and, in the exceptional instance where a vote is called, each Member has one vote. As such, decision-making within the WTO seems to ensure the participation of all Members, including developing-country Members and, hence, appears democratic. Every Member formally enjoys an equal say. Nevertheless, many developing-country Members feel marginalised within the WTO decision-making process.

2.6.4.1. Marginalisation of developing-country Members

As discussed above, it will often be impossible for Members, and especially developing-country Members, to block consensus decision-making when a critical mass of other Members favours the decision.[308] Moreover, it is obviously not possible or practical to involve all 151 Members in discussions aimed at reaching deals on controversial issues. It is likely that such broad participation would

---

[306] Mark Pearson, *Assisting the LDCs in WTO Trade Negotiations, A Personal Assessment*, dated December 2005, available at rtfp.africonnect.com/media/assisting_the_ldcs_mp_dec_05.pdf, visited on 1 December 2007.
[307] See above, pp. 91–2.   [308] See above, pp. 139, 145–6.

make these discussions ineffective. As Robert Keohane and Joseph Nye observed in 2001, the legitimacy of international organisations flows not only from 'inputs' in the form of procedures and accountability, but also from 'outputs', that is, their capacity to deliver results.[309] Mechanisms have, therefore, been developed to reduce the number of countries actively participating in the deliberations in the WTO and to allow the WTO to come to decisions. One such mechanism, already discussed above, is the green room meetings (i.e. inner circle meetings).[310] This mechanism brings the major trading powers and a select group of developing-country Members together to try to reach preliminary agreements which are then presented to the rest of the membership. As noted above, this mechanism was much criticised at the ill-fated Seattle Session of the Ministerial Conference.[311] Peter Sutherland wrote in this respect:

> Ironically, in Seattle, WTO Director-General Mike Moore and US Trade Representative Charlene Barshefsky, the co-chairs of the Ministerial Meeting, made a concerted, good-faith effort to broaden the participation of delegations in the negotiations. They divided the Ministerial agenda into several sections, created working groups for each, and invited all delegations to participate in all the working groups. Their goal was to keep Green Rooms to a minimum. But developing country delegations, in particular, had difficulty covering all of the working groups, and as the Ministerial week proceeded and agreements remained elusive, the temptation to pull together smaller groups of countries for harder bargaining – Green Rooms, in other words – understandably grew. In communiqués released towards the end of the week, large groupings of African and Latin American countries denounced what they described as the Ministerial's exclusive and non-democratic negotiating structure.[312]

A small group of influential developing-country Members, including of course Brazil, China, and India, undoubtedly participate in a very effective manner in the work of the WTO.[313] However, many other developing and low-income countries lack the staff and expertise to participate effectively in the many, often highly specialised meetings and discussions within the WTO. These countries are frequently confronted with 'take-it-or-leave-it' decisions agreed upon during informal meetings of a select group of developed and developing countries, such as green room meetings.

2.6.4.2. *The 'internal transparency' debate*

In the first half of 2000, after the debacle of the Seattle Session of the Ministerial Conference in 1999, Members conducted intensive consultations on what was

---

[309] See R. Keohane and J. Nye, 'The Club Model of Multilateral Cooperation and the World Trade Organization: Problems of Democratic Legitimacy', in R. Porter, P. Sauvé, A. Subramanian (eds.), *Efficiency, Equity and Legitimacy: The Multilateral Trading System at the Millennium* (Brookings Institution Press, 2001), 286. [310] See above, pp. 128–9.

[311] See R. Keohane and J. Nye, 'The Club Model of Multilateral Cooperation and the World Trade Organization: Problems of Democratic Legitimacy', in R. Porter, P. Sauvé, A. Subramanian (eds.), *Efficiency, Equity and Legitimacy: The Multilateral Trading System at the Millennium* (Brookings Institution Press, 2001), 286.

[312] P. Sutherland, J. Sewell and D. Weiner, 'Challenges Facing the WTO and Policies to Address Global Governance', in G. Sampson (ed.), *The Role of the World Trade Organization in Global Governance* (United Nations University Press, 2001), 87–8. [313] See above, pp. 106–7.

referred to as the issue of 'internal transparency', i.e. the issue of the effective participation of developing countries in WTO decision-making. At the General Council meeting of 17–19 July 2000, the Chairman of the General Council summarised the outcome of the consultations as follows:

> First, within the framework of the WTO Agreement it seemed that Members generally did not see the need for any major institutional reform which could alter the basic character of the WTO as a Member-driven organization and its decision-making process. There was also a strong commitment of the Members to reaffirm the existing practice of taking decisions by consensus. Second, Members seemed to recognize that interactive open-ended informal consultation meetings played an important role in facilitating consensus decision-making. As a complement to, but in no way a replacement of this open-ended consultation process, consultations might also take place with individual Members or groups of Members.[314]

The consultations of 2000 on internal transparency did not result in any formal change to the WTO's institutional structure or its decision-making process. They did, however, serve to 'clear the air' and rebuild a degree of confidence in the process. In order to ensure that consultations taking place in groups of Members contribute to the achievement of genuine consensus among all Members, it was recognised that there was a need:

- to inform all Members of consultations conducted by a select group of Members;
- to allow all interested Members to make their views known in such consultations;
- not to make any assumptions on the representation of Members by other Members in such consultations; and
- to report back promptly on the results of the consultations to all Members.[315]

The consultations on internal transparency also made clear that the WTO needed:

- to schedule its meetings carefully so as to avoid overlapping meetings as much as possible; and
- to ensure prompt and efficient dissemination of information and documents to Members, and, in particular, to non-resident Members and Members with small missions.

Since 2000, improvements along these lines have been made to the WTO decision-making process. The success of the Doha Session of the Ministerial Conference and the launch of the Doha Development Round is testimony to the progress made since the Seattle debacle. Nevertheless, the improvements made still fall short of the expectations of some Members. Members continue the discussion with a view to identifying and agreeing on further improvements in the decision-making process within the WTO. In 2002, Members held consultations on internal transparency and effective participation of Members in sessions of

---

[314] General Council, *Minutes of Meeting*, WT/GC/M/57, dated 14 September 2000, para. 134.   [315] See *ibid*.

the Ministerial Conference and the preparatory process leading up to these sessions.[316] The main challenge is to *balance* the interests of inclusiveness with the
interests of efficiency. Disparities in economic and political power will of course
always affect, if not determine, the weight of Members in the WTO decision-
making process. No institutional mechanism can ever totally 'undo' these differences. Neither would this be desirable. It is clear that an obvious response to the
problem of the 'marginalisation' of many developing-country Members in the
WTO is technical assistance and human capacity-building. As discussed above,
considerable efforts in that respect are currently undertaken as part of the Doha
Development Agenda.[317]

Furthermore, as Rubens Ricupero, a former Ambassador of Brazil to the GATT
and Chairman of the GATT Council as well as former Secretary-General of
UNCTAD, noted:

> developing countries needed to draw up a 'positive agenda' in which they would system-
> atically identify their interests and set realistic objectives with respect to all issues, not
> only those where they were *demandeurs*, and would pursue these objectives by formulat-
> ing explicit and technically sound proposals in alliance with other like-minded countries.
> This would be a concrete way of both strengthening the multilateral trading system and
> enhancing the participation of developing countries in the decision-making process.[318]

By developing a common 'positive agenda' and coordinating their actions, it is possible for developing-country Members to exercise considerable influence in the
WTO through their numbers and their growing importance in the world economy.

The Doha Ministerial Declaration of November 2001 stated:

> Recognizing the challenges posed by an expanding WTO membership, we confirm our
> collective responsibility to ensure internal transparency and the effective participation of
> all Members.[319]

The success of the Doha Development Round depends, to a large extent, on
whether Members will be able to meet that collective responsibility of ensuring
internal transparency and the effective participation of all Members.

Questions and Assignments 2.22

Can developing-country Members effectively participate in the WTO
decision-making process? If not, why? What are green room meetings?
Could the WTO function without green room or similar meetings? How
can the effective participation of developing-country Members best be
ensured?

---

[316] See General Council, *Minutes of Meetings*, WT/GC/M/73, dated 11 March 2002; WT/GC/M/74, dated 1 July
2002; WT/GC/M/75, dated 27 September 2002; and WT/GC/M/77, dated 13 February 2002. See also
Communication from Cuba, Dominican Republic, Egypt, Honduras, India, Indonesia, Jamaica, Kenya,
Malaysia, Mauritius, Pakistan, Sri Lanka, Tanzania, Uganda and Zimbabwe, *Preparatory Process in Geneva
and Negotiating Procedure at the Ministerial Conferences*, WT/GC/W/471, dated 24 April 2002.
[317] See above, pp. 99–102.
[318] R. Ricupero, 'Rebuilding Confidence in the Multilateral Trading System: Closing the Legitimacy Gap', in
G. Sampson (ed.), *The Role of the World Trade Organization in Global Governance* (United Nations University
Press, 2001), 39–40.   [319] WT/MIN(01)/DEC/1, dated 20 November 2001, para. 10.

2.6.5. Involvement of NGOs

The WTO is portrayed, by many, as a secretive organisation in which the governments (of a few major trading nations), unsupervised by parliaments or civil society, set the agenda and push through rules that affect the welfare of people worldwide. WTO decision-making has been described as undemocratic and lacking transparency.

2.6.5.1. Requirements of democratic decision-making

To the extent that rule-making, as a result of globalisation, is shifting from the national to the international level, international rule-making must meet the standards of democratic decision-making. For decision-making to be democratic, it must, as Markus Krajewski argued, involve either directly, or more likely through representation, those that will be affected by the decisions taken. Furthermore, decisions must be reached as a result of an open and transparent exchange of rational arguments which allows those represented to 'watch-dog' the representatives.[320]

If these standards of democratic decision-making are applied to WTO decision-making, one could argue that, in a narrow, formal sense, those affected by WTO decisions are involved, through representation, in the decision-making process. At least for democratic WTO Members, it is true that diplomats act in the WTO under the instructions of their governments, and that these governments are controlled by parliaments which represent the people. In practice, however, the so-called 'legitimacy chain', the chain between those affected by the decision and those making the decision, is too long and not transparent.[321] Parliamentary participation in, and control over, WTO processes is very weak in most Members (including democratic Members).

With regard to the other standard of democratic decision-making, namely, that decisions are reached as a result of an open and transparent exchange of rational arguments, the WTO's performance is particularly poor. WTO decision-making is characterised by its non-transparent, selective and secretive nature. Moreover, it has been said that WTO decision-making is dominated by bargaining (and sometimes irrational trade-offs) instead of arguing (and exchanging rational arguments).[322]

2.6.5.2. Article V:2 of the WTO Agreement

Over the last decade, NGOs have demanded a greater role in WTO decision-making in order to make this process more democratic and to give it more legitimacy. As was discussed above, Article V:2 of the *WTO Agreement* empowers the General Council to:

---

[320] See M. Krajewski, 'Democratic Legitimacy and Constitutional Perspectives of WTO Law', *Journal of World Trade*, 2001, 167–86.   [321] See *ibid.*, 170.   [322] See *ibid.*, 177.

make appropriate arrangements for consultations and cooperation with non-governmental organizations concerned with matters related to those of the WTO.[323]

It is interesting to note that the 1948 *Havana Charter for an International Trade Organization* contained a similarly worded provision.[324] As discussed above, the ITO never became operational, and the GATT 1947 filled the gap left by the ITO for almost fifty years. The GATT, however, did not have any provision relating to cooperation with NGOs. Under the GATT, informal and *ad hoc* contacts existed with NGOs.[325] However, NGOs were denied accreditation and access to meetings and conferences. That was also the case for the Marrakesh Conference at which the *WTO Agreement* was signed. NGOs as such were not invited to Marrakesh; those NGOs present were registered as members of the press.

2.6.5.3. *The pros and cons of greater NGO involvement*

The debate on the desirability of greater involvement of NGOs in the work of the WTO is multifaceted, as the abundant literature on the issue clearly shows. Summarising that literature, this section gives a brief overview of the arguments for and against greater involvement of NGOs.

There are four arguments *in favour* of greater NGO involvement. First, NGO participation will enhance the WTO decision-making process because NGOs will provide information, arguments and perspectives that governments do not bring forward. NGOs have a wealth of specialised knowledge, resources and analytical capacity. As Daniel Esty noted, NGOs can and should function as 'intellectual competitors' to governments in the quest for optimal policies.[326] In fact, governments often lack the resources and the specific expertise necessary to investigate certain issues. NGOs may frequently be of help, enhancing the resources and expertise available and enriching the policy debate.

Secondly, NGO participation will increase the legitimacy of the WTO. Public confidence in the WTO will increase when NGOs have the opportunity to be heard and to observe the decision-making process. NGOs will contribute to ensuring that decisions result from the open and transparent exchange of rational arguments rather than from shady bargaining. Moreover, NGOs can play an important role in disseminating information at the national level, ensuring broader public support and understanding.

Thirdly, transnational interests and concerns may not be adequately represented by any national government. By allowing NGO involvement in WTO discussions, the WTO would hear about important issues which are international in nature.

---

[323] See above, pp. 97–8.
[324] See Article 87.2 of the Final Act of the United Nations Conference on Trade and Employment (the *Havana Charter for an International Trade Organization*).
[325] The GATT did allow business NGOs to participate in GATT working parties in the 1950s. See S. Charnovitz, 'Two Centuries of Participation: NGOs and International Governance', *Michigan Journal of International Law*, 1997, 255.
[326] See D. Esty, 'Non-Governmental Organizations at the World Trade Organization: Cooperation, Competition, or Exclusion', *Journal of International Economic Law*, 1998, 136 (reproduced by permission of Oxford University Press).

Finally, civil society participation in the debate at the national level is only an option for those WTO Members with open and democratic processes at the national level. This is not the case in all WTO Members. Hearing NGOs at the WTO can compensate for the fact that NGOs are not always and everywhere heard at the national level.

There are equally four main arguments *against* greater involvement of NGOs in the work of the WTO. First, NGO involvement may lead the decision-making process to be captured by special interests.[327] Trade liberalisation produces diffuse and hard-to-quantify benefits for the general public while producing visible harm to specific and well-organised interests.[328] The NGOs seeking access to the WTO are often entities representing special interests, not the interests of the general public. Thus, special interests may gain undue influence.[329]

Secondly, many NGOs lack legitimacy. They are neither accountable to an electorate nor representative in a general way. NGOs typically advocate relatively narrow interests. Unlike governments, they do not balance all of society's interests. It is legitimate to ask questions regarding the actual constituency of an NGO and its financial backing.

Thirdly, most developing-country Members object to greater involvement of NGOs in the WTO because they view most NGOs, and in particular NGOs focusing on environmental or labour issues, as inimical to their interests. Moreover, NGOs of industrialised Members tend to be well organised and well financed. Allowing NGOs a bigger role may therefore further marginalise developing-country Members within the WTO decision-making process. In other words, it may tilt the negotiating balance further to their disadvantage.[330]

Finally, WTO decision-making, with its consensus requirement, is already very difficult. NGO involvement will make negotiations and decision-making even more difficult. Further transparency will enable private interest groups to frustrate the negotiating powers of governments in WTO fora. Gary Sampson noted in this respect:

> national representatives must on occasion subordinate certain national interests in order to achieve marginally acceptable or sub-optimal compromises that, by definition, require trade-offs. Doubt is expressed whether such a system could continue to work effectively if these trade-offs were open to scrutiny by precisely those special interest groups that would have opposed them.[331]

2.6.5.4. The 'external transparency' debate

In the autumn of 2000, one year after the Seattle debacle, the General Council held informal but intensive consultations on what was referred to as the issue of

---

[327] See J. Dunoff, 'The Misguided Debate over NGO Participation at the WTO', *Journal of International Economic Law*, 1998, 437 (reproduced by permission of Oxford University Press).   [328] See above, pp. 9–15.
[329] See Dominic Eagleton, 'Under the Influence: Exposing Undue Corporate Influence over Policy-making at the World Trade Organization', 24 January 2006, Actionaid International, available at www.actionaid.org/docs/under_the_influence.pdf, visited on 1 December 2007.
[330] This argument has in recent years lost some of its validity as some NGOs based in developed countries have become effective champions of the cause of developing countries.
[331] G. Sampson, 'Overview', in G. Sampson (ed.), *The Role of the World Trade Organization in Global Governance* (United Nations University Press, 2001), 11.

'external transparency', i.e. the issue of the participation of civil society/NGOs in the work of the WTO. A number of Members, including the European Communities, the United States, Canada, Australia and Hong Kong, submitted position papers for these informal consultations. From these position papers, it is clear that no Member wishes to undermine the government-to-government, or intergovernmental, character of the WTO. Moreover, most, if not all, Members are of the opinion that the dialogue with civil society is first and foremost a responsibility for Member governments. The primary responsibility for synthesising the views and concerns of all domestic stakeholders (NGOs, special interest groups, etc.) into an overall national position must fall on the national governments. However, on whether NGOs can and should play a more important role in the work of the WTO, the positions of Members differ significantly. On the one hand, the position championed by many of the industrialised Members is that the involvement of NGOs in the work of the WTO should be a 'two-way street'. The involvement of NGOs should be a 'give and take' relationship; it involves not only informing NGOs about the work and activities of the WTO but also being informed by NGOs on issues of relevance to the WTO. On the other hand, the position of many developing-country Members, a position well reflected in the submission of Hong Kong, is that the relationship between the WTO and NGOs can only be a 'one-way street'. Hong Kong insists that a distinction is made between enhancing transparency to the civil society (i.e. informing the public about the WTO) *and* making provision for their direct participation in the decision-making process (including a right to put forward their views in WTO meetings and thus influence the outcome of discussions). Hong Kong is 'not convinced of the desirability of adopting proposals which seek to make provisions for direct participation of civil society'.[332]

The United States takes the most radical position in favour of participation of NGOs in the work of the WTO. It has argued that some of the WTO council and committee meetings should be opened to NGOs. It has proposed that WTO bodies would hold an annual meeting to which NGOs would be invited and at which they would be allowed to make submissions. The United States has also suggested opening the meetings of the Trade Policy Review Body to the public, perhaps by webcasting these meetings. Finally, the United States has proposed organising symposia and other forms of informal dialogue with civil society on a broader range of WTO issues and on a more regular basis.[333] Along the same lines but less radical, the European Communities has proposed that the meetings of the Trade Policy Review Body be opened (on a voluntary basis) to parliamentarians and NGOs of the Member reviewed. It has also suggested that the WTO could hold an annual open meeting at ministerial or senior official level combined with a symposium for dialogue with civil society as well as a meeting of parliamentarians of WTO Members. As already mentioned above, the

---

[332] Submission from Hong Kong, *General Council Informal Consultations on External Transparency*, WT/GC/W/418, dated 31 October 2000, para. 9.
[333] See Submission from the United States, *General Council Informal Consultations on External Transparency*, WT/GC/W/413/Rev.1, dated 13 October 2000.

European Communities has also proposed the establishment of a WTO Parliamentary Consultative Assembly as a forum for inter-parliamentary dialogue on WTO issues.[334]

Stepping on thin ice, the then WTO Director-General, Mike Moore, noted in March 2002 with regard to the role of NGOs in the WTO:

> We plan special workshops where both critics and friends will have time put aside to make their case. This includes the environmentalists, the ICFTU, the Chamber of Commerce, the Third World Network, other development NGOs like Oxfam, Parliamentarians, and hopefully Party Political Internationals. I believe these kinds of exchanges are all very healthy and can be a constructive opportunity to learn and improve upon our performance, the better to serve our Member Governments and the people.
>
> The WTO will always remain an Inter-governmental organization, because ultimately it is always our member Governments and Parliaments that must ratify any agreements we conclude. We need to encourage better-focused and more constructive inputs from civil society. *They should be given a voice, but not a vote.* But in return, we should seek from civil society and its representatives a formal code of conduct, and much greater transparency and accountability from them to us and to their membership.[335]
>
> [Emphasis added]

2.6.5.5. Modes of interaction between the WTO and NGOs

Pursuant to Article V:2 of the *WTO Agreement*, the General Council adopted a set of Guidelines, in July 1996, regarding the relations of the WTO with non-governmental organisations.[336] In deciding on these Guidelines, Members recognised 'the role NGOs can play to increase the awareness of the public in respect of WTO activities'.[337] Members agreed to improve transparency by making documents available more promptly. NGOs were recognised to be 'a valuable resource' that can 'contribute to the accuracy and richness of the public debate'.[338] In the 1996 Guidelines, it was agreed that interaction with NGOs should be developed through various means such as:

- the organisation of symposia for NGOs on specific WTO-related issues;
- informal arrangements to receive the information NGOs may wish to make available for consultation by interested delegations;
- the continuation of the past practice of the WTO Secretariat of responding to requests for general information and briefings about the WTO; and
- participation of chairpersons of WTO councils and committees in discussions and meetings with NGOs in their personal capacity.

The 1996 Guidelines also make the limits of NGO involvement clear. In the last paragraph of the Guidelines, the General Council refers to the special character of the WTO as both a legally binding intergovernmental treaty of rights and

---

[334] See Discussion Paper from the European Community to the WTO General Council on *Improving the Functioning of the WTO System*, WT/GC/W/412, dated 6 October 2000.

[335] M. Moore, *How Trade Liberalization Impacts on Employment*, Speech to the International Labour Organization, 18 March 2002, available at www.wto.org/english/news_e/spmm_e/spmm80_e.htm, visited on 19 September 2007.

[336] General Council, *Guidelines for Arrangements on Relations with Non-Governmental Organizations*, WT/L/162, dated 23 July 1996.   [337] *Ibid.*, para. II. See also above, p. 153.   [338] *Ibid.*, para. IV.

obligations among its Members *and* a forum for negotiations. The General Council then concludes:

> As a result of extensive discussions, there is currently a broadly held view that it would not be possible for NGOs to be directly involved in the work of the WTO or its meetings. Closer consultation and cooperation with NGOs can also be met constructively through appropriate processes at the national level where lies primary responsibility for taking into account the different elements of public interest which are brought to bear on trade policy-making.[339]

In 1996, the position of the General Council was clearly that NGOs could not, and should not, be *directly* involved in the work of the WTO.

Subsequent to the adoption of the 1996 Guidelines, the External Relations Division was created within the WTO Secretariat to deal with contacts with civil society and NGOs in particular. Another, albeit modest, 'breakthrough' of sorts in the relationship between the WTO and NGOs was realised in Singapore in December 1996, when NGOs were invited to attend the plenary meetings of the First Session of the Ministerial Conference and an NGO Centre with facilities for organising gatherings and workshops was set up alongside the official Conference Centre. However, the 108 NGOs that attended did not have observer status. They were not allowed to make any statements and could only attend the plenary meetings of the Session. The WTO Secretariat accredited all non-profit organisations that could point to activities related to those of the WTO and did not examine the representativeness and/or legitimacy of the NGOs wishing to attend the Ministerial Conference. Since the Singapore Session, the number of NGOs attending the sessions of the Ministerial Conference has increased with each session, with the exception of the Doha Session when limited local facilities did not allow for a large number of NGOs. At these sessions, the participation of NGOs remained limited to attending the plenary meetings at which heads of government and trade ministers merely read out short prepared statements and which are now also webcasted. Access to the working meetings is denied. During the sessions, NGOs are kept informed about the issues under discussion through regular briefings by the WTO Secretariat.

Figure 2.5 Trend in NGO representation at Ministerial Conference sessions[340]

Ministerial	Number of eligible NGOs	NGOs who attended	Number of participants
Singapore 1996	159	108	235
Geneva 1998	153	128	362
Seattle 1999	776	686	approx. 1,500
Doha 2001	651	370	370
Cancún 2003	961	795	1,578
Hong Kong 2005	1,065	811	1,596

[339] *Ibid.*, para. VI.　[340] See WTO Secretariat, *WTO Annual Report 2007*, available at www.wto.org/english/res_e/booksp_e/anrep_e/anrep07_e.pdf, visited on 20 September 2007.

Over the years, the WTO Secretariat has also organised a number of symposia for NGOs and Members on specific topics. More recently the WTO Secretariat has organised a yearly WTO Public Symposium or, as it has been called since 2006, a WTO Public Forum, with a very broad agenda of topics of interest to a wide range of NGOs. The 2007 WTO Public Forum on 'How Can the WTO Help Harness Globalization?' was held at the WTO in Geneva on 4 and 5 October 2007.[341] In his opening remarks, Director-General Pascal Lamy stated:

> Today, I am proud to announce that 1,750 participants from across the globe have registered for this Forum – in and of itself an indicator of the extent of globalization! This number testifies to the relevance of the WTO to the wider world, and it is precisely for this reason that the WTO must continue to consult that wider world on how best it can meet its needs and aspirations. Registered today are various types of non-governmental organizations – from environmental, to human rights, to labour rights groups; numerous parliamentarians; various academic institutions; members of the business community; journalists; lawyers; representatives of other international organizations; and students. It is precisely this very broad spectrum of society that the WTO was hoping to tap into. So thank you all for coming in such record numbers, and thank you for helping us make this year's event successful.[342]

As with the 2006 Public Forum on 'What WTO for the XXIst Century?' and the 2005 Public Symposium on 'WTO After 10 Years: Global Problems and Multilateral Solutions', the 2007 Public Forum was well attended and generally considered to make a valuable contribution to the 'dialogue' between the WTO and civil society.

With respect to access to official documents, WTO Members agreed in May 2002, after years of discussion, to accelerate the de-restriction of official WTO documents. Pursuant to the Decision of the General Council of 14 May 2002 on *Procedures for the Circulation and De-restriction of WTO Documents*, most WTO documents are now immediately available to the public and those documents that are initially restricted are de-restricted much faster.[343]

Since 1998, the WTO website has a special section for NGOs, 'For NGOs', containing information on WTO activities and initiatives for, or of interest to, NGOs.[344] More generally, on the WTO website and the access for civil society to online information about the WTO, the One World Trust, a British NGO, reported in its *Global Accountability Report 2003* as follows:

> Information on the WTO's trade activities is excellent. The WTO provides access to the legal texts of its agreements by topic, alongside a full, non-technical description of the law. This is very important given the technical nature of much of the work it covers. The public are able to review the extent to which members have implemented agreements

---

[341] See www.wto.org/english/forums_e/public_forum2007_e/programme_e.htm, visited on 20 November 2007.   [342] See www.wto.org/english/news_e/sppl_e/sppl73_e.htm, visited on 4 October 2007.

[343] See General Council, *Procedures for the Circulation and De-restriction of WTO Documents*, WT/L/452, dated 16 May 2002. These Procedures replaced the *Decision on De-restriction* of the General Council of July 1996, which introduced the principle of immediate, unrestricted circulation of WTO documents, but subjected this principle to important exceptions. Minutes of WTO meetings and WTO Secretariat background papers were de-restricted only after the lapse of eight to nine months. Under the 2002 Procedures, the time period for de-restriction has been reduced to an average of six to twelve weeks.

[344] See www.wto.org/english/forums_e/ngo_e/ngo_e.htm, visited on 16 September 2007.

and view the process and documentation surrounding any decisions taken by the disputes panel. The information available from the committees is standardised. Each committee produces an annual report of its work for the General Council outlining its activities.[345]

Note that the WTO Secretariat compiles a monthly list of position papers of NGOs received by the Secretariat. Members can obtain a copy of these papers from the Secretariat or on the WTO website.[346] In September 1998, the WTO Secretariat also initiated regular briefings for NGOs on specific issues. Building on these efforts, the WTO Secretariat started in 2007 a series of issue-specific dialogues with civil society. These dialogues offer an opportunity to Geneva-based NGOs, WTO Members and Secretariat staff to exchange – in an informal manner and off the record – information and views on specific issues. The first of these dialogues took place in April 2007 and related to the *Development Component of the Doha Development Round.*[347]

Questions and Assignments 2.23

Describe how the WTO currently interacts with civil society and the role NGOs play within the WTO. How would the United States and the European Communities like to change this role? Would the WTO benefit from a greater role for NGOs in WTO decision-making processes?

2.6.6. Form and legal basis of WTO decisions

Having addressed the two most controversial issues regarding WTO decision-making, namely, the effective participation of developing-country Members and the role of NGOs in the process of WTO decision-making, this section finally examines an aspect of WTO decision-making which is often overlooked: the form and legal basis of WTO decisions. Consistency regarding the form of WTO decisions and the systematic and reasoned reference in decisions to their legal basis would enhance the transparency of WTO decision-making and contribute to the democratic accountability of the WTO.

However, the old GATT legacy of diplomacy and pragmatism is still clearly visible in the formal aspects of the decisions taken by WTO bodies. As Pieter-Jan Kuijper, then Director of the WTO Legal Affairs Division, noted:

> [I]t is very often unclear whether any decision in the legal sense of the term has been taken. The WTO presently abounds in 'decisions' which have no legal basis whatsoever, are not presented in a standard legal format, but nevertheless purport to be 'decisions'. Many of such decisions are taken by a mere tap of the gavel. Moreover, the WTO organs are somewhat addicted to Chairman's statements. It must be admitted that they often present a useful way out of a dilemma. The Chairman pronounces them from the chair, usually after painstaking consultations with many delegations, but in principle

---

[345] H. Kovach, C. Neligan and S. Burall, *Power Without Accountability: The Global Accountability Report 2003* (One World Trust, 2003), 15.
[346] See www.wto.org/english/forums_e/ngo_e/pospap_e.htm, visited on 16 September 2007.
[347] See www.wto.org/english/forums_e/ngo_e/ngo_dialogue_e.htm, visited on 20 November 2007.

they are not fully negotiated. Nobody contradicts them, but nobody has accepted them either and everybody can live in the illusion that this statement is the Chair's responsibility alone, does not really represent a true consensus or decision but, as if by magic, will still be followed and respected by everyone. Except in the end, of course, in the dispute settlement procedure, as the Appellate Body made only too clear when it treated the various 'decisions' and 'Chairman's statements' in the Foreign Sales Corporation case.[348]

To avoid the demise of such 'decisions' at the hands of panels or of the Appellate Body, Pieter-Jan Kuijper suggested that it would be useful to have a clear distinction between:

- *decisions* which have binding legal effect and which should be based on a specific legal basis giving the power for such binding decisions; and
- *recommendations* which are just that: mere recommendations with no binding effect.

Furthermore, Kuijper suggested that it might also be useful to make a distinction between:

- *decisions with external effect*, i.e. imposing legal obligations or legal rights on Members; and
- *decisions with internal effect*, i.e. binding only the WTO organs.[349]

Kuijper has also pointed out that it is often unclear *who* takes the decision. General Council decisions in certain instances still begin with the words, 'the Members'. Kuijper argued:

Showing clearly that WTO decisions, though as a political matter of course still taken by the Members, are legal acts of the Ministerial Conference or one of the Councils is the simple consequence of the fact that an international organization like the WTO has a separate (legal) life from that of its Members.[350]

Finally, it is quite obvious that in the past little attention was given to the legal form of the text of decisions. As a result:

decisions are highly variegated in this respect: some state no legal basis, some have the legal basis at the beginning, some at the end of the preamble, sometimes there is no consistent reference to proposals made or reports forming the basis of the decision, often there is no consistent pattern of building the reasoning (the *motifs*) underpinning the decision, etc.; a consistent way of presenting the operational clauses is also often lacking.[351]

Recently, some degree of uniformity with respect to the legal form of the text of decisions has been achieved. This is an important step towards more transparency and accountability of WTO decision-making. However, much work remains to be done.

---

[348] P. J. Kuijper, 'Some Institutional Issues Presently Before the WTO', in D. Kennedy and J. Southwick (eds.), *The Political Economy of International Trade Law: Essays in Honor of Robert E. Hudec* (Cambridge University Press, 2002), 106.   [349] See *ibid.*, 106–7.   [350] *Ibid.*, 107.   [351] *Ibid.*

Questions and Assignments 2.24
Does the WTO give sufficient attention to the form and legal basis of its decisions? If not, how could this be improved and why would such improvement be welcome?

2.7. OTHER ISSUES

2.7.1. Status of the WTO

Article VIII of the *WTO Agreement* states:

1. The WTO shall have legal personality, and shall be accorded by each of its Members such legal capacity as may be necessary for the exercise of its functions.
2. The WTO shall be accorded by each of its Members such privileges and immunities as are necessary for the exercise of its functions.
3. The officials of the WTO and the representatives of the Members shall similarly be accorded by each of its Members such privileges and immunities as are necessary for the independent exercise of their functions in connection with the WTO.
4. The privileges and immunities to be accorded by a Member to the WTO, its officials, and the representatives of its Members shall be similar to the privileges and immunities stipulated in the Convention on the Privileges and Immunities of the Specialised Agencies, approved by the General Assembly of the United Nations on 21 November 1947.
5. The WTO may conclude a headquarters agreement.

The *WTO Headquarters Agreement* with Switzerland addresses the matter of the privileges and immunities of the WTO, its officials and the representatives of WTO Members in great detail.[352]

It deserves to be mentioned that the WTO is *not* part of the UN 'family'. It is a fully independent international organisation with its own particular 'corporate' culture. John Jackson noted with regard to the question of 'specialised agency of the UN' status for the WTO, that this question:

was explicitly considered and explicitly rejected by the WTO members, possibly because of the skepticism of some members about the UN budgetary and personnel policies and their alleged inefficiencies.[353]

2.7.2. The WTO budget

The total WTO budget for 2007 amounted to almost 182 million Swiss francs.[354] In recent years, the WTO budget has been increased to allow the WTO

---

[352] For the *WTO Headquarters Agreement*, see WT/GC/1 and Add.1.
[353] J. Jackson, *The World Trade Organization: Constitution and Jurisprudence* (Royal Institute of International Affairs, 1998), 52.
[354] See www.wto.org/english/thewto_e/secre_e/budget07_e.htm, visited on 15 September 2007. CHF182 million is equivalent to €110 million.

Secretariat to give more technical assistance to developing countries and contribute more to capacity-building in these countries. However, in comparison with the annual budget of other international organisations or some NGOs, the WTO's annual budget remains quite modest. In 2001, the then WTO Director-General, Mike Moore, noted that the World Wildlife Fund had three times the resources of the WTO.[355] The modest budget of the WTO reflects the small size of the Secretariat and the relatively limited scope of the WTO's activities outside Geneva. Peter Sutherland has, however, criticised the limited size of the WTO budget:

> Lacking either the courage of their own convictions or confidence in their ability to prevail over domestic opposition, the chief financial backers of the WTO have failed to provide adequate funding for a WTO Secretariat (by far the smallest of all the major multilateral institutions) that is already overburdened by technical assistance demands as well as dispute settlement cases and new accessions.[356]

Article VII:1 of the *WTO Agreement* sets out the basic rules applicable to the draft WTO budget presented by the Director-General:

> The Director-General shall present to the Committee on Budget, Finance and Administration the annual budget estimate and financial statement of the WTO. The Committee on Budget, Finance and Administration shall review the annual budget estimate and the financial statement presented by the Director-General and make recommendations thereon to the General Council. The annual budget estimate shall be subject to approval by the General Council.

With respect to the financial contributions to be made by Members to the budget of the WTO, Article VII:2 of the *WTO Agreement* states:

> The Committee on Budget, Finance and Administration shall propose to the General Council financial regulations which shall include provisions setting out:
>
> a. the scale of contributions apportioning the expenses of the WTO among its Members; and
> b. the measures to be taken in respect of Members in arrears.

Pursuant to Article VII:4 of the *WTO Agreement*, each Member shall promptly contribute to the WTO its share in the expenses of the WTO in accordance with the financial regulations adopted by the General Council. In November 1995, the General Council adopted the WTO *Financial Regulations* and the *Financial Rules*.[357]

The contributions of Members to the WTO budget are established according to a formula based on their share of international trade in goods and services for the last three years for which data are available. Members whose share in the total international trade of all WTO Members is less than 0.015 per cent make a

---

[355] Reported by F. Lewis, 'The Anti-Globalization Spoilers Are Going Global', *International Herald Tribune*, 6 July 2001.

[356] P. Sutherland, J. Sewell and D. Weiner, 'Challenges Facing the WTO and Policies to Address Global Governance', in G. Sampson (ed.), *The Role of the World Trade Organization in Global Governance* (United Nations University Press, 2001), 82.

[357] Both the *Financial Regulations* and the *Financial Rules* were revised in 2007. For the *Financial Regulations*, see WT/L/156/Rev.2, dated 21 May 2007; for the *Financial Rules*, see WT/L/157/Rev.1, dated 21 May 2007.

minimum contribution to the budget of 0.015 per cent. The Member States of the European Union are by far the largest contributors to the WTO budget. The European Communities itself does not contribute to the WTO budget. In the calculation of the contribution of the EU Member States, the intra-Community trade is also taken into account, which explains the high level of their contributions. Altogether, the EU Member States contributed, in 2007, 42 per cent of the WTO budget; the United States 14.9 per cent; Japan 5.8 per cent; China 4.7 per cent; Canada 3.7 per cent; Hong Kong 3 per cent; Korea 2.5 per cent; Mexico 2.2 per cent; Singapore 2.1 per cent; Chinese Taipei 1.9 per cent; Malaysia 1.3 per cent; Australia 1.1 per cent; Brazil 0.9 per cent; India 0.8 per cent; and Indonesia 0.8 per cent.[358]

As already discussed, Article VII:3 of the *WTO Agreement* provides that the annual budget and the financial regulations, setting out the contributions to be paid, are adopted by the General Council by a two-thirds majority comprising more than half of the Members of the WTO.[359]

In addition to the annual budget, the WTO also manages a number of trust funds, which have been contributed to by Members. Trust funds such as the Doha Development Agenda Global Trust Fund are used in support of special activities for technical cooperation and training meant to enable least-developed and developing countries to make better use of the WTO and draw greater benefit from the multilateral trading system.

Questions and Assignments 2.25

How is the WTO financed? How is the decision on the annual budget and on the contributions of Members to that budget taken? Who is the biggest contributor to the WTO budget?

2.8. SUMMARY

The WTO is a young international organisation with a long history. The origins of the WTO lie in the GATT 1947, which for almost fifty years was – after the 'still-birth' of the ITO in the late 1940s – the *de facto* international organisation for trade. While the GATT was successful with respect to the reduction of tariffs, effectively addressing the problems of international trade in goods and services in the era of economic globalisation would require a more 'sophisticated' institutional framework. The Uruguay Round negotiations resulted, in December 1993, in an agreement on the establishment of the World Trade Organization which was subsequently signed in Marrakesh, Morocco, in April 1994. The WTO has been operational since 1 January 1995.

---

[358] The actual contributions of each member to the budget can be found at www.wto.org/english/thewto_e/secre_e/contrib07_e.htm, visited on 1 December 2007.   [359] See above, pp. 122, 144.

Pursuant to the Preamble to the *WTO Agreement*, the ultimate objectives of the WTO are:

- the increase of standards of living;
- the attainment of full employment;
- the growth of real income and effective demand; and
- the expansion of production of, and trade in, goods and services.

However, it is clear from the Preamble that, in pursuing these objectives, the WTO must take into account the need for sustainable development and the needs of developing countries. The two main instruments, or means, to achieve the objectives of the WTO are:

- the reduction of trade barriers; and
- the elimination of discrimination.

The primary function of the WTO is to provide the common institutional framework for the conduct of trade relations among its Members. More specifically, the WTO has been assigned six widely defined functions:

- to facilitate the implementation, administration and operation of the WTO agreements;
- to be a forum for negotiations of new trade agreements;
- to settle trade disputes between its Members;
- to review the trade policies of its Members;
- to cooperate with other international organisations and non-governmental organisations; and
- to give technical assistance to developing-country Members to allow them to integrate into the world trading system and reap the benefits from international trade.

Since the accession of the People's Republic of China in December 2001, the WTO has been a quasi-universal organisation. Its 151 Members account for almost all international trade. Three out of every four WTO Members are developing countries. It is noteworthy that not only States but also autonomous customs territories can be, and are, Members of the WTO. Equally noteworthy is that both the European Communities *and* all Member States of the European Union are Members of the WTO. Accession to the WTO is a difficult process since candidates for membership have to negotiate an 'entrance ticket' of market access concessions, in addition to bringing their national legislation and practice into conformity with the obligations under the *WTO Agreement*. Members can, and do, in exceptional circumstances obtain temporary, partial waivers of their WTO obligations; they can also, but have not done so to date, withdraw from the WTO. With one exception of minor importance, the *WTO Agreement* does not provide for the possibility to expel Members from the WTO, even Members which systematically act inconsistently with their obligations under the WTO agreements or which are guilty of systematic gross violations of human rights or acts of aggression.

The WTO has a complex institutional structure which includes:

- at the *highest* level, the Ministerial Conference, which is in session only for a few days every two years;
- at a *second* level, the General Council, which exercises the powers of the Ministerial Conference in between its sessions; and the Dispute Settlement Body (DSB) and the Trade Policy Review Body (TPRB), which are both emanations of the General Council; and
- at *lower* levels, specialised councils and manifold committees and working parties.

The current Doha Development Round negotiations are conducted in special sessions of existing WTO bodies and in two, specially created, negotiating groups. The conduct of these negotiations is supervised by the Trade Negotiations Committee (TNC), which regularly reports to the General Council. Furthermore, the institutional structure of the WTO includes quasi-judicial and other non-political bodies as well as the WTO Secretariat, headed by the WTO Director-General. The WTO is a 'Member-driven' organisation. The Members – and not the Director-General or the WTO Secretariat – set the agenda, make proposals and take decisions. The Director-General and the WTO Secretariat act primarily as an 'honest broker' in, or a 'facilitator' of, the political decision-making processes in the WTO. Unlike other international organisations, the WTO does not have a permanent body through which the 'dialogue' between the WTO and civil society can take place. Furthermore, all WTO bodies (except for the non-political bodies) comprise all 151 Members of the WTO. Unlike other international organisations with a large membership, the WTO does not have an executive body, comprising only core WTO Members, to facilitate the process of deliberation and decision-making. To date, proposals for the establishment of a WTO consultative body, comprising representatives of civil society, and/or a WTO executive body, comprising core WTO Members, have received little support from WTO Members.

With respect to decision-making by WTO bodies, one can distinguish between the normal decision-making procedure, which applies as the default procedure, and a number of special procedures for specific decisions. In theory, WTO Members, under both the normal and most of the special procedures, take decisions by consensus, and, if that is not possible, by majority voting. Every Member has one vote, except the European Communities which has as many votes as the European Union has Member States. In practice, however, the WTO seldom resorts to voting. WTO decisions are made almost exclusively by consensus. Decision-making by consensus is at the heart of the WTO system and is regarded as a fundamental democratic guarantee. However, the consensus requirement renders decision-making by the WTO difficult and susceptible to paralysis.

While decision-making by consensus should, in principle, ensure the participation in the decision-making process of all Members, including developing-country Members, many developing-country Members feel marginalised. The effective participation of developing-country Members in WTO decision-making has become one of the principal institutional challenges of the WTO. It is gener-ally recognised that it is not possible to negotiate effectively in bodies compris-ing all 151 WTO Members. Therefore, in the GATT and now the WTO, informal mechanisms have been developed that allow for negotiations on difficult issues among a restricted number of Members. While they are indispensable, these mechanisms, and in particular the green room meetings, have triggered much criticism from developing-country Members. Discussions among WTO Members since the ill-fated Seattle Session of the Ministerial Conference in 1999 have led to informal agreement on a number of checks on negotiations among a restricted number of Members. Furthermore, it has been recognised that to ensure a more effective involvement of developing-country Members in WTO decision-making, the lack of expertise and resources of these Members has to be addressed. At present, a considerable effort to help developing-country Members with capacity-building is being undertaken by the WTO as well as by individual developed-country Members.

Apart from the effective involvement of developing-country Members, another aspect of WTO decision-making that has given rise to considerable con-troversy is the role of NGOs in the decision-making process. Over the last decade, NGOs have demanded a bigger role in the WTO decision-making process in order to make this process more democratic and to give it more legitimacy. The response of Members to the demands of NGOs has been mixed. No Member wishes to undermine the intergovernmental character of the WTO. Most, if not all, Members are of the opinion that the dialogue with civil society is first and foremost a responsibility of Member governments and needs to be conducted at the national level. However, a number of developed-country Members have sup-ported NGOs in their demand for a bigger role at the international level. They have campaigned for more transparency in the work of the WTO and for some degree of direct involvement of NGOs in the WTO decision-making process. On the other hand, many developing-country Members have strongly objected to NGO involvement. They fear that granting NGOs a bigger role may further mar-ginalise developing-country Members within the WTO decision-making process. Positions on the appropriate role of NGOs in the WTO decision-making process thus sharply diverge. In recent years, however, NGOs have been given more of a voice through WTO public symposia or fora organised for and with NGOs and through the systematic transfer by the WTO Secretariat of NGO position papers to WTO Members. Furthermore, public access to WTO official documents and information on WTO policies and activities has been enhanced by the 2002 Decision on De-restriction and by improvements to the WTO website. Also, the regular briefings of NGOs by the WTO Secretariat and frequent, informal con-tacts between the Secretariat and NGOs have contributed to the dialogue between the WTO and civil society.

WTO Members acknowledge the institutional problems confronting the WTO:

- the effective participation of developing-country Members; and
- the 'dialogue' of the WTO with civil society, and in particular NGOs.

They realise that, if left unaddressed, these problems will undermine the legitimacy and/or the effectiveness of the WTO as an international organisation to promote trade, to balance trade with other societal values and interests, and to advance the integration of developing countries in the world trading system.

2.9. EXERCISE: TO JOIN OR NOT TO JOIN?

The Parliament of the Republic of Newland has approved – by a narrow margin – the Government's plans to start negotiations on accession to the WTO. However, the opposition continues its campaign against Newland's accession to the WTO in the hope of turning public opinion in Newland against WTO membership. In a series of interviews and speeches the charismatic leader of the opposition claims that:

- for many years Newland's best diplomats and negotiators will be caught up in never-ending, very complex negotiations on accession;
- Newland will have to make many amendments to its domestic legislation;
- should Newland be unable to meet some of its obligations under the *WTO Agreement*, it will have no other option than to withdraw from the WTO;
- as a Member, Newland will have to grant market access to goods and services from Evilland, an original WTO Member, but a country with a notoriously bad human rights record;
- the WTO is controlled by the European Communities (which holds no less than twenty-seven votes) and the United States;
- Newland, as a developing country, will not be able to participate effectively in WTO decision-making;
- the WTO is directed by a powerful group of faceless international bureaucrats, headed by the WTO Director-General, who is handpicked by the Quad;
- the confidentiality of government-to-government negotiations on trade matters is not guaranteed as special interest groups have access to meetings of WTO bodies and have immediate access to all official documents; and
- NGOs, none of which is friendly to the economic and trade interests of Newland, have a voice in WTO decision-making.

A recent poll showed that the opposition's campaign against WTO accession is succeeding and that public opinion in Newland is turning against accession. To reverse the tide, Newland's Government decides to engage in a debate with the opposition in Parliament. The Minister of Foreign Affairs has taken it upon herself to reply to each of the claims of the opposition leader. She wishes to do so with legal, rather than political, arguments. You have been instructed to prepare speaking notes for the Minister.

WTO dispute settlement

Contents

3.1. INTRODUCTION

The WTO agreements provide for many wide-ranging rules concerning international trade in goods, trade in services and trade-related aspects of intellectual property rights.[1] In view of the importance of their impact, economic and otherwise, it is not surprising that WTO Members do not always agree on the correct interpretation and application of these rules. Members frequently argue about whether or not a particular law or practice of a Member constitutes a violation of a right or obligation provided for in a WTO agreement. The WTO has a remarkable system to settle such disputes between WTO Members concerning their rights and obligations under the WTO agreements.

The WTO dispute settlement system has been operational for thirteen years now. In that period it has arguably been the most prolific of all international dispute settlement systems. Between 1 January 1995 and 1 December 2007, a total of 369 disputes had been brought to the WTO for resolution.[2] That is more than were brought to the GATT, the WTO's predecessor, in the forty-seven years between 1948 and 1995.[3] In almost a quarter of the disputes brought to the WTO for resolution, the parties were able to reach an amicable solution through consultations, or the dispute was otherwise resolved without recourse to adjudication.[4] In other disputes, parties have resorted to adjudication.[5] The WTO dispute settlement system has been used by developed-country Members and developing-country Members alike.[6]

Some of the disputes brought to the WTO dispute settlement system have triggered considerable controversy and public debate and have attracted much media attention. This has been the case, for example, for disputes on national legislation for the protection of public health or the environment, such as:

- the *EC – Hormones* dispute on the European Communities' import ban on meat from cattle treated with growth hormones;[7]
- the *US – Shrimp* dispute on the US import ban on shrimp harvested with nets that kill sea turtles;[8]
- the *EC – Asbestos* dispute on a French ban on asbestos and asbestos-containing products;[9] and

---

[1] For an overview, see above, pp. 42–51.

[2] I.e. the number of requests for consultations notified to the DSB until 1 December 2007. See below, pp. 269–74, and see www.worldtradelaw.net/dsc/database/searchcomplaints.asp, visited on 1 December 2007.

[3] Between 1948 and 1994, a total of 132 GATT dispute settlement reports were issued, while since 1995 a total of 103 WTO panel reports issued. See WT/DS/OV/31, dated 22 August 2007.

[4] Note that the group of otherwise resolved disputes also includes those where measures have been terminated and/or panel requests withdrawn. See below, pp. 173, 219–25.   [5] *Ibid.*

[6] The most active user of the system has been the United States, closely followed by the European Communities. The system has, however, also been used 'against' the United States more often than against any other Member, the European Communities being a distant second in this respect. For statistics on complainants and respondents in the WTO dispute settlement system, see www.worldtradelaw.net.   [7] *EC – Hormones*, complaints by the US and Canada. See below, pp. 848–52.

[8] *US – Shrimp*, complaint by India, Malaysia, Pakistan and Thailand. See below, pp. 181–2.

[9] *EC – Asbestos*, complaint by Canada. See below, pp. 374–82.

- the *EC – Approval and Marketing of Biotech Products* dispute on measures affecting the approval and marketing of genetically modified products in the European Union.[10]

Also the *EC – Bananas III* dispute on the European Communities' preferential import regime for bananas was, for many years, headline news.[11] Other highly 'sensitive' disputes include the *EC and Certain Member States – Large Civil Aircraft* and *US – Large Civil Aircraft* disputes concerning subsidies to Airbus and Boeing respectively.[12]

The WTO dispute settlement system, which has been in operation since 1 January 1995, was not established out of the blue. It is not an entirely novel system. On the contrary, this system is based on, and has taken on board, almost fifty years of experience in the resolution of trade disputes in the context of the GATT 1947. Article 3.1 of the DSU states:

> Members affirm their adherence to the principles for the management of disputes heretofore applied under Articles XXII and XXIII of GATT 1947, and the rules and procedures as further elaborated and modified herein.

The GATT 1947 contained only two brief provisions on dispute settlement (Articles XXII and XXIII), which neither explicitly referred to 'dispute settlement' nor provided for detailed procedures to handle disputes.[13] However, the GATT Contracting Parties 'transformed', in a highly pragmatic manner over a period of five decades, what was initially a rudimentary, power-based system for settling disputes through diplomatic negotiations into an elaborate, rules-based system for settling disputes through adjudication. While quite successful in resolving disputes to the satisfaction of the parties,[14] the GATT dispute settlement had some serious shortcomings which became ever more acute in the course of the 1980s. The most important shortcoming related to the fact that the findings and conclusions of the panels of experts adjudicating disputes only became legally binding when adopted *by consensus* by the GATT Council. The responding party could thus prevent any unfavourable conclusions from becoming legally binding upon it. As discussed in this chapter, the WTO dispute settlement system, negotiated during the Uruguay Round and provided for in

---

[10] *EC – Approval and Marketing of Biotech Products*, complaint by the United States, Canada and Argentina. See below, pp. 835–7. Note also the recent *Brazil – Retreaded Tyres* dispute on a Brazilian ban on the import of retreaded tyres for environmental reasons. This measure was challenged by the European Communities. See below, pp. 622–8.

[11] *EC – Bananas III*, complaint by Ecuador, Guatemala, Honduras, Mexico and the United States.

[12] *EC and Certain Member States – Large Civil Aircraft*, Complaint by the United States, and *US – Large Civil Aircraft*, Complaint by the European Communities. This dispute has been called the 'biggest trade conflict handled by the WTO'. See Kevin Done, 'WTO to Hear of 'Lavish' Boeing aid' *Financial Times*, 22 March 2007. See also Edward Alden, Caroline Daniel, Raphael Minder, *et al.*, 'Dogfight at the WTO: The US and EU Step Up their Battle over Aircraft Subsidies', *Financial Times*, 8 October 2004. At the time of writing, both these disputes were pending before their respective Panels.

[13] As explained in chapter 2 of this book, the GATT 1947 was to be the first substantive agreement concluded in the context of the ITO. The *ITO Charter* contained an extensive chapter regarding the settlement of disputes arising from the agreements concluded in the context of the ITO. See above, pp. 77–80.

[14] Robert Hudec's statistical analysis of the results of GATT dispute settlement until the end of the 1980s indicated an overall success rate of almost 90 per cent (see R. Hudec *et al.*, 'A Statistical Profile of GATT Dispute Settlement Cases: 1948–1989', *Minnesota Journal of Global Trade*, 1993, 285–7). Hudec has also been quoted as saying with regard to the success of the GATT dispute settlement system that 'accomplishments to this point, if not unique, are at least rare in the history of international legal institutions'.

the *Understanding on Rules and Procedures for the Settlement of Disputes*, commonly referred to as the *Dispute Settlement Understanding* or DSU, remedied this and a number of other shortcomings of the GATT dispute settlement system. The DSU is attached to the *WTO Agreement* as Annex 2 and is generally considered to be one of the most important achievements of the Uruguay Round negotiations.[15]

This chapter discusses:

- the principles of WTO dispute settlement;
- the institutions of WTO dispute settlement; and
- WTO dispute settlement proceedings.

3.2. PRINCIPLES OF WTO DISPUTE SETTLEMENT

The WTO possesses a remarkable system for the resolution of trade disputes between its Members. This section deals with the basic principles of WTO dispute settlement. It examines:

- the object and purpose of the WTO dispute settlement system;
- the various methods of WTO dispute settlement;
- the jurisdiction of the WTO dispute settlement system;
- access to the WTO dispute settlement system;
- the steps in, and timeframe for, the WTO dispute settlement process;
- rules on interpretation and the burden of proof applicable in WTO dispute settlement;
- the confidentiality of, and rules of conduct for, WTO dispute settlement;
- remedies for breach of WTO law; and
- special rules and assistance for developing-country Members.

3.2.1. Object and purpose of the WTO dispute settlement system

The prime object and purpose of the WTO dispute settlement system is the prompt settlement of disputes between WTO Members concerning their respective rights and obligations under WTO law. As stated in Article 3.3 of the DSU, the prompt settlement of such disputes is:

> essential to the effective functioning of the WTO and the maintenance of a proper balance between the rights and obligations of Members.

Article 3.2 of the DSU states:

> The dispute settlement system of the WTO is a central element in providing security and predictability to the multilateral trading system. The Members recognize that it serves to preserve the rights and obligations of Members under the covered agreements, and to clarify the existing provisions of those agreements in accordance with customary rules of interpretation of public international law.

---

[15] On the Uruguay Round negotiations, see above, pp. 82–4.

According to the Panel in *US – Section 301 Trade Act*, the DSU is one of the most important *instruments* of the WTO in protecting the security and predictability of the multilateral trading system.[16]

3.2.1.1. Settlement of disputes through multilateral procedures

The object and purpose of the dispute settlement system is for Members to settle disputes with other Members through the *multilateral* procedures of the DSU, rather than through *unilateral* action.[17] Article 23.1 of the DSU states:

> When Members seek the redress of a violation of obligations or other nullification or impairment of benefits under the covered agreements or an impediment to the attainment of any objective of the covered agreements, they shall have recourse to, and abide by, the rules and procedures of this Understanding.

According to the Appellate Body in *US – Certain EC Products*, Article 23.1 of the DSU imposes a general obligation to redress a violation of WTO law through the multilateral DSU procedures, and not through unilateral action.[18] Pursuant to Article 23.2 of the DSU, WTO Members may not make a *unilateral* determination that a violation of WTO law has occurred and may not take retaliation measures *unilaterally* in the case of a violation of WTO law.[19] The Panel in *EC – Commercial Vessels* held that:

> the obligation to have recourse to the DSU when Members 'seek the redress of a violation . . .' covers *any act of a Member* in response to what it considers to be a violation of a WTO obligation by another Member whereby that first Member attempts unilaterally to restore the balance of rights and obligations.[20] [Emphasis added]

It is important to note that concerns regarding unilateral actions by the United States against what it considered to be violations of GATT law under Section 301 of the US Trade Act of 1974, and even more so under the 'Super 301' created by the Trade and Competitiveness Act of 1988, were a driving force behind the negotiations of the DSU. The other GATT Contracting Parties were greatly alarmed by the 'vigilante justice' of the United States in the field of international trade. They

---

[16] See Panel Report, *US – Section 301 Trade Act*, para. 7.75.   [17] See Article 23 of the DSU.

[18] Appellate Body Report, *US – Certain EC Products*, para. 111. The Panel in the same case noted: 'An important reason why Article 23 of the DSU must be interpreted with a view to prohibiting any form of unilateral action is because such unilateral actions threaten the stability and predictability of the multilateral trade system, a necessary component for 'market conditions conducive to individual economic activity in national and global markets' which, in themselves, constitute a fundamental goal of the WTO. Unilateral actions are, therefore, contrary to the essence of the multilateral trade system of the WTO.' Panel Report, *US – Certain EC Products*, para. 6.14. See also Panel Report, *US – Section 301 Trade Act*, para. 7.71.

[19] The Panel in *US – Section 301 Trade Act*, noted: 'There is a great deal more State conduct which can violate the general obligation in Article 23.1 to have recourse to, and abide by, the rules and procedures of the DSU than the instances especially singled out in Article 23.2.' Panel Report, *US – Section 301 Trade Act*, para. 7.45. The Panel gave two examples: not notifying mutually agreed solutions to the DSB as required in Article 3.6 of the DSU; and not abiding by the requirements for a request for consultations or for establishment of a panel as elaborated in Articles 4 and 6 of the DSU. See *ibid.*, footnote 656.

[20] Panel Report, *EC – Commercial Vessels*, para. 7.207. The act at issue in this case was an EC regulation adopted in response to Korea's alleged failure to abide by the terms of an agreement between Korea and the European Communities on subsidies for shipbuilding. According to the Panel, the European Communities sought to achieve results unilaterally through adopting a regulation where it should have used the DSU, therefore the regulation was found to be inconsistent with Article 23.1. See Panel Report, *Korea – Commercial Vessels*, para. 7.220.

demanded that the United States change its legislation which allowed for much unilateral action. The United States, however, argued that the existing GATT dispute settlement system, as a result of the consensus requirement, was too weak to protect US trade interests effectively. Robert Hudec noted:

> This United States counter-attack against the procedural weaknesses of the existing dispute settlement system led other governments to propose a deal. In exchange for a US commitment not to employ its Section 301-type trade restrictions, the other GATT governments would agree to create a new and procedurally tighter dispute settlement system that would meet US complaints.[21]

In this way, agreement was eventually reached on the current dispute settlement system, a key feature of which is the insistence on the resolution of disputes through multilateral procedures as reflected in Article 23 of the DSU.

3.2.1.2. Settlement of disputes through consultations if possible

Article 3.7 of the DSU states, in relevant part:

> The aim of the dispute settlement mechanism is to secure a positive solution to a dispute. A solution mutually acceptable to the parties to a dispute and consistent with the covered agreements is clearly to be preferred.

The DSU thus expresses a clear preference for solutions mutually acceptable to the parties reached through negotiations, rather than solutions resulting from adjudication. Accordingly, each dispute settlement proceeding must start with consultations (or an attempt to have consultations) between the parties to the dispute.[22] To resolve disputes through consultations is obviously cheaper and more satisfactory for the long-term trade relations with the other party to the dispute than adjudication by a panel. Note that any mutually agreed solution reached through consultations needs to be consistent with WTO law.[23]

In 16 per cent of disputes, it has been possible to resolve the dispute amicably as the parties succeeded in reaching a solution acceptable to all. In 8 per cent, the dispute was otherwise amicably resolved without resort to adjudication.[24] In other disputes, however, recourse to adjudication was necessary in order to secure actual resolution of the dispute.[25]

3.2.1.3. Settlement of disputes and the clarification of WTO law

Article 3.2 of the DSU, as quoted above, states that the dispute settlement system serves not only 'to preserve the rights and obligations of Members under the

---

[21] Robert Hudec, 'The New WTO Dispute Settlement Procedure', *Minnesota Journal of Global Trade*, 1999, 13.
[22] The Appellate Body in *US – Certain EC Products*, upholding the Panel's finding of violation of Article 3.7 of the DSU, stated that if a Member has violated Articles 22.6 and 23.2(c) of the DSU, it has also acted contrary to Article 3.7 thereof. See Appellate Body Report, *US – Certain EC Products*, paras. 116–21.
[23] See Articles 3.5 and 3.7 of the DSU.
[24] See below, pp. 273–4. In addition, in five disputes (*EC – Butter, EC – Scallops (complaint by Canada) and (complaint by Peru and Chile), Japan – Quotas on Laver* and *US – DRAMS (Article 21.5 – Korea)*) panel proceedings were initiated, but a mutually agreed solution was reached during these proceedings. See above, p. 169
[25] Data calculated on the basis of the number of requests for consultations which have led to adopted reports or mutually agreed solutions or were otherwise settled or inactive.

covered agreements', but also 'to clarify the existing provisions of those agreements'. As the covered agreements are full of gaps and 'constructive ambiguity', there is much need for clarification of the existing provisions. However, the last sentence of Article 3.2 provides:

> Recommendations and rulings of the DSB cannot add to or diminish the rights and obligations provided in the covered agreements.

Article 19.2 of the DSU states:

> In accordance with paragraph 2 of Article 3, in their findings and recommendations, the panel and Appellate Body cannot add to or diminish the rights and obligations provided in the covered agreements.

While allowing the WTO dispute settlement system to clarify WTO law, Articles 3.2 and 19.2 explicitly preclude the system from adding to or diminishing the rights and obligations of Members. The DSU thus explicitly cautions the WTO dispute settlement system against 'judicial activism', i.e. against taking on the role of 'legislator'.[26] Furthermore, as noted in chapter 2, pursuant to Article IX:2 of the *WTO Agreement*, it is the exclusive competence of the Ministerial Conference and the General Council to adopt 'authoritative' interpretations of the provisions of the *WTO Agreement* and the Multilateral Trade Agreements.[27] Article 3.9 of the DSU stipulates that the provisions of the DSU are without prejudice to the rights of Members to seek such 'authoritative' interpretation. In *US – Certain EC Products*, the Appellate Body held:

> we observe that it is certainly not the task of either panels or the Appellate Body to amend the DSU or to adopt interpretations within the meaning of Article IX:2 of the WTO Agreement. Only WTO Members have the authority to amend the DSU or to adopt such interpretations. Pursuant to Article 3.2 of the DSU, the task of panels and the Appellate Body in the dispute settlement system of the WTO is 'to preserve the rights and obligations of Members under the covered agreements, and to *clarify the existing provisions* of those agreements in accordance with customary rules of interpretation of public international law.' Determining what the rules and procedures of the DSU ought to be is not our responsibility nor the responsibility of panels; it is clearly the responsibility solely of the Members of the WTO.[28] (Emphasis added)

Note that in *Chile – Alcoholic Beverages*, Chile argued before the Appellate Body that the Panel had acted inconsistently with Articles 3.2 and 19.2 of the DSU as it had added to the rights and obligations of Members. The Appellate Body found, however that:

> We have difficulty in envisaging circumstances in which a panel could add to the rights and obligations of a Member of the WTO if its conclusions reflected a correct interpretation and application of provisions of the covered agreements.[29]

---

[26] Referring to Article 19.2 as well as to the task of a panel under Article 11 of the DSU, the Panel in *India – Patents (EC)* held that 'the Panel is required to base its findings on the language of the DSU. We simply cannot make a ruling *ex aequo et bono* to address a systemic concern divorced from explicit language of the DSU.' Panel Report, *India – Patents (EC)*, para. 7.23.   [27] See above, pp. 141–2.

[28] Appellate Body Report, *US – Certain EC Products*, para. 92.

[29] Appellate Body Report, *Chile – Alcoholic Beverages*, para. 79. See also Appellate Body Report, *US – Oil Country Tubular Goods Sunset Reviews (Article 21.5 – Argentina)*, footnote 370 to para. 175.

Accusations of judicial activism are frequently raised by the party losing a dispute. By way of example, note the reactions to the Appellate Body Report in *US – Zeroing (Japan)*, a report unfavourable to the United States. *BRIDGES* reported:

> Sander Levin, a senior Congressional Democrat from Michigan, said that the Appellate Body was overstepping its mandate, 'changing the rules in the middle of the game.' He added that 'the Appellate Body is required to apply obligations that the United States and other WTO Members have negotiated – not create obligations out of thin air.'[30]

3.2.1.4. *Settlement of disputes in good faith*

Finally, Article 3.10 of the DSU provides that the use of the dispute settlement procedures:

> should not be intended or considered as contentious acts

and that all Members must:

> engage in these procedures in good faith in an effort to resolve the dispute.

Engaging in dispute settlement *in good faith*, i.e. with the genuine intention to see the dispute resolved, is part of the object and purpose of the WTO dispute settlement system.

In *US – FSC*, the Appellate Body found that the United States had failed to act in good faith, by failing to bring procedural deficiencies 'seasonably and promptly' to the attention of the complainant and the Panel, so that corrections, if needed, could have been made.[31] In *Argentina – Poultry Anti-Dumping Duties*, Argentina argued that Brazil failed to act in good faith by first challenging Argentina's anti-dumping measure before a MERCOSUR *Ad Hoc* Tribunal and then, having lost that case, challenging the same measure in WTO dispute settlement proceedings. The Panel, referring to the findings of the Appellate Body in *US – Offset Act (Byrd Amendment)*, held:

> we consider that two conditions must be satisfied before a Member may be found to have failed to act in good faith. First, the Member must have violated a substantive provision of the WTO agreements. Second, there must be something 'more than mere violation'.[32]

As Argentina had not argued that Brazil had violated any substantive provision of the WTO agreements in bringing its case, the first requirement was not met, and the Panel did not find a violation of the principle of good faith.[33] In *EC – Export Subsidies on Sugar*, the Appellate Body held that in the context of determining whether a Member has engaged in dispute settlement proceedings in good faith 'estoppel' may be examined.[34]

---

[30] *BRIDGES Weekly Trade News Digest*, 17 January 2007.
[31] See Appellate Body Report, *US – FSC*, para. 166. See also below, p. 276.
[32] Panel Report, *Argentina – Poultry Anti-Dumping Duties*, para. 7.36. See also Appellate Body Report, *US – Offset Act (Byrd Amendment)*, para. 298.   [33] See Panel Report, *Argentina – Poultry Anti-Dumping Duties*, para. 7.36.
[34] See Appellate Body, *EC – Export Subsidies on Sugar*, para. 307. Note that in *EC – Export Subsidies on Sugar*, the Panel referred to the definition of 'estoppel' by J. P. Müller and T. Cottier, *Encyclopaedia of Public*

Questions and Assignments 3.1

What is the object and purpose of the WTO dispute settlement system? What is the WTO dispute settlement system's preferred method of dispute settlement? Is it part of the object and purpose of the WTO dispute settlement system to 'make law'? Does Article 23 of the DSU prohibit *any* form of unilateral conduct by Members when seeking redress of a violation of WTO obligations or does it prohibit only the unilateral suspension of concessions or other obligations? When can a Member be found to have failed to act in good faith when engaging in dispute settlement?

3.2.2. Methods of WTO dispute settlement

The DSU provides for more than one method to settle disputes between WTO Members. In fact, the DSU provides for:

- consultations or negotiations;
- adjudication by panels and the Appellate Body;
- arbitration; and
- good offices, conciliation and mediation.

As noted above, the DSU expresses a clear preference for resolving disputes through *consultations*, i.e. negotiations, between the parties to the dispute. Therefore, consultations, or at least an attempt to have consultations, must always precede resort to adjudication. The rules and procedures for consultations are set out in Article 4 of the DSU.[35]

If consultations fail to resolve the dispute, the complaining party may resort to *adjudication* by a panel and, if either party to the dispute appeals the findings of the panel, adjudication by the Appellate Body. The rules and procedures for adjudication by a panel and the Appellate Body are set out in Articles 6 to 20 of the DSU.[36]

The dispute settlement methods provided for in Articles 4 and 6 to 20 of the DSU (consultations and adjudication by panels and the Appellate Body) are by far the methods most frequently used. However, the WTO dispute settlement system provides for expeditious *arbitration* as an alternative means of dispute settlement.[37] Pursuant to Article 25 of the DSU, parties to a dispute arising under a covered agreement may decide to resort to arbitration, rather than follow the procedure set out in Articles 4 and 6 to 20 of the DSU. In that case, the parties must clearly define the issues referred to arbitration and agree on the particular procedure to be followed.[38] The parties must also agree to abide by the arbitration

Footnote *(cont.)*

International Law (Ed. Max Planck Institute, 1992), 116, which states: 'It is generally agreed that the party invoking estoppel "must have been induced to undertake legally relevant action or abstain from it by relying in good faith upon clear and unambiguous representations by the other State".' Panel Report, *EC – Export Subsidies on Sugar*, para. 7.61. See also Appellate Body Report, *Guatemala – Cement II*, footnote 105 to para. 5.42.   [35] For a detailed discussion of consultations, see below, pp. 269–74.
[36] For a detailed discussion of panel and appellate review proceedings, see below, pp. 275–97.
[37] See Article 25 of the DSU.   [38] See Articles 25.1 and 25.2 of the DSU.

award.[39] Pursuant to Article 3.5 of the DSU, the arbitration award must be consistent with the WTO agreements. In the latter part of 2001, WTO Members used the Article 25 arbitration procedure for the first and thus far only time. In that case, the Arbitrators set the appropriate level of compensation which the United States and the European Communities could not agree on after the failure of the United States to comply with the Panel Report in *US – Section 110(5) Copyright Act*.[40] The DSU also provides for arbitration in Articles 21.3(c) and 22.6, but this arbitration is not 'an alternative means of dispute settlement' within the meaning of Article 25 of the DSU. As discussed below, these arbitrations concern specific issues that may arise in the *context* of a dispute, such as the determination of the reasonable period of time for implementation (Article 21.3(c) of the DSU)[41] and the appropriate level of retaliation (Article 22.6 of the DSU).[42]

Finally, the DSU also provides, in Article 5, for the possibility for the parties to a dispute – if they all agree to do so – to use good offices, conciliation or mediation to settle a dispute. Good offices, conciliation or mediation may be requested by any party at any time. Also, they may begin and be terminated at any time.[43] If the parties agree, procedures for good offices, conciliation or mediation may continue while the panel process proceeds.[44] Before requesting consultations with the European Communities with regard to the WTO-consistency of its new 'tariff-only' banana import regime in *EC – Bananas III (Article 21.5 – Ecuador)*, Ecuador tried to resolve the matter by means of a negotiated solution with the European Communities using the good offices of Norway's foreign minister, Jonas Gahr Store. As reported in *BRIDGES*:

> sources close to the proceedings suggest that though the process was useful for building trust between the parties, it did not produce concrete developments, prompting Ecuador to look elsewhere for a solution.[45]

The Director-General may, acting in an *ex officio* capacity, offer under Article 5 of the DSU good offices, conciliation or mediation with a view to assisting Members to settle a dispute.[46] In July 2001, the Director-General reminded Members of his availability to help settle disputes through good offices, mediation or conciliation.[47] On 4 September 2002, the Philippines, Thailand and the European Communities jointly requested – albeit formally speaking not on the basis of Article 5 of the DSU – mediation by the Director-General, or by a

---

[39] See Article 25.3 of the DSU.
[40] Award of the Arbitrators, *US – Section 110(5) Copyright Act (Article 25.3)*, recourse to arbitration under Article 25 of the DSU, WT/DS160/ARB25/1, 9 November 2001.   [41] See below, pp. 298–9.
[42] See below, pp. 305–6. The Decision of the Ministerial Conference on the Cotonou waiver also contained an arbitration procedure. See Ministerial Conference, *Decision on the Waiver for the European Communities – The ACP – EC Partnership Agreement*, WT/MIN(01)/15, dated 14 November 2001. This procedure was used (twice) to determine the appropriate level of compensation due as a result of the changes by the European Communities to its tariff binding on bananas. On 1 August 2005, the Arbitrator issued its award in *European Communities – The ACP-EC Partnership Agreement – Recourse to Arbitration Pursuant to the Decision of 14 November 2001*, WT/L/616 and, on 27 October 2005, the Arbitrator issued its Award in *European Communities – The ACP–EC Partnership Agreement – Second Recourse to Arbitration Pursuant to the Decision of 14 November 2001*, WT/L/625. On arbitration on compensation due as a result of changes in Services Schedules, see below, pp. 490–1.   [43] See Article 5.3 of the DSU.   [44] See Article 5.5 of the DSU.
[45] See *BRIDGES Weekly Trade News Digest*, 22 November 2006.   [46] See Article 5.6 of the DSU.
[47] Communication from the Director-General, *Article 5 of the Dispute Settlement Understanding*, WT/DSB/25, dated 17 July 2001.

mediator designated by him with their agreement, in a matter concerning the tariff treatment of canned tuna.[48] The requesting Members had held three rounds of consultations, but could not reach a mutually acceptable solution. The Director-General accepted the request for mediation and, with the agreement of the requesting Members, nominated Deputy Director-General Rufus Yerxa as mediator. The mediator was asked to examine the extent to which the preferential tariff treatment granted by the European Communities to other Members unduly impaired the legitimate export interests of the Philippines and Thailand, and possibly to propose a solution. On 20 December 2002, Yerxa informed the Director-General that he had completed his work.[49] He also informed the Director-General that the requesting Members had agreed that the mediator's conclusions would remain confidential.[50] In July 2003, the European Communities, the Philippines and Thailand informed the Director-General that an amicable outcome had been reached based on the mediator's conclusions.[51]

Questions and Assignments 3.2

Briefly discuss the various dispute settlement methods provided for in the DSU.

3.2.3. Jurisdiction of the WTO dispute settlement system

The WTO dispute settlement system stands out by virtue of the broad scope of its jurisdiction as well as by the compulsory, exclusive and contentious nature of that jurisdiction. This section examines these two aspects – scope and nature – of the jurisdiction of the WTO dispute settlement system.

3.2.3.1. *One integrated system for all WTO disputes*

The WTO dispute settlement system has jurisdiction over any dispute between WTO Members arising under the 'covered agreements'.[52] Article 1.1 of the DSU states, in relevant part:

> The rules and procedures of this Understanding shall apply to disputes brought pursuant to the consultation and dispute settlement provisions of the agreements listed in Appendix 1 to this Understanding (referred to in this Understanding as the 'covered agreements').

[48] Note that the request stated that the requesting Members did not consider the matter at issue to be a 'dispute' within the terms of the DSU, but nevertheless agreed that the WTO Director-General or the mediator designated by him could be guided by procedures similar to those envisaged for mediation under Article 5 of the DSU. See Communication from the Director-General, *Request for Mediation by the Philippines, Thailand and the European Communities*, WT/GC/66, dated 16 October 2002. See also www.wto.org/english/tratop_e/dispu_e/disp_settlement_cbt_e/c8s1p2_e.htm#txt3, visited on 27 November 2007.
[49] See Communication from the Director-General, *Request for Mediation by the Philippines, Thailand and the European Communities, Addendum*, WT/GC/66/Add.1, dated 23 December 2002.   [50] See *ibid.*
[51] See WT/GC/71, dated 1 August 2003.   [52] For the concept of 'covered agreements', see below, p. 179.

The covered agreements, listed in Appendix 1 to the DSU, include the *WTO Agreement*, the GATT 1994 and all other multilateral agreements on trade in goods, the GATS, the *TRIPS Agreement* and the DSU.[53]

The DSU provides for a *single, coherent system* of rules and procedures for dispute settlement, applicable to disputes arising under any of the covered agreements.[54] However, some of the covered agreements provide for a few special and additional rules and procedures 'designed to deal with the particularities of dispute settlement relating to obligations arising under a specific covered agreement'.[55] Article 1.2 of the DSU provides, in relevant part:

> The rules and procedures of this Understanding shall apply subject to such special or additional rules and procedures on dispute settlement contained in the covered agreements as are identified in Appendix 2 to this Understanding.

Pursuant to Article 1.2 of the DSU, these special or additional rules and procedures *prevail* over the DSU rules and procedures to the extent that there is a 'difference' between them. The Appellate Body in *Guatemala – Cement I* ruled:

> if there is no 'difference', then the rules and procedures of the DSU apply *together with* the special or additional provisions of the covered agreement. In our view, it is only where the provisions of the DSU and the special or additional rules and procedures of a covered agreement *cannot* be read as *complementing* each other that the special or additional provisions are to *prevail*. A special or additional provision should only be found to *prevail* over a provision of the DSU in a situation where adherence to the one provision will lead to a violation of the other provision, that is, in the case of a *conflict* between them.[56]

The special and additional rules and procedures of a particular covered agreement combine with the generally applicable rules and procedures of the DSU 'to form a comprehensive, integrated dispute settlement system for the *WTO Agreement*'.[57]

Questions and Assignments 3.3

The WTO dispute settlement system has been defined as 'an integrated dispute settlement system'. What does this mean and why is this important? Which of the agreements forming part of the *WTO Agreement*

---

[53] The only multilateral trade agreement which is not a covered agreement is the *Trade Policy Review Mechanism*, Annex 3 to the *WTO Agreement*. Whether plurilateral trade agreements are covered agreements is subject to the adoption of a decision by the parties to these agreements setting out the terms for the application of the DSU (see Appendix 1 to the DSU). Of the two plurilateral agreements currently in force, only the *Agreement on Government Procurement* is a covered agreement.

[54] The Appellate Body stated in *Guatemala – Cement I* that Article 1.1 of the DSU establishes 'an integrated dispute settlement system' which applies to all the covered agreements. See Appellate Body Report, *Guatemala – Cement I*, para. 64.   [55] *Ibid.*, para. 66.

[56] *Ibid.*, para. 65. The Appellate Body reaffirmed its narrow definition of 'conflict' in *US – Hot-Rolled Steel*, where it ruled that 'we see no 'conflict'' between Article 17.6(i) of the *Anti-Dumping Agreement* and Article 11 of the DSU' and that 'although the second sentence of Article 17.6(ii) of the *Anti-Dumping Agreement* imposes obligations on panels which are not found in the DSU, we see Article 17.6(ii) as supplementing, rather than replacing, the DSU, and Article 11 in particular'. Appellate Body Report, *US – Hot-Rolled Steel*, paras. 55 and 62. See also below, p. 556.

[57] Appellate Body Report, *Guatemala – Cement I*, para. 66. See also Appellate Body Report, *US – FSC*, para. 159, with regard to Article 4.2 of the *SCM Agreement*; Appellate Body Report, *US – Lead and Bismuth II*, para. 45, with regard to standard of review; and Appellate Body Report, *US – Hot-Rolled Steel*, para. 51, with regard to standard of review under Article 17.6 of the *Anti-Dumping Agreement* and Article 11 of the DSU.

are not 'covered agreements'? Identify the special or additional rules and procedures contained in the *Anti-Dumping Agreement* and discuss whether these rules and procedures prevail over the rules and procedures of the DSU.

3.2.3.2. Compulsory jurisdiction

The jurisdiction of the WTO dispute settlement system is compulsory in nature. Article 23.1 of the DSU states:

> When Members seek the redress of a violation of obligations or other nullification or impairment of benefits under the covered agreements or an impediment to the attainment of any objective of the covered agreements, they shall have recourse to, and abide by, the rules and procedures of this Understanding.

Pursuant to this provision, a complaining Member is obliged to bring any dispute arising under the covered agreements to the WTO dispute settlement system. On the other hand, a responding Member has, as a matter of law, no choice but to accept the jurisdiction of the WTO dispute settlement system. With regard to the latter, we note that Article 6.1 of the DSU states:

> *If* the complaining party *so requests*, a *panel* shall *be established* at the latest at the DSB meeting following that at which the request first appears as an item on the DSB's agenda, unless at that meeting the DSB decides by consensus not to establish
>
> [Emphasis added

Unlike in other international dispute settlement systems, there is no need for the parties to a dispute, arising under the covered agreements, to accept, in a separate declaration or separate agreement, the jurisdiction of the WTO dispute settlement system to adjudicate that dispute. Membership of the WTO constitutes consent to, and acceptance of, the compulsory jurisdiction of the WTO dispute settlement system.

3.2.3.3. Exclusive jurisdiction

The Panel in *US – Section 301 Trade Act* ruled that Article 23.1 of the DSU (as quoted above):

> imposes on all Members [a requirement] to 'have recourse to' the multilateral process set out in the DSU when they seek the redress of a WTO inconsistency. In these circumstances, Members have to have recourse to the DSU dispute settlement system to the exclusion of any other system, in particular a system of unilateral enforcement of WTO rights and obligations. This, what one could call 'exclusive dispute resolution clause', is an important new element of Members' rights and obligations under the DSU.[58]

Members shall thus have recourse to the WTO dispute settlement system to the exclusion of any other system. Article 23.1 of the DSU both ensures the

---

[58] Panel Report, *US – Section 301 Trade Act*, para. 7.43.

exclusivity of the WTO vis-à-vis other international fora *and* protects the multi-lateral system from unilateral conduct.[59] As Article 23.2(a) of the DSU provides, Members are prohibited from making a determination to the effect that a viola-tion has occurred, that benefits have been nullified or impaired, or that the attainment of any objective of the covered agreements has been impeded, *except* through recourse to dispute settlement in accordance with the rules and proce-dures of the DSU.[60]

3.2.3.4. *Contentious jurisdiction*

The WTO dispute settlement system has only contentious, and not advisory, jurisdiction. In *US – Wool Shirts and Blouses*, the Appellate Body held:

> Given the explicit aim of dispute settlement that permeates the DSU, we do not consider that Article 3.2 of the DSU is meant to encourage either panels or the Appellate Body to 'make law' by clarifying existing provisions of the WTO Agreement *outside the context of resolving a particular dispute*.[61]
>
> [Emphasis added]

The WTO dispute settlement system is called upon to clarify WTO law only in the context of an actual dispute. In *EC – Commercial Vessels* the Panel declined to address a matter before it because it did not consider that 'an abstract ruling on hypothetical future measures' was either necessary or helpful to the resolution of that dispute.[62]

Questions and Assignments 3.4

Could a WTO Member refuse to submit to the jurisdiction of the WTO dispute settlement system? Could a WTO Member submit a dispute arising under one of the covered agreements to the International Court of Justice? In your opinion, would it be useful for the WTO dispute settlement system to have advisory jurisdiction?

3.2.4. Access to the WTO dispute settlement system

Access to, or the use of, the WTO dispute settlement system is limited to Members of the WTO. The Appellate Body ruled in *US – Shrimp*:

> It may be well to stress at the outset that access to the dispute settlement process of the WTO is limited to Members of the WTO. This access is not available, under the *WTO Agreement* and the covered agreements as they currently exist, to individuals or

---

[59] See Panel Report, *EC – Commercial Vessels*, para. 7.193.
[60] Article 23.2 also stipulates that, to determine the reasonable period of time for implementation (see below, pp. 298–9) or to determine the level of suspension of concessions or other obligations and to obtain DSB authorisation for such suspension (see below, pp. 305–6), Members must also follow the rules and procedures set out in the DSU. See also above, p. 172, footnote 19.
[61] Appellate Body Report, *US – Wool Shirts and Blouses*, 340.
[62] See Panel Report, *EC – Commercial Vessels*, para. 7.30.

international organizations, whether governmental or non-governmental. Only Members may become parties to a dispute of which a panel may be seized, and only Members 'having a substantial interest in a matter before a panel' may become third parties in the proceedings before that panel. Thus, under the DSU, only Members who are parties to a dispute, or who have notified their interest in becoming third parties in such a dispute to the DSB, have a *legal right* to make submissions to, and have a *legal right* to have those submissions considered by, a panel.[63]

The WTO dispute settlement system is a *government-to-government* dispute settlement system for disputes concerning rights and obligations of WTO Members. Only WTO Members are entitled to initiate proceedings against breaches of WTO law. The WTO Secretariat cannot prosecute breaches of WTO law on its own motion nor are individuals, international organisations, non-governmental organisations or industry associations entitled to do so.[64]

This section discusses when Members can use the WTO dispute settlement system. It looks at the causes of action, i.e. the grounds for action, in WTO dispute settlement. Furthermore, this section examines what types of measures can be challenged. In this context three questions arise: first, whether measures by private parties can be challenged; second, whether measures no longer in force can be challenged; and, third, whether legislation *as such*, i.e. independent from its application in specific cases, can be challenged and found to be inconsistent with WTO law. This section also addresses the controversial issue of *amicus curiae* briefs submitted to panels and the Appellate Body by legal and natural persons seeking some degree of access to the WTO dispute settlement system. Finally, this section discusses the 'indirect' access that companies and industry associations have to the WTO dispute settlement system.

3.2.4.1. Causes of action

Each covered agreement contains one or more consultation and dispute settlement provisions. These provisions set out when a Member can have recourse to the WTO dispute settlement system. For the GATT 1994, the relevant provisions are Articles XXII and XXIII. Of particular importance is Article XXIII:1 of the GATT 1994, which states:

If any Member should consider that any benefit accruing to it directly or indirectly under this Agreement is being nullified or impaired or that the attainment of any objective of the Agreement is being impeded as the result of

(a) the failure of another Member to carry out its obligations under this Agreement, or
(b) the application by another Member of any measure, whether or not it conflicts with the provisions of this Agreement, or
(c) the existence of any other situation,

the Member may, with a view to the satisfactory adjustment of the matter, make written representations or proposals to the other Member or Members which it considers to be concerned.

[63] Appellate Body Report, *US – Shrimp*, para. 101.
[64] On 'indirect' access to WTO dispute settlement, see below, pp. 197–8.

In *India – Quantitative Restrictions*, the Appellate Body held:

> This dispute was brought pursuant to, *inter alia*, Article XXIII of the GATT 1994. According to Article XXIII, any Member which considers that a benefit accruing to it directly or indirectly under the GATT 1994 is being nullified or impaired as a result of the failure of another Member to carry out its obligations, may resort to the dispute settlement procedures of Article XXIII. The United States considers that a benefit accruing to it under the GATT 1994 was nullified or impaired as a result of India's alleged failure to carry out its obligations regarding balance-of-payments restrictions under Article XVIII:B of the GATT 1994. Therefore, the United States was entitled to have recourse to the dispute settlement procedures of Article XXIII with regard to this dispute.[65]

The consultation and dispute settlement provisions of most other covered agreements incorporate, by reference, Articles XXII and XXIII of the GATT 1994. For example, Article 11.1 of the *SPS Agreement*, entitled 'Consultations and Dispute Settlement', states:

> The provisions of Articles XXII and XXIII of GATT 1994 as elaborated and applied by the Dispute Settlement Understanding shall apply to consultations and the settlement of disputes under this Agreement, except as otherwise specifically provided herein.

As was the case in *India – Quantitative Restrictions*, the nullification or impairment of a benefit (or the impeding of the realisation of an objective) may, and most often will, be the result of a violation of an obligation prescribed by a covered agreement. Nullification or impairment may, however, also be the result of 'the application by another Member of any measure, whether or not it conflicts with the provisions' of a covered agreement.[66] Nullification or impairment may equally be the result of 'the existence of any other situation'.[67]

Unlike other international dispute settlement systems, the WTO system thus provides for three types of complaint:

- 'violation' complaints;
- 'non-violation' complaints; and
- 'situation' complaints.[68]

In the case of a 'non-violation' complaint or a 'situation' complaint, the complainant must demonstrate that there is nullification or impairment of a benefit or that the achievement of an objective is impeded.[69] The Panel in *Japan – Film* stated with regard to non-violation claims that:

---

[65] Appellate Body Report, *India – Quantitative Restrictions*, para. 84.
[66] Article XXIII:1(b) of the GATT 1994 and Article 26.1 of the DSU.
[67] Article XXIII:1(c) of the GATT1994 and Article 26.2 of the DSU.
[68] Pursuant to Article XXIII:3 of the GATS, situation complaints are not possible in disputes arising under the GATS. Non-violation complaints and situation complaints are currently not possible in disputes arising under the *TRIPS Agreement*. See below, pp. 800–1.
[69] See Articles 26.1 (for non-violation complaints) and 26.2 (for situation complaints) of the DSU. Articles 26.1 and 26.2 set out a few special rules for these types of complaint. The Panel in *EC – Asbestos* rejected the argument by the European Communities that the rules on non-violation nullification apply only if the measure in question does not fall under other provisions of the GATT 1994. The Panel noted that both Article XXIII:1(b) of the GATT 1994 and Article 26.1 of the DSU apply 'whether or not' the measure conflicts with a particular provision. See Panel Report, *EC – Asbestos*, paras. 8.260–8.265. The Appellate Body upheld the Panel's findings on this issue. See Appellate Body Report, *EC – Asbestos*, paras. 186–90.

> it must be demonstrated that the competitive position of the imported products subject to and benefiting from a relevant market access (tariff) concession is being *upset by* ('nullified or impaired . . . as the result of') the application of a measure not reasonably anticipated.[70]

In that case, the United States, the complainant, failed to prove such causal link.[71] According to the Panel in *EC – Asbestos*, nullification or impairment would exist, in the case before it, if the measure:

> ha[s] the effect of upsetting the competitive relationship between Canadian asbestos and products containing it, on the one hand, and substitute fibres and products containing them, on the other.[72]

In the case of a 'violation' complaint, however, there is a presumption of nullification or impairment when the complainant demonstrates the existence of the 'violation'.[73] Article 3.8 of the DSU states:

> In cases where there is an infringement of the obligations assumed under a covered agreement, the action is considered *prima facie* to constitute a case of nullification or impairment. This means that there is normally a presumption that a breach of the rules has an adverse impact on other Members parties to that covered agreement, and in such cases, it shall be up to the Member against whom the complaint has been brought to rebut the charge.

In only a few cases to date has the respondent argued that the alleged violation of WTO law did not nullify or impair benefits accruing to the complainant.[74] In no case has the respondent been successful in rebutting the presumption of nullification or impairment. For instance in *EC – Export Subsidies on Sugar*, the Appellate Body upheld the Panel's finding that the European Communities did not rebut the presumption of nullification or impairment. The Appellate Body noted that the European Communities also on appeal did not try to rebut this presumption:

> The European Communities, instead, appears to suggest that, to rebut the presumption of nullification or impairment, it need only demonstrate that the Complaining Parties 'could

---

70 Panel Report, *Japan – Film*, para. 10.82.
71 *Ibid.* paras. 10.347–10.348. With regard to what a complainant must show in a non-violation complaint, see *ibid.*, para. 9.5.
72 Panel Report, *EC – Asbestos*, para. 8.288. With respect to non-violation complaints, see also Appellate Body Report, *EC – Asbestos*, paras. 38 and 185–6.
73 Note, for example, that the Appellate Body in *EC – Export Subsidies on Sugar* upheld the Panel's finding that the European Communities' violations of the *Agreement on Agriculture* nullified or impaired the benefits accruing to the complainants under this agreement, noting that '[u]nless a Member demonstrates that there are no adverse trade effects arising as a consequence of WTO-inconsistent export subsidies, we do not believe that a complaining Member's expectations would have a bearing on a finding pursuant to Article 3.8 of the DSU'. Appellate Body Report, *EC – Export Subsidies on Sugar*, paras. 293–300. In *US – Offset Act (Byrd Amendment)*, the Appellate Body concluded pursuant to Article 3.8 of the DSU that to the extent that it had found the measure to be inconsistent with Article 18.1 of the *Anti-Dumping Agreement* and Article 32.1 of the *SCM Agreement*, 'the [Offset Act] nullifies or impairs benefits accruing to the appellees in this dispute under those Agreements'. Appellate Body Report, *US – Offset Act (Byrd Amendment)*, paras. 300–4. See also Panel Report, *Guatemala – Cement II*, paras. 8.105–8.112; Panel Report, *Turkey – Textiles*, paras. 9.193–9.206; Appellate Body Report, *EC – Bananas III*, paras. 249–54; and Panel Reports, *EC – Bananas III*. para. 7.398 (complaint by Ecuador); para. 7.398 (complaint by Guatemala/Honduras); para. 7.398 (complaint by Mexico) and para. 7.398 (complaint by US).
74 See Appellate Body Report, *EC – Bananas III*, paras. 250–3, in which the Appellate Body referred to the GATT Panel Report, *US – Superfund*, para. 5.1.9. See also Panel Report, *Turkey – Textiles*, para. 9.204; and Panel Report, *Guatemala – Cement II*, para. 8.25.

not have expected that the EC would take any measure to reduce its exports of C sugar.'[75]

It is in fact doubtful whether this presumption is rebuttable.

Violation complaints are by far the most common type of complaint. To date, there have been few non-violation complaints.[76] Note that the Appellate Body stated in *EC – Asbestos* that:

> the ['non-violation' nullification or impairment] remedy . . . 'should be approached with caution and should remain an exceptional remedy'.[77]

None of the non-violation complaints brought to the WTO to date has been successful.[78] Moreover, there have never been any situation complaints. The difference between the WTO system and other international dispute settlement systems with regard to causes of action is, therefore, 'of little practical significance'.[79]

There is no explicit provision in the DSU requiring a Member to have a 'legal interest' in order to have recourse to the WTO dispute settlement system. It has been held that such a requirement is not implied either in the DSU or in any other provision of the *WTO Agreement*.[80] In *EC – Bananas III*, the Appellate Body held:

> we believe that a Member has broad discretion in deciding whether to bring a case against another Member under the DSU. The language of Article XXIII:1 of the GATT 1994 and of Article 3.7 of the DSU suggests, furthermore, that a Member is expected to be largely self-regulating in deciding whether any such action would be 'fruitful'.[81]

The Appellate Body explicitly agreed with the statement of the Panel in *EC – Bananas III* that:

> with the increased interdependence of the global economy, . . . Members have a greater stake in enforcing WTO rules than in the past since any deviation from the negotiated balance of rights and obligations is more likely than ever to affect them, directly or indirectly.[82]

Note that in *EC – Bananas III*, the Appellate Body decided that the United States could bring a claim under the GATT 1994 despite the fact that the United States does not export bananas. In coming to this decision, the Appellate Body considered the fact that the United States is a producer and a potential exporter of

---

[75] Appellate Body Report, *EC – Export Subsidies on Sugar*, para. 298.
[76] See e.g. Panel Report, *Japan – Film*; Panel Report, *Korea – Procurement*; Panel Report, *EC – Asbestos*; and Panel Report, *US – Offset Act (Byrd Amendment)* (with regard to non-violation complaints under the SCM Agreement).
[77] Appellate Body Report, *EC – Asbestos*, para. 186. This was reiterated by the Panel in *US – Offset Act (Byrd Amendment)* with regard to non-violation complaints under the SCM Agreement. See Panel Report, *US – Offset Act (Byrd Amendment)*, para. 7.125.
[78] Note, however, that in *Korea – Procurement*, *EC – Asbestos* and *US – Offset Act (Byrd Amendment)*, the violation claims, brought together with the non-violation claims, were successful.
[79] F. Feliciano and P. Van den Bossche, 'The Dispute Settlement System of the World Trade Organization: Institutions, Process and Practice', in N. Blokker and H. Schermers (eds.), *Proliferation of International Organizations* (Kluwer Law International, 2001), 308.
[80] See Appellate Body Report, *EC – Bananas III*, paras. 132 and 133.   [81] *Ibid.*, para. 135.
[82] *Ibid.*, para. 136. Here the Appellate Body referred to Panel Reports, *EC – Bananas III*, para. 7.50.

bananas, the effects of the EC banana regime on the US internal market for bananas and the fact that the US claims under the GATS and the GATT 1994 were inextricably interwoven. The Appellate Body subsequently concluded:

> Taken together, these reasons are sufficient justification for the United States to have brought its claims against the EC banana import regime under the GATT 1994.[83]

The Appellate Body added, however, that:

> This does not mean, though, that one or more of the factors we have noted in this case would necessarily be dispositive in another case.[84]

In *Mexico – Corn Syrup (Article 21.5 – US)*, the Appellate Body ruled with respect to recourse by Members to the WTO dispute settlement system:

> Given the 'largely self-regulating' nature of the requirement in the first sentence of Article 3.7, panels and the Appellate Body must presume, whenever a Member submits a request for establishment of a panel, that such Member does so in good faith, having duly exercised its judgement as to whether recourse to that panel would be 'fruitful'. Article 3.7 neither requires nor authorizes a panel to look behind that Member's decision and to question its exercise of judgement.[85]

A Member's decision to start WTO dispute settlement proceedings is thus largely beyond judicial review. Note, however, that it is apparent from the 'success rate' of complainants in WTO dispute settlement that Members do indeed duly exercise their judgement as to whether recourse to WTO dispute settlement will be *'fruitful'*. In 89 per cent of all reports, panels agree with the complainant that the respondent acted inconsistently with WTO law.[86]

Questions and Assignments 3.5

Who has access to the WTO dispute settlement system? When do WTO Members have access to the WTO dispute settlement system? List the different causes of action provided for in Article XXIII:1 of the GATT 1994. Can the presumption of nullification or impairment, provided for in Article 3.8 of the DSU, be rebutted? In your opinion, why have there been so few 'non-violation' complaints? Can a Member bring a case against another Member regardless of its 'interest' in the outcome of the case?

3.2.4.2. *Measures subject to WTO dispute settlement*

This section examines the scope of the measures that can be challenged in WTO dispute settlement proceedings and focuses on three 'atypical' measures: first,

---

[83] *Ibid.*, para. 138.   [84] *Ibid.*
[85] Appellate Body Report, *Mexico – Corn Syrup (Article 21.5 – US)*, para. 74. The Appellate Body here referred to its earlier finding, quoted above, in *EC – Bananas III*, para. 135.
[86] See www.worldtradelaw.net/dsc/database/violationcount.asp, visited on 28 November 2007.

measures by private parties; second, measures that are no longer in force; and third, legislation *as such* rather than the actual application of this legislation.

The question whether measures by private parties, the first category of 'atypical' measures mentioned above, can be challenged in WTO dispute settlement arises because the WTO agreements, as is traditionally the case with international agreements, bind the States that are party to them, not private parties. As clearly stated by the Panel in *Japan – Film*:

> As the WTO Agreement is an international agreement, in respect of which only national governments and separate customs territories are directly subject to obligations, it follows by implication that the term *measure* in Article XXIII:1(b) and Article 26.1 of the DSU, as elsewhere in the WTO Agreement, refers only to policies or actions of governments, not those of private parties.[87]

Nevertheless, the Panel recalled that various GATT panels have had to deal with the question whether

> what appear on their face to be private actions may nonetheless be attributable to a government because of some governmental connection to or endorsement of those actions.[88]

For private actions to be attributed to a government – and therefore potentially be subject to WTO dispute settlement – there has to be a certain level of government intervention in the private action.[89] The Panel in *Japan – Film* ruled in this respect:

> past GATT cases demonstrate that the fact that an action is taken by private parties does not rule out the possibility that it may be deemed to be governmental if there is sufficient government involvement with it. It is difficult to establish bright-line rules in this regard, however. Thus, that possibility will need to be examined on a case-by-case basis.[90]

Therefore, each case will have to be examined on its facts to determine whether the level of government involvement in actions of private parties is sufficient to make these actions challengeable measures.

The second category of 'atypical' measures where the question arises whether they may be challenged in WTO dispute settlement proceedings is that of

---

[87] Panel Report, *Japan – Film*, para. 10.52.
[88] *Ibid.* The first GATT Panel report to address this issue was GATT Panel Report *Review Pursuant to Article XVI:5*, para. 12. Here the GATT Panel found private party schemes concerning subsidies to be subject to the notification obligation in GATT Article XVI:1 whenever such schemes were 'dependent for their enforcement on some form of government action'. *Ibid.*
[89] Note that once sufficient government intervention by a Member has been established, the presence of some element of private choice will not relieve the Member of its responsibility. See, for example, *Korea – Various Measures on Beef*, where the measure at issue was a scheme instituted by Korea whereby retailers had to choose to sell either domestic or imported beef. Many retailers stopped selling imported beef. The Appellate Body noted: 'In these circumstances, the intervention of some element of private choice does not relieve Korea of responsibility under the GATT 1994 for the resulting establishment of competitive conditions less favourable for the imported product than for the domestic product.' Appellate Body Report, *Korea – Various Measures on Beef*, para. 146.
[90] Panel Report, *Japan – Film*, para. 10.56. Note that more recently, in *Argentina – Hides and Leather*, the Panel reiterated the findings in *Japan – Film* and noted that in its view it does not follow 'from that panel's statement or from the text or context of Article XI:1 that Members are under an obligation to exclude any possibility that governmental measures may enable private parties, directly or indirectly, to restrict trade, where those measures themselves are not trade restrictive.' Panel Report, *Argentina – Hides and Leather*, para. 11.19.

measures that are no longer in force. In *Indonesia – Autos*, Indonesia notified the Panel that it had terminated its disputed National Car Programme. Nevertheless, the Panel decided to examine the claims with regard to the programme. After mentioning that Indonesia had notified the termination after the deadline set for the submission of new facts, the Panel stated:

> [i]n any event, taking into account our terms of reference, and noting that any revocation of a challenged measure could be relevant to the implementation stage of the dispute settlement process, we consider that it is appropriate for us to make findings in respect of the National Car programme. In this connection, we note that in previous GATT/WTO cases, where a measure included in the terms of reference was otherwise terminated or amended after the commencement of the panel proceedings, panels have nevertheless made findings in respect of such a measure. We shall therefore proceed to examine all of the claims of the complainants.[91]

In *US – Upland Cotton*, the Appellate Body stated:

> Whether or not a measure is still in force is not dispositive of whether that measure is currently affecting the operation of any covered agreement. Therefore, we disagree with the United States' argument that measures whose legislative basis has expired are incapable of affecting the operation of a covered agreement in the present and that, accordingly, expired measures cannot be the subject of consultations under the DSU. In our view, the question of whether measures whose legislative basis has expired affect the operation of a covered agreement currently is an issue that must be resolved on the facts of each case. The outcome of such an analysis cannot be prejudged by excluding it from consultations and dispute settlement proceedings altogether.[92]

The Appellate Body thus explicitly confirmed that measures that are no longer in force can be the subject of consultations or examination by panels, if they currently affect the operation of a covered agreement. However, it noted that the fact that a measure has expired may affect the recommendations a panel may make under Article 19.1 of the DSU.[93] The current legal position on this matter was neatly summarised by the Panel in *EC – Selected Customs Matters*, which stated:

> as a general principle, a panel is competent to make findings and recommendations on measures in existence at the time of establishment of the panel, assuming that the request for establishment of a panel covers those measures. Nevertheless, a panel may also be competent to make findings and make recommendations on measures that have expired or are not yet in existence at the time of establishment, assuming again that the request covers those measures. More specifically, we understand that, to the extent that expired measures affect the operation of a covered agreement at the time of establishment of a panel, they may properly be the subject of findings and recommendations by a panel, particularly if such findings and recommendations are necessary to secure a positive solution to the dispute. Further, measures that are not in existence at the time of establishment may be the subject of findings and recommendations by a panel when they come into

---

[91] Panel Report, *Indonesia – Autos*, para. 14.9. In the omitted footnote, the Panel refers to various WTO and GATT cases in which measures were withdrawn or amended but where the measures as they originally stood were examined nonetheless. See *ibid.*, footnote 642 to para. 14.9.

[92] Appellate Body Report, *US – Upland Cotton*, para. 262.

[93] See *ibid.*, para. 272. Recent case law follows this line of reasoning. See, for example, Panel Report, *Turkey – Rice*, paras. 7.180 and 8.4; Panel Report, *EC – Selected Customs Matters*, para. 7.36; and Panel Reports, *EC – Approval and Marketing of Biotech Products*, paras. 7.1650–7.1652.

> existence provided that they do not change the essential nature of the complaining Member's case as reflected in its request for establishment of a panel.[94]

The third category of 'atypical' measures refers to challenges to legislation *as such*. It is clear that the WTO consistency of the actual application of specific national legislation can be challenged in WTO dispute settlement proceedings. However, can national legislation as such, i.e. independently from its application in specific cases, be challenged in WTO dispute settlement procedures? In *US – 1916 Act*, the Appellate Body recalled the GATT practice in this respect as follows:

> Prior to the entry into force of the *WTO Agreement*, it was firmly established that Article XXIII:1(a) of the GATT 1947 allowed a Contracting Party to challenge legislation as such, independently from the application of that legislation in specific instances. While the text of Article XXIII does not expressly address the matter, panels consistently considered that, under Article XXIII, they had *the jurisdiction* to deal with claims against legislation as such. In *examining* such claims, panels developed the concept that mandatory and discretionary legislation should be distinguished from each other, reasoning that only legislation that mandates a violation of GATT obligations can be found as such to be inconsistent with those obligations.[95]

The practice of GATT panels was summed up in *US – Tobacco* as follows:

> panels had consistently ruled that legislation which mandated action inconsistent with the General Agreement could be challenged as such, whereas legislation which merely gave the discretion to the *executive authority* of a contracting party to act inconsistently with the General Agreement could not be challenged as such; only the actual application of such legislation inconsistent with the General Agreement could be subject to challenge.[96]
>
> [Emphasis added]

WTO panels, as well as the Appellate Body, have followed the same practice.[97] However, the Panel in *US – Section 301 Trade Act* 'refined' the existing jurisprudence. The Panel in that case rejected the presumption, implicit in the argument of the United States, that no WTO provision ever prohibits discretionary legislation. The Panel explicitly stated that, in rejecting this presumption, it did not imply a reversal of the classic test in the existing jurisprudence that only legislation mandating a WTO inconsistency or precluding WTO consistency could, as such, violate WTO provisions.[98] On the contrary, that was the very test which the Panel applied. The Panel argued, however, that:

> It simply does not follow from this test, as sometimes has been argued, that legislation with discretion could never violate the WTO. If, for example, it is found that the specific obligations in Article 23 [of the DSU] prohibit a certain type of legislative discretion, the existence of such discretion in the statutory language of Section 304 would presumptively preclude WTO consistency.[99]

---

[94] Panel Report, *EC – Selected Customs Matters*, para. 7.36.
[95] Appellate Body Report, *US – 1916 Act*, para. 60. In a footnote, the Appellate Body referred, for example, to the GATT Panel Reports in *US – Superfund*, *US – Section 337*, *Thailand – Cigarettes* and *US – Malt Beverages*.
[96] GATT Panel Report, *US – Tobacco*, para. 118.
[97] See e.g. Panel Report, *US – Zeroing (EC)*, paras 7.37–7.69; Panel Report, *Korea – Commercial Vessels*, paras. 7.57–7.67; Panel Reports, *Canada – Wheat Exports and Grain Imports;* paras. 6.184–6.186 and 6.27; Panel Report, *US – Corrosion-Resistant Steel Sunset Review*, paras. 7.124–7.127; Panel Report, *US – Carbon Steel*, paras. 8.85–8.107; Panel Report, *US – Carbon Steel*, para. 8.102; and Appellate Body Report, *US – Carbon Steel*, paras. 154–63.
[98] See Panel Report, *US – Section 301 Trade Act*, para. 7.54.   [99] Ibid.

The Panel then examined Article 23 of the DSU, the obligation at issue, in great detail. In this examination, the Panel observed with regard to the nature of the obligation of Article 23 of the DSU:

> It may have been plausible if one considered a strict Member–Member matrix to insist that the obligations in Article 23 [of the DSU] do not apply to legislation that threatens unilateral determinations but does not actually mandate them. It is not, however, plausible to construe Article 23 in this way if one interprets it in the light of the indirect effect such legislation has on individuals and the market-place, the protection of which is one of the principal objects and purposes of the WTO.
>
> To be sure, in the cases referred to above, whether the risk materialised or not depended on certain market factors such as fluctuating reference prices on which the taxation of the imported product was based by virtue of the domestic legislation. In this case, whether the risk materializes depends on a decision of a government agency. From the perspective of the individual economic operator, however, this makes little difference. Indeed, it may be more difficult to predict the outcome of discretionary government action than to predict market conditions, thereby exacerbating the negative economic impact of the type of domestic law under examination here.
>
> When a Member imposes unilateral measures in violation of Article 23 in a specific dispute, serious damage is created both to other Members and the market-place. However, in our view, the creation of damage is not confined to actual conduct in specific cases. A law reserving the right for unilateral measures to be taken contrary to DSU rules and procedures, may – as is the case here – constitute an ongoing threat and produce a 'chilling effect' causing serious damage in a variety of ways.[100]

According to the Panel, the duty of Members under Article 23 to abstain from unilateral determinations of inconsistency is meant to guarantee Members, as well as the marketplace and those who operate in it, that no such determinations in respect of WTO rights and obligations will be made.[101] The Panel subsequently ruled with regard to the measure at issue:

> The *discretion* given to the [US Trade Representative] to make a determination of inconsistency creates a real risk or threat for both Members and individual economic operators that determinations prohibited under Article 23.2(a) will be imposed. The USTR's *discretion* effectively to make such determinations removes the guarantee which Article 23 is intended to give not only to Members but indirectly also to individuals and the market-place.[102]
>
> [Emphasis added]

The Panel concluded, therefore, that the statutory language of Section 304 of the Trade Act of 1974, although it was not mandatory but discretionary in nature, was *prima facie* inconsistent with Article 23 of the DSU (in view of the particular nature of the obligation in Article 23).[103] The Panel report in *US – Section 301 Trade Act* was not appealed.

Questions and Assignments 3.6

Can a Member challenge the WTO consistency of a measure by a private party? Can a Member challenge the WTO consistency of the measure that is no longer in force? Can a Member challenge national legislation as

---

[100] *Ibid.*, paras. 7.86–7.88.   [101] See *ibid.*, para. 7.95.   [102] *Ibid.*, para. 7.96.   [103] See *ibid.*, para. 7.97.

such, i.e. independently from any application of this legislation in specific cases? Does the Panel in *US – Section 301 Trade Act* deviate from the established GATT/WTO practice on this issue?

3.2.4.3. *The amicus curiae brief issue*

As noted above, the WTO dispute settlement system is a government-to-government dispute settlement system for disputes concerning rights and obligations of WTO Members. Individuals, companies, international organisations and non-governmental organisations (including environmental and human rights NGOs, labour unions and industry associations) have no direct access to the WTO dispute settlement system.[104] They cannot bring claims of violation of WTO rights or obligations. Under the current rules, they do not have the *right* to be heard or to participate in the proceedings. However, under Appellate Body case law, panels and the Appellate Body have the authority to accept and consider written briefs submitted by individuals, companies or organisations. The acceptance by panels and the Appellate Body of these briefs, which are commonly referred to as *amicus curiae* briefs ('friend of the court' briefs), has been controversial and criticised by most WTO Members.[105]

In *US – Shrimp*, the Appellate Body noted with respect to the authority of panels to accept and consider *amicus curiae* briefs:

> The comprehensive nature of the authority of a panel to 'seek' information and technical advice from 'any individual or body' it may consider appropriate, or from 'any relevant source', should be underscored. This authority embraces more than merely the choice and evaluation of the *source* of the information or advice which it may seek. A panel's authority includes the authority to decide *not to seek* such information or advice at all. We consider that a panel also has the authority to *accept or reject* any information or advice which it may have sought and received, or to *make some other appropriate disposition* thereof. It is particularly within the province and the authority of a panel to determine *the need for information and advice* in a specific case, to ascertain the *acceptability* and *relevancy* of information or advice received, and to decide *what weight to ascribe to that information or advice* or to conclude that no weight at all should be given to what has been received.
>
> It is also pertinent to note that Article 12.1 of the DSU authorizes panels to depart from, or to add to, the Working Procedures set forth in Appendix 3 of the DSU, and in effect to develop their own Working Procedures, after consultation with the parties to the dispute. Article 12.2 goes on to direct that '[p]anel procedures should provide *sufficient flexibility* so as to *ensure high-quality panel reports* while *not unduly delaying the panel process*'. [Emphasis added]
>
> The thrust of Articles 12 and 13, taken together, is that the DSU accords to a panel established by the DSB, and engaged in a dispute settlement proceeding, ample and

---

[104] On 'indirect' access to the WTO dispute settlement system, see below, pp. 197–8.

[105] Only *amicus curiae* briefs that were attached to the submissions of the parties or third parties have generally been accepted. This is logical since it is of course for a party to determine for itself what to include in its submission. See e.g. Panel Report, *US – Shrimp*, para. 7.8; Appellate Body Report, *US – Shrimp*, para. 81–91; Panel Report, *US – Shrimp (Article 21.5 – Malaysia)*, paras. 5.14–5.16; Panel Report, *EC – Asbestos*, para. 8.12; Panel Report, *US – Softwood Lumber IV*, para. 7.1 and Panel Report, *US – Softwood Lumber VI*, para. 7.10. In *Brazil – Retreaded Tyres*, the Panel received two unsolicited *amicus curiae* briefs, one from the Humane Society International and one from a group of environmental NGOs. Both *amicus curiae* briefs were made part of Brazil's exhibits, at the request of Brazil in the first substantive meeting. See Panel Report, *Brazil – Retreaded Tyres*, para. 1.8.

> extensive authority to undertake and to control the process by which it informs itself both of the relevant facts of the dispute and of the legal norms and principles applicable to such facts. That authority, and the breadth thereof, is indispensably necessary to enable a panel to discharge its duty imposed by Article 11 of the DSU to 'make an objective assessment of the matter before it, including an *objective assessment of the facts of the case* and the *applicability of and conformity with the relevant covered agreements . . .*'.
>
> [Emphasis added][106]

On the basis of Articles 13, 12 and 11 of the DSU, the Appellate Body thus came to the conclusion that panels have the authority to accept and consider *amicus curiae* briefs, and reversed the Panel's finding to the contrary. A few panels in later disputes did, on the basis of this ruling of the Appellate Body in *US – Shrimp*, accept and consider *amicus curiae* briefs. This was the case, for example, in *Australia – Salmon (Article 21.5 – Canada)*, in which the Panel accepted and considered a letter from 'Concerned Fishermen and Processors' in South Australia. This letter addressed the treatment by Australia of, on the one hand, imports of pilchard for use as bait or fish feed and, on the other hand, imports of salmon. The Panel considered the information submitted in the letter as relevant to the dispute before it and accepted this information as part of the record.[107] In many other disputes, however, panels refused to accept or consider *amicus curiae* briefs submitted to them.[108]

In *US – Lead and Bismuth II*, the Appellate Body ruled with respect to its own authority to accept and consider *amicus curiae* briefs submitted in appellate review proceedings:

> In considering this matter, we first note that nothing in the DSU or the *Working Procedures* specifically provides that the Appellate Body may accept and consider submissions or briefs from sources other than the participants and third participants in an appeal. On the other hand, neither the DSU nor the *Working Procedures* explicitly prohibit acceptance or consideration of such briefs. However, Article 17.9 of the DSU provides:
>
>> Working procedures shall be drawn up by the Appellate Body in consultation with the Chairman of the DSB and the Director-General, and communicated to the Members for their information.

---

[106] Appellate Body Report, *US – Shrimp*, paras. 104, 105 and 106.

[107] See Panel Report, *Australia – Salmon (Article 21.5 – Canada)*, paras. 7.8–7.9. In *US – Softwood Lumber III*, the Panel accepted for consideration one unsolicited *amicus* brief that was submitted before the first substantive meeting with the parties. The other three *amicus* briefs were rejected 'for reasons relating to the timing of these submissions'. See Panel Report, *US – Softwood Lumber III*, para. 7.2.

[108] See Panel Report, *US – Lead and Bismuth II*, para. 6.3 (where the *amicus curiae* brief was rejected as its late submission gave rise to due process concerns); Panel Report, *US – Section 110(5) Copyright Act*, para. 6.8 (where the panel disregarded a letter copied to it by the US that 'essentially duplicate[d] information already submitted by the parties'; Panel Report, *EC – Bed Linen*, para. 6.1, footnote 10 (where the Panel did not find it necessary to take the *amicus* submission into account in reaching its decision); Panel Report, *US – Zeroing (Japan)*, para. 1.7 (where the Panel invited the parties and third parties to express their views on how it should handle an *amicus curiae* brief from the Committee to Support US Trade Laws (CSUSTL), and on that basis decided 'that it would not further consider the arguments in the CSUSTL brief except to the extent that the parties reflected those arguments in their written submissions and/or oral statements'; Panel Reports, *EC – Export Subsidies on Sugar*, paras 2.20 and 7.76- 7.85 (where the *amicus* submission was based on confidential information in a party's submission and the breach of confidentiality, in the Panel's view, disqualified the credibility of the authors); Panel Reports, *EC – Approval and Marketing of Biotech Products*, paras. 7.10–7.11 (in which the Panel did accept such briefs into the record but did not consider it necessary to take them into account); and Panel Report, *EC – Selected Customs Matters*, para. 7.76, footnote 209 (where the Panel refused to admit an *amicus curiae* brief as part of the Panel's record 'because, *inter alia*, it was filed too late and its admission would have unduly delayed the Panel's proceedings').

> This provision makes clear that the Appellate Body has broad authority to adopt procedural rules which do not conflict with any rules and procedures in the DSU or the covered agreements. Therefore, we are of the opinion that as long as we act consistently with the provisions of the DSU and the covered agreements, we have the legal authority to decide whether or not to accept and consider any information that we believe is pertinent and useful in an appeal.[109]

In this case, the Appellate Body did not find it necessary to take the two *amicus curiae* briefs filed into account in rendering its decision.[110]

In October 2000, the Appellate Body Division hearing the appeal in *EC – Asbestos* adopted an Additional Procedure to deal with *amicus curiae* briefs which the Division expected to receive in great numbers in that dispute.[111] This Additional Procedure, which was adopted pursuant to Rule 16(1) of the *Working Procedures for Appellate Review* in the interests of fairness and orderly procedure in the conduct of this appeal, stipulated:

> 2. Any person, whether natural or legal, other than a party or a third party to this dispute, wishing to file a written brief with the Appellate Body, must apply for leave to file such a brief from the Appellate Body *by noon* on *Thursday, 16 November 2000*.
> 3. An application for leave to file such a written brief shall:
> . . .
>   d. specify the nature of the interest the applicant has in this appeal;
>   e. identify the specific issues of law covered in the Panel Report and legal interpretations developed by the Panel that are the subject of this appeal, as set forth in the Notice of Appeal (WT/DS135/8) dated 23 October 2000, which the applicant intends to address in its written brief;
>   f. state why it would be desirable, in the interests of achieving a satisfactory settlement of the matter at issue, in accordance with the rights and obligations of WTO Members under the DSU and the other covered agreements, for the Appellate Body to grant the applicant leave to file a written brief in this appeal; and indicate, in particular, in what way the applicant will make a contribution to the resolution of this dispute that is not likely to be repetitive of what has been already submitted by a party or third party to this dispute; . . .
> 4. The Appellate Body will review and consider each application for leave to file a written brief and will, without delay, render a decision whether to grant or deny such leave.

With regard to briefs filed by applicants granted leave to do so, the Additional Procedure further stipulated:

> 5. The grant of leave to file a brief by the Appellate Body does not imply that the Appellate Body will address, in its Report, the legal arguments made in such a brief.
> 6. Any person, other than a party or a third party to this dispute, granted leave to file a written brief with the Appellate Body, must file its brief with the Appellate Body Secretariat *by noon* on *Monday, 27 November 2000*.
> 7. A written brief filed with the Appellate Body by an applicant granted leave to file such a brief shall:
> . . .

---

[109] Appellate Body Report, *US – Lead and Bismuth II*, para. 39. In support of its reasoning, the Appellate Body referred, in a footnote to this paragraph, to Rule 16(1) of the *Working Procedures for Appellate Review*. Rule 16(1) allows a Division hearing an appeal to develop an appropriate procedure in certain specified circumstances where a procedural question arises that is not covered by the *Working Procedures*. See below, p. 289.   [110] See *ibid.*, para. 42.

[111] See Appellate Body Report, *EC – Asbestos*, paras. 51–2. Note that the Division adopted this Additional Procedure after consultations among all Members of the Appellate Body.

b. be concise and in no case longer than 20 typed pages, including any appendices; and

c. set out a precise statement, strictly limited to legal arguments, supporting the applicant's legal position on the issues of law or legal interpretations in the Panel Report with respect to which the applicant has been granted leave to file a written brief.

The Appellate Body received eleven applications for leave to file a written brief in the *EC – Asbestos* appeal within the time limits specified in paragraph 2 of the Additional Procedure. It reviewed and considered each of these applications in accordance with the Additional Procedure and, in each case, decided to deny leave to file a written brief for failure to comply sufficiently with all the requirements set forth in paragraph 3 of the Additional Procedure.

While, in the end, the Appellate Body did not accept and consider any *amicus curiae* brief in the *EC – Asbestos* appeal, many WTO Members were infuriated by the Appellate Body's adoption of the Additional Procedure and its apparent willingness to accept and consider *amicus curiae* briefs where certain requirements are fulfilled. On 20 November 2000, a Special Meeting of the General Council was convened to discuss this issue. The discussion at this meeting reflected the deep division between the vast majority of WTO Members opposing the Appellate Body's case law on this issue and the United States, which fully supported this case law. At the end of this tumultuous meeting, the Chairman of the General Council made the following observations:

> There was a broad agreement that the rights and obligations under the DSU belonged to WTO Members. It had been repeatedly stated that the WTO was a Member-driven organization. Therefore, most delegations had concluded that since there was no specific provision regarding *amicus* briefs such briefs should not be accepted. Some delegations were of the view that *amicus* briefs could be used in some cases and there was at least one delegation who believed that there was both a legal and a substantive reason to use *amicus* briefs. There was no agreement on this point.
>
> . . . [M]any Members had made reference to the shrimp case and the decision to interpret Article 13 of the DSU in such a way so as to accept *amicus* briefs. The majority of delegations had stated that they did not agree with that decision which served as a basis for subsequent decisions on *amicus* briefs by panels and the Appellate Body. At the same time, at least one delegation had stated that there was nothing wrong with that kind of procedure.
>
> Finally, many Members had made the point that the issue under discussion was not a transparency issue, but rather a legal issue and concerned the question of who should participate in the legal system.[112]

The Chairman of the General Council concluded that he believed that there had been a large sentiment, expressed by almost all delegations, that there was a need to put clear rules in place for *amicus curiae* briefs. He called for further consultations on both the substantive content of the rules and what procedure should be used for putting them in place. The Chairman finally also stated:

> in light of the views expressed and in the absence of clear rules, he believed that the Appellate Body should exercise extreme caution in future cases until Members had considered what rules were needed.[113]

---

[112] General Council, *Minutes of the Meeting of 22 November 2000*, WT/GC/M/60, dated 23 January 2001, paras. 114–15 and 118.   [113] *Ibid.*, para. 120.

There are two main reasons for the antagonism of many Members, especially developing-country Members, against *amicus curiae* briefs. First, Members fear that the need to consider and react to *amicus curiae* briefs will take up scarce legal resources and will further bend the WTO dispute settlement procedures in favour of Members with more legal resources at their disposal. Secondly, developing-country Members, in particular, note that the most vocal and best funded NGOs (such as Greenpeace, WWF and labour unions) often take positions that are considered 'unfriendly' to the interests and policies of developing-country Members.[114]

To date, WTO Members have been unable to adopt any clear rules on *amicus curiae* briefs.[115] The Appellate Body has repeatedly confirmed its case law on the authority of panels and the Appellate Body to accept and consider *amicus curiae* briefs. In no appellate proceedings thus far, however, has the Appellate Body considered it useful in deciding on an appeal to accept or consider *amicus curiae* briefs submitted to it.[116]

Note that in *US – Steel Safeguards* the Appellate Body ruled, in response to a question from the European Communities whether the Appellate Body intended to accept and take account of the *amicus curiae* brief from the American Institute of International Steel, that this determination would be made after the Appellate Body had considered all submissions by the participants in the appeal, including the submissions at the oral hearing.[117]

The *amicus curiae* brief filed by Morocco in the appellate proceedings in *EC – Sardines* is of particular interest. Morocco was the first WTO Member to file an *amicus curiae* brief. Peru, the complainant in *EC – Sardines*, argued that the Appellate Body should not accept or consider this brief. In considering the issue, the Appellate Body first recalled its case law on *amicus curiae* briefs and then noted:

---

[114] Note that it has also been argued that persons submitting an *amicus curiae* brief would have more rights than third parties. This argument is mistaken. In fact, persons submitting an *amicus curiae* brief have no right to have this brief considered (see above, p. 191). By contrast, third parties do have a right to have their brief considered (see above, pp. 181–2). See also Appellate Body Report, *US – Steel Safeguards*, para. 268.

[115] The issue of *amicus curiae* briefs has been addressed in the DSU reform negotiations. See the Proposal by the African Group, TN/DS/W/15, dated 15 September 2002, 5; and Proposal by India *et al.* TN/DS/W/18, dated 7 October 2002, 2. Both proposals want to include in the DSU an explicit prohibition on acceptance of *amicus curiae* briefs. See *contra*, the Communication from the European Communities, TN/DS/W/1, dated 13 March 2002, 11. The European Communities pleads for admittance of *amicus curiae* briefs if they provide information directly relevant to issues under consideration. None of these proposals were taken up in the Chairman's Text. See below, pp. 309–10.

[116] For examples of where the Appellate Body did not consider it necessary to take unsolicited *amicus curiae* briefs into account, see Appellate Body Report, *Mexico – Taxes on Soft Drinks*, para. 8; Appellate Body Report, *EC – Chicken Cuts*, para. 12; Appellate Body Report, *EC – Export Subsidies on Sugar*, para. 9; Appellate Body Report, *US – Softwood Lumber IV*, para. 9; Appellate Body Report, *US – Steel Safeguards*, para. 268; Appellate Body Report, *US – Lead and Bismuth II*, para. 42; Appellate Body Report, *Brazil – Retreaded Tyres*, para. 7; and Appellate Body Report, *Thailand – H-Beams*, para.78 (in this case the rejection was partly due to a breach of confidentiality whereby Thailand's submission had been disclosed to the relevant NGO). Even in *US – Certain EC Products*, a complaint by the EC, in which both the complainant and the respondent explicitly agreed that the Appellate Body had the authority to accept and consider an *amicus curiae* brief from an industry association received in the course of the appeal, the Appellate Body decided not to take the brief into account 'as we do not find it to be of assistance in this appeal'. Appellate Body Report, *US –Certain EC Products*, paras. 10 and 76.

[117] See Appellate Body Report, *US – Steel Safeguards*, paras. 9 and 10.

> We have been urged by the parties to this dispute not to treat Members less favourably than non-Members with regard to participation as *amicus curiae*. We agree. We have not. And we will not. As we have already determined that we have the authority to receive an *amicus curiae* brief from a private individual or an organization, *a fortiori* we are entitled to accept such a brief from a WTO Member, provided there is no prohibition on doing so in the DSU. We find no such prohibition.[118]

The Appellate Body therefore concluded that it was entitled to accept the *amicus curiae* brief submitted by Morocco, and consider it.[119] However, the Appellate Body emphasised that, in accepting the brief filed by Morocco in this appeal, it was not suggesting that each time a Member filed such a brief it would be required to accept and consider it. The Appellate Body noted:

> To the contrary, acceptance of any *amicus curiae* brief is a matter of discretion, which we must exercise on a case-by-case basis. We recall our statement that:
>
>> The procedural rules of WTO dispute settlement are designed to promote . . . the fair, prompt and effective resolution of trade disputes.
>
>> Therefore, we could exercise our discretion to reject an *amicus curiae* brief if, by accepting it, this would interfere with the 'fair, prompt and effective resolution of trade disputes.' This could arise, for example, if a WTO Member were to seek to submit an *amicus curiae* brief at a very late stage in the appellate proceedings, with the result that accepting the brief would impose an undue burden on other participants.[120]

Having concluded that it had the authority to accept the *amicus curiae* brief filed by Morocco, the Appellate Body then considered whether this brief could assist it in this appeal. Morocco's *amicus curiae* brief provided mainly factual information.[121] The Appellate Body therefore ruled on the relevance of these parts of Morocco's brief:

> As Article 17.6 of the DSU limits an appeal to issues of law and legal interpretations developed by the panel, the factual information provided in Morocco's *amicus curiae* brief is not pertinent in this appeal.[122]

Morocco also put forward arguments relating to legal issues.[123] However, the Appellate Body decided not to make findings on these specific issues and, therefore, Morocco's arguments on these issues did not assist the Appellate Body in this appeal.[124] If the Appellate Body had made findings on these issues, it would arguably have accepted and considered the relevant part of Morocco's *amicus curiae* brief.

Questions and Assignments 3.7

Do panels and the Appellate Body have the authority to accept and consider *amicus curiae* briefs? Do NGOs have a right to submit *amicus*

---

[118] Appellate Body Report, *EC – Sardines*, para. 164.
[119] See *ibid.*, para. 167. The quote cited by the Appellate Body comes from Appellate Body Report, *US – FSC*, para 166.   [120] Appellate Body Report, *EC – Sardines*, para. 167.
[121] Morocco's brief referred to the scientific differences between *Sardina pilchardus Walbaum* and ('*Sardinops sagax*'), and it also provided economic information about the Moroccan fishing and canning industries.
[122] Appellate Body Report, *EC – Sardines*, para. 169.
[123] Morocco's brief contained arguments relating to Article 2.1 of the *TBT Agreement* and the GATT 1994.
[124] See Appellate Body Report, *EC – Sardines*, para. 314.

curiae briefs? Should an *amicus curiae* brief filed by a WTO Member be treated differently from briefs filed by NGOs? Did panels and the Appellate Body ever consider *amicus curiae* briefs in their deliberations? Why are most WTO Members highly critical of the Appellate Body's approach to the *amicus curiae* brief issue? Do you consider their criticism justified?

3.2.4.4. 'Indirect access' for private parties

Many, if not most, of the disputes heard by the WTO are disputes brought by governments *at the instigation of* an industry or a company. It is well known that in *Japan – Film*, it was Kodak which masterminded and actively supported the US claims against Japan. In *EC – Bananas III*, Chiquita played a central role in the United States' involvement in this dispute. As Quentin Peel reported in the *Financial Times*:

> Even in the incestuous world of trade politics in Washington, where deals are done behind closed doors and lobbyists reign supreme, they talk of Carl Lindner in hushed tones.
>
> If the present words between the US and the European Union over bananas come to real blows, his influence will certainly be seen as critical. This veteran financier, 80 next year, has succeeded almost single-handedly in turning a row about someone else's exports, and other people's jobs, into an issue of principle for the US Government, and the possible cause of a serious rift in relations with its biggest trading partner.
>
> And yet no one admits to surprise. 'It is a textbook case of how trade policy works in this city', says a diplomat closely involved in trade talks. 'It is driven by very narrow interest groups. And nobody is prepared to stand up to this.'
>
> Mr Lindner is a banana baron, although a thoroughly unlikely one. He is chairman and chief executive of Chiquita Brands International, the largest banana producer and trader in the world, with some 26 per cent of the market.
>
> In 1993, the EU introduced new rules to discriminate in favour of buying Caribbean bananas, and therefore squeezed the share of Chiquita's 'dollar bananas' from one of its most lucrative markets. Since then, Mr Lindner has lined up a remarkable bipartisan battery of political heavy-weights to gun for him in the capital.
>
> Headed by Bob Dole, the former Senate majority leader, and Trent Lott, his successor as majority leader, it includes Newt Gingrich, the former Speaker of the House of Representatives, Senator John Glenn of Ohio and space fame, and Congressman Richard Gephardt, the House Democratic leader. All wrote letters to President Bill Clinton and Mickey Kantor, then US Trade Representative, urging tough counter-measures against the EU. They also tried to bring down the wrath of the US on any Central American country that dared to break ranks and join the EU cartel.[125]

Companies or industry associations will not only lobby governments to bring dispute settlement cases to the WTO, they (and their law firms) will often also play an important, 'behind-the-scenes' role in planning the legal strategy and drafting the submissions.

The legal system of some WTO Members explicitly provides for the possibility for industry associations and/or companies to bring a violation of WTO

---

[125] Quentin Peel, 'Man in the News Carl Lindner, Banana Republican', *Financial Times*, 14–15 November 1998.

obligations, by another WTO Member, to the attention of their government and to 'induce' their government to start WTO dispute settlement proceedings against that Member. In EC law, this possibility is provided for under the Trade Barriers Regulation;[126] in US law, under Section 301 of the 1974 Trade Act;[127] and in Chinese law, under the Investigation Rules of Foreign Trade Barriers.[128] In many other Members, the process of lobbying the government to bring WTO cases has not been regulated and institutionalised in the same manner, but the process is no less present. In this respect, industry associations and individual companies have 'indirect' access to the WTO dispute settlement system.

Questions and Assignments 3.8

Consult the EC Trade Barriers Regulation, Section 301 of the US Trade Act of 1947 and the Chinese Investigation Rules of Foreign Trade Barriers. Determine who can make use of the procedures set out in these legislative acts.

3.2.5. The WTO dispute settlement process

3.2.5.1 Steps in the WTO dispute settlement process

The WTO dispute settlement process entails four major steps:

- consultations;
- panel proceedings;
- appellate review proceedings; and
- implementation and enforcement.

As already indicated above, the process always starts with *consultations*, or at least an attempt by the complainant to involve the respondent in consultations, to resolve the dispute amicably.[129] If that is not possible, the complainant can refer the dispute to a panel for adjudication. The *panel proceedings* will result in a panel report.[130] This report can be appealed to the Appellate Body. The *appellate review proceedings* will result in an Appellate Body report upholding, modifying or

---

[126] Council Regulation (EC) No. 3286/94 on Community procedures for the exercise of rights under international trade rules, in particular those established under the WTO, OJ 1994, L349, 71, as amended by Council Regulation (EC) No. 356/95, OJ 1995, L41, 3. The European Community's Trade Barriers Regulation creates a mechanism whereby individuals and firms that have suffered adverse effects from a WTO-inconsistent measure of another WTO Member can complain to the Commission and request it to take appropriate action, including the initiation of WTO dispute settlement proceedings. See P. J. Kuijper, 'From Initiating Proceedings to Ensuring Implementation: The Links with the Community Legal Order' in G. Sacerdoti, A. Yanovich and J. Bohanes (eds.), *The WTO at Ten: The Contribution of the Dispute Settlement System* (Cambridge University Press, 2006), 273.

[127] Section 301(a)(1) of the Trade Act 1974, 19 USC 2411(a)(1).

[128] Investigation Rules of Foreign Trade Barriers, entered into force on 1 March 2005. The English translation of these rules is available on the official website of the Ministry of Commerce of China. See http://english.mofcom.gov.cn/aarticle/policyrelease/domesticpolicy/200503/20050300029640.html, visited on 13 August 2007.

[129] See above, p. 173. For a detailed discussion on the initiation, conduct and possible outcome of consultations, see below, pp. 269–74.

[130] For a detailed discussion of panel proceedings, see below, pp. 275–88.

Figure 3.1 Flowchart of the WTO dispute settlement process[131]

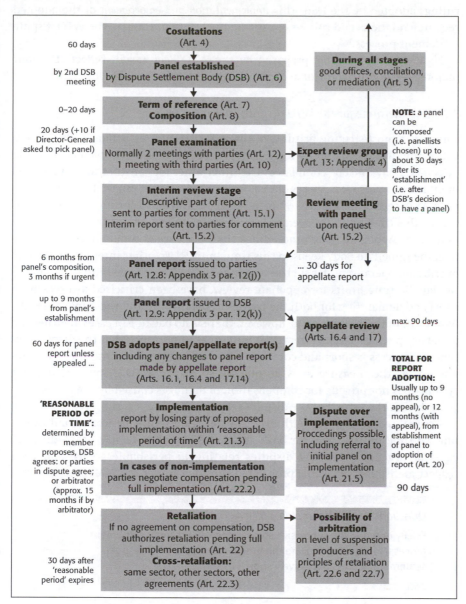

reversing the panel report.[132] The panel report, or in the case of an appeal, the Appellate Body report *and* the panel report, will be adopted by the Dispute Settlement Body. After the adoption of the reports, the respondent, if found to

---

[131] See www.wto.org/english/thewto_e/whatis_e/tif_e/disp2_e.htm, visited on 8 August 2007. Note that in this flowchart the length of each step in the process reflects the minimum or maximum indicated in the DSU, and not the actual practice. See below, p. 200.

[132] For a detailed discussion of appellate review proceedings, see below, pp. 288–97.

be in breach of WTO law, will have to implement the recommendations and rulings adopted by the DSB. This *implementation and enforcement* of the adopted recommendations and rulings constitute the last major step in the WTO dispute settlement process.[133]

Figure 3.1, a flowchart prepared by the WTO Secretariat, reflects the four major steps, adding additional elements which are discussed below.[134]

3.2.5.2. Timeframe for the WTO dispute settlement process

One of the most striking features of the WTO dispute settlement system is the short timeframes within which the proceedings of both panels and the Appellate Body must be completed. The timeframes for consultations and implementation are also strictly regulated. In principle, panel proceedings should in no case exceed nine months.[135] In practice, however, panel proceedings often exceed this time limit. On average, panel proceedings last approximately twelve months.[136] Appellate Body proceedings shall not exceed ninety days.[137] In practice, the Appellate Body keeps to this time limit.[138] No other international court or tribunal operates under such severe time limits. These time limits, and in particular the time limits for appellate review, have been criticised as excessively short and demanding for both the parties to the dispute and the Appellate Body. As a result of these time limits, however, there is no backlog of cases at either the panel or appellate level. Moreover, it is of great importance that the dispute settlement process is short and comes to a determination regarding the WTO consistency of the measure at issue quickly since the WTO dispute settlement system does not provide for compensation of damages caused by the measure at issue during the time that the dispute settlement process is running.[139]

Accelerated procedures with even shorter time limits (generally half of the normal time limits) apply for both panel and appellate review proceedings in cases of urgency (including disputes relating to perishable goods) and with respect to disputes regarding prohibited subsidies under the *SCM Agreement*.[140]

Questions and Assignments 3.9

Briefly describe the successive steps in the WTO dispute settlement process. In your opinion, are the time limits on the WTO dispute settlement process excessively short?

---

[133] For a detailed discussion of implementation and enforcement proceedings, see below, pp. 298–307.
[134] See above, p. 199.   [135] See Article 12.9 of the DSU.
[136] See the WTO website, www.wto.org/english/thewto_e/whatis_e/tif_e/disp1_e.htm, visited on 8 August 2007. For a detailed discussion on the duration of the panel proceedings and the reasons for delays in these proceedings, see below, pp. 287–8.   [137] See Article 17.5 of the DSU.
[138] For a detailed discussion on the duration of the appellate review proceedings, see below, p. 297.
[139] For a detailed discussion on the remedies available in case of breach of WTO law, see below, pp. 218–31.
[140] See Articles 4.9, 12.8 and 17.5 of the DSU and Article 4 of the *SCM Agreement*. Under Article 4.6 of the *SCM Agreement*, a panel must, for example, circulate its report within ninety days of the date of its composition Pursuant to Article 7 of the *SCM Agreement*, disputes regarding actionable subsidies are also subject to some specific deadlines. A panel must, for example, circulate its report to all Members within 120 days of the date of its composition. See Article 7.5 of the *SCM Agreement*.

3.2.6. Rules of interpretation and burden of proof

Central to any dispute settlement system are the rules of interpretation and the rules on burden of proof. This section discusses these rules as applied in WTO dispute settlement.

3.2.6.1. Rules of interpretation

Article 3.2 of the DSU stipulates in relevant part that the dispute settlement system serves:

> to clarify the existing provisions of [the covered] agreements in accordance with *customary rules of interpretation of public international law.*
>
> [Emphasis added]

In *US – Gasoline*, the Appellate Body noted:

> The 'general rule of interpretation' [set out in Article 31(1) of the *Vienna Convention on the Law of Treaties*] has attained the status of a rule of customary or general international law. As such, it forms part of the 'customary rules of interpretation of public international law' which the Appellate Body has been directed, by Article 3(2) of the *DSU*, to apply in seeking to clarify the provisions of the *General Agreement* and the other 'covered agreements' of the *Marrakesh Agreement Establishing the World Trade Organization* (the '*WTO Agreement*'). That direction reflects a measure of recognition that the *General Agreement* is not to be read in clinical isolation from public international law.[141]

In *Japan – Alcoholic Beverages II*, the Appellate Body added:

> There can be no doubt that Article 32 of the *Vienna Convention,* dealing with the role of supplementary means of interpretation, has also attained the same status [of a rule of customary international law].[142]

Article 31 of the *Vienna Convention on the Law of Treaties*, entitled 'General Rule of Interpretation', states:

> 1. A treaty shall be interpreted in good faith in accordance with the ordinary meaning to be given to the terms of the treaty in their context and in the light of its object and purpose.
> 2. The context for the purpose of the interpretation of a treaty shall comprise, in addition to the text, including its preamble and annexes:
>   a. any agreement relating to the treaty which was made between all the parties in connection with the conclusion of the treaty;
>   b. any instrument which was made by one or more parties in connection with the conclusion of the treaty and accepted by the other parties as an instrument related to the treaty.
> 3. There shall be taken into account together with the context:
>   a. any subsequent agreement between the parties regarding the interpretation of the treaty or the application of its provisions;
>   b. any subsequent practice in the application of the treaty which establishes the agreement of the parties regarding its interpretation;

---

[141] Appellate Body Report, *US – Gasoline*, 16.
[142] Appellate Body Report, *Japan – Alcoholic Beverages II*, 104.

> c. any relevant rules of international law applicable in the relations between the parties.
> 4. A special meaning shall be given to a term if it is established that the parties so intended.

Article 32 of the *Vienna Convention*, entitled 'Supplementary Means of Interpretation', states:

> Recourse may be had to supplementary means of interpretation, including the preparatory work of the treaty and the circumstances of its conclusion, in order to confirm the meaning resulting from the application of article 31, or to determine the meaning when the interpretation according to article 31:
> a. leaves the meaning ambiguous or obscure; or
> b. leads to a result which is manifestly absurd or unreasonable.

Consequently, panels and the Appellate Body interpret provisions of the covered agreements in accordance with the ordinary meaning of the words of the provision taken in their context and in the light of the object and purpose of the agreement involved. If necessary and appropriate, panels and the Appellate Body have recourse to supplementary means of interpretation.[143] As the Panel in *US – Section 301 Trade Act* observed:

> Text, context and object-and-purpose correspond to well established textual, systemic and teleological methodologies of treaty interpretation, all of which typically come into play when interpreting complex provisions in multilateral treaties. For pragmatic reasons the normal usage, and we will follow the normal usage, is to start the interpretation from the ordinary meaning of the 'raw' text of the relevant treaty provisions and then seek to construe it in its context and in the light of the treaty's object and purpose. However, the elements referred to in Article 31 – text, context and object-and-purpose as well as good faith – are to be viewed as one holistic rule of interpretation rather than a sequence of separate tests to be applied in a hierarchical order. Context and object-and-purpose may often appear simply to confirm an interpretation seemingly derived from the 'raw' text. In reality it is always some context, even if unstated, that determines which meaning is to be taken as 'ordinary' and frequently it is impossible to give meaning, even 'ordinary meaning', without looking also at object-and-purpose.[144]

The Panel in *US – Section 301 Trade Act* thus stressed that the elements of Article 31 of the *Vienna Convention* – text, context and object-and-purpose – constitute 'one holistic rule of interpretation', and not 'a sequence of separate tests to be applied in a hierarchical order'.[145] To determine the ordinary meaning of a term, it makes sense to start with the dictionary meaning of that term but, as the Appellate Body noted more than once, a term often has several dictionary meanings and dictionary meanings thus leave many interpretative questions open.[146] The ordinary meaning of a term cannot be determined outside the context in which the term is used and without consideration of the object and purpose of the agreement at issue.

---

[143] Note that the Appellate Body Report in *EC – Chicken Cuts* contains useful clarification of the concepts of 'ordinary meaning' (see paras. 170–87); 'context' including additional context under Article 31.2(a) (see paras. 188–235); 'object and purpose' (see paras. 236–50); 'subsequent practice' (see paras. 251–76); and 'circumstances of [a treaty's] conclusion' (see paras. 277–346).

[144] Panel Report, *US – Section 301 Trade Act*, para. 7.22.   [145] *Ibid.*

[146] See Appellate Body Report, *Canada – Aircraft*, para. 153; and Appellate Body Report, *EC – Asbestos,* para. 92.

In *Japan – Alcoholic Beverages II*, the Appellate Body stated:

> Article 31 of the *Vienna Convention* provides that the words of the treaty form the foundation for the interpretive process: 'interpretation must be based above all upon the text of the treaty'. The provisions of the treaty are to be given their ordinary meaning in their context. The object and purpose of the treaty are also to be taken into account in determining the meaning of its provisions.[147]

The duty of an interpreter is to examine the words of the treaty to determine the *common* intentions of the parties to the treaty.[148] This is also the case with respect to Members' Schedules of Concessions or Commitments under the GATT 1994 or GATS as these are an integral part of the respective agreements and therefore subject to the same rules of interpretation.[149]

The Panel in *US – Corrosion-Resistant Steel Sunset Review* declined to consider Japan's arguments regarding the object and purpose of the *Anti-Dumping Agreement* on the basis that:

> Article 31 of the *Vienna Convention* requires that the text of the treaty be read in light of the object and purpose of the treaty, not that object and purpose alone override the text.[150]

One of the corollaries of the 'general rule of interpretation' of Article 31 of the *Vienna Convention* is that interpretation must give meaning and effect to *all* the terms of a treaty (i.e. the interpretive principle of effectiveness). An interpreter is not free to adopt a reading that would result in reducing whole clauses or paragraphs of a treaty to redundancy or inutility.[151] Furthermore, the Appellate Body in *EC – Hormones* cautioned interpreters as follows:

> The fundamental rule of treaty interpretation requires a treaty interpreter to read and interpret the words actually used by the agreement under examination, not words the interpreter may feel should have been used.[152]

In *India – Patents (US)*, the Appellate Body ruled that the principles of treaty interpretation 'neither require nor condone' the importation into a treaty of 'words that are not there' or 'concepts that were not intended'.[153]

The importance of other international law in the interpretation of WTO agreements is evident from Article 31.3(c) of the *Vienna Convention on the Law of Treaties*. In *US – Shrimp*, the Appellate Body referred to this provision and noted that its task:

> is to interpret the language of the chapeau [of Article XX of the GATT 1994], seeking additional interpretative guidance, as appropriate, from the general principles of international law.[154]

---

[147] Appellate Body Report, *Japan – Alcoholic Beverages II*, 104.

[148] See e.g. Appellate Body Report, *India – Patents (US)*, para. 45; and Appellate Body Report, *EC – Computer Equipment*, para. 84. Note that, in both these cases, the Appellate Body rejected the relevance of the 'legitimate expectations' of one of the parties in the interpretation of the meaning of the provision at issue.

[149] This was held for the first time, with respect to GATT Schedules, by the Appellate Body in *EC – Computer Equipment*, para. 109, and, with respect to GATS Schedules, by the Appellate Body in *US – Gambling*, paras. 159–60. See further below, pp. 489–90.

[150] Panel Report, *US – Corrosion-Resistant Steel Sunset Review*, para. 7.44.

[151] See Appellate Body Report, *US – Gasoline*, 21.   [152] Appellate Body Report, *EC – Hormones*, para. 181.

[153] Appellate Body Report, *India – Patents (US)*, para. 45.   [154] Appellate Body Report, *US – Shrimp*, para. 158.

Following its earlier ruling that WTO law is not to be read 'in clinical isolation from public international law',[155] the Appellate Body followed an evolutionary interpretation of the relevant treaty terms, taking into account the 'contemporary concerns of the community of nations' as reflected in other treaties.[156] The mandatory nature of the directive in Article 31.3(c) of the *Vienna Convention on the Law of Treaties* to have regard to other rules of international law was pointed out by the Panel in *EC – Approval and Marketing of Biotech Products*. This Panel noted:

> It is important to note that Article 31(3)(c) mandates a treaty interpreter to take into account other rules of international law ('[t]here shall be taken into account'); it does not merely give a treaty interpreter the option of doing so. It is true that the obligation is to 'take account' of such rules, and thus no particular outcome is prescribed. However, Article 31(1) makes clear that a treaty is to be interpreted 'in good faith'. Thus, where consideration of all other interpretative elements set out in Article 31 results in more than one permissible interpretation, a treaty interpreter following the instructions of Article 31(3)(c) in good faith would in our view need to settle for that interpretation which is more in accord with other applicable rules of international law.[157]

The Panel in *EC – Approval and Marketing of Biotech Products* addressed the meaning of the phrase 'any relevant rules of international law applicable in the relations between the parties' in Article 31.3(c) of the *Vienna Convention on the Law of Treaties*. It held:

> Textually, this reference seems sufficiently broad to encompass all generally accepted sources of public international law, that is to say, (i) international conventions (treaties), (ii) international custom (customary international law), and (iii) the recognized general principles of law. In our view, there can be no doubt that treaties and customary rules of international law are 'rules of international law' within the meaning of Article 31(3)(c).[158]

Further, the Panel noted that in *US – Shrimp*, the Appellate Body had made clear that general principles of international law also fall under Article 31.3(c).[159] However, the Panel pointed out that Article 31.3(c) of the *Vienna Convention* contains an important limitation, namely that only those rules of international law 'applicable in the relations between the parties' are to be taken into account. It held 'the parties' to mean those States that have consented to be bound by the treaty being interpreted (i.e. *all* WTO Members).[160] According to the Panel, a treaty interpreter is not *required* to have regard to treaties signed by only some WTO Members as context under Article 31.3(c) of the *Vienna Convention*, but would have the *discretion* to use such treaties as informative tools in establishing the ordinary meaning of the words used.[161] However, the Panel's finding limiting

---

[155] Appellate Body Report, *US – Gasoline*, p.16, cited above.

[156] Appellate Body Report, *US – Shrimp*, paras. 129–30.

[157] Panel Reports, *EC – Approval and Marketing of Biotech Products*, para. 7.69. The Panel noted that '[R]equiring that a treaty be interpreted in the light of other rules of international law which bind the States parties to the treaty ensures or enhances the consistency of the rules of international law applicable to these States and thus contributes to avoiding conflicts between the relevant rules.' *Ibid.*, para. 7.70.

[158] *Ibid.* para. 7.67.

[159] The Panel here referred to the finding of the Appellate Body in *US – Shrimp*, para. 158 and note 157.

[160] Panel Reports, *EC – Approval and Marketing of Biotech Products*, para. 7.68.

[161] See *ibid.*, constitute paras 7.92–7.93.

Article 31.3(c) to treaties applicable between *all* WTO Members is possibly not correct.[162] Note that this finding of the Panel in *EC – Approval and Marketing of Biotech Products* has been expressly criticised in the Report of the Study Group on the Fragmentation of International Law, set up by the United Nations International Law Commission (ILC). This Report observed that:

> Bearing in mind the unlikeliness of a precise congruence in the membership of most important multilateral conventions, it would become unlikely that *any* use of conventional international law could be made in the interpretation of such conventions. This would have the ironic effect that the more the membership of a multilateral treaty such as the WTO covered agreements expanded, the more those treaties would be cut off from the rest of international law. In practice, the result would be the isolation of multilateral agreements as 'islands' permitting no references *inter se* in their application.[163]

With regard to the concept of 'subsequent practice' within the meaning of Article 31.3(b) of the *Vienna Convention* and its relevance in the interpretation of WTO provisions, the Appellate Body stated in *Japan – Alcoholic Beverages II*:

> in international law, the essence of subsequent practice in interpreting a treaty has been recognized as a 'concordant, common and consistent' sequence of acts or pronouncements which is sufficient to establish a discernble pattern implying the agreement of the parties regarding its interpretation. An isolated act is generally not sufficient to establish subsequent practice; it is a sequence of acts establishing the agreement of the parties that is relevant.[164]

With regard to the use of 'supplementary means of interpretation' within the meaning of Article 32 of the *Vienna Convention*, the Appellate Body held in *EC – Computer Equipment*:

> The application of . . . [the] rules in Article 31 of the *Vienna Convention* will usually allow a treaty interpreter to establish the meaning of a term. However, if after applying Article 31 the meaning of the term remains ambiguous or obscure, or leads to a result which is manifestly absurd or unreasonable, Article 32 allows a treaty interpreter to have recourse to
>
> . . . supplementary means of interpretation, including the preparatory work of the treaty and the circumstances of its conclusion.
>
> With regard to 'the circumstances of [the] conclusion' of a treaty, this permits, in appropriate cases, the examination of the historical background against which the treaty was negotiated.[165]

In this case, the Appellate Body considered that the tariff classification practice in the European Communities during the Uruguay Round was part of 'the

---

162 See also the Panel in *Argentina – Poultry Anti-Dumping Duties*, which stated that 'it is not clear to us that a rule applicable between only several WTO Members would constitute a relevant rule of international law applicable in the relations between the "parties" '. Panel Report, *Argentina – Poultry Anti-Dumping Duties*, footnote 64 to para. 7.41.

163 International Law Commission, 58th Session, *Fragmentation of International Law: Difficulties Arising from the Diversification and Expansion of International Law*, Report of the Study Group of the International Law Commission, finalised by Martti Koskenniemi, A/CN.4/L.682, 13 April 2006, para. 471.

164 Appellate Body Report, *Japan – Alcoholic Beverages II*, 105–6. See also above, p. 58, and Panel Report, *US – FSC*, para. 7.75; Panel Report, *Canada – Patent Term*, paras. 5.5 and 6.89 footnote 48; and Appellate Body Report, *Chile – Price Band System*, para. 272.

165 Appellate Body Report, *EC – Computer Equipment*, para. 86. See also Appellate Body Report, *Canada – Dairy*, para. 138.

circumstances of [the] conclusion' of the *WTO Agreement* and could therefore be used as a supplementary means of interpretation within the meaning of Article 32 of the *Vienna Convention*.[166] In *EC – Poultry*, the Appellate Body considered a pre-WTO bilateral agreement between the parties to the dispute (i.e. the Oilseeds Agreement) to be part of the historical background to be taken into account when interpreting the provision at issue.[167] In *Canada – Dairy*, the Appellate Body based its interpretation of the scope of the tariff quota commitment by Canada on its 'reading of the circumstances surrounding the conclusion of the *WTO Agreement*'.[168] In *US – Gambling*, the Appellate Body used two documents drawn up by the Secretariat during the Uruguay Round services negotiations to assist Members in drafting their GATS Schedules of Specific Commitments as supplementary means of interpretation with regard to the United States' Services Schedule.[169]

In *US – Corrosion-Resistant Steel Sunset Review*, the Panel noted that:

> [Article 32] of the *Vienna Convention* limits recourse to the negotiating history of a treaty to two instances: (i) to confirm the meaning of the treaty's provisions or in cases where either a meaning cannot be derived from the treaty; or (ii) where the interpretation would lead to absurd results.[170]

As neither of those instances was the case in the matter before it, the Panel declined to have recourse to the negotiating history of the *Anti-Dumping Agreement* in interpreting one of its provisions.[171]

With regard to the degree of 'flexibility' and 'interpretability' of the *WTO Agreement*, the Appellate Body noted in *Japan – Alcoholic Beverages II*:

> WTO rules are reliable, comprehensible and enforceable. WTO rules are not so rigid or so inflexible as not to leave room for reasoned judgements in confronting the endless and ever-changing ebb and flow of real facts in real cases in the real world. They will serve the multilateral trading system best if they are interpreted with that in mind. In that way, we will achieve the 'security and predictability' sought for the multilateral trading system by the Members of the WTO through the establishment of the dispute settlement system.[172]

Questions and Assignments 3.10

Why are Articles 31 and 32 of the *Vienna Convention on the Law of Treaties* relevant to the interpretation and clarification of the provisions of the covered agreements? How do panels and the Appellate Body have to interpret provisions of the covered agreements? Can panels or the Appellate Body base their interpretation of a provision of the covered agreements on the 'legitimate expectations' of one of the parties to the dispute? What does the 'principle of effectiveness' require panels and the

---

[166] See Appellate Body Report, *EC – Computer Equipment*, para. 92.
[167] See Appellate Body Report, *EC – Poultry*, para. 83. [168] Appellate Body Report, *Canada – Dairy*, para. 139.
[169] See Appellate Body Report, *US – Gambling*, para. 196. In this regard, the Appellate Body disagreed with the Panel that these documents were part of the 'context' for interpretation of the United States' Schedule, under Article 31.3(c) of the *Vienna Convention*.
[170] Panel Report, *US – Corrosion-Resistant Steel Sunset Review*, para. 7.84. [171] See *ibid.*
[172] Appellate Body Report, *Japan – Alcoholic Beverages II*, 122–3.

Appellate Body to do when they interpret provisions of the covered agreements? What is the relevance of non-WTO agreements and general international law in the interpretation of provisions of the covered agreements? What can panels and the Appellate Body use as supplementary means of interpretation and when can they do so?

3.2.6.2. Burden of proof

The DSU does not contain any specific rules concerning the burden of proof in the WTO dispute settlement system. However, in *US – Wool Shirts and Blouses*, the Appellate Body noted:

> we find it difficult, indeed, to see how any system of judicial settlement could work if it incorporated the proposition that the mere assertion of a claim might amount to proof. It is, thus, hardly surprising that various international tribunals, including the International Court of Justice, have generally and consistently accepted and applied the rule that the party who asserts a fact, whether the claimant or the respondent, is responsible for providing proof thereof. Also, it is a generally accepted canon of evidence in civil law, common law and, in fact, most jurisdictions, that the burden of proof rests upon the party, whether complaining or defending, who asserts the affirmative of a particular claim or defence. If that party adduces evidence sufficient to raise a presumption that what is claimed is true, the burden then shifts to the other party, who will fail unless it adduces sufficient evidence to rebut the presumption.[173]

The burden of proof in WTO dispute settlement proceedings is thus on the party, the complainant *or* the respondent, that asserts the affirmative of a particular claim or defence.[174] The burden of proof shifts to the other party when sufficient evidence is adduced to raise a presumption that what is claimed is true. Precisely how much and precisely what kind of evidence is required to establish such a presumption 'will necessarily vary from measure to measure, provision to provision, and case to case'.[175]

In *EC – Hormones*, the Appellate Body further clarified the burden of proof in WTO dispute settlement proceedings and stated with respect to disputes under the *SPS Agreement*:

> The initial burden lies on the complaining party, which must establish a *prima facie* case of inconsistency with a particular provision of the *SPS Agreement* on the part of the

---

[173] Appellate Body Report, *US – Wool Shirts and Blouses*, 335. See also Panel Report, *Argentina – Textiles and Apparel*, para. 6.35; and Panel Report, *Turkey – Textiles*, para. 9.57.

[174] Note that the Appellate Body in *Japan – Apples* stated: 'It is important to distinguish, on the one hand, the principle that the complainant must establish a prima facie case of inconsistency with a provision of a covered agreement from, on the other hand, the principle that the party that asserts a fact is responsible for providing proof thereof. In fact, the two principles are distinct.' Appellate Body Report, *Japan – Apples*, para. 157.

[175] Appellate Body Report, *US – Wool Shirts and Blouses*, 335. The rule on burden of proof identified by the Appellate Body in *US – Wool Shirts and Blouses* has since been consistently applied by panels, the Appellate Body and arbitrators. For recent examples, see Panel Report, *US –Shrimp (Ecuador)*, paras. 7.7–7.11; Panel Report, *Mexico – Taxes on Soft Drinks*, paras. 8.16–8.20; Decision by the Arbitrators, *US – 1916 Act (EC) (Article 22.6)*, paras. 3.2–3.3; and the Award of the Arbitrator, *EC – Export Subsidies on Sugar (Article 21.3(c))*, para. 59.

> defending party, or more precisely, of its SPS measure or measures complained about. When that *prima facie* case is made, the burden of proof moves to the defending party, which must in turn counter or refute the claimed inconsistency.
>
>   . . . It is also well to remember that a *prima facie* case is one which, in the absence of effective refutation by the defending party, requires a panel, as a matter of law, to rule in favour of the complaining party presenting the *prima facie* case.[176]

With regard to the concept of a '*prima facie* case', the Appellate Body further stated in *US – Gambling*:

> A *prima facie* case must be based on 'evidence *and* legal argument' put forward by the complaining party in relation to each of the elements of the claim. A complaining party may not simply submit evidence and expect the panel to divine from it a claim of WTO-inconsistency. Nor may a complaining party simply allege facts without relating them to its legal arguments.
>
>   . . . The evidence and arguments underlying a *prima facie* case, therefore, must be sufficient to identify the challenged measure and its basic import, identify the relevant WTO provision and obligation contained therein, and explain the basis for the claimed inconsistency of the measure with that provision.[177]

In *Canada – Wheat Exports and Grain Imports*, the Appellate Body stated with regard to the establishment of a *prima facie* case:

> In our view, it is incumbent upon a party to identify in its submissions the relevance of the provisions of legislation – the evidence – on which it relies to support its arguments. It is not sufficient merely to file an entire piece of legislation and expect a panel to discover, on its own, what relevance the various provisions may or may not have for a party's legal position.[178]

The above should not be understood as imposing a requirement on panels to make an explicit ruling on whether the complainant has established a *prima facie* case of violation before a panel may proceed to examine the respondent's defence and evidence.[179] The jurisprudence of the Appellate Body regarding the rules on burden of proof is well summarised by the Panel in *US – Section 301 Trade Act*, where it is stated:

> In accordance with this jurisprudence, both parties agreed that it is for the EC, as the complaining party, to present arguments and evidence sufficient to establish a *prima facie* case in respect of the various elements of its claims regarding the inconsistency of Sections 301–310 with US obligations under the WTO. Once the EC has done so, it is for the US to rebut that *prima facie* case. Since, in this case, both parties have submitted extensive facts and arguments in respect of the EC claims, our task will essentially be to balance all evidence on record and decide whether the EC, as party bearing the original burden of proof, has convinced us of the validity of its claims. In case of uncertainty, i.e. in case all the evidence and arguments remain in equipoise, we have to give the benefit of the doubt to the US as defending party.[180]

---

[176] Appellate Body Report, *EC – Hormones*, paras. 98 and 104.
[177] Appellate Body Report, *US – Gambling*, paras. 140–1.
[178] Appellate Body Report, *Canada – Wheat Exports and Grain Imports*, para. 191.
[179] See Appellate Body Report, *Korea – Dairy*, para. 145. In *Thailand – H-Beams*, the Appellate Body ruled that a panel is not required to make a separate and specific finding, in each and every instance, that a party has met its burden of proof in respect of a particular claim, or that a party has rebutted a *prima facie* case. See Appellate Body Report, *Thailand – H-Beams*, para. 134.
[180] Panel Report, *US – Section 301 Trade Act*, para. 7.14.

As stated by the Panel in *US – Section 301 Trade Act*, the task of a panel is essentially to *balance all evidence* on record and decide whether the party bearing the original burden of proof has convinced it of the validity of its claims. The Panel in the same case furthermore noted that:

> the party that alleges a specific fact – be it the EC or the US – has the burden to prove it. In other words, it has to establish a *prima facie* case that the fact exists. Following the principles set out in the previous paragraph, this *prima facie* case will stand unless sufficiently rebutted by the other party.
>
> The factual findings in this Report were reached [by] applying these principles. Of course, when it comes to deciding on the correct interpretation of the covered agreements a panel will be aided by the arguments of the parties but not bound by them; its decisions on such matters must be in accord with the rules of treaty interpretation applicable to the WTO.[181]

With regard to the burden of establishing the correct legal interpretation of provisions of the covered agreements, the Appellate Body further clarified in *EC – Tariff Preferences*:

> Consistent with the principle of *jura novit curia*, it is not the responsibility of the European Communities to provide us with the legal interpretation to be given to a particular provision in the Enabling Clause; instead, the burden of the European Communities is to adduce sufficient evidence to substantiate its assertion that the Drug Arrangements comply with the requirements of the Enabling Clause.[182]

Thus, the burden of establishing what the applicable rule of WTO law is, and how that rule must be interpreted, is not on the parties but on the panel and the Appellate Body. In *India – Quantitative Restrictions*, the Appellate Body upheld the Panel's findings and conclusions and disagreed with India's argument that the Panel had erred in allocating to India the burden of proof with respect to the proviso of Article XVIII:11 of the GATT 1994. The Appellate Body stated the following:

> We consider that the invocation of the proviso to Article XVIII:11 does not give rise to a burden of proof issue insofar as it relates to the interpretation of what policies may constitute a 'development policy' within the meaning of the proviso. However, we do not exclude the possibility that a situation might arise in which an assertion regarding development policy does involve a burden of proof issue. Assuming that the complaining party has successfully established a *prima facie* case of inconsistency with Article XVIII:11 and the Ad Note, the responding party may, in its defence, either rebut the evidence adduced in support of the inconsistency or invoke the proviso. In the latter case, it would have to demonstrate that the complaining party violated its obligation not to require the responding party to change its development policy. This is an assertion with respect to which the responding party must bear the burden of proof. We,

---

[181] *Ibid.*, paras. 7.15 and 7.16.
[182] Appellate Body Report, *EC – Tariff Preferences*, para. 105. In a footnote, the Appellate Body added that the principle of *jura novit curia* was articulated by the International Court of Justice as follows: 'it being the duty of the Court itself to ascertain and apply the relevant law in the given circumstances of the case, the burden of establishing or proving rules of international law cannot be imposed upon any of the parties, for the law lies within the judicial knowledge of the Court'. International Court of Justice, Merits, *Case Concerning Military and Paramilitary Activities in and against Nicaragua (Nicaragua v. United States of America)*, 1986 ICJ Reports, 14, para. 29.

therefore, agree with the Panel that the burden of proof with respect to the proviso is on India.[183]

As the Appellate Body pointed out in *EC – Hormones*, the complainant cannot avoid its duty to show the inconsistency of the measure concerned with the provision at issue – before the burden of showing the consistency thereof moves to the respondent – by simply describing such provision as 'an exception'.[184] However, an exception often operates as an affirmative defence. In *Dominican Republic – Import and Sale of Cigarettes*, Honduras, the complainant, claimed that the foreign exchange fee at issue constituted an 'other duty or charge' and was hence inconsistent with Article II:1(b) of the GATT 1994. The Dominican Republic, however, argued that this fee was an exchange restriction justified under Article XV:9(a) of the GATT 1994. During the proceedings both parties put forward the argument that Article XV is an exception or an affirmative defence. The Panel agreed with both parties and further stated:

> The Panel agrees with this characterization of Article XV. That means that it serves as a justification for inconsistency with other provisions of the GATT. If there is no inconsistency with other GATT provisions in the first place, there is no need to have recourse to any affirmative defence for justification.[185]

Further, the Panel also clarified that:

> Although the two concepts are not identical, an exception can often be invoked as an affirmative defence. It is well established that under an exception provision, the burden is on the defending party to justify the consistency of its measure under the exception provision it invoked.[186]

Note that in *EC – Tariff Preferences*, the Appellate Body introduced the concept of the legal responsibility to *raise* a defence as an issue in dispute settlement proceedings. With regard to the Enabling Clause, and in view of the specific characteristics of the Enabling Clause,[187] the Appellate Body ruled that:

---

[183] Appellate Body Report, *India – Quantitative Restrictions*, para. 136. Note also the Appellate Body's ruling with regard to India's assertion that the Panel had not made a finding on whether the burden of proof in respect of the Note *Ad* Article XVIII:11 was on India or the United States. The Appellate Body stated that while it did not consider that a panel has an obligation to state '*expressly*' which party bears the burden of proof with regard to every claim put forward, *in casu*, the Panel had allocated the burden of proof with respect to the *Ad* Note to the United States. See *ibid.*, paras. 137–8.

[184] See Appellate Body Report, *EC – Hormones*, para. 104. In any event, in the case at hand the provision relied upon, Article 3.3 of the *SPS Agreement*, was found not to be an exception. Note that in *EC – Sardines*, the Panel deviated from the Appellate Body's ruling, asserting that the Appellate Body's finding in *EC – Hormones* did not have a 'direct bearing' on the matter under analysis. The Appellate Body disagreed with this assertion and found that there were important conceptual similarities between the two cases. It allocated the burden of proof to the complainant, Peru, which had the duty to show the inconsistency of the measure adopted by the European Communities with Article 2.4 of the *TBT Agreement*. See Appellate Body Report, *EC – Sardines*, paras. 272–3 and 282.

[185] Panel Report, *Dominican Republic – Import and Sale of Cigarettes*, para. 7.107.   [186] *Ibid.*, para. 7.131.

[187] The Appellate Body noted that every measure undertaken pursuant to the Enabling Clause would necessarily be inconsistent with Article I, if assessed on that basis alone, but it would be exempted from compliance with Article I because it meets the requirements of the Enabling Clause. The Appellate Body noted that: 'under these circumstances, we are of the view that a complaining party challenging a measure taken pursuant to the Enabling Clause must allege more than mere inconsistency with Article I:1 of the GATT 1994, for to do only that would not convey the 'legal basis of the complaint sufficient to present the problem clearly'. In other words, it is insufficient in WTO dispute settlement for a complainant to allege inconsistency with Article I:1 of the GATT 1994 if the complainant seeks also to argue that the measure is not justified under the Enabling Clause.' See Appellate Body Report, *EC – Tariff Preferences*, para. 110.

although a responding party must defend the consistency of its preference scheme with the conditions of the Enabling Clause and must prove such consistency, a *complaining* party has to define the parameters within which the *responding* party must make that defence.[188]

The Appellate Body thus concluded that it is the responsibility of the complaining party to identify those provisions of the Enabling Clause with which the scheme is allegedly inconsistent. The Appellate Body emphasised, however, that the responsibility of the complaining party in such an instance should not be overstated. The Appellate Body noted that the responsibility of the complaining party:

is merely to *identify* those provisions of the Enabling Clause with which the scheme is allegedly inconsistent, without bearing the burden *of establishing* the facts necessary to support such inconsistency.[189]

The latter burden remains on the responding party invoking the Enabling Clause as a defence.

Finally, note that the Panel in *EC – Approval and Marketing of Biotech Products* addressed the question of when a provision should be characterised as an exception to another provision, and when it should instead be characterised as a right creating an exemption from the scope of application of another provision.[190] Referring to the findings of the Appellate Body in *EC – Tariff Preferences*,[191] the Panel in *EC – Approval and Marketing of Biotech Products* found that a provision can be characterised as a right (rather than as an exception) in relation to another provision if the relationship between them is one:

where one provision permits, in certain circumstances, behaviour that would otherwise be inconsistent with an obligation in another provision, [where] one of the two provisions refers to the other provision, [and] where one of the provisions suggests that the obligation is not applicable to the said measure.[192]

Otherwise, the permissive provision is characterised as an exception or defence. The Panel in *EC – Approval and Marketing of Biotech Products* subsequently addressed the implications for the burden of proof of regarding a provision as embodying a right rather than an exception. According to the Panel, in cases where the complainant claims a violation of a provision embodying a *right* creating an exemption from the scope of application of another provision, it is incumbent on the complainant, and not the respondent, to prove that the challenged measure is also inconsistent with at least one of the requirements of the provision creating the exemption. As the Panel stated:

If such non-compliance is demonstrated, then, and only then, does the relevant obligation . . . apply to the challenged . . . measure.[193]

---

[188] Appellate Body Report, *EC – Tariff Preferences*, para. 114.   [189] *Ibid.*, para. 115.
[190] See Panel Reports, *EC – Approval and Marketing of Biotech Products*, para. 7.2985.
[191] See Appellate Body Report, *EC – Tariff Preferences*, para. 88.
[192] Panel Reports, *EC – Approval and Marketing of Biotech Products*, para. 7.2985.   [193] *Ibid.*, para. 7.2976.

The relationship between the rules on burden of proof, discussed here, and the authority of panels to seek expert advice is examined in detail below.[194]

Questions and Assignments 3.11

Who has the burden of proof in WTO dispute settlement proceedings? Does the burden of proof ever shift between the parties? When has a *prima facie* case of inconsistency been made? Will a panel consider the arguments and evidence advanced by the respondent before the complainant has made a *prima facie* case with respect to its claims? Is an exception to a WTO obligation an affirmative defence, and if so, on whom rests the burden of proof that the exception applies? How does one distinguish between an exception to another WTO provision *and* a right creating an exemption from the scope of application of another WTO provision? What are the implications for the burden of proof of this distinction? When and why does the complainant have the responsibility 'to raise a defence' in WTO dispute settlement proceedings?

3.2.7. Confidentiality and Rules of Conduct

This section discusses the confidential – some say secretive – nature of WTO dispute settlement. It also examines the rules of conduct that apply to all those involved in WTO dispute settlement.

3.2.7.1. *Confidentiality of the proceedings*

The WTO dispute settlement proceedings are characterised by their confidentiality. Consultations, panel proceedings and appellate review proceedings are all confidential. The meetings of the DSB also take place behind closed doors.[195] All written submissions to a panel or to the Appellate Body by the parties and third parties to a dispute are confidential.[196] Parties *may* only make their *own* submissions available to the public.[197] While a few Members do so in a systematic manner (e.g. the United States and the European Communities), most parties choose to keep their submissions confidential. The DSU provides that a party to a dispute must, upon request of any WTO Member, provide a non-confidential summary of the information contained in its submissions to the panel that could be disclosed to the public.[198] However, this provision does not provide for a deadline by which such a non-confidential summary must be made available. In the few instances in which WTO Members requested such a summary, it was usually made available too late to be of any practical relevance.

---

[194] See below, pp. 281–3.   [195] See above, p. 122, and below, p. 237.
[196] See Articles 18.2 and 17.10 of, and Appendix 3, para. 3 to, the DSU.
[197] See Panel Report, *Argentina – Poultry Anti-Dumping Duties*, paras. 7.13–7.16, regarding an additional complexity relating to this issue.   [198] See Article 18.2 of the DSU.

The interim report of the panel and the final panel report, as long as it has only been issued to the parties to the dispute, are also confidential. The final panel report only becomes a public document when it is circulated to all WTO Members. In reality, however, the interim report and the final report issued to the parties are often 'leaked' to the media.[199] In *US – Gambling* the Panel regretted the breach of the duty of confidentiality by the parties and stated that 'disregard for the confidentiality requirement contained in the DSU affects the credibility and integrity of the WTO dispute settlement process, of the WTO and of WTO Members and is, therefore, unacceptable'.[200]

Unlike panel reports, Appellate Body reports are not first issued to the parties and then, weeks later, circulated to all WTO Members. In principle, they are issued to the parties and circulated to all WTO Members at the same time and are as of that moment a public document.

Recognising that parties have a legitimate interest in protecting sensitive and confidential business information submitted to a panel, the Panels in *Canada – Aircraft* and *Brazil – Aircraft* adopted special procedures, governing confidential business information that go beyond the protection afforded by Article 18.2 of the DSU.[201] Whether panels consider the adoption of special procedures for the protection of business confidential information appropriate, however, varies from case to case. In *EC – Export Subsidies on Sugar*, for example, the Panel rejected a request for special procedures noting that normal DSU confidentiality rules were sufficient, while in *Korea – Commercial Vessels* and in *Canada – Wheat Exports and Grain Imports*, the Panels did adopt special procedures to protect business confidential information.[202] In *Canada – Aircraft*, the Appellate Body ruled, after carefully considering all the confidentiality requirements already provided for in the DSU, and in particular in Articles 17.10 and 18.2:

---

[199] An infamous example of leaked interim panel reports were the Reports in *EC – Approval and Marketing of Biotech Products*. The Panel in that case expressed its grave concern about the effect of such breaches on the integrity of the WTO dispute settlement system. It referred specifically to the adverse effect this may have on the willingness of private parties to make available business confidential information that may be crucial to the resolution of a dispute, and to the possibility that, as a result of the public discussion of the interim findings, the Panel or Secretariat may be exposed to political pressure. See Panel Reports, *EC – Approval and Marketing of Biotech Products*, paras. 6.179–6.182 and 7.43. These concerns were expressed in more detail in a communication of the Chairman of the Panel, Christian Häberli, to the Chairman of the Dispute Settlement Body when the final Panel Reports were circulated. See Communication from the Chairman of the Panel, *EC – Approval and Marketing of Biotech Products*, WT/DS291/32, WT/DS292/26, WT/DS293/26, circulated on 29 September 2006. Interestingly, the Panel took the unprecedented step of explaining some of its findings in a letter to the parties, as it was concerned that certain aspects of the leaked findings had 'inadvertently or on purpose' been misconstrued in the civil society discussion of the interim reports. This letter is appended to the Panel Reports as Annex K. The Panel Reports state, however, that the letter 'is not part of the Panel's findings and is not intended to modify them in any way'. Panel Reports, *EC – Approval and Marketing of Biotech Products*, para. 6.3, footnote 170.

[200] Panel Report, *US – Gambling*, paras. 5.3–5.13. Note that further concerns were put forward by the Panel in *US – Gambling (Article 21.5 – Antigua and Barbuda)*, where, according to the Panel by the United States seemed to imply that the leak would have taken place in Geneva, as a breach of confidentiality by the Panel or the WTO Secretariat, assertions that the Panel rejected 'forcefully'. See Panel Report, *US – Gambling (Article 21.5 – Antigua and Barbuda)*, paras. 5.2–5.10.

[201] See Panel Report, *Canada – Aircraft*, Annex 1; and Panel Report, *Brazil – Aircraft*, Annex 1. For a further discussion of the special procedures, see below, pp. 284–5.

[202] See Panel Report, *EC – Export Subsidies on Sugar*, paras. 2.10–2.19; Panel Report, *Korea – Commercial Vessels*, para. 1.15; and Panel Reports, *Canada – Wheat Exports and Grain Imports*, paras. 6.8–6.9.

> we do not consider that it is necessary, under all the circumstances of this case, to adopt *additional* procedures for the protection of business confidential information in these appellate proceedings.[203]

The Appellate Body considered the protection offered by the confidentiality requirements of Articles 17.10 and 18.2 of the DSU more than sufficient.

The meetings of the panel with the parties as well as the hearings of the Appellate Body generally take place behind closed doors.[204] As a rule nobody except the parties themselves and the officials of the WTO Secretariat, assisting the panel, are allowed to attend all meetings of the panel with the parties. Third parties are usually invited to attend only one session of the first substantive panel meeting.[205] The hearings of the Appellate Body may only be attended by the participants and third participants in the appellate review proceedings as well as the staff of the Appellate Body Secretariat. The 2004 Sutherland Report noted in this respect that:

> the degree of confidentiality of the current dispute settlement proceedings can be seen as damaging to the WTO as an institution[206]

The Report therefore recommended that, as a matter of course, the panel meetings and Appellate Body hearings should generally be open to the public.[207] Certain WTO Members share this view, as evidenced by the recent opening of panel meetings to the general public in a few disputes involving the European Communities, the United States and Canada.[208] At the request of the parties, the Panel in *Canada – Continued Suspension* and *US – Continued Suspension*[209] authorised in September and October 2006 the closed-circuit broadcast of its meetings with experts and the parties to a separate viewing room at WTO Headquarters in Geneva.[210] In July 2007, the Panel in *EC and Certain Member States – Large Civil*

---

[203] Appellate Body Report, *Canada – Aircraft*, para. 147. See also Appellate Body Report, *Brazil – Aircraft*, para. 125.   [204] See Appendix 3, para. 2 to, and Article 17.10 of, the DSU.   [205] See below, p. 279.

[206] Consultative Board to the Director-General Supachai Panitchpakdi, *The Future of the WTO: Addressing Institutional Challenges in the New Millennium* (the 'Sutherland Report') (WTO, 2004), para. 261 (emphasis omitted).   [207] See *ibid.*, para. 262.

[208] Note that in 1999 in *US – Lead and Bismuth II*, a dispute involving the United States and the European Communities, the United States requested that the Panel allow observers into the Panel meetings. In response to this request, the Panel held: 'Since it is up to each party to decide whether or not it chooses to forego its right to confidentiality for its written and oral submissions to a panel, we are obliged to seek the agreement of each party before implementing Working Procedures that might undermine the confidentiality of a party's written and oral submissions. By its 14 June response to the US request of 11 June 1999, the EC effectively withheld such agreement. As a result, we are not in a position to develop any Working Procedures that might jeopardise the confidentiality of the EC written and oral submissions to the Panel. Accordingly, we are unable to grant the US request to open this meeting to observers.' Panel Report, *US – Lead and Bismuth II*, para. 6.2. Note also that, in the ongoing negotiations on DSU reform, both the EC and Canada have proposed allowing panel and Appellate Body meetings to be open to the public, provided that the parties to the dispute agree, in order to enhance the transparency of the dispute settlement system. See Communication from the European Communities, TN/DS/W/1, dated 13 March 2003, 6; and Communication from Canada, TN/DS/W/42, dated 24 January 2003, 5.

[209] These cases were brought by the European Communities to secure the lifting of retaliation measures applied by the United States and Canada in the *EC – Hormones* dispute. See below, p. 306.

[210] The meeting with the experts took place on 27–28 September 2006 and with the parties on 2–3 October 2006. The 200 places reserved for the public were allocated on a first-come-first-served basis upon receipt of the completed application form. However, despite the frequent calls by civil society for increased transparency of dispute settlement proceedings, few attended the open hearings. See Communication from the Chairman of the Panels, *Canada–Continued Suspensing* and *US – Continued Suspension*, WT/DS320/8, WT/DS321/8, dated 2 August 2005. See also WTO News Item, 'Hormones Panels to open Proceedings with

Aircraft was more cautious (because of concerns regarding the protection of business confidential information) and merely allowed its second meeting with the parties to be video-taped and broadcast in an edited version two days later in Geneva.[211] In November 2007, the Panel in *EC – Bananas III (Article 21.5 – US)* decided to allow the delegates of WTO Members and members of the general public to observe the Panel's meeting with the parties from the public gallery above the meeting room. As only a limited number of places was available, prior registration with either party in this dispute, the United States or the European Communities, was required to secure a seat.[212] Note that in *Brazil – Retreaded Tyres*, the Centre for International Environmental Law (CIEL) requested the Panel to allow the webcasting of the first meeting of the Panel with the parties. After consultations with the parties, Brazil and the European Communities, and in light of the views expressed by them, the Panel informed CIEL that its meetings with the parties would be held in closed sessions in accordance with the Working Procedures adopted by the Panel at the beginning of the proceedings.[213]

The DSU does not explicitly address the issue of representation of the parties before panels or the Appellate Body. In *EC – Bananas III*, the issue arose whether private counsel, not employed by government, may represent a party or third party (such as Saint Lucia) before the Appellate Body. In its ruling, the Appellate Body noted that nothing in the *WTO Agreement* or the DSU, or in customary international law or the prevailing practice of international tribunals, prevents a WTO Member from determining the composition of its own delegation in WTO dispute settlement proceedings.[214] A party can, therefore, decide that private counsel forms part of its delegation and will represent it in WTO dispute settlement proceedings. While the ruling of the Appellate Body concerned the proceedings before this body, the reasoning of this ruling is equally relevant for panel proceedings. This was confirmed in the Panel Report in *Indonesia – Autos*, adopted one year after the Appellate Body Report in *EC – Bananas III*. The Panel in *Indonesia – Autos* rejected the request of the United States to exclude Indonesia's private lawyers from the Panel meetings, stating:

> it is for the Government of Indonesia to nominate the members of its delegation to meetings of this Panel, and we find no provision in the WTO Agreement or the DSU, including the standard rules of procedure included therein, which prevents a WTO Member from determining the composition of its delegation to WTO panel meetings.[215]

Private counsel now routinely appear in panel as well as appellate review proceedings as part of the delegation of a party or third party. The parties and third parties are responsible for all members of their delegations and must ensure

---

Parties to the Public', dated 4 August 2005, available at www.wto.org/english/news_e/news05_e.htm, visited on 8 August 2007. See also F. Williams, 'WTO Opens Hearing to Public', *Financial Times*, 13 September 2005.

[211] See www.ustr.gov/assets/Trade_Agreements/Monitoring_Enforcement/WTO_Airbus_Case/asset_upload_file81_13158.pdf, visited on 24 November 2007. The delayed broadcasting allowed the Panel to verify that no business confidential information would be inadvertently disclosed in showing the videotape.

[212] WTO News Item: 'WTO Hearings on Banana Dispute Opened to the Public', 29 October 2007.

[213] See Panel Report, *Brazil – Retreaded Tyres*, para. 1.9.

[214] See Appellate Body Report, *EC – Bananas III*, para. 10.   [215] Panel Report, *Indonesia – Autos*, para. 14.1.

that all members of the delegation, private counsel included, act in accordance with the rules of the DSU and the Working Procedures of the panel, particularly with respect to the confidentiality of the proceedings.[216]

With respect to concerns regarding the protection of business confidential information, note that in *Korea – Certain Paper*, a dispute concerning anti-dumping duties on paper from Indonesia, Korea had requested that representatives of the Indonesian paper industry who were part of the Indonesian delegation leave the room for confidentiality reasons. Moreover, Korea wanted to withdraw its written submissions and provide non-confidential versions to Indonesia. In response, the Panel ruled with regard to the presence of the representatives of the Indonesian paper industry that, as provided in paragraph 15 of its Working Procedures, Indonesia was entitled to determine the composition of its delegation in the proceedings. The Panel noted that, in accordance with Article 18.2 of the DSU and paragraph 15 of its Working Procedures, Indonesia assumed responsibility for its delegation, including respect for the confidentiality of the submissions made by Korea in those proceedings.[217] With regard to Korea's proposal to withdraw its existing submissions and submit non-confidential versions of those submissions to Indonesia, the Panel in *Korea – Certain Paper* ruled as follows:

> considering the fact that Article 18.1 of the DSU precludes *ex parte* communications between the Panel and a party, we stated that while we would entertain any request by Korea to withdraw its submissions or to redact from them certain information, in such a case the submissions withdrawn or information redacted would no longer be before the Panel.[218]

Questions and Assignments 3.12

Under WTO law, do citizens have a right of access to the submissions made by their and other governments to panels and the Appellate Body? Do WTO Members have a right of access to the submissions made by other Members in panel or Appellate Body proceedings? Are meetings of panels or the hearings of the Appellate Body open to the public? Are they open to WTO Members that are not a party to the dispute? In your opinion, should panel meetings and Appellate Body hearings be open to the public? In your opinion, should confidential business information, submitted by the parties to a panel or the Appellate Body, be given *additional* protection? Are panel and Appellate Body reports confidential documents? Can WTO Members be represented by private counsel in WTO dispute settlement proceedings?

---

[216] See, in this respect, Appellate Body Report, *Thailand – H-Beams*, paras. 62–78. In this case, Hogan & Hartson LLP withdrew as Poland's legal counsel after Thailand's appellant submission had been 'leaked' and the Appellate Body had instituted an investigation into this breach of the confidentiality of the appellate review proceedings.   [217] See Panel Report, *Korea – Certain Paper*, para. 7.11.
[218] Panel Report, *Korea – Certain Paper*, para. 7.17.

3.2.7.2. Rules of Conduct

When hearing and deciding a WTO dispute, panellists, arbitrators and Appellate Body members are subject to the *Rules of Conduct for the Understanding on Rules and Procedures Governing the Settlement of Disputes* (the 'Rules of Conduct').[219] To preserve the integrity and impartiality of the WTO dispute settlement system, the *Rules of Conduct* require that panellists, arbitrators and Appellate Body members:

> shall be independent and impartial, shall avoid direct or indirect conflicts of interest and shall respect the confidentiality of proceedings.[220]

Also the staff of the WTO Secretariat and the staff of the Appellate Body Secretariat as well as experts consulted by panels are subject to these *Rules of Conduct*.

To ensure compliance with the *Rules of Conduct*, all persons to whom the rules apply must disclose:

> the existence or development of any interest, relationship or matter that person could reasonably be expected to know and that is likely to affect, or give rise to justifiable doubts as to, that person's independence or impartiality.[221]

This disclosure obligation includes information on financial, professional and other active interests as well as considered statements of personal opinion on issues relevant to the dispute and employment or family interests.[222]

Parties can request the disqualification of a panellist on the ground of *material* violation of the obligations of independence, impartiality, confidentiality or the avoidance of direct or indirect conflicts of interest.[223] The evidence of such material violation is provided to the Chairman of the DSB, who will, in consultation with the Director-General of the WTO and the chairpersons of the relevant WTO bodies, decide whether a material violation has occurred. If it has, the panellist is replaced. Parties can also request the disqualification of an Appellate Body Member on the ground of a material violation of the obligations of the *Rules of Conduct*. It is, however, for the Appellate Body, and not for the Chairman of the DSB, to decide whether a material violation has occurred and, if so, to take appropriate action.[224] To date, no panellist or Appellate Body Member has ever been found to have committed a material violation of the *Rules of Conduct*. However, in a few instances, a panellist withdrew, on his or her own initiative, after a party raised concerns about a possible conflict of interest.

With respect to the issue of the rules of conduct applicable to private counsel acting for a party or third party, note that in *EC – Tariff Preferences*, the European Communities objected to the 'joint representation' by the Advisory Centre on WTO Law (ACWL) of both India, the complainant, and Paraguay, a third party. The Panel was therefore confronted with the question of whether the same legal counsel could represent simultaneously a complaining party and a third party.[225] In response to this question, the Panel first noted that:

---

[219] WT/DSB/RC/1, dated 11 December 1996.　　[220] Para. II(1) of the *Rules of Conduct*.
[221] Para. III(1) of the *Rules of Conduct*.　　[222] See Annex 2 to the *Rules of Conduct*.
[223] See Para. VIII of the *Rules of Conduct*.　　[224] See *ibid*.　　[225] See Panel Report, *EC – Tariff Preferences*, para. 7.3.

the WTO has not itself elaborated any rules governing the ethical conduct of legal counsel representing WTO Members in particular disputes.[226]

The Panel subsequently noted, however, that:

As a general matter . . . it is the responsibility of legal counsel to ensure that it is not placing itself in a position of actual or potential conflict of interest when agreeing to represent, and thereafter representing, one or more WTO Members in a dispute under the DSU.[227]

As the Panel observed, bar associations in many jurisdictions have elaborated rules of conduct dealing explicitly with conflicts of interest through joint representation. Common to all such ethical rules of conduct are:

- the principle that counsel shall not accept or continue representation of more than one client in a matter in which the interests of the clients actually or potentially conflict;
- the possibility for clients, when faced with counsel being subject to actual or potential conflicts of interest as the result of joint representation, to consent to such joint representation, but only following full disclosure by counsel; and
- that counsel shall nevertheless discontinue such joint representation at such time as counsel becomes aware that the interests of the two (or more) clients are directly adverse.[228]

As India and Paraguay had been fully informed about their joint representation by the ACWL and had given their written consent to such representation, the Panel did not see any problem with the joint representation in this case.[229]

Questions and Assignments 3.13

To whom do the *Rules of Conduct* apply? What are the key obligations under the *Rules of Conduct?* Can panellists and Appellate Body members be disqualified? If so, by whom and on what grounds? What rules of conduct apply to private counsel representing WTO Members in dispute settlement proceedings?

3.2.8. Remedies for breach of WTO law

The DSU provides for three types of remedy for breach of WTO law:

- one final remedy, namely, the withdrawal (or amendment) of the WTO-inconsistent measure; and

---

[226] *Ibid.*, para. 7.5.   [227] *Ibid.*, para. 7.9.   [228] See *ibid.*, para. 7.10.
[229] See *ibid.*, para. 7.13. The European Communities also raised the question of whether the ACWL's joint representation of a party and a third party may be inconsistent with the DSU rules on confidentiality. As the Panel in this case granted the third parties 'additional rights' (see below, p. 279), the Panel found that the confidentiality issue did not arise in this dispute. See Panel Report, *EC – Tariff Preferences*, para. 7.17.

- two temporary remedies which can be applied awaiting the withdrawal (or amendment) of the WTO-inconsistent measure, namely, compensation *and* suspension of concessions or other obligations (commonly referred to as 'retaliation').

This section discusses these three types of remedy. It also briefly examines whether other types of remedy may be available.

3.2.8.1. *Withdrawal of the WTO-inconsistent measure*

Article 3.7 of the DSU states, in relevant part:

> In the absence of a mutually agreed solution, the first objective of the dispute settlement mechanism is usually to secure the withdrawal of the measures concerned if these are found to be inconsistent with the provisions of any of the covered agreements.

Furthermore, Article 3.7 suggests that the withdrawal of the WTO-inconsistent measure should normally be 'immediate'.[230]
Article 19.1 of the DSU provides:

> Where a panel or the Appellate Body concludes that a measure is inconsistent with a covered agreement, it shall recommend that the Member concerned bring the measure into conformity with that agreement . . .[231]

Such a recommendation, once adopted by the DSB, is legally binding on the Member concerned.[232] With regard to recommendations and rulings adopted by the DSB, Article 21.1 of the DSU provides that:

> *Prompt* compliance with recommendations or rulings of the DSB is essential in order to ensure effective resolution of disputes to the benefit of all Members.
>
> [Emphasis added]

While Article 3.7 of the DSU refers to the withdrawal of the measure found to be WTO-inconsistent, the withdrawal or the amendment of the WTO-inconsistent aspects or elements of such a measure usually suffices to bring the measure into conformity with WTO law pursuant to the recommendations or rulings of the DSB.[233] Prompt or immediate compliance with the DSB recommendations and rulings, i.e. prompt or immediate withdrawal or amendment of the WTO-inconsistent measure, is essential to the effective functioning of the WTO and is the primary obligation. However, if it is impracticable to comply immediately with

[230] As discussed below, Article 3.7 provides: 'The provision of compensation should be resorted to only if the immediate withdrawal of the measure is impracticable . . .'
[231] Note that several panels have emphasised that, pursuant to Article 19.1 of the DSU, they can 'only' recommend that the Member concerned bring its measure into WTO conformity. They cannot order that the measure is terminated immediately. See Panel Report, *Korea – Certain Paper*, paras. 9.1–9.4; and Panel Report, *EC – Commercial Vessels*, paras. 7.24–7.25.   [232] See below, p. 255.
[233] While it is appropriate for panels and the Appellate Body to rule on the WTO-consistency of measures that are no longer in force, it is not appropriate for them to recommend that a measure that is no longer in force be brought into conformity. In *Dominican Republic – Import and Sale of Cigarettes*, the Appellate Body upheld the Panel's ruling to this effect. See Appellate Body Report, *Dominican Republic – Import and Sale of Cigarettes*, para. 129. On measures at issue that are no longer in force, see also above, pp. 187–9.

the recommendations and rulings, and this may often be the case, the Member concerned has, pursuant to Article 21.3 of the DSU, a reasonable period of time in which to do so. The 'reasonable period of time for implementation' may be:

- determined by the DSB;
- agreed on by the parties to the dispute; or
- determined through binding arbitration at the request of either party.[234]

The parties to the dispute often succeed in agreeing on what constitutes a 'reasonable period of time for implementation'. In forty-nine cases to date, the parties were able to agree on the reasonable period of time for implementation.[235] The average length of the reasonable period of time agreed on is nine months and one week.[236] Parties agreed on the 'reasonable period of time for implementation' in, for example, *Canada – Periodicals* (fifteen months), *India – Patents (US)* (fifteen months), *US – Shrimp* (thirteen months), *Japan – Agricultural Products II* (nine months and twelve days), *US – DRAMS* (eight months), *Chile – Price Band System* (fourteen months), *US – Gambling* (eleven months and two weeks) and *EC – Export Subsidies on Sugar* (twelve months and three days).[237]

In twenty-one cases to date, the 'reasonable period of time for implementation' was decided through binding arbitration under Article 21.3(c) of the DSU.[238] The latter provision states:

> In such arbitration, a guideline for the arbitrator should be that the reasonable period of time to implement panel or Appellate Body recommendations should not exceed 15 months from the date of the adoption of a panel or Appellate Body report. However, that time may be shorter or longer, depending upon the particular circumstances.

The Arbitrator in *US – Hot-Rolled Steel* explained the following with regard to the 'reasonable period of time for implementation':

> It is useful to recall the essential principle and rule that WTO Members are committed to 'prompt compliance' with DSB recommendations and rulings and that 'prompt compliance' translates into 'immediate' compliance. When, however, such 'immediate' compliance is '*impracticable*', then the Member bound to comply becomes entitled to 'a reasonable period of time' within which to comply. It is similarly salutary to recall that the 15-month period mentioned in Article 21.3(c) of the DSU is expressly designated as 'a *guideline* for the arbitrator': the 'reasonable period of time' to implement panel or Appellate Body recommendations 'should not exceed 15 months' from the date of adoption of the panel or Appellate Body Report, which period may, however, be 'shorter or longer', 'depending upon the particular circumstances'. I do not see any basis for reading the 15-month guideline as establishing a fixed maximum or '*outer* limit' for 'a reasonable period of time'. Neither, of course, does the 15-month guideline constitute *a floor* or '*inner* limit' of 'a reasonable period of time'.[239]

> [Emphasis added]

---

[234] See Article 21.3(a), (b) and (c) of the DSU. See below, pp. 298–9.
[235] See www.worldtradelaw.net/dsc/database/implementationprovision.asp, visited on 1 December 2007.
[236] See www.worldtradelaw.net/dsc/database/implementationaverage.asp, visited on 1 December 2007.
[237] Note that, to date, the reasonable period of time has never been determined by the DSB pursuant to Article 21.3(a) of the DSU.
[238] See www.worldtradelaw.net/dsc/database/rptawards.asp,visited on 18 October 2007.
[239] Award of the Arbitrator, *US – Hot-Rolled Steel (Article 21.3 (c))*, para. 25.

In *EC – Hormones*, the Arbitrator ruled that the 'reasonable period of time for implementation', as determined under Article 21.3(c), should be:

> the shortest period possible within the legal system of the Member to implement the recommendations and rulings of the DSB.[240]

While this has become the core rule in establishing the reasonable period of time for implementation, the Arbitrator in *US – Gambling* stated:

> Yet, it is useful to recall that the DSU does not refer to the 'shortest period possible for implementation within the legal system' of the implementing Member. Rather, this is a convenient phrase that has been used by previous arbitrators to describe their task. I do not, however, view this standard as one that stands in isolation from the text of the DSU. In my view, the determination of the 'shortest period possible for implementation' can, and must, also take due account of the two principles that are expressly mentioned in Article 21 of the DSU, namely reasonableness and the need for prompt compliance. Moreover, as differences in previous awards involving legislative implementation by the United States have shown, and as the text of Article 21.3(c) prescribes, each arbitrator must take account of 'particular circumstances' relevant to the case at hand. Strict insistence on the 'shortest period possible for implementation within the legal system' of the implementing Member would, in my view, tie an arbitrator's hands and prevent him or her from properly identifying and weighing the particular circumstances that are determinative of 'reasonableness' in each individual case.[241]

Moreover, as the Arbitrator in *Korea – Alcoholic Beverages* ruled, a Member is not required to utilise extraordinary legislative procedures, rather than the normal procedure, in order to shorten the period of implementation.[242] In *EC – Hormones*, the Arbitrator also noted that, when implementation does not require changes in legislation but can be effected by administrative means, the reasonable period of time 'should be considerably less than 15 months'.[243] In *Canada – Pharmaceutical Patents*, the Arbitrator listed a number of other 'particular circumstances' that can influence what the shortest period possible for implementation may be within the legal system of the implementing Member. Apart from the means of implementation (legislative or administrative), this Arbitrator referred to the complexity of the proposed implementation[244] and the legally binding, as opposed to the discretionary, nature of the component steps in the process leading to implementation.[245] In situations where compliance can be

---

[240] Award of the Arbitrator, *EC – Hormones (Article 21.3 (c))*, para. 26.

[241] Award of the Arbitrator, *US – Gambling (Article 21.3(c))*, para. 44.

[242] See Awards of the Arbitrator, *Korea – Alcoholic Beverages (Article 21.3(c))*, para. 42; *US – Offset Act (Byrd Amendment) (Article 21.3(c))*, paras. 43, 74; *EC – Export Subsidies on Sugar (Article 21.3(c))* para. 79; and *EC – Tariff Preferences (Article 21.3(c))*, para. 42. In *Canada – Autos*, the Arbitrator held that the question whether a Member could take 'extraordinary action' to bring about compliance was not even relevant to the determination of the reasonable period of time. See Award of the Arbitrator, *Canada – Autos (Article 21.3(c))*, para. 53.

[243] Award of the Arbitrator, *EC – Hormones (Article 21.3(c))*, para. 25. See also Awards of the Arbitrator, *Australia – Salmon (Article 21.3(c))*, para. 38; and *EC – Chicken Cuts (Article 21.3(c))*, para. 67.

[244] This may only be an 'in principle' relevant factor. As the Arbitrator in *US – Offset Act (Byrd Amendment) (Article 21.3(c))* noted, if every analysis distinguishing WTO-consistency and inconsistency that will precede implementing legislation were *per se* to be considered complex, then 'complexity' would not be a 'particular circumstance', but a 'standard aspect of every implementation': see Award of the Arbitrator, *US – Offset Act (Byrd Amendment) (Article 21.3(c))*, paras. 60–1. For yet another failed 'complexity' argument, see Award of the Arbitrator, *EC – Export Subsidies on Sugar (Article 21.3(c))*, para. 88.

[245] See Award of the Arbitrator, *Canada – Pharmaceutical Patents (Article 21.3(c))*, paras. 48–52.

brought about through government regulatory policy or administrative action instead of legislation,[246] or even where legislation would be required, when there is sufficient flexibility in legislative procedures the reasonable period of time awarded will be shorter than otherwise.[247] The legislative calendar of Members will have a bearing on the reasonable period on a case-by-case basis.[248] Also the time taken for previous legislation on the same subject-matter to pass through parliament would be relevant before an Article 21.3(c) arbitration.[249]

The domestic political or economic situation in the Member concerned is not relevant in determining the 'reasonable period of time for implementation'. The absence of a political majority to adopt implementing measures or economic hardship resulting from implementation, for example, are not taken into consideration by the arbitrator in determining the 'reasonable period of time for implementation'.[250] The need for consultations with government departments and stakeholders is in itself not a reason for more time for implementation.[251] Note that the Arbitrator in *EC – Tariff Preferences* considered that the EU enlargement was a relevant factor in the determination of the reasonable period of time for implementation in that case. The same Arbitrator, however, did not consider the election of a new European Parliament and a new European Commission to be of relevance.[252] The Arbitrator in *US – Offset Act (Byrd Amendment)* explicitly stated that the economic harm suffered by foreign exporters did not, and could not, impact on what the reasonable period of time for implementation was in that case.[253]

Members should make good use of the time following an adverse DSB ruling to bring about compliance as the obligation to implement starts at the moment of the adoption of the report(s) and *not* at the moment of the arbitrator's award setting the reasonable period of time. The implementing Member bears the burden of proof that the period of time it seeks is a reasonable period of time within the meaning of Article 21.3 of the DSU.[254]

---

[246] See Award of the Arbitrator, *Canada – Autos (Article 21.3(c))*, paras. 47–8.

[247] At least regarding US legislative procedure and practice, it is now generally accepted that there is considerable inherent flexibility. See Awards of the Arbitrator, *US – Section 110(5) Copyright Act (Article 21.3(c))*, paras. 38–9, 46, *US – 1916 Act (Japan) (Article 21.3(c))*, para. 39, *US – Offset Act (Byrd Amendment) (Article 21.3(c))*, para. 64; and *US – Gambling (Article 21.3(c))*, paras. 49–50. See also Awards of the Arbitrator, *Chile – Price Band System (Article 21.3(c))*, para. 39; *EC – Export Subsidies on Sugar (Article 21.3(c))*, paras. 76–77, 85, 95; *EC – Chicken Cuts*, para. 80; and *EC – Tariff Preferences*, para. 36.

[248] See Awards of the Arbitrator, *US – Gambling (Article 21.3(c))*, para. 52; and *Canada – Patent Term (Article 21.3(c))*, paras. 65–6.

[249] See Award of the Arbitrator, *US – Gambling (Article 21.3(c))*, para. 55. However, the time periods fixed under previous arbitrations concerning a Member's legislative measures will not be relevant to fixing the reasonable period of time. See Award of the Arbitrator, *EC – Export Subsidies on Sugar (Article 21.3(c))*, para. 97.

[250] Note, however, that the Arbitrator in *Chile – Price Band System* considered that the unique role and *impact* of the Price Band System on the Chilean society was a relevant factor in his determination of the reasonable period of time for implementation. See Award of the Arbitrator, *Chile – Price Band System (Article 21.3(c))*, para. 48.

[251] See Award of the Arbitrator, *Canada – Autos (Article 21.3(c))*, para. 49. See also Award of the Arbitrator, *US – Section 110(5) Copyright Act (Article 21.3(c))*, paras. 41–2. For a more liberal view of the need for consultations, see Award of the Arbitrator, *Chile – Price Band System (Article 21.3(c))*, paras. 41–2. The need for 'serious debate' and the 'political contentiousness' of the proposed measure are however not grounds for a longer compliance period. See Award of the Arbitrator, *EC – Export Subsidies on Sugar (Article 21.3(c))*, paras. 89–90.

[252] See Award of the Arbitrator, *EC – Tariff Preferences (Article 21.3(c))*, para. 54.

[253] See Award of the Arbitrator, *US – Offset Act (Byrd Amendment) (Article 21.3(c))*, para. 79.

[254] See Award of the Arbitrator, *EC – Export Subsidies on Sugar (Article 21.3(c))*, para. 59.

The mandate of an Article 21.3(c) arbitrator relates exclusively to determining the reasonable period of time for implementation.[255] The mandate of the arbitrator does not relate to the type or kind of measure that must be taken to implement the recommendations and rulings of the DSB. As the Arbitrator in *EC – Chicken Cuts* stated:

> a Member's prerogative to select the means of implementation is particularly strong, and it is appropriate in that situation for an arbitrator to refrain from questioning whether another, perhaps shorter, means of implementation is available within that legal system.[256]

Article 21.2 of the DSU requires that, in determining the 'reasonable period of time for implementation', particular attention should be paid to matters affecting the interests of developing-country Members. On that legal basis, the Arbitrator in *Indonesia – Autos* ruled:

> Indonesia is not only a developing country; it is a developing country that is currently in a dire economic and financial situation. Indonesia itself states that its economy is 'near collapse'. In these very particular circumstances, I consider it appropriate to give full weight to matters affecting the interests of Indonesia as a developing country pursuant to the provisions of Article 21.2 of the DSU. I, therefore, conclude that an additional period of six months over and above the six-month period required for the completion of Indonesia's domestic rule-making process constitutes a reasonable period of time for implementation of the recommendations and rulings of the DSB in this case.[257]

In *EC – Export Subsidies on Sugar*, for the first time, an arbitrator authoritatively held that Article 21.2 directs an arbitrator to pay attention to matters affecting the interests of *both* complaining and implementing developing-country Members.[258] Previously, there was considerable doubt as to which developing-country Member the provision pertained to.[259] Agreeing with the Arbitrator in *US – Gambling*,[260] the Arbitrator in *EC – Export Subsidies on Sugar* ruled that there was nothing in the text of Article 21.2 of the DSU that suggested that the developing-country Member referred to therein could only be an *implementing*

---

[255] See Award of the Arbitrator, *Korea – Alcoholic Beverages (Article 21.3(c))*, para. 45. See also below, p. 299.

[256] See Award of the Arbitrator, *EC – Chicken Cuts*, para. 51. Note, however, that the situation in *EC – Chicken Cuts* was atypical as the Member concerned sought to implement the DSB recommendations and rulings by decision-making processes outside its domestic legal order.

[257] Award of the Arbitrator, *Indonesia – Autos (Article 21.3(c))*, para. 24. However, note that the Arbitrator in para. 23 concluded that the fact that the Indonesian domestic industry had to adjust to the withdrawal or modification of the measure was not something that pertained only to a developing-country Member and was therefore not a ground by itself to award a longer period for implementation. See also Awards of the Arbitrator, *Argentina – Hides and Leather (Article 21.3(c))*, paras. 50–1; and, *Chile – Alcoholic Beverages (Article 21.3(c))*, para. 45, in which the Arbitrator noted: 'It is not necessary to assume that the operation of Article 21.2 will essentially result in the application of "criteria" for the determination of "the reasonable period of time" . . . that would be "qualitatively" different for developed and for developing-country Members.

[258] Awards of the Arbitrator, *EC – Export Subsidies on Sugar (Article 21.3(c))*, para. 99. The complaining developing-country member in *EC – Exports Subsides on Sugar*, of which the interest had to be taken into account, was Brazil.

[259] For a lead to disputes that previously touched upon this question (or applied Article 21.2 to implementing Members), see Award of the Arbitrator, *EC – Export Subsidies on Sugar (Article 21.3(c))*, footnote 192 to para. 99. Note, however, that the question as to whether the 'developing-country Member' could even be a Member not party to the dispute was not addressed, *ibid*.

[260] See Award of the Arbitrator, *US – Gambling (Article 21.3(c))*, para. 59. This was a mere *obiter* statement; the Arbitrator did not rule on the scope of Article 21.2 since he did not reach that far in his analysis. See also Awards of the Arbitrator, *EC – Chicken Cuts (Article 21.3(c))*, para. 82; and *US – Offset Act (Byrd Amendment) (Article 21.3(c))*, para. 81.

Member. Note, however, that the fact that the parties to a dispute are developing-country Members does not *ipso facto* affect the determination of the period of implementation unless these Members are able to substantiate why the otherwise normal period for implementation should cause them hardship (as either implementing or complaining Members).[261]

The 'reasonable period of time for implementation' determined through arbitration to date ranges between six months (*Canada – Pharmaceutical Patents*) and fifteen months and one week (*EC – Bananas III*) from the date of adoption of the report(s) by the DSB.[262] The average time granted for compliance as a 'reasonable period' under Article 21.3 arbitrations to date is just under twelve months, meaning that Members generally have a year to comply with a DSB ruling from the date of the adoption of the panel and/or Appellate Body Report(s).[263]

Note that, in more than four out of five disputes in which the responding party had to bring its challenged measure or legislation into conformity with WTO law, this was done within the 'reasonable period of time for implementation'. In most cases, therefore, the responding party implements the recommendations and rulings adopted by the DSB in a timely and correct manner. The media and academic interest tends to focus on disputes in which this was, or is, not the case, such as *EC – Bananas III*, *EC – Hormones*, *US – FSC*, and *US – Offset Act (Byrd Amendment)*. However, the overall record of compliance with the recommendations and rulings adopted by the DSB is quite positive and encouraging.[264] One can conclude on the basis of this record of compliance that the WTO dispute settlement system 'works'. Nevertheless, it is useful to consider the following sobering story regarding the *US – Cotton Yarn* dispute between Pakistan and the United States in which the United States implemented the recommendations and rulings of the DSB within the reasonable period of time:

> Finally, complying with the recommendations of the DSB and the Appellate Body of the WTO, the US government in November 2001 lifted the quota restriction on Pakistani imports, much to the relief of the Pakistani manufacturers and exporters. The whole process, from the day the quota restraints were imposed to the day they were lifted, lasted for almost two years and nine months, covering almost the entire period of the three-year transitional safeguard measure-quota restraint employed by the United States. The following comment by Akbar Sheikh after being congratulated by Ambassador Don Johnson for winning the case aptly summarizes the feeling at that time.
>
> > At the end of the day both parties won, Pakistan because it got a decision in its favour and the United States because it was able to keep the quota restraints for almost the entire three-year period, thanks to the duration of the case.[265]

---

[261] See Awards of the Arbitrator, *US – Offset Act (Byrd Amendment) (Article 21.3(c))*, para. 81; *EC – Tariff Preferences*, para. 59; and *US – Oil Country Tubular Goods Sunset Review*, para. 52.

[262] See Awards of the Arbitrator, *Canada – Pharmaceutical Patents (Article 21.3(c))*, paras. 62–4; and *EC – Bananas III (Article 21.3(c))*, paras. 18–20.

[263] See www.worldtradelaw.net/dsc/database/implementaverage.asp, visited on 20 February 2008.

[264] See B. Wilson, 'Compliance by WTO Members with Adverse WTO Dispute Settlement Rulings: The Record to Date', *Journal of International Economic Law*, 2007, 397.

[265] T. Hussain, 'Victory in Principle: Pakistan's Dispute Settlement Case on Combed Cotton Yarn Exports to the United States', in P. Gallagher, P. Low and A. Stoler (eds.), *Managing the Challenges of WTO Participation: 45 Case Studies* (Cambridge University Press, 2005), 469. Hussain nevertheless observed that: 'The positive and effective role played by the dispute settlement mechanism of the WTO in resolving this trade dispute between two unequal partners helped reinvigorate the confidence of the local business players in the

---

Questions and Assignments 3.14

What are the remedies for breach of WTO law? Must Members comply with the recommendations and rulings adopted by the DSB 'immediately' or within a 'reasonable period of time'? Who determines the 'reasonable period of time for implementation'? How is the 'reasonable period of time for implementation' determined?

3.2.8.2. Compensation and retaliation

Only the withdrawal (or amendment) of the WTO-inconsistent measure constitutes a final remedy for breach of WTO law. However, if a Member has not withdrawn or amended the WTO-inconsistent measure by the end of the 'reasonable period of time for implementation', the DSU provides for the possibility of recourse to *temporary* remedies:

- compensation; or
- suspension of concessions or other obligations.

Article 22.1 of the DSU states, in relevant part:

> Compensation and the suspension of concessions or other obligations are temporary measures available in the event that the recommendations and rulings are not implemented within a reasonable period of time. However, neither compensation nor the suspension of concessions or other obligations is preferred to full implementation of a recommendation to bring a measure into conformity with the covered agreements.

The DSU leaves no doubt that compensation and/or the suspension of concessions or other obligations are *not* alternative remedies which Members may want to apply *instead of* complying with the recommendations and rulings.[266] Compensation and suspension of concessions are remedies which are only applied until implementation takes place.[267]

Compensation within the meaning of Article 22 of the DSU is voluntary and forward looking, i.e. both parties have to agree on the compensation and the compensation concerns only damages that will be suffered in the future. Compensation must be consistent with the covered agreements.[268] To date, parties have been able to agree on compensation in very few cases. In *Japan – Alcoholic Beverages II*, for example, the parties agreed on compensation which

---

global trading environment. According to Akbar Sheikh it also helped in improving the image of the WTO at the level of both the government and business and enhanced its credibility as an institution aimed at fostering free and fair trade.' *Ibid.*

[266] The 2004 Sutherland Report noted: 'It has even been argued by some that a WTO Member finding itself in a losing position in the WTO dispute settlement system has a free choice on whether or not to actually implement the obligations spelled out in the adopted Appellate Body or panel reports: the alternatives being simply to provide compensation or endure retaliation. This is an erroneous belief.' Consultative Board to the Director-General Supachai Panitchpakdi, *The Future of the WTO: Addressing Institutional Challenges in the New Millennium* (the 'Sutherland Report') (WTO, 2004), para. 241.

[267] See Articles 22.1 and 22.8 of the DSU.   [268] See Article 22.1 of the DSU.

took the form of temporary, additional market access concessions for certain products of export interest to the original complainants.

The suspension of concessions or other obligations – commonly referred to as 'retaliation' – is very different in nature from compensation. There is no need for the parties to agree. When the 'reasonable period of time for implementation' has expired and the parties have not been able to agree on compensation, the injured party may request authorisation from the DSB to retaliate against the offending party by suspending concessions or other obligations with respect to that offending party. Since the DSB decides on such a request by reverse consensus, the granting of authorisation is quasi-automatic.[269]

Retaliation often takes the form of a drastic increase in the customs duties on strategically selected products of export interest to the offending party.[270] Retaliation thus puts economic and political pressure on the offending party to comply with the recommendations and rulings. The producers and traders of the products hit by the increased duties – typically not beneficiaries of the WTO-inconsistent measure – will lobby furiously for the withdrawal or amendment of the WTO-inconsistent measure.

With regard to the concessions or other obligations that may be suspended, Article 22.3 of the DSU provides, in relevant part:

> In considering what concessions or other obligations to suspend, the complaining party shall apply the following principles and procedures:
>
> a. the general principle is that the complaining party should first seek to suspend concessions or other obligations with respect to the same sector(s) as that in which the panel or Appellate Body has found a violation or other nullification or impairment;
> b. if that party considers that it is not practicable or effective to suspend concessions or other obligations with respect to the same sector(s), it may seek to suspend concessions or other obligations in other sectors under the same agreement;
> c. if that party considers that it is not practicable or effective to suspend concessions or other obligations with respect to other sectors under the same agreement, and that the circumstances are serious enough, it may seek to suspend concessions or other obligations under another covered agreement.[271]

In other words, if the violation of WTO law concerns an obligation regarding trade in goods, or regarding trade in financial services, or regarding the protection of patents, suspension of concessions or other obligations should first be sought in the *same* sector. If this is not 'practicable' or 'effective', then suspension may be sought in another sector or under another agreement. This is known as 'cross-retaliation'. Cross-retaliation is seldom requested. In *EC – Bananas III*, Ecuador requested and the DSB authorised the suspension of concessions or other obligations under another agreement (the *TRIPS Agreement*) than the agreements at issue in that dispute (the GATT 1994 and the GATS).[272] In

---

[269] See below, p. 236.
[270] In *EC – Bananas III*, for example, the United States increased the customs duties on carefully selected products from the European Communities to 100 per cent *ad valorem*. See Panel Report, *EC – Bananas III (Article 21.5 – EC)*, para. 2.3.
[271] For definitions of, for example, the concept of 'sectors', and further rules, see Article 22.3(d) – (g) of the DSU.   [272] See Decision by the Arbitrators, *EC – Bananas III (Ecuador) (Article 22.6 – EC)*, para. 1.

US – Gambling, a dispute in which the Panel and the Appellate Body found that the United States' measures at issue were inconsistent with the GATS, Antigua and Barbuda, hereinafter referred to as Antigua, requested authorisation to suspend concessions or other obligations under the GATS and the *TRIPS Agreement*.[273] As reported in *BRIDGES*:

> Antigua observed that retaliating against US goods or services would have a 'disproportionate adverse impact' on its own population: 48.9 percent of the country's goods and services imports come from the US, but total bilateral trade accounts for less than 0.02 percent of the US' total exports. It thus argued that retaliating in services alone – for instance, by barring some US services companies from operating in the country – would be vastly inadequate to recoup the over USD 3.4 billion in losses it claims to have suffered . . . Antigua argued that cross-retaliation was necessary, since its gaming industry and overall economy would continue to suffer serious losses unless the US withdrew its gambling restrictions. It thus asked for authorisation to suspend its WTO obligations to protect US copyrights, trademarks, industrial designs, patents, and data protection, as well as to suspend liberalisation commitments in the communication services sector. Some legal scholars suggest that cross-retaliation against intellectual property might give small countries more leverage at large economies to comply with WTO rulings. However, even if Antigua were to be allowed to legally break US patents, trademarks, and copyrights, the legitimate copies thus produced would only be eligible for sale in the country's tiny internal market. It is not clear whether Antigua could, for instance, export copied drugs to say, the EU, without breaching international or domestic rules.[274]

Note that Antigua requested authorisation to suspend concessions or other obligations for an amount of $3.4 billion a year.[275] With regard to the level of suspension of concessions or other obligations, Article 22.4 of the DSU provides:

> The level of the suspension of concessions or other obligations authorized by the DSB shall be equivalent to the level of the nullification or impairment.

Disputes between the parties on the level of suspension or on whether the rules set out in Article 22.3 have been complied with are resolved through arbitration by the original panel.[276] This arbitration will also review whether a retaliating Member has:

> considered the necessary facts objectively and whether, on the basis of these facts, it could plausibly arrive at the conclusion that it was not practicable or effective to seek suspension within the same sector under the same agreements, or only under another agreement.[277]

---

[273] See *Recourse by Antigua and Barbuda to Article 22.2 of the DSU*, WT/DS/285/22, dated 22 June 2007.

[274] *BRIDGES, Weekly Trade News Digest*, 4 July 2007.

[275] On 21 December 2007, the Arbitrator under Article 22.6 of the DSU (see below, pp. 305–6) decided that Antigua may request the DSB authorisation to suspend obligations under the *TRIPS Agreement* at a level not exceeding US$21 million per year. See Decision by the Arbitrator, *US – Gambling (Article 22.6 – US)*, para 6.1.

[276] See below, pp. 305–6. In *US – Offset Act (Byrd Amendment)*, the Arbitrators determined that the level of nullification or impairment suffered in a particular year by the original complainant could be deemed to be equal to the illegal disbursements for the preceding year multiplied by a certain coefficient. On the problems that arise when the suspension takes the form of a suspension of obligations rather than a suspension of concessions, see Decision by the Arbitrators, *US – 1916 Act (EC)(Article 22.6 – US)*.

[277] Decision by the Arbitrators, *EC – Bananas III (Ecuador)(Article 22.6 – EC)*, para. 52.

In the period from January 1995 to October 2007, the DSB authorised the taking of retaliation measures in seven cases.[278] In four out of the seven cases in which the DSB authorised retaliation, the injured parties actually suspended concessions or other obligations. This was the case in *EC – Bananas III* (retaliation by the United States for an amount of US$191.4 million a year), in *EC – Hormones* (retaliation by the United States and Canada for an amount of US$116.8 million and C$11.3 million a year respectively), in *US – FSC* (retaliation by the European Communities for an amount of US$4,043 million per year), and in *US – Offset Act (Byrd Amendment)* (retaliation by the European Communities, Canada and Japan for an amount of US$27.8 million, 11.2 million and 52.1 million, respectively per year).[279]

As noted above, retaliation measures often take the form of a drastic *increase* in the customs duties (e.g. an increase up to 100 per cent *ad valorem*) on selected products of export interest to the offending party.[280] In *US – FSC*, however, the European Communities opted for retaliation measures on selected products consisting of an additional customs duty of 5 per cent, increased each month by 1 per cent up to a maximum of 17 per cent. Retaliation measures can also take the form of the suspension of 'obligations' rather than the suspension of tariff 'concessions'.[281]

Retaliation measures are *trade destructive* and the injured party imposing these measures is also negatively affected by these measures. In particular for developing-country Members, applying retaliation measures is often not a genuine option. In *EC – Bananas III*, Ecuador was authorised to apply (cross-sector) retaliation measures for an amount of US$201.6 million a year but found it impossible to make use of this possibility without causing severe damage to its own economy. Also consider the observations made above concerning the retaliation of Antigua against the United States in *US – Gambling*.[282] When Chile failed to implement the recommendations and rulings of the Panel and the Appellate Body in *Chile – Price Band System*, it was reported that:

> Faced with no prospect for compensation and with an accumulated loss of US$50 million, both business and government agents [in Argentina] considered the question of retaliating against Chilean products. But retaliation was a completely inadequate solution. From the business angle, retaliation could not offset the losses. From the government perspective, retaliation was likely to poison overall relations with Chile.[283]

---

[278] See *Update of WTO Dispute Settlement Cases*, WT/DS/OV/31, dated 22 August 2007. The DSB authorised retaliatory measures in *EC – Bananas III* (US and Ecuador), *EC – Hormones* (US and Canada), *Brazil – Aircraft* (Canada), *US – FSC* (EC) and *Canada – Aircraft Credits and Guarantees* (Brazil), *US – 1916 Act* (EC) and *US – Offset Act (Byrd Amendment)* (Brazil, Canada, Chile, EC, India, Japan, Korea and Mexico).

[279] See www.wto.org/english/tratop_e/dispu_e/cases_e/ds234_e.htm, visited on 20 October 2007.

[280] The fact that the retaliation measures imposed by the complainant can hit producers that have nothing to do with the conflict has given rise to public criticism. As reported in *BRIDGES Weekly Trade News Digest*: 'Protesting punitive tariffs imposed on EU products by the US in the context of the dispute over EU banning imports of US hormone-treated beef, farmers in southwest France dumped 10 tonnes of nectarines in front of a McDonald's on 20 August, followed the next day by farmers in Arles and Martigues dumping tonnes of fruit, vegetables and manure in front of McDonald's there. These protests follow similar incidents by French farmers throughout the month.' *BRIDGES Weekly Trade News Digest*, 30 August 1999.   [281] See Decision by the Arbitrators, *US – 1916 Act (EC) (Article 22.6 – US)*.

[282] See above, p. 227.

[283] D. Tussie and V. Delich, 'Dispute Settlement between Developing Countries: Argentina and Chilean Price Bands', in P. Gallagher *et al.* (eds.), *Managing the Challenges of WTO Participation: 45 Case Studies* (Cambridge University Press, 2005), 35.

Doubts thus exist as to the effectiveness of retaliation as a (temporary) remedy for breach of WTO law. However, in *EC – Bananas III* and in *US – FSC*, the retaliation measures imposed by the United States on the European Communities and imposed by the European Communities on the United States respectively, have arguably led to 'some degree of compliance' with the recommendations and rulings in those disputes.[284]

It is much debated whether a Member authorised to take retaliation measures may periodically (e.g. every six months) rotate, i.e. change, the products or services on which these retaliation measures are applied. This issue, commonly referred to as the 'carousel' issue, arose because US legislation provides for a periodic shift in the focus of retaliation measures to maximise their impact. To date, the United States has not applied this legislation. It is clear that rotation that will have the effect of, for example, covering a wider section of exporters of the Member concerned and will add to the pressure on that Member to comply with WTO law, thus being consonant with a purposive interpretation of Article 22.1 of the DSU. It has been argued, however, that a periodic rotation in the products and services 'hit' by the retaliation measure cannot be allowed since it would result in retaliation measures going beyond the level of nullification or impairment caused.[285]

Questions and Assignments 3.15

What are the rules applicable to compensation within the meaning of Article 22 of the DSU? What are the rules applicable to the suspension of concessions or other obligations? Has the suspension of concessions or other obligations been an effective temporary remedy for breach of WTO law?

3.2.8.3. *Other remedies for breach of WTO law*

Under general international law, a breach of an international obligation leads to responsibility entailing certain legal consequences. The first legal consequence of international responsibility is the obligation to cease the illegal conduct.[286] According to the ILC Articles on State Responsibility, the injured State is furthermore entitled to claim 'full reparation' in the form of:

---

[284] In both disputes, the implementing measures taken 'under pressure' from retaliation were later challenged and found WTO-inconsistent. See *EC – Bananas III (Article 21.5 – Ecuador)*; and *US – FSC (Article 21.5 II)*.

[285] It is to be noted that in *US – Offset Act (Byrd Amendment)*, the European Communities and Japan have notified the DSB on a yearly basis of the new list of products that will be subject to retaliation. See, however, Decision by the Arbitrator, *US – Offset Act (Byrd Amendment) (Article 22.6 –US)*, where the Arbitrator noted that the concept of 'inducing compliance', the object of which was to fix nullification/impairment at levels that would bring a Member to comply, was not the exclusive object of Article 22 of the DSU and that this 'benchmark for the selection of the most appropriate approach [in determining the level of suspension] run[s] the risk of losing sight of the requirement of Article 22.4 that the level of suspension be *equivalent* to the level of nullification or impairment'. Decision by the Arbitrator, *US – Offset Act (Byrd Amendment) Article 22.6–US)*, para. 3.74 (emphasis in original).

[286] See ILC Articles on State Responsibility, Part 2, Article 6.

- restitution in kind;
- compensation;
- satisfaction; and,
- assurances and guarantees of non-repetition.[287]

Restitution in kind means that the wrong-doing State has to re-establish the situation that existed before the illegal act was committed.[288] If restitution in kind is not available, compensation for the damage caused by the act must be paid. Compensation covers any economically assessable damage suffered by the injured State and may include interest, and also, under certain circumstances, lost profits.[289] The DSU does not explicitly provide for the compensation of damage suffered.[290] However, the question is whether the rules of general international law on State responsibility, as reflected in the ILC Articles, apply to breaches of WTO law. Are the only possible remedies for breaches of WTO law the remedies explicitly provided for in the provisions of the DSU quoted above? Or, in the absence of a specific rule in the DSU on the compensation of damage suffered, is the general international law rule on compensation applicable? It could be argued that by providing a detailed set of rules regarding the legal consequences of a breach of WTO law, the DSU has contracted out of general international law on State responsibility and that the rule on compensation for damage suffered would thus not apply.[291] Most, if not all, WTO Members seem to share this view. This issue is part of the larger issue of the relationship between WTO law and other international law, discussed in chapter 1 of this book.[292]

While controversial, in very specific circumstances, repayment of sums illegally received may also constitute a remedy for breach of WTO law. Article 4.7 of the *SCM Agreement* states that, if a measure is found to be a prohibited subsidy, the panel shall recommend that the subsidising Member withdraw the subsidy without delay. In *Australia – Automotive Leather II (Article 21.5 – US)*, the Panel examined whether the recommendation to 'withdraw the subsidy' in Article 4.7 of the *SCM Agreement* can properly be understood to encompass repayment. The Panel concluded that:

> in the circumstances of this case, repayment is necessary in order to 'withdraw' the prohibited subsidies found to exist. As discussed above, we do not find any basis for repayment of anything less than the full subsidy. We therefore conclude that repayment in full of the prohibited subsidy is necessary in order to 'withdraw the subsidy' in this case.
>
> In our view, the required repayment does not include any interest component. We believe that withdrawal of the subsidy was intended by the drafters of the SCM

---

[287] See *ibid.*, Article 6 *bis*.

[288] See *ibid.*, Article 7. Restitution in kind is not required in a number of situations set out in this provision, such as the situation in which the restitution would 'seriously jeopardize the political independence or economic stability of the State which has committed the internationally wrongful act, whereas the injured State would not be similarly affected if it did not obtain restitution in kind'.

[289] See *ibid.*, Article 8. See also P. Malanczuk, *Akehurst's Modern Introduction to International Law*, 7th revised edition (Routledge, 1997), 269–71.

[290] Compensation under Article 22 of the DSU concerns only damages that will be suffered in the future. See above, p. 225.   [291] See also above, pp. 55–6.

[292] See above, pp. 59–63. For a better appreciation of WTO law and rules of State responsibility, see, B. Simma and D. Pulkowski, 'Of Planets and the Universe: Self-contained Regimes in International Law', *European Journal of International Law*, 2006, 483, 519–23.

> Agreement to be a specific and effective remedy for violations of the prohibition in Article 3.1(a). However, we do not understand it to be a remedy intended to fully restore the *status quo ante* by depriving the recipient of the prohibited subsidy of the benefits it may have enjoyed in the past. Nor do we consider it to be a remedy intended to provide reparation or compensation in any sense. A requirement of interest would go beyond the requirement of repayment encompassed by the term 'withdraw the subsidy', and is therefore, we believe, beyond any reasonable understanding of that term.[293]

The Panel insisted on the specificity of this ruling by stating:

> That a 'retrospective' remedy might not be permissible under Article 19.1 of the DSU (a question which we do not here decide) does not preclude us from concluding, on the basis of the text of Article 4.7 of the SCM Agreement, that 'withdraw the subsidy' is not limited to purely prospective action, but may encompass repayment of prohibited subsidies.[294]

The Panel's ruling that, at least with regard to prohibited subsidies, the DSU not only provides for a 'prospective' but also for a 'retrospective' remedy was criticised by many WTO Members, including *both* parties to this dispute.[295]

Questions and Assignments 3.16

Do WTO rules on remedies deviate from general international law on remedies? If so, does general international law nevertheless apply? In your opinion, should a Member that causes significant damage to the economy of another Member as a result of a breach of WTO law compensate this damage? Should customs duties which were imposed in violation of obligations under WTO law be repaid to the importer?

3.2.9. Special rules and assistance for developing-country Members

As noted above, developing-country Members have made much use of the WTO dispute settlement system. In 1995 and in every year since 2000 (except in 2006),[296] developing-country Members, as a group, have brought more disputes to the WTO than developed-country Members.[297] To date, Brazil (twenty-three complaints), India (seventeen complaints), Mexico (seventeen complaints), Argentina (fourteen complaints), Thailand (twelve complaints) and Chile (ten complaints) are among the biggest users of the system.[298] The 2004 Sutherland Report observed with regard to the record of complainants under the WTO dispute settlement system:

> One of the interesting facets of this record of complaints is a much greater participation of developing countries than was the case in the GATT dispute settlement system. Of

---

[293] Panel Report, *Australia – Automotive Leather II (Article 21.5 – US)*, paras. 6.48 and 6.49.
[294] *Ibid.*, para. 6.42.
[295] The Panel Report was not appealed because the parties to this dispute, the United States and Australia, had agreed at the start of the Article 21.5 panel proceedings not to appeal the panel report.
[296] To date, the United States has filed eighty-eight complaints and the European Communities seventy-six. See www.worldtradelaw.net/dsc/database/complaintscomplainant.asp, visited on 23 November 2007.
[297] See www.worldtradelaw.net/dsc/database/classificationcount.asp, visited on 23 November 2007.
[298] See www.worldtradelaw.net/dsc/database/complaintscomplainant.asp, visited on 23 November 2007.

course, the major trading powers continue to act either as complainant or respondent in a very large number of cases. Given their large amount of trade with an even greater number of markets, it could hardly be otherwise. Yet, developing countries – even some of the poorest (when given the legal assistance now available to them) – are increasingly taking on the most powerful. That is how it should be.[299]

Developing-country Members have used the WTO dispute settlement system to bring cases against the economic superpowers and have done so successfully. *US – Underwear*, a complaint by Costa Rica, and even more so *US – Gambling*, a complaint by Antigua (population 67,000), are well-known examples of successful 'David versus Goliath' use of the system.[300] Developing-country Members have also used the system against other developing-country Members. Examples of such use of the system are *Chile – Price Band System*, a complaint by Argentina, and *Egypt – Import Prohibition on Canned Tuna with Soybean Oil*, a complaint by Thailand.

Thus far, least-developed-country Members have used the WTO dispute settlement system only once. In February 2004, Bangladesh requested consultations with India on the imposition of anti-dumping duties by India on batteries from Bangladesh.[301] To date, the WTO dispute settlement system has never been used 'against' least-developed-country Members. Note in this respect that Article 24.1 of the DSU requires Members to 'exercise due restraint' in using the WTO dispute settlement system in disputes involving a least-developed-country Member.

The DSU contains a number of other provisions providing for special treatment or consideration for developing-country Members involved in WTO dispute settlement. This section examines these provisions. It also discusses the legal assistance available to developing-country Members involved in WTO dispute settlement.

3.2.9.1. *Special rules for developing-country Members*

The DSU recognises the difficulties developing-country Members may encounter when they are involved in WTO dispute settlement. Therefore, the DSU contains some special rules for developing-country Members. Such special DSU rules are found in Article 3.12 (regarding the application of the 1966 Decision),[302]

---

[299] Consultative Board to the Director-General Supachai Panitchpakdi, *The Future of the WTO: Addressing Institutional Challenges in the New Millennium* (the 'Sutherland Report') (WTO, 2004), para. 222.

[300] As observed by J. Breckenridge, 'when Costa Rica initiated its case [in 1995], no small developing country had brought a case against a large developed country. Many observers viewed confronting the United States as a risky strategy – not only for Costa Rica, but also for the DSU process in general. How would the United States respond to a ruling against it? Unwillingness by the United States to abide by such a ruling could undermine the credibility of the entire process.' J. Breckenridge, 'Costa Rica's Challenge to US Restrictions on the Import of Underwear', in P. Gallagher, *et al.* (eds.), *Managing the Challenges of WTO Participation: 45 Case Studies* (Cambridge University Press, 2005), 180. These concerns were shown to be unfounded.

[301] Request for Consultations by Bangladesh, *India – Anti-Dumping Measure on Batteries from Bangladesh*, WT/DS306/1, dated 2 February 2004. On 20 February 2006, the parties informed the DSB that a mutually satisfactory solution to the matter had been achieved. The anti-dumping measure addressed in the request for consultations had been terminated by India. See Notification of Mutually Satisfactory Solution, *India – Anti-Dumping Measure on Batteries from Bangladesh*, WT/DS306/3, dated 23 February 2006.

[302] Decision of 5 April 1966 on Procedures under Article XXIII, BISD 14S/18. Article 3.12 of the DSU allows a developing-country Member that brings a complaint against a developed-country Member to invoke the

Article 4.10 (regarding consultations), Article 8.10 (regarding the composition of panels), Article 12.10 (regarding consultations and the time to prepare and present arguments), Article 12.11 (regarding the content of panel reports), Article 24 (regarding least-developed countries) and Article 27 (on the assistance of the WTO Secretariat). For the most part, however, these special rules have not been used much to date. Developing-country Members criticise the fact that many of these provisions are merely hortatory in nature.[303] A number of these provisions will be discussed in greater detail below.[304]

3.2.9.2. *Legal assistance for developing-country Members*

Many developing-country Members do not have the 'in-house' legal expertise to participate effectively in WTO dispute settlement. As discussed above, since the Appellate Body ruling in *EC – Bananas III*, it is clear that WTO Members can be assisted and represented by private counsel in WTO dispute settlement proceedings. The Appellate Body noted in its ruling:

> that representation by counsel of a government's own choice may well be a matter of particular significance – especially for developing-country Members – to enable them to participate fully in dispute settlement proceedings.[305]

However, assistance and representation by private counsel has its costs, and these costs may be quite burdensome for developing-country Members.[306]

---

provisions of the Decision of 5 April 1966 of the GATT Contracting Parties. These provisions may be invoked as an 'alternative' to the provisions contained in Articles 4, 5, 6 and 12 of the DSU. To date, the provisions of the 1966 Decision have been 'invoked' only once, on 21 March 2007, in a complaint brought by Colombia against the European Communities' new 'tariff-only' regime for bananas applied from 1 January 2006. In its request for consultations, Colombia stated: 'Should these consultations not lead to a satisfactory settlement, Colombia will consider referring the matter to the Director General pursuant to Article 3.12 of the DSU and the Decision of 5 April 1966 (BISD 14S/18) in the hope that his good offices will facilitate a rapid solution to this dispute and, if necessary, request the establishment of a panel in accordance with applicable accelerated procedures.' Request for Consultations by Colombia, *European Communities – Regime for the Importation of Bananas*, WT/DS/361/1. The reason for the lack of enthusiasm for the provisions of the 1966 Decision is undoubtedly that the DSU provisions afford developing-country complaining parties treatment at least as favourable as, if not more favourable than, the treatment afforded by the 1966 Decision.

[303] Various proposals have been made in the DSU reform negotiations to replace language of special and differential treatment provisions from 'should' to 'shall' to strengthen these provisions. Most have found their way into the Chairman's Text. Furthermore, proposals on the strengthening of developing-country Members' rights regarding issues such as panel composition and the timetable for panel proceedings have been included in the Chairman's Text. See below, p. 309.   [304] See below, pp. 233, 245, 255, 274, 278.

[305] Appellate Body Report, *EC – Bananas III*, para. 12.

[306] While the 'litigation costs' are undoubtedly an important factor in explaining the reluctance of most developing-country Members to engage in WTO dispute settlement, H. Nordström and G. Shaffer wrote: 'We wish to stress that the issue is not just litigation costs. It is also a country's perceptions of litigation costs (including in terms of internal agency time) under uncertainty regarding the results from litigation, including the defendant's compliance with a decision in a meaningful manner – i.e. one that actually results in increased market access. The costs are also difficult to estimate in advance since it depends on what the counterpart does. If the other party decides not to settle and the case goes to a panel after an unsuccessful consultation, the price will go up. If the other party decides to appeal the ruling, the price will increase further. If the choice is to litigate further over compliance, the price continues to rise. Finally, if the opposing side does not comply with a ruling, then the entire litigation can be for naught'. H. Nordström and G. Shaffer, *Access to Justice in the World Trade Organization: The Case for a Small Claims Procedure. A Preliminary Analysis* (ICTSD Project on Dispute Settlement, June 2007), 10. Note that a Chinese proposal to allow panels and the Appellate Body to award 'an amount for litigation costs' has been included in the Chairman's Text. See below, p. 309.

The WTO Secretariat assists all Members in respect of dispute settlement when they so request. However, the DSU recognises that there may be a need to provide additional legal advice and assistance to developing-country Members.[307] To meet this additional need, Article 27.2 of the DSU requires that the WTO Secretariat make qualified legal experts available to help any developing-country Member that so requests. The extent to which the Secretariat can assist developing-country Members is, however, limited by the requirement that the Secretariat's experts give assistance in a manner 'ensuring the continued impartiality of the Secretariat'.[308]

Effective legal assistance for developing-country Members, in dispute settlement proceedings, is given by the Geneva-based Advisory Centre on WTO Law (ACWL). The ACWL is an independent, intergovernmental organisation (fully independent from the WTO), which functions essentially as a law office specialising in WTO law, providing legal services and training exclusively to developing-country and economy-in-transition members of the ACWL and *all* least-developed countries. The ACWL provides support at all stages of WTO dispute settlement proceedings at discounted rates. The ACWL currently has thirty-seven members: ten developed countries and twenty-seven developing countries and economies-in-transition.[309] The services of the ACWL are at present available to a total of sixty-nine countries, representing approximately 40 per cent of the WTO membership.

On the occasion of the official opening of the ACWL on 5 October 2001, Mike Moore, then WTO Director-General, said:

> The International Court of Justice has a small fund out of which costs of legal assistance can be paid for countries who need such help. But today marks the first time a true legal aid centre has been established within the international legal system, with a view to combating the unequal possibilities of access to international justice as between States.[310]

At the same occasion, Claus-Dieter Ehlermann, then Chairman of the Appellate Body, noted:

> By providing low-cost, high-quality legal services, the Centre will enable the greater participation of developing-country Members. The Centre will, therefore, benefit its Members. It will benefit panels, the Appellate Body, and the WTO. Ultimately, the Centre will benefit the 'rules-based' multilateral trading system, and strengthen the notion that the dispute settlement system of the WTO is available to the economically weak as much as it is available to the economically strong.[311]

A significant success for the ACWL thus far was the *EC – Sardines* dispute in which the ACWL represented Peru, the complainant in this dispute. In the span of a few years, the ACWL has become a major player in WTO dispute settlement. During the period from 2001 to 2007, the ACWL provided support in twenty-nine WTO dispute settlement proceedings, i.e. one fifth of all WTO dispute settlement proceedings during that period.[312] In 2007, the ACWL received 110 requests for

---

[307] See Article 27.2 of the DSU.   [308] Article 27.2, final sentence, of the DSU.
[309] For up-to-date information on the ACWL, see www.acwl.ch, visited on 1 December 2007.   [310] *Ibid.*
[311] *Ibid.*
[312] See ACWL, *Report on Operations 2007*, available at www.acwl.ch/pdf/opr_2007.pdf, visited on 1 December 2007.

legal opinions, provided support in six dispute settlement proceedings and received two new requests for support.[313] The 2006 Report of the Task Force established by the ACWL's General Assembly to develop a financial plan for the ACWL made the following findings regarding the activities of the ACWL to date:

> Both developing countries and LDCs indicated that they have little or no legal expertise of the kind available through the ACWL in their own countries. All ACWL Members and LDCs that have used the ACWL not only recognize it as a centre of excellence with regard to the services it provides, but would also strongly recommend it to other LDCs and developing countries. It is expected that there will be increased demand for the services of the ACWL over the coming years.[314]

Questions and Assignments 3.17

Does the DSU take the particular situation of developing-country Members into account? Do developing-country Members involved in WTO dispute settlement benefit from legal assistance? By whom and under what conditions is this assistance granted?

3.3. INSTITUTIONS OF WTO DISPUTE SETTLEMENT

Among the institutions involved in WTO dispute settlement, one can distinguish between *political institutions*, such as the Dispute Settlement Body, and independent, *judicial-type institutions*, such as the dispute settlement panels and the standing Appellate Body. While the WTO has entrusted the adjudication of disputes at the first instance to panels, and at the appellate level to the Appellate Body, the Dispute Settlement Body continues to play an active role in the WTO dispute settlement system. This section examines the Dispute Settlement Body, the panels and the Appellate Body.

3.3.1. The Dispute Settlement Body

The WTO dispute settlement system is administered by the Dispute Settlement Body (DSB).[315] Article IV:3 of the *WTO Agreement* states, in relevant part:

> The General Council shall convene as appropriate to discharge the responsibilities of the Dispute Settlement Body provided for in the Dispute Settlement Understanding. The Dispute Settlement Body may have its own chairman and shall establish such rules of procedure as it deems necessary for the fulfilment of those responsibilities.

As already noted in chapter 2, the DSB is an emanation, or an *alter ego*, of the WTO's General Council.[316] When the General Council administers the WTO dispute

---

[313] See *ibid.*
[314] See ACWL, *Report on Operations 2006*, available at www.acwl.ch/pdf/opz_2006, visited on 20 Novenber 2007.
[315] See Article 2.1 of the DSU.   [316] See above, pp. 122–3.

settlement system, it convenes and acts as the DSB. Like the General Council, the DSB is composed of ambassador-level diplomats of all WTO Members.[317]

With respect to the functions of the DSB, Article 2.1 of the DSU broadly defines these functions as the administration of the dispute settlement system and then specifies them by stating:

> Accordingly, the DSB shall have the authority to establish panels, adopt panel and Appellate Body reports, maintain surveillance of implementation of rulings and recommendations, and authorize suspension of concessions and other obligations under the covered agreements.

However, the administration of the dispute settlement system is not limited to these functions. It also includes, for example, the appointment of the Members of the Appellate Body[318] and the adoption of the Rules of Conduct for WTO dispute settlement.[319]

Article 2.4 of the DSU stipulates that, where the DSU provides for the DSB to take a decision, such a decision is always taken by consensus.[320] It is important to note, however, that, for some key decisions, such as:

* the decision on the establishment of panels,
* the adoption of panel and Appellate Body reports and
* the authorisation of suspension of concession and other obligations,

the consensus requirement is in fact a 'reverse' or 'negative' consensus requirement.[321] With respect to the DSB's decision to adopt an Appellate Body report for example, Article 17.14 of the DSU states, in relevant part:

> An Appellate Body report shall be adopted by the DSB . . . unless the DSB decides by consensus not to adopt the Appellate Body report within 30 days following its circulation to the Members.

The 'reverse' consensus requirement means that the DSB is deemed to take a decision unless there is a consensus among WTO Members *not* to take that decision. Since there will usually be at least one Member with a strong interest in the establishment of a panel, the adoption of the panel and/or Appellate Body reports or the authorisation to suspend concessions, it is unlikely that there will be a consensus *not* to adopt these decisions.[322] As a result, decision-making by the DSB on these matters is, for all practical purposes, automatic and a matter of course. Furthermore, it should be noted that the DSU provides for strict time-frames within which decisions on these matters must be taken.[323]

---

[317] See Article IV:2 of the *WTO Agreement*. Where the DSB administers the dispute settlement provisions of a WTO plurilateral trade agreement, only those WTO Members that are parties to that agreement may participate in the decisions or actions taken by the DSB with respect to that dispute. See Article 2.1 of the DSU.   [318] See below, pp. 258–9.   [319] See above, pp. 217–18.

[320] Footnote 1 to the DSU states: 'The DSB shall be deemed to have decided by consensus on a matter submitted for its consideration, if no Member, present at the meeting of the DSB when the decision is taken, formally objects to the proposed decision.'

[321] See Articles 6.1, 16.4, 17.14 and 22.6 of the DSU. Other decisions of the DSB, such as the appointment of the Members of the Appellate Body, are taken by 'normal' consensus.

[322] Note, however, that, in very exceptional circumstances, it is possible that no Member puts the adoption of the report on the agenda of the DSB and that the report therefore remains unadopted. This happened with the Panel Report, *EC – Bananas III (Article 21.5 – EC)*, circulated on 12 April 1999.

[323] For example, the decision to adopt an Appellate Body report shall be taken within thirty days following its circulation to the Members (see Article 17.14 of the DSU). If there is no meeting of the

Figure 3.2 Agenda of the DSB meeting of 24 July 2007[324]

I.   Surveillance of implementation of recommendations adopted by the DSB
     (a)   United States – Section 211 Omnibus Appropriations Act of 1998: Status report by the
        United States
     (b)   United States – Anti-dumping measures on certain hot-rolled steel products from Japan:
        Status report by the United States
     (c)   United States – Section 110(5) of the US copyright act: Status report by the United States
     (d)   United States – Laws, regulations and methodology for calculating dumping margins
        ('zeroing'): Status report by the United States

II.   United States – Continued Dumping and Subsidy Offset Act of 2000: Implementation of the
    recommendations adopted by the DSB
     (a)   Statements by Canada, the European Communities and Japan

III.   Brazil – Anti-dumping measures on imports of certain resins from Argentina
     (a)   Request for the establishment of a panel by Argentina

IV.   China – Certain measures granting refunds, reductions or exemptions from taxes and other
    payments
     (a)   Request for the establishment of a panel by the United States

V.   China – Certain measures granting refunds, reductions or exemptions from taxes and other
    payments
     (a)   Request for the establishment of a panel by Mexico

VI.   United States – Measures affecting the cross-border supply of gambling and betting services
     (a)   Recourse to Article 22.2 of the DSU by Antigua and Barbuda

VII.   Mexico – Anti-dumping duties on steel pipes and tubes from Guatemala
     (a)   Report of the panel

VIII. Proposed nomination for the indicative list of governmental and non-governmental panellists
Other Business

The DSB meets as often as necessary to carry out its functions within the time-frames provided in the DSU. In practice, the DSB has one scheduled meeting per month and, in addition, special meetings convened when the need for a meeting arises. In 2006, the DSB met twenty-two times.[325] By way of example, consider the agenda of the DSB meeting of 24 July 2007, as shown in figure 3.2. Meetings of the DSB are always held in Geneva, usually last a few hours and are well attended. About fifty WTO Members will normally attend, and these Members will often be represented by their highest-ranking resident diplomat, the Permanent Representative of that Member in Geneva. In February 2008, Ambassador Mario Matus of Chile was elected as Chairperson for 2008. With minor deviations regarding Observers (Chapter IV) and the Chairperson (Chapter V), the Rules of Procedure for the General Council apply to the meetings of the DSB.

As a result of the fact that the DSB takes the core dispute settlement decisions referred to above by reverse consensus, the DSB's impact on, and influence over, WTO dispute settlement is limited. The involvement of the DSB is, to a large extent, a legacy of the past in which trade dispute settlement was more

DSB scheduled during this period, such a meeting shall be held for this purpose (see footnote 8 to the DSU).   [324] See WT/DSB/W/355, dated 20 July 2007.
[325] WTO Secretariat, *Annual Report* 2007, 34, available at
www.wto.org/english/res_e/booksp_e/anrep_e/anrep07_e.pdf, visited on 13 September 2007.

diplomatic and political than judicial in nature.[326] Nevertheless, the involvement of the DSB in each major step of a dispute fulfils two useful purposes:

- it keeps all WTO Members directly informed of WTO dispute settlement; and
- it gives WTO Members a designated political forum in which issues arising from the use of the dispute settlement system can be debated.

Questions and Assignments 3.18

What are the functions of the DSB in the WTO dispute settlement system? Is it common for political institutions to play an active role in dispute settlement systems? Does the DSB play a significant role in WTO dispute settlement or is its role more a 'symbolic' one? Explain.

3.3.2. WTO dispute settlement panels

The actual adjudication of disputes brought to the WTO is carried out, at the first-instance level, by *ad hoc* dispute settlement panels. This section discusses:

- the request for the establishment of a panel;
- the establishment of a panel;
- the composition of a panel;
- a panel's terms of reference;
- the standard of review applied by panels;
- the exercise of judicial economy by panels;
- characteristics of a panel report; and
- the role of the WTO Secretariat in supporting panels.

3.3.2.1. Request for the establishment of a panel

WTO dispute settlement panels are not standing bodies. They are *ad hoc* bodies established for the purpose of adjudicating a particular dispute and are dissolved once they have accomplished this task. The complainant must request the DSB to establish a panel. Pursuant to Article 6.2 of the DSU, the 'request for the establishment of a panel', also referred to as the 'panel request', must be made in writing and must:

- indicate *whether* consultations were held;[327]
- identify the *specific* measures at issue; and
- provide a brief summary of the legal basis of the complaint *sufficient* to present the problem clearly.[328]

---

[326] See above, p. 170.
[327] On the relationship between the request for consultations and the panel request, see below, pp. 270–1.
[328] Article 6.2 of the DSU. Note that Article 6.2 of the DSU also applies to requests for the establishment of a panel under Article 21.5 of the DSU, but it needs to be interpreted in the light thereof, and, as a result, its requirements need to be adapted to compliance proceedings. See Appellate Body Report, *US – FSC (Article 21.5 – EC II)*, paras. 52–69. See also below, p. 300.

In *EC – Bananas III*, the Appellate Body found that:

> It is important that a panel request be sufficiently precise for two reasons: first, it often forms the basis for the terms of reference of the panel pursuant to Article 7 of the DSU; and, second, it informs the defending party and the third parties of the legal basis of the complaint.[329]

The Appellate Body also held that a failure to make a claim in the panel request cannot be 'subsequently "cured" by a complaining party's argumentation in its first written submission to the panel or in any other submission or statement made later in the panel proceeding'.[330]

Addressing the nature of the obligation to indicate in the panel request whether consultations were held, and the consequences of a failure to do so, the Appellate Body in *Mexico – Corn Syrup (Article 21.5 – US)* held:

> The purpose of the requirement seems to be primarily informational – to inform the DSB and Members as to whether consultations took place. We also recall that the DSU expressly contemplates that, in certain circumstances, a panel can deal with and dispose of the matter referred to it even if no consultations took place. Similarly, the authority of the panel cannot be invalidated by the absence, in the request for establishment of the panel, of an indication 'whether consultations were held'. Indeed, it would be curious if the requirement in Article 6.2 to inform the DSB whether consultations were held was accorded more importance in the dispute settlement process than the requirement actually to hold those consultations.[331]

An example of a straightforward application of Article 6.2 of the DSU is provided by *US – Hot-Rolled Steel*. The Panel in this case held that Japan's failure to make a claim in its panel request challenging 'general [US] practice' regarding safeguards, meant that the claim was not within the Panel's terms of reference.[332] Another instance is *US – Carbon Steel*, where the Appellate Body upheld the Panel's conclusion that the European Communities' panel request referring to 'certain aspects of the [US] sunset review procedure as well as US statutory and regulatory provisions related to sunset reviews' was not sufficient to indicate the *specific measures* at issue, namely matters relating to the submission of evidence in a sunset review.[333]

Whether or not the 'specific measure at issue' is sufficiently identified in the panel request depends on the ability of the respondent to defend itself given the actual reference to the measure at issue.[334] In *Canada – Wheat Exports and Grain*

---

[329] Appellate Body Report, *EC – Bananas III*, para. 142.   [330] Appellate Body Report, *EC – Bananas III*, para. 143.

[331] Appellate Body Report, *Mexico – Corn Syrup (Article 21.5 – US)*, para. 70.

[332] See Panel Report, *US – Hot-Rolled Steel*, paras. 7.16–7.23. See also Panel Report, *Australia – Salmon*, paras. 8.26–8.28.

[333] Appellate Body Report, *US – Carbon Steel*, para. 171. See also Panel Report, *US – Upland Cotton*, paras. 7.129–7.152 and 7.172–7.181; Panel Report, *US – Corrosion-Resistant Steel Sunset Review*, paras. 7.47–7.54 and 7.189–7.191; and Panel Report, *EC – Trademarks and Geographical Indications (Australia)*, paras. 7.37–7.43 and 7.46–7.50.

[334] See Panel Report, *Japan – Film*, para. 10.8; Panel Report, *Argentina – Footwear (EC)*, para. 8.35 (on subsidiary or implementing measures or later modifications to measures which were not explicitly identified); Appellate Body Report, *EC – Computer Equipment*, para. 70; Panel Report, *Korea – Alcoholic Beverages*, paras. 10.4–10.16; Panel Report, *Turkey – Textiles*, paras. 9.2–9.3; Panel Report, *US – FSC*, paras. 7.23–7.32; Appellate Body Report, *Dominican Republic – Import and Sale of Cigarettes*, paras. 116–27; Appellate Body Report, *EC – Chicken Cuts*, paras. 150–62 (on the identification of the products to which the measure at issue applied);

Imports, the Panel distinguished between particular actions and measures of general application and noted that whether a measure of general application is sufficiently identified,

> will depend . . . on whether the information provided serves the purposes of Article 6.2, and in particular its due process objective, as well as the specific circumstances of each case, including the type of measure that is at issue.[335]

The Panel went on to articulate a legal proposition that:

> the fact that a panel request does not specify by name, date of adoption, etc. the relevant law, regulation or other legal instrument to which a claim relates does not necessarily render the panel request inconsistent with Article 6.2, provided that the panel request contains sufficient information that effectively identifies the precise measures at issue.[336]

In a few cases the question has arisen whether the requirement of Article 6.2 to 'identify the specific measures at issue' also means that the specific *products* at issue must be identified in the panel request. The Appellate Body noted in *EC – Computer Equipment* that:

> 'measures' within the meaning of Article 6.2 of the DSU . . . also can be the application of tariffs by customs authorities.[337]
>
> Article 6.2 of the DSU does *not* explicitly require that the products to which the 'specific measures at issue' apply be identified. However, with respect to certain WTO obligations, in order to identify 'the specific measures at issue', it may also be necessary to identify the products subject to the measures in dispute.[338]

More recently, the Appellate Body found in *EC – Chicken Cuts*:

> Article 6.2 of the DSU does not refer to the identification of the products at issue; rather, it refers to the identification of the specific measures at issue. Article 6.2 contemplates that the identification of the products at issue must flow from the specific measures identified in the panel request. Therefore, the identification of the product at issue is generally not a separate and distinct element of a panel's terms of reference; rather, it is a consequence of the scope of application of the specific measures at issue. In other words, it is the *measure* at issue that generally will define the *product* at issue.[339]

Footnote (*cont.*)

   Panel Report, *Canada – Aircraft*, paras. 9.34–9.35; and Panel Report, *Canada – Aircraft Credits and Guarantees*, paras. 7.21–7.55 (on an umbrella term used in a request sufficing to indicate more precise matters and general commercial terms used to identify specific measures).

[335] Panel Reports, *Canada – Wheat Exports and Grain Imports*, para. 6.10, point 20. With reference to the distinction in this finding between measures of general application and particular actions, the Panel in *EC – Approval and Marketing of Biotech Products* held that: 'another appropriate distinction is that between formal (*de jure*) governmental measures and informal (*de facto*) governmental measures. In our view, the informal nature of a governmental measure may affect the degree of precision with which such a measure can be set out in a panel request. Notably, it will often not be possible to identify informal measures by their name, date of adoption and/or legal status.' See Panel Reports, *EC – Approval and Marketing of Biotech Products*, para. 7.47 point 22.

[336] Panel Reports, *Canada – Wheat Exports and Grain Imports*, para. 6.10, point 36. Accordingly, the Panel allowed Canada's challenge in respect of one of the claims of the United States and dismissed two others. See also in this respect, Appellate Body Report, *US – Oil Country Tubular Goods Sunset Review*, paras. 172–3, advising complainants to be specific about their 'as such' challenges to the municipal law of Members. Note, however, that Article 6.2 does not demand that 'specific aspects' of 'specific measures' be contained in panel requests. See Panel Report, *EC – Trademarks and Geographical Indications (Australia)*, para. 7.2.

[337] Appellate Body Report, *EC – Computer Equipment*, para. 65.   [338] *Ibid.*, para. 67.

[339] Appellate Body Report, *EC – Chicken Cuts*, para. 165. Note, however, that in some instances the products covered in a panel request can have the effect of potentially qualifying the scope of substantive measures before the panel. See, for example, Panel Report, *Dominican Republic – Import and Sale of Cigarettes*, paras. 7.94–7.103.

With regard to the requirement that the panel request must 'provide a brief summary of the legal basis of the complaint sufficient to present the problem clearly', the Appellate Body noted that the DSU demands only a *brief* summary of the legal basis of the complaint.[340] The summary must, however, be one 'sufficient to present the problem clearly'.[341] The claims, but not the arguments,[342] must all be specified sufficiently in the panel request.[343] In *EC – Bananas III*, the Appellate Body found that, in view of the particular circumstances of that case, the listing of the articles of the agreements alleged to have been breached satisfied the minimum requirement of Article 6.2 of the DSU.[344] In *Korea – Dairy*, however, the Appellate Body noted that, where the articles listed establish not one single, distinct obligation but, rather, multiple obligations, the listing of articles of an agreement, in and of itself, may fall short of the standard of Article 6.2 of the DSU.[345] The Appellate Body held that the question of whether the mere listing of the articles suffices must be examined on a case-by-case basis. Furthermore, it ruled that, in resolving that question:

> we take into account whether the ability of the respondent to defend itself was prejudiced, given the actual course of the panel proceedings, by the fact that the panel request simply listed the provisions claimed to have been violated.[346]

The Appellate Body thus set forth the standard of the 'ability of the respondent to defend itself'. In *EC – Tube or Pipe Fittings*, the Panel examined whether the respondent's ability to defend itself was prejudiced by an alleged lack of specificity in the text of the panel request. The Panel found that it was evident from the participation of the European Communities in asserting its views in various phases of the panel proceedings that the ability of the European Communities to defend itself had not been prejudiced over the course of the proceedings.[347]

The Appellate Body ruled in *US – Carbon Steel* that:

> in considering the sufficiency of a panel request, submissions and statements made during the course of the panel proceedings may be consulted in order to confirm the meaning of the words used in the panel request.[348]

[340] See Appellate Body Report, *Korea – Dairy*, para. 120.   [341] *Ibid.*

[342] The *arguments* are set out and progressively clarified in the written submissions to the panel and at the panel meetings.

[343] See Appellate Body Report, *EC – Bananas III*, para. 143. Note that the Appellate Body ruled in *EC – Tariff Preferences* that in the particular circumstances of that case 'a complaining party challenging a measure taken pursuant to the Enabling Clause must allege more than mere inconsistency with Article I:1 of the GATT 1994, for to do only that would not convey the "legal basis of the complaint sufficient to present the problem clearly" '. See Appellate Body Report, *EC – Tariff Preferences*, para. 110. See also above, pp. 210–11.

[344] See Appellate Body Report, *EC – Bananas III*, para. 141.

[345] See Appellate Body Report, *Korea – Dairy*, para. 129. See also Panel Report, *Thailand – H-Beams*, paras. 7.18, 7.27, and Panel Report, *US – Certain EC Products (Article 21.5 – EC)*, para. 7.50. The Panel in *Korea – Various Measures on Beef* held that a mere listing of articles may suffice to cover other provisions or annexures not expressly mentioned in the request, if the nature of the legal determination of the issues covered by the enumerated provisions would be 'inextricably linked' to a consideration of consistencies under such other provisions or annexures. See Panel Report, *Various Measures on Beef*, paras. 813–15, upheld in Appellate Body Report, *Korea – Various Measures on Beef*, paras. 76–89. See also Panel Report, *Egypt – Steel Rebar*, para. 7.29; and Panel Report, *EC – Trademarks and Geographical Indications (Australia)*, paras. 7.32–7.34. For decisions that found a claim in the panel request not to be 'integrally linked' or 'not related in any self-evident way' with another provision that was argued only in the written submissions, see Panel Report, *US – Line Pipe*, paras. 7.116–7.126; and Panel Report, *Egypt – Steel Rebar*, para. 7.31.

[346] Appellate Body Report, *Korea – Dairy*, para. 127.

[347] See Panel Report, *EC – Tube or Pipe Fittings*, paras. 7.22–7.24.

[348] Appellate Body Report, *US – Carbon Steel*, para. 127.

In *Mexico – Anti-Dumping Measures on Rice*, the Panel held that the listing of provisions allegedly violated had to be taken '*together with the narrative*' that accompanied the list, in order to determine whether the request was sufficient to present the problem clearly to the responding Member.[349] However, it should be emphasised as the Appellate Body ruled in *EC – Bananas III* and as already discussed above, that a panel request cannot be 'cured' by a complaining party's argumentation in subsequent submissions.[350] Note that the Panel in *US – FSC (Article 21.5 – EC II)* ruled that:

> In assessing whether the United States may be prejudiced by any apparent defects in the EC's panel request, we consider whether the EC Panel request identified the measures with sufficient clarity to allow the United States to defend itself. In this regard, we are mindful that defects in a panel request cannot be 'cured' in a subsequent submission of a complainant during a panel proceeding. Nevertheless, a complainant's first written submission may confirm the meaning of the words used in the panel request.[351]

Questions and Assignments 3.19

What are the requirements that a panel request must meet? Why is it important that a panel request is sufficiently precise? How does one determine whether a panel request is sufficiently precise?

3.3.2.2. Establishment of a panel

The panel is established *at the latest* at the DSB meeting following the meeting at which the request for the establishment first appeared as an item on the agenda. At this stage, the panel is established *unless* the DSB decides by consensus *not* to establish a panel ('reverse consensus').[352] Since this is unlikely, the establishment of a panel by the DSB is 'quasi-automatic'. A panel can be, and occasionally is, established at the first DSB meeting at which the panel request is considered. At this meeting, the establishment of the panel requires a 'normal consensus' decision of the DSB. The panel can thus only be established at the first DSB meeting if the respondent does not object to its establishment. Often, however, the respondent objects to the establishment of the panel at the first DSB meeting,

---

[349] See Panel Report, *Mexico – Anti-Dumping Measures on Rice*, para. 7.30. For a case where even when read with the narrative, the mere listing was not sufficient to identify the 'problem', see Panel Report, *Japan – DRAMs (Korea)*, para. 7.21.

[350] See above, p. 239. See also the Panel's ruling in *Japan – DRAMS (Korea)*, which stated that 'consideration of an actual prejudice suffered during the panel process undermines the due process objective, since it allows a Member to correct any lack of clarity in its request during the panel proceedings, even though the request may not have been sufficiently clear for the respondent to begin preparing its defence at the beginning of the panel process'. Panel Report, *Japan – DRAMS (Korea)*, para. 7.9.

[351] Panel Report, *US – FSC (Article 21.5–EC II)*, para. 7.83.

[352] Article 6.1 of the DSU. See also above, p. 236. Note that Japan and the EC have proposed that a panel be established by reverse consensus at the meeting at which the panel request first appears on the DSB's agenda. The Chairman's Text of May 2003 included this proposal, with the qualification that, where a case against a developing-country Member is concerned, the establishment will be postponed if the developing-country Member so requests. See the amended version of the Chairman's Text in the annex to Special Session of the Dispute Settlement Body. Report by the Chairman to the Trade Negotiations Committee, TN/DS/9, dated 6 June 2003. The Chairman's Text is discussed further below, p. 309.

arguing that it 'hopes' and 'believes' that a mutually agreed solution to the dispute can still be found.

The decision of the DSB on the establishment of a panel is usually preceded by short statements by the parties to the dispute setting forth their respective positions. Decisions to establish a panel very seldom give rise to much debate within the DSB. A practice has evolved whereby, immediately after the DSB's decision to establish the panel (or within ten days of this decision), other Members may notify their interest in the dispute and reserve their third party rights.[353]

Where more than one Member requests the establishment of a panel related to the same matter, Article 9.1 of the DSU states that:

> a single panel may be established to examine these complaints taking into account the rights of all Members concerned.

Whenever feasible, a single panel *should* be established to examine such complaints.[354] Note, however, that the Panel in *India – Patents (EC)* observed in this regard that Article 9.1 of the DSU is not intended to limit the rights of WTO Members, one of which is the 'freedom to determine whether and when to pursue a complaint under the DSU'.[355]

In *US – Steel Safeguards*, the DSB at first established multiple panels to hear and decide similar complaints by the European Communities, Japan, Korea, China, Switzerland, Norway, New Zealand and Brazil. Subsequently, the United States and the complainants reached an agreement on the establishment of a single panel, under Article 9.1, to hear the matter at issue. The United States, however, requested that the Panel issue eight separate reports rather than one single report.[356] On the basis of Article 9.2, which explicitly provides for the right of parties to have separate reports, the Panel decided 'to issue its Reports in the form of one document constituting eight Panel Reports' with a common cover page and a common descriptive part.[357]

Note that in *US – Offset Act (Byrd Amendment)* concerning complaints by Australia, Brazil, Chile, the European Communities, India, Indonesia, Japan, Korea and Thailand, the Appellate Body upheld the Panel's refusal to issue, at

---

[353] See below, p. 279.   [354] See Article 9.1 of the DSU.

[355] Panel Report, *India – Patents (EC)*, para. 7.15. In *India – Patents (EC)*, the European Communities, which had been a third party to the dispute in *India – Patents (US)*, brought a complaint on the same matter after the Panel Report was issued. India argued that this was in violation of Article 9.1 of the DSU, which it viewed as imposing on 'both the WTO and its membership' a 'duty to submit multiple complaints to a single panel whenever feasible'. Panel Report, *India – Patents (EC)*, para. 7.12. Referring to the word 'should' and the term 'whenever feasible', the Panel pointed out that the ordinary meaning of the terms of Article 9.1 is 'directory or recommendatory, not mandatory'. It held: 'Article 9.1 is clearly a code of conduct for the DSB because its provisions pertain to the establishment of a panel, the authority for which is exclusively reserved for the DSB. As such, Article 9.1 should not affect substantive and procedural rights and obligations of individual Members under the DSU.' Panel Report, *India – Patents (EC)*, para. 7.14.

[356] The United States argued that by doing so it wanted to protect its rights under the DSU, including the right to seek a solution with one or more of the complainants without adoption of a report or without an appeal.

[357] Separate panel reports were also issued as a single document in *EC – Approval and Marketing of Biotech Products*, and *Canada – Wheat Exports and Grain Imports*. Separate panel reports were issued in different documents in, for example, *EC – Chicken Cuts*, *EC – Trademarks and Geographical Indications*, *EC – Export Subsidies on Sugar* and *EC – Bananas III*.

the request of the United States, a separate report for the complaint brought by Mexico because the United States filed that request too late. The United States had made its request for a separate report two months after the issuance of the descriptive part of the Panel Report and more than seven months after the Panel had been composed. As the Appellate Body observed, Article 9.2 of the DSU refers to the rights of *all* the parties to the dispute and the Panel correctly based its decision on an assessment of the rights of *all* the parties, including the rights of the complainants.[358]

In cases in which it is not possible to establish a single panel to examine complaints relating to the same matter, Article 9.3 of the DSU requires that – to the extent possible – the same persons shall serve as panellists on each of the separate panels and that the timetable for the panel process in such disputes shall be harmonised. This was done in *EC – Hormones* and *US – 1916 Act*.[359]

The DSU does not deal with situations that could involve multiple respondents. Therefore a Member is free to decide which Member to challenge before the dispute settlement system even if the measure at issue has been imposed by several Members or several Members bear some responsibility for the measure at issue.[360] In all but one case to date, there was or is only *one* respondent. The exception referred to is *EC and Certain Member States – Large Civil Aircraft*, which the United States brought against the European Communities as well as certain Member States of the European Union.

Another situation not provided for in the DSU is the situation in which a Member files a second panel request on the same matter to clarify and/or extend the scope of its first panel request. This happened, for example, in *Canada – Wheat Exports and Grain Imports* and *EC and Certain Member States – Large Civil Aircraft*. In both cases the United States filed a second panel request. In *Canada – Wheat Exports and Grain Imports*, it was decided that the panellists that composed the panel established pursuant to the first panel request would also compose the panel established pursuant to the second panel request, and that the proceedings of both Panels would be harmonised pursuant to Article 9.3 of the DSU.[361] In *EC and Certain Member States – Large Civil Aircraft*, only one panel was established.

Questions and Assignments 3.20

Who establishes a panel? How are panels established? What happens in case more than one Member requests the establishment of a panel related to the same matter?

---

[358] See Appellate Body Report, *US – Offset Act (Byrd Amendment)*, paras. 305–17. The Appellate Body also considered that the United States was not claiming that it suffered any prejudice as a result of the Panel's denial of its request.

[359] See Panel Report, *EC – Hormones (US)* and Panel Report, *EC – Hormones (Canada)*; and Panel Report, *US – 1916 Act (EC)* and Panel Report, *US – 1916 Act (Japan)*.   [360] See e.g. Panel Report, *Turkey – Textiles*, para. 9.4.

[361] See Panel Reports, *Canada – Wheat Exports and Grain Imports*, paras 1.11–1.12.   [362] Article 8.1 of the DSU.

3.3.2.3. *Composition of a panel*

As set forth in Article 8.5 of the DSU, panels are normally composed of three persons. The parties to the dispute can agree, within ten days from the establishment of the panel, to a panel composed of five panellists. However, to date, this has never occurred.

Pursuant to Article 8.1 of the DSU, panels must be composed of well-qualified governmental and/or non-governmental individuals. By way of guidance, the DSU indicates that these individuals can be:

> persons who have served on or presented a case to a panel, served as a representative of a Member or of a contracting party to GATT 1947 or as a representative to the Council or Committee of any covered agreement or its predecessor agreement, or in the Secretariat, taught or published on international trade law or policy, or served as a senior trade policy official of a Member.[362]

Article 8.2 of the DSU stipulates that panellists should be selected with a view to ensuring their independence, providing a sufficiently diverse background and a wide spectrum of experience. Nationals of Members that are parties or third parties to the dispute shall not serve on a panel concerned with that dispute unless the parties to the dispute agree otherwise.[363] While this is not common, parties have in some cases agreed on a panellist who is a national of one of the parties.[364] When a dispute occurs between a developing-country Member and a developed-country Member, the panel shall, if the developing-country Member so requests, include at least one panellist from a developing-country Member.[365] In many panels dealing with disputes involving a developing-country Member, at least one of the panellists has indeed been a national of a developing-country Member.

Panellists are predominantly current or retired government trade officials with a background in law. Many among them are Geneva-based diplomats of WTO Members. The DSU explicitly provides, however, that panellists shall serve in their individual capacities and not as government representatives. Members shall therefore not give government officials serving as panellists any instructions nor seek to influence them as individuals with regard to matters before a panel.[366] In recent years, there has been an increase in the number of academics and legal practitioners serving as panellists. It is also significant that at least half of the panellists have already served on a GATT or WTO panel before. In other words, many panellists serve more than once as panellists.[367]

Once a panel is established by the DSB, the parties to the dispute will try to reach an agreement on the composition of the panel. The Secretariat shall propose nominations for the panel to the parties to the dispute. The DSU requires the parties to the dispute not to oppose nominations except for compelling

---

[363] See Article 8.3 of the DSU. As the European Communities and the United States are involved in many cases, either as parties or as third parties, their nationals do not often serve as panellists.

[364] In *US – Zeroing (EC)*, a dispute between the European Communities and the United States, the Panel included William Davey from the US and Hans-Friedrich Beseler from Germany.

[365] See Article 8.10 of the DSU.   [366] See Article 8.9 of the DSU.

[367] For a list of all persons who served as panellists to date and the panels on which they served, see www.worldtradelaw.net/dsc/database/panelistcountry.asp, visited on 1 December 2007.

reasons.[368] However, parties often reject the nominations initially proposed by the WTO Secretariat without much justification. In practice, the composition of the panel is often a difficult and contentious process, which may take many weeks. If the parties are unable to agree on the composition of the panel within twenty days of its establishment by the DSB, either party *may* request the Director-General of the WTO to determine the composition of the panel.[369] Within ten days of such a request, the Director-General shall – after consulting the parties to the dispute and the Chair of the DSB and of the relevant council or committee – appoint the panellists whom he considers most appropriate.[370] In recent years, the Director-General has determined the composition of about half of the panels.

To assist in the selection of panellists, the Secretariat maintains a list of governmental and non-governmental individuals possessing the required qualifications to serve as panellists.[371] Members periodically suggest names of individuals for inclusion on this list, and those names are added to the list upon approval by the DSB. However, this list is merely *indicative* and individuals not included in this list may be selected as panellists. In fact, most first-time panellists were not on the list at the time of their selection.

Note that in the context of the DSU reform negotiations, the European Communities has proposed to move from the current system of *ad hoc* panellists to a system of permanent panellists.[372] According to the European Communities, such a change will lead to faster procedures and increase the quality of the panel reports.[373] While the introduction of a system of permanent panellists seems a logical next step in the evolution of the WTO dispute settlement system, the proposal of the European Communities has received little support to date.

Questions and Assignments 3.21

Who decides on the composition of panels? Describe the relevant procedure. What are the required qualifications for a panellist? Is it, in your opinion, inappropriate for a national of a party or third party to the dispute to sit on the panel?

---

[368] See Article 8.6 of the DSU.
[369] See Article 8.7 of the DSU. Often, however, parties will allow more time to reach an agreement on the composition of a panel instead of requesting the Director-General to decide on the composition.
[370] Interestingly, WTO Director-General Pascal Lamy waived his right to decide on the composition of the panels in the *EC and Certain Member States – Large Civil Aircraft* and the *US – Large Civil Aircraft* disputes, in which the United States and the European Communities challenged each other's subsidies to Airbus and Boeing, respectively. It is reported that 'Mr Lamy felt he was too close to the issue' due to his previous position as EU Trade Commissioner. Instead, Deputy Director-General Alejandro Jara composed the panels in these disputes. See A. Beattie, 'Lamy Waives Right to Name WTO Panel', *Financial Times*, 8 October 2005.   [371] See Article 8.4 of the DSU.
[372] Communication from the European Union, TN/DS/W/1, dated 13 March 2002, 3; and Communication from the European Union, TN/DS/W/38, dated 23 January 2003, 3.
[373] In the opinion of the European Communities, there is currently a growing quantitative discrepancy between the need for panellists and the availability of qualified *ad hoc* panellists. Not only is the number of disputes much higher than under the old GATT, the actual conduct of a dispute settlement procedure has become much more sophisticated than before. The workload of panellists has substantially increased since the substance of the cases, from both a factual and a legal point of view, has become significantly more complex. The European Communities is therefore of the view that it is necessary to introduce a system of permanent panellists. These permanent panelists would serve on panels as appointed by the Director-General on a random basis.

3.3.2.4. *Terms of reference of a panel*

Article 7.1 of the DSU states that, unless the parties agree otherwise within twenty days from the establishment of the panel, a panel is given the following *standard* terms of reference:

> To examine in the light of the relevant provisions in (name of the covered agreement(s) cited by the parties to the dispute), the matter referred to the DSB by (name of party) in document . . . and make such findings as will assist the DSB in making the recommendations or in giving the rulings provided for in that/those agreement(s).

The document referred to in these standard terms of reference is the panel request. Hence, a claim falls within the panel's terms of reference, i.e. within the mandate of the panel, only if that claim is identified in the panel request.[374] In *EC – Tube or Pipe Fittings*, the Panel found that Brazil's claims under Articles 6.9, 6.13, 9.3 and 12.1 of the *Anti-Dumping Agreement* were not within its terms of reference as these provisions 'do not appear in the list of provisions' in the panel request, 'nor are they referred to in the ensuing description of allegations in that document'.

As the Appellate Body stated in *Brazil – Desiccated Coconut*, the terms of reference of the panel are important for two reasons:

> First, terms of reference fulfil an important due process objective – they give the parties and third parties sufficient information concerning the claims at issue in the dispute in order to allow them an opportunity to respond to the complainant's case. Second, they establish the jurisdiction of the panel by defining the precise claims at issue in the dispute.[375]

A panel may consider only those claims that it has authority to consider under its terms of reference.[376] Therefore, a panel is *bound* by its terms of reference.[377] Within twenty days of the establishment of the panel, the parties to the dispute *can* agree on special terms of reference for the panel.[378] However, this rarely occurs.[379] In establishing a panel, the DSB may authorise its Chairperson to draw up the terms of reference of the panel in consultation with the parties to the dispute.[380] However, if no agreement on special terms of reference is reached within twenty days of the establishment of the panel, the panel shall have standard terms of reference.

Note that, in case of a broadly phrased panel request, it may be necessary to examine the complainant's submissions closely to determine precisely which claims have been made and fall under the terms of reference of the panel.[381]

As stated by the Appellate Body in *Brazil – Desiccated Coconut*, the terms of reference establish the jurisdiction of a panel. With regard to the question whether

---

[374] Note that in *EC and Certain Member States – Large Civil Aircraft*, the United States asked the DSB to decide that its claims in its second panel request (see above, p. 244) be included in the terms of reference of the original Panel. See WT/DS316/8, dated 15 May 2006.

[375] Appellate Body Report, *Brazil – Desiccated Coconut*, 186.

[376] See Appellate Body Report, *India – Patents (US)*, para. 92. A panel cannot assume jurisdiction that it does not have. See *ibid*.   [377] See *ibid*., para. 93.   [378] See Article 7.1 of the DSU.

[379] See e.g. Panel Report, *Brazil – Desiccated Coconut*, para. 9.   [380] See Article 7.3 of the DSU.

[381] See Appellate Body Report, *Chile – Price Band System*, para. 165. However, as discussed above, later submissions and statements cannot cure any defects in the panel request. See above, pp. 239, 242.

a panel could decline to exercise jurisdiction which it has according to its terms of reference, the Appellate Body in *Mexico – Taxes on Soft Drinks* held:

> A decision by a panel to decline to exercise validly established jurisdiction would seem to 'diminish' the right of a complaining Member to 'seek the redress of a violation of obligations' within the meaning of Article 23 of the DSU, and to bring a dispute pursuant to Article 3.3 of the DSU. This would not be consistent with a panel's obligations under Articles 3.2 and 19.2 of the DSU. We see no reason, therefore, to disagree with the Panel's statement that a WTO panel 'would seem . . . not to be in a position to choose freely whether or not to exercise its jurisdiction.'[382]

Questions and Assignments 3.22

What are, and where do we find, the terms of reference of a panel? Why are the terms of reference of a panel important?

3.3.2.5. *Standard of review for panels*

A panel is called upon to review the consistency of a challenged measure with WTO law. Both the measure at issue and the relevant provisions of WTO law allegedly violated are determined by the terms of reference of the panel. But what is the standard of review a panel has to apply in reviewing the WTO consistency of the challenged measure? Article 11 of the DSU stipulates:

> The function of panels is to assist the DSB in discharging its responsibilities under this Understanding and the covered agreements. Accordingly, a panel should make an objective assessment of the matter before it, including an objective assessment of the facts of the case and the applicability of and conformity with the relevant covered agreements, and make such other findings as will assist the DSB in making the recommendations or in giving the rulings provided for in the covered agreements.

In *EC – Hormones*, the Appellate Body noted that Article 11 of the DSU:

> articulates with great succinctness but with sufficient clarity the appropriate standard of review for panels in respect of both the ascertainment of facts and the legal characterization of such facts under the relevant agreements.[383]

As far as fact-finding is concerned, the appropriate standard is neither a '*de novo* review' of the facts nor 'total deference' to the factual findings of national authorities. One example of '*de novo* review' is that identified by the Appellate Body in *US – Cotton Yarn*, where it stated:

> a panel must not consider evidence which did not exist *at that point in time* [i.e. the time that the measure at issue was taken] . . . If a panel were to examine such evidence, the

---

[382] Appellate Body Report, *Mexico – Taxes on Soft Drinks*, para. 53. Note, however, that the Appellate Body in paragraph 54 of its Report was careful to stress that it was not expressing any views on whether there may be other circumstances in which legal impediments could exist that would preclude a panel from ruling on the merits of the claims before it. See *ibid.*, para. 54. In view of the scope of Mexico's appeal it was not necessary for the Appellate Body to express a view on this issue.

[383] Appellate Body Report, *EC – Hormones*, para. 116. See also Panel Report, *US – Underwear*, paras. 7.10, 7.12 and 7.13; and Panel Report, *US – Wool Shirts and Blouses*, paras. 7.16 and 7.17.

panel would, in effect, be conducting a de novo review . . . In our view, this would be inconsistent with the standard of a panel's review under Article 11 of the DSU.[384]

Rather, pursuant to Article 11 of the DSU, panels have 'to make an objective assessment of the facts'. With regard to legal questions, i.e. the consistency or inconsistency of a Member's measure with the specified provisions of the relevant agreement, Article 11 imposes the same standard on panels, i.e. 'to make an objective assessment' of the applicability of and conformity with the relevant covered agreement.[385]

In a number of appeals from panel reports, the Appellate Body addressed the question of whether a panel had failed to discharge its duty under Article 11 of the DSU 'to make an objective assessment of the matter before it'. Certain statements made by the Appellate Body indicate that the threshold for a finding that a panel has not made an objective assessment of the matter is high. In *EC – Hormones*, the Appellate Body explained that:

> not every error in the appreciation of the evidence (although it may give rise to a question of law) may be characterized as a failure to make an objective assessment of the facts . . . The duty to make an objective assessment of the facts is, among other things, an obligation to consider the evidence presented to a panel and to make factual findings on the basis of that evidence. The deliberate disregard of, or refusal to consider, the evidence submitted to a panel is incompatible with a panel's duty to make an objective assessment of the facts. The wilful distortion or misrepresentation of the evidence put before a panel is similarly inconsistent with an objective assessment of the facts. 'Disregard' and 'distortion' and 'misrepresentation' of the evidence, in their ordinary signification in judicial and quasi-judicial processes, imply not simply an error of judgment in the appreciation of evidence but rather an egregious error that calls into question the good faith of a panel.[386]

In *Brazil – Retreaded Tyres*, the Appellate Body ruled in paragraph 185 of its Report that an 'objective assessment' within the meaning of Article 11 'implies, among other things, that a panel must consider all the evidence presented to it, assess its credibility, determine its weight, and ensure that its factual findings have a proper basis in that evidence'. According to the Appellate Body in *EC – Hormones*, not every error in the appreciation of evidence can necessarily be characterised as a failure to make an objective assessment. A panel must make an *egregious* error in the assessment of the evidence before the Appellate Body will come to the conclusion that the panel failed to make an objective assessment of the facts. As the Appellate Body noted in *EC – Poultry*:

---

[384] Appellate Body Report, *US – Cotton Yarn*, para. 78.

[385] See Appellate Body Report, *Chile – Price Band System*, para. 172; and Appellate Body Report, *Dominican Republic – Import and Sale of Cigarettes*, para. 105. Note the very *unusual* situation that arose in *US – Shrimp (Ecuador)*, where the United States did not contest any of the claims of inconsistency made by Ecuador but the parties had not, however, characterised their shared view of the substantive aspects of the dispute as a 'mutually agreed solution'. The Panel held: 'Given that, notwithstanding their common view as to how the dispute should be resolved, the parties have not reached a mutually agreed solution (which would require us only to "report . . . that a solution has been reached"), we understand that our responsibility is as set forth in Article 11 DSU.' It therefore proceeded to make an objective assessment of the matter. See Panel Report, *US – Shrimp (Ecuador)*, paras. 7.1–7.6.

[386] Appellate Body Report, *EC – Hormones*, para. 133. See also Appellate Body Report, *Japan – Agricultural Products II*, para. 141; and Appellate Body Report, *Korea – Dairy*, paras. 137–8.

> An allegation that a panel has failed to conduct the 'objective assessment of the matter before it' required by Article 11 of the DSU is a very serious allegation. Such an allegation goes to the very core of the integrity of the WTO dispute settlement process itself.[387]

The party losing a case may be tempted to argue that the panel failed to make an objective assessment. However, as the Appellate Body observed in *Korea – Alcoholic Beverages*, it is not an error, let alone an egregious error, for a panel to fail to accord to the evidence the weight that one of the parties believes should be accorded to it.[388]

In *US – Wheat Gluten*, the Appellate Body considered the following:

> in view of the distinction between the respective roles of the Appellate Body and panels, we have taken care to emphasize that a panel's appreciation of the evidence falls, in principle, 'within the *scope of the panel's discretion as the trier of facts*' (emphasis added). In assessing the panel's appreciation of the evidence, we cannot base a finding of inconsistency under Article 11 simply on the conclusion that we might have reached a different factual finding from the one the panel reached. Rather, we must be satisfied that the panel has exceeded the bounds of its discretion, as the trier of facts, in its appreciation of the evidence. As is clear from previous appeals, we will not interfere lightly with the panel's exercise of its discretion.[389]

For the Appellate Body to find that a panel has acted inconsistently with Article 11 of the DSU, it must be satisfied that the panel has *exceeded the bounds of its discretion* in adjudicating the facts. Aptly summarising its earlier case law, the Appellate Body ruled in *US – Carbon Steel*:

> Article 11 requires panels to take account of the evidence put before them and forbids them to wilfully disregard or distort such evidence. Nor may panels make affirmative findings that lack a basis in the evidence contained in the panel record. Provided that panels' actions remain within these parameters, however, we have said that 'it is generally within the discretion of the Panel to decide which evidence it chooses to utilize in making findings' and, on appeal, we 'will not interfere lightly with a panel's exercise of its discretion'.[390]

To date, the Appellate Body has found that the relevant Panels had acted inconsistently with their obligations under Article 11 in, for example, *US – Wheat Gluten*, *US – Lamb*, *US – Cotton Yarn*, *Chile – Price Band System*, *US – Oil Country Tubular Goods Sunset Reviews*, *EC – Export Subsidies on Sugar*, *US – Countervailing Duty Investigation on DRAMS* and *US – Anti-dumping Measures on Oil Country Tubular Goods*.[391] However, in most cases, the Appellate Body rejected the claim

---

[387] Appellate Body Report, *EC – Poultry*, para. 133. See also Appellate Body Report, *US – Zeroing (EC)*, paras. 253–4.   [388] See Appellate Body Report, *Korea – Alcoholic Beverages*, para. 164.

[389] Appellate Body Report, *US – Wheat Gluten*, para. 151, citing Appellate Body Report, *EC – Hormones*, para. 132. See also Appellate Body Report, *EC – Sardines*, para. 299. Appellate Body Report, *EC – Asbestos*, para. 177; Appellate Body Report, *Japan – Apples*, paras. 221, 222; Appellate Body Report, *Canada – Wheat Exports and Grain Imports*, para. 186; Appellate Body Report, *US – Gambling*, paras. 329–34, 363–4; and Appellate Body Report, *Dominican Republic – Import and Sale of Cigarettes*, para. 111.

[390] Appellate Body Report, *US – Carbon Steel*, para. 142.

[391] See Appellate Body Report, *US – Wheat Gluten*, paras. 152–5 and 156–63; Appellate Body Report, *US – Lamb*, paras. 140–149; Appellate Body Report, *US – Cotton Yarn*, paras. 68–80; Appellate Body Report, *Chile – Price Band System*, paras. 169–77; Appellate Body Report, *US – Oil Country Tubular Goods Sunset Reviews*, paras. 209–15; Appellate Body Report, *EC – Export Subsidies on Sugar*, paras. 329–35; Appellate Body Report, *US – Countervailing Duty Investigation on DRAMS*, paras. 176–90; and Appellate Body Report, *US – Anti-Dumping Measures on Oil Country Tubular Goods*, paras. 202–10.

of the appellant that the Panel had acted inconsistently with Article 11 of the DSU.[392]

In *US – Steel Safeguards*, the Appellate Body noted that a challenge under Article 11 of the DSU 'must not be vague or ambiguous', but, rather, must be clearly articulated and substantiated with specific arguments.[393] A claim that a panel failed to conduct an objective assessment of the matter is, according to the Appellate Body:

> not to be made lightly, or merely as a subsidiary argument or claim in support of a claim of a panel's failure to construe or apply correctly a particular provision of a covered agreement.[394]

A claim of inconsistency with Article 11 of the DSU 'must stand by itself and be substantiated, as such, and not as subsidiary to another alleged violation'.[395] Most claims of inconsistency with Article 11 of the DSU are rejected by the Appellate Body.

Article 11 of the DSU sets forth the appropriate standard of review for panels for disputes under all but one of the covered agreements. Only for disputes under the *Anti-Dumping Agreement* is there a special standard of review, which is set out in Article 17.6 of the *Anti-Dumping Agreement* and discussed in chapter 6 of this book.[396]

Questions and Assignments 3.23

What is the standard of review a panel has to apply in reviewing the WTO consistency of a measure challenged by the complainant? When does a panel not meet the requirement of Article 11 of the DSU to make an objective assessment of the matter before it?

3.3.2.6. Judicial economy and acts ultra petita

Complainants often assert numerous violations under various agreements. It is well-established case law that panels are not required to examine each and every one of the legal claims that a complainant makes. The aim of dispute settlement is to secure a positive solution to a dispute. The Appellate Body in *US – Wool Shirts and Blouses* ruled that panels:

> need only address those claims which must be addressed in order to resolve the matter in issue in the dispute.[397]

---

[392] See e.g. Appellate Body Report, *US – Zeroing (Japan)*, paras. 78–96; Appellate Body Report, *EC – Selected Customs Matters*, paras. 255–6; Appellate Body Report, *Mexico – Taxes on Soft Drinks*, paras. 82–3; Appellate Body Report, *EC – Chicken Cuts*, paras. 177–86 and 324; Appellate Body Report, *Dominican Republic – Import and Sale of Cigarettes*, paras. 75–85 and 101–15; Appellate Body Report, *US – Gambling*, paras. 268–76, 278–84, 328–34 and 358–66; Appellate Body Report, *US – Upland Cotton*, paras. 658–63; Appellate Body Report, *Canada –Wheat Exports and Grain Imports*, paras. 164–78 and 179–96; and Appellate Body Report, *Japan – Apples*, paras. 217–424.   [393] See Appellate Body Report, *US – Steel Safeguards*, para. 498.
[394] *Ibid.*   [395] *Ibid.*   [396] See below, pp. 556–7.
[397] Appellate Body Report, *US – Wool Shirts and Blouses*, 340.

A panel has discretion to determine the claims it must address in order to resolve the dispute between the parties effectively.[398] The Appellate Body has, however, cautioned panels to be careful when exercising judicial economy. To provide only a partial resolution of a dispute may be false judicial economy since the issues that are not resolved may well give rise to a new dispute.[399] As the Appellate Body stated in *Australia – Salmon*, a panel has to address:

> those claims on which a finding is necessary in order to enable the DSB to make sufficiently precise recommendations and rulings so as to allow for prompt compliance by a Member with those recommendations and rulings 'in order to ensure effective resolution of disputes to the benefit of all Members'.[400]

In *Argentina – Preserved Peaches*, Chile insisted that the Panel rule on all the claims presented 'in order to ensure that Argentina does not continue to violate these agreements as it has done'. The Panel observed, however, that Chile did not offer any explanation as to why ruling on *all* claims would achieve this objective. Having concluded that the measure at issue was inconsistent with various WTO provisions and that further findings on the other Chilean claims would not alter that conclusion and would not further assist the DSB in making sufficiently precise recommendations (to allow for prompt compliance by Argentina), the Panel chose to exercise judicial economy on these other claims.[401] Panels frequently exercise judicial economy with regard to claims before them.[402] However, in some instances panels may decide to continue their legal analysis and to make factual findings beyond those that are strictly necessary to resolve the dispute because this 'may assist the Appellate Body should it later be called upon to complete the analysis'.[403]

In 2007, in *Brazil – Retreaded Tyres*, the Appellate Body reminded the Panel that:

> a panel's discretion to decline the rule on different claims of inconsistency adduced in relation to the same measure is limited by its duty to make findings that will allow the

---

[398] See Appellate Body Report, *India – Patents (US)*, para. 87. A panel is never required to exercise judicial economy (see Appellate Body Report, *US – Lead and Bismuth II*, para. 71; and Appellate Body Report, *US – Gambling*, paras. 343–4), but when it does exercise judicial economy, it should state so explicitly for the purposes of transparency and fairness to the parties (see Appellate Body Report, *Canada – Autos*, para. 117).

[399] The Appellate Body found that the panels had erred in exercising judicial economy in, for example, Appellate Body Report, *Japan – Agricultural Products II* and Appellate Body Report, *Australia – Salmon*.

[400] Appellate Body Report, *Australia – Salmon*, para. 223. See also Appellate Body Report, *Japan – Agricultural Products II*, para. 111; Appellate Body Report, *US – Wheat Gluten*, para. 183; and Appellate Body Report, *US – Lamb*, para. 194.

[401] See Panel Report, *Argentina – Preserved Peaches*, paras. 7.141–7.142. See, for similar conclusions, Panel Report, *EC – Sardines*, paras. 7.147–7.152; Panel Report, *US – Steel Safeguards*, paras. 10.700–10.715; Panel Report, *Japan – Apples*, paras. 8.293–8.304; Appellate Body Report, *US – Anti-Dumping Measures on Oil Country Tubular Goods*, para. 178; Appellate Body Report, *US – Zeroing (EC)*, para. 250; and Panel Report, *Mexico – Steel Pipes and Tubes*, para. 7.400.

[402] See e.g. Panel Report, *EC – Export Subsidies on Sugar*, paras. 7.375–7.387 (complaint by Australia), paras. 7.375–7.387 (complaint by Brazil) and paras. 7.375–387 (complaint by Thailand), as upheld in Appellate Body Report, *EC – Export Subsidies on Sugar*, paras. 321–35; and Panel Report, *US – Zeroing (EC)*, paras 6.9–6.10, as upheld in Appellate Body Report, *US – Zeroing (EC)*, paras. 223–5, 244–50 and 136–47. Note that in *US – Gambling* the Panel exercised judicial economy with respect to Antigua and Barbuda's claim under Article XI of the GATS because it considered that 'there is not sufficient material on record to enable us to undertake a meaningful analysis of this provision and its specific application to the facts of this case with respect to Antigua and Barbuda's claim under [GATS] Article XI'. See Panel Report, *US – Gambling*, paras. 6.438–6.442.

[403] Appellate Body Report, *US – Gambling*, para. 344. On the 'completing of the legal analysis' by the Appellate Body, see below, pp. 266–8.

DSB to make sufficiently precise recommendations and rulings 'in order to ensure effective resolution of disputes to the benefit of all Members'.[404]

As long as it is clear in a panel report that a panel has reasonably considered a claim, the fact that a particular *argument* relating to that claim is not addressed is not inconsistent with Article 11 of the DSU.[405] In *Dominican Republic – Import and Sale of Cigarettes*, the Appellate Body ruled that:

> there is no obligation upon a panel to consider each and every argument put forward by the parties in support of their respective cases, so long as it completes an objective assessment of the matter before it, in accordance with Article 11 of the DSU.[406]

A different situation is where a panel makes a finding on a claim that does not fall within its terms of reference, i.e. acts *ultra petita*. In such a case, the panel does not make an objective assessment of *the matter before it*, and thus acts inconsistently with Article 11 of the DSU.[407] However, if the panel's finding relates to a *claim* which does fall within its terms of reference, it is not restricted to considering only those *legal arguments* made by the parties to the dispute.[408] The Appellate Body ruled in *EC – Hormones* that:

> nothing in the DSU limits the faculty of a panel freely to use arguments submitted by any of the parties – or to develop its own legal reasoning – to support its own findings and conclusions on the matter under its consideration.[409]

A panel which uses arguments or reasoning that have not been submitted or developed by any of the parties to the dispute does not act *ultra petita*. Panels are restricted to the claims falling within their terms of reference but they are not restricted to the legal arguments and reasoning submitted or developed by the parties.[410]

Questions and Assignments 3.24

Does a panel have to address and decide on every claim of the complainant? Can the panel ignore an explicit request of the complainant to rule on a particular claim? Can a panel develop an 'original' legal reasoning in its report that is not in any way based on legal arguments made by any of the parties to the dispute?

---

[404] Appellate Body Report, *Brazil – Retreated Tyres*, para. 257.
[405] See Appellate Body Report, *EC – Poultry*, para. 135.
[406] Appellate Body Report, *Dominican Republic – Import and Sale of Cigarettes*, para. 125. The Appellate Body referred in a footnote to Appellate Body Report, *EC – Poultry*, para. 135. On this matter, see also Appellate Body Report, *US – Anti-Dumping Measures on Oil Country Tubular Goods*, paras. 131–6.
[407] See Appellate Body Report, *Chile – Price Band System*, para. 173. In *Chile – Price Band System*, the Panel made findings regarding Article II:1(b), second sentence of the GATT 1994, while Argentina, the complainant, had not made any claim of inconsistency with that provision. On Article II:1(b), second sentence of the GATT 1994, see below, pp. 439–43.
[408] Also note, however, in this respect, the rules on the burden of proof. See above, pp. 207–12.
[409] Appellate Body Report, *EC – Hormones*, para. 156. See also Panel Report, *Australia – Automotive Leather II (Article 21.5 – US)*, para. 6.19.   [410] See *ibid.*

3.3.2.7. Characteristics of a panel report

A panel submits its findings and conclusions on the WTO consistency of the measure at issue in the form of a written report to the DSB. This report typically includes a section on the following:

- procedural aspects of the dispute;
- factual aspects of the dispute (in which the measure at issue is discussed);
- the claims of parties;
- summary of the arguments of the parties and third parties;[411]
- the interim review;
- the panel's findings; and
- the panel's conclusions.

As required by Article 12.7, second sentence, of the DSU, a panel report must, at a minimum, set out the findings of fact, the applicability of relevant provisions and the basic rationale behind any findings and recommendations that it makes.[412] As discussed above, in 89 per cent of all panel reports circulated to date, the panel found at least one inconsistency with WTO law.[413] In *Mexico – Corn Syrup (Article 21.5 – US)*, the Appellate Body stated that Article 12.7 sets a 'minimum standard' for the basic rationale with which Panels must support their findings and recommendations.[414] The Appellate Body explained further:

> In our view, the duty of panels under Article 12.7 of the DSU to provide a 'basic rationale' reflects and conforms with the principles of fundamental fairness and due process that underlie and inform the provisions of the DSU. In particular, in cases where a Member has been found to have acted inconsistently with its obligations under the covered agreements, that Member is entitled to know the reasons for such finding as a matter of due process. In addition, the requirement to set out a 'basic rationale' in the panel report assists such Member to understand the nature of its obligations and to make informed decisions about: (i) what must be done in order to implement the eventual rulings and recommendations made by the DSB; and (ii) whether and what to appeal. Article 12.7 also furthers the objectives, expressed in Article 3.2 of the DSU, of promoting security and predictability in the multilateral trading system and of clarifying the existing provisions of the covered agreements, because the requirement to provide 'basic' reasons contributes to other WTO Members' understanding of the nature and scope of the rights and obligations in the covered agreements.[415]

---

[411] The practice on this point varies. Most panels have included a summary of the arguments drafted on the basis of an 'executive summary' of the arguments provided by the parties and third parties. Other panels have not included a separate section in their report summarising the arguments but have attached the executive summaries received from the parties and third parties to the report. Some panels have attached the submissions of the parties and third parties in full to the panel report. In *EC – Tube or Pipe Fittings*, Brazil, the complainant, requested that the complete text of its first and second written submissions, rather than its executive summaries, be included in Annexes A and C to the Panel Report. The Panel rejected this request as it had been provided for in the *ad hoc* working procedures that the 'executive summary approach' would be followed. See Panel Report, *EC – Tube or Pipe Fittings*, paras. 7.48–7.55.

[412] Note the special requirements for panel reports in cases where parties have reached a mutually acceptable solution during the panel proceedings (see Article 12.7 of the DSU). See e.g. Panel Report, *Japan – Quotas on Laver*.   [413] See above, p. 186.

[414] See Appellate Body Report, *Mexico – Corn Syrup (Article 21.5 – US)*, para. 106.   [415] *Ibid.*, para. 107.

In the same dispute, the Appellate Body clarified:

> We do not believe that it is either possible or desirable to determine, in the abstract, the minimum standard of reasoning that will constitute a 'basic rationale' for the findings and recommendations made by a panel. Whether a panel has articulated adequately the 'basic rationale' for its findings and recommendations must be determined on a case-by-case basis, taking into account the facts of the case, the specific legal provisions at issue, and the particular findings and recommendations made by a panel.[416]

In a few cases to date, parties have challenged a panel report before the Appellate Body for lack of a basic rationale behind the panel's findings and recommendations. In *Argentina – Footwear (EC)*, the Appellate Body found as follows:

> In this case, the Panel conducted *extensive* factual and legal analyses of the competing claims made by the parties, set out numerous factual findings based on detailed consideration of the evidence before the Argentine authorities as well as other evidence presented to the Panel, and provided extensive explanations of how and why it reached its factual and legal conclusions. Although Argentina may not agree with the rationale provided by the Panel, and we do not ourselves agree with all of its reasoning, we have no doubt that the Panel set out, in its Report, a 'basic rationale' consistent with the requirements of Article 12.7 of the DSU.[417]

In *Chile – Price Band System (Article 21.5 – Argentina)*, the Appellate Body curtly observed that:

> The mere fact that Chile disagrees with the substance of [the Panel's] reasoning cannot suffice to establish a violation of Article 12.7.[418]

In a dispute involving a developing-country Member, the panel report must explicitly indicate how the panel has taken account of any special or differential treatment provision that the developing-country Member has invoked before the panel. In *India – Quantitative Restrictions*, for example, the Panel specifically referred to this requirement and noted:

> In this instance, we have noted that Article XVIII:B as a whole, on which our analysis throughout this section is based, embodies the principle of special and differential treatment in relation to measures taken for balance-of-payments purposes. This entire part G therefore reflects our consideration of relevant provisions on special and differential treatment, as does Section VII of our report (suggestions for implementation).[419]

Where a panel concludes that a Member's measure is inconsistent with a covered agreement, it shall recommend that the Member concerned bring that measure into conformity with that agreement.[420] The recommendations and rulings of a panel are *not* legally binding by themselves. They become legally binding only when they are adopted by the DSB and thus have become the recommendations and rulings of the DSB.[421] In addition to making recommendations and rulings, the panel may suggest ways in which the Member concerned could implement

---

[416] *Ibid.*, para 108. See also Appellate Body Report, *Korea – Alcoholic Beverages*, para. 168; Appellate Body Report, *Chile – Alcoholic Beverages*, para. 78; and Appellate Body Report, *US – Upland Cotton*, paras. 275–7.

[417] Appellate Body Report, *Argentina – Footwear (EC)*, para. 149.

[418] Appellate Body Report, *Chile – Price Band System (Article 21.5 – Argentina)*, para. 247. See also Appellate Body Report, *US – Steel Safeguards*, para. 507.   [419] Panel Report, *India – Quantitative Restrictions*, para. 5.157.

[420] See Article 19.1 of the DSU.

[421] On the adoption of panel reports, see above, p. 236, and below, pp. 286–7.

those recommendations.[422] These suggestions are not legally binding on the Member concerned (even after the report is adopted). However, because the panel making the suggestions might later be called upon to assess the sufficiency of the implementation of the recommendations, such suggestions are likely to have a certain impact.[423] To date, few panels have made use of this authority to make suggestions regarding implementation of their recommendations.[424]

Panellists can express a separate opinion in the panel report, be it dissenting or concurring. However, if they do, they must do so anonymously.[425] To date, there have been few panel reports setting out a separate opinion of one of the panellists.[426]

Panel reports are always circulated to WTO Members, and made available to the public, in English, French and Spanish. Reports are not circulated until all three language versions are available. Most reports are written in English and then translated into French and Spanish. However, there have been a few panel reports written in Spanish and at least one written in French.[427]

Questions and Assignments 3.25

What are the (formal) requirements that a panel report must meet under the DSU? Can a panellist have his or her dissenting opinion noted in the panel report? What is the difference between a recommendation of a panel and a suggestion of a panel?

3.3.2.8. Role of the WTO Secretariat

Pursuant to Article 27.1 of the DSU, the WTO Secretariat has the responsibility of assisting panels, especially on the legal, historical and procedural aspects of the

---

[422] See Article 19.1 of the DSU.   [423] See below, pp. 300–4.

[424] See e.g. Panel Report, *US – Underwear*, paras. 8.1–8.3; Panel Report, *India – Quantitative Restrictions*, paras. 7.1–7.7; Panel Report, *Guatemala – Cement II*, paras. 9.3–9.7; Panel Report, *Argentina – Poultry Anti-Dumping Duties*, paras. 8.3–8.7; and Panel Report, *Mexico – Steel Pipes and Tubes*, paras. 8.12–8.13. In the latter three cases the Panels have suggested the revocation of the inconsistent measures and have justified their suggestions by referring to the fundamental and pervasive nature of the violations of the *Anti-Dumping Agreement* in those cases. In *EC – Exports Subsidies on Sugar*, the Panel suggested that 'in bringing its exports of sugar into conformity with its obligations under Articles 3.3 and 8 of the *Agreement on Agriculture*, the European Communities consider[s] measures to bring its production of sugar more into line with domestic consumption whilst fully respecting its international commitments with respect to imports, including its commitments to developing countries'. Panel Report, *EC – Export Subsidies on Sugar*, paras. 8.6–8.8 (complaint by Australia); paras. 8.6–8.8 (complaint by Brazil); and paras. 8.6–8.8 (complaint by Thailand). Panels often decline the request to make suggestions with regard to the implementation of their recommendations and rulings. See e.g. Panel Report, *EC – Tariff Preferences*, para. 8.3. The Panel in this case stated: 'in light of the fact that there is more than one way that the European Communities could bring its measures into conformity with its obligations under GATT 1994 and the fact that the European Communities has requested a waiver which is still pending, the Panel does not consider it appropriate to make any particular suggestions to the European Communities as to how the European Communities should bring its inconsistent measures into conformity with its obligations under GATT 1994'. *Ibid.*

[425] See Article 14.3 of the DSU. Note that some WTO Members have proposed that the requirement of anonymity of separate opinions should be abolished; and that each panellist must deliver a fully reasoned opinion on all issues.

[426] See e.g. Panel Report, *EC – Poultry*, paras. 289–92; Panel Report, *EC – Tariff Preferences*, paras. 9.1–9.21; Panel Report *US – Zeroing (EC)*, paras. 7.285 and 9.1–9.62; Panel Report, *US – Softwood Lumber V*, paras. 9.1–9.24; Panel Report, *US – Carbon Steel*, paras. 10.1–10.15; and Panel Report, *US – Certain EC Products*, paras. 6.60–6.61.   [427] See e.g. Panel Report, *EC – Asbestos*.

matters dealt with, and of providing secretarial and technical support. The Legal Affairs Division and the Rules Division are the main divisions of the WTO Secretariat that assist dispute settlement panels. However, a significant number of staff from other 'operational divisions' of the WTO Secretariat are also involved.

Depending on the agreement principally at issue in the dispute, a panel will be assisted by an interdisciplinary team (i.e. economists and lawyers) drawn from the Legal Affairs Division and other divisions of the WTO Secretariat. For example, for a dispute concerning an SPS measure, a team composed of staff from the Agriculture and Commodities Division and staff from the Legal Affairs Division will assist the panel. Panels considering cases relating to State trading, subsidies, countervailing duties and anti-dumping duties are assisted by staff from the Rules Division. As already noted above, officials of the WTO Secretariat assigned to assist panels are also subject to the *Rules of Conduct* and bound by the obligations of independence, impartiality, confidentiality and the avoidance of direct or indirect conflicts of interest.[428]

Questions and Assignments 3.26

What is the role of the WTO Secretariat in panel proceedings? In your opinion, can this role be problematic? If so, how?

3.3.3. The Appellate Body

Article 17.1 of the DSU provides for the establishment of an Appellate Body to hear appeals from reports of panels. The DSB established the Appellate Body in February 1995.[429] Unlike panels, the Appellate Body is a standing, i.e. permanent, international tribunal.[430] This section discusses:

- the membership of the Appellate Body;
- the institutional structure of the Appellate Body;
- access to appellate review;
- the scope of appellate review; and
- the mandate of the Appellate Body.

3.3.3.1. *Membership of the Appellate Body*

The Appellate Body is composed of seven persons referred to as 'Members' of the Appellate Body.[431] With respect to the required qualifications of Members of the Appellate Body, Article 17.3 of the DSU states in relevant part:

---

[428] See above, pp. 217–18.
[429] See Dispute Settlement Body, *Decision Establishing the Appellate Body*, 10 February 1995, WT/DSB/1, dated 19 June 1995.   [430] See Article 17.1 of the DSU.
[431] Note that in the context of the DSU reform negotiations, the EC has proposed providing the DSB with the power to modify the number of Appellate Body Members, when necessary, to deal with the workload.

> The Appellate Body shall comprise persons of recognized authority, with demonstrated expertise in law, international trade and the subject matter of the covered agreements generally. They shall be unaffiliated with any government.

It is understood that the expertise of Appellate Body Members should be of a type that allows them to resolve 'issues of law covered in the panel report and legal interpretations developed by the panel'.[432] While the overriding concern is to provide highly qualified members for the Appellate Body,[433] Article 17.3 also requires that:

> The Appellate Body membership shall be broadly representative of membership in the WTO.

Therefore, factors such as different geographical areas, levels of development and legal systems are taken into account.[434] In its *Decision Establishing the Appellate Body*, the DSB stated:

> The success of the WTO will depend greatly on the proper composition of the Appellate Body, and persons of the highest calibre should serve on it.[435]

At the end of 2007, the composition of the Appellate Body was as follows:[436]

- Mr Georges Abi-Saab (Egypt)[437]
- Mr Luiz Olavo Baptista (Brazil)
- Ms Lilia Bautista (Philippines)
- Mr Arumugamangalam Venkatachalam Ganesan (India)[438]
- Ms Jennifer Hillman (United States)
- Mr Giorgio Sacerdoti (Italy)
- Mr David Unterhalter (South Africa)

Appellate Body Members are not required to reside permanently or continuously in Geneva and most do not. However, Article 17.3 of the DSU requires that they 'be available at all times and on short notice'.[439] To this end, Members keep the Appellate Body Secretariat informed of their whereabouts at all times.[440]

Article 17.2 of the DSU states with respect to the appointment of Appellate Body Members and their term of office:

---

[432] Dispute Settlement Body, *Decision establishing the Appellate Body*, 10 February 1995, WT/DSB/1, dated 19 June 1995, para. 5.   [433] See *ibid.*, para. 6.   [434] See *ibid.*   [435] *Ibid.*, para. 4.

[436] For biographical information on the current and former Members of the Appellate Body and their respective terms of office, see www.wto.org/english/tratop_e/dispu_e/ab_members_descrp_e.htm, visited on 23 November 2007.

[437] The term of office of Mr Georges Abi-Saab (Egypt) and Mr Arumugamangalam V. Ganesan (India) expires on 1 June 2008; pursuant to the decision of the DSB of 27 November 2007, Mr Shotaro Oshima (Japan) and Ms Yuejiao Zhang (China) will join the Appellate Body as of that date. See below, p. 259.

[438] See above, footnote 437.

[439] Note that Appellate Body Members have 'part-time' appointments. This arrangement reflects the expectation on the part of WTO Members, in 1995, that the Appellate Body would not be so 'busy' as to justify a full-time employment arrangement. Since 1998, however, Appellate Body membership has often been more than a full-time job. The demands of the job have been such that it is difficult, and at times impossible, for Appellate Body Members to pursue other professional activities. In 2001, the employment arrangement of Appellate Body Members came under review by the DSB to determine whether a move to full-time employment was warranted. WTO Members failed, however, to agree on such a change. See WT/DSB/M/101, dated 8 April 2001, para. 119.   [440] See Rule 2(4) of the *Working Procedures*.

> The DSB shall appoint persons to serve on the Appellate Body for a four-year term, and each person may be reappointed once . . . Vacancies shall be filled as they arise. A person appointed to replace a person whose term of office has not expired shall hold office for the remainder of the predecessor's term.

The Members of the Appellate Body thus serve a term of four years which can be renewed once.[441] Pursuant to Article 2.4 of the DSU, the DSB takes the decision on the appointment of Appellate Body Members by consensus.[442] It takes this decision on the recommendation of a Selection Committee, composed of the chairpersons of the General Council, the DSB, the Councils for Goods and for Services, the TRIPS Council and the WTO Director-General. The Selection Committee selects among candidates nominated by WTO Members.

As already noted, Appellate Body Members must not be affiliated with any government.[443] They must exercise their office without accepting or seeking instructions from any international, governmental or non-governmental organisation or any private source.[444] During their term of office, Members must not accept any employment nor pursue any professional activity that is inconsistent with their duties and responsibilities.[445] As already noted above, the Members of the Appellate Body are subject to the *Rules of Conduct* and are required 'to disclose the existence or development of any interest, relationship or matter' that is 'likely to affect, or give rise to justifiable doubts' as to their 'independence or impartiality'.[446] They may not participate in the consideration of any appeal that would create a direct or indirect conflicts of interest.

Questions and Assignments 3.27

How and by whom are Members of the Appellate Body appointed? Is the current composition of the Appellate Body consistent with the relevant DSU provisions? What requirements apply to Appellate Body Members during their term in office?

3.3.3.2. *Institutional structure of the Appellate Body*

The Appellate Body does not hear or decide appeals *en banc*. It hears and decides appeals in divisions of three Members.[447] Rule 6 of the *Working Procedures for Appellate Review* (the '*Working Procedures*'), entitled 'Divisions', provides:

---

[441] Note that in the context of the DSU Reform negotiations, India has proposed to replace this renewable four-year term with a non-renewable term of six years.

[442] Note that at the DSB meeting of 19 November 2007, Chinese Taipei blocked the appointment of the new Members to replace Members whose term of office expires in December 2007 or June 2008. Chinese Taipei objected to the agenda item pertaining to the appointment because it reportedly had 'deep concerns on the question of impartiality and qualification of one of the recommended candidates to serve the Appellate Body'. While Chinese Taipei did not mention any candidate by name or nationality, it is clear that it objected to the appointment of Ms Yuejiao Zhang (China). See http://ilreports.blogspot.com/2007/11/wto-appointment-of-appellate-body.html, visited on 23 November 2007. As noted in footnote 437 the DSB took the decision on the appointment of the new Appellate Body Members (including the appointment of Ms Zhang) at its meeting of 27 November 2007.

[443] See Article 17.3 of the DSU.   [444] See Rule 2(3) of the *Working Procedures*.

[445] See Rule 2(2) of the *Working Procedures*   [446] See above, pp. 217–18.

[447] See Article 17.1 of the DSU and Rule 6(1) of the *Working Procedures*.

1. In accordance with paragraph 1 of Article 17 of the DSU, a division consisting of three Members shall be established to hear and decide an appeal.
2. The Members constituting a division shall be selected on the basis of rotation, while taking into account the principles of random selection, unpredictability and opportunity for all Members to serve regardless of their national origin.
3. A Member selected pursuant to paragraph 2 to serve on a division shall serve on that division, unless
   i. he/she is excused from that division pursuant to Rules 9 or 10;
   ii. he/she has notified the Chairman and the Presiding Member that he/she is prevented from serving on the division because of illness or other serious reasons pursuant to Rule 12; or
   iii. he/she has notified his/her intentions to resign pursuant to Rule 14.

Pursuant to Rule 6 of the *Working Procedures*, the Members constituting the division hearing and deciding a particular appeal are thus selected on the basis of *rotation*, taking into account the principles of random selection and unpredictability and opportunity for all Members to serve, regardless of their nationality.[448] Unlike in the process for panellist selection, the nationality of Appellate Body Members is irrelevant. Appellate Body Members can, and will, sit in cases to which their countries of origin are party.

The Members of a division select their Presiding Member.[449] Pursuant to Rule 7(2) of the *Working Procedures*, the responsibilities of the Presiding Member shall include:

- coordinating the overall conduct of the appeal proceeding;
- chairing all oral hearings and meetings related to that appeal; and
- coordinating the drafting of the appellate report.

Decisions relating to an appeal are taken by the division assigned to that appeal. However, to ensure consistency and coherence in its case law and to draw on the individual and collective expertise of all seven Members, the division responsible for deciding an appeal exchanges views with the other Members on the issues raised by the appeal.[450] This exchange of views, which may take two to three days, is held before the division has come to any definitive views on the issues arising in the appeal.

A division makes every effort to take its decision on the appeal by consensus. However, if a decision cannot be reached by consensus, the *Working Procedures* provide that the matter at issue be decided by a majority vote.[451] Individual Members may express dissenting opinions in the report. However, Article 17.11 of the DSU requires in this respect:

Opinions expressed in the Appellate Body report by individuals serving on the Appellate Body shall be anonymous.

[448] A Member unable to serve on a division for a reason set out in Rule 6(3) shall be replaced by another Member selected pursuant to Rule 6(2). In *US – Softwood Lumber IV* and *US – Offset Act (Byrd Amendment)*, for example, Professor G. Sacerdoti was selected to replace Mr Arumugamangalam V. Ganesan, who had to step down for 'serious personal reasons'. See Appellate Body Report, *US – Softwood Lumber IV*, para. 10; and Appellate Body Report, *US – Offset Act (Byrd Amendment)*, para. 8.   [449] See Rule 7(1) of the *Working Procedures*.
[450] See Rule 4(3) of the *Working Procedures*. Each Member therefore receives all documents filed in an appeal. A Member who has a conflict of interest shall not take part in the exchange of views.
[451] See Rule 3(2) of the *Working Procedures*.

To date, only twice, in *EC – Asbestos* and *EC – Tariff Preferences*, did an Appellate Body Member express an individual opinion in an Appellate Body report.[452]

In addition to their meetings to exchange views on each appeal, all seven Appellate Body Members also convene on a regular basis to discuss matters of policy, practice and procedure.[453] These meetings are usually held either before or after the exchange of views in an appeal. If the Appellate Body is called upon to take a decision, it will try to do so by consensus. However, if it fails to reach a consensus, the decision will be taken by majority vote.

Each year the Appellate Body Members elect a Chairperson from among them.[454] Rule 5(3) of the *Working Procedures* states that:

> The Chairman shall be responsible for the overall direction of the Appellate Body business. His/her responsibilities shall include:
>
> - the supervision of the internal functioning of the Appellate Body; and
> - any such other duties as the Members may agree to entrust to him/her.

The Appellate Body has its own Secretariat which is separate and independent from the WTO Secretariat.[455] The Appellate Body Secretariat provides the Appellate Body with legal and administrative support.[456] As noted above, the *Rules of Conduct* and their requirements of independence, impartiality and confidentiality apply to the staff of the Appellate Body Secretariat.[457] The Appellate Body Secretariat has its offices in the Centre William Rappard, the lakeside premises of the WTO Secretariat in Geneva. All meetings of the Appellate Body or of divisions of the Appellate Body, as well as the oral hearings in appeals, are also held on these premises.

Questions and Assignments 3.28

How are the Appellate Body divisions that hear and decide particular appeals composed? In your opinion, is it appropriate that a Member of the Appellate Body with the nationality of one of the participants may sit on the division hearing and deciding the appeal? How has the Appellate Body been able to maintain consistency in its case law in spite of the fact that appeals are never heard or decided *en banc*?

---

[452] On the separate opinion in *EC – Asbestos*, see below, pp. 378–9.

[453] See Rule 4 of the *Working Procedures*.

[454] See Rule 5(1) of the *Working Procedures*. While the term of office of the Chairperson is one year, the Appellate Body may decide to extend the term of office for an additional period of up to one year. However, in order to ensure rotation of the chairmanship, no Member can serve as Chairperson for more than two consecutive terms. To date, Mr Julio Lacarte-Muro (1996, 1997) and Mr James Bacchus (2002, 2003) have each served two years as Chairman.

[455] See Dispute Settlement Body, *Decision Establishing the Appellate Body*, 10 February 1995, WT/DSB/1, dated 19 June 1995, para. 17.

[456] Article 17.7 of the DSU. While for many years notoriously understaffed, the Appellate Body Secretariat now consists of a director who heads a team of ten lawyers and four support staff. See www.wto.org/english/tratop_e/dispu_e/ab_secretariat_bio_e.htm, visited on 23 November 2007.

[457] See above, p. 217.

3.3.3.3. Access to appellate review

Only parties to the dispute may appeal a panel report.[458] Third parties or other WTO Members cannot appeal a panel report. However, third parties, i.e. WTO Members which have notified the DSB of a substantial interest in the dispute at the time of the establishment of the panel,[459] can participate in the appellate review proceedings.[460]

In appellate review proceedings, the parties are referred to as 'participants'. The participant that appeals a panel report is called the 'appellant', while the participant responding to an appeal is called the 'appellee'. Once one of the participants has appealed certain aspects of a panel report, it is not uncommon for other participants to 'cross-appeal' other aspects of the report. A participant cross-appealing is known as an 'other appellant'. Third parties choosing to participate in the appellate review proceedings are referred to as 'third participants'.

During the first years of the WTO dispute settlement system, all panel reports were appealed. The first panel report *not* appealed was the report in *Japan – Film*, circulated on 31 March 1998. Of all panel reports circulated since 1995, 68 per cent have been appealed to date.[461]

This high rate of appeal is not necessarily a reflection of the quality of the panel reports but rather of the fact that appealing an unfavourable panel report does not 'cost' the appellant anything. On the contrary, an appeal – even if eventually unsuccessful – will allow a party, found to have acted inconsistently with WTO law, to delay the moment at which it has to bring its measure into consistency. An appeal will also demonstrate to domestic constituencies that a Member has exhausted all legal means available.

Questions and Assignments 3.29

Can third parties or other WTO Members which are directly and adversely affected by a panel report appeal that report? What is an 'other appellant'? What explains the high rate of appeals of panel reports?

3.3.3.4. Scope of appellate review

The scope of review in appeals to the WTO Appellate Body is defined primarily in Article 17.6 of the DSU, which states:

> An appeal shall be limited to issues of law covered in the panel report and legal interpretations developed by the panel.

---

[458] See Article 17.4 of the DSU.   [459] Or within ten days of the establishment of the panel.
[460] For a detailed discussion, see below, pp. 295–6.
[461] See www.worldtradelaw.net/dsc/database/appealcount.asp, visited on 23 November 2007.

In *EC – Hormones*, the Appellate Body found that factual findings of panels are, in principle, excluded from the scope of appellate review. The Appellate Body stated:

> Under Article 17.6 of the DSU, appellate review is limited to appeals on questions of law covered in a panel report and legal interpretations developed by the panel. Findings of fact, as distinguished from legal interpretations or legal conclusions, by a panel are, in principle, not subject to review by the Appellate Body.[462]

In some cases, the characterisation of specific issues before the panel as issues of fact, rather than as issues of law or legal interpretations, is fairly straightforward. In *EC – Hormones*, the Appellate Body noted that:

> The determination of whether or not a certain event did occur in time and space is typically a question of fact.[463]

In that case, the Appellate Body found that the Panel's findings regarding whether or not international standards had been adopted by the Codex Alimentarius Commission were findings on issues of fact and were, therefore, not subject to appellate review.

In other cases, the task of distinguishing between issues of fact and issues of law can be a complex exercise. The Appellate Body has made it clear, however, that findings involving the application of a legal rule to a specific fact or a set of facts are findings on issues of law and thus fall within the scope of appellate review. As stated in *EC – Hormones*:

> The consistency or inconsistency of a given fact or set of facts with the requirements of a given treaty provision is . . . a legal characterization issue. It is a legal question.[464]

The Appellate Body used similar reasoning in *Canada – Periodicals* to explain why the panel's determination of 'like products', for the purposes of Article III:2 of the GATT 1994, was reviewable:

> The determination of whether imported and domestic products are 'like products' is a process by which legal rules have to be applied to facts.[465]

As a panel's factual determinations are, in principle, not subject to appellate review, a panel's weighing and assessment of evidence before it is also, in principle, not subject to appellate review.[466] In *EC – Hormones*, the Appellate Body found:

---

[462] Appellate Body Report, *EC – Hormones*, para. 132. See also Appellate Body Report, *EC – Bananas III*, para. 239.   [463] Appellate Body Report, *EC – Hormones*, para. 132.

[464] *Ibid.* Considerable reliance has been placed by later decisions on this proposition. In *US – Anti-Dumping Measures on Oil Country Tubular Goods*, the Appellate Body held that the qualitative assessment of facts against a legal requirement is a 'legal characterization of [those] facts', and, as held in *EC – Hormones*, thus subject to appellate review. See Appellate Body Report, *US – Anti-Dumping Measures on Oil Country Tubular Goods*, para. 195, citing Appellate Body Report, *EC – Hormones*, para. 116. Similarly, in *US – Softwood Lumber V*, the Appellate Body found that the question as to whether the particular approach adopted by a domestic authority was fair and even-handed was a 'legal characterization' of facts, thus unencumbered by Article 17.6. See Appellate Body Report, *US – Softwood Lumber V*, para. 163.

[465] Appellate Body Report, *Canada – Periodicals*, 468.

[466] Note that in *US – Offset Act (Byrd Amendment)*, Canada argued on appeal that Article 17.6 of the DSU prohibited the United States from challenging 'the credibility and weight the Panel attached' to two

> Determination of the credibility and weight properly to be ascribed to (that is, the appreciation of) a given piece of evidence is part and parcel of the fact finding process and is, in principle, left to the discretion of a panel as the trier of facts.[467]

In *Korea – Alcoholic Beverages*, in which Korea sought to cast doubt on certain studies relied on by the Panel in that case, the Appellate Body stated:

> The Panel's examination and weighing of the evidence submitted fall, in principle, within the scope of the Panel's discretion as the trier of facts and, accordingly, outside the scope of appellate review. This is true, for instance, with respect to the Panel's treatment of the Dodwell Study, the Sofres Report and the Nielsen Study. We *cannot second-guess* the Panel in appreciating either the evidentiary value of such studies or the consequences, if any, of alleged defects in those studies. Similarly, it is not for us to review the relative weight ascribed to evidence on such matters as marketing studies.[468]

> [Emphasis added]

Panels thus have wide-ranging discretion in the consideration and weight they give to the evidence before them.[469]

However, a Panel's discretion in the consideration and weight it gives to evidence is *not* unlimited.[470] A panel's factual determinations must be consistent with Article 11 of the DSU. Article 11, which is quoted and discussed above, defines the mandate of panels.[471] As noted by the Appellate Body in *EC – Hormones*:

> Whether or not a panel has made an objective assessment of the facts before it, as required by Article 11 of the DSU, is also a legal question which, if properly raised on appeal, would fall within the scope of appellate review.[472]

Therefore, a factual finding may be subject to appellate review when the appellant alleges that this finding was not reached in a manner consistent with the requirements of Article 11 of the DSU. Also the scope and content of the municipal law of a Member, as determined by a Panel, for the purpose of ascertaining the Member's compliance with WTO obligations, is a question of law which the Appellate Body can review.[473]

Note that, in *US – Offset Act (Byrd Amendment)*, the Appellate Body held that, as Article 17.6 of the DSU is clear in limiting the scope of appellate review to issues of law and legal interpretations, the Appellate Body has no authority to consider 'new facts' on appeal, even if these new facts are contained in documents that

---

Footnote 466 (*cont.*)
   letters that had been in evidence before it. The Appellate Body, however, rejected Canada's claim. It found that the comments by the United States formed part of the latter's challenge to the Panel's legal findings. Whether these findings were supported by those letters was, according to the Appellate Body, an issue of law on which it had the authority to rule. See Appellate Body Report, *US – Offset Act (Byrd Amendment)*, para. 220.   [467] Appellate Body Report, *EC – Hormones*, para. 132.
[468] Appellate Body Report, *Korea – Alcoholic Beverages*, para. 161.
[469] See also Appellate Body Report, *Australia – Salmon*, para. 261; Appellate Body Report, *India – Quantitative Restrictions*, para. 143; and Appellate Body Report, *Korea – Dairy*, para. 137.
[470] See Appellate Body Report, *Korea – Alcoholic Beverages*, para. 162.   [471] See above, pp. 248–51.
[472] Appellate Body Report, *EC – Hormones*, para. 132. See also Appellate Body Report, *Korea – Alcoholic Beverages*, para. 162.
[473] See Appellate Body Report, *US – Section 211 Appropriations Act*, paras. 105–6, relying on Appellate Body Report, *India – Patents*, paras. 65–6, 68.

are 'available on the public record'.[474] In *US – Softwood Lumber V*, Canada asked that the United States be requested to submit certain documents to the Appellate Body. The Appellate Body declined to do so, arguing that:

> the materials at issue constituted new factual evidence and, therefore, pursuant to Article 17.6 of the DSU, fall outside the scope of the appeal.[475]

However, evidence need not be presented to the Appellate Body in *precisely* the same manner as before the panel. If the data presented on appeal can be clearly traced to the data in the panel record and the way in which such data has been converted can be readily understood, the evidence presented on appeal will not amount to 'new evidence', excluded by Article 17.6.[476]

With regard to 'new arguments', the Appellate Body held in *Canada – Aircraft* that 'new arguments' on appeal cannot be rejected 'simply because they are new'. However, the Appellate Body acknowledged that the possibility for the Appellate Body to *decide* on a new argument that would involve reviewing new facts is foreclosed by Article 17.6 of the DSU. According to the Appellate Body in *Canada – Aircraft*:

> to rule on [the] new argument [at issue], we would have to solicit, receive and review new facts that were not before the Panel, and were not considered by it. In our view, Article 17.6 of the DSU manifestly precludes us from engaging in any such enterprise.[477]

In *US – FSC*, the United States asked the Appellate Body to address a matter that it had not argued before the Panel. The Appellate Body ruled:

> In our view, [the] examination of the substantive issues raised . . . would be outside the scope of our mandate under Article 17.6 of the DSU, as this argument does not involve either an 'issue of law covered in the panel report' or 'legal interpretations developed by the panel'. The Panel was simply not asked to address the issues raised by the United States' new argument. Further, the new argument now made before us would require us to address legal issues quite different from those which confronted the Panel and which may well require proof of new facts.[478]

The Appellate Body had occasion in *EC – Poultry* to note that Article 17.6, read together with Article 17.13, discussed below, precludes from appellate review comments[479] or statements[480] by the panel (as opposed to legal findings and conclusions).

Questions and Assignments 3.30

What can be appealed? How does one distinguish between issues of law and issues of fact? Can factual findings ever be the subject of appeal?

---

[474] See Appellate Body Report, *US – Offset Act (Byrd Amendment)*, paras. 221–2. Note, however, that a new fact in a document that is publicly available may *in principle* be considered on appeal if the document is expressly referred to in the measure in question and its contents were discussed before the Panel. The other party may have to establish prejudice in entertaining such a document so as to render it inadmissible before the Appellate Body. See Appellate Body Report, *Chile – Price Band System*, para. 13.

[475] Appellate Body Report, *US – Softwood Lumber*, para. 9.

[476] See Appellate Body Report, *Chile – Price Band System*, para. 13. See also Appellate Body Report, *EC – Export Subsidies on Sugar*, para. 242.   [477] Appellate Body Report, *Canada – Aircraft*, para. 211.

[478] Appellate Body Report, *US – FSC*, para. 103.   [479] See Appellate Body Report, *EC – Poultry*, para. 107.

[480] See Appellate Body Report, *US – Wool Shirts and Blouses*, 338.

Can the weighing of evidence by a panel be reviewed by the Appellate
Body? Can the Appellate Body consider 'new facts' and/or 'new
arguments' in the course of appellate review proceedings?

3.3.3.5. *The mandate of the Appellate Body*

The mandate of the Appellate Body is primarily set out in Article 17.13 of the
DSU, which states:

> The Appellate Body may uphold, modify or reverse the legal findings and conclusions of
> the panel.

When the Appellate Body agrees with both the panel's reasoning and the conclusion regarding the WTO-consistency of a measure, it *upholds* the relevant findings. When the Appellate Body agrees with the conclusion but not with the
reasoning leading to that conclusion, it *modifies* the relevant findings. If the
Appellate Body disagrees with the conclusion regarding the WTO-consistency of
a measure, it *reverses* the relevant findings.[481]

In some panel reports appealed, the Appellate Body upheld all findings
appealed and thus upheld the panel report as a whole. The Appellate Body
agreed with all the panel's reasoning and with its conclusions. In very few panel
reports appealed the Appellate Body found such fundamental error that it could
not but reverse the whole report.[482] In most appeals, the results of the appellate
review were mixed. Some of the findings appealed were upheld, some modified
and/or reversed. The panel report as a whole therefore was modified.

Although Article 17.13 of the DSU allows the Appellate Body only to uphold,
modify or reverse the panel's findings appealed, the Appellate Body has, in a
number of cases, gone beyond that mandate. In those cases, the Appellate Body
has, explicitly or implicitly, 'completed the legal analysis'.[483] As noted above, a
complainant often makes claims of violation of multiple provisions of WTO law
with regard to the measure at issue. After the panel has found a violation of one
or some of these provisions, the panel may decide, for reasons of judicial
economy, not to make findings with respect to the claims of violation of other
provisions. However, if the panel report is appealed and the Appellate Body
reverses the panel's findings of violation, the question arises as to what the
Appellate Body can do with regard to the claims of violation which the panel, in
its exercise of judicial economy, did not address. A similar question arises in
cases in which a panel concludes that a provision or provisions of WTO law (e.g.

---

[481] The distinction between 'upholding' and 'modifying' a panel's finding has not always been clear.
Occasionally, the Appellate Body has 'upheld' a panel's finding while criticising and disagreeing to some
extent with the panel's reasoning. See e.g. Appellate Body Report, *US – Hot-Rolled Steel*, paras. 90 and 158;
and Appellate Body Report, *US – Lamb*, para. 188.

[482] For examples of panel reports reversed, see e.g. the reports in *Guatemala – Cement I* and *Canada – Dairy
(Article 21.5 – New Zealand and US)*.

[483] The Appellate Body has completed the legal analysis of one or more issues in, for example, *Canada –
Periodicals*, *EC – Hormones*, *EC – Poultry*, *US – Shrimp*, *Japan – Agricultural Products II*, *US – FSC*, *Canada – Aircraft
(Article 21.5 – Brazil)*, *US – Wheat Gluten* and *EC – Asbestos*.

the *TBT Agreement* as was the case in *EC – Asbestos*) is not applicable in the case at hand but in which, on appeal of this finding of inapplicability, the Appellate Body comes to the opposite conclusion. What can the Appellate Body subsequently do in such situation?

In many domestic judicial systems, the appeals court would in similar situations 'remand' the case to the court of first instance. However, the DSU does not provide the Appellate Body with the authority to remand a dispute to the panel.[484] In the absence of a remand authority, the Appellate Body is left with two options:

- either to leave the dispute unresolved; or
- to go on to 'complete the legal analysis'.

In *Canada – Periodicals*, the Appellate Body stated:

> We believe the Appellate Body *can, and should,* complete the analysis of Article III:2 of the GATT 1994 in this case by examining the measure with reference to its consistency with the second sentence of Article III:2, *provided that there is a sufficient basis in the Panel Report to allow us to do so.*[485]
>
> [Emphasis added]

In the circumstances of that case, the Appellate Body considered that it would be 'remiss in not completing the analysis of Article III:2'.[486] However, the Appellate Body has 'completed the legal analysis' only in cases in which there were sufficient factual findings in the panel report or undisputed facts in the panel record to enable it to carry out the legal analysis.[487] In practice, the Appellate Body has often found it impossible to 'complete the legal analysis' due to insufficient factual findings in the panel report or a lack of undisputed facts in the panel record. In *US – Zeroing (EC)*, the Appellate Body was asked to complete the analysis on the validity of the 'zeroing' methodology of the United States in *administrative reviews* under the *Anti-Dumping Agreement*. The Appellate Body found, however, that the Panel's findings were limited to the existence and consistency of 'zeroing' in *original investigations alone*. As a result, the Appellate Body came to the conclusion that there were no adequate factual findings on which it could complete the analysis as requested.[488] In *EC – Selected Customs Matters*, the Appellate Body held that the 'general observations' of the Panel on the EC's administration of customs did not accord a sufficient basis for it to complete its analysis by entertaining the United States' broad claim that pertained to European customs institutions and mechanisms.[489] Similarly, highly contested and complicated facts will discourage the Appellate Body from completing the analysis.[490] In addition, the Appellate Body has also declined to complete the

---

[484] In the context of the DSU reform negotiations, Jordan and the European Communities tabled proposals to provide the Appellate Body with remand authority. See below, p. 309.

[485] Appellate Body Report, *Canada – Periodicals*, 469.   [486] *Ibid.*

[487] See Appellate Body Report, *Australia – Salmon*, para. 118. See also Appellate Body Report, *EC – Export Subsidies on Sugar*, para. 340.   [488] See Appellate Body Report, *US – Zeroing (EC)*, paras. 228, 243.

[489] See Appellate Body Report, *EC – Selected Customs Matters*, paras. 278–87.

[490] See Appellate Body Report, *US – Softwood Lumber VI (Article 21.5 – Canada)*, paras. 157–61.

legal analysis because of the novel character of the claims which the Panel did not address. Claims are 'novel' when they concern issues which have not yet been dealt with in the WTO case law. In *EC – Asbestos*, the Appellate Body stated:

> In light of their novel character, we consider that Canada's claims under the *TBT Agreement* have not been explored before us in depth. As the Panel did not address these claims, there are no 'issues of law' or 'legal interpretations' regarding them to be analyzed by the parties, and reviewed by us under Article 17.6 of the DSU. We also observe that the sufficiency of the facts on the record depends on the reach of the provisions of the *TBT Agreement* claimed to apply – a reach that has yet to be determined.[491]

The Appellate Body will also decline to complete the legal analysis when a Panel is thought to have improperly excluded evidence, or erred in its assessment of evidence, and the Appellate Body would have to examine the evidence in order to complete the legal analysis.[492] The Appellate Body will also not complete the legal analysis if the completion will not be decisive for the outcome of the dispute. In *US – Steel Safeguards*, the Appellate Body refused to address a substantive issue that arose as a result of reversing a Panel reasoning because addressing that issue would in no event have disturbed the Panel's ultimate finding.[493]

Questions and Assignments 3.31

When does the Appellate Body uphold, when does it modify and when does it reverse the legal findings and conclusions of the panel under appellate review? Why and when does the Appellate Body 'complete the legal analysis'? In your opinion, should the Appellate Body have the power to remand cases to the panel?

3.3.4. Other bodies and persons involved in WTO dispute settlement

Apart from the DSB, panels and the Appellate Body, there are a number of other bodies and persons involved in the WTO's efforts to resolve disputes between its Members. These bodies and persons include, in no particular order:

- arbitrators under Articles 21.3, 22.6 and 25 of the DSU;[494]
- the Permanent Group of Experts under Article 4.5 of the *SCM Agreement*;[495]
- the Facilitator under Annex V.4 of the *SCM Agreement*;
- experts under Articles 13.1 and 13.2 of the DSU, Article 11.2 of the *SPS Agreement* and Article 14 of the *TBT Agreement*;[496]
- Expert Review Groups under Article 13.2 of and Appendix 4 to the DSU;[497]
- Technical Expert Groups under Article 14.3 of and Annex 2 to the *TBT Agreement*;[498]

---

[491] Appellate Body Report, *EC – Asbestos*, para. 82.   [492] See Appellate Body Report, *US – DRAMS*, para. 196.
[493] See Appellate Body Report, *US – Steel Safeguards*, paras. 430–1.
[494] See above, pp. 176–8 and below, pp. 298–9, 305–6.   [495] See below, pp. 575–6.
[496] See below, pp. 281–3.   [497] See below, pp. 282–3.   [498] See below, pp. 829–30.

- the Chairman of the DSB;[499] and
- the WTO Director-General.[500]

Note also the role of the WTO Secretariat, the Appellate Body Secretariat and the Advisory Centre on WTO Law, as discussed above.[501]

3.4. WTO DISPUTE SETTLEMENT PROCEEDINGS

In WTO dispute settlement proceedings four separate stages can be distinguished:

- consultations;
- panel proceedings;
- appellate review proceedings; and
- implementation and enforcement of the recommendations and rulings of the panel and/or the Appellate Body, as adopted by the DSB.

In this section, each of these stages of the WTO dispute settlement proceedings will be examined.

3.4.1. Consultations

As noted above, the DSU expresses a clear preference for resolving disputes amicably rather than through adjudication.[502] To that end, WTO dispute settlement proceedings always start with consultations (or, at least, an attempt to have consultations) between the parties to the dispute.[503] In *Mexico – Corn Syrup (Article 21.5 – US)*, the Appellate Body stressed the importance of consultations in WTO dispute settlement as follows:

> Through consultations, parties exchange information, assess the strengths and weaknesses of their respective cases, narrow the scope of the differences between them and, in many cases, reach a mutually agreed solution in accordance with the explicit preference expressed in Article 3.7 of the DSU. Moreover, even where no such agreed solution is reached, consultations provide the parties an opportunity to define and delimit the scope of the dispute between them. Clearly, consultations afford many benefits to complaining and responding parties, as well as to third parties and to the dispute settlement system as a whole.[504]

As already noted, the resolution of disputes, through consultations, is obviously more cost-effective and more satisfactory for the long-term trade relations with the other party to the dispute than adjudication by a panel.[505] Consultations enable the disputing parties to understand better the factual situation and the

---

[499] See above, pp. 217–18, 237, 246, 247, 259, and below, pp. 274, 279.
[500] See above, pp. 177, 217, 246, 259 and below, pp. 289, 298.
[501] See above, pp. 132–8, 256–7 (on the WTO Secretariat), p. 261 (on the Appellate Body Secretariat) and p. 234 (on the ACWL). Recall that the ACWL is not a WTO body or institution.
[502] See above, p. 173.
[503] See Article 4 of the DSU. Note in particular Article 4.5 but also Articles 4.3 and 4.7 of the DSU.
[504] Appellate Body Report, *Mexico – Corn Syrup (Article 21.5 – US)*, para. 54.   [505] See above, p. 173.

legal claims in respect of the dispute. Such understanding may allow them to resolve the matter without further proceedings and, if not, will at least allow a party to learn more about the facts and the legal arguments that the other party is likely to use when the dispute goes to adjudication. In this way, the consultations *can* serve as an informal pre-trial discovery mechanism. Their primary object and purpose, however, is to settle the dispute amicably.

This section discusses the following issues that arise with respect to consultations:

- initiation of consultations;
- conduct of consultations; and
- outcome of consultations.

3.4.1.1. Initiation of consultations

Any WTO Member considering that a benefit accruing to it under the *WTO Agreement* is being impaired or nullified by measures taken by another WTO Member may request consultations with that other Member. WTO Members are required to accord sympathetic consideration to, and afford adequate opportunity for, consultations.[506] A request for consultations, giving the reasons for the request, must be submitted in writing and must identify:

- the measure at issue; and
- the legal basis for the complaint.[507]

The request for consultations circumscribes the scope of the dispute.[508] As held by the Appellate Body in *India – Patents (US)*:

> All parties engaged in dispute settlement under the DSU must be fully forthcoming from the very beginning both as to the claims involved in a dispute and as to the facts relating to those claims. Claims must be stated clearly. Facts must be disclosed freely. This must be so in consultations as well as in the more formal setting of panel proceedings. In fact, the demands of due process that are implicit in the DSU make this especially necessary during consultations. For the claims that are made and the facts that are established during consultations do much to shape the substance and the scope of subsequent panel proceedings.[509]

All requests for consultations are to be notified to the DSB (and the relevant councils and committees) by the Member requesting consultations.[510]

With respect to the relationship between the request for consultations and the later request for the establishment of a panel, the Appellate Body noted, in *Brazil – Aircraft*, that Articles 4 and 6 of the DSU do not require a precise and exact identity between the specific measures and claims of WTO-inconsistency that were the subject of consultations and the specific measures and claims of WTO-inconsistency that were identified in the request for the establishment of a

---

[506] See Article 4.2 of the DSU.   [507] See Article 4.4 of the DSU.
[508] See Appellate Body Report, *Mexico – Corn Syrup (Article 21.5 – US)*, para. 54.
[509] Appellate Body Report, *India – Patents (US)*, para. 94.   [510] See Article 4.4 of the DSU.

panel. What is important is that the essence of the challenged measures and claims has not changed.[511]

Note that in *US – Certain EC Products*, the Appellate Body found that one of the measures challenged by the European Communities was not properly before the Panel. The Appellate Body explained that, although the panel request referred to the measure, it was not possible for it to conclude 'on this basis *alone*' that the measure was within the Panel's terms of reference. It noted that the European Communities' request for consultations did not refer to the measure and that the European Communities acknowledged that the measure was not the subject of the consultations.[512] Also note that, as the Appellate Body ruled in *US – Upland Cotton*, the scope of the consultations is determined by the request for consultations rather than by what actually happened, i.e. what actually was discussed, during the consultations.[513]

Questions and Assignments 3.32

Apart from settling the dispute amicably, what is the purpose of consultations? What must be contained in the request for consultations? How do requests for consultations relate to panel requests, and what is the importance of this relationship for the terms of reference of a panel?

3.4.1.2. *Conduct of consultations*

Parties have broad discretion as regards the manner in which consultations are to be conducted. The DSU provides few rules on the conduct of consultations. The consultation process is essentially a *political–diplomatic process*, 'without prejudice to the rights of any Member in further legal proceedings'.[514]

---

[511] See Appellate Body Report, *Brazil – Aircraft*, para. 132. See also Appellate Body Report, *US – Zeroing (Japan)*, paras. 89–96 (finding that the description of the measure in the consultations request was sufficient to cover 'the use of "zeroing procedures" in the context of all types and stages of antidumping proceedings, and regardless of the comparison methodology used.' *Ibid.*, para. 94. The same logic applies with respect to the relationship between the legal basis identified in the request for consultations and the legal basis of the complaint. In *Mexico – Anti-Dumping Measures on Rice*, the Appellate Body ruled that 'it is not necessary that the provisions referred to in the request for consultations be identical to those set out in the panel request, provided that the "legal basis" in the panel request may reasonably be said to have evolved from the "legal basis" that formed the subject of consultations. In other words, the addition of provisions must not have the effect of changing the essence of the complaint.' Appellate Body Report, *Mexico – Anti-Dumping Measures on Rice*, para. 138. See also Appellate Body Report, *US – DRAMS*, paras. 89–101.
[512] See Appellate Body Report, *US Upland Cotton*, footnote 244 to para. 285, summarising the relevant findings in Appellate Body Report, *US – Certain EC Products*, paras. 69–75.
[513] See Appellate Body Report, *US – Upland Cotton*, para. 286–7. The Appellate Body in this case stated that: 'Examining what took place in the consultations would seem contrary to Article 4.6 of the DSU, which provides that "[c]onsultations shall be confidential, and without prejudice to the rights of any Member in any further proceedings".' Appellate Body Report, *US – Upland Cotton*, para. 287.
[514] Article 4.6 of the DSU. Therefore, evidence pertaining to settlement offers made during the consultations is 'of no legal consequence to the later stages' of WTO dispute settlement proceedings. On this basis, the Panel in *US – Underwear* refused to consider as evidence the settlement proposals made by the United States during consultations, which had been submitted to it by Costa Rica, emphasising that 'Article 4.6 of the DSU makes it clear that offers made in the context of consultations are, in case a mutually agreed solution is not reached, of no legal consequence to the later stages of dispute settlement, as far as the rights of the parties to the dispute are concerned.' Panel Report, *US – Underwear*, para. 7.27.

Unless otherwise agreed, the Member to which a request for consultations is made must *reply* to the request within ten days of the date of its receipt, and enter into consultations within a period of no more than thirty days after the date of receipt of the request.[515] It must enter into consultations in good faith and with a view to reaching a mutually satisfactory solution. If the Member does not respond within ten days after the date of receipt of the request, or does not enter into consultations within a period of no more than thirty days (or a period otherwise mutually agreed), then the Member that requested the consultations may proceed directly to request the establishment of a panel. As the Appellate Body noted in *Mexico – Corn Syrup (Article 21.5 – US)*, in such a case the respondent, by its own conduct, relinquishes the potential benefits that could be derived from consultations.[516]

While the request for consultations is notified to the DSB and posted on the WTO websites as a WT/DS document, the consultations themselves are confidential.[517] Generally, consultations are held in Geneva and involve Geneva-based diplomats as well as capital-based trade officials and private lawyers of the parties to the dispute.[518] The WTO Secretariat is neither present at, nor in any other way associated with, the consultations. As the Appellate Body noted in *US – Upland Cotton*:

> There is no public record of what actually transpires during consultations and parties will often disagree about what, precisely, was discussed.[519]

Note that the requirement of confidentiality does not mean that information acquired during consultations may not be used during panel proceedings between the same parties on the same matter. It means that the information acquired may not be disclosed to anyone not involved in the consultations.[520]

---

[515] See Article 4.3 of the DSU. In cases of urgency, Article 4.8 of the DSU provides that Members shall enter into consultations within a period of no more than ten days after the date of receipt of the request, and, if consultations are unsuccessful within twenty days, the complainant may request the establishment of a panel. On 21 March 2007, Colombia relied on this expedited procedure in its complaint against the European Communities concerning its 'tariff-only' regime for the importation of bananas that has applied since 1 January 2006. Colombia argued: 'As a developing country heavily dependent on its exports of bananas, Colombia can ill-afford yet another lengthy dispute settlement proceeding conducted according to standard time frames. Accordingly, Colombia requests the EC to hold consultations within the time frame set out in Article 4.8 of the DSU for cases of urgency, that is within 10 days after the date of receipt of this request.' Colombia stated that if consultations or the good offices of the Director-General were not successful in resolving the dispute, it might resort to the accelerated procedure for the establishment of a panel. See *Request for Consultations by Colombia, European Communities – Regime for the Importation of Bananas*, WT/DS361/1. See also *BRIDGES Weekly Trade News Digest*, 28 March 2007.   [516] See Appellate Body Report, *Mexico – Corn Syrup (Article 21.5 – US)*, para. 59.

[517] See Article 4.6 of the DSU. In *Canada – Wheat Exports and Grain Imports*, the Panel granted Canada's request in the interim review stage that specific references to discussions and events that occurred during consultations between the parties be deleted from the final panel report. See Panel Report, *Canada – Wheat Exports and Grain Imports*, paras. 5.4–5.10.

[518] Note that the LDC Group, the group of least-developed country Members, proposed in the context of the DSU reform negotiations a change regarding the location of consultations when least developed countries are involved. According to this proposal, such consultations must be held in the capital city of the least developed country involved should there be a request.

[519] Appellate Body Report, *US – Upland Cotton*, para. 287.

[520] See Panel Report, *Korea – Alcoholic Beverages*, para. 10.23; Panel Report, *EC – Bed Linen*, paras. 6.39–6.40; and Panel Report, *Australia – Automotive Leather II*, paras. 9.31–9.35. As third parties are subject to the same requirement to maintain the confidentiality of panel proceedings as are parties, information obtained during consultations may be included in the written submission of a party provided to a third party in

Consultations can be requested:

- pursuant to Article XXII of the GATT 1994, or the corresponding provisions in other covered agreements; *or*
- pursuant to Article XXIII of the GATT 1994, or the corresponding provisions in other covered agreements.

The Member requesting consultations is free to choose either type of consultations. There is only one difference, albeit a significant one, between these two types of consultations. Only in the context of consultations pursuant to Article XXII or corresponding provisions can a Member other than the consulting Members be allowed to participate in the consultations. A Member that considers that it has a 'substantial trade interest' may notify the consulting Members and the DSB of such interest within ten days after the date of the circulation of the request for consultations.[521] Provided that the respondent to the dispute agrees that the claim of substantial interest is well founded, this Member shall join in the consultations. If consultations are instead conducted pursuant to Article XXIII, or corresponding provisions, it is not possible for other Members to join in the consultations.

Occasionally, respondents have argued that the consultations held had not been adequate or meaningful or that the complainant had not engaged in consultations in good faith.[522] The Panel in *Korea – Alcoholic Beverages* ruled in this respect that it was not for panels to assess the 'adequacy' of consultations.[523] Consultations are a matter reserved for the parties. What takes place in these consultations is not the concern of panels. Panels may only ascertain whether consultations were held or at least were requested.[524] Note that, if a panel were to find that consultations had *not* been held or requested prior to its establishment, it would have to conclude that it has no authority to hear and decide the dispute.[525]

3.4.1.3. Outcome of consultations

If consultations are successful and lead to a mutually agreed solution to the dispute, this solution must be notified to the DSB.[526] Any Member may raise any point relating to this notified solution at meetings of the DSB.[527] Note that

---

the subsequent panel proceedings even if that third party did not participate in the consultations. See Panel Report, *Mexico – Corn Syrup*, para. 7.41.

[521] See Article 4.11 of the DSU. Several proposals on ways to facilitate the joining of consultations have been submitted in the context of the DSU reform negotiations.

[522] See the requirements in Articles 3.10 and 4.2 of the DSU. Also note Article 4.10 of the DSU, which provides that during consultations Members 'should' give special attention to the particular problems and interests of developing-country Members.

[523] See Panel Report, *Korea – Alcoholic Beverages*, para. 10.19.

[524] See Panel Reports, *EC – Bananas III*, para. 7.19.

[525] The lack of prior consultations is, however, not a defect that a panel must examine on its own motion. See Appellate Body Report, *Mexico – Corn Syrup (Article 21.5 – US)*, para. 64.

[526] See Article 3.6 of the DSU. The mutually agreed solutions must also be notified to other relevant bodies, such as the TRIPS Council in a dispute concerning rights and obligations of Members under the *TRIPS Agreement*.

[527] See *ibid*. Any Member may also raise any point relating to notified solutions at meetings of other relevant WTO bodies.

mutually agreed solutions must be consistent with WTO law.[528] As discussed above, consultations have frequently been successful in resolving disputes.[529]

If consultations between the parties fail to settle the dispute within sixty days of the receipt of the request for consultations, the complainant may request the DSB to establish a panel to adjudicate the dispute.[530] In many cases, however, the complainant will not, immediately upon the expiration of the sixty-day period, request the establishment of a panel but will allow for more time to settle the dispute through consultations.

For consultations involving a measure taken by a developing-country Member, Article 12.10 of the DSU explicitly provides that the parties may agree to extend the sixty-day period. If, after the sixty-day period has elapsed, the consulting parties cannot agree that the consultations have concluded, the Chairman of the DSB shall decide, after consultation with the parties, whether to extend this period and, if so, for how long.

Consultations between the parties with the aim of settling the dispute can, and do, continue *during* the panel proceedings.[531] The DSU provides that panels should consult the parties to the dispute regularly and give them an adequate opportunity to develop a mutually satisfactory solution.[532] There have been a number of disputes in which a mutually agreed solution was reached while the dispute was already before a panel.[533] In such a case, Article 12.7 of the DSU provides that the panel report 'shall be confined to a brief description of the case and to reporting that a solution has been reached'.

Questions and Assignments 3.33

What is the 'sanction' for not holding (or requesting) consultations before requesting the establishment of a panel? Will consultations always last at least sixty days? Can consultations last longer than sixty days? Can a panel find that the complainant did not engage in consultation in good faith as required by Article 3.10 of the DSU? Can other Members join consultations between the parties to a dispute? May WTO Members resolve a dispute amicably by *agreeing* to a solution which deviates from the *WTO Agreement*? Does the DSU provide any special rules for developing-country Members engaged in consultations?

---

[528] See Article 3.5 of the DSU.   [529] See above, p. 173.

[530] The complainant may request a panel *during* the sixty-day period if the consulting parties jointly consider that consultations have failed to settle the dispute. See Article 4.7 of the DSU. Note that in the context of the DSU reform negotiations, several WTO Members proposed a shortening of the minimum time period for consultations from sixty to thirty days. This proposal did not find its way into the Chairman's Text due to a lack of support. However, a maximum time limit for consultations of eighteen months, proposed by the EC and Jordan, has been included.

[531] Note that a senior US trade official reportedly said the day after the United States had requested the establishment of a panel in *EC and Certain Member States – Large Civil Aircraft* that the United States was still 'prepared to negotiate even as the litigation goes forward', adding, however, that 'We will only suspend litigation if we get an assurance that launch aid will be ended completely – not one euro more.' See R. Minder and E. Alden, 'War of Aircraft Titans Gives WTO Biggest Case', *Financial Times*, 1 June 2005.

[532] See Article 11 of the DSU.

[533] See e.g. *EC – Scallops*, complaints by Canada, Peru and Chile; *EC – Butter*, complaint by New Zealand; *US – DRAMS (Article 21.5 – Korea)*, complaint by Korea; and *Japan – Quotas on Laver*, complaint by Korea.

3.4.2. Panel proceedings

As outlined above, when consultations are unsuccessful, the complainant may request the establishment of a panel. As discussed earlier in this chapter, the DSB will usually establish the panel by reverse consensus at the meeting following that at which the panel request first appeared on the DSB's agenda.[534] Subsequently, the parties will agree on the composition of the panel or, if they fail to do so, the composition of the panel will be decided on by the WTO Director-General.[535] This section discusses the following issues which arise with respect to panel proceedings:

- working procedures for panel proceedings;
- written submissions and substantive panel meetings;
- rights of third parties;
- submission and admission of evidence;
- use of experts;
- protection of confidential business information;
- panel deliberations and interim review;
- adoption or appeal of the panel report; and
- duration of panel proceedings.

3.4.2.1. *Working procedures for panel proceedings*

The basic rules governing panel proceedings are set out in Article 12 of the DSU. Article 12.1 of the DSU directs a panel to follow the *Working Procedures* contained in Appendix 3 to the DSU, while at the same time authorising a panel to do otherwise after consulting the parties to the dispute. While Article 12.1 of the DSU merely requires that the panel 'consults' the parties, panels will often be hesitant to deviate from the Working Procedures contained in Appendix 3 without the 'consent' of the parties. Moreover, panels usually agree to requests on procedural issues tabled by the parties jointly.[536] In *EC – Hormones*, the Appellate Body noted that panels enjoy:

> a margin of discretion to deal, always in accordance with due process, with specific situations that may arise in a particular case.[537]

In *India – Patents (US)*, however, the Appellate Body cautioned panels as follows:

> Although panels enjoy some discretion in establishing their own working procedures, this discretion does not extend to modifying the substantive provisions of the DSU. To be sure, Article 12.1 of the DSU says: Panels shall follow the Working Procedures in Appendix 3 unless the panel decides otherwise after consulting the parties to the dispute.' Yet that is *all* that it says. Nothing in the DSU gives a panel the authority either to disregard or to modify other explicit provisions of the DSU.[538]

---

[534] See above, pp. 242, 244.   [535] See above, pp. 245–6.
[536] Note, however, that the discretion of panels is limited in that panels cannot modify the rules set out in the DSU itself. See below, p. 276.   [537] Appellate Body Report, *EC – Hormones*, footnote 138.
[538] Appellate Body Report, *India – Patents (US)*, para. 92. In this case, the Appellate Body reversed a decision by the Panel that it would consider all claims made prior to the end of the first substantive meeting. All parties had agreed with this Panel decision.

Article 12.2 of the DSU requires that panel procedures provide sufficient flexibility so as to ensure high-quality panel reports while not unduly delaying the panel process. Since the *Working Procedures* contained in Appendix 3 to the DSU are rudimentary, most panels now find it useful, if not necessary, to adopt more detailed *ad hoc* working procedures.[539]

Appendix 3 to the DSU provides for 'a proposed timetable for panel work'.[540] On the basis of this proposed timetable, the panel will – whenever possible within a week of its composition – fix the timetable for its work.[541] The panel may at that time also decide on detailed *ad hoc* working procedures. The panel will do so after consulting the parties to the dispute at what is called the 'organisational meeting'.[542]

Generally speaking, the parties to a dispute enjoy a high degree of discretion to argue before panels in the manner they deem appropriate. This discretion, however, does not detract from their obligation under the DSU to engage in dispute settlement proceedings 'in good faith in an effort to resolve the dispute'.[543] Both the complaining and the responding Members must comply with the requirements of the DSU in good faith. In *US – FSC*, the Appellate Body held:

> By good faith compliance, complaining Members accord to the responding Members the full measure of protection and opportunity to defend, contemplated by the letter and spirit of the procedural rules. The same principle of good faith requires that responding Members seasonably and promptly bring claimed procedural deficiencies to the attention of the complaining Member, and to the DSB or the Panel, so that corrections, if needed, can be made to resolve disputes. The procedural rules of WTO dispute settlement are designed to promote, not the development of litigation techniques, but simply the fair, prompt and effective resolution of trade disputes.[544]

Note that, in *EC – Tube or Pipe Fittings*, Brazil's first written submission did not contain paragraph or line numbering. The Panel noted in this respect that it 'would appreciate efforts on the part of the parties to facilitate the task of the Panel in examining the matter referred to [it]', and 'invite[d] Brazil to submit a paragraph-numbered version of its first submission to facilitate referencing by the Panel and the parties'.[545] Brazil accordingly submitted a revised, paragraph-numbered version of its first written submission to the Panel.[546]

Questions and Assignments 3.34

Who decides on the working procedures for the panels and on the timetable for the panel's work? Which requirements do the working procedures and the timetable have to meet? Is a panel free to deviate

---

[539] For an example of such *ad hoc* panel Working Procedures, see Panel Report, *US – Steel Safegaurds*, para. 6.1.
[540] See para. 12 of Appendix 3 to the DSU.
[541] See Article 12.3 of the DSU. The timetable includes precise deadlines for written submissions by the parties, which the parties must respect (see Article 12.5 of the DSU). In determining the timetable, the panel must provide sufficient time for the parties to prepare their submissions (see Article 12.4 of the DSU).   [542] See Articles 12.3 and 12.5 of the DSU.   [543] Article 3.10 of the DSU.
[544] Appellate Body Report, *US – FSC*, para. 166. See also Appellate Body Report, *US – Lamb*, para. 115.
[545] Panel Report, *EC – Tube or Pipe Fittings*, para. 7.40.   [546] See *ibid.*, para. 7.41.

from Appendix 3 to the DSU as well as other provisions of the DSU if all parties to the dispute agree? How much discretion do parties enjoy regarding the manner in which they argue before panels?

3.4.2.2. *Written submissions and substantive panel meetings*

Each of the parties to a dispute submits two written submissions to the panel:

- a 'first written submission'; and
- a 'rebuttal submission'.

In their first written submissions, the parties present the facts of the case as they see them and their arguments relating to the alleged inconsistencies with WTO law.[547] In their rebuttal submissions, they reply to the argument and evidence submitted by the other party.[548] As the Appellate Body ruled in *US – Shrimp*, the parties have a *legal right* to make the above-mentioned submissions to the panel, and the panel in turn is *obliged in law* to accept and give due consideration to these submissions.[549]

After the first written submissions of the parties have been filed, the panel holds its first substantive meeting with the parties.[550] At this meeting, the panel asks the complainant to present its case. At the same meeting, the respondent is also asked to present its point of view.[551] The panel holds a second substantive meeting with the parties after the rebuttal submissions have been filed.[552] While not mandatory, panel meetings are always held on the premises of the WTO Secretariat in Geneva. A panel meeting may take one or more days. While initially far less formal and less 'court-like' than the oral hearings of the Appellate Body, WTO panel meetings have become increasingly formal and 'court-like' in recent years.[553] All *ex parte* communications with the panel, on matters under consideration, are explicitly proscribed.[554] As already discussed, the panel usually meets in closed session with only the delegations of the parties present.[555]

The panel may, at any time, put questions to the parties and ask them for explanations either in the course of a meeting or in writing.[556] The DSU provides panels

---

[547] Note that, even if the complainant fails to include any arguments on certain claims in its first written submission, these claims, if properly identified in the panel request, remain within the terms of reference of the panel. See Appellate Body Report, *EC – Bananas III*, para. 145.

[548] The first written submission of the complainant is usually filed two to three weeks in advance of the first written submission of the respondent. The rebuttal submissions are filed simultaneously. See Article 12.6 of, and para. 12 of Appendix 3 to, the DSU. On the 'late' submission of evidence, see below, pp. 280–1.

[549] See Appellate Body Report, *US – Shrimp*, para. 101. This is also the case for submissions by third parties but not for submissions by any other Member or person (*amicus curiae* briefs). See above, pp. 191–6.

[550] See para. 4 of Appendix 3 to the DSU.　　[551] See para. 5 of Appendix 3 to the DSU.

[552] Additional meetings with the parties may be scheduled if required. Para. 12 of Appendix 3 to the DSU. In practice, however, very few panels have had additional meetings with the parties.

[553] See below, p. 294.

[554] See Article 18.1 of the DSU. As already mentioned, in *Turkey – Rice*, the respondent, Turkey, proposed that it would provide certain information to the Panel on the condition that these documents would not be made available to the complainant, the United States. The Panel refused this condition, as it would violate Article 18.1 of the DSU. See Panel Report, *Turkey – Rice*, para. 7.100. See also Panel Report, *Korea – Certain Paper*, paras. 7.13–7.18.　　[555] See above, pp. 212–16.

[556] See para. 8 of Appendix 3 to the DSU. During panel meetings, parties may also question each other. This does not happen during hearings of the Appellate Body.

with discretionary authority to request and obtain information from *any* Member, including *a fortiori* a Member which is a party to a dispute before the panel.[557] The parties are under an obligation to provide the panel with the information or the documents that the panel requests. Article 13.1 of the DSU states, in relevant part:

> A Member *should* respond promptly and fully to any request by a panel for such information as the panel considers necessary and appropriate.
>
> [Emphasis added]

In *Canada – Aircraft*, the Appellate Body ruled that the word 'should' in Article 13.1 is used in a normative sense.[558] As held by the Appellate Body in this case, it is within the discretion of panels to draw adverse inferences from the fact that a party has refused to provide information requested by the panel. However, the Appellate Body stressed that panels must draw inferences on the basis of all the facts of record (and not only the refusal to provide information).[559]

For the benefit of a developing-country Member, Article 12.10 of the DSU provides, in relevant part:

> in examining a complaint against a developing-country Member, the panel shall accord sufficient time for the developing country to prepare and present its argumentation.

In *India – Quantitative Restrictions*, India requested additional time from the Panel in order to prepare its first written submission. Noting the DSU's strict time-frame for the panel process, the United States objected to this request. Referring to Article 12.10, the Panel ruled as follows:

> In light of this provision, and considering the administrative reorganization taking place in India as a result of the recent change in government, the Panel has decided to grant an additional period of time to India to prepare its submission. However, bearing in mind also the need to respect the time frames of the DSU and in light of the difficulties of rescheduling the meeting of 7 and 8 May, the Panel considers that an additional period of ten days would represent 'sufficient time' within the meaning of Article 12.10 of the DSU. India is therefore granted until 1 May 1998 (5 p.m.) to submit its first written submission to the Panel. The original date of the first meeting remains unchanged as 7 and 8 May.[560]

Questions and Assignments 3.35

Briefly describe the content of the various written submissions of the parties to the panel. When does the panel meet with the parties? Are *ex parte* communications with the panel allowed? Are parties to a dispute obliged to provide the panel with the information or the documents that

---

[557] See Article 13.1 of the DSU. On the discretionary nature of this authority to request information, see e.g. Panel Report, *EC – Bed Linen (Article 21.5 – India)*, paras. 165–7; Panel Report, *EC – Selected Customs Matters*, paras. 7.77–7.83; Panel Report, *US – Wheat Gluten*, paras. 8.7–8.12; and Panel Report, *US – Lead and Bismuth II*, paras. 6.4–6.7.   [558] See Appellate Body Report, *Canada – Aircraft*, para. 187.

[559] See Appellate Body Report, *Canada – Aircraft*, paras. 204–5; and Appellate Body Report, *US – Wheat Gluten*, paras. 173–6. In *US – Upland Cotton*, the United States responded in part to the request of the Panel to provide certain information and also argued that other information could not be provided. The Panel ultimately, based on all of the information before it, determined that it was not necessary to draw adverse inferences in respect of information allegedly not submitted by the United States. See Panel Report, *US – Upland Cotton*, paras. 7.20–7.42 and 7.609–7.633. See also Panel Report, *Canada – Aircraft Credits and Guarantees*, paras. 7.379–7.386.   [560] Panel Report, *India – Quantitative Restrictions*, para. 5.10.

the panel requests? What are the consequences of a failure or refusal to provide information or documents requested by a panel? Can developing-country Members request additional time to prepare their written submissions?

3.4.2.3. *Rights of third parties*

As discussed above, any WTO Member having a substantial interest in a matter before a panel and having notified its interest in a timely manner to the DSB shall have an opportunity to be heard by the panel and to make written submissions to the panel.[561] These third parties to the dispute are invited by the panel to present their views during a special session of the first substantive meeting.[562] Their written submissions to the panel are given to the parties to the dispute.[563] Third parties, however, only receive the first written submissions of the parties.[564] It is clear from the above that the rights of third parties to participate in the panel proceedings are, as a rule, quite limited.[565]

In some cases, however, third parties have sought and obtained enhanced third party rights. In *EC – Bananas III*, for example, third party developing-country Members having a major interest in the outcome of this case were allowed to attend the entire first and second substantive meetings of the panel with the parties as well as make statements at both meetings. Third parties were also granted enhanced third party rights in, for example, *EC – Hormones*, *EC – Tariff Preferences* and *EC – Export Subsidies on Sugar*.[566] Note that the grant of enhanced third party rights is within 'the sound discretion' of the panel, although '[s]uch discretionary authority is, of course, not unlimited and is circumscribed, for example, by the requirements of due process'.[567] Third

---

[561] See Article 10.2 of the DSU. See also above, pp. 181–2, 243.

[562] See Article 10.2 of, and para. 6 of Appendix 3 to, the DSU.

[563] Article 10.2 of the DSU. These submissions are reflected in, or attached to, the panel report. See above, p. 254.   [564] See Article 10.3 of the DSU.

[565] Following a number of proposals on this point in the DSU reform negotiations, the Chairman's Text contains a proposal to allow third parties to participate in all substantive panel meetings and to receive a copy of all written submissions to the panel. See below, p. 309.

[566] The Panel in *EC – Hormones*, however, refused the third parties participation in the interim review process: see Panel Reports, *EC – Bananas III*, para. 7.9. In *EC – Hormones*, enhanced third party rights were granted due to the fact that the third parties in the two disputes were complainants in a parallel panel procedure concerning the same EC measure, to be dealt with by the same panellists. See Panel Report, *EC – Hormones (US)*, para. 8.15 and Panel Report, *EC – Hormones (Canada)*, paras. 8.12–8.20 (upheld by the Appellate Body, see Appellate Body Report, *EC – Hormones*, paras. 150–4). The Panel in *EC – Tariff Preferences* allowed third parties some participation in the interim review process by allowing them to review the summary of their respective arguments in the draft descriptive part of the Panel Report. See Panel Report, *EC – Tariff Preferences*, para. 1.10. In this case, eleven of the eighteen third parties had requested enhanced third party rights. The Panel decided to grant additional rights to *all* third parties. It noted, amongst others, two considerations in its ruling, namely that '[a]s a matter of due process, it is appropriate to provide the same procedural rights to all third parties in this dispute' and that 'in granting any additional rights to third parties, it is important to guard against an inappropriate blurring of the distinction drawn in the DSU between parties and third parties'. Panel Report, *EC – Tariff Preferences*, Annex A, para. 7. The same two considerations were reiterated in Panel Reports, *EC – Export Subsidies on Sugar*, paras. 2.5–2.9, where, following a request for enhanced third party rights by the fourteen ACP sugar-producing third parties, the Panel decided to grant additional rights to *all* third parties.

[567] Appellate Body Report, *US – 1916 Act*, paras. 149 and 150. In this case, the Appellate Body upheld the Panel's decision not to grant enhanced third party rights.

parties were refused enhanced third party rights in, for example, *US – Upland Cotton*.[568]

Questions and Assignments 3.36

What are the rights of third parties in panel proceedings?

3.4.2.4. *Submission and admissibility of evidence*

The DSU does not establish precise rules or deadlines for the submission of evidence by a party to the dispute. In *Argentina – Textiles and Apparel*, the Panel allowed the United States to submit certain evidence two days before the second substantive meeting. Argentina appealed the Panel's decision to admit this evidence. The Appellate Body rejected the appeal on the basis of the following reasoning:

> Article 11 of the DSU does not establish time limits for the submission of evidence to a panel. Article 12.1 of the DSU directs a panel to follow the Working Procedures set out in Appendix 3 of the DSU, but at the same time authorizes a panel to do otherwise after consulting the parties to the dispute. The Working Procedures in Appendix 3 also do not establish precise deadlines for the presentation of evidence by a party to the dispute. It is true that the Working Procedures 'do not prohibit' submission of additional evidence after the first substantive meeting of a panel with the parties.[569]

The Appellate Body recognised that the DSU clearly contemplates two distinguishable stages in panel proceedings: a first stage during which the parties should set out their case in chief, including a full presentation of the facts on the basis of submission of supporting evidence; and a second stage which is generally designed to permit 'rebuttals' by each party of the arguments and evidence submitted by the other party.[570] Nevertheless, unless specific deadlines for the submission of evidence are set out in the *ad hoc* working procedures of the panel, parties can submit new evidence as late as the second meeting with the panel.[571] The panel must, of course, always be careful to observe due process

---

[568] In *US – Upland Cotton*, the Panel agreed to provide a certain Panel communication to the third parties, 'in order to enable them to participate, as necessary and appropriate, in any second session of the first substantive meeting in a full and meaningful fashion'. While it denied the European Communities' two requests for additional third party rights, it 'directed the parties to the dispute to make best efforts to ensure that their submissions to any second session of the first meeting were understandable either on their own or in conjunction with the submissions to the first session of the meeting'. See Panel Report, *US – Upland Cotton*, paras. 7.11–7.13.

[569] See Appellate Body Report, *Argentina – Textiles and Apparel*, para. 79. See also Panel Report, *Canada – Aircraft*, paras. 9.75–9.78.

[570] See Appellate Body Report, *Argentina – Textiles and Apparel*, para. 79. See also Panel Report, *Korea – Commercial Vessels*, paras. 7.277–7.279.

[571] In *EC – Selected Customs Matters*, the Appellate Body upheld the Panel's decision to exclude evidence contained in exhibits provided by the European Communities at the interim review stage. The Appellate Body noted that: 'the interim review stage is not an appropriate time to introduce new evidence'. Appellate Body Report, *EC – Selected Customs Matters*, paras. 248, 250 and 259. See also Panel Reports, *EC – Approval and Marketing of Biotech Products*, paras. 6.134 and 6.162–6.164. However, note that the Panel in *US – Anti-Dumping Measures on Oil Country Tubular Goods* saw 'no harm' in accepting a letter from the United States drawing the Panel's attention to the Appellate Body Report in *US – Gambling*, circulated after the interim report was issued. See Panel Reports, *US – Anti-Dumping Measures on Oil Country Tubular Goods*, paras. 7.24–7.25.

which, *inter alia*, entails providing the parties with adequate opportunity to respond to the evidence submitted.[572] Most panels now have *ad hoc* working procedures that set out precise deadlines for the submission of evidence.[573]

With regard to temporal limitations on the evidence submitted, the Appellate Body ruled in *EC – Customs Matters* that while there are temporal limitations on the measures that may be within a panel's terms of reference, 'such limitations do not apply in the same way to evidence'. The Appellate Body found that '[e]vidence in support of a claim challenging measures that are within a panel's terms of reference may pre-date or post-date the establishment of the panel'.[574]

The Panel in *EC – Trademarks and Geographical Indications* (Australia) rejected a request by Australia to exclude certain evidence submitted by the European Communities on the grounds that it is not 'relevant'. The Panel ruled that this evidence 'form[s] part of the respondent's submission', and '[t]o the extent that [it] lack[s] evidentiary worth, [it] will suffer from that defect and the Panel will disregard [it]'.[575]

Questions and Assignments 3.37

Can parties submit new evidence to the panel at any stage of the panel proceedings?

3.4.2.5. *Use of experts*

Disputes brought to panels for adjudication often involve complex factual, technical and scientific issues. These issues frequently play a central role in WTO dispute settlement proceedings. Article 13 of the DSU gives a panel the authority to seek information and technical advice from any individual or body which it deems appropriate.[576] Panels may consult experts to obtain their opinion on certain aspects of the matter under consideration. As the Appellate Body ruled in *Argentina – Textiles and Apparel*, '[t]his is a grant of discretionary authority'.[577] In *US – Shrimp*, the Appellate Body further stated:

---

[572] Appellate Body Report, *Argentina – Textiles and Apparel*, paras. 80–1; and Appellate Body Report, *Australia – Salmon*, para. 272.

[573] Under these rules, the submission of evidence after the deadline will nevertheless be allowed when there is 'good cause' to do so. The Panel in *US – Offset Act (Byrd Amendment)* accepted evidence submitted after the deadline, stating that 'good cause' for acceptance existed. See Panel Report, *US – Offset Act (Byrd Amendment)*, para. 7.2.

[574] Appellate Body Report, *EC – Selected Customs Matters*, paras. 177–89 and 249–54. See also Panel Report, *Japan – Apples*, paras. 8.55–8.56.

[575] Panel Report, *EC – Trademarks and Geographical Indications (Ausrtalia)*, paras. 7.83–7.84. See also Panel Report, *Japan – Apples*, paras. 8.55–8.56.

[576] In addition to Article 13 of the DSU, panels have either the possibility or the obligation to consult experts under a number of other covered agreements: see Article XV:2 of the GATT 1994; Article 11.2 of the *SPS Agreement*; Articles 14.2 and 14.3 of the *TBT Agreement*; Articles 19.3 and 19.4 of, and Annex II to, the *Agreement on Customs Valuation*; and Articles 4.5 and 24.3 of the *SCM Agreement*.

[577] Appellate Body Report, *Argentina – Textiles and Apparel*, para. 84. This case concerned the question whether the Panel was obliged to consult the IMF with regard to Argentina's imposition of import surcharges. The Appellate Body noted that the only provision that *requires* consultation of the IMF is Article XV:2 of the GATT (dealing with problems of monetary reserves, balances of payments or foreign exchange arrangements).

> a panel . . . has the authority to *accept or reject* any information or advice which it may have sought and received, or to *make some other appropriate disposition* thereof. It is particularly within the province and the authority of a panel to determine the *need for information and advice* in a specific case, to ascertain the *acceptability* and *relevancy* of information or advice received, and to decide *what weight to ascribe to that information or advice* or to conclude that no weight at all should be given to what has been received.[578]

This authority is 'indispensably necessary' to enable a panel to discharge its duty under Article 11 of the DSU to 'make an objective assessment of the matter before it'.[579]

To date, panels have consulted experts in, for example, *EC – Hormones*, *Australia – Salmon*, *Japan – Agricultural Products II*, *EC – Asbestos*, *Japan – Apples* and *EC – Approval and Marketing of Biotech Products*, which were all disputes involving complex scientific issues. In these cases, the panels typically selected the experts in consultation with the parties; presented the experts with a list of questions to which each expert individually responded in writing; and finally called a special meeting with the experts at which these and other questions were discussed with the panellists and the parties. The panel report usually contained both the written responses of the experts to the panel's questions as well as a transcript of the discussions at the meeting with the panel. However, confidential information which is provided must not be revealed without formal authorisation from the individual, body or authorities of the Member providing the information.

Under Article 13 of the DSU, a panel may not only consult individual experts and scientists; it may also consult specialised international organisations.[580] In *EC – Approval and Marketing of Biotech Products*, the Panel sought information from the Secretariat of the Convention on Biological Diversity, the Codex Alimentarius Commission, the Food and Agriculture Organization, the International Plant Protection Convention, the International Organization for Epizootics, the UN Environment Programme and the World Health Organization.[581] In *EC – Chicken Cuts*, the Panel sought information from the World Customs Organization.[582] In *Dominican Republic – Import and Sale of Cigarettes*, the Panel consulted with the International Monetary Fund[583] and in *EC – Trademarks and Geographical Indications*, the Panel requested the World Intellectual Property Organization for 'assistance in the form of any factual information available to it relevant to the interpretation of certain provisions of the *Paris Convention for the Protection of Industrial Property*'.[584]

Apart from consulting individual experts and international organisations, a panel can, with respect to a factual issue concerning a scientific or other technical

---

[578] Appellate Body Report, *US – Shrimp*, para. 104.   [579] *Ibid.*, para. 106.
[580] Such consultations of specialised international organisations are also possible under the other legal bases for consultations listed in footnote 576.
[581] See Panel Reports, *EC – Approval and Marketing of Biotech Products,* paras. 7.19 and 7.31–7.32.
[582] See Panel Report, *EC – Chicken Cuts*, paras. 7.52–7.53 (complaint by Brazil) and paras. 7.52–7.53 (complaint by Thailand).
[583] See Panel Report, *Dominican Republic – Import and Sale of Cigarettes*, paras. 1.8 and 7.138–7.154.
[584] Panel Report, *EC – Trademarks and Geographical Indications*, paras. 2. 16–2.18 (complaint by Australia) and paras. 2.16–2.18 (complaint by the US).

matter, request a report in writing from an expert review group.[585] Rules for the establishment of such a group and its procedures are set forth in Appendix 4 to the DSU. Expert review groups are under the authority of the panel and report to the panel. The panel decides their terms of reference. The report of an expert review group is advisory only; it does not bind the panel. To date, panels have made no use of this possibility to request an advisory report from an expert review group. Panels have preferred to seek information from experts directly and on an individual basis.[586]

It should be noted that, while a panel has broad authority to consult experts to help it to understand and evaluate the evidence submitted and the arguments made by the parties, a panel may not – with the help of its experts – make the case for one or the other party. In *Japan – Agricultural Products II*, the Appellate Body held:

> Article 13 of the DSU and Article 11.2 of the *SPS Agreement* suggest that panels have a significant investigative authority. However, this authority cannot be used by a panel to rule in favour of a complaining party which has not established a *prima facie* case of inconsistency based on specific legal claims asserted by it. A panel is entitled to seek information and advice from experts and from any other relevant source it chooses, pursuant to Article 13 of the DSU and, in an SPS case, Article 11.2 of the *SPS Agreement*, to *help it to understand and evaluate the evidence* submitted and the arguments made by the parties, but not to make the case for a complaining party.[587]
>
> [Emphasis added]

In *Japan – Apples*, Japan referred to this finding by the Appellate Body to challenge on appeal the Panel's use of experts. Japan argued that the US had not made claims or submitted evidence in respect of the risk of transmission of fire blight by apples other than mature symptomless apples, yet the Panel had made findings of fact with regard to these 'other' apples. Japan claimed that the Panel had thus exceeded the bounds of its investigative authority. The Appellate Body rejected Japan's argument, finding that the Panel had acted within the limits of its investigative authority, as:

> it did nothing more than assess the relevant allegations of fact asserted by Japan, in the light of the evidence submitted by the parties and the opinions of the experts.[588]

It thus clarified that a panel may use the evidence of its experts to assist it in assessing not only the claims of the complaining Member, but also the allegations of the responding Member. In doing so, it cannot be said to be exceeding its authority.

---

[585] See Article 13.2 of the DSU.
[586] The DSU also leaves it to the sound discretion of a panel to determine whether the establishment of an expert review group is necessary or appropriate. See Appellate Body Report, *EC – Hormones*, para. 147.
[587] Appellate Body Report, *Japan – Agricultural Products II*, para. 129. In *Japan – Agricultural Products II*, the Panel was correct to seek information and advice from experts to help it to understand and evaluate the evidence submitted and the arguments made by the United States and Japan with regard to the alleged violation of Article 5.6 of the *SPS Agreement*. The Panel erred, however, when it used that expert information and advice as the basis for a finding of inconsistency with Article 5.6 based on claims relating to the 'determination of sorption levels', since the United States did not establish a *prima facie* case of inconsistency with Article 5.6 based on such claims. The United States did not even argue that the 'determination of sorption levels' is an alternative measure which meets the three elements under Article 5.6. See Appellate Body Report, *Japan – Agricultural Products II*, para. 130. See further Appellate Body Report, *Japan – Apples*, para. 158.   [588] Appellate Body Report, *Japan – Apples*, para. 158.

Questions and Assignments 3.38

When can panels make use of experts? Which experts may panels consult? Who selects the experts? Do panels have broad investigative authority? What are the limits of this authority? Find in a panel report a section dealing with the testimony and questioning of experts.

3.4.2.6. *Protection of confidential business information*

As mentioned above, panel proceedings are confidential. However, the Panels in *Canada – Aircraft* and *Brazil – Aircraft* considered that parties had a legitimate interest in additional protection for sensitive business information submitted to the Panels. Thus, special procedures governing this information were adopted.[589] Under the Procedures Governing Business Confidential Information adopted by the Panel in *Canada – Aircraft*, the confidential business information was to be stored in a safe in a locked room at the premises of the relevant Geneva missions, with restrictions imposed on access. The Procedures also provided for either party to visit the other party's Geneva mission and review the proposed location of the safe and suggest any changes. Finally, the Procedures adopted by the Panel in *Canada – Aircraft* provided for the return or the destruction of the confidential business information after completion of the panel process. In spite of these Procedures, Canada refused to submit certain confidential business information because they did not, according to Canada, provide the requisite level of protection.[590]

While panels are willing to provide additional protection of business confidential information, the Panel in *Canada – Dairy (Article 21.5 – New Zealand and United States)* made it clear that the party invoking procedures governing business confidential information must at least explain to the Panel the nature of the information it seeks to protect and justify the insufficiency of the standard confidentiality requirements.[591] Also note that the party that has concerns about the protection of business confidential information must *request* the panel to adopt special procedures to handle such information. In other words, parties cannot just invoke the business confidential nature of certain information as a 'justification' for not submitting the information without having at least requested the panel to adopt special procedures. In *Turkey – Rice*, Turkish officials informed the Panel that they '[did] not feel comfortable in risking information leaks and possible criminal accusations of violation of Turkish law on confidentiality'.[592] The Panel noted, however, that Turkey neither requested the adoption of special procedures for handling confidential information through the Panel proceedings, nor was there such a request from Turkey after the complainant, the United States, suggested this possibility.[593]

---

[589] See Panel Report, *Canada – Aircraft*, Annex 1; and Panel Report, *Brazil – Aircraft*, Annex 1.
[590] On the consequences of such a refusal to submit information requested by the Panel, see above, p. 278.
[591] See Panel Report, *Canada – Dairy (Article 21.5 – New Zealand and United States)*, paras. 2.20–2.21.
[592] Panel Report, *Turkey – Rice*, para. 7.92.   [593] See *ibid.*, para. 7.103.

The protection of business confidential information has been – or currently is – an important issue in, *inter alia, EC – Approval and Marketing of Biotech Products, EC – Export Subsidies on Sugar, Korea – Commercial Vessels, Canada – Wheat Exports and Grain Imports, EC – Tube or Pipe Fittings, US – Large Civil Aircraft* and *EC and Certain Member States – Large Civil Aircraft*.[594]

Questions and Assignments 3.39

Which documents are confidential in panel proceedings? Describe the additional procedures adopted by the Panel in *EC and Certain Member States – Large Civil Aircraft* to protect confidential business information. In your opinion, is there a need for such procedures?

3.4.2.7. *Panel deliberations and interim review*

As with a court or tribunal, panel deliberations are confidential.[595] The reports of panels are drafted without the presence of the parties to the dispute; they are drafted in the light of the information provided and the statements made during the proceedings.[596]

Having completed a draft of the descriptive (i.e. facts and argument) sections of its report, the panel issues this draft to the parties for their comments.[597] Following the expiration of the time period for comments, the panel subsequently issues an interim report to the parties, including both the descriptive sections and the panel's findings and conclusions.[598] A party may submit a written request to the panel to review particular aspects of the interim report. At the request of a party, the panel may hold a further meeting with the parties on the issues identified in the written comments.[599] The final panel report must include a discussion of the arguments made at the interim review stage.[600]

The comments made by the parties at the interim review stage frequently give rise to corrections of technical errors or unclear drafting. Until recently panels seldom changed the conclusions reached in their reports in any substantive way as a result of the comments made by parties. In a few recent cases, however, the panel did alter its conclusions in the light of comments made by the parties.

In *EC – Approval and Marketing of Biotech Products*, the Panel had found in its interim report that the European Communities' general moratorium on the approval of biotech products had ceased to exist and therefore declined to make any recommendations on this issue. In its final report, however, the Panel

---

[594] See e.g. Panel Reports, *EC – Approval and Marketing of Biotech Products*, paras. 6.179–6.182; Panel Report, *EC – Export Subsidies on Sugar*, paras. 2.10–2.19; Panel Report, *Korea – Commercial Vessels*, paras. 1.15–1.17; Panel Reports, *Canada – Wheat Exports and Grain Imports*, paras. 6.8–6.9; and Panel Report, *EC – Tube or Pipe Fittings*, para. 7.45.   [595] See Article 14.1 of the DSU.   [596] See Article 14.2 of the DSU.

[597] See Article 15.1 of the DSU. Note that recently some panels attached the submissions, the written versions of oral statements and answers to questions to their report, rather than include a summary of these documents in the descriptive sections of the report. See e.g. Panel Report, *US – Lead and Bismuth II*. See also above, pp. 254–6.   [598] See Article 15.2 of the DSU.   [599] See *ibid.*

[600] See Article 15.3 of the DSU. If no comments are received from any party within the comment period, the interim report shall be considered the final panel report. See Article 15.3 of the DSU.

declined to rule on whether the moratorium had ceased to exist or not. The Panel followed the arguments of the United States made at the interim review stage that the question of whether the moratorium had ceased to exist *after* the date of establishment of the Panel was outside the Panel's terms of reference.[601]

In *Korea – Certain Paper*, the Panel revisited some of its findings and conclusions and made additional substantive findings which were absent in its interim report in response to comments received from Indonesia during the interim review process.[602] Also in *US – Carbon Steel*, the Panel revisited substantive findings in response to comments made by the United States during the interim review process.[603] In the light of these developments, disregard for the confidentiality of the interim report is a matter of systemic concern. In a letter from the Chairman of the Panel in *EC – Approval and Marketing of Biotech Products* to the Chairman of the DSB, the Panel sharply criticised two NGOs, Friends of the Earth Europe and the Institute of Agriculture and Trade Policy, for having posted the interim report on their websites. It is clear that the interim report in this case was leaked in order to bring political pressure to bear on the Panel during the interim review process.[604]

Interim review is an unusual feature in judicial or quasi-judicial dispute settlement procedures. The need for and utility of this interim review procedure has been the subject of debate.

Questions and Assignments 3.40

In your opinion, is interim review of panel reports useful and/or appropriate in the current WTO dispute settlement system? Discuss the importance of the confidentiality of the interim report.

3.4.2.8. Adoption or appeal of the panel report

The final panel report is first issued to the parties to the dispute, and some weeks later, once the report is available in the three working languages of the WTO, it is circulated to the general WTO membership. Once circulated to WTO Members, the panel report is an unrestricted document available to the public. On the day of its circulation, a panel report is posted on the WTO's website as a WT/DS document. Panel reports are also included in the official WTO *Dispute Settlement Reports*, published by Cambridge University Press.

Within sixty days after the date of circulation of the panel report to the Members, the report is adopted at a DSB meeting unless:

- a party to the dispute formally notifies the DSB of its decision to appeal; or

---

[601] Eventually, the Panel made the qualified recommendation that the European Communities bring the general moratorium into line with the *SPS Agreement*, 'if, and to the extent that, that measure has not already ceased to exist'. Panel Reports, *EC – Approval and Marketing of Biotech Products*, para. 8.18 (with regard to the US complaint) and para. 8.36 (with regard to the Canadian complaint).
[602] See Panel Report, *Korea – Certain Paper*, paras. 6.3–6.5 and 7.106–7.112.
[603] See Panel Report, *US – Carbon Steel*, paras. 7.24 and 8.120–8.145.   [604] See also above, p. 213.

- the DSB decides by consensus not to adopt the report.[605]

If a panel report is appealed, it is not discussed by the DSB until the appellate review proceedings are completed and the Appellate Body report – together with the panel report – comes before the DSB for adoption.

When the DSB does consider and debate a panel report, all Members have the right to comment on the report. In order to provide sufficient time for the Members to review panel reports, the reports shall not be considered for adoption by the DSB until twenty days after they have been circulated. The parties have the right to participate fully in the consideration of panel reports by the DSB, and their views shall be fully recorded.[606]

Questions and Assignments 3.41

Is a panel report that is appealed, considered by the DSB for adoption? Do parties have an opportunity to comment on a panel report prior to its adoption by the DSB? Within what period can and must a panel report be adopted or rejected by the DSB? Can the adoption of a panel report be blocked? Look up what Members had to say on the Panel report in *US – Shrimp*.

3.4.2.9. Duration of panel proceedings

The period in which a panel must conduct its examination, from the date that the composition and terms of reference of the panel have been agreed upon until the date the final report is issued to the parties, shall, as a general rule, not exceed six months.[607] When a panel considers that it cannot issue its report within six months, it shall inform the DSB in writing of the reasons for the delay, together with an estimate of the period within which it will issue its report. In no case should the period from the establishment of the panel to the circulation of the report to the Members exceed nine months.[608]

---

[605] See Article 16.4 of the DSU. Interestingly, in a couple of cases, the parties to a dispute have reached a procedural agreement to request the DSB to extend the sixty-day deadline for the adoption or appeal of a panel report to take account of holiday periods that could cause scheduling difficulties in the appeal procedure. The DSB has granted such requests. For example, in *EC – Export Subsidies on Sugar*, Australia, Brazil, Thailand and the European Communities jointly requested the DSB to extend the period for the adoption or appeal of the Panel Report in order to take account of the end of year period, and to avoid inconveniencing the appeal procedure. See WT/DS265/24; WT/DS266/24 and WT/DS283/5. Similarly, in *Brazil – Retreaded Tyres*, at the joint request of the parties to the dispute, Brazil and the European Communities, due to scheduling difficulties regarding the appeal procedure, the DSB agreed to extend the deadline for the adoption or appeal of the Panel Report. See WT/DS332/8 and www.wto.org/english/news_e/news07_e/dsb_10aug07_e.htm, visited on 13 August 2007.

[606] See Articles 16.1 and 16.3 of the DSU.

[607] See Article 12.8 of the DSU. In cases of urgency, including those relating to perishable goods, the panel aims to issue its report to the parties within three months and makes every effort to accelerate the proceedings to the greatest extent possible. See Articles 12.9 and 4.9 of the DSU. In *Canada – Patent Term*, the Panel was unable to accelerate the proceedings as requested by the US under Article 4.9 of the DSU, due to scheduling problems among the panellists. However, with Canada's consent, it limited the schedule to the minimum periods suggested in Appendix 3 of the DSU, and 'undertook to make every effort to issue its report as soon as possible after the second substantive meeting'. Panel Report, *Canada – Patent Term*, para. 1.5.   [608] See Article 12.9 of the DSU.

In practice, however, the panel process often exceeds this time limit. On average, a panel process – from the establishment of the panel until the circulation of the panel report – lasts 404 days.[609] The reasons for exceeding the nine-month time limit include: the complexity of the case; the need to consult experts; the availability of experts; problems with scheduling meetings; and the time taken to translate the report. The longest panel proceeding to date has been that in *EC – Approval and Marketing of Biotech Products*, which lasted 1,127 days.[610]

Note that, at the request of the complaining party, the panel may, at any time during the panel proceedings, suspend its work for a maximum period of twelve months.[611] While not common, this does happen occasionally.[612] The authority of the panel lapses if the work of the panel is suspended for more than twelve months.[613]

Questions and Assignments 3.42

Describe the various steps in panel proceedings. Do you consider the rules on the duration of panel proceedings too strict or too liberal? Can panel proceedings be suspended indefinitely?

3.4.3. Appellate review

Almost 70 per cent of the panel reports circulated to date were appealed to the Appellate Body.[614] This section discusses key aspects of the appellate review proceedings and issues that arise with respect to these proceedings:

- working procedures for appellate review;

---

[609] See www.worldtradelaw.net/dsc/database/paneltiming.asp, visited on 24 November 2007. The period between the establishment of the panel and the adoption of the panel report by the DSB (in cases where there is no appeal) is on average 462 days. See www.worldtradelaw.net/dsc/database/adoptiontiming1.asp, visited on 24 November 2007.

[610] See www.worldtradelaw.net/dsc/database/adoptiontiming1.asp, visited on 24 November 2007. The exceptionally long delay in this case was an issue of systemic concern raised by the Chairman of the Panel in his communication to the Chairman of the DSB. He explained that the delay was due to the unprecedented number of claims in this dispute, and the immense record before the Panel. Other factors mentioned by the Chairman were the EC's delays in submitting information, the procedural and substantive complexity of the case, the lengthy procedure to select experts to advise the Panel, and the reduced availability of Secretariat staff because of the Hong Kong Ministerial Conference preparations. The Chairman concluded that 'this quite simply means that panels are unable to complete proceedings concerning such disputes within the 6–9 month timeframe laid down in Article 12.9 of the DSU, without additional resources being made available to the Secretariat for this purpose'. Communication from the Chairman of the Panel, *EC – Approval and Marketing of Biotech Products*, WT/DS291/32, WT/DS292/26 and WT/DS293/26, dated 29 September 2006, para. 1.   [611] See Article 12.12 of the DSU.

[612] See e.g. Panel Report, *EC – Butter*, para. 12, in which New Zealand requested the Panel to suspend its work. See also *India – Wines and Spirits*, in which the European Communities requested the Panel to suspend its work after India had agreed to remove a series of taxes on wines and spirits. See Communication from the Chairman of the Panel, *India – Wines and Spirits*, WT/DS352/6, 17 July 2007. The European Commission has reportedly stated that during the suspension period it will 'continue to monitor the situation on the ground to make sure that no new discriminations appear at state level'. See *BRIDGES Weekly Trade News Digest*, 25 July 2007.

[613] The authority of the panel lapsed in, for example, *US – The Cuban Liberty and Democratic Solidarity Act (Helms–Burton Act)*, complaint by the EC. Note that it is for the complainant to request the panel to resume its work.

[614] On 24 November 2007, exact percentage of panel reports appealed was 67.65 per cent. See www.worldtradelaw.net/dsc/database/appealcount.asp, visited on 24 November 2007.

- initiation of appellate review;
- withdrawal of an appeal;
- written submissions and the oral hearing;
- rights of third participants;
- exchange of views, deliberations and the adoption of the Appellate Body report; and
- duration of appellate review proceedings.

3.4.3.1. Working procedures for appellate review

In contrast to panels, the Appellate Body has detailed standard working procedures set out in the *Working Procedures for Appellate Review* (the 'Working Procedures').[615] Pursuant to Article 17.9 of the DSU, these *Working Procedures* were drawn up by the Appellate Body itself, in consultation with the Chairman of the DSB and the WTO Director-General. In addition, where a procedural question arises that is not covered by the *Working Procedures*, the division hearing the appeal may, 'in the interest of fairness and orderly procedure in the conduct of the appeal', adopt an appropriate procedure for the purpose of that appeal.[616] The Additional Procedure adopted in the context of the *EC – Asbestos* case in respect of the filing of *amicus curiae* briefs, partially quoted and discussed above, is the best-known example of the use of this authority.[617]

Questions and Assignments 3.43

How are the *Working Procedures for Appellate Review* established? What can a division hearing an appeal do when a procedural question arises that is not covered by the *Working Procedures*?

3.4.3.2. Initiation of appellate review

Pursuant to Rule 20(1) of the *Working Procedures*, appellate review proceedings commence with a party's notification in writing to the DSB of its decision to appeal *and* the simultaneous filing of a notice of appeal with the Appellate Body. The notice of appeal must adequately identify the findings or legal interpretations of the panel which are being appealed as erroneous. In addition to the title of the panel report under appeal, the name of the appellant and the service address, Rule 20(2)(d) states that a notice of appeal will include:

> (i) identification of the alleged errors in the issues of law covered in the panel report and legal interpretations developed by the panel;

---

[615] *Working Procedures for Appellate Review*, WT/AB/WP/W/9, dated 7 October 2004. This is a consolidated, revised version of the original *Working Procedures for Appellate Review*, WT/AB/WP/1, dated 15 February 1996.
[616] Rule 16(1) of the *Working Procedures*. Such procedure must, however, be consistent with the DSU, the other covered agreements and the *Working Procedures*.
[617] See above, p. 193. See also Appellate Body Report, *US – Lead and Bismuth II*, footnote 33 to para. 39.

> (ii) a list of the legal provision(s) of the covered agreements that the panel is alleged to have erred in interpreting or applying; and
>
> (iii) without prejudice to the ability of the appellant to refer to other paragraphs of the panel report in the context of its appeal, an indicative list of the paragraphs of the panel report containing the alleged errors.[618]

In *US – Certain EC Products*, the Appellate Body ruled with respect to this requirement:

> [O]ur previous rulings have underscored the important balance that must be maintained between the right of Members to exercise the right of appeal meaningfully and effectively, and the right of appellees to receive notice through the Notice of Appeal of the findings under appeal, so that they may exercise their right of defence effectively . . . The additional requirements under Rule 20(2) serve to ensure that the appellee also receives notice, albeit brief, of the 'nature of the appeal' and the 'allegations of errors' by the panel.[619]

The underlying rationale of Rule 20(2)(d) is thus to require the appellant to provide notice of the alleged error that the appellant intends to argue on appeal.[620] The notice of appeal is not expected to contain the reasons why the appellant regards those findings or interpretations as erroneous.[621] Citing the relevant parts of the challenged panel report and basing claims on specifically identified legal provisions is sufficient to indicate the 'nature of the appeal' to which the other party must respond.[622] In *EC – Export Subsidies on Sugar*, Australia contended that the Notice of Appeal of the European Communities did not satisfy the 'due process requirements' of Rule 20(2)(d) of the *Working Procedures*. The Appellate Body noted, however, that:

> In its Notice of Appeal, the European Communities 'seeks review' of six 'conclusion[s]' and 'related legal findings and interpretations' set out in certain specified paragraphs of the Panel Reports. The European Communities summarizes the substance of each contested conclusion and the related legal findings and interpretations. The Notice of Appeal also contains a list of the legal provisions of the covered agreements that the Panel is alleged to have erred in interpreting or applying. In our view, the Notice of Appeal gives adequate notice to the Complaining Parties of the content of its appeal so as to allow them to make a proper defence, as required by Rule 20(2)(d) of the *Working Procedures*.[623]

---

[618] Rule 20(2)(d) of the *Working Procedures* was amended in 2004 and has been in force as quoted here since 1 January 2005. For case law on the scope of this requirement as in force before 2005, see Appellate Body Report, *US – Shrimp*, paras. 92–7; and Appellate Body Report, *EC – Bananas III*, paras. 151–2. Note that Rule 23 *bis* of the *Working Procedures* provides for the possibility of amending a notice of appeal, if authorised by the division.

[619] Appellate Body Report, *US – Certain EC Products*, para. 62. Note that the requirements of Rule 20(2) discussed by the Appellate Body in *US – Certain EC Products* were still less specific and detailed than the requirements introduced per 1 January 2005 and quoted above. The Appellate Body's statement on the purpose of Rule 20(2) remains, however, valid.

[620] See Appellate Body Report, *US – Offset Act (Byrd Amendment)*, para. 195.

[621] The legal arguments in support of the allegations of error are to be set out and developed in the appellant's submission. See Appellate Body Report, *US – Shrimp*, paras. 92–7; and Appellate Body Report, *EC – Bananas III*, paras. 148–52. Note the special situation of a claim that the panel has violated Article 11 of the DSU. See *US – Offset Act (Byrd Amendment)*, paras. 199–201.

[622] See Appellate Body Report, *US – DRAMS*, para. 97, and Appellate Body Report, *EC – Export Subsidies on Sugar*, para. 344. However, note that 'a Notice of Appeal that refers simply to the paragraph numbers found in the 'Conclusions and Recommendations' section of a panel report, or that quotes them in full, will be insufficient to provide adequate notice of the allegations of error on appeal, and, hence, will fall short of the requirements set out in Rule 20(2)(d)'. Appellate Body Report, *US – Certain EC Products*, para. 70.

[623] Appellate Body Report, *EC – Export Subsidies on Sugar*, para. 344.

The Appellate Body subsequently concluded that the Notice of Appeal of the European Communities in *EC – Export Subsidies on Sugar* satisfied the requirements of Rule 20(2)(d) of the *Working Procedures*.[624]

If the notice of appeal fails to give the appellee sufficient notice of a claim of error, that claim cannot and will not be considered by the Appellate Body.[625] In *US – Upland Cotton*, the Appellate Body found that the Notice of Appeal 'did not provide adequate notice' to Brazil, as contemplated by Rule 20(2) of the *Working Procedures*, that the United States intended to make a claim of error under Article 12.7 of the DSU with respect to certain of the Panel's findings. The Appellate Body, therefore, 'decline[d] to rule on these findings'.[626]

It is important that all claims intended to be made on appeal are *expressly* and *exhaustively* covered in the notice of appeal. In *US – Upland Cotton*, the Appellate Body held:

> We acknowledge that the wording . . . of the United States' Notice of Appeal (and, in particular, the use of the words 'for example') suggests that the findings listed . . . are simply *examples* of findings challenged . . . [being] an illustrative rather than exhaustive list of the findings that the United States intends to challenge. [A]n illustrative list is not conclusive as to whether the Notice of Appeal contains a sufficient reference to the Panel's findings . . . for us to conclude that these findings are included in the United States' appeal.[627]
>
> [Emphasis in original]

Note, however, that the Appellate Body, in *US – Offset Act (Byrd Amendment)*, held that the issue of a panel's jurisdiction is so

> fundamental that it is appropriate to consider claims that a panel has exceeded its jurisdiction even if such claims were not raised in the Notice of Appeal.[628]

In the interest of due process, it would of course be preferable for the appellant to raise such important issues in the notice of appeal. A party can appeal a panel report as soon as the report is circulated to WTO Members, and it can do so as long as the report has not yet been adopted by the DSB. In practice, parties usually appeal shortly before the meeting of the DSB that would consider the adoption of the report.

---

[624] See *ibid.*, para. 345.
[625] See e.g. Appellate Body Report, *US – Offset Act (Byrd Amendment)*, para. 206. A particular situation arises with regard to claims of error based on Article 11 of the DSU. A party wishing to raise an Article 11 violation, albeit dependent on another substantive claim which the Appellate Body must endorse, should still indicate in its notice of appeal that it wishes to raise an Article 11 argument, and, if so, in relation to which substantive claim(s). In *Japan – Apples*, the Appellate Body found that the appellee could not have been aware that the appellant intended to raise an Article 11 challenge with respect to certain findings of the Panel because the notice of appeal did not refer to Article 11 or to the 'objective assessment' standard with respect to these findings. The Appellate Body therefore concluded that the Article 11 claim of error was not reviewable in this appeal. See Appellate Body Report, *Japan – Apples*, paras. 120–8. See also Appellate Body Report, *Chile – Price Band System*, paras. 151–65. In *Chile – Price Band System*, another interesting issue arose concerning Chile's challenge of the 'order of analysis' that the Panel adopted on Argentina's arguments in the dispute. The Appellate Body held that the claim on the Panel's order of analysis did not amount to a *separate* 'allegation of error' which by itself could have had any legal basis. Rather, the order of analysis issue was a *legal argument* supporting other substantive claims in Chile's written submissions, and was not itself a *claim* that necessarily had to be included in the notice of appeal. See Appellate Body Report, *Chile – Price Band System*, para. 182.
[626] Appellate Body Report, *US – Upland Cotton*, paras. 494–5.
[627] Appellate Body Report, *US – Upland Cotton*, para. 495.
[628] Appellate Body Report, *US – Offset Act (Byrd Amendment)*, para. 208.

Upon the commencement of an appeal, the Appellate Body division responsible for deciding the appeal draws up an appropriate working schedule in accordance with the time periods stipulated in the *Working Procedures*.[629] The working schedule sets forth precise dates for the filing of documents and includes a timetable of the division's work.[630] In exceptional circumstances, where strict adherence to a time period would result in manifest unfairness, a party or third party to the dispute may request modification of that time period. This possibility is provided for in Rule 16(2) of the *Working Procedures* and has been used occasionally.[631]

If the other party to the dispute decides to 'cross appeal' pursuant to Rule 23 of the *Working Procedures*, it must file a 'notice of other appeal' within twelve days of the first notice. The notice of other appeal must meet the same requirements as the first notice.[632]

Questions and Assignments 3.44

How and when can an appellate review proceeding be initiated? At what point in time are appellate review proceedings most frequently initiated? When is a notice of appeal sufficiently precise?

3.4.3.3. Withdrawal of an appeal

A Member may not only initiate an appeal, it may – pursuant to Rule 30(1) of the *Working Procedures* – also withdraw that appeal at any stage of the appellate review process. Such a withdrawal leads normally to the termination of the appellate review. This was the case in *India–Autos*, where the Appellate Body issued, subsequent to the withdrawal, a brief report on the procedural history and the reason for not having completed its work due to India's withdrawal.[633]

However, in some cases, parties withdraw their appeals in order to submit new ones. This happened, for example, in *EC – Sardines*. In this case, Peru contended that the appeal of the European Communities was insufficiently clear. In response, the European Communities withdrew its appeal and filed a more detailed one. The Appellate Body rejected Peru's claim that the withdrawal of

---

[629] See Rule 26(1) of the *Working Procedures*. The Appellate Body Secretariat shall serve forthwith a copy of the working schedule on the appellant, the parties to the dispute and any third parties. See Rule 26(4) of the *Working Procedures*.

[630] See Rule 26(2) of the *Working Procedures*.

[631] Instances of extension have been where a Member has a deadline for written submission or a hearing in another WTO dispute, very close to the initial date set for filing of submissions (see Appellate Body Report, *Chile – Price Band System (Article 21.5 – Argentina)*, para. 11); where lead counsel for a party had prior commitments (see Appellate Body Report, *US – Softwood Lumber VI (Article 21.5 – Canada)*, para. 13); and where suspected bioterrorist attacks prevent internal consultations in legislative circles of a Member (see Appellate Body Report, *US – FSC (Article 21.5 – EC)*, para. 8). A hearing can also be brought forward if parties do not object (see Appellate Body Report, *US – Softwood Lumber V (Article 21.5 – Canada)*, footnote 29 to para. 9). While translation of documents is a valid ground for extension (see Appellate Body Report, *Guatemala – Cement I*, para. 4), it will not be unfair to decline a request for extension where documents requiring translation would be made available earlier than expected (see Appellate Body Report, *Mexico – Anti-Dumping Measures on Rice*, paras. 9–10).   [632] See Rule 23(2) of the *Working Procedures*.

[633] See Appellate Body Report, *India – Autos,* paras. 14–18

the European Communities' appeal was invalid and clarified that there was no indication in Rule 30 that the right of withdrawal only encompasses unconditional withdrawal. Conditions are allowed as long as they do not undermine the fair, prompt and effective resolution of the dispute and as long as the disputing party involved acts in good faith.[634]

In *US – Softwood Lumber IV*, the United States filed a notice of appeal on 2 October 2003 and withdrew this notice the following day 'for scheduling reasons'. The withdrawal was conditional upon the right to re-file the notice of appeal at a later date, and, on 21 October 2003, the United States re-filed a 'substantively identical' notice of appeal.[635] The Appellate Body ruled in this regard in *EC – Sardines*:

> While it is true that nothing in the text of Rule 30(1) explicitly permits an appellant to exercise its [Rule 30(1)] right subject to conditions, it is also true that nothing in the same text prohibits an appellant from doing so.[636]

The Appellate Body thus allows an appellant to attach conditions to the withdrawal of its notice of appeal, saving its right to file a replacement notice. This is permissible under Rule 30(1) of the *Working Procedures*. In *US – Line Pipe* and *US – FSC*, the Division and the appellees had prior knowledge of, and agreed to, the United States' reservation that it would file a fresh notice of appeal on withdrawing its initial notice under Rule 30(1).[637] However, as the Appellate Body ruled in *EC – Sardines*, such prior notice or agreement is not a precondition and a requirement for validity of every withdrawal and replacement.[638]

3.4.3.4. *Written submissions and the oral hearing*

Within seven days after filing the notice of appeal the appellant must file a written submission.[639] This written submission sets out a precise statement of the grounds of appeal, including the specific allegations of legal errors in the panel report, and the legal arguments in support of these allegations.[640] Within fifteen days of the filing of the notice of appeal, the parties to the dispute that have filed a notice of other appeal (before day 12) must file an 'other appellant's submission'.[641] Within twenty-five days of the filing of the notice of appeal, any

---

[634] See Appellate Body Report, *EC – Sardines*, para. 141.
[635] See Appellate Body Report, *US – Softwood Lumber IV*, para. 6.
[636] Appellate Body Report, *EC – Sardines*, para. 141. The Appellate Body continued, saying: 'Rule 30(1) permits conditional withdrawals, unless the condition imposed undermines the "fair, prompt and effective resolution of trade disputes", or unless the Member attaching the condition is not "engag[ing] in [dispute settlement] procedures in good faith in an effort to resolve the dispute".' Therefore, it is necessary to examine any such conditions attached to withdrawals on a case-by-case basis to determine whether, in fact, the particular condition in a particular case in any way obstructs the dispute settlement process, or in some way diminishes the rights of the appellee or other participants in the appeal. *Ibid.*
[637] See Appellate Body Report, *US – Line Pipe*, para. 13; and Appellate Body Report, *US – FSC*, para. 4.
[638] See Appellate Body Report, *EC – Sardines*, para. 138, footnote 31.
[639] See Rule 21(1) of the *Working Procedures*.
[640] See Rule 21(2) of the *Working Procedures*. The submission also includes the nature of the decision or ruling sought.
[641] See Rule 23(1) of the *Working Procedures*. Rule 23 *bis* of the *Working Procedures* further envisages the possibility of amending a notice of other appeal, if authorised by the division.

party that wishes to respond to allegations of legal errors, whether raised in the submission of the original appellant or in the submission(s) of other appellants, may file an appellee's submission.[642] The appellee's submission sets out a precise statement of the grounds for opposing the specific allegations of legal errors raised in the (other) appellant's submission and includes legal arguments in support thereof.[643] Should a participant fail to file a submission within the required time periods, the division, after hearing the views of the participants, issues such order, including dismissal of the appeal, as it deems appropriate.[644]

The division responsible for deciding the appeal holds an oral hearing. According to the *Working Procedures*, the oral hearing is, as a general rule, held between thirty-five and forty-five days after the notice of appeal is filed.[645] The purpose of the oral hearing is to provide participants with an opportunity to present and argue their case before the division, in order to clarify the legal issues in the appeal. At the hearing, the appellant(s) and appellee(s) first make brief oral presentations focusing on the core legal issues raised in the appeal.[646] After the oral presentations, the participants answer detailed questions posed by Members of the division regarding the issues raised in the appeal. At the end of the oral hearing, the participants are given the opportunity to make a brief concluding statement. The oral hearing is usually completed in one day. In complex cases, however, the oral hearing may take longer. In *EC – Bananas III* and *EC – Hormones*, for example, the oral hearing took two-and-a-half days and two days, respectively.

At any time during the appellate proceedings, the division may address questions to, or request additional memoranda from, any participant or third participant and specify the time periods by which written responses or memoranda shall be received.[647] Any such questions, responses or memoranda are made available simultaneously to the other participants and third participants in the appeal who are then given an opportunity to respond.[648] Neither the DSU nor any other covered agreement explicitly grants the Appellate Body the authority to appoint and consult experts. However, to the extent advice from experts

---

[642] See Rules 22(1) and 23(3) of the *Working Procedures*. Note that Rule 18(5) provides for the correction of clerical errors (such as 'typographical mistakes, errors of grammar, or words or numbers placed in the wrong order') in the documents submitted by parties and third parties. All other participants are given the right to respond in writing to the request and the division makes its decision thereafter. These requests for the correction of clerical errors are almost always granted. See e.g. Appellate Body Report, *EC – Export Subsidies on Sugar*, para. 10; Appellate Body Report, *EC – Chicken Cuts*, para. 11; Appellate Body Report, *EC – Selected Customs Matters*, para. 13; and Appellate Body Report, *US – Zeroing (Japan)*, para. 5. There have been cases where requests were allowed, when the other party to the dispute did not object, for corrections sought on matters not strictly clerical (see Appellate Body Report, *Mexico – Taxes on Soft Drinks*, para. 7), or after the thirty-day period for requesting corrections had expired (see Appellate Body Report, *US – Softwood Lumber VI (Article 21.5 – Canada)*, para. 15).

[643] For written submissions of third participants, see below, pp. 295–6.

[644] See Rule 29 of the *Working Procedures*. To date, there has been no need for such an order.

[645] See Rule 27(1) of the *Working Procedures*.

[646] See Rule 27(3) of the *Working Procedures*. Any third participant may also make an oral presentation and may be questioned at the oral hearing. See below, p. 296. The Presiding Member may, as necessary, set time limits for oral arguments. See Rule 27(4) of the *Working Procedures*. Typically, the appellant and appellee are given thirty minutes each and the third participants ten to fifteen minutes each for their oral arguments. Any time limit imposed is strictly enforced.

[647] See Rule 28(1) of the *Working Procedures*.

[648] See Rule 28(2) of the *Working Procedures*. See also Appellate Body Report, *US – Section 211 Appropriations Act*, para. 13.

would be necessary to comprehend better the arguments made by the participants and to decide the appeal, such authority is implied and cannot be denied to the Appellate Body.

Throughout the proceedings, the participants and third participants are precluded from having *ex parte* communications with the Appellate Body in respect of matters concerning the appeal. Neither a division nor any of its Members may meet with or contact a participant or third participant in the absence of the other participants and third participants.[649]

Questions and Assignments 3.45

Briefly describe the written submissions of the participants in appellate review proceedings. When does the Appellate Body meet with the participants in the appeal? Briefly describe the organisation of an oral hearing of the Appellate Body. Are *ex parte* communications with the Appellate Body allowed? Can the Appellate Body – like panels – consult experts? Can participants, and in particular developing-country participants, request additional time to prepare their written submissions in appellate review proceedings? Can an appeal be withdrawn in order to file a new appeal?

3.4.3.5. Rights of third participants

As discussed above, the rights of third parties in panel proceedings are limited. Normally, third parties only attend, and are heard at, a special session of the first substantive meeting of the panel, and receive the first written submissions of the parties only. Third participants, i.e. third parties participating in appellate review proceedings, have much broader rights.

In appellate review proceedings, all third parties have a right to file a written submission, within twenty-five days of the date of the filing of the notice of appeal, containing the grounds and legal arguments in support of their position.[650] A third party has the right to participate in the oral hearing when:

- it has filed a written submission; or
- it has notified the Appellate Body Secretariat of its intention to participate in the oral hearing within twenty-five days of the notice of appeal.[651]

A third party that has neither filed a written submission nor notified its intention to participate in the oral hearing within twenty-five days may still participate in

---

[649] See Article 18.1 of the DSU and Rule 19(1) of the *Working Procedures*. Also, a Member of the Appellate Body who is not assigned to the division hearing the appeal shall not discuss any aspect of the subject matter of the appeal with any participant or third participant (Rule 19(3) of the *Working Procedures*).

[650] See Rule 24(1) of the *Working Procedures*. A third party may not seek extension of time for filing submissions when the same would significantly reduce the time the division would have to consider the arguments of the parties: see Appellate Body Report, *US – Softwood Lumber IV*, para. 7, or where exceptional circumstances do not exist see Appellate Body Report, *EC – Bananas III*, para. 4.

[651] See Rule 27(2) of the *Working Procedures*. Third participants are encouraged to file written submissions to facilitate their positions being taken into account. See Rule 24(3) of the *Working Procedures*.

the oral hearing. It may, at the discretion of the division and taking into account the requirements of due process, be allowed to make an oral statement at the hearing and respond to questions asked by the division.[652]

Questions and Assignments 3.46

Compare the rights of third parties in panel proceedings with the rights of third participants in appellate review proceedings.

3.4.3.6. *Exchange of views, deliberations and the adoption of the report*

As noted above, the division responsible for deciding an appeal will exchange views on issues raised by the appeal with the other Members of the Appellate Body, before finalising its report.[653] The exchange of views puts into practice the principle of collegiality set out in the *Working Procedures*.[654] Depending on the number and complexity of the issues under discussion, this process usually takes place over two or more days.

Following the exchange of views, the division continues its deliberations and drafts the report. When finalised, the report is signed by the three Members of the division. The report is then translated so that it is available in all three languages of the WTO.[655] After translation, the report is circulated to the WTO Members as an unrestricted document available to the public. The Appellate Body report is posted on the WTO website as a WT/DS document.

Within thirty days following circulation of the Appellate Body report, the Appellate Body report *and* the panel report as upheld, modified or reversed by the Appellate Body are adopted by the DSB *unless* the DSB decides by consensus not to adopt the reports.[656] The adopted Appellate Body report must be accepted unconditionally by the parties to the dispute. The adoption procedure is, however, without prejudice to the right of Members to express their views on an Appellate Body report.[657] WTO Members often take full advantage of this opportunity to comment on the reports at the meeting of the DSB at which they are adopted. Generally, the winning party briefly praises the Appellate Body (and the panel) while the losing party is more critical, often repeating the arguments submitted to, but rejected by, the Appellate Body (and the panel). The views of WTO Members on the Appellate Body report (and the panel report) are fully recorded in the minutes of the DSB meeting.

---

[652] See Rule 27(3)(b) and (c) of the *Working Procedures*.   [653] See above, p. 260.
[654] See Rule 4 of the *Working Procedures*.
[655] During the period 1995–2007, in all appellate review proceedings English has been the working language of the Appellate Body, and the Appellate Body reports were all drafted in English and then translated into French and Spanish. In a few appellate review proceedings, participants or third participants filed submissions or made oral statements in French or Spanish. When requested, interpretation is provided at the oral hearing.
[656] See Article 17.14 of the DSU. On the reverse consensus requirement, see above, pp. 236–7.
[657] See *ibid*.

Questions and Assignments 3.47

When is an Appellate Body report considered by the DSB for adoption? Is a panel report that has been reversed by the Appellate Body adopted by the DSB? Look up what Members had to say at the time of DSB adoption of the Appellate Body and panel reports in *US – Shrimp*.

3.4.3.7. Duration of appellate review proceedings

With regard to the appellate review proceedings, the DSU provides that, as a general rule, the proceedings shall not exceed sixty days from the date a party to the dispute formally notifies its decision to appeal to the date the Appellate Body circulates its report.[658] When the Appellate Body believes that it cannot render its report within sixty days, it shall inform the DSB in writing of the reasons for the delay together with an estimate of the period within which it will submit its report. In no case shall the proceedings exceed ninety days.[659] In practice, the Appellate Body has, in most cases, taken more than sixty days to complete the appellate review.[660] In all but seven cases, however, the Appellate Body has been able to complete the proceedings within the ninety-day time limit.[661] The reasons for the delay in the appellate review proceedings included the complexity of the appeal, an overload of work, a delay in translation of the submissions or the report, and the death of an Appellate Body Member hearing the appeal.[662]

Questions and Assignments 3.48

Describe the various steps in appellate review proceedings. Do you consider the rules on the duration of appellate review proceedings too strict or too liberal?

---

[658] See Article 17.5 of the DSU. In cases of urgency, including those which concern perishable foods, the Appellate Body makes every effort to accelerate the proceedings to the greatest extent possible. See Articles 17.5 and 4.9 of the DSU. Also, for disputes involving prohibited subsidies, there are accelerated proceedings. See below, p. 575.

[659] See Article 17.5 of the DSU. Note that this ninety-day time limit also includes the time needed for translation.

[660] Especially during the first years of its operation, the Appellate Body succeeded a few times in completing appellate review proceedings within the sixty-day time limit. See e.g. *Japan – Alcoholic Beverages II*, *US – Wool Shirts and Blouses*, *Canada – Periodicals*, *Brazil – Aircraft (Article 21.5 – Canada)* and *Canada – Aircraft (Article 21.5 – Brazil)*. It has not done so again since May 2000[0]. For *India – Autos*, see above, p. 292. Currently the average duration of appellate proceedings, from the notice of appeal to the circulation of the Appellate Body report, is 89.17 days. See www.worldtradelaw.net/dsc/database/abtiming.asp, visited on 24 November 2007.

[661] The seven cases in which the ninety-day time limit was exceeded were *EC – Hormones* (114 days), *US – Lead and Bismuth II* (104 days), *EC – Asbestos* (140 days), *Thailand – H-Beams* (140 days), *US – Upland Cotton* (136 days), *EC – Export Subsidies on Sugar* (105 days) and *Mexico – Anti-Dumping Measures on Rice* (132 days). Notwithstanding the fact that the Appellate Body generally succeeds in staying within the ninety-day time limit, the US and Chile have proposed in the context of the DSU reform negotiations an extension of the timeframe for appellate review from ninety to a hundred and twenty days.

[662] This happened in *US – Lead and Bismuth II* where Mr Christopher Beeby, a Member of the Appellate Body Division hearing the appeal, died six days after the completion of the oral hearing. After reconstitution of the Division under Rule 13 of the *Working Procedures*, another oral hearing was held pursuant to Rule 16(1) of the *Working Procedures*, and the timeframe for the circulation of the Report was extended by two weeks. See Appellate Body Report, *US – Lead and Bismuth II*, para. 8.

3.4.4. Implementation and enforcement

At a DSB meeting held within thirty days of the adoption of the panel and/or Appellate Body report, the Member concerned must inform the DSB of its intentions in respect of the implementation of the recommendations and rulings.[663] This section discusses the following procedural issues which arise with respect to the implementation and enforcement of recommendations and rulings:

- arbitration on the 'reasonable period of time for implementation';
- the surveillance of implementation by the DSB;
- disagreement on implementation;
- arbitration on, and authorisation of, suspension of concessions or other obligations; and
- the 'sequencing' issue.

3.4.4.1. Arbitration on the 'reasonable period of time for implementation'

As discussed above, prompt or immediate compliance with the recommendations and rulings adopted by the DSB, i.e. prompt or immediate withdrawal or amendment of the WTO-inconsistent measure, is essential for the effective functioning of the WTO and the primary obligation of the Member concerned.[664] However, if it is impracticable to comply with the recommendations and rulings immediately – and this may often be the case – the Member concerned has, pursuant to Article 21.3 of the DSU, a reasonable period of time in which to do so.[665]

If no agreement between the parties can be reached on the 'reasonable period of time for implementation' within forty-five days of the adoption of the recommendations and rulings, the original complainant can refer the matter to arbitration under Article 21.3(c) of the DSU.[666] The parties must agree on an arbitrator. In most cases they are able to do so. However, if they cannot agree on an arbitrator within ten days, either party may request the Director-General of the WTO to appoint an arbitrator.[667] The Director-General will consult the parties and appoint an arbitrator within ten days. The DSU does not provide for any rule or guideline as to the professional or other requirements persons should meet to serve as an Article 21.3(c) arbitrator. However, a practice has developed that Members or former Members of the Appellate Body serve as Article 21.3(c) arbitrators.[668] They do so not as Appellate Body Members but in a personal capacity.

---

[663] See Article 21.3 of the DSU.   [664] See above, pp. 219–20.   [665] See Article 21.3(a), (b) and (c) of the DSU.
[666] In a few instances, the parties reached an agreement on the reasonable period of time for implementation *during* the Article 21.3(c) proceedings. In those cases the arbitrator issues a short report of proceedings, not an award. See e.g Reports of the Arbitrator in *Dominican Republic – Import and Sale of Cigarettes, US – Line Pipe, US – Softwood Lumber V* and *US – Zeroing (Japan)*.
[667] In all but eight out of twenty-five cases, up to November 2007, the parties agreed on the arbitrator. In the remaining eight cases the Director-General appointed the arbitrator.
[668] Until 2005, all Article 21.3(c) arbitrators were at the time of their appointment Members of the Appellate Body. In *EC – Hormones*, the Director-General initially appointed two arbitrators: an Appellate Body Member and a senior diplomat of a WTO Member. However, for reasons unrelated to the arbitration, the senior diplomat withdrew at the start of the arbitration proceedings. In *US – Gambling Services* and *EC – Chicken Cuts*, the arbitrators were Claus-Dieter Ehlermann and James Bacchus respectively. Both are former Appellate Body Members.

While not set out in the DSU, the arbitration proceedings involve the filing of written submissions and a meeting of the parties with the arbitrator. The DSU does require that the arbitration proceedings do not exceed ninety days commencing on the date of the adoption of the panel and Appellate Body reports by the DSB. As this requirement is often not realistic, it is – with the express agreement of the parties – commonly set aside.

The mandate of an Article 21.3(c) arbitrator is narrow in scope. The Arbitrator in *Korea – Alcoholic Beverages* stated as follows:

> My mandate in this arbitration relates exclusively to determining the reasonable period of time for implementation under Article 21.3(c) of the DSU. It is not within my mandate to suggest ways and means to implement the recommendations and rulings of the DSB.[669]

It is not for the Article 21.3(c) arbitrator to rule on the WTO-consistency of the proposed implementing measures.[670]

The arbitration award indicating the 'reasonable period of time for implementation' is issued to the parties and circulated to all WTO Members. Note that, unlike panel or Appellate Body reports, an Article 21.3(c) arbitration award is *not* adopted by the DSB. An arbitration award is posted as a WT/DS document on the WTO website.

Questions and Assignments 3.49

Who can serve as an Article 21.3(c) arbitrator? Briefly discuss the steps in Article 21.3(c) proceedings. What is the mandate of Article 21.3(c) arbitrators? Find the Article 21.3(c) award in *EC – Hormones*. What was the ruling of the Arbitrator in that case?

3.4.4.2. *Surveillance of implementation by the DSB*

During the 'reasonable period of time for implementation', the DSB keeps the implementation of adopted recommendations and rulings under surveillance.[671] At any time following adoption of the recommendations or rulings, any WTO Member may raise the issue of implementation at the DSB. Starting six months after establishment of the reasonable period of time, the issue of implementation is placed on the agenda of each DSB meeting and remains on the DSB's agenda until the issue is resolved. At least ten days prior to such a DSB meeting, the Member concerned must provide the DSB with a status report on its progress in the implementation of the recommendations or rulings.[672]

---

[669] Award of the Arbitrator, *Korea – Alcoholic Beverages*, para. 45. See also above, p. 223.
[670] See Award of the Arbitrator, *Canada – Pharmaceutical Patents*, para. 41.
[671] See Article 21.6 of the DSU. Note also that, after the DSB has authorised retaliation measures (see below, pp. 305–6), the DSB shall 'continue to keep under surveillance the implementation of adopted recommendations or rulings'. See Article 22.8 of the DSU.
[672] See Article 21.6 of the DSU. The status reports under Article 21.6 of the DSU are posted on the WTO website as WT/DS documents. For the debate on these reports, see the minutes of the relevant DSB meeting (WT/DSB/M/ . . .).

Questions and Assignments 3.50

Find the latest Article 21.6 status report in *EC – Hormones.* How did the
United States react to this report?

3.4.4.3. *Disagreement on the implementation*

Before the expiry of the reasonable period of time, the respondent must withdraw
or amend the measure that was found to be WTO-inconsistent. In other words, the
respondent must take the appropriate implementing measures. It is, however, not
uncommon for the original complainant and respondent to disagree on whether
any implementing measure was taken or whether the implementing measure is
WTO-consistent. Article 21.5 of the DSU provides that such disagreement as to the
existence, or consistency with WTO law, of implementing measures shall be
decided:

> through recourse to these dispute settlement procedures, including wherever possible
> resort to the original panel.[673]

Recourse to 'these dispute settlement procedures' means recourse to the procedures set out in Articles 4 to 20 of the DSU.[674] The normal procedures discussed
in previous sections apply with one important exception.[675] Article 21.5 requires
that the panel circulate its report within ninety days after the date of the refer-
ral of the matter to it. However, this timeframe is not realistic, as is demonstrated by the fact that the average duration of an Article 21.5 compliance
procedure is now 215 days, i.e. more than double the time allowed.[676]

The issue of which measures fall within the scope of jurisdiction of a 'compliance' panel has been addressed in a number of cases. The question when a
measure is a 'measure taken to comply with the recommendations and rulings'
was addressed in *US – Softwood Lumber IV (Article 21.5 – Canada).* According to the
United States in that case, the measure at issue, the First Assessment Review, was
not an implementing measure. The Panel, therefore, lacked jurisdiction under
Article 21.5 to consider Canada's claim of inconsistency with regard to this
measure. After a careful analysis of Article 21.5, the Appellate Body noted that
this provision strikes a balance between competing considerations:

---

[673] In the context of the DSU reform negotiations, the EC and Japan have proposed the inclusion of a new
Article 21 *bis.* The proposed Article incorporates, clarifies and elaborates on the current practice under
Article 21.5. This proposal has been taken up in the Chairman's Text. See below, p. 309.

[674] While Article 21.5 refers to 'these procedures', there was initially considerable disagreement among
Members as to which procedures were included. It is now generally accepted that 'these procedures'
include appellate review pursuant to Article 17 of the DSU. Note that in *US – FSC (Article 21.5 – EC II),* the
Appellate Body ruled that the rules of Article 6.2 with regard to the request for the establishment of a
panel (and the sufficiency thereof) applied in the context of an Article 21.5 procedure, albeit that Article
6.2 needs to be interpreted in the light of Article 21.5. See Appellate Body Report, *US – FSC (Article 21.5 – EC
II),* para. 59, and see also above p. 238. It is still disputed by some WTO Members that 'these procedures'
also include consultations pursuant to Article 4 of the DSU.

[675] Another exception is that the complainant and respondent will each file only one submission to the
panel and the panel will have only one meeting with the parties.

[676] See www.worldtradelaw.net/dsc/database/paneltiming1.asp, visited on 24 November 2007.

On the one hand, it seeks to promote the prompt resolution of disputes, to avoid a complaining Member having to initiate dispute settlement proceedings afresh when an original measure found to be inconsistent has not been brought into conformity with the recommendations and rulings of the DSB, and to make efficient use of the original panel and its relevant experience. On the other hand, the applicable time-limits are shorter than those in original proceedings, and there are limitations on the types of claims that may be raised in Article 21.5 proceedings. This confirms that the scope of Article 21.5 proceedings logically must be narrower than the scope of original dispute settlement proceedings. This balance should be borne in mind in interpreting Article 21.5 and, in particular, in determining the measures that may be evaluated in proceedings pursuant to that provision.[677]

The Appellate Body noted that the limits on the claims that can be raised in Article 21.5 proceedings 'should not allow circumvention by Members by allowing them to comply through one measure, while, at the same time, negating compliance through another'. Therefore, what constitutes a 'measure taken to comply' is not determined exclusively by the implementing Member. Ultimately it is for the panel to determine the scope of its jurisdiction.[678] After considering how the panels in other disputes handled this question,[679] the Appellate Body in *US – Softwood Lumber IV (Article 21.5 – Canada)* concluded:

Taking account of all of the above, our interpretation of Article 21.5 of the DSU confirms that a panel's mandate under Article 21.5 of the DSU is not necessarily limited to an examination of an implementing Member's measure declared to be 'taken to comply' . . . Some measures with a particularly close relationship to the declared 'measure taken to comply', and to the recommendations and rulings of the DSB, may also be susceptible to review by a panel acting under Article 21.5. Determining whether this is the case requires a panel to scrutinize these relationships, which may, depending on the particular facts, call for an examination of the timing, nature, and effects of the various measures. This also requires an Article 21.5 panel to examine the factual and legal background against which a declared 'measure taken to comply' is adopted. Only then is a panel in a position to take a view as to whether there are sufficiently close links for it to characterize such an other measure as one 'taken to comply' and, consequently, to assess its consistency with the covered agreements in an Article 21.5 proceeding.[680]

In brief, for a new measure to be an 'implementing measure' within the meaning of Article 21.5 of the DSU, there have to be 'sufficiently close links' between the original measure and the new measure so that the latter can be characterised as 'taken to comply' with the recommendations and rulings concerning the original measure.

---

[677] Appellate Body Report, *US – Softwood Lumber IV (Article 21.5 – Canada)*, para. 72.   [678] See *ibid.*, para. 73.

[679] The Appellate Body noted in *US – Softwood Lumber IV (Article 21.5 – Canada)* that in both *Australia – Salmon (Article 21.5 – Canada)* and *Australia – Automotive Leather II (Article 21.5 – US)*, the relevant Panel examined a measure that the implementing Member maintained was not a measure taken to comply, because its nature and timing indicated that it was 'inextricably linked' to the measure the respondent stated it had taken to comply. See Appellate Body Report, *US – Softwood Lumber IV (Article 21.5 – Canada)*, paras. 74–5. The Appellate Body held: 'The fact that Article 21.5 mandates a panel to assess "existence" and "consistency" tends to weigh against an interpretation of Article 21.5 that would confine the scope of a panel's jurisdiction to measures that move in the direction of, or have the objective of achieving, compliance.' Ibid., para. 67.

[680] Appellate Body Report, *US – Softwood Lumber IV (Article 21.5 – Canada)*, para. 77.

The mandate of an Article 21.5 'compliance' panel is to examine the WTO-consistency of implementing measures.[681] The examination under Article 21.5 involves a consideration of the 'new measure in its totality' and the fulfilment of that task requires that a panel consider both the measure itself and the measure's application.[682] It is important to note that as the Appellate Body ruled in *Canada – Aircraft (Article 21.5 – Brazil)*:

> in carrying out its review under Article 21.5 of the DSU, a panel is not confined to examining the 'measures taken to comply' from the perspective of the claims, arguments and factual circumstances that related to the measure that was the subject of the original proceedings. Although these may have some relevance in proceedings under Article 21.5 of the DSU, Article 21.5 proceedings involve, in principle, not the original measure, but rather a new and different measure which was not before the original panel.[683]

If an Article 21.5 panel were restricted to examining the new measure from the perspective of the claims, arguments and factual circumstances that related to the original measure, the effectiveness of an Article 21.5 review would be seriously undermined because an Article 21.5 panel would then be unable to examine fully the 'consistency with a covered agreement of the measures taken to comply', as required by Article 21.5 of the DSU.[684] The Appellate Body accordingly ruled in *Canada – Aircraft (Article 21.5 – Brazil)* that the Panel was not merely mandated to see if the revised subsidy programme of Canada had dropped the WTO-inconsistent aspects that the original dispute pertained to, but was also mandated to consider Brazil's new claim that the revised programme was inconsistent with Article 3.1(a) of the *SCM Agreement*. Inconsistency with Article 3.1(a) of the *SCM Agreement* had not been an issue before the original Panel but this did not prevent the Article 21.5 Panel from examining this claim. In *EC – Bed Linen (Article 21.5 – India)*, the Appellate Body found that:

> [N]ew claims, arguments, and factual circumstances different from those raised in the original proceedings [may be raised], because a 'measure taken to comply' may be *inconsistent* with WTO obligations *in ways different* from the original measure . . . an Article 21.5 panel could not properly carry out its mandate to assess whether a 'measure taken to comply' is *fully consistent* with WTO obligations if it were precluded from examining claims additional to, and different from, the claims raised in the original proceedings.[685]

---

[681] See Appellate Body Report, *Canada – Aircraft (Article 21.5 – Brazil)*, para. 36.
[682] Appellate Body Report, *US – Shrimp (Article 21.5 – Malaysia)*, para. 87. See also Panel Report, *US – Certain EC Products (Article 21.5 – EC)*, paras. 7.20–7.21.
[683] Appellate Body Report, *Canada – Aircraft (Article 21.5 – Brazil)*, para. 41.
[684] See *ibid*. See also Panel Report, *Australia – Salmon (Article 21.5 – Canada)*, in which the panel stated: 'Article 21.5 is not limited to consistency of certain measures *with the DSB recommendations and rulings* adopted as a result of the original dispute; nor to consistency with those covered agreements or specific provisions thereof that fell within the <u>mandate of the original panel</u>; nor to consistency with specific WTO provisions <u>under which the original panel found violations</u>. . . The *rationale* behind this is obvious: a complainant, after having prevailed in an original dispute, should not have to go through the entire DSU process once again if an implementing Member in seeking to comply with DSB recommendations under a covered agreement is breaching, inadvertently or not, its obligations under other provisions of covered agreements.' See Panel Report, *Australia – Salmon (Article 21.5 – Canada)*, para. 7.10(9).
[685] Appellate Body Report, *EC – Bed Linen (Article 21.5 – India)*, para. 79.

In *Chile – Price Band System (Article 21.5 – Argentina)*, the Panel considered, as *obiter dicta*, three conditions that shall be met in order to examine a new claim of WTO-inconsistency in the context of an Article 21.5 procedure:

> First, that the claim is identified by the complainant in its request for the establishment of the compliance panel. Second, that the claim concerns a new measure, adopted by the respondent allegedly to comply with the recommendations and rulings of the DSB. Third, that the claim does not relate to aspects of the original measure that remain unchanged in the new measure and were not challenged in the original proceedings or, if challenged, were addressed in those proceedings and not found to be WTO-inconsistent.[686]

The question of the *existence* of an implementing measure was addressed by the Article 21.5 Panel in *US – Gambling (Article 21.5 – Antigua and Barbuda)*. In this case, the United States requested that the 'compliance' Panel re-examine the WTO-consistency of its original measure 'based on new evidence and arguments not previously available to the Panel or the Appellate Body'.[687] The Panel rejected this request of the United States. The Panel found that compliance entails a *change* relevant to the measure. This may take various forms, including the repeal or amendment of the measure at issue, a change in the way the measure is applied, or changes in the factual or legal background that modify the effects of the measure.[688] In this case no such changes had occurred.[689] The Panel made clear that the respondent's original defence cannot be re-litigated in an Article 21.5 proceeding on the basis of new arguments or evidence. It stated:

> The recommendation of the DSB was that the United States bring its measures into conformity, not to bring the assessment of the conformity of those measures into conformity. Therefore, the recommendation requires a change that eliminates the inconsistency of those measures with the covered agreements.
>
> The context within Article 21 of the DSU confirms this interpretation. As part of Article 21, a proceeding under Article 21.5 is a procedure for surveillance of the implementation of recommendations and rulings. It is not an opportunity to reassess claims and defences that led to those recommendations and rulings. Article 21 as a whole deals with events subsequent to the DSB's adoption of recommendations and rulings in a particular dispute. The Panel considers this is true not just of the timing of the proceeding under Article 21, but also of the matter that an Article 21.5 panel is mandated to assess.[690]

---

[686] Panel Report, *Chile – Price Band System (Article 21.5 – Argentina)*, para. 7.141. According to the Panel, the first two conditions were already addressed by the Appellate Body in *US – Shrimp (Article 21.5 – Malaysia)*, *Canada – Aircraft (Article 21.5 – Brazil)* and *EC – Bed Linen (Article 21.5 – India)*. The third condition only partially has been addressed by the Appellate Body to date. According to the Panel, this third requirement also relates to the findings of the Article 21.5 Panel in *US – Certain EC Products (Article 21.5 – EC)*. The Panel noted: 'In our view, while this third condition has not been fully addressed yet by the Appellate Body, it is an essential requirement to prevent the misuse of the special expedited procedures contemplated in Article 21.5 of the DSU.' See Panel Report, *Chile – Price Band System (Article 21.5 – Argentina)*, para. 7.142.   [687] See Panel Report, *US – Gambling (Article 21.5 – Antigua and Barbuda)*, para. 6.40.

[688] *Ibid.*, paras.6.20–6.22.

[689] See *ibid.*, para. 6.27. Antigua and Barbuda argued before this Panel that the United States had taken no measures to comply with the DSB rulings as the measures challenged in the original proceeding had not been amended, supplanted or otherwise changed. The US countered that the 'measures taken to comply' can be the same measures at issue in the original proceeding. By bringing new evidence that these measures satisfy the requirements of the chapeau of Article XIV, the US submitted that it had complied with the DSB rulings. See *ibid.*, para. 6.4.

[690] *Ibid.*, paras. 6.15–6.16. The Panel referred in a footnote to Appellate Body Report, *US – Shrimp (Article 21.5 – Malaysia)*, para. 97; Appellate Body Report, *Mexico – Corn Syrup (Article 21.5 – United States)*, para. 79; and Appellate Body Report, *US – Softwood Lumber IV (Article 21.5 – Canada)*, para. 70.

To re-assess the consistency of the original measure would, according to the Panel, mean that the original conclusion in the Appellate Body report was not final, and be contrary to the obligation on parties to a dispute, under Article 17.14 of the DSU, 'unconditionally' to accept an Appellate Body report that has been adopted by the DSB.[691]

To date, thirty-six Article 21.5 'compliance' procedures have been initiated;[692] and twenty-four Article 21.5 panel reports have been circulated.[693] In three disputes, there were two successive Article 21.5 'compliance' procedures.[694] In most Article 21.5 procedures thus far, the original panel served as the compliance panel.[695] Fourteen of the twenty-four Article 21.5 panel reports were appealed.[696]

Like 'normal' panel and Appellate Body reports, Article 21.5 compliance panel and Appellate Body reports become legally binding on the parties only after adoption by the DSB. The DSB adopts these reports by reverse consensus.

An important difference between the recommendations and rulings of 'normal' reports and Article 21.5 reports is that the respondent does not benefit from a reasonable period of time to implement the recommendations and rulings of Article 21.5 reports. Immediately after the adoption of these report(s), the complainant can request authorisation from the DSB to suspend the application of concessions or other obligations to the respondents.

Questions and Assignments 3.51

When will an Article 21.5 procedure be initiated? What are the differences between the 'normal' DSU proceedings and the Article 21.5 proceedings? Which measures can be the subject of an Article 21.5 procedure? What is the mandate of an Article 21.5 'compliance' panel? To what extent can 'new' claims of WTO-inconsistency be made in an Article 21.5 procedure? Will an Article 21.5 'compliance' panel examine whether the respondent has adopted a measure which implements the recommendations and rulings of the DSB or a measure which is

---

[691] See Panel Report, *US – Gambling (Article 21.5 – Antigua and Barbuda)*, paras. 6.55 and 6.57. The Panel referred to the Appellate Body Report in *US – Shrimp (Article 21.5 – Malaysia)*, followed in *EC – Bed Linen (Article 21.5 – India)*, which held that 'Appellate Body Reports that are adopted by the DSB are, as Article 17.14 provides, ". . . unconditionally accepted by the parties to the dispute", and, therefore, *must be treated by the parties to a particular dispute as a final resolution to that dispute*. In this regard, we recall, too, that Article 3.3 of the DSU states that the "prompt settlement" of disputes "is essential to the effective functioning of the WTO".' Appellate Body Report, *US – Shrimp (Article 21.5 – Malaysia)*, para. 97, quoted in Appellate Body Report, *EC – Bed Linen (Article 21.5 – India)*, para. 90. (emphasis added by the Appellate Body).

[692] See www.worldtradelaw.net/dsc/database/searchcomplaintscompliance.asp, visited on 24 November 2007.

[693] See www.worldtradelaw.net/dsc/database/wtopanels.asp, visited on 24 November 2007.

[694] See *Canada – Dairy (Article 21.5 – New Zealand and US II)* and *US – FSC (Article 21.5 – EC II)* and *Brazil-Aircraft (Article 21.5 – Canada II)*. In *EC – Bananas III*, both Ecuador and the US requested a second Article 21.5 panel (in November 2006 and June 2007 respectively) to examine whether the European Communities' new tariff-only regime for bananas eliminates the discrimination against MFN banana suppliers that do not benefit from preferences. Both cases are still pending.

[695] Note, however, that in, for example, *US – Softwood Lumber IV (Article 21.5 – Canada)* and *Chile – Price Band System (Article 21.5 – Argentina)* certain panellists of the original panel were replaced because they had the nationality of third parties in the Article 21.5 procedure.

[696] See www.worldtradelaw.net/dsc/database/abreports.asp, visited on 24 November 2007.

consistent with WTO law? Can an Article 21.5 procedure function as a kind of appeal procedure?

3.4.4.4. *Arbitration on, and authorisation of, suspension of concessions or other obligations*

If the respondent fails to implement the recommendations and rulings adopted by the DSB correctly within the reasonable period of time agreed by the parties or determined by an arbitrator, the respondent will, at the request of the complainant, enter into negotiations with the latter party in order to come to an agreement on mutually acceptable compensation.[697] If satisfactory compensation is not agreed upon within twenty days of the expiry of the reasonable period of time, the complainant may request authorisation from the DSB to suspend the application of concessions or other obligations to the respondent, under the covered agreements.[698] In other words, it may seek authorisation to retaliate. The DSB must decide on the authorisation to retaliate within thirty days of the expiry of the reasonable period of time.[699] As discussed above, the DSB decides on the authorisation to retaliate by reverse consensus; the authorisation is thus quasi-automatic.[700]

However, if the non-complying Member objects to the level of suspension proposed, or claims that the principles and procedures for suspension have not been followed, the matter may be referred to arbitration before the DSB takes a decision.[701] This arbitration under Article 22.6 of the DSU is carried out by the original panel, if the same members are available, or by an arbitrator appointed by the Director-General.[702]

The arbitration must be completed within sixty days of expiry of the reasonable period of time,[703] and a second arbitration or appeal is not possible.[704] The

---

[697] See Article 22.2 of the DSU. On compensation under Article 22, see above, pp. 225–6.

[698] See Article 22.2 of the DSU. On the specificity of the request for authorisation to suspend, note that such request must specify the amount of concessions or other obligations that a Member proposes to suspend (i.e. the proposed level of retaliation) and also the agreement(s) and sector(s) to which the retaliation will pertain See e.g. Decision by the Arbitrators, *EC – Hormones (US) (Article 22.6 – EC)*, para. 16; Decision by the Arbitrators, *EC – Bananas III (Ecuador) (Article 22.6 – EC)*, para. 24; Decision by the Arbitrator, *US – Offset Act (Byrd Amendment) (Article 22.6 – US)*, para. 2.18. The proposed level of retaliation must be stated in 'economically quantifiable terms'. A Member may not request authorisation for a 'qualitatively' similar retaliation (such as enacting the same WTO-inconsistent measure). See Decision by the Arbitrators, *US – 1916 Act (EC) (Article 22.6 – US)*, paras. 5.17–5.36. Members are not required to supply information as to *which* obligations and concessions they propose to suspend. See e.g. Decision by the Arbitrator, *US – 1916 Act (EC) (Article 22.6 – US)*, paras. 3.10–3.11; and Decision by the Arbitrator, *US – Offset Act (Byrd Amendment) (Article 22.6 – US)*, paras. 2.29, 2.32. Note that there is a requirement in Article 22.7 that the arbitration should not concern itself with the 'nature' of the concessions and obligations to be suspended. See Decision by the Arbitrator, *US – 1916 Act (EC) (Article 22.6 – US)*, para. 5.40, relying on Decision by the Arbitrators, *EC – Hormones (Article 22.6 – EC)*, paras. 18–19. However, where an issue that pertains to the nature of to-be-suspended concessions/obligations would also be 'closely linked' to the *level* of those suspensions, it would be within the arbitrator's mandate. See Decision by the Arbitrators, *Brazil – Aircraft (Article 22.6 – Brazil)*, para. 3.17.

[699] See Article 22.6 of the DSU.   [700] See above, p. 226.

[701] See Article 22.6 of the DSU. On the appropriate level of suspension and on the principles and procedures of suspension, see above, pp. 226–9.   [702] See Article 22.6 of the DSU.

[703] See Article 22.6 of the DSU. In *EC – Bananas III (US) (Article 22.6 – EC)*, the sixty-day period was exceeded to give parties time to submit the additional information requests by the Arbitrators, as the Arbitrators considered it imperative to achieve the greatest degree of clarity possible to avoid future disagreements

DSB is informed promptly of the decision of the arbitrator and grants, by reverse consensus, the requested authorisation to suspend concessions or other obligations where the request is consistent with the decision of the arbitrator.[705] Decisions by the arbitrators under Article 22.6 of the DSU are circulated to WTO Members, and posted on the WTO website as WT/DS documents.

Note that the DSU currently does not provide for a procedure for the withdrawal or termination of the authorisation to retaliate.[706] The lack of such procedure is of course not a problem when the original complainant is satisfied that the respondent has withdrawn or amended the WTO-inconsistent measure. A problem arises, however, when the original complainant is not satisfied that the respondent has withdrawn or amended the WTO-inconsistent measure and thus maintains the retaliation measure. This situation arose in *EC –Hormones*, and led the European Communities to initiate new dispute settlement proceedings against the United States and Canada in an effort to secure the lifting of their retaliation measures.[707]

Questions and Assignments 3.52

When *must* the respondent enter into negotiations on compensation? When may the complainant request the DSB to authorise retaliation measures? How is the level of retaliation decided on?

3.4.4.5. The 'sequencing' issue

As discussed above, if the respondent fails to implement the recommendations and rulings within the 'reasonable period of time' and agreement on compensation cannot be reached, the complainant may request the DSB authorisation to retaliate.[708] However, it is clear that such retaliation is *only* called for when the respondent has indeed failed to implement the recommendations and rulings, i.e. has failed to take a WTO-consistent implementing measure. As also discussed above, the complainant and the respondent may disagree on whether such implementing measure exists or whether it is WTO-consistent. To resolve such disagreements, the DSU provides for the Article 21.5 procedure. However, due to 'sloppy' drafting of the DSU, there is a conflict between the timeframe

---

Footnote 703 (*cont.*)
   between parties, in view of the fact that Article 22.6 decisions cannot as appealed. See Decision by the Arbitrators, EC –*Bananas III (US) (Article 22.6)*, para 2.12.   [704] See Article 22.7 of the DSU.
[705] See Article 22.7 of the DSU. Note that the Decision of the Arbitrator under Article 22.6 is notified to the DSB but is not adopted by it.
[706] At the meeting of the Special Session of the DSB of 22 May 2006, negotiators discussed the proposal of Argentina, Brazil, Canada, India, New Zealand and Norway setting out possible procedures to govern the withdrawal of the authorisation to retaliate, as well as what to do when the respondent Member has already taken steps to comply with the ruling. However no clear consensus was reached on any of the proposed changes. See *BRIDGES Weekly Trade News Digest*, 24 May 2006.
[707] See *Canada – Continued Suspension*, WT/DS/321, and *US – Continued Suspension*, WT/DS/320.
[708] See above, pp. 225–9.

for this Article 21.5 procedure and the timeframe within which authorisation for the suspension of concessions and other obligations must be requested and obtained from the DSB. Pursuant to Article 22.6, the authorisation for retaliation must be granted by the DSB within thirty days of the expiry of the reasonable period of time. It is clear that it is not possible to obtain authorisation for retaliation within thirty days, in cases where the complainant must first submit the disagreement on implementation to an Article 21.5 'compliance' panel. In *EC – Bananas III*, this inconsistency led to a serious institutional crisis in which the United States insisted on its right to obtain authorisation for retaliation and the European Communities asserted that an Article 21.5 'compliance' panel first had to establish that the implementing measures taken by the European Communities were not WTO-consistent. Eventually, a pragmatic compromise was found to unblock the situation. However, the problem of the relationship between these two procedures (often referred to as the 'sequencing issue') remains, and a change to the DSU is required to resolve the problem. In the meantime, parties commonly agree, on an *ad hoc* basis, that the procedure of examining the WTO-consistency of the implementing measures will need to be terminated before the authorisation for retaliation measures may be granted.[709] As the European Communities noted in a communication of March 2002:

> In light of the practice followed consistently since [1999], it would appear that Members now broadly agree that completing the procedure established under Article 21.5 DSU is a pre-requisite for invoking the provisions of Article 22 DSU, in case of disagreement among the parties about implementation.[710]

However, this does not mean that the DSU does not need to be amended on this point in order to ensure legal certainty and predictability of the system for all its Members.[711]

Questions and Assignments 3.53

Explain briefly what the so-called 'sequencing issue' is and how it is 'handled' now. In your opinion, can the DSB authorise the suspension of concessions or other obligations before a panel, under Article 21.5 of the DSU, has established that there has not been proper implementation?

---

[709] See e.g. *Canada – Aircraft (Article 21.5 – Brazil)*, para. 1.7 and *Brazil – Aircraft (Article 21.5 – Canada)*, para. 1.5.

[710] Communication from the European Communities, *Contribution of the European Communities and its Member States to the Improvement of the WTO Dispute Settlement Understanding*, TN/DS/W/1, dated 13 March 2002, 4.

[711] Therefore, in the same Communication, the EC proposed an amendment of Article 22 of the DSU to stipulate that a request for retaliation can only be made after the compliance panel finds that the respondent has failed to bring its measures into conformity with the WTO agreements. Japan submitted a similar proposal. These proposals can be found in the Chairman's Text. See below, p. 309.

3.5. MAIN CHALLENGE TO THE WTO DISPUTE SETTLEMENT SYSTEM

The WTO system for resolving trade disputes between WTO Members has been a remarkable success in many respects. The 2004 Sutherland Report on *The Future of the WTO* stated:

> The current WTO dispute settlement procedures – constructed with painstaking, innovative, hard work during the Uruguay Round – are to be admired, and are a very significant and positive step forward in the general system of rules-based international trade diplomacy. In many ways, the system has already achieved a great deal, and is providing some of the necessary attributes of 'security and predictability,' which traders and other market participants need, and which is called for in the Dispute Settlement Understanding (DSU), Article 3.[712]

The WTO dispute settlement system makes an important contribution to the objective that within the WTO 'right prevails over might'. The WTO dispute settlement system offers an opportunity for economically weak Members, such as Antigua and Barbuda, to challenge trade measures taken by economically much stronger Members, such as the United States.[713] As demonstrated by the frequent and broad use of the WTO dispute settlement system by developed as well as developing-country Members, the current system is well regarded by Members. The system works to the advantage of all Members, but it especially gives security to the weaker Members that have often, in the past, lacked the political or economic clout to enforce their rights and to protect their interests.[714] Special dispute settlement rules and procedures for developing-country Members and the Advisory Centre on WTO Law aim to help developing-country Members to make use of this opportunity.[715] While the current system can undoubtedly be further improved, the Sutherland Report cautioned Members against 'dramatic changes'.[716] According to the Report, two considerations should be kept in mind when discussing potential changes to the system:

> First, while there are some grounds for criticism and reform of the dispute settlement system, on the whole, there exists much satisfaction with its practices and performance. Second, in appraising ideas for reform or improvement, the most important principle is to 'do no harm'.[717]

Negotiations on the further improvement of the WTO dispute settlement system have in one form or another been conducted ever since 1998.[718]

---

[712] Consultative Board to the Director-General Supachai Panitchpakdi, *The Future of the WTO: Addressing Institutional Challenges in the New Millennium* (the 'Sutherland Report') (WTO, 2004), para. 213. In 2002 Peter Sutherland stated that the WTO dispute settlement system is 'the greatest advance in multilateral governance since Bretton Woods'. See G. de Jonquieres, 'Rules to Fight By', *Financial Times*, 25 March 2002.

[713] See above, p. 232 and below, p. 489.

[714] J. Lacarte and P. Gappah, 'Developing Countries and the WTO Legal and Dispute Settlement System', *Journal of International Economic Law*, 2000, 400.   [715] See above, pp. 233–5.

[716] Consultative Board to the Director-General Supachai Panitchpakdi, *The Future of the WTO: Addressing Institutional Challenges in the New Millennium* (the 'Sutherland Report') (WTO, 2004), para. 214.

[717] *Ibid*. The report stresses these points again in para. 254.

[718] As agreed at the time of the adoption of the *WTO Agreement*, the WTO Members reviewed the DSU in 1998 and 1999. This first review of the DSU was concluded in July 1999 without agreement on any

Currently, DSU reform negotiations take place in the context of the Doha Development Round. This chapter contains several references in footnotes to proposals for amendment to the DSU made by Members in these negotiations.[719] In May 2003, the Chair of the DSB circulated a document, commonly referred to as the Chairman's Text, which contained proposals for reform on a significant number of issues, including:

- the extension of third party rights;
- improved conditions for Members seeking to join consultations;
- the introduction of remand and interim review in appellate review proceedings;
- the 'sequencing' issue and other problems concerning the suspension of concessions or other obligations;
- the enhancement of compensation as a temporary remedy for breach of WTO law;
- the strengthening of notification requirements for mutually agreed solutions; and
- the strengthening of special and differential treatment for developing-country Members.[720]

In the absence of a sufficiently high level of support, other proposals by Members were not included in the Chairman's Text. These 'rejected' proposals included proposals on:

- accelerated procedures for certain disputes;
- a list of permanent panellists or a permanent panel body;
- increased control of Members over panel and Appellate Body reports;
- the treatment of *amicus curiae* briefs; and
- collective and monetary retaliation.

amendment to the DSU. Discussions on amendments to the DSU continued on an informal basis in the run-up to the Seattle Session of the Ministerial Conference in December 1999. These discussions resulted in a proposal for reform focused primarily on resolving the 'sequencing' issue. See WT/MIN(99)/8 and above, p. 307. At the Seattle Session of the Ministerial Conference, agreement on this proposal might have been possible, but fell victim to the overall failure of that Session. In 2000 and 2001, informal efforts, outside the DSB, to reach agreement on amendments to the DSU continued. These efforts resulted in October 2001 in a revised proposal for amending the DSU tabled by a group of fourteen WTO Members, chaired by Japan but not including the European Communities or the United States. See WT/GC/W/410/Rev.1, dated 26 October 2001. This proposal again focused on the 'sequencing' issue but also addressed the timeframes for panel proceedings, third party rights and the 'carousel' retaliation issue. However, Members failed to reach agreement on this proposal. In November 2001, at the Doha Session of the Ministerial Conference, Members decided to open formal negotiations on the DSU in January 2002. See Ministerial Conference, *Doha Ministerial Declaration*, WT/MIN(01)/DEC/1, dated 20 November 2001, para. 30.

[719] See footnotes 115, 303, 484, 565, 673 and 711. Note that some of the proposals for reform made by Members would, if adopted, further strengthen the judicial, rules-based nature of the WTO dispute settlement system, while other proposals would weaken that nature.

[720] An amended version of the 'Chairman's Text' can be found in the annex to Special Session of the Dispute Settlement Body, *Report by the Chairman to the Trade Negotiations Committee*, TN/DS/9, dated 6 June 2003. For an analysis of the proposals for reform contained in the Chairman's Text, see P. Van den Bossche, 'Reform of the WTO Dispute Settlement System: What to Expect from the Doha Development Round?', in S. Charnovitz, D. Steger and P. Van den Bossche, *Law in the Service of Human Dignity: Essays in Honour of Florentino Feliciano* (Cambridge University Press, 2005), 103–26.

Members have generally welcomed the Chairman's Text but were unable to *agree* to the proposals for reform it contained. Certain Members had conceptual problems with some of these proposals or objected to the fact that other proposals had been excluded from the Chairman's Text.[721] New proposals have been tabled since the circulation of the Chairman's Text in 2003. The 2007 Annual Report gave the following account of the DSU reform negotiations since 2005:

> At the end of 2005, at the Hong [Kong] Ministerial Conference, Ministers 'direct[ed] the Special Session [of the DSB] to continue to work towards a rapid conclusion of the negotiations' [on DSU reform]. Accordingly, in the first half of 2006 the Special Session held a number of meetings under the chairmanship of Ambassador Ronald Saborío Soto of Costa Rica. Continuing the bottom-up approach based on Members' drafting proposals, the meetings of the Special Session discussed Members' new and revised drafting proposals, including on third party rights, strictly confidential information, measures under review, post-retaliation, transparency, remand and issues relating to special and differential (S&D) treatment. In addition, some Members indicated that they were working on other drafting proposals. In December 2006, the Chairman held consultations to prepare the more intensive continuation of the negotiations in early 2007.[722]

To date, Members have not been able to reach agreement on the reform of the DSU.

While further improvement of the WTO dispute settlement system would be useful, such improvement is not the main challenge to the system in the years to come. The main challenge relates to the genuine danger that Members overburden, and thus undermine, the dispute settlement system as a result of their inability to agree on (clearer) rules governing politically sensitive issues concerning international trade. Since 1995, the WTO dispute settlement system has been severely put to the test by politically sensitive disputes on issues touching on public health (e.g. *EC – Hormones*, *EC – Asbestos* and *EC – Approval and Marketing of Biotech Products*); environmental protection (e.g. *US – Gasoline*, *US – Shrimp* and *Brazil – Retreaded Tyres*); public morals and public order (e.g. *US – Gambling*), cultural identity (e.g. *Canada – Periodicals*); taxation (e.g. *Chile – Alcoholic Beverages*, *US – FSC* and *Mexico – Taxes on Soft Drinks*), foreign and development policy (*EC – Bananas III* and *EC – Tariff Preferences*) and industrial policy (e.g. *India – Autos*, *Indonesia – Autos*, *Brazil – Aircraft*, *EC and Certain Member States – Large Civil Aircraft* and *US – Large Civil Aircraft*). Although the WTO dispute settlement system has performed very well so far,[723] the task may become steadily more difficult as the WTO is drawn more deeply into politically controversial issues. Some observers fear that the system may be overwhelmed. Claude Barfield of the Washington-based American Enterprise Institute has stirred keen debate in the international trade policy community by suggesting that the WTO dispute settlement system is 'sub-

---

[721] See Special Session of the Dispute Settlement Body, *Report by the Chairman to the Trade Negotiations Committee*, TN/DS/9, dated 6 June 2003, paras. 10 and 11.

[722] WTO Secretariat, *2007 Annual Report*, 48.

[723] As discussed in this chapter, the WTO dispute settlement system has been widely used by developed as well as developing-country Members (see above, pp. 169, 231–2). In 85 per cent of the disputes in which a WTO-inconsistent measure had to be withdrawn or amended, the Member concerned did so within a reasonable period of time (see above, pp. 219–24). The conclusions of the Appellate Body have generally been well received and accepted by the WTO membership.

stantively and politically unsustainable'. Barfield suggested that governments may only continue to obey its rulings if its powers are curbed.[724] While disagreeing with Barfield's prescription, others have also warned against excessive reliance by WTO Members on adjudication, instead of political solutions, to resolve problems arising in trade relations. Claus-Dieter Ehlermann, a former Chairman of the Appellate Body, has noted that the system is threatened by a dangerous imbalance between the WTO's highly efficient judicial arm and its far less effective political arm.[725] As noted in the Sutherland Report, every judicial institution has some measure of 'gap-filling responsibility' as part of its efforts to resolve ambiguity. However, the Report emphasised that:

> it can also reasonably be argued that WTO obligations should generally be the product of negotiations among Members, not juridical proceedings. In recent years, Members have successfully negotiated very little: the Doha Round, it is to be profoundly hoped, will eventually correct the imbalance between law-making and any tendency towards creative law enforcement through the dispute settlement system. Likewise, improvement in the various decision-making processes of the WTO to avoid what sometimes appears to be stalemate situations or other inability to act (sometimes attributed to the consensus rule), would considerably diminish the incentive to bring situations to the dispute settlement system, rather than work out agreed solutions through the diplomatic process.[726]

To preserve the effectiveness and efficiency of the WTO dispute settlement system, Members will need to improve the ability of the political institutions of the WTO to address the major issues confronting the multilateral trading system. As Hugo Paemen, a former senior EU trade negotiator and EU Ambassador to the United States, noted:

> the strains on the system can be relieved only if governments seek to deal with conflicts through more active diplomacy, rather than expecting disputes adjudicators to do the job for them.[727]

3.6. SUMMARY

The WTO dispute settlement system is based on the dispute settlement system of the GATT. The latter system evolved between the late 1940s and the early 1990s from a system that was primarily a power-based system of dispute settlement through diplomatic negotiations, into a rules-based system of dispute settlement through adjudication. The WTO dispute settlement system, one of the most significant achievements of the Uruguay Round, is a further step in that process of progressive 'judicialisation' of the settlement of international trade disputes.

---

[724] See C. Barfield, *Free Trade, Sovereignty, Democracy: The Future of the World Trade Organization* (American Enterprise Institute Press, 2001), 111–48.

[725] See C. D. Ehlermann, *Some Personal Experiences as Member of the Appellate Body of the WTO*, Policy Papers, RSC No. 02/9 (European University Institute, 2002), 14.

[726] Consultative Board to the Director-General Supachai Panitchpakdi, *The Future of the WTO: Addressing Institutional Challenges in the New Millennium* (the 'Sutherland Report', (WTO, 2004), para. 247.

[727] As quoted by G. de Jonquières, 'Rules to Fight By', *Financial Times*, 25 March 2002.

Since January 1995, the WTO dispute settlement system has been widely used and its 'output', in terms of the number of dispute settlement reports, has been remarkable. Both developed and developing-country Members have frequently used the system to resolve their trade disputes, and these disputes have concerned a very broad range of matters under WTO law.

The prime object and purpose of the WTO dispute settlement system is the prompt settlement of disputes through multilateral proceedings. The system prefers WTO Members to resolve a dispute through consultations rather than adjudication. The WTO dispute settlement system serves to preserve the rights and obligations of Members under the covered agreements, and to clarify the existing provisions of those agreements. The system may not, however, add to or diminish the rights and obligations of the WTO Members. The DSU provides for four different methods to settle disputes between WTO Members: consultations or negotiations (Article 4 of the DSU); adjudication by panels and the Appellate Body (Articles 6 to 20 of the DSU); arbitration (Articles 21.3(c), 22.6 and 25 of the DSU); and good offices, conciliation and mediation (Article 5 of the DSU).

The jurisdiction of the WTO dispute settlement system is very broad in scope. It covers disputes arising under the *WTO Agreement*, the DSU, all multilateral agreements on trade in goods, the GATS and the *TRIPS Agreement* (i.e. the covered agreements). Furthermore, the jurisdiction of the WTO dispute settlement system is compulsory, exclusive and contentious in nature.

Access to the WTO dispute settlement system is limited to WTO Members. A WTO Member can use the system when it claims that a benefit accruing to it under one of the covered agreements is nullified or impaired. A complainant will almost always argue that the respondent violated a provision of WTO law (violation complaint). If the violation is shown, there is a presumption of nullification or impairment of a benefit. NGOs, industry associations or individuals have no access to the WTO dispute settlement system. However, it should be noted that most disputes are brought to the WTO system for resolution at the instigation of companies and industry associations. Moreover, panels and the Appellate Body have the right to accept and consider *amicus curiae* briefs submitted by NGOs.

The WTO dispute settlement process entails four major steps: consultations; the panel proceedings; appellate review proceedings; and implementation and enforcement of the recommendations and rulings adopted by the DSB. The WTO dispute settlement process is subject to strict time limits.

WTO dispute settlement bodies interpret provisions of the covered agreements in accordance with the ordinary meaning of the words of the provision taken in their context and in the light of the object and purpose of the agreement involved. If necessary and appropriate, they have recourse to supplementary means of interpretation. The burden of proof in WTO dispute settlement proceedings is on the party, the complainant or the respondent, that asserts the affirmative of a particular claim or defence.

The WTO dispute settlement proceedings are characterised by their confidentiality. Written submissions by the parties are confidential. Panel meetings (with a few exceptions since 2006) and the oral hearing of the Appellate Body take place behind closed doors. The *Rules of Conduct* require panellists and Appellate Body Members to be independent and impartial, to avoid direct and indirect conflicts of interest and to respect the confidentiality of proceedings.

The DSU provides for three types of remedy for breach of WTO law: one final remedy, namely, the withdrawal (or amendment) of the WTO-inconsistent measure; and two temporary remedies, namely, compensation and suspension of concessions or other obligations (commonly referred to as 'retaliation'). Compliance with the recommendations or rulings of the DSB must be immediate, or, if that is impracticable, within a 'reasonable period of time'. In most disputes, the Member concerned complies with the recommendations and rulings in a timely and correct fashion. If not, the DSB will, by reverse consensus, authorise the original complainant to take retaliation measures when requested. Retaliation measures (usually in the form of a drastic increase in the customs duties on strategically selected products) put economic and political pressure on Members to withdraw or amend their WTO-inconsistent measures. However, doubts exist as to the effectiveness of retaliation as a temporary remedy for breach of WTO law.

In recognition of the difficulties developing-country Members may encounter when they are involved in WTO dispute settlement, the DSU contains some special rules for developing-country Members. Most of these rules are, however, of limited significance. Effective legal assistance to developing-country Members in dispute settlement proceedings is given by the Geneva-based Advisory Centre on WTO Law (ACWL), an independent, international organisation that offers legal advice and representation to its developing-country Members and to least-developed countries.

Among the institutions involved in WTO dispute settlement one must distinguish between a political institution, the Dispute Settlement Body or DSB, and two independent, judicial-type institutions, the dispute settlement panels and the Appellate Body. The DSB, which is composed of all WTO Members, administers the dispute settlement system. It has the authority to establish panels, adopt panel and Appellate Body reports, and authorise suspension of concessions or other obligations under the covered agreements. It takes decisions on these important matters by *reverse consensus*. As a result, the DSB decisions on these matters are, for all practical purposes, quasi-automatic.

The actual adjudication of disputes brought to the WTO is done, at the first-instance level, by dispute settlement panels and, at the appellate level, by the standing Appellate Body. Panels are *ad hoc* bodies established for the purpose of adjudicating a particular dispute and are dissolved once they have accomplished this task. Panels are established by the DSB at the request of the complainant. At the second DSB meeting at which the panel request is discussed, the panel is established by reverse consensus. The parties decide on the composition of the panel. However, if they fail to do so within twenty days after the establishment of the panel, the complainant can ask the Director-General of the WTO to appoint the panellists. As a rule, panels are composed of three well-qualified governmental and/or non-governmental individuals, who are not nationals of the parties or third parties to the dispute. Almost all panels have standard terms of reference, which refer back to the complainant's request to establish a panel. Hence, a claim falls within the panel's terms of reference, i.e. within the mandate of the panel, only if that claim is identified in the panel request. The standard of review of panels, as set forth in Article 11 of the DSU, is 'to make an objective assessment of the matter'. Panels may exercise judicial economy; they need only address those claims which must be addressed in order to resolve the matter at issue in the dispute. A panel report must, at a minimum, set out the findings of fact, the applicability of relevant provisions and the basic rationale behind any findings and recommendations it makes. Where a panel concludes that a Member's measure is inconsistent with WTO law, it shall recommend that the Member concerned bring that measure into conformity with WTO law. The recommendations and rulings of the panel are *not* legally binding by themselves. They become legally binding only when they are adopted – by reverse consensus – by the DSB.

The Appellate Body is a standing, i.e. permanent, international tribunal of seven independent individuals of recognised authority, appointed by the DSB for a term of four years. The composition of the Appellate Body is representative of WTO membership. The Appellate Body hears and decides appeals in divisions of three of its Members. Only parties to the dispute can appeal a panel report. An appeal is limited to issues of law covered in the panel report and legal interpretations developed by the panel. Issues of fact cannot be appealed. However, the treatment of the facts or evidence by a panel may raise the question of whether the panel acted consistently with Article 11 of the DSU. This is a legal issue and can therefore be examined by the Appellate Body. The Appellate Body may uphold, modify or reverse the legal findings and conclusions of the panel that were appealed. On occasion, the Appellate Body has also – in the absence of the authority to remand a case to the panel – felt compelled to 'complete the legal analysis' on issues not addressed by the panel.

WTO dispute settlement proceedings always begin with consultations (or, at least, an attempt to have consultations) between the parties to the dispute. The consultations enable the disputing parties to understand the factual situation and the legal claims in respect of the dispute better. Parties have broad discretion regarding the manner in which consultations are to be conducted. The consultation process is essentially a *political–diplomatic* process and has often been successful in resolving disputes. However, if consultations do not resolve the dispute within sixty days after the request for consultations, the complainant may request the DSB to establish a panel.

The basic rules governing panel proceedings are set out in Article 12 of the DSU. Article 12.1 of the DSU directs a panel to follow the *Working Procedures* contained in Appendix 3 to the DSU, but at the same time authorises a panel to do otherwise. A panel will – whenever possible within one week of its composition – fix the timetable for its work and decide on detailed *ad hoc* working procedures. Each party to a dispute normally submits two written submissions to the panel: a 'first written submission' and a 'rebuttal submission'. During the proceedings, the panel will meet with the parties twice, first after the filing of the 'first written submissions' and then after the filing of the 'rebuttal submissions'. Unless specific deadlines for the submission of evidence are set out in the *ad hoc* working procedures of the panel, parties can submit new evidence as late as the second meeting with the panel. The panel must of course always be careful to observe due process. Panels have the discretionary authority to seek information and technical advice from experts in order to help them to understand and evaluate the evidence submitted and the arguments made by the parties. The parties are under an obligation to provide the panel with the information or the documents that the panel requests at any time during the proceedings. The rights of third parties to participate in the panel proceedings are quite limited. Panels submit their draft reports to the parties for a so-called 'interim review'. After this interim review, the panel finalises the report, issues it to the parties and eventually – when the report is available in the three official languages – makes the report public by circulating it to all WTO Members. Panel proceedings in theory should not exceed nine months, but in practice panel proceedings take, on average, twelve months. Within sixty days of its circulation, a panel report is either adopted by the DSB or appealed to the Appellate Body.

In contrast to panels, the Appellate Body has detailed standard working procedures set out in the *Working Procedures for Appellate Review*. Appellate review proceedings are initiated by a notice of appeal. A party to the dispute other than the original appellant may also appeal alleged legal errors in the panel report by filing a notice of other appeal within twelve days of the filing of the notice of appeal. The appellant's submission, the other (or cross) appellants' submission(s) and the appellee's submission(s) are due within, respectively seven, fifteen and twenty-five days after the date of the notice of appeal. An oral hearing generally takes place between day 35 and day 45 of the appellate review process. Unlike in panel proceedings, third parties have broad rights to participate in appellate review proceedings. After the oral hearing and before finalising its report, the division responsible for deciding an appeal will always exchange views on the issues raised by the appeal with the Members of the Appellate Body not sitting on the division. When the report is available in the three official languages, it is circulated to all WTO Members and made public. Appellate review proceedings shall not exceed ninety days, and, to date, they have exceeded this time limit in only seven cases. Within thirty days of its circulation, the Appellate Body report, together with the panel report, as upheld, modified or reversed by the Appellate Body, is adopted by the DSB by reverse consensus.

Recommendations and rulings of panels and/or the Appellate Body, as adopted by the DSB, must be implemented promptly. If that is impracticable, the Member concerned must implement them within a 'reasonable period of time'. If the parties are unable to agree on the duration of that period, it can – at the request of either party – be determined through binding arbitration (under Article 21.3(c) of the DSU). During the 'reasonable period of time for implementation', the DSB keeps the implementation of adopted recommendations and rulings under surveillance. If the respondent fails to implement the recommendations and rulings within the 'reasonable period of time' and agreement on compensation cannot be reached, the complainant may request authorisation from the DSB to suspend the application of concessions or other obligations to the respondent. If there is disagreement as to the existence or the WTO-consistency of the implementing measures, a practice has developed under which the complainant will first resort to the Article 21.5 compliance procedure before obtaining authorisation from the DSB to retaliate. Under the Article 21.5 compliance procedure, disagreement as to the existence or consistency with WTO law of implementing measures shall be decided through recourse to the DSU dispute settlement procedures, including, wherever possible, resort to the original panel. If the respondent did indeed fail to implement or adopt WTO-inconsistent implementing measures, the DSB can at the request of the complainant authorise the suspension of concessions or other obligations by reverse consensus. If the non-complying Member objects to the level of suspension proposed or claims that the principles and procedures for suspension have not been followed, the matter may be referred to arbitration (under Article 22.6 of the DSU) before the DSB takes a decision.

The WTO system for resolving trade disputes between WTO Members has been a remarkable success in many respects. However, the current system can undoubtedly be further improved. In the context of the Doha Development Round, WTO Members are currently negotiating on proposals for the clarification and amendment of the DSU. The main challenge to the WTO dispute settlement system is, however, not its further improvement but the dangerous imbalance between the WTO's highly efficient judicial arm and its far less effective political arm.

3.7. EXERCISE: NEWLAND SEEKS JUSTICE

To protect its ailing steel industry from import competition, the Kingdom of Richland, a WTO Member, imposed a quota on imports of steel from the Republic of Newland, a recently acceded WTO Member. After intense lobbying by FerMetal, Newland's major steel producer, and the Newland Brotherhood of Steel Workers, the Government of Newland decided to challenge the WTO consistency of Richland's import quota.

As a lawyer in the Brussels-based law firm Dupont, Bridge & Brucke, you have been asked by the Government of Newland to advise on the procedural and systemic issues arising in the course of the dispute settlement proceedings in Geneva. In the course of the proceedings, the following situations arise on which your advice is requested:

- To mitigate the damage to Newland's steel exports and employment in the steel industry, it is important to act quickly against Richland's steel quota. Newland's Minister of Foreign Affairs therefore instructs Newland's Permanent Representative to the WTO, Ambassador Rita Montesdeoca de

Murillo, to request the establishment of a panel at the next meeting of the DSB. Does Newland act in accordance with the DSU by requesting the establishment of a panel in this way? If not, could the DSB refuse to establish the panel?

- Richland's Permanent Representative to the WTO, Ambassador Dr Heinrich Schiller, reportedly receives instructions from his Government to block or, if that is impossible, to delay the establishment *and* composition of a panel as much as possible. What can the Permanent Representative of Richland do? Can he refuse to accept the jurisdiction of the WTO to settle this dispute and suggest that Richland and Newland take the dispute to the International Court of Justice?

- The Government of Richland announces that it will insist that the panel includes five members, of which at least one is a national of Richland and none are nationals of developing-country Members. Among the five panellists, it wants two economists and one engineer. None of the panellists should be a former or current Geneva diplomat. The instructions of the Government of Richland are not to agree to a panel the composition of which does not meet these 'requirements'. The Government of Newland cannot agree to Richland's 'requirements' and instructs its Permanent Representative to expedite the process of establishing *and* composing the panel. What can the Permanent Representative of Newland do?

- Poorland, a neighbour of Newland and a WTO Member, would like to be a third party in this dispute. Is this possible? Can Richland prevent Poorland from becoming a third party in this dispute?

- In the interest of transparency, the Government of Richland would like the meetings of the Panel with the parties to be open to other WTO Members as well as to the general public. Newland would prefer to hold the meetings with the Panel behind closed doors. What will and/or can the Panel do?

- In its first written submission, Newland requests the Panel to examine not only the quota on steel (the measure at issue identified in the panel request) but also an import quota on cement that was also recently introduced by Richland. Moreover, Newland wants the Panel to find that the import quota on steel is not only in breach of Article XIX of the GATT 1994 and the *Agreement on Safeguards* (as it had stated in its panel request) but also in violation of the *Agreement on Import Licensing Procedures*. Finally, Newland calls upon the Panel to examine *de novo* whether the imports of steel from Newland did indeed cause or threaten to cause serious injury to the domestic steel industry of Richland. How will the Panel react to these demands by Newland?

- Newland also argues in its first written submission that the burden is on Richland to demonstrate that it has acted consistently with its obligations under Article XIX of the GATT 1994 since Article XIX constitutes an exception to the basic prohibition of quantitative restrictions set out in Article XI of the GATT 1994. On whom does the burden of proof rest in this dispute?

- The Newland Brotherhood of Steel Workers, the National Association of Steel Producers of Richland and 'Fair Deal', a non-governmental organisation that focuses on the problems of developing countries, all send *amicus curiae* briefs to the Chairman of the Panel. The brief of the National Association of Steel Producers of Richland was published in the *Financial Times* and the *Wall Street Journal* a week earlier and received a lot of attention. The Chairman of the Panel also receives a brief from Southland, a developing-country Member with important interests in steel. What should the Panel do with these unsolicited briefs? The Newland Brotherhood of Steel Workers and the National Association of Steel Producers of Richland have expressed a wish to receive all the briefs submitted by the parties to the Panel and to attend the panel meetings. Is this possible? Will you, as a private lawyer, be allowed to attend the panel meetings and speak for Newland?

- Newland argues in its rebuttal submission that the Panel should interpret the provisions of the *Agreement on Safeguards* in the light of the object and purpose of the *WTO Agreement* and in the light of the alleged intention of the negotiators to limit the use of safeguard measures. Can the Panel follow the interpretative approach suggested by Newland?

- One week before the second substantive meeting with the Panel, Newland submits to the Panel a 100-page document on the Uruguay Round negotiations, which it claims supports its position. The Panel would like to get the advice of a number of eminent international trade law scholars and of former Uruguay Round negotiators on this issue. What can the Panel do?

- In its interim report, the Panel finds in favour of Newland and recommends that the DSB requests that Richland bring the measure at issue in this dispute into conformity with its obligations under the GATT 1994 and the *Agreement on Safeguards*. The Panel suggests that this can best be achieved by prompt removal of the quota. Richland's Minister of Trade denounces the Panel's ruling as a legal travesty and announces that Richland will appeal as soon as possible. Is Richland's Minister of Trade allowed to make such statement? When and how can Richland appeal the panel report?

- Richland appeals the Panel's interpretation of Article XIX of the GATT 1994 and several provisions of the *Agreement on Safeguards*. It also appeals the Panel's finding that the imports of steel from Newland did not cause or threaten to cause serious injury to the domestic steel industry of Richland. In its notice of appeal, Richland also calls upon the Appellate Body 'to complete the legal analysis when required'. Does the Appellate Body have the mandate to review the findings appealed by Richland? Can the Appellate Body complete the legal analysis?

- Newland objects to the composition of the division of the Appellate Body that hears the appeal. One of the Appellate Body Members is a national of Richland and has acted in the past as counsel to a Richland steel company. What can Newland do?

- While the Panel ruled in its favour, Newland is not 'happy' with some of the Panel's legal findings and would like to appeal these findings. Can it still do so once Richland has initiated appellate review proceedings?

- Newland insists that it needs more time to prepare its appellee's submission and argues that the date set for the oral hearing is not convenient. What can Newland do? When can it expect to receive Richland's appellant's submission? Under what circumstances will also Richland need to submit an appellee's submission? When can the parties expect the report of the Appellate Body?
- The Appellate Body upholds the Panel report. After the DSB adopts the Appellate Body Report and the Panel Report as upheld, Richland announces that it will comply with the DSB's recommendations and rulings but that it is unable to do so immediately. Newland contends that it is possible to withdraw the quota promptly. What can Newland do next?
- After the expiry of the reasonable period of time for implementation (determined at five months), Richland claims that it has implemented the recommendations and rulings of the Panel. Newland is baffled by this claim since the import quota is still in force. Can Newland take retaliatory measures?

Principles of non-discrimination

Contents

4.1. INTRODUCTION

Non-discrimination is a key concept in WTO law and policy. As already noted in chapter 1, there are two main principles of non-discrimination in WTO law: the most-favoured-nation (MFN) treatment obligation and the national treatment obligation. In simple terms, the MFN treatment obligation prohibits a country from discriminating *between* other countries; the national treatment obligation prohibits a country from discriminating *against* other countries. This chapter examines these two principles of non-discrimination as they apply to trade in goods and trade in services.[1]

Discrimination between, as well as against, other countries was an important characteristic of the protectionist trade policies pursued by many countries during the Great Depression of the 1930s. Historians now regard these discriminatory policies as an important contributing cause of the economic and political crises that resulted in the Second World War. Discrimination in trade matters breeds resentment among the countries, manufacturers, traders and workers discriminated against. Such resentment poisons international relations and may lead to economic and political confrontation and conflict. In addition, discrimination makes scant economic sense, generally speaking, since it distorts the market in favour of products and services that are more expensive and/or of a lower quality. Eventually, it is the citizens of the discriminating country that end up 'paying the bill' for the discriminatory trade policies pursued.

The importance of eliminating discrimination in the context of the WTO is highlighted in the Preamble to the *WTO Agreement*, where the 'elimination of discriminatory treatment in international trade relations' is identified as one of the two main means by which the objectives of the WTO may be attained.[2]

The key provisions of the GATT 1994 dealing with non-discrimination in trade in goods are:

- Article I, on the MFN treatment obligation; and
- Article III, on the national treatment obligation.

The key provisions on non-discrimination in trade in services in the GATS are:

- Article II, on the MFN treatment obligation; and
- Article XVII, on the national treatment obligation.

The MFN and national treatment obligations of the GATT 1994 and the GATS prohibit discrimination on the basis of the 'national origin or destination' of a product or a service, or on the basis of the 'nationality' of a service supplier. It should be noted, however, that, in a few situations, WTO law also prohibits discrimination based on criteria other than 'nationality' or 'national origin or destination'. Most notable in this respect is Article X:3(a) of the GATT 1994, which requires that laws, regulations, judicial decisions and administrative rulings of

---

[1] As discussed in chapter 8, these principles of non-discrimination are also relevant in the context of the protection of intellectual property rights. See below, pp. 752–3.   [2] See above, pp. 38–9, 86.

general application pertaining to trade be administered in 'a uniform, impartial and reasonable manner'. It has been suggested that this requirement of Article X:3(a) has the effect of imposing a general non-discrimination obligation.[3] In the GATS, Article VI:1 arguably provides for a similar obligation. This chapter, however, focuses exclusively on the MFN treatment obligation and the national treatment obligation.[4]

As noted in chapter 1, WTO law provides for exceptions to its basic rules, including the MFN treatment obligation and the national treatment obligation. These exceptions are important in WTO law and policy because they allow for the 'reconciliation' of trade liberalisation with other economic and non-economic values and interests. This chapter explores the obligations of non-discrimination but does not address the exceptions thereto. The exceptions to the obligations of MFN treatment and national treatment are dealt with in detail in chapter 7.[5]

4.2. MOST-FAVOURED-NATION TREATMENT UNDER THE GATT 1994

Article I of the GATT 1994, entitled 'General Most-Favoured-Nation Treatment', states in paragraph 1:

> With respect to customs duties and charges of any kind imposed on or in connection with importation or exportation or imposed on the international transfer of payments for imports or exports, and with respect to the method of levying such duties and charges, and with respect to all rules and formalities in connection with importation and exportation, and with respect to all matters referred to in paragraphs 2 and 4 of Article III, any advantage, favour, privilege or immunity granted by any [Member] to any product originating in or destined for any other country shall be accorded immediately and unconditionally to the like product originating in or destined for the territories of all other [Members].[6]

The GATT 1994 contains a number of other provisions requiring MFN or MFN-like treatment:

- Article III:7 (regarding internal quantitative regulations);
- Article V (regarding freedom of transit);
- Article IX:1 (regarding marking requirements);
- Article XIII (regarding the non-discriminatory administration of quantitative restrictions); and
- Article XVII (regarding State trading enterprises).

---

[3] Note by the GATT Director-General, L/3149, dated 11 November 1968. See also below, p. 324, footnote 17.

[4] Article X:3(a) of the GATT 1994 and Article VI:1 of the GATS are discussed in chapter 5 of this book. See below, pp. 466–70, 494–5.

[5] See below, pp. 614–739. The relevant exceptions to the MFN treatment obligation and the national treatment obligation dealt with in chapter 7 are the general exceptions (Article XX of the GATT 1994 and Article XIV of the GATS), the security exceptions (Article XXI of the GATT 1994 and Article XIV bis of the GATS), the regional integration exceptions (Article XXIV of the GATT 1994 and Article V of the GATS) and the economic development exception (Enabling Clause).

[6] Article I:2 to I:4 of the GATT 1994 deals with so-called colonial preferences and allows the continuation of such preferences albeit within certain limits. While important and controversial when the GATT 1947 was negotiated, these colonial preferences are now of very little significance and will therefore not be discussed.

Article XX of the GATT 1994, the 'general exceptions' provision, also contains an MFN-like obligation.[7] The very existence of these MFN-type clauses demonstrates the pervasive character of the MFN principle of non-discrimination.[8] Other multilateral agreements on trade in goods such as the *TBT Agreement*, the *SPS Agreement* and the *Agreement on Import Licensing Procedures* likewise require MFN treatment.[9] However, this section is only concerned with the MFN treatment obligation set out in Article I:1 of the GATT 1994.

4.2.1. Nature of the MFN treatment obligation of Article I:1 of the GATT 1994

As the Appellate Body stated in *EC – Tariff Preferences*, it is well settled that the MFN treatment obligation set out in Article I:1 of the GATT 1994 is a 'cornerstone of the GATT' and 'one of the pillars of the WTO trading system'.[10] In *US – Section 211 Appropriations Act*, the Appellate Body ruled:

> For more than fifty years, the obligation to provide most-favoured-nation treatment in Article I of the GATT 1994 has been both central and essential to assuring the success of a global rules-based system for trade in goods.[11]

The importance of the MFN treatment obligation to the multilateral trading system is undisputed. However, as discussed in chapter 7 of this book, the proliferation of customs unions, free trade agreements and other preferential arrangements in the last fifteen years has led to a situation in which much of world trade is not conducted in accordance with the MFN treatment obligation.[12] As noted on the WTO website:

> By July 2005, only one WTO Member – Mongolia – was not party to a regional trade agreement. The surge in these agreements has continued unabated since the early 1990s. By July 2005, a total of 330 had been notified to the WTO (and its predecessor, GATT). Of these: 206 were notified after the WTO was created in January 1995; 180 are currently in force; several others are believed to be operational although not yet notified.[13]

Considering this reality of widespread preferential treatment in trade relations between WTO Members, the 2004 Sutherland Report on *The Future of the WTO* arrived, not without some pathos, at the following conclusion regarding the MFN treatment obligation:

> [N]early five decades after the founding of the GATT, MFN is no longer the rule; it is almost the exception. Certainly, much trade between the major economies is still conducted on an MFN basis. However, what has been termed the 'spaghetti bowl' of customs unions, common markets, regional and bilateral free trade areas, preferences and an

---

[7] See below, pp. 643–9.   [8] See Appellate Body Report, *Canada – Autos*, para. 82.
[9] See below, pp. 817–18, 847–8 and 459–60.   [10] Appellate Body Report, *EC – Tariff Preferences*, para. 101.
[11] Appellate Body Report, *US – Section 211 Appropriations Act*, para. 297. See also Appellate Body Report, *Canada – Autos*, para. 69; and Appellate Body Report, *EC – Tariff Preferences*, para. 101.
[12] With regard to the application of, for example, MFN tariffs by the European Communities, see below, pp. 410–11.
[13] See WTO website, *Regionalism: Friends or Rivals?*, available at www.wto.org/english/thewto_e/whatis_e/tif_e/bey1_e.htm, visited on 11 November 2007.

> endless assortment of miscellaneous trade deals has almost reached the point where MFN
> treatment is exceptional treatment.[14]

It is clear that MFN treatment is in practice less prevalent than one might expect of the 'cornerstone of the GATT' and 'one of the pillars of the WTO trading system'.[15] Subject to the exceptions discussed in chapter 7 of this book, MFN treatment is, and remains, however, a principal obligation for WTO Members.

Article I:1 of the GATT 1994 prohibits discrimination *between* like products originating in, or destined for, different countries.[16] The principal purpose of the MFN treatment obligation is to ensure *equality of opportunity* to import from, or to export to, all WTO Members. In *EC – Bananas III*, the Appellate Body stated, with respect to WTO non-discrimination obligations (such as the obligation set out in Article I:1):

> The essence of the non-discrimination obligations is that like products should be treated equally, irrespective of their origin. As no participant disputes that all bananas are like products, the non-discrimination provisions apply to *all* imports of bananas, irrespective of whether and how a Member categorizes or subdivides these imports for administrative or other reasons.[17]

In *EC – Bananas III*, the measure at issue was the import regime for bananas of the European Communities under which bananas from Latin American countries ('dollar bananas') were treated less favourably than bananas from, broadly speaking, former European colonies ('ACP bananas').

Article I:1 covers not only 'in law', or *de jure*, discrimination but also 'in fact', or *de facto*, discrimination.[18] In other words, Article I:1 applies not only to 'origin-based' measures (which are discriminatory by definition), but also to measures which, on their face, appear 'origin-neutral' but are *in fact* discriminatory. In *Canada – Autos*, the Appellate Body rejected, as the Panel had done, Canada's argument that Article I:1 does not apply to measures which appear, on their face, to be 'origin-neutral'.[19] Measures which appear, on their face, to be 'origin-neutral' can give certain countries more opportunity to trade than others and can, therefore, be in violation of the non-discrimination obligation of Article I:1. The measure at issue in *Canada – Autos* was an import duty exemption accorded by Canada to imports of motor vehicles by certain manufacturers. Formally speaking, there were no restrictions on the origin of the motor vehicles that were eligible for this exemption. In practice, however, the manufacturers imported only their own make of motor vehicle and those of related companies.

---

[14] Report by the Consultative Board to the Director-General Supachai Panitchpakdi, *The Future of the WTO: Addressing Institutional Challenges in the New Millennium* (the 'Sutherland Report') (WTO, 2004), para. 60.

[15] See *ibid*.   [16] See Appellate Body Report, *Canada – Autos*, para. 84.

[17] Appellate Body Report, *EC – Bananas III*, para. 190. Note that the Appellate Body also referred to the non-discrimination obligations set out in Articles X:3(a) and XIII of the GATT 1994 and Article 1.3 of the *Import Licensing Agreement*.

[18] A measure may be said to discriminate in law (or *de jure*) in a case in which it is clear from reading the text of the law, regulation or policy that it discriminates. If the measure does not appear on the face of the law, regulation or policy to discriminate, it may still be determined to discriminate *de facto* if, on reviewing all the facts relating to the application of the measure, it becomes clear that it discriminates in practice or in fact.   [19] See Appellate Body Report, *Canada – Autos*, para. 78.

As a result, only motor vehicles originating in a small number of countries benefited *de facto* from the exemption.

Previously, the GATT Panel in *EEC – Imports of Beef* found that EC regulations, making the suspension of an import levy conditional on the production of a certificate of authenticity, were inconsistent with the MFN treatment obligation of Article I:1 after it was established that the only certifying agency authorised to produce a certificate of authenticity was an agency in the United States.[20]

Questions and Assignments 4.1

What is the principal purpose of the MFN treatment obligation of Article I:1 of the GATT 1994? Does Article I:1 cover both *de jure* and *de facto* discrimination? Give two examples of *de facto* discrimination from the WTO/GATT case law.

4.2.2. MFN treatment test of Article I:1 of the GATT 1994

Article I:1 of the GATT 1994 sets out a three-tier test of consistency. There are three questions which must be answered to determine whether there is a violation of the MFN treatment obligation of Article I:1, namely:

- whether the measure at issue confers a trade 'advantage' of the kind covered by Article I:1;
- whether the products concerned are 'like products'; and
- whether the advantage at issue is granted 'immediately and unconditionally' to all like products concerned.

4.2.2.1. 'Any advantage with respect to . . .'

The MFN treatment obligation concerns 'any advantage, favour, privilege or immunity' granted by any Member to any product originating in, or destined for, any other country with respect to: (1) customs duties; (2) charges of any kind imposed *on* importation or exportation (e.g. import surcharges or consular taxes); (3) charges of any kind imposed *in connection with* importation or exportation (e.g. customs fees or quality inspection fees); (4) charges imposed on the international transfer of payments for imports or exports; (5) the method of levying such duties and charges, such as the method of assessing the base value on which the duty or charge is levied; (6) all rules and formalities in connection with importation and exportation; (7) internal taxes or other internal charges (i.e. the matters referred to in Article III:2 of the GATT 1994); and (8) laws, regulations and requirements affecting internal sale, offering for sale, purchase, transportation, distribution or use of any product (i.e. the matters referred to in Article III:4 of the GATT 1994).

---

[20] GATT Panel Report, *EEC – Imports of Beef from Canada*, paras. 4.2 and 4.3.

In brief, the MFN treatment obligation concerns any advantage granted by any Member with respect to:

- customs duties, other charges on imports and exports and other customs matters;
- internal taxes; and
- internal regulations affecting the sale, distribution and use of products.

Generally, there has been little debate about the kind of measures covered by Article I:1. Both panels and the Appellate Body have recognised that Article I:1 clearly casts a very wide net.[21] In *US – MFN Footwear*, also referred to as *US – Non-Rubber Footwear*, the Panel found:

> the rules and formalities applicable to countervailing duties, including those applicable to the revocation of countervailing duty orders, are rules and formalities imposed in connection with importation, within the meaning of Article I:1.[22]

The Panel in *US – Customs User Fee* stated:

> The merchandise processing fee was a 'charge imposed on or in connection with importation' within the meaning of Article I:1. Exemptions from the fee fell within the category of 'advantage, favour, privilege or immunity' which Article I:1 required to be extended unconditionally to all other contracting parties.[23]

As already mentioned, in *EEC – Imports of Beef*, the Panel applied Article I:1 to EC regulations making the suspension of an import levy conditional on the production of a certificate of authenticity.[24]

In *EC – Bananas III*, the European Communities contended before the Appellate Body that the Panel had erred in concluding that the EC's 'activity function rules' for the allocation of import licences for bananas violated Article I:1. The Appellate Body upheld the Panel's finding of a violation of Article I:1 as follows:

> the Panel found that the procedural and administrative requirements of the activity function rules for importing third-country and non-traditional ACP bananas differ from, and go significantly beyond, those required for importing traditional ACP bananas. This is a factual finding. Also, a broad definition has been given to the term 'advantage' in Article I:1 of the GATT 1994 by the panel in *United States – Non-Rubber Footwear* . . . For these reasons, we agree with the Panel that the activity function rules are an 'advantage' granted to bananas imported from traditional ACP States, and not to bananas imported from other Members, within the meaning of Article I:1.[25]

Also, the 'unbound customs duties' at issue in *Spain – Unroasted Coffee*,[26] the 'additional bonding requirements' at issue in *US – Certain EC Products*,[27] the 'tax and customs duty benefits' at issue in *Indonesia – Autos*[28] and the concessions

---

[21] In August 1948, the Contracting Parties had adopted a ruling by the Chairman that consular taxes would be covered by the phrase 'charges of any kind' in Article I:1 of the GATT 1947. See BISDII/12.
[22] GATT Panel Report, *US – MFN Footwear*, para. 6.8.   [23] GATT Panel Report, *US – Customs User Fee*, para. 122.
[24] See above, p. 325.   [25] Appellate Body Report, *EC – Bananas III*, para. 206.
[26] See GATT Panel Report, *Spain – Unroasted Coffee*, para. 4.3. See also below, p. 331.
[27] See Panel Report, *US – Certain EC Products*, para. 6.54.   [28] See Panel Report, *Indonesia – Autos,* para. 14.147.

contained in a Member's Schedule pertaining to tariff rate quotas at issue in *EC –Poultry*[29] have all been found to be 'advantages' within the meaning of Article I:1 of the GATT 1994.

In *Canada – Autos*, the Appellate Body usefully clarified the scope of Article I:1 by ruling:

> Article I:1 requires that '*any advantage*, favour, privilege or immunity granted by any Member to *any product* originating in or destined for any other country shall be accorded immediately and unconditionally to the like product originating in or destined for the territories of *all other Members*'. [Emphasis added] The words of Article I:1 refer not to *some* advantages granted 'with respect to' the subjects that fall within the defined scope of the Article, but to '*any advantage*'; not to *some* products, but to '*any product*'; and not to like products from *some* other Members, but to like products originating in or destined for '*all other*' Members.[30]

In other words, the MFN treatment obligation requires that *any* advantage granted by a Member to any product from or for another country be granted to *all* like products from or for *all other* Members.

In the past, there has been some debate on the applicability of Article I:1 to safeguard measures, anti-dumping duties and countervailing duties. With regard to safeguard measures, the *Agreement on Safeguards* makes it clear that the MFN treatment obligation normally applies to safeguard measures. However, the *Agreement* does allow, under certain conditions, the discriminatory use of safeguard measures.[31] With regard to anti-dumping duties and countervailing duties which are, in principle, within the scope of Article I:1, it should be noted that the facts concerning dumped or subsidised exports will more often than not differ from country to country. However, where all the relevant facts are the same, anti-dumping duties and countervailing duties should be applied without discrimination.[32] In a 1960 Report of the Group of Experts on Anti-Dumping and Countervailing Duties, it is stated:

> In equity, and having regard to the most-favoured-nation principle, the Group considered that where there was dumping to the same degree from more than one source and where that dumping caused or threatened material injury to the same extent, the importing country ought normally to be expected to levy anti-dumping duties equally on all the dumping imports.[33]

Article I:1 applies also, in principle, to advantages granted under the Plurilateral Agreements. Advantages granted by a party to other parties to the *Agreement on Civil Aircraft* or to the *Agreement on Government Procurement* should, pursuant to Article I:1, at least in principle, be accorded 'immediately and unconditionally' to all WTO Members.

While the net cast by Article I:1 of the GATT 1994 is very wide, the Panel in *EC – Commercial Vessels* made it clear that the scope of application of Article I:1 is not unlimited. This dispute concerned an EC Regulation which allowed for

---

[29] See Appellate Body Report, *EC – Poultry*, para. 99.   [30] Appellate Body Report, *Canada – Autos*, para. 79
[31] See below, pp. 687–8.   [32] See below, pp. 547, 596.
[33] Report of the Group of Experts on Anti-Dumping and Countervailing Duties, BISD 9S/194 at 198.

subsidies to domestic shipyards. Korea claimed, *inter alia*, that these subsidies were inconsistent with Article I:1. As noted above, Article I:1 applies to 'all matters referred to in paragraphs 2 and 4 of Article III'. According to Korea, the EC Regulation at issue (known as the 'TDM Regulation') was a measure within the meaning of Article III:4 and therefore covered by Article I:1. However, before addressing the claim of inconsistency with Article I:1, the Panel had rejected Korea's claim of inconsistency with Article III:4 because it found that the subsidies granted under the EC Regulation were covered by Article III:8(b) and that Article III:4 therefore did not apply.[34] The question before the Panel in *EC – Commercial Vessels* was thus:

> whether our conclusion that the TDM Regulation is covered by Article III:8(b) and hence not inconsistent with Article III:4 means that the TDM Regulation is also outside the scope of the MFN obligation in Article I:1 as applied to 'all matters referred to in paragraphs 2 and 4 of Article III'.[35]

In replying to this question, the Panel stated:

> the phrase 'matters referred to in . . .' in Article I:1 refers to the subject matter of those provisions in terms of their substantive legal content. Understood in this sense, it is clear to us that the 'matters referred to in paragraphs 2 and 4 of Article III' cannot be interpreted without regard to limitations that may exist regarding the scope of the substantive obligations provided for in these paragraphs. If it is explicitly provided that a particular measure is not subject to the obligations of Article III, that measure in our view does not form part of the 'matters referred to' in Articles III:2 and 4. Thus, since Article III:8(b) provides that Article III 'shall not prevent the payment of subsidies exclusively to domestic producers', such subsidies are not part of the subject matter of Article III:4 and cannot be covered by the expression 'matters referred to in paragraphs 2 and 4 of Article III' in Article I:1.[36]

As measures covered by Article III:8(b) (i.e. subsidies to domestic producers) fall outside the scope of application of Article III:2 and 4, these measures also fall outside the scope of application of Article I:1.

Finally, note that the MFN treatment obligation concerns not only advantages granted to other WTO Members, but also advantages granted to all other countries (including non-WTO Members). If a Member grants an advantage to a non-Member, Article I:1 obliges the Member to grant that advantage also to all WTO Members. Now that trade between WTO Members comprises 95 per cent of all world trade and all large economies (except Russia) are WTO Members, this aspect of the MFN treatment obligation has become less important than it was in the past.

Questions and Assignments 4.2

What are the constituent elements of the MFN treatment test of Article I:1 of the GATT 1994? To which kind of 'advantages', generally speaking, does Article I:1 apply? Does Article I:1 apply to 'advantages' granted to

---

[34] Panel Report, *EC – Commercial Vessels*, para. 7.75. On Article III:8(b) of the GATT 1994, see below, p. 344.
[35] *Ibid.*, para. 7.81.   [36] *Ibid.*, para. 7.83.

non-WTO Members? Does the MFN treatment obligation apply to safeguard measures, anti-dumping duties, countervailing duties and/or subsidies to domestic producers?

4.2.2.2. 'Like products'

Article I:1 concerns any product originating in or destined for any other country and requires that an advantage granted to such products shall be accorded to 'like products' originating in or destined for the territories of all other Members. It is only between 'like products' that the MFN treatment obligation applies and discrimination within the meaning of Article I:1 of the GATT 1994 may occur. Products that are not 'like' may be treated differently. Are four-door cars 'like' two-door cars? Is orange juice 'like' tomato juice? Are portable computers 'like' desktop computers? Is pork 'like' beef? Is alcohol-free beer 'like' regular beer?

The concept of 'like products' is used not only in Article I:1 but also in Articles II:2(a), III:2, III:4, VI:1(a), IX:1, XI:2(c), XIII:1, XVI:4 and XIX:1 of the GATT 1994.[37] Nevertheless, the concept of 'like products' is not defined in the GATT 1994. In its examination of the concept of 'like products' under Article III:4, the Appellate Body in *EC – Asbestos* considered that the dictionary meaning of 'like' suggests that 'like products' are products that share a number of identical or similar characteristics. The reference to 'similar' as a synonym of 'like' also echoes the language of the French version of Article III:4, '*produits similaire*', and the Spanish version, '*productos similares*'.[38] However, as the Appellate Body noted in *Canada – Aircraft*, 'dictionary meanings leave many interpretative questions open'.[39] With regard to the concept of 'like products', there are three questions of interpretation that need to be resolved:

(1) which characteristics or qualities are important in assessing 'likeness';
(2) to what degree or extent must products share qualities or characteristics in order to be 'like products'; and
(3) from whose perspective 'likeness' should be judged.[40]

It is generally accepted that the concept of 'like products' has a different meaning in the different contexts in which it is used. In *Japan – Alcoholic Beverages II*, the Appellate Body illustrated the possible differences in the scope of the concept of 'like products' in different provisions of the *WTO Agreement* by evoking the image of an accordion:

> The accordion of 'likeness' stretches and squeezes in different places as different provisions of the *WTO Agreement* are applied. The width of the accordion in any one of those

---

[37] The concept of 'like product' is also used in the *Anti-Dumping Agreement*, the *SCM Agreement* and the *Agreement on Safeguards*. See below, pp. 517–18, 578–9, 679–80.

[38] See Appellate Body Report, *EC – Asbestos*, para. 91. Note that the French and Spanish versions of the GATT 1994 are equally authentic.

[39] Appellate Body Report, *Canada – Aircraft*, para. 153. See also Appellate Body Report, *EC – Asbestos*, para. 92.

[40] See Appellate Body Report, *EC – Asbestos*, para. 92.

> places must be determined by the particular provision in which the term 'like' is encoun-
> tered as well as by the context and the circumstances that prevail in any given case to
> which that provision may apply.[41]

In other words, products such as orange juice and tomato juice may be 'like' under one provision of the GATT 1994 and not 'like' under another provision.[42]

The meaning of the phrase 'like products' in Article I:1 was addressed in a few GATT working party and panel reports.[43] In *Spain – Unroasted Coffee*, the Panel had to decide whether various types of unroasted coffee ('Colombian mild', 'other mild', 'unwashed Arabica', 'Robusta' and 'other') were 'like products' within the meaning of Article I:1. Spain did not apply customs duties on 'Colombia mild' and 'other mild', while it imposed a 7 per cent customs duty on the other three types of unroasted coffee. Brazil, which exported mainly 'unwashed Arabica', claimed that the Spanish tariff regime was inconsistent with Article I:1. In examining whether the various types of unroasted coffee were 'like products' to which the MFN treatment obligation applied, the Panel considered:

- the characteristics of the products;
- their end-use; and
- tariff regimes of other Members.

The Panel stated as follows:

> The Panel examined all arguments that had been advanced during the proceedings for the justification of a different tariff treatment for various groups and types of unroasted coffee. It noted that these arguments mainly related to organoleptic differences resulting from geographical factors, cultivation methods, the processing of the bean, and the genetic factor. The Panel did not consider that such differences were sufficient reason to allow for a different tariff treatment. It pointed out that it was not unusual in the case of agricultural products that the taste and aroma of the end-product would differ because of one or several of the above-mentioned factors.
>
> The Panel furthermore found relevant to its examination of the matter that unroasted coffee was mainly, if not exclusively, sold in the form of blends, combining various types of coffee, and that coffee in its end-use, was universally regarded as a well-defined and single product intended for drinking.
>
> The Panel noted that no other contracting party applied its tariff regime in respect of unroasted, non-decaffeinated coffee in such a way that different types of coffee were subject to different tariff rates.
>
> In the light of the foregoing, the Panel concluded that unroasted, non-decaffeinated coffee beans listed in the Spanish Customs Tariff . . . should be considered as 'like products' within the meaning of Article I:1.[44]

---

[41] Appellate Body Report, *Japan – Alcoholic Beverages II*, 114.   [42] See also below, p. 374.

[43] See e.g. Working Party Report, *Australian Subsidy on Ammonium Sulphate*, para. 8; and GATT Panel Report, *EEC – Animal Feed Proteins*, para. 4.2. See also GATT Panel Report, *Canada/Japan – Tariff on Imports of Spruce, Pine, Fir (SPF) Dimension Lumber*, paras. 5.13 and 5.14.

[44] GATT Panel Report, *Spain – Unroasted Coffee*, paras. 4.6–4.9. In *EEC – Animal Feel Proteins*, the Panel decided, on the basis of such factors as 'the number of products and tariff items carrying different duty rates and tariff bindings, the varying protein contents and the different vegetable, animal and synthetic origins of the protein products', that the various protein products at issue could not be considered as 'like products' within the meaning of Articles I and III of the GATT 1947. GATT Panel Report, *EEC – Measures on Animal Feed Proteins*, para. 4.2

In addition to the characteristics of the products, their end-use and the tariff regimes of other Members (the criteria used by the GATT Panel in *Spain – Unroasted Coffee*), a WTO panel examining whether products are 'like' within the meaning of Article I:1 would now definitely consider consumers' tastes and habits. Since the case law on 'likeness' within the meaning of Article I:1 of the GATT 1994 is limited, the case law on 'likeness' within the meaning of Article III of the GATT 1994 , discussed below, should be considered carefully, even though the scope of the concept may differ.[45]

It is much debated whether, under current WTO law, a product's process and production method (PPM) is relevant in determining whether products are 'like' if the PPM by which a product is made does *not* affect the physical characteristics of the product. The prevailing view is that such non-product related processes and production methods (NPR PPMs) are not relevant.[46] Consequently, products produced in an environmentally unfriendly manner cannot be treated differently from products produced in an environmentally friendly manner on the sole basis of the difference in PPMs.

Finally, note that Article I:1 also applies to products that are not subject to a tariff binding.[47] As the Panel in *Spain – Unroasted Coffee* ruled, Article I:1 applies equally to bound and unbound tariff items.[48]

Questions and Assignments 4.3

According to the Appellate Body in *EC – Asbestos*, which three questions of interpretation need to be answered to clarify the concept of 'likeness'? Is there *one* concept of 'likeness' in WTO law? What criteria have been used by GATT panels to determine whether products were 'like' within the meaning of Article I:1? Are differences in the way in which products are produced (e.g. an environmentally friendly versus a polluting production method, or production involving child labour versus production not involving child labour) relevant to the determination of the 'likeness' of products under Article I:1? Is beef from cattle kept, fed, transported and slaughtered in accordance with animal welfare requirements 'like' beef from cattle treated in a less 'humane' manner?

4.2.2.3. Advantage granted 'immediately and unconditionally'

Article I:1 of the GATT 1994 requires that any advantage granted by a WTO Member to imports from any country must be granted 'immediately and

---

[45] See Panel Report, *Indonesia – Autos*, para. 14.141. On the meaning of 'like products' in Article III, see below, pp. 351–6, 374–82. Note, however, the warning by Petros Mavroidis 'against "lock, stock and barrel" transfers of interpretations reached in Article III GATT, into the four corners of Article I GATT'. See P. Mavroidis, *The General Agreement on Tariffs and Trade: A Commentary* (Oxford University Press, 2005), 119.

[46] Note, however, the discussion of the concept of 'likeness' in Article III:4 in the context of the *EC – Asbestos* dispute. See below, pp. 374–82.   [47] See below, pp. 422–5.

[48] See GATT Panel Report, *Spain – Unroasted Coffee*, para. 4.3.

unconditionally' to imports from all other WTO Members.[49] Once a WTO Member has granted an advantage to imports from a country, it cannot make the granting of that advantage to imports of other WTO Members conditional upon those other WTO Members 'giving something in return' or 'paying' for the advantage.[50] The granting of an advantage within the meaning of Article I:1 may also not be conditional on whether a Member has certain characteristics, has certain legislation in place or undertakes certain action. In *Belgium – Family Allowances*, a 1952 dispute concerning a Belgian law providing for a tax exemption for products purchased from countries which had a system of family allowances similar to that of Belgium, the Panel held that the Belgian law at issue:

> introduced a discrimination between countries having a given system of family allowances and those which had a different system or no system at all, and made the granting of the exemption dependent on certain conditions.[51]

The Panel concluded that the advantage – the exemption from a tax – was not granted 'unconditionally' and that the Belgian law was therefore inconsistent with the MFN treatment obligation of Article I:1.

In *Indonesia – Autos*, the Panel found in its 1998 Report with respect to the requirement under Article I:1 that advantages shall be granted 'immediately and unconditionally', as follows:

> under the February 1996 car programme the granting of customs duty benefits to parts and components is conditional to their being used in the assembly in Indonesia of a National Car. The granting of tax benefits is conditional and limited to the only Pioneer company producing National Cars. And there is also a third condition for these benefits: the meeting of certain local content targets. Indeed under all these car programmes, customs duty and tax benefits are conditional on achieving a certain local content value for the finished car. The existence of these conditions is inconsistent with the provisions of Article I:1 which provides that tax and customs duty advantages accorded to products of one Member (here on Korean products) be accorded to imported like products from other Members 'immediately and unconditionally'.[52]

According to the Panel in *Indonesia – Autos*, under Article I:1 of the GATT 1994, trade advantages – *in casu* tax and customs duty benefits – could not:

> be made conditional on any criteria that [are] not related to the imported product itself.[53]

In support of this statement, the Panel referred to the Report in *Belgium – Family Allowances*.[54] Note, however, that the Panel in *Canada – Autos* found in its 2000 Report as follows:

---

[49] Note that Article I:1 also requires that any advantage granted by a WTO Member to exports to any country must be accorded 'immediately and unconditionally' to exports to all other WTO Members. This has, however, seldom been a problem.

[50] See in this respect, the Working Party Report on the *Accession of Hungary*, L/3889, adopted on 30 July 1973, BISD 20S/34, para. 12.   [51] GATT Panel Report, *Belgium – Family Allowances*, para. 3.

[52] Panel Report, *Indonesia – Autos*, para. 14.146.   [53] *Ibid.*, para. 14.143.

[54] *Ibid.*, para. 14.144. Note that the GATT Panel in *EEC – Imports of Beef from Canada* and the GATT Working Party Report on *Accession of Hungary* took a similar (strict) approach to the requirement that advantages shall be granted 'unconditionally'.

we believe that the panel decisions and other sources referred to by Japan do not support the interpretation of Article I:1 advocated by Japan in the present case according to which the word 'unconditionally' in Article I:1 must be interpreted to mean that subjecting an advantage granted in connection with the importation of a product to conditions not related to the imported product itself is per se inconsistent with Article I:1, regardless of whether such conditions are discriminatory with respect to the origin of products. Rather, they accord with the conclusion from our analysis of the text of Article I:1 that whether conditions attached to an advantage granted in connection with the importation of a product offend Article I:1 depends upon whether or not such conditions discriminate with respect to the origin of products.[55]

The Panel in *Canada – Autos* found that the term 'unconditionally' does not mean that all conditions are prohibited. The imposition of conditions that do not discriminate between products on the basis of their origin is not inconsistent with Article I:1. According to the Panel, 'unconditionally' refers to the obligation that MFN treatment towards another WTO Member shall not be conditional on reciprocal conduct by that other Member. The Panel stated:

[I]t appears to us that there is an important distinction to be made between, on the one hand, the issue of whether an advantage within the meaning of Article I:1 is subject to conditions, and, on the other, whether an advantage, once it has been granted to the product of any country, is accorded 'unconditionally' to the like product of all other Members. An advantage can be granted subject to conditions without necessarily implying that it is not accorded 'unconditionally' to the like product of other Members.[56]

The Panel in *EC – Tariff Preferences* opted in its 2003 Report for a stricter meaning of the term 'unconditionally'. The measure at issue was the additional tariff preferences granted under the Drug Arrangements of the EC Generalized System of Preferences (GSP) to developing countries that are experiencing grave problems relating to the production of, and the traffic in, illegal drugs. According to the complainant, India, 'the term "unconditionally" in Article I:1 means that any such advantage must be accorded to like products of all other Members regardless of their situation or conduct'.[57] According to the European Communities, 'unconditionally' means that 'any advantage granted may not be subject to conditions requiring compensation'.[58] The Panel did not agree with the European Communities, and stated that:

the term 'unconditionally' in Article I:1 has a broader meaning than simply that of not requiring compensation. While the Panel acknowledges the European Communities' argument that conditionality in the context of traditional MFN clauses in bilateral treaties may relate to conditions of trade compensation for receiving MFN treatment, the Panel does not consider this to be the full meaning of 'unconditionally' under Article I:1. Rather, the

---

[55] Panel Report, *Canada – Autos*, para. 10.29.
[56] *Ibid.*, para. 10.24. Note that the Appellate Body in *Canada – Autos* found: 'The measure maintained by Canada accords the import duty exemption to certain motor vehicles entering Canada from certain countries. These privileged motor vehicles are imported by a limited number of designated manufacturers who are required to meet certain performance conditions. In practice, this measure does not accord the same import duty exemption immediately and unconditionally to like motor vehicles of *all* other Members, as required under Article I:1 of the GATT 1994. The advantage of the import duty exemption is accorded to some motor vehicles originating in certain countries without being accorded to like motor vehicles from *all* other Members. Accordingly, we find that this measure is not consistent with Canada's obligations under Article I:1 of the GATT 1994.' See Appellate Body Report, *Canada – Autos*, para. 85.
[57] Panel Report, *EC – Tariff Preferences*, para. 7.55.   [58] *Ibid.*, para. 7.56.

> Panel sees no reason not to give that term its ordinary meaning under Article I:1, that is, 'not limited by or subject to any conditions'.[59]

As the tariff preferences at issue in *EC – Tariff Preferences* were limited by or subject to conditions, the Panel concluded that they were not granted 'unconditionally' and thus were inconsistent with Article I:1.[60] These different meanings given by the respective Panels to the term 'unconditionally' clearly indicate the need for future clarification by the Appellate Body.

Questions and Assignments 4.4

Give a few examples of disputes in which panels found that an advantage was not accorded 'unconditionally' to like products of all WTO Members.

4.3. MOST-FAVOURED-NATION TREATMENT UNDER THE GATS

As mentioned above, the MFN treatment obligation is also one of the basic provisions of the GATS. This section examines:

- the nature of the MFN treatment obligation provided for in Article II:1 of the GATS;
- the test of consistency of Article II:1; and
- the exemptions from the MFN treatment obligation under the GATS.

4.3.1. Nature of the MFN treatment obligation of Article II:1 of the GATS

Article II:1 of the GATS prohibits discrimination *between* like services and service suppliers from different countries. Accordingly:

> With respect to any measure covered by this Agreement, each Member shall accord immediately and unconditionally to services and service suppliers of any other Member treatment no less favourable than that it accords to like services and service suppliers of any other country.[61]

As is the case with the MFN treatment obligation under the GATT 1994, the principal purpose of the MFN treatment obligation of Article II:1 of the GATS is to ensure *equality of opportunity*, *in casu*, for services and service suppliers from *all* WTO Members. Article II:1 is supplemented by a number of other MFN or MFN-like provisions found elsewhere in the GATS:

---

[59] *Ibid*., para. 7.59.
[60] Note that the European Communities did not appeal this finding by the Panel. See Appellate Body Report, *EC – Tariff preferences*, para. 124, footnote 259.   [61] Article II:1 of the GATS.

- Article VII (regarding recognition)
- Article VIII (regarding monopolies and exclusive service suppliers)
- Article X (regarding future rules on emergency safeguard measures)
- Article XII (regarding balance of payments measures)
- Article XVI (regarding market access) and
- Article XXI (regarding the modification of schedules).[62]

Article XIV of the GATS, the 'general exceptions' provision, also contains an MFN-like obligation.[63]

The Appellate Body in *EC – Bananas III* found that the MFN treatment obligation of Article II:1 of the GATS applies both to *de jure* and to *de facto* discrimination.[64] The Appellate Body disagreed with the European Communities, which had argued that if the negotiators of the GATS had wanted Article II:1 to cover also *de facto* discrimination, they would have explicitly said so.[65] The Appellate Body ruled:

> The obligation imposed by Article II is unqualified. The ordinary meaning of this provision does not exclude *de facto* discrimination. Moreover, if Article II was not applicable to *de facto* discrimination, it would not be difficult – and, indeed, it would be a good deal easier in the case of trade in services, than in the case of trade in goods – to devise discriminatory measures aimed at circumventing the basic purpose of that Article.[66]

In *EC – Bananas III*, various rules for the allocation of import licences for bananas were at issue. According to the complainants, these rules, which on their face were origin-neutral, discriminated against distributors of Latin American and non-traditional ACP bananas in favour of distributors of EC and traditional ACP bananas.

Questions and Assignments 4.5

Are the MFN clauses of the GATS and of the GATT 1994 similar in wording? Are they similar in nature? Does Article II:1 of the GATS also prohibit *de facto* discrimination? Explain.

---

[62] See also Article 5(a) of the GATS *Annex on Telecommunications* and the Preamble of the GATS *Understanding on Commitments in Financial Services.*   [63] See below, pp. 652–3.

[64] With respect to the concepts of *de jure* and *de facto* discrimination, see above, p. 324, footnote 18.

[65] The European Communities noted that, unlike Article II:1, Article XVII of the GATS on the national treatment obligation states explicitly that it applies both to *de jure* and to *de facto* discrimination (see below, p. 341).

[66] Appellate Body Report, *EC – Bananas III*, para. 233. While the Appellate Body agreed with the Panel that Article II of the GATS also covers *de facto* discrimination, it found the Panel's reasoning on this issue 'to be less than fully satisfactory' (Appellate Body Report, *EC – Bananas III*, para. 231). The Panel interpreted Article II of the GATS in the light of panel reports interpreting the national treatment obligation of Article III of the GATT. The Panel also referred to Article XVII of the GATS, which is also a national treatment obligation. The Appellate Body observed, however, that Article II of the GATS relates to MFN treatment, not to national treatment. Therefore, provisions elsewhere in the GATS relating to national treatment obligations, and previous GATT practice relating to the interpretation of the national treatment obligation of Article III of the GATT 1994, are not necessarily relevant to the interpretation of Article II of the GATS. According to the Appellate Body, the Panel would have been on safer ground had it compared the MFN obligation in Article II of the GATS with the MFN and MFN-type obligations in the GATT 1994. The Appellate Body referred, in particular, to the GATT Panel Report in *EEC – Imports of Beef*, See Appellate Body Report, *EC – Bananas III*, paras. 231 and 232. For comments on *EEC – Imports of Beef*, see above, p. 325.

4.3.2. MFN treatment test of Article II:1 of the GATS

As is the case with Article I:1 of the GATT 1994, Article II:1 of the GATS sets out a three-tier test of consistency. There are three questions which need to be answered to determine whether or not a measure violates the MFN treatment obligation of Article II:1 of the GATS, namely:

- whether the measure at issue is a measure covered by the GATS;
- whether the services or service suppliers concerned are 'like services' or 'like service suppliers'; and
- whether less favourable treatment is accorded to the services or service suppliers of a Member.

4.3.2.1. 'Measures covered by this Agreement'

Article I:1 of the GATS states:

> This Agreement applies to measures by Members affecting trade in services.

For a measure to be covered by the GATS, that measure must therefore be:

- a measure by a Member; and
- a measure affecting trade in services.

A 'measure by a Member' is a very broad concept. As stated in Article I:3(a) of the GATS, a 'measure by a Member' is not limited to measures taken by the central government or central government authorities. Measures taken by regional or local governments and authorities are also 'a measure by a Member' within the meaning of Article I:1 of the GATS. Measures taken by non-governmental bodies are 'a measure by a Member' when these measures are taken in the exercise of powers delegated by governments or authorities.[67] A 'measure by a Member' can be a law, regulation, rule, procedure, decision or administrative action, but can also take any other form.[68] A 'measure by a Member' within the meaning of Article I:1 can therefore be a national parliamentary law as well as municipal decrees or rules adopted by professional bodies.[69]

The concept of a 'measure affecting the trade in services' has been clarified by the Appellate Body in *Canada – Autos*. The measure at issue in that case was an import duty exemption accorded by Canada to imports of motor vehicles by certain manufacturers. The complainants, the European Communities and Japan, argued that this measure was inconsistent with Article II:1 of the GATS as it accorded 'less favourable treatment' to certain Members' services and service suppliers than to those of other Members. The Panel found that the import duty

---

[67] See Article I:3(a) of the GATS. It follows that measures of private persons, companies or organisations, which do not exercise any delegated governmental powers, will not be considered to be a 'measure by a Member'.

[68] See Article XXVIII(a) of the GATS.

[69] Note that, pursuant to Article I:3(a) of the GATS, Members have the obligation to take all reasonable measures to ensure that 'sub-national' levels of government and non-governmental bodies with delegated governmental powers comply with the obligations under the GATS. See also above, pp. 63–4.

exemption was indeed inconsistent with Article II:1 of the GATS. Canada appealed this finding of inconsistency and, in addition, as a threshold matter, appealed the Panel's finding that the measure at issue fell within the scope of Article II:1 of the GATS. According to Canada, the measure at issue was not a measure 'affecting trade in services'. The Appellate Body stated that two key issues must be examined to determine whether a measure is one 'affecting trade in services', namely:

- whether there is 'trade in services' in the sense of Article I:2; and
- whether the measure in issue 'affects' such trade in services within the meaning of Article I:1.[70]

With respect to the question of whether there is 'trade in services', note that the GATS does not define what a service is. Article I:3(b) of the GATS, however, states that the term 'services' includes:

> any service in any sector except services supplied in the exercise of governmental authority.

'Services supplied in the exercise of governmental authority' are defined as any services which are supplied neither on a commercial basis nor in competition with one or more service suppliers.[71] Examples of such services may be health care, police protection, penitentiary services and basic education. However, in a growing number of Members, some of the services that are traditionally considered to be services supplied in the exercise of governmental authority have in recent years been subject to privatisation and may now fall within the scope of the GATS.[72]

While the GATS does not define 'services', Article I:2 thereof defines 'trade in services' as 'the supply of a service' through one of four defined 'modes of supply'. Article I:2 states:

> For the purpose of this Agreement, trade in services is defined as the supply of a service:
>
> (a) from the territory of one Member into the territory of any other Member;
> (b) in the territory of one Member to the service consumer of any other Member;
> (c) by a service supplier of one Member, through commercial presence in the territory of any other Member;
> (d) by a service supplier of one Member, through presence of natural persons of a Member in the territory of any other Member.

These four modes of supply of services are commonly referred to as:

- the '*cross border*' mode of supply (for example, legal advice given by a lawyer established in country A to a client in country B);

---

[70] Appellate Body Report, *Canada – Autos*, para. 155. Note that the Appellate Body eventually reversed the Panel's conclusion that the import duty exemption was inconsistent with the requirements of Article II:1 of the GATS. However, it did so, not because it came to the conclusion that Canada acted consistently with its MFN treatment obligation, but because the Panel failed to substantiate its conclusion that the import duty exemption was inconsistent with Article II:1 of the GATS. See Appellate Body Report, *Canada – Autos*, paras. 182 and 184.   [71] See Article I:3(c) of the GATS.

[72] Note also that many measures affecting services in the air transport sector do not fall within the scope of application of the GATS. See GATS *Annex on Air Transport Services*, para. 2.

- the '*consumption abroad*' mode of supply (for example, medical treatment given by a doctor established in country A to a patient from country B who comes to country A for medical treatment);
- the '*commercial presence*' mode of supply (for example, financial services supplied in country B by a bank from country A through a branch office established in country B);[73] and
- the '*presence of natural persons*' mode of supply (for example, the programming services supplied in country B by a computer programmer from country A, who travels to country B to supply his services).[74]

Clearly, the concept of 'trade in services' within the meaning of Article I:1 is very broad. The Panel in *Mexico – Telecoms* defined two of these modes of supply, namely 'cross-border supply' and 'commercial presence'. The question in *Mexico – Telecoms* was whether telecommunication services, provided by a United States service provider to consumers in Mexico without operating or being present in Mexico, could be considered services supplied 'cross-border' within the meaning of Article I:2(a) of the GATS. The Panel found that Article I:2(a) does not require the presence of the supplier in the territory of the country where the service is provided. The Panel then clarified the definition of 'cross-border supply' in Article I:2(a) as follows:

> The ordinary meaning of the words of this provision indicate that the *service* is supplied from the territory of one Member into the territory of another Member. Subparagraph (a) is silent as regards the *supplier* of the service. The words of this provision do not address the service supplier or specify where the service supplier must operate, or be present in some way, much less imply any degree of presence of the supplier in the territory into which the service is supplied. The silence of subparagraph (a) with respect to the supplier suggests that the place where the supplier itself operates, or is present, is not directly relevant to the definition of cross-border supply.[75]

The Panel also had occasion to examine the definition of supply through 'commercial presence'. It clarified this definition, stating:

> The definition of services supplied through a commercial presence makes explicit the location of the service supplier. It provides that a service supplier has a commercial presence – any type of business or professional establishment – *in the territory* of any other Member. The definition is silent with respect to any other territorial requirement (as in cross-border supply under mode 1) or nationality of the service consumer (as in consumption abroad under mode 2). Supply of a service through commercial presence would therefore not exclude a service that originates in the territory in which a commercial presence is established (such as Mexico), but is delivered into the territory of any other Member (such as the United States).[76]

---

[73] Note that, pursuant to Article XXVIII(d) of the GATS, 'commercial presence' means any type of business or professional establishment, including through the constitution, acquisition or maintenance of a juridical person, or the creation or maintenance of a branch or a representative office, within the territory of a Member for the purpose of supplying a service.

[74] It is estimated that cross-border supply of services and supply of services through commercial presence each represent around 40 per cent of total world trade in services; consumption abroad represents around 20 per cent. Supply through the presence of natural persons is, to date, insignificant. See WTO Secretariat, *Market Access: Unfinished Business*, Special Studies Series 6 (WTO, 2001), 105.

[75] Panel Report, *Mexico – Telecoms*, para. 7.30.   [76] *ibid.*, para. 7.375.

With respect to the question of whether the measure at issue *affects* trade in services within the meaning of Article I:1, the Appellate Body clarified in *EC – Bananas III* the term 'affecting' as follows:

> In our view, the use of the term 'affecting' reflects the intent of the drafters to give a broad reach to the GATS. The ordinary meaning of the word 'affecting' implies a measure that has 'an effect on', which indicates a broad scope of application. This interpretation is further reinforced by the conclusions of previous panels that the term 'affecting' in the context of Article III of the GATT is wider in scope than such terms as 'regulating' or 'governing'.[77]

For a measure to affect trade in services, this measure is not required to regulate or govern the trade in, i.e. the supply of, services. A measure is covered by the GATS if it *affects* trade in services, even though the measure may regulate other matters.[78] A measure affects trade in services when the measure bears upon 'the conditions of competition in supply of a service'.[79]

Article XXVIII(c) of the GATS gives a number of examples of 'measures by Members affecting trade in services'. This non-exhaustive list includes measures in respect of:

(i) the purchase, payment or use of a service;
(ii) the access to and use of – in connection with the supply of a service – services which are required by those Members to be offered to the public generally; and
(iii) the presence, including commercial presence, of persons of a Member for the supply of a service in the territory of another Member;

In brief, the concept of 'measures by Members affecting trade in services' is, in all respects, a concept with a broad meaning. Consequently, the scope of measures covered by the GATS, i.e. the scope of measures to which the MFN treatment obligation applies, is likewise broad.

Questions and Assignments 4.6

What are the constituent elements of the MFN treatment test of Article II:1 of the GATS? What measures are covered by the GATS and therefore subject to the MFN treatment obligation under Article II:1 of the GATS? What measures are not covered? In your opinion, are measures affecting basic education and health care in your country subject to the MFN treatment obligation of Article II:1 of the GATS? Give an example (other than those given above) of each mode of supply of services. Can an import prohibition on products containing asbestos be a measure covered by the GATS?

---

[77] Appellate Body Report, *EC – Bananas III*, para. 220.   [78] See Panel Reports, *EC – Bananas III*, para. 7.285.
[79] See *ibid.*, para. 7.281. Regarding the question whether measures adopted by regional and local governments and authorities can 'affect the supply of a service', see Panel Report, *US – Gambling*, para. 6.252. With regard to the function of the term 'affecting' in the context of Article I:1 of the GATS, see Appellate Body Report, *US – FSC (Article 21.5 – EC)*, para. 209.

4.3.2.2. 'Like services or service suppliers'

Once it has been established that the measure at issue is covered by the GATS, the second element of the three-tier test of Article II:1 of the GATS concerning MFN treatment comes into play. Namely, it must be determined whether the services or service suppliers concerned are 'like services' or 'like service suppliers'. It is only between 'like services' or 'like service suppliers' that the MFN treatment obligation applies and that discrimination within the meaning of Article II:1 of the GATS may occur. Services or service suppliers that are not 'like' may be treated differently. Are classical ballet performances 'like' jazz dance? Are French *advocats* and US attorneys 'like service suppliers'? Are internet gambling services and gambling services provided in brick-and-mortar casinos 'like services'?

As noted above, the term 'services' is not defined in the GATS, but Article I:3(c) states that 'services' includes 'any service in any sector except services supplied in the exercise of governmental authority'. The concept of 'service supplier' is defined in the GATS. Article XXVIII(g) provides that a 'service supplier' is 'any person who supplies a service', including natural and legal persons as well as service suppliers providing their services through forms of commercial presence, such as a branch or a representative office. The concepts of '*like* services' and '*like* service suppliers' are not defined in the GATS and, to date, there is almost no relevant case law on the meaning of these terms.[80] A determination of the 'likeness' of services and service suppliers should clearly be based – among other relevant factors – on:

- the characteristics of the service or the service supplier;
- the classification and description of the service in the United Nations Central Product Classification (CPC) system; and
- consumer habits and preferences regarding the service or the service supplier.

Note that two service suppliers that supply a like service are not necessarily 'like service suppliers'. Factors such as the size of the service suppliers, their assets, their use of technology and the nature and extent of their expertise must all be taken into account.[81]

Determining whether services or service suppliers are 'like' for the purpose of article II:1 of the GATS, in essence calls for a determination of the nature and the extent of the competition relationship between the services or service suppliers concerned. The case law on the concept of 'like products' used in the GATT 1994 can serve as a useful source of inspiration but it is clear that the concepts of 'like services' and 'like service suppliers' raise much more difficult conceptual problems than does the concept of 'like products'.

---

[80] See Panel Report, *EC – Bananas III*, para. 7.322; and Panel Report, *Canada – Autos*, para. 10.248.
[81] Note, however, that the Panel in *Canada – Autos* found that to the extent that the service suppliers concerned supplied the same services, they should, in that particular case, be considered 'like'. See Panel Report, *Canada – Autos*, para. 10.248.

Questions and Assignments 4.7

How does one determine whether services or service suppliers are 'like' within the meaning of Article II:1 of the GATS? Are all banking services 'like services'? Are all doctors 'like service suppliers'?

4.3.2.3. *Treatment no less favourable*

The third and final element of the MFN treatment test of Article II:1 of the GATS concerns the treatment accorded to 'like services' or 'like service suppliers'. Members must accord, immediately and unconditionally,[82] to services or service suppliers of Members 'treatment no less favourable' than the treatment they accord to 'like services' or 'like service suppliers' of any other country. Article II of the GATS does not provide any guidance as to the meaning of the concept of 'treatment no less favourable'. However, as discussed below, Article XVII of the GATS on the national treatment obligation contains guidance on the meaning of the concept of 'treatment no less favourable'.[83] Article XVII:3 states:

> Formally identical or formally different treatment shall be considered to be less favourable if it modifies the conditions of competition in favour of services or service suppliers of the Member compared to the like services or service suppliers of any other Member.

In the context of Article XVII, a measure constitutes less favourable treatment if it *modifies* the *conditions of competition*. The Appellate Body ruled in *EC – Bananas III* that, in interpreting Article II:1, and in particular the concept of 'treatment no less favourable', it should not be assumed that the guidance of Article XVII equally applies to Article II. However, as noted above, the Appellate Body has already concluded that the concept of 'treatment no less favourable' in Article II:1 and Article XVII of the GATS should be interpreted to include both *de facto* as well as *de jure* discrimination although only Article XVII states so explicitly.[84] Moreover, note that the Panel in *EC – Bananas III (Article 21.5 – Ecuador)* held that:

> Ecuador has established a presumption that the revised licence allocation system prolongs – at least in part – less favourable treatment in the meanings of Articles II and XVII for wholesale service suppliers of Ecuadorian origin. Ecuador has also shown that its service suppliers do not have opportunities to obtain access to import licences on terms equal to those enjoyed by service suppliers of EC/ACP origin under the revised regime and carried on from the previous regime. Accordingly, it was for the EC to adduce sufficient evidence to rebut this presumption. In light of our evaluation of the factual and legal arguments presented, we conclude that the European Communities has not succeeded in doing so.[85]

---

[82] As noted by Footer and George, 'unconditionally' means that MFN treatment must be given to all other Members regardless of whether reciprocal concessions are provided by those Members. See M. E. Footer and C. George, 'The General Agreement on Trade in, Services' in P. F. J. Macrory, A. E. Appleton and M. G. Plummer (eds), *The World Trade Organization: Legal, Economic and Political Analysis* (Springer, 2005), 828.
[83] See below, pp. 394–5.   [84] See Appellate Body Report, *EC – Bananas III*, para. 234. See also above, p. 335.
[85] Panel Report, *EC – Bananas III (Article 21.5 – Ecuador)*, para. 6.133.

Questions and Assignments 4.8

When is treatment accorded to services or service suppliers of a Member *less favourable* than that accorded to like services or like service suppliers of any other country? Can formally identical treatment be considered to be *less favourable* treatment within the meaning of Article II:1 of the GATS?

4.3.3. Exemptions from the MFN treatment obligation under the GATS

Unlike under the GATT 1994, the GATS allows Members to schedule exemptions from the MFN treatment obligation of Article II:1. Article II:2 of the GATS provides:

> A Member may maintain a measure inconsistent with paragraph 1 provided that such a measure is listed in, and meets the conditions of, the Annex on Article II Exemptions.

Members could list measures in the Annex on Article II Exemptions *until* the date of entry into force of the *WTO Agreement*, i.e. 1 January 1995.[86] Around two-thirds of WTO Members have listed MFN exemptions. In total over 400 exemptions have been granted. The exemptions concern mainly transport (especially maritime), communications (mostly audiovisual), financial and business services.[87]

A Member's notification of an exemption had to contain:

- a description of the sector or sectors in which the exemption applies;
- a description of the measure, indicating why it is inconsistent with Article II;
- the country or countries to which the measure applies;
- the intended duration of the exemption;[88] and
- the conditions creating the need for the exemption.

It is important to note that the exemption list may not identify Members that would not benefit from MFN treatment; the exemption list may only identify Members that would benefit from more market access than other Members. Note, by way of example, that the European Communities included the following exemptions from the MFN treatment obligation in the Annex on Article II Exemptions:

- with regard to audiovisual services (production and distribution of television programmes and cinematographic works), measures granting the benefit of support programmes (such as the Action Plan for Advanced Television Services, MEDIA and EURIMAGES) to audiovisual works and suppliers of such works, meeting certain European origin criteria;

---

[86] Since 1 January 1995, a Member can only exempt a measure from the application of the MFN obligation under Article II:1 by obtaining a waiver from the MFN obligation pursuant to Article IX:3 of the *WTO Agreement* (see paragraph 2 of the Annex on Article II Exemptions). On waivers, see above, pp. 114–15, 142–3.

[87] WTO Secretariat, *Market Access: Unfinished Business*, Special Studies Series 6 (WTO, 2001), 100.

[88] In spite of this requirement, most exemptions have no definitive date for termination.

- with regard to publishing, foreign participation in Italian companies exceeding 49 per cent of the capital and voting rights, subject to a condition of reciprocity; and
- with regard to inland waterways transport, regulations implementing the Mannheim Convention on Rhine Shipping.[89]

Paragraph 6 of the Annex on Article II Exemptions states that, in principle, the exemptions should not exceed ten years. Therefore, all exemptions under Article II:2 should have come to an end by January 2005. However, this did not happen. Relying on the language of paragraph 6 (which merely states that 'in principle' exemptions 'should not' exceed ten years), many Members continue to apply the exemptions they listed in the Annex on Article II Exemptions.[90]

Pursuant to paragraph 3 of the Annex on Article II Exemptions, all exemptions granted for a period of more than five years are reviewed by the Council for Trade in Services. As stated in paragraph 4 of the Annex, the Council examines whether the conditions that created the need for the exemption still prevail and sets a date for any further review. If the Council concludes that these conditions are no longer present, the Member concerned would arguably be obliged to accord MFN treatment in respect of the measure previously exempted from this obligation. The first review of Article II exemptions by the Council for Trade in Services took place in 2000.[91] This review was conducted on a sector-by-sector basis through a question-and-answer process, but the Services Council did not find any exemption no longer justified. The Services Council undertook the second review of MFN exemptions in 2004–5.[92] This review was conducted in the same manner as the 2000 review and also did not result in any finding that an exemption was no longer justified.[93] The Services Council concluded the review by deciding that the next review should start no later than June 2010.[94]

The lists of measures which individual Members have included in the Annex on Article II Exemptions can be found on the WTO's website.[95]

Questions and Assignments 4.9

Can Members exempt measures affecting trade in services from the application of the MFN treatment obligation under Article II:1 of the GATS? Give examples of measures of the United States and India which are exempted from the MFN treatment obligation pursuant to Article II:2 of the GATS.

---

[89] See European Communities and Their Members States, *Final List of Article II (MFN) Exemptions*, GATS/EL/31, dated 15 April 1994.

[90] Note that some Members explicitly stated in their exemption lists that particular exemptions would last for more than ten years. Also note that where a Member indicated, with regard to a specific exemption, the date of its termination, the exemption shall in any case terminate on that date. See para. 5 of the Annex on Article II Exemptions.   [91] See S/C/M/44, dated 21 June 2000.

[92] See S/C/M/76, dated 4 February 2005, S/C/M/78, dated 17 May 2005 and S/C/M/79, dated 16 August 2005.

[93] In view of the fact that the Services Council in practice makes its decisions by consensus, it is 'unlikely' that the Council will ever make such a finding without the consent of the Member concerned. On WTO decision-making, see above, pp. 138–40.   [94] See S/C/M/79, dated 16 August 2005, para. 60.

[95] See www.wto.org/english/tratop_e/serv_e/serv_commitments_e.htm, visited on 12 November 2007.

4.4. NATIONAL TREATMENT UNDER THE GATT 1994

Article III of the GATT 1994, entitled 'National Treatment on Internal Taxation and Regulation', states, in relevant part:

1. The [Members] recognize that internal taxes and other internal charges, and laws, regulations and requirements affecting the internal sale, offering for sale, purchase, transportation, distribution or use of products, and internal quantitative regulations requiring the mixture, processing or use of products in specified amounts or proportions, should not be applied to imported or domestic products so as to afford protection to domestic production.
2. The products of the territory of any [Member] imported into the territory of any other [Member] shall not be subject, directly or indirectly, to internal taxes or other internal charges of any kind in excess of those applied, directly or indirectly, to like domestic products. Moreover, no [Member] shall otherwise apply internal taxes or other internal charges to imported or domestic products in a manner contrary to the principles set forth in paragraph 1.
3. . . .
4. The products of the territory of any [Member] imported into the territory of any other [Member] shall be accorded treatment no less favourable than that accorded to like products of national origin in respect of all laws, regulations and requirements affecting their internal sale, offering for sale, purchase, transportation, distribution or use.

The other paragraphs of Article III deal with particular measures such as internal quantitative regulations relating to the mixture, processing or use of products in specific amounts (paragraphs 5 to 7); government procurement (paragraph 8(a)); subsidies to domestic producers (paragraph 8(b)); internal maximum price control measures (paragraph 9); and internal quantitative regulations relating to cinematographic films (paragraph 10). This chapter does not discuss the rules relating to these specific measures in any detail. It is sufficient to mention here that, pursuant to paragraph 5, local content requirements are prohibited.[96] Pursuant to paragraph 8(a), the national treatment obligation does not apply to laws, regulations or requirements governing government procurement. Pursuant to paragraph 8(b), the national treatment obligation does not prevent the payment of subsidies exclusively to domestic producers.[97]

The provisions of Article III, quoted above, should always be read together with the provisions of the Note *Ad* Article III contained in Annex I, entitled 'Notes and Supplementary Provisions', of the GATT 1994.

Other multilateral agreements on trade in goods, such as the *TBT Agreement*, the *SPS Agreement* and the *Agreement on Trade-Related Investment Measures*, also

---

[96] Local content requirements are direct or indirect requirements that any specific amount or proportion of any product must be supplied from domestic sources.
[97] With regard to subsidies to domestic producers, it should be noted that the GATT Panel in *Italy – Agricultural Machinery* in 1958 had already given a narrow interpretation to the Article III:8(b) exemption from the MFN treatment obligation. If this provision were to be interpreted broadly, any discrimination against imports could be qualified as a subsidy to domestic producers and thus render the discipline of Article III meaningless. The Panel in *US – Malt Beverages* found that the words 'payment of subsidies' in Article III:8(b) refer only to direct subsidies involving a payment, not to other subsidies, such as tax credits or tax reductions. See Panel Report, *US – Malt Beverages*, para. 5.8. Also note that while the payment of a subsidy to domestic producers escapes the disciplines of Article III of the GATT 1994, the disciplines of the *SCM Agreement* are likely to apply. See below, pp. 557–605. On Article III:8(b), see also Panel Report, *EC – Commercial Vessels*, paras. 7.55–7.75.

require national treatment.[98] However, this section is only concerned with the national treatment obligation set out in Article III of the GATT 1994.

4.4.1. Nature of the national treatment obligation of Article III of the GATT 1994

4.4.1.1. The object and purpose of Article III

Article III of the GATT 1994 prohibits discrimination against imported products. Generally speaking, it prohibits Members from treating imported products less favourably than like domestic products once the imported product has entered the domestic market. In a 1958 dispute concerning an Italian law providing special conditions for the purchase on credit of Italian-produced agricultural machinery, the Panel in *Italy – Agricultural Machinery* stated with regard to Article III:

> that the intention of the drafters of the Agreement was clearly to treat the imported products in the same way as the like domestic products once they had been cleared through customs. Otherwise indirect protection could be given.[99]

In *US – Section 337*, the Panel noted that:

> the purpose of Article III . . . is to ensure that internal measures 'not be applied to imported or domestic products so as to afford protection to domestic production' (Article III:1).[100]

In *Japan – Alcoholic Beverages II*, the Appellate Body stated with respect to the purpose of the national treatment obligation of Article III:

> The broad and fundamental purpose of Article III is to avoid protectionism in the application of internal tax and regulatory measures, More specifically, the purpose of Article III 'is to ensure that internal measures "not be applied to imported or domestic products so as to afford protection to domestic producers"'. Toward this end, Article III obliges Members of the WTO to provide equality of competitive conditions for imported products in relation to domestic products. '[T]he intention of the drafters of the Agreement was clearly to treat the imported products in the same way as the like domestic products once they had been cleared through customs. Otherwise indirect protection could be given'.[101]

In *Korea – Alcoholic Beverages*, the Appellate Body identified the objectives of Article III as 'avoiding protectionism, requiring equality of competitive conditions and protecting expectations of equal competitive relationships'.[102]

---

[98] See below, pp. 752–8, 817–18 and 847–8. Note that Article XX of the GATT 1994 also contains a 'national treatment-like' obligation. See below, p. ##.   [99] GATT Panel Report, *Italy – Agricultural Machinery*, para. 11.
[100] GATT Panel Report, *US – Section 337*, para. 5.10.
[101] Appellate Body Report, *Japan – Alcoholic Beverages II*, 109. In a footnote, the Appellate Body refers to GATT Panel Report, *US – Section 337*, para. 5.10 (for the first quote); GATT Panel Report, *US – Superfund*, para. 5.1.9; Panel Report, *Japan – Alcoholic Beverages II*, para. 5.5(b); and GATT Panel Report, *Italy – Agricultural Machinery*, para. 11 (for the second quote). See also Appellate Body Report, *Korea – Alcoholic Beverages*, para. 119; Appellate Body Report, *Chile – Alcoholic Beverages*, para. 67; Appellate Body Report, *EC – Asbestos*, para. 97; and Panel Report, *Indonesia – Autos*, para. 14.108.
[102] Appellate Body Report, *Korea – Alcoholic Beverages*, para. 120. In *Canada – Periodicals*, the Appellate Body stated: 'The fundamental purpose of Article III of the GATT 1994 is to ensure equality of competitive conditions between imported and like domestic products.' See Appellate Body Report, *Canada – Periodicals*, 464 See also Panel Report, *Argentina – Hides and Leather*, para. 11.182.

Panels and scholars have affirmed that one of the main purposes of Article III is to guarantee that internal measures of WTO Members do not undermine their commitments regarding tariffs under Article II.[103] Note, however, that the Appellate Body stressed in *Japan – Alcoholic Beverages II* that the purpose of Article III is broader. The Appellate Body stated:

> The broad purpose of Article III of avoiding protectionism must be remembered when considering the relationship between Article III and other provisions of the *WTO Agreement*. Although the protection of negotiated tariff concessions is certainly one purpose of Article III, the statement in Paragraph 6.13 of the Panel Report that 'one of the main purposes of Article III is to guarantee that WTO Members will not undermine through internal measures their commitments under Article II' should not be overemphasized. The sheltering scope of Article III is not limited to products that are the subject of tariff concessions under Article II. The Article III national treatment obligation is a general prohibition on the use of internal taxes and other internal regulatory measures so as to afford protection to domestic production. This obligation clearly extends also to products not bound under Article II. This is confirmed by the negotiating history of Article III.[104]

In brief, the national treatment obligation of Article III of the GATT 1994 is an obligation of general application that applies both to products with regard to which Members have made tariff concessions and to products with regard to which Members have not done so.[105]

4.4.1.2. *De jure and de facto discrimination*

Article III of the GATT 1994 covers not only 'in law' or *de jure* discrimination; it also covers 'in fact' or *de facto* discrimination.[106] An example of an 'origin-based' measure to which the non-discrimination obligation of Article III has been applied is the measure at issue in *Korea – Various Measures on Beef*.[107] In that case, the disputed measure was a dual retail distribution system for the sale of beef under which *imported* beef was, *inter alia*, to be sold in specialist stores selling only imported beef or in separate sections of supermarkets. An example of an allegedly 'origin-neutral' measure to which the non-discrimination obligation of Article III has been applied is the measure at issue in *Japan – Alcoholic Beverages II*.[108] In that case, the disputed measure was tax legislation that provided for higher taxes on vodka (domestic and imported) than on shochu (domestic and imported).

4.4.1.3. *Internal measures versus border measures*

Article III only applies to internal measures, not to border measures. Other GATT provisions, such as Article II on tariff concessions and Article XI on quantitative

---

[103] See e.g. Panel Report, *Japan – Alcoholic Beverages II*, para. 6.13.
[104] Appellate Body Report, *Japan – Alcoholic Beverages II*, 16
[105] Note the difference with the national treatment obligation of Article XVII of the GATS. See below, pp. 391–2
[106] For definitions of *de jure* and *de facto* discrimination see above, p. 324.   [107] See below, p. 384.
[108] See below, p. 349. Another example is the ban on asbestos and asbestos-containing products at issue in *EC – Asbestos*.

restrictions, apply to border measures. Since Articles III and Articles II and XI provide for very different rules, it is important to determine whether a measure is an internal or a border measure. It is not always easy to distinguish an internal measure from a border measure when the measure is applied to imported products at the time or point of importation. The Note *Ad* Article III clarifies:

> Any internal tax or other internal charge, or any law, regulation or requirement of the kind referred to in paragraph 1 which applies to an imported product and to the like domestic product and is collected or enforced in the case of the imported product at the time or point of importation, is nevertheless to be regarded as an internal tax or other internal charge, or a law, regulation or requirement of the kind referred to in paragraph 1, and is accordingly subject to the provisions of Article III.

It follows that if the import of a product is barred at the border because that product fails, for example, to meet a public health or consumer safety requirement that applies also to domestic products, the consistency of this import ban with the GATT is to be examined under Article III.[109] However, the Note *Ad* Article III, quoted above, leaves it unclear whether Article XI could also apply to such measure.

In *India – Autos*, the Panel noted on the relationship between Article III and Article XI of the GATT 1994 that:

> it . . . cannot be excluded *a priori* that different aspects of a measure may affect the competitive opportunities of imports in different ways, making them fall within the scope either of Article III (where competitive opportunities on the domestic market are affected) or of Article XI (where the opportunities for importation itself, i.e. entering the market, are affected), or even that there may be, in perhaps exceptional circumstances, a potential for overlap between the two provisions, as was suggested in the case of state trading.[110]

According to the Panel, it is possible that one and the same measure is an internal measure (to which Article III applies) *and* a border measure (to which Article XI applies). The Panel in *India – Autos* consequently found that:

> The fact that the measure applies only to imported products need not [be], in itself, an obstacle to its falling within the purview of Article III. For example, an internal tax, or a product standard conditioning the sale of the imported but not of the like domestic product, could nonetheless 'affect' the conditions of the imported product on the market and could be a source of less favorable treatment. Similarly, the fact that a requirement is imposed as a condition on importation is not necessarily in itself an obstacle to its falling within the scope of Article III:4.[111]

4.4.1.4. *Articles III:1, III:2 and III:4*

As stated above, and as explicitly noted by the Appellate Body in *Japan – Alcoholic Beverages II*, Article III:1 articulates a general principle that internal measures should not be applied so as to afford protection to domestic production. According to the Appellate Body in *Japan – Alcoholic Beverages II*:

---

[109] See Panel Report, *Canada – FIRA*, para. 5.14   [110] Panel Report, *India – Autos*, para. 7.224.
[111] *Ibid.* para. 7.306. The Panel applied this finding subsequently to the 'indigenization' condition, at issue in this case. See *ibid.*, paras. 7.307–7.315.

> This general principle informs the rest of Article III. The purpose of Article III:1 is to establish this general principle as a guide to understanding and interpreting the specific obligations contained in Article III:2 and in the other paragraphs of Article III, while respecting, and not diminishing in any way, the meaning of the words actually used in the texts of those other paragraphs.[112]

The general principle that internal measures should not be applied so as to afford protection to domestic production is elaborated on in Article III:2 with regard to internal taxation and in Article III:4 with regard to internal regulation. In Article III:2, two non-discrimination obligations can be distinguished: one obligation is set out in the first sentence of Article III:2, relating to internal taxation of 'like products'; and the other obligation is set out in the second sentence of Article III:2, relating to internal taxation of 'directly competitive or substitutable products'. The sections below will discuss:

- the national treatment test for internal taxation on like products under Article III:2, first sentence of the GATT 1994;
- the national treatment test for internal taxation on directly competitive or substitutable products, contained in Article III:2, second sentence of the GATT 1994; and
- the national treatment test for internal regulation under Article III:4 of the GATT 1994.

Questions and Assignments 4.10

What is the purpose of the national treatment obligation set out in Article III of the GATT 1994? Does Article III apply to border measures? How does one distinguish between border measures and internal measures? What is the function of Article III:1?

4.4.2. National treatment test for internal taxation on like products

Article III:2, first sentence of the GATT 1994 states:

> The products of the territory of any [Member] imported into the territory of any other [Member] shall not be subject, directly or indirectly, to internal taxes or other internal charges of any kind in excess of those applied, directly or indirectly, to like domestic products.

This provision sets out a two-tier test for the GATT-consistency of internal taxation. In *Canada – Periodicals*, the Appellate Body found:

> [T]here are two questions which need to be answered to determine whether there is a violation of Article III:2 of the GATT 1994: (a) whether imported and domestic products are like products; and (b) whether the imported products are taxed in excess of the domestic products. If the answers to both questions are affirmative, there is a violation of Article III:2, first sentence.[113]

---

[112] Appellate Body Report, *Japan – Alcoholic Beverages II*, 111. See also Appellate Body Report, *EC – Bananas III*, para. 216.   [113] Appellate Body Report, *Canada – Periodicals*, 468.

In brief, the two-tier test for the consistency of internal taxation with Article III:2, first sentence, therefore requires the examination of:

- whether the imported and domestic products are *like products*; and
- whether the imported products are *taxed in excess* of the domestic products.

Recall that Article III:1 provides that internal taxation must not be applied so as to afford protection to domestic production. However, according to the Appellate Body in *Japan – Alcoholic Beverages II*, the presence of a protective application need not be established separately from the *specific* requirements of Article III:2, first sentence. The Appellate Body stated:

> Article III:1 informs Article III:2, first sentence, by establishing that if imported products are taxed in excess of like domestic products, then that tax measure is inconsistent with Article III. Article III:2, first sentence does not refer specifically to Article III:1. There is no specific invocation in this first sentence of the general principle in Article III:1 that admonishes Members of the WTO not to apply measures so as to afford protection. This omission must have some meaning. We believe the meaning is simply that the presence of a protective application need not be established separately from the specific requirements that are included in the first sentence in order to show that a tax measure is inconsistent with the general principle set out in the first sentence. However, this does not mean that the general principle of Article III:1 does not apply to this sentence. To the contrary, we believe the first sentence of Article III:2 is, in effect, an application of this general principle.[114]

The presence of a protective application thus need be established neither separately nor together with the specific requirements contained in Article III:2, first sentence. Whenever imported products from one Member are subject to taxes in excess of those applied to like domestic products in another Member, this is deemed to 'afford protection to domestic production' within the meaning of Article III:1.[115] However, before applying the test under Article III:2, first sentence, it has to be determined whether the measure at issue is an 'internal tax or other internal charge of any kind' within the meaning of that provision.

Questions and Assignments 4.11

What are the constituent elements of the national treatment test of Article III:2, first sentence of the GATT 1994?

4.4.2.1. 'Internal tax . . .'

Article III:2, first sentence of the GATT 1994 concerns 'internal taxes and other charges of any kind' which are applied 'directly or indirectly' on products. Examples of such internal taxes on products are value added taxes (VAT), sales taxes and excise duties. Income taxes or import duties are not covered since they

---

[114] Appellate Body Report, *Japan – Alcoholic Beverages II*, 111–12.
[115] See also Panel Report, *Argentina – Hides and Leather*, para. 11.137.

are not *internal* taxes on *products*.[116] The words 'applied *directly or indirectly* on products' should be understood to mean 'applied *on or in connection with* products'. It has been suggested that a tax applied 'indirectly' is a tax applied, not on a product as such, but on the processing of the product.[117] The word 'indirectly' has also been considered to cover taxes that are imposed on inputs.[118] The Panel in *Mexico – Taxes on Soft Drinks* found that non-cane sugar sweeteners were 'indirectly' subject to the soft drink tax when they were used for the production of soft drinks and syrups.[119]

In *US – Tobacco*, the Panel examined the question of whether penalty provisions under US law, consisting of a non-refundable marketing assessment and a requirement to purchase additional quantities of domestic burley and flue-cured tobacco, could be qualified as 'internal taxes or other charges of any kind' within the meaning of Article III:2, first sentence. The Panel stated:

> It was thus the Panel's understanding that the US Government treated these DMA [Domestic Marketing Assessment] provisions as penalty provisions for the enforcement of a domestic content requirement for tobacco, not as separate fiscal measures, and that such interpretation corresponded to the ordinary meaning of the terms used in the relevant statute and proposed rules. Further, it appeared that these penalty provisions had no separate raison d'être in the absence of the underlying domestic content requirement. The above factors suggested to the Panel that it would not be appropriate to analyze the penalty provisions separately from the underlying domestic content requirement.[120]

According to the Panel in *US – Tobacco*, a penalty provision for the enforcement of a domestic law is not an 'internal tax or charge of any kind' within the meaning of Article III:2, first sentence. Such a financial penalty provision is an internal regulation within the meaning of Article III:4 of the GATT 1994, as discussed below.[121]

Also, the Panel in *EEC – Animal Feed Proteins* did not consider a security deposit to be a fiscal measure although this deposit accrued to the EEC when the buyers of vegetable proteins failed to fulfil the obligation to purchase milk powder. The Panel considered the security deposit, including any associated cost, to be only an enforcement mechanism for the purchase requirement and, as such, it should be examined with the purchase obligation.[122]

The issue of border tax adjustment must also be mentioned in this context. Border tax adjustments are:

> any fiscal measures which put into effect, in whole or in part, the destination principle (i.e. which enable exported products to be relieved of some or all of the tax charged in the exporting country in respect of similar domestic products sold to consumers on the home market and which enable imported products sold to consumers to be charged with some or all of the tax charged in the importing country in respect of similar domestic products).[123]

---

[116] Note that an income tax regulation can be considered to be an internal regulation and thus to fall within the scope of Article III:4 of the GATT 1994, discussed below, pp. 367–90. See also Panel Report, *US – FSC (Article 21.5 – EC)*, para. 8.145.   [117] *Analytical Index: Guide to GATT Law and Practice* (WTO, 1995), 141.
[118] See GATT Panel Report, *Japan – Alcoholic Beverages I*, para. 5.8.
[119] See Panel Report, *Mexico – Taxes on Soft Drinks*, para. 8.45.   [120] GATT Panel Report, *US – Tobacco*, para. 80.
[121] See below, p. ##.   [122] See GATT Panel Report, *EEC – Animal Feed Proteins*, para. 4.4.
[123] 1970 Report of the Working Party on *Border Tax Adjustments*, BISD 18S/97, para. 4.

Such a fiscal measure involving the *imposition of taxes* by the importing country is obviously a fiscal measure which falls within the scope of application of Article III:2. This was confirmed by the Working Party on *Border Tax Adjustments* which found that:

> there was convergence of views to the effect that taxes directly levied on products were eligible for tax adjustment. Examples of such taxes comprised specific excise duties, sales taxes and cascade taxes and the tax on value added.[124]

Note that the regulatory objective pursued by the tax measure is of no relevance to the question of whether the measure is an internal tax within the meaning of Article III:2 and the consistency of that measure with the national treatment requirement. In *Japan – Alcoholic Beverages II*, the Appellate Body stated that Members may pursue through their tax measures any given policy objective *provided* they do so in compliance with Article III:2. In *Argentina – Hides and Leather*, the Panel rejected Argentina's contention that the tax legislation at issue in that case was designed to achieve efficient tax administration and collection and as such did not fall under Article III:2. The Panel stated:

> We agree that Members are free, within the outer bounds defined by such provisions as Article III:2, to administer and collect internal taxes as they see fit. However, if, as here, such 'tax administration' measures take the form of an internal charge and are applied to products, those measures must, in our view, be in conformity with Article III:2. There is nothing in the provisions of Article III:2 to suggest a different conclusion. If it were accepted that 'tax administration' measures are categorically excluded from the ambit of Article III:2, this would create a potential for abuse and circumvention of the obligations contained in Article III:2.[125]

In *US – Malt Beverages*, a measure preventing imported products from being sold in a manner that would enable them to avoid taxation was considered to be a measure within the scope of Article III:2, first sentence, because it assigned a higher tax rate to the imported products.[126]

Questions and Assignments 4.12

Does income tax fall within the scope of application of Article III:2 of the GATT 1994? What is border tax adjustment and does it fall within the scope of application of Article III:2? Does Article III:2 affect the freedom of Members to administer and collect internal taxes on products as they see fit?

4.4.2.2. 'Like products'

Similar to the concept of 'like products' in Article I:1 of the GATT 1994, the concept of 'like products' in Article III:2, first sentence, is not defined in the

---

[124] *Ibid.*, para. 14.   [125] Panel Report, *Argentina – Hides and Leather*, para. 11.144.
[126] See GATT Panel Report, *US – Malt Beverages*, paras. 5.21 and 5.22.

GATT 1994. There are, however, a considerable number of GATT and WTO dispute settlement reports that shed light on the meaning of the concept of 'like products' in Article III:2, first sentence.

Under the Japanese tax system at issue in *Japan – Alcoholic Beverages II*, the internal tax imposed on domestic shochu was the same as that imposed on imported shochu; the higher tax imposed on imported vodka was also imposed on domestic vodka. Identical products (not considering brand differences) were thus taxed identically. However, the question was whether shochu and vodka should be considered to be 'like products'. If shochu and vodka were found to be 'like', vodka could not be taxed in excess of shochu. The Appellate Body in *Japan – Alcoholic Beverages II* addressed the scope of the concept of 'like products' within the meaning of Article III:2, first sentence. The Appellate Body first stated that this concept should be interpreted narrowly because of the existence of the concept of 'directly competitive or substitutable products' used in the second sentence of Article III:2. The Appellate Body ruled:

> Because the second sentence of Article III:2 provides for a separate and distinctive consideration of the protective aspect of a measure in examining its application to a broader category of products that are not 'like products' as contemplated by the first sentence, we agree with the Panel that the first sentence of Article III:2 must be construed narrowly so as not to condemn measures that its strict terms are not meant to condemn. Consequently, we agree with the Panel also that the definition of 'like products' in Article III:2, first sentence, should be construed narrowly.[127]

Subsequently, the Appellate Body expressly agreed with the basic approach for determining 'likeness' set out in the 1970 Report of the Working Party on *Border Tax Adjustments*.[128] This Working Party found that:

> the interpretation of the term should be examined on a case-by-case basis. This would allow a fair assessment in each case of the different elements that constitute a 'similar' product. Some criteria were suggested for determining, on a case-by-case basis, whether a product is 'similar': the product's end-uses in a given market; consumers' tastes and habits, which change from country to country; the product's properties, nature and quality.[129]

This basic approach was followed in almost all post-1970 GATT panel reports involving a GATT provision in which the concept of 'like products' was used.[130] According to the Appellate Body in *Japan – Alcoholic Beverages II*, this approach should be helpful in identifying on a case-by-case basis the range of 'like products' that falls within the limits of Article III:2, first sentence, of the GATT 1994. However, the Appellate Body added:

> Yet this approach will be most helpful if decision makers keep ever in mind how narrow the range of 'like products' in Article III:2, first sentence is meant to be as opposed to the

---

[127] Appellate Body Report, *Japan – Alcoholic Beverages II*, 112–13.
[128] The Working Party considered the concept of 'like' or 'similar' products as used throughout the GATT.
[129] Report of the Working Party on *Border Tax Adjustments*, BISD 18S/97, para. 18.
[130] See e.g. GATT Panel Report, *Australia – Ammonium Sulphate*; GATT Panel Report, *EEC – Animal Proteins*; GATT Panel Report, *Spain – Unroasted Coffee*; GATT Panel Report, *Japan – Alcoholic Beverages I*; and GATT Panel Report, *US – Superfund*.

> range of 'like' products contemplated in some other provisions of the GATT 1994 and other Multilateral Trade Agreements of the *WTO Agreement*. In applying the criteria cited in [the report of the Working Group on] Border Tax Adjustments to the facts of any particular case, and in considering other criteria that may also be relevant in certain cases, panels can only apply their best judgement in determining whether in fact products are 'like'. This will always involve an unavoidable element of individual, discretionary judgement.[131]

The criteria listed in the Report of the Working Party on *Border Tax Adjustments* did not include the tariff classification of the products concerned. Yet tariff classification has been used as a criterion for determining 'like products' in several panel reports.[132] The Appellate Body acknowledged in *Japan – Alcoholic Beverages II* that uniform classification in tariff nomenclatures based on the Harmonised System can be of help in determining 'likeness', but cautioned against the use of tariff bindings since there are sometimes very broad bindings that do not necessarily indicate similarity of the products covered by those bindings.[133] Rather, tariff bindings represent the results of trade concessions negotiated among WTO Members.[134]

To determine whether beet sugar and cane sugar are 'like' products with the meaning of Article III:2, first sentence, the Panel in *Mexico – Taxes on Soft Drinks* stated that it would consider:

> on the basis of the evidence presented by the parties, the products' properties, nature and quality; their end-uses in a given market; consumers' tastes and habits; and the tariff classification of the products based on the Harmonized System. It will construe the test of likeness in a narrow manner, as has been consistently done under the first sentence of Article III:2 of the GATT 1994.[135]

Having considered these factors, the Panel concluded that beet sugar and cane sugar are 'like' products within the meaning of Article III:2, first sentence, as sweeteners in the production of soft drinks and syrups.[136]

The Panel in *Dominican Republic – Import and Sale of Cigarettes* agreed with the Dominican Republic that quality is a factor in the determination of 'likeness'. However, the Panel then stated that:

> it does not think that values declared by importers for customs purposes can be the only factor used in order to determine the quality of a product. The Dominican Republic admits that the imported *Viceroy* cigarettes had the same retail selling price as the domestic *Líder* cigarettes. The Panel believes that, if prices of a product are to be considered as a function of their quality, then the actual price of the product in the marketplace should be in principle more relevant than the value declared in customs.[137]

---

[131] Appellate Body Report, *Japan – Alcoholic Beverages II*, 113–14. The Appellate Body disagreed with the Panel's observation in para. 6.22 of the Panel Report that distinguishing between 'like products' and 'directly competitive or substitutable products' under Article III:2 is 'an arbitrary decision'. According to the Appellate Body, it is 'a discretionary decision that must be made in considering the various characteristics of products in individual cases'. Appellate Body Report, *Japan – Alcoholic Beverages II*, 114.

[132] Note that the tariff classification of the products concerned by other countries was a factor considered by the GATT Panel in *Spain – Unroasted Coffee*. See above, pp. 330–1. Also, the Panel in *US – Gasoline* referred to the tariff classification in its determination of 'likeness'.

[133] On the Harmonised System and the concept of 'tariff bindings', see below, pp. 428–31 and 417–18.

[134] See Appellate Body Report, *Japan – Alcoholic Beverages II*, 114–15.

[135] Panel Report, *Mexico – Taxes on Soft Drinks*, para. 8.29.   [136] *Ibid*, para. 8.36.

[137] Panel Report, *Dominica Republic – Import and Sale of Cigarettes*, para. 7.333.

The Panel in *Dominican Republic – Import and Sale of Cigarettes* thus concluded that in examining whether the Selective Consumption Tax was consistent with Article III:2, first sentence, it would consider:

> as products 'alike' to the imported cigarettes, those domestic cigarettes that were sold at a similar price and, more specifically, will consider that *Viceroy* cigarettes imported in the Dominican Republic are alike to domestic *Líder* cigarettes.[138]

The actual price at which products are sold on the market of the importing country is thus a factor – in addition to the factors identified in the report of the Working Party on *Border Tax Adjustments* – to be considered when determining whether products are 'like' within the meaning of Article III:2, first sentence.

In *US – Malt Beverages*, the Panel held that national legislation giving special tax exemptions to products of small firms (whether domestic or foreign) would constitute discrimination against imports from a larger foreign firm and therefore infringe Article III because its products would be treated less favourably than the like products of a small domestic firm.[139] According to the Panel in *US – Malt Beverages*, the fact that products were produced by small or large firms, i.e. a process and production method (PPM) of the products concerned, was irrelevant in the determination of their 'likeness'.[140]

The same Panel also considered, however, with regard to the determination of 'likeness' that:

> the like product determination under Article III:2 also should have regard to the purpose of the Article . . . The purpose is . . . not to prevent contracting parties from using their fiscal and regulatory powers for purposes other than to afford protection to domestic production. Specifically, the purpose of Article III is not to prevent contracting parties from differentiating between different product categories for policy purposes unrelated to the protection of domestic production . . . Consequently, in determining whether two products subject to different treatment are like products, it is necessary to consider whether such product differentiation is being made 'so as to afford protection to domestic production'.[141]

The Panel found domestic wine containing a particular local variety of grape to be 'like' imported wine not containing this variety of grape after considering that the purpose of differentiating between the wines was to afford protection to the local production of wine. The Panel noted that the United States did not advance any alternative policy objective for the differentiation. According to the Panel in *US – Malt Beverages*, the reason for the product differentiation was to be considered when deciding on the 'likeness' of products. This Panel thus introduced into the case law the 'regulatory intent' approach, more commonly referred to as the 'aim-and-effect' approach, to the determination of 'likeness' of products.

In a dispute concerning, *inter alia*, special tax levels for luxury vehicles, *US – Taxes on Automobiles*, the Panel elaborated on this approach to determining 'likeness'.[142] The United States imposed a retail excise tax on cars over US$30,000 and

---

[138] *Ibid.*, para. 7.336.   [139] See GATT Panel Report, *US – Malt Beverages*, para. 5.19   [140] See above, p. 331.
[141] GATT Panal Report, US – *Malt-Beverages paras*. 5.24–5.25.
[142] GATT Panel Report, *US – Taxes on Automobiles*, paras. 5.8 ff.

the Panel had to determine whether cars with prices above and below US$30,000 were 'like products'. The complainant in this dispute, the European Communities, argued before the Panel that 'likeness' should be determined on the basis of factors such as the end-use of the products, their physical characteristics and tariff classification. The United States contended that the key factor in determining 'likeness' should be whether the measure was applied 'so as to afford protection to domestic industry'. The Panel reasoned that the determination of 'likeness' would, in all but the most straightforward cases, have to include an examination of the *aims and effects* of the particular tax measure. According to the Panel in *US – Taxes on Automobiles*, 'likeness' should be examined in terms of whether the less favourable treatment was based on a regulatory distinction made so as to afford protection to domestic production. *In casu*, the Panel decided that the luxury tax was not implemented to afford protection to the domestic production of cars and that cars above and below US$30,000 could not, for the purpose of the luxury tax, be considered as 'like products' under Article III:2, first sentence.[143]

The 'aim-and-effect' test for determining 'likeness' was, however, explicitly rejected in 1996 by the Panel in *Japan – Alcoholic Beverages II*. The Panel found as follows:

> The Panel noted, in this respect, that the proposed aim-and-effect test is not consistent with the wording of Article III:2, first sentence. The Panel recalled that the basis of the aim-and-effect test is found in the words 'so as to afford protection' contained in Article III:1. The Panel further recalled that Article III:2, first sentence, contains no reference to those words. Moreover, the adoption of the aim-and-effect test would have important repercussions on the burden of proof imposed on the complainant. The Panel noted in this respect that the complainants, according to the aim-and-effect test, have the burden of showing not only the effect of a particular measure, which is in principle discernible, but also its aim, which sometimes can be indiscernible. The Panel also noted that very often there is a multiplicity of aims that are sought through enactment of legislation and it would be a difficult exercise to determine which aim or aims should be determinative for applying the aim-and-effect test. Moreover, access to the complete legislative history, which according to the arguments of the parties defending the aim-and-effect test, is relevant to detect protective aims, could be difficult or even impossible for a complaining party to obtain. Even if the complete legislative history is available, it would be difficult to assess which kinds of legislative history (statements in legislation, in official legislative reports, by individual legislators, or in hearings by interested parties) should be primarily determinative of the aims of the legislation.[144]

In support of its rejection of the aim-and-effect test in determining 'likeness' in the context of Article III:2, the Panel in *Japan – Alcoholic Beverages II* further noted:

> the list of exceptions contained in Article XX of GATT 1994 could become redundant or useless because the aim-and-effect test does not contain a definitive list of grounds justifying departure from the obligations that are otherwise incorporated in Article III. The purpose of Article XX is to provide a list of exceptions, subject to the conditions that they 'are not applied in a manner which would constitute a means of arbitrary or unjustifiable discrimination between countries where the same conditions prevail, or a disguised restriction of international trade', that could justify deviations from the obligations

---

[143] Note that the GATT Panel Report in *US – Taxes on Automobiles* was never adopted by the Contracting Parties.   [144] Panel Report, *Japan – Alcoholic Beverages II*, para. 6.16.

imposed under GATT. Consequently, in principle, a WTO Member could, for example, invoke protection of health in the context of invoking the aim-and-effect test. The Panel noted that if this were the case, then the standard of proof established in Article XX would effectively be circumvented. WTO Members would not have to prove that a health measure is 'necessary' to achieve its health objective. Moreover, proponents of the aim-and-effect test even shift the burden of proof, arguing that it would be up to the complainant to produce a *prima facie* case that a measure has both the aim and effect of affording protection to domestic production and, once the complainant has demonstrated that this is the case, only then would the defending party have to present evidence to rebut the claim. In sum, the Panel concluded that for reasons relating to the wording of Article III as well as its context, the aim-and-effect test proposed by Japan and the United States should be rejected.[145]

The Appellate Body in *Japan – Alcoholic Beverages II* implicitly affirmed the Panel's rejection of the 'aim-and-effect' (or 'regulatory intent') approach to determining whether products are 'like'.[146]

Questions and Assignments 4.13

Why must the concept of 'like products' in Article III:2, first sentence, of the GATT 1994 be interpreted narrowly? What is the basic approach followed by most panels and the Appellate Body in determining 'likeness' within the meaning of Article III:2, first sentence? Can it be that products considered to be 'like' under Article I:1 are not 'like' under Article III:2, first sentence? Why did the Panel in *Japan – Alcoholic Beverages II* reject the 'aim and effect' approach, or 'regulatory intent' approach, to the determination of whether products are 'like'?

4.4.2.3. Taxes 'in excess of'

Pursuant to Article III:2, first sentence, of the GATT 1994, internal taxes on imported products should not be 'in excess of' the internal taxes applied to 'like' domestic products. In *Japan – Alcoholic Beverages II*, the Appellate Body established a strict benchmark for the 'in excess of' requirement. The Appellate Body ruled:

> Even the smallest amount of 'excess' is too much. The prohibition of discriminatory taxes in Article III:2, first sentence, is not conditional on a 'trade effects test' nor is it qualified by a *de minimis* standard.[147]

On the absence of a 'trade-effects-test', the Appellate Body stated in the same case, *Japan – Alcoholic Beverages II*:

> it is irrelevant that the 'trade effects' of the tax differential between imported and domestic products, as reflected in the volumes of imports, are insignificant or even non-existent;

---

[145] *Ibid.*, para. 6.17.
[146] Appellate Body Report, *Japan – Alcoholic Beverages II*, 115. The Appellate Body stated: 'With these modifications to the legal reasoning in the Panel Report, we affirm the legal conclusions and the findings of the Panel with respect to 'like products' in all other respects.'
[147] *Ibid.* See also Panel Report, *Argentina – Hides and Leather*, para. 11.244; and Panel Report, *Mexico – Taxes on Soft Drinks*, para. 8.52.

> Article III *protects expectations* not of any particular trade volume but rather of the *equal competitive relationship* between imported and domestic products.[148]
>
> [Emphasis added]

With respect to the absence of a *de minimis* standard, note that the Panel in *US – Superfund* had already ruled in 1987:

> The rate of tax applied to the imported products is 3.5 cents per barrel higher than the rate applied to the like domestic products . . . The tax on petroleum is . . . inconsistent with the United States' obligations under Article III:2, first sentence.[149]

In *Argentina – Hides and Leather*, the Panel rejected Argentina's argument that the tax burden differential between imported and domestic products was *de minimis* because it would only exist for a thirty-day period.[150] Furthermore, the Panel ruled that the identity and circumstances of the persons involved in sales transactions could not serve as a justification for tax burden differentials.[151]

In the same case, the Panel also emphasised that Article III:2, first sentence, requires a comparison of *actual* tax burdens rather than merely of *nominal* tax burdens. The Panel ruled:

> It is necessary to recall the purpose of Article III:2, first sentence, which is to ensure 'equality of competitive conditions between imported and like domestic products'. Accordingly, Article III:2, first sentence, is not concerned with taxes or charges as such or the policy purposes Members pursue with them, but with their economic impact on the competitive opportunities of imported and like domestic products. It follows, in our view, that what must be compared are the tax burdens imposed on the taxed products.
>
> We consider that Article III:2, first sentence, requires a comparison of actual tax burdens rather than merely of nominal tax burdens. Were it otherwise, Members could easily evade its disciplines. Thus, even where imported and like domestic products are subject to identical tax rates, the actual tax burden can still be heavier on imported products. This could be the case, for instance, where different methods of computing tax bases lead to a greater actual tax burden for imported products.[152]

The Panel in *Japan – Alcoholic Beverages I* stated:

> in assessing whether there is tax discrimination, account is to be taken not only of the rate of the applicable internal tax but also of the taxation methods (e.g. different kinds of internal taxes, direct taxation of the finished product or indirect taxation by taxing the raw materials used in the product during the various stages of its production) and of the rules for the tax collection (e.g. basis of assessment).[153]

A Member which applies higher taxes on imported products in some situations but 'balances' this by applying lower taxes on the imported products in other situations also acts inconsistently with the national treatment obligation of Article III:2, first sentence. The Panel in *Argentina – Hides and Leather* ruled:

---

[148] Appellate Body Report, *Japan – Alcoholic Beverages II*, 110.
[149] GATT Panel Report, *US – Superfund*, para. 5.1.1.
[150] See Panel Report, *Argentina – Hides and Leather*, para. 11.245.
[151] See *ibid.*, para. 11.220. See also Panel Report, *US – Gasoline*, para. 6.11. As the Panel in *Argentina – Hides and Leather* noted in a footnote, the disciplines of Article III:2, first sentence, are of course subject to whatever exceptions a Member may justifiably invoke.
[152] Panel Report, *Argentina – Hides and Leather*, paras. 11.182–11.183.
[153] GATT Panel Report, *Japan – Alcoholic Beverages I*, para. 5.8.

> Article III:2, first sentence, is applicable to each individual import transaction. It does not permit Members to balance more favourable tax treatment of imported products in some instances against less favourable tax treatment of imported products in other instances.[154]

If differences in taxes are based only upon the nationality of producers or the origin of the parts and components contained in the products, these tax differences are – as the Panel in *Indonesia – Autos* found – necessarily inconsistent with the national treatment obligation of Article III:2, first sentence.[155] Note, however, that Article III:2, first sentence, also covers *de facto* discrimination.[156] An example of *de facto* discrimination under Article III:2, first sentence, can be found in *Dominican Republic – Import and Sale of Cigarettes*. Here, the Panel started with an examination of the legislation on the basis of which the added tax on cigarettes was determined, only to find that the legislation itself was not discriminatory.[157] It went on to look at the actual practice, however, and concluded that there was sufficient evidence to indicate that imported cigarettes were, in fact, taxed in excess of Dominican Republic cigarettes, in violation of Article III:2, first sentence.[158]

Questions and Assignments 4.14

Is the size of the tax differential important under Article III:2, first sentence, of the GATT 1994? Does Article III:2, first sentence, require equality of the nominal or the actual tax burden on like products? Does Article III:2, first sentence, allow balancing more favourable tax treatment of imported products in some instances against less favourable tax treatment of imported products in other instances?

4.4.3. National treatment test for internal taxation on directly competitive or substitutable products

The second sentence of Article III:2 of the GATT 1994 states:

> Moreover, no Member shall otherwise apply internal taxes or other internal charges to imported or domestic products in a manner contrary to the principles set forth in paragraph 1.

As discussed above, the relevant leading principle set forth in Article III:1 is that internal taxes and other internal charges:

> should not be applied to imported or domestic products so as to afford protection to domestic production.

Furthermore, the Note *Ad* Article III provides with respect to Article III:2:

---

[154] Panel Report, *Argentina – Hides and Leather*, para. 11.260. See also in GATT Panel Report, *US – Tobacco*, para. 98.   [155] See Panel Report, *Indonesia – Autos*, para. 14.112.   [156] See above, p. 346 .
[157] See Panel Report, *Dominican Republic – Import and Sale of Cigarettes*, paras. 7.345–7.353.
[158] See *ibid.*, paras. 7.354–7.358.

> A tax conforming to the requirements of the first sentence of paragraph 2 would be considered to be inconsistent with the provisions of the second sentence only in cases where competition was involved between, on the one hand, the taxed product and, on the other hand, a directly competitive or substitutable product which was not similarly taxed.

The relationship between the first and the second sentence of Article III:2 was addressed by the Appellate Body in *Canada – Periodicals*, a dispute concerning, *inter alia*, a Canadian excise tax on magazines. The Appellate Body considered:

> there are two questions which need to be answered to determine whether there is a violation of [the first sentence of] Article III:2 of the GATT 1994: (a) whether imported and domestic products are like products; and (b) whether the imported products are taxed in excess of the domestic products. If the answers to both questions are affirmative, there is a violation of Article III:2, first sentence.
>
> If the answer to one question is negative, there is a need to examine further whether the measure is consistent with Article III:2, second sentence.[159]

As the Appellate Body stated in *Japan – Alcoholic Beverages II* and again in *Canada – Periodicals*, Article III:2, second sentence, contemplates a 'broader category of products' than Article III:2, first sentence.[160] Furthermore, Article III:2, second sentence, sets out a different test of inconsistency. In *Japan – Alcoholic Beverages II*, the Appellate Body stated:

> Unlike that of Article III:2, first sentence, the language of Article III:2, second sentence, specifically invokes Article III:1. The significance of this distinction lies in the fact that whereas Article III:1 acts implicitly in addressing the two issues that must be considered in applying the first sentence, it acts explicitly as an entirely separate issue that must be addressed along with two other issues that are raised in applying the second sentence. Giving full meaning to the text and to its context, three separate issues must be addressed to determine whether an internal tax measure is inconsistent with Article III:2, second sentence. These three issues are whether:
>
> (1) the imported products and the domestic products are 'directly competitive or substitutable products' which are in competition with each other;
> (2) the directly competitive or substitutable imported and domestic products are 'not similarly taxed'; and
> (3) the dissimilar taxation of the directly competitive or substitutable imported and domestic products is 'applied . . . so as to afford protection to domestic production'.
>
> Again, these are three separate issues. Each must be established separately by the complainant for a panel to find that a tax measure imposed by a Member of the WTO is inconsistent with Article III:2, second sentence.[161]

In brief, the national treatment test for internal taxation under Article III:2, second sentence, of the GATT 1994 thus requires an examination of:

- whether the imported and domestic products are *directly competitive or substitutable*;
- whether these products are *not similarly taxed*; and

---

[159] Appellate Body Report, *Canada – Periodicals*, 468.

[160] *Ibid.*, 470; and Appellate Body Report, *Japan – Alcoholic Beverages II*, p. 112.

[161] Appellate Body Report, *Japan – Alcoholic Beverages II*, 116. This part was later cited and endorsed by the Appellate Body, in Appellate Body Report, *Canada – Periodicals*, 23; and in Appellate Body Report, *Chile – Alcoholic Beverages*, para. 47.

- whether the dissimilar taxation is *applied so as to afford protection* to domestic production.

However, before this test of consistency of internal taxation can be applied, it must be established that the measure at issue is an 'internal tax or other internal charge' within the meaning of Article III:2, second sentence.

Questions and Assignments 4.15

What are the constituent elements of the national treatment test under Article III:2, second sentence, of the GATT 1994? What is the relationship between the first and the second sentence of Article III:2?

4.4.3.1. 'Internal taxes . . .'

As is the case with Article III:2, first sentence, Article III:2, second sentence, of the GATT 1994 is also concerned with 'internal taxes or other internal charges'. For a discussion on the meaning and the scope of these concepts, recall the discussion above in the section dealing with Article III:2, first sentence.[162] With regard to this constituent element of the national treatment test, there is no difference between the first and the second sentence of Article III:2.

4.4.3.2. 'Directly competitive or substitutable products'

The national treatment obligation of Article III:2, second sentence of the GATT 1994 applies to 'directly competitive or substitutable products'. The relevant case law to date provides us with a number of examples of products that panels and/or the Appellate Body have found to be 'directly competitive or substitutable' on the market of a particular Member. In *Canada – Periodicals*, the 'directly competitive or substitutable products' are the imported split-run periodicals and domestic non-split-run periodicals at issue in that case.[163] In *Japan – Alcoholic Beverages II* and *Korea – Alcoholic Beverages*, shochu and soju respectively were found to be 'directly competitive or substitutable' with imported liquors, such as whisky, vodka, brandy, cognac, rum, genever and liqueurs.[164] In *Chile – Alcoholic Beverages*, the domestically produced pisco was considered 'directly competitive or substitutable' with imported distilled spirits, such as whisky, brandy and cognac.[165] In *Mexico – Taxes on Soft Drinks*, the 'directly competitive or substitutable products'

---

[162] See above, pp. 348–58.

[163] See Appellate Body Report, *Canada – Periodicals*, 474. A split-run periodical is a periodical with different editions distributed in different countries, in which part of the editorial material is the same or substantially the same as editorial material that appears in other editions but in which advertisements differ (as they are focused on the local market of a specific edition). The Appellate Body found split-run and non-split-run periodicals to be directly competitive or substitutable products in so far as they are part of the same segment of the Canadian market for periodicals.

[164] See Panel Report, *Japan – Alcoholic Beverages II*, para. 6.32 ('whisky, brandy, rum, gin, genever, and liqueurs', para. 6.28); and Panel Report, *Korea – Alcoholic Beverages*, para. 10.98 ('vodka, whiskies, rum, gin, brandies, cognac, liqueurs, tequila and ad-mixtures', para. 10.57).

[165] See Appellate Body Report, *Chile – Alcoholic Beverages*, para. 7.83.

were soft drinks that were domestically produced with cane sugar and foreign soft drinks that were produced with high fructose corn syrup.[166] Note that in this case, domestic soft drinks produced with cane sugar and imported soft drinks produced with beet sugar were considered 'like' under Article III:2, first sentence.

In *Canada – Periodicals*, the Appellate Body ruled that to be 'directly competitive or substitutable' within the meaning of Article III:2, second sentence, products do not – contrary to what Canada had argued – have to be perfectly substitutable. The Appellate Body noted:

> A case of perfect substitutability would fall within Article III:2, first sentence, while we are examining the broader prohibition of the second sentence.[167]

With regard to the relationship between the concept of 'like products' of Article III:2, first sentence, and the concept of 'directly competitive or substitutable' products of Article III:2, second sentence, the Appellate Body stated in *Korea – Alcoholic Beverages*:

> 'Like' products are a subset of directly competitive or substitutable products: all like products are, by definition, directly competitive or substitutable products, whereas not all 'directly competitive or substitutable' products are 'like'. The notion of like products must be construed narrowly but the category of directly competitive or substitutable products is broader. While perfectly substitutable products fall within Article III:2, first sentence, imperfectly substitutable products can be assessed under Article III:2, second sentence.[168]

As to the meaning of the concept of 'directly competitive or substitutable products', the Appellate Body stated in *Korea – Alcoholic Beverages*:

> The term 'directly competitive or substitutable' describes a particular type of relationship between two products, one imported and the other domestic. It is evident from the wording of the term that the essence of that relationship is that the products are in competition. This much is clear both from the word 'competitive' which means 'characterized by competition', and from the word 'substitutable' which means 'able to be substituted'. The context of the competitive relationship is necessarily the marketplace since this is the forum where consumers choose between different products. Competition in the marketplace is a dynamic, evolving process. Accordingly, the wording of the term 'directly competitive or substitutable' implies that the competitive relationship between products is *not* to be analyzed *exclusively* by reference to *current* consumer preferences. In our view, the word 'substitutable' indicates that the requisite relationship *may* exist between products that are not, at a given moment, considered by consumers to be substitutes but which are, nonetheless, *capable* of being substituted for one another.[169]

The Appellate Body also noted:

> according to the ordinary meaning of the term, products are competitive or substitutable when they are interchangeable or if they offer, as the Panel noted, 'alternative ways of satisfying a particular need or taste'. Particularly in a market where there are regulatory barriers to trade or to competition, there may well be latent demand.

---

[166] See Panel Report, *Mexico – Taxes on Soft Drinks*, para. 8.78.
[167] Appellate Body Report, *Canada – Periodicals*, 473.
[168] Appellate Body Report, *Korea – Alcoholic Beverages*, para. 118. In a footnote, the Appellate Body referred to the Appellate Body Report, *Japan – Alcoholic Beverages II* and Appellate Body Report, *Canada – Periodicals*.
[169] Appellate Body Report, *Korea – Alcoholic Beverages*, para. 114.

> The words 'competitive or substitutable' are qualified in the *Ad* Article by the term 'directly'. In the context of Article III:2, second sentence, the word 'directly' suggests a degree of proximity in the competitive relationship between the domestic and the imported products. The word 'direct' does not, however, prevent a panel from considering both latent and extant demand.[170]

In brief, the Appellate Body considers products to be 'directly competitive or substitutable' when they are interchangeable or when they offer alternative ways of satisfying a particular need or taste. The Appellate Body also considers that, in examining whether products are 'directly competitive or substitutable', an analysis of *latent* as well as *extant* demand is required since 'competition in the marketplace is a dynamic, evolving process'.[171] As the Appellate Body in *Korea – Alcoholic Beverages* stated, in justification of its dynamic view of the concept of 'directly competitive or substitutable products':

> In view of the objectives of avoiding protectionism, requiring equality of competitive conditions and protecting expectations of equal competitive relationships, we decline to take a static view of the term 'directly competitive or substitutable'. The object and purpose of Article III confirms that the scope of the term 'directly competitive or substitutable' cannot be limited to situations where consumers *already* regard products as alternatives. If reliance could be placed only on current instances of substitution, the object and purpose of Article III:2 could be defeated by the protective taxation that the provision aims to prohibit.[172]

Past panels have acknowledged that consumer behaviour might be influenced, in particular, by protectionist internal taxation. Citing the Panel in *Japan – Alcoholic Beverages I*,[173] the Panel in *Japan – Alcoholic Beverages II* observed:

> a tax system that discriminates against imports has the consequence of creating and even freezing preferences for domestic goods.[174]

The same Panel also stated:

> consumer surveys in a country with . . . a [protective] tax system would likely understate the degree *of potential* competitiveness between substitutable products.[175]
>
> [Emphasis added]

The Appellate Body in *Korea – Alcoholic Beverages* thus concluded that it may be highly relevant to examine latent demand.[176] The competitive relationship between products is clearly not to be analysed by reference to *current* consumer preferences only.[177]

With respect to the factors to be taken into account in establishing whether products are 'directly competitive or substitutable', the Appellate Body in *Japan – Alcoholic Beverages II* agreed with the Panel in that case that these factors include, in addition to their physical characteristics, common end-use and tariff classifications, the nature of the compared products and the competitive conditions in the relevant market.[178] The Appellate Body held:

---

[170] *Ibid.*, paras. 115–16.   [171] *Ibid.*, para. 120.   [172] *Ibid.*
[173] GATT Panel Report, *Japan – Alcoholic Beverages I*, para. 5.9.
[174] Panel Report, *Japan – Alcoholic Beverages II*, para. 6.28.   [175] *Ibid.*
[176] See Appellate Body Report, *Korea – Alcoholic Beverages*, para. 120.   [177] See *ibid.*, para. 114.
[178] See Appellate Body Report *Japan – Alcoholic Beverages II*, 117.

> The GATT 1994 is a commercial agreement, and the WTO is concerned, after all, with markets. It does not seem inappropriate to look at competition in the relevant markets as one among a number of means of identifying the broader category of products that might be described as 'directly competitive or substitutable'.
>
> Nor does it seem inappropriate to examine elasticity of substitution as one means of examining those relevant markets.[179]

The Appellate Body thus considered an examination of the cross-price elasticity of demand in the relevant market, as a means of establishing whether products are 'directly competitive or substitutable' in that market. In *Korea – Alcoholic Beverages*, the Appellate Body further clarified:

> studies of cross-price elasticity, which in our Report in *Japan – Alcoholic Beverages* were regarded as one means of examining a market, involve an assessment of latent demand. Such studies attempt to predict the change in demand that would result from a change in the price of a product following, *inter alia*, from a change in the relative tax burdens on domestic and imported products.[180]

However, in that case, *Korea – Alcoholic Beverages*, the Appellate Body was careful to stress that cross-price elasticity of demand for products is not the decisive criterion in determining whether these products are 'directly competitive or substitutable'. The Appellate Body agreed with the Panel's emphasis on the 'quality' or 'nature' of competition rather than the 'quantitative overlap of competition'. The Appellate Body shared the Panel's reluctance to rely unduly on quantitative analyses of the competitive relationship. In its view, an approach that focused solely on the quantitative overlap of competition would, in essence, make cross-price elasticity the decisive criterion in determining whether products are 'directly competitive or substitutable'.[181]

In establishing whether products are 'directly competitive or substitutable', the market situation in *other* Members may be relevant and can be taken into consideration. In *Korea – Alcoholic Beverages*, the Appellate Body stated:

> It is, of course, true that the 'directly competitive or substitutable' relationship must be present in the market at issue, in this case, the Korean market. It is also true that consumer responsiveness to products may vary from country to country. This does not, however, preclude consideration of consumer behaviour in a country other than the one at issue. It seems to us that evidence from other markets may be pertinent to the examination of the market at issue, particularly when demand on that market has been influenced by regulatory barriers to trade or to competition. Clearly, not every other market will be relevant to the market at issue. But if another market displays characteristics similar to the market at issue, then evidence of consumer demand in that other market may have some relevance to the market at issue. This, however, can only be determined on a case-by-case basis, taking account of all relevant facts.[182]

The question has arisen as to whether, in examining whether products are 'directly competitive or substitutable', it is necessary to examine products on an item-by-item basis or whether it is permitted to group products together for the purpose of this examination.

---

[179] *Ibid.*   [180] Appellate Body Report, *Korea – Alcoholic Beverages*, para. 121.   [181] See *ibid.*, para. 134.
[182] *Ibid.*, para. 137.

In *Korea – Alcoholic Beverages*, the Panel compared distilled and diluted soju (the domestic Korean liquor at issue in this case) with imported liquor products (vodka, whiskies, rum, gin, brandies, cognac, liqueurs, tequila and ad-mixtures) on a group basis, rather than on an item-by-item basis. The Appellate Body, rejecting Korea's appeal of the Panel's method of comparison, ruled:

> Whether, and to what extent, products can be grouped is a matter to be decided on a case-by-case basis. In this case, the Panel decided to group the imported products at issue on the basis that:
>
> > . . . on balance, all of the imported products specifically identified by the complainants have sufficient common characteristics, end-uses and channels of distribution and prices. . .
>
> As the Panel explained in the footnote attached to this passage, the Panel's subsequent analysis of the physical characteristics, end-uses, channels of distribution and prices of the imported products confirmed the correctness of its decision to group the products for analytical purposes. Furthermore, where appropriate, the Panel did take account of individual product characteristics. It, therefore, seems to us that the Panel's grouping of imported products, complemented where appropriate by individual product examination, produced the same outcome that individual examination of each imported product would have produced. We, therefore, conclude that the Panel did not err in considering the imported beverages together.[183]

Questions and Assignments 4.16

When are products 'directly competitive or substitutable' within the meaning of Article III:2, second sentence, of the GATT 1994? In determining whether products are 'directly competitive or substitutable', does one consider only extant demand or also latent demand? What factors can be taken into account in determining whether products are 'directly competitive or substitutable'? How important is the 'cross-price elasticity of demand' of products in determining whether such products are 'directly competitive or substitutable'?

4.4.3.3. 'Not similarly taxed'

The next element or requirement of the national treatment test under Article III:2, second sentence, of the GATT 1994 is whether the products at issue are 'not similarly taxed'. While under Article III:2, first sentence, even the slightest tax differential leads to the conclusion that the internal tax imposed on imported products is inconsistent with the national treatment obligation, under Article III:2, second sentence, the tax differential has to be more than *de minimis* to support a conclusion that the internal tax imposed on imported products is GATT-inconsistent. In *Japan – Alcoholic Beverages II*, the Appellate Body explained:

> To interpret 'in excess of' and 'not similarly taxed' identically would deny any distinction between the first and second sentences of Article III:2. Thus, in any given case, there may be some amount of taxation on imported products that may well be 'in excess of' the tax

---

[183] *Ibid.*, paras. 143–4.

> on domestic 'like products' but may not be so much as to compel a conclusion that 'directly competitive or substitutable' imported and domestic products are 'not similarly taxed' for the purposes of the *Ad* Article to Article III:2, second sentence. In other words, there may be an amount of excess taxation that may well be more of a burden on imported products than on domestic 'directly competitive or substitutable products' but may nevertheless not be enough to justify a conclusion that such products are 'not similarly taxed' for the purposes of Article III:2, second sentence. We agree with the Panel that this amount of differential taxation must be more than *de minimis* to be deemed 'not similarly taxed' in any given case. And, like the Panel, we believe that whether any particular differential amount of taxation is *de minimis* or is not *de minimis* must, here too, be determined on a case-by-case basis. Thus, to be 'not similarly taxed', the tax burden on imported products must be heavier than on 'directly competitive or substitutable' domestic products, and that burden must be more than *de minimis* in any given case.[184]

The 'not similarly taxed' requirement is met even if only some imported products are not taxed similarly to domestic products, while other imported products are taxed similarly. The Appellate Body stated in *Canada – Periodicals* that:

> dissimilar taxation of even some imported products as compared to directly competitive or substitutable domestic products is inconsistent with the provisions of the second sentence of Article III:2.[185]

To support this conclusion, the Appellate Body referred to the Panel in *US – Section 337*, which found:

> that the 'no less favourable' treatment requirement of Article III:4 has to be understood as applicable to each individual case of imported products. The Panel rejected any notion of balancing more favourable treatment of some imported products against less favourable treatment of other imported products.[186]

Questions and Assignments 4.17

Is the size of the tax differential important under Article III:2, second sentence, of the GATT 1994?

4.4.3.4. 'So as to afford protection to domestic production'

The last element or requirement of the test under Article III:2, second sentence, of the GATT 1994 is whether the dissimilar taxation is applied 'so as to afford protection to domestic production'. This requirement must be distinguished from the second requirement of 'not similarly taxed'. In *Japan – Alcoholic Beverages II*, the Appellate Body noted:

> [T]he Panel erred in blurring the distinction between [the issue of whether the products at issue were 'not similarly taxed'] and the entirely separate issue of whether the tax measure in question was applied 'so as to afford protection'. Again, these are separate

---

[184] Appellate Body Report, *Japan – Alcoholic Beverages II*, 118. On the *de minimis* standard, see also Appellate Body Report, *Canada – Periodicals*, 474; Appellate Body Report, *Chile – Alcoholic Beverages*, para. 49; and Panel Report, *Indonesia – Autos*, para. 14.115.

[185] Appellate Body Report, *Canada – Periodicals*, 474.

[186] GATT Panel Report, *US – Section 337*, para. 5.14. See below, p. 383.

issues that must be addressed individually. If 'directly competitive or substitutable products' are *not* 'not similarly taxed', then there is neither need nor justification under Article III:2, second sentence, for inquiring further as to whether the tax has been applied 'so as to afford protection'. But if such products are 'not similarly taxed', a further inquiry must necessarily be made.[187]

As to how to establish whether a tax measure was applied so as to afford protection to domestic production, the Appellate Body noted in *Japan – Alcoholic Beverages II*:

> As in [the GATT Panel Report on *Japan – Customs Duties, Taxes and Labelling Practices on Imported Wines and Alcoholic Beverages*, BISD 34S/83], we believe that an examination in any case of whether dissimilar taxation has been applied so as to afford protection requires a comprehensive and objective analysis of the structure and application of the measure in question on domestic as compared to imported products. We believe it is possible to examine objectively the underlying criteria used in a particular tax measure, its structure, and its overall application to ascertain whether it is applied in a way that affords protection to domestic products.
>
> Although it is true that the aim of a measure may not be easily ascertained, nevertheless its protective application can most often be discerned from the design, the architecture, and the revealing structure of a measure.[188]

To determine whether the application of a tax measure affords protection to domestic production, it is the application criteria, the structure and the overall application rather than the subjective intent of the legislator or regulator that must be examined. For example, if the tax measure operates in such a way that the lower tax brackets cover primarily domestic production, whereas the higher tax brackets embrace primarily imported products, the implication is that the tax measure is applied so as to afford protection to domestic production.

As the Appellate Body acknowledged in *Japan – Alcoholic Beverages II*, the very magnitude of the tax differential may be evidence of the protective application of a tax measure. Most often, however, other factors will also be considered.

With regard to the relevance of the intent of the legislator or regulator, the Appellate Body in *Japan – Alcoholic Beverages II* noted:

> [Whether a tax measure is applied so as to afford protection to domestic production] is not an issue of intent. It is not necessary for a panel to sort through the many reasons legislators and regulators often have for what they do and weigh the relative significance of those reasons to establish legislative or regulatory intent. If the measure is applied to imported or domestic products so as to afford protection to domestic production, then it does not matter that there may not have been any desire to engage in protectionism in the minds of the legislators or the regulators who imposed the measure. It is irrelevant that protectionism was not an intended objective if the particular tax measure in question is nevertheless, to echo Article III:1, '*applied* to imported or domestic products so as to afford protection to domestic production'. This is an issue of how the measure in question is *applied*.[189]

In *Chile – Alcoholic Beverages*, Chile argued that the internal taxation on alcoholic beverages at issue in that case was aimed at, among other things, reducing

---

[187] Appellate Body Report, *Japan – Alcoholic Beverages II*, 119.   [188] *Ibid.*, 120.   [189] *Ibid.*, 119.

the consumption of alcoholic beverages with higher alcohol content. The Appellate Body held:

> We recall once more that, in *Japan – Alcoholic Beverages*, we declined to adopt an approach to the issue of 'so as to afford protection' that attempts to examine 'the many reasons legislators and regulators often have for what they do'. We called for examination of the design, architecture and structure of a tax measure precisely to permit identification of a measure's objectives or purposes as revealed or objectified in the measure itself. Thus, we consider that a measure's purposes, objectively manifested in the design, architecture and structure of the measure, *are* intensely pertinent to the task of evaluating whether or not that measure is applied so as to afford protection to domestic production. In the present appeal, Chile's explanations concerning the structure of the New Chilean System – including, in particular, the truncated nature of the line of progression of tax rates, which effectively consists of two levels (27 per cent *ad valorem* and 47 per cent *ad valorem*) separated by only 4 degrees of alcohol content – might have been helpful in understanding what *prima facie* appear to be anomalies in the progression of tax rates. The conclusion of protective application reached by the Panel becomes very difficult to resist, in the absence of countervailing explanations by Chile. The mere statement of the four objectives pursued by Chile does not constitute effective rebuttal on the part of Chile.[190]

Note, however, that, in *Canada – Periodicals*, the Appellate Body did seem to give at least some importance to statements of representatives of the Canadian Government about the policy objectives of the tax measure at issue.[191]

Questions and Assignments 4.18

How does one establish whether internal taxes on directly competitive or substitutable products have been applied so as to afford protection to domestic production? Is the intent of the legislator relevant in deciding whether an internal tax is inconsistent with the national treatment obligation of Article III:2, second sentence, of the GATT 1994?

4.4.4. National treatment test for internal regulation

The national treatment obligation under Article III of the GATT 1994 does not only concern internal taxation dealt with in Article III:2. Article III also concerns internal regulation, dealt with primarily in Article III:4. Article III:4 states, in relevant part:

---

[190] Appellate Body Report, *Chile – Alcoholic Beverages*, para. 71. The Panel in this case found that approximately 75 per cent of all *domestic* production of the distilled alcoholic beverages at issue will be located in the *lowest* tax bracket, whereas approximately 95 per cent of the directly competitive or substitutable *imported* products will be found in the *highest* tax bracket. See Panel Report, *Chile – Alcoholic Beverages*, para. 7.158.

[191] See Appellate Body Report, *Canada – Periodicals*, 475–6 *In casu* these statements of Canadian officials confirmed that the tax measure was indeed applied so as to afford protection to domestic production. The Appellate Body took these explicit statements into account together with the demonstrated actual protective effect of the measure, as a basis for its finding that the design and structure of the Canadian measure was so as to afford protection to the production of Canadian periodicals.

> The products of the territory of any [Member] imported into the territory of any other [Member] shall be accorded treatment no less favourable than that accorded to like products of national origin in respect of all laws, regulations and requirements affecting their internal sale, offering for sale, purchase, transportation, distribution or use.

This provision sets out a three-tier test for the consistency of internal regulation. In *Korea – Various Measures on Beef*, the Appellate Body stated:

> For a violation of Article III:4 to be established, three elements must be satisfied: that the imported and domestic products at issue are 'like products'; that the measure at issue is a 'law, regulation, or requirement affecting their internal sale, offering for sale, purchase, transportation, distribution, or use'; and that the imported products are accorded 'less favourable' treatment than that accorded to like domestic products.[192]

In other words, the three-tier test of consistency of internal regulation with Article III:4 requires the examination of whether:

- the measure at issue is a *law, regulation or requirement* covered by Article III:4;
- the imported and domestic products are *like products*; and
- the imported products are accorded *less favourable treatment*.

In *EC – Bananas III*, the Appellate Body, in its examination of the constituent elements of Article III:4, ruled with regard to the phrase 'so as afford protection to domestic production' of Article III:1 as follows:

> Article III:4 does *not* specifically refer to Article III:1. Therefore, a determination of whether there has been a violation of Article III:4 does *not* require a separate consideration of whether a measure 'afford[s] protection to domestic production'.[193]

As the Appellate Body found in *EC – Asbestos*, Article III:1, nevertheless, has 'particular contextual significance in interpreting Article III:4, as it sets forth the "general principle" pursued by that provision'.[194]

Questions and Assignments 4.19

What are the constituent elements of the national treatment test of Article III:4 of the GATT 1994? In this context, what is the importance of the general principle, set out in Article III:1, that internal measures may not be applied so as to afford protection to domestic production?

4.4.4.1. 'Laws, regulations and requirements . . .'

Article III:4 concerns 'all laws, regulations and requirements affecting [the] internal sale, offering for sale, purchase, transportation, distribution or use [of products]'. Broadly speaking, the national treatment obligation of Article III:4

---

[192] Appellate Body Report, *Korea – Various Measures on Beef*, para. 133. See also Panel Report, *Dominican Republic – Import and Sale of Cigarettes*, para. 7.272; and Panel Report, *EC – Trademarks and Geographical Indications (Australia)*, para. 7.262.   [193] Appellate Body Report, *EC – Bananas III*, para. 216.
[194] Appellate Body Report, *EC – Asbestos*, para. 93.

applies to regulations affecting the sale and use of products. In 1958, the Panel in *Italy – Agricultural Machinery* ruled:

> the text of paragraph 4 referred both in English and French to laws and regulations and requirements *affecting* internal sale, purchase, etc., and not to laws, regulations and requirements governing the conditions of sale or purchase. The selection of the word 'affecting' would imply, in the opinion of the Panel, that the drafters of the Article intended to cover in paragraph 4 not only laws and regulations which directly governed the conditions of sale or purchase but also any laws or regulations which might adversely modify the conditions of competition between the domestic and imported products on the internal market.[195]

The Panel thus interpreted the scope of application of Article III:4 broadly as including all measures that may modify the conditions of competition. While affirming this broad – interpretation of the term 'affecting',[196] the Appellate Body in *US – FSC (Article 21.5 – EC)* stressed the important function of this term in the context of Article III:4. The Appellate Body observed that:

> the clause in which the word 'affecting' appears – 'in respect of all laws, regulations and requirements *affecting* their internal sale, offering for sale, purchase, transportation, distribution or use' – serves to define the scope of application of Article III:4. (emphasis added) Within this phrase, the word 'affecting' operates as a link between identified types of government action ('laws, regulations and requirements') and specific transactions, activities and uses relating to products in the marketplace ('internal sale, offering for sale, purchase, transportation, distribution or use'). It is, therefore, not any 'laws, regulations and requirements' which are covered by Article III:4, but only those which 'affect' the specific transactions, activities and uses mentioned in that provision. Thus, the word 'affecting' assists in defining the types of measure that must conform to the obligation not to accord 'less favourable treatment' to like imported products, which is set out in Article III:4.[197]

Later panels built on the broad interpretation of the scope of Article III:4.[198] In *US – Section 337*, for example, the Panel, referring back to the paragraph from *Italy – Agricultural Machinery* quoted above, addressed the issue of whether only substantive laws, regulations and requirements *or* also procedural laws, regulations and requirements can be regarded as 'affecting' the internal sale of imported goods. The Panel in *US – Section 337* found:

> In the Panel's view, enforcement procedures cannot be separated from the substantive provisions they serve to enforce. If the procedural provisions of internal law were not covered by Article III:4, contracting parties could escape the national treatment standard by enforcing substantive law, itself meeting the national treatment standard, through

---

[195] GATT Panel Report, *Italy – Agricultural Machinery*, para. 12.
[196] See Appellate Body Report, *US – FSC (Article 21.5 – EC)*, para. 210.   [197] *Ibid.*, para. 208.
[198] It has been suggested that Article III:4 might *not* apply to 'laws, regulations . . .' making distinctions based on extra-territorial policy considerations not affecting the characteristics or properties of the products concerned. See G. Marceau and J. Trachtmann, 'A Map of the World Trade Organization Law of Domestic Regulation of Goods', in G. A. Bermann and P. C. Mavroidis (eds.), *Trade and Human Health and Safety* (Cambridge University Press, 2006), 55. An example would be a law prohibiting a product produced by child labour or produced in an environmentally unfriendly manner. Such laws regulating non-product related process and production methods (NPR PPMs) would fall under the scope of application of the prohibition of quantitative restrictions under Article XI of the GATT 1994 rather than the national treatment obligation of Article III:4 of the GATT 1994. See above, p. 354. However, the broad scope of application given to Article III:4 in the case law to date strongly pleads against the exclusion of measures regulating NPR PPMs from the scope of application of Article III:4.

procedures less favourable to imported products than to like products of national origin. The interpretation suggested by the United States would therefore defeat the purpose of Article III, which is to ensure that internal measures 'not be applied to imported or domestic products so as to afford protection to domestic production' (Article III:1).[199]

According to GATT and WTO case law, Article III:4 applies, *inter alia*, to:

- minimum price requirements applicable to domestic and imported beer (*Canada – Provincial Liquor Boards (US)*);[200]
- limitations on points of sale for imported alcoholic beverages (*Canada – Provincial Liquor Boards (EEC)*);[201]
- limiting 'listing' of imported beer to the six-pack size (*Canada – Provincial Liquor Boards (US)*);[202]
- the requirement that imported beer and wine be sold only through in-State wholesalers or other middlemen (*US – Malt Beverages*);[203]
- a ban on cigarette advertising (*Thailand – Cigarettes*);[204]
- additional marking requirements such as an obligation to add the name of the producer or the place of origin or the formula of the product (*Certificates of Origin, Marks of Origin, Consular Formalities*);[205]
- practices concerning internal transportation of beer (*US – Malt Beverages*);[206]
- trade-related investment measures (*Canada – FIRA*);[207]
- requirements that imported cigarettes cannot leave the bonded warehouse unless the tax stamps are affixed to each cigarette packet in the presence of a tax inspector (*Dominican Republic – Import and Sale of Cigarettes*);[208]
- regulation resulting in higher railway transportation costs for imported grain (*Canada – Wheat Exports and Grain Imports*);[209]
- regulation providing that foreign grain was not allowed into Canadian grain elevators without prior authorisation (*Canada – Wheat Exports and Grain Imports*);[210]
- regulation prohibiting storage of grain of foreign origin in grain elevators containing domestic grain (*Canada – Wheat Exports and Grain Imports*);[211]
- legislation setting down (additional) requirements of equivalence and reciprocity for the registration of geographical indications for agricultural

---

[199] GATT Panel Report, *US – Section 337*, para. 5.10.
[200] See GATT Panel Report, *Canada – Provincial Liquor Boards (US)*, para. 5.30.
[201] See GATT Panel Report, *Canada – Provincial Liquor Boards (EEC)*, para. 4.26. Note that the Panel found it unnecessary to decide if there was a violation of Article III:4 but held that 'Article III:4 was also applicable to state trading enterprises at least when the monopoly of the importation and monopoly of the distribution in the domestic markets were combined, as was the case of the provincial liquor boards in Canada.' *Ibid.*
[202] See GATT Panel Report, *Canada – Provincial Liquor Boards (US)*, para. 5.4. Suppliers of domestic or imported beer, wine or spirits wishing to sell the product in a Canadian province had to obtain a 'listing', i.e. an authorisation to sell, from the provincial marketing agency. A listing request was assessed on the basis of criteria such as quality, price, marketability, etc. and could be subject to conditions under which the product in question could be sold in the province (e.g. minimum sales quotas, bottle/package sizes).
[203] See GATT Panel Report, *US – Malt Beverages*, para. 5.32.
[204] See GATT Panel Report, *Thailand – Cigarettes*, para. 77.
[205] See Working Party Report, *Certificates of Origin, Marks of Origin, Consular Formalities*, para. 13.
[206] See GATT Panel Report, *US – Malt Beverages*, para. 5.50. See also GATT Panel Report, *Canada – Provincial Liquor Boards (US)*, para. 5.12.   [207] See GATT Panel Report, *Canada – FIRA*, paras. 5.12 and 6.1.
[208] See Panel Report, *Dominican Republic – Import and Sale of Cigarettes*, paras. 7.170–7.171.
[209] See Panel Reports, *Canada – Wheat Exports and Grain Imports*, paras. 6.331–6.332.
[210] See *ibid.*, para. 6.165.   [211] See *ibid.*, para. 6.262.

products and foodstuffs of other WTO Members (*EC – Trademarks and Geographical Indications (Australia)*);[212]

- a prohibition on the 'marketing' of retreaded tyres (*Brazil – Retreaded Tyres*);[213] and
- an obligation to dispose of ten used tyres as a prerequisite for the importation of one retreaded tyre (*Brazil – Retreaded Tyres*).[214]

In *EC – Bananas III*, the Appellate Body agreed with the Panel that Article III:4 was applicable to the EC import licensing requirements at issue. This was contested by the European Communities on the ground that import licensing was a border measure and not an internal measure within the scope of Article III:4. However, the Appellate Body ruled:

> At issue in this appeal is not whether *any* import licensing requirement, as such, is within the scope of Article III:4, but whether the EC procedures and requirements for the *distribution* of import licences for imported bananas among eligible operators *within* the European Communities are within the scope of this provision . . . These rules go far beyond the mere import licence requirements needed to administer the tariff quota for third-country and non-traditional ACP bananas or Lomé Convention requirements for the importation of bananas. These rules are intended, among other things, to cross-subsidize distributors of EC (and ACP) bananas and to ensure that EC banana ripeners obtain a share of the quota rents. As such, these rules affect 'the internal sale, offering for sale, purchase . . .' within the meaning of Article III:4, and therefore fall within the scope of this provision.[215]

The Panel in *Canada – Wheat Exports and Grain Imports* addressed the question of whether one of the measures at issue, Section 57(c) of the Canada Grain Act, affects 'distribution' within the meaning of Article III:4 of the GATT 1994. The Panel noted:

> the GATT 1994 does not contain a definition of 'distribution'. The New Shorter Oxford English Dictionary defines 'distribution' to mean, *inter alia*, 'the dispersal of commodities among consumers effected by commerce'. We take this to mean that 'distribution' entails, *inter alia*, the supply of goods to consumers or to on-sellers.[216]

The Panel subsequently found that since Section 57(c) of the Canada Grain Act directly affects access to the Canadian bulk grain handling system, described by Canada itself as a 'distribution channel', Section 57(c) is a measure affecting internal 'distribution' of foreign grain in Canada.[217]

In *Canada – Autos*, the Panel held that a measure can be considered to be a measure affecting, i.e. having an effect on, the internal sale or use of imported products even if it is not shown that *under the current circumstances* the measure has an impact on the decisions of private parties to buy imported products. The Panel noted:

> With respect to whether the CVA [Canadian Value Added] requirements affect the 'internal sale . . . or use' of products, we note that, as stated by the Appellate Body, the

---

[212] See Panel Report, *EC – Trademarks and Geographical Indications* (Australia) para. 7.263.
[213] See Panel Report, *Brazil – Retreaded Tyres*, para. 7.419.   [214] See *ibid.*, para. 7.433.
[215] Appellate Body Report, *EC – Bananas III*, para. 211.
[216] Panel Reports, *Canada – Wheat Exports and Grain Imports,* para. 6.171.   [217] See *ibid.*, para. 6.172.

ordinary meaning of the word 'affecting' implies a measure that has 'an effect on' and thus indicates a broad scope of application. The word 'affecting' in Article III:4 of the GATT has been interpreted to cover not only laws and regulations which directly govern the conditions of sale or purchase but also any laws or regulations which *might* adversely modify the conditions of competition between domestic and imported products . . .

The idea that a measure which distinguishes between imported and domestic products can be considered to affect the internal sale or use of imported products only if such a measure is shown to have an impact *under current circumstances* on decisions of private firms with respect to the sourcing of products is difficult to reconcile with the concept of the 'no less favourable treatment' obligation in Article III:4 as an obligation addressed to governments to ensure effective equality of competitive opportunities between domestic and imported products, and with the principle that a showing of trade effects is not necessary to establish a violation of this obligation.[218]

[Emphasis added]

While, to date, most cases involving Article III:4 have concerned *generally applicable* 'laws' and 'regulations', i.e. measures that apply across the board, Article III:4 also covers 'requirements' which may apply to *isolated cases only*.[219] The Panel in *Canada – FIRA* noted:

The Panel could not subscribe to the Canadian view that the word 'requirements' in Article III:4 should be interpreted as 'mandatory rules applying across-the-board' because this latter concept was already more aptly covered by the term 'regulations' and the authors of this provision must have had something different in mind when adding the word 'requirements' . . . The Panel also considered that, in judging whether a measure is contrary to obligations under Article III:4, it is not relevant whether it applies across-the-board or only in isolated cases. Any interpretation which would exclude case-by-case action would, in the view of the Panel, defeat the purposes of Article III:4.[220]

While Article III:2 concerns internal taxation and Article III:4 internal regulation, the Panel in *Mexico – Taxes on Soft Drinks* found that:

The soft drink tax, the distribution tax and the bookkeeping requirements may be considered as measures that affect the internal use in Mexico of non-cane sugar sweeteners, such as beet sugar and [high fructose corn syrup], within the meaning of Article III:4 of the GATT 1994.[221]

Taxes can thus be measures subject to Article III:4.

The question has arisen whether a 'requirement' within the meaning of Article III:4 necessarily needs to be a government-imposed requirement, or whether an action by a private party can constitute a 'requirement' to which Article III:4 applies. In *Canada – Autos*, the Panel examined commitments by Canadian car manufacturers to increase the value added to cars in their Canadian plants. These commitments were communicated in letters addressed

---

[218] Panel Report, *Canada – Autos*, paras. 10.80 and 10.84. In a footnote to para. 10.80, the Panel referred to Appellate Body Report, *EC – Bananas III*, para. 220. Note that the Appellate Body in this report did not discuss the word 'affecting' within the meaning of Article III:4 but within the meaning of Article I:1 of the GATS. The Panel in *Canada – Autos* also referred to GATT Panel Report, *Italy – Agricultural Machinery*, para. 12, quoted above.   [219] See GATT Panel Report, *Canada – FIRA*.

[220] *Ibid.*, para. 5.5. The measures at issue in *Canada – FIRA* were written undertakings by investors to purchase goods of Canadian origin in preference to imported goods or in specified amounts or proportions, or to purchase goods from Canadian sources.   [221] Panel Report, *Mexico – Taxes on Soft Drinks*, para. 8.113.

to the Canadian Government. The Panel qualified these commitments as 'requirements' subject to Article III:4.[222] The Panel found:

> To qualify a private action as a 'requirement' within the meaning of Article III:4 means that in relation to that action a Member is to provide no less favourable treatment to imported products than to domestic products. A determination of whether private action amounts to a 'requirement' under Article III:4 must therefore necessarily rest on a finding that there is a nexus between that action and the action of a government such that the government must be held responsible for that action. We do not believe that such a nexus can exist only if a government makes undertakings of private parties legally enforceable, as in the situation considered by the Panel on *Canada – FIRA*, or if a government conditions the grant of an advantage on undertakings made by private parties, as in the situation considered by the Panel on *EEC – Parts and Components* . . . The word 'requirements' in its ordinary meaning and in light of its context in Article III:4 clearly implies government action involving a demand, request or the imposition of a condition but in our view this term does not carry a particular connotation with respect to the legal form in which such government action is taken. In this respect, we consider that, in applying the concept of 'requirements' in Article III:4 to situations involving actions by private parties, it is necessary to take into account that there is a broad variety of forms of government action that can be effective in influencing the conduct of private parties.[223]

In brief, private action can be a 'requirement' within the meaning of Article III:4 if, and only if, there is such a *nexus*, i.e. a close link, between that action and the action of a government, that the government must be held responsible for that private action. Such nexus may exist, for example, when a Member makes the grant of an advantage conditional upon the private action concerned.[224]

Note that the *Agreement on Trade-Related Investment Measures* contains an illustrative list of trade-related investment measures that are inconsistent with Article III:4.[225] The illustrative list includes, for example, measures that:

- are mandatory or enforceable under domestic law or compliance with which is necessary to obtain an advantage; and
- require the purchase or use by an enterprise of products of domestic origin; or require that an enterprise's purchases or use of imported products be limited to an amount related to the volume or value of local products that it exports.

Questions and Assignments 4.20

What laws, regulations and requirements fall within the scope of application of Article III:4 of the GATT 1994? Can a measure be

---

[222] The question whether actions of private parties can qualify as 'requirements' within the meaning of Article III:4 was previously addressed in GATT Panel Report, *Canada – FIRA*, para. 5.4 and GATT Panel Report, *EEC – Parts and Components*, para. 5.21. The Panel in *Canada – Autos* explicitly referred to this case law and took it further. Note that, in *Canada – FIRA*, Canada argued that the purchase undertakings should be considered as private contractual obligations of particular foreign investors *vis-à-vis* the Canadian Government. The Panel felt, however, that, even if this was so, private contractual obligations entered into by investors should not adversely affect the rights which Members possess under Article III:4 of the GATT. See GATT Panel Report, *Canada – FIRA*, para. 5.6.

[223] Panel Report, *Canada – Autos*, paras. 10.106–10.107.

[224] On the general question whether actions by private parties can be challenged before panels and the Appellate Body, see above, pp. 186–7.

[225] See Article 2.2 of, and the Annex to, the *Agreement on Trade-Related Investment Measures*.

considered to be a measure affecting the internal sale of imported products within the meaning of Article III:4 if it is not shown that *under current circumstances* the measure has an impact on the decisions of private parties to buy imported products? Is the national treatment obligation of Article III:4 also applicable to measures that apply only to isolated cases? Can an action by a private person, company or organisations constitute a measure within the meaning of Article III:4? Does the national treatment obligation of Article III apply to regulations concerning government procurement or to subsidies to domestic producers? Can internal taxes within the meaning of Article III:2 be subject to the national treatment requirement of Article III:4?

4.4.4.2. 'Like products'

As with Articles I:1 and III:2, first sentence, both discussed above, the non-discrimination obligation of Article III:4 only applies to 'like products'. So once again questions arise such as whether four-door cars are 'like' two-door cars; orange juice is 'like' tomato juice; portable computers are 'like' desktop computers; pork is 'like' beef; and alcohol-free beer is 'like' regular beer. As discussed above, the answer to these questions may be different in the context of Article III:4 of the GATT 1994 than in the context of other non-discrimination provisions of the GATT 1994.[226]

The Appellate Body considered the meaning of the concept of 'like products' in Article III:4 in *EC – Asbestos*. In its report in that case, the Appellate Body first noted that the concept of 'like products' was also used in Article III:2, first sentence, and that, in previous reports, it had held that the scope of 'like products' was to be construed 'narrowly' in that provision.[227] The Appellate Body then examined whether this interpretation of 'like products' in Article III:2 could be taken to suggest a similarly narrow reading of 'like products' in Article III:4, since both provisions form part of the same Article. The Appellate Body reasoned as follows:

> we observe that, although the obligations in Articles III:2 and III:4 both apply to 'like products', the text of Article III:2 differs in one important respect from the text of Article III:4. Article III:2 contains *two separate* sentences, each imposing *distinct* obligations: the first lays down obligations in respect of 'like products', while the second lays down obligations in respect of 'directly competitive or substitutable' products. By contrast, Article III:4 applies only to 'like products' and does not include a provision equivalent to the second sentence of Article III:2.[228]

The Appellate Body considered that this textual difference between Article III:2 and Article III:4 had considerable implications for the meaning of the concept of 'like products' in these two provisions. The Appellate Body recalled:

---

[226] On the 'accordion of likeness', see above, pp. 329–30.
[227] The Appellate Body referred in a footnote to Appellate Body Report, *Japan – Alcoholic Beverages II*, 112 and 113, and Appellate Body Report, *Canada – Periodicals*, 473.   [228] Appellate Body Report, *EC – Asbestos*, para. 94.

In *Japan – Alcoholic Beverages*, we concluded, in construing Article III:2, that the two separate obligations in the two sentences of Article III:2 must be interpreted in a harmonious manner that gives meaning to *both* sentences in that provision. We observed there that the interpretation of one of the sentences necessarily affects the interpretation of the other. Thus, the scope of the term 'like products' in the first sentence of Article III:2 affects, and is affected by, the scope of the phrase 'directly competitive or substitutable' products in the second sentence of that provision. We said in *Japan – Alcoholic Beverages*:

> Because the second sentence of Article III:2 provides for a separate and distinctive consideration of the protective aspect of a measure in examining its application to a broader category of products that are not 'like products' as contemplated by the first sentence, we agree with the Panel that the first sentence of Article III:2 must be construed narrowly so as not to condemn measures that its strict terms are not meant to condemn. Consequently, we agree with the Panel also that the definition of 'like products' in Article III:2, first sentence, should be construed narrowly.[229]

The Appellate Body, after considering the reasoning underlying its interpretation of 'like products' in Article III:2, first sentence, subsequently observed:

> In construing Article III:4, the same interpretive considerations do not arise, because the 'general principle' articulated in Article III:1 is expressed in Article III:4, not through two distinct obligations, as in the two sentences in Article III:2, but instead through a single obligation that applies solely to 'like products'. Therefore, the harmony that we have attributed to the two sentences of Article III:2 need not and, indeed, cannot be replicated in interpreting Article III:4. Thus, we conclude that, given the textual difference between Articles III:2 and III:4, the 'accordion' of 'likeness' stretches in a different way in Article III:4.[230]

Having distinguished the concept of 'like products' in Article III:4 from the concept in Article III:2, first sentence, the Appellate Body then proceeded to examine the meaning of this concept in Article III:4. It first recalled that, in *Japan – Alcoholic Beverages II*, it had ruled that the broad and fundamental purpose of Article III is to avoid protectionism in the application of internal tax and regulatory measures. As is explicitly stated in Article III:1, the purpose of Article III is to ensure that internal measures 'not be applied to imported and domestic products so as to afford protection to domestic production'. To this end, Article III obliges Members of the WTO to provide *equality of competitive conditions for imported products in relation to domestic products*.[231] This 'general principle' is not explicitly invoked in Article III:4. Nevertheless, it does 'inform' that provision.[232] The Appellate Body in *EC – Asbestos* thus reasoned that the term 'like product' in Article III:4 must be interpreted to give proper scope and meaning to the anti-protectionism principle of Article III:1.[233] It is clear that an internal regulation can *only* afford protection to domestic production if the internal regulation addresses domestic and imported products that are in a competitive relationship. In the absence of a competitive relationship between the domestic and imported products, internal regulation cannot be applied to these products so as to afford protection of domestic production.

---

[229] *Ibid.*, para. 95.   [230] *Ibid.*, para. 96.
[231] See Appellate Body Report, *Japan – Alcoholic Beverages II*, 109–10.   [232] *Ibid.*, 111.
[233] Appellate Body Report, *EC – Asbestos*, para. 98.

The Appellate Body thus came to the following conclusion with respect to the meaning of 'like products' in Article III:4:

> [A] determination of 'likeness' under Article III:4 is, fundamentally, a determination about the nature and extent of a competitive relationship between and among products. In saying this, we are mindful that there is a spectrum of degrees of 'competitiveness' or 'substitutability' of products in the marketplace, and that it is difficult, if not impossible, in the abstract, to indicate precisely where on this spectrum the word 'like' in Article III:4 of the GATT 1994 falls. We are not saying that *all* products which are in *some* competitive relationship are 'like products' under Article III:4. In ruling on the measure at issue, we also do not attempt to define the precise scope of the word 'like' in Article III:4. Nor do we wish to decide if the scope of 'like products' in Article III:4 is co-extensive with the combined scope of 'like' and 'directly competitive or substitutable' products in Article III:2 . . . In view of [the] different language [of Articles III:2 and III:4], and although we need not rule, and do not rule, on the precise product scope of Article III:4, we do conclude that the product scope of Article III:4, although broader than the *first* sentence of Article III:2, is certainly *not* broader than the *combined* product scope of the *two* sentences of Article III:2 of the GATT 1994.[234]

In brief, the determination of whether products are 'like products' under Article III:4 is, in essence, a determination about the nature and extent of the competitive relationship between these products. Note that the Appellate Body refers to both the nature *and* the extent of the competitive relationship. A mere economic analysis of the cross-price elasticity of demand for the products at issue will not suffice to determine whether these products are 'like'. 'Likeness' is a matter of judgement – qualitatively as well as quantitatively.[235] Precisely what the nature and extent of the competitive relationship needs to be for products to be 'like' within the meaning of Article III:4 cannot be indicated in the abstract. Nevertheless, it can be said that the concept of 'like products' in Article III:4 has a relatively broad scope. According to the Appellate Body in *EC – Asbestos*, its scope is broader than that of the concept of 'like products' in Article III:2, first sentence. However, it is not broader than the combined scope of the concepts of 'like product' and 'directly competitive or substitutable products' under Article III:2, first and second sentence, respectively. In line with this reasoning, the Panel in *Mexico – Taxes on Soft Drinks* concluded that, as it had found soft drinks sweetened with cane sugar and beet sugar to be 'like' under Article III:2, first sentence, these products could also be considered 'like' under Article III:4.[236] Furthermore, the Panel concluded that soft drinks sweetened with cane sugar and high fructose corn syrup, which were considered 'directly competitive or substitutable' within the meaning of Article III:2, second sentence, were in a close competitive relationship and could thus be considered 'like' products within the meaning of Article III:4.[237]

In *EC – Asbestos*, the Appellate Body after having reached a conclusion on the meaning and the scope of the concept of 'like products' under Article III:4,

---

[234] *Ibid.*, para. 99.
[235] See R. Howse and E. Türk, 'The WTO Impact on Internal Regulations: A Case Study of the *Canada – EC Asbestos* Dispute', in G. A. Bermann and P. C. Mavroidis (eds.), *Trade and Human Health and Safety*, (Cambridge University Press, 2006), 91.   [236] See Panel Report, *Mexico – Taxes on Soft Drinks*, para. 8.105.
[237] See *ibid.*, para. 8.106.

turned to the question of *how* it should determine whether products are 'like' within the meaning of Article III:4. The Appellate Body noted:

> As in Article III:2, in this determination, '[n]o one approach . . . will be appropriate for all cases'. Rather, an assessment utilizing 'an unavoidable element of individual, discretionary judgement' has to be made on a case-by-case basis. The Report of the Working Party on Border Tax Adjustments outlined an approach for analyzing 'likeness' that has been followed and developed since by several panels and the Appellate Body. This approach has, in the main, consisted of employing four general criteria in analyzing 'likeness': (i) the properties, nature and quality of the products; (ii) the end-uses of the products; (iii) consumers' tastes and habits – more comprehensively termed consumers' perceptions and behaviour – in respect of the products; and (iv) the tariff classification of the products. We note that these four criteria comprise four categories of 'characteristics' that the products involved might share: (i) the physical properties of the products; (ii) the extent to which the products are capable of serving the same or similar end-uses; (iii) the extent to which consumers perceive and treat the products as alternative means of performing particular functions in order to satisfy a particular want or demand; and (iv) the international classification of the products for tariff purposes.[238]

The Appellate Body in *EC – Asbestos* hastened to add, however, that, while these general criteria, or groupings of potentially shared characteristics, provide a framework for analysing the 'likeness' of particular products, they are 'simply tools to assist in the task of sorting and examining the relevant evidence'.[239] The Appellate Body stressed that these criteria are 'neither a treaty-mandated nor a closed list of criteria that will determine the legal characterisation of products'.[240] In each case, *all* pertinent evidence, whether related to one of these criteria or not, must be examined and considered by panels to determine whether products are 'like'. With regard to these general criteria, the Appellate Body in *EC – Asbestos* finally noted:

> under Article III:4 of the GATT 1994, the term 'like products' is concerned with competitive relationships between and among products. Accordingly, whether the *Border Tax Adjustments* framework is adopted or not, it is important under Article III:4 to take account of evidence which indicates whether, and to what extent, the products involved are – or could be – in a competitive relationship in the marketplace.[241]

In its appeal in *EC – Asbestos*, the European Communities argued that the Panel had erred in its consideration of 'likeness', in particular because it: (1) had adopted an exclusively 'commercial or market access approach' to the comparison of allegedly 'like products'; (2) had placed excessive reliance on a single criterion, namely, end-use; and (3) had failed to include consideration of the health 'risk' factors relating to asbestos.[242]

---

[238] Appellate Body Report, *EC – Asbestos*, para. 101. In a footnote, the Appellate Body referred to Appellate Body Report, *Japan – Alcoholic Beverages II*, 113 and 114; it also referred to Panel Report, *US – Gasoline*, para. 6.8, where the approach set out in the *Border Tax Adjustments report* was adopted in a dispute concerning Article III:4 of the GATT 1994. The Appellate Body noted in a footnote that the fourth criterion, tariff classification, was not mentioned by the Working Party on *Border Tax Adjustments*, but was included by subsequent panels (see e.g. GATT Panel Report, *EEC – Animal Feed Proteins*, para. 4.2; and GATT Panel Report, *Japan – Alcoholic Beverages I*, para. 5.6).
[239] Appellate Body Report, *EC – Asbestos*, para. 102.   [240] *Ibid.*   [241] *Ibid.*, para. 103.
[242] The European Communities was an 'other appellant' pursuant to Rule 23(1) of the *Working Procedures for Appellate Review*. See above, p. 293.

The Appellate Body was highly critical of the manner in which the Panel examined the 'likeness' of chrysotile asbestos fibres *and* PCG fibres[243] as well as the 'likeness' of cement-based products containing chrysotile asbestos fibres *and* cement-based products containing PCG fibres.[244] The Appellate Body criticised the Panel for not examining each of the criteria set forth in the Report of the Working Party on *Border Tax Adjustments*[245] and for not examining these criteria separately.[246] The Appellate Body also disagreed with the Panel's refusal to consider the health risks posed by asbestos in the determination of 'likeness', stating:

> neither the text of Article III:4 nor the practice of panels and the Appellate Body suggest that any evidence should be excluded *a priori* from a panel's examination of 'likeness'. Moreover, as we have said, in examining the 'likeness' of products, panels must evaluate *all* of the relevant evidence. We are very much of the view that evidence relating to the health risks associated with a product may be pertinent in an examination of 'likeness' under Article III:4 of the GATT 1994. We do not, however, consider that the evidence relating to the health risks associated with chrysotile asbestos fibres need be examined under a *separate* criterion, because we believe that this evidence can be evaluated under the existing criteria of physical properties, and of consumers' tastes and habits.[247]

In the opinion of the Appellate Body, the carcinogenic or toxic nature of chrysotile asbestos fibres constitutes a defining aspect of the physical properties of those fibres and must therefore be considered when determining 'likeness' under Article III:4.[248] According to the Appellate Body, 'evidence relating to health risks may be relevant in assessing the *competitive relationship in the marketplace* between allegedly "like" products'.[249]

In a separate concurring opinion, one of the Members of the Appellate Body in *EC – Asbestos* went further and considered that, in view of the nature and the quantum of the scientific evidence showing that the physical properties and qualities of chrysotile asbestos fibres include or result in carcinogenicity, there is ample basis for a 'definitive characterisation' of such fibres as not 'like' PCG fibres. The Member suggested that this 'definitive characterisation' may and should be made even in the absence of evidence concerning end-uses and consumers' tastes and habits. As this Member explained:

> It is difficult for me to imagine what evidence relating to economic competitive relationships as reflected in end-uses and consumers' tastes and habits could outweigh and set at naught the undisputed deadly nature of chrysotile asbestos fibres, compared with PCG fibres, when inhaled by humans, and therefore compel a characterisation of 'likeness' of chrysotile asbestos and PCG fibres.[250]

The Member who wrote this separate opinion clearly did not share the position taken by the two other Appellate Body Members that the competitive

---

[243] PCG fibres are PVA, cellulose and glass fibres.   [244] Appellate Body Report, *EC – Asbestos*, para. 109.
[245] The Panel declined to examine the third criterion (consumers' tastes and habits) and dismissed the fourth criterion (tariff classification) as non-decisive.
[246] In the course of the examination of the first criterion (the properties, nature and quality of the products), the Panel relied on the second criterion (end-use) to come to the 'conclusion' that the products were like.
[247] Appellate Body Report, *EC – Asbestos*, para. 113.   [248] See *ibid.*, para. 114.   [249] *Ibid.*, para. 115.
[250] *Ibid.*, para. 152.

relationship in the market is decisive in the determination of the 'likeness' of products under Article III:4.[251] This Member stated:

> the necessity or appropriateness of adopting a 'fundamentally' economic interpretation of the 'likeness' of products under Article III:4 of the GATT 1994 does not appear to me to be free from substantial doubts.[252]

The separate opinion reflects a very significant and fundamental difference of views on how to interpret the concept of 'likeness' under Article III:4.

With regard to the second and third criteria set out in the Report of the Working Party on *Border Tax Adjustments*, i.e. end-uses and consumers' tastes and habits, the Appellate Body found in *EC – Asbestos*:

> Evidence of this type is of particular importance under Article III of the GATT 1994, precisely because that provision is concerned with competitive relationships in the marketplace. If there is – or could be – *no* competitive relationship between products, a Member cannot intervene, through internal taxation or regulation, to protect domestic production. Thus, evidence about the extent to which products can serve the same end-uses, and the extent to which consumers are – or would be – willing to choose one product instead of another to perform those end-uses, is highly relevant evidence in assessing the 'likeness' of those products under Article III:4 of the GATT 1994.
>
> We consider this to be especially so in cases where the evidence relating to properties establishes that the products at issue are physically quite different. In such cases, in order to overcome this indication that products are *not* 'like', a higher burden is placed on complaining Members to establish that, despite the pronounced physical differences, there is a competitive relationship between the products such that *all* of the evidence, taken together, demonstrates that the products are 'like' under Article III:4 of the GATT 1994.[253]

With respect to end-uses, the Appellate Body found that, while it is certainly relevant that products have similar end-uses for a 'small number of . . . applications', a panel must also consider the other, *different* end-uses for products. As the Appellate Body stated in *EC – Asbestos*:

> It is only by forming a complete picture of the various end-uses of a product that a panel can assess the significance of the fact that products share a limited number of end-uses.[254]

With respect to consumers' tastes and habits, the Appellate Body was very critical of the Panel for declining to examine this criterion because, as the Panel stated, 'this criterion would not provide clear results'.[255] Furthermore, the Appellate Body noted that, in its opinion, consumers' tastes and habits regarding asbestos fibres or PCG fibres, even in the case of commercial parties such as manufacturers, are very likely to be shaped by the health risks associated with a product which is known to be highly carcinogenic (as asbestos fibres are).[256]

After reversing the Panel's findings, in *EC – Asbestos*, on the 'likeness' of chrysotile asbestos fibres and PCG fibres, the Appellate Body itself examined the 'likeness' of these products and came to the conclusion that the evidence was certainly far from sufficient to satisfy the complainant's burden of proving that chrysotile asbestos fibres are 'like' PCG fibres under Article III:4. The Appellate

---

[251] See *ibid.*, para. 153.   [252] *Ibid.*, para. 154.   [253] *Ibid.*, paras. 117 and 118.   [254] *Ibid.*, para. 119.
[255] Panel Report, *EC – Asbestos*, para. 8.139.   [256] See Appellate Body Report, *EC – Asbestos*, para. 122.

Body considered that the evidence tended rather to suggest that these products are not 'like products'.[257]

As the Appellate Body stated in *Japan – Alcoholic Beverages II*, the concept of 'like products' in WTO law is indeed like an accordion whose width varies depending on the provision under which the term is interpreted. As discussed above, the interpretation of the concept of 'like product' in Article III:4 is relatively broad. However, it is not so broad that chrysotile asbestos fibres and PCG fibres would be 'like products'. On the one hand, the Appellate Body in *EC – Asbestos* confirmed the prior case law by upholding the market-based, economic interpretation of the concept of 'likeness' (and thus confirmed the 'marketplace approach to determining 'likeness'). On the other hand, the Appellate Body remedied the narrowness of this case law by allowing non-economic interests and values to be considered in the determination of 'likeness'.

Two additional observations on the determination of 'likeness' under Article III:4 of the GATT 1994 are called for: one observation regarding the 'regulatory intent' or 'aim-and-effect' approach discussed above in the context of Article III:2, first sentence of the GATT 1994;[258] and one observation regarding the relevance of processes and production methods (PPMs) discussed above in the context of Article I of the GATT 1994.[259] With regard to the former, note that in 1992, in *US – Malt Beverages*, the Panel considered the regulatory intent (or aim) of the measure in determining whether low alcohol beer and high alcohol beer should be considered 'like products' within the meaning of Article III:4. In this regard, the Panel recalled its earlier statement on like product determinations under Article III:2, first sentence,[260] and considered that:

> in the context of Article III, it is essential that such determinations be made not only in the light of such criteria as the products' physical characteristics, but also in the light of the purpose of Article III, which is to ensure that internal taxes and regulations 'not be applied to imported or domestic products so as to afford protection to domestic production'.[261]

The Panel noted that, on the basis of their 'physical characteristics', low and high alcohol beers were 'similar'. However, in order to determine whether low and high alcohol beers were 'like products' under Article III:4, the Panel considered that it had to examine whether the purpose of the distinction between low and high alcohol beers was 'to afford protection to domestic production'. The Panel noted that the United States argued that the distinction was made to encourage the consumption of low rather than high alcohol beer. The Panel eventually concluded that the purpose of the regulatory distinction was not to afford protection to domestic production and that low and high alcoholic beers were, therefore, not 'like products'.[262]

For reasons discussed above, this 'regulatory intent' or 'aim-and-effect' approach to the determination of 'likeness' has been discredited and abandoned

---

[257] See *ibid.*, para. 141. Also, with regard to the products containing asbestos and PCG fibres, the Appellate Body concluded that Canada had not satisfied the burden of proof that these products were 'like'. See *ibid.*, para. 147.   [258] See above, pp. 354–6.   [259] See above, p. 331.   [260] See above, p. 354.
[261] GATT Panel Report, *US – Malt Beverages*, para. 5.71.   [262] See *ibid.*, paras. 5.25–5.26 and 5.71–5.76.

by WTO panels and the Appellate Body.[263] A first indication that WTO panels would not follow this approach was given in *US – Gasoline*, in which the Panel found that chemically identical imported and domestic gasoline were 'like products' because 'chemically identical imported and domestic gasoline by definition have exactly the same physical characteristics, end-uses, tariff classification, and are perfectly substitutable'.[264] The intent or the aim of the regulatory distinction made was not given any consideration in determining 'likeness'.

With regard to the processes and production methods which do not affect the characteristics or properties of the products concerned (NPR PPMs), note that the Panel in *US – Tuna (Mexico)* found that differences in NPR PPMs are not relevant in determining 'likeness'. The Panel stated:

> Article III:4 calls for a comparison of the treatment of imported tuna *as a product* with that of domestic tuna *as a product*. Regulations governing the taking of dolphins incidental to the taking of tuna could not possibly affect tuna as a product. Article III:4 therefore obliges the United States to accord treatment to Mexican tuna no less favourable than that accorded to United States tuna, whether or not the incidental taking of dolphins by Mexican vessels corresponded to that of United States vessels.[265]

However, as reflected above, the thinking on the concept of 'likeness' has evolved since the 1991 *US – Tuna (Mexico)* case. The question of whether NPR PPMs may be of relevance in the determination of 'likeness' now requires a more nuanced answer than that given by the Panel in *US – Tuna (Mexico)*. It should be noted that NPR PPMs may have an impact on consumer preferences and tastes, and thus on the nature and the extent of the competitive relationship between products. If carpets made by children are shunned by the consumers in a particular market, a situation may arise in which there is in fact no (or only a weak) competitive relationship between these carpets and carpets made by adults. In the light of the nature and the extent of the competitive relationship between them, carpets made by children and carpets made by adults could in such a situation be found to be not 'like'. However, it seems unlikely that this type of situation will often arise as consumers in most markets are, in their choice between products, primarily guided by the price and other aspects that are *not* related to the conditions (e.g. environmental, labour or animal welfare conditions) under which the products were produced. Some commentators have argued, however, that:

> the prevailing anti-PPM rationale in Geneva – and in the trade community more generally – has grown out of sync with market realities, namely, the interest of significant numbers of consumers in the environmental consequences of how a product is produced.[266]

[263] See above, pp. 355–6.   [264] Panel Report, *US – Gasoline*, para. 6.9.
[265] GATT Panel Report, *US – Tuna (Mexico)*, para. 5.15. Note that this report was never adopted.
[266] R. Howse, P. van Bork and C. Hedebrand, 'WTO Disciplines and Biofuels, Opportunities and Constraints in the Creation of a Global Marketplace', *IPC Discussion Paper*, October 2006, referring to M. Araya, 'WTO Negotiations on Environmental Goods and Services: Maximizing Opportunities', Global Environmental and Trade Study, Yale Center for Environmental Law and Policy, June 2003, 1–2. Note in this respect a Zogby poll of consumers in the United States in 2000, which showed that 75.4 per cent of respondents found it unacceptable to induce moulting in laying hens by withholding feed, and 80.7 per cent said they would be willing to pay more for eggs from hens raised in a 'humane manner'. A UK survey revealed that 79 per cent of respondents supported legislation to phase out battery cages in the EU, and 87 per cent

Finally, it should be noted that in spite of the importance of the issue of 'likeness', there have been disputes involving Article III:4 in which 'likeness' was not a problematic issue. 'Likeness' typically was, and is, not problematic in disputes concerning 'origin-based' measures (or in other words, in disputes concerning *de jure* discrimination). In *Canada – Wheat Exports and Grain Imports*, for example, the measures at issue provided either for requirements to which *only* foreign grain was subject[267] or benefits *only* granted to domestic products.[268] 'Likeness' was therefore not a problematic issue in *Canada – Wheat Exports and Grain Imports*.[269] The same was true in *Brazil – Retreaded Tyres*. Brazil prohibited the sale of imported retreaded tyres while allowing the sale of domestic retreaded tyres.[270] However, in disputes concerning *de facto* discrimination, such as *EC – Asbestos* and *Mexico – Taxes on Soft Drinks* (where the measures at issue were, on their face, 'origin-neutral'), the 'likeness' of the domestic and imported products concerned is usually at the core of the dispute.[271]

Questions and Assignments 4.21

Should the concept of 'like products' in Article III:4 of the GATT 1994 be interpreted in the same manner as in Article III:2, first sentence? What is the relevance of the general principle of Article III:1 to the interpretation of the concepts of 'like products' in Article III:4? How do the scopes of the concept of 'likeness' in Article III:2 and Article III:4 compare? Which factors should be taken into account in determining whether products are 'like' within the meaning of Article III:4? What is the ultimate basis for determining the 'likeness' of products? Can two products that have totally different physical characteristics be 'like products' within the meaning of Article III:4? Would the Appellate Body Member who wrote the 'concurring opinion' in *EC – Asbestos* agree? Explain why the issue of 'likeness' is typically not a problematic issue in disputes concerning *de*

Footnote 266 (*cont.*)
  indicated that they were willing to pay more for eggs from non-battery cage hens. See A. B. Thiermann and S. Babcock, 'Animal Welfare and International Trade', *Revue Scientifique et Technique Office International des Epizooties*, 2005, 751.
[267] Under Section 57(c) of the *Canada Grain Act* foreign grain was prohibited from entering Canadian grain elevators unless authorisation was first obtained from the Canada Grain Commission. Thus, by its terms, Section 57(c) only applied to foreign grain and by virtue merely of its origin, domestic grain was not subject to the authorisation requirement. Panel Reports, *Canada – Wheat Exports and Grain Imports*, para. 6.165.
[268] Under Section 56(1) of the *Canada Grain Regulations*, a standing authorisation was granted to operators of transfer elevators to allow mixing of grain other than foreign and Western Canadian grain. This draws an origin-based distinction between Eastern Canadian grain, on the one hand, and foreign and Western Canadian grain, on the other hand for the granting of an advantage (the mixing authorisation). Further under Sections 150(1) and 150(2) of the *Canada Transportation Act*, the annual revenue that relevant Canadian railroads may collect for transporting Western Canadian grain was capped and a requirement was laid down that railroads must refund, with penalties, any revenues received in excess of the cap. Thus, these railroads had an incentive to hold their rates for the transportation of Western Canadian grain at a level that would ensure that they did not exceed the revenue cap whereas no comparable incentive existed for setting the rates charged for the transport of imported grain. Panel Reports, *Canada – Wheat Exports and Grain Imports*, paras. 6.262 and 6.331- 6.332.
[269] See *ibid.*, paras. 6.164, 6.264 and 6.333.
[270] See Panel Report, *Brazil – Retreaded Tyres*, para. 7.432. See also Panel Reports, *EC – Trademarks and Geographical Indications*, para. 7.265 (Australia) and para. 7.229 (US).
[271] For *EC – Asbestos*, see above, p. 374; and for *Mexico – Taxes on Soft Drinks*, see Panel Report, *Mexico – Taxes on Soft Drinks*, paras. 8.116–8.122.

jure discrimination, and why the opposite is true in disputes concerning *de facto* discrimination.

4.4.4.3. 'Treatment no less favourable'

The fact that a measure distinguishes between 'like products' does not suffice to conclude that this measure is inconsistent with Article III:4.[272] As the Appellate Body noted in *EC – Asbestos*:

> there is a second element that must be established before a measure can be held to be inconsistent with Article III:4 . . . A complaining Member must still establish that the measure accords to the group of 'like' *imported* products 'less favourable treatment' than it accords to the group of 'like' *domestic* products.[273]

The Panel in *US – Section 337* explained the 'treatment no less favourable' element of the Article III:4 test as follows:

> the 'no less favourable' treatment requirement set out in Article III:4 is unqualified. These words are to be found throughout the General Agreement and later Agreements negotiated in the GATT framework as *an expression of the underlying principle of equality of treatment* of imported products as compared to the treatment given either to other foreign products, under the most favoured nation standard, or to domestic products, under the national treatment standard of Article III. The words 'treatment no less favourable' in paragraph 4 call for *effective equality of opportunities* for imported products in respect of the application of laws, regulations and requirements affecting the internal sale, offering for sale, purchase, transportation, distribution or use of products. This clearly sets a minimum permissible standard as a basis.[274]
>
> [Emphasis added]

The Panel in *US – Section 337* thus interpreted 'treatment no less favourable' as requiring 'effective equality of competitive opportunities'.[275] In later GATT and WTO reports, the Appellate Body and panels have consistently interpreted 'treatment no less favourable' in the same way.[276]

In *US – Gasoline*, a dispute concerning legislation designed to prevent and control air pollution, the Panel found that the measure at issue afforded less favourable treatment to imported gasoline than to domestic gasoline because, for domestic refiners of gasoline, an individual baseline (representing the

---

[272] Regulatory distinctions between 'like products' are not necessarily inconsistent with Article III:4 of the GATT 1994. See below, p. 384.

[273] Appellate Body Report, *EC – Asbestos*, para. 100. Note that Howse and Türk argue that while the Appellate Body has rejected the 'aim-and-effect' test with respect to likeness (see above, pp. 355–6), it has in effect brought this test back in at this stage of considering whether there is less favourable treatment. See R. Howse and E. Türk, 'The WTO Impact on Internal Regulations: A Case Study of the *Canada – EC Asbestos* Dispute', in G. Bermann and P. Mavroidis, (eds.) *Trade and Human Health and Safety* (Cambridge University Press, 2006), 91.   [274] GATT Panel Report, *US – Section 337*, para. 5.11.

[275] Note that the examination of whether the measure at issue provides for 'effective equality of competitive opportunities' need not be based on the actual effects of the measure in the marketplace. See Appellate Body Report, *US – FSC (Article 21.5 – EC)*, para. 215.

[276] See e.g. GATT Panel Report, *Canada – Provincial Liquor Boards (US)*, paras. 5.12–5.14 and 5.30–5.31; GATT Panel Report, *US – Malt Beverages*, para. 5.30; Panel Report, *US – Gasoline*, para. 6.10; Panel Reports, *EC – Bananas III*, paras. 7.179–7.180; and Panel Report, *Japan – Film*, para. 10.379.

quality of gasoline produced by that refiner in 1990) was established while, for importers of gasoline, the more onerous statutory baseline applied. Recalling the ruling of the Panel in *US – Section 337* that the words 'treatment no less favourable' in Article III:4 call for effective equality of opportunities for imported products, the Panel in *US – Gasoline* found:

> since, under the baseline establishment methods, imported gasoline was effectively pre-vented from benefiting from as favourable sales conditions as were afforded domestic gasoline by an individual baseline tied to the producer of a product, imported gasoline was treated less favourably than domestic gasoline.[277]

Although in *EC – Asbestos* the Appellate Body was not called upon to examine the 'no less favourable treatment' finding of the Panel, the Appellate Body noted:

> The term 'less favourable treatment' expresses the general principle, in Article III:1, that internal regulations 'should not be applied . . . so as to afford protection to domestic pro-duction'. If there is 'less favourable treatment' of the group of 'like' imported products, there is, conversely, 'protection' of the group of 'like' domestic products.[278]

In *Korea – Various Measures on Beef*, a dispute concerning a dual retail distribu-tion system for the sale of beef under which *imported* beef was, *inter alia*, to be sold in specialised stores selling only imported beef or in separate sections of supermarkets, the Panel ruled that 'any regulatory distinction that is based exclusively on criteria relating to the nationality or the origin of the products is incompatible with Article III:4 of the GATT 1994'.[279] The Appellate Body dis-agreed with the Panel and reversed this ruling. According to the Appellate Body, the formal difference in treatment between domestic and imported products is neither necessary nor sufficient for a violation of Article III:4. Formally different treatment of imported products did not necessarily constitute less favourable treatment while the absence of formal difference in treatment did not necessar-ily mean that there was no less favourable treatment.[280] The Appellate Body stated in *Korea – Various Measures on Beef*:

> We observe . . . that Article III:4 requires only that a measure accord treatment to imported products that is 'no less favourable' than that accorded to like domestic prod-ucts. A measure that provides treatment to imported products that is *different* from that accorded to like domestic products is not necessarily inconsistent with Article III:4, as long as the treatment provided by the measure is no 'less favourable'. According treat-ment 'no less favourable' means, as we have previously said, according *conditions of competition* no less favourable to the imported product than to the like domestic product.
>
> This interpretation, which focuses on the *conditions of competition* between imported and domestic like products, implies that a measure according formally *different* treatment to imported products does not *per se*, that is, necessarily, violate Article III:4.[281]

---

[277] Panel Report, *US – Gasoline*, para. 6.10.
[278] Appellate Body Report, *EC – Asbestos*, para. 100. The Appellate Body did not examine the requirement of 'treatment no less favourable' any further since the Panel's findings on this requirement had not been appealed.   [279] Panel Report, *Korea – Various Measures on Beef*, para. 627.
[280] See also GATT Panel Report, *US – Section 337*, para. 5.11; and Panel Report, *US – Gasoline*, para. 6.25.
[281] Appellate Body Report, *Korea – Various Measures on Beef*, paras. 135–6. See also, for example, Panel Report, *India – Autos*, para. 7.199.

The Appellate Body recalled that this point was persuasively made in *US – Section 337*. The Panel in that case had to determine whether United States patent enforcement procedures, which were formally different for imported and for domestic products, violated Article III:4. The Panel ruled:

> On the one hand, contracting parties may apply to imported products *different* formal legal requirements if doing so would accord imported products more favourable treatment. On the other hand, it also has to be recognised that there may be cases where the application of formally *identical* legal provisions would in practice accord less favourable treatment to imported products and a contracting party might thus have to apply different legal provisions to imported products to ensure that the treatment accorded them is in fact no less favourable. For these reasons, the mere fact that imported products are subject under Section 337 to legal provisions that are different from those applying to products of national origin is in itself not conclusive in establishing inconsistency with Article III:4.[282]
>
> [Emphasis added]

From this, the Appellate Body concluded in *Korea – Various Measures on Beef*:

> A formal difference in treatment between imported and like domestic products is thus neither necessary, nor sufficient, to show a violation of Article III:4. Whether or not imported products are treated 'less favourably' than like domestic products should be assessed instead by examining whether a measure modifies the *conditions of competition* in the relevant market to the detriment of imported products.[283]

In *US – Gasoline*, the Panel rejected the US argument that the requirements of Article III:4 were met because imported gasoline was treated similarly to domestic gasoline from *similarly situated* domestic parties.[284] The Panel pointed out, *inter alia*, that '[the] wording [of Article III:4] does not allow less favourable treatment dependent on the characteristics of the producer'.[285] Note also that when establishing whether there is 'treatment less favourable', what is to be compared is the treatment given to the group of imports as a whole and the treatment given to the group of domestic products as a whole.[286] In *US – Gasoline*, the Panel also rejected the US contention that the regulation at issue treated imported products 'equally overall' and was therefore not inconsistent with Article III:4.[287] The Panel noted that:

---

[282] GATT Panel Report, *US – Section 337*, para. 5.11.

[283] Appellate Body Report, *Korea – Various Measures on Beef*, para. 137.

[284] See Panel Report, *US – Gasoline*, para. 6.11. The Appellate Body did not address this finding of the Panel.

[285] *Ibid.*

[286] See Appellate Body Report, *EC – Asbestos*, para. 100. Note, however, that the GATT Panel in *US – Malt Beverages* held that the national treatment obligation requires that treatment accorded to imported products be no less favourable than that accorded to *any* like domestic product, *whatever the domestic origin*. Article III consequently requires treatment of imported products no less favourable than *that accorded to the most favoured domestic products*. See GATT Panel Report, *US – Malt Beverages*, para. 5.17. Similarly, in *Canada – Wheat Exports and Grain Imports*, the Panel held that, 'where an origin-based difference in regulatory treatment is made between products originating in one area, region or administrative unit of a country and all other like products – that is, like products originating in other areas of the same country or originating in foreign countries – Article III:4 requires that the foreign product be granted treatment no less favourable than that accorded to the *most-favoured domestic product*'. (Emphasis added). Thus, as Canada had conferred a certain advantage (a standing authorisation of mixture) only on Eastern Canadian grain, and another advantage (a cap on rail transportation revenue) only on Western Canadian grain, Canada had to accord like imported grain treatment that is at least as favourable as the treatment afforded respectively to Eastern or Western Canadian grain. Panel Reports, *Canada – Wheat Exports and Grain Imports*, paras. 6.294 and 6.350.   [287] See Panel Report, *US – Gasoline*, para. 6.14.

> the argument that on average the treatment provided was equivalent amounted to arguing that less favourable treatment in one instance could be offset provided that there was correspondingly more favourable treatment in another. This amounted to claiming that less favourable treatment of particular imported products in some instances would be balanced by more favourable treatment of particular products in others.[288]

Under Article III:4, as under Articles I:1 and III:2, 'balancing' less favourable treatment with more favourable treatment does not 'excuse' the less favourable treatment.[289]

Note that in *Canada – Wheat Exports and Grain Imports*, the Panel stated that the measures at issue (i.e. a prohibition to enter foreign grain in Canadian grain elevators unless specifically authorised, the granting of a standing mixing authorisation for Eastern Canadian grain only, and the application of a revenue cap for rail transportation of Western Canadian grain only) would appear to be inconsistent with Article III:4 of the GATT 1994 because imported grain is treated less favourably than like domestic grain.[290] However, as the Panel noted, Canada argued that the measure at issue:

> does not adversely affect the conditions of competition for imported grain as compared with like domestic grain. More particularly, Canada argues that the authorization process is not onerous; that elevator operators are very familiar with the process; that authorizations are consistently granted; that the CGC [Canadian Grain Commission] has discretion to always authorize receipt of foreign grain; and that advance authorization may be obtained.[291]

The Panel recognised that there may be legitimate reasons for Canada to treat domestic grain and 'like' imported grain differently, for example because the latter has not been subjected to the Canadian quality assurance system, which imposes certain restrictions and conditions on Canadian grain, including with respect to production.[292] However, it was not clear to the Panel how the arguments put forward by Canada to justify the difference in treatment between domestic grain and 'like' imported grain could support the conclusion that the measure at issue treated imported grain 'no less favourably' than 'like' domestic grain. The Panel, therefore, found as follows with regard to the authorisation requirement for foreign grain to enter grain elevators:

---

[288] *Ibid.*   [289] See GATT Panel Report, *US – Section 337*, para. 5.14.

[290] See Panel Reports, *Canada – Wheat Exports and Grain Imports*, paras. 6.186–6.187 (with regard to the authorisation requirement for foreign grain to enter grain elevators), para. 6.187 (with regard to the standing mixing authorisation for Eastern Canadian grain only) and para. 6.352 (with regard to the revenue cap on rail transportation of Western Canadian grain).

[291] *Ibid.*, para. 6.188. Similarly, with respect to the standing mixing authorisation for Eastern Canadian grain, Canada argued that foreign producers are not obliged to use Canadian transfer elevators and may deliver their grain directly to Canadian end-users and that mixing restrictions do not apply outside the bulk grain handling system. *Ibid.*, para. 6.295. With regard to the revenue cap on rail transportation of Western Canadian grain, Canada argued that the revenue cap has never been met and is unlikely to be met in the future, and that the revenue cap has no relevance or effect for movements of imported grain that originate and/or terminate outside the geographic parameters of the revenue cap. *Ibid.*, paras. 6.353–6.358.

[292] See *ibid.*, para. 6.209 (with regard to the authorisation requirement for foreign grain to enter grain elevators), para. 6.212 (with regard to the standing mixing authorisation for Eastern Canadian grain only). Legitimate reasons were not discussed with regard to the revenue cap on rail transportation of Western Canadian grain.

> In conclusion, since the Panel is not persuaded by the defences put forward by Canada to suggest that the additional regulatory requirement imposed on imported grain pursuant to Section 57(c) of the *Canada Grain Act* does not impose any burden on imported grain or, at least, does not impose a burden that is not also borne by like domestic grain, the Panel confirms its provisional conclusion above at paragraph 6.187 that Section 57(c) of the *Canada Grain Act* is, as such, inconsistent with Article III:4 of the GATT 1994.[293]

In *Dominican Republic – Import and Sale of Cigarettes*, the Panel found with respect to the tax stamp to be affixed to all cigarette packets marketed in the Dominican Republic that:

> although the tax stamp requirement is applied in a formally equal manner to domestic and imported cigarettes, it does modify the conditions of competition in the marketplace to the detriment of imports. The tax stamp requirement imposes additional processes and costs on imported products. It also leads to imported cigarettes being presented to final consumers in a less appealing manner.[294]

Subsequently, the Panel noted:

> [I]n this case, the differences in the conditions between imported and domestic products mean that the Dominican Republic should not apply the tax stamp requirement in a formally identical manner that does not take those differences into account, since this would, in practice, accord less favourable treatment to imported products. On the contrary, the Dominican Republic could have chosen to apply the requirement in a different manner to imported products, to ensure that the treatment accorded to them is *de facto* not less favourable.[295]

The Panel in *Dominican Republic – Import and Sale of Cigarettes*, however, found that Honduras failed to establish that a requirement that importers and domestic producers post a bond of 5 million Dominican pesos (RD) accorded less favourable treatment to imported cigarettes than that accorded to like domestic products, in a manner inconsistent with Article III:4 of the GATT 1994.[296] The Appellate Body upheld this ruling on appeal. The reasoning underlying the rejection of this claim of inconsistency by Honduras introduced a new element in the case law on 'less favourable treatment' within the meaning of Article III:4. As the Appellate Body recalled in its Report, Honduras argued that the requirement to post a bond of RD$5 million accorded 'less favourable treatment' to imported cigarettes because, as the sales of domestic cigarettes are greater than those of imported cigarettes on the Dominican Republic market, the per unit cost of the bond requirement for imported cigarettes is higher than for domestic products.[297] As discussed above, the Appellate Body ruled in *Korea – Various Measures on Beef* that imported products are treated less favourably than like products if a measure modifies the conditions of competition in the relevant market *to the detriment of imported products*.[298] In *Dominican Republic – Import and*

---

[293] *Ibid.*, para. 6.214. Similar findings were made with regard to Canada's defences relating to the advantage of standing mixing authorisation it granted to Eastern Canadian grain only and relating to the revenue cap on rail transportation of Western Canadian grain. See *ibid.*, paras. 6.297 and 6.359.

[294] Panel Report, *Dominican Republic – Import and Sale of Cigarettes*, para. 7.196.   [295] *Ibid.*, para. 7.197.

[296] See *ibid.*, paras. 7.311 and 7.316; and Appellate Body Report, *Dominican Republic – Import and Sale of Cigarettes*, para. 96.

[297] See Appellate Body Report, *Dominican Republic – Import and Sale of Cigarettes*, para. 96.

[298] See above, p. 384.

Sale of Cigarettes, the Appellate Body elaborated on its ruling in *Korea – Various Measures on Beef* as follows:

> However, the existence of a detrimental effect on a given imported product resulting from a measure does not necessarily imply that this measure accords less favourable treatment to imports if the detrimental effect *is explained by factors or circumstances unrelated to the foreign origin of the product*, such as the market share of the importer in this case. In this specific case, the mere demonstration that the per-unit cost of the bond requirement for imported cigarettes was higher than for some domestic cigarettes during a particular period is not, in our view, *sufficient* to establish 'less favourable treatment' under Article III:4 of the GATT 1994. Indeed, the difference between the per-unit costs of the bond requirement alleged by Honduras is explained by the fact that the importer of Honduran cigarettes has a smaller market share than two domestic producers (the per-unit cost of the bond requirement being the result of dividing the cost of the bond by the number of cigarettes sold on the Dominican Republic market). In this case, the difference between the per-unit costs of the bond requirement alleged by Honduras *does not depend on the foreign origin of the imported cigarettes*. Therefore, in our view, the Panel was correct in dismissing the argument that the bond requirement accords less favourable treatment to imported cigarettes because the per-unit cost of the bond was higher for the importer of Honduran cigarettes than for two domestic producers.[299]
>
> [Emphasis added]

In brief, the Appellate Body ruled in *Dominican Republic – Import and Sale of Cigarettes* that if the less favourable treatment can be explained by factors or circumstances unrelated to the foreign origin of the product (such as the market share of the importer), this less favourable treatment would *not* be inconsistent with Article III:4.

In line with this ruling of the Appellate Body, the Panel in *EC – Approval and Marketing of Biotech Products*, rejected Argentina's claim of inconsistency with Article III:4, stating that:

> Argentina has not adduced argument and evidence sufficient to raise a presumption that the alleged less favourable treatment is explained by the foreign origin of the relevant biotech products.[300]

In the opinion of the Panel, Argentina, one of the complainants in *EC – Approval and Marketing of Biotech Products*, failed to demonstrate that the (alleged) less favourable treatment was less favourable treatment within the meaning of Article III:4 of the GATT 1994. Argentina did not demonstrate that this less favourable treatment is explained by the foreign origin of the imported product concerned.

It is therefore no longer sufficient to demonstrate inconsistency with Article III:4 that a measure adversely affects the conditions of competition for the imported product. Since the Appellate Body Report in *Dominican Republic – Import and Sale of Cigarettes*, it must also be shown that the adverse effects are explained by the foreign origin of the product. If the adverse effect has a different explanation, the measure cannot be found inconsistent with the national treatment obligation of Article III:4.

---

[299] Appellate Body Report, *Dominican Republic – Import and Sale of Cigarettes*, para. 96.
[300] Panel Report, *EC – Approval and Marketing of Biotech Products*, para. 7.2514.

GATT and WTO panels and the Appellate Body have found a wide variety of measures inconsistent with the national treatment obligation of Article III:4. In addition to the measures at issue in *US – Section 337*, *US – Gasoline*, *Korea – Various Measures on Beef* and *Canada – Wheat Exports and Grain Imports*, all discussed above, measures found to be inconsistent include:

- minimum price requirements (*Canada – Provincial Liquor Boards (US)*);
- a general ban on cigarette advertising (*Thailand – Cigarettes*);
- regulations concerning internal transportation (*US – Malt Beverages*); and
- exemption from the soft drink tax, the distribution tax and the bookkeeping requirements for producers using cane sugar as a sweetener in the production of soft drinks and syrups (*Mexico – Taxes on Soft Drinks*).

With respect to minimum price requirements, it deserves to be noted that the Panel in *Canada – Provincial Liquor Boards (US)* ruled in 1992 that:

> minimum prices applied equally to imported and domestic beer did not necessarily accord equal conditions of competition to imported and domestic beer. Whenever they prevented imported beer from being supplied at a price lower than that of domestic beer, they accorded in fact treatment to imported beer less favourable than that accorded to domestic beer: when they were set at the level at which domestic brewers supplied beer – as was presently the case in New Brunswick and Newfoundland – they did not change the competitive opportunities accorded to domestic beer but did affect the competitive opportunities of imported beer which could otherwise be supplied below the minimum price.[301]

With respect to a general ban on cigarette advertising, the Panel in *Thailand – Cigarettes* noted:

> It might be argued that such a general ban on all cigarette advertising would create unequal competitive opportunities between the existing Thai supplier of cigarettes and new, foreign suppliers and was therefore contrary to Article III:4.[302]

The Panel in *US – Malt Beverages* found with regard to regulations concerning internal transportation that:

> the requirement for imported beer and wine to be transported by common carrier, whereas domestic in-state beer and wine is not so required, may result in additional charges to transport these imported products and therefore prevent imported products from competing on an equal footing with domestic like products.[303]

In *Mexico – Taxes on Soft Drinks*, the Panel concluded with regard to the exemption from the soft drink tax, the distribution tax and the bookkeeping requirements at issue in that case:

> The challenged measures create an economic incentive for producers to use cane sugar as a sweetener in the production of soft drinks and syrups, instead of other non-cane sugar

---

[301] GATT Panel Report, *Canada – Provincial Liquor Boards (US)*, para. 5.30.
[302] GATT Panel Report, *Thailand – Cigarettes*, para. 78. Note that such a general ban on cigarette advertising was not the measure at issue in this case but a suggested alternative measure of which the Panel considered the GATT-consistency. The Panel further stated: 'Even if this argument were accepted, such an inconsistency would have to be regarded as unavoidable and therefore necessary within the meaning of Article XX(b) because additional advertising rights would risk stimulating demand for cigarettes.' See below, p. 624.   [303] GATT Panel Report, *US – Malt Beverages*, para. 5.50.

sweeteners such as beet sugar or HFCS. This incentive is created by conferring an advantage (the exemption from the soft drink tax, the distribution tax and the bookkeeping requirements) on those producers that use cane sugar instead of non-cane sugar sweeteners, such as beet sugar or HFCS. These measures do not legally impede producers from using non-cane sugar sweeteners, such as beet sugar or HFCS. However, they significantly modify the conditions of competition between cane sugar, on the one hand, and non-cane sugar sweeteners, such as beet sugar or HFCS, on the other. Indeed, there is evidence that the imposition of these measures reverted the trend that was seemingly under way in the Mexican market towards the replacement of cane sugar as an industrial sweetener in the production of soft drinks and syrups, for non-cane sugar sweeteners, such as HFCS.[304]

Note, however, that in *US – FSC (Article 21.5 – EC)*, the Appellate Body cautioned Members and panels as follows:

> The examination of whether a measure involves 'less favourable treatment' of imported products within the meaning of Article III:4 of the GATT 1994 must be grounded in close scrutiny of the 'fundamental thrust and effect of the measure itself'. This examination cannot rest on simple assertion, but must be founded on a careful analysis of the contested measure and of its implications in the marketplace.[305]

Questions and Assignments 4.22

Can a Member treat 'like' products differently without acting inconsistently with Article III:4 of the GATT 1994? What does 'treatment no less favourable' require? Give three examples of internal regulations which panels and/or the Appellate Body found to be inconsistent with Article III:4 of the GATT 1994.

4.5. NATIONAL TREATMENT UNDER THE GATS

Article XVII of the GATS, which is entitled 'National Treatment', states, in paragraph 1:

> In the sectors inscribed in its Schedule, and subject to any conditions and qualifications set out therein, each Member shall accord to services and service suppliers of any other Member, in respect of all measures affecting the supply of services, treatment no less favourable than that it accords to its own like services and service suppliers.

This section first explores the nature of the national treatment obligation of Article XVII of the GATS and then discusses the test of consistency with this obligation.[306]

---

[304] Panel Report, *Mexico – Taxes on Soft Drinks*, para. 8.117.
[305] Appellate Body Report, *US – FSC (Article 21.5 – EC)*, para. 215.
[306] On the relationship between the national treatment obligation of Article XVII of the GATS and the market access obligation of Article XVI of the GATS, see below, p. 488.

4.5.1. Nature of the national treatment obligation of Article XVII of the GATS

The national treatment obligation of Article XVII of the GATS is different from the national treatment obligation of Article III of the GATT 1994. As discussed above, the national treatment obligation of Article III of the GATT 1994 has *general* application to all trade in goods.[307] On the contrary, the national treatment obligation for trade in services of Article XVII of the GATS does not have such general application; it does not apply generally to all measures affecting trade in services. The national treatment obligation applies only to the extent that WTO Members have explicitly committed themselves to grant 'national treatment' in respect of specific service sectors.[308] Members set out such commitments in the national treatment column of their 'Schedule of Specific Commitments'. These specific commitments to grant national treatment are often made subject to certain conditions, qualifications and limitations, which are also set out in the Schedules. Members can, for example, grant national treatment in a specific service sector only with respect to certain modes of supply (such as cross-border supply) and not others (such as commercial presence).[309] Typical national treatment limitations included in Schedules relate to:

- nationality or residence requirements for executives of companies supplying services;
- requirements to invest a certain amount of assets in local currency;
- restrictions on the purchase of land by foreign service suppliers;
- special subsidy or tax privileges granted only to domestic suppliers; and
- differential capital requirements and special operational limits applying only to operations of foreign suppliers.[310]

Note, by way of example, the national treatment column of the Schedule of the European Communities and its Member States with respect to higher education services, as included in Figure 4.1. It appears from this Schedule that the European Communities and its Member States have agreed to accord national treatment to higher education services supplied in mode 1 ('cross-border supply') (with a qualification by Italy), mode 2 ('consumption abroad') and mode 3 ('commercial presence'). However, no commitment to accord national treatment was made with regard to mode 4 ('presence of natural persons'), except the commitment made for all service sectors.

The Schedules of Specific Commitments of Members can be found on the WTO website.[311] Overall, most Members, especially developing-country Members, have not made national treatment commitments with regard to many

---

[307] See above, p. 346.
[308] On the concept of 'service sectors', see below, pp. 485–6. A list of the service sectors is contained in GATT Secretariat, *Note by the Secretariat, Services Sectoral Classification List*, MTN.GNS/W/120, dated 10 July 1991.
[309] On the modes of supply of services, see above, pp. 337–8.
[310] See WTO Secretariat, *Market Access: Unfinished Business*, Special Series Studies 6 (WTO, 2001), 103.
[311] See www.wto.org/english/tratop_e/serv_e/serv_commitments_e.htm, visited on 17 November 2007. For an explanation on how to 'read' Services Schedules, see below, pp. 486–8.

Figure 4.1 Excerpt from the Schedule of Specific Commitments of the European Communities and its Member States[312]

Sector or Sub-Sector	Limitations on Market Access	Limitations on National Treatment	Additional Commitments	Notes
C. Higher Education Services (CPC 923)	5. PRIVATELY FUNDED EDUCATION SERVICES 1) F: Condition of nationality. However, third country antionals can have authorization from competent authorities to establish and direct an education institution and to teach. 2) None 3) E, I: Needs test for opening of private universities authorised to issue recognised diplomas or degrees; producere involves an advice of the Parliment. GR: Unbound for education institutions granting recognised State diplomas. 4) Unbound except as indicated in the horizontal section and subject to the following specific limitations: DK: Condition of nationality for professors. F: Condition of nationality. However, third country nationals may obtain authorization from competent authorities to establish and direct an education institution and to teach. I: Condition of nationality for service providers to be authorised to issue state recognised diplomas.	1) I: Condition of nationality for service providers to be authorised to issue state recognised diplomas. 2) None 3) None 4) Unbound except as indicated in the horizontal section		

service sectors and when commitments are made, they are often accompanied by extensive limitations. Negotiations on more ambitious national treatment commitments are a substantial element of the ongoing negotiations on trade in services in the context of the Doha Development Round.

To determine the scope of the national treatment obligation of a Member, or to determine whether, in respect of a specific service, a Member must grant national treatment to services and service suppliers of other Members, it is necessary to examine the commitments, conditions, qualifications and limitations set out in the Member's Schedule very carefully.

Questions and Assignments 4.23

In your country, are measures affecting basic education and health care subject to the national treatment obligation of Article XVII:1 of the GATS? Are they in the United States, China, India and Brazil?

4.5.2. National treatment test of Article XVII of the GATS

In the sectors inscribed in its Schedule and subject to the conditions, qualifications and limitations set out therein, a Member must accord to services and service suppliers of any other Member treatment no less favourable than that it accords to its own like services and service suppliers. This obligation exists in respect of all measures by Members affecting the supply of services. In

---

[312] GATS/SC/31, dated 15 April 1994.

its analysis of the consistency of the EC licensing regime for the importation of bananas with the national treatment obligation under Article XVII of the GATS in *EC – Bananas III*, the Panel noted:

> In order to establish a breach of the national treatment obligation of Article XVII, three elements need to be demonstrated: (i) the EC has undertaken a commitment in a relevant sector and mode of supply; (ii) the EC has adopted or applied a measure affecting the supply of services in that sector and/or mode of supply; and (iii) the measure accords to service suppliers of any other Member treatment less favourable than that it accords to the EC's own like service suppliers.[313]

Article XVII of the GATS sets out a three-tier test of consistency with the national treatment obligation of Article XVII of the GATS. After first having established that a national treatment commitment was made in respect of the relevant service sector, this three-tier test of consistency under Article XVII of the GATS requires the examination of:

- whether the measure at issue is a measure by a Member affecting trade in services;
- whether the foreign and domestic services or service suppliers are 'like services' or 'like service suppliers'; and
- whether the foreign services or service suppliers are granted treatment no less favourable.

4.5.2.1. *'Measures by Members affecting trade in services'*

As discussed above in the context of the MFN treatment obligation of Article II of the GATS, the concept of a 'measure by a Member' is broad, including not only measures of central government or authorities but also measures of regional and local governments and authorities as well as – in specific circumstances – measures of non-governmental bodies.[314] The concept of a 'measure affecting trade in services' has been clarified by the Appellate Body in *Canada – Autos*, where it stated that two key issues must be examined to determine whether a measure is one 'affecting trade in services', namely:

- first, whether there is 'trade in services' in the sense of Article I:2; and
- secondly, whether the measure at issue 'affects' such trade in services within the meaning of Article I:1.[315]

Recall, with respect to the first question, the broad scope of the concept of 'trade in services', including all services except services supplied in the exercise of governmental authority. Trade in services includes services supplied in any of the four distinct modes of supply (cross-border supply, consumption abroad, commercial presence and the presence of natural persons).[316] With respect to

---

[313] Panel Reports, *EC – Bananas III*, para. 7.314. See also *EC – Bananas III (Article 21.5 – Ecuador)*, para. 6.100.
[314] See above, p. 336.   [315] See Appellate Body Report, *Canada – Autos*, para. 155. See above, pp. 336–7.
[316] See above, pp. 337–8.

the second question, recall that, for a measure to 'affect' trade in services, this measure need not regulate or govern the trade in, i.e. the supply of, services. A measure affects trade in services when the measure bears 'upon the conditions of competition in supply of a service'.[317]

4.5.2.2. 'Like services and service suppliers'

The second element of the national treatment test of Article XVII of the GATS is whether the foreign and domestic services or service suppliers are 'like services' or 'like service suppliers'. The concept of 'like services' or 'like service suppliers' is discussed above in the context of the MFN treatment obligation of Article II of the GATS. As is the case for 'likeness' under Article II, there is almost no relevant case law to date on the meaning of 'likeness' under Article XVII.[318] However, a determination of the 'likeness' of services and service suppliers should clearly be based, among other relevant factors, on:

- the characteristics of the service or the service supplier;
- the classification and description of the service in the United Nations Central Product Classification (CPC) system; and
- consumers' habits and preferences regarding the service or the service supplier.

As also stated above in the context of Article II of the GATS, determining whether services or service suppliers are 'like' for the purposes of Article XVII of the GATS in essence calls for a determination of the nature and the extent of the competitive relationship between the services or service suppliers concerned.[319]

Note that also under Article XVII of the GATS, two service suppliers that supply a like service are not *necessarily* 'like service suppliers'.[320] Factors such as the size of the companies, their assets, their use of technology and the nature and extent of their expertise must all be taken into account.

4.5.2.3. 'Treatment no less favourable'

The third and final element of the national treatment test of Article XVII:1 of the GATS is whether the foreign services or service suppliers are granted treatment no less favourable. Paragraphs 2 and 3 of Article XVII clarify the requirement of 'treatment no less favourable' set out in paragraph 1 by stating:

2. A Member may meet the requirement of paragraph 1 by according to services and service suppliers of any other Member, either formally identical treatment or formally different treatment to that it accords to its own like services and service suppliers.
3. Formally identical or formally different treatment shall be considered to be less favourable if it modifies the conditions of competition in favour of services or service suppliers of the Member compared to like services or service suppliers of any other Member.

---

317 See above, p. 339.   318 Note Panel Report, *EC – Bananas III*, para. 7.322. See above, p. 340.
319 See above, p. 340.   320 See above, p. 340.

It follows that a Member that gives formally identical treatment to foreign and domestic services or service suppliers may nevertheless be in breach of the national treatment obligation. This happens if that Member, by giving formally identical treatment, modifies the conditions of competition in favour of the domestic services or service suppliers. Also, a Member that gives formally *different* treatment to foreign and domestic services or service suppliers does not act in breach of the national treatment obligation if that Member, by giving formally *different* treatment, does not modify the conditions of competition in favour of the domestic services and service suppliers. The latter would obviously be the case if the different treatment would be in favour of the foreign services or service suppliers but it may also be that a formally different treatment has no impact on the conditions of competition. Note that the Panel in *EC – Bananas III (Article 21.5 – Ecuador)* found that certain EC measures accorded Ecuadorian service suppliers *de facto* less favourable conditions of competition than like EC service suppliers within the meaning of Article XVII of the GATS.[321]

With respect to inherent competitive disadvantages resulting from the fact that the service or service supplier is foreign and not domestic, footnote 10 to Article XVII states:

> Specific commitments assumed under this Article shall not be construed to require any Member to compensate for any inherent competitive disadvantages which result from the foreign character of the relevant services or service suppliers.

The Panel in *Canada – Autos*, however, stressed the limited scope of this provision as follows:

> Footnote 10 to Article XVII only exempts Members from having to compensate for disadvantages due to the foreign character in the application of the national treatment provision; it does not provide cover for actions which might modify the conditions of competition against services or service suppliers which are already disadvantaged due to their foreign character.[322]

Questions and Assignments 4.24

What are the elements of the national treatment test of Article XVII:1 of the GATS? Which measures are 'measures affecting trade in services'? How does one determine whether services or service suppliers are 'like' within the meaning of Article XVII:1? Are all banking services 'like services' within the meaning of Article XVII:1? Are all law firms 'like service suppliers' within the meaning of Article XVII:1? When is there 'treatment less favourable' within the meaning of Article XVII:1? Can a measure which grants a subsidy to both domestic and foreign service suppliers be in breach of the national treatment obligation of Article XVII:1 of the GATS?

---

[321] See Panel Report, *EC – Bananas III (Article 21.5 – Ecuador)*, para. 6.126.
[322] Panel Report, *Canada – Autos*, para. 10.300.

4.6. SUMMARY

There are two main principles of non-discrimination in WTO law: the most-favoured-nation (MFN) treatment obligation and the national treatment obligation. In simple terms, the MFN treatment obligation prohibits a country from discriminating *between* other countries; the national treatment obligation prohibits a country from discriminating *against* other countries. These principles of non-discrimination apply – albeit not in the same manner – with respect to trade in goods, as well as trade in services. The key provisions of the GATT 1994 that deal with non-discrimination in trade in goods are Article I, on the MFN treatment obligation, and Article III, on the national treatment obligation. The key provisions on non-discrimination in the GATS are Article II, on the MFN treatment obligation, and Article XVII, on the national treatment obligation.

The principal purpose of the MFN treatment obligation of Article I of the GATT 1994 is to ensure *equality of opportunity* to import from, or to export to, *all* WTO Members. There are three questions which must be answered to determine whether or not there is a violation of the MFN treatment obligation of Article I:1 of the GATT 1994, namely:

- whether the measure at issue confers a trade 'advantage' of the kind covered by Article I:1;
- whether the products concerned are 'like products'; and
- whether the advantage at issue is granted 'immediately and unconditionally' to all like products concerned.

As is the case with the MFN treatment obligation under the GATT 1994, the principal purpose of the MFN treatment obligation of Article II:1 of the GATS is to ensure *equality of opportunity*, *in casu*, for services and service suppliers of *all* other WTO Members. There are three questions which must be answered to determine whether or not a measure violates the MFN treatment obligation of Article II:1 of the GATS, namely:

- whether the measure at issue is a measure covered by the GATS, i.e. a measure by a Member affecting trade in services;
- whether the services or service suppliers concerned are 'like services' or 'like service suppliers'; and
- whether less favourable treatment is accorded to the services or service suppliers of a Member.

The principal purpose of the national treatment obligations of Article III of the GATT 1994 is to *avoid protectionism* in the application of internal tax and regulatory measures. As is explicitly stated in Article III:1, the purpose of Article III is to ensure that internal measures 'not be applied to imported and domestic products so as to afford protection to domestic production'. To this end, Article III obliges Members of the WTO to provide *equality of competitive conditions* for imported products in relation to domestic products. The test of consistency of internal taxation with the national treatment obligation of Article III:2, first sentence of the GATT 1994 requires the examination of:

- whether the measure at issue is an 'internal tax';
- whether the imported and domestic products are 'like products'; and
- whether the imported products are not taxed in excess of the domestic products.

Article III:2, second sentence, also concerns national treatment with respect to internal taxation, but it contemplates a 'broader category of products' than Article III:2, first sentence. It applies to 'directly competitive or substitutable products'. Article III:2, second sentence of the GATT 1994 sets out a different test of consistency, which requires the examination of:

- whether the measure at issue is an 'internal tax';
- whether the imported and domestic products are 'directly competitive or substitutable';
- whether these products are 'not similarly taxed'; and
- whether the dissimilar taxation is applied so as to afford protection to domestic production.

The national treatment obligation of Article III of the GATT 1994 concerns not only internal taxation, but also internal regulation. The national treatment obligation for internal regulation is set out in Article III:4. To determine whether a measure is consistent with the national treatment obligations of Article III:4 of the GATT 1994, there is a three-tier test which requires the examination of:

- whether the measure at issue is a law, regulation or requirement covered by Article III:4;
- whether the imported and domestic products are 'like products'; and
- whether the imported products are accorded 'treatment no less favourable'.

The national treatment obligation, with respect to measures affecting trade in services, is set out in Article XVII of the GATS. The national treatment obligation of Article XVII is different from the national treatment obligation of Article III of the GATT 1994. While the national treatment obligation of Article III of the GATT 1994 has general application to all trade in goods, the national treatment obligation for trade in services of Article XVII of the GATS applies only to the extent WTO Members have explicitly committed themselves to grant 'national treatment' in respect of specific service sectors. Often such national treatment commitments are subject to conditions and qualifications limiting the scope of the commitment. Where a Member has made a specific commitment to grant 'national treatment', it must fulfil the 'national treatment' obligations of Article XVII of the GATS. To determine whether a measure is consistent with the national treatment obligation of Article XVII of the GATS, there is a three-tier test which requires the examination of:

- whether the measure at issue is a measure covered by the GATS, i.e. a measure by a Member affecting trade in services;

- whether the foreign and domestic services or service suppliers are 'like services' or 'like service suppliers'; and
- whether the foreign services or service suppliers are granted 'treatment no less favourable'.

The non-discrimination obligations of Articles I:1, III:2, first sentence, and III:4 of the GATT 1994 and Articles II:1 and XVII:1 of the GATS only apply to products, services or service suppliers which are 'like'. As the Appellate Body noted, the concept of 'like products' is like an accordion whose width varies depending on the provision under which the term is interpreted. However, the determination of whether products are 'like products' is, in essence, a determination of the nature and extent of the competitive relationship between these products. The same can be said of the determination of whether services or service suppliers are 'like'. The factors that must be considered in determining 'likeness' are, among other relevant factors:

- the characteristics of the products, services and service suppliers;
- the classification of the products, services and service suppliers;
- consumer tastes and habits regarding the products, services and service suppliers; and
- for products, their end-use.

4.7. EXERCISE: BEER IN NEWLAND

Traditionally, Newland is a wine-drinking country. However, recent market research has shown that demand for beer in Newland is steadily growing. Superbrew Inc. of Richland, one of the world's largest beer producers, therefore wants to increase its exports of low alcohol beer, high alcohol beer and non-alcoholic beer to Newland. Before its accession to the WTO, Newland limited the importation of beer of any kind to a meagre 50,000 hectolitres per year. This quantitative restriction was put into place in the late 1950s to protect the many winegrowers in Newland from competition from imported beer. The National Association of Wineries (NAW) was, and still is, a powerful lobby in Newland politics. On accession to the WTO, Newland abolished the quantitative restriction on the importation of beer and introduced customs duties instead.

Since 1995, Newland as imposed the following *ad valorem* customs duties:

- 10 per cent on wine;
- 20 per cent on low alcohol beer and non-alcoholic beer; and
- 30 per cent on high alcohol beer.

Newland has exempted the following beverages from customs duties:
- high alcohol beer produced in the United States; and
- high alcohol beer produced in micro-breweries.

Since last year, when a case of serious customs fraud was discovered, Newland has required that all beer be imported through two designated ports only. This requirement does not apply, however, to beer imported from neighbouring Nearland, a country currently negotiating accession to the WTO.

Shortly after Newland joined the WTO, it also revised its tax regime for alcoholic and non-alcoholic beverages. The following VAT rates now apply:

- 2 per cent on domestically produced non-alcoholic beverages and non-alcoholic beverages produced in the United States; and
- 5 per cent on all other imported non-alcoholic beverages.

The following excise tax rates apply:

- 15 per cent on wine;
- 15.5 per cent on low alcohol beer and non-alcoholic beer; and
- 30 per cent on high alcohol beer.

In Newland, beer, whether domestic or imported, may only be sold by licensed beer merchants and may not be sold in supermarkets. No such restrictions exist on the sales of domestic or imported beer and wine. In addition, they do not apply to Australian beer.

Superbrew Inc. not only wants to sell its beer in Newland's supermarkets, it also wants to establish a wholesale trade company in Newland as well as a network of retail shops to handle the distribution of its beer. Superbrew has been told it can do neither.

Pursuant to the Fair Competition Act of 1991, imported as well as domestic beer is subject to a minimum price requirement, annually set by the Ministry of Commerce of Newland. Furthermore, Newland prohibits the use of additives in low alcohol beer while leaving the use of additives in high alcohol beer unregulated.

In support of the national wine industry, Newland's National Federation of Restaurateurs, a government-sponsored organisation, has instructed its 10,000 members not to serve beer with traditional Newland dishes. Municipal authorities in Newland's main wine-producing region prohibit serving beer on weekends. Note also that, since the Armed Forces Reform Act of 1996, the armed forces of Newland are required by law to buy domestic alcoholic beverages.

Finally, CoolBrew Inc., a subsidiary of Superbrew Inc. specialising in the maintenance of beer-cooling installations, wants to employ in Newland engineers from Richland for short-term repair jobs. However, CoolBrew Inc. has been informed that, under Newland's Regulated Professions Act of 1997, only engineers with a degree obtained in Newland or the United States are allowed to work in Newland.

Note that Newland's Schedule of Specific Commitments contains national treatment commitments for 'wholesale trade' services and 'maintenance and repair of equipment' services with respect to all modes of supply. For 'wholesale trade' services, however, 'commercial presence' is subject to the limitation that foreigners may never own more than 70 per cent of wholesale trade companies established in Newland. Newland's Schedule does not refer to retailing services. Finally, Newland did not include any measures relating to distribution or other business services in the Annex on Article II Exemptions.

You are an associate with the Brazilian law firm, Nogueira Neto Avogados. Your firm has been hired by Superbrew Inc. to give legal advice on all the issues raised above. You have been instructed to limit your legal brief to the question of whether there are violations of the non-discrimination obligations under WTO law. At present, you will not address the question of whether a possible violation can be justified under the 'general' or other exceptions provided for in the GATT 1994 or the GATS as discussed in chapter 7 of this book.

Rules on market access

Contents

5.1. INTRODUCTION

There can be no international trade without access to the domestic markets of other countries. It is important for countries, traders and service suppliers to have secure, predictable and growing access to markets of other countries. Rules on market access are, therefore, at the core of WTO law.

Market access for goods and services from other countries is impeded or restricted in various ways. There are two main categories of barriers to market access:

- tariff barriers; and
- non-tariff barriers.

The category of tariff barriers primarily includes customs duties, i.e. tariffs. Tariff barriers are particularly relevant for trade in goods; they are of marginal importance for trade in services. The category of non-tariff barriers includes quantitative restrictions (such as quotas) and 'other non-tariff barriers' (such as lack of transparency of trade regulation, unfair and arbitrary application of trade regulation, customs formalities, technical barriers to trade and government procurement practices). These 'other non-tariff barriers' undoubtedly constitute the largest and most diverse sub-category of non-tariff barriers.

As set out in the Preamble to the *WTO Agreement*, WTO Members pursue the objectives of higher standards of living, full employment, growth and sustainable economic development by:

> entering into reciprocal and mutually advantageous arrangements directed to the substantial reduction of tariffs and other barriers to trade.

The substantial reduction of tariff and non-tariff barriers to market access is, together with the elimination of discrimination, the key instrument of the WTO to achieve its overall objectives.[1] Few economists and trade policy-makers dispute that further trade liberalisation can make a significant contribution to the economic development of most developed and developing countries.[2] The WTO calculated that if all customs duties were eliminated, the resulting economic benefits would range between US$80 billion and US$500 billion.[3] The estimates of the share of these economic benefits going to developing countries range from 40 to 60 per cent. Potential gains from the liberalisation of trade in services are estimated to be between two and four times the gains from liberalising trade in goods.

As already noted in chapter 1, some barriers to market access, such as quantitative restrictions on goods, are prohibited, while other barriers, such as customs duties, are allowed in principle and are only limited to the extent of a Member's specific agreement. Different rules apply to different forms of barriers. This difference in rules reflects a difference in the negative effects they have on trade and on the economy.[4]

This chapter on the rules on market access addresses the rules on:

- tariff barriers to trade in goods;
- non-tariff barriers to trade in goods; and
- barriers to trade in services.

---

[1] See above, p. 321.   [2] See above, pp. 15–20.
[3] See *Some Facts for the 'Fifth'*, Cancún WTO Ministerial 2003 Briefing Notes, available at www.wto.org/english/thewto_e/minist_e/min03_e/brief_e/brief24_e.htm, visited on 10 May 2003.
[4] See below, pp. 445–6.

5.2. TARIFF BARRIERS TO TRADE IN GOODS

The most common and widely used barrier to market access for goods is customs duties, also referred to as tariffs. Furthermore, market access for goods is impeded by other duties and charges. This section discusses:

- customs duties or tariffs;
- negotiations on tariff reductions;
- tariff concessions or bindings and Schedules of Concessions;
- protection of tariff concessions;
- modification or withdrawal of tariff concessions;
- the imposition of customs duties; and
- duties and charges other than customs duties.

Since tariffs are normally not imposed on trade in services, this section only addresses tariffs on trade in goods.

5.2.1. Customs duties or tariffs

5.2.1.1. Definition and types

A customs duty, or tariff, is a financial charge, in the form of a tax, imposed on products at the time of, and/or because of, their importation.[5] Market access is conditional upon the payment of the customs duty.

Customs duties are specific, *ad valorem* or mixed. A specific customs duty on a product is an amount based on the weight, volume or quantity of that product, for example a duty of €100 per hectolitre of vegetable oil or a duty of €3,000 on each car. An *ad valorem* customs duty on a good is an amount based on the value of that good. It is a percentage of the value of the imported product, for example a 15 per cent *ad valorem* duty on computers. In that case, the duty on a computer worth €1,000 will be €150. A mixed, or compound, duty is a customs duty comprising an *ad valorem* duty to which a specific duty is added or, less frequently, subtracted: for example, a customs duty on wool of 10 per cent *ad valorem* and €50 per tonne. In that case, the duty on three tonnes of wool worth €1,000 per tonne will be €450.

Ad valorem customs duties are by far the most common type of customs duties. They are preferable to specific and mixed duties for several reasons. First, *ad valorem* duties are more transparent than specific duties. The protectionist impact and the negative effect on prices for consumers are easier to assess for *ad valorem* duties than for specific duties. The lack of transparency of specific

---

[5] Note that governments can also impose customs duties on products at the time of, and/or because of, their exportation. However, this is uncommon and, therefore, not addressed in this chapter. Note that the European Communities has been advocating in the context of the ongoing Doha Development Round negotiations a prohibition on export taxes. To date it has been unsuccessful in garnering much support. Developing countries wish to keep the right to use export taxes to encourage the development of their domestic processing industries. See F. Williams, 'EU Aims to Curb Export Taxes in Doha Talks', *Financial Times*, 30 March 2006.

duties makes it easier for special interest groups to obtain governmental support for high levels of protection.[6] Secondly, by definition, *ad valorem* customs duties are indexed. In times of inflation, the government's tariff revenue will keep up with price increases and the level of protection will remain the same. By contrast, specific duties will constantly have to be increased to maintain the same real tariff revenue or maintain the same level of protection.[7] Overall, with respect to industrial products specific duties as well as mixed duties are unusual.[8] With respect to agricultural products, however, non-*ad valorem* duties, and in particular mixed duties, are still common.[9]

Ad valorem, specific or mixed customs duties can be MFN duties, preferential duties or neither of the two. *MFN duties* are the 'standard' customs duties applicable to all other WTO Members in compliance with the non-discrimination MFN treatment obligation of Article I:1 of the GATT 1994.[10] *Preferential duties* are customs duties applied to specific countries pursuant to conventional or autonomous arrangements under which products from these countries are subject to duties lower than MFN duties. For example, the customs duties currently still applied by the European Communities to products from ACP countries under the terms of the *Cotonou Agreement* are conventional preferential duties.[11] The customs duties applied by the European Communities on products from developing countries under the EC's Generalised System of Preferences (GSP) are autonomous preferential duties.[12] Finally, there are customs duties that are neither MFN duties nor preferential duties. These are the duties applicable to goods from countries which are not WTO Members and do not benefit from MFN treatment.[13] The number of such countries is small and the latter category of customs duties is therefore of limited importance.

5.2.1.2. *Purpose of customs duties or tariffs*

Customs duties or tariffs serve three different purposes. First, customs duties are a source of revenue for governments. This purpose is less important for

---

[6] See WTO Secretariat, *Market Access: Unfinished Business*, Special Studies Series 6 (WTO, 2001), 9.

[7] Note that specific customs duties have the advantage that they are easier to impose as they do not require customs authorities to determine the value of the imported products. See below, pp. 431–4.

[8] Switzerland, and to a lesser extent Sri Lanka and Thailand, is an exception in this respect. Over 80 per cent of Switzerland's customs duties are non-*ad valorem* duties. See WTO Secretariat, *Market Access: Unfinished Business*, Special Studies Series 6 (WTO, 2001), 9. Note that the General Council, in its Decision of 1 August 2004 on the Doha Work Programme, decided that 'all non-*ad valorem* duties shall be converted to *ad valorem* equivalents on the basis of a methodology to be determined' (WT/L/579, dated 2 August 2004, Annex B, para. 5).

[9] WTO Secretariat, *Market Access: Unfinished Business*, Special Studies Series 6 (WTO, 2001), 46 and 47.

[10] See above, pp. 322–34.

[11] See *Partnership Agreement between the Members of the African, Caribbean and Pacific Group of States of the One Part and the European Community and Its Member States, of the Other Part*, signed in Cotonou, Benin, on 23 June 2000. Under Article 1 of Annex V to the Agreement, industrial products from ACP countries shall be imported into the European Communities free of customs duties; agricultural products benefit from a lower rate than normal. On 1 January 2008, this preferential tariff treatment will come to an end and is expected to be replaced by preferential tariff treatment provided for under the Economic Partnership Agreements concluded between the EC and regional groupings of ACP countries.

[12] See below, pp. 726–8.

[13] Note that non-WTO Members may benefit from MFN treatment under the terms of bilateral or regional trade agreements.

industrialised countries with a well-developed system of direct and indirect taxation. For many developing countries, however, customs duties are an important source of government revenue. In comparison with income taxes and sales taxes, customs duties are easy to collect. Imports are relatively easy to monitor and the collection of customs duties can be concentrated in a few ports of entry. Secondly, customs duties are used to protect domestic industries. The customs duties imposed on imported products make the 'like' domestic products relatively cheaper, giving them a price advantage and thus some degree of protection from import competition. Thirdly, customs duties can be used to promote a *rational* allocation of scarce foreign exchange. To promote the use of foreign exchange for the importation of capital goods (e.g. industrial machinery) and discourage its use for the importation of luxury goods (e.g. luxury cars), a country can impose low customs duties on the former and higher customs duties on the latter. Customs duties can thus be an instrument of an economic development policy.

5.2.1.3. National tariff

As stated above, the terms 'customs duties' and 'tariffs' are synonyms. However, the term 'tariff' has a second meaning. A 'tariff' is also a structured list of product descriptions and their corresponding customs duty. The customs duties or tariffs, which are due on importation, are set out in a country's tariff. Most national tariffs now follow or reflect the structure set out in the Harmonised Commodity Description and Coding System, usually referred to as the 'Harmonised System' or 'HS' discussed in detail later in this chapter.[14]

The national tariff of the European Communities is referred to as the Common Customs Tariff.[15] Its structure follows the HS but is more detailed, as is the case for the tariffs of many industrialised countries. Every year the European Commission adopts a Regulation reproducing a complete version of the Common Customs Tariff, taking into account Council and Commission amendments of that year. The Regulation is published in the *Official Journal of the European Communities* no later than 31 October. It applies from 1 January of the following year.[16]

The national tariff of the United States is structured in the same manner as the EC Common Customs Tariff; both follow the Harmonised System.

The excerpt from India's First Schedule to the Customs Tariff Act, reproduced as figure 5.1, shows that the customs duties on cocoa are 30 per cent *ad valorem*. India's customs duties on some products are still higher than 30 per cent while on other products they are lower. The customs duty on, for example, tariff item

---

[14] See below, pp. 428–31.
[15] See Council Regulation (EEC) No. 2658/87 of 23 July 1987 on the tariff and statistical nomenclature and on the Common Customs Tariff, OJ 1987, L256, 7 September 1987. In addition to the applicable customs duties, the Common Customs Tariff is usually understood to include also all other Community legislation that has an effect on the level of customs duty payable on a particular import. Note that the Member States of the European Union, as constituent members of the customs union of the European Union, do not have separate national tariffs. Their common external tariff is the Common Customs Tariff.
[16] For 2008, see Commission Regulation (EC) No. 1214/2007 of 20 September 2007 amending Annex I to Council Regulation (EEC) No. 2658/87 on the tariff and statistical nomenclature and on the Common Customs Tariff, OJ 2007, L286, 31 October 2007.

Figure 5.1: Excerpt from India's First Schedule to the Customs Tariff Act[17]

Section-IV   *Chapter-18*

CHAPTER 18
Cocoa and cocoa preparations

Notes:

1. This Chapter does not cover the preparations of headings 0403, 1901, 1904, 1905, 2105, 2202, 2208, 3003, or 3004.

2. Heading 1806 includes sugar confectionery containing cocoa and, subject to Note 1 to this Chapter, other food preparations containing cocoa.

Tariff Item		Description of goods	Unit	Rate of duty	
				Standard	Preferential Areas
(1)		(2)	(3)	(4)	(5)
1801 00 00		COCOA BEANS, WHOLE OR BROKEN, RAW OR ROASTED	kg.	30%	–
1802 00 00		COCOA SHELLS, HUSKS, SKINS AND OTHER COCOA WASTE	kg.	30%	–
1803		COCOA PASTE, WHETHER OR NOT DEFATTED			
1803 10 00	–	Not defatted	kg.	30%	–
1803 20 00	–	Wholly or partly defatted	kg.	30%	–
1804 00 00		COCOA BUTTER, FAT AND OIL	kg.	30%	–
1805 00 00		COCOA POWDER, NOT CONTAINING ADDED SUGAR OR OTHER SWEETENING MATTER	kg.	30%	–
1806		CHOCOLATE AND OTHER FOOD PREPARATIONS CONTAINING COCOA			
1806 10 00	–	Cocoa powder, containing added sugar or other sweetening matter	kg.	30%	–
1806 20 00	–	Other preparations in blocks, slabs or bars weighing more than 2 kg. or in liquid, paste, powder, granular or other bulk form in containers or immediate packings, of a content exceeding 2 kg.	kg.	30%	–
	–	*Other, in blocks, slabs or bars:*			
1806 31 00	–	Filled	kg.	30%	–
1806 32 00	–	Not filled	kg.	30%	–
1806 90	–	*Other:*			
1806 90 10	–	Chocolate and chocolate products	kg.	30%	–
1806 90 20	–	Sugar confectionary containing cocoa	kg.	30%	–
1806 90 30	–	Spreads containing cocoa	kg.	30%	–
1806 90 40	–	Preparations containing cocoa for making beverages	kg.	30%	–
1806 90 90	–	Other	kg.	30%	–

---

[17] See www.cbec.gov.in/customs/cst-0708/cst-main.htm visited on 2 December 2007.

1704 10 00 ('Chewing gum . . .') is 45 per cent *ad valorem* and the customs duty on tariff item 8703 21 10 ('Vehicles principally designed for the transport of more than seven persons, including the driver') is 100 per cent *ad valorem*. The customs duty on tariff item 2501 00 10 ('Common salt . . .') is 12.5 per cent *ad valorem*. When compared to the customs duties imposed by the European Communities and the United States, the duties imposed by India are definitely high.[18] Note, however, that India reduced its overall applied rate between 2001/2 and 2006/7 from 32.3 per cent to 15.8 per cent.[19]

Many WTO Members have an online database of the customs duties they apply. The website of the World Customs Organization, www.wcoomd.org, gives easy access to a number of these databases, including the TARIC database of the European Communities.[20] Alternatively, the EU Market Access Database, a service offered by the Directorate-General for Trade of the European Commission, also gives up-to-date information on the customs duties imposed by about ninety other countries or customs territories.[21] This database also includes a convenient link to the TARIC database.

Questions and Assignments 5.1

What are specific customs duties and how do they differ from *ad valorem* customs duties? What are MFN customs duties? What is a tariff? Why do countries impose customs duties on imports? Find out and compare the MFN customs duties imposed by the European Communities, the United States, China, South Africa, Bangladesh and Poland on cocoa powder and road tractors. If you are a national of a WTO Member other than those Members referred to in this section, find out what the MFN customs duties which your government imposes on cocoa powder and tractors are.

5.2.2. Negotiations on tariff reductions

5.2.2.1. *Tariffs as a lawful instrument of protection*

In principle, WTO Members are free to impose customs duties on imported products. WTO law, and in particular, the GATT 1994, does not prohibit the

---

[18] See e.g. for chewing gum, the European Communities' Common External Tariff, available at http://ec.europa.eu/taxation_customs/dds/tarhome_en.htm, visited on 1 November 2007.

[19] WTO Secretariat, *Trade Policy Review Report – India, Revision*, WT/TPR/S/182/Rev.1, dated 24 July 2007, vii, para. 2.

[20] See http://ec.europa.eu/taxation_customs/dds/en/tarhome.htm, visited on 1 December 2007. The TARIC database shows the various arrangements applying to specific products when imported into the European Union. Apart from the MFN duties, it also incorporates tariff quotas; preferential customs duties (under the EC's Generalised System of Preferences, under the *Cotonou Agreement* for ACP countries, under the *European Economic Area Agreement* for Iceland, Liechtenstein and Norway, and under a number of bilateral trade agreements with, for example, Algeria, Egypt, Israel, the Occupied Palestinian Territory and South Africa). The TARIC database also incorporates anti-dumping and countervailing duties, import prohibitions and import restrictions. See OJ 2003, C103, 30 April 2003.

[21] See http://mkaccdb.eu.int, visited on 21 November 2007. This database also gives information on non-tariff barriers to trade maintained by other countries, general information on the trade policies of these countries and statistics on trade.

imposition of customs duties. This is in sharp contrast to the general prohibition on quantitative restrictions.[22] Customs duties, unlike quantitative restrictions, represent an instrument of protection against imports generally allowed by the GATT 1994. The reasons behind the GATT's preference for customs duties are discussed below.[23]

5.2.2.2. A call for tariff negotiations

While WTO law does not prohibit customs duties, it does recognise that customs duties constitute an obstacle to trade. Article XXVIII *bis* of the GATT 1994, therefore, calls upon WTO Members to negotiate the reduction of customs duties. This article provides, in relevant part:

> thus negotiations on a reciprocal and mutually advantageous basis, directed to the substantial reduction of the general level of tariffs and other charges on imports and exports and in particular to the reduction of such high tariffs as discourage the importation even of minimum quantities, and conducted with due regard to the objectives of this Agreement and the varying needs of individual [Members], are of great importance to the expansion of international trade. The [Members] may therefore sponsor such negotiations from time to time.

Note that Article XXXVII:1 of the GATT 1994 calls upon developed-country Members to accord, in the interest of the economic development of developing-country Members:

> high priority to the reduction and elimination of barriers to products currently or potentially of particular export interest to [developing-country Members] . . . [24]

5.2.2.3. Success of past tariff negotiations

Under the GATT 1947, negotiations on the reduction of tariff duties took place primarily in the context of eight successive 'Rounds' of trade negotiations. In fact, the first five of these Rounds (Geneva, Annecy, Torquay, Geneva and Dillon) were exclusively dedicated to the negotiation of the reduction of tariffs. The sixth, seventh and eighth Rounds (Kennedy, Tokyo and Uruguay) had an increasingly broader agenda, although the negotiation of tariff reductions remained an important element on the agenda of these Rounds.

The eight GATT Rounds of trade negotiations were very successful in reducing customs duties. In the late 1940s, the average duty on industrial products imposed by developed countries was about 40 per cent *ad valorem*. As a result of the eight GATT Rounds, the average duty of developed-country Members on industrial products is now as low as 3.9 per cent *ad valorem*.[25]

---

[22] See below, pp. 447–50.   [23] See below, pp. 409, 411, 445, 446.
[24] Note, however, that Article XXXVII qualifies its call to give high priority to the reduction and elimination of barriers with the words 'except when compelling reasons . . . make it impossible'.
[25] See WTO Trade Policy Review Division, *Multilateral Approaches to Market Access Negotiations*, Staff Working Paper TPRD-98-02 (WTO, 1998), 2.

Figure 5.2: Fifty years of tariff reduction negotiations[26]

Implementation period	Round covered	Weighted tariff reduction of all duties
1948–63	First five GATT rounds (1947–62)	–36
1968–72	Kennedy Round (1964–7)	–37
1980–7	Tokyo Round (1973–1979)	–33
1995–9	Uruguay Round (1986–94)	–38

5.2.2.4. *Customs duties remain important trade barriers*

Economists often consider a customs duty, or tariff, below 5 per cent to be a nuisance rather than a barrier to trade. Nevertheless, customs duties remain an important barrier in international trade for several reasons. First, most developing-country Members still maintain high customs duties. See figure 5.3. Many of them have an average duty for industrial products ranging between 25 and 50 per cent *ad valorem*.[27] Second, developed-country Members still have high, to very high, duties on specific groups of 'sensitive' industrial and agricultural products. With respect to industrial products, these so-called 'tariff peaks'[28] are quite common for textiles and clothing, leather and, to a lesser extent, transport equipment.[29] With respect to agricultural products, under the *WTO Agreement on Agriculture* all non-tariff barriers to trade have been eliminated and substituted by customs duties at often very high levels.[30] Third, in very competitive markets and in trade between neighbouring countries, a very low duty may still constitute a barrier.

In addition, customs duties may also impede the economic development of developing-country Members to the extent that duties increase with the level of processing that products have undergone. The duties on processed and semi-processed products are often higher than the duties on non-processed products and raw materials. This phenomenon is referred to as 'tariff escalation'. Tariff escalation discourages manufacturing or processing in developing countries.[31] The customs duties of Canada and Australia increase at each production stage. US customs duties increase significantly only between raw materials and

---

[26] See www.wto.org/english/thewto_e/minist_e/min99_e/english/about_e/22fact_e.htm, visited on 22 November 2007. The tariff reductions concern MFN tariffs of developed countries on industrial products, excluding petroleum.

[27] See WTO Secretariat, *Market Access: Unfinished Business*, Special Studies Series 6 (WTO, 2001), 10. The concept of 'average duty' refers to the 'simple average bound customs duty'.

[28] Tariff peaks are tariffs that exceed a selected reference level. The OECD distinguishes between 'national peaks' and 'international peaks'. 'National peaks' are tariffs which are three times or more the national mean tariff. 'International peaks' are tariffs of 15 per cent or more. See *ibid.*, 12.

[29] See *ibid.*, 12. Note that the European Communities does not have tariff peaks in the textiles and clothing sector.   [30] See below, pp. 450–1.

[31] Note that Article XXXVII of the GATT 1994 calls upon developed-country Members to accord 'high priority to the reduction and elimination of barriers to products currently or potentially of particular export interest to [developing-country Members], including customs duties and other restrictions *which differentiate unreasonably between such products in their primary and in their processed forms*' (emphasis added). See, in this respect, however, also p. 408, footnote 24

Figure 5.3 Simple average MFN applied tariffs for some non-agricultural products (non-Ag) and some agricultural products (Ag)[32]

Import markets	Wood, paper (No-Ag)	Clothing (No-Ag)	Leather and footwear (No-Ag)	Minerals and metals (No-Ag)	Electrical machinery (No-Ag)	Fish and fish products (No-Ag)	Dairy Products (Ag)	Cotton (Ag)	Sugars and confectionary (Ag)	Other agricultural products (Ag)
Developing countries										
Brazil	11.0	20	14.7	9.9	14.1	10.1	18.3	6.9	16.5	7.7
Mexico	12.3	35	18.1	11.4	11.3	16.6	23.5	9.3	70.5	9.8
Hong Kong, China	0.0	0.0	0.0	0.0	0.0	0.0	0.0	0.0	0.0	0.0
India	13.5	22.4	15.4	15.4	12.3	30.0	35.0	17.0	48.4	27.1
South Africa	7.7	37.9	13.7	4.2	5.2	4.2	23.0	5.5	5.4	2.1
Developed countries										
Canada	1.1	17.0	5.6	1.7	2.4	1.0	248.6	0.5	5.7	6.9
United States	0.4	11.5	4.3	1.7	1.7	1.1	25.0	5.2	20.5	1.1
European Union	1.1	11.5	4.2	1.9	2.5	10.3	53.8	0.0	32.9	5.3
Australia	3.4	15.4	5.6	2.7	3.0	0.0	4.3	0.0	1.9	0.2
Japan	0.9	9.2	15.0	1.0	0.2	5.7	178.1	0.0	27.3	6.3

32 Data collected from *World Tariff Profiles 2006* (WTO/ITC, 2007).

semi-processed products. The same holds true for the customs duties of Japan. In general, the customs duties of the European Communities appear to de-escalate, i.e. they are higher on raw materials than on semi-processed or processed products.[33] However, consider that the European Communities imposes:

- zero duties on cocoa beans;
- an *ad valorem* duty of 9.6 per cent on cocoa paste; and
- a mixed duty of 8 per cent and €31.40 per 100 kg net on cocoa powder containing added sugar.[34]

Questions and Assignments 5.2

Is the imposition of customs duties or tariffs on products imported into the territory of a Member prohibited under WTO law? What does Article XXVIII *bis* of the GATT 1994 provide for? Have past efforts to reduce customs duties through negotiations been successful? Are customs duties still a major barrier to trade? What is 'tariff escalation' and why is it a problem?

5.2.2.5. *Basic principles and rules governing tariff negotiations*

As noted above, Article XXVIII *bis* of the GATT 1994 calls for '[tariff] negotiations on a reciprocal and mutually advantageous basis'. As discussed in chapter 4 of this book, Article I:1 of the GATT 1994 requires that '[w]ith respect to customs duties . . . any advantage . . . granted by any [Member] to any product originating in . . . any other country shall be accorded immediately and unconditionally to the like product originating in . . . all other [Members]'. The basic principles and rules governing tariff negotiations are thus:

- the principle of reciprocity and mutual advantage; and
- the most-favoured-nation (MFN) treatment obligation.

The principle of reciprocity and mutual advantage, as applied in tariff negotiations, entails that when a Member requests another Member to reduce its customs duties on certain products, it must be ready to reduce its own customs duties on products which the other Member exports, or wishes to export. For tariff negotiations to succeed, the tariff reductions requested must be considered to be of equivalent value to the tariff reductions offered. There is no agreed method to establish or measure reciprocity. Each Member determines for itself whether the economic value of the tariff reductions received is equal to the value of the tariff reductions granted. Although some Members apply rather sophisticated economic methods to measure reciprocity, in general the methods

---

[33] See WTO Secretariat, *Market Access: Unfinished Business*, Special Studies Series 6 (WTO, 2001), 12 and 13.
[34] See the TARIC database, available at http://ec.europa.eu/taxation_customs/dds/en/tarhome.htm, visited on 1 December 2007.

applied are basic. The final assessment of the 'acceptability' of the outcome of tariff negotiations is primarily political in nature.[35]

The principle of reciprocity does not apply, at least not to its full extent, to tariff negotiations between developed and developing-country Members. Article XXXVI:8 of Part IV ('Trade and Development') of the GATT 1994 provides:

> [Developed-country Members] do not expect reciprocity for commitments made by them in trade negotiations to reduce or remove tariffs and other barriers to the trade of [developing-country Members].

This is further elaborated on in the 1979 Tokyo Round Decision on Differential and More Favourable Treatment, Reciprocity and Fuller Participation of Developing Countries, commonly referred to as the Enabling Clause, which provides, in paragraph 5:

> [Developed-country Members] shall ... not seek, neither shall [developing-country Members] be required to make, concessions that are inconsistent with the latter's development, financial and trade needs.

In tariff negotiations between developed- and developing-country Members, the principle of *relative* reciprocity applies. In tariff negotiations with developed-country Members, developing-country Members are expected to 'reciprocate' only to the extent consistent with their development, financial and trade needs.

With respect to least-developed-country Members, paragraph 6 of the Enabling Clause furthermore instructs developed-country Members to exercise the 'utmost restraint' in seeking any concessions for commitments made by them to reduce or remove tariffs.

Note, however, that paragraph 7 of the Enabling Clause states, in pertinent part:

> [Developing-country Members] expect that their capacity to make contributions or negotiated concessions ... would improve with the progressive development of their economies and improvement in their trade situation and they would accordingly expect to participate more fully in the framework of rights and obligations under the General Agreement.

Because of the principle of relative reciprocity, few developing-country Members agreed to any reductions of their customs duties up to and including the Tokyo Round. Before the Uruguay Round, tariff negotiations were, in practice, primarily conducted between developed-country Members. This changed in the Uruguay Round when almost all developing-country Members agreed to a reduction of their customs duties, albeit that this reduction – in accordance with the principle of relative reciprocity – was smaller than the reduction agreed to by developed-country Members.

The increased willingness of developing-country Members to participate actively in tariff reduction negotiations during the Uruguay Round can be

---

[35] Note that the principle of reciprocity applies not only to tariff negotiations adopting a product-by-product request-and-offer approach but also to tariff negotiations adopting a linear reduction approach, a harmonisation formula approach or a sector approach. See below, pp. 414–17.

attributed to two factors. First, a number of developing-country Members had made significant progress in their economic development. Secondly, a fundamental change had occurred in the trade policy of many developing-country Members. In the 1980s, many developing-country Members moved away from protectionist trade policies to open and liberal trade policies.[36]

As noted above, tariff negotiations are governed not only by the principle of reciprocity (full or relative), but also by the MFN treatment obligation set out in Article I:1 of the GATT 1994. Any tariff reduction a Member would grant to any country as the result of tariff negotiations with that country must be granted to all other Members, immediately and unconditionally. This considerably complicates tariff negotiations. Member A, interested in exporting product *a* to Member B, will request Member B to reduce its customs duties on product *a*. In return for such a reduction, Member A will offer Member B, interested in exporting product *b* to Member A, a reduction of its customs duties on product *b*. As a result of the MFN treatment obligation, the tariff reductions to which Members A and B would agree would also benefit all other Members. However, Members A and B will be hesitant to give other Members the benefit of the tariff reductions 'without getting something in return'. Member A is therefore likely to put a hold on the agreement to reduce the customs duty on product *b* until it has been able 'to get something in return' from, for example, Member C which also exports product *b* to Member A and would thus also benefit from the reduction of the customs duty on product *b*. Likewise, Member B will be hesitant to reduce the customs duty on product *a* as long as Member D, which also has an interest in exporting product *a* to Member B, has not given Member B 'something in return' for this reduction. In tariff negotiations, Members may try to benefit from tariff reductions agreed between other Members without giving anything in return. If their export interests are small, they are likely to succeed and will therefore be 'free-riders'. The free-rider problem can be mitigated by opting for an approach to tariff negotiations other than the product-by-product request-and-offer approach. Other approaches to tariff negotiations include the linear reduction approach, the harmonisation formula approach and the sector approach, all discussed below.[37]

Questions and Assignments 5.3

What are the basic principles and rules governing tariff negotiations? Does the principle of reciprocity also apply to tariff negotiations between developed- and developing-country Members? Why does the MFN treatment obligation complicate tariff negotiations? What does the term 'free-rider' refer to in tariff negotiations?

---

[36] See *Business Guide to the World Trading System*, 2nd edition (International Trade Centre/Commonwealth Secretariat, 1999), 59.

[37] In fact, the increasing complexity of multilateral (as opposed to bilateral) tariff negotiations has led to the abandonment of the product-by-product request-and-offer approach to multilateral tariff negotiations. Note, however, that the principle of reciprocity (full or relative) and the MFN treatment obligation continue to be the underlying principles governing the negotiations. See below, pp. 414–17.

5.2.2.6. *Organisation of tariff negotiations*

Tariff negotiations can be organised in different ways. As Article XXVIII *bis* of the GATT 1994 provides, tariff negotiations may be carried out:

- on a selective product-by-product basis; or
- by the application of such multilateral procedures as may be accepted by the Members concerned.

During the first GATT Rounds (up to and including the 1961–2 Dillon Round), negotiators opted for a *product-by-product request-and-offer approach* to tariff negotiations. Under this approach, each of the participants in the tariff negotiations submits first its request list and then its offer list, identifying respectively the products with regard to which it is seeking and is willing to make tariff reductions. The negotiations take place between the principal suppliers and importers of each product. However, the product-by-product approach has one major disadvantage. For practical reasons, the number of products that can be subject to this kind of tariff negotiation is necessarily limited, and the product coverage of the tariff reductions that can be achieved is thus 'restricted'.

The product-by-product request-and-offer approach to tariff negotiations is still used, in bilateral or plurilateral negotiations outside a Round, both for Article XXVIII re-negotiations and for tariff negotiations in the context of the accession of new Members to the WTO. However, since the 1963–7 Kennedy Round, the product-by-product request-and-offer approach has no longer been used in multilateral tariff negotiations. A *linear reduction approach* to tariff negotiations was adopted for the Kennedy Round tariff negotiations. Under this approach, the negotiations aim at agreeing on a reduction of customs duties across the board, i.e. a reduction of the customs duties on all products, by for example 50 per cent. By agreement, certain products are excluded from the linear reduction, and, with respect to these products, the tariff negotiations are conducted on a product-by-product request-and-offer basis. While successful, the linear reduction approach also presented problems. Members with low customs duties on average argued that it was not reasonable to expect them to cut these duties by the same percentage as Members with high customs duties. It is clear that a 50 per cent reduction of a customs duty of 40 per cent still leaves a 20 per cent customs duty in place, i.e. a significant degree of protection from import competition. However, a 50 per cent reduction of a customs duty of 10 per cent leaves only a 5 per cent customs duty. To mitigate this problem, the negotiators in the Tokyo Round (1973–9) applied a *harmonisation formula approach* to tariff negotiations. A harmonisation formula approach is a non-linear reduction approach which requires larger cuts of higher customs duties than of lower customs duties. The negotiations aim at reaching agreement on the formula *and* on the products excluded from the application of the formula.

In the Uruguay Round tariff negotiations (1986–94), both old and new approaches to tariff negotiations were applied. Under the new *sector elimination approach*, the negotiators aimed at the elimination (or harmonisation) of customs duties in a given sector (such as the pharmaceutical, construction equipment, medical equipment and beer sectors).[38] Other approaches applied in the Uruguay Round tariff negotiations were the harmonisation formula approach, a 50 per cent reduction in tariff peaks and a linear reduction of 33 per cent on residual products.

Between the end of the Uruguay Round and the start of the current Doha Development Round, a group of WTO Members agreed to eliminate all customs duties on information technology products (i.e. computers, telecommunications equipment, semiconductors, etc.). At the Singapore Session of the Ministerial Conference in 1996, twenty-nine Members adopted the *Ministerial Declaration on Trade in Information Technology Products* and thus agreed to the *Agreement on Trade in Information Technology Products* (ITA) attached to the Ministerial Declaration.[39] The ITA provided for participants to eliminate duties completely on information technology products by 1 January 2000. The ITA entered into force in 1997 when forty Members had adopted the agreement, and the agreement covered more than 90 per cent of world trade in information technology products.[40] As a result of the ITA, almost all trade in information technology products is now free from customs duties. Over the last ten years world exports of information technology products have grown at an average rate of 8.5 per cent, and amounted to US$1.450 billion in 2005.[41]

The Doha Ministerial Declaration of November 2001, in which the WTO Members agreed to start the Doha Development Round, provided little guidance with respect to the approach to be taken to tariff negotiations in the Doha Development Round. The Doha Ministerial Declaration states, in relevant part:

> We agree to negotiations which shall aim, *by modalities to be agreed*, to reduce or as appropriate eliminate tariffs, including the reduction or elimination of tariff peaks, high tariffs, and tariff escalation, as well as non-tariff barriers, in particular on products of export interest to developing countries. Product coverage shall be comprehensive and without *a priori* exclusions. The negotiations shall take fully into account the special needs and interests of developing and least-developed country participants, including through less than full reciprocity in reduction commitments.[42]
>
> [Emphasis added]

The approach to be taken to the tariff negotiations in the context of the Doha Development Round – negotiations commonly referred to as negotiations on non-agricultural market access or NAMA negotiations – was further clarified by the General Council in its Decision of 1 August 2004 and by the Ministerial Conference at its session in Hong Kong in December 2005.[43] In its Decision of 1 August 2004, the General Council stated:

---

[38] See A. Hoda, *Tariff Negotiations and Renegotiations under the GATT and the WTO: Procedures and Practice* (WTO/Cambridge University Press, 2001), 37.

[39] Ministerial Conference, *Singapore Ministerial Declaration on Trade in Information Technology Products*, WT/MIN(96)/16, dated 13 December 1996.

[40] To date, seventy countries have joined the ITA and they represent '97 per cent of world trade in IT products'. See WTO: 2007 News Items: *Lamy says ITA success is inspiration to Doha negotiators*, 28 March 2007, available at www.wto.org/english/news_e/news07_e/symp_ita_march07_e.htm, visited on 20 November 2007.   [41] *Ibid.*

[42] Ministerial Conference, *Doha Ministerial Declaration*, WT/MIN(1)/DEC/1, dated 20 November 2001, para. 16.

[43] Ministerial Conference, *Hong Kong Ministerial Declaration*, WT/MIN(05)/DEC, dated 22 December 2005, 4–5.

> We recognize that a formula approach is key to reducing tariffs, and reducing or eliminating tariff peaks, high tariffs, and tariff escalation. We agree that the Negotiating Group should continue its work on a non-linear formula applied on a line-by-line basis which shall take fully into account the special needs and interests of developing and least-developed country participants, including through less than full reciprocity in reduction commitments.
>
> We recognize that a sectoral tariff component, aiming at elimination or harmonization is another key element to achieving the objectives of paragraph 16 of the Doha Ministerial Declaration with regard to the reduction or elimination of tariffs, in particular on products of export interest to developing countries.[44]

In July 2007, Ambassador Don Stephenson, the Chair of the Negotiating Group on Non-Agricultural Market Access (NAMA), proposed the 'NAMA Draft Modalities' with regard to the tariff negotiations on non-agricultural products.[45] The Chair proposed to conduct the tariff reduction negotiations primarily on the basis of a formula, commonly referred to as the *Swiss formula*. According to this formula, which applies on a line-by-line basis, the tariff reductions will be calculated as follows:

$$t_1 = \frac{(a \text{ or } b) \times t_0}{(a \text{ or } b) + t_0}$$

where,

t_1 = final bound rate of duty

t_0 = base rate of duty

a = [8–9] = coefficient for developed Members

b = [19–23] = coefficient for developing Members[46]

Note that the *Swiss formula* provides for different coefficients for developed- and developing-country Members.[47] Least-developed-country Members would not be required to undertake tariff reduction commitments.

The Chair's July 2007 proposals for tariff negotiations on non-agricultural products were not received with much enthusiasm. Many developing-country Members have grave concerns regarding both the *Swiss formula* approach and the sector elimination approach. They consider that the specific interests of developing countries are not sufficiently taken into account. The *Financial Times* reported on the reaction of developing-country Members to the Chair's proposals, as follows:

[44] See General Council, *Doha Work Programme, Framework for Establishing Modalities in Market Access for Non-Agricultural Products*, WT/L/579, dated 2 August 2004, Annex B, paras. 4 and 7. See paras. 5, 6 and 8–13 for further details on the 'initial elements' for future work on the modalities for the Doha Development Round tariff negotiations.

[45] Negotiationg Group on Market Access, *Draft NAMA Modalities*, JOB(07)/126, dated 17 July 2007. This draft was revised by the Chair in February 2008. See Negotiating Group on Market Access, *Draft Modalities for Non-Agricultural Market Access*, TN/MA/W/103, dated 8 February 2008.

[46] Negotiating Group on Market Access, *Draft NAMA Modalities*, JOB(07)/126, dated 17 July 2007, para. 5.

[47] As an exception, the Chair proposed that developing-country Members with a binding coverage of non-agricultural tariff lines of less than 35 per cent would be exempted from making tariff reductions through the formula. Instead, they would be expected to bind 90 per cent of non-agricultural tariff lines at an average level that does not exceed the overall average of bound tariffs for all developing countries after full implementation of current concessions (28.5 per cent). The developing countries concerned are: Cameroon; Congo; Côte d'Ivoire; Cuba; Ghana; Kenya; Macao; China; Mauritius; Nigeria; Sri Lanka; Suriname; and Zimbabwe. See *ibid.*, para. 8.

Serious opposition emerged . . . to new proposals to cut manufacturing tariffs in the trou-
bled Doha round of trade talks, with a group of developing countries saying the draft
agreement was unacceptable.

The group, led by South Africa and including Argentina and Venezuela, wants to continue protecting its industry against imports . . .

Mr Stephenson's [Canadian Ambassador] paper, released this week . . . suggested a
ceiling of 19–23 per cent for developing country industrial tariffs.

The group wanted a ceiling of more than 30 per cent. In a statement to the manufacturing negotiating committee, it said: 'The hallmark of a good text is one that has the potential to build genuine engagement, negotiation and ultimately consensus . . . this text does
not meet this objective.'

The statement also said the draft industrial goods text demanded far bigger cuts than its
farming equivalent, thus undermining the aim of the Doha round to focus on agriculture
as the issue of most concern to developing countries.

. . .

Other developing countries privately accused India and Brazil of failing to take their
views into account.[48]

Developed-country Members are also dissatisfied with the Chair's proposals, as
these proposals are not, in their opinion, sufficiently ambitious in reducing
customs duties.

Questions and Assignments 5.4

Discuss the different approaches to tariff negotiations applied since 1947.
Which approach to tariff negotiations is applied in the Doha
Development Round tariff negotiations?

5.2.3. Tariff concessions and Schedules of Concessions

5.2.3.1. *Tariff concessions or tariff bindings*

The results of tariff negotiations are referred to as 'tariff concessions' or 'tariff
bindings'. A tariff concession, or a tariff binding, is a commitment not to raise the
customs duty on a certain product above an agreed level. As a result of the
Uruguay Round tariff negotiations, all, or almost all, customs duties imposed by
developed-country Members are now 'bound', i.e. are subject to a maximum
level.[49] Most Latin American developing-country Members have bound all customs
duties; however, for Asian and African developing-country Members the situation
is more varied.[50] While Members such as Indonesia and South Africa have bound
more than 95 per cent of their customs duties on non-agricultural products, India

---

[48] See A. Beattie, 'Attack on Doha Talks Plan to Cut Tariffs', *Financial Times*, 25 July 2007.
[49] For the European Communities, 100 per cent of the tariff lines for both agricultural products and
industrial products are bound. For the United States, 100 per cent of the tariff lines for agricultural
products and 99.9 per cent of the tariff lines for industrial products are bound. See WTO Secretariat,
Market Access: Unfinished Business, Special Studies Series 6 (WTO, 2001), 49.
[50] Note that many Latin American Members apply a 'uniform ceiling binding', i.e. they have bound
their customs duties to a single maximum level. For Chile, for example, this uniform maximum level is
25 per cent.

and Thailand have bound about 70 per cent; Hong Kong, China, 37.5 per cent; Bangladesh 15 per cent; Zimbabwe, 9 per cent; and Cameroon, 0.1 per cent.[51] Cameroon has made tariff concessions with regard to only three products.

5.2.3.2. Schedules of Concessions

The tariff concessions or bindings of a Member are set out in that Member's Schedule of Concessions. Each Member of the WTO has a schedule, except when the Member is part of a customs union, in which case the Member has a common schedule with the other members of the customs union.[52] The Schedules resulting from the Uruguay Round negotiations are all annexed to the *Marrakesh Protocol* to the GATT 1994. Pursuant to Article II:7 of the GATT 1994, the Schedules of Members are an integral part of the GATT 1994. The Schedules of Concessions can be consulted on the WTO website.[53] See, for example, China's Schedule of Concessions in figure 5.4.

Each Schedule of Concessions contains four parts. The most important part, Part I, sets out the MFN concessions with respect to agricultural products (tariffs (Section 1A) and tariff quotas (Section 1B)) and with respect to non-agricultural products (tariffs only (Section 2)). Furthermore, a Schedule sets out preferential concessions (Part II), concessions on non-tariff measures (Part III) and specific commitments on domestic support and export subsidies on agricultural products (Part IV).

It is not possible for Members to agree in their Schedules to treatment which is inconsistent with the basic GATT obligations. In *EC – Bananas III*, the Appellate Body addressed the question of whether the allocation of tariff quotas agreed to and inscribed in the EC's Schedule was inconsistent with Article XIII of the GATT 1994. The Appellate Body referred first to the Report of the Panel in *US – Sugar*, which stated, *inter alia*:

> Article II permits contracting parties to incorporate into their Schedules acts yielding rights under the General Agreement but not acts diminishing obligations under that Agreement.[54]

Subsequently, the Appellate Body ruled in *EC – Bananas III*:

> This principle is equally valid for the market access concessions and commitments for agricultural products contained in the Schedules annexed to the GATT 1994. The ordinary meaning of the term 'concessions' suggests that a Member may yield rights and grant benefits, but it cannot diminish its obligations.[55]

All Schedules are structured according to the Harmonised Commodity Description and Coding System ('Harmonised System' or 'HS'), discussed below,

---

[51] See WTO Secretariat, *Market Access: Unfinished Business*, Special Studies Series 6 (WTO, 2001), 7 and 8. Note that these percentages are not weighted according to trade volume or value. Note, with regard to Hong Kong, China, that, while a high percentage of customs duties is unbound, the applied duties are zero.

[52] E.g. the twenty-seven Member States of the European Union do not have their 'own' individual schedule. Their common schedule is the Schedule of the European Communities.

[53] See www.wto.org/english/tratop_e/schedules_e/goods_schedules_table_e.htm, visited on 15 November 2007.   [54] GATT Panel Report, *US – Sugar*, para. 5.2.

[55] Appellate Body Report, *EC – Bananas III*, para. 154. The Appellate Body confirmed this ruling in Appellate Body Report, *EC – Poultry*, para. 98.

Figure 5.4: Excerpt from Chapter 18 of the Schedule of Concessions of China (cocoa and cocoa preparations)[56]

HS	Description	Bound rate at date of accession	Final bound rate	Implementation	Present concession established	INR	Concession first incorporated in a GATT Schedule	Earlier INRs	ODCs
1801	Cocoa beans, whole or broken, raw or roasted:								
18010000	Cocoa beans, whole or broken, raw or roasted	9.2	8	2004		BO,CO,DO,EC,HN,MY, NI,PA,US			0
1802	Cocoa shells, husks, skins and other cocoa waste:								
18020000	Cocoa shells, husks, skins and other cocoa waste	10				US			0
1803	Cocoa paste, whether or not defatted:								
18031000	- Not defatted	10				US			0
18032000	- Wholly or partly defatted	10				SG,US			0
1804	Cocoa butter, fat and oil:								
18040000	Cocoa butter, fat and oil	29.8	22	2004		MY,US			0
1805	Cocoa powder, not containing added sugar or other sweetening matter:								
18050000	Cocoa powder, not containing added sugar or other sweetening matter	18	15	2004		MY,US			0
1806	Chocolate and other food preparations containing cocoa:								
18061000	- Cocoa powder, containing added sugar or other sweetening matter	10				CO,MY,US			0
18062000	- Other preparations in blocks, slabs or bars weighing more than 2kg or in liquid, paste, powder, granular or other bulk form in containers or immediate packings, of a content exceeding 2 kg	11.2	10	2004		AU,CH,US			0
	- Other, in blocks, slabs or bars:								
18063100	— Filled	10.4	8	2004		AU,CH,EC,LV,US			0
18063200	— Not filled	11.2	10	2004		CH,LV,US			0
18069000	- Other	10.4	8	2004		AU,CH,EC,JP,LV,SG,US			0

56 Schedule CLII, People's Republic of China, WT/ACC/CHN/49/Add.1, WT/MIN(01)/3/Add.1, available at www.mofcom.gov.cn/table/wto/02B.doc, visited on 15 November 2007.

and contain the following information for each product subject to tariff concessions:

- HS tariff item number;
- description of the product;
- rate of duty;
- present concession established;
- initial negotiating rights (INR);[57]
- other duties and charges;[58] and
- for agricultural products only, special safeguards.[59]

Note that the Schedules of the major trading entities such as the European Communities and the United States, which have made tariff concessions on virtually all products, are lengthy and detailed. The file containing the Schedule of the European Communities on the WTO's website is 759KB in size. By contrast, the Schedules of many developing-country Members are short. The files containing the Schedules of Botswana and the Dominican Republic are only 12 and 13KB respectively.[60]

5.2.3.3. *Interpretation of tariff schedules and concessions*

Since the tariff schedules are an integral part of the GATT 1994, they constitute a 'covered agreement' under the DSU. Article 3.2 of the DSU applies to the interpretation of tariff schedules and the concessions set out therein. As discussed in chapter 3 of this book, Article 3.2 of the DSU provides that the provisions of the covered agreements are to be clarified in accordance with customary rules of interpretation of public international law.[61] Accordingly, the tariff schedules and tariff concessions must be interpreted in accordance with the customary rules of interpretation of public international law as codified in Articles 31 and 32 of the *Vienna Convention on the Law of Treaties*. In *EC – Computer Equipment*, at issue was a dispute between the United States and the European Communities on whether the EC's tariff concessions regarding automatic data-processing equipment applied to local area network (LAN) computer equipment.[62] The Panel based its interpretation of the EC's tariff concessions on the 'legitimate expectations' of the exporting Member, *in casu*, the United States. On appeal, the Appellate Body rejected this approach to the interpretation of tariff concessions, ruling as follows:

> The purpose of treaty interpretation under Article 31 of the *Vienna Convention* is to ascertain the *common* intentions of the parties. These *common* intentions cannot be ascertained

---

[57] See below, pp. 426–8.   [58] See below, pp. 438–43.   [59] See below, pp. 670–1.
[60] See www.wto.org/english/tratop_e/schedules_e/goods_schedules_e.htm, visited on 18 September 2007.
[61] See above, pp. 201–6.
[62] In the context of the Uruguay Round tariff negotiations, the European Communities agreed to a tariff binding for automatic data processing equipment of 4.9 per cent (to be reduced to 2.5 per cent for some products or duty-free for others). According to the United States, during and shortly after the Uruguay Round, the European Communities classified LAN computer equipment as automatic data processing equipment. Later, however, it started classifying LAN computer equipment as telecommunications equipment, a product category subject to generally higher duties, in the range of 4.6 to 7.5 per cent (to be reduced to 3 to 3.6 per cent).

> on the basis of the subjective and unilaterally determined 'expectations' of *one* of the parties to a treaty. Tariff concessions provided for in a Member's Schedule – the interpretation of which is at issue here – are reciprocal and result from a mutually advantageous negotiation between importing and exporting Members. A Schedule is made an integral part of the GATT 1994 by Article II:7 of the GATT 1994. Therefore, the concessions provided for in that Schedule are part of the terms of the treaty. As such, the only rules which may be applied in interpreting the meaning of a concession are the general rules of treaty interpretation set out in the *Vienna Convention*.[63]

The Appellate Body furthermore noted with respect to the lack of clarity of tariff concessions and tariff schedules:

> Tariff negotiations are a process of reciprocal demands and concessions, of 'give and take'. It is only normal that importing Members define their offers (and their ensuing obligations) in terms which suit their needs. On the other hand, exporting Members have to ensure that their corresponding rights are described in such a manner in the Schedules of importing Members that their export interests, as agreed in the negotiations, are guaranteed . . . [T]he fact that Members' Schedules are an integral part of the GATT 1994 indicates that, while each Schedule represents the tariff commitments made by *one* Member, they represent a common agreement among *all* Members.
>
> For the reasons stated above, we conclude that the Panel erred in finding that 'the United States was not required to clarify the scope of the European Communities' tariff concessions on LAN equipment'. We consider that any clarification of the scope of tariff concessions that may be required during the negotiations is a task for *all* interested parties.[64]

Note that, at the very end of the Uruguay Round, a special arrangement was made to allow the negotiators to check and control, through consultations with their negotiating partners, the scope of tariff concessions agreed to. This 'process of verification' took place from 15 February to 25 March 1994.[65]

As discussed above, all schedules are structured according to the Harmonised System. The Uruguay Round tariff negotiations were held on the basis of the Harmonised System's nomenclature; requests for, and offers of, concessions were normally made in terms of this nomenclature. For that reason, the Appellate Body expressed surprise in *EC – Computer Equipment* that neither the European Communities nor the United States argued before the Panel that the Harmonised System and its Explanatory Notes were relevant in the interpretation of Schedule LXXX of the European Communities. The Appellate Body ruled:

> We believe . . . that a proper interpretation of Schedule LXXX should have included an examination of the *Harmonized System* and its *Explanatory Notes*.[66]

According to the Appellate Body, decisions of the World Customs Organization regarding the Harmonised System may also be relevant to the interpretation of tariff concessions and should therefore be examined.[67]

Finally, note that the consistent classification practice at the time of the tariff negotiations is also relevant to the interpretation of tariff concessions.[68] As the

---

[63] Appellate Body Report, *EC – Computer Equipment*, para. 84. [64] *Ibid.*, paras. 109 and 110.
[65] See MTN.TNC/W/131, dated 21 January 1994.
[66] Appellate Body Report, *EC – Computer Equipment*, para. 89. [67] See *ibid.*, para. 90.
[68] On tariff classification, see below, pp. 428–31.

Appellate Body noted in *EC – Computer Equipment*, the classification practice during the Uruguay Round is part of 'the circumstances of [the] conclusion' of the *WTO Agreement*. Therefore, this practice may be used as a supplementary means of interpretation within the meaning of Article 32 of the *Vienna Convention*.[69]

Questions and Assignments 5.5

What are tariff concessions or tariff bindings? Where can you find the tariff concessions or tariff bindings agreed to by a Member? Do Argentina, Mali, Thailand and the Netherlands each have a tariff schedule? Find out what, if any, is the tariff binding of your country on cocoa powder and on road tractors. How are tariff schedules and tariff concessions to be interpreted? Whose obligation is it to ensure that the scope of tariff concessions is unambiguous?

5.2.4. Protection of tariff concessions

As noted above, under WTO law customs duties are not prohibited. This does not mean, however, that there are no rules on customs duties. WTO rules on customs duties relate primarily to the protection of tariff concessions or bindings agreed to in the context of tariff negotiations. The basic rules are set out in Article II:1 of the GATT 1994.

5.2.4.1. Articles II:1(a) and II:1(b), first sentence, of the GATT 1994

Article II:1 of the GATT 1994 states:

> a. Each [Member] shall accord to the commerce of the other [Members] treatment no less favourable than that provided for in the appropriate Part of the appropriate Schedule annexed to this Agreement.
> b. The products described in Part I of the Schedule relating to any [Member], which are the products of territories of other [Members], shall, on their importation into the territory to which the Schedule relates, and subject to the terms, conditions or qualifications set forth in that Schedule, be exempt from ordinary customs duties in excess of those set forth and provided therein . . .

Article II:1(a) provides that Members shall accord to products imported from other Members *treatment no less favourable* than that provided for in their Schedule. Article II:1(b), first sentence, provides that products described in Part I of the Schedule of any Member shall, on importation, be *exempt from ordinary customs duties in excess of* those set out in the Schedule. This means that products may not be subjected to customs duties above the tariff concessions or bindings. With respect to the relationship between Article II:1(a) and Article II:1(b), first sentence, the Appellate Body noted in *Argentina – Textiles and Apparel*:

---

[69] See above, pp. 201–6. See also Appellate Body Report, *EC – Computer Equipment*, paras. 92 and 95. Note that, while the prior classification practice of only *one* of the parties may be relevant, it is clearly of more limited value than the practice of all parties. See *ibid.*, para. 93.

> Paragraph (a) of Article II:1 contains a general prohibition against according treatment less favourable to imports than that provided for in a Member's Schedule. Paragraph (b) prohibits a specific kind of practice that will always be inconsistent with paragraph (a): that is, the application of ordinary customs duties in excess of those provided for in the Schedule.[70]

The requirement of Article II:1(b), first sentence, that a Member may not impose customs duties *in excess of* the duties set out in its Schedule was at issue in *Argentina – Textiles and Apparel*. In its Schedule, Argentina has bound its customs duties on textiles and apparel to 35 per cent *ad valorem*. In practice, however, these products were subject to the higher of *either* a 35 per cent *ad valorem* duty *or* a minimum specific import duty (the so-called 'DIEM'). The Panel found the DIEM to be inconsistent with Argentina's obligations under Article II:1(b) of the GATT 1994 for two reasons:

- first, because Argentina applied a different *type* of import duty (a specific duty) than that set out in its Schedule (an *ad valorem* duty); and
- secondly, because the DIEM would, in certain cases, be in excess of the binding of 35 per cent *ad valorem*.

On appeal, the Appellate Body agreed with the Panel that the DIEM was inconsistent with Argentina's obligations under Article II:1(b), but it considerably modified the Panel's reasoning. The Appellate Body first noted:

> The principal obligation in the first sentence of Article II:1(b) . . . requires a Member to refrain from imposing ordinary customs duties *in excess of* those provided for in that Member's Schedule. However, the text of Article II:1(b), first sentence, does not address whether applying a *type* of duty different from the *type* provided for in a Member's Schedule is inconsistent, in itself, with that provision.[71]

According to the Appellate Body, the application of a type of duty different from the type provided for in a Member's Schedule is only inconsistent with Article II:1(b) *to the extent that* it results in customs duties being imposed in excess of those set forth in that Member's Schedule.[72] In *Argentina – Textiles and Apparel*, the Appellate Body concluded:

> In this case, we find that Argentina has acted inconsistently with its obligations under Article II:1(b), first sentence, of the GATT 1994, because the DIEM regime, by its structure and design, results, with respect to a certain range of import prices in any relevant tariff category to which it applies, in the levying of customs duties in excess of the bound rate of 35 per cent *ad valorem* in Argentina's Schedule.[73]

As Article II:1(b), first sentence, explicitly states, the obligation to exempt products from customs duties in excess of those set forth in the Schedule is 'subject to the terms, conditions or qualifications set forth in that Schedule'. In *Canada – Dairy*, the Appellate Body ruled in this respect:

> In our view, the ordinary meaning of the phrase 'subject to' is that such concessions are without prejudice to and are *subordinated to*, and are, therefore, *qualified by*, any 'terms,

---

[70] Appellate Body Report, *Argentina – Textiles and Apparel*, para. 45.   [71] *Ibid.*, para. 46.
[72] See *ibid.*, para. 55.   [73] *Ibid.*

> conditions or qualifications' inscribed in a Member's Schedule . . . A strong presumption arises that the language which is inscribed in a Member's Schedule under the heading, 'Other Terms and Conditions', has some *qualifying* or *limiting* effect on the substantive content or scope of the concession or commitment.[74]

Some of the disputes under Article II:1(a) and (b), first sentence, of the GATT 1994 do not directly stem from duties or charges imposed in excess of those contained in the Schedules of Concessions. In *EC – Chicken Cuts*, the European Communities did not deviate from the customs duties as contained in its Schedule of Concessions. It did, however, reclassify a certain type of chicken meat, namely frozen boneless chicken cuts impregnated with salt, under a different tariff heading (heading 02.07 'Meat and edible offal, of the poultry of heading No. 0105, fresh, chilled or frozen').[75] Under that particular tariff heading, the customs duty imposed was higher than under the heading that applied according to the complainants in the case (heading 02.10 'Meat and edible meat offal, salted, in brine, dried, smoked; edible flours and meals of meat or meat offal'). As in *EC – Computer Equipment*, discussed above, the outcome of the *EC – Chicken Cuts* dispute depended on the interpretation of the tariff headings, and, in this case more specifically, on the interpretation of the term 'salted'. According to the European Communities, the key element under heading 02.10 was preservation and therefore the term 'salted' implied that the meat should be impregnated with salt sufficient to ensure long-term preservation. The complainants, Thailand and Brazil, contended that 'salted' did not imply long-term preservation and that the chicken cuts thus fell within heading 02.10. The Panel and Appellate Body followed the customary rules of treaty interpretation as codified in Articles 31 and 32 of the *Vienna Convention on the Law of Treaties*.[76] Both the Panel and the Appellate Body came to the conclusion that 'salted' did not imply long-term preservation in any way and that therefore the chicken cuts did fall under the more favourable tariff heading 02.10. The European Communities had acted inconsistently with Article II:1(a) and (b) by wrongly classifying the chicken cuts, which resulted in treatment less favourable than that provided for in its Schedule.[77]

---

[74] Appellate Body Report, *Canada – Dairy*, para. 134. At issue in *Canada – Dairy* was a tariff quota (see below, p. 446) for fluid milk of 64,500 tonnes included in Canada's Schedule. In the column 'Other Terms and Conditions' of Canada's Schedule, it states that 'this quantity [64,500 tonnes] represents the estimated annual cross-border purchases imported by Canadian consumers'. In practice, Canada restricted imports under the 64,500 tonnes tariff quota to dairy products for the personal use of the importer and his household not exceeding C\$20 in value for each importation. The United States contested that the restriction of access to imports for personal use not exceeding C\$20 in value constituted a violation of Article II:1(b) of the GATT 1994. The Panel agreed with the United States. The Panel found that the 'condition' in Canada's Schedule is *descriptive* and does not establish restrictions on access to the tariff quota for fluid milk. The Appellate Body disagreed with the Panel that the 'condition' was merely descriptive, and concluded that the limitation of cross-border purchases to 'Canadian consumers' referred to in Canada's Schedule justifies Canada's effective limitation of access to the tariff quota to imports for 'personal use'.   [75] See Panel Report, *EC – Chicken Cuts*, paras. 7.46–7.47.

[76] Note, however, that the Appellate Body reversed the Panel's conclusion that: 'the European Communities' practice of classifying, between 1996 and 2002, the products at issue under heading 02.10 of the EC Schedule "amounts to subsequent practice" within the meaning of Article 31(3)(b) of the *Vienna Convention*', Appellate Body Report, *EC – Chicken Cuts*, para. 276.

[77] See *ibid.*, paras. 346, 347(b)(i),(ii),(iii) and 347 (c)(i),(ii),(iii).

5.2.4.2. *Tariff concessions and customs duties actually applied*

Finally, a note on the difference between tariff concessions or bindings and the customs duties actually applied. As the Appellate Body noted in *Argentina – Textiles and Apparel*:

> A tariff binding in a Member's Schedule provides an upper limit on the amount of duty that may be imposed, and a Member is permitted to impose a duty that is less than that provided for in its Schedule.[78]

For many Members, tariff bindings for industrial products are considerably higher than the customs duties actually applied to these products. This means that the customs duties applied are significantly lower than the maximum levels agreed upon. For example, the simple average bound tariff of Costa Rica is about 42.8 per cent, while its average applied tariff is 5.9 per cent.[79] Likewise, the simple average bound tariff of Turkey is around 28.4 per cent, while its average applied tariff is 9.6 per cent.[80] The simple average bound tariff of India is 49.2 per cent. The applied rates of India, however, are on average 19.2 per cent.[81] To the extent that this reflects a unilateral lowering of tariff barriers and thus allows for more trade, the difference between bound tariffs and the lower applied tariffs is to be welcomed. However, this difference also gives the importing Members concerned ample opportunity to increase the applied tariffs, namely, up to the level of the tariff binding. The tariff bindings thus do not give exporting Members and traders much security and predictability with respect to the level of the customs duties that will actually be applied on the imported products. *The Economist* reported on this issue in June 2007 as follows:

> In WTO negotiations, countries haggle not over tariffs, but over tariff ceilings. In many cases, however, these mutually agreed ceilings give countries much more latitude than they choose to use. Brazil, for example, has pledged not to raise its duties on industrial goods above about 30% on average. But the duties it actually imposes average less than 13%.
>
> The gap between these two numbers is known as 'water' in WTO-speak. After the liberalising wave of the past two decades, in which countries decided to open their economies without waiting for others to do likewise, there are now big gaps between actual tariffs and allowable ones. Exporters fear the Doha round will amount to little more than a mangle, squeezing water out of the trading system.
>
> For example, Brazil, Argentina and others have offered to lower their ceilings by over 40%. But this proposal would trim the tariffs Brazil and Argentina actually impose by less than a percentage point, the WTO has calculated. Even the more ambitious efforts urged by America and the EU would shave only about three percentage points off the South Americans' average.
>
> Why all the fuss then? Behind these averages lies a lot of variation. A handful of industries cowers behind barriers that brush close to the WTO ceilings. For example, South Africa's garment-makers enjoy a tariff of about 40%; its carmakers one of 30%.[82]

---

[78] Appellate Body Report, *Argentina – Textiles and Apparel*, para. 46.
[79] See *World Tariff Profiles 2006* (WTO/ITC, 2007), 64, available at www.wto.org/english/tratop_e/tariffs_e/tariff_profiles_2006_e/tariff_profiles_2006_e.pdf, visited on 5 November 2007.   [80] See *ibid.*, 106.   [81] See *ibid.*, 92.
[82] 'Global Trade Talks Suffer a Familiar Outcome, but for an Unfamiliar Reason', *The Economist*, 28 June 2007.

Questions and Assignments 5.6

Which provisions of the GATT 1994 prohibit the imposition of customs duties higher than the tariff concession? What is the relationship between Article II:1(a) and Article II:1(b), first sentence? Is the application of a type of duty different from the type provided for in a Member's Schedule inconsistent with Article II:1(b), first sentence? Can tariff concessions be subject to terms and conditions? If so, give a concrete example of such a term or condition. Can a Member impose customs duties lower than the tariff concession? Is this a problem?

5.2.5. Modification or withdrawal of tariff concessions

As discussed above, Members may not apply customs duties above the tariff concessions or bindings agreed to in tariff negotiations. However, the GATT 1994 provides a procedure for the modification or withdrawal of the agreed tariff concessions. Article XXVIII:1 of the GATT 1994 states, in pertinent part:

> a [Member] . . . may, by negotiation and agreement . . . modify or withdraw a concession included in the appropriate schedule annexed to this Agreement.

The negotiations on the modification or withdrawal of tariff concessions are to be conducted with:

- the Members that hold so-called 'Initial Negotiating Rights' (INRs); and
- any other Member that has a 'principal supplying interest'.

The Members holding INRs are those Members with which the concession was bilaterally negotiated, initially. As mentioned above, INRs are commonly specified in the Schedule of the Member granting the concession but can also be determined on the basis of the negotiation records. Due to the approach to tariff negotiations adopted during the Uruguay Round,[83] most tariff concessions did not result from bilateral negotiations and thus INRs are virtually nonexistent in respect of concessions agreed during the Uruguay Round.[84] It was therefore agreed in the Uruguay Round *Understanding on Article XXVIII* that:

> Any Member having a principal supplying interest . . . in a concession which is modified or withdrawn shall be accorded an initial negotiating right.[85]

A Member has a 'principal supplying interest' if, as provided in Note *Ad* Article XXVIII, paragraph 1.4:

> that [Member] has had, over a reasonable period of time prior to the negotiations, a larger share in the market of the applicant [Member] than a Member with which the concession was initially negotiated or would . . . have had such a share in the absence of discriminatory quantitative restrictions maintained by the applicant [Member].

---

[83] See above, pp. 414–15.
[84] See A. Hoda, *Tariff Negotiations and Renegotiations under the GATT and the WTO: Procedures and Practice* (WTO/Cambridge University Press, 2001), 136.
[85] *Understanding on the Implementation of Article XXVIII of the GATT 1994*, para. 7.

Furthermore, the Note *Ad* Article XXVIII, paragraph 1.5, states:

> the [Ministerial Conference] may exceptionally determine that a [Member] has a princi-
> pal supplying interest if the concession in question affects trade which constitutes a major
> part of the total exports of such [Member].

Finally, the *Understanding on Article XXVIII*, paragraph 1, provides with respect to the concept of 6 'principal supplying interest':

> the Member which has the highest ratio of exports affected by the concession (i.e. exports
> of the product to the market of the Member modifying or withdrawing the concession) to
> its total exports shall be deemed to have a principal supplying interest if it does not
> already have an initial negotiating right or a principal supplying interest as provided for in
> paragraph 1 of Article XXVIII.

Pursuant to Article XXVIII, the *negotiations* on the modification or withdrawal of a tariff concession are to be conducted only with the Members holding INRs or those having a principal supplying interest. However, the Member wishing to modify or withdraw a tariff concession must *consult* any other Member that has a substantial interest in such concession.[86] The Note *Ad* Article XXVIII, paragraph 1.7, states:

> The expression 'substantial interest' is not capable of a precise definition and accordingly
> may present difficulties . . . It is, however, intended to be construed to cover only those
> [Members] which have, or in the absence of discriminatory quantitative restrictions
> affecting their exports could reasonably be expected to have, a significant share in the
> market of the [Member] seeking to modify or withdraw the concession.

A 'significant share', required to claim a 'substantial interest', has generally been considered to be 10 per cent of the market of the Member seeking to modify or withdraw a tariff concession.

With respect to the objective of the negotiations and agreement on the modification or withdrawal of tariff concessions, Article XXVIII:2 provides:

> In such negotiations and agreement . . . the [Members] concerned shall endeavour to
> maintain a general level of reciprocal and mutually advantageous concessions not less
> favourable to trade than that provided for in this Agreement prior to such negotiations.

When a tariff concession is modified or withdrawn, compensation in the form of new concessions needs to be granted to maintain a general level of concessions not less favourable to trade.[87]

It follows from the above that the modification or withdrawal of a tariff binding is based on the principle of renegotiation and compensation. However, if the negotiations fail to lead to an agreement, Article XXVIII:3(a) provides, in relevant part, that:

> the [Member] which proposes to modify or withdraw the concession shall, nevertheless,
> be free to do so.

---

[86] See Article XXVIII:1 of the GATT 1994. The Ministerial Conference determines which Members have a
'substantial interest': see *ibid*.

[87] See Award of the Arbitrator, *EC–ACP Partnership Agreement – Recourse to Arbitration Pursuant to the Decision of
14 November 2001*. See above, p. 177.

In that case, any Member holding an INR, any Member having a principal supplying interest *and* any Member having a substantial interest shall be free to
withdraw substantially equivalent concessions.[88]

Questions and Assignments 5.7

Can tariff concessions or bindings, set forth in a Member's Schedule, be
modified or withdrawn? Which Members hold INRs? Which Members
have a 'principal supplying interest' and which Members have a
'substantial interest' in the concession to be modified or withdrawn? Why
is this important? Can a tariff concession or binding be modified or
withdrawn without agreement on compensation?

5.2.6. Imposition of customs duties

In addition to rules for the protection of tariff concessions, WTO law also provides for rules on the manner in which customs duties must be imposed. The
imposition of customs duties may require three determinations to be made:

- the determination of the proper classification of the imported good;
- the determination of the customs value of the imported good; and
- the determination of the origin of the imported good.

The need for these determinations follows from the fact that customs duties
differ from good to good; are usually *ad valorem* duties and thus calculated on
the basis of the value of the products concerned; and may differ depending on
the exporting country.

5.2.6.1. *Customs classification*

As illustrated above, when discussing *EC – Computer Equipment* and *EC – Chicken
Cuts*, the imposition of customs duties requires the determination of the proper
customs classification of the imported good.[89] WTO law does not *specifically*
address the issue of customs classification. In *Spain – Unroasted Coffee*, the Panel
ruled:

> that there was no obligation under the GATT to follow any particular system for classify-
> ing goods, and that a contracting party had the right to introduce in its customs tariff new
> positions or sub-positions as appropriate.[90]

However, in classifying products for customs purposes, Members have of course
to consider their general obligations under the WTO agreements, such as the
MFN treatment obligation. As discussed in chapter 4 of this book, the Panel in
Spain – Unroasted Coffee ruled that:

---

[88] See Article XXVIII:3 of the GATT 1994.   [89] See above, p. 424.
[90] GATT Panel Report, *Spain – Unroasted Coffee*, para. 4.4.

whatever the classification adopted, Article I:1 required that the same tariff treatment be applied to 'like products'.[91]

Specific rules on classification can be found in the *International Convention on the Harmonised Commodity Description and Coding System*, which entered into force on 1 January 1988 and to which most WTO Members are a party.[92] The Harmonised Commodity Description and Coding System, commonly referred to as the 'Harmonised System' or 'HS', is an *international commodity classification system*, developed under the auspices of the Brussels-based Customs Cooperation Council (CCC), known today as the World Customs Organization (WCO).[93]

The Harmonised System consists of 21 sections covering 99 chapters, 1,241 headings and over 5,000 commodity groups. The sections and chapters are:

- Section I (Chapters 1–5, live animals and animal products);
- Section II (Chapters 6–14, vegetable products);
- Section III (Chapter 15, animal or vegetable fats and oils);
- Section IV (Chapters 16–24, prepared foodstuffs, beverages and spirits, tobacco);
- Section V (Chapters 25–7, mineral products);
- Section VI (Chapters 28–38, chemical products);
- Section VII (Chapters 39–40, plastics and rubber);
- Section VIII (Chapters 41–3, leather and travel goods);
- Section IX (Chapters 44–6, wood, charcoal, cork);
- Section X (Chapters 47–9, wood pulp, paper and paperboard articles);
- Section XI (Chapters 50–63, textiles and textile products);
- Section XII (Chapters 64–7, footwear, umbrellas, artificial flowers);
- Section XIII (Chapters 68–70, stone, cement, ceramic, glass);
- Section XIV (Chapter 71, pearls, precious metals);
- Section XV (Chapters 72–83, base metals);
- Section XVI (Chapters 84–5, electrical machinery);
- Section XVII (Chapters 86–9, vehicles, aircraft, vessels);
- Section XVIII (Chapters 90–2, optical instruments, clocks and watches, musical instruments);
- Section XIX (Chapter 93, arms and ammunition);
- Section XX (Chapters 94–6, furniture, toys, miscellaneous manufactured articles); and
- Section XXI (Chapter 97, works of art, antiques).[94]

In the Harmonised System, each commodity group has a six-digit HS code. For example, the HS Code for 'Electric trains, including tracks, signals and other

---

[91] *Ibid.* See also above, pp. 329–31; and GATT Panel Report, *Canada/Japan – Tariff on Imports of Spruce, Pine, Fir (SPF) Dimension Lumber*, para. 5.9.

[92] *International Convention on the Harmonised Commodity Description and Coding System*, Brussels, 14 June 1983, as amended by the Protocol of Amendment of 24 June 1986, available at www.wcoomd.org/home_wco_topics_hsoverviewboxes_hsconvention.htm, visited on 1 December 2007.

[93] The Harmonised System was developed not only for customs classification purposes, but also for the collection of trade statistics and for use in the context of various types of transactions in international trade (such as insurance and transport).

[94] Chapters 98 and 99 are reserved for special use by contracting parties.

accessories therefore; reduced-size (scale) model assembly kits' is 95030030. Of this code, the first two digits refer to the Chapter, in this case Chapter 95 ('Toys, games and sport requisites; parts and accessories thereof'), while the first four digits refer to the heading, in this case Heading 95.03 ('Tricycles, scooters, pedal cars and similar wheeled toys; dolls' carriages; dolls; other toys; reduced-size (scale) models and similar recreational models working or not; puzzles of all kinds'.)

To keep the Harmonised System up to date, to include new products (resulting from new technologies) and to take account of new developments in international trade, the Harmonised System is revised every four to six years.[95]

To allow for a systematic and uniform classification of goods, the Harmonised System not only provides for a structured list of commodity descriptions but also includes:

- General Rules for the Interpretation of the Harmonised System; and
- Explanatory Notes.

The General Rules for the Interpretation of the Harmonised System provide that the classification of goods shall be governed, *inter alia*, by the following principles:

- Incomplete or unfinished goods are classified as finished goods (in the event that they do not have their own line) when the goods already have the essential character of the complete or finished goods.[96]
- When goods are, *prima facie*, classifiable under two or more headings, classification shall be effected as follows:

    a. the heading which provides the most specific description shall be preferred to headings providing a more general description;[97]
    b. when goods cannot be classified as provided under (a), mixtures, composite goods consisting of different materials or made up of different components, and goods put up in sets for retail sale, shall be classified as if they consisted of the material or component which gives them their essential character;[98]
    c. when goods cannot be classified as provided under (a) or (b), they shall be classified under the heading which occurs last in numerical order among those which equally merit consideration.[99]

- Goods which cannot be classified in accordance with the above rules shall be classified under the heading appropriate to the goods to which they are most akin, i.e. with which they bear most likeness.[100]

The Explanatory Notes give the official interpretation of the Harmonised System as agreed by the WCO.[101]

---

[95] See Article 16 of the *International Convention on the Harmonised System.* To date, there have been revisions in 1992, 1996, 2002 and 2007.
[96] See General Rules for the Interpretation of the Harmonised System, para. 2(a).
[97] *Ibid.*, para. 3(a).   [98] *Ibid.*, para. 3(b).   [99] *Ibid.*, para. 3(c).   [100] *Ibid.*, para. 4.
[101] They are published in four volumes in English and French but are also available on CD-ROM, as part of a database giving the HS classification of more than 200,000 goods.

WTO Members are not obliged under the GATT 1994, or under any other WTO agreement, to adopt the Harmonised System. However, as already noted, most WTO Members are a party to the *International Convention on the Harmonised System*. Article 3.1(a) of this Convention provides, in relevant part, that a party to the Convention:

> undertakes that, in respect of its customs tariff and statistical nomenclatures:
>
> i.   it shall use all the headings and subheadings of the Harmonized System without addition or modification, together with their related numerical codes;
> ii. it shall apply the General Rules for the Interpretation of the Harmonized System and all the Section, Chapter and Subheading Notes, and shall not modify the scope of the Sections, Chapters, headings or subheadings of the Harmonized System; and
> iii. it shall follow the numerical sequence of the Harmonized System.

Consequently, most WTO Members use the Harmonised System, its General Rules for the Interpretation of the Harmonised System and its Explanatory Notes in their national tariffs and for the customs classification of goods.

Although the Harmonised System is not part of WTO law, it can be relevant to the interpretation and application of WTO obligations. As discussed above, in *EC – Computer Equipment*, the Appellate Body expressed surprise that:

> Neither the European Communities nor the United States argued before the Panel that the *Harmonized System* and its *Explanatory Notes* were relevant in the interpretation of the terms of Schedule LXXX. We believe, however, that a proper interpretation of Schedule LXXX should have included an examination of the *Harmonized System* and its *Explanatory Notes*.[102]

Disputes between the importer and the relevant customs authorities on proper classification are resolved by national courts or tribunals.[103] Parties to the *International Convention on the Harmonised System* may bring a dispute to the WCO for settlement.

Questions and Assignments 5.8

Are there any WTO rules on tariff classification? What is the Harmonised System? Discuss the key principles that govern the classification of goods set forth in the General Rules for the Interpretation of the Harmonised System. Are these rules of any relevance in disputes on WTO rights and obligations?

5.2.6.2. *Valuation for customs purposes*

As previously explained, most customs duties are *ad valorem*. The customs administrations must therefore determine the value of the imported goods in order to be able to calculate the customs duty due.

---

[102] Appellate Body Report, *EC – Computer Equipment*, para. 89. See above, pp. 420–2.
[103] Article X of the GATT 1994 concerns the access to national courts and tribunals. See below, p. 470.

Unlike for customs classification, the WTO agreements provide for rules on customs valuation. These rules are set out in:

- Article VII of the GATT 1994, entitled 'Valuation for Customs Purposes';
- the Note *Ad* Article VII; and
- the WTO *Agreement on the Implementation of Article VII of the GATT 1994*.[104]

The latter agreement, commonly referred to as the *Customs Valuation Agreement*, elaborates the provisions of Article VII in order to provide greater uniformity and certainty in their implementation.

The core provision of Article VII on customs valuation is found in paragraph 2(a), which states:

> The value for customs purposes of imported merchandise should be based on the *actual value* of the imported merchandise on which duty is assessed, or of like merchandise, and should *not* be based on the value of merchandise of national origin or on arbitrary or fictitious values.
>
> [Emphasis added]

Paragraph 2(b) of Article VII defines the concept of the 'actual value' of goods as the price at which such or like goods are sold or offered for sale in the ordinary course of trade under fully competitive conditions.

Elaborating on and elucidating Article VII:2 of the GATT 1994, Article 1.1 of the *Customs Valuation Agreement* provides:

> The customs value of imported goods shall be the *transaction value*, that is the price actually paid or payable for the goods when sold for export to the country of importation adjusted in accordance with the provisions of Article 8 . . . [105]
>
> [Emphasis added]

The primary basis for the customs value is thus the 'transaction value' of the imported goods, i.e. the price actually paid or payable for the goods. This price is normally shown in the invoice, contract or purchase order.[106] Article 1.1 is to be read together with Article 8, which provides for *adjustments* to be made to the price actually paid or payable, as discussed below.

Articles 2 to 7 of the *Customs Valuation Agreement* provide methods for determining the customs value whenever it cannot be determined under the provisions of

---

[104] The WTO *Agreement on the Implementation of Article VII of the GATT 1994* replaced the 1979 Tokyo Round *Agreement on the Implementation of Article VII of the GATT*, but is not significantly different from this 1979 Agreement.

[105] Note that, in the proviso to Article 1.1, a number of situations are identified in which the transaction value cannot be used to determine the customs value. This is, for example, the case when there are certain restrictions on the use or disposition of the goods. Furthermore, as a rule, the buyer and seller should not be related (within the meaning of Article 15) but, if they are, the use of the transaction value is still acceptable if this relationship did not influence the price (see Article 1.2(a)) or the transaction value closely approximates a test value (see Article 1.2(b)).

[106] Pursuant to Article 17 of the *Customs Valuation Agreement*, customs administrations have the right to 'satisfy themselves as to the truth or accuracy of any statement, document or declaration'. In cases of doubt as to the truth or accuracy, customs administrations will first request the importer to provide further information and clarification. If reasonable doubt persists, the customs administration will not determine the customs value on the basis of the transaction value but will apply a different method of valuation (see below, pp. 432–3).

Article 1. These methods to determine the customs value, other than the 'transaction value' method of Article 1, are:

- the transaction value of identical goods (Article 2);[107]
- the transaction value of similar goods (Article 3);[108]
- the deductive value method (Article 5);
- the computed value method (Article 6); and
- the fall-back method (Article 7).

These methods to determine the customs value of imported goods are to be applied in the above order.[109] Under the *deductive value method*, the customs value of imported goods is determined on the basis of the unit price at which the imported goods, or identical or similar imported goods, are sold at the greatest aggregate quantity to an unrelated buyer in the country of importation. The greatest aggregate quantity is the greatest number of units sold at one price.[110] Under the *computed value method*, the customs value is determined on the basis of the computed value. The computed value is the sum of the production cost (i.e. the cost of materials and fabrication), profit and general expenses and other expenses (e.g. transport costs to the place or port of importation).[111]

The *fall-back method*, set out in Article 7, applies when the customs value cannot be determined under any of the other four methods. Under this method, the customs value shall be:

> determined using reasonable means consistent with the principles and general provisions of this Agreement and of Article VII of the GATT 1994 and on the basis of the data available in the country of importation.[112]

However, the customs value of imported goods may never be determined on the basis of, for example:

- the selling price in the country of importation of goods produced in that country;
- the price of goods on the domestic market of the country of exportation;
- minimum customs values; or
- arbitrary or fictitious values.[113]

---

[107] Goods are 'identical' if they are the same in all respects, including physical characteristics, quality and reputation. 'Similar goods' means goods which, although not alike in all respects, have like characteristics and like component materials which enable them to perform the same functions and to be commercially interchangeable. In addition, goods shall not be regarded as 'similar' or 'identical' unless they are produced in the same country as the goods being valued. See Article 15.2 of the *Customs Valuation Agreement*.   [108] Ibid.

[109] See Article 4 of, and Annex I, General Note, to, the *Customs Valuation Agreement*. Note, however, that at the request of the importer the order of application of the deductive method (Article 5) and the computed method (Article 6) may be reversed (*ibid*.).

[110] See Article 5 of, and Annex I, Note to Article 5, to, the *Customs Valuation Agreement*. Since the deductive value method uses the sale price in the country of importation as a basis for the calculation of the customs value, a number of deductions (for profits, general expenses, transport, etc.) are necessary to reduce the sale price to the relevant customs value.

[111] See Article 6 of, and Annex I, Note to Article 6, to, the *Customs Valuation Agreement*.

[112] Article 7.1 of the *Customs Valuation Agreement*.   [113] See Article 7.2 of the *Customs Valuation Agreement*.

As mentioned above, the customs value of imported goods is – if possible and, usually, this is possible – determined on the basis of the transaction value of these goods. This transaction value must, however, be adjusted as provided for in Article 8 of the *Customs Valuation Agreement*. Pursuant to Article 8.1, the following costs and values, for example, must be added to the price actually paid or payable for the imported products:

- commissions and brokerage;[114]
- the cost of packing;[115]
- royalties and licence fees related to the goods being valued that the buyer must pay;[116] and
- the value of any part of the proceeds of any subsequent resale that accrues to the seller.[117]

Pursuant to Article 8.2, each Member is free either to include or to exclude from the customs value of imported goods:

- the cost of transport to the port or place of importation;
- loading, unloading and handling charges associated with the transport to the port or place of importation; and
- the cost of insurance.

Note in this respect that most Members take the CIF price as the basis for determining the customs value, while the United States takes the (lower) FOB price.[118]

Questions and Assignments 5.9

Why must customs administrations determine the value of imported goods? Which provisions set out the WTO rules on customs valuation? What is the principal, and most common, method for determining the customs value of imported goods? Briefly discuss other methods for determining the customs value of imported products. Must the cost of the packaging and/or the cost of transport to the port or place of importation be included in the customs value of imported goods?

5.2.6.3. Determination of origin

The customs duties applied to imported goods may differ depending on the country from which the goods were exported. For example, goods *from* developing-country Members commonly benefit from lower import duties

---

[114] See Article 8.1(a)(i) of the *Customs Valuation Agreement*.
[115] See Article 8.1(a)(iii) of the *Customs Valuation Agreement*.
[116] See Article 8.1(c) of the *Customs Valuation Agreement*.
[117] See Article 8.1(d) of the *Customs Valuation Agreement*.
[118] CIF (cost, insurance and freight) and FOB (free on board) are International Commercial terms (INCO terms). CIF means that the seller must pay the costs, insurance and freight involved in bringing the goods to the named port of destination. FOB means that the buyer has to bear all costs and risks of loss of, or damage to, the goods from the point that the goods pass the ship's rail at the named port of shipment.

in developed-country Members than goods from other developed-country Members; and on goods *from* Members that are a party to the same free trade agreement, no customs duties apply. Moreover, only the goods *from* WTO Members benefit under WTO law from MFN treatment with respect to customs duties. It is, therefore, important to determine the origin of imported goods and, surprisingly perhaps, this is not always an easy determination to make. Many industrial products, available on the market today, are produced in more than one country. For example, in the case of cotton shirts, it is possible that the cotton used in their production is manufactured in country A, the textile woven, dyed and printed in country B, the cloth cut and stitched in country C and the shirts packed for retail in country D before being exported to country E.[119]

The rules to determine the origin of imported goods differ from Member to Member and many Members use different rules of origin depending on the purpose for which the origin is determined.[120] However, generally speaking, the rules of origin currently applied by Members are based on:

- the principle of value added; or
- the principle of change in tariff classification.

Under rules of origin based on the principle of value added, an imported good will be considered to have originated in country X if in that country a specified percentage (for example, 50 per cent) of the value of the good was added. Under rules of origin based on the principle of change in tariff classification, a good will be considered to have originated in country X, if, as a result of processing in that country, the tariff classification of the product changes.

The GATT 1947 had no specific rules on the determination of the origin of imported goods, and the GATT 1994 still provides no specific rules on this matter. However, the negotiators during the Uruguay Round recognised the need for multilateral disciplines on rules of origin in order to prevent these rules from being a source of uncertainty and unpredictability in international trade.

The consensus on the need for such disciplines resulted in the WTO *Agreement on Rules of Origin*. This Agreement makes a distinction between:

- non-preferential rules of origin; and
- preferential rules of origin.

Pursuant to Article 1 of the *Agreement on Rules of Origin*, most of the multilateral disciplines set forth therein (i.e. Parts I to IV) concern only *non-preferential* rules of origin. Non-preferential rules of origin are rules of origin used in non-preferential trade policy instruments (relating to, *inter alia*, MFN treatment, anti-dumping and countervailing duties, safeguard measures, origin marking or tariff quotas).[121]

---

[119] See *Business Guide to the World Trading System*, 2nd edition (International Trade Centre/Commonwealth Secretariat, 1999), 155.
[120] E.g. whether the origin of imported products is determined for the imposition of ordinary customs duties, anti-dumping or countervailing duties or the administration of country-specific tariff quota shares.   [121] See Article 1.2 of the *Agreement on Rules of Origin*.

However, Annex II to the *Agreement on Rules of Origin* provides some multilateral disciplines for *preferential* rules of origin. Preferential rules of origin are rules of origin applied by Members to determine whether goods qualify for preferential treatment under contractual or autonomous trade regimes (leading to the granting of tariff preferences going beyond the application of the MFN treatment obligation).[122] Note that around 45 per cent of world trade is conducted on a preferential basis.[123]

With respect to *non-preferential* rules of origin, the *Agreement on Rules of Origin* provides for a work programme on the harmonisation of these rules.[124] Pursuant to Article 9.2 of the *Agreement on Rules of Origin*, this Harmonisation Work Programme should have been completed by July 1998. However, due to the complexity of the matter, the WTO Members failed to meet this deadline. In fact, work on the harmonisation of non-preferential rules of origin is still not completed.[125]

The failure of WTO Members to agree, to date, on harmonised rules of origin does not mean, however, that no WTO disciplines apply to non-preferential rules of origin. Article 2 of the *Agreement on Rules of Origin* contains a rather extensive list of multilateral disciplines for rules of origin already applicable during the 'transition period', i.e. the period until the Harmonisation Work Programme is completed. These multilateral disciplines applicable during the transitional period include:

- a transparency requirement: the rules of origin must clearly and precisely define the criteria they apply (Article 2(a));
- a prohibition on using rules of origin as instruments to pursue trade objectives (Article 2(b));
- a requirement that rules of origin shall not themselves create restrictive, distorting or disruptive effects on international trade (Article 2(c));
- a national treatment requirement, namely, that the rules of origin applied to imported products shall not be more stringent than the rules of origin applied to determine whether or not a good is domestic (Article 2(d));
- an MFN requirement, namely, that rules of origin shall not discriminate between other Members, irrespective of the affiliation of the manufacturers of the good concerned (Article 2(d));
- a requirement that rules of origin shall be administered in a consistent, uniform, impartial and reasonable manner (Article 2(e));
- a requirement that rules of origin state what *does* confer origin (positive standard) rather than state what does *not* confer origin (negative standard) (Article 2(f));
- a requirement to publish laws, regulations, judicial decisions, etc., relating to rules of origin (Article2(g));

---

[122] See Article 1.1 of, and Annex II.2 to, the *Agreement on Rules of Origin*.
[123] See above, p. 404, and below, pp. 699–709, 726–30.
[124] See Article 9.1 of the *Agreement on Rules of Origin*. This work programme is to be undertaken in conjunction with the WCO.
[125] See WTO Secretariat, *Twelfth Annual Review of the Implementation and Operation of the Agreement on Rules of Origin, Note by the Secretariat*, G/RO/63, dated 3 November 2006; and WTO Secretariat, *WTO Annual Report 2007*, 25.

- requirements regarding the issuance of assessments of origin (no later than 150 days after the request) and the validity of the assessments (in principle, three years) (Article 2(h));
- a prohibition on the retroactive application of new or amended rules of origin (Article 2(i));
- a requirement that any administrative action relating to the determination of origin is reviewable promptly by independent tribunals (Article 2(j)); and
- a requirement to respect the confidentiality of information provided on a confidential basis (Article 2(k)).

Note that most of these disciplines are in fact the specific application of general GATT obligations (such as Articles I, III and X of the GATT 1994) to national non-preferential rules on the determination of origin.

To date, there has only been one dispute before a panel dealing with rules of origin. In *US – Textiles Rules of Origin*, India claimed that the United States applied rules of origin on textiles and certain other products that were inconsistent with several obligations under Article 2 of the *Agreement on Rules of Origin*. The Panel in *US – Textiles Rules of Origin* noted that Article 2 does not provide what WTO Members must do, but rather what they should not do,[126] and that:

> By setting out what Members cannot do, these provisions leave for Members themselves discretion to decide what, within those bounds, they can do. In this regard, it is common ground between the parties that Article 2 does not prevent Members from determining the criteria which confer origin, changing those criteria over time, or applying different criteria to different goods.[127]

Once the Harmonisation Work Programme is completed, all Members will apply only one set of non-preferential rules of origin for all purposes.[128] As provided for in Article 3 of the *Agreement on Rules of Origin*, the disciplines set out in Article 2, already applicable, will continue to apply.[129] As an instruction to Members for the negotiations under the Harmonisation Work Programme, Article 3 provides that Members must ensure that under the harmonised rules of origin:

> the country to be determined as the origin of a particular good is either the country where the good has been wholly obtained or, when more than one country is concerned in the production of the good, the country where the last substantial transformation has been carried out.[130]

---

[126] See Panel Report, *US – Textiles Rules of Origin*, para. 6.23.
[127] *Ibid.*, para. 6.24. India argued that rules of origin applied by the United States on its textiles imports were inconsistent with Article 2(b) (prohibition 'to pursue trade objectives directly or indirectly'); Article 2(c), first sentence (prohibition to 'create [themselves] restrictive, distorting or disruptive effects on international trade'); Article 2(c), second sentence (prohibition to 'pose unduly strict requirements'); and Article 2(d), second clause ('shall not discriminate between Members, irrespective of the affiliation of the manufacturers') of the *Agreement on Rules of Origin*. The Panel found with regard to all claims that India did not adduce sufficient evidence to make a *prima facie* case of inconsistency. See Panel Report, *US – Textiles Rules of Origin*, paras. 6.118; 6.190–6.191, 6.221 and 6.231; and 6.271–6.272.
[128] See Article 3(a) of the *Agreement on Rules of Origin*.
[129] See Article 3(c) to (i) and Article 9(c) to (g) of the *Agreement on Rules of Origin*.
[130] Article 3(b) of the *Agreement on Rules of Origin*.

Under the harmonised rules, WTO Members must therefore be required to determine as the country of origin of imported goods:

- the country where the goods have been wholly obtained; or
- the country where the last substantial transformation to the goods has been carried out.

To date, Members have been unsuccessful in achieving consensus either on detailed rules regarding the requirements for a good to be 'wholly obtained' in one country,[131] or on the criteria for a 'substantial transformation' (a change in tariff classification and/or a specific percentage of value added).

The disciplines on rules of origin discussed above concern, pursuant to Article 1 of the *Agreement on Rules of Origin*, only non-preferential rules of origin. However, as already noted, Annex II to the *Agreement on Rules of Origin* provides – in the form of a 'Common Declaration' – for some multilateral disciplines applicable to preferential rules of conduct. Pursuant to Annex II, the general principles and requirements set out in the *Agreement on Rules of Origin* in respect of transparency, positive standards, administrative assessments, judicial review, non-retroactivity of changes and confidentiality apply also to *preferential* rules of origin. The results of the Harmonisation Work Programme, however, will not apply to preferential rules of origin.

Questions and Assignments 5.10

Why is it important to determine the origin of imported goods? How do Members commonly determine the origin of goods? Why is there a need for multilateral disciplines on rules of origin? Are there any WTO rules on the determination of the origin of goods? Briefly describe the disciplines currently applicable to non-preferential rules of origin. Discuss the rules which will be applicable once the Harmonisation Work Programme is completed. Are there any multilateral disciplines applicable on preferential rules of origin?

5.2.7. Other duties and charges

In addition to 'ordinary customs duties', tariff barriers can also take the form of 'other duties and charges'.

5.2.7.1. Definition and types

'Other duties and charges' are financial charges, *other than* ordinary customs duties, imposed on, or in the context of, the importation of a good. 'Other duties and charges' form a residual category encompassing financial charges that are

---

[131] Under debate is, for example, the question of which minimal operations or processes can and cannot, by themselves, confer origin on a good.

not 'ordinary customs duties'. Unfortunately, the GATT 1994 does not define the concept of 'ordinary customs duties' and the relevant case law is not very helpful. In *Chile – Price Band System*, the Panel found that 'ordinary customs duties':

> always relate to either the value of the imported goods, in the case of *ad valorem* duties, or the volume of the imported goods, in the case of specific duties. Such ordinary customs duties, however, do not appear to involve the consideration of any other, exogenous, factors, such as, for instance, fluctuating world market prices. We therefore consider that . . . an 'ordinary' customs duty, that is, a customs duty *senso strictu*, is to be understood as referring to a customs duty which is not applied on the basis of factors of an exogenous nature.[132]

On appeal, the Appellate Body disagreed with the Panel and reversed its finding that the concept of 'ordinary customs duty' is to be understood as referring to a customs duty which is not applied on the basis of factors of an exogenous nature.[133] The Appellate Body, however, did not give an alternative definition of 'ordinary customs duties'.

Examples of 'other duties and charges' identified in GATT/WTO case law are:

- an import surcharge, i.e. a duty imposed on an imported product in addition to the ordinary customs duty;[134]
- a security deposit to be made on the importation of goods;[135]
- a statistical tax imposed to finance the collection of statistical information;[136]
- a customs fee, i.e. a financial charge imposed for the processing of imported goods by the customs authorities;[137]
- a transitional surcharge for economic stabilisation imposed on imported goods;[138] and
- a foreign exchange fee imposed on imported goods.[139]

5.2.7.2. Rules regarding 'other duties or charges'

To protect the tariff bindings set forth in the Schedules and to prevent 'circumvention' of the prohibition of Article II:1(b), first sentence, of the GATT 1994, to impose ordinary customs duties in excess of the bindings, WTO law provides for rules on 'other duties and charges'. With regard to products subject to a tariff binding, Article II:1(b), second sentence, of the GATT 1994 states:

> Such products shall also be exempt from all other duties or charges of any kind imposed on or in connection with the importation in excess of those imposed on the date of this Agreement or those directly and mandatorily required to be imposed thereafter by legislation in force in the importing territory on that date.

Article II:1(b), second sentence, thus requires that, on products subject to a tariff binding, *no* other duties or charges may be imposed *in excess of* those duties or charges:

---

[132] Panel Report, *Chile – Price Band System*, para. 7.52. See also *ibid.*, para. 7.104.
[133] See Appellate Body Report, *Chile – Price Band System*, para. 278.
[134] See e.g. *Korea – Beef (Australia)*.   [135] See e.g. *EEC – Minimum Import Prices* and *EEC – Animal Feed Proteins*.
[136] See e.g. *Argentina – Textiles and Apparel*.   [137] See e.g. *United States – Customs User Fee*.
[138] See e.g. *Dominican Republic – Import and Sale of Cigarettes*.   [139] *Ibid.*

- already imposed at the 'date of this Agreement'; or
- provided for in mandatory legislation in force on that date.

However, under the GATT 1947 regime, the 'date of this Agreement' was not necessarily the date of the GATT 1947, i.e. 30 October 1947, but could also be the date of a later tariff protocol to the GATT 1947.[140] As is explained in the *Analytical Index: Guide to GATT Law and Practice*:

> in the GATT 1947, each concession would have its own 'date of this Agreement' for the purpose of the binding on 'other duties and charges' under Article II:1(b) . . . and in a Schedule with a number of concessions there could be a number of different and coexisting such 'dates of this Agreement'.[141]

As a result, there was considerable uncertainty and confusion regarding the maximum level of 'other duties or charges' that could be imposed. Therefore, the Uruguay Round negotiators agreed on the *Understanding on the Interpretation of Article II:1(b) of the GATT 1994*, commonly referred to as the *Understanding on Article II:1(b)*. This Understanding states, in relevant part:

> In order to ensure transparency of the legal rights and obligations deriving from paragraph 1(b) of Article II, the nature and level of any 'other duties or charges' levied on bound tariff items, as referred to in that provision, shall be recorded in the Schedules of Concessions annexed to GATT 1994 against the tariff item to which they apply.[142]

The *Understanding on Article II:1(b)* thus requires Members to record in their Schedules all 'other duties or charges' imposed on products subject to a tariff binding. As noted above, the Uruguay Round Schedules have a special column for 'other duties or charges'.[143] The 'other duties or charges' must be recorded in the Schedules at the levels applying on 15 April 1994.[144] The 'other duties or charges' are 'bound' at these levels.[145]

It follows from Article II:1(b), second sentence, and from the *Understanding on Article II:1(b)*, that Members may:

- impose only 'other duties and charges' that have been properly recorded in their Schedules; and
- impose 'other duties and charges' only at a level that does not exceed the level recorded in their Schedules.

In *Chile – Price Band System*, the Panel, having found that the Chilean Price Band System (PBS) duties were not 'ordinary customs duties' but were 'other

---

[140] See *Analytical Index: Guide to GATT Law and Practice* (WTO, 1995), 84.   [141] *Ibid.*, 85.

[142] *Understanding on the Interpretation of Article II:1(b) of the GATT 1994* (hereinafter '*Understanding on Article II:1(b)*'), para. 1.   [143] See above, pp. 418–20.

[144] *Understanding on Article II:1(b)*, para. 2. Note, however, that paragraph 4 of the *Understanding on Article II:1(b)* states: 'Where a tariff item has previously been the subject of a concession, the level of "other duties or charges" recorded in the appropriate Schedule shall not be higher than the level obtaining at the time of the first incorporation of the concession in that Schedule.'

[145] Note that paragraph 1 of the *Understanding on Article II:1(b)* states that the recording in the Schedules does not change the legal character of the 'other duties or charges' and that paragraphs 4 and 5 provide that – with certain restrictions in time – the Members can challenge the GATT-consistency of recorded 'other duties or charges'. See Panel Report, *Argentina – Textiles and Apparel*, para. 6.81.

duties or charges', examined whether these duties were inconsistent with Article II:1(b), second sentence. The Panel ruled:

> Pursuant to the Uruguay Round Understanding on the Interpretation of Article II:1(b), such other duties or charges had to be recorded in a newly created column 'other duties and charges' in the Members' Schedules . . .
>
> Other duties or charges must not exceed the binding in this 'other duties and charges' column of the Schedule. If other duties or charges were not recorded but are nevertheless levied, they are inconsistent with the second sentence of Article II:1(b), in light of the Understanding on the Interpretation of Article II:1(b). We note that Chile did not record its PBS in the 'other duties and charges' column of its Schedule.
>
> We therefore find that the Chilean PBS duties are inconsistent with Article II:1(b) of GATT 1994.[146]

In *Dominican Republic – Import and Sale of Cigarettes*, the Panel found that the two 'other duties or charges' at issue in this case, namely the transitional surcharge for economic stabilisation and the foreign exchange fee imposed on imported products, had not been recorded in a legally valid manner in the Schedule of Concessions of the Dominican Republic.[147] With regard to the transitional surcharge for economic stabilisation, the Panel came to the following conclusion:

> For all legal and practical purposes, what was notified by the Dominican Republic in document G/SP/3 is equivalent to 'zero' in the Schedule. The Panel finds that the surcharge as an 'other duty or charge' measure is applied in excess of the level 'zero' pursuant to the Schedule. Therefore, the surcharge measure is inconsistent with Article II:1(b) of the GATT 1994.[148]

With regard to the foreign exchange fee, the Panel came to the same conclusion.[149]

On the legal effects of the scheduling of 'other duties or charges', note that in *Argentina – Textiles and Apparel*, Argentina argued that since its 3 per cent statistical tax was included in its Schedule of Concessions (Schedule LXIV), there was no violation of Article II:1(b) of the GATT 1994. The Panel disagreed with Argentina and noted that:

> The provisions of the WTO Understanding on the Interpretation of Article II:1(b) of GATT 1994, dealing with 'other duties and charges', make clear that including a charge in a schedule of concessions in no way immunizes that charge from challenge as a violation of an applicable GATT rule.[150]

5.2.7.3. Exceptions to the rule

There are a number of exceptions to the rule that Members may not impose 'other duties or charges' unless recorded and not in excess of the recorded level.

---

[146] Panel Report, *Chile – Price Band System*, paras. 7.105 and 7.107–7.108. On appeal, the Appellate Body found that the Panel's finding on Article II:1(b), second sentence, related to a claim that had not been made, and this finding was therefore in violation of Article 11 of the DSU. As a result, the Appellate Body reversed the finding. See above, p. 439.

[147] The Panel ruled that the recording of the Selective Consumption Tax, i.e. an internal tax, could not be used as legal basis to justify the current transitional surcharge or the foreign exchange fee. See Panel Report, *Dominican Republic – Import and Sale of Cigarettes*, para. 7.86.   [148] *Ibid.*, para. 7.89.

[149] See *ibid.*, para. 7.121.

[150] Panel Report, *Argentina – Textiles and Apparel*, para. 6.81. See also above, p. 423.

Pursuant to Article II:2 of the GATT 1994, Members may – despite their obligations under Article II:1(b), second sentence – impose on imported products:

- any financial charge that is not in excess of the internal tax imposed on the like domestic product (border tax adjustment);[151]
- WTO-consistent anti-dumping or countervailing duties; or
- fees or other charges 'commensurate' with, i.e. matching, the cost of the services rendered.

With respect to the latter category of 'other duties or charges', note that the requirement that these fees or other charges are commensurate with the cost of the services is also reflected in Article VIII:1(a) of the GATT 1994. This Article requires that:

> All fees and charges of whatever character (other than import or export duties and other than taxes within the purview of Article III) imposed by [Members] on or in connection with importation or exportation shall be limited in amount to the approximate cost of services rendered and shall not represent an indirect protection to domestic products or a taxation of imports or exports for fiscal purposes.[152]

The fees and charges for services rendered within the meaning of Articles II:2(c) and VIII:1(a) include, pursuant to Article VIII:4, fees and charges relating to:

- consular transactions, such as consular invoices and certificates;
- quantitative restrictions;
- licensing;
- exchange control;
- statistical services;
- documents, documentation and certification;
- analysis and inspection; and
- quarantine, sanitation and fumigation.

With respect to the concept of 'services' used in this context, the GATT Panel in *US – Customs User Fee* stated, not without wit:

> Granted that some government regulatory activities can be considered as 'services' in an economic sense when they endow goods with safety or quality characteristics deemed necessary for commerce, most of the activities that governments perform in connection with the importation process do not meet that definition. They are not desired by the importers who are subject to them. Nor do they add value to the goods in any commercial sense. Whatever governments may choose to call them, fees for such government regulatory activities are, in the Panel's view, simply taxes on imports. It must be presumed, therefore, that the drafters meant the term 'services' to be used in a more artful political sense, i.e. government activities closely enough connected to the processes of customs entry that they might, with no more than the customary artistic licence accorded to taxing authorities, be called a 'service' to the importer in question.[153]

---

[151] On the concept of 'border tax adjustment', see above, pp. 350–1.
[152] Note that there is a slight difference in wording between the two 'cost of services' limitations stated in Articles II:2(c) and VIII:1(a), i.e. 'commensurate with the cost of services rendered' and 'limited in amount to the approximate cost of services rendered'. However, the GATT Panel in *US – Customs User Fee*, after reviewing both the drafting history and the subsequent application of these provisions, concluded that no difference of meaning had been intended.   [153] GATT Panel Report, *US – Customs User Fee*, para. 77.

In *US – Customs User Fee*, the financial charge at issue was a merchandise-processing fee, in the form of an *ad valorem* charge without upper limits. The complainants, the European Communities and Canada, challenged the GATT-consistency of an *ad valorem* charge without upper limit. Before turning to the specific claim of inconsistency, the Panel noted that the requirement of Article VIII:1(a) that a fee or charge be 'limited in amount to the approximate cost of services rendered' is in fact a dual requirement:

- the fee or charge in question must first involve a 'service' rendered; and
- the level of the charge must not exceed the approximate cost of that service.[154]

With respect to the first element of this dual requirement, the Panel further clarified that the fee or charge in question must involve a 'service' rendered to the *individual* importer in question.[155] Services rendered to foreign trade operators in general and foreign trade as an activity *per se* would fail to meet this first element of the dual requirement.[156] With respect to the second element of the dual requirement, the Panel stated:

> that the term 'cost of services rendered' in Articles II:2(c) and VIII:1(a) must be interpreted to refer to the cost of the customs processing for the individual entry in question and accordingly that the *ad valorem* structure of the United States merchandise processing fee was inconsistent with the obligations of Articles II:2(c) and VIII:1(a) to the extent that it caused fees to be levied in excess of such costs.[157]

In *Argentina – Textiles and Apparel*, the Panel found that Argentina's 3 per cent *ad valorem* statistical tax on imports was inconsistent with Article VIII:1(a) of the GATT 1994

> to the extent it results in charges being levied in excess of the approximate costs of the services rendered.[158]

As the Panel explained, an *ad valorem* charge with no maximum limit, as was the case with Argentina's statistical tax,

> by its very nature, is not 'limited in amount to the approximate cost of services rendered'. For example, high-price items necessarily will bear a much higher tax burden than low-price goods, yet the service accorded to both is essentially the same. An unlimited *ad valorem* charge on imported goods violates the provisions of Article VIII because such a charge cannot be related to the cost of the service rendered.[159]

Note that the Panel in *Argentina – Textiles and Apparel* also found that the statistical tax was inconsistent with Article VIII:1(a) because this tax – according to Argentina's own admission – was imposed for 'fiscal purposes', which is explicitly prohibited under Article VIII:1(a).

---

[154] See *ibid.*, para. 69. See also Panel Report, *Argentina – Textiles and Apparel*, para. 6.74; and Panel Report, *US – Certain EC Products*, para. 6.69.   [155] See GATT Panel Report, *US – Customs User Fee*, para. 80.

[156] See Panel Report, *Argentina – Textiles and Apparel*, para. 6.74.

[157] GATT Panel Report, *US – Customs User Fee*, para. 86 (underlining in the original replaced with italics).

[158] Panel Report, *Argentina – Textiles and Apparel*, para. 6.80.   [159] *Ibid.*, para. 6.75.

Questions and Assignments 5.11

What are 'other duties or charges' within the meaning of Article II:1(b), second sentence, of the GATT 1994? Give three examples of such 'other duties or charges'. Are 'other duties or charges' permitted in the same way as customs duties are? Which 'other duties or charges' are permitted under the GATT 1994? Find an example of a product on which the country of which you are a national imposes an 'other duty or charge'. Which 'other duties or charges' are allowed on imported products irrespective of a Member's obligations under Article II:1(b), second sentence, of the GATT 1994? When are customs fees or charges covered by Article II:2(c) of the GATT 1994?

5.3. NON-TARIFF BARRIERS TO TRADE IN GOODS

Trade in goods is not only restricted by customs duties and other duties and charges, but also by non-tariff barriers. This section deals with both main categories of non-tariff barriers, i.e. quantitative restrictions and other non-tariff barriers. It discusses:

- quantitative restrictions;
- rules on quantitative restrictions;
- the administration of quantitative restrictions; and
- other non-tariff barriers.

5.3.1. Quantitative restrictions

5.3.1.1. Definition and types

A quantitative restriction, also referred to as a 'QR', is a measure that *limits the quantity* of a product that may be imported or exported. There are different types of quantitative restriction:

- a *prohibition*, or ban, on a product; such a prohibition may be absolute or conditional, i.e. only applicable when certain defined conditions are *not* fulfilled;
- a *quota*, i.e. a measure indicating the quantity that may be imported or exported; a quota can be a global quota, a global quota allocated among countries or a bilateral quota;
- automatic and non-automatic *licensing*;[160] and
- *other* quantitative restrictions, such as a quantitative restriction made effective through State trading operations; a mixing regulation; a minimum price, triggering a quantitative restriction; and a voluntary export restraint.[161]

---

[160] See below, pp. 458–60.
[161] For an illustrative list of quantitative restrictions, see Council for Trade in Goods, *Decision on Notification Procedures for Quantitative Restrictions*, G/L/59, dated 10 January 1996, Annex.

A typical example of a quantitative restriction, and in particular a quota, is a measure allowing the importation of a maximum of 1,000 tonnes of cocoa powder a year or a measure allowing the importation of a maximum of 450 tractors a year. While usually based on the number of units, weight or volume, quantitative restrictions can also be based on value, for example a limit on the importation of flowers to the value of €12 million per year.

WTO Members are required to notify the WTO Secretariat of any quantitative restrictions which they maintain and of any changes in these restrictions, as and when they occur.[162] The notifications must indicate:

- the products affected by the QR;
- the type of QR (prohibition, quota, licensing, etc.);
- an indication of the grounds and WTO justification for the QR; and
- a statement on the trade effects of the QR.

With this information, the WTO Secretariat maintains a QR database, which Members may consult.[163]

5.3.1.2. *Customs duties versus quantitative restrictions*

The WTO has a clear preference for customs duties over quantitative restrictions and this preference is reflected in the relevant provisions of the GATT 1994.[164] In comparing customs duties with quantitative restrictions, the Panel in *Turkey – Textiles* noted:

> A basic principle of the GATT system is that tariffs are the preferred and acceptable form of protection . . . The prohibition against quantitative restrictions is a reflection that tariffs are GATT's border protection 'of choice'.[165]

The reasons for this preference are both economic and political in nature. First, customs duties are more transparent. The economic impact of customs duties on imported products, i.e. how much more expensive imported products are as a result of customs duties, is immediately clear. Quantitative restrictions also increase the price of the imported products. As supply of the imported product is limited, the price increases. However, it is not immediately clear by how much quantitative restrictions increase the price of imported products. Secondly, while the price increase resulting from customs duties goes to the government, the price increase resulting from quantitative restrictions ordinarily benefits the importers. The importers will be able to sell at higher prices because of the limits on the supply of the product. The 'extra profit' is commonly referred to as the 'quota rent' and, unless a quota is auctioned (which is seldom done), no part of this quota rent goes to the

---

[162] See *ibid*.   [163] This database is not accessible to the general public.
[164] See below, pp. 447–50. See also above, p. 408.   [165] Panel Report, *Turkey – Textiles*, para. 9.63.

government. Thirdly, the administration of quantitative restrictions is more open to corruption than the administration of customs duties. This is because quantitative restrictions, and, in particular, quotas, are usually administered through an import licensing system and decisions by government officials to award an import licence are not necessarily based on the general interest.[166] Fourthly, and arguably most importantly, quantitative restrictions impose absolute limits on imports, while customs duties do not. While customs duties are surmountable (at least, if they are not set at prohibitively high levels), quantitative restrictions cannot be surmounted. If a foreign producer is sufficiently more efficient than a domestic producer, the customs duty will not prevent imported products from competing with domestic products. By contrast, once the limit of a quantitative restriction is reached, no more products can be imported. Even the most efficient foreign producer cannot 'overcome' the quantitative restriction. Above the quota, domestic products have no competition from imported products.

5.3.1.3. Tariff quotas

A tariff (rate) quota, or 'TRQ', is *not* a quota; it is *not* a quantitative restriction.[167] A tariff quota is a quantity which can be imported at a certain duty. The Panel in *US – Line Pipe* stated that a tariff quota involves the 'application of a higher tariff rate to imported goods after a specific quantity of the item has entered the country at a lower prevailing rate'.[168] Any quantity above the quote is subject to a higher tariff. For example, a Member may allow the importation of 5,000 tractors at 10 per cent *ad valorem* and any tractor imported above this quantity at 30 per cent *ad valorem*. Tariff quotas are not quantitative restrictions since they do not directly prohibit or restrict the quantity of imports. They only subject the imports to varying duties. The European Communities' intricate import regime for bananas, at issue in *EC – Bananas III*, provided for tariff quotas. Under this regime, the European Communities granted, for example, duty-free access to 90,000 tonnes of non-traditional ACP bananas; the out-of-quota tariff rate for these same bananas was 693 ECU per tonne.

Questions and Assignments 5.12

What is a quantitative restriction? Discuss the different types of quantitative restriction. Why does the WTO prefer customs duties to quantitative restrictions? Are tariff quotas quantitative restrictions or quotas?

---

[166] On import licensing procedures, see below, pp. 458–60.
[167] See the unadopted GATT Panel Report, *EEC – Bananas II*, paras. 138–9.
[168] Panel Report, *US – Line Pipe*, para. 7.18.

5.3.2. Rules on quantitative restrictions

5.3.2.1. *General prohibition on quantitative restrictions*

Article XI:1 of the GATT 1994, entitled 'General Elimination of Quantitative Restrictions', sets out a general prohibition on quantitative restrictions, whether on imports or exports. As the Panel in *Turkey – Textiles* stated:

> The prohibition on the use of quantitative restrictions forms one of the cornerstones of the GATT system.[169]

Article XI:1 provides, in relevant part:

> No prohibitions or restrictions other than duties, taxes or other charges, whether made effective through quotas, import or export licences or other measures, shall be instituted or maintained by any [Member] on the importation of any product of the territory of any other [Member] or on the exportation or sale for export of any product destined for the territory of any other [Member].

As the Panel in *Japan – Semi-Conductors* noted, the wording of Article XI:1

> was comprehensive: it applied to *all measures* instituted or maintained by a contracting party *prohibiting or restricting* the importation, exportation or sale for export of products *other than* measures that take the form of duties, taxes or other charges.[170]
>
> [Emphasis added]

In *India – Autos*, India argued that the term 'restrictions . . . on importation' within the meaning of Article XI:1 of the GATT 1994 applies only to border measures. The Panel rejected this argument and noted that the reference to 'other measures' in Article XI:1 suggests a broad scope as to the kind of measures covered by Article XI:1.[171] The Panel stated that it is:

> the nature of the measure as a restriction *in relation to importation* which is the key factor to consider in determining whether a measure may properly fall within the scope of Article XI:1.[172]

As an illustration of the broad scope of the prohibition on quantitative restrictions, consider the following examples of measures that were found to be inconsistent with Article XI:1:

- In *US – Shrimp*, the Panel found that the United States acted inconsistently with Article XI:1 by imposing an import ban on shrimp and shrimp products harvested by vessels of foreign nations not certified by the US authorities as using methods not leading to the accidental killing of sea turtles above certain levels.[173]

---

[169] Panel Report, *Turkey – Textiles*, para. 9.63.   [170] GATT Panel Report, *Japan – Semi-Conductors*, para. 104.
[171] See Panel Report, *India – Autos*, para. 7.246.   [172] *Ibid.*, para.7.261.
[173] See Panel Report, *US – Shrimp*, paras. 7.17 and 8.1. Previous GATT Panels in *US – Tuna (EEC)*, para. 5.10, and *US – Tuna (Mexico)*, paras. 5.17–5.18, found similar measures also to be 'restrictions' within the meaning of Article XI.

- In *EEC – Minimum Import Prices*, the Panel found that the prohibition on quantitative restrictions in Article XI:1 applied to a system of minimum import prices.[174]
- In *Japan – Agricultural Products I*, the Panel ruled that the prohibition of Article XI:1 applied to import restrictions made effective through an import monopoly, or more broadly through State trading operations.[175]
- In *India – Quantitative Restrictions*, the Panel held that non-automatic import licensing systems are import restrictions prohibited by Article XI:1.[176]

Unlike other GATT provisions, Article XI refers not to laws or regulations but more broadly to measures. A measure instituted or maintained by a Member which restricts imports or exports is covered by Article XI, *irrespective* of the legal status of the measure.[177] In *Japan – Semi-Conductors*, the Panel therefore ruled that *non-mandatory* measures of the Japanese Government, restricting the export of certain semi-conductors at below-cost price, were nevertheless 'restrictions' within the meaning of Article XI:1.[178]

Note that, in addition, quantitative restrictions which do not *actually* impede trade are nevertheless prohibited under Article XI:1 of the GATT 1994.[179] The Panel in *EEC – Oilseeds I* ruled in this respect in 1990:

> the CONTRACTING PARTIES have consistently interpreted the basic provisions of the General Agreement on restrictive trade measures as provisions establishing conditions of competition. Thus they decided that an import quota constitutes an import restriction within the meaning of Article XI:1 whether or not it actually impeded imports.[180]

On the other hand, the Panel in *EEC – Minimum Import Prices* found in 1978 that automatic import licensing does not

> constitute a restriction of the type meant to fall under the purview of Article XI:1.[181]

---

[174] See GATT Panel Report, *EEC – Minimum Import Prices*, para. 4.14. Also, restrictions on exports below a certain price fall within the scope of application of Article XI:1. See GATT Panel Report, *Japan – Semi-Conductors*, para. 117.

[175] See GATT Panel Report, *Japan – Agricultural Products I*, para. 5.2.2.2. The Panel noted that its finding was confirmed by the Note *Ad* Articles XI, XII, XIII, XIV and XVIII, according to which the concept of 'import restrictions' throughout these Articles covers restrictions made effective through State trading operations. Note, however, that the mere fact that imports are affected through State trading enterprises does not in itself constitute a restriction within the meaning of Article XI. For such a restriction to be found to exist, it should be shown that the operation of this State trading entity is such as to result in a restriction. See Panel Report, *India – Quantitative Restrictions*, para. 5.134.

[176] See Panel Report, *India – Quantitative Restrictions*, para. 5.130. For an explanation of a 'non-automatic import licensing system', see below, p. 460.

[177] See GATT Panel Report, *Japan – Semi-Conductors*, para. 106.

[178] *Ibid.*, paras. 104–17. The Panel considered that, in order to determine whether the *non-mandatory* measures were measures falling within the scope of Article XI, it needed to be satisfied on two essential criteria: first, there were reasonable grounds to believe that sufficient incentives or disincentives existed for non-mandatory measures to take effect; second, the operation of the measures was essentially dependent on government action or intervention. The Panel considered that, if these two criteria were met, the measures would be operating in a manner equivalent to mandatory requirements such that the difference between the measures and mandatory requirements was only one of form and not one of substance, and that there could therefore be no doubt that they fell within the scope of Article XI:1.

[179] Such non-biting quotas, i.e. quotas above current levels of trade, cause increased transaction costs and create uncertainties which could affect investment plans. See GATT Panel Report, *Japan – Leather II (US)*, para. 55.   [180] GATT Panel Report, *EEC – Oilseeds I*, para. 150.

[181] GATT Panel Report, *EEC – Minimum Import Prices*, para. 4.1.

In *EC – Asbestos*, the question arose whether a French ban on the manufacturing, import and export, and domestic sales and transfer of certain asbestos and asbestos-containing products fell within the scope of the prohibition of quantitative restrictions in Article XI or the national treatment obligation of Article III. Recall in this respect the discussion on the respective scopes of Articles III and XI of the GATT 1994 in chapter 4 of this book.[182]

Recently, in *Brazil – Retreaded Tyres*, the European Communities claimed, *inter alia*, that the imposition of fines on the importation, marketing, transportation, storage, keeping and warehousing of imported retreaded tyres was inconsistent with Article XI:1 of the GATT 1994.[183] In addressing this claim, the Panel considered whether these fines, imposed by Brazil as an enforcement measure of the import prohibition, constituted a restriction on importation within the meaning of Article XI:1. The Panel reached the following conclusion:

> what is important in considering whether a measure falls within the types of measures covered by Article XI:1 is the nature of the measure. In the present case, we note that the fines as a whole, including that on marketing, have the effect of penalizing the act of 'importing' retreaded tyres by subjecting retreaded tyres already imported and existing in the Brazilian internal market to the prohibitively expensive rate of fines. To that extent, we consider that the fact that the fines are not administered at the border does not alter their nature as a restriction on importation within the meaning of Article XI:1. In addition, the level of the fines – R$ 400 per unit, which significantly exceeds the average prices of domestically produced retreaded tyres for passenger cars (R$ 100–280) – is significant enough to have a restrictive effect on importation.[184]

Finally, note that restrictions of a *de facto* nature are also prohibited under Article XI:1 of the GATT 1994. A quantitative restriction within the meaning of Article XI:1 is thus not necessarily a measure that sets an explicit numerical ceiling. Also, a measure which has in fact that effect is a quantitative restriction within the meaning of Article XI:1. In *Argentina – Hides and Leather*, the issue arose whether Argentina violated Article XI:1 by authorising the presence of domestic tanners' representatives in the customs inspection procedures for hides destined for export operations. According to the European Communities, the complainant in this case, Argentina imposed a *de facto* restriction on the exportation of hides inconsistent with Article XI:1. The Panel ruled:

> There can be no doubt, in our view, that the disciplines of Article XI:1 extend to restrictions of a *de facto* nature.[185]

However, the Panel concluded with respect to the Argentinian regulation providing for the presence of the domestic tanners' representatives in the customs inspection procedures that there was insufficient evidence that this regulation really operated as an export restriction inconsistent with Article XI:1 of the GATT 1994.[186]

---

[182] See above, pp. 346–7.
[183] See Panel Report, *Brazil – Retreaded Tyres*, para. 7.361. This finding was not appealed.
[184] *Ibid.*, para. 7.372.
[185] Panel Report, *Argentina – Hides and Leather*, para. 11.17. In support of this finding, the Panel referred to the GATT Panel Report in *Japan – Semi-Conductors*, paras. 105–9.
[186] See Panel Report, *Argentina – Hides and Leather*, para. 11.55.

The general prohibition on quantitative restrictions set out in Article XI:1 of the GATT 1994 is, however, not without exceptions. The many and broad exceptions discussed in chapter 7 of this book are most important in this respect.[187] In addition, note that Article XI itself provides for a few exceptions in its second paragraph. Note in particular Article XI: 2(a) which allows for export prohibitions or restrictions temporarily applied to prevent or relieve critical shortages of foodstuffs or other products essential to the exporting Member.[188]

Questions and Assignments 5.13

Are quantitative restrictions allowed under WTO law? To which measures does Article XI:1 of the GATT 1994 apply? Is the scope of application of Article XI:1 limited to mandatory measures? Give four examples of quantitative restrictions which panels and/or the Appellate Body have found to be inconsistent with Article XI:1. Is a quantitative restriction which does not actually impede trade inconsistent with Article XI:1? Give an example of a *de facto* quantitative restriction. Is such a restriction consistent with Article XI:1? Can a WTO Member in times of a national or international food crisis prohibit the export of foodstuffs?

5.3.2.2. *Rules on quantitative restrictions on specific products*

Under the GATT 1947, the prohibition against quantitative restrictions was often *not* respected. The Panel in *Turkey – Textiles* noted:

> From early in the GATT, in sectors such as agriculture, quantitative restrictions were main-tained and even increased . . . In the sector of textiles and clothing, quantitative restrictions were maintained under the Multifibre Agreement . . . Certain contracting parties were even of the view that quantitative restrictions had gradually been tolerated and accepted as negotiable and that Article XI could not be, and had never been considered to be, a provision prohibiting such restrictions irrespective of the circumstances specific to each case.[189]

However, the overall detrimental effect of these quantitative restrictions in the sectors of agriculture and textiles was generally recognised. Therefore, the elimination of these quantitative restrictions was high on the agenda of the Uruguay Round negotiations (1986–93). As a result, the *Agreement on Agriculture* and the *Agreement on Textiles and Clothing* contain specific rules regarding the elimination of quantitative restrictions on agricultural products and textile products respectively.

The *Agreement on Agriculture* provides that quantitative import restrictions and voluntary export restraints, *inter alia*, must be converted into tariffs and that no

---

[187] See below, pp. 614–739.
[188] To the extent Article XI:2 allows the use of quantitative restrictions on the *importation* of agricultural products, this provision has been set aside by Article 4.2 of the *Agreement on Agriculture* (see Article 21.1 of the *Agreement on Agriculture*).
[189] Panel Report, *Turkey – Textiles*, para. 9.64. Note that the argument of certain Contracting Parties that Article XI could not be a provision prohibiting quantitative restrictions irrespective of the circumstances in which they were imposed, in a specific case, was explicitly rejected by the GATT Panel in *EEC – Import Restrictions*.

new restrictions of this kind can be adopted. Article 4.2 of the *Agreement on Agriculture* states:

> Members shall not maintain, resort to, or revert to any measures of the kind which have been required to be converted into ordinary customs duties, except as otherwise provided for in Article 5 and Annex 5.

In footnote 1 to this provision, the measures which had to be converted into tariffs (or tariff quotas) were identified as: quantitative import restrictions, variable import levies, minimum import prices, discretionary import licensing, non-tariff measures maintained through State trading enterprises, voluntary export restraints, and similar border measures other than ordinary customs duties.[190] The process of converting these non-tariff measures into tariffs is commonly referred to as the 'tariffication process'. As this process provided for the replacement of non-tariff measures with a tariff which afforded *an equivalent level of protection*, many of the tariffs resulting from the 'tariffication process' are very high.[191] However, by introducing a system of tariff quotas, it was possible to guarantee:

- that the quantities imported before Article 4.2 of the *Agreement on Agriculture* took effect could continue to be imported; and
- that some new quantities were subject to tariffs that were not prohibitive.

Under this system of tariff quotas, lower tariffs applied to specified quantities (in-quota quantities), while higher (often prohibitive) tariffs applied to quantities that exceed the quota (over-quota quantities).[192]

With respect to the relationship between Article 4.2 of the *Agreement on Agriculture* and Article XI of the GATT 1994, the Panel in *Korea – Various Measures on Beef* stated that:

> when dealing with measures relating to agricultural products which should have been converted into tariffs or tariff-quotas, a violation of Article XI of GATT . . . would necessarily constitute a violation of Article 4.2 of the *Agreement on Agriculture* and its footnote.[193]

As mentioned above, trade in textiles and clothing largely 'escaped' from the GATT 1947 rules and disciplines, and in particular the prohibition of Article XI on quantitative restrictions. Under the *Multifibre Agreement* (MFA), in effect from 1974, developed and developing countries, respectively importing and exporting textiles, entered into bilateral agreements requiring the exporting developing countries to limit their exports of certain categories of textiles and clothing. In

---

[190] Note that measures maintained under balance-of-payments provisions or under other general, non-agriculture-specific provisions of the GATT 1994 or of the other Multilateral Trade Agreements in Annex 1A to the *WTO Agreement* did not need to be converted into tariffs.

[191] The tariffs resulting from the 'tariffication process' concern, on average, one-fifth of the total number of agricultural tariff lines in the tariffs of developed-country Members.

[192] Note that developed-country Members also agreed during the Uruguay Round negotiations to reduce all tariffs on agricultural products (and the over-quota tariffs in the case of tariff quotas) by an average of 36 per cent, in equal steps over six years. Developing-country Members agreed to reduce these tariffs by 24 per cent over ten years. See Uruguay Round Schedules of Concessions.

[193] Panel Report, *Korea – Various Measures on Beef*, para. 7.62.

1995, the main importing countries had eighty-one such restraint agreements with exporting countries, comprising over a thousand individual quotas.[194] The MFA, which was negotiated within the framework of the GATT, provided a 'legal cover' for the GATT-inconsistency of these quotas.[195] The *Agreement on Textiles and Clothing* (ATC) negotiated during the Uruguay Round sought to address this situation and contained specific rules for quantitative restrictions on textiles and clothing. The Panel in *US –Underwear* stated:

> the overall purpose of the ATC is to integrate the textiles and clothing sector into GATT 1994. Article 1 of the ATC makes this point clear. To this effect, the ATC requires notification of all existing quantitative restrictions (Article 2 of the ATC) and provides that they will have to be terminated by the year 2004 (Article 9 of the ATC).[196]

The 'integration process', provided for in the ATC, was to be carried out in four stages. At each stage, products amounting to a certain minimum percentage of the volume of a Member's 1990 imports of textiles and clothing were made fully subject to the disciplines of the GATT 1994, including the prohibition on quantitative restrictions of Article XI.[197] Moreover, the level of the remaining QR was to be increased annually.[198] Note, however, that this integration process applied to *all* textile products listed in the ATC, including products on which there were no quantitative restrictions. This allowed the United States and the European Communities, during the first stages, to integrate mainly products on which there were *no* quantitative restrictions into the GATT 1994.[199] To the discontent and disappointment of the textile-exporting Members, the two major importing Members could at least initially meet their obligations under the ATC without significantly removing quantitative restrictions. The United States and the European Communities removed most of the quantitative restrictions only in the fourth and last stage, ending on 1 January 2005.

As the last stage of the implementation of the ATC drew to an end in 2004, a number of smaller, textile-producing developing-country Members, which had thus far enjoyed guaranteed quota access, feared that they would encounter serious adjustment problems as their textile exports could not compete with the textile exports of the large textile-producing developing-country Members, such

---

[194] In addition, there were also a number of non-MFA (*Multifibre Agreement*) agreements or unilateral measures restricting the imports of textiles and clothing. See *Business Guide to the World Trading System*, 2nd edition (International Trade Centre/ Commonwealth Secretariat, 1999), 164.   [195] *Ibid.*, 165.

[196] Panel Report, *US – Underwear*, para. 7.19.

[197] The minimum percentages of the volume of imports that must be made subject to the GATT 1994 disciplines are:

- 16 per cent on the date of entry into force of the Agreement on Textiles and Clothing (1 January 1995);
- 17 per cent at the end of the third year (1 January 1998);
- 18 per cent at the end of the seventh year (1 January 2002); and
- the balance, up to 49 per cent, at the end of the tenth year (1 January 2005).

See Articles 2.6 and 2.7 of the *Agreement on Textiles and Clothing*.

[198] The quotas were increased by 16 per cent per year from 1995 to 1997, by 25 per cent per year from 1998 to 2001 and by 27 per cent per year from 2002 to 2004. In 2005, all quotas were terminated. See Articles 2.13 and 2.14 of the *Agreement on Textiles and Clothing*.

[199] Note that the percentage of imports of products on which there were no quantitative restrictions in the reference year, 1990, was 34 per cent for the United States and 37 per cent for the European Communities. See *Business Guide to the World Trading System*, 2nd edition (International Trade Centre/Commonwealth Secretariat, 1999), 165.

as China, India and Brazil. Their fears have proven to be justified. While the integration process of the ATC has been successfully completed and quantitative restrictions on textiles terminated, the benefits of this return to GATT discipline have been unevenly spread. The *Financial Times* reported in 2005 on the situation after the liberalisation of the international trade in textiles as follows:

> China and India have been the main beneficiaries so far of the scrapping of global quotas for textiles and clothing . . .
>
> The main losers since the lifting of quotas have been smaller textile and clothing producers in Africa, the Americas and Europe, according to the ILO's analysis of developments in the first half of 2005. The decades-old Multi-Fibre Arrangement came to an end on December 31, 2004, after a 10-year phase-out . . .
>
> China, the world's dominant exporter of both textiles and clothing, boosted its exports of textiles by 20 per cent and of clothing by nearly 23 per cent in the first seven months of this year, pushing its share of global clothing trade to 28 per cent . . .
>
> [Like China] Bangladesh, Pakistan, Sri Lanka, Cambodia and India also saw higher export deliveries to the US market, though there were losses for South Korea, Taiwan, Mauritius, Lesotho and Costa Rica.
>
> Clothing exports to the EU showed a slightly different pattern. India increased its deliveries by a quarter in the first half of 2005, but the other countries with positive growth rates were mainly EU members such as Austria, Denmark and Germany.
>
> Overall, in the world clothing market, the main losers this year have been South Korea, Taiwan . . .
>
> Most Latin American textile and clothing producers have also lost market share, the ILO report says.[200]

When several developing-country Members, including Jordan, Morocco, Tunisia and Turkey, suggested that the WTO should address the problems of small developing-country Members adversely affected by the elimination of quotas (problems including low world prices, fierce competition from China and India and the risk of losing market share in the EU and US), China, Brazil, India and Hong Kong objected to the inclusion of this issue on the agenda of the Council for Trade in Goods.[201] As reported in *BRIDGES Weekly Trade News Digest*:

> The Chinese responded forcefully against the idea of continued work in the Goods Council on textiles, noting that the quota system, which expired with the Agreement on Textiles and Clothing on 1 January 2005, discriminated against China and hurt the Chinese people. The WTO's job, argued China, was to promote trade competition, not to stabilise market prices. Indian diplomats also said that their country opposed special measures for particular industries.[202]

5.3.2.3. Voluntary export restraints

Voluntary export restraints (VERs) are actions taken by exporting countries involving a self-imposed *quantitative restriction* of exports. VERs are taken either unilaterally or under the terms of an agreement or arrangement between two or

---

[200] F. Williams, 'China and India Gain from End of Quotas', *Financial Times*, 25 October 2005.
[201] See *BRIDGES Weekly Trade News Digest*, 18 May 2005.
[202] *BRIDGES Weekly Trade News Digest*, 22 June 2005.

more countries. As the term indicates, in theory, VERs are entered into on a voluntary basis, i.e. the exporting country *voluntarily* limits the volume of its exports. However, in reality, this is usually not the case. A 1984 GATT report correctly observed:

> It appeared . . . that exporting countries which accepted so-called 'grey-area' actions did so primarily because . . . they felt that they had little choice and that the alternative was, or would have been, unilateral action in the form of quantitative restrictions, harassment by anti-dumping investigations, countervailing action . . . involving greater harm to their exports in terms of quantity or price.[203]

Under the GATT 1947, the legality of voluntary export restraints was a much-debated issue. Since the entry into force of the *WTO Agreement*, this issue has been definitively decided. The WTO *Agreement on Safeguards* specifically prohibits voluntary export restraints.[204] Article 11.1(b) of the *Agreement on Safeguards* provides:

> a Member shall not seek, take or maintain any voluntary export restraints, orderly marketing arrangements or any other similar measures on the export or the import side.[205]

Article 11.1(b) of the *Agreement on Safeguards* furthermore provides:

> Any such measure in effect on the date of entry into force of the WTO Agreement shall be brought into conformity with this Agreement or phased out in accordance with paragraph 2.

Pursuant to Article 11.2, all voluntary export restraints had to be phased out (or brought into compliance with the *Agreement on Safeguards*) before the end of 1999.

5.3.3. Administration of quantitative restrictions

Article XI:1 of the GATT 1994 prohibits quantitative restrictions. There are, however, as noted above, many exceptions to this prohibition of Article XI:1. Article XIII of the GATT 1994 bears testimony to this by setting out rules on the *administration* of quantitative restrictions. This section will address:

- the rule of non-discrimination;
- the rules on the distribution of trade; and
- the rules on import licensing procedures.

While tariff quotas are not quantitative restrictions, the rules on the administration of quantitative restrictions set out in Article XIII, and discussed in this section, also apply to the administration of tariff quotas. Article XIII:5 of the GATT 1994 states, in relevant part:

> The provisions of this Article shall apply to any tariff quota instituted or maintained by any [Member].[206]

---

[203] Report of the Chairman of the Safeguards Committee, BISD 30S/216, 218.
[204] For a detailed discussion of the *Agreement on Safeguards*, see below, pp. 670–92.
[205] Footnote 4 to this provision contains an illustrative list of 'similar measures', including export moderation, export-price or import-price monitoring systems, export or import surveillance, compulsory import cartels and discretionary export or import licensing schemes, any of which afford protection.
[206] See also Panel Report, *US – Line Pipe*, para. 7.58.

Note that many of the disputes on Article XIII were in fact related to the administration of tariff quotas.[207] This section therefore includes some examples of tariff quotas applied by the European Communities.

5.3.3.1. *Rule of non-discrimination*

Article XIII:1 of the GATT 1994 provides that quantitative restrictions, when applied, should be administered in a non-discriminatory manner. Article XIII:1 states:

> No prohibition or restriction shall be applied by any [Member] on the importation of any product of the territory of any other [Member] or on the exportation of any product destined for the territory of any other [Member], unless the importation of the like product of all third countries or the exportation of the like product to all third countries is *similarly prohibited or restricted*.
>
> [Emphasis added]

What Article XIII:1 requires is that, if a Member imposes a quantitative restriction on products to or from another Member, products to or from all other countries are 'similarly prohibited or restricted'. This requirement of Article XIII:1 is an MFN-like obligation. As the Appellate Body noted in *EC – Bananas III*, the essence of the non-discrimination obligations of Articles I:1 *and* XIII of the GATT 1994 is that:

> like products should be treated equally, irrespective of their origin.[208]

The GATT Panel in *EEC – Apples I (Chile)* found that the European Communities had acted inconsistently with the non-discrimination obligation of Article XIII:1. The importation of apples from Argentina, Australia, New Zealand and South Africa had been restricted through voluntary restraint agreements negotiated and concluded with these countries. The European Communities tried to reach agreement on a similar voluntary restraint agreement with Chile but the negotiations failed. The European Communities subsequently adopted measures restricting the importation of Chilean apples to approximately 42,000 tonnes. The Panel in *EEC – Apples I (Chile)* found that the measures applied to imports from Chile by the European Communities were *not* a restriction *similar* to the voluntary restraint agreements negotiated with the other countries and therefore were a violation of Article XIII:1. The Panel came to this conclusion primarily on the basis that:

- there was a difference in transparency between the two types of action;
- there was a difference in the administration of the restrictions, the one being an import restriction, the other an export restraint; and
- the import restriction was unilateral and mandatory while the other was voluntary and negotiated.[209]

---

[207] See e.g. the controversial administration of the tariff quotas under the EC's import regime for bananas (*EC – Bananas III*) or for poultry (*EC – Poultry*). See also the tariff quotas at issue in *US – Line Pipe*.
[208] Appellate Body Report, *EC – Bananas III*, para. 190.
[209] See GATT Panel Report, *EEC – Apples I (Chile)*, para. 4.11.

5.3.3.2. Rules on the distribution of trade

If quantitative restrictions, other than a prohibition or ban, are applied on the importation of a product, the question arises how the trade that is still allowed will be distributed among the different Members exporting that product. The chapeau of Article XIII:2 of the GATT 1994 provides in this respect:

> In applying import restrictions to any product, [Members] shall aim at a distribution of trade in such product approaching as closely as possible the shares which the various [Members] might be expected to obtain in the absence of such restrictions.

In *EC – Bananas III*, the reallocation of non-utilised tariff quotas only among those countries that concluded the Banana Framework Agreement with the European Communities was found to be inconsistent with Article XIII:2, as the reallocation failed to approximate, in the administration of tariff quotas, the relative trade flows which would exist in the absence of the tariff quotas.[210]

The GATT 1994 thus favours a distribution of trade as close as possible to that which would have been the distribution of trade in the absence of the quantitative restriction. Furthermore, Article XIII:2 sets out a number of requirements to be met when imposing quantitative restrictions. Article XIII:2(a) states:

> Wherever practicable, quotas representing the total amount of permitted imports (whether allocated among supplying countries or not) shall be fixed, and notice given of their amount in accordance with paragraph 3(b) of this Article.

When imposing a quantitative restriction, a quota – whether global or allocated among the supplying countries – is preferred.[211] In cases in which a quota is allocated among supplying countries, Article XIII:2(d) provides:

> the [Member] applying the restrictions may seek agreement with respect to the allocation of shares in the quota with all other [Members] having a substantial interest in supplying the product concerned.

However, when this method of allocating the shares in the quota 'is not reasonably practicable', i.e. when no agreement can be reached with *all* the Members having a substantial interest, the Member applying the quota:

> shall allot to [Members] having a substantial interest in supplying the product shares based upon the proportions, supplied by such [Members] during a previous representative period, of the total quantity or value of imports of the product, due account being taken of any special factors which may have affected or may be affecting the trade in the product.

In other words, if no agreement can be reached, the quota must be allocated among the Members having a substantial interest on the basis of their share of the trade during a previous representative period. It is normal GATT practice to

---

[210] See Appellate Body Report, *EC – Bananas III*, para. 163.
[211] In cases in which a quota is not practicable, Article XIII:2(b) provides that the quantitative restrictions may be applied by means of import licences or permits without a quota.

use a three-year period prior to the imposition of the quota as the 'representative period'.[212] The Panel in *US – Line Pipe* found:

> There is nothing in the record before the Panel to suggest that the line pipe measure was based in any way on historical trade patterns in line pipe, or that the United States otherwise 'aim[ed] at a distribution of trade . . . approaching as closely as possible the shares which the various Members might be expected to obtain in the absence of' the line pipe measure. Instead, as noted by Korea, 'the in-quota import volume originating from Korea, the largest supplier historically to the US market, was reduced to the same level as the smallest – or even then non-existent – suppliers to the US market (9,000 short tons)'. For this reason, we find that the line pipe measure is inconsistent with the general rule contained in the chapeau of Article XIII:2.[213]

Quotas allocated among supplying countries *must* be allocated among all Members having a *substantial interest* in supplying the product.[214] There is no additional obligation to allocate a part of the quota to Members *without* a substantial interest in supplying the product concerned. While the requirement of Article XIII:2(d) is not expressed as an exception to the basic non-discrimination requirement of Article XIII:1, it may be regarded, to the extent that its practical application is inconsistent with it, as a *lex specialis*.[215] It allows for the discrimination between Members with and Members without a substantial interest in supplying the product at issue. Their imports of that product are not 'similarly' restricted.

In *EC – Bananas III*, the Panel addressed the question of whether quota shares or tariff quota shares (as they were *in casu*) can also be allocated to Members that do not have a substantial interest in supplying the product at issue. According to the Panel, quota shares and tariff quota shares *can* be allocated to Members with minor market shares. The Panel ruled:

> we note that the first sentence of Article XIII:2(d) refers to allocation of a quota 'among supplying countries'. This could be read to imply that an allocation may also be made to Members that do not have a substantial interest in supplying the product.[216]

However, if a Member wishes to allocate quota shares or tariff quota shares to some Members with minor market shares, then such shares must be allocated to all such Members. If not, imports from Members would not be 'similarly restricted' as required by Article XIII:1 of the GATT 1994.[217] Moreover, the same method as was used to allocate the shares to the Members having a substantial interest in supplying the product would be required to be used. Otherwise, the non-discrimination obligation of Article XIII:1 would not be met.[218]

If a Member wishes to allocate a part of the quota or tariff quota to Members with minor market shares, then this is best done by providing – next to country-specific quota shares for Members with a substantial interest – for an 'others'

---

[212] See GATT Panel Report, *EEC – Apples I (Chile)*, para. 4.16; and GATT Panel Report, *EEC – Dessert Apples*, para. 12.22.   [213] Panel Report, *US – Line Pipe*, para. 7.55.

[214] As discussed above, a share of 10 per cent of the market of the Member applying the quota has generally been considered to be a 'significant share' of the market, required to claim a 'substantial interest'. See above, p. 427.   [215] See Panel Reports, *EC – Bananas III*, para. 7.75.   [216] *Ibid.*, para. 7.73.

[217] See above, pp. 454–5.   [218] See *ibid.*

category for all Members not having a substantial interest in supplying the product.[219] The use of an 'others' category is in conformity with the object and purpose of Article XIII (as expressed in the chapeau of Article XIII:2) to achieve a distribution of trade as close as possible to that which would have been the distribution of trade in the absence of the quantitative restriction.[220] The Panel in *EC – Bananas III* noted:

> When a significant share of a tariff quota is assigned to 'others', the import market will evolve with a minimum amount of distortion. Members not having a substantial supplying interest will be able, if sufficiently competitive, to gain market share in the 'others' category and possibly achieve 'substantial supplying interest' status . . . New entrants will be able to compete in the market, and likewise have an opportunity to gain 'substantial supplying interest' status.[221]

Questions and Assignments 5.14

How should quantitative restrictions be administered? Are the rules set out in Article XIII also applicable to the administration of measures other than quantitative restrictions? If the importation of a product is subject to a quota, how then shall the trade that is still allowed be distributed among the different Members exporting that product? Can a Member applying a quota, or tariff quota, allocate part of that quota, or tariff quota, to Members with minor market shares? If so, how is this done best? Give two examples other than those referred to above of the administration of tariff quotas by allocating country-specific tariff quota shares.

5.3.3.3. *Import-licensing procedures*

Quotas and tariff quotas are habitually administered through import-licensing procedures. Article 1.1 of the *Agreement on Import Licensing Procedures*, commonly referred to as the *Import Licensing Agreement*, defines import-licensing procedures as:

> administrative procedures . . . requiring the submission of an application or other documentation (other than that required for customs purposes) to the relevant administrative body as a prior condition for importation into the customs territory of the importing Member.[222]

A trader who wishes to import a product that is subject to a quota or tariff quota must apply for an import licence, i.e. a permit to import. Whether this

---

[219] The alternative is to allocate to all supplying countries, including Members with minor market shares, country-specific tariff quota shares. This method, however, is more likely to lead to a long-term freezing of market shares and a less competitive market. See also Panel Report, *EC – Bananas III*, para. 7.76.

[220] See *ibid.*, para. 7.76.   [221] *Ibid.*, para. 7.76.

[222] While Article 1.1 of the *Import Licensing Agreement* does not explicitly state that import licensing procedures for tariff quotas are import licensing procedures within the meaning of Article 1.1, the Appellate Body in *EC – Bananas III* ruled that a careful reading of that provision 'leads inescapably to that conclusion'. As the Appellate Body noted, import licensing procedures for tariff quotas require 'the submission of an application' for import licences as 'a prior condition for importation' of a product at the lower in-quota tariff rate. See Appellate Body Report, *EC – Bananas III*, para. 193.

import licence will be granted depends on whether the quota is already filled or not, and on whether the trader meets the requirements for an import licence.[223]

Economists agree that a first-come, first-served distribution rule for import licences is the most economically efficient licensing method.[224] However, import-licensing rules and procedures are often much more complex, as was illustrated by the import licensing system for bananas at issue in *EC – Bananas III*.[225]

Article 1 of the *Import Licensing Agreement* sets out rules on the *application* and *administration* of import-licensing rules. The most important of these rules is set out in Article 1.3, which reads:

> The rules for import licensing procedures shall be neutral in application and administered in a fair and equitable manner.[226]

Moreover, Article 1.4 of the *Import Licensing Agreement* requires that the rules and all information concerning procedures for the submission of applications for import licences must be published in such a manner as to enable Members and traders to become acquainted with them.[227] In no event shall such a publication be later than the date on which the licence requirement becomes effective.[228] Any exceptions, derogations or changes in or from the rules concerning licensing procedures or the list of products subject to import licensing shall also be published in the same manner and within the same period.[229] In *EC – Poultry*, Brazil argued that frequent changes to the EC licensing rules and procedures regarding the poultry tariff quota made it difficult for Members and traders to become familiar with the rules, contrary to the provisions of Article 1.4 and other provisions of the *Import Licensing Agreement*. The Panel rejected this complaint as follows:

> We note that the transparency requirement under the cited provisions is limited to publication of rules and other information. While we have sympathy for Brazil regarding the difficulties caused by the frequent changes to the rules, we find that changes in rules *per se* do not constitute a violation of Articles 1.4, 3.3, 3.5(b), 3.5(c) or 3.5(d).[230]

Articles 1.7 and 1.8 of the *Import Licensing Agreement* require that, in the administration and application of licensing rules, 'common sense' prevails. Small errors or variations may not have major adverse consequences. For example, an application for an import licence shall not be refused for minor documentation errors, which do not alter basic data contained therein.[231]

---

[223] This would be an example of non-automatic import licensing. As discussed below, there is also automatic import licensing, but this would not occur with respect to the importation of a product that is subject to a quota or tariff quota. See below, p. 460.

[224] See e.g. P. Lindert and T. Pugel, *International Economics*, 10th edition (McGraw Hill, 1996).

[225] See Panel Reports, *EC – Bananas III*, paras. 7.142–7.273.

[226] On this provision, see Appellate Body Report, *EC – Bananas III*, para. 197.

[227] See Article 1.4(a) of the *Import Licensing Agreement*. The rules and information concerned include rules and information on the eligibility of persons, firms and institutions to make such applications and the administrative body(ies) to be approached.

[228] See *ibid*. Whenever practicable, the publication shall take place twenty-one days prior to the effective date.   [229] See *ibid*.   [230] Panel Report, *EC – Poultry*, para. 246.

[231] See Article 1.7 of the *Import Licensing Agreement*.

The *Import Licensing Agreement* distinguishes between automatic and non-automatic import licensing. *Automatic import licensing* is defined as import licensing where approval of the application is granted *in all cases*.[232] Automatic import licensing may be maintained to collect statistical and other information on imports. Article 2.2 of the *Import Licensing Agreement* requires that automatic import-licensing procedures shall not be administered in such a manner as to have 'restricting effects on imports subject to automatic licensing'. *Non-automatic import licensing* is import licensing where approval is *not* granted in all cases. Import-licensing procedures for quotas and tariff quotas are by definition non-automatic import-licensing procedures. Note, for example, that Saudi Arabia requires non-automatic import licences for certain 'distillation equipment' due to the fact that the latter has been used to produce alcoholic beverages in the past. Since alcohol is generally prohibited in Saudi Arabia it has decided therefore to establish an import licence requirement for certain distillation equipment. Those are granted by the Ministry of Commerce and Industry.[233] Article 3.2 of the *Import Licensing Agreement* requires that:

> Non-automatic licensing shall not have trade-restrictive or distortive effects on imports additional to those caused by the imposition of the restriction.

Other requirements relating to non-automatic import licensing concern:

- the non-discrimination among applicants for import licences;[234]
- the obligation to give reasons for refusing an application;[235]
- the right of appeal or review of the decisions on applications;[236]
- time-limits for processing applications;[237]
- the validity of import licences;[238] and
- the desirability of issuing licences for products in economic quantities.[239]

Questions and Assignments 5.15

What are import-licensing procedures and how do they relate to quotas and tariff quotas? How are import licensing rules to be applied and administered? What is the difference between automatic and non-automatic import licensing? Are they subject to different requirements?

5.3.4. Other non-tariff barriers

In addition to customs duties and other duties and charges (i.e. tariff barriers) and quantitative restrictions (i.e. the first subcategory of non-tariff barriers), trade in goods is also impeded by 'other non-tariff barriers'. As the term

---

[232] See Article 2.1 of the *Import Licensing Agreement*.
[233] See Report of the Working Party on the Accession of the Kingdom of Saudi Arabia to the WTO, WT/ACC/SAU/61, dated November 2005, para. 149.   [234] See Article 3.5(e) of the *Import Licensing Agreement*.
[235] See *ibid*.   [236] See *ibid*.   [237] See Article 3.5(f) of the *Import Licensing Agreement*.
[238] See Article 3.5(g) of the *Import Licensing Agreement*.   [239] See Article 3.5(h) of the *Import Licensing Agreement*.

indicates, this is a *residual* category of measures and actions that restrict, to various degrees and in different ways, market access for goods.[240] The category of 'other non-tariff barriers' covers numerous rather different measures and actions, such as technical barriers to trade, customs formalities and procedures, and government procurement practices. With regard to technical barriers to trade, one must distinguish between:

- the general category of technical barriers to trade, including technical regulations, standards and conformity assessment procedures for which rules have been set out in the *TBT Agreement*; and
- a special category of technical barriers to trade, namely, sanitary and phytosanitary measures, for which rules are provided in the *SPS Agreement*.

Not only action but also the absence of action, and in particular the failure to inform about the applicable trade laws, regulations, procedures and practices, promptly and accurately, may constitute a formidable barrier to trade. Also the unfair and arbitrary application of trade measures may constitute an important barrier to trade.

This section addresses the following other 'non-tariff barriers' to trade in goods:

- lack of transparency;
- unfair and arbitrary application of trade measures;
- customs formalities and procedures; and
- other measures or actions, such as preshipment inspection, marks of origin, government procurement practices and measures relating to transit shipments.

The rules on technical barriers to trade (technical regulations, standards, conformity assessment procedures and sanitary and phytosanitary measures are discussed in chapter 8.

5.3.4.1. Lack of transparency

As discussed above, ignorance, uncertainty or confusion with respect to the trade laws, regulations and procedures applicable in actual or potential export markets is an important barrier to trade. Therefore, WTO law provides for rules and procedures to ensure a high level of transparency of its Members' trade laws, regulations and procedures.

There are four kinds of relevant WTO rules and procedures:

- the *publication* requirement;
- the *notification* requirement;
- the requirement to establish *enquiry points*; and
- the trade policy *review* process.

---

[240] See e.g. *Table of Contents of the Inventory of Non-Tariff Measures*, Note by the Secretariat, TN/MA/S/5/Rev.1, dated 28 November 2003.

Article X of the GATT 1994, entitled 'Publication and Administration of Trade Regulations', states in its first paragraph:

> Laws, regulations, judicial decisions and administrative rulings of general application, made effective by any [Member], pertaining to the classification or the valuation of products for customs purposes, or to rates of duty, taxes or other charges, or to requirements, restrictions or prohibitions on imports or exports or on the transfer of payments therefor, or affecting their sale, distribution, transportation, insurance, warehousing, inspection, exhibition, processing, mixing or other use, shall be published promptly in such a manner as to enable governments and traders to become acquainted with them. Agreements affecting international trade policy which are in force between the government or a governmental agency of any [Member] and the government or governmental agency of any other [Member] shall also be published.

Article X:1 of the GATT 1994 thus requires Members to publish their laws, regulations, judicial decisions, administrative rulings of general application and international agreements relating to trade matters. Article X:1 does not prescribe in any detail how the laws, regulations, etc. have to be published but it does state that they have to be published 'promptly' and 'in such a manner as to enable governments and traders to become acquainted with them'.[241] In *EEC – Apples (US)*, the United States claimed that the European Communities acted inconsistently with, *inter alia*, Article X:1 by not giving 'adequate public notice' of the import quotas on the product at issue, apples. These import quotas applied to the period from 15 February to 31 August 1988, but the European Communities adopted the regulation setting forth these import quotas only on 20 April 1988 and published the regulation on the following day.[242] The Panel noted that:

> the EEC had observed the requirement of Article X:1 to publish the measures under examination 'promptly in such a manner as to enable governments and traders to become acquainted with them' through their publication in the Official Journal of the European Communities. It noted that no lapse of time between publication and entry into force was specified by this provision.[243]

The Panel, however, subsequently interpreted the requirements of Article X:2 of the GATT 1994, discussed below, as prohibiting backdated quotas, and concluded therefore that the European Communities had acted inconsistently with

---

[241] Note that these requirements do not explicitly apply to the publication of the international agreements, but it may be assumed that they also apply in this context. Moreover, note that Article X:1 does not require Members to disclose confidential information which would impede law enforcement or otherwise be contrary to the public interest or which would prejudice the legitimate commercial interests of particular enterprises, public or private. See Article X:1, last sentence, of the GATT 1994.

[242] See GATT Panel Report, *EEC – Apples (US)*, para. 3.41.

[243] *Ibid.*, para. 5.21. In *Canada – Provincial Liquor Boards (US)*, the Panel noted that Article X:1 required the prompt publication of trade regulations but did not require the publication of trade regulations *in advance* of their entry into force. The Panel also noted that Article X:1 did not require that information affecting trade be made available to domestic and foreign suppliers at the same time. See GATT Panel Report, *Canada – Provincial Liquor Boards (US)*, para. 5.34. Note that Article 2.12 of the *TBT Agreement* requires that 'Members shall allow a reasonable interval between the publication of technical regulations and their entry into force in order to allow time for producers in exporting Members . . . to adapt their products or methods of production to the requirement of the importing Member.' A similar provision is found in Annex B.2 of the *SPS Agreement*, see also Article X:2 of the GATT 1994, discussed below.

Article X:2 since it gave public notice of the quotas only about two months after the quota period had begun.[244]

With regard to the concept of 'administrative ruling of general application', note that, to the extent that an administrative ruling is addressed to a specific company or applied to a specific shipment, it cannot be qualified as an administrative ruling of general application. However, to the extent that an administrative ruling affects an unidentified number of economic operators, it can be qualified as a ruling of general application. The fact that a measure is country-specific does not preclude the possibility of it being an administrative ruling of general application.[245]

The Panel in *Dominican Republic – Import and Sale of Cigarettes* examined whether the surveys needed to make the tax determination for cigarettes were 'administrative rulings of general application'. It considered that the surveys themselves were not laws or regulations. However, if they had been used, they would have provided the basis for the administrative determination of the tax and as such were covered by the phrase 'administrative rulings of general application'.[246] As these surveys had not been published, the Panel found that the Dominican Republic had acted inconsistently with Article X:1.[247]

In addition to Article X:1, Article X:2 of the GATT 1994 also concerns the publication of trade measures of general application. Article X:2 provides:

> No measure of general application taken by any [Member] effecting an advance in a rate of duty or other charge on imports under an established and uniform practice, or imposing a new or more burdensome requirement, restriction or prohibition on imports, or on the transfer of payments therefor, shall be enforced before such measure has been officially published.

Pursuant to Article X:2, publication is therefore a condition of enforcement. Members may not enforce trade measures of general application, imposing restraints, requirements or other burdens, *before* they are published. Such measures will only take effect *after* publication.[248] With respect to the rationale of Article X:2, the Appellate Body noted in *US – Underwear*:

> Article X:2, *General Agreement*, may be seen to embody a principle of fundamental importance – that of promoting full disclosure of governmental acts affecting Members

---

[244] The Panel's reasoning was in fact based on its interpretation of Article XIII:3(b) and (c) as prohibiting backdated quotas. The Panel merely stated that it interpreted Article X:1 'likewise'. See GATT Panel Report, *EEC – Apples (US)*, para. 5.23.

[245] See Appellate Body Report, *US – Underwear*, 29. See also Appellate Body Report, *EC – Poultry*, paras. 111–13. Note that the Panel in *Japan – Film* stated that: 'it stands to reason that inasmuch as the Article X:1 requirement applies to all administrative rulings of general application, it also should extend to administrative rulings in individual cases where such rulings establish or revise principles or criteria applicable in future cases'. See Panel Report, *Japan – Film*, para. 10.388.

[246] See Panel Report, *Dominican Republic – Import and Sale of Cigarettes*, paras. 7.402–7.408.

[247] See *ibid.*, paras. 7.412–7.414.

[248] Note that, with respect to the issue of the retroactive effect of measures, the Appellate Body ruled in *US – Underwear* that prior publication as required by Article X:2 of the GATT 1994 cannot, in and of itself, justify the retroactive effect of a trade-restrictive measure. Article X:2 does not speak to, and hence does not resolve, the permissibility of giving retroactive effect to trade-restrictive measures. Where no authority exists to give retroactive effect to a trade-restrictive measure, that deficiency is not cured by publishing the measure some time before its actual application. See Appellate Body Report, *US – Underwear*, 29.

> and private persons and enterprises, whether of domestic or foreign nationality. The relevant policy principle is widely known as the principle of transparency and has obviously due process dimensions. The essential implication is that Members and other persons affected, or likely to be affected, by governmental measures imposing restraints, requirements and other burdens, should have a reasonable opportunity to acquire authentic information about such measures and accordingly to protect and adjust their activities or alternatively to seek modification of such measures.[249]

Note that the GATT 1994 and other WTO agreements also require Members to publish, or give public notice of, certain *specific* trade measures of general application.[250]

As noted above, WTO law also provides for a *notification* requirement. Almost all WTO agreements require Members to notify the WTO of measures or actions covered by these agreements. A typical example of such a notification requirement is found in Article 12.6 of the *Agreement on Safeguards*, which states:

> Members shall notify promptly the Committee on Safeguards of their laws, regulations and administrative procedures relating to safeguard measures as well as any modifications made to them.

A number of WTO agreements also provide for the possibility for a Member to notify measures or actions of other Members, which the latter failed to notify. Article 12.8 of the *Agreement on Safeguards*, for example, provides:

> Any Member may notify the Committee on Safeguards of all laws, regulations, administrative procedures and any measures or actions dealt with in this Agreement that have not been notified by other Members that are required by this Agreement to make such notifications.

The following list, annexed to the *Decision on Notification Procedures* of 1993,[251] contains measures and actions which Members must notify to the WTO:

- tariffs (including range and scope of bindings, GSP provisions, rates applied to members of free trade areas/customs unions, other preferences);
- tariff quotas and surcharges;
- quantitative restrictions, including voluntary export restraints and orderly marketing; arrangements affecting imports;
- other non-tariff measures such as licensing and mixing requirements; variable levies;
- customs valuation;
- rules of origin;
- government procurement;
- technical barriers;
- safeguard actions;

---

[249] *Ibid.*

[250] See e.g. Article XIII:3 of the GATT 1994 (concerning quotas and tariff quotas) and Article 2.11 of the *TBT Agreement* (concerning technical regulations).

[251] *Decision on Notification Procedures*, adopted by the Trade Negotiations Committee on 15 December 1993 and annexed to the Final Act Embodying the Results of the Uruguay Round of Multilateral Trade Negotiations, in *The Legal Texts: Results of the Uruguay Round of Multilateral Trade Negotiations* (Cambridge University Press, 1999), 388.

- anti-dumping actions;
- countervailing actions;
- export taxes;
- export subsidies, tax exemptions and concessionary export financing;
- free trade zones, including in-bond manufacturing;
- export restrictions, including voluntary export restraints and orderly marketing arrangements;
- other government assistance, including subsidies, tax exemptions;
- role of State trading enterprises;
- foreign exchange controls related to imports and exports;
- government-mandated countertrade; and
- any other measure covered by the Multilateral Trade Agreements in Annex 1A to the *WTO Agreement*.[252]

To improve the operation of the WTO notification requirements and thereby contribute to the transparency of Members' trade policies and measures, a *central registry of notifications* has been established under the responsibility of the WTO Secretariat. This central registry records the measures notified and the information provided by Members with respect to the purpose of the measure, its trade coverage and the requirement under which it has been notified. The central registry cross-references its records of notifications by Members and their obligations.[253] Information in the central registry regarding individual notifications is made available, on request, to any Member entitled to receive the notification concerned. The central registry informs each Member annually of the regular notification obligations to which that Member will be expected to respond in the course of the following year. It must be noted that many Members, and specially developing-country Members, fail to comply with one or more of their notification requirements. Often this failure is due to a lack of administration capacity and WTO expertise within the relevant ministries of the Members concerned.

In addition to a publication requirement and a notification requirement, some WTO agreements also require Members to establish national *enquiry points* where further information on certain trade laws and regulations can be obtained. Article 10.1 of the *TBT Agreement*, for example, provides:

> Each Member shall ensure that an enquiry point exists which is able to answer all reasonable enquiries from other Members and interested parties in other Members as well as to provide the relevant documents regarding:
>
> . . . any technical regulations adopted or proposed . . .
> . . . any standards adopted or proposed . . .
> . . . any conformity assessment procedures, or proposed conformity assessment procedures . . .

Note also that Article 10.4 of the *TBT Agreement* requires that Members take all reasonable measures available to them to ensure that where *copies of documents*

---

[252] See *ibid.*, 390.   [253] See *ibid.*, 388.

are requested by other Members or by interested parties, they are supplied, and are supplied at an equitable price (if any).

Finally, the transparency of Members' trade policies, legislation and procedures is also advanced considerably by the periodic trade policy reviews under the *Trade Policy Review Mechanism*. This mechanism is discussed in detail in chapter 2 of this book.[254]

Questions and Assignments 5.16

Why is the lack of transparency with respect to a country's trade laws, regulations and other measures of general application, a formidable barrier to trade in goods? How does WTO law seek to ensure transparency with respect to its Members' trade measures of general application?

5.3.4.2. *Unfair and arbitrary application of trade measures*

It is clear that the unfair and arbitrary application of national trade measures, and the degree of uncertainty and unpredictability this generates for other Members and traders, constitutes significant barriers to trade – in the same way as the lack of transparency discussed above. To ensure a fair and correct application of national trade measures, WTO law provides for:

- a requirement of uniform, impartial and reasonable administration of national trade rules; and
- a requirement for procedures for the objective and impartial review of the administration of national customs rules.

Article X:3(a) of the GATT provides:

> Each [Member] shall administer in a uniform, impartial and reasonable manner all its laws, regulations, decisions and rulings of the kind described in paragraph 1 of this Article.

As the words of Article X:3(a) clearly indicate, the requirements of 'uniformity, impartiality and reasonableness' do not apply to the laws, regulations, decisions and rulings *themselves*, but rather to the *administration* of those laws, regulations, decisions and rulings.[255] To the extent that the laws, regulations, decisions and rulings themselves are discriminatory, they may be found inconsistent with, for example, Articles I:1, III:2 or III:4 of the GATT 1994.[256] Note,

---

[254] See above, pp. 93–5.
[255] See Appellate Body Report, *EC – Bananas III*, para. 200. In *US – Corrosion-Resistant Steel Sunset Review*, Japan had claimed that US law 'as such' and 'as applied' was inconsistent with Article X:3(a). The Panel noted, however, that the 'as such' claim regarded content rather than administration of the law; and that the 'as applied' claim had not shown actual impact on the overall administration of US sunset review law. See Panel Report, *US – Corrosion-Resistant Steel Sunset Review*, paras. 7.284–7.310. In *US – Offset Act (Byrd Amendment)*, the Panel concluded that the measure was substantive in nature and therefore did not fall within the scope of Article X:3(a). See Panel Report, *US – Offset Act (Byrd Amendment)*, para. 7.145.
[256] See above, pp. 322–34, 344–90.

however, that the Appellate Body in *EC – Selected Customs Matters* reversed the Panel's finding that:

> *without exception*, Article X:3(a) of the GATT 1994 always relates to the application of laws and regulations, but not to laws and regulations as such.[257]
>
> [Emphasis added]

Nonetheless, it upheld the Panel's conclusion that:

> substantive differences in penalty laws and audit procedures among the member States of the European Communities alone do not constitute a violation of Article X:3(a) of the GATT 1994.[258]

Moreover, Article X:3(a) applies *not only* in situations where it is established that a Member, in the administration of its trade laws, regulations, decisions and rulings, discriminates between *Members*. In fact, the test under Article X:3(a) generally will not be whether there has been discriminatory treatment in favour of imports to, or exports from, one Member relative to another.[259] According to the Panel in *Argentina – Hides and Leather*:

> the focus is on the treatment accorded by government authorities to the *traders* in question.[260]
>
> [Emphasis added]

In *Argentina – Hides and Leather*, the Panel also found that the substance of administrative regulations, i.e. regulations providing for a certain manner of applying substantive rules, *can* be challenged under Article X:3(a).[261] At issue in that case was an Argentinian regulation providing for the participation of representatives of the domestic tanners' association, ADICMA, [262] in the customs inspection procedures for hides destined for export operations.[263] The representatives of ADICMA 'assisted' Argentina's customs authorities in the application and enforcement of the rules on customs classification, valuation and export duties. The European Communities, the complainant in *Argentina – Hides and Leather*, claimed that the presence of 'partial and interested' representatives of the domestic tanning industry made the application of the Argentinian customs rules in a 'uniform, impartial and reasonable manner' impossible.[264] The Panel first noted that:

> Article X:3(a) requires an examination of the real effect that a measure might have on traders operating in the commercial world. This, of course, does not require a showing of trade damage, as that is generally not a requirement with respect to violations of the GATT 1994. But it can involve an examination of whether there is a possible *impact on the competitive situation* due to alleged partiality, unreasonableness or lack of uniformity in the application of customs rules, regulations, decisions, etc.[265]
>
> [Emphasis added]

---

[257] Appellate Body Report, *EC – Selected Custom Matters*, para. 309(b)(i).   [258] *Ibid.*
[259] See Panel Report, *Argentina – Hides and Leather*, para. 11.76.   [260] *Ibid.*   [261] *Ibid.*, paras. 11.71–11.72.
[262] ADICMA stands for 'Association of Industrial Producers of Leather, Leather Manufactures and Related Products'.
[263] See also above, pp. 447–50.   [264] Panel Report, *Argentina – Hides and Leather*, para. 11.58.
[265] *Ibid.*, para. 11.77.

With regard to the requirement that national trade rules be applied in a uniform manner (the requirement of 'uniform administration'), the Panel found that there was no evidence that Argentina had applied the regulation at issue in a non-uniform manner with respect to hides.[266]

However, with respect to the requirement that national trade rules be applied in a reasonable manner (the requirement of 'reasonable administration'), the Panel found that:

> a process . . . which inherently contains the possibility of revealing confidential business information, is an unreasonable manner of administering the laws, regulations and rules identified in Article X:1 and therefore is inconsistent with Article X:3(a).[267]

Note that in *Dominican Republic – Import and Sale of Cigarettes*, the Panel found that the Dominican Republic had applied the provisions regarding the determination of the tax base for the imposition of tax on cigarettes in an unreasonable manner. According to the Panel:

> The fact that the Dominican Republic authorities did not support its decisions regarding the determination of the tax base for imported cigarettes by resorting to the rules in force at the time and that they decided to disregard retail selling prices of imported cigarettes, is not 'in accordance with reason', 'having sound judgement', 'sensible', 'within the limits of reason', nor 'articulate'.[268]

With respect to the requirement that national trade rules be applied in an impartial manner (the requirement of 'impartial administration'), the Panel in *Argentina – Hides and Leather* found:

> Whenever a party with a contrary commercial interest, but no relevant legal interest, is allowed to participate in an export transaction such as this, there is an inherent danger that the Customs laws, regulations and rules will be applied in a partial manner so as to permit persons with adverse commercial interests to obtain confidential information to which they have no right.[269]

While adequate safeguards could remedy such a situation, these safeguards were – according to the Panel – not in place. The Panel, therefore, ruled that the regulation at issue could not be considered an impartial administration of the customs laws and was, also for that reason, inconsistent with Article X:3(a) of the GATT 1994.

In *US – Stainless Steel*, Korea, the complainant, argued that the United States had violated Article X:3(a) by departing from its own established policy with respect to an important aspect of its anti-dumping investigation. The Panel rejected this claim of inconsistency. The Panel held that Article X:3(a) is:

> not . . . intended to function as a mechanism to test the consistency of a Member's particular decisions or rulings with the Member's own domestic law and practice; that is a function reserved for each Member's domestic judicial system.[270]

---

[266] See *ibid.*, para. 11.85. Note that the Panel stated in this context that Article X:3(a) should not be read as a broad anti-discrimination provision. According to the Panel, this provision does not require that all products be treated identically. There are many variations in products that might require differential treatment. See *ibid.*, para. 11.84.   [267] *Ibid.*, para. 11.94.

[268] Panel Report, *Dominican Republic – Import and Sale of Cigarettes*, para. 7.388.

[269] Panel Report, *Argentina – Hides and Leather*, para. 11.100.   [270] Panel Report, *US – Stainless Steel*, para. 6.50.

With regard to the requirements of 'uniform administration' and 'reasonable administration', the Panel in *US – Stainless Steel* stated:

> the requirement of uniform administration of laws and regulations must be understood to mean uniformity of treatment in respect of persons similarly situated; it cannot be understood to require identical results where relevant facts differ. Nor do we consider that the requirement of reasonable administration of laws and regulations is violated merely because, in the administration of those laws and regulations, different conclusions were reached based upon differences in the relevant facts.[271]

In *US – Shrimp*, the Appellate Body found:

> It is also clear to us that Article X:3 of the GATT 1994 establishes certain minimum standards for transparency and procedural fairness in the administration of trade regulations which, in our view, are not met here. The non-transparent and *ex parte* nature of the internal governmental procedures applied by the competent officials in the Office of Marine Conservation, the Department of State, and the United States National Marine Fisheries Service throughout the certification processes under Section 609, as well as the fact that countries whose applications are denied do not receive formal notice of such denial, nor of the reasons for the denial, and the fact, too, that there is no formal legal procedure for review of, or appeal from, a denial of an application, are all contrary to the spirit, if not the letter, of Article X:3 of the GATT 1994.[272]

Finally, note that the Appellate Body in *US – Oil Country Tubular Goods Sunset Reviews* cautioned WTO Members on bringing a case under Article X:3(a):

> We observe, first, that allegations that the conduct of a WTO Member is biased or unreasonable are serious under any circumstances. Such allegations should not be brought lightly, or in a subsidiary fashion. A claim under Article X:3(a) of the GATT 1994 must be supported by solid evidence; the nature and the scope of the claim, and the evidence adduced by the complainant in support of it, should reflect the gravity of the accusations inherent in claims under Article X:3(a) of the GATT 1994.[273]

The requirements of uniform, impartial and reasonable administration with regard to specific trade rules are also reflected in WTO agreements other than the GATT 1994. Article 1.3 of the *Import Licensing Agreement*, for example, provides:

> The rules for import licensing procedures shall be neutral in application and administered in a fair and equitable manner.[274]

The Appellate Body ruled in *EC – Bananas III* that Article 1.3 of the *Import Licensing Agreement* and Article X:3(a) of the GATT 1994 have 'identical coverage'.[275] In disputes involving the administration of import licensing procedures, Article 1.3 of the *Import Licensing Agreement* should be applied *first* since the *Import Licensing Agreement* deals specifically, and in detail, with the administration of import licensing procedures.[276]

---

[271] *Ibid.*, para. 6.51.   [272] Appellate Body Report, *US – Shrimp*, para. 183.
[273] Appellate Body Report, *US – Oil Country Tubular Goods Sunset Reviews*, para. 217.
[274] See also above, pp. 458–60.
[275] Appellate Body Report, *EC – Bananas III*, para. 203. The Appellate Body noted the difference in wording between Article 1.3 of the *Import Licensing Agreement* and Article X:3(a) of the GATT 1994, but considered that 'the two phrases are, for all practical purposes, interchangeable'.   [276] See *ibid.*, para. 204.

Apart from the requirements of Article X:3(a) that national trade rules be administered in a uniform, impartial and reasonable manner, WTO law contains – as noted above – a second rule to ensure the fair and correct application of national trade rules, namely, the requirement of procedures for the *objective and impartial review*, and possible correction, of the administration of national customs rules. Article X:3(b) of the GATT 1994 provides:

> Each [Member] shall maintain, or institute as soon as practicable, judicial, arbitral or administrative tribunals or procedures for the purpose, *inter alia*, of the prompt review and correction of administrative action relating to customs matters.

Article X:3(b) requires that these tribunals or procedures be independent of the agencies entrusted with administrative enforcement.[277] Their decisions must be implemented by, and shall govern the practice of, administrative enforcement agencies (unless an appeal is lodged with a court or tribunal of superior jurisdiction).[278]

In *EC – Selected Customs Matters*, the United States challenged the EC's administration of several laws and regulations concerning the valuation and classification of products for customs purposes because the procedures for review varied from EU Member State to EU Member State. The United States contested that it was not possible to obtain review of a customs decision within the meaning of Article X:3(b) of the GATT 1994 unless the importer or other interested party had exhausted review by national (i.e. EU Member State) administrative and/or judicial tribunals. The Panel in *EC – Selected Customs Matters* did *not* consider that:

> it would be reasonable to infer that first instance independent review tribunals and bodies, whose jurisdiction in most legal systems is normally limited in substantive and geographical terms, should have the authority to bind all agencies entrusted with administrative enforcement throughout the territory of a Member.[279]

Note that Article X:3(b) refers to 'administrative action relating to customs matters', i.e. the administration of *customs rules*, and not to the administration of the broader category of 'laws, regulations, decisions and rulings relating to trade matters' or, in short, the administration of *trade rules*. However, it could be argued that, with respect to trade rules other than customs rules, Members should also provide for procedures for the objective and impartial review of the administration of these rules.

5.3.4.3. *Customs formalities and procedures*

Another important type of 'other non-tariff barrier' to trade is customs formalities and procedures, i.e. administrative barriers to trade. The losses that traders suffer through delays at borders, complicated and/or unnecessary documentation requirements and lack of automation of customs trade procedures are estimated

---

[277] For situations in which the procedures are not fully or formally independent of the agencies entrusted with administrative enforcement, see Article X:3(c) of the GATT 1994.
[278] See Article X:3(b) of the GATT 1994.   [279] Panel Report, *EC – Selected Customs Matters*, para. 7.538.

to exceed, in many cases, the costs of tariffs. A 2001 UNCTAD study estimated that the average customs transaction involves:

- 20–30 different parties;
- 40 documents;
- 200 data elements (30 of which are repeated at least 30 times); and
- the re-keying of 60–70 per cent of all data at least once.[280]

At present, many small and medium-size companies are not active players in international trade and it is argued that this has more to do with red tape than with tariff barriers.[281] The administrative barriers for companies, who do not regularly export large quantities, are often simply too high to make foreign markets appear attractive.[282] Article VIII:1(c) of the GATT 1994 states:

> The [Members] . . . recognize the need for minimizing the incidence and complexity of import and export formalities and for decreasing and simplifying import and export documentation requirements.

Nevertheless, WTO law currently contains few rules on customs formalities and procedures aimed at mitigating their adverse impact on trade. Article VIII:2 requires Members, in very general terms, to 'review' the operation of their laws and regulations in the light of the acknowledged need for:

- minimising the incidence and complexity of customs formalities; and
- decreasing and simplifying documentation requirements.

Article VIII:3 of the GATT 1994 furthermore requires penalties for breaches of customs regulations and procedural requirements to be *proportional*. Article VIII:3 provides:

> No [Member] shall impose substantial penalties for minor breaches of customs regulations or procedural requirements. In particular, no penalty in respect of any omission or mistake in customs documentation which is easily rectifiable and obviously made without fraudulent intent or gross negligence shall be greater than necessary to serve merely as a warning.

In view of the paucity of substantive WTO rules with respect to customs formalities and procedures, the Ministerial Conference directed the Council for Trade in Goods at its Singapore Session in 1996, 'to undertake exploratory and analytical work . . . on the simplification of trade procedures in order to assess the scope for WTO rules in this area'.[283] In 2001, at its Doha Session, the Ministerial Conference agreed with regard to the simplification of trade procedures, commonly referred to as 'trade facilitation':

---

[280] See *Trade Facilitation: Cutting Red Tape at the Border*, Briefing Note, Ministerial Conference, December 2001, available at www.wto.org/english/thewto_e/minist_e/min01_e/brief_e/brief15_e.htm, visited on 15 November 2007.

[281] Note that, in many economies, small and medium-sized companies account for up to 60 per cent of GDP creation.

[282] See *Trade Facilitation: Cutting Red Tape at the Border*, Briefing Note, Ministerial Conference, December 2001, available at www.wto.org/english/thewto_e/minist_e/min01_e/brief_e/brief15_e.htm, visited on 15 November 2007.

[283] Ministerial Conference, *Singapore Ministerial Declaration*, adopted 13 December 1996, WT/MIN(96)/DEC, para. 21.

> that negotiations will take place after the Fifth Session of the Ministerial Conference on the basis of a decision to be taken, by explicit consensus, at that session on modalities of negotiations.[284]

However, at the Fifth Session of the Ministerial Conference, i.e. the Cancún Session in September 2003, Members failed to agree on the modalities of negotiations on any of the Singapore issues, including trade facilitation. Only in the summer of 2004 were Members able to agree on including trade facilitation on the agenda of the Doha Development Round.[285] Note that many developing-country Members are very hesitant to take on new WTO obligations regarding customs formalities and procedures. They are worried that, without a substantial increase of technical assistance to strengthen their administrative capacities and to support their national reform efforts, additional WTO rules on customs formalities and procedures will exceed their implementation capacities. The negotiations on trade facilitation in the context of the Doha Development Round have not yet produced any results.

Questions and Assignments 5.17

Are customs procedures and formalities significant barriers to trade? Are there any *specific* WTO rules on customs procedures and formalities? Does the Doha Development Round include negotiations on multilateral rules on customs procedures and formalities?

5.3.4.4. Other measures or actions

In addition to *technical barriers to trade*,[286] lack of transparency, unfair and arbitrary application of trade rules and customs formalities and procedures, the category of 'other non-tariff barriers' to trade in goods also includes many other measures or actions, or the lack thereof. This section briefly addresses the following 'other non-tariff barriers':

- preshipment inspection;
- marks of origin;
- government procurement practices; and
- measures relating to transit shipments.[287]

Preshipment inspection is the practice of employing private companies to check the price, quantity, quality and/or the customs classification of goods *before* their shipment to the importing country.[288] Preshipment inspection is primarily used

---

[284] Ministerial Conference, *Doha Ministerial Declaration*, adopted 14 November 2001, WT/MIN(01)/DEC/1, para. 27.
[285] See General Council, *Doha Work Programme*, Decision adopted on 1 August 2004, WT/L/579, dated 2 August 2004, para. 1(g).   [286] Note that technical barriers to trade are discussed in chapter 8.
[287] In addition, exchange controls or exchange restrictions (see Article XV:9 of the GATT 1994) and the operations of State trading enterprises (see Article XVII of the GATT 1994) can also constitute or create barriers to trade.   [288] See Article 1 of the *Agreement on Preshipment Inspection*.
[289] See Articles 2.1 and 2.2 of the *Agreement on Preshipment Inspection*.

by developing-country Members to prevent commercial fraud and evasion of customs duties. Preshipment inspection is used to compensate for inadequacies in national customs administrations. While certainly beneficial, the problem with preshipment inspection is that it may give rise to unnecessary delays or unequal treatment, and thus constitute a barrier to trade. The WTO *Agreement on Preshipment Inspection* sets out obligations for both importing Members using pre-shipment inspection and the exporting Members on whose territory the inspection is carried out. The importing Members using preshipment inspection must ensure, *inter alia*, that:

- preshipment inspection activities are carried out in a non-discriminatory manner;[289]
- preshipment inspection activities are carried out in a transparent manner;[290]
- the companies carrying out the inspection respect the confidentiality of business information received in the course of the preshipment inspection;[291] and
- the companies carrying out the inspection avoid unreasonable delays in the inspection of shipments.[292]

The exporting Members on whose territory the preshipment inspection is carried out must ensure non-discrimination and transparency with regard to their laws and regulations relating to preshipment inspection activities.[293] The *Agreement on Preshipment Inspection* also provides for rules on procedures for independent review of disputes between the companies carrying out the inspection and the exporters.[294]

With respect to *marks of origin* 'attached' to imported goods, Article IX:2 of the GATT 1994 states:

> The [Members] recognize that, in adopting and enforcing laws and regulations relating to marks of origin, the difficulties and inconveniences which such measures may cause to the commerce and industry of exporting countries should be *reduced to a minimum*, due regard being had to the necessity of protecting consumers against fraudulent or misleading indications.
>
> [Emphasis added]

Note that marking requirements are, of course, subject to all relevant WTO rules and disciplines, such as the MFN treatment obligation.

National laws and/or practices relating to the *procurement of goods* by a government for its own use are often significant barriers to trade. Under such laws or practices, governments frequently buy domestic products rather than imported products.[295] However, as discussed above, the national treatment

---

[290] See Articles 2.5 to 2.8 of the *Agreement on Preshipment Inspection*.
[291] See Articles 2.9 to 2.13 of the *Agreement on Preshipment Inspection*.
[292] See Articles 2.15 to 2.19 of the *Agreement on Preshipment Inspection*.
[293] See Articles 3.1 and 3.2 of the *Agreement on Preshipment Inspection*. These Members must also provide to user Members, if requested, technical assistance directed towards the achievement of the objectives of this agreement on mutually agreed terms. See Article 3.3 of the *Agreement on Preshipment Inspection*.
[294] See Article 4 of the *Agreement on Preshipment Inspection*.
[295] It is undisputed that a government can most effectively ensure 'best value for money' by purchasing goods (and services) through an open and non-discriminatory procurement process. However, governments often use public procurement to support the domestic industry or to promote employment.

obligation of Article III:4 of the GATT 1994 does not apply to government procurement laws and practices.[296] As government procurement typically represents between 10 and 15 per cent of GDP, it is clear that the absence of this and other multilateral disciplines represents a significant gap in the multilateral trading system and leaves a considerable source of barriers to trade unaddressed.

The plurilateral WTO *Agreement on Government Procurement* provides for some disciplines with respect to government procurement. However, it does so only for the forty Members that are currently a party to this Agreement.[297] The *Agreement on Government Procurement* applies to the laws, regulations, procedures and practices regarding procurement by the government bodies which a party listed in Appendix I to the Agreement.[298] Furthermore, for the Agreement to apply, the government procurement contract must be worth more than a specified threshold value.[299] The key discipline provided for in the plurilateral *Agreement on Government Procurement* is non-discrimination. Article III of the *Agreement on Government Procurement*, entitled 'National Treatment and Non-Discrimination', states, in paragraph 1:

> With respect to all laws, regulations, procedures and practices regarding government procurement covered by this Agreement, each Party shall provide immediately and unconditionally to the products, services and suppliers of other Parties offering products or services of the Parties, treatment no less favourable than:
>
> a. that accorded to domestic products, services and suppliers; and
> b. that accorded to products, services and suppliers of any other Party.

Furthermore, in order to ensure that the national treatment and MFN treatment obligations under Articles III:1 (a) and (b) quoted above are abided by, the plurilateral *Agreement on Government Procurement* provides for procedures to ensure that laws, regulations, procedures and practices regarding government procurement are transparent.[300] However, it deserves to be stressed again that all of these disciplines and rules only apply to the forty Members which are a party to the *Agreement on Government Procurement*.

At the Singapore Session in 1996, the Ministerial Conference agreed to establish a working group to conduct a study on transparency in government procurement practices and, based on this study, to develop elements for inclusion

---

[296] See Article III:8(a) of the GATT 1994; and above, p. 344.

[297] The parties to the *Agreement on Government Procurement* currently are Austria, Belgium, Bulgaria, Canada, Cyprus, Czech Republic, Denmark, Estonia, the European Communities, Finland, France, Germany, Greece, Hong Kong China, Hungary, Iceland, Ireland, Israel, Italy, Japan, Korea, Latvia, Liechtenstein, Lithuania, Luxembourg, Malta, the Netherlands, the Netherlands with respect to Aruba, Norway, Poland, Portugal, Romania, Singapore, Slovak Republic, Slovenia, Spain, Sweden, Switzerland, the United Kingdom and the United States. Accession negotiations are under way with Albania, Georgia, Jordan, the Kyrgyz Republic, Moldova, Panama and Chinese Taipei. See www.wto.org/english/tratop_e/gproc_e/memobs_e.htm#parties, visited on 28 August 2007.

[298] See, in this respect, Panel Report, *Korea – Procurement*, in which the question arose whether the Korean Airport Construction Authority, the Korean Airports Authority and the Inchon International Airport Corporation were within the scope of Korea's list of 'central government entities' as specified in Korea's Schedule in Appendix I to the *Agreement on Government Procurement*.

[299] See Article I.4 of the *Agreement on Government Procurement*. In Appendix I to the Agreement, each party specifies relevant thresholds.   [300] See Articles VII to XVI of the *Agreement on Government Procurement*.

in an appropriate *multilateral* agreement.[301] In 2001, in Doha, the Ministerial Conference expressly recognised the case for a *multilateral* agreement on transparency in government procurement and agreed:

> that negotiations will take place after the Fifth Session of the Ministerial Conference on the basis of a decision to be taken, by explicit consensus, at that session on modalities of negotiations.[302]

It is important to note that these negotiations would be:

> limited to the *transparency aspects* and therefore will not restrict the scope for countries to give preference to domestic supplies and suppliers.[303]
>
> [Emphasis added]

As discussed above, the current plurilateral *Agreement on Government Procurement* prohibits discrimination and limits the scope for preference for domestic goods. The wished-for *multilateral agreement* would thus be far less 'ambitious' than the current plurilateral agreement (which will continue to exist in parallel). The new agreement would focus on transparency as such, rather than on transparency as a vehicle for monitoring market access commitments (as does the current plurilateral agreement).[304]

Between the 2001 Doha Session and the 2003 Cancún Session of the Ministerial Conference, Members prepared the start of the negotiations in the Working Group on Transparency in Government Procurement. However, as already discussed, the Members failed to agree on the modalities of the negotiations on any of the Singapore issues, including government procurement, at the Cancún Session. In the summer of 2004, the General Council eventually decided *not* to start negotiations on transparency in government procurement in the context of the Doha Development Round.[305] Although Members have explicitly committed themselves in the Doha Ministerial Declaration 'to ensuring adequate technical assistance and support for capacity-building both during the negotiations and after their conclusion',[306] many developing-country Members were concerned about their ability to engage 'successfully' in negotiations and to implement the new international commitments resulting from these negotiations.

Finally, with respect to measures concerning *traffic in transit*, Article V of the GATT 1994, entitled 'Freedom of Transit', sets out a number of obligations on Members not to impede this traffic. Traffic in transit is the traffic of goods from country A to country C, through the territory of country B. It is clear that any restriction or impediment that country B would impose on the transit of the

---

[301] See Ministerial Conference, *Singapore Ministerial Declaration*, adopted 13 December 1996, WT/MIN(96)/DEC, para. 21.

[302] Ministerial Conference, *Doha Ministerial Declaration*, adopted 14 November 2001, WT/MIN(01)/DEC/1, para. 26.   [303] *Ibid.*

[304] See *Transparency in Government Procurement: Applying the Fundamental WTO Principle of Transparency to How Governments Buy Goods and Services*, Briefing Note, Ministerial Conference, December 2001, available at www.wto.org/english/thewto_e/minist_e/min01_e/brief_e/brief14_e.htm, visited on 15 November 2007.

[305] See General Council, *Doha Work Programme*, Decision adopted on 1 August 2004, WT/L/579, dated 2 August 2004, para. 1(g).

[306] Ministerial Conference, *Doha Ministerial Declaration*, adopted 14 November 2001, WT/MIN(01)/DEC/1, para. 26.

goods concerned would constitute a barrier to trade. Article V:2 of the GATT 1994 provides:

> There shall be freedom of transit through the territory of each [Member], via the routes most convenient for international transit, for traffic in transit to or from the territory of other [Members]. No distinction shall be made which is based on the flag of vessels, the place of origin, departure, entry, exit or destination, or on any circumstances relating to the ownership of goods, of vessels or of other means of transport.

Traffic in transit shall not be subject to any unnecessary delays or restrictions and shall be exempt from customs duties and from all transit duties or other charges imposed in respect of transit, except charges for transportation or those commensurate with administrative expenses entailed by transit or with the cost of services rendered.[307] All charges, regulations and formalities in connection with transit shall be reasonable and be subject to the MFN treatment obligation.[308]

Questions and Assignments 5.18

Explain how government procurement laws and practices, marks of origin, measures relating to traffic in transit and preshipment inspection can constitute barriers to trade in goods. In your opinion, which of these measures or actions is the most significant barrier to trade? Does WTO law regulate these types of other non-tariff barriers? Name at least two other measures or actions, not discussed in this chapter, that may constitute other non-tariff barriers to trade in goods.

5.4. BARRIERS TO TRADE IN SERVICES

This chapter on barriers to trade has dealt thus far with tariff and non-tariff barriers to trade in *goods*. This section deals with barriers to trade in *services*. As already discussed, the production and consumption of services are a principal economic activity in virtually all countries, developed and developing, alike. Financial, telecommunication and transport services are the backbone of a modern economy, and economic development and prosperity are dependent on the availability and efficiency of these and other services.[309]

Services play an increasingly central role in the world economy. They represent approximately 68 per cent of world GDP.[310] However, the importance of services in the world economy is *not* reflected in their share of world trade.[311] Services account for no more than 20 per cent of global cross-border trade.[312]

---

[307] See Article V:3 of the GATT 1994.   [308] See Article V:4 and 5 of the GATT 1994.
[309] See WTO Secretariat, *Market Access: Unfinished Business*, Special Studies Series 6 (WTO, 2001), 98.
[310] See Pascal Lamy, *Doha Success Will Need Positive Outcome in Services*, Speech at the European Services Forum and the London School of Economics conference on 15 October 2007, available at www.wto.org/english/news_e/sppl_e/sppl77_e.htm, visited on 21 October 2007.
[311] World exports in services amounted to close to $2.8 trillion in 2006. See *ibid*.
[312] See WTO Secretariat, *Market Access: Unfinished Business*, Special Studies Series 6 (WTO, 2001), 98.

Trade in services is often subject to restrictions. For trade in services, unlike trade in goods, trade-restrictive measures applied at the border are barely significant. The production and consumption of services are subject to a vast range of domestic regulations. Barriers to trade in services are primarily the result of these domestic regulations. Examples of such domestic regulations that may constitute barriers to trade in services are:

- a restriction on the number of drugstores allowed within a geographical area;
- an obligation for all practising lawyers to be a member of the local bar association;
- sanitation standards for restaurants;
- technical safety requirements for airline companies;
- a requirement that all professional services be offered in the national language;
- professional qualification requirements for accountants; and
- a prohibition on banks selling life insurance.

WTO law, and the GATS in particular, provides for rules and disciplines on barriers to trade in services. Note, however, that – as explained below – most domestic regulation of services does not constitute a GATS-inconsistent barrier to trade in services.[313] The production and consumption of services are often subject to domestic regulation for good reasons, including the protection of consumers and the protection of public health and safety. The Preamble to the GATS explicitly recognises:

> the right of Members to regulate, and to introduce new regulations on, the supply of services within their territories in order to meet national policy objectives.

It is important to stress that the objective of the GATS is *not* the *deregulation* of services.

This section addresses:

- the GATS rules on market access barriers; and
- the GATS rules on other barriers to trade in services.[314]

5.4.1. Market access barriers to trade in services

The GATS provides for specific rules on market access barriers and their progressive reduction. This section discusses:

- the definition and types of market access barriers;
- rules on market access barriers;
- negotiations on market access;
- schedules of specific commitments;

---

[313] See below, pp. 495–6.
[314] Recall that chapter 4 already discussed the scope of application of the GATS and the GATS non-discrimination provisions, i.e. Article II (MFN) and Article XVII (national treatment). See above, pp. 334–43, 390–5.

- interpretation of Services Schedules;
- modification and withdrawal of commitments; and
- market access commitments agreed to thus far.

5.4.1.1. *Definition and types of market access barriers*

The GATS does not explicitly define the concept of 'market access barriers'. However, Article XVI:2 (a) to (f) of the GATS provides an *exhaustive* list of such measures.[315] This list comprises:

- limitations on the *number of service suppliers* whether in the form of numerical quotas, monopolies, exclusive service suppliers or the requirements of an economic needs test (see Article XVI:2(a)); for example, licences for fast food restaurants subject to an economic needs test based on population density;
- limitations on the *total value of service transactions* or assets in the form of numerical quotas or the requirement of an economic needs test (see Article XVI:2(b)); for example, limitation of the activities of subsidiaries of foreign insurance companies to 40 per cent of the domestic insurance market;
- limitations on the *total number of service operations* or on the *total quantity of service* output expressed in terms of designated numerical units in the form of quotas or the requirement for an economic needs test (see Article XVI:2(c)); for example, restrictions on the broadcasting time available for foreign movies;
- limitations on the *total number of natural persons* that may be employed in a particular service sector or that a service supplier may employ and who are *necessary* for, and directly related to, the *supply of a specific service* in the form of numerical quotas or the requirement of an economic needs test (see Article XVI:2(d)); for example, a cap on the percentage of foreign workers employed by construction companies;
- measures which restrict or require *specific types of legal entity or joint venture* through which a service supplier may supply a service (see Article XVI:2(e)); for example, a law requires that all foreign subsidiaries must be in the form of a joint venture with domestic partners; and
- limitations on the *participation of foreign capital* in terms of maximum percentage limits on foreign shareholding or the total value of individual or aggregate foreign investment (see Article XVI:2(f)); for example, an investment law stipulating that foreign banks may never hold more than 49 per cent of the capital of domestic banks.

In short, the market access barriers listed in Article XVI:2 of the GATS include:

- five types of quantitative restrictions;[316] and
- limitations on forms of legal entity.[317]

---

[315] The Panel in *US – Gambling* confirmed that the list of Article XVI:2 is exhaustive. It came to this conclusion based on the text of the provision, its context and the 1993 Scheduling Guidelines. See Panel Report, *US – Gambling*, paras. 6.293–6.298. Antigua appealed this finding. The Appellate Body, however, chose not to deal with this issue. See Appellate Body Report, *US – Gambling*, para. 256.
[316] See Article XVI:2(a) to (d) and (f) of the GATS.   [317] See Article XVI:2(e) of the GATS.

These market access barriers can be discriminatory *or* non-discriminatory with respect to foreign services or service suppliers. Of the examples included above, a restriction on the broadcasting time available for foreign movies is obviously a *discriminatory* market access barrier, while a licence for a fast food restaurant subject to an economic needs test based on population density is a *non-discriminatory* market access barrier.[318] Article XVI:2 covers both discriminatory and non-discriminatory market access barriers.

Note that four of the five types of quantitative restrictions referred to in Article XVI:2(a) can be expressed numerically, *or* through the criteria specified in these provisions, such as an economic needs test. It is important to note, however, that these criteria do *not* relate:

- to the quality of the service supplied; or
- to the ability of the supplier to supply the service (i.e. technical standards or qualification of the supplier).[319]

A requirement, for example, that services be offered in the national language or a requirement for engineers to have specific professional qualifications may impede trade in services but is *not* a market access barrier within the meaning of Article XVI:2 of the GATS.

Also note that the quantitative restrictions specified in sub-paragraphs (a) to (d) refer to *maximum* limitations. Minimum requirements such as those common to licensing criteria (for example, minimum capital requirements for the establishment of a corporate entity) do not fall within the scope of Article XVI of the GATS.[320]

In *US – Gambling*, the Panel found that by maintaining measures that *prohibit* the supply of certain services, the United States effectively limited to zero the service suppliers and service operations relating to that service. According to the Panel, such a zero quota constituted a limitation 'on the number of service suppliers . . . in the form of numerical quotas' within the meaning of Article XVI:2(a) and a limitation 'on the total number of service operations . . . in the form of quotas' within the meaning of Article XVI:2(c).[321] On appeal, the United States argued that the Panel had ignored the fact that Article XVI:2(a) and (c) refer to measures in the *form* of numerical quotas and not to measures having the *effect* of numerical quotas. According to the United States, the measures concerned were not market access barriers within the meaning of Article XVI:2. The Appellate Body disagreed with the United States and upheld the relevant findings of the Panel.[322]

---

[318] See *Guidelines for the Scheduling of Specific Commitments under the General Agreement on Trade in Services (GATS)*, adopted by the Council for Trade in Services on 23 March 2001, S/L/92, dated 28 March 2001, para. 12. As stated in an explanatory note, these Guidelines were based on two documents which were produced and circulated during the Uruguay Round negotiations: MTN.GNS/W/164, *Scheduling of Initial Commitments in Trade in Services: Explanatory Note*, dated 3 September 1993; and MTN.GNS/W/164, Add.1, *Scheduling of Initial Commitments in Trade in Services: Explanatory Note, Addendum*, dated 30 November 1993. See *ibid.*, footnote 1.

[319] *Guidelines for the Scheduling of Specific Commitments under the General Agreement on Trade in Services (GATS)*, S/L/92, dated 28 March 2001, para. 8.   [320] See *ibid.*, para.11.

[321] See Panel Report, *US–Gambling*, para. 6.332.   [322] See Appellate Body Report, *US–Gambling*, para. 250.

5.4.1.2. Rules on market access barriers

The GATS does not provide for a general prohibition on the market access barriers discussed in the above paragraphs. Whether a Member may maintain or adopt these market access barriers with regard to a specific service depends on whether, and if so to what extent, that Member has, in its Services Schedule, made market access commitments with regard to that service or the relevant service sector. This is commonly referred to as the 'positive list' or 'bottom-up' approach to the liberalisation of trade in services.

Article XVI of the GATS, entitled 'Market Access', provides, in paragraph 1:

> With respect to market access through the modes of supply identified in Article I, each Member shall accord services and service suppliers of any other Member *treatment no less favourable* than that provided for under the terms, limitations and conditions agreed and specified in its Schedule.
>
> [Emphasis added]

Furthermore, the chapeau of Article XVI:2 of the GATS states:

> In sectors where market-access commitments are undertaken, the measures which a Member shall not maintain or adopt either on the basis of a regional subdivision or on the basis of its entire territory, unless otherwise specified in its Schedule, are defined as: . . .

Paragraphs (a) to (f) of Article XVI:2 then provide for the list of market access barriers discussed above. In other words, when a Member has undertaken a market access commitment in a service sector, it may not maintain or adopt any of the listed market access barriers with regard to trade in services in that sector, unless otherwise specified in its Schedule. A Member can specify in its Schedule that it maintains, or reserves the right to adopt, certain market access barriers.

When a Member makes a market access commitment, it *binds* the level of market access specified in the Schedule (see Article XVI:1) and agrees not to impose any market access barrier that would restrict access to the market beyond the level specified (see Article XVI:2). In the *US – Gambling* case, the United States had inscribed the term 'none' in its Schedule with respect to market access limitations for 'other recreational services (excluding sporting)', which was interpreted to include gambling and betting services.[323] Both the Panel and the Appellate Body confirmed that this means that the United States has committed itself to providing full market access in that sector.[324]

Questions and Assignments 5.19

Are the following measures inconsistent with Article XVI of the GATS: a governmental measure prohibiting the broadcasting of American and Australian television soaps; a law limiting the number of foreign workers

---

[323] See below, p. 489.
[324] See Panel Report, *US – Gambling*, paras. 6.267–6.279; and Appellate Body Report, *US – Gambling*, paras. 214–15.

employed by construction companies; a law requiring that only plumbers speaking the national language may do repairs in private households; a law stating that foreign banks may not hold more than 49 per cent of the capital of domestic banks; a government measure limiting the number of pubs to one for every 5,000 people? What must you know in order to answer these questions?

5.4.1.3. Negotiations on market access

The GATS aims at achieving *progressively* higher levels of liberalisation of trade in services through *successive* rounds of negotiations. The Uruguay Round negotiations on the liberalisation of trade in services were only a first step in what will definitely be a long process of progressive liberalisation. Article XIX of the GATS, entitled 'Negotiation of Specific Commitments', states, in its first paragraph:

> In pursuance of the objectives of this Agreement, Members shall enter into successive rounds of negotiations . . . with a view to achieving a progressively higher level of liberalization.

With regard to the negotiations on the progressive liberalisation of trade in services, Article XIX:1 furthermore provides:

> Such negotiations shall be directed to the reduction or elimination of the adverse effects on trade in services of measures as a means of providing effective market access. This process shall take place with a view to promoting the interests of all participants on a mutually advantageous basis and to securing an overall balance of rights and obligations.

The objective of the negotiations is thus to provide effective *market access* for services. In these market access negotiations, Members strive for a 'mutually advantageous' outcome, i.e. 'reciprocity'.[325] The approach to negotiations on the liberalisation of services is a request-and-offer approach.[326] At the initial stage of negotiations, Members first make requests for the liberalisation of trade in specific services.[327] The exchange of requests, as a process, is purely bilateral. It is simply a process of letters being addressed from the requesting participants to their negotiating partners.[328] After Members participating in the negotiations have made requests, they submit offers.[329] A Member submits an offer in response to all the requests that it has received, but does not necessarily have to

---

[325] Note, in this respect, that, while perhaps economically dubious, striving for 'reciprocity' in market access negotiations is 'one of the most deep-rooted . . . compulsions in international trade policy-making'. See WTO Secretariat, *Market Access: Unfinished Business*, Special Studies Series 6 (WTO, 2001), 99.
[326] On approaches to tariff negotiations, see above, pp. 411–17.
[327] There are possibly four types of contents in a request, which are not mutually exclusive: (i) the addition of new service sectors; (ii) the removal of existing limitations or the introduction of bindings in modes which have so far been unbound; (iii) the undertaking of additional commitments under Article XVIII; and (iv) the termination of MFN exemptions. See *Technical Aspects of Requests and Offers*, Summary of Presentation by the WTO Secretariat at the WTO Seminar on the GATS, 20 February 2002,1, available at www.wto.org/english/tratop_e/serv_e/requests_offers_approach_e.doc, visited on 21 November 2007. For further clarification, see below, pp. 484–8.   [328] See *ibid.*
[329] In terms of content, offers normally address the same four types referred to in footnote 327 above.

address each element contained in those requests in its offer.[330] Unlike a request, which is usually presented in the form of a letter, an offer is normally presented in the form of a draft schedule of commitments.[331] While requests are addressed bilaterally to negotiating partners, offers are circulated multilaterally.[332] Offers are to be open to consultations and negotiation by all negotiating partners; not only to those who have made requests to the Member concerned but also any other participant in the negotiations.[333] In fact, offers are a signal of the real start of the advanced stage of bilateral negotiations, i.e. when negotiators come to Geneva to hold many bilateral talks with various different delegations. The submission of offers may also trigger the submission of further requests and then the process continues and becomes a succession of requests and offers.[334]

Article XIX:2 of the GATS explicitly requires that the process of liberalisation of trade in services takes place with due respect for:

- national policy objectives; and
- the level of development of individual Members, both overall and in individual sectors.

Consequently, Article XIX:2 further provides with respect to the position of developing-country Members in the negotiations on the liberalisation of trade in services that:

> There shall be appropriate flexibility for individual developing-country Members for opening fewer sectors, liberalizing fewer types of transactions, progressively extending market access in line with their development situation and, when making access to their markets available to foreign service suppliers, attaching to such access conditions aimed at achieving the objectives referred to in Article IV.

It is thus accepted that developing-country Members undertake fewer and more limited market access commitments than developed-country Members. 'Full reciprocity' is not required from developing-country Members. These Members are only expected to undertake market access commitments commensurate with their level of development.

As provided in Article XIX:3 of the GATS, for each round of multilateral negotiations on the liberalisation of trade in services, negotiating guidelines and procedures shall be established.[335] For the current negotiations, initiated pursuant to Article XIX:1 of the GATS in January 2000 and now conducted in the context of the Doha Development Round, the *Guidelines and Procedures for the Negotiations on Trade in Services* were adopted on 28 March 2001 by the Council for Trade in

---

[330] See *Technical Aspects of Requests and Offers*, Summary of Presentation by the WTO Secretariat at the WTO Seminar on the GATS, 20 February 2002, 3, available at www.wto.org/english/tratop_e/serv_e/requests_offers_approach_e.doc, visited on 21 November 2007.   [331] See *ibid*.

[332] See *ibid*. The multilateral circulation is useful not only from a transparency point of view but also from a functional point of view since, in an offer, a participant is actually responding to *all* the requests that it has received.   [333] See *ibid*.   [334] See *ibid*.

[335] For the purposes of establishing such guidelines, the Council for Trade in Services carries out an assessment of trade in services in overall terms and on a sectoral basis with reference to the objectives of the GATS. Negotiating guidelines, *inter alia*, establish modalities for the treatment of liberalisation undertaken autonomously by Members since previous negotiations, as well as for the special treatment for least-developed-country Members. See Article XIX:3 of the GATS.

Services.[336] The Doha Ministerial Declaration of November 2001 stated with respect to the current negotiations:

> The negotiations on trade in services shall be conducted with a view to promoting the economic growth of all trading partners and the development of developing and least-developed countries. We recognize the work already undertaken in the negotiations, initiated in January 2000 under Article XIX of the General Agreement on Trade in Services, and the large number of proposals submitted by members on a wide range of sectors and several horizontal issues, as well as on movement of natural persons. We reaffirm the Guidelines and Procedures for the Negotiations adopted by the Council for Trade in Services on 28 March 2001 as the basis for continuing the negotiations.[337]

Members have been exchanging bilateral initial requests since 30 June 2002, and between 31 March and 30 October 2003, thirty-nine Members submitted initial offers.[338] However, there is widespread disappointment regarding the progress made in the negotiations. In April 2004, the Chairman of the Special Session of the Council for Trade in Services reported to the Trade Negotiations Committee as follows:

> there was a feeling among Members that, in the light of the passage of one year since the benchmark date for the circulation of initial offers, far too few offers had been submitted and that the minimalist character of many of these offers was disappointing.[339]

In its Decision of 1 August 2004 on the *Doha Work Programme*, the General Council reaffirmed the Members' commitment to progress in this area of the negotiations in line with the Doha mandate. A deadline of May 2005 was set for tabling revised offers.[340]

In an attempt to achieve a breakthrough in the negotiations, the Members adopted in March 2006 a 'plurilateral' approach to the negotiations. Under this approach, a group of Members requesting market access, commonly referred to as 'demandeurs', start negotiations with targeted Members on the basis of a collective request. In March 2006, a total of twenty-two collective requests relating to a variety of sectors and modes of supply were tabled.[341]

Developing countries are often hesitant to engage in further liberalisation of trade in services. However, consider the following report on the liberalisation of retail services in India:

> Global brands such as Reebok, Nokia, Louis Vuitton and Gucci will for the first time be able to own and operate their own stores in India after the country's communist-backed government last night approved a liberalisation of foreign direct investment rules. Consent to permit 51 per cent foreign investment in single brand retail operations was the

---

[336] Council for Trade in Services, *Guidelines and Procedures for the Negotiations on Trade in Services*, S/L/93, dated 29 March 2001.

[337] Ministerial Conference, *Doha Ministerial Declaration*, adopted 14 November 2001, WT/MIN(01)/DEC/1, dated 20 November 2001, para. 15.

[338] On the request-and-offer approach to the negotiations on trade in services, see above, p. 481.

[339] Council for Trade in Services, *Report by the Chairman to the Trade Negotiations Committee*, TN/S/15, dated 14 April 2004, para. 5.

[340] See General Council, *Doha Work Programme*, Decision adopted on 1 August 2004, WT/L/579, dated 2 August 2004, para. 1(e). The General Council adopted the recommendations agreed by the Special Session, set out in Annex C to the General Council Decision, based on which further progress in the services negotiations will be pursued.   [341] *BRIDGES Weekly Trade News Digest*, 22 March 2006.

> most striking among a package of measures aimed at signalling the Indian government's determination to kick-start a stalled programme of economic reforms . . .
>
> International retailers have until now been able to operate in India only through franchise arrangements with local partners, in contrast to China, which has thrown open its high streets to foreign investors[342]

Resistance to further liberalisation sometimes also comes from Members that usually champion further liberalisation:

> The US has been asked by several trading partners to open up its port services to international competition, a longstanding request given more significance by the dispute over the takeover of P&O by Dubai Ports World. The request, made in the World Trade Organization 'Doha round' of global trade negotiations, stands almost no chance of success. The proposal is not new, and the US has already ruled out liberalising any port services in the Doha round. But it underlines the sensitivity that even rich nations can have to liberalising service industries, which often leads to foreign companies buying up domestic providers . . .
>
> The US has long been protective of its shipping and other maritime companies: the Jones Act, a longstanding piece of legislation, stipulates that all merchandise shipped between two US ports must be carried in a vessel built, owned and crewed by Americans.[343]

Questions and Assignments 5.20

What is the objective of negotiations pursuant to Article XIX of the GATS? How are these negotiations conducted? How is the special situation of developing-country Members taken into consideration in these negotiations?

5.4.1.4. *Schedules of Specific Commitments*

The terms, limitations and conditions on market access agreed to in the negotiations on the liberalisation of trade in services are set out in Schedules of Specific Commitments, already referred to above as Services Schedules.[344] As discussed elsewhere in this and the previous chapter, the conditions and qualifications on national treatment and undertakings relating to additional commitments are also set out in the Schedules of Specific Commitments.[345] Each Member has a Schedule of Specific Commitments. In fact, each Member *must* have a Schedule, albeit that there is no minimum requirement as to the scope or depth of the commitments set out in that Schedule. All Schedules of Specific Commitments are annexed to the GATS and form an integral part thereof.[346] The online WTO Services Database gives information on all commitments undertaken by all Members that joined the WTO before 2000.[347] All Schedules of Specific Commitments are also available on the WTO website.[348]

---

[342] J. Johnson, 'India Sets Out its Stall for Global Retailers', *Financial Times*, 24 January 2006.
[343] A. Beattie, 'Trading Partners Request Access to US Ports', *Financial Times*, 5 March 2006.
[344] See above, p. 481.   [345] See above, pp. 390–2, and below, pp. 485–8.   [346] Article XX:3 of the GATS.
[347] WTO Services Database Online, available at http://tsdb.wto.org/wto/WTOHomepublic.htm, visited on 22 November 2007.
[348] See www.wto.org/english/tratop_e/serv_e/serv_commitments_e.htm, visited on 20 November 2007.

Schedules of Specific Commitments have two parts:

* a part containing the *horizontal commitments*; and
* a part containing the *sectoral commitments*.

Horizontal commitments apply to all sectors included in the Schedule. Schedules include horizontal commitments to *avoid repeating* in relation to each sector contained in the Schedule the same information regarding limitations, conditions or qualifications of commitments.[349] They often concern two modes of supply in particular, namely, supply through commercial presence (mode 3) and supply through the presence of natural persons (mode 4).[350] For example, the Schedule of Specific Commitments of the European Communities and their Member States mentions with regard to mode 4 supply of all services scheduled:

> Unbound except for measures concerning the entry into and temporary stay within a Member State, without requiring compliance with an economic needs test, of the following categories of natural persons providing services: . . .[351]

Sectoral commitments, or sector-specific commitments, are, as the term indicates, commitments made regarding specific service sectors or sub-sectors. For scheduling commitments, WTO Members distinguish twelve broad service sectors:

* business services;
* communication services;
* construction and related engineering services;
* distribution services;
* educational services;
* environmental services;
* financial services;
* health-related and social services;
* tourism and travel-related services;
* recreational, cultural and sporting services;
* transport services; and
* other services not included elsewhere.

These twelve broad service sectors are further divided into more than 150 sub-sectors. For example, the 'business services' sector includes:

* professional services (including, for example, legal services, accounting, architectural services, engineering services, and medical and dental services);

---

[349] Horizontal commitments are found at the beginning of a schedule. The concept of 'horizontal commitments' is misleading since 'horizontal commitments' are often, in fact, horizontal limitations, i.e. limitations applicable to all commitments.

[350] On the four modes of supply of services (cross-border supply, consumption abroad, supply through commercial presence and supply through the presence of natural persons), see above, pp. 336–9.

[351] GATS/SC/31, dated 15 April 1994, 7–10. For the categories of persons subsequently listed (including intra-corporate transferees and representatives of a service supplier seeking temporary entry for the purpose of negotiating for the sale of services), the measures concerning entry and temporary stay will not require compliance with an economic needs test. However, all other requirements of Community and Member States' laws and regulations regarding entry, stay, work and social security measures continue to apply, including regulations concerning the period of stay, minimum wages as well as collective wage agreements.

- computer and related services;
- research and development services;
- real estate services;
- rental/leasing services without operators; and
- other business services (including, for example, building cleaning services and publishing).

The 'communication services' sector includes:

- postal services;
- courier services;
- telecommunications services (including, for example, voice telephone services, electronic mail, voice mail and electronic data interchange); and
- audiovisual services (including, for example, motion picture and video tape production and distribution services, radio and television services and sound recording).

This WTO classification of service sectors, set out in the Services Sectoral Classification List of the WTO Secretariat,[352] is based on the Central Product Classification (CPC) of the United Nations. In the Secretariat's List each sector is identified by the corresponding CPC number. The CPC gives a detailed explanation of the services covered by each of the sectors and sub-sectors.[353]

In scheduling their commitments, most Members follow the WTO Services Sectoral Classification List. Thus, most Schedules have the same structure. A service sector or sub-sector is of course only included in a Member's Services Schedule if that Member undertakes commitments in that sector or sub-sector.

Services Schedules have four columns:

1. first column identifying the services sector or sub-sector which is the subject of the commitment;
2. second column containing the terms, limitations and conditions on market access;
3. third column containing the conditions and qualifications on national treatment; and
4. fourth column for undertakings relating to additional commitments.

With regard to market access commitments, Members indicate, in the second column of their Schedule, the presence or absence of limitations on market access. They do so for each service sector scheduled and with regard to each of the four modes of supply:

- cross-border supply (mode 1);
- consumption abroad (mode 2);

---

[352] See MTN.GNS/W/120, dated 10 July 1991.

[353] A breakdown of the CPC, including explanatory notes for each sub-sector, is contained in the UN Provisional Central Product Classification, available at http://unstats.un.org/unsd/cr/registry/regcst.asp?Cl=16&Lg=1, visited 20 November 2007. To determine the coverage of the service sectors and sub-sectors of the WTO Services Sectoral Classification List, the detailed explanation of the CPC system can be used. Entries in Schedules often include CPC numbers.

Figure 5.5 Excerpt form the Schedule of Specific Commitments of Brazil (engineering services)[354]

Modes of supply: (1) Cross-border supply (2) Consumption abroad (3) Commercial presence (4) Presence of natural persons

Sector or sub-sector	Limitations on market access	Limitations on national treatment	Additional commitments
e) Engineering Services			
Advisory and consultative engineering services (CPC 86721)	1. Unbound 2. Unbound 3. Same conditions as in Architectural services 4. Unbound except as indicated in the horizontal section	1. Unbound 2. Unbound 3. None 4. Unbound except as indicated in the horizontal section	
Industrial engineering (CPC 86725)	1. Unbound 2. Unbound 3. Same conditions as in Architectural services 4. Unbound except as indicated in the horizontal section	1. Unbound 2. Unbound 3. None 4. Unbound except as indicated in the horizontal section	
Engineering design (CPC 86722, CPC 86723, CPC 86724)	1. Unbound 2. Unbound 3. Same conditions as in Architectural services 4. Unbound except as indicated in the horizontal section	1. Unbound 2. Unbound 3. None 4. Unbound except as indicated in the horizontal section	
Other engineering services (CPC 86729)	1. Unbound 2. Unbound 3. Same conditions as in Architectural services 4. Unbound except as indicated in the horizontal section	1. Unbound 2. Unbound 3. None 4. Unbound except as indicated in the horizontal section	

- supply through commercial presence (mode 3); and
- supply through presence of natural persons (mode 4).

For each market access commitment with respect to each mode of supply, four different situations can occur:[355]

- *full commitment*, i.e. the situation in which a Member does not seek in any way to limit market access in a given sector and mode of supply through market access barriers within the meaning of Article XVI:2; a Member in this situation records in the second column of its Schedule the word 'none';[356]
- *commitment with limitations*, i.e. the situation in which a Member wants to limit market access in a given sector and mode of supply through market access barriers within the meaning of Article XVI:2; a Member in this situation describes in the second column of its Schedule the market access barrier(s) that is/are maintained;[357]
- *no commitment*, i.e. the situation in which a Member wants to remain free in a given sector and mode of supply to introduce or maintain market access

[354] GATS/SC/13, dated 15 April 1994, 7.
[355] See Council for Trade in Services, *Guidelines for the Scheduling of Specific Commitments under the General Agreement on Trade in Services (GATS)*, adopted by the Council for Trade in Services on 23 March 2001, S/L/92, dated 28 March 2001.
[356] Note, however, that any relevant limitations listed in the 'horizontal commitments' part of the Schedule apply. See above, pp. 484–5.
[357] Two main possibilities can be envisaged in such a situation: the first is the binding of an existing situation ('standstill'); the second is the binding of a more liberal situation where some, but not all, of the access barriers inconsistent with Article XVI:2 will be removed ('rollback').

barriers within the meaning of Article XVI:2; a Member in this situation records in the second column of its Schedule the word 'unbound';[358] and

- *no commitment technically feasible*, i.e. the situation in which a particular mode of supply is not technically possible, such as the cross-border supply of hair-dressing services; a Member in this situation records in the second column of its Schedule 'unbound*'.[359]

As discussed in chapter 4, and as is evident from the excerpt from the Services Schedule of Brazil, national treatment commitments and limitations thereof are inscribed in the third column of the Schedules in the same way as market access commitments and limitations thereof are inscribed. It is possible that a measure is both a market access barrier prohibited under Article XVI:2 and a measure inconsistent with the national treatment obligation of Article XVII. For this type of situation, Article XX:2 of the GATS provides that:

> Measures inconsistent with both Articles XVI and XVII shall be inscribed in the column relating to Article XVI. In this case the inscription will be considered to provide a condition or qualification to Article XVII as well.

Some scholars and other experts are critical of the 'positive list' or 'bottom-up' approach of the GATS to scheduling market access and other commitments regarding trade in services. The Sutherland Report on *The Future of the WTO* stated:

> Scheduling cannot be practical in all areas. It is hard to apply, for instance, in the rule-making areas such as anti-dumping and subsidies. There are other drawbacks. In particular, the multiplicity of individual national commitments can be a complication for traders and investors that are active on a global scale. That said, any enforceable and predictable commitment made in the WTO might be seen as preferable to no commitment and constantly changing market or regulatory conditions.[360]

Questions and Assignments 5.21

What is the difference between horizontal and sectoral commitments? What is the function of the WTO Services Sectoral Classification List? Examine the Schedules of Specific Commitments of the European Communities and their Member States, the United States, Brazil, China and India and draw conclusions as to the extent of market access commitments in the engineering services sector. Find out whether Mexico, Indonesia and South Africa, as well as the WTO Member of which you are a national, have made market access commitments in the engineering services sector.

---

[358] Note that this situation will only occur when a Member made a commitment in a sector with respect to at least one mode of supply. Where all modes of supply are 'unbound', and no additional commitments have been undertaken in the sector, the sector should not appear in the Schedule.

[359] The asterisk refers to a footnote which states: 'Unbound due to lack of technical feasibility'.

[360] Report by the Consultative Board to the Director-General Supachai Panitchpakdi, *The Future of the WTO: Addressing Institutional Challenges in the New Millennium* (the 'Sutherland Report') (WTO, 2004), para. 302.

[361] On the interpretation of tariff schedules, see above, pp. 420–2.

5.4.1.5. Interpretation of Services Schedules

Just as Goods Schedules are an integral part of the GATT 1994,[361] Services Schedules are an integral part of the GATS. Article XX:3 of the GATS states:

> Schedules of specific commitments shall be annexed to this Agreement and shall form an integral part thereof.

The issue of interpretation of Services Schedules arose in *US – Gambling*. In this case the Panel had to interpret the Services Schedule of the United States. The question was:

> whether the US Schedule includes specific commitments on gambling and betting services notwithstanding the fact that the words 'gambling and betting services' do not appear in the US Schedule.[362]

The United States had inscribed 'other recreational services (except sporting)' in its Schedule, and had recorded *no* limitations on market access in mode 1 (cross-border supply of services). It argued, however, that the term 'sporting' includes gambling and betting and that it thus had excluded gambling and betting services from its specific commitments.

Referring to the finding of the Appellate Body in *EC – Computer Equipment* (with regard to the interpretation of Goods Schedules), that scheduled commitments 'are reciprocal and result from mutually advantageous negotiations between importing and exporting Members',[363] the Panel noted that:

> The United States has repeated several times in these proceedings that it did not intend to schedule a commitment for gambling and betting services. This may well be true, given that the legislation at issue in this dispute predates by decades, not only the GATS itself, but even the notion of 'trade in services' as embodied therein. We have, therefore, some sympathy with the United States' point in this regard. However, the scope of a specific commitment cannot depend upon what a Member intended or did not intend to do at the time of the negotiations.[364]

What matters, according to the Panel, is the *common* intent of all negotiating parties. To determine this common intent with regard to the specific commitment at issue in this case, the Panel applied – as did the Appellate Body in *EC – Computer Equipment* – the rules of interpretation set out in Articles 31 and 32 of the *Vienna Convention*.[365]

On appeal, the Appellate Body agreed with the Panel's reliance on the rules of interpretation of the *Vienna Convention* to ascertain the meaning of the Services Schedule of the United States. However, it applied these rules differently.[366] The Appellate Body concluded as follows:

---

[362] Panel Report, *US – Gambling*, para. 6.41.   [363] Appellate Body Report, *EC – Computer Equipment*, para. 84.
[364] Panel Report, *US – Gambling*, para. 6.136.
[365] See Appellate Body Report, *EC – Computer Equipment*, para. 84.
[366] Note that while the Panel relied upon two documents drafted by the Secretariat in the context of the Uruguay Round services negotiations as *context*, under Article 31.2(a) or (b) of the *Vienna Convention*, for the interpretation of the United States' Schedule, the Appellate Body saw them only as *supplementary means of interpretation*. See Panel Report, *US – Gambling*, para. 6.80 and Appellate Body Report, *US – Gambling*, para. 197. For a critical view of the Appellate Body's approach, see F. Ortino, 'Treaty Interpretation and the WTO Appellate Body Report in *US – Gambling*: A Critique', *Journal of International Economic Law*, 2006, 117–48.

> . . . we reject the United States' argument that, by excluding 'sporting' services from the scope of its commitment in subsector 10.D, the United States excluded gambling and betting services from the scope of that commitment. Accordingly, we uphold, albeit for different reasons, the Panel's finding, in paragraph 7.2(a) of the Panel Report, that:
>
> > . . . the United States' Schedule under the GATS includes specific commitments on gambling and betting services under subsector 10.D.[367]

This finding has raised systemic concerns. As reported in *BRIDGES, Monthly Review* in October 2007:

> While it may be fashionable to bash the US for the manoeuvres it is trying to perpetrate presently, the gambling dispute raises several questions about the broader systemic implications for scheduling commitments in services. If the US – with all its resources and relatively advanced understanding of the GATS and the nuanced technicalities of inscribing commitments in its schedule – could make such a mistake during the Uruguay Round, scheduling services sectors or activities that it did not in fact intend to commit to market access liberalisation, then what of other Members, particularly smaller and poorer developing countries that are only now beginning to comprehend the full extent of the GATS? What kind of 'mistakes' might they have made in scheduling commitments in the Uruguay Round when GATS commitments were even more of a novelty for them? Or, put another way, as these countries seek to adapt to and take advantage of the growing relevance of service trade in their economies, do they have the space to evolve and put in place regulations without necessarily breaching commitments that they had not foreseen? From this perspective, it would seem that the looser the strings around a Member seeking to use Article XXI, the more beneficial it may be for countries seeking to break ground in pursuit of their sustainable development objectives.[368]

5.4.1.6. Modification or withdrawal of commitments

As is the case with tariff concessions for goods, market access commitments for services can also be modified or withdrawn.[369] According to Article XXI of the GATS, a Member may modify or withdraw any commitment in its Schedule, at any time after three years have elapsed from the date on which that commitment entered into force, in accordance with the provisions of this Article.[370] A Member wishing to 'unbind' a market access commitment must first notify its intention to do so to the Council for Trade in Services. Subsequently, it must — if so requested — enter into negotiations with a view to reaching agreement on any necessary compensatory adjustment. The purpose of these negotiations on compensatory adjustment is to maintain a general level of mutually advantageous commitments not less favourable to trade than that provided for in the Schedule.

If no agreement on compensatory adjustment can be reached between the modifying Member and any affected Member, the affected Member may refer the matter to arbitration.[371] Recall that this possibility to refer to arbitration is not

---

[367] Appellate Body Report, *US – Gambling*, para. 213.
[368] *BRIDGES Monthly Review*, 'Assessing the Implications of the Gambling Dispute', June–July 2007, available at www.ictsd.org/monthly/bridges/Bridges%2011–4.pdf, visited on 31 October 2007.
[369] On tariff concessions, see Article XXVIII of the GATT 1994, and above, pp. 426–8.
[370] In certain exceptional circumstances, the period of three years is reduced to one year. See Article X of the GATS.
[371] See Article XXI:3(a) of the GATS. Any affected Member that wishes to enforce a right that it may have to compensation must participate in the arbitration. See *ibid.*

provided for in the context of the modification or withdrawal of tariff concessions.[372] If no arbitration is requested, the modifying Member is free to implement the intended modification or withdrawal.[373] If arbitration is requested, however, the modifying Member may not modify or withdraw its commitment until it has made compensatory adjustments in conformity with the findings of the arbitration.[374] In case the modifying Member does not comply with the findings of the arbitration, any affected Member that participated in the arbitration may modify or withdraw *substantially equivalent benefits* in conformity with those findings.[375]

Note that any compensatory adjustment made by the Member 'unbinding' a commitment must be made on an MFN basis. However, the modification or withdrawal of substantially equivalent benefits by affected Members in case of non-compliance with the arbitration findings may be implemented solely with respect to the modifying Member.[376]

In May 2007, the United States announced that it would not comply with the 2005 Panel and Appellate Body recommendations and rulings in *US – Gambling*, discussed above, but was modifying its market access commitments in the sector of 'recreational services', the service sector at issue in *US – Gambling*. In May 2007, *BRIDGES Weekly Trade News Digest* reported:

> The US claims that the dispute dates back to misunderstandings from the 1993–1994 Uruguay Round negotiations. Deputy United States Trade Representative John Verneau on 4 May stated that the US never intended to include cross-border gambling, 'it didn't occur to us that this could include gambling until Antigua brought this case in 2003.' The US further issued a statement that it was 'clarifying' its commitment to cross-border internet gambling and betting. Washington believes this clarification will 'dispose of the matter.'
> According to Article XXI of the GATS, Members are permitted to file modifications to their original schedule of commitments. This procedure has only been applied once before in the case of the EU's expansion from 15 to 25 member countries. Under this process, an affected country can claim compensation, subject to WTO arbitration.
> According to GATS procedures, Antigua and Barbuda have 45 days from the US's notification of its intent to modify its commitment to file a claim seeking compensation.[377]

Before the 22 June 2007 deadline, seven other WTO Members joined Antigua in notifying their intent to seek compensation from the US.[378]

Questions and Assignments 5.22

Can market access commitments for services be modified or withdrawn? If so, how?

---

[372] See above, pp. 426–8.   [373] See Article XXI:3(b) of the GATS.   [374] See Article XXI:4(a) of the GATS.
[375] See Article XXI:4(b) of the GATS.
[376] See Article XXI:2(b) of the GATS (for the compensatory adjustment) and Article XXI:4(b) of the GATS (for the modification or withdrawal of substantially equivalent benefits).
[377] *BRIDGES Weekly Trade News Digest*, 9 May 2007.
[378] The Members reportedly seeking compensation from the United States are Antigua, the European Communities, Costa Rica, India, Canada, Macau, Australia and Japan. See *BRIDGES Weekly Trade Digest*, 4 July 2007.

5.4.1.7. Market access commitments agreed to thus far

The market access commitments agreed to during the Uruguay Round negotiations on the liberalisation of trade in services are, in general, modest. On average, WTO Members have only undertaken market access commitments on about twenty-five sub-sectors, i.e. 15 per cent of the total.[379] Only one-third of the Members have undertaken commitments on more that sixty-one sub-sectors.[380] Furthermore, the market access commitments rarely go beyond the *status quo*, i.e. they bind the degree of market access already existing. The value of these bindings, also referred to as standstill bindings, is that they give traders and investors a degree of security and predictability with respect to market access in the service sectors of interest to them.

In a number of important sectors, such as financial services, telecommunications and maritime transport, and with respect to the movement of natural persons, the Uruguay Round negotiators were unable to complete the market access negotiations and the GATS made provision for further negotiations. These further negotiations led in 1997 to agreements providing for significant market access commitments in the sectors of basic telecommunications and financial services.[381] Further negotiations on market access for maritime transport failed, while further negotiations on the movement of natural persons were completed in July 1995 with very modest results. To the dissatisfaction of developing-country Members, the agreement reached on the movement of natural persons was largely confined to business visitors (to establish business contacts or negotiate contracts) and intra-corporate transfers of managers and technical staff.

Thus far, tourism has been the service sector in which most market access commitments have been made, followed by financial and business services. In the health and education sectors, Members have made the fewest market access commitments, but few commitments were also made in the sector of distribution services.

On the whole, developed-country Members have made market access commitments with regard to nearly all sectors, except health and education. Note, however, that the United States did not make any market access commitments with respect to maritime transport services; and that the European Communities, Canada and Switzerland made no commitments with regard to audiovisual services.[382]

Market access commitments with respect to 'consumption abroad' (mode 2) are much less subject to limitations than market access commitments with

---

[379] See WTO Secretariat, *Market Access: Unfinished Business*, Special Studies Series 6 (WTO, 2001), 104.
[380] See *ibid.* This group of Members includes Australia, Canada, the European Communities, Hong Kong, Japan, Korea, Mexico, New Zealand, Norway, South Africa, Switzerland, Thailand, Turkey and the United States (*ibid.*, 106). According to the World Bank study, this group also includes a number of developing-country Members and least-developed-country Members (the Gambia, Lesotho and Sierra Leone). This study also noted that the Kyrgyz Republic and Georgia, two countries that recently acceded to the WTO, have undertaken broader commitments, in terms of sector coverage, than any participant in the Uruguay Round negotiations. See B. Hoekman, A. Mattoo and P. English (eds.), *Development, Trade, and the WTO: A Handbook* (World Bank, 2004), 262.   [381] See above, p. 89.
[382] See WTO Secretariat, *Market Access: Unfinished Business*, Special Studies Series 6 (WTO, 2001), 104.

respect to other modes of supply of services.[383] Presumably, governments feel no need to restrict their nationals' consumption abroad or consider it impracticable to enforce such restrictions.[384] Market access commitments with respect to 'supply through the presence of natural persons' (mode 4), however, are usually subject to broad limitations. Many Members have horizontal commitments with respect to mode 4, providing for limitations to market access applicable to all scheduled sectors. Members, developed and developing alike, are clearly hesitant to undertake any commitments involving the entry of natural persons onto their territory. They are unwilling to expose their labour markets to competition from foreign workers.

Questions and Assignments 5.23

Discuss the extent of market access commitments for trade in services agreed to in the context of the WTO thus far.

5.4.2. Other barriers to trade in services

In addition to the market access barriers, discussed above, trade in services can also be impeded by a wide array of other barriers. With regard to a number of these other barriers, WTO law, and in particular the GATS, provides for specific rules. Some of these rules have general application.[385] Other rules apply only in sectors where specific market access commitments were made.[386] This section discusses:

- lack of transparency;
- unfair or arbitrary application of measures affecting trade in services;
- domestic regulation;
- lack of recognition of diplomas and professional certificates; and
- other measures and actions.

5.4.2.1. Lack of transparency

Ignorance, uncertainty or confusion with respect to the relevant laws and regulations applicable in actual or potential foreign markets are formidable barriers to trade in services. Effective market access is impossible without transparency regarding the laws and regulations affecting the services concerned. Service suppliers must have accurate information concerning the rules with which they must comply.

---

[383] On the relative importance of each of the four modes of supply in the total world services trade, see above, p. 338, footnote 74.

[384] See WTO Secretatiat, *Market Access: Unfinished Business*, Special Studies Series 6 (WTO, 2001), 105.

[385] For example, the requirement that Members maintain or institute as soon as practicable judicial, arbitral or administrative tribunals for the prompt review of decisions affecting trade in services. See Article VI:2(a) of the GATS, and below, p. 494.

[386] For example, the requirement to administer measures affecting trade in services in a reasonable, objective and impartial manner. See Article VI:1 of the GATS, and below, p. 494.

As in Article X of the GATT 1994, Article III of the GATS requires that Members *publish* all measures of general application affecting trade in services.[387] Publication must take place promptly and at the latest by the time the measure enters into force.[388]

Since the end of 1997, each Member has been required to establish one or more *enquiry points* to provide information on laws and regulations affecting trade in services.[389] Members have an obligation to respond promptly to all requests by any other Member for specific information on any of its measures of general application.[390] For the benefit of developing-country Members, developed-country Members have a special obligation to establish 'contact points' to facilitate the access of service suppliers from developing-country Members to information of special interest to them.[391]

Article III of the GATS also requires a Member to *notify* the Council for Trade in Services of any new, or any changes to, laws, regulations or administrative guidelines, which significantly affect trade in sectors where that Member has made specific commitments. Members must do so at least once a year.[392]

Note that the transparency of Members' measures affecting trade in services is also advanced by the trade policy reviews under the *Trade Policy Review Mechanism*.[393]

5.4.2.2. *Unfair and arbitrary application of measures affecting trade in services*

In sectors where specific commitments are undertaken, Article VI:1 of the GATS requires a Member to ensure:

> that all measures of general application affecting trade in services are administered in a reasonable, objective and impartial manner.

This obligation is the counterpart of Article X:3(a) of the GATT 1994, discussed above, for trade in services.[394]

In all service sectors, including those in which no specific commitments are undertaken, Article VI:2(a) of the GATS requires Members to maintain procedures which allow service suppliers to challenge administrative decisions affecting them. These procedures may be administrative or judicial but must be objective and impartial. Moreover, they must provide for prompt review and, where necessary, appropriate remedies.[395]

Where authorisation is required for the supply of a service on which a commitment has been made, the competent authorities of a Member must, within a

---

[387] Where publication is not practicable, the information must be made otherwise publicly available (see Article III:2 of the GATS). The publication requirement exists also for measures affecting trade in services with regard to which a Member has not made specific commitments.

[388] See Article III:1 of the GATS. This obligation can be waived in emergency situations. This publication obligation also applies to international agreements pertaining to or affecting trade in services to which a Member is a signatory.   [389] See Article III:4 of the GATS.   [390] See *ibid*.

[391] See Article IV:2 of the GATS. Such information includes information on registration, recognition and obtaining of professional qualifications; and the availability of services technologies.

[392] See Article III:3 of the GATS. Members are not required, however, to supply confidential information. See Article III *bis* of the GATS.   [393] See above, pp. 93–5.   [394] See above, pp. 466–70.

[395] See Article VI:2(a) of the GATS.

reasonable period of time, inform the applicant of the decision concerning the application.[396]

5.4.2.3. *Domestic regulation*

As discussed above, trade in services is primarily impeded or restricted by domestic regulation. For scheduled services, certain domestic regulations may constitute market access barriers within the meaning of Article XVI:2 of the GATS and, as discussed above, are prohibited unless otherwise specified in the Schedule.[397] However, most domestic regulations do not constitute market access barriers within the meaning of Article XVI:2.[398] Examples of such domestic regulations include qualification requirements, technical standards and licensing requirements for services or service suppliers as well as price controls imposing minimum or maximum prices on services.[399] Apart from the rules concerning transparency and the rules on unfair and arbitrary application, discussed above, the GATS does not provide for rules on domestic regulations in general. Nevertheless, it is clear that domestic regulations of the sort described here can seriously undermine any market access commitments made with regard to a service sector. Therefore, Article VI:5(a) of the GATS provides:

> In sectors in which a Member has undertaken specific commitments . . . the Member shall not apply licensing and qualification requirements and technical standards that nullify or impair such specific commitments in a manner which:
>
> i. does not comply with the criteria outlined in subparagraphs 4(a), (b) or (c); and
> ii. could not reasonably have been expected of that Member at the time the specific commitments in those sectors were made.

According to the criteria of Article VI:4(a), (b) and (c) to which the above provision refers, licensing requirements, qualification requirements and technical standards relating to service sectors in which specific commitments are undertaken must:

- be based on objective and transparent criteria such as competence and the ability to supply the service;
- not be more burdensome than necessary to ensure the quality of the service; and
- in the case of licensing procedures, not be, in themselves, a restriction on the supply of the service.

If licensing requirements, qualification requirements or technical standards relating to service sectors, in which specific commitments are undertaken, do

---

[396] See Article VI:3 of the GATS.   [397] See above, pp. 477–9.

[398] Note that the Panel in *US – Gambling* stated: 'Under Article VI and Article XVI, measures are either of the type covered by the disciplines of Article XVI or are domestic regulations relating to qualification requirements and procedures, technical standards and licensing requirements subject to the specific provisions of Article VI. Thus, Articles VI:4 and VI:5 on the one hand and XVI on the other hand are mutually exclusive.' Panel Report, *US – Gambling*, para. 6.305.

[399] For the scope of the concept of 'market access barrier' within the meaning of Article XVI:2 of the GATS, see above, pp. 477–9.

not meet these criteria *and*, furthermore, nullify or impair the specific commitments undertaken in a manner which could not reasonably have been expected at the time the commitments were made, the Member acts inconsistently with its obligations under Article VI:5(a) of the GATS.[400] The Member must then amend the licensing requirement, qualification requirement or technical standard at issue.

Note that Article VI:4 of the GATS gives the Council for Trade in Services a broad and ambitious mandate to develop the multilateral disciplines necessary to ensure that licensing requirements, qualification requirements and procedures and technical standards do not constitute *unnecessary barriers* to trade in services. To date, such disciplines have only been successfully developed with regard to accountancy.[401]

Note also that Article XVIII, entitled 'Additional Commitments', provides:

> Members may negotiate commitments with respect to measures affecting trade in services not subject to scheduling under Articles XVI or XVII, including those regarding qualifications, standards or licensing matters. Such commitments shall be inscribed in a Member's Schedule.

Members may therefore make commitments with respect to measures which are neither market access barriers (Article XVI) nor inconsistent with the national treatment obligation (Article XVII). These additional commitments are recorded in the fourth column of a Member's Schedule. In practice, such commitments are exceptional.

5.4.2.4. *Lack of recognition of foreign diplomas and professional certificates*

Foreign service suppliers such as doctors, engineers, nurses, lawyers and accountants will usually have obtained their diplomas and professional certificates in their country of origin and will not have diplomas or professional certificates of the country in which they wish to be active. Members are required to provide for adequate procedures, in sectors where specific commitments regarding professional services are undertaken, to *verify the competence* of professionals from any other Member.[402] However, it is clear that even with these procedures, having only a foreign diploma or professional certificate may constitute an important impediment for persons to supply services in other Members.

WTO law does not require that Members recognise foreign diplomas or professional certificates. However, the GATS *encourages the recognition* of foreign diplomas and professional certificates, by allowing Members to deviate, under certain conditions, from the basic MFN treatment obligation of Article II of the GATS. Article VII:1 of the GATS provides in relevant part:

---

[400] Note that, in determining whether a Member is in conformity with the obligation under Article VI:5(a), account shall be taken of international standards of relevant international organisations applied by that Member. See Article VII:5(b) of the GATS.

[401] See Council for Trade in Services, *Disciplines on Domestic Regulation in the Accountancy Sector*, adopted on 14 December 1998, S/L/64, dated 17 December 1998.   [402] See Article VII:6 of the GATS.

> a Member may recognize the education or experience obtained, requirements met, or
> licences or certifications granted in *a particular country*.
>
> [Emphasis added]

Pursuant to Article VII:1, such recognition:

- may be achieved through harmonisation *or* otherwise; and
- may be based upon an agreement with the country concerned *or* may be accorded autonomously.

However, the recognition must be based on objective criteria, and may not discriminate among Members where similar conditions prevail. Members who are parties to recognition agreements are required to afford adequate opportunity for other interested Members to negotiate their accession to such agreements or negotiate comparable agreements with them. If recognition is accorded on an autonomous basis, the Member concerned must give adequate opportunity for any other Member concerned to demonstrate that qualifications acquired in its territory should be recognised. Members must notify the Council for Trade in Services of all existing recognition measures.[403]

In the long term, Members aim at adopting common standards for the recognition of diplomas and professional qualifications. A first effort in this respect has been the *Guidelines for Mutual Recognition Agreements or Arrangements in the Accountancy Sector*, agreed upon by the Council for Trade in Services in May 1997.[404]

5.4.2.5. *Other measures and actions*

In addition to lack of transparency, unfair or arbitrary application of measures affecting trade in services, domestic regulation and lack of recognition, trade in services is impeded by a number of other measures or actions. This section briefly addresses the following:

- monopolies and exclusive service providers;
- international payments and transfers; and
- government procurement laws and practices.

While *monopolies* or the *exclusive right* to supply a service can obviously impede trade in services, they are not prohibited by WTO law in general or by the GATS in particular. It is common for governments to grant entities an exclusive right to supply certain services, such as rail transport, telecommunications, sanitation, etc. However, pursuant to Article VIII:1 of the GATS, a Member must ensure that:

---

[403] See Article VII:4 of the GATS. They must also inform the Council of the opening of negotiations on a recognition agreement in order to give any other Member the opportunity to indicate an interest in participating in the negotiations.

[404] See S/L/38, dated 28 May 1997. Negotiations on these guidelines were conducted in the WTO Working Party on Professional Services. See WPPS/W/12/Rev.1, dated 20 May 1997.

> any monopoly supplier of a service in its territory does not, in the supply of the monopoly service in the relevant market, act in a manner inconsistent with that Member's obligations under Article II and specific commitments.

A Member must also ensure that, when a monopoly supplier competes in the supply of a service outside the scope of its monopoly rights, the Member does not *abuse* its monopoly position inconsistent with its commitments regarding that service.[405]

Business practices, other than monopolies, may also hinder competition and thereby restrict trade in services. Article IX of the GATS requires Members, at the request of any other Member, to enter into consultations with a view to eliminating such practices.

It is obvious that restrictions on *international transfers and payments for services* can constitute a barrier to trade in services. Article XI of the GATS requires Members to allow international transfers and payments relating to services covered by specific commitments. A Member is also required to allow incoming transfers related to the establishment of commercial presence whenever a commitment is undertaken with respect to that mode of supply.

As discussed above in the context of trade in goods, *government procurement laws and practices* often constitute significant barriers to trade as governments give preferences to domestic services or service suppliers over foreign services or service suppliers. The GATS, like the GATT 1994 with regard to government procurement of goods, does not set forth any multilateral disciplines on the procurement of services for governmental purposes. Article XIII:1 of the GATS provides:

> Articles II, XVI and XVII shall not apply to laws, regulations or requirements governing the procurement by governmental agencies of services purchased for governmental purposes and not with a view to commercial resale or with a view to use in the supply of services for commercial sale.

The general MFN treatment obligation (of Article II) and specific commitments on market access and national treatment (of Articles XVI and XVII respectively) do not, generally speaking, apply to laws, regulations or requirements governing public procurement of services.

Note, however, that the plurilateral WTO *Agreement on Government Procurement* discussed above applies not only to government procurement of goods but also to government procurement of services. The plurilateral disciplines set forth in that Agreement also apply to laws and regulations on the government procurement of services.[406]

Questions and Assignments 5.24

Briefly describe the GATS rules on transparency and the unfair and arbitrary application of measures affecting trade in services. Does the

---

[405] See Article VIII:2 of the GATS.   [406] See above, pp. 472–6.

GATS lay down rules with respect to domestic regulation other than market access barriers? Are there any GATS rules regarding the recognition of diplomas and professional qualifications? Are there any WTO rules on government procurement of services?

5.5. SUMMARY

Market access for goods and services from other countries can be, and frequently is, impeded or restricted in various ways. There are two main categories of barriers to market access for trade in goods:

- tariff barriers; and
- non-tariff barriers.

The category of tariff barriers includes customs duties (i.e. tariffs) and other duties and charges. The category of non-tariff barriers includes quantitative restrictions (such as quotas) and other non-tariff barriers (such as lack of transparency of trade regulation, unfair and arbitrary application of trade regulation, customs formalities, technical barriers to trade and government procurement practices). Different rules apply to the different forms of barriers. This difference in rules reflects a difference in the negative effects the barriers have on trade and on the economy.

A customs duty, or tariff, is a financial charge, i.e. a tax, imposed on products at the time of, and/or because of, their importation. Market access is conditional upon the payment of the customs duty. Customs duties are either specific, *ad valorem* or mixed. *Ad valorem* customs duties are by far the most common type of customs duties. The customs duties or tariffs, which are due on importation, are set out in a country's tariff. Most national tariffs follow or reflect the structure set out in the Harmonised Commodity Description and Coding System, usually referred to as the 'Harmonised System'.

WTO law and, in particular, the GATT 1994, does not prohibit the imposition of customs duties. Customs duties, unlike quantitative restrictions, represent an instrument of protection against imports generally allowed by the GATT 1994. Article XXVIII *bis* of the GATT 1994 does, however, call upon WTO Members to negotiate the reduction of customs duties. The eight GATT Rounds of trade negotiations have been very successful in reducing customs duties. Nevertheless, customs duties remain an important barrier in international trade and further negotiations on the reduction of tariffs are therefore necessary. The basic principles and rules governing tariff negotiations are:

- the principle of reciprocity and mutual advantage; and
- the most-favoured-nation (MFN) treatment obligation.

The principle of reciprocity does not apply in full to tariff negotiations between developed and developing-country Members. Members can adopt different approaches to tariff negotiations, including the product-by-product request-and-offer approach, the linear reduction approach, the formula approach and the sectoral elimination approach.

The results of tariff negotiations are referred to as 'tariff concessions' or 'tariff bindings'. A tariff concession, or tariff binding, is a commitment not to raise the customs duty on a certain product above an agreed level. The tariff concessions or bindings of a Member are set out in that Member's Schedule of Concessions. The Schedules resulting from the Uruguay Round negotiations are all annexed to the *Marrakesh Protocol* to the GATT 1994 and are an integral part thereof. Therefore, the tariff schedules and tariff concessions must be interpreted in accordance with the general rules of interpretation set out in the *Vienna Convention on the Law of Treaties*.

Article II:1(a) of the GATT 1994 provides that Members shall accord to products imported from other Members *treatment no less favourable* than that provided for in their Schedules. Article II:1(b), first sentence, of the GATT 1994 provides that products described in Part I of the Schedule of any Member shall, on importation, be *exempt from ordinary customs duties in excess of* those set out in the Schedule. This means that products may not be subjected to customs duties above the tariff concessions or bindings. Note, however, that Article XXVIII of the GATT 1994 provides a procedure for the modification or withdrawal of the agreed tariff concessions.

In addition to the rules to protect tariff concessions, WTO law also provides for some rules on the manner in which customs duties must be imposed. The imposition of customs duties may require three determinations to be made:

- the determination of the proper classification of the imported good;
- the determination of the customs value of the imported good; and
- the determination of the origin of the imported good.

The WTO agreements do not specifically address the issue of customs classification. However, in classifying products for customs purposes, Members have of course to consider their general obligations under the WTO agreements, such as the MFN treatment obligation. *Specific* rules on classification can be found in the *International Convention on the Harmonised Commodity Description and Coding System*, to which most WTO Members are a party.

Unlike for customs classification, the *WTO Agreement* provides for rules on customs valuation. These rules are set out in: Article VII of the GATT 1994; the Note *Ad* Article VII; and the WTO *Customs Valuation Agreement*. The primary basis for the customs value is the 'transaction value' of the imported goods, i.e. the price actually paid or payable for the goods. This price is normally shown in the invoice, contract or purchase order, albeit that a number of adjustments usually have to be made. If the customs value cannot be established in this manner, it must be established pursuant to the alternative methods set out in the *Customs Valuation Agreement*.

The GATT 1994 provides no specific disciplines on rules of origin. However, the negotiators during the Uruguay Round recognised the need for multilateral disciplines on rules of origin in order to prevent these rules from being a source of uncertainty and unpredictability in international trade. The consensus on the need for such disciplines resulted in the WTO *Agreement on Rules of Origin.* With respect to *non-preferential* rules of origin, the *Agreement on Rules of Origin* provides for a work programme on the harmonisation of these rules. Until the successful completion of this work programme, Article 2 of the *Agreement on Rules of Origin* contains a rather extensive list of multilateral disciplines on the application and administration of rules of origin applicable during the current 'transition period'. After harmonised rules of origin have been agreed on, these disciplines will continue to apply. With respect to *preferential* rules of origin, Annex 2 to the Agreement on Rules of Origin provides for a more modest list of multilateral disciplines on the application and administration of rules of origin.

In addition to 'ordinary customs duties', tariff barriers can also take the form of 'other duties and charges'. 'Other duties and charges' are financial charges, *other than* ordinary customs duties, imposed on, or in the context of, the importation of a good. Pursuant to Article II:1(b), second sentence, of the GATT 1994 and the *Understanding on Article II:1(b)*, Members may:

- impose only 'other duties and charges' that have been properly recorded in their Schedules; and
- impose 'other duties and charges' only at a level that does not exceed the level recorded in their Schedules.

There are, however, a number of exceptions to the rule that Members may not impose 'other duties or charges' in excess of the recorded level. Pursuant to Article II:2 of the GATT 1994, Members may – in spite of their obligations under Article II:1(b), second sentence – impose on imported products:

- any financial charge that is not in excess of the internal tax imposed on the like domestic product (border tax adjustment);
- WTO-consistent anti-dumping or countervailing duties; or
- fees or other charges 'commensurate' with, i.e. matching, the cost of the services rendered.

Trade in goods is not only restricted by customs duties and other duties and charges, but also by non-tariff barriers, i.e. quantitative restrictions and other non-tariff barriers. A quantitative restriction is a measure which *limits the quantity* of a product that may be imported or exported. Article XI:1 of the GATT 1994 sets out a general prohibition on quantitative restrictions, whether on imports or exports. Unlike other GATT provisions, Article XI refers not to laws or regulations but more broadly to measures. A measure instituted or maintained by a Member which restricts imports or exports is covered by Article XI, *irrespective* of the legal status of the measure. Furthermore, quantitative restrictions which do not *actually* impede trade are nevertheless prohibited under Article XI:1 of the GATT 1994. According to firmly established case law, the basic provisions of the GATT on restrictive trade measures are 'provisions establishing equality of conditions of competition'. Also note that restrictions of a *de facto* nature are also prohibited under Article XI:1 of the GATT 1994.

While quantitative restrictions are, as a rule, prohibited, there are many exceptions to this prohibition. Article XIII of the GATT 1994 sets out rules on the *administration* of these GATT-consistent quantitative restrictions (and tariff quotas). Article XIII:1 of the GATT 1994 provides that quantitative restrictions, when applied, should be administered in a non-discriminatory manner. According to Article XIII:2 of the GATT 1994, the distribution of trade still allowed should be as close as possible to what would have been the distribution of trade in the absence of the quantitative restriction (or tariff quota). Furthermore, Article XIII:2 sets out a number of requirements to be met when imposing quotas (or tariff quotas). Article XIII:2(d) provides that, if no agreement can be reached with all Members having a substantial interest in supplying the product concerned, the quota (or tariff quota) must be allocated among these Members on the basis of their share of the trade during a previous representative period.

Quotas and tariff quotas are habitually administered through import licensing procedures. A trader who wishes to import a product that is subject to a quota or tariff quota must apply for an import licence, i.e. a permit to import. The *Import Licensing Agreement* sets out rules on the *application* and *administration* of import licensing rules. The most important of these rules, set out in Article 1.3, is that the rules for import-licensing procedures shall be neutral in application and administered in a fair and equitable manner.

In addition to customs duties and other duties and charges (i.e. tariff barriers) and quantitative restrictions (i.e. the first category of non-tariff barriers), trade in goods is also impeded by 'other non-tariff barriers', including:

- technical barriers to trade in goods (which are discussed in chapter 8 of this book)
- lack of transparency;
- unfair and arbitrary application of trade laws and regulations; and
- customs formalities and procedures.

Ignorance, uncertainty or confusion with respect to the trade laws, regulations and procedures applicable in actual or potential export markets is an important barrier to trade in goods. To ensure a high level of transparency of its Members' trade laws, regulations and procedures, WTO law requires their *publication* and *notification* as well as the establishment of *enquiry points*. The unfair and arbitrary application of national trade measures, and the degree of uncertainty and unpredictability this generates for other Members and traders, also constitutes a significant barrier to trade in goods. Therefore, WTO law provides for:

- a requirement of uniform, impartial and reasonable administration of national trade rules; and
- a requirement of procedures for the objective and impartial review of the administration of national customs rules.

The losses that traders suffer through delays at borders and complicated and/or unnecessary documentation requirements and other customs procedures and formalities are estimated to exceed the costs of tariffs in many cases. However, WTO law currently contains few rules on customs formalities and procedures aimed at mitigating their adverse impact on trade.

As with trade in goods, trade in services is also often subject to restrictions. Unlike for trade in goods, however, trade-restrictive measures applied at the border are barely significant for trade in services. The production and consumption of services are subject to a vast range of domestic regulations. Barriers to trade in services primarily result from these domestic regulations. WTO law, and the GATS in particular, provides for rules and disciplines on barriers to trade in services. A distinction must be made between market access barriers and other barriers to trade in services.

Article XVI:2 of the GATS contains an *exhaustive* list of *market access barriers*. This list includes:

- five types of quantitative restrictions (Article XVI:2(a) to (d) and (f)); and
- limitations on forms of legal entity (Article XVI:2(e)).

These market access barriers can be discriminatory or non-discriminatory with regard to foreign services or service suppliers. Note that four of the five types of quantitative restrictions referred to in Article XVI:2 can be expressed numerically, or through the criteria specified in these provisions, such as an economic needs test. It is important, however, that these criteria do not relate:

- to the quality of the service supplied; or
- to the ability of the supplier to supply the service (i.e. technical standards or qualification of the supplier).

Also note that the quantitative restrictions specified in Article XVI:2(a) to (d) refer to *maximum* limitations.

The GATS does not provide for a general prohibition of these market access barriers. Whether a Member may maintain or adopt such market access barriers with regard to a specific service depends on whether, and if so to what extent, that Member has made market access commitments with regard to the relevant service sector in its Schedule of Specific Commitments. When a Member makes a market access commitment, it *binds* the level of market access specified in the Schedule (see Article XVI:1) and agrees not to impose any market access barrier that would restrict access to the market beyond the level specified (see Article XVI:2).

To achieve *progressively* higher levels of liberalisation of trade in services, the GATS provides for *successive* rounds of negotiations. The approach to negotiations on the liberalisation of services is a request-and-offer approach. It is accepted that developing-country Members undertake fewer and more limited market access commitments than developed-country Members. The terms, limitations and conditions on *market access* agreed to in the negotiations on the liberalisation of trade in services are set out in the second column of the Schedules of

Specific Commitments. Each Member has a Schedule of Specific Commitments, and these Schedules, all annexed to the GATS, form an integral part thereof. Like tariff concessions for goods, market access commitments for services can also be modified or withdrawn. To do so, the procedure set out in Article XXI of the GATS must be followed.

In addition to market access barriers, trade in services can also be impeded by a wide array of other barriers. With regard to a number of these other barriers, WTO law, and in particular the GATS, provides for specific rules. The GATS requires the prompt *publication* of all measures of general application affecting trade in services. It also requires Members to establish *enquiry points* to provide information on laws and regulations affecting trade in services. Furthermore, the GATS requires Members to ensure that all measures of general application affecting trade in services are administered in a *reasonable, objective and impartial* manner. As noted above, trade in services is primarily impeded or restricted by domestic regulation. Most domestic regulation does not constitute market access barriers within the meaning of Article XVI:2. Apart from the rules concerning transparency and the rules on unfair and arbitrary application, the GATS does not provide for general rules on domestic regulation. The GATS, however, does provide for certain disciplines for licensing and qualification requirements and technical standards relating to service sectors in which specific commitments are undertaken. These requirements and standards must:

- be based on objective and transparent criteria such as competence and the ability to supply the service;
- not be more burdensome than necessary to ensure the quality of the service; and
- in the case of licensing procedures, not be, in themselves, a restriction on the supply of the service.

Finally, note that the GATS encourages and facilitates the recognition of diplomas and professional certificates of foreign service suppliers.

5.6. EXERCISE: CARLIE® GOES TO EUROPE

Dolls Я Us is a toy manufacturer from Goldtown, Richland, with production facilities in both Richland and Newland. Dolls Я Us produces a wide range of toys but is best known for a doll named Carlie®. In view of its success in the United States, Dolls Я Us wants to explore the possibility of marketing Carlie® in the United Kingdom. However, Dolls Я Us does not merely want to export Carlie® to the United Kingdom. It also wants to distribute its dolls to retail shops in the United Kingdom and set up its own chain of Carlie® shops for the London area. In the United States, a daughter company of Dolls Я Us, BuyItNow, has acquired significant expertise in advertising Carlie® and it intends to offer advertising services to UK toy retailers, either via the internet or by sending its experts to the UK.

Carlie® is a Barbie-like doll with a plastic body, artificial hair and three sets of clothes. The plastic body parts, the hair and the clothes are produced in Newland. Carlie® is only assembled and packaged in Richland. It is expected to sell at £10 per doll in the United Kingdom.

Her Majesty's Customs Service has informed Dolls Я Us that the customs duty on Carlie® will amount to 15 per cent *ad valorem* and that the value will be determined on the basis of the sales price on the domestic market in Richland. Dolls Я Us challenges both the level of the duty and the manner in which the Customs Service intends to determine the value of the dolls for customs purposes. It also disagrees with the Customs Service that the country of origin of Carlie® is Richland and not Newland. Furthermore, Dolls Я Us considers that Carlie® is not really a toy but rather a collector's item. Finally, it wonders whether, for the customs classification of Carlie®, it makes a difference whether Carlie® is imported as a finished product or in parts still to be assembled.

The Customs Service also informed Dolls Я Us that the European Communities only allows the importation of 500,000 dolls per year. This quota has been divided among China (400,000 dolls), Vietnam (90,000 dolls) and others (10,000 dolls). In the past, neither Richland nor Newland has been a significant exporter of dolls to the European Communities. Dolls Я Us, however, hopes to sell at least 100,000 dolls per year in the United Kingdom within two years.

Finally, Her Majesty's Customs Service informs Dolls Я Us that all dolls must be imported through the port of Plymouth and that a special customs-handling fee of 0.2 per cent *ad valorem* is imposed on foreign toys upon their importation. This fee goes to the Customs Service's Fund for Disfavoured Children.

With respect to Dolls Я Us' plans to distribute Carlie® to retail shops in the United Kingdom itself and to set up – for the London area – a chain of Carlie® shops, the UK Ministry of Trade and Industry informed Dolls R Us that:

- under the Toys Act of 1935, foreign companies are not allowed to act as wholesale distributors of toys in the United Kingdom; and
- under the Small Shopkeepers Protection Act of 1976, the number of retail shops in a specific area is limited on the basis of an economic needs test.

The Ministry of Trade and Industry also informs Dolls Я Us that only persons holding European professional qualifications or qualifications recognised as equivalent by the United Kingdom can supply advertising services in the United Kingdom.

Dolls Я Us is very disappointed by the information received from the Customs Service and the Ministry of Trade and Industry. It has asked its law firm, Gandhi, Rao & Ganesan, an Indian law firm with offices in London, to contact both the Customs Service and the Ministry of Trade and Industry to discuss the information given by them. Dolls Я Us considers that much of the legislation at issue in this case is not transparent and that its application is arbitrary and unfair. Dolls Я Us has announced that, if it is not allowed to market Carlie® in the United Kingdom on more 'favourable' terms, it will lobby the governments of Richland

and Newland to bring a case against the European Communities *and* the United Kingdom at the WTO in Geneva.

You are a lawyer working at Gandhi, Rao & Ganesan and you have been asked to prepare a legal brief on all the issues raised above.

You have been advised to consult the Goods and Services Schedules of the European Communities and the TARIC database.

Contents

6.1. INTRODUCTION

While professing support for trade liberalisation, trade policy-makers often insist that international trade should at the same time be 'fair'. 'Unfair' trade comes in many forms and guises. Unfair trade practices include cartel agreements, price fixing and the abuse of a dominant position on the market.[1] WTO law, at present, does not provide for rules on these and many other particular forms of unfair trade. It does provide, however, for relatively detailed rules with respect to dumping and certain types of subsidisation – two specific practices commonly considered to be unfair trade practices. This chapter examines the WTO rules on dumping and subsidisation.[2]

6.2. DUMPING AND ANTI-DUMPING MEASURES

As discussed in chapter 1, 'dumping' is the bringing of a product onto the market of another country (or customs territory) at a price less than the normal value of that product.[3] In WTO law, dumping is not prohibited.[4] However, dumping is to be 'condemned' if it causes injury to the domestic industry of the importing country. The essence of the WTO rules on dumping is that Members are allowed to take certain measures, which are otherwise WTO-inconsistent, to protect their domestic industry from the injurious effects of dumping.

During the first half of 2007, thirteen Members initiated a total of forty-nine anti-dumping investigations. This represents a sharp decline as compared to the corresponding period in 2006, when ninety-two investigations were initiated.[5] Sixteen Members imposed a total of fifty-seven new definitive anti-dumping measures against exports from other countries or customs territories: a slight decrease as compared to seventy-one in the corresponding period in 2006.[6]

The overall use of anti-dumping measures fluctuates from year to year. In the period since the establishment of the WTO, the number of anti-dumping measures taken by Members has been on average 162 per year.[7] From 1995 to 2006, India was the most frequent user of the anti-dumping instrument, with a total of 331 measures.[8] The United States was second, with 239 measures and the European Communities was third with 231.[9] In the first half of 2007, India imposed the most new measures (sixteen), followed by Argentina (seven), the European Communities (six), China (five), Pakistan (four), and Canada, Colombia, Turkey and the United States (three each).[10] These figures make clear that the days when anti-dumping measures were taken almost exclusively by

---

[1] The concept of 'unfair trade' is also commonly used to refer to trade on terms and conditions which are disadvantageous for developing countries in general and small companies, workers and farmers in these countries in particular.

[2] The section on dumping and anti-dumping measures, as it appeared in the first edition of this book, was written in collaboration with Dr Julie Soloway. I am much indebted to Dr Soloway for her contribution to this chapter.   [3] See above, p. 40. For a more detailed definition, see below, pp. 515–26.

[4] See below, p. 513.

[5] See www.wto.org/english/news_e/pres07_e/pr497_e.htm, visited on 30 October 2007.   [6] See *ibid.*

[7] Note that in the final years of the GATT, this number was considerably higher.

[8] India has indeed been a frequent user of anti-dumping measures. Between January 2002 and December 2005, India initiated 176 anti-dumping investigations and imposed final measures in 163 of them; 20 new investigations were initiated in the first half of 2006, with final measures taken in 8 cases. See WTO Secretariat, *Trade Policy Review Report – India*, WT/TPR/S/182, dated 18 April 2007, para. 44.

[9] See www.wto.org/english/tratop_e/adp_e/adp_stattab7_e.pdf, visited on 17 August 2007.

[10] See www.wto.org/english/news_e/pres07_e/pr497_e.htm, visited on 30 October 2007.

developed-country Members are gone. Developing-country Members have 'discovered' this trade policy instrument and some have become avid users.

China has been by far the biggest target of anti-dumping measures, with 375 such measures having been taken against it between 1995 and 2006.[11] Also, in the first half of 2007, exports from China were the subject of the largest number of new anti-dumping measures (twenty-two, compared with fifteen during the corresponding period in 2006).[12] Chinese Taipei ranked second with four measures on its exports, followed by India, Indonesia, Korea and Thailand (each subject to three new measures).[13]

Anti-dumping law is one of the most controversial and politically sensitive areas of WTO law. WTO Members are often put under severe pressure by their 'domestic industry' to impose anti-dumping measures, or by foreign producers and importers *not* to impose those measures, as the following excerpt makes clear:

> Peter Mandelson, EU trade commissioner, has become embroiled in a 'fridge war' with electrical goods makers in Europe after he took an eleventh-hour decision not to levy anti-dumping duties on certain Korean imports. Mr Mandelson is accused by Whirlpool, the US home appliance maker with operations in Europe, of succumbing to 'devious lobbying activity' and of 'a serious breach in procedures'. It claims that his decision not to impose punitive tariffs on Korean 'three-door side-by-side' fridges would have 'direct and very significant consequences for the European industry'.[14]

Exerting public pressure on civil servants is indeed common practice, as the full-page advertisement of ANCI, the National Association of Italian Shoe Factories, illustrates in Figure 6.1.[15]

The shoe-spat also exemplifies the highly controversial and political character of anti-dumping cases:

> After months of contentious discussions, EU member states narrowly voted on 4 October to slap anti-dumping duties on shoes imported from China and Vietnam . . . The decision had badly split EU members. Mediterranean states, led by Italy, generally supported the measures, in the face of active opposition from the Scandinavian countries and Germany. The UK was another of the 12 countries that voted against the new tariffs – just one short of the majority that would have been necessary to block them. On 7 October, the EU started imposing extra duties of 16.5 percent on leather shoes from China, and 10 percent on those from Vietnam. These replace higher provisional duties that had been in place since April. Under a compromise brokered by France, they will remain in force for two years, though the European Commission had originally sought five. Brussels claims that there is 'compelling evidence of serious state intervention' in the footwear sector in China and Vietnam – in the form of cheap finance, tax holidays, favourable land rental and electricity rates, and the like – which allow them to 'dump' goods on the EU market at unfairly low prices.[16]

However, Werner Haizmann, President of the Federation of European Sporting Goods Retail Associations, and Horst Widmann, President of the Federation of

---

[11] See www.wto.org/english/tratop_e/adp_e/adp_stattab6_e.pdf, visited on 17 August 2007.
[12] See www.wto.org/english/news_e/pres07_e/pr497_e.htm, visited on 30 October 2007.   [13] See *ibid.*
[14] G. Parker, 'Mandelson Embroiled in "Fridge War" ', *Financial Times*, 27 July 2006.
[15] See *Financial Times*, 31 January 2006.
[16] *BRIDGES Weekly Trade News Digest*, 11 October 2006. See also A. Bounds, 'Deal Ends EU Impasse on Asian Shoe Tarrifs', *Financial Times*, 5 October 2006.

Figure 6.1 Advertisement of the National Association of Italian Shoe Factories (ANCI)

THIS IS AN ADVERTISEMENT PLACED BY ANCI

APPEAL TO COMMISSIONER PETER MANDELSON

Mr Mandelson,
Here are the reasons for implementing antidumping measures
on leather-footwear imports from China and Vietnam:

Imports of footwear from China to EU25:
- 2002–2003: +19%; 2004: +39%;
- First 10 months 2005: +300% leather footwear no longer subject to quotas;
average price: –25%.
Leather footwear is being imported at a price that is lower
than the net cost of the raw materials.

The European footwear industry gives work directly or through suppliers to **over 600,000
people**. More than **75,000 jobs were lost in 2005**. Thousands of footwear firms
are going out of business in Italy and across Europe, and **tens of thousands
of workers are losing their jobs.**
In extreme situations, the reactions must be firm, bold and swift.

Mr Mandelson, yours is a very delicate role.
The EU has an interest in defending those who produce
real wealth and create jobs in Europe.

The **antidumping process** has but one purpose: **to defend manufacturing.**
Six months have gone by since it was officially launched and it **is time to conclude
the procedures.** All types of leather footwear must be covered by the measures,
including STAF, Special Technology Athletic Footwear, which is made throughout Europe.

The **Italian and European footwear manufacturers are not afraid of
competition, but we are defenceless against those who practise dumping
in order to sell their products.** The state of the industry **is getting worse day
by day** and we cannot wait any longer.

These are the criteria on which you should base your decisions.
We trust that your intervention will be bold and swift.

A.N.C.I. Servizi S.r.l.

European Sporting Goods Industries, noted with regard to the use of anti-dumping measures:

> [W]e fail to see how duties would serve Europe's interest, given that they will raise prices for consumers and add costs and barriers for retailers, while benefiting no one.
> Anti-dumping policy cannot be used to offer once-protected European sectors respite from global competition. It would be extremely damaging for Europe's relations with China as well as a bad signal to other European sectors facing global competition if anti-dumping became a protectionist tool rather than a targeted measure founded on strict legal and economic criteria.[17]

Furthermore, the use of anti-dumping measures is increasingly at odds with contemporary tendencies of outsourcing, one of the characteristics of the

---

17 W. Haizmann and H. Widmann, 'Letters to the Editor: Anti-dumping not the Right EU Step in Chinese Shoe Trade', *Financial Times*, 6 February 2006.

globalised economy. Peter Mandelson, the EU Trade Commissioner, noted in this respect:

> [A]nti-dumping tariffs and quotas could harm Europe's own manufacturers, which have increasingly outsourced the production of shoes, textiles, lightbulbs and other goods, aiming to maintain a competitive edge against cheaper Asian rivals . . . While Europe should tackle unfair trade, globalisation means the definitions of what is European-made have become blurred . . . 'If producing cheaply in China helps generate profits and jobs in Europe, how should we treat these companies when disputes over unfair trading arise?'[18]

Note that from 1995 until December 2007, anti-dumping measures imposed by WTO Members have given rise to twenty-seven disputes, which resulted in a panel report or in both a panel and an Appellate Body report.[19]

This section on the WTO rules on dumping and anti-dumping measures addresses:

- the basic elements of the WTO anti-dumping regime;
- the determination of dumping;
- the determination of injury;
- the demonstration of a causal link;
- the national procedures for taking anti-dumping measures;
- anti-dumping measures;
- special and differential treatment for developing-country Members; and
- the standard of review in anti-dumping disputes.

Questions and Assignments 6.1

What is the essence of the WTO rules on dumping? Is all dumping to be 'condemned'? How has the use of anti-dumping measures evolved over the years? Does the use of anti-dumping measures make political and/or economic sense?

6.2.1. Basic elements of WTO law on dumping

Before entering into a more detailed, and often technical, discussion of the rules on dumping and anti-dumping measures, this section addresses in general terms:

- the history of the law on dumping;
- the concept of 'dumping';
- WTO treatment of dumping; and
- the response to injurious dumping.

6.2.1.1. History of the law on dumping

Current WTO law on dumping and anti-dumping measures is set out in Article VI of the GATT 1994 and in the WTO *Agreement on Implementation of Article VI of the*

---

[18] A. Bounds, 'Mandelson Warns Over Extra Taxes on Asian Imports', *Financial Times*, 4 September 2007.
[19] See www.worldtradelaw.net/dsc/database/ad.asp, visited on 31 December 2007.

GATT 1994, commonly referred to as the *Anti-Dumping Agreement*. When the GATT was negotiated in 1947, participants could at first not agree on whether a provision allowing anti-dumping duties should even be included.[20] However, largely at US insistence, Article VI was included to provide a basic framework as to how nations could respond to cases of dumping.[21] In the years following its negotiation, Article VI by itself proved to be inadequate in dealing with the anti-dumping issue. The Article was vague and was interpreted and applied in an inconsistent manner.[22] Many GATT contracting parties began to feel that other contracting parties were applying anti-dumping laws in a manner that effectively raised new barriers to trade.[23] The inadequacies of Article VI dictated that it would have to be fleshed out in further agreements. This was done, in 1967, by the Kennedy Round *Anti-Dumping Code*, which was later replaced, in 1979, by the Tokyo Round *Anti-Dumping Code*. However, in spite of the clarification and elaboration of Article VI by the Tokyo Round *Anti-Dumping Code*, there was even more criticism of the anti-dumping regime in the 1980s. At that time, there was a genuine proliferation of anti-dumping activity, with developed countries being the dominant users of the regime and developing countries a significant target.[24] Not surprisingly, therefore, the anti-dumping regime was one of the most controversial issues on the agenda of the Uruguay Round. The positions taken by the participants in the negotiations varied greatly. Some participants wanted to facilitate the taking of anti-dumping measures (the United States and the European Communities), while others wanted to impose stricter disciplines (Japan, Korea and Hong Kong, China). At the end of the Uruguay Round, a compromise was reached which found its reflection in the WTO *Anti-Dumping Agreement* and which, together with Article VI of the GATT 1994, sets out the current rules on dumping and anti-dumping measures. As will be noted in this chapter, the conflicting, and sometimes even opposing, interests at stake in the negotiations resulted in provisions with ambiguous language. Some of these provisions have been 'clarified' by the case law. Others still await clarification.

In the Doha Ministerial Declaration of November 2001, WTO Members agreed to place anti-dumping rules on the agenda of the Doha Development Round:

> In the light of experience and of the increasing application of these instruments by Members, we agree to negotiations aimed at clarifying and improving disciplines under the Agreements on Implementation of Article VI of the GATT 1994 and on Subsidies and Countervailing Measures, while preserving the basic concepts, principles and effectiveness of these

---

[20] The United Kingdom and others argued that anti-dumping laws were a hindrance to free trade and that the GATT should actually prohibit the imposition of anti-dumping duties. See B. Blonigen and T. Prusa, *Antidumping* (July 2001), NBER Working Paper No. W8398, available at: http://ssrn.com/abstract=278031, visited on 22 October 2007.

[21] The United States was one of the few countries at this time with anti-dumping legislation in place. Apart from the well-known Anti-Dumping Act of 1916, there was the Anti-Dumping Act of 1921 and the Tariff Act of 1930.

[22] See M. Trebilcock and R. Howse, *The Regulation of International Trade* (Routledge, 1999), 167.

[23] See J. Jackson, *The World Trading System: Law and Policy of International Economic Relations*, 2nd edition (Massachusetts Institute of Technology, 1997), 256.

[24] Between July 1980 and June 1988, nearly 1,200 anti-dumping actions were initiated. See M. Trebilcock and R. Howse, *The Regulation of International Trade* (Routledge, 1999), 166.

Agreements and their instruments and objectives, and taking into account the needs of developing and least-developed participants.[25]

In November 2007, the Chair of the Negotiating Group on Rules, Ambassador Guilleromo Valles Galmés, circulated among WTO Members the Draft Consolidated Chair Text of the *Anti-Dumping Agreement*.[26]

6.2.1.2. *Concept of 'dumping'*

'Dumping' is a situation of *international price discrimination* involving the price and cost of a product in the exporting country in relation to its price in the importing country. Article VI of the GATT 1994 and Article 2.1 of the *Anti-Dumping Agreement* define dumping as the introduction of a product into the commerce of another country at less than its 'normal value'.[27] Thus, a product can be considered 'dumped' where the export price of that product is less than its normal value, that is, the comparable price, in the ordinary course of trade, for the 'like product' destined for consumption in the exporting country.[28]

6.2.1.3. *WTO treatment of dumping*

WTO law does *not* prohibit dumping. In fact, since prices of products are ordinarily set by private companies, 'dumping' in and of itself is *not* regulated by WTO law. As discussed above, WTO law in general only imposes obligations on, and regulates the measures and actions of, WTO Members. It does not directly regulate the actions of private companies. Therefore, WTO law does not prohibit dumping. However, as dumping may cause injury to the domestic industry of the importing country, Article VI of the GATT 1994 states, in relevant part, that:

> The [Members] recognize that dumping . . . is to be *condemned* if it causes or threatens material injury to an established industry in the territory of a [Member] or materially retards the establishment of a domestic industry.
>
> [Emphasis added]

Consequently, Article VI of the GATT 1994 and the *Anti-Dumping Agreement* provide a framework of substantive and procedural rules to govern how a Member may counteract or 'remedy' dumping, through the imposition of 'anti-dumping' measures.

It is not mandatory for a WTO Member to enact anti-dumping legislation or to have in place a system for conducting anti-dumping investigations and imposing anti-dumping measures. However, if the government of a Member makes the

---

[25] Ministerial Conference, *Doha Ministerial Declaration*, WT/MIN(01)/DEC/1, dated 20 November 2001, para. 28.
[26] Negotiating Group on Rules, *Draft Consolidated Chair Texts of the AD and SCM Agreements*, TN/RL/W/213, dated 30 November 2007.
[27] Note that the Appellate Body in *US – Zeroing (Japan)* stated that Article 2.1 of the *Anti-Dumping Agreement* and Article VI:1 of the GATT 1994 are 'definitional provisions' and do not impose independent obligations. See Appellate Body Report, *US – Zeroing (Japan)*, para. 140.
[28] See Article 2.1 of the *Anti-Dumping Agreement*. For a more detailed analysis of the concept of dumping, see below, pp. 515–26.

policy choice to have the option of imposing anti-dumping measures, Article 1 of the *Anti-Dumping Agreement* specifies that:

> An anti-dumping measure shall be applied only under the circumstances provided for in Article VI of GATT 1994 and pursuant to investigations initiated and conducted in accordance with the provisions of this Agreement. The following provisions govern the application of Article VI of GATT 1994 in so far as action is taken under anti-dumping legislation or regulations.

Pursuant to Article VI of the GATT 1994 and the *Anti-Dumping Agreement*, WTO Members are entitled to impose anti-dumping measures if, after an investigation initiated and conducted in accordance with the Agreement, on the basis of pre-existing legislation that has been properly notified to the WTO, a determination is made that:

- there is dumping;
- the domestic industry producing the like product in the importing country is suffering injury; and
- there is a causal link between the dumping and the injury.

6.2.1.4. *Response to injurious dumping*

In response to injurious dumping, Members may take anti-dumping measures. However, Article VI, and in particular Article VI:2, read in conjunction with the *Anti-Dumping Agreement*, limits the permissible responses to dumping to:

- provisional measures;
- price undertakings; and
- definitive anti-dumping duties.[29]

Article 18.1 of the *Anti-Dumping Agreement* provides:

> No specific action against dumping of exports from another Member can be taken except in accordance with the provisions of GATT 1994, as interpreted by this Agreement.[30]

In *US – 1916 Act*, the Appellate Body indicated that this provision clarifies the scope of application of Article VI of the GATT 1994. This provision requires that any 'specific action against dumping' be in accordance with the provisions of Article VI of the GATT 1994 concerning dumping, as those provisions are interpreted by the *Anti-Dumping Agreement*. Article VI of the GATT 1994 is thus applicable to any:

> 'specific action against dumping' of exports, i.e., action that is taken in response to situations presenting the constituent elements of 'dumping'.[31]

---

[29] See Appellate Body Report, *US – 1916 Act*, para. 137.

[30] Footnote 24 to this provision reads: 'This is not intended to preclude action under other relevant provisions of GATT 1994, as appropriate.'

[31] Appellate Body Report, *US – 1916 Act*, para. 126. In *US – Offset Act (Byrd Amendment)*, the Appellate Body found that a measure is a 'specific action against dumping' when that measure is inextricably linked to, or has a strong correlation with, a determination of dumping. See Appellate Body, *US – Offset Act (Byrd Amendment)*, para. 239. See also Panel Report, *Mexico – Anti-Dumping Measures on Rice*, para. 7.278.

In *US – 1916 Act*, the Appellate Body upheld the Panel's findings that the United States legislation at issue – which provided for civil and criminal proceedings and penalties for conduct which presented the constituent elements of dumping – fell within the scope of application of Article VI of the GATT 1994 and the *Anti-Dumping Agreement* and was inconsistent with Article VI:2 and the *Anti-Dumping Agreement* to the extent that it provided for 'specific action against dumping' in the form of civil and criminal proceedings and penalties.[32]

In *US – Offset Act (Byrd Amendment)*, the measure at issue was the United States Continued Dumping and Subsidy Offset Act of 2000 (CDSOA).[33] This Act provided, in relevant part, that the United States Customs shall *distribute* duties assessed pursuant to an anti-dumping duty order to 'affected domestic producers' for 'qualifying expenditures'.[34] Recalling its ruling in *US – 1916 Act* that Article VI:2, read in conjunction with the *Anti-Dumping Agreement*, limits the permissible responses to dumping to definitive anti-dumping duties, provisional measures and price undertakings,[35] the Appellate Body concluded in *US – Offset Act (Byrd Amendment)*:

> As CDSOA offset payments are not definitive anti-dumping duties, provisional measures or price undertakings, we conclude, in the light of our finding in *US – 1916 Act*, that the CDSOA is not 'in accordance with the provisions of the GATT 1994, as interpreted by' the *Anti-Dumping Agreement*. It follows that the CDSOA is inconsistent with Article 18.1 of that Agreement.[36]

Questions and Assignments 6.2

Has the WTO *Anti-Dumping Agreement* set aside and replaced Article VI of the GATT 1947? What is 'dumping' in simple terms? Why does WTO law not prohibit dumping? Is it mandatory for WTO Members to enact anti-dumping legislation? To which measures do Article VI of the GATT 1994 and the *Anti-Dumping Agreement* apply? What forms can an anti-dumping measure take? Is it WTO-consistent for a measure against dumping to take the form of civil and criminal proceedings and penalties? What was the Appellate Body's ruling in *US – Offset Act (Byrd Amendment)*?

6.2.2. Determination of dumping

As discussed above, Article VI:1 of the GATT 1994 and Article 2.1 of the *Anti-Dumping Agreement* define 'dumping' as the introduction of a product into the

---

[32] Civil and criminal proceedings and penalties are not among the permissible responses to dumping exhaustively listed in Article VI:2 as interpreted by the *Anti-Dumping Agreement*.

[33] The CDSOA amends Title VII of the US Tariff Act of 1930 by adding a new Section 754 entitled 'Continued Dumping and Subsidy Offset' and is often referred to as the 'Byrd Amendment'.

[34] See Appellate Body Report, *US – Offset Act (Byrd Amendment)*, para. 12. On the concepts of 'affected domestic producer' and 'qualifying expenditure', see Section 754(b)(1) and (4) of the US Tariff Act of 1930 respectively.   [35] See above, p. 514.

[36] Appellate Body Report, *US – Offset Act (Byrd Amendment)*, para. 265. See also Panel Report, *Mexico – Anti-Dumping Measures on Rice*, para. 7.278. In the latter case, the measure at issue was fines imposed on importers of products on which anti-dumping investigations were under way.

commerce of another country at less than its 'normal value'. In other words, 'dumping' exists where the 'normal value' of the product exceeds the 'export price'. This section explains:

- how the 'normal value' of the product concerned is determined;
- how the relevant 'export price' is determined;
- how the existence of dumping is determined; and
- how the 'dumping margin' is calculated.

Ordinarily, dumping is discerned through a price-to-price comparison of the 'normal value' with the 'export price'. However, the *Anti-Dumping Agreement* envisages circumstances in which such a straightforward price-to-price comparison may not be possible or appropriate, and, therefore, provides for alternative methods for determining the existence of dumping in such cases.

Before engaging in this discussion of how to determine the existence of dumping, it is important to recall that only dumping causing injury is condemned and potentially subject to anti-dumping measures under Article VI of the GATT 1994 and the *Anti-Dumping Agreement*. However, in determining whether dumping exists, the injurious effect that 'dumping' may have on a Member's domestic industry is not a constituent element of 'dumping'.[37] In addition, the intent of the persons engaging in 'dumping' is irrelevant in the determination of whether dumping exists.[38]

6.2.2.1. Determination of the 'normal value'

Article 2.1 of the *Anti-Dumping Agreement* defines the 'normal value' of a product as:

> the comparable price, in the ordinary course of trade, for the like product when destined for consumption in the exporting country.

In other words, the 'normal value' is the price of the like product in the home market of the exporter or producer. According to the Appellate Body in *US – Hot-Rolled Steel*, the text of Article 2.1 expressly imposes four conditions on domestic sales transactions so that they may be used to determine 'normal value':

- first, the sale must be 'in the ordinary course of trade';
- secondly, the sale must be of the 'like product';
- thirdly, the product must be 'destined for consumption in the exporting country'; and
- fourthly, the price must be 'comparable'.[39]

The first of the four conditions imposed on sales transactions so that they may be used to determine the 'normal value' is that the sale must be 'in the

---

[37] See Appellate Body Report, *US – 1916 Act*, para. 107.   [38] See *ibid*.

[39] See Appellate Body Report, *US – Hot-Rolled Steel*, para. 165. Other provisions in the *Anti-Dumping Agreement*, such as Article 2.4, discussed below, permit the domestic investigating authorities to take account of considerations that may not be expressly identified in Article 2.1, such as the identity of the seller in a particular sales transaction.

ordinary course of trade'. The decision as to whether sales in the domestic market of the exporting Member are made 'in the ordinary course of trade' can be a complex one. There are many situations that *may* form a reason to determine that transactions were not made 'in the ordinary course of trade', such as:

- sales to affiliated parties;
- aberrationally high priced sales, or abnormally low priced sales; or
- sales below cost.[40]

Sales not made in the ordinary course of trade may be *disregarded* in determining normal value, which would then be determined on the basis of the remaining sales.[41] As the Appellate Body stated in *US – Hot-Rolled Steel*:

> Article 2.1 requires investigating authorities to exclude sales not made 'in the ordinary course of trade', from the calculation of normal value, precisely to ensure that normal value is, indeed, the 'normal' price of the like product, in the home market of the exporter.[42]

As the Appellate Body found in *US – Hot-Rolled Steel*, the *Anti-Dumping Agreement* affords WTO Members discretion to determine how to ensure that normal value is not distorted through the inclusion of sales that are not 'in the ordinary course of trade'. However, the Appellate Body noted at the same time that this discretion is not without limits. The Appellate Body ruled:

> In particular, the discretion must be exercised in an *even-handed* way that is fair to all parties affected by an anti-dumping investigation. If a Member elects to adopt general rules to prevent distortion of normal value through sales between affiliates, those rules must reflect, even-handedly, the fact that both high and low-priced sales between affiliates might not be 'in the ordinary course of trade'.[43]

The second of the four conditions imposed on sales transactions so that they may be used to determine the 'normal value' is that the sale must be of the 'like product'. The determination of what constitutes a 'like product' involves:

- first examining the imported product or products that is or are alleged to be dumped; and
- then establishing the product that is 'like'.

Article 2.6 of the *Anti-Dumping Agreement* defines the 'like product' as:

> a product which is identical, i.e. alike in all respects to the product under consideration, or in the absence of such a product, another product which, although not alike in all respects, has characteristics closely resembling those of the product under consideration.[44]

---

[40] See Article 2.2.1 of the *Anti-Dumping Agreement*. Note that pricing below cost alone is not sufficient. Such sales must be made within an extended period of time, in substantial quantities, and at prices which do not provide for recovery of costs within a reasonable period of time. With regard to the second of these criteria, see Panel Report, *EC – Salmon (Norway)*, paras. 7.231–7.279.

[41] See Appellate Body Report, *US – Hot-Rolled Steel*, para. 139. However, where the exclusion of such below-cost sales results in a level of sales that is so low as not to permit a proper comparison with export price, an alternative method of calculation may be used.   [42] *Ibid.*, para. 140.   [43] *Ibid.*, para. 148.

[44] Article 2.6 explicitly states that this definition applies 'throughout this Agreement', i.e. throughout the *Anti-Dumping Agreement*. See also Panel Report, *Korea – Certain Paper*, para. 7.219, as discussed below, p. 518.

A 'like product' is thus an identical product or a product with a close resemblance to the product under consideration.[45]

The Panel in *EC – Salmon (Norway)*, found:

> It is important to note that the assessment of whether goods are 'like' in the sense of Article 2.6 entails first a consideration of whether goods are identical. Only if there are no goods which are identical to the product under consideration does Article 2.6 allow an investigating authority to consider whether there is some other good which 'has characteristics closely resembling those of the product under consideration'.[46]

In response to Norway's argument that, in defining the 'like product', Article 2.6 requires an assessment of 'likeness' in respect of the product under consideration as a whole, and that this requires a comparison of all product categories the product under consideration each other and with all product categories considered as potentially 'like products'. The Panel noted that:

> while the AD Agreement specifically defines 'like product' by requiring a comparison between domestically-produced (or foreign) goods and the imported products that are the subject of the investigation, there is no specific definition of 'product under consideration'. In our view, the very fact that there is a definition of like product in the AD Agreement indicates that Members were well able to define terms carefully and precisely when considered necessary. The absence of a definition of product under consideration indicates that no effort was undertaken in that regard. In our view, this consideration supports the conclusion that it would be absurd to impose the definition of like product from Article 2.6 onto the undefined term product under consideration. We simply see no basis in the text of Articles 2.1 and 2.6 for the obligations Norway seeks to impose on investigating authorities with respect to product under consideration.[47]

Moreover, the Panel found that:

> contrary to Norway's claim, Articles 2.1 and 2.6 of the AD Agreement do not establish an obligation on investigating authorities to ensure that where the product under consideration is made up of categories of products, all such categories of products must individually be 'like' each other, thereby constituting a single 'product'.[48]

Recall that the third and fourth conditions imposed on sales transactions, so that they may be used to determine the 'normal value', are that the product must be 'destined for consumption in the exporting country' *and* that the price must be 'comparable'. With respect to the latter condition, note that Article 2.4 of the *Anti-Dumping Agreement* requires that a 'fair comparison' be made between export price and normal value. This comparison 'shall be made at the same level of trade, normally at the ex-factory level'. In making a 'fair comparison', 'Article 2.4 mandates that due account be taken of "differences which affect price comparability", such as differences in the "levels of trade" at which normal value and the export price are calculated.'[49]

---

[45] Compare with the concept of 'like products' as used in the GATT 1994 (see above, pp. 329–31) and in the *SCM Agreement* (see below, pp. 578–9).   [46] Panel Report, *EC – Salmon (Norway)*, para. 7.52.
[47] *Ibid.*, para. 7.59.   [48] *Ibid.*, para. 7.68.   [49] Appellate Body Report, *US – Hot-Rolled Steel*, para. 167.

Questions and Assignments 6.3

What is the 'normal value' of a product within the meaning of Article 2.1 of the *Anti-Dumping Agreement*? What four conditions must sales transactions fulfil in order to be used to determine the 'normal value'? What is the 'ordinary course of trade' and why is it important? What is a 'like product' within the meaning of the *Anti-Dumping Agreement*? What differences may, according to Article 2.4 of the *Anti-Dumping Agreement*, affect the price comparability and what should be done about this?

6.2.2.2. *Alternative rules for the determination of the 'normal value'*

The *Anti-Dumping Agreement* acknowledges that in certain circumstances consideration of the domestic price in the exporting country does not produce an appropriate 'normal value' for the purposes of comparison with the export price. Such circumstances may arise when there are no sales of the like product in the 'ordinary course of trade' in the domestic market of the exporting country; or when, because of the low volume of sales in that market, such sales do not permit a proper comparison.[50] The *Anti-Dumping Agreement* also recognises that the domestic price in the exporting country market may not produce an appropriate normal value for the purposes of comparison with the export price because of 'a particular market situation', but does not offer any criteria to aid domestic investigating authorities in determining whether such a particular market situation exists.[51] The second Supplementary Provision to paragraph 1 of Article VI of the GATT 1994, to which Article 2.7 of the *Anti-Dumping Agreement* also refers, acknowledges that a straight comparison with the home market price may not always be appropriate in the case of imports from a country which has a complete or substantially complete monopoly of its trade and where all domestic prices are fixed by the State, often referred to as a 'non-market economy'.

Where the domestic price in the exporting country market may not produce an appropriate normal value for the purposes of comparison with the export price, Article 2.2 of the *Anti-Dumping Agreement* provides that an importing Member may select one of two alternative methods for determining an appropriate normal value for comparison with the export price:

- using a third country price as the normal value; or
- constructing the normal value.

---

[50] Footnote 2 to Article 2.2 of the *Anti-Dumping Agreement* provides that the volume of sales in the domestic market of the exporting country shall normally be considered 'sufficient' for the purposes of calculating normal value if such sales constitute 5 per cent or more of the sales of the like product under consideration to the importing Member.

[51] A panel established under the Tokyo Round *Anti-Dumping Code*, when considering a similar provision in that Code, found that the combined circumstance created by hyper-inflation and a frozen exchange rate in Brazil did not constitute such a particular market situation and therefore did not render home market prices an inappropriate basis for normal value. See Panel Report, *EEC – Cotton Yarn*, para. 479.

No preference or hierarchy between these alternatives is expressed in the Agreement.

First, Article 2.2 of the *Anti-Dumping Agreement* permits the determination of 'normal value' through consideration of the comparable price of the like product when exported to an 'appropriate' third country, provided that this price is representative. Note, however, that the Agreement does not offer any criteria for determining whether a third country is 'appropriate'.

Secondly, Article 2.2 of the *Anti-Dumping Agreement* permits a Member to construct the normal value on the basis of:

> the cost of production in the country of origin plus a reasonable amount for administrative, selling and general costs and for profits.

The amounts for administrative, selling and general costs and for profits shall be based on actual data pertaining to production and sales in the ordinary course of trade of the like product by the exporter or producer under investigation.[52]

Questions and Assignments 6.4

Under what circumstances does consideration of the domestic price in the exporting country market not produce an appropriate normal value? In such cases, how can the 'normal value' be determined?

6.2.2.3. Determination of the 'export price'

The export price is ordinarily based on the transaction price at which the producer in the exporting country sells the product to an importer in the importing country.

However, the *Anti-Dumping Agreement* recognises that the transaction price may not be an appropriate export price. For example, there may be no export price where the transaction involves an internal transfer or barter. Additionally, an association or a compensatory arrangement between the exporter and the importer or a third party may affect the transaction price.

Article 2.3 of the *Anti-Dumping Agreement* therefore provides for an alternative method to calculate, or 'construct', an appropriate export price. The 'constructed export price' is based on the price at which the product is first sold to an independent buyer. Where it is not possible to construct the export price on this basis, the investigating authorities may determine a reasonable basis on which to calculate the export price.

---

[52] Article 2.2.2 of the *Anti-Dumping Agreement*. If the amounts for administrative, selling and general costs and for profits cannot be determined in this way, they may be determined in one of the three ways discussed in Article 2.2.2(i) to (iii) of the *Anti-Dumping Agreement*. On the interpretation and application of these provisions, see Panel Report, *EC – Bed Linen*, paras. 6.59–6.62; and Appellate Body Report, *EC – Bed Linen*, paras. 74–83.

Questions and Assignments 6.5

How is the 'export price' normally determined? When is the transaction price at which the producer in the exporting country sells to the importer in the importing country not an appropriate export price? In such a case, how is the export price to be determined?

6.2.2.4. Comparison between the 'export price' and the 'normal value'

To determine whether dumping, as defined above, exists, the export price is compared with the normal value. Article 2.4 of the *Anti-Dumping Agreement* provides in relevant part:

> A fair comparison shall be made between the export price and the normal value. This comparison shall be made at the same level of trade, normally at the ex-factory level, and in respect of sales made at as nearly as possible the same time.

In order to ensure a fair comparison between the export price and normal value, Article 2.4 of the *Anti-Dumping Agreement* requires that adjustments be made to the normal value, the export price or both. Thus, Article 2.4 requires that:

> Due allowance shall be made in each case, on its merits, for differences which affect price comparability, including differences in conditions and terms of sale, taxation, levels of trade, quantities, physical characteristics, and any other differences which are also demonstrated to affect price comparability.[53]

As the reference to 'any other differences' indicates, this provision does not exhaustively identify differences which may affect price comparability. One difference that is identified is a difference 'in conditions and terms of sale', which refers to such considerations as, for example, transport costs or credit terms associated with particular transactions involving the product concerned. In *US – Stainless Steel*, the question arose as to whether differences resulting from the unforeseen bankruptcy of a customer and consequent failure to pay for certain sales fell within 'differences in the conditions and terms of sale' for which due allowance is to be made. The Panel in this case stated that:

> the requirement to make due allowance for differences that affect price comparability is intended to neutralise differences in a transaction that an exporter could be expected to have reflected in his pricing. A difference that could not reasonably have been anticipated and thus taken into account by the exporter when determining the price to be charged for the product in different markets or to different customers is not a difference that affects the comparability of *prices* within the meaning of Article 2.4.[54]

The Panel in *US – Stainless Steel* therefore ruled that an unanticipated failure of a customer to pay for certain sales cannot be considered to be a 'difference in

---

[53] Footnote 7 to the *Anti-Dumping Agreement* notes that: 'It is understood that some of the above factors may overlap, and authorities shall ensure that they do not duplicate adjustments that have been already made under this provision.'   [54] Panel Report, *US – Stainless Steel*, para. 6.77.

conditions and terms of sale', requiring adjustment to the export price, the normal value or both, to ensure price comparability.[55] In *US – Hot-Rolled Steel*, the United States used downstream sales prices to make a comparison without making any allowances. The Appellate Body ruled in this case that:

> Article 2.4 of the *Anti-Dumping Agreement* requires that appropriate 'allowances' be made to any downstream sales prices which are used to calculate normal value in order to ensure a 'fair comparison' between export price and normal value. If those proper 'allowances' were not, in fact, made in this case, the comparison made by USDOC between export price and normal value was, by definition, not 'fair', and not consistent with Article 2.4 of the *Anti-Dumping Agreement*.[56]

The Appellate Body also recalled that Article 2.4 requires that allowances are made not only for the differences explicitly mentioned in Article 2.4 (i.e. differences in conditions and terms of sale, taxation, levels of trade, etc.) but for *any other differences* which are also demonstrated to affect price comparability.[57] The Panel in *US – Softwood Lumber V*, agreeing with the Panel in *EC – Tube or Pipe Fittings*, found that:

> the requirement to make due allowance for such differences, in each case on its merits, means that the authority must *at least* evaluate identified differences – in this case, differences in dimension – with a view to determining whether or not an adjustment is required to ensure a fair comparison between normal value and export price under Article 2.4, and make an adjustment where it determines this to be necessary on the basis of its evaluation. We consider that Article 2.4 does *not* require that an adjustment be made automatically in all cases where a difference is found to exist, but only where – based on the merits of the case – that difference is demonstrated to affect price comparability.[58]

In *US – Zeroing (EC)*, the Appellate Body stated:

> Article 2.4 also applies *a contrario*: this sentence implies that allowances should not be made for differences that do not affect price comparability.[59]

Where the export price is constructed, Article 2.4 of the *Anti-Dumping Agreement* contains special rules regarding adjustments. An allowance should be made for costs, including duties and taxes, incurred *between* the importation of the product and its resale to the first independent purchaser, as well as for profits.[60] Where the comparison of the 'normal value' with the export price requires conversion of currency, Article 2.4.1 of the *Anti-Dumping Agreement* provides specific rules governing that conversion.[61]

---

[55] See *ibid*.   [56] Appellate Body Report, *US – Hot-Rolled Steel*, para. 176.   [57] *Ibid.*, para. 177.

[58] Panel Report, *US – Softwood Lumber V*, para. 7.165. See also Panel Report, *EC – Tube or Pipe Fittings*, para. 7.157.

[59] Appellate Body Report, *US – Zeroing (EC)*, para. 156. Note that the Appellate Body subsequently stated that: 'adjustments or allowances made in relation to *differences in price* between export transactions and domestic transactions – such as zeroing – cannot be adjustments or allowances covered by the third sentence of Article 2.4, including its *a contrario* application'. Appellate Body Report, *US – Zeroing (EC)*, para. 157. See also below, p. 525.

[60] On the non-mandatory nature of these adjustments, see Panel Report, *US – Stainless Steel*, para. 6.93.

[61] See on the interpretation of this provision, Panel Report, *US – Stainless Steel*, paras. 6.11–6.12. The Panel in that case concluded that it was inconsistent with Article 2.4.1 of the *Anti-Dumping Agreement* to undertake currency conversions in instances where the prices being compared were in the same currency. See also on the currency conversion rules of Article 2.4.1. of the *Anti-Dumping Agreement*, Panel Report, *EC – Tube or Pipe Fittings*, paras. 7.198–7.199.

The question of making a *fair* comparison between the 'normal value' and the 'export price' is often one of the most contentious aspects of an anti-dumping investigation as there will always be adjustments that arguably should be made. Frequently the extent of the adjustments allowed will have an important impact on the outcome of the anti-dumping investigation. Note that while it is incumbent upon the investigating authorities to ensure a fair comparison, the interested parties must substantiate their assertions concerning the need for adjustments as constructively as possible.[62]

Questions and Assignments 6.6

Which differences may affect price comparability and may therefore require adjustment of the 'export price', the 'normal value' or both? How can price comparability be ensured?

6.2.2.5. Calculation of the margin of dumping

The margin of dumping is the difference between the export price and the 'normal value'. This would appear simple enough. However, the methodology to be applied when calculating the difference between the export price and the 'normal value' may raise difficult and controversial issues.

As provided in Article 2.4.2, first sentence, of the *Anti-Dumping Agreement*, the calculation of the dumping margin *generally* requires:

* either the *comparison of the weighted average* 'normal value' to the weighted average of prices of all comparable export transactions; or
* a *transaction-to-transaction comparison* of 'normal value' and export price.

However, as provided in Article 2.4.2, second sentence, a comparison of the weighted average normal value to export prices in individual transactions may occur if:

* there is 'targeted dumping' (i.e. a pattern of export prices differing significantly among different purchasers, regions or time periods); and
* the investigating authorities provide an explanation as to why such differences cannot be taken into account appropriately in weighted-average-to-weighted-average or transaction-to-transaction comparisons.[63]

As the Appellate Body noted in *US – Softwood Lumber V (Article 21.5 – Canada)*:

> the methodology in the second sentence of Article 2.4.2 is an exception. Article 2.4.2 clearly provides that investigating authorities 'shall normally' use one of the two methodologies set out in the first sentence of that provision.[64]

---

[62] See Panel Report, *US – Softwood Lumber V*, para. 7.158.   [63] See Article 2.4.2 of the *Anti-Dumping Agreement*.
[64] Appellate Body Report, *US – Softwood Lumber V (Article 21.5 – Canada)*, para. 97.

With regard to the calculation of 'weighted average value', the Panel in *Argentina – Poultry Anti-Dumping Duties* found that Argentina had acted inconsistently with 2.4.2 of the *Anti-Dumping Agreement* as it had established the weighted average normal value on the basis of statistical *samples* of domestic sales transactions rather than on the basis of *all* domestic transactions.[65]

Significant questions have arisen with regard to the calculation of margins of dumping under Article 2.4.2. Specifically, the practice of 'zeroing' has been challenged several times in anti-dumping disputes. The practice of zeroing was explained by the Appellate Body in *EC – Bed Linen* as follows:

> [F]irst, the European Communities identified with respect to the product under investigation – cotton-type bed linen – a certain number of different 'models' or 'types' of that product. Next, the European Communities calculated, for each of these models, a *weighted average* normal value and a *weighted average* export price. Then, the European Communities compared the weighted average normal value with the weighted average export price for each model. For some models, normal value was *higher* than export price; by subtracting export price from normal value for these models, the European Communities established a '*positive* dumping margin' for each model. For other models, normal value was *lower* than export price; by subtracting export price from normal value for these other models, the European Communities established a '*negative* dumping margin' for each model. Thus, there is a 'positive dumping margin' where there *is* dumping, and a 'negative dumping margin' where there *is not*. The 'positives' and 'negatives' of the amounts in this calculation are an indication of precisely *how much* the export price is above or below the normal value. Having made this calculation, the European Communities then added up the amounts it had calculated as 'dumping margins' for each model of the product in order to determine an *overall* dumping margin for the product *as a whole*. However, in doing so, the European Communities treated any 'negative dumping margin' as zero – hence the use of the word 'zeroing'. Then, finally, having added up the 'positive dumping margins' and the zeroes, the European Communities divided this sum by the cumulative total value of all the export transactions involving all types and models of that product. In this way, the European Communities obtained an overall margin of dumping for the product under investigation.[66]

The effect of zeroing, as the Appellate Body pertinently noted in *US – Corrosion-Resistant Steel Sunset Review*, is that apart from artificially inflating the dumping margin for the product as a whole, it may turn a negative margin of dumping into a positive margin, introducing an 'inherent bias'.[67] Examining this practice of the European Communities under Article 2.4.2 of the *Anti-Dumping Agreement*, the Appellate Body in *EC – Bed Linen* stated:

> We see nothing in Article 2.4.2 or in any other provision of the *Anti-Dumping Agreement* that provides for the establishment of 'the existence of margins of dumping' for *types* or *models* of the product under investigation; to the contrary, all references to the establishment of 'the existence of margins of dumping' are references to the *product* that is the subject of the investigation . . . Whatever the method used to calculate the margins of dumping, in our view, these margins must be, and can only be, established for the *product* under investigation as a whole.[68]

[65] See Panel Report, *Argentina – Poultry Anti-Dumping Duties*, paras. 7.272–7.275.
[66] Appellate Body Report, *EC – Bed Linen*, para. 47.
[67] Appellate Body Report, *US – Corrosion-Resistant Steel Sunset Review*, para. 135. See also paras. 127–8, 130.
[68] Appellate Body Report, *EC – Bed Linen*, para. 53.

The Appellate Body in *EC – Bed Linen* thus held that the practice where an investigating authority does not offset the difference between the export price and the normal value in cases where the export price is *above* the normal value, and treats the difference as 'zero', is incompatible with Article 2.4.2 of the *Anti-Dumping Agreement*. The conclusions of the Appellate Body were limited to the first of the methods of calculating the dumping margin outlined in Article 2.4.2, first sentence, of the *Anti-Dumping Agreement*, i.e. the weighted-average-to-weighted-average method, and related to so-called 'model zeroing'. The United States adopted a similar practice of margin determination, which was at issue in *US – Softwood Lumber V*. Again, the Appellate Body held that:

> If an investigating authority has chosen to undertake multiple comparisons, the investigating authority necessarily has to take into account the results of *all* those comparisons in order to establish margins of dumping for the product as a whole under Article 2.4.2.[69]

The Appellate Body in *US – Zeroing (EC)* later supported this view that:

> there is no justification for 'taking into account the "results" of only some multiple comparisons in the process of calculating margins of dumping, while disregarding other "results"'.[70]

In fact, the consistency of this line of reasoning was pertinently highlighted by the Panel in *US – Shrimp (Ecuador)*, which stated:

> [I]n our view, there is now a consistent line of Appellate Body Reports, from *EC – Bed Linen* to *US – Zeroing (EC)* that holds that 'zeroing' in the context of the weighted average-to-weighted average methodology in original investigations . . . is inconsistent with Article 2.4.2.[71]

It is now well-established case law that zeroing also amounts to a violation of the 'fair comparison' requirement set out in Article 2.4. An inflated margin of dumping, because it violates Article 2.4.2, cannot qualify as being the result of a 'fair' comparison under Article 2.4. As noted by the Appellate Body in *US – Softwood Lumber V (Article 21.5 – Canada)*:

> Article 2.4.2 begins with the phrase '[s]ubject to the provisions governing fair comparison in paragraph 4'. Thus, the application of the comparison methodologies set out in Article 2.4.2 of the *Anti-Dumping Agreement*, including the transaction-to-transaction methodology . . . is expressly made subject to the 'fair comparison' requirement set out in Article 2.4.[72]

A new question arose for consideration in *US – Softwood Lumber V (Article 21.5 – Canada)*, namely the legality of zeroing when the second methodology for the calculation of the dumping margin articulated in Article 2.4.2, first sentence – the transaction-to-transaction methodology – is used. The Appellate Body found

---

[69] Appellate Body Report, *US – Softwood Lumber V*, para. 98 (emphasis in the original).
[70] Appellate Body Report, *US – Zeroing (EC)*, para. 126, citing Appellate Body Report, *US – Softwood Lumber V*, para. 98.   [71] Panel Report, *US – Shrimp (Ecuador)*, para. 7.40.
[72] Appellate Body Report, *US – Softwood Lumber V (Article 21.5 – Canada)*, para. 132. See also Appellate Body Report, *US – Zeroing (EC)*, para. 146, for a similar argument on the pervasiveness of the 'fair comparison' requirement in Article 2.4 and its role in the interpretation of Article 2.4.2.

in this case that the practice of zeroing in the transaction-to-transaction methodology was equally impermissible under Article 2.4.2 and Article 2.4. This has been reiterated more recently by the Appellate Body in *US – Zeroing (Japan)*, reversing the findings of the Panel which had found that the United States had not acted inconsistently by maintaining zeroing procedures.[73]

A further question with regard to zeroing surfaced in *US – Zeroing (EC)*. This pertained to the correctness of zeroing vis-à-vis the application of Article 2.4.2 in administrative reviews under Article 9.3 of the *Anti-Dumping Agreement*.[74] The Panel had come to a finding that zeroing in administrative reviews was not in contravention of Article 2.4.2.[75] However, the Appellate Body in *US – Zeroing (Japan)* held that zeroing in administrative reviews was in contravention of Article 2.4.2.[76]

The current state of the law is that in the case of the calculation of the dumping margin by a weighted-average-to-weighted-average comparison, or by a transaction-to-transaction comparison, the *entirety of the prices* for all comparable transactions involving the product that is the subject of the investigation must be included in the calculation of the dumping margin. The practice of zeroing has been categorically rejected by the Appellate Body. It has been reported that:

> Some trade observers who oppose zeroing as a form of unfair protectionism have described the Appellate Body's rulings as a contribution to free trade that would have been difficult to achieve in negotiations. Talks on changing WTO anti-dumping rules have faltered alongside other issues in the Doha Round, with the US particularly reluctant to accept reforms that would have made it harder to impose extra duties.[77]

Questions and Assignments 6.7

How is the dumping margin to be calculated under the *Anti-Dumping Agreement*? Explain the practice of 'zeroing' as applied by the European Communities and the United States. Why did the Appellate Body in *EC – Bed Linen* consider this practice to be inconsistent with Article 2.4.2 of the *Anti-Dumping Agreement*? Is the case law on the question of the WTO consistency of the practice of 'zeroing' clear and consistent?

6.2.3. Determination of injury

As noted above, only dumping that causes, or threatens to cause, injury to the domestic industry is condemned and potentially subject to anti-dumping

---

[73] Appellate Body Report, *US – Zeroing (Japan)*, para. 138. This Report extends the zeroing prohibition to yet other stages of anti-dumping procedures, such as periodic reviews and new shipper reviews.

[74] On the concept of 'administrative reviews', see below, p. 550.

[75] Panel Report, *US – Zeroing (EC)*, para. 8.1(d). Note that the Panel differentiated between 'model zeroing' and 'simple zeroing'; 'model zeroing' was found to be inconsistent with Article 2.4.2, while 'simple zeroing' was not. Note that in this case the Appellate Body explicitly refrained from endorsing the Panel's interpretation on this point. Appellate Body Report, *US – Zeroing (EC)*, para. 164.

[76] See Appellate Body Report, *US – Zeroing (Japan)*, para. 156.

[77] 'Appellate Body Condemns US for "Zeroing" on Anti-Dumping Duties', *BRIDGES Weekly Trade News Digest*, 17 January 2007.

measures under Article VI of the GATT 1994 and the *Anti-Dumping Agreement*. Therefore, after having determined the existence of dumping, the competent authorities must establish:

- the existence, or threat, of injury to the domestic industry; and
- the causal link between the dumping and the injury.

This section addresses the determination of injury to the domestic industry.

6.2.3.1. Concept of 'domestic industry'

The concept of 'domestic industry' flows from the definition of the 'like product'. It establishes who may file a petition requesting the initiation of an anti-dumping investigation.[78] It also delineates the scope of the data to be taken into account in the injury determination, in that the domestic industry with respect to which injury is considered and determined must be the domestic industry defined in accordance with Article 4.1.[79] Article 4.1 of the *Anti-Dumping Agreement* defines the 'domestic industry' generally as:

> the domestic producers as a whole of the like products or . . . those of them whose collective output of the products constitutes a major proportion of the total domestic production of those products.[80]

The 'domestic industry' need therefore not be the domestic producers as a whole; the domestic producers whose output makes up a *major* proportion of the domestic production can also be considered to be the 'domestic industry'.[81] In *Argentina – Poultry Anti-Dumping Duties*, the Panel stated that:

> an interpretation that defines the domestic industry in terms of domestic producers of an important, serious or significant proportion of total domestic production is permissible.[82]

The Panel in this case also noted that:

> Article 4.1 does not define the 'domestic industry' in terms of producers of the major proportion of total domestic production. Instead, Article 4.1 refers to producers of a major proportion of total domestic production. If Article 4.1 had referred to the major proportion, the requirement would clearly have been to define the 'domestic industry' as producers constituting 50+ per cent of total domestic production. However, the reference to a major proportion suggests that there may be more than one 'major proportion' for the purpose of defining 'domestic industry'. In the event of multiple 'major proportions', it is inconceivable that each individual 'major proportion' could – or must – exceed 50 per cent.[83]

---

[78] See below, pp. 539–41.

[79] See Panel Report, *Mexico – Steel Pipes and Tubes*, paras. 7.320 ff.

[80] In *Argentina – Poultry Anti-Dumping Duties*, the United States argued that Article 4.1 merely contains a definition of 'domestic industry' and that this provision did not impose an obligation on WTO Members to use this definition. The Panel resolutely rejected this argument. See Panel Report, *Argentina – Poultry Anti-Dumping Duties*, para. 7.338; and Panel Report, *EC – Salmon (Norway)*, para. 7.119.

[81] As the Panel in *Mexico – Steel Pipes and Tubes* stated, the text of Article 4.1 of the *Anti-Dumping Agreement* indicates 'no hierarchy of preference between these two options'. The investigating authorities are not allowed, however, to switch back and forth between these two possibilities in the course of a single investigation. See Panel Report, *Mexico – Steel Pipes and Tubes*, para. 7.322.

[82] Panel Report, *Argentina – Poultry Anti-Dumping Duties*, para. 7.341.   [83] *Ibid.*

The Panel thus found that Article 4.1 of the *Anti-Dumping Agreement* does not require Members to define the 'domestic industry' in terms of domestic producers representing the majority, or 50+ per cent, of total domestic production.[84]

The domestic industry may presumably consist of one *or* multiple producers. The Panel in *EC – Bed Linen* stated:

> Article 4.1 of the [Anti-Dumping] Agreement defines the domestic industry in terms of 'domestic producers' in the plural. Yet we consider it indisputable that a single domestic producer may constitute the domestic industry under the [Anti-Dumping] Agreement, and that the provisions concerning domestic industry under Article 4 continue to apply in such a factual situation.[85]

Article 4.1 of the *Anti-Dumping Agreement* recognises that it may not be appropriate to include *all* producers of the like product in the domestic industry when producers are 'related' to the exporters or importers or are themselves importers of the allegedly dumped product.[86] Related producers may not entirely share the interests of purely domestic producers. A producer is deemed to be 'related' to exporters or importers only if:

- one of them directly or indirectly controls the other; or
- both of them are directly or indirectly controlled by a third person; or
- together they directly or indirectly control a third person,

provided that there are grounds for believing or suspecting that the effect of the relationship is such as to cause the producer concerned to behave differently from non-related producers.[87]

The Panel in *EC – Salmon (Norway)* made it clear that the text of Article 4.1 of the *Anti-Dumping Agreement* does not support the notion that there is any other circumstance in which the domestic industry can be interpreted, from the outside, as not including certain categories of producers of the like product, other than those set out in Article 4.1(1).[88] Note that, in limited circumstances, a *regional industry*, instead of the total domestic industry, may be defined as the basis for the injury analysis.[89]

Questions and Assignments 6.8

What is the 'domestic industry' within the meaning of Article 4 of the *Anti-Dumping Agreement*? Must the 'domestic industry' consist of all producers, or at least those producers representing more than 50 per cent of the domestic production? Which producers, established in a

---

[84] See *ibid. In casu*, the 'domestic industry' was made up of domestic producers representing 46 per cent of the total domestic production of the like product. *Ibid.*, para. 7.342.
[85] Panel Report, *EC – Bed Linen*, para. 6.72.   [86] See Article 4.1(i) of the *Anti-Dumping Agreement*.
[87] See footnote 11 to the *Anti-Dumping Agreement*. Note that one is deemed to control another 'when the former is legally or operationally in a position to exercise restraint or direction over the latter'.
[88] See Panel Report, *EC – Salmon (Norway)*, para. 7.112.
[89] See Article 4.1(ii) of the *Anti-Dumping Agreement*. On the application of anti-dumping measures in that case, see Article 4.2 of the *Anti-Dumping Agreement*.

Member, may be excluded from the relevant 'domestic industry' of that Member?

6.2.3.2. Determination of injury

An affirmative determination of injury to the domestic industry is a fundamental pre-condition for the imposition of anti-dumping measures, along with a determination of the causal link between the dumped imports and the injury. The *Anti-Dumping Agreement* defines 'injury' to mean one of three things:

- material injury, i.e. genuine injury, to a domestic industry;
- threat of material injury to a domestic industry; or
- material retardation of the establishment of a domestic industry.[90]

The *Anti-Dumping Agreement* provides further details and guidance relating to the consideration of material injury and threat of material injury, but provides no further specific guidance on the consideration of material retardation of the establishment of a domestic industry.

Article 3.1 of the *Anti-Dumping Agreement* requires that a determination of injury to the domestic industry:

> be based on positive evidence and involve an objective examination of both *(a)* the volume of dumped imports and the effect of the dumped imports on prices in the domestic market for like products, and *(b)* the consequent impact of these imports on domestic producers of such products.

In *Thailand – H-Beams*, the Appellate Body referred to Article 3.1 as an overarching provision that sets forth a Member's fundamental, substantive obligation with respect to the determination of injury.[91] Article 3.1 informs the more detailed obligations in succeeding paragraphs. These obligations concern:

- the determination of the volume of dumped imports, and their effect on prices (Article 3.2);
- investigations of imports from more than one country (Article 3.3);
- the impact of dumped imports on the domestic industry (Article 3.4);
- causality between dumped imports and injury (Article 3.5);
- the assessment of the domestic production of the like product (Article 3.6); and
- the determination of the threat of material injury (Articles 3.7 and 3.8).

The Appellate Body in *Thailand – H-Beams* emphasised that the focus of Article 3 is thus on *substantive* obligations that a Member must fulfil in making an injury determination.[92]

---

[90] See footnote 9 to Article 3 of the *Anti-Dumping Agreement*. Note that the *Anti-Dumping Agreement*, like the *SCM Agreement*, requires *material* injury or threat thereof, rather than *serious* injury as required under the *Agreement on Safeguards*. See below, pp. 678–81. The Appellate Body in *US – Lamb* noted that the standard of 'serious injury' is higher than that of 'material injury'. See Appellate Body Report, *US – Lamb*, para. 124.
[91] Appellate Body Report, *Thailand – H-Beams*, para. 106.   [92] See *ibid*.

In *US – Hot-Rolled Steel*, the Appellate Body held that the thrust of the investigating authorities' obligation, in Article 3.1, lies in the requirement that they:

- base their determination on 'positive evidence'; and
- conduct an 'objective examination'.

According to the Appellate Body, the concept of 'positive evidence' relates to the quality of the evidence that authorities may rely on in making a determination. It focuses on the facts underpinning and justifying the injury determination. The word 'positive' means that the evidence must be of an affirmative, objective and verifiable character, and that it must be credible.[93] The concept of 'objective examination' aims at a different aspect of the investigating authorities' determination. It is concerned with the investigation process itself. The word 'objective', which qualifies the word 'examination', indicates essentially that the 'examination' process must conform to the dictates of the basic principles of good faith and fundamental fairness.[94] In short, an 'objective examination' requires that the domestic industry, and the effects of dumped imports, be investigated in an unbiased manner, without favouring the interests of any interested party, or group of interested parties, in the investigation.[95] If an examination is to be 'objective', the identification, investigation and evaluation of the relevant factors must be *even-handed*. Thus, investigating authorities are not entitled to conduct their investigation in such a way that it becomes more likely that, because of the fact-finding or evaluation process, they will determine that the domestic industry is injured.[96] In *Mexico – Anti-Dumping Measures on Rice*, the Panel found that Mexico's investigating authority had acted inconsistently with Article 3.1 of the *Anti-Dumping Agreement*:

- by choosing to base its determination of injury on a period of investigation which ended more than fifteen months before the initiation of the investigation;
- by excluding six months of data from each year of the investigation period; and
- by using assumptions in its evaluation of export volumes and price effects.[97]

The Appellate Body upheld the Panel's findings of inconsistency. It stated that,

> [b]ecause the conditions to impose an anti-dumping duty are to be assessed with respect to the current situation, the determination of whether injury exists should be based on data that provide indications of the situation prevailing when the investigation takes place.[98]

---

[93] See Appellate Body Report, *US – Hot-Rolled Steel*, para. 192.   [94] See *ibid.*, para. 193.   [95] See *ibid.*

[96] See *ibid.*, para. 196. Note that the Appellate Body in *US – Hot-Rolled Steel* ruled that an examination of only certain parts of a domestic industry does not ensure a proper evaluation of the state of the domestic industry as a whole, and does not, therefore, satisfy the requirements of 'objectiv[ity]' in Article 3.1 of the *Anti-Dumping Agreement*. See Appellate Body Report, *US – Hot-Rolled Steel*, para. 206.

[97] See Panel Report, *Mexico – Anti-Dumping Measures on Rice*, paras. 7.50–7.65, 7.66–7.87 and 7.89–7.116. See also Panel Report, *Mexico – Steel Pipes and Tubes*, paras. 7.211 ff.

[98] Appellate Body Report, *Mexico – Anti-Dumping Measures on Rice*, para. 165.

The Panel in *Mexico – Steel Pipes and Tubes* stated that the data considered by the investigating authority should include, to the extent practicable, the most recent information possible, 'taking into account the inevitable delay caused by the need for an investigation, as well as any practical problems of data collection in a particular case'.[99] As the Appellate Body stated in *Mexico – Anti-Dumping Measures on Rice*:

> Articles 3.1 and 3.2 do not prescribe a methodology that must be followed by an investigating authority in conducting an injury analysis. Consequently, an investigating authority enjoys a certain discretion in adopting a methodology to guide its injury analysis. Within the bounds of this discretion, it may be expected that an investigating authority might have to rely on reasonable assumptions or draw inferences. In doing so, however, the investigating authority must ensure that its determinations are based on 'positive evidence'. . . . An investigating authority that uses a methodology premised on unsubstantiated assumptions does not conduct an examination based on positive evidence. An assumption is not properly substantiated when the investigating authority does not explain why it would be appropriate to use it in the analysis.[100]

As noted above, Article 3.1 requires that a determination of injury to the domestic market must involve an examination of both:

- the volume of dumped imports and the effect of the dumped imports on prices in the domestic market for like products (first requirement); and
- the consequent impact of these imports on domestic producers of such products (second requirement).

With regard to the first requirement, the Appellate Body in *EC – Bed Linen (Article 21.5 – India)* made clear that imports from those *exporters* who were not found to be dumping may *not* be included in the volume of dumped imports from a country:

> It is clear from the text of Article 3.1 that investigating authorities must ensure that a 'determination of injury' is made on the basis of 'positive evidence' and an 'objective examination' of the volume and effect of imports that *are dumped* – and to the exclusion of the volume and effect of imports that *are not dumped*. It is clear from the text of Article 3.2 that investigating authorities must consider whether there has been a significant increase in *dumped* imports, and that they must examine the effect of *dumped* imports on prices resulting from price undercutting, price depression, or price suppression.[101]

After also considering Article 3.5 of the *Anti-Dumping Agreement*, the Appellate Body concluded:

> None of these provisions of the *Anti-Dumping Agreement* can be construed to suggest that Members may include in the volume of *dumped* imports the imports from producers that are *not* found to be dumping.[102]

---

[99] Panel Report, *Mexico – Steel Pipes and Tubes*, para. 7.228.
[100] Appellate Body Report, *Mexico – Anti-Dumping Measures on Rice*, paras. 204–5.
[101] Appellate Body Report, *EC – Bed Linen (Article 21.5 – India)*, para. 111.
[102] Appellate Body Report, *EC – Bed Linen (Article 21.5 – India)*, para. 112. In *Argentina – Poultry Anti-Dumping Duties*, Brazil claimed that Argentina violated Article 3 of the *Anti-Dumping Agreement* because it had in its injury determination included the imports from two companies (Nicolini and Seara) which had been

With regard to the first requirement, note also that the injury enquiry focuses on developments in the domestic market of the importing Member. Article 3.2 of the *Anti-Dumping Agreement* requires the investigating authorities to consider whether there has been a *significant increase* in the dumped imports, either in absolute terms or relative to production or consumption, in the domestic market. The investigating authorities must also consider whether there has been *significant price undercutting* by the dumped imports as compared with the price of a like product of the importing Member, or whether the effect is otherwise to *depress prices to a significant degree* or prevent price increases, which would otherwise have occurred, to a significant degree.[103]

With regard to the second requirement referred to above, Article 3.4 of the *Anti-Dumping Agreement* states:

> The examination of the impact of the dumped imports on the domestic industry concerned shall include an evaluation of all relevant economic factors.

Article 3.4 then lists the following fifteen relevant economic factors that must be evaluated:

- factors and indices having a bearing on the state of the industry (such as an actual or potential decline in sales, profits, output, market share, productivity, return on investments, or utilisation of capacity);
- factors affecting the domestic prices;
- the magnitude of the margin of dumping; and
- actual or potential negative effects on cash flow, inventories, employment, wages, growth, ability to raise capital, or investments.

Article 3.4 of the *Anti-Dumping Agreement* explicitly states that this list is not exhaustive. It also stresses that one or more of these factors, no matter how pronounced, will not necessarily give decisive guidance as to the existence of injury to the domestic industry or lack thereof.

While not exhaustive, it is widely accepted that the list of factors in Article 3.4 is a *mandatory* minimum, and that investigating authorities must therefore collect and analyse data relating to each of these individual enumerated factors.[104] In addition, investigating authorities must also collect and analyse

Footnote 102 (*cont.*)
found not to have dumped. Referring to the Appellate Body Report in *EC – Bed Linen (Article 21.5 – India)*, the Panel found that the term 'dumped imports' excludes imports from producers/exporters found in the course of the investigation not to have dumped and that the imports from Nicolini and Seara should thus have been 'excluded outright' from the injury analysis. See Panel Report, *Argentina – Poultry Anti-Dumping Duties*, paras. 7.303–7.306.

[103] See Panel Report in *EC – Tube or Pipe Fittings*, para. 7.276, in which the Panel found that there is no requirement under Article 3.2 of the *Anti-Dumping Agreement* to 'establish one single margin of undercutting on the basis of an examination of every transaction involving the product concerned and the like product'. However, the investigating authorities must, of course, conduct an unbiased and even-handed price undercutting analysis. The Panel concluded, in para. 7.279, that the EC's methodology for an injury determination – a zeroing methodology that offsets 'undercutting prices' with 'overcutting prices' – does not contravene Articles 3.1 and 3.2 to the extent that the application of this methodology reflects the full impact of price undercutting on the domestic industry.

[104] See Panel Report, *Thailand – H-Beams*, paras. 7.224–7.225. The Appellate Body upheld this aspect of the Panel Report, stating: 'We agree with the Panel's analysis in its entirety, and with the Panel's interpretation of the mandatory nature of the factors mentioned in Article 3.4 of the *Anti-Dumping*

data relating to *any other relevant factors* that may have a bearing on the state of a domestic industry in a particular case.[105] The Panel in *Korea – Certain Paper* considered:

> that the IA's obligation to evaluate all relevant economic factors under Article 3.4 shall be read in conjunction with the overarching obligation to carry out an 'objective examination' on the basis of 'positive evidence' as set out under Article 3.1. Therefore, the obligation to analyse the mandatory list of fifteen factors under Article 3.4 is not a mere 'checklist obligation' consisting of a mechanical exercise to make sure that each listed factor has somehow been addressed by the IA. We recognize that the relevance of each one of these injury factors may vary from one case to the other. The fact remains, however, that Article 3.4 requires the IA to carry out a reasoned analysis of the state of the industry. This analysis cannot be limited to a mere identification of the 'relevance or irrelevance' of each factor, but rather must be based on a thorough evaluation of the state of the industry. The analysis must explain in a satisfactory way why the evaluation of the injury factors set out under Article 3.4 lead[s] to the determination of material injury, including an explanation of why factors which would seem to lead in the other direction do not, overall, undermine the conclusion of material injury.[106]

Article 3.1 of the *Anti-Dumping Agreement* permits an investigating authority, making an injury determination, to base its determination on all relevant reasoning and facts before it, including all confidential and non-confidential information on the record of the investigation.[107]

Questions and Assignments 6.9

What does the term 'injury' in the *Anti-Dumping Agreement* mean? What is the thrust of the investigating authorities' obligation under Article 3 of the *Anti-Dumping Agreement* relating to the determination of injury? What is 'positive evidence' and an 'objective examination' within the meaning of Article 3.1 of the *Anti-Dumping Agreement*? Can the total volume of dumped imports legally include imports from exporters that were not found to be dumping? What is the role and importance of the list of economic factors contained in Article 3.4?

6.2.3.3. *Determination of a threat of material injury*

As discussed above, the term 'injury' in the *Anti-Dumping Agreement* refers not only to material injury but also to the threat of material injury. Article 3.7 of the *Anti-Dumping Agreement* relates to the determination of a threat of material injury. It provides:

> A determination of a threat of material injury shall be based on facts and not merely on allegation, conjecture or remote possibility. The change in circumstances which would create a situation in which the dumping would cause injury must be clearly foreseen and imminent.

Agreement.' Appellate Body Report, *Thailand – H-Beams*, para. 125. See also Panel Report, *Argentina – Poultry Anti-Dumping Duties*, para. 7.314.   [105] See Panel Report, *Thailand – H-Beams*, para. 7.225.

[106] Panel Report, *Korea – Certain Paper*, para. 7.272. 'IA' stands for 'investigating authority'.

[107] See Appellate Body Report, *Thailand – H-Beams*, para. 111.

Article 3.7 further provides that, in making a determination regarding the existence of a threat of material injury, the investigating authorities should consider, *inter alia*, such factors as:

- a significant rate of increase of dumped imports into the domestic market indicating the likelihood of substantially increased importation;
- sufficient freely disposable, or an imminent substantial increase in, capacity of the exporter indicating the likelihood of substantially increased dumped exports to the importing Member's market, taking into account the availability of other export markets to absorb any additional exports;
- whether imports are entering at prices that will have a significant depressing or suppressing effect on domestic prices, and would be likely to increase demand for further imports; and
- inventories of the product being investigated.[108]

However, no one of these factors by itself can necessarily give decisive guidance. The totality of the factors considered must lead to the conclusion that further dumped exports are imminent and that, unless protective action is taken, material injury would occur.[109] As the Panel in *US – Softwood Lumber VI* concluded:

> What is critical, however, is that it be clear from the determination that the investigating authority has evaluated how the future will be different from the immediate past, such that the situation of no present material injury will change in the imminent future to a situation of material injury, in the absence of measures.[110]

In respect of the nature of the analysis required under Article 3.7 of the *Anti-Dumping Agreement*, the Panel in *Mexico – Corn Syrup* considered whether a specific analysis of the consequent impact of the dumped imports on the domestic industry is required in a 'threat of injury' determination. Referring to Article 3.7, the Panel stated that:

> This language, in our view, recognizes that factors other than those set out in Article 3.7 itself will necessarily be relevant to the determination.[111]

The Panel in *Mexico – Corn Syrup* further stated that it is clear that in making a determination regarding the threat of material injury, investigating authorities must conclude that *material injury would occur* in the absence of an anti-dumping measure. However, a determination that material injury would occur cannot be made solely on the basis of consideration of the Article 3.7 factors. Therefore, the Panel in *Mexico – Corn Syrup* ruled that:

---

[108] Note that the Panel in *US – Softwood Lumber VI* found that consideration of the factors set out in Articles 3.7 and 15.7 of the *Anti-Dumping Agreement* 'must go beyond a mere recitation of the facts in question, and put them into context'. The Panel did, however, consider that 'the investigating authorities are not required by Articles 3.7 and 15.7 to make an explicit "finding" or "determination" with respect to the factors considered'. Panel Report, *US – Softwood Lumber VI*, para. 7.67.

[109] See Article 3.7 of the *Anti-Dumping Agreement*.   [110] Panel Report, *US – Softwood Lumber VI*, para. 7.58.

[111] Panel Report, *Mexico – Corn Syrup*, para. 7.124.

consideration of the Article 3.4 factors in examining the consequent impact of imports is required in a case involving threat of injury in order to make a determination consistent with the requirements of Articles 3.1 and 3.7.[112]

The Appellate Body ruled in *Mexico – Corn Syrup (Article 21.5 – US)* that:

In determining the existence of a *threat* of material injury, the investigating authorities will necessarily have to make assumptions relating to 'the occurrence of future events' since such *future* events 'can never be definitively proven by facts'. Notwithstanding this intrinsic uncertainty, a 'proper establishment' of facts in a determination of threat of material injury must be based on events that, although they have not yet occurred, must be 'clearly foreseen and imminent', in accordance with Article 3.7 of the *Anti-Dumping Agreement*.[113]

Not surprisingly, Article 3.8 of the *Anti-Dumping Agreement* requires that the application of anti-dumping measures shall be considered and decided with 'special care' where a determination of threat of material injury is involved. While the provision offers no further guidance as to the meaning of 'special care', it is clear that the provision cautions against the 'automatic' imposition of measures in such cases.[114] The Panel in *US – Softwood Lumber VI* stated:

The adjective 'special' is defined as, *inter alia*, 'Exceptional in quality or degree; unusual; out of the ordinary'. The noun 'care' is defined, *inter alia*, as 'Serious attention, heed; caution, pains, regard'. Thus, it seems clear to us that a degree of attention over and above that required of investigating authorities in all anti-dumping and countervailing duty injury cases is required in the context of cases involving threat of material injury.[115]

Questions and Assignments 6.10

When does a 'threat of material injury' within the meaning of Article 3.7 of the *Anti-Dumping Agreement* exist? Which factors should investigating authorities consider in order to establish a 'threat of material injury'?

6.2.3.4. *Determination of material retardation*

Beyond specifying that the term 'injury' as used in the *Anti-Dumping Agreement* also includes 'material retardation', the Agreement contains no further specific language pertaining to this concept. Some guidance may perhaps be derived from the 1967 *Anti-Dumping Code*,[116] which refers to the retardation of the establishment of a new industry, and indicates that a finding must be based on 'convincing evidence' that such a new industry is actually forthcoming. Examples of such evidence include plans for an industry being at an advanced stage, a

---

[112] *Ibid.*, para. 7.127. See also Panel Report, *US – Softwood Lumber VI*, para. 7.105.

[113] Appellate Body Report, *Mexico – Corn Syrup (Article 21.5 – US)*, para. 85.

[114] See also the concern of the Appellate Body regarding statements of the Panel in *US – Softwood Lumber VI (Article 21.5 – Canada)*, which seemed to imply 'a greater likelihood of panels upholding a *threat* of injury determination, as compared to a determination of *current* material injury, when those determinations rest on the same level of evidence'. Appellate Body Report, *US – Softwood Lumber VI (Article 21.5 – Canada)*, para. 110.   [115] Panel Report, *US – Softwood Lumber VI*, para. 7.33   [116] See above, p. 512.

factory under construction or new capital equipment already having been ordered.

6.2.4. Demonstration of a causal link

Article 3.5 of the *Anti-Dumping Agreement* requires the demonstration of a *causal link* between:

- the dumped imports; and
- the injury to the domestic industry.

As with the determinations of dumping and injury to the domestic industry, the demonstration of a causal link between these two elements shall be based on an examination of all relevant evidence before the investigating authorities. Article 3.5 also contains a *'non-attribution' requirement*. According to this requirement, investigating authorities must examine any known factors other than the dumped imports that are injuring the domestic industry at the same time *and* they must not attribute the injury caused by these other factors to the dumped imports. It is important to note that the *Anti-Dumping Agreement* does *not* require that the dumped imports are the *principal cause* of the injury to the domestic injury.[117] The *Anti-Dumping Agreement* only requires that the dumped imports be a cause of the injury and that other causes of injury not be attributed to the dumping.

6.2.4.1. *Relevant factors*

Article 3.5 of the *Anti-Dumping Agreement* identifies several factors which 'may be relevant' in demonstrating a causal link between dumped imports and injury *and* in ensuring non-attribution to the dumped imports of injury being caused by other factors. These factors include:

- the volume and prices of imports not sold at dumping prices;
- contraction in demand or changes in the patterns of consumption;
- trade-restrictive practices of and competition between the foreign and domestic producers;
- developments in technology; and
- the export performance and productivity of the domestic industry.

However, Article 3.5 does not *require* examination of any particular factors or *give clear guidance* on the manner in which the investigating authorities should evaluate relevant evidence in order to establish the causal link *and* to ensure non-attribution to the dumped imports of injury being caused by other factors. As the Appellate Body ruled in *US – Hot-Rolled Steel* and confirmed in *EC – Tube or Pipe Fittings*:

---

[117] Note that this was the requirement under Article 3 of the Kennedy Round *Anti-Dumping Code*, BISD 15S/74. As discussed above, the Kennedy Round *Anti-Dumping Code* was superseded by the Tokyo Round *Anti-Dumping Code* in which this requirement was already dropped. See also Panel Report, *EC – Bed Linen (Article 21.5 – India)*, para. 6.233.

> provided that an investigating authority does not attribute the injuries of other causal factors to dumped imports, it is free to choose the methodology it will use in examining the 'causal relationship' between dumped imports and injury.[118]

The Panel in *Thailand – H-Beams* made clear its view that, in contrast to the mandatory list of factors in Article 3.4, the list of factors in Article 3.5 was merely *illustrative*. Thus, while the listed factors in Article 3.5 might be relevant in many cases, and while the list contains useful guidance as to the kinds of factors other than imports that might cause injury to the domestic industry, the specific list in Article 3.5 is not itself mandatory.[119]

6.2.4.2. 'Non-attribution' requirement

The Appellate Body in *US – Hot-Rolled Steel* clarified the 'non-attribution' requirement of Article 3.5 of the *Anti-Dumping Agreement* as follows:

> The non-attribution language in Article 3.5 of the *Anti-Dumping Agreement* applies solely in situations where dumped imports and other known factors are causing injury to the domestic industry *at the same time*. In order that investigating authorities, applying Article 3.5, are able to ensure that the injurious effects of the other known factors are not 'attributed' to dumped imports, they must appropriately assess the injurious effects of those other factors. Logically, such an assessment must involve separating and distinguishing the injurious effects of the other factors from the injurious effects of the dumped imports. If the injurious effects of the dumped imports are not appropriately separated and distinguished from the injurious effects of the other factors, the authorities will be unable to conclude that the injury they ascribe to dumped imports is actually caused by those imports, rather than by the other factors. Thus, in the absence of such separation and distinction of the different injurious effects, the investigating authorities would have no rational basis to conclude that the dumped imports are indeed causing the injury which, under the *Anti-Dumping Agreement*, justifies the imposition of anti-dumping duties.[120]

In short, in order to comply with the 'non-attribution' requirement of Article 3.5, investigating authorities must make an appropriate *assessment* of the injury caused to the domestic industry by the other known factors, and they must *separate and distinguish* the injurious effects of the dumped imports from the injurious effects of those other factors.[121] With respect to the 'other known factors', the Appellate Body noted in *EC – Tube or Pipe Fittings* that the *Anti-Dumping Agreement*:

> . . . does not expressly state how such factors should become 'known' to the investigating authority, or if and in what manner they must be raised by interested parties, in order to qualify as 'known'.[122]

---

[118] Appellate Body Report, *EC – Tube or Pipe Fittings*, para. 188.
[119] See Panel Report, *Thailand – H-Beams*, para. 7.274.
[120] Appellate Body Report, *US – Hot-Rolled Steel*, para. 223. Claims of violation of the non-attribution requirement were *inter alia* rejected by the Panels in *Korea – Certain Paper*, para. 7.288, and *Mexico – Steel Pipes and Tubes*, para. 7.61.   [121] See Panel Report, *EC – Salmon (Norway)*, paras. 7.660 and 7.668–7.669.
[122] Appellate Body Report, *EC – Tube or Pipe Fittings*, para. 176. The Appellate Body added to this: 'In our view, a factor is either "known" to the investigating authority, or it is not "known"; it cannot be "known" in one stage of the investigation and unknown in a subsequent stage.' *Ibid.*, para. 178.

Note that, under the GATT 1947 practice, there was no need to 'identify' the injury caused by the other factors. According to the GATT Panel in *US – Norwegian Salmon AD*, such separate identification of the injurious effects of the other causal factors was not required.[123] The Appellate Body in *US – Hot-Rolled Steel* reversed this case law although it did recognise that the different causal factors operating on a domestic industry may interact, and their effects may well be interrelated, such that they produce a *combined* effect on the domestic industry. Therefore, it may not be easy, as a practical matter, to separate and distinguish the injurious effects of different causal factors. The Appellate Body noted:

> However, although this process may not be easy, this is precisely what is envisaged by the non-attribution language. If the injurious effects of the dumped imports and the other known factors remain lumped together and indistinguishable, there is simply no means of knowing whether injury ascribed to dumped imports was, in reality, caused by other factors. Article 3.5, therefore, requires investigating authorities to undertake the process of assessing appropriately, and separating and distinguishing, the injurious effects of dumped imports from those of other known causal factors.[124]

6.2.4.3. Cumulation

A cumulative analysis is the consideration of the effects of dumped imports from more than one country in determining whether dumped imports are causing injury to the domestic industry. As such an analysis will necessarily increase the volume of imports whose impact is being considered, it will clearly augment the possibility of an affirmative injury determination. A controversial negotiation topic in the Uruguay Round, the conditions for cumulative analysis of the effects of imports from more than one country are now set forth in Article 3.3 of the *Anti-Dumping Agreement*. Cumulation is *not mandatory* under any circumstances but is *permitted*, be it only under the conditions set forth in Article 3.3. In *EC – Tube or Pipe Fittings*, the Appellate Body stated that:

> The text of Article 3.3 expressly identifies three conditions that must be satisfied before an investigating authority is permitted under the *Anti-Dumping Agreement* to assess cumulatively the effects of imports from several countries. These conditions are:
>
> (a) the dumping margin from each individual country must be more than *de minimis*;
> (b) the volume of imports from each individual country must not be negligible; and
> (c) cumulation must be appropriate in the light of the conditions of competition
>   (i) between the imported products; and
>   (ii) between the imported products and the like domestic product.
>
> By the terms of Article 3.3, it is 'only if' the above conditions are established that an investigating authority 'may' make a cumulative assessment of the effects of dumped imports from several countries.[125]

---

[123] See GATT Panel Report, *US – Norwegian Salmon AD*, para. 550.
[124] Appellate Body Report, *US – Hot-Rolled Steel*, para. 228.
[125] Appellate Body Report, *EC – Tube or Pipe Fittings*, para. 109.

Questions and Assignments 6.11

Does the *Anti-Dumping Agreement* require that the dumped imports are the principal cause of the injury to the domestic industry? What does the 'non-attribution' requirement of Article 3.5 entail? What is the purpose or relevance of the list of economic factors contained in Article 3.5 of the *Anti-Dumping Agreement*? Why must the investigating authorities separate and distinguish the injurious effects of dumped imports from those of other known causal factors of the injury? What is a cumulative analysis within the meaning of Article 3.3 of the *Anti-Dumping Agreement*? Are investigating authorities permitted to apply such analysis?

6.2.5. Anti-dumping investigation

The *Anti-Dumping Agreement* sets out, in considerable detail, how investigating authorities of WTO Members have to initiate and conduct an anti-dumping investigation. This section addresses:

- the initiation of an anti-dumping investigation;
- the period of an investigation; and
- the conduct of an investigation.

6.2.5.1. *Initiation of an investigation*

Article 5 of the *Anti-Dumping Agreement* contains numerous requirements concerning the initiation of an anti-dumping investigation. The domestic investigating authorities can instigate an investigation on their own initiative. However, the *Anti-Dumping Agreement* specifies that investigations must *generally* be initiated on the basis of a written application submitted 'by or on behalf of' a domestic industry as defined in Article 4 of the *Anti-Dumping Agreement*.[126] Sufficient support for the application must therefore exist among domestic producers to warrant initiation.[127] The *Anti-Dumping Agreement* contains guidance relating to the required contents of the initiation request, including:

- evidence of dumping;
- evidence of injury to the domestic industry; and
- evidence of a causal link between the dumped imports and the injury to the domestic industry.

---

[126] In *US – 1916 Act (Japan)*, the Panel found that there was a violation of Articles 4 and 5 of the *Anti-Dumping Agreement* as the 1916 Act did not require 'a minimum representation of a US industry in applications for the initiation of proceedings under the 1916 Act'. Panel Report, *US – 1916 Act (Japan)*, paras. 6.255–6.261. See also Panel Report, *US – 1916 Act (EC)*, paras. 6.212–6.214.

[127] An application is considered to have been made 'by or on behalf of the domestic industry' if it is supported by those domestic producers whose collective output makes up over 50 per cent of the total production of the like product produced by that portion of the domestic industry expressing support for or opposition to the application, *and* the domestic producers supporting the application account for at least 25 per cent of total domestic production of the like product. See Article 5.4 of the *Anti-Dumping Agreement*.

As the Panel in *Mexico – Corn Syrup* stated and the Panel in *Thailand – H-Beams* affirmed:

> Article 5.2 does not require an application to contain analysis, but rather to contain information, in the sense of evidence, in support of allegations.[128]

The application must contain information that is 'reasonably available' to the applicant in accordance with Article 5.2.[129] Simple assertion, unsubstantiated by relevant evidence, cannot be considered to meet the requirements of this provision.[130] In considering the nature and extent of the information that must be provided in an application pursuant to Article 5.2(iv), the Panel in *Mexico – Corn Syrup* stated:

> Obviously, the quantity and quality of the information provided by the applicant need not be such as would be required in order to make a preliminary or final determination of injury. Moreover, the applicant need only provide such information as is 'reasonably available' to it with respect to the relevant factors. Since information regarding the factors and indices set out in Article 3.4 concerns the state of the domestic industry and its operations, such information would generally be available to applicants. Nevertheless, we note that an application which is consistent with the requirements of Article 5.2 will not necessarily contain sufficient evidence to justify initiation under Article 5.3.[131]

Article 5.3 of the *Anti-Dumping Agreement* requires that the investigating authorities examine the accuracy and adequacy of the evidence provided in the application to determine whether there is sufficient evidence to justify the initiation of the investigation.[132] Statements and assertions unsubstantiated by any evidence do not constitute sufficient evidence within the meaning of Article 5.3 of the *Anti-Dumping Agreement*.[133] However, in determining whether there is sufficient evidence to initiate an investigation, the investigating authorities are not limited to the information contained in the application. The Panel in *Guatemala – Cement II* noted:

> We have expressed the view that Articles 5.2 and 5.3 contain different obligations. One of the consequences of this difference in obligations is that investigating authorities need not content themselves with the information provided in the application but may gather information on their own in order to meet the standard of sufficient evidence for initiation in Article 5.3.[134]

With respect to the nature and extent of the evidence required to initiate an anti-dumping investigation, the Panel in *Guatemala – Cement II* ruled:

---

[128] Panel Report, *Thailand – H-Beams*, para. 7.75, citing Panel Report, *Mexico – Corn Syrup*, para. 7.76.

[129] As the Panel in *US – Softwood Lumber V* found, this provision is not intended to require an applicant to submit *all* information that is reasonably available to it. The 'reasonably available' language is intended to avoid putting an undue burden on the applicant to submit information which is *not* reasonably available to it. See Panel Report, *US – Softwood Lumber V*, para. 7.54.

[130] See Panel Report, *US – Softwood Lumber V*, para. 7.52.   [131] Panel Report, *Mexico – Corn Syrup*, para. 7.74.

[132] The Panel in *Mexico – Steel Pipes and Tubes* found that although there is no express reference to evidence of 'dumping' or 'injury' or 'causation' in Article 5.3 of the *Anti-Dumping Agreement*, reading Article 5.3 in the context of Article 5.2 makes clear that the evidence to which Article 5.3 refers is the evidence in the application concerning dumping, injury and causation. See Panel Report, *Mexico – Steel Pipes and Tubes*, para. 7.21.

[133] See Panel Report, *Argentina – Poultry Anti-Dumping Duties*, para. 7.60; See also Panel Report, *US – Softwood Lumber V*, para. 7.79; and Panel Report, *Mexico – Steel Pipes and Tubes*, para. 7.24.

[134] Panel Report, *Guatemala – Cement II*, para. 8.62. See also Panel Report, *US – Softwood Lumber V*, para. 7.75.

We do not of course mean to suggest that an investigating authority must have before it at the time it initiates an investigation evidence of dumping within the meaning of Article 2 of the quantity and quality that would be necessary to support a preliminary or final determination. An anti-dumping investigation is a process where certainty on the existence of all the elements necessary in order to adopt a measure is reached gradually as the investigation moves forward. However, the evidence must be such that an unbiased and objective investigating authority could determine that there was sufficient evidence of dumping within the meaning of Article 2 to justify initiation of an investigation.[135]

The same is true for the evidence on injury to the domestic industry and the causal link between the dumped imports and the injury.[136]

Article 5.5 of the *Anti-Dumping Agreement* requires that the investigating authorities 'avoid, unless a decision has been made to initiate an investigation, any publicizing of the application for the initiation of an investigation'. However, 'after receipt of a properly documented application and before proceeding to initiate an investigation, the authorities shall notify the government of the exporting Member concerned'.[137] There are also public notice requirements concerning the initiation of an investigation in Article 12.1 of the *Anti-Dumping Agreement*.[138]

An application to initiate an anti-dumping investigation shall be rejected, and an investigation shall be terminated *promptly*, as soon as the investigating authorities are satisfied that there is not enough evidence either of dumping or of injury.[139] Moreover, in order to ensure that an unwarranted investigation is not continued, Article 5.8 provides for prompt termination of investigations in the event that:

- the margin of dumping is *de minimis* (i.e. less than 2 per cent of the export price); and
- the volume of imports from each country is *negligible* (i.e. normally less than 3 per cent of imports of the like product in the importing Member, unless countries accounting for less than 3 per cent *individually* account *collectively* for more than 7 per cent of imports of the like product in the importing Member).[140]

6.2.5.2. *Period of investigation*

It is the common practice of WTO Members to conduct an anti-dumping investigation using data from a fixed 'period of investigation' which precedes the date

---

[135] Panel Report, Guatemala – Cement II, para. 8.35. See also Panel Report, *US – Softwood Lumber V*, para 7.84; and Panel Report, *Mexico – Steel Pipes and Tubes*, para. 7.22.

[136] Where an investigation is self-initiated by the authorities, the authorities may proceed only if they have sufficient evidence of dumping, injury and a causal link to justify the initiation of the investigation. See Article 5.6 of the *Anti-Dumping Agreement*.

[137] See Article 5.5 of the *Anti-Dumping Agreement*. Several panels (*Thailand – H-Beams*; *Guatemala – Cement I*; *Guatemala – Cement II*; *US – 1916 Act (EC)*) have considered the nature and extent of the obligation imposed by Article 5.5. See also *Recommendation Concerning the Timing of the Notification under Article 5.5*, adopted by the Committee on Anti-Dumping Practices on 29 October 1998, G/ADP/5, dated 3 November 1998.

[138] See below, pp. 553–4.

[139] See Article 5.8 of the *Anti-Dumping Agreement*. See e.g. Panel Report, *Mexico – Steel Pipes and Tubes*, para. 7.61; Panel Report, *Mexico – Corn Syrup*, para. 7.99; Panel Report, *Guatemala – Cement II*, para. 8.75; Panel Report, *Argentina – Poultry Anti-Dumping Duties*, para. 7.112; and Appellate Body Report, *Mexico – Anti-Dumping Measures on Rice*, para. 208.

[140] See Appellate Body Report, *Mexico – Anti-Dumping Measures on Rice*, paras. 217 ff and 305 ff.

of initiation of an investigation. Measures are then imposed on the basis of the determinations on dumping and injury made using the data from the 'period of investigation'. The *Anti-Dumping Agreement* refers to the concept of a 'period of investigation', and the use of such a period appears to be implicit in several provisions of the Agreement.[141] As discussed above, the Panel in *Mexico – Anti-Dumping Measures on Rice* concluded that by choosing to base its determination of injury on a period of investigation which ended more than fifteen months before the initiation of the investigation, Mexico acted inconsistently with the obligation in Article 3.1 of the *Anti-Dumping Agreement* to make a determination of injury which is based on an objective examination of positive evidence.[142]

The WTO Committee on Anti-Dumping Practices has adopted a *Recommendation Concerning the Periods of Data Collection for Anti-Dumping Investigations*.[143] Pursuant to this Recommendation, the period of data collection for *dumping investigations* normally should not exceed twelve months and, in any case, be no less than six months, ending as close to the date of initiation as is practicable. Furthermore, the period of data collection for *injury investigations* normally should be at least three years, unless a party from whom data is being gathered has existed for a shorter period, and should include the entirety of the period of data collection for the dumping investigation.[144]

Questions and Assignments 6.12

How is an anti-dumping investigation initiated? On what basis do the investigating authorities of a Member decide to initiate an investigation? How does the *Anti-Dumping Agreement* ensure that unwarranted investigations are not continued? What is the 'period of investigation' in anti-dumping investigations? Can or should the period of investigation differ from case to case depending on the facts?

6.2.5.3. *Conduct of the investigation*

Article 6 of the *Anti-Dumping Agreement* contains detailed rules concerning the process of the investigation, including evidentiary, informational and procedural elements. The Appellate Body in *EC – Tube or Pipe Fittings* stated:

> we wish to underscore the importance of the obligations contained in Article 6 of the *Anti-Dumping Agreement*. This Article 'establishes a framework of procedural and due process obligations'. Its provisions 'set out evidentiary rules that apply *throughout* the course of the anti-dumping investigation, and provide also for due process rights that are enjoyed by "interested parties" *throughout* such an investigation'.[145]

---

[141] For example, Articles 2.4.2 and 2.2.1 of the *Anti-Dumping Agreement*.
[142] See Panel Report, *Mexico – Anti-Dumping Measures on Rice*, para. 7.65. See also above, p. 530.
[143] G/ADP/6, adopted by the Committee on Anti-Dumping Practices on 5 May 2000.
[144] While it reflects common practice of Members, the Recommendation has no binding effect. See E. Vermulst, *The WTO Anti-Dumping Agreement: A Commentary* (Oxford University Press, 2006), 82–3.
[145] Appellate Body Report, *EC – Tube or Pipe Fittings*, para. 138.

Article 6.1 requires that all interested parties in an anti-dumping investigation be given *notice* of the information which the authorities require as well as ample *opportunity to present* in writing all evidence which they consider relevant in respect of the investigation.[146] In practice, investigating authorities typically send interested parties questionnaires in which they identify the information that they require in order to conduct the investigation. Article 6.1 sets 'flexible' thirty-day minimum time limits for submissions and responses to questionnaires from interested parties.[147]

Pursuant to Article 6.6 of the *Anti-Dumping Agreement*, investigating authorities must *generally* satisfy themselves as to the accuracy of the information supplied by interested parties upon which their findings are based.[148] The investigating authorities will often verify the information supplied by on-site visits to review the records of the companies involved.[149] In this regard, the Panel in *US – DRAMS* stated the following in support of its position that the text of Article 6.6 does *not* explicitly require verification of all information relied upon:

> Article 6.6 simply requires Members to 'satisfy themselves as to the accuracy of the information'. In our view, Members could 'satisfy themselves as to the accuracy of the information' in a number of ways without proceeding to some type of formal verification, including for example reliance on the reputation of the original source of the information. Indeed, we consider that anti-dumping investigations would become totally unmanageable if investigating authorities were required to actually verify the accuracy of all information relied on.[150]

The Panel questioned, for example, 'whether investigating authorities should be required to verify import statistics from a different government office' and 'whether investigating authorities should be required to verify "official" exchange rates obtained from a central bank'.[151]

To ensure the transparency of the anti-dumping investigation and proceedings, the investigating authorities must, according to Article 6.4 of the *Anti-Dumping Agreement*, provide timely opportunities for all interested parties to see all relevant information.[152] Note, however, that Article 6.5 of the *Anti-Dumping Agreement* requires that investigating authorities preserve the confidentiality of

---

[146] On the requirement to give notice, see Panel Report, *Egypt – Steel Rebar*, para. 7.96; and Appellate Body Report, *Mexico – Anti-Dumping Measures on Rice*, para. 251. On the requirement to give ample opportunity to present evidence, see Panel Report, *Guatemala – Cement II*, paras. 8.119, 8.178 and 8.237–8.239; Panel Report, *US – Corrosion-Resistant Steel Sunset Review*, paras. 6.257–6.263; Panel Report, *US – Oil Country Tubular Goods Sunset Reviews*, paras. 7.107–7.128; Appellate Body Report, *US – Oil Country Tubular Goods Sunset Reviews*, para. 241; and Panel Report, *US – Oil Country Tubular Goods Sunset Reviews (Article 21.5 – Argentina)*, paras. 7.109–7.120.

[147] See Appellate Body Report, *US – Hot-Rolled Steel*, paras. 73–5, where the Appellate Body stated that Article 6.1.1 establishes that investigating authorities may impose time limits for questionnaire responses, that these time limits are not necessarily absolute and immutable and that in appropriate circumstances these time limits must be extended. See also Panel Report, *Egypt – Steel Rebar*, para. 7.279; Panel Report, *Argentina – Poultry Anti-Dumping Duties*, paras. 7.144–7.145; and Appellate Body Report, *Mexico – Anti-Dumping Measures on Rice*, para. 283.   [148] See Panel Report, *Guatemala – Cement II*, paras. 8.173–8.174.

[149] See Annex I to the *Anti-Dumping Agreement* on 'Procedures for on-the-spot investigations pursuant to paragraph 7 of Article 6'.   [150] Panel Report, *US – DRAMS*, para. 6.78.

[151] Ibid., para. 6.78, footnote 513.

[152] Article 6.4 of the *Anti-Dumping Agreement* defines what information is 'relevant' for the purposes of this provision. See Panel Report, *Guatemala – Cement II*, paras. 8.158; Appellate Body Report, *EC – Tube or Pipe Fittings*, paras. 148–50; and Panel Report, *Korea – Certain Paper*, paras. 7.199–7.201 and 7.299–7.303.

sensitive business information relating to the exporting firms and the domestic industry involved in the investigation.[153] The Panel in *Mexico – Steel Pipes and Tubes* noted:

> We are aware that the designation of information as 'confidential' might affect the ability of interested parties to have full access to that information, and therefore might affect their ability to defend their interests in the course of an anti-dumping investigation. We are further aware of the potential for abuse of the possibility to designate information as confidential so as to consciously place other interested parties at a disadvantage in the investigation. We consider that the conditions set out in Article 6.5, chapeau, and 6.5.1 are of critical importance in preserving the balance between the interests of confidentiality and the ability of another interested party to defend its rights throughout an anti-dumping investigation.[154]

The investigating authority has the responsibility to review whether a request for confidentiality is, or is not, warranted.[155]

All interested parties enjoy certain rights to participate in the proceedings and to make presentations.[156] In addition, investigating authorities must provide opportunities for industrial users of the product under investigation and for representative consumer organisations, in cases where the product is commonly sold at the retail level, to provide information which is relevant to the investigation regarding dumping, injury and causation.[157]

Hardly surprisingly, the *Anti-Dumping Agreement* prefers investigating authorities to base their determinations on 'first-hand information'. The Agreement does not, however, allow any party to hold an investigating authority hostage by not providing the necessary information, and thus provides that 'second-best information' from secondary sources may be used in certain well-defined circumstances.[158] Article 6.8 of, and Annex II to, the *Anti-Dumping Agreement* identify the circumstances in which investigating authorities may overcome a lack of information, in the responses of the interested parties, by using 'facts' which are otherwise 'available' to the investigating authorities, i.e. the 'best information available'.[159] As the Appellate Body noted in *Mexico – Anti-Dumping Measures on Rice*:

> [W]e understand that an investigating authority in an anti-dumping investigation may rely on the facts available to calculate margins for a respondent that failed to provide some or

---

[153] Article 6.5 of the *Anti-Dumping Agreement* protects information which is by its nature confidential (i.e. information of which the disclosure would, for example, be of significant competitive advantage to a competitor or would have a significantly adverse effect upon a person supplying the information) or information which has been supplied on a confidential basis by the parties to the investigation. However, regardless of the type of confidential information, to provide confidential treatment good cause must be shown. See Panel Report, *Guatemala – Cement II*, paras. 8.219–8.221; and Panel Report, *Korea – Certain Paper*, paras. 7.334–7.335.   [154] Panel Report, *Mexico – Steel Pipes and Tubes*, para. 7.380.

[155] See *ibid.*, para. 7.382. The Panel in *Guatemala – Cement II* rejected a claim by Mexico that Article 6.5.2 of the *Anti-Dumping Agreement* does not require a party to provide justification for confidential treatment. See Panel Report, *Guatemala – Cement II*, para. 8.209.

[156] Article 6.13 of the *Anti-Dumping Agreement* requires investigating authorities to take due account of the difficulties interested parties, in particular small companies, may experience in supplying information. Investigating authorities must provide interested parties with any assistance practicable.

[157] See Article 6.12 of the *Anti-Dumping Agreement*.

[158] See Panel Report, *Mexico – Anti-Dumping Measures on Rice*, para. 7.238.

[159] If the producer submits information meeting the requirements of Annex II, para. 3, no use may be made of 'best information available' under Article 6.8. See Panel Report, *EC – Salmon (Norway)*, paras. 7.371–7.372.

> all of the necessary information requested by the agency. In so doing, however, the agency must first have made the respondent aware that it may be subject to a margin calculated on the basis of the facts available because of the respondent's failure to provide necessary information. Furthermore, assuming a respondent acted to the best of its ability, an agency must generally use, in the first instance, the information the respondent did provide, if any.[160]

Moreover, in *US – Hot-Rolled Steel*, the Appellate Body held:

> According to Article 6.8, where the interested parties do not 'significantly impede' the investigation, recourse may be had to facts available only if an interested party fails to submit necessary information 'within a reasonable period'. Thus, if information is, in fact, supplied 'within a reasonable period', the investigating authorities cannot use facts available, but must use the information submitted by the interested party.[161]

Paragraph 7 of Annex II to the *Anti-Dumping Agreement* indicates that a lack of 'cooperation' by an interested party may, by virtue of the use made of facts available, lead to a result that is 'less favourable' to the interested party than would have been the case had that interested party cooperated. In *US – Hot-Rolled Steel*, the Appellate Body cautioned, however, that investigating authorities should not arrive at a 'less favourable' outcome simply because an interested party fails to furnish requested information if, in fact, the interested party has 'cooperated' with the investigating authorities. Parties may very well 'cooperate' to a high degree, even though the requested information is, ultimately, not obtained.[162] The Appellate Body noted:

> In order to complete their investigations, investigating authorities are entitled to expect a very significant degree of effort – to the 'best of their abilities' – from investigated exporters. At the same time, however, the investigating authorities are not entitled to insist upon *absolute* standards or impose *unreasonable* burdens upon those exporters.[163]

Article 5.10 of the *Anti-Dumping Agreement* specifies that an anti-dumping investigation must be completed within one year, and in no cases more than eighteen months, after initiation.

Questions and Assignments 6.13

How are interested parties involved in an anti-dumping investigation? Are there any specific rules on the involvement of consumer organisations? When may investigating authorities make use of 'best information available' within the meaning of Article 6.8 of, and Annex II to, the *Anti-Dumping Agreement*? Is it recommendable for an interested party not to cooperate with the investigating authorities in the context of

---

[160] Appellate Body Report, *Mexico – Anti-Dumping Measures on Rice*, para. 288.
[161] Appellate Body Report, *US – Hot-Rolled Steel*, para. 77. See also Panel Report, *Guatemala – Cement II*, para. 8.255, in which the Panel found that recourse to the 'best information available' was not warranted because the exporter had *not* impeded the investigation. See also Panel Report, *US – Steel Plate*, para. 7.55; Panel Report *Egypt – Steel Rebar*, para. 7.147; Panel Report *Argentina – Poultry Anti-Dumping Duties*, para. 7.187; Panel Report, *Korea – Certain Paper*, para. 7.75, and Appellate Body Report *Mexico – Anti-Dumping Measures on Rice*, para. 259.   [162] See Appellate Body Report, *US – Hot-Rolled Steel*, para. 99.
[163] *Ibid.*, para. 102.

an anti-dumping investigation? Within what timeframe must investigating authorities complete an anti-dumping investigation?

6.2.6. Anti-dumping measures

The *Anti-Dumping Agreement* provides for three kinds of anti-dumping measures:

- provisional measures;
- price undertakings; and
- definitive anti-dumping duties.

This section will discuss the rules on the imposition of each of these measures. It will also address the issues of the duration, termination and review of anti-dumping measures.

6.2.6.1. Imposition of provisional anti-dumping measures

Article 7 of the *Anti-Dumping Agreement* contains rules relating to the imposition of provisional measures. To apply a provisional anti-dumping measure, investigating authorities must make a *preliminary* affirmative determination of dumping, injury and causation.[164] Furthermore, the investigating authorities must judge that such a measure is *necessary* to prevent injury being caused during the investigation.[165] A provisional measure cannot be applied earlier than sixty days following the initiation of the investigation.[166] Provisional measures may take the form of a provisional duty or, preferably, a security, by cash deposit or bond, equal to the amount of the preliminarily determined margin of dumping.[167]

With regard to the time period for application of the provisional measure, Article 7.4 of the *Anti-Dumping Agreement* states that it:

> shall be limited to as short a period as possible, not exceeding four months or, on decision of the authorities concerned, upon request by exporters representing a significant percentage of the trade involved, to a period not exceeding six months.

Where the Member applies the 'lesser duty rule' in its administration of anti-dumping duties, the period of provisional application is generally six months, with the possibility of extension to nine months upon request of the exporters.[168]

6.2.6.2. Price undertakings

Article 8 of the *Anti-Dumping Agreement* provides for the possibility of offering and accepting price undertakings as an alternative to the imposition of anti-dumping duties. Undertakings to revise prices or cease exports at the dumped price may be

---

[164] See Article 7.1(ii) of the *Anti-Dumping Agreement*.   [165] See Article 7.1(iii) of the *Anti-Dumping Agreement*.
[166] See Article 7.3 of the *Anti-Dumping Agreement*.   [167] See Article 7.2 of the *Anti-Dumping Agreement*.
[168] On the 'lesser duty rule', see below, p. 547. On the question of the allowable duration of a provisional measure, see Panel Report, *Mexico – Corn Syrup*, paras. 7.182–7.183.

entered into only after the investigating authorities have made an affirmative preliminary determination of dumping, injury and causation. Such undertakings are voluntary on the part of both exporters and investigating authorities.[169] An exporter may request the continuation of an investigation after the acceptance of an undertaking. The undertaking would then automatically lapse in the event of a negative final determination of dumping, injury or causation.[170]

Questions and Assignments 6.14

When can provisional anti-dumping measures be imposed according to the *Anti-Dumping Agreement*? What form can these provisional measures take? For how long can provisional anti-dumping measures be applied? What are price undertakings within the meaning of Article 8 of the *Anti-Dumping Agreement*? When can such price undertakings be made?

6.2.6.3. *Imposition and collection of anti-dumping duties*

Article 9 of the *Anti-Dumping Agreement* governs the imposition and collection of anti-dumping duties. This provision establishes the general principle that 'it is desirable' that, even where all the requirements for imposition of duties have been fulfilled, the imposition of anti-dumping duties remains *optional*. Article 9 also contains the so-called 'lesser duty rule', under which 'it is desirable' that the duty imposed be *less* than the margin of dumping *if* such lesser duty would be *adequate* to remove the injury to the domestic industry.[171]

Members are required to collect duties on a *non-discriminatory* basis on imports from all sources found to be dumped and causing injury.[172] The MFN treatment obligation thus applies to the collection of anti-dumping duties.[173] The competent national authorities should name the supplier or suppliers of the products affected by the anti-dumping duty. However, if several suppliers from the same country are involved, and it is impracticable to name all these suppliers, the authorities may just name the supplying country concerned. If several suppliers from more than one country are involved, the authorities may either name all the suppliers involved or, if this is impracticable, all the supplying countries involved.[174]

---

[169] Exporters and investigating authorities may enter into price undertakings over the opposition of the domestic industry. See Panel Report, *US – Offset Act (Byrd Amendment)*, paras. 7.79 ff.

[170] Article 8.6 of the *Anti-Dumping Agreement* sets out what happens in case of violation of an undertaking.

[171] The European Communities applies the 'lesser duty rule'; the United States does not. See P. F. J. Macrory, 'The Anti-Dumping Agreement', in P. Macrory, A. Appleton and M. Plummer (eds.), *The World Trade Organization: Legal, Economic and Political Analysis* (Springer, 2005), 519.

[172] See Article 9.2 of the *Anti-Dumping Agreement*. On non-discrimination between exporting States after a positive finding of dumping in particular products, see Mutually Agreed Solution, *European Communities – Anti-Dumping Duties on Certain Flat Rolled Iron or Non-Alloy Steel Products from India*, WT/DS313/2, dated 27 October 2004. Note, however, that the anti-dumping duty will not be applied to imports from sources with regard to which a price undertaking has been put in place. See *ibid.* [173] See above, p. 327.

[174] See Article 9.2 of the *Anti-Dumping Agreement*.

The anti-dumping duty collected *shall not exceed* the dumping margin.[175] As the Appellate Body stated in *US – Zeroing (Japan)*:

> The *Anti-Dumping Agreement* is neutral as between different systems for levy and collection of anti-dumping duties. The Agreement lays down the 'margin of dumping' as the *ceiling* for collection of duties regardless of the duty assessment system adopted by a WTO Member, and provides for a refund if the ceiling is exceeded.[176]
>
> [Emphasis added]

When anti-dumping duties are imposed, the investigating authorities must, in principle, calculate a dumping margin for each exporter.[177] However, the *Anti-Dumping Agreement* recognises that this may not always be possible.[178] When it is not possible to calculate a dumping margin for each exporter, the investigating authorities may limit the number of exporters considered individually (i.e. sampling). In accordance with Article 9.4 of the *Anti-Dumping Agreement*, an anti-dumping duty is then imposed on *uninvestigated* sources on the basis of the *weighted average dumping margin* actually established for investigated sources (sometimes referred to as the 'all others' rate).[179] However, the investigating authorities:

- must not include in this weighted average calculation any dumping margins that are *de minimis*, zero or based on the 'facts available';[180] and
- must calculate an individual margin for any exporter or producer who provides the necessary information during the course of the investigation.[181]

With respect to the 'all others' rate applied to uninvestigated sources, the Appellate Body stated in *US – Hot-Rolled Steel*:

> Article 9.4 does not prescribe any method that WTO Members must use to establish the 'all others' rate that is actually applied to exporters or producers that are not investigated. Rather, Article 9.4 simply identifies a maximum limit, or ceiling, which investigating authorities '*shall not exceed*' in establishing an 'all others' rate.[182]

---

[175] See Article 9.3 of the *Anti-Dumping Agreement*.

[176] Appellate Body Report, *US – Zeroing (Japan)*, para. 163. Which mechanism a Member opts to use will depend on whether the Member collects the anti-dumping duties on a prospective basis (i.e. where a Member collects the duty at the time of importation – as is the case for the European Communities) or on a retrospective basis (i.e. where a Member calculates a specific amount of anti-dumping duty to be paid only after permitting importation and collecting an estimated duty – as the United States does). See further, Articles 9.3.1 and 9.3.2 of the *Anti-Dumping Agreement*. See also Panel Report, *Argentina – Poultry Anti-Dumping Duties*, para. 7.364, in which the Panel concluded that the variable anti-dumping duties imposed by Argentina were not inconsistent with Article 9.3 of the *Anti-Dumping Agreement* because 'they are collected by reference to a margin of dumping established at the time of collection'.

[177] See Article 6.10 of the *Anti-Dumping Agreement*.

[178] This will be the case when the number of exporters, producers, importers or types of products concerned is considerable. See Article 6.10 of the *Anti-Dumping Agreement*.

[179] Note in this context, Panel Report, *Korea – Certain Paper*, para. 7.171.

[180] Also when a dumping margin was calculated, only to a very limited extent, on the basis of 'facts available' pursuant to Article 6.8 of the *Anti-Dumping Agreement*, this dumping margin may not be used to calculate the 'all others' rate. See Appellate Body Report, *US – Hot-Rolled Steel*, paras. 122–3.

[181] See Article 9.4 of the *Anti-Dumping Agreement*. Note that Article 9.4 of the *Anti-Dumping Agreement* does not expressly address the issue of how the 'all others' rate should be calculated in the event that all margins are to be excluded from the calculation, under the prohibitions. See Appellate Body Report, *US – Hot-Rolled Steel*, para. 126.

[182] Appellate Body Report, *US – Hot-Rolled Steel*, para. 116. Article 9.4 of the *Anti-Dumping Agreement* seeks to prevent exporters who were not asked to cooperate in the investigation from being prejudiced by gaps or shortcomings in the information supplied by the investigated exporters. See *ibid.*, para. 123.

With respect to the individual margin of dumping for producers or exporters who were not sources of imports considered during the period of investigation (i.e. 'new shippers'), Article 9.5 of the *Anti-Dumping Agreement* provides that:

> the authorities shall promptly carry out a review for the purpose of determining individual margins of dumping.

The investigating authorities must therefore conduct an expedited review to determine a specific margin of dumping for exports from such 'new shippers'. No anti-dumping duties may be levied on imports from such exporters or producers while the review is being carried out.[183]

Article 10 of the *Anti-Dumping Agreement* establishes the general principle that both provisional and definitive duties may be applied only as of the date on which the preliminary or final determinations of dumping, injury and causation have been made.[184] *Retroactive application* of anti-dumping duties is thus, in principle, prohibited. However, Article 10 contains rules for the retroactive application of anti-dumping duties in specific circumstances. According to Article 10.2, where the imposition of the anti-dumping duty is based on a determination of material injury – as opposed to a threat thereof, or material retardation – the duties may be collected as of the date of imposition of the provisional measures.[185] If provisional duties were collected in an amount greater than the amount of the final duty or if the imposition of duties is based on a finding of threat of material injury or of material retardation, a refund of provisional duties is necessary.[186] Article 10.6 also permits retroactive application of final anti-dumping duties in exceptional circumstances. These exceptional circumstances involve:

- a history of dumping which caused injury; *or* a situation in which the importer was, or should have been, aware that the exporter practises injurious dumping, *and*
- the injury is caused by massive dumped imports in a short time which is likely to undermine the remedial effect of the definitive anti-dumping duty (this may be the case because of a rapid and massive build-up of stocks of the imported product).[187]

In these circumstances, Article 10.6 permits retroactive application of final duties to a date not more than ninety days prior to the application of provisional measures.[188]

---

[183] See Article 9.5 of the *Anti-Dumping Agreement*. The authorities may, however, withhold appraisal and/or request guarantees to ensure that, if necessary, anti-dumping duties can be levied retroactively to the date of the initiation of the review. See Article 9.5 of the *Anti-Dumping Agreement*. See also Appellate Body Report, *Mexico – Anti-Dumping Measures on Rice*, paras. 323–4.

[184] See Article 10.1 of the *Anti-Dumping Agreement*.

[185] Also in the case of a final determination of a threat of injury, where the effect of the dumped imports would, in the absence of the provisional measures, have led to a determination of injury, the anti-dumping duties may be applied retroactively for the period for which provisional measures, if any, have been applied. See Article 10.2 of the *Anti-Dumping Agreement*.

[186] See Article 10.3 of the *Anti-Dumping Agreement*. Note, however, that if the final anti-dumping duty is higher than the provisional duty the difference may *not* be collected.

[187] See Article 10.6 of the *Anti-Dumping Agreement*.

[188] Note that Article 10.7 of the *Anti-Dumping Agreement* provides that: 'The authorities may, after initiating an investigation, take such measures . . . *as may be necessary to collect* anti-dumping duties retroactively,

Questions and Assignments 6.15

What is the 'lesser duty rule' of Article 9 of the *Anti-Dumping Agreement*? Are Members required to collect anti-dumping duties on imports from all sources found to be dumped and causing injury? Will the competent authority name the supplier or suppliers of the products affected by the anti-dumping duty *or* will it name the supplying country concerned? Must investigating authorities calculate a dumping margin for each exporter? What is the maximum anti-dumping duty that may, pursuant to Article 9.4 of the *Anti-Dumping Agreement*, be imposed on 'uninvestigated sources'? Can anti-dumping duties be applied retroactively? Can anti-dumping duties be levied prior to the date of initiation of an anti-dumping investigation?

6.2.6.4. *Duration, termination and review of anti-dumping measures*

Responding to the concern of some Members that some countries were leaving anti-dumping measures in place indefinitely, Article 11 of the *Anti-Dumping Agreement* establishes rules governing the duration of anti-dumping measures and a requirement for the periodic review of any continuing necessity for the imposition of anti-dumping measures.

With respect to the duration of anti-dumping duties, Article 11.1 of the *Anti-Dumping Agreement* provides:

> An anti-dumping duty shall remain in force only as long as and to the extent necessary to counteract dumping which is causing injury.

The Panel in *US – DRAMS* stated that:

> the need for the continued imposition of the duty must be demonstrable on the basis of the evidence adduced.[189]

With respect to the periodic review of anti-dumping duties applied, Article 11.2, first sentence, requires the competent authorities to:

> review the need for the continued imposition of the duty, where warranted, on their own initiative or, provided that a reasonable period of time has elapsed since the imposition of the definitive anti-dumping duty, upon request by any interested party which submits positive information substantiating the need for a review.[190]

The second sentence of Article 11.2 requires investigating authorities to examine whether the 'continued imposition' of the duty is necessary to offset dumping.

Footnote 189 (*cont.*)

as provided for in paragraph 6 . . .' (emphasis added). Once the authorities have 'sufficient evidence' that the conditions of Article 10.6 are satisfied, they may take the conservatory or precautionary measures provided for in Article 10.7. On what constitutes 'sufficient evidence', and other issues relating to Articles 10.6 and 10.7, see Panel Report, *US – Hot-Rolled Steel*, paras. 7.143–7.144; and Panel Report, *Mexico – Corn Syrup*, paras. 7.190–7.191.   [189] Panel Report, *US – DRAMS*, para. 6.42.

[190] The determination of whether or not good and sufficient grounds exist for the self-initiation of a review necessarily depends upon the factual situation in a given case and will vary from case to case. See Panel Report, *EC – Tube or Pipe Fittings*, para. 7.115.

The Panel in *US – DRAMS* interpreted this requirement as follows:

> The word 'continued' covers a temporal relationship between past and future. In our view, the word 'continued' would be redundant if the investigating authority were restricted to considering only whether the duty was necessary to offset *present* dumping. Thus, the inclusion of the word 'continued' signifies that the investigating authority is entitled to examine whether imposition of the duty may be applied henceforth to offset dumping.[191]

Furthermore, with regard to injury, Article 11.2, second sentence, provides for a review of 'whether the injury would be likely to continue or recur if the duty were removed or varied'. The Panel in *US – DRAMS* stated in this respect that:

> In conducting an Article 11.2 injury review, an investigating authority may examine the causal link between injury and dumped imports. If, in the context of a review of such a causal link, the only injury under examination is injury that may recur following revocation (i.e., future rather than present injury), an investigating authority must necessarily be examining whether that future injury would be caused by dumping with a commensurately prospective timeframe. To do so, the investigating authority would first need to have established a status regarding the prospects of dumping. For these reasons, we do not agree that Article 11.2 precludes *a priori* the justification of continued imposition of anti-dumping duties when there is no present dumping.
>
> In addition, we note that there is nothing in the text of Article 11.2 of the [Anti-Dumping] Agreement that explicitly limits a Member to a 'present' analysis, and forecloses a prospective analysis, when conducting an Article 11.2 review.[192]

In other words, Article 11.2 does not preclude *a priori* continued imposition of anti-dumping duties in the *absence* of present dumping. However, it may also be clear from the plain meaning of the text of Article 11.2 that the continued imposition must still satisfy the 'necessity' standard, even where the need for the continued imposition of an anti-dumping duty is tied to the *recurrence* of dumping.[193] Note also that the Panel in *US – DRAMS* found that, with regard to injury, an absence of dumping during the preceding three years and six months is not in and of itself indicative of the likely state of the relevant domestic industry if the duty were removed or varied. Likewise, with regard to causality, an absence of dumping during the preceding three years and six months is not in and of itself indicative of causal factors other than the absence of dumping.[194]

If, as a result of the review, the authorities determine that the anti-dumping duty is no longer warranted, it shall be terminated immediately.[195]

In any case, pursuant to Article 11.3 of the *Anti-Dumping Agreement* (the so-called 'sunset clause'), any definitive anti-dumping duty shall be *terminated* on a date not later than *five years* from its imposition,[196] *unless* the authorities determine, in a review initiated before that date, that the expiry of the duty 'would be likely to lead to continuation or recurrence of dumping and injury'.[197] Such a review is commonly referred to as a 'sunset review'. It can be initiated:

---

[191] Panel Report, *US – DRAMS*, para. 6.27.   [192] See *ibid.*, paras. 6.28–6.29.   [193] See *ibid.*, para. 6.43.
[194] See *ibid.*, para. 6.59.   [195] See Article 11.2 of the *Anti-Dumping Agreement*.
[196] Or, alternatively, from the date of the most recent review under Article 11.2, if that review has covered both dumping and injury, or the date of the most recent review under Article 11.3.
[197] The duty may remain in force pending the outcome of such a review. See Article 11.3 of the *Anti-Dumping Agreement*.

- at the initiative of the competent authorities; or
- upon a duly substantiated request made by or on behalf of the domestic industry.[198]

Any such review shall be carried out expeditiously and shall normally be concluded within twelve months of the date of initiation of the review.[199]

The Panel in *US – DRAMS* made the following observations with regard to the 'sunset review' under Article 11.3 of the *Anti-Dumping Agreement*:

> We note that Article 11.3 provides for termination of a definitive anti-dumping duty five years from its imposition. However, such termination is conditional. First, the terms of Article 11.3 itself lay down that this should occur unless the authorities determine that the expiry would be 'likely to lead to continuation or recurrence of dumping and injury'. Where there is a determination that both are likely, the duty may remain in force, and the five year clock is reset to start again from that point. Second, Article 11.3 provides also for another situation whereby this five year period can be otherwise effectively extended, viz in a situation where a review under paragraph 2 covering both dumping and injury has taken place. If, for instance, such a review took place at the four year point, it could effectively extend the sunset review until 9 years from the original determination. In the first case, we note that the provisions of Article 11.3 explicitly conditions the prolongation of the five year period on a finding that there is *likelihood* of dumping and injury continuing or recurring. In the second case, where there is reference to review under Article 11.2, there is no such explicit reference.[200]

However, since both instances of review (i.e. review and sunset review) have the same practical effect of prolonging the application of anti-dumping duties beyond five years, the Panel in *US – DRAMS* argued that the investigating authorities are entitled to apply the same test concerning the likelihood of recurrence or the continuation of dumping for both Article 11.2 and Article 11.3 reviews. With respect to both Article 11.2 and Article 11.3 reviews, the Panel in *US – DRAMS* noted that:

> 'likelihood' or 'likely' carries with it the ordinary meaning of 'probable'. That being so, it seems to us that a 'likely standard' amounts to the view that where recurrence of dumping is found to be *probable* as a consequence of revocation of an anti-dumping duty, this probability would constitute a proper basis for entitlement to maintain that anti-dumping duty in force.[201]
>
> [Emphasis added]

Note that the sunset review in Article 11.3 has recently been the subject of several WTO disputes, such as *US – Corrosion-Resistant Steel Sunset Review* and the *US – Oil Country Tubular Goods Sunset Reviews*.

Questions and Assignments 6.16

How long can an anti-dumping duty remain in force? When, and on whose initiative, will the national investigating authorities review the

---

[198] See *ibid.*

[199] See Article 11.4 of the *Anti-Dumping Agreement*. The provisions of Article 6 of the *Anti-Dumping Agreement* regarding evidence and procedure shall apply to any review carried out under Article 11.

[200] Panel Report, *US – DRAMS*, para. 6.48, footnote 494.   [201] *Ibid.*

continued need for the imposition of an anti-dumping duty? On what basis will the investigating authorities decide on the continued need for the imposition of an anti-dumping duty? What is a 'sunset review'? Describe two ways in which the imposition of an anti-dumping duty can be prolonged beyond the period of five years provided for in Article 11.3 of the *Anti-Dumping Agreement*.

6.2.6.5. *Problem of circumvention of anti-dumping duties*

As explained above, anti-dumping duties are typically levied on a specific product of a specific exporter or producer from a specific country. An exporter or producer may try to change the characteristics of the product concerned so that it no longer responds to the characteristics of the product subjected to an anti-dumping duty. An exporter or producer also may move part of its assembly or manufacturing operations to the importing country or to a third country so that the product arguably no longer originates in the country the products of which are subjected to an anti-dumping duty. In short, the exporter or producer may attempt to avoid or 'circumvent' the anti-dumping duties imposed. Members have different ways of handling this problem and of answering the question to what extent the 'new' products may be subjected to the existing anti-dumping duties.[202] The problem of circumvention and anti-circumvention measures was on the agenda of the Uruguay Round but no agreement on specific rules was reached. The matter was referred to the WTO Committee on Anti-Dumping Practices for resolution.[203]

6.2.6.6. *Public notice and judicial review*

In order to increase the transparency of the determinations made by the investigating authorities and to encourage solid and thorough reasoning underlying such determinations, Article 12 of the *Anti-Dumping Agreement* contains detailed requirements for public notice by investigating authorities of the initiation of an investigation, preliminary and final determinations and price undertakings. For example, the public notice of a final determination *must* set forth, or otherwise make available through a separate report, in sufficient detail, the findings and conclusions reached on all issues of fact and law considered material by the investigating authorities.[204] In particular, the notice or report *must* contain:

- the names of the suppliers, or, when this is impracticable, the supplying countries involved;

---

[202] The rules of the European Communities on anti-circumvention were found inconsistent with Article III:2 of the GATT 1947 because they provided for an internal tax not applied to like products of EC origin and inconsistent with Article III:4 of the GATT 1947 because they made the grant of an advantage dependent on an undertaking to limit the use of Japanese parts or materials. See GATT Panel Report, *EEC – Parts and Components*, paras. 5.9 and 5.21.   [203] See the Uruguay Round *Decision on Anti-Circumvention*.
[204] See Article 12.2.2 of the *Anti-Dumping Agreement*. Note, however, that Article 12.2.2 does require that due regard be paid to the requirement of the protection of confidential information.

- a description of the product which is sufficient for customs purposes;
- the margins of dumping established and a full explanation of the reasons for the methodology used in the establishment and comparison of the export price and the normal value under Article 2;
- considerations relevant to the injury determination as set out in Article 3; and
- the main reasons leading to the determination.[205]

Furthermore, the notice or report *must* set out the reasons for the acceptance or rejection of relevant arguments or claims made by the exporters and importers.[206] The consistency of notices or reports with the requirements of Article 12.2 of the *Anti-Dumping Agreement* has been an issue in many disputes.[207] In *EC – Tube or Pipe Fittings*, for example, the Panel found that the European Communities acted inconsistently with Articles 12.2 and 12.2.2 of the *Anti-Dumping Agreement*:

> in that it is not directly discernible from the published Provisional or Definitive Determination that the European Communities addressed or explained the lack of significance of certain listed Article 3.4 factors.[208]

As provided for in Article 13 of the *Anti-Dumping Agreement*, entitled 'Judicial Review', each Member whose national legislation contains provisions on anti-dumping measures must maintain judicial, arbitral or administrative tribunals or procedures for the purpose, *inter alia*, of the prompt review of administrative actions relating to final determinations and reviews of determinations. Such tribunals or procedures must be independent of the authorities responsible for the determination or review in question.[209] Although judicial review in some WTO Members, such as the European Communities, takes notoriously long, thus far this has not been challenged under the 'prompt' review provision.

6.2.7. Special and differential treatment for developing-country Members

As with many other WTO agreements, the *Anti-Dumping Agreement* contains a provision relating to special and differential treatment for developing-country Members. Article 15 of the *Anti-Dumping Agreement* states:

> It is recognized that special regard must be given by developed country Members to the special situation of developing country Members when considering the application of anti-dumping measures under this Agreement. Possibilities of constructive remedies provided for by this Agreement shall be explored before applying anti-dumping duties where they would affect the essential interests of developing country Members.

---

[205] See Article 12.2.2 in conjunction with Article 12.2.1 of the *Anti-Dumping Agreement*.
[206] Article 12.2.2 of the *Anti-Dumping Agreement*.
[207] See e.g. Panel Report, *Korea – Certain Paper*, paras. 7.207 ff; Panel Report, *US – Oil Country Tubular Goods Sunset Reviews*, paras. 7.252 ff; Panel Report, *EC – Tube or Pipe Fittings*, paras. 7.417 ff; Panel Report, *US – Steel Plate*, paras. 6.1 ff; and Panel Report, *Mexico – Corn Syrup*, para. 7.198.
[208] Panel Report, *EC – Tube or Pipe Fittings*, para. 7.435.   [209] See Article 13 of the *Anti-Dumping Agreement*.

The Panel in *EC – Tube or Pipe Fittings* characterised Article 15 as follows:

> [T]here is no requirement for any specific outcome set out in the first sentence of Article 15. We are furthermore of the view that, even assuming that the first sentence of Article 15 imposes a general obligation on Members, it clearly contains no operational language delineating the precise extent or nature of that obligation or requiring a developed country Member to undertake any specific action. The second sentence serves to provide operational indications as to the nature of the specific action required. Fulfilment of the obligations in the second sentence of Article 15 would therefore necessarily, in our view, constitute fulfilment of any general obligation that might arguably be contained in the first sentence.[210]

Examining the nature of the obligation contained in the second sentence of Article 15, the Panel in *EC – Bed Linen* interpreted the term 'explore' as follows:

> In our view, while the exact parameters of the term are difficult to establish, the concept of 'explore' clearly does not imply any particular outcome. We recall that Article 15 does not require that 'constructive remedies' must be explored, but rather that the 'possibilities' of such remedies must be explored, which further suggests that the exploration may conclude that no possibilities exist, or that no constructive remedies are possible, in the particular circumstances of a given case. Taken in its context, however, and in light of the object and purpose of Article 15, we do consider that the 'exploration' of possibilities must be actively undertaken by the developed country authorities with a willingness to reach a positive outcome. Thus, in our view, Article 15 imposes no obligation to actually provide or accept any constructive remedy that may be identified and/or offered. It does, however, impose an obligation to actively consider, with an open mind, the possibility of such a remedy prior to imposition of an anti-dumping measure that would affect the essential interests of a developing country.[211]

There is no obligation to accept or apply a 'constructive remedy'. There is merely an obligation to 'explore' possibilities of constructive remedies, in particular, where the possibility of an undertaking has already been broached by the developing country concerned.[212] A developed-country Member that fails to acknowledge the willingness of a developing-country Member to enter into a price undertaking would fail to 'explore constructive remedies'.

With respect to the meaning of the phrase 'constructive remedies provided for by this Agreement' in the second sentence of Article 15, the Panel in *EC – Bed Linen* rejected the argument that a 'constructive remedy' might be a decision not to impose anti-dumping duties at all. The Panel stated that:

> Article 15 refers to 'remedies' in respect of injurious dumping. A decision not to impose an anti-dumping duty, while clearly within the authority of a Member under Article 9.1 of the [Anti-Dumping] Agreement, is not a 'remedy' of any type, constructive or otherwise.[213]

Addressing what the phrase 'constructive remedies provided for by this Agreement' might encompass, the Panel in *EC – Bed Linen* stated:

> The Agreement provides for the imposition of anti-dumping duties, either in the full amount of the dumping margin, or desirably, in a lesser amount, or the acceptance of

---

[210] Panel Report, *EC – Tube or Pipe Fittings*, para. 7.68. On the meaning of the first sentence of Article 15, see also Panel Report, *US – Steel Plate*, para. 7.110.
[211] *Ibid.*, para. 6.233. See also Panel Report, *EC – Tube or Pipe Fittings*, para. 7.72.
[212] See Panel Report, *EC – Bed Linen*, para. 6.238.   [213] Panel Report, *EC – Bed Linen*, para. 6.228.

> price undertakings, as a means of resolving an anti-dumping investigation resulting in a final affirmative determination of dumping, injury, and causal link. Thus, in our view, imposition of a lesser duty, or a price undertaking would constitute 'constructive remedies' within the meaning of Article 15. We come to no conclusions as to what other actions might in addition be considered to constitute 'constructive remedies' under Article 15, as none have been proposed to us.[214]

The Panel in *EC – Bed Linen* understood the phrase 'before applying anti-dumping duties' to mean before the application of definitive (as opposed to provisional) anti-dumping measures, at the end of the investigative process.[215]

At the Doha Session of the Ministerial Conference in November 2001, WTO Members recognised the following, concerning Article 15 of the *Anti-Dumping Agreement*:

> while Article 15 . . . is a mandatory provision, the modalities for its application would benefit from clarification. Accordingly, the Committee on Anti-Dumping Practices is instructed, through its working group on implementation, to examine this issue and to draw up appropriate recommendations within twelve months on how to operationalize this provision.[216]

Questions and Assignments 6.17

What does the 'special and differential treatment' provision of Article 15 of the *Anti-Dumping Agreement* require from developed-country Members?

6.2.8. Standard of review for WTO panels in anti-dumping disputes

Pursuant to Article 17.1 of the *Anti-Dumping Agreement*, disputes between Members on the consistency of anti-dumping measures with the obligations under this Agreement are subject to the normal rules on WTO dispute settlement contained in the DSU, *except as otherwise provided*. As discussed in chapter 3 of this book, Article 11 of the DSU sets forth the appropriate standard of review for panels: the 'objective assessment' standard.[217] Article 17.6 of the *Anti-Dumping Agreement*, however, provides for two special rules with regard to the standard of review for panels hearing disputes concerning anti-dumping measures. The first of these special rules is set out in Article 17.6(i) of the *Anti-Dumping Agreement*, which provides that:

> (i) in its assessment of the facts of the matter, the panel shall determine whether the authorities' establishment of the facts was proper and whether their evaluation of those facts was unbiased and objective. If the establishment of the facts was proper and the evaluation was unbiased and objective, even though the panel might have reached a different conclusion, the evaluation shall not be overturned.

---

[214] Ibid., para. 6.229. See also Panel Report, *EC – Tube or Pipe Fittings*, paras. 7.71–7.72.
[215] See Panel Report, *EC – Bed Linen*, paras. 6.231–6.232.
[216] Ministerial Conference, *Decision on Implementation-Related Issues and Concerns of 14 November 2001*, WT/MIN(01)/17, dated 20 November 2001, para. 7.2.   [217] See above, pp. 248–51.

This provision requires a panel not to engage in a 'new and independent fact-finding exercise',[218] or to conduct a *de novo* review of the evidence before an investigating authority.[219] Rather, the mandate of the panel is confined to examining whether the evaluation of the evidence by the investigating authority was 'unbiased and objective'.[220] In doing so, a panel should consider all information, *both* confidential and non-confidential, that was *before* the investigating authority.[221] Read with Article 11 of the DSU, panels under Article 17.6(i) should make an *objective* review of the investigating authority's establishment and evaluation of facts.[222]

The second special rule regarding the standard of review is set out in Article 17.6(ii) of the *Anti-Dumping Agreement*. It requires that where a panel finds that a relevant provision of the Agreement – when interpreted in accordance with customary rules of interpretation of public international law – admits of more than one permissible interpretation, the panel shall find the authoritiy's measure to be in conformity with the Agreement *if* it rests upon one of those permissible interpretations.[223]

6.3. SUBSIDIES AND COUNTERVAILING MEASURES

In addition to rules on dumping and anti-dumping measures, WTO law also includes rules on another unfair trade practice, subsidisation. Subsidies are a very sensitive matter in international trade relations. On the one hand, subsidies are evidently used by governments to pursue and promote important and fully legitimate objectives of economic and social policy. On the other hand, subsidies may have adverse effects on the interests of trading partners whose industry may suffer, in its domestic or export markets, from the unfair competition from subsidised products. According to a 2006 WTO study, agricultural and other subsidies in 2003 totalled US$300 billion. Of this, around US$250 billion, or 83 per cent, was spent in (and by) twenty-one developed countries.[224] This study emphasised that:

> subsidies can distort trade flows if they give an artificial competitive advantage to exporters or import-competing industries.[225]

---

[218] Appellate Body Report, *Mexico – Corn Syrup (Article 21.5 – US)*, para. 84.

[219] See Panel Report, *US – Steel Plate*, para. 7.6; and Panel Report, *Egypt – Steel Rebar*, paras. 7.8 and 7.14.

[220] See Panel Report, *Mexico – Corn Syrup*, para. 7.94; Panel Report, *Guatemala – Cement II*, para. 8.19; Panel Report, *Thailand – H-Beams*, para. 7.51; Panel Report, *US – Stainless Steel*, para. 6.3; and Panel Report, *US – Hot-Rolled Steel*, para. 7.26.

[221] See Appellate Body Report, *Thailand – H-Beams*, paras. 113–20. See also Panel Report, *EC – Tube or Pipe Fittings*, para. 7.45.

[222] See Appellate Body Report, *US – Hot-Rolled Steel*, paras. 55, 62; Panel Report, *US – Steel Plate*, para. 7.5; Appellate Body Report, *Mexico – Corn Syrup (Article 21.5 – US)*, para. 130; and Panel Report, *Korea – Certain Paper*, paras. 6.1–6.3.

[223] See Article 17.6(ii) of the *Anti-Dumping Agreement*. See e.g. Panel Report, *US – Softwood Lumber V (Article 21.5 – Canada)*, para. 5.66. The Panel in this case found that two permissible interpretations existed and accepted, therefore, the respondent's interpretation. However, the Appellate Body reversed the finding that two interpretations were permissible. See Appellate Body Report, *US – Softwood Lumber V (Article 21.5 – Canada)*, para. 123.

[224] WTO Secretariat, *World Trade Report 2006: Exploring the Links between Subsidies, Trade and the WTO* (WTO, 2006), xxx, available at www.wto.org/english/res_e/booksp_e/anrep_e/world_trade_report06_e.pdf, visited on December 2007.　　[225] *Ibid.*, xxii.

Disputes about subsidies, and in particular subsidies to 'strategic sectors' of the economy of Members, have been prominent on the GATT/WTO agenda. Most noteworthy at present are the *EC and Certain Member States – Large Civil Aircraft* and *US – Large Civil Aircraft* disputes, both pending before a WTO dispute settlement panel.[226] With regard to these disputes, *The Economist* noted in 2005:

> Like Kaiser Wilhelm's army in the summer of 1914, the United States Trade Representative's office is rumbling inexorably down the track to war: it seems too late to stop the conflict that looms. Immediately after America filed its complaint to the World Trade Organisation (WTO) at the end of May about European subsidies to Airbus, the European Union (EU) followed with a counter complaint about federal and state subsidies to Boeing in America . . . The Americans accuse Airbus of receiving subsidies worth $17 billion in launch loans alone over the past 35 years. The Europeans counter that Boeing has enjoyed R&D subsidies worth $23 billion in the past 13 years.
>
>   The nightmare for America and Europe is that both WTO suits succeed . . . the threat of countervailing import duties being applied to new Airbus and Boeing planes would cast a pall over the aviation industry and could even ignite a disastrous transatlantic trade war.[227]

As discussed in chapter 1, subsidies are subject to an intricate set of rules.[228] Some subsidies, such as export subsidies, are, as a rule, prohibited, while other subsidies are not prohibited but must be withdrawn (or their adverse effects removed) when they cause adverse effects to the interests of other Members. Furthermore, if a subsidy causes or threatens to cause material injury to the domestic industry of a Member, that Member is authorised to impose countervailing duties on the subsidised products to offset the subsidisation.

In the period from 1 July 2005 to 30 June 2006, three definitive countervailing duties were imposed: the United States, Japan and Mexico each imposed one.[229] On 30 June 2006, a total of seventy-nine definitive countervailing measures were in force, of which forty-five were taken by the United States and fourteen by the European Communities.[230]

Questions and Assignments 6.18

Compare the use made of countervailing duties with that made of anti-dumping duties.

6.3.1. Basic elements of WTO law on subsidies and subsidised trade

Before entering into a more detailed, and often technical, discussion of the rules on subsidies and countervailing measures, this section addresses in general terms:

---

[226] See *EC and Certain Member States – Large Civil Aircraft*, complaint by the United States, WT/DS316/1, and *US – Large Civil Aircraft*, complaint by the European Communities, WT/DS317/1.
[227] 'Boeing v Airbus: Nose to Nose', *The Economist*, 23 July 2005.   [228] See above, p. 40.
[229] See WTO Secretariat, *WTO Annual Report 2007*, 31, available at www.wto.org/english/res_e/booksp_e/anrep_e/anrep07_e.pdf, visited on 1 December 2007.   [230] See *ibid*.

- the history of the law on subsidies and subsidised trade;
- the concept of 'subsidies';
- WTO treatment of subsidies; and
- the response to injurious subsidised trade.

6.3.1.1. The history of the law on subsidies and subsidised trade

The WTO rules on subsidies and subsidised trade are set out in Articles VI and XVI of the GATT 1994 but also, and more importantly, in the WTO *Agreement on Subsidies and Countervailing Measures*, commonly referred to as the *SCM Agreement*. The GATT 1947 did not contain clear and comprehensive rules on subsidies. In fact, Article XVI of the GATT 1947, entitled 'Subsidies', did not even define the concept of 'subsidies'. Moreover, with regard to subsidies in general, Article XVI merely provided that Contracting Parties to the GATT should notify subsidies that have an effect on trade and should be prepared to discuss limiting such subsidies if they cause serious damage to the interests of other Contracting Parties.[231] With regard to export subsidies, Article XVI provided that Contracting Parties were to 'seek to avoid' using subsidies on exports of primary products.[232] In 1962, Article XVI was amended to add a provision prohibiting Contracting Parties from granting export subsidies to non-primary products which would reduce the sales price on the export market below the sales price on the domestic market.[233] Note, however, that this amendment did not apply to developing countries. In addition, Article VI of the GATT 1947, which dealt with measures taken to offset any subsidy granted to an imported product (i.e. countervailing duties), did not provide for clear and comprehensive rules. In order to elaborate on the GATT rules on subsidies and countervailing duties and to provide greater uniformity and certainty in their implementation, the GATT Contracting Parties, during the Tokyo Round (1973–9), negotiated and concluded the *Agreement on Interpretation and Application of Articles VI, XVI and XXIII of the General Agreement*, commonly referred to as the Tokyo Round *Subsidies Code*.[234] Fewer than twenty-five Contracting Parties accepted this plurilateral agreement, including the European Communities and the United States.[235] The *Subsidies Code* certainly did not bring the degree of clarification and elaboration of the rules on subsidies and countervailing duties sought by some of the Contracting Parties. During the 1980s, the lack of clear rules on subsidies and countervailing duties led to many disputes between the GATT Contracting Parties. It was therefore not surprising that the Punta del Este Ministerial Declaration on the Uruguay Round of September 1986 instructed the negotiators to review Articles VI and XVI of the GATT 1947 as well as the Tokyo Round *Subsidies Code*:

---

[231] See Article XVI:1 of the GATT 1947.
[232] See Article XVI:3 of the GATT 1947. Contracting Parties 'should not' give a subsidy which results in the exporting country gaining 'more than an equitable share of world export trade in that product'.
[233] See Article XVI:4 of the GATT 1947, as amended.   [234] See BISD 26S/56.
[235] See the list of acceptances of Tokyo Round agreements in *Analytical Index: Guide to GATT Law and Pratice* (WTO, 1995), 1147–50.

with the objective of improving GATT disciplines relating to all subsidies and counter-vailing measures that affect international trade.[236]

The Uruguay Round negotiations eventually resulted in the *SCM Agreement*, which forms part of Annex 1A to the *WTO Agreement*. The multilateral rules on subsidies and subsidised trade are now set out in Articles VI and XVI of the GATT 1994 and, most importantly, in the *SCM Agreement*. With respect to the object and purpose of this Agreement, the Panel in *Brazil – Aircraft* clarified that:

> The object and purpose of the SCM Agreement is to impose multilateral disciplines on subsidies which distort international trade.[237]

The Panel in *Canada – Aircraft* further clarified that:

> The object and purpose of the SCM Agreement could more appropriately be summarised as the establishment of multilateral disciplines 'on the premise that some forms of government intervention distort international trade [or] have the potential to distort [international trade]'.[238]

Questions and Assignments 6.19

Briefly discuss the origins of the *SCM Agreement*. What is the object and purpose of the *SCM Agreement*?

6.3.1.2. The concept of 'subsidy'

The *SCM Agreement* contains, for the first time in the GATT/WTO context, a detailed and comprehensive definition of the concept of 'subsidy'. As the Panel in *US – FSC* stated:

> the inclusion of this detailed and comprehensive definition of the term 'subsidy' is generally considered to represent one of the most important achievements of the Uruguay Round in the area of subsidy disciplines.[239]

Broadly speaking, Article 1.1 of the *SCM Agreement* defines a subsidy as a financial contribution by a government or public body, which confers a benefit.[240] Furthermore, Article 1.2 of the *SCM Agreement* provides that the WTO rules on subsidies and subsidised trade only apply to 'specific' subsidies, i.e. subsidies granted to an enterprise or industry, or a group of enterprises or industries. The concepts of 'subsidy' and 'specificity' are examined in detail below.[241]

---

[236] *Punta del Este Ministerial Declaration on the Uruguay Round*, BISD 33S/25.
[237] Panel Report, *Brazil – Aircraft*, para. 7.26.   [238] Panel Report, *Canada – Aircraft*, para. 9.119.
[239] Panel Report, *US – FSC*, para. 7.80. The Panel in *US – Softwood Lumber III* noted that this definition constituted 'one of the most important achievements in the development of the law on subsidies'. Panel Report, *US – Softwood Lumber III*, para. 7.24.
[240] On this definition and its constituent elements, see below, pp. 562–70. See also Panel Report, *US – Export Restraints*, paras. 8.22–8.24.   [241] See below, pp. 562–70.

6.3.1.3. WTO treatment of subsidies

Article XVI of the GATT 1994 and Articles 3 to 9 of the *SCM Agreement* deal with the WTO treatment of subsidies.[242] As discussed above, dumping is not prohibited. It is merely 'condemned' if it causes injury. The WTO treatment of subsidies is different. Certain subsidies are prohibited, and many other subsidies, at least when they are specific rather than general, may be challenged when they cause adverse effects to the interests of other Members.[243] WTO law distinguishes between prohibited subsidies, actionable subsidies and non-actionable subsidies. Each of these kinds of subsidy has its own substantive and procedural rules.[244] Moreover, subsidies on agricultural products are subject to certain rules set out in the *Agreement on Agriculture*.

6.3.1.4. Response to injurious subsidised trade

Article VI of the GATT 1994 and Articles 10 to 23 of the *SCM Agreement* concern the manner in which WTO Members may respond to subsidised trade which causes injury to the domestic industry. Members may, in these situations, impose countervailing duties on the subsidised imports to offset the subsidisation. However, comparable to the anti-dumping measures discussed above, countervailing duties may only be imposed when it is properly established that there are subsidised imports, that there is injury to a domestic industry and that there is a causal link between the subsidised imports and the injury. As with the conduct of anti-dumping investigations, the conduct of countervailing investigations is also subject to relatively strict procedural requirements. Note that the substantive and procedural rules on the imposition and maintenance of countervailing measures are similar to (albeit somewhat less detailed than) the rules on anti-dumping measures.

Questions and Assignments 6.20

Explain briefly how WTO law regulates subsidisation and the response to injurious subsidised trade.

---

[242] On the relationship between Article XVI of the GATT 1994 and the provisions of the *SCM Agreement*, note that the obligations and procedures set out in Article XVI of the GATT 1994 must be read and applied together with the *SCM Agreement*. As the Appellate Body concluded in *Brazil – Desiccated Coconut*, Article XVI of the GATT 1994 cannot be invoked independently from the *SCM Agreement*. See Appellate Body Report, *Brazil – Desiccated Coconut*, 182–3. In fact, the provisions of the *SCM Agreement* are so wide and detailed that they leave very little scope for application of the provisions of Article XVI of the GATT 1994.
[243] For a full discussion of the WTO treatment of subsidies, see below, pp. 571–85.
[244] With regard to the third category of subsidies, the non-actionable subsidies, Article 8.1 of the *SCM Agreement* distinguishes between non-specific subsidies and other types of subsidies listed in Article 8.2. Note that by virtue of the operation of Article 31 of the *SCM Agreement*, the specific provisions on non-actionable subsidies listed in Article 8.2 have lapses and these subsidies have become 'actionable' (see below, pp. 577–85). Also note that by virtue of Article 1.2 of the *SCM Agreement*, no discipline of the *SCM Agreement* is applicable to non-specific subsidies.

6.3.2. Determination of subsidisation

Article 1.1 of the *SCM Agreement* provides, in relevant part:

> For the purpose of this Agreement, a subsidy shall be deemed to exist if:
>
> (a)(1) there is a financial contribution by a government or any public body within the ter-
>   ritory of a Member . . . or
> (a)(2) there is any form of income or price support in the sense of Article XVI of GATT
>   1994 and
> (b)   a benefit is thereby conferred.

Article 1.2 of the *SCM Agreement* furthermore provides:

> A subsidy as defined in paragraph 1 shall be subject to the provisions of Part II or shall be
> subject to the provisions of Part III or V only if such a subsidy is specific in accordance
> with the provisions of Article 2.

This section first examines the three constituent elements of the concept of 'subsidy':

- a *financial contribution*;
- a financial contribution *by a government or any public body*; and
- a financial contribution *conferring a benefit*.

Subsequently, this section discusses the concept of 'specificity'.

6.3.2.1. Financial contribution

For a measure to be a subsidy within the meaning of Article 1.1 of the *SCM Agreement*, that measure must constitute a 'financial contribution' or take the form of income or price support in the sense of Article XVI of the GATT 1994. Article 1.1 provides for an exhaustive list of types of financial contributions. This list includes:

- direct transfers of funds, such as grants, loans and equity infusions (Article 1.1(a)(1)(i));
- potential direct transfers of funds or liabilities, such as loan guarantees (Article 1.1(a)(1)(i));
- government revenue, otherwise due, that is foregone or not collected (Article 1.1(a)(1)(ii));
- the provision by a government of goods or services other than general infra-structure (Article 1.1(a)(1)(iii));
- the purchase by a government of goods (Article 1.1(a)(1)(iii)); and
- government payments to a funding mechanism or entrustment or direction of a private body (Article 1.1(a)(1)(iv)).

A financial contribution exists not only when a direct transfer of funds or a potential direct transfer of funds has actually been effectuated. Pursuant to Article 1.1(a)(1)(i), it is sufficient that there is a 'government practice' involving the transfer of funds. The Panel in *Brazil – Aircraft* noted in this respect:

> If subsidies were deemed to exist only once a direct or potential direct transfer of funds had actually been effectuated, the Agreement would be rendered totally ineffective and even the typical WTO remedy (i.e. the cessation of the violation) would not be possible.[245]

As provided in Article 1.1(a)(1)(ii), government revenue, otherwise due, that is foregone or not collected is also a financial contribution within the meaning of Article 1.1. In *US – FSC*, the Appellate Body held:

> In our view, the *'foregoing'* of revenue *'otherwise* due' implies that less revenue has been raised by the government than would have been raised in a different situation, or, that is, 'otherwise'. Moreover, the word 'foregone' suggests that the government has given up an entitlement to raise revenue that it could 'otherwise' have raised. This cannot, however, be an entitlement in the abstract, because governments, in theory, could tax *all* revenues. There must, therefore, be some defined, normative benchmark against which a comparison can be made between the revenue actually raised and the revenue that would have been raised 'otherwise'. We, therefore, agree with the Panel that the term 'otherwise due' implies some kind of comparison between the revenues due under the contested measure and revenues that would be due in some other situation. We also agree with the Panel that the basis of comparison must be the tax rules applied by the Member in question . . . A Member, in principle, has the sovereign authority to tax any particular categories of revenue it wishes. It is also free *not* to tax any particular categories of revenues. But, in both instances, the Member must respect its WTO obligations. What is 'otherwise due', therefore, depends on the rules of taxation that each Member, by its own choice, establishes for itself.[246]

The term 'otherwise', as used in 'government revenue, otherwise due, that was foregone', refers to a normative benchmark as established by the tax rules applied by the Member concerned.[247] The Panel in *US – FSC* explained that the term 'otherwise due' refers to the situation that would prevail *but for* the measure at issue.[248]

Note that the Panels in *Korea – Commercial Vessels* and *Japan – DRAMs (Korea)* found that interest reductions and deferrals, interest/debt forgiveness and debt-for-equity swaps were 'financial contributions' within the meaning of Article 1.1 of the *SCM Agreement*.[249] The Panel in *US – Softwood Lumber III* found that the Canadian Provincial Stumpage programme constituted a 'financial contribution' as this programme, under which harvesting companies were allowed by the Government to cut trees, amounted to the 'supply' by the Government of a particular good, namely standing timber.[250] The Panel in *EC – Countervailing Measures on DRAM Chips* found that an export insurance guarantee and the purchase of corporate bonds were 'financial contributions' within the meaning of

---

[245] Panel Report, *Brazil – Aircraft*, para. 7.13. [246] Appellate Body Report, *US – FSC*, para. 90.

[247] The Appellate Body in *US – FSC (Article 21.5 – EC)* clarified that Article 1.1(a)(1)(ii) does not require panels to identify a general rule of taxation and exceptions to that general rule, but rather they should compare the domestic fiscal treatment of 'legitimately' comparable income 'to determine whether the contested measure involves the foregoing of revenue that is "otherwise due" '. Appellate Body Report, *US – FSC (Article 21.5 – EC)*, para. 91.

[248] See Panel Report, *US – FSC*, para. 7.45. Note, however, that the Appellate Body stated that, although the Panel's 'but for' test works in this case, it may not work in other cases. The Appellate Body had 'certain abiding reservations' about applying any legal standard, such as this 'but for' test, in place of the actual treaty language. See Appellate Body Report, *US – FSC*, para. 91.

[249] See Panel Report, *Korea – Commercial Vessels*, para. 7.31; and Panel Report, *Japan – DRAMs (Korea)*, para. 7.446.

[250] See Panel Report, *US – Softwood Lumber III*, para. 7.30.

Article 1.1 of the *SCM Agreement*.[251] In *US – Upland Cotton* the Panel found that user marketing payments to domestic users and exporters, marketing loan programme payments, crop insurance payments and cotton seed payments were grants that undoubtedly constituted financial contributions.[252] While the list in Article 1.1 of types of financial contributions is exhaustive, it is clear that the concept of 'financial contributions' is broad. Note, however, that the Panel in *US – Export Restraints*, considering the negotiating history of Article 1 of the *SCM Agreement*, held that the inclusion of the term 'financial contributions' was intended to make sure that not all governmental measures that confer some sort of benefit would fall within the scope of the *SCM Agreement*.[253]

Questions and Assignments 6.21

Give five examples of 'financial contributions' within the meaning of the *SCM Agreement*. When does the non-taxation of income constitute a 'financial contribution'? Is a temporary waiver of environmental standards for a company in financial and economic difficulty a 'financial contribution' within the meaning of Article 1.1(a) of the *SCM Agreement*?

6.3.2.2. *A financial contribution by a government*

For a financial contribution to be a subsidy within the meaning of Article 1.1 of the *SCM Agreement*, the financial contribution must be made by a government or a public body, including regional and local authorities as well as State-owned companies. The question of what constitutes a 'public body' was addressed by the Panel in *Korea – Commercial Vessels* as follows:

> In our view, an entity will constitute a 'public body' if it is controlled by the government (or other public bodies). If an entity is controlled by the government (or other public bodies), then any action by that entity is attributable to the government, and should therefore fall within the scope of Article 1.1(a)(1) of the *SCM Agreement*.[254]

In *Korea – Commercial Vessels*, the Panel considered that the body at issue, KEXIM, was controlled by the Korean Government because it was 100 per cent owned by the Government or other public bodies, its President was appointed (and could be dismissed) by the President of Korea, the senior staff of KEXIM were appointed by the Minister of Finance and Economy, and the Annual Operations Programme of KEXIM was subject to ministerial approval.[255]

Pursuant to Article 1.1(a)(1)(iv), a financial contribution made by a *private body* is considered to be a 'financial contribution by a government' when the

---

[251] See Panel Report, *EC – Countervailing Measures on DRAM Chips*, paras. 7.87 and 7.92.
[252] See Panel Report, *US – Upland Cotton*, paras. 7.1153–7.1155.
[253] See Panel Report, *US – Export Restraints*, paras. 8.65 and 8.73.
[254] Panel Report, *Korea – Commercial Vessels*, para. 7.50. Note that the Panel in *Korea – Commercial Vessels* firmly rejected Korea's argument that whether an entity is a public body should depend on whether this entity acts pursuant to commercial principles. See Panel Report, *Korea – Commercial Vessels*, para. 7.44.
[255] See *ibid.*

government entrusts or directs the private body to carry out one or more of the type of functions illustrated in Article 1.1(a)(1)(i) to (iii).[256] The Appellate Body in *US – Countervailing Duty Investigation on DRAMS* explained that:

> 'entrustment' occurs where a government gives responsibility to a private body, and 'direction' refers to situations where the government exercises its authority over a private body. In both instances, the government uses a private body as proxy to effectuate one of the types of financial contributions listed in paragraphs (i) through (iii).[257]

The involvement of some form of 'threat' or 'inducement' could serve as evidence of entrustment or direction.[258]

Questions and Assignments 6.22

How can one distinguish between private and public bodies for the purpose of Article 1.1 of the *SCM Agreement*? Can a financial contribution by a local authority or a private body be a 'subsidy' within the meaning of Article 1.1 of the *SCM Agreement*? Is financial assistance given by an NGO to cotton growers in African countries a 'financial contribution by a government'?

6.3.2.3. *A financial contribution conferring a benefit*

A financial contribution by a government or a public body is a subsidy within the meaning of Article 1.1 of the *SCM Agreement* only if the financial contribution *confers a benefit*. If a government gives a sum of money to a company, it seems clear that this financial contribution would generally confer a benefit. However, it may be less clear whether a government loan to that same company, the purchase of goods or services by the government from the company or an equity infusion by the government in the company confer a benefit. In *Canada – Aircraft*, Canada argued that 'cost to government' is one way of conceiving of 'benefit'. The Appellate Body rejected this argumentation as follows:

> A 'benefit' does not exist in the abstract, but must be received and enjoyed by a beneficiary or a recipient. Logically, a 'benefit' can be said to arise only if a person, natural or legal, or a group of persons, has in fact received something. The term 'benefit', therefore, implies that there must be a recipient. This provides textual support for the view that the focus of the inquiry under Article 1.1(b) of the *SCM Agreement* should be on the recipient and not on the granting authority. The ordinary meaning of the word 'confer', as used in Article 1.1(b), bears this out. 'Confer' means, *inter alia*, 'give', 'grant' or 'bestow'. The use of the past participle 'conferred' in the passive form, in conjunction with the word 'thereby', naturally calls for an inquiry into *what was conferred on the recipient*. Accordingly, we believe that Canada's argument that 'cost to government' is one way of conceiving of 'benefit' is at odds with the ordinary meaning of Article 1.1(b), which

---

[256] See above, pp. 562–4. In *US – Export Restraints*, the Panel stated that the ordinary meanings of 'entrusts' and 'directs' require an explicit and affirmative action of delegation or command. See Panel Report, *US – Export Restraints*, para. 8.44.
[257] Appellate Body Report, *US – Countervailing Duty Investigation on DRAMS*, para. 116.   [258] See *ibid.*

focuses on the *recipient* and not on the *government* providing the 'financial contribution'.[259]

This reading of the term 'benefit' is confirmed by Article 14 of the *SCM Agreement*, which sets forth guidelines for calculating the amount of a subsidy in terms of 'the benefit to the recipient'.[260] The guidelines set forth in Article 14 apply to the calculation of the 'benefit to the recipient conferred pursuant to paragraph 1 of Article 1'. The reference to 'benefit to the recipient' in Article 14 also implies that the word 'benefit', as used in Article 1.1, is concerned with the 'benefit to the recipient' and not with the 'cost to government'.[261]

In *Canada – Aircraft*, the Appellate Body further held with regard to the term 'benefit' that:

> the word 'benefit', as used in Article 1.1(b), implies some kind of comparison. This must be so, for there can be no 'benefit' to the recipient unless the 'financial contribution' makes the recipient 'better off' than it would otherwise have been, absent that contribution. In our view, the marketplace provides an appropriate basis for comparison in determining whether a 'benefit' has been 'conferred', because the trade-distorting potential of a 'financial contribution' can be identified by determining whether the recipient has received a 'financial contribution' on terms more favourable than those available to the recipient in the market.[262]

In brief, a 'benefit' arises if the recipient has received a 'financial contribution' on terms more favourable than those available to any recipient in the market.[263] In other words, a government loan is a financial contribution conferring a benefit, i.e. a subsidy, *only* if the terms of the loan are more favourable than the terms of a comparable commercial loan. In *Canada – Aircraft Credits and Guarantees*, the Panel thus found that since the Canada Account financing to Air Wisconsin was at rates better than those available commercially, it therefore conferred a benefit and was a subsidy under Article 1.1(b) of the *SCM Agreement*.[264] In *EC – Countervailing Measures on DRAM Chips*, the Panel found:

> very relevant the fact that in total ten banks participated in the Syndicated Loan and extended loans on similar terms to Hynix [i.e. the recipient of the financial contribution]. Of these banks, the Final Determination discusses the KDB, KEB and KFB, and leaves unmentioned the seven others. Among the remaining seven banks, a certain number such as, for example, Citibank, the KorAm Bank and Chohung Bank were not considered to be public bodies by the EC in its investigation . . . If a number of parties provide the same type of financing as the public body, such as in the case of the Syndicated Loan, their participation is an obvious aspect of a benefit analysis.[265]

---

[259] Appellate Body Report, *Canada – Aircraft*, para. 154.

[260] See *ibid.*, para. 155. Although Article 14 explicitly states that its guidelines apply '[f]or the purposes of Part V' of the *SCM Agreement*, which relates to 'countervailing measures', the Appellate Body was of the opinion that Article 14, nonetheless, constitutes a relevant context for the interpretation of 'benefit' in Article 1.1(b).   [261] See *ibid.*   [262] *Ibid.*, para. 157.

[263] See also Panel Report, *US – Lead and Bismuth II*, para. 6.66; Panel Report, *Japan – DRAMs (Korea)*, para. 7.256; Panel Report, *EC – Countervailing Measures on DRAM Chips*, para. 7.176; Panel Report, *Canada – Aircraft Credits and Guarantees*, paras. 7.67 and 7.144; Panel Report *Canada – Aircraft*, para. 9.112; and Appellate Body Report, *Canada – Aircraft*, para. 157.

[264] See Panel Report, *Canada – Aircraft Credits and Guarantees*, para. 7.150.

[265] Panel Report, *EC – Countervailing Measures on DRAM Chips*, para. 7.183.

The Panel immediately added that this is of course not the end-point of such an analysis, as it will need to be determined whether the behaviour of these banks is so distorted by government intervention that they can no longer serve as a benchmark.[266]

With regard to the question of whether a benefit within the meaning of Article 1.1(b) is 'passed through' when goods are sold by a subsidised upstream producer to a downstream producer, the Panel in *US – Softwood Lumber III* found that when the producers are not related and the goods are sold at an arm's-length price, i.e. the fair market value, it cannot be assumed that the benefit that the upstream producer has received is passed through to the downstream producers.[267]

On the issue of privatisation of a State-owned producer and the 'passing through' of benefits, the Appellate Body in *US – Countervailing Measures on Certain EC Products* stated that, if 'fair market value' is paid in a privatisation transaction, the subsidies previously provided to the State-owned producer *may* extinguish the benefit to the privatised producer.[268]

The *SCM Agreement* leaves Members wide discretion in deciding on the particular method used to calculate the subsidy in terms of the benefit that the recipient has received. However, Article 14 of the *SCM Agreement*, referred to above, provides, *inter alia*, for the following guidelines:

- government provision of equity capital shall not be considered as conferring a benefit when the investment decision can be regarded as consistent with the usual investment practice of private investors;[269]
- governmental loans shall not be considered as conferring a benefit, unless (and to the extent that) there is a difference between the amount that the firm receiving the loan pays on the government loan and the amount the firm would pay on a comparable commercial loan which the firm could actually obtain on the market;[270] and
- the provision of goods or services or the purchase of goods by a government shall not be considered as conferring a benefit unless the provision is made for less than adequate remuneration, or the purchase is made for more than adequate remuneration.[271]

Questions and Assignments 6.23

Why is 'cost to government' an invalid method of conceiving of 'benefit' within the meaning of Article 1.1 of the *SCM Agreement*? When does a

---

[266] See *ibid*. [267] See Panel Report, *US – Softwood Lumber III*, para. 7.71.
[268] Note, however, that the Appellate Body reversed the Panel's finding that a fair market value privatisation 'must' lead to the conclusion that there is no benefit anymore. See Appellate Body Report, *US – Countervailing Measures on Certain EC Products*, paras. 103–5. On this issue, see also Panel Report, *US – Softwood Lumber IV*, para. 7.91. [269] See Article 14(a) of the *SCM Agreement*.
[270] See Article 14(b) of the *SCM Agreement*. The same is true for loan guarantees. See Article 14(c) of the *SCM Agreement*.
[271] See Article 14(d) of the *SCM Agreement*. The adequacy of the remuneration shall be determined in relation to prevailing market conditions for the good or service in question in the country of provision or purchase (including price, quality, availability, marketability, transportation and other conditions of purchase or sale).

> financial contribution confer a benefit? When is a government loan or the purchase of goods by the government a subsidy within the meaning of Article 1.1 of the *SCM Agreement*?

6.3.2.4. Requirement of 'specificity' of the subsidy

The WTO rules on subsidies do not apply to all 'financial contributions by a government that confer a benefit'. In other words, these rules do not apply to all subsidies. They apply only to *specific* subsidies. Article 1.2 of the *SCM Agreement*, quoted above, states:

> A subsidy as defined in paragraph 1 shall be subject to the provisions of Part II or shall be subject to the provisions of Part III or V only if such a subsidy is specific in accordance with the provisions of Article 2.

According to Article 2, a subsidy is *specific* when it has been specifically provided to an enterprise, an industry or a group of enterprises or industries. A subsidy that is widely available within an economy is presumed not to distort the allocation of resources within that economy and, therefore, does not require or justify any action.

The *SCM Agreement* distinguishes between four types of specificity:

- *enterprise specificity*, i.e. a situation in which a government targets a particular company or companies for subsidisation;[272]
- *industry specificity*, i.e. a situation in which a government targets a particular sector or sectors for subsidisation;[273]
- *regional specificity*, i.e. a situation in which a government targets producers in specified parts of its territory for subsidisation;[274] and
- *prohibited subsidies*, i.e. a situation in which a government targets export goods or goods using domestic inputs for subsidisation.[275]

For a subsidy to fall within the scope of application of the *SCM Agreement*, it has to be *specific* in one of the above four ways.

If the criteria and conditions governing eligibility for, and the amount of, a subsidy are objective, the subsidy is *not specific*, provided that eligibility is automatic and the criteria and conditions are strictly applied.[276] Pursuant to footnote 2 to the *SCM Agreement*, objective criteria and conditions are:

> criteria or conditions which are neutral, which do not favour certain enterprises over others, and which are economic in nature and horizontal in application, such as number of employees or size of enterprise.

---

[272] See Article 2.1 of the *SCM Agreement*.   [273] See *ibid*.   [274] See Article 2.2 of the *SCM Agreement*.
[275] See Article 2.3 of the *SCM Agreement*. Article 2.3 states that prohibited subsidies (see below, p. 571) shall be deemed to be specific. See also Panel Report, *Korea – Commercial Vessels*, para. 7.192; Panel Report, *US – Upland Cotton*, para. 7.1153; and Panel Report, *Indonesia – Autos*, para. 14.155.
[276] See Article 2.1(b) of the *SCM Agreement*.

Often, a subsidy may not be specific, on its face, but, in fact, operates in a specific manner. The *SCM Agreement* applies to both *de jure* and *de facto* specific subsidies. Article 2.1(c) of the *SCM Agreement* states:

> If, notwithstanding any appearance of non-specificity resulting from the application of the principles laid down in subparagraphs (a) and (b), there are reasons to believe that the subsidy may in fact be specific, other factors may be considered.

These 'other factors' on the basis of which *de facto* subsidies may be identified include:

- the use of a subsidy programme by a limited number of certain enterprises;
- the predominant use of a subsidy programme by certain enterprises;
- the granting of disproportionately large subsidies to certain enterprises; and
- the manner in which discretion has been exercised by the granting authority in the decision to grant a subsidy; the frequency with which applications for a subsidy are refused or approved and the reasons for such decisions are of particular relevance in this context.[277]

The extent of diversification of economic activities within the jurisdiction of the granting authority and the length of time during which the subsidy programme has been in operation will also be taken into account when determining whether a subsidy, which is not specific *de jure*, is specific *de facto*.[278]

The Panel in *Japan – DRAMs (Korea)* clarified that an individual transaction under a general support programme would not become 'specific' within the meaning of Article 2.1 of the *SCM Agreement* 'simply because it was provided to a specific company'.[279] According to the Panel in this case, an individual transaction would, however, become 'specific' if:

> it resulted from a framework programme whose normal operation (1) does not generally result in financial contributions, and (2) does not predetermine the terms on which any resultant financial contributions might be provided, but rather requires (a) conscious decisions as to whether or not to provide the financial contribution (to one applicant or another), and (b) conscious decisions as to how the terms of the financial contribution should be tailored to the needs of the recipient company.[280]

The Panel in *EC – Countervailing Measures on DRAM Chips* made the following findings in evaluating the EC's determination that the subsidy at issue was specific:

> The EC determined that (1) the subsidy programme was used by a very limited number of companies, as only six out of an eligible two hundred companies used the programme; (2) that it was predominantly used by the Hyundai group companies among which Hynix; and (3) that a disproportionate 41 per cent of the total subsidy amount of KRW 2.9 trillion was granted to Hynix. These figures are uncontested and clearly constitute 'positive evidence'. In addition, the EC pointed out that, after the participants to the programmes had

---

[277] See Article 2.1(c) of, and footnote 3 to, the *SCM Agreement*. See Panel Report, *EC – Countervailing Measures on DRAM Chips*, para. 7.226. See also Panel Report, *US – Softwood Lumber IV*, para. 7.123, on the fact that there is no obligation on the investigating authorities to examine the 'other factors' referred to in Article 2.1(c) of the *SCM Agreement*. Article 2.1(c) states that these factors 'may' be considered.

[278] See Article 2.1(c) of the *SCM Agreement*. See Panel Report, *US – Softwood Lumber IV*, para. 7.124.

[279] Panel Report, *Japan – DRAMs (Korea)*, para. 7.374.   [280] *Ibid.*

been announced, there was a lot of criticism within Korea from companies in similarly difficult situations complaining about the lack of transparency and the eligibility criteria. These criticisms indicate that the EC also considered the manner in which discretion was exercised in admitting companies to the KDB Debenture Programme.

In sum, the EC's conclusion is based on the disproportionate use of the Programme's funds for Hynix, which led it to the reasonable conclusion that the KDB Debenture Programme, as applied, constituted a *de facto* specific subsidy to Hynix.[281]

In *US – Softwood Lumber IV*, Canada argued with regard to the specificity of the subsidy at issue – the supply of standing timber by the government – that a subsidy is specific only when the government deliberately limits access to this subsidy to certain enterprises within the group of enterprises eligible or naturally apt to use the subsidy.[282] The Panel in this case rejected Canada's argument as follows:

We note that the availability of a subsidy which is limited by the inherent characteristics of the good cannot be considered to have been limited by 'objective' criteria in the sense of footnote 2 to Article 2.1(b) SCM Agreement, i.e. 'criteria or conditions which are neutral, which do not favour certain enterprises over others, and which are economic in nature and horizontal in application, such as number of employees or size of enterprise'.[283]

In *US – Upland Cotton*, the Panel concluded that since no technical definition is given by Article 2 of the *SCM Agreement* on how broad or narrow the interpretation of the concept of 'industry' shall be, it was not necessary to determine a fixed scope of that concept. The Panel held:

To us, the concept of an 'industry' relates to producers of certain products. The breadth of this concept of 'industry' may depend on several factors in a given case. At some point that is not made precise in the text of the agreement, and which may modulate according to the particular circumstances of a given case, a subsidy would cease to be specific because it is sufficiently broadly available throughout an economy as not to benefit a particular limited group of producers of certain products. The plain words of Article 2.1 indicated that specificity is a general concept, and the breadth or narrowness of specificity is not susceptible to rigid quantitative definition. Whether a subsidy is specific can only be assessed on a case-by-case basis.[284]

Questions and Assignments 6.24

Do the rules of the *SCM Agreement* apply to all 'financial contributions by the government that confer a benefit'? Discuss the various types of 'specificity' within the meaning of Article 2.1 of the *SCM Agreement*. When is a subsidy not specific? Does the *SCM Agreement* apply also to *de facto* specific subsidies? How is a *de facto* specific subsidy identified?

---

[281] Panel Report, *EC – Countervailing Measures on DRAM Chips*, paras. 7.226–7.227.
[282] See Panel Report, *US – Softwood Lumber IV*, para. 7.116.   [283] *Ibid.*, para. 7.116, footnote 179.
[284] Panel Report, *US – Upland Cotton*, para. 7.1142.

6.3.2.5. *Transparency and notification requirement*

As transparency is essential for the effective operation of the *SCM Agreement*, Article 25 requires that Members notify all specific subsidies by 30 June of each year. Currently, there is an understanding in the SCM Committee that there is an emphasis on new and full subsidy notifications to be submitted every two years, while updating notifications in the interim years are de-emphasised. As of October 2006, thirty-nine Members[285] had submitted their 2005 new and full notifications indicating that they provided specific subsidies within the meaning of the *SCM Agreement*. Thirteen Members had notified that they provided no notifiable specific subsidies. Seventy-two Members did not submit any notification.[286]

6.3.3. Prohibited subsidies

The *SCM Agreement* distinguishes between prohibited subsidies, actionable subsidies and non-actionable subsidies.[287] This section will discuss the rules relating to prohibited subsidies.

Article 3 of the *SCM Agreement*, entitled 'Prohibition', states, in its first paragraph:

> Except as provided in the Agreement on Agriculture, the following subsidies, within the meaning of Article 1, shall be prohibited:
>
> a.   subsidies contingent, in law or in fact, whether solely or as one of several conditions, upon export performance, including those illustrated in Annex I;
> b.   subsidies contingent, whether solely or as one of several conditions, upon the use of domestic over imported products.

In short, WTO Members may not grant or maintain:

* export subsidies; or
* import substitution subsidies.[288]

These subsidies, which are often referred to as 'red light' subsidies, are prohibited because they aim to affect trade and are most likely to cause adverse effects to other Members.

6.3.3.1. *Export subsidies*

As defined in Article 3.1(a) of the *SCM Agreement*, quoted above, export subsidies are subsidies contingent upon export performance. Annex I to the *SCM Agreement* contains an 'Illustrative List of Export Subsidies'. This non-exhaustive list includes eleven types of export subsidy, including:

---

[285] For this purpose, the European Communities and the Member States of the European Union were counted as a single Member.

[286] The 2005 notifications may be found in document series G/SCM/N/123/. See also *Report (2006) of the Committee on Subsidies and Countervailing Measures*, G/L/798, dated 8 November 2006, 5.

[287] Note, however, that, since 1 January 2000, the category of 'non-actionable subsidies' only contains non-specific subsidies, to which the *SCM Agreement* does not apply. See above, p. 561, footnote 244, and below, p. 585.   [288] See Article 3.2 of the *SCM Agreement*.

- direct export subsidies;
- export retention schemes which involve a bonus on exports;
- export-related exemption, remission or deferral of direct taxes and social welfare charges;
- excess exemption or remission, in respect of the production and distribution of exported products, of indirect taxes in excess of those levied in respect of the production and distribution of like products when sold domestically;
- provision of goods or services for use in the production of exported goods on terms more favourable than those for the production of goods for domestic consumption; and
- provision of certain forms of export financing extended at rates below those which the government actually had to pay for the funds (subject to certain considerations).

Article 3.1(a) of the *SCM Agreement* prohibits subsidies contingent upon export performance. The meaning of 'contingent' in this provision is 'conditional' or 'dependent for its existence on something else'.[289] Article 3.1(a) prohibits both subsidies that are contingent *de jure* and subsidies that are contingent *de facto* on exports. In *Canada – Aircraft*, the Appellate Body stated:

> The Uruguay Round negotiators have, through the prohibition against export subsidies that are contingent *in fact* upon export performance, sought to prevent circumvention of the prohibition against subsidies contingent *in law* upon export performance.[290]

Pursuant to footnote 4 to the *SCM Agreement*, a subsidy is contingent *de facto* upon export performance:

> when the facts demonstrate that the granting of a subsidy, without having been made legally contingent upon export performance, is in fact tied to actual or anticipated exportation or export earnings. The mere fact that a subsidy is granted to enterprises which export shall not for that reason alone be considered to be an export subsidy within the meaning of this provision.

While the legal standard expressed by the term 'contingent' is the same for both *de jure* and *de facto* contingency, there is an important difference in what evidence may be employed to demonstrate that a subsidy is export contingent.[291] *De jure* export contingency is demonstrated on the basis of the words of the relevant legislation, regulation or other legal instrument. In *Canada – Autos*, the Appellate Body held:

> The simplest, and hence, perhaps, the uncommon, case is one in which the condition of exportation is set out expressly, in so many words, on the face of the law, regulation or other legal instrument. We believe, however, that a subsidy is also properly held to be *de jure* export contingent where the condition to export is clearly, though implicitly, in the instrument comprising the measure.[292]

---

[289] See Appellate Body Report, *Canada – Aircraft*, para. 166. See also Panel Report, *Australia – Automotive Leather II*, para. 9.55.   [290] Appellate Body Report, *Canada – Aircraft*, para. 167.   [291] See *ibid*.
[292] Appellate Body Report, *Canada – Autos*, para. 100.

According to the Appellate Body, for a subsidy to be *de jure* export contingent, the underlying law, regulation or other legal instrument does *not* have to provide *expressis verbis* that the subsidy is available only upon the fulfilment of the condition of export performance.[293] The *de jure* export contingency can also 'be derived by necessary implication from the words actually used in the measure'.[294]

With respect to *de facto* export contingency, footnote 4 to the *SCM Agreement* states that the standard of 'in fact' contingency is met if the facts demonstrate that the subsidy is:

> in fact tied to actual or anticipated exportation or export earnings.[295]

As the Panel in *Australia – Automotive Leather II* established, *de facto* export contingency requires there to be a 'close connection' between the granting of, or maintenance of, a subsidy *and* export performance.[296]

De facto export contingency is much more difficult to demonstrate than *de jure* export contingency.[297] The Appellate Body stated in *Canada – Aircraft* that satisfaction of the standard for determining *de facto* export contingency set out in footnote 4 requires proof of three different substantive elements:

- first, the '*granting* of a subsidy';
- second, 'is . . . *tied to* . . .';[298] and
- third, 'actual or anticipated exportation or export earnings'.[299]

De facto export contingency must be inferred from the *total* configuration of the facts constituting and surrounding the granting of the subsidy.[300] None of these facts on its own is likely to be decisive. In combination, however, they may lead to the conclusion that there is *de facto* export contingency in a given case.

According to the Panel in *Australia – Automotive Leather II*, *in certain circumstances a Member's awareness that its domestic market is too small to absorb domestic production of a subsidised product may indicate that the subsidy is granted on the condition that it be exported.*[301] Note, however, that a subsidy to an export-oriented company is not *per se* an export subsidy. The export orientation of a recipient may be taken into account but it will be only one of several facts which are

---

[293] See *ibid*.   [294] *Ibid*.
[295] The Panel in *Australia – Automotive Leather II* noted that the ordinary meaning of 'tied to' is 'restrain or constrain to or from an action; limit or restrict as to behaviour, location, conditions, etc.'. Panel Report, *Australia – Automotive Leather II*, para. 9.55. For a further discussion of the concept of 'tied to', see Appellate Body Report, *Canada – Aircraft*, para. 171.
[296] See Panel Report, *Australia – Automotive Leather II*, para. 9.55.
[297] As noted above, the Appellate Body stressed in *Canada – Aircraft* that the legal standard expressed by the word 'contingent' is the same for both *de jure* and *de facto* contingency. The difference is in what evidence may be employed to prove that a subsidy is export contingent. See Appellate Body Report, *Canada – Aircraft*, para. 167.
[298] In *US – Upland Cotton*, the Appellate Body pointed out that this is one of the most essential factors to be examined in order to confirm export contingency. See Appellate Body Report, *US – Upland Cotton*, para. 572. See also Appellate Body Report, *Canada – Aircraft (Article 21.5 – Brazil)*, para. 47.
[299] See Appellate Body Report, *Canada – Aircraft*, para. 169. The Appellate Body subsequently worked out each of these elements in paras. 170–3.   [300] See *ibid*.
[301] See Panel Report, *Australia – Automotive Leather II*, para. 9.67.

considered and cannot be the only fact supporting a finding of *de facto* export contingency.[302]

To illustrate the wide scope of the prohibition on export subsidies, consider the subsidies at issue in, for example, *Brazil – Aircraft*, *Australia – Automotive Leather II* and *US – FSC*. The WTO-inconsistent export subsidies at issue in these disputes concerned:

- payments by the Government of Brazil, related to the export of regional aircraft, which cover, at most, the difference between the interest charges contracted with the buyer and the cost to the financing party of raising the required funds; these payments were made under the interest rate equalisation component of the 'PROEX', an export financing programme (*Brazil – Aircraft*);
- grants for a total of A$30 million and a loan of A$25 million (on 'noncommercial' terms) provided by the Australian Government to Howe, the only producer and exporter of automotive leather in Australia (*Australia –Automotive Leather II*); and
- exemption from United States income tax of a portion of export-related income of 'foreign sales corporations' (FSCs), i.e. foreign corporations in charge of specific activities with respect to the sale or lease of goods produced in the United States for export outside the United States (*US – FSC*).

Questions and Assignments 6.25

Which subsidies are 'prohibited' under the *SCM Agreement*? Define an export subsidy. Give three examples of an export subsidy. When is a subsidy *de jure* contingent on export performance? Is a subsidy that is *de facto* export contingent an export subsidy? How is *de facto* export contingency demonstrated?

6.3.3.2. *Import substitution subsidies*

In addition to export subsidies, the category of prohibited subsidies also includes import substitution subsidies. As defined in Article 3.1(b) of the *SCM Agreement*, quoted above, import substitution subsidies are subsidies contingent upon the use of domestic over imported goods.[303] The Appellate Body in *Canada – Autos* ruled that the prohibition of import substitution subsidies of Article 3.1(b) covers both *de jure* and *de facto* contingency upon the use of domestic over imported goods. The Panel in that case had found that 'contingency' under

---

[302] See footnote 4, second sentence, to the *SCM Agreement*; and Panel Report, *Australia – Automotive Leather II*, para. 9.56. On the facts taken into account when determining whether a subsidy is *de facto* export contingent, see Appellate Body Report, *Canada – Aircraft*, para. 175; and Panel Report, *Canada – Aircraft Credits and Guarantees*, paras. 7.376–7.378.

[303] 'Import substitution subsidies' are also referred to as 'local content subsidies'. Note the relationship of this concept to the cornerstone principle of national treatment in Article III of the GATT 1994. Note, in particular, Article III:5 of the GATT 1994: see above, p. 344.

Article 3.1(b) extended only to *de jure* contingency.[304] Reversing this finding of the Panel, the Appellate Body held:

> we believe that a finding that Article 3.1(b) extends only to contingency 'in law' upon the use of domestic over imported goods would be contrary to the object and purpose of the *SCM Agreement* because it would make circumvention of obligations by Members too easy.[305]

In *US – Upland Cotton*, the Panel (and the Appellate Body on appeal) concluded that the subsidies at issue in that case, namely payments to domestic users of US upland cotton, were subsidies contingent upon the use of domestic over imported goods and were, therefore, inconsistent with Article 3.1(b) of the *SCM Agreement*.[306]

Questions and Assignments 6.26

Define an import substitution subsidy. How does the import substitution concept relate to the national treatment obligation in Article III of the GATT 1994? Is a subsidy that is *de facto* contingent on import substitution a prohibited subsidy?

6.3.3.3. *Multilateral remedies for prohibited subsidies*

The multilateral remedies for prohibited subsidies, be they export subsidies or import substitution subsidies, are set out in Article 4 of the *SCM Agreement*. Pursuant to Article 4, consultations may be requested with any Member believed to be granting or maintaining a prohibited subsidy. If such consultations fail to resolve the dispute, the dispute may be referred to a dispute settlement panel, and then to the Appellate Body, for adjudication. The rules applicable to consultations and adjudication are primarily those of the DSU, discussed in detail in chapter 3 above.[307] However, Article 4 of the *SCM Agreement* sets out a number of 'special or additional rules and procedures' which prevail over the DSU rules in cases of conflict.[308] The most notable difference between the rules and procedures of Article 4 of the *SCM Agreement* and the DSU rules and procedures relates to timeframes. The timeframes under Article 4 are half as long as the timeframes provided for under the DSU.[309] For example, the timeframe for 'ordinary' panel proceedings is six months;[310] under Article 4 of the *SCM Agreement* the time limit for panel proceedings concerning prohibited subsidies is three months. Note also that a panel established for a 'prohibited subsidy' dispute may ask a

---

[304] In making this finding, the Panel relied on the wording of Article 3.1(b), which, unlike Article 3.1(a), did not refer explicitly to both subsidies contingent 'in law or in fact'. See Panel Report, *Canada – Autos*, paras. 10.220–10.222.   [305] Appellate Body Report, *Canada – Autos*, para. 142.

[306] See Panel Report, *US – Upland Cotton*, paras. 7.1088 and 7.1097–7.1098, and Appellate Body Report, *US – Upland Cotton*, para. 552.   [307] See above, pp. 171–235.   [308] See above, pp. 178–9.

[309] Note, however, that parties can, and regularly do, agree on an extension of these special timeframes. See Article 4.12 of the *SCM Agreement*. Also, when a complainant brings claims under both the *SCM Agreement* and other WTO agreements, the shorter timeframes under the *SCM Agreement* do not apply.

[310] See Article 12.8 of the DSU. See also above, pp. 287–8.

Permanent Group of Experts (PGE) whether the measure at issue is a prohibited subsidy.[311] The determination of the PGE is binding on the panel. To date, panels have not yet made use of this possibility.

If a panel finds a measure to be a prohibited subsidy, Article 4.7 of the *SCM Agreement* states that:

> the panel shall recommend that the subsidizing Member withdraw the subsidy without delay. In this regard, the panel shall specify in its recommendation the time-period within which the measure must be withdrawn.

Prohibited subsidies must therefore be withdrawn without delay. As the Appellate Body clarified in *Brazil – Aircraft (Article 21.5 – Canada)*, withdrawal of the prohibited subsidy involves the removal of the subsidy.[312] The Panel in *Australia – Automotive Leather II (Article 21.5 – US)* concluded that the obligation to withdraw the prohibited subsidy, in that case, could only be met by repayment of the subsidy received. In general, remedies for breaches of WTO law are only prospective, but, according to the Panel in *Australia – Automotive Leather II (Article 21.5 – US)*, Article 4.7 of the *SCM Agreement* provides for a retrospective remedy and requires the company that received a one-time prohibited subsidy to repay that subsidy to the subsidising Member. The Panel in *Australia – Automotive Leather II (Article 21.5 – US)* reasoned as follows:

> We believe it is incumbent upon us to interpret 'withdraw the subsidy' so as to give it effective meaning. A finding that the term 'withdraw the subsidy' may not encompass repayment would give rise to serious questions regarding the efficacy of the remedy in prohibited subsidy cases involving one-time subsidies paid in the past whose retention is not contingent upon future export performance.[313]

This ruling of the Panel in *Australia – Automotive Leather II (Article 21.5 – US)* was heavily criticised by WTO Members because of its retroactive character (and because it was felt to violate the principle of *non ultra petita*).[314] To date, no other panel has followed this ruling.[315]

Panels in 'prohibited subsidy' disputes specify the time period within which the prohibited subsidy must be withdrawn, i.e. they specify what is meant by 'withdraw without delay' as required by Article 4.7 of the *SCM Agreement*.[316] Note by way of example the conclusion reached by the Panel in *Korea – Commercial Vessels*:

---

[311] See Article 4.5 of the *SCM Agreement*. See also above, p. 131.

[312] See Appellate Body Report, *Brazil – Aircraft (Article 21.5 – Canada)*, para. 45.

[313] Panel Report, *Australia – Automotive Leather II (Article 21.5 – US)*, para. 6.35.

[314] See Dispute Settlement Body, *Minutes of the DSB Meeting of 11 February 2000*, WT/DSB/M/75. See also above, pp. 230–1. Note that the United States, the original complainant in this dispute, had not requested the repayment of the export subsidy at issue.

[315] Note that the Panels in *Canada – Aircraft (Article 21.5 – Brazil)* and *Brazil – Aircraft (Article 21.5 – Canada)* did not rule on the repayment of subsidies because repayment had not been requested by the complainants and the Panels considered that their findings should be restricted to the scope of the disagreement between the parties. See Panel Report, *Canada – Aircraft (Article 21.5 – Brazil)*, para. 5.48; and Panel Report, *Brazil – Aircraft (Article 21.5 – Canada)*, footnote 17.

[316] Recall that 'ordinary' panels do not set a time period within which a WTO-inconsistent measure must be brought into consistency. The reasonable period of time for implementation is agreed on by the parties or is determined through binding arbitration under Article 21.3(c) of the DSU. See above, pp. 298–9.

> Taking into account the procedures that may be required to implement our recommendation on the one hand, and the requirement that Korea withdraw its subsidies 'without delay' on the other, we recommend that Korea withdraw the individual APRG and PSL subsidies within 90 days.[317]

To date, several panels have specified a period of three months for the withdrawal of a prohibited subsidy. In *US – FSC*, however, the Panel specified a period of more than a year to allow the United States to adopt the necessary fiscal legislation.[318]

If a recommendation for withdrawal is not followed within the time period set by the panel, the DSB must, upon the request of the original complainant(s) and by reverse consensus, authorise 'appropriate countermeasures'. In 'prohibited subsidies' disputes, these 'appropriate countermeasures' replace the suspension of concessions or other obligations, i.e. retaliation measures, available in case of non-implementation in other WTO disputes.[319] 'Appropriate countermeasures' and 'retaliation measures' may differ in that the level of 'appropriate countermeasures' could be the amount of the prohibited subsidy rather than the level of any trade effects or the nullification or impairment that has been caused.[320]

Questions and Assignments 6.27

What happens when a panel finds that a subsidy granted by a Member is an export or import substitution subsidy within the meaning of Article 3 of the *SCM Agreement*?

6.3.4. Actionable subsidies

Unlike export subsidies and import substitution subsidies, most subsidies are not prohibited but are 'actionable', i.e. they are subject to challenge in the event that they cause adverse effects on the interests of another Member. To the extent that these subsidies do not cause adverse effects, or the adverse effects are removed, they cannot, or can no longer, be challenged. Article 5 of the *SCM Agreement* provides:

> No Member should cause, through the use of any subsidy referred to in paragraphs 1 and 2 of Article 1, adverse effects to the interests of other Members.

---

[317] Panel Report, *Korea – Commercial Vessels*, para. 8.5.   [318] See Panel Report, *US – FSC*, para. 8.8.
[319] See above, pp. 225–9.
[320] The Arbitrators in *Brazil – Aircraft (Article 22.6 – Brazil)* accepted the view of the parties that the term 'countermeasures', as used in these provisions, includes suspension of concessions or other obligations. Furthermore, it was concluded that, when dealing with a prohibited export subsidy, an amount of countermeasures that corresponds to the total amount of the subsidy is appropriate. See Decision by the Arbitrator, *Brazil – Aircraft (Article 22.6 – Brazil)*, paras. 3.28, 3.29 and 3.33–3.40. See also Decision by the Arbitrator, *US – FSC (Article 22.6 – US)*. There, the Arbitrator held that the amount of the countermeasures proposed exhibited a manifest relationship of proportionality with regard to the amount of the export subsidy granted. The Arbitrator also observed that trade effects are not *a priori* to be ruled out as relevant in a particular case.

The Panel in *US – Offset Act (Byrd Amendment)* interpreted this to mean that a subsidy is actionable if it is 'specific' and its use causes 'adverse effects'.[321]

Article 5(a) to (c) distinguishes between three types of 'adverse effect' on the interests of other Members:

- *injury* to the domestic industry of another Member (Article 5(a));
- *nullification or impairment* of benefits accruing directly or indirectly to other Members under the GATT 1994 (Article 5(b)); and
- *serious prejudice*, including a threat thereof, to the interests of another Member (Article 5(c)).

Questions and Assignments 6.28
When is a subsidy 'actionable' under the *SCM Agreement*?

6.3.4.1. Subsidies causing injury

Subsidies have adverse effects on the interests of other Members within the meaning of Article 5(a) of the *SCM Agreement* – and are therefore 'actionable' – when the subsidised imports cause injury to the domestic industry producing the like product. This section examines, in turn, the concepts of 'like product', 'domestic industry', 'injury' and causation as generally applied in the *SCM Agreement*.[322]

The concept of 'like product' is defined in footnote 46 to the *SCM Agreement* as:

> a product which is identical, i.e. alike in all respects to the product under consideration, or in the absence of such a product, another product which, although not alike in all respects, has characteristics closely resembling those of the product under consideration.[323]

When compared to the definitions of 'like products' resulting from the case law on Articles I and III of the GATT 1994 or the definition of 'like products' in the *Agreement on Safeguards*, the definition in the *SCM Agreement* seems narrower. The approach to establishing 'likeness' under the *SCM Agreement* is, however, in fact similar to the approach under the GATT 1994.[324] In *Indonesia – Autos*, the Panel found:

> Although we are required in this dispute to interpret the term 'like product' in conformity with the specific definition provided in the SCM Agreement, we believe that useful guidance can nevertheless be derived from prior analysis of 'like product' issues under other provisions of the WTO Agreement.[325]

---

[321] See Panel Report, *US – Offset Act (Byrd Amendment)*, para. 7.106.

[322] Note that footnote 11 to the *SCM Agreement* stipulates that the term 'injury to the domestic industry' is used in Article 5(a) in the same sense as it is used in Part V of that Agreement. They are addressed here together, although it may be important to note that considerations may differ under certain provisions of Part III and Part V of the Agreement. See below, p. 581.

[323] Note that this definition applies throughout the *SCM Agreement* and not merely in the context of the determination of material injury. It also applies, for example, in the context of the serious prejudice determination of Article 6 of the *SCM Agreement* (see below, pp. 583–4).

[324] See above, pp. 329–31, 351–6, 374–82.   [325] Panel Report, *Indonesia – Autos*, para. 14.174.

The provisions of the *WTO Agreement* referred to are, of course, Articles I:1, III:2 and III:4 of the GATT 1994. In establishing 'likeness', the same elements (physical characteristics as well as end-uses, consumer habits and preferences and tariff classification) will be of importance. In *Indonesia – Autos*, in which the product, allegedly subsidised by Indonesia, was a car called the 'Timor', the Panel noted:

> we do not see that the SCM Agreement precludes us from looking at criteria other than physical characteristics, where relevant to the like product analysis. The term 'characteristics closely resembling' in its ordinary meaning includes but is not limited to physical characteristics, and we see nothing in the context or object and purpose of the SCM Agreement that would dictate a different conclusion.[326]

In *Indonesia – Autos*, the European Communities argued before the Panel that *all* passenger cars should be considered 'like products' to the Timor. The Panel disagreed and ruled:

> While it is true that all passenger cars 'share the same basic physical characteristics and share an identical end-use', we agree with Indonesia that passenger cars are highly differentiated products . . . [A]ll drivers know that passenger cars may differ greatly in terms of size, weight, engine power, technology, and features. The significance of these extensive physical differences, both in terms of the cost of producing the cars and in consumer perceptions regarding them, is manifested in huge differences in price between brands and models. It is evident that the differences, both physical and non-physical, between a Rolls Royce and a Timor are enormous, and that the degree of substitutability between them is very low. Viewed from the perspective of the SCM Agreement, it is almost inconceivable that a subsidy for Timors could displace or impede imports of Rolls Royces, or that any meaningful analysis of price undercutting could be performed between these two models. In short, we do not consider that a Rolls Royce can reasonably be considered to have 'characteristics closely resembling' those of the Timor.[327]

The Panel eventually decided that the Ford Escort, Peugeot 306 and Opel Optima were 'like products' to the Timor within the meaning of footnote 46 to the *SCM Agreement*.[328]

The definition of 'domestic industry' in the *SCM Agreement* is quite similar to the definition of that concept in the *Anti-Dumping Agreement*.[329] Article 16.1 of the *SCM Agreement* defines the 'domestic industry' as:

> the domestic producers as a whole of the like products or . . . those of them whose collective output of the products constitutes a major proportion of the total domestic production of those products.

There are two exceptions to this definition of 'domestic industry'. First, domestic producers that are related to exporters or importers or which themselves import the subsidised products may be excluded from the relevant 'domestic industry'.[330] Secondly, in exceptional circumstances, the territory of a Member may be divided into two or more competitive markets and the producers within each

---

[326] *Ibid.*, para. 14.173.   [327] *Ibid.*, para. 14.175.
[328] See *ibid.*, para. 14.193. For the purposes of its further analysis, the Panel assumed, *arguendo*, that the Chrysler Neon is also a 'like product' to the Timor.   [329] See above, pp. 527–8.
[330] See Article 16.1 of the *SCM Agreement*.

market may be regarded as a separate industry. A regional industry then constitutes the relevant 'domestic industry'.[331]

The concept of 'injury' to a domestic industry in the *SCM Agreement* covers:

- material injury, i.e. genuine injury, to a domestic industry;[332]
- a threat of material injury to a domestic industry; and
- material retardation of the establishment of a domestic industry.[333]

The determination of 'injury' to the domestic industry must, pursuant to Article 15.1 of the *SCM Agreement*, be based on positive evidence and involve an objective examination of:

- the volume of the subsidised imports and the effect of the subsidised imports on prices in the domestic market for like products; and
- the consequent impact of these imports on the domestic producers of such products.[334]

With respect to the volume of the subsidised imports, it must be examined whether there has been a significant increase of the subsidised imports.[335] With respect to the effect of the subsidised imports on prices, it must be examined whether there has been a significant price undercutting by the subsidised imports, or whether these imports otherwise depress or suppress prices to a significant degree.[336] The examination of the consequent impact of the subsidised imports on the domestic industry must include an evaluation of all *relevant economic factors and indices* having a bearing on the state of the industry.[337] Article 15.4 lists the following specific factors:

- an actual and potential decline in the output, sales, market share, profits, productivity, return on investments or utilisation of capacity;
- factors affecting domestic prices; and
- actual and potential negative effects on cash flow, inventories, employment, wages, growth or the ability to raise capital or investments.[338]

The examination of all factors on this list is mandatory in each case.[339] However, this list is not exhaustive and *other* relevant factors must also be considered.

---

[331] See Article 16.2 of the *SCM Agreement*.

[332] Note that the *SCM Agreement*, like the *Anti-Dumping Agreement*, requires *material injury*, or a threat thereof, rather than serious injury as required under the *Agreement on Safeguards*. As already mentioned, the Appellate Body in *US – Lamb* noted that the standard of 'serious injury' is higher than that of 'material injury'. See above, pp. 529–33, and below, pp. 678–81.   [333] See footnote 45 to the *SCM Agreement*.

[334] Note in this regard that the Panel in *US – Softwood Lumber VI* recalled the definitions of the Appellate Body with respect to 'positive evidence' and 'objective examination' under the *Anti-Dumping Agreement* (as in *US – Hot-Rolled Steel*). See Panel Report, *US – Softwood Lumber VI*, para. 7.28, referring to Appellate Body Report, *US – Hot-Rolled Steel*, paras. 192–7.

[335] See Article 15.2 of the *SCM Agreement*. This increase may be an increase in absolute terms or relative to production or consumption in the importing country.

[336] See Article 15.2 of the *SCM Agreement*. Note that to 'suppress' prices is to prevent price increases that would otherwise occur.   [337] See Article 15.4 of the *SCM Agreement*.

[338] Note that, in the case of agriculture, the investigating authorities must also consider whether there has been an increased burden on government support programmes.

[339] The existence of an obligation to examine all the factors of the Article 15.4 list can be established by analogy to panel and Appellate Body reports interpreting similar provisions in the *Anti-Dumping Agreement* and the *Agreement on Safeguards*. See above, pp. 531–3, and below, pp. 679–81.

Furthermore, note that no single factor, or combination of factors, listed in Article 15.4 necessarily gives decisive guidance.[340]

As indicated above, the concept of 'injury' to a domestic industry in the *SCM Agreement* covers not only 'material injury' but also 'threat of material injury'. The determination of a 'threat of material injury' must be based on facts and not merely on allegations, conjecture or remote possibility.[341] For there to be a 'threat of material injury':

> the change in circumstances which would create a situation in which the subsidy would cause injury must be clearly foreseen and imminent.[342]

Article 15.7 lists a number of factors to be considered in making a determination regarding the existence of a 'threat of material injury'. This non-exhaustive list of factors includes *inter alia*:

- the nature of the subsidy and the trade effects likely to arise from it;
- a significant rate of increase of subsidised imports; and
- whether imports are entering at prices that will have a significant depressing or suppressing effect on domestic prices.[343]

All relevant factors (including the injury factors listed in Article 15.4, discussed above)[344] must be considered in order to establish whether further subsidised imports are imminent and whether, unless protective action is taken, material injury would occur.[345] In addition, as in the case of dumping, Article 15.8 requires 'special care' when considering and deciding on the application of countervailing measures in the case of a threat of material injury. In this regard, the Panel in *US – Softwood Lumber VI* considered the phrase 'special care' to mean:

> a degree of attention over and above that required of investigating authorities in all [other] anti-dumping and countervailing duty injury cases.[346]

When the subsidised imports originate in several countries and several countries are therefore subject to the anti-subsidy investigations, the effects of the subsidised imports may be assessed *cumulatively* for the purpose of establishing injury to the domestic industry.[347] It is quite common for WTO Members to apply a cumulative assessment of the effects of subsidised imports. However, pursuant to Article 15.3 of the *SCM Agreement* such cumulative assessment is only allowed when:

---

[340] See Article 15.4 of the *SCM Agreement*.　　[341] See Article 15.7 of the *SCM Agreement*.

[342] Article 15.7, second sentence, of the *SCM Agreement*.

[343] See the factors mentioned in Article 15.7(i), (ii) and (iv) of the *SCM Agreement*.

[344] See, by analogy, Panel Report, *Mexico – Corn Syrup*, para. 7.133, which concerned an identical provision in the *Anti-Dumping Agreement*. See above, pp. 533–5.

[345] See Article 15.7, last sentence, of the *SCM Agreement*. Note that the Panel in *US – Softwood Lumber VI* stated that a threat determination is made against the background of an evaluation of the condition of the industry in light of the Article 15.4 factors. Once such an analysis has been carried out in the context of an investigation of material injury, however, the Panel said that none of the relevant provisions of Article 15 require a second analysis of the injury factors in cases involving a threat of material injury. See Panel Report, *US – Softwood Lumber VI*, paras. 7.97–7.112.　　[346] Panel Report, *US – Softwood Lumber VI*, para. 7.33.

[347] Article 15.3 of the *SCM Agreement*.

- the amount of subsidisation is more than *de minimis* (i.e. more than 1 per cent *ad valorem*);[348]
- the volume of the imports of each country is not negligible; and
- the cumulative assessment of the effects of the imports is appropriate in light of the conditions of competition between the imported products and the conditions of competition between the imported products and the like domestic products.[349]

Finally, an observation is necessary on the need for a causal link between the subsidised imports and the injury to the domestic industry. Article 15.5 of the *SCM Agreement* provides:

> It must be demonstrated that the subsidized imports are, through the effects of subsidies, causing injury within the meaning of this Agreement.

A causal link between the subsidised imports and the injury to the domestic industry must therefore be established. The injury suffered by the domestic industry may be caused not only by the subsidised imports. Other factors may also cause injury to the domestic industry, including: the volumes and prices of non-subsidised imports of the product in question; a contraction in demand or changes in the patterns of consumption; trade-restrictive practices of, and competition between, the foreign and domestic producers; developments in technology; and the export performance and productivity of the domestic industry. The injury caused by these other factors may not be attributed to the subsidised imports.

Questions and Assignments 6.29

What are 'like products' in the context of the *SCM Agreement*? What is the relevant 'domestic industry' in the context of the *SCM Agreement*? What does the concept of 'injury', within the meaning of Article 15 of the *SCM Agreement*, cover? How is 'injury' to the domestic industry established? When is there a 'threat of material injury'? May the effects of subsidised imports from different countries be assessed *cumulatively* for the purpose of establishing injury to the domestic industry? Explain the non-attribution requirement provided for in Article 15.5 of the *SCM Agreement*.

6.3.4.2. *Subsidies causing nullification or impairment*

Subsidies have adverse effects on the interests of other Members within the meaning of Article 5(b) of the *SCM Agreement* – and are therefore 'actionable' – when the subsidised imports cause the nullification or impairment of benefits accruing directly or indirectly to other Members under the GATT 1994. This may be the case, in particular, with respect to the benefits from tariff concessions

---

[348] See Article 11.9 of the *SCM Agreement*. The amount of the subsidy is considered *de minimis* if the subsidy is less than 1 per cent of the value of the subsidised product.   [349] See Article 15.3 of the *SCM Agreement*.

bound under Article II:1 of the GATT 1994. Subsidisation may undercut improved market access resulting from a tariff concession.[350]

6.3.4.3. *Subsidies causing serious prejudice*

Subsidies have adverse effects on the interests of other Members within the meaning of Article 5(c) of the *SCM Agreement* – and are therefore 'actionable' – when the subsidised imports cause serious prejudice to the interests of another Member. Pursuant to Article 6.3 of the *SCM Agreement*, 'serious prejudice' *may* arise where a subsidy has one or more of the following effects:[351]

- the subsidy displaces or impedes imports of a like product of another Member into the market of the subsidising Member (Article 6.3(a));
- the subsidy displaces or impedes the export of a like product of another Member from a third country market (Article 6.3(b));
- the subsidy results in a significant price undercutting by the subsidising product in comparison to the like product of another Member in the same market, or significant price suppression, price depression or lost sales in the same market (Article 6.3(c)); or
- the subsidy leads to an increase in the world market share of the subsidising Member in a particular primary product or commodity in comparison to the average share it had during the previous period of three years (Article 6.3(d)).[352]

If a complaining Member can show that a subsidy has any of these effects, then 'serious prejudice' may be found to exist.[353] On the other hand, if the subsidising Member can show that subsidies do not result in any of these effects, these subsidies will *not* be found to cause serious prejudice.[354] Note that the concept of 'serious prejudice' includes a 'threat of serious prejudice', i.e. a situation in which the serious prejudice is imminent.[355]

The existence of serious prejudice must be determined on the basis of the information submitted to, or obtained by, the panel. Specific procedures for developing information on serious prejudice are set out in Annex V to the *SCM*

---

[350] The existence of nullification or impairment is established in accordance with the practice of application of Article XXIII of the GATT 1994. See footnote 12 of the *SCM Agreement*. However, in *US – Offset Act (Byrd Amendment)*, Mexico, one of the complainants, had argued that since the Panel had already found that the CDSOA was inconsistent with, *inter alia*, Articles 11.4 and 32.1, there was pursuant to Article 3.8 of the DSU a presumption of nullification or impairment. According to Mexico, this nullification or impairment was sufficient to demonstrate nullification or impairment for the purpose of Article 5(b) of the *SCM Agreement*. The Panel rejected this argument and stated that, for the purpose of Article 5(b) of the *SCM Agreement*, Mexico must show that the *use* of the subsidy caused nullification or impairment. See Panel Report, *US – Offset Act (Byrd Amendment)*, para. 7.119. The Panel subsequently referred to the Panel Report in *Japan – Film* on the three elements that must be established in order to uphold a claim of nullification or impairment. See above, pp. 183–4.

[351] Note that Article 6.1 of the *SCM Agreement* listed several situations in which subsidies are *deemed* to cause 'serious prejudice'. However, this provision lapsed on 31 December 1999. See Article 31 of the *SCM Agreement*.

[352] Note that the Panel in *Indonesia – Autos* considered that products not originating in a complaining Member cannot be the subject of a claim of serious prejudice and that Members cannot bring a claim that another Member has suffered serious prejudice. See Panel Report, *Indonesia – Autos*, paras. 14.201–14.202.

[353] There is as yet no ruling on whether the list of Article 6.3 is illustrative and non-exhaustive. If so, it may be possible to establish serious prejudice on grounds other than those in the list.

[354] Article 6.2 of the *SCM Agreement*.   [355] See footnote 13 to the *SCM Agreement*.

Agreement. If a Member fails to cooperate in the information-gathering process, the panel may rely on the 'best information available', and it may draw adverse inferences from the lack of cooperation.[356]

Questions and Assignments 6.30

When will a subsidy be found to cause 'serious prejudice' within the meaning of Article 6 of the *SCM Agreement*? Can a WTO Member bring a claim that *another* Member has suffered serious prejudice?

6.3.4.4. *Multilateral remedies for actionable subsidies*

The multilateral remedies for actionable subsidies are set out in Article 7 of the *SCM Agreement*. Like the remedies for prohibited subsidies, the remedies for actionable subsidies also differ from the remedies provided for in the DSU. Compared with the remedies for prohibited subsidies, however, the timeframes are longer and the Permanent Group of Experts is not involved.[357] If a panel concludes that a subsidy causes adverse effects to the interests of another Member (be it injury, nullification or impairment, or serious prejudice), the subsidising Member must:

> take appropriate steps to remove the adverse effect or . . . withdraw the subsidy.[358]

The subsidising Member must do so within six months from the adoption of the report by the DSB.[359] Instead of withdrawing the subsidy at issue or removing its adverse effects, the subsidising Member can also agree with the complaining Member on compensation.[360] If, within six months from the adoption of the report, the subsidy is not withdrawn, its adverse effects are not removed or no agreement on compensation is reached, the DSB must, at the request of the complaining Member and by reverse consensus, grant authorisation to the complaining Member to take countermeasures. These countermeasures must be commensurate with the degree and nature of the adverse effects of the subsidies granted.[361]

Questions and Assignments 6.31

What happens when a panel finds that a subsidy granted by a Member causes adverse effects to the interests of other Members?

---

[356] See Annex V, paras. 6 and 7, to the *SCM Agreement*.
[357] Several of the timeframes provided for under Article 7 are, however, still shorter than the 'ordinary' timeframes provided for in the DSU. For example, the timeframe for the panel proceedings is four months. See Article 7.5 of the *SCM Agreement*.   [358] Article 7.8 of the *SCM Agreement*.
[359] See Article 7.9 of the *SCM Agreement*.
[360] See *ibid*. Note that, in this specific context, compensation is a permanent alternative for bringing the measure into consistency with WTO law. This is not the case under the DSU. See above, pp. 225–6.
[361] Article 7.9 of the *SCM Agreement*. The contrast between 'appropriate countermeasures' in Article 4.10 and 'countermeasures. . . commensurate with the degree and nature of the adverse effects' was emphasised by the Arbitators in *Brazil – Aircraft (Article 22.6 – Brazil)*, para. 3.49, and the Arbitrators in *US – FSC (Article 22.6 – US)*, paras. 4.24–4.26.

6.3.4.5. *Note on non-actionable subsidies*

As already mentioned, in addition to prohibited subsidies and actionable subsidies, the *SCM Agreement* identifies a third category of subsidies: non-actionable subsidies.[362] This group of subsidies now only includes non-specific subsidies, to which, as discussed above, the disciplines of the *SCM Agreement* do not apply.[363] Until 31 December 1999, this category of non-actionable subsidies also included certain types of specific subsidy listed in Article 8.2 of the *SCM Agreement*, such as certain narrowly defined regional subsidies, environmental subsidies and research and development subsidies. As from 1 January 2000, however, these subsidies, provided that they are specific, are actionable.[364]

6.3.5. Countervailing measures

Prohibited and actionable subsidies which cause injury to the domestic industry can not only be challenged multilaterally but can also, alternatively, be offset by the application of a countervailing measure.[365] A Member whose domestic industry is injured because of subsidised imports has the choice between:

- challenging the subsidy concerned *multilaterally*, pursuant to Article 4 or 7 of the *SCM Agreement*, as discussed in detail above; and
- *unilaterally* imposing countervailing duties on the subsidised imports.

A countervailing duty is defined in Article VI of the GATT 1994 and footnote 36 to the *SCM Agreement* as:

> a special duty levied for the purpose of offsetting . . . any subsidy bestowed, directly, or indirectly, upon the manufacture, production or export of any merchandise.

Article 10 of the *SCM Agreement* provides with respect to countervailing duties:

> Members shall take all necessary steps to ensure that the imposition of a countervailing duty on any product of the territory of any Member imported into the territory of another Member is in accordance with the provisions of Article VI of GATT 1994 and the terms of this Agreement. Countervailing duties may only be imposed pursuant to investigations initiated and conducted in accordance with the provisions of this Agreement and the Agreement on Agriculture.

This section examines:

- under what conditions countervailing duties may be imposed on subsidised imports;
- how the investigations leading up to the imposition of countervailing duties should be conducted; and
- how countervailing duties must be applied.

---

[362] See above, p. 561, footnote 244.   [363] See above, pp. 568–70.   [364] See Article 31 of the *SCM Agreement*.
[365] A countervailing measure is also sometimes referred to as an 'anti-subsidy measure'.

6.3.5.1. Conditions for the imposition of countervailing duties

It follows from Article VI of the GATT 1994 and Articles 10 and 32.1 of the *SCM Agreement* that WTO Members may only impose countervailing duties when three conditions are fulfilled, namely:

- there are *subsidised imports*, i.e. imports of products from producers who benefited from specific subsidies within the meaning of Articles 1, 2 and 14 of the *SCM Agreement*, as discussed in detail above;[366]
- there is *injury* to the domestic industry of the like products within the meaning of Articles 15 and 16 of the *SCM Agreement*, as discussed in detail above;[367] and
- there is a *causal link* between the subsidised imports and the injury to the domestic industry *and* injury caused by other factors is *not attributed* to the subsidised imports.[368]

As noted by the Panel in *US – Countervailing Duty Investigation on DRAMS*, claims under Articles 10 and 32.1 are dependent on claims of violation of other provisions of the *SCM Agreement* or Article VI of the GATT.[369] Most successful claims under Article 10 of the *SCM Agreement* have been based on the fact that countervailing duties have been imposed or maintained on the basis of a calculation of a 'benefit' in a manner inconsistent with the *SCM Agreement*.[370]

Questions and Assignments 6.32

When may a Member impose countervailing duties under the terms of the *SCM Agreement*? Compare the conditions for imposing countervailing duties on subsidised imports to the conditions for a successful multilateral challenge of subsidies pursuant to Article 4 or 7 of the *SCM Agreement*.

6.3.5.2. Conduct of countervailing investigations

The *SCM Agreement* provides for detailed procedural requirements regarding the initiation and conduct of a countervailing investigation by the competent authorities of the Member imposing the countervailing duties on the subsidised

---

[366] On the concept of 'subsidies' and the specificity of subsidies, see above, pp. 562–71.
[367] On the concepts of 'like products', 'domestic industry' and 'injury' (including 'material injury', 'threat of material injury' and 'material retardation'), see above, pp. 578–82.
[368] See above, pp. 581–2. All the conditions for the imposition of countervailing duties, including the causal link and non-attribution requirements, are discussed above.
[369] See Panel Report, *US – Countervailing Duty Investigation on DRAMS*, para. 7.424.
[370] An example of a case where a violation of Article 10 of the *SCM Agreement* and Article VI of the GATT was found due to an incorrect calculation of a 'subsidy' is *US – Softwood Lumber IV (Article 21.5 – Canada)*. Here USDOC had included in its numerator transactions for which it had not demonstrated that the benefit of subsidised log inputs had passed through to the processed product. The Panel held that this resulted in the imposition of countervailing duties in a manner inconsistent with Articles 10 and 32.1 of the *SCM Agreement*, and Article VI:3 of the GATT. See Panel Report, *US – Softwood Lumber IV (Article 21.5 – Canada)*, para. 4.115.

imports. These requirements are set out in Articles 11 to 13 of the *SCM Agreement*. The main objective of these requirements is to ensure that:

- the investigations are conducted in a transparent manner;
- all interested parties have the opportunity to defend their interests; and
- the investigating authorities adequately explain the basis for their determinations.

The Appellate Body and panels have interpreted these requirements strictly. Note that the procedural requirements for countervailing investigations set out in the *SCM Agreement* are largely the same as the procedural requirements for anti-dumping investigations set out in the *Anti-Dumping Agreement* and discussed above.[371] This is true, in particular, for that part of the investigation dealing with injury and the general notification and explanation requirements. The rest of the investigation, not dealing with injury, of course has a different substantive focus. In a countervailing investigation, the focus is on establishing the extent to which countervailable subsidies are granted and the measurement of the amount of such subsidisation, while in an anti-dumping investigation, the focus is on the measurement of a dumping margin.

A countervailing investigation normally starts with the submission of a so-called application, i.e. a written complaint that injurious subsidisation is taking place. This application is submitted by, or on behalf of, the domestic industry allegedly injured by the subsidised imports.[372] A countervailing investigation shall not be initiated unless the investigating authorities have determined, on the basis of an examination of the degree of support for, or opposition to, the application, that the application has been made 'by or on behalf of' the domestic industry.[373] Pursuant to Article 11.2 of the *SCM Agreement*, the application must contain sufficient evidence of the existence of:

- a subsidy and, if possible, its amount;
- injury to the domestic industry; and
- a causal link between the subsidised imports and the alleged injury.[374]

Simple assertion, unsubstantiated by relevant evidence, is not considered to meet the requirement of 'sufficient evidence' under Article 11.2 of the *SCM Agreement*. Before initiating a countervailing investigation, the investigating authorities must examine the adequacy and accuracy of the evidence in the application to determine whether this evidence justifies the initiation of an investigation.[375]

---

[371] See above, pp. 539–45.   [372] See Article 11.1 of the *SCM Agreement*.

[373] As is set out in Article 11.4 of the *SCM Agreement*, the application shall be considered to have been made 'by or on behalf of the domestic industry' if it is supported by those domestic producers whose collective output constitutes more than 50 per cent of the total production of the like product produced by that portion of the domestic industry expressing either support for *or* opposition to the application. However, no investigation shall be initiated when domestic producers expressly supporting the application account for less than 25 per cent of total production of the like product produced by the domestic industry.

[374] Article 11.2 of the *SCM Agreement* sets out in significant detail the information the application must contain.

[375] See Article 11.3 of the *SCM Agreement*. Note, however, that Article 11.3 of the *SCM Agreement* does not specify how this examination is to be carried out. Note also that 'sufficient evidence' is, of course, not the same as 'full proof'; it is clearly a lower standard.

If the investigating authorities concerned are satisfied that there is not sufficient evidence of either subsidisation or injury to justify proceeding with the case, they must reject the application for the initiation of an investigation, or, if the investigation has already been initiated, promptly terminate that investigation.[376] There shall be immediate termination in cases where the amount of a subsidy is *de minimis* (i.e. less than 1 per cent *ad valorem*), or where the volume of subsidised imports, actual or potential, or the injury, is negligible.[377] The nature of the *de minimis* rule set forth in Article 11.9 was explored by the Appellate Body in *US – Carbon Steel*. According to the Panel in *US – Carbon Steel*, the *de minimis* requirement establishes a certain threshold, below which subsidisation is always non-injurious.[378] The Appellate Body disagreed:

> To us, there is nothing in Article 11.9 to suggest that its *de minimis* standard was intended to create a special category of '*non-injurious*' subsidization, or that it reflects a concept that subsidization at less than a *de minimis* threshold *can never* cause injury. For us, the *de minimis* standard in Article 11.9 does no more than lay down an agreed rule that if *de minimis* subsidization is found to exist in an original investigation, authorities are obliged to terminate their investigation, with the result that no countervailing duty can be imposed in such cases.[379]

Article 11.9 was furthermore considered in *Mexico – Anti-Dumping Measures on Rice*. At issue was a Mexican regulation which enabled a Mexican investigating authority to carry out a review of final countervailing measures *ex officio* or at the request of a third party with respect to parties that had been found not to have received countervailable subsidies during the original period of investigation. The Panel held that:

> [Article 11.9 of the *SCM Agreement*] requires the termination of the investigation with regard to such exporters found not to have [received actionable subsidies] above *de minimis* levels, and requires that such exporters be excluded from the measures imposed. The *logical consequence* of such an exclusion of producers found not to have [received actionable subsidies] is that they can not subsequently be subjected to administrative or changed circumstances reviews . . . We therefore find that Article 68 of the Act is as such inconsistent with [Article 11.9 of the *SCM Agreement*].[380]
>
> [Emphasis added]

On appeal, Mexico argued *inter alia* that Article 11.9 of the *SCM Agreement* only applies to 'events subsequent to the original investigation, including reviews' and that the Panel had as such erred in its finding.[381] The Appellate Body, however, upheld the Panel's 'logical consequence' rationale:

> We have already indicated that the Panel was correct in finding that Article [11.9 of the *SCM Agreement*] requires an investigating authority to terminate the investigation 'in respect of' an exporter found not to have [a subsidy] above *de minimis*, and that the exporter consequently must be excluded from the definitive [countervailing measure] . . .

---

[376] See Article 11.9 of the *SCM Agreement*.   [377] See *ibid*.   [378] See Panel Report, *US – Carbon Steel*, para. 8.79.
[379] Appellate Body Report, *US – Carbon Steel*, para. 83.
[380] Panel Report, *Mexico – Anti-Dumping Measures on Rice*, para. 7.251. It must be mentioned that the Panel's text relates to Article 5.8 of the *Anti-Dumping Agreement*, but the Panel notes in para. 7.251 that its reasoning applies *mutatis mutandis* to Article 11.9 of the *SCM Agreement*.
[381] See Appellate Body Report, *Mexico – Anti-Dumping Measures on Rice*, para. 302.

> We therefore agree with the Panel that the 'logical consequence' of this approach is that such exporters cannot be subject to administrative and changed circumstances reviews, because such reviews examine . . . 'the need for the *continued imposition* of the duty'. Were an investigating authority to undertake a review of exporters that were excluded from the [countervailing measure] by virtue of their *de minimis* [subsidies], those exporters effectively would be made subject to the [countervailing measure], inconsistent with [Article 11.9 of the *SCM Agreement*].[382]

Hence, when a company has been found not to have received countervailable subsidies above *de minimis* levels during the original period of investigation, it necessarily follows from Article 11.9 of the *SCM Agreement* that such companies can no longer be made subject to administrative and changed circumstances reviews.

In special circumstances, domestic authorities can also initiate countervailing investigations of their own accord.[383] However, they may only do so when they have sufficient evidence of the existence of a subsidy, injury and causal link to justify the initiation of an investigation.

When the investigating authorities decide to initiate an investigation, be it at the request of the domestic industry or of their own accord, several obligations must then be fulfilled to provide adequate protection for those potentially affected by such an investigation. First, a public notice of the initiation must be issued,[384] and as soon as the investigation is initiated,[385] the application for the initiation of an investigation must be made available to the known exporters of the subsidised products and the exporting Member.[386] Secondly, interested Members and all interested parties in the investigation, including, of course, the exporter(s) of the subsidised products and the domestic producer(s) of the like product,[387] must be given:

- notice of the information which the authorities require; and
- ample opportunity to present in writing all evidence which they consider relevant.[388]

Thirdly, Members and interested parties must then be given at least thirty days to reply to the questionnaire they receive from the investigating authorities.[389] In *Mexico – Anti-Dumping Measures on Rice*, the Appellate Body made clear that the thirty-day period must be accorded to '*all* exporters and foreign producers receiving a questionnaire, to be counted, "[a]s a general rule", from the date of receipt

---

[382] Appellate Body Report, *Mexico – Anti-Dumping Measures on Rice*, para. 305.
[383] See Article 11.6 of the *SCM Agreement*.
[384] See Article 22.1 of the *SCM Agreement*. Article 22.2 sets out the information which this public notice must contain.
[385] Note that, before the investigation is actually initiated, the investigating authorities must invite the subsidising Member for consultations. Such consultations will continue throughout the investigation. See Articles 13.1 and 13.2 of the *SCM Agreement*.
[386] See Article 12.1.3 of the *SCM Agreement*. The application shall also be made available, upon request, to other interested parties involved.
[387] For a definition of 'interested parties', see Article 12.9 of the *SCM Agreement*. Note that domestic or foreign parties other than those mentioned above may be considered to be 'interested parties'.
[388] See Article 12.1 of the *SCM Agreement*.
[389] See Article 12.1.1 of the *SCM Agreement*. Where cause is shown, a thirty-day extension period should be granted whenever practicable.

of the questionnaire',[390] and not only, as Mexico had argued, to exporters and foreign producers which were made known to the investigating authorities *at the outset* of an investigation.[391] It is hence contrary to Article 12.1.1 of the *SCM Agreement* to exclude from the thirty-day period exporters and foreign producers that make themselves known to the investigating authority, or become known to the investigating authority as a result of its own enquiry, at some point after the outset of the investigation.[392] The Appellate Body furthermore made clear that it observes the thirty-day period strictly: a period of twenty-eight working days following the date of publication of the initiating resolution does not suffice.[393]

Fourthly, the investigating authorities must provide opportunities for industrial users of the product under investigation, and for representative consumer organisations in cases where the product is commonly sold at the retail level, to provide information.[394] Fifthly, all interested parties must be invited to participate in the hearings held by the investigating authorities.[395] Finally, the investigating authorities are obliged to make all information that is not confidential available to all interested Members and interested parties.[396] However, any information the disclosure of which would be of significant competitive advantage to a competitor or would have significant adverse effects on those supplying the information (i.e. any confidential information or other information which is provided on a confidential basis), must, where good cause is shown, be treated as confidential by the investigating authorities.[397] Such confidential information may only be disclosed with the specific permission of the party submitting it.[398]

During the course of an investigation, the investigating authorities must satisfy themselves as to the accuracy of the information supplied by interested Members or interested parties upon which their findings are based.[399]

Investigating authorities which, in spite of their best efforts, fail to obtain all relevant information, may take decisions on the basis of the 'best information available'. Article 12.7 of the *SCM Agreement* provides:

> In cases in which any interested Member or interested party refuses access to, or otherwise does not provide, necessary information within a reasonable period or significantly impedes the investigation, preliminary and final determinations, affirmative or negative, may be made on the basis of the facts available.

---

[390] Appellate Body Report, *Mexico – Anti-Dumping Measures on Rice*, para. 280.

[391] See *ibid.*, para. 278.

[392] See *ibid.*, para. 280. It is, however, very possible that a notification of interest comes at such a late stage that a grant of the thirty-day period would cause an investigating authority to fail to comply with its time limits under the *SCM Agreement*. In this regard the Appellate Body has held on several occasions that the 'due process rights in [Article 12 of the *SCM Agreement*] . . ."cannot extend indefinitely" but, instead, are limited by the investigating authority's need "to 'control the conduct' of its inquiry and to 'carry out the multiple steps' required to reach a timely completion" of the proceeding'. *Ibid.*, para. 282.

[393] See Appellate Body Report, *Mexico – Anti-Dumping Measures on Rice*, para. 283.

[394] See Article 12.10 of the *SCM Agreement*.

[395] See Article 12.2 of the *SCM Agreement*. Note, however, that any decision of the investigating authorities can only be based on such information and arguments as were on the written record of these authorities. Therefore, information provided orally must also be submitted in writing.

[396] See Article 12.3 of the *SCM Agreement*.   [397] See Article 12.4 of the *SCM Agreement*.

[398] See *ibid*. Investigating authorities may, however, be asked to provide non-confidential summaries that provide a reasonable understanding of the substance of the information submitted in confidence. See Article 12.4.1 of the *SCM Agreement*. See also Panel Report, *US – Oil Country Tubular Goods Sunset Reviews (Article 21.5 – Argentina)*, para. 7.135.   [399] Article 12.5 of the *SCM Agreement*.

According to the Panel in *EC – Countervailing Measures on DRAM Chips*, Article 12.7 of the *SCM Agreement* 'identifies the circumstances in which investigating authorities may overcome a lack of information, in the response of the interested parties, by using "facts" which are otherwise "available" to the investigating authority'.[400] Article 12.7 of the *SCM Agreement* was further clarified by the Appellate Body in *Mexico – Anti-Dumping Measures on Rice*. It drew a comparison with Article 6.8 of the *Anti-Dumping Agreement*, which also 'permits an investigating authority, under certain circumstances, to fill in gaps in the information necessary to arrive at a conclusion as to subsidization (or dumping) and injury'.[401] While the Appellate Body recognised that Article 6.8 of the *Anti-Dumping Agreement* contains far more detailed rules as regards the use of 'facts available' by an investigating authority, it considered that:

> it would be anomalous if Article 12.7 of the *SCM Agreement* were to permit the use of 'facts available' in countervailing duty investigations in a manner markedly different from that in anti-dumping investigations.[402]

Hence, according to the Appellate Body, similar limitations apply to Article 12.7 of the *SCM Agreement*. It held that:

> recourse to facts available does not permit an investigating authority to use any information in whatever way it chooses. First, such recourse is not a licence to rely on only part of the evidence provided. To the extent possible, an investigating authority using the 'facts available' in a countervailing duty investigation must take into account all the substantiated facts provided by an interested party, even if those facts may not constitute the complete information requested of that party. Secondly, the 'facts available' to the agency are generally limited to those that may reasonably replace the information that an interested party failed to provide. In certain circumstances, this may include information from secondary sources.[403]

This possibility for investigating authorities is important to avoid investigations being frustrated and deadlocked because of the lack of cooperation from an interested party holding the relevant information. However, this possibility may evidently also potentially give rise to abuse on the part of investigating authorities.

Note that Article 12.7 speaks of 'interested parties'. Article 12.9 of the *SCM Agreement* provides in this respect:

> For the purposes of this Agreement, 'interested parties' shall include:
>
> - an exporter or foreign producer or the importer of a product subject to investigation, or a trade or business association a majority of the members of which are producers, exporters or importers of such product; and
> - a producer of the like product in the importing Member or a trade and business association a majority of the members of which produce the like product in the territory of the importing Member.
>
> This list shall not preclude Members from allowing domestic or foreign parties other than those mentioned above to be included as interested parties.

---

[400] Panel Report, *EC – Countervailing Measures on DRAM Chips*, para. 7.245.
[401] Appellate Body Report, *Mexico – Anti-Dumping Measures on Rice*, para. 291.   [402] *Ibid.*, para. 295.
[403] *Ibid.*, para. 294.

In *Japan – DRAMs (Korea)*, a Panel had to address the question whether the inclusion of a party as an 'interested party' in an investigation requires a prior establishment that that party has an interest in the outcome of an investigation.[404] Korea had argued that such a requirement was implied in the language of Article 12.9.[405] The Panel disagreed. According to the Panel, Article 12.9 does not provide an exhaustive list as to which parties 'can be taken to be "interested parties"'.[406] Furthermore, the Panel also considered this issue in the light of the task of the investigating authorities, and noted that:

> previous Appellate Body and panel reports have underscored the important role that Article 12.7 serves in ensuring that investigating authorities are able to obtain the information necessary to make proper determinations. Requiring an investigating authority to establish that a party has an interest in the outcome of an investigation as a precondition for treating that party as an 'interested party' could preclude investigating authorities from making proper determinations. In our view, the scope of the right of investigating authorities to include parties as 'interested parties' in investigations must be interpreted with a view to ensuring that investigating authorities are able to obtain the 'necessary information' needed to arrive at a determination. Therefore, we do not believe that Article 12.7 gives rise to the necessary implication that an investigating authority must establish that a party has an interest in the outcome of an investigation in order to include that party as an 'interested party' in the investigation.[407]

Investigations must normally be concluded within one year,[408] and in no case should an investigation take longer than eighteen months.[409]

Questions and Assignments 6.33

Describe the key features of a countervailing investigation. What is the main objective of the procedural requirements set out in Articles 11 to 13 of the *SCM Agreement*? How is a countervailing investigation initiated? When are investigating authorities obliged to terminate a countervailing investigation immediately? How does the *SCM Agreement* ensure all interested parties get a chance to be heard in a countervailing investigation? Who is an 'interested party' within the meaning of Article 12.7 of the *SCM Agreement*? Discuss how confidential information is handled in a countervailing investigation. Can investigating authorities base their conclusions on the 'best information available'?

6.3.5.3. *Application of countervailing measures*

The *SCM Agreement* provides for three types of countervailing measure:

- provisional countervailing measures;
- voluntary undertakings; and
- definitive countervailing duties.

---

[404] See Panel Report, *Japan – DRAMs (Korea)*, para. 7.385.   [405] See *ibid.*, para. 7.386.   [406] *Ibid.*, para. 7.388.
[407] *Ibid.*, para. 7.392.   [408] See Article 11.11 of the *SCM Agreement*.   [409] See *ibid.*

After making a preliminary determination that a subsidy is causing or threatening to cause injury to a domestic industry, an importing Member can impose *provisional countervailing measures* on the subsidised imports if the authorities judge such measures necessary to prevent injury being caused during the investigation.[410] Provisional countervailing measures may take the form of provisional countervailing duties guaranteed by cash deposits or bonds equal to the amount of the provisionally calculated amount of subsidisation.[411] However, such provisional countervailing measures cannot be applied earlier than sixty days from the date of initiation of the investigation. Furthermore, their application must be limited to as short a period as possible and in no case may they be applied for more than four months.[412] In *US – Softwood Lumber III*, the Panel found that the United States had violated Articles 17.3 and 17.4 of the *SCM Agreement* as it had imposed provisional countervailing measures on imports of softwood lumber prior to the lapse of the sixty-days' period after the date of initiation and had exceeded the four-months' maximum length by three months.[413]

Investigations may be suspended or terminated without the imposition of provisional measures or countervailing duties upon receipt of satisfactory *voluntary undertakings* under which:

- the government of the exporting Member agrees to eliminate or limit the subsidy or to take other measures concerning its effects; or
- the exporter agrees to revise its prices so that the investigating authorities are satisfied that the injurious effect of the subsidy is eliminated.[414]

Note that, pursuant to Article 18.2 of the *SCM Agreement*, undertakings may not be sought or accepted unless the investigating authorities have made a preliminary affirmative determination of subsidisation and injury caused by such subsidisation. In case of undertakings from exporters, the consent of the exporting Member must be obtained. Article 18.4 of the *SCM Agreement* provides that, if an undertaking is accepted, the investigation of subsidisation and injury shall nevertheless be completed if the exporting Member so desires or the importing Member so decides.[415]

Members may impose *definitive countervailing duties* only after making a final determination that:

- a countervailable subsidy exists; and
- the subsidised imports cause, or threaten to cause, injury to the domestic industry.[416]

Note that Article 32.1 of the *SCM Agreement* states:

---

[410] See Article 17 of the *SCM Agreement*.   [411] See Article 17.2 of the *SCM Agreement*.
[412] See Articles 17.3 and 17.4 of the *SCM Agreement*.
[413] See Panel Report, *US – Softwood Lumber III*, para. 7.101.   [414] See Article 18.1 of the *SCM Agreement*.
[415] Article 18.6 of the *SCM Agreement* sets out what happens in case of violation of an undertaking.
[416] See Article 19.1 of the *SCM Agreement*. Before a final determination is made, the investigating authorities inform all interested Members and interested parties of the essential facts under consideration which form the basis for the decision whether to apply definitive measures. Such disclosure should take place in sufficient time for the parties to defend their interests. See Article 12.8 of the *SCM Agreement*.

No specific action against a subsidy of another Member can be taken except in accordance with the provisions of GATT 1994, as interpreted by this Agreement.[417]

In *US – Offset Act (Byrd Amendment)*, the Appellate Body ruled that it follows from this provision that the response to a countervailable subsidy must be in one of the four forms provided for in provisions of the GATT 1994 or the *SCM Agreement*.[418] As discussed above, the GATT 1994 and the *SCM Agreement* provide four responses to a countervailable subsidy: definitive countervailing duties; provisional measures; price undertakings; and multilaterally sanctioned countermeasures under the dispute settlement system. No other response to subsidisation is permitted. In *US – Offset Act (Byrd Amendment)*, the measure at issue was the United States Continued Dumping and Subsidy Offset Act of 2000 (CDSOA).[419] This Act provided, in relevant part, that the United States Customs shall *distribute* duties assessed pursuant to a countervailing duty order to 'affected domestic producers' for 'qualifying expenditures'.[420] The Appellate Body concluded:

As the CDSOA does not correspond to any of the responses to subsidization envisaged by the GATT 1994 and the *SCM Agreement*, we conclude that it is not in accordance with the provisions of the GATT 1994, as interpreted by the *SCM Agreement*, and that, therefore, the CDSOA is inconsistent with Article 32.1 of the *SCM Agreement*.[421]

More recently, the Panel in *Mexico – Anti-Dumping Measures on Rice* held that the provision in a Mexican regulation imposing fines against importers importing products subject to countervailing duty investigations was a form of 'specific action' against a subsidy, that fines were not provided for in the GATT 1994 or the *SCM Agreement*, and that the fines at issue were thus inconsistent with Article 32.1 of the *SCM Agreement*.[422]

With respect to the amount of the countervailing duty imposed on subsidised imports, Article 19.4 of the *SCM Agreement* provides:

No countervailing duty shall be levied on any imported product in excess of the amount of the subsidy found to exist, calculated in terms of subsidization per unit of the subsidized and exported product.

Thus, a countervailing duty must never exceed the amount of the subsidy. Moreover, if the amount of the injury caused is less than the amount of the subsidy, the definitive countervailing duty should *preferably* be limited to the

---

[417] The Appellate Body established in *US – Offset Act (Byrd Amendment)* the following test to determine whether a measure constitutes 'a specific action': 'a measure that may be taken only when the constituent elements of . . . a subsidy are present, is a "specific action" in response to. . . subsidization within the meaning of Article 32.1 of the *SCM Agreement*. In other words, the measure must be inextricably linked to, or have a strong correlation with, the constituent elements of dumping or of a subsidy. Such link or correlation may . . . be derived from the text of the measure itself'. See Appellate Body Report, *US – Offset Act (Byrd Amendment)*, para. 239.

[418] Appellate Body Report, *US – Offset Act (Byrd Amendment)*, para. 269.   [419] See *ibid.*, paras. 11–14.

[420] See *ibid.*   [421] *Ibid.*, para. 273.

[422] See Panel Report, *Mexico – Anti-Dumping Measures on Rice*, para. 7.278. See also Panel Report, *EC – Commercial Vessels*, where the Panel ruled that a European regulation on shipbuilding constituted a form of 'specific action', but was not directed 'against' a subsidy, meaning that Article 32.1 of the *SCM Agreement* was not violated.

[423] See Article 19.2 of the *SCM Agreement*. Moreover, a Member may even decide not to impose countervailing duties at all. See also Article 19.2 of the *SCM Agreement*.

amount necessary to counteract the injury caused.[423] This is also commonly referred to as the 'lesser duty' rule.[424] As discussed above, Members have a wide discretion in deciding on the method used to calculate the amount of the subsidy. Article 14 of the *SCM Agreement* requires: first, that the method used shall be provided for in national legislation or implementing regulations; second, that the application of the method to each particular case shall be transparent and adequately explained; and third, that the method must be consistent with the guidelines set out in Article 14 (a)–(d).[425]

In *Japan – DRAMs (Korea)*, the issue was raised whether subsidisation must be 'found to exist' – as is stated in Article 19.4 of the *SCM Agreement* – at the time of imposition of the countervailing duty, or whether a determination that a subsidy was 'found to exist' during some prior period suffices.[426] The Panel found that 'countervailing duties may only be imposed if there is present subsidization at the time of duty imposition'.[427] According to the Panel, this does not, however, exclude the possibility for an investigating authority to rely on previous data. It held that:

> countervailing duties may be imposed on the basis of the investigating authority's review of a past period of investigation. We are not suggesting that an investigating authority is somehow required to conduct a new investigation at the time of imposition, in order to confirm the continued existence of the subsidization found to exist during the period of investigation. That would defeat the very purpose of using periods of investigation in the first place.[428]

Nonetheless, the Panel urged the need to establish present subsidisation, stating that:

> the use of a past period of investigation does not negate the need for an investigating authority to be satisfied that there is present subsidization. Rather, the historical data from the period of investigation 'is being used to draw conclusions about the current situation,' '[b]ecause the conditions to impose [a duty] are to be assessed with respect to the current situation'. In this sense, the situation during the period of investigation is used as a proxy for the situation pertaining 'current[ly]', at the time of imposition. In the case of non-recurring subsidies, if the review of the period of investigation indicates that the subsidy will no longer exist at the time of imposition, the existence of subsidization during the period of investigation will not suffice to demonstrate 'current' subsidization at the time of imposition.[429]

Countervailing duties must be collected on a non-discriminatory basis. Article 19.3 of the *SCM Agreement* states:

> When a countervailing duty is imposed in respect of any product, such countervailing duty shall be levied . . . on a non-discriminatory basis on imports of such product from all sources found to be subsidized and causing injury.

---

[424] See above, p. 547.   [425] See above, p. 567.   [426] See Panel Report, *Japan – DRAMs (Korea)*, para. 7.351.
[427] *Ibid.*, para. 7.355.   [428] *Ibid.*, para. 7.356.
[429] Panel Report, *Japan – DRAMs (Korea)*, para. 7.357. The Panel refers in quote to Panel Report, *Mexico – Anti-Dumping Measures on Rice*, para. 7.28 and Appellate Body Report, *Mexico – Anti-Dumping Measures on Rice*, para. 165.

As discussed above, the MFN treatment obligation applies to countervailing duties.[430]

Note that any exporter whose exports are subject to a definitive countervailing duty but who was not actually investigated is entitled to an expedited review so that the investigating authorities can promptly establish an individual countervailing duty rate for that exporter.[431]

Countervailing duties, in principle, may not be applied retroactively, i.e. they may only be applied to products imported after the decision to impose countervailing duties entered into force.[432] Where a final determination is negative, any cash deposit made during the period of the application of provisional measures shall be refunded and any bonds released in an expeditious manner.[433]

With respect to the duration, magnitude and purpose of countervailing duties, Article 21.1 of the *SCM Agreement* states as a rule:

> A countervailing duty shall remain in force only as long as and to the extent necessary to counteract subsidization which is causing injury.

The Appellate Body held in *US – Carbon Steel* that it considered Article 21.1 of the *SCM Agreement* to be:

> a general rule that, after the imposition of a countervailing duty, the continued application of that duty is subject to certain disciplines. These disciplines relate to the *duration* of the countervailing duty ('only as long as . . . necessary'), its *magnitude* ('only . . . to the extent necessary'), and its *purpose* ('to counteract subsidization which is causing injury'). Thus, the general rule of Article 21.1 underlines the requirement for periodic review of countervailing duties and highlights the factors that must inform such reviews.[434]

Upon a request from an interested party or upon their own initiative where warranted, the investigating authorities shall review the need for the continued application of the duty.[435]

Interested parties may request such review once a reasonable period has elapsed since the imposition of the definitive countervailing duty. The interested parties requesting a review must submit positive information substantiating the need for a review.[436] During the review, the investigating authorities examine at the request of the interested party:

---

[430] See above, p. 327. The MFN treatment obligation also applies to anti-dumping duties. See above, p. 547. Note that countervailing duties shall not be applied to imports from sources which have renounced any subsidies in question or sources from which undertakings have been accepted. See Article 19.3 of the *SCM Agreement*.

[431] See Article 19.3 of the *SCM Agreement*. This does not apply to exporters for which no individual countervailing duty was established due to their refusal to cooperate with the investigating authorities.

[432] See Article 20.1 of the *SCM Agreement*. Note, however, that in specific circumstances the retroactive application of countervailing duties is possible. See Articles 20.2 and 20.6 of the *SCM Agreement*.

[433] See Article 20.5 of the *SCM Agreement*. However, if the definitive countervailing duty is higher than the amount guaranteed by the cash deposit or bond, the difference shall not be collected. See Article 20.3 of the *SCM Agreement*.   [434] Appellate Body Report, *US – Carbon Steel*, para. 70.

[435] See Article 21.2 of the *SCM Agreement*. With regard to administrative reviews, i.e. reviews upon the initiative of the investigating authorities, see Appellate Body Report, *US – Lead and Bismuth II*, para. 53. See also Panel Report, *US – Softwood Lumber III*, para. 7.151. The Panel in this case noted that Article 21.2 does *not* impose an obligation to establish a yearly administrative review procedure as was undertaken by the United States in its retrospective duty assessment system.

[436] See Article 21.2 of the *SCM Agreement*.

- whether the continued imposition of the duty is necessary to offset subsidisation; and/or
- whether the injury would be likely to continue or recur if the duty were removed or varied.[437]

The Appellate Body in *Mexico – Anti-Dumping Measures on Rice* found that Members are not allowed to subject the right of interested parties to a review to requirements other than those set out in Article 21.2 of the *SCM Agreement*.[438]

In *US – Lead and Bismuth II*, the Appellate Body noted the following with regard to the determination an investigating authority must make under an Article 21.2 review:

> [o]n the basis of its assessment of the information presented to it by interested parties, as well as of other evidence before it relating to the period of review, the investigating authority must determine whether there is a continuing need for the application of countervailing duties. The investigating authority is not free to ignore such information. If it were free to ignore this information, the review mechanism under Article 21.2 would have no purpose.[439]

As regards the establishment of a 'benefit' under an Article 21.2 review, the Appellate Body held in *US – Lead and Bismuth II*:

> We do not agree with the Panel's implied view that, in the context of an administrative review under Article 21.2, an investigating authority must *always* establish the existence of a 'benefit' during the period of review *in the same way as* an investigating authority must establish a 'benefit' in an original investigation . . . In an original investigation, the investigating authority must establish that *all* conditions set out in the *SCM Agreement* for the imposition of countervailing duties are fulfilled. In an administrative review, however, the investigating authority must address those issues which have been raised before it by the interested parties or, in the case of an investigation conducted on its own initiative, those issues which warranted the examination.[440]

The Appellate Body hence draws a clear distinction between the original investigation procedure which is concerned with the initial imposition of a countervailing duty *and* the review procedure of Article 21.2.[441]

If the investigating authorities, as a result of a review, come to the conclusion that the countervailing duty at issue is no longer warranted, it shall be

---

[437] See *ibid*. The review must be conducted pursuant to the same procedural rules as those that applied to the original investigation. See Article 21.4 of the *SCM Agreement*.

[438] See Appellate Body Report, *Mexico – Anti-Dumping Measures on Rice*, para. 314.

[439] Appellate Body Report, *US – Lead and Bismuth II*, para. 61.   [440] *Ibid*., paras. 62–3.

[441] The extent of the obligations of the investigating authorities in the context of a review procedure was clarified by the Appellate Body in *US – Countervailing Measures on Certain EC Products*. The measure at issue in this case was an administrative practice employed by the United States in review procedures following a change in ownership.

 The Appellate Body tested the consistency of this practice, referred to as the 'same person' method, with Article 21.2 and found that: 'under the "same person" method, when the USDOC determines that no new legal person is created as a result of privatization, the USDOC will conclude from this determination, *without any further analysis*, and irrespective of the price paid by the new owners for the newly privatized enterprise, that the newly-privatized enterprise continues to receive the benefit of a previous financial contribution. This approach is contrary to the obligation in Article 21.2 of the *SCM Agreement* that the investigating authority must take into account in an administrative review "positive information substantiating the need for a review" '. For this reason, the Appellate Body held the 'same person method' as such inconsistent with Article 21.2. See Appellate Body Report, *US – Countervailing Measures on Certain EC Products*, para. 146.

terminated immediately.[442] Should the investigating authorities conclude that the countervailing duty remains warranted, it will continue to apply, albeit possibly at a different level.

Article 21.3 of the *SCM Agreement* provides for a so-called 'sunset' clause under which all definitive countervailing duties must be terminated, at the latest, five years after their imposition or latest review. However, where the investigating authorities determine that the expiry of the countervailing duty would be likely to lead to continuation or recurrence of subsidisation and injury, the duty will not be terminated.[443] Investigating authorities may come to that determination in the context of a review that is commonly referred to as a 'sunset review'. A sunset review may be undertaken by the investigating authorities at their own initiative *or* upon a duly substantiated request made by, or on behalf of, the domestic industry.[444] The provisions of Article 12 of the *SCM Agreement*, setting out rules on evidence and procedure with regard to the original investigation, also apply to the sunset reviews.[445] Sunset reviews shall be carried out expeditiously and shall normally be concluded within twelve months of their initiation.[446]

Questions and Assignments 6.34

Discuss briefly the three types of countervailing measure. When can a Member impose a provisional countervailing measure? When can a Member impose a definitive countervailing duty? Is a Member allowed to impose a countervailing duty in excess of the subsidy found to exist? Is a Member allowed to impose a countervailing duty in excess of the amount necessary to counteract the injury caused? Discuss whether the MFN treatment obligation applies to countervailing duties. Can countervailing duties be applied retroactively? What is the maximum duration of a countervailing duty? What is the object and purpose of the review procedure of Article 21.2 of the *SCM Agreement*? What is a 'sunset review' within the meaning of Article 21.3 of the *SCM Agreement*?

6.3.5.4. *Public notice and judicial review*

In order to increase the transparency of decisions taken by investigating authorities and to encourage solid and thorough reasoning underlying such decisions, Article 22 of the *SCM Agreement* contains detailed requirements for public notice

---

[442] See Article 21.2 of the *SCM Agreement*.　　[443] See Article 21.3 of the *SCM Agreement*.

[444] See Article 21 of the *SCM Agreement*. Note that a request for a sunset review must be made within a reasonable period of time prior to the expiry of the countervailing duties and that the investigating authorities must initiate the review before that date. Note also that Article 21.3, unlike Article 11.9, does not impose a *de minimis* standard for the initiation of a sunset review. The Appellate Body held in *US – Carbon Steel* that the *de minimis* requirement of Article 11.9 is also *not implied* in Article 21.3. See Appellate Body Report, *US – Carbon Steel*, para. 92. See also above, p. 588. With regard to sunset reviews initiated by investigating authorities, the Appellate Body in *US – Carbon Steel* held that there are no evidentiary standards for self-initiation of sunset reviews. See Appellate Body Report, *US – Carbon Steel*, para. 112.

[445] See Article 21.4 of the *SCM Agreement*.

[446] See *ibid*. During a sunset review, the countervailing duties may remain in force. See Article 21.3 of the *SCM Agreement*.

by investigating authorities of decisions on the initiation of an investigation, provisional countervailing measures, voluntary undertakings or definitive countervailing duties. For example, the public notice issued when the investigating authorities decide to impose a definitive countervailing duty *must* set forth, or otherwise make available through a separate report, all relevant information on the matters of fact, law and reasons which have led to the imposition of the countervailing duty.[447] In particular, the notice or report *must* contain:

- the names of the suppliers or, when this is impracticable, the supplying countries involved;
- a description of the product which is sufficient for customs purposes;
- the amount of subsidy established and the basis on which the existence of a subsidy has been determined;
- considerations relevant to the injury determination as set out in Article 15 and discussed above; and
- the main reasons leading to the determination.[448]

Furthermore, the notice or report *must* set out the reasons for the acceptance or rejection of relevant arguments or claims made by interested Members and by the exporters and importers.[449]

As provided for in Article 23 of the *SCM Agreement*, entitled 'Judicial Review', each Member whose national legislation contains provisions on countervailing measures must maintain judicial, arbitral or administrative tribunals or procedures for the purpose of, *inter alia*, the prompt review of administrative actions relating to final determinations and reviews of determinations. Such tribunals or procedures must be independent of the authorities responsible for the determination or review in question, and must provide all interested parties who participated in the administrative proceeding, and are affected directly and individually by the administrative actions, with access to review.[450]

6.3.5.5. *Countervailing duties or countermeasures*

Note that the provisions relating to prohibited and actionable subsidies, discussed above, may be invoked, and relied upon, *in parallel with* the provisions relating to countervailing duties. However, with regard to the effects of a particular subsidy, only *one* form of remedy (either a countervailing duty *or* a countermeasure) may be applied.[451]

Questions and Assignments 6.35

Why is the public notice requirement of Article 22 of the *SCM Agreement* important? What must the public notice, issued when the investigating

---

[447] See Article 22.5 of the *SCM Agreement*. Note, however, that Article 22.5 requires that due regard be paid to the requirement for the protection of confidential information.
[448] See Article 22.5 of the *SCM Agreement*, referring to Article 22.4 thereof.
[449] See Article 22.5 of the *SCM Agreement*.   [450] See Article 23 of the *SCM Agreement*.
[451] See footnote 35 to the *SCM Agreement*.

authorities decide to impose a definitive countervailing duty, set forth, or otherwise make available through a separate report? What does Article 23 of the *SCM Agreement* require from Members? Can countervailing duties and countermeasures be applied simultaneously with regard to the same instance of subsidisation?

6.3.6. Agricultural subsidies

Agricultural subsidies have traditionally been, and continue to be, a very contentious issue in international trade. Agricultural subsidies were a central issue during the Uruguay Round and are currently one of the major stumbling blocks in the Doha Development Round. Allen Beattie of the *Financial Times* described the issue as follows:

> Cutting domestic farm subsidies is one of the most pressing subjects for trade ministers . . . to rescue the crisis-hit Doha round of global trade talks. But though it will affect millions of farmers around the world, the subject is as arcane as it is important. Its astonishing complexity recalls the remark made by Lord Palmerston, the 19th-century British foreign secretary, of an intractable European diplomatic puzzle known as the Schleswig-Holstein Question. Only three people had ever understood it, he said, of whom one was mad, one was dead and the third, Palmerston himself, had forgotten.[452]

Agricultural export subsidies and domestic agricultural support measures are indispensable instruments of agricultural policy of a number of developed-country Members. At the same time, the trade interests and the economic development of many other Members are severely affected by these agricultural subsidies. The economic absurdity of agricultural subsidisation is well illustrated by the following excerpt from *The Economist* on US cotton subsidies:

> The absurdity of America's cotton subsidies is well known. Uncle Sam spends over $4 billion a year propping up cotton farmers, with the bulk of the money going to those whose operations are much larger than Mr Evans's [a family farmer near the west Texas town of Kress]. Cotton receives far more government cash per acre than other crops – in 2001, four or five times that of maize or wheat, according to a recent paper by the National Centre for Policy Analysis, a conservative think-tank. The losers are not just American taxpayers but some of the world's poorest farmers, as America's subsidised production pushes down world prices. Cotton prices have halved since the mid-1990s as America's subsidies have doubled.[453]

Developing countries in particular are seriously harmed by agricultural subsidies. As *The Economist* noted with regard to the EC's sugar subsidies:

> Subsidising sugar producers is not just economically stupid, it is morally indefensible, too. For Europe's subsidies are not merely a quaint way to keep a few farmers in business. They cause so much sugar to be produced that the stuff is exported to poor countries, hurting farmers who might otherwise earn a living by growing it themselves – and perhaps even exporting it to Europe . . . Brazil loses around $500m a year, and Thailand

[452] A. Beattie, 'Doha Negotiators Boxed in by Farm Subsidies', *Financial Times*, 23 July 2006.
[453] 'Cotton, a Tangle of Troubles', *The Economist*, 20 July 2006.

about $151m, even though these two countries are the most efficient sugar producers in the world. Even less efficient, and poorer, African countries lose out. Mozambique will lose $38m in 2004 – as much as it spends on agriculture and rural development. The costs to Ethiopia equal the sums it spends on HIV/AIDS programmes.[454]

According to the *2006 World Trade Report* of the WTO:

the bulk of agricultural domestic support is provided by three Members, the EU, the US and Japan. Between 1995 and 2001 the EU spent an average of USD 96.1 billion, the US spent USD 66.2 billion and Japan USD 41.8 billion. Nevertheless, it did point to a downward trend in rich country farm subsidies.[455]

The particularly sensitive nature of the issue of agricultural subsidies explains why the rules of the *SCM Agreement* do not apply *in full* to agricultural subsidies.[456] The *Agreement on Agriculture* provides for special rules on agricultural subsidies and, in case of conflict, these special rules prevail over the rules of the *SCM Agreement*.[457] This section briefly discusses the special rules of the *Agreement on Agriculture* on:

• agricultural export subsidies; and
• domestic agricultural support measures.

Questions and Assignments 6.36

Do the rules of the *SCM Agreement* apply to agricultural subsidies? In your opinion, should WTO law provide special rules on agricultural subsidies?

6.3.6.1. Agricultural export subsidies

The *SCM Agreement's* prohibition on export subsidies applies to agricultural export subsidies except as provided otherwise in the *Agreement on Agriculture*. In *US – FSC*, the Appellate Body found that the *Agreement on Agriculture* and the *SCM Agreement* use exactly the same words to define 'export subsidies' and that although there are differences between the disciplines established under the two Agreements, those differences do not, according to the Appellate Body, 'affect the common substantive requirements relating to export contingency'.[458] The Appellate Body thus concluded that it is appropriate to apply the interpretation of export contingency adopted under the *SCM Agreement* to the interpretation of export contingency under the *Agreement on Agriculture*.[459]

---

[454] 'Oh, Sweet Reason', *The Economist*, 15 April 2004.
[455] WTO Secretariat, *World Trade Report 2006: Exploring the Links between Subsidies, Trade and the WTO* (WTO, 2006), 135, available at www.wto.org/english/res_e/booksp_e/anrep_e/world_trade_report06_e.pdf, visited on 24 October 2007.   [456] See also above, p. 561.
[457] See Article 21 of the *Agreement on Agriculture*, which states: 'The provisions of GATT 1994 and of other Multilateral Trade Agreements in Annex 1A to the WTO Agreement shall apply subject to the provisions of this Agreement.'
[458] Appellate Body Report, *US – FSC*, para. 141. See also Panel Report, *US – Upland Cotton*, para. 7.754
[459] See Appellate Body Report, *US – FSC*, para. 141. See also Panel Report, *US – Upland Cotton*, para. 7.700.

While export subsidies on non-agricultural products are prohibited, with respect to export subsidies on agricultural products a distinction must be made between export subsidies on:

- agricultural products that are specified in Section II of Part IV of a Member's GATT Schedule of Concessions; and
- agricultural products that are not specified in that section.

With respect to agricultural products *not* specified in the relevant section of their Schedule, Members shall not provide any export subsidies.[460]

With respect to the agricultural products specified in the relevant section of their Schedule, Members have agreed – pursuant to Article 9 of the *Agreement on Agriculture* – to subject all export subsidies, defined in paragraphs (a) to (f) of Article 9(1), to reduction commitments.[461] As set out in the relevant section of their Schedule, developed-country Members agreed to reduce the export subsidies on these products by an average of 36 per cent by value (budgetary outlay) and 21 per cent by volume (subsidised quantities). Developing-country Members agreed to reduce the export subsidies by an average of 24 per cent by value and 14 per cent by volume. Members may *not* provide listed export subsidies *in excess of* the budgetary outlay and quantitative commitment levels specified in their Schedules.[462] Note that the Panel in *EC – Export Subsidies on Sugar* held:

> In the Panel's view, to comply with Article 3.3 of the *Agreement on Agriculture*, a Member that exports a scheduled product must comply with two distinct requirements: (1) its subsidized exports must be within the quantity limitation specified in its schedule; *and* (2) its corresponding budgetary outlays must also be within its commitments. The Panel considers that Article 3.3 (and Article 9.2(b)(iv)) makes it clear that the level of commitment of export subsidies on specified products must be scheduled both in terms of quantity and in terms of budgetary outlays, as the level of reduction of any such export subsidies apply to both their quantity and to their budgetary outlays: 'a Member shall not provide export subsidies . . . in excess of the budgetary outlay *and* quantity commitment levels specified [in its Schedule].'
>
> [Emphasis added][463]

In *Canada – Dairy*, the measure at issue was a government scheme under which the price for milk used in manufacturing dairy products destined for export was set at a lower level than the price for milk destined for domestic consumption. On appeal, the Appellate Body upheld the Panel's finding that Canada acted:

> inconsistently with its obligations under Article 3.3 and Article 8 of the *Agreement on Agriculture* by providing export subsidies as listed in Article 9.1(c) of that Agreement in excess of the quantity commitment levels specified in Canada's Schedule.[464]

Pursuant to Article 10.1 of the *Agreement on Agriculture*, Members shall not apply export subsidies that are not listed in Article 9.1 of the *Agreement on Agriculture* in a

---

[460] See Article 3.3 of the *Agreement on Agriculture*.   [461] *Ibid.*

[462] *Ibid.* See also Article 8 of the *Agreement on Agriculture*, which states that a Member must undertake not to provide export subsidies otherwise than in conformity with the Agreement and with the commitments as specified in that Member's Schedule.   [463] Panel Reports, *EC – Subsidies on Sugar*, para. 7.137.

[464] Appellate Body Report, *Canada – Dairy*, para. 144.

manner which results in or threatens to lead to circumvention of export subsidy commitments. This effectively prohibits any other export subsidies.

Questions and Assignments 6.37

Are agricultural export subsidies prohibited under the *Agreement on Agriculture*?

6.3.6.2. *Domestic agricultural support measures*

With respect to domestic agricultural support measures, Members have agreed – pursuant to Article 6 of the *Agreement on Agriculture* – to reduce the level of support. Under the terms of the *Agreement on Agriculture*, developed-country Members agreed to reduce between 1995 and 2000 their 'aggregate measurement of support', or 'AMS', by 20 per cent.[465] Developing-country Members agreed to reduce their AMS by 13.3 per cent in the period 1995–2004.[466] The commitments of Members on the reduction of domestic agricultural support measures are set out in Part IV of their GATT Schedule of Concessions. Members may *not* provide domestic support *in excess of* the commitment levels specified in their Schedules.[467]

Domestic agricultural support measures that do not have the effect of providing price support to producers are, under certain conditions, exempt from the reduction commitments. These exempted domestic support measures are commonly referred to as 'green box' and 'blue box' measures.[468] 'Green box' measures include support for agricultural research and infrastructure, training and advisory services, domestic food aid and environmental programmes.[469] 'Blue box' subsidies include certain developing-country subsidies designed to encourage agricultural production, certain *de minimis* subsidies, and certain direct payments aimed at limiting agricultural production.[470] The conditions which these subsidies must fulfil to be exempted from the reduction commitments are set out in the *Agreement on Agriculture* in Annex 2 (for 'green box' subsidies) and in Article 6(2), 6(4) and 6(5) (for 'blue box' subsidies).

Questions and Assignments 6.38

What are the obligations of Members with respect to domestic agricultural support measures? What are 'amber box', 'green box' and 'blue box' measures?

---

[465] On the calculation of the AMS, see Annex 3 to the *Agreement on Agriculture*.
[466] See Article 15.2 of the *Agreement on Agriculture*. Least-developed-country Members are not required to undertake reduction commitments. See *ibid.*   [467] See Article 3.2 of the *Agreement on Agriculture*.
[468] Note that domestic support measures that are subject to reduction commitments are commonly referred to as 'amber box' subsidies.
[469] See Annex 2 to the *Agreement on Agriculture*. Article 7 provides that Members must ensure that any 'green box' subsidies are maintained in conformity with the criteria set out in Annex 2, which justify their exemption from reduction commitments.   [470] See Article 6 of the *Agreement on Agriculture*.

6.3.6.3. Note on the 'peace' clause

Until the end of the nine-year implementation period,[471] agricultural export subsidies that conformed fully to the requirements of the *Agreement on Agriculture*, and domestic agricultural support that was within commitment levels and fulfilled certain other conditions, benefited from the 'due restraint' or 'peace' clause of Article 13 of the *Agreement on Agriculture*.[472] Pursuant to Article 13, the consistency of many agricultural subsidies with the *SCM Agreement* could not be challenged. Furthermore, 'green box' subsidies could not be subjected to countervailing duties.

In *US – Upland Cotton*, where Brazil challenged United States' domestic subsidies on cotton during the implementation period in which Article 13 applied, the Appellate Body upheld the Panel's finding that those measures were not entitled to the exemption provided by the peace clause from actions under Article XVI:1 of the GATT 1994 and Articles 5 and 6 of the *SCM Agreement*. This was due to the fact that the US subsidies did not comply with the requirement in Article 13(b)(ii) that non-green box domestic support measures must not 'grant support to a specific commodity in excess of that decided during the 1992 marketing year', if such measures are to enjoy exemption.[473]

Since the end of the implementation period in 2004, however, the 'peace' clause no longer applies. The consistency of agricultural subsidies with the *SCM Agreement* can be challenged and countervailing duties can be imposed on 'green box' subsidies. As mentioned above, in case of conflict between the rules of the *SCM Agreement* and those of the *Agreement on Agriculture*, the rules of the *Agreement on Agriculture* prevail.

6.3.7. Special and differential treatment for developing-country Members

Subsidies can play an important role in the economic development programmes of developing-country Members. Article 27 of the *SCM Agreement* recognises this and provides for some rules and disciplines for developing-country Members that are less strict than the general rules and disciplines.

Pursuant to Article 27, the prohibition on export subsidies under Article 3 of the *SCM Agreement* does not apply to least-developed countries and to countries with a per capita annual income of less than US$1,000.[474] The remedies available

---

[471] This period began in 1995. By virtue of Article 1(i) of the *Agreement on Agriculture*, the term 'year' refers to the calendar, financial or marketing year specified in the Schedule relating to that Member.

[472] With respect to the requirements to be fulfilled for agricultural export subsidies, see Articles 9, 10 and 11 of the *Agreement on Agriculture*; for 'amber box' subsidies, see Article 7 (not in excess of the reduction commitments); for 'green box' subsidies, see Annex 2; and for 'blue box' subsidies, see Article 6.

[473] See Appellate Body Report, *US – Upland Cotton*, paras. 391–4.

[474] See Article 27.2 of the *SCM Agreement*. Note that, until 2003, the prohibition on export subsidies did not apply to the remaining developing-country Members either, albeit that these Members had to phase out their export subsidies progressively. Their export subsidies could not be increased and had to come to an end even before 2003 if their use had become inconsistent with the Member's development needs. See Article 27.4 of the *SCM Agreement* and the Panel and Appellate Body Reports in *Brazil – Aircraft*. The SCM Committee was empowered, under certain conditions and for certain countries, to extend the period of

against these export subsidies are those available against actionable subsidies as set out in Article 7 of the *SCM Agreement*.[475]

Furthermore, certain subsidies which are normally actionable are not actionable when granted by developing-country Members in the context of privatisation programmes. This is the case, for example, for direct forgiveness of debts and subsidies to cover social costs.[476]

With respect to countervailing duties, Article 27.2 of the *SCM Agreement* provides that any countervailing investigation of a product originating in a developing-country Member must be terminated as soon as the investigating authorities determine that:

- the overall level of subsidies granted upon the product in question does not exceed 2 per cent *ad valorem*; or
- the volume of the subsidised imports represents less than 4 per cent of the total imports of the like product of the importing Member.

Note, however, that the latter rule does not apply when the imports from developing-country Members whose individual shares of total imports represent less than 4 per cent, collectively account for more than 9 per cent of the total imports of the like product of the importing Member.[477]

Questions and Assignments 6.39

To what extent does the *SCM Agreement* provide special and differential treatment for developing-country Members?

6.4. SUMMARY

WTO law provides for detailed rules with respect to dumping and subsidisation – two specific practices commonly considered to be unfair trade practices.

'Dumping' is the bringing of a product onto the market of another country at a price less than the normal value of that product. In WTO law, dumping is not prohibited. However, WTO Members are allowed to take measures to protect their domestic industry from the injurious effects of dumping. Pursuant to

---

non-application of the prohibition export subsidies of Article 3 beyond 2003. Accordingly, in 2002, the SCM Committee granted extensions of the transition period for exemption from the prohibition on export subsidies in respect of a number of programmes of twenty-one developing-country Members. These extensions are time limited and programme-specific. They were granted on the basis of Article 27.4, in most cases in conjunction with procedures (G/SCM/39) endorsed by Ministers at the Doha Session of the Ministerial Conference and/or paragraph 10.6 of the *Doha Decision on Implementation Issues* (WT/MIN(01)/17). The SCM Committee granted continuations of some of these extensions in 2003. Note that the prohibition on import substitution subsidies has applied to least-developed-country Members since 2003 and to other developing-country Members since 2000. See Article 27.3 of the *SCM Agreement*.

[475] See above, p. 584
[476] See Article 27.13 of the *SCM Agreement*. Note also the limitation in Article 27.9 of the *SCM Agreement* on remedies for actionable subsidies granted by developing countries.
[477] See Article 27.10 of the *SCM Agreement*.

Article VI of the GATT 1994 and the *Anti-Dumping Agreement*, WTO Members are entitled to impose anti-dumping measures if three conditions are fulfilled.

The first condition for the imposition of an anti-dumping measure is that there is dumping. Dumping is generally determined through a price-to-price comparison of the 'normal value' with the 'export price'. The 'normal value' is the price of the like product in the domestic market of the exporter or producer. Where this price in the exporting country market is not an 'appropriate' normal value, an importing Member may determine the normal value by:

- using the export price to an appropriate third country as the normal value; or
- constructing the normal value.

The export price is ordinarily based on the transaction price at which the producer in the exporting country sells the product to an importer in the importing country. Where the transaction price is not an 'appropriate' export price, the importing Member may calculate, or 'construct', an export price. In order to ensure a fair comparison between the export price and normal value, the *Anti-Dumping Agreement* requires that adjustments be made to either the normal value, the export price or both.

The dumping margin is the difference between the export price and the 'normal value'. The calculation of the dumping margin *generally* requires:

- either the comparison of the weighted average 'normal value' to the weighted average of prices of all comparable export transactions; or
- a transaction-to-transaction comparison of 'normal value' and export price.

However, in particular circumstances, a comparison of the weighted average normal value to export prices in individual transactions may be used.

The second condition for the imposition of an anti-dumping measure is that the domestic industry producing the like product in the importing country must be suffering injury. The *Anti-Dumping Agreement* defines 'injury' to mean one of three things:

- material injury, i.e. genuine injury, to a domestic industry;
- the threat of material injury to a domestic industry; or
- material retardation of the establishment of a domestic industry.

The *Anti-Dumping Agreement* defines the 'domestic industry' generally as 'the domestic producers as a whole of the like products or . . . those of them whose collective output of the products constitutes a major proportion of the total domestic production of those products'. The *Anti-Dumping Agreement* requires that a determination of injury to the domestic industry be based on positive evidence and involve an objective examination of both:

- the volume of dumped imports and the effect of the dumped imports on prices in the domestic market for like products; and
- the consequent impact of these imports on domestic producers of such products.

A determination of a threat of material injury shall be based on facts and not merely on allegation, conjecture or remote possibility. A threat of material injury exists when a change in circumstances, creating a situation in which the dumping would cause injury, is clearly foreseen and imminent.

The third and last condition for the imposition of an anti-dumping measure is that there is a causal link between:

- the dumped imports; and
- the injury to the domestic industry.

According to the *'non-attribution' requirement*, investigating authorities must examine any known factors other than the dumped imports that are injuring the domestic industry at the same time and must not attribute the injury caused by these other factors to the dumped imports.

The *Anti-Dumping Agreement* contains detailed rules on the initiation of an anti-dumping investigation, the process of the investigation (including evidentiary issues) and requirements for public notice. The main objectives of these procedural rules are to ensure that:

- the investigations are conducted in a transparent manner;
- all interested parties have the opportunity to defend their interests; and
- the investigating authorities adequately explain the basis for their determinations.

The *Anti-Dumping Agreement* provides for three kinds of anti-dumping measure:

- provisional anti-dumping measures;
- price undertakings; and
- definitive anti-dumping duties.

To apply a provisional anti-dumping measure, investigating authorities must make a *preliminary* affirmative determination of dumping, injury and causation. Furthermore, the investigating authorities must judge that such a measure is *necessary* to prevent injury being caused during the investigation.

The *Anti-Dumping Agreement* provides for an alternative to the imposition of anti-dumping duties, by affording exporters the possibility to offer, and investigating authorities the possibility to accept, price undertakings. These voluntary undertakings to revise prices or cease exports at the dumped price may be entered into only after the investigating authorities have made an affirmative preliminary determination of dumping, injury and causation.

Where a final determination is made of the existence of dumping, injury and causation, a final anti-dumping duty may be imposed. The amount of the anti-dumping duty *may not exceed* the dumping margin, although it may be a lesser amount. Members are required to collect duties, on a *non-discriminatory* basis, on imports from all sources found to be dumped and causing injury. When anti-dumping duties are imposed, the investigating authorities must, in principle, calculate a dumping margin for each exporter. However, the *Anti-Dumping Agreement* recognises that this may not always be possible. When it is not possible to calculate a dumping margin for each exporter, the investigating authorities may limit the number of exporters considered individually. The anti-dumping duty imposed on uninvestigated exporters is based on the weighted average dumping margin actually established for investigated exporters.

An anti-dumping duty shall remain in force only as long as and to the extent necessary to counteract dumping which is causing injury. The need for the continued imposition of an anti-dumping duty must be periodically reviewed by the competent authorities, where warranted, on their own initiative or upon a request by any interested party. In any case, any definitive anti-dumping duty shall be *terminated* at a date not later than *five years* from its imposition, *unless* the authorities determine – in the context of a sunset review – that the expiry of the duty 'would be likely to lead to continuation or recurrence of dumping and injury'.

As with many other WTO agreements, the *Anti-Dumping Agreement* contains a provision relating to special and differential treatment for developing-country Members. Article 15 of the *Anti-Dumping Agreement* requires developed-country Members to explore 'possibilities of constructive remedies' provided for by the *Anti-Dumping Agreement* before applying anti-dumping duties, where such duties would affect the essential interests of developing-country Members.

In addition to rules on dumping, WTO law also includes rules on subsidies and subsidised trade. The *SCM Agreement* defines a subsidy as a financial contribution by a government or public body which confers a benefit. Both the *SCM Agreement* and the case law work out and clarify each element of this definition. Furthermore, the *SCM Agreement* provides that the WTO rules on subsidies and subsidised trade only apply to 'specific' subsidies.

Article XVI of the GATT 1994 and Parts II, III and IV of the *SCM Agreement* concern the WTO treatment of subsidies. The WTO treatment of subsidies is different from the treatment of dumping. Under WTO law, certain subsidies are prohibited and many other subsidies may be challenged as WTO-inconsistent when they cause adverse effects to the interests of other Members. Article VI of the GATT 1994 and Part V of the *SCM Agreement* concern the manner in which WTO Members may respond to subsidised trade which causes injury to the domestic industry. Members may, in these situations, impose countervailing duties on the subsidised imports to offset, i.e. to cancel out, the subsidisation.

The *SCM Agreement* distinguishes between prohibited subsidies and actionable subsidies. The prohibited subsidies are:

- export subsidies; and
- import substitution subsidies.

Export subsidies are subsidies contingent upon export performance. Annex I of the *SCM Agreement* contains an 'Illustrative List of Export Subsidies'. Import substitution subsidies are subsidies contingent upon the use of domestic over imported goods. Both export subsidies and import substitution subsidies are prohibited regardless of whether the subsidy is contingent *de jure* or *de facto* upon exportation or the use of domestic over imported goods.

The rules applicable to consultations and adjudication concerning allegedly prohibited subsidies are primarily those of the DSU. However, the timeframes under Article 4 of the *Anti-Dumping Agreement* are half as long as the timeframes provided for under the DSU. Moreover, if a panel finds a measure to be a prohibited subsidy, that subsidy must be withdrawn, i.e. removed, without delay. If a recommendation for withdrawal is not followed within the time period set by the panel, the DSB must, upon the request of the original complainant(s) and by reverse consensus, authorise 'appropriate countermeasures'.

Unlike export subsidies and import substitution subsidies, most subsidies are not prohibited but are 'actionable', i.e. they are subject to challenge in the event that they cause adverse effects to the interests of another Member. There are three types of 'adverse effect' to the interests of other Members:

- *injury* to the domestic industry of another Member;
- *nullification or impairment* of benefits accruing directly or indirectly to other Members under the GATT 1994; and
- *serious prejudice*, including a threat thereof, to the interests of another Member.

The concept of 'injury' to a domestic industry covers:

- material injury, i.e. genuine injury, to a domestic industry;
- a threat of material injury to a domestic industry; and
- material retardation of the establishment of a domestic industry.

The definition of 'domestic industry' in the *SCM Agreement* is quite similar to the definition of this concept in the *Anti-Dumping Agreement*. There is also a high degree of similarity between the concepts of 'material injury' and the 'threat of material injury' in the *Anti-Dumping Agreement* and the *SCM Agreement*. Note that it must be demonstrated that the subsidised imports are causing injury to the domestic industry (the 'causal link' requirement) and that injury caused by other factors may not be attributed to the subsidised imports (the 'non-attribution' requirement).

The adverse effects of subsidies on the interests of other Members can also take the form of 'serious prejudice'. 'Serious prejudice' *may arise* where a subsidy has one or more of the effects described in the *SCM Agreement*, including the impediment of imports of another Member into the market of the subsidising Member or the significant price undercutting by the subsidised product in comparison to the like product of another Member in the same market. If a complaining Member can show that a subsidy has any of the effects listed in the *SCM Agreement*, serious prejudice may be found to exist. Note that the concept of 'serious prejudice' includes a 'threat of serious prejudice', i.e. a situation in which the serious prejudice is imminent.

As is the case with multilateral remedies for prohibited subsidies, the multilateral remedies for actionable subsidies are principally, but not entirely, the remedies for breach of WTO law provided for in the DSU. If a panel concludes that a subsidy causes adverse effects to the interests of another Member (be it injury, nullification or impairment, or serious prejudice), the subsidising Member must take appropriate steps to remove the adverse effect or withdraw the subsidy. The subsidising Member must do so within six months from the adoption of the report by the DSB. Instead of withdrawing the subsidy at issue or removing its adverse effects, the subsidising Member can also agree with the complaining Member on compensation. If within six months from the adoption of the report, the subsidy is not withdrawn, its adverse effects are not removed or no agreement on compensation is reached, the DSB shall, at the request of the complaining Member and by reverse consensus, grant authorisation to the complaining Member to take countermeasures commensurate with the degree and nature of the adverse effects of the subsidy.

Prohibited and actionable subsidies which cause injury to the domestic industry not only can be challenged multilaterally but also can be offset by the application of a countervailing duty. WTO Members may impose countervailing duties when three conditions are fulfilled:

- there are *subsidised imports*, i.e. imports of products from producers who benefited from specific subsidies;
- there is *injury* to the domestic industry; and
- there is a *causal link* between the subsidised imports and the injury to the domestic industry *and* injury caused by other factors is *not attributed* to the subsidised imports.

The *SCM Agreement* provides for detailed procedural requirements regarding the initiation and conduct of a countervailing investigation by the competent authorities of the Member imposing the countervailing duties on the subsidised imports. Note that the procedural requirements for countervailing investigations set out in the *SCM Agreement* are largely the same as the procedural requirements for anti-dumping investigations set out in the *Anti-Dumping Agreement*. The main objectives of these requirements are also the same.

The *SCM Agreement* provides for three types of countervailing measure:

- provisional countervailing measures;
- voluntary undertakings; and
- definitive countervailing duties.

After making a preliminary determination that a subsidy is causing or threatening to cause injury to a domestic industry, an importing Member can impose *provisional countervailing measures* on the subsidised imports. Investigations may be suspended or terminated without the imposition of provisional measures or countervailing duties upon receipt of satisfactory *voluntary undertakings* under which:

- the government of the exporting Member agrees to eliminate or limit the subsidy or take other measures concerning its effects; or
- the exporter agrees to revise its prices so that the investigating authorities are satisfied that the injurious effect of the subsidy is eliminated.

Members may impose *definitive countervailing duties* only after making a final determination that a countervailable subsidy exists; and that the subsidy causes, or threatens to cause, injury to the domestic industry. The amount of a countervailing duty must never exceed the amount of the subsidy. Moreover, if the amount of the injury caused is less than the amount of the subsidy, the definitive countervailing duty should preferably be limited to the amount necessary to counteract the injury caused.

Countervailing duties must be collected on a non-discriminatory basis. Note that any exporter whose exports are subject to a definitive countervailing duty but who was not actually investigated is entitled to an expedited review so that the investigating authorities promptly establish an individual countervailing duty rate for that exporter.

Countervailing duties may not be applied retroactively, except in certain specific circumstances.

A countervailing duty shall remain in force only as long as and to the extent necessary to counteract subsidisation which is causing injury. Upon their own initiative or upon a request from an interested party, the investigating authorities shall review the need for the continued imposition of the duty. All definitive countervailing duties must be terminated, at the latest, five years after their imposition or the latest review. However, where the investigating authorities determine – in the context of a sunset review – that the expiry of the countervailing duty would be likely to lead to a continuation or recurrence of subsidisation and injury, the duty will not be terminated.

Note that countervailing duties and countermeasures cannot be applied simultaneously with regard to the same instance of subsidisation.

The *Agreement on Agriculture* provides for special rules on agricultural export subsidies and domestic agricultural support measures. In case of conflict, these special rules prevail over the rules of the *SCM Agreement*. Export subsidies on agricultural products not specified in Section II of Part IV of a Member's GATT Schedule of Concessions are prohibited under the terms of the *Agreement on Agriculture*. Export subsidies on agricultural products specified in Section II of Part IV of a Member's GATT Schedule of Concessions and listed in Article 9(1) of the *Agreement on Agriculture* are not prohibited but are subject to reduction commitments. Members may *not* provide these export subsidies *in excess of* the budgetary outlay and quantitative commitment levels specified in the Schedule. Also with respect to domestic agricultural support measures, Members have agreed to reduce the level of support. Members may *not* provide domestic support *in excess of* the commitment levels specified in their Schedules. However, domestic agricultural support measures that do not have the effect of providing price support to producers (i.e. 'green box' and 'blue box' subsidies) are exempt from the reduction commitments.

Subsidies can play an important role in the economic development programmes of developing-country Members. Article 27 of the *SCM Agreement*, therefore, provides some rules and disciplines for developing-country Members that are less strict than the general rules on subsidies of the *SCM Agreement*.

6.5. EXERCISE: DIRTY PLAY, BUT BY WHOM?

Newland has three important manufacturers of furniture, AEKI, Schoeder and StyleMark. Together, they represent 70 per cent of the domestic furniture industry. Many small manufacturers make up the rest of the industry. Over the last few years, all manufacturers of furniture in Newland have been exporting an ever increasing part of their production to Richland, as the trendy but cheap furniture from Newland is quite popular with consumers in Richland.

The furniture industry in Richland is not happy with this development. The market share of the domestic furniture manufacturers has steadily decreased over recent years and many of the smaller manufacturers are going out of business. The six major furniture manufacturers, which together represent about 49 per cent of total furniture production in Richland, want to take action against the imports of furniture from Newland. They want the government of Richland to impose anti-dumping and/or countervailing duties on the furniture imported from Newland or to take any other action that would reduce the flow of furniture from Newland. They are convinced that the furniture from Newland is sold on the market of Richland at prices far below the cost of production. They claim that this is the case in particular for bedroom furniture produced by AEKI and StyleMark. They also note that the furniture manufacturers of Newland get electricity from the state-owned Newland Power Corporation at preferential rates. In addition, the small furniture manufacturers of Newland get a significant tax rebate if they hire a number of unemployed workers each year. Small manufacturers can also get technical advice and financial support from the Export Promotion Board of Newland, a government agency, to market their furniture abroad.

Alarmed by reports in the *Financial Times* on the calls of the Richland furniture industry for action against imports of furniture from Newland, the Government of Newland turns to the Advisory Centre on WTO Law (ACWL) for legal advice on whether, and under what conditions, Richland may, consistent with WTO law:

- impose anti-dumping duties;
- impose countervailing duties; or
- take any other action (in particular against the alleged subsidies).

Newland also wants to know what procedures WTO law prescribes for the imposition of anti-dumping or countervailing duties.

Should Richland be allowed to impose such duties, Newland wants to know:

- whether duties may be imposed on all furniture imported from Newland;
- the maximum level of duties that may be applied; and
- the maximum length of time duties may be imposed.

The Executive Director of the ACWL has instructed you, a junior lawyer at the Centre, to prepare a presentation for a group of Newland trade officials and representatives of the Newland furniture industry addressing the concerns and queries put forward by the Government of Newland. Because of budgetary constraints you should not spend more than five hours on this assignment.

7

Trade liberalisation versus other societal values and interests

Contents

7.1. INTRODUCTION

The promotion and protection of public health, consumer safety, the environ-ment, employment, economic development and national security are *core* tasks of governments. Often, trade liberalisation and the resulting availability of better and cheaper products and services facilitate the promotion and protec-tion of these and other societal values and interests. Through trade, environ-mentally friendly products or life-saving medicines, that would not be available otherwise, become available to consumers and patients respectively. At a more general level, trade generates the degree of economic activity and economic welfare indispensable for the effective promotion and protection of the societal values and interests referred to above.

In order to protect and promote these societal values and interests, however, governments also frequently adopt legislation or take measures that inadver-tently or deliberately constitute barriers to trade. Members are often politically and/or economically 'compelled' to adopt legislation or measures which are inconsistent with rules of WTO law and, in particular, with the principles of non-discrimination and the rules on market access discussed in chapters 4 and 5. Trade liberalisation, and its principles of non-discrimination and rules on market access, often conflicts with other important societal values and interests. Therefore, WTO law provides for a set of rules to reconcile trade liberalisation with other societal values and interests. As the Sutherland Report noted:

> Neither the WTO nor the GATT was ever an unrestrained free trade charter. In fact, both were and are intended to provide a structured and functionally effective way to harness the value of open trade to principle and fairness. In so doing they offer the security and predictability of market access advantages that are sought by traders and investors. But the rules provide checks and balances including mechanisms that reflect political realism as well as free trade doctrine. It is not that the WTO disallows market protection, only that it sets some strict disciplines under which governments may choose to respond to special interests.[1]
>
> [Emphasis omitted]

This chapter addresses the wide-ranging *exceptions* to the basic WTO rules, allowing Members to adopt trade-restrictive legislation and measures that

---

[1] Report by the Consultative Board to the Director-General Supachai Panitchpakdi, *The Future of the WTO: Addressing Institutional Challenges in the New Millennium* (the 'Sutherland Report') (WTO, 2004), para. 39.

pursue the promotion and protection of other societal values and interests. This chapter deals with:

- the 'general exceptions' of Article XX of the GATT 1994 and Article XIV of the GATS;
- the 'security exceptions' of Article XXI of the GATT 1994 and Article XIV *bis* of the GATS;
- the 'economic emergency exceptions' of Article XIX of the GATT 1994 and the *Agreement on Safeguards*;
- the 'regional integration exceptions' of Article XXIV of the GATT 1994 and Article V of the GATS;
- the 'balance of payments exceptions' of Articles XII and XVIII:B of the GATT 1994 and Article XII of the GATS; and
- the 'economic development exceptions' of Article XVIII:A of the GATT 1994 and the 'Enabling Clause'.

These exceptions differ in scope and nature. Some allow deviation from all other GATT or GATS obligations; others allow deviation from specific obligations only; some are of indefinite duration; others temporary; some can be invoked by all Members; others only by a specific category of Members. However, while different in scope and nature, all the exceptions have something in common: they allow Members, under specific conditions, to adopt and maintain legislation and measures that promote or protect other important societal values and interests, even though this legislation or these measures are inconsistent with substantive disciplines imposed by the GATT 1994 or the GATS. These exceptions clearly allow Members, under specific conditions, to give *priority* to certain societal values and interests over trade liberalisation.

7.2. GENERAL EXCEPTIONS UNDER THE GATT 1994

Article XX of the GATT 1994, entitled 'General Exceptions', states:

> Subject to the requirement that such measures are not applied in a manner which would constitute a means of arbitrary or unjustifiable discrimination between countries where the same conditions prevail, or a disguised restriction on international trade, nothing in this Agreement shall be construed to prevent the adoption or enforcement by any [Member] of measures:
>
> a. necessary to protect public morals;
> b. necessary to protect human, animal or plant life or health;
> c. . . .
> d. necessary to secure compliance with laws or regulations which are not inconsistent with the provisions of this Agreement, including those relating to customs enforcement, the enforcement of monopolies operated under paragraph 4 of Article II and Article XVII, the protection of patents, trade marks and copyrights, and the prevention of deceptive practices;
> e. relating to the products of prison labour;
> f. imposed for the protection of national treasures of artistic, historic or archaeological value;

> g. relating to the conservation of exhaustible natural resources if such measures are made effective in conjunction with restrictions on domestic production or consumption; . . .

Thus, Article XX allows for, *inter alia*, the protection of some important non-economic societal values, such as public health and the environment. Note that paragraphs (c), (h), (i) and (j) are not included above. These paragraphs relate to trade in gold and silver; obligations under international commodities agreements; efforts to ensure essential quantities of materials to a domestic processing industry; and products in general or local short supply. These paragraphs have been, and still are, of less importance in international trade law and practice than the other paragraphs of Article XX. Therefore, they are not discussed in this chapter.

7.2.1. The nature and function of Article XX of the GATT 1994

The Panel in *US – Section 337* noted, with respect to the nature and function of Article XX:

> that Article XX is entitled 'General Exceptions' and that the central phrase in the introductory clause reads: 'nothing in this Agreement shall be construed to prevent the adoption or enforcement . . . of measures . . .'. Article XX(d) thus provides for a limited and conditional exception from obligations under other provisions. The Panel therefore concluded that Article XX(d) applies only to measures inconsistent with another provision of the General Agreement, and that, consequently, the application of Section 337 has to be examined first in the light of Article III:4. If any inconsistencies with Article III:4 were found, the Panel would then examine whether they could be justified under Article XX(d).[2]

In general, Article XX is relevant and will be invoked by a Member only when a measure of that Member has been found to be inconsistent with another GATT provision. In such a case, Article XX will be invoked to justify the GATT-inconsistent measure. As the Panel in *US – Section 337* noted, the central phrase in the first sentence of Article XX is that 'nothing in this Agreement shall be construed to prevent the adoption or enforcement by any Member of measures . . .'. Measures satisfying the conditions set out in Article XX are thus permitted, even if they are inconsistent with other provisions of the GATT 1994. As noted by the Panel in *US – Section 337*, Article XX provides, however, for *limited and conditional exceptions* from obligations under other GATT provisions. The exceptions are 'limited' as the list of exceptions in Article XX is exhaustive. The exceptions are 'conditional' in that Article XX only provides for justification of an otherwise illegal measure when the conditions set out in Article XX – and discussed in detail below – are fulfilled. While Article XX allows Members to adopt or maintain measures promoting or protecting other important societal values, it provides an exception to, or limitation of, affirmative commitments under the GATT 1994. In this light, it is not surprising that Article XX has played a central role in many GATT and WTO disputes.

---

[2] GATT Panel Report, *US – Section 337*, para. 5.9.

While it could be argued that it is an accepted principle of interpretation that exceptions are to be construed narrowly (*singularia non sunt extendenda*) and that Article XX should, therefore, be construed narrowly, the Appellate Body has not adopted this approach. Instead, it has advocated in *US – Gasoline* and *US – Shrimp* a kind of balancing between the general rule and the exception. It stated, with regard to Article XX(g), the exception at issue in these cases:

> The context of Article XX(g) includes the provisions of the rest of the *General Agreement*, including in particular Articles I, III and XI; conversely, the context of Articles I and III and XI includes Article XX. Accordingly, the phrase 'relating to the conservation of exhaustible natural resources' may not be read so expansively as seriously to subvert the purpose and object of Article III:4. Nor may Article III:4 be given so broad a reach as effectively to emasculate Article XX(g) and the policies and interests it embodies. The relationship between the affirmative commitments set out in, e.g. Articles I, III and XI, and the policies and interests embodied in the 'General Exceptions' listed in Article XX, can be given meaning within the framework of the *General Agreement* and its object and purpose by a treaty interpreter only on a case-to-case basis, by careful scrutiny of the factual and legal context in a given dispute, without disregarding the words actually used by the WTO Members themselves to express their intent and purpose.[3]

Clearly, therefore, the Appellate Body considers a *narrow* interpretation of the exceptions of Article XX, i.e. the exceptions allowing for, *inter alia*, trade-restrictive measures to protect public health or the environment, to be inappropriate. The Appellate Body advocates a *balance* between trade liberalisation and other societal values.

With regard to the kind of measure that can be justified under Article XX, the Panel in *US – Shrimp* ruled that Article XX could not justify measures that 'undermine the WTO multilateral trading system',[4] and that a measure of a Member 'conditioning access to its market for a given product upon the adoption by the exporting Member of certain policies' would undermine the multilateral trading system.[5] On appeal, however, the Appellate Body categorically rejected this ruling by the Panel on the scope of measures that Article XX could justify. The Appellate Body held:

> conditioning access to a Member's domestic market on whether exporting Members comply with, or adopt, a policy or policies unilaterally prescribed by the importing Member may, to some degree, be a common aspect of measures falling within the scope of one or another of the exceptions (a) to (j) of Article XX. Paragraphs (a) to (j) comprise measures that are recognized as *exceptions to substantive obligations* established in the GATT 1994, because the domestic policies embodied in such measures have been recognized as important and legitimate in character. It is not necessary to assume that requiring from exporting countries compliance with, or adoption of, certain policies (although covered in principle by one or another of the exceptions) prescribed by the importing country, renders a measure *a priori* incapable of justification under Article XX. Such an interpretation renders most, if not all, of the specific exceptions of Article XX inutile, a result abhorrent to the principles of interpretation we are bound to apply.[6]

---

[3] Appellate Body Report, *US – Gasoline*, 16–17.   [4] Panel Report, *US – Shrimp*, para. 7.44.
[5] *Ibid.*, para. 7.45.   [6] Appellate Body Report, *US – Shrimp*, para. 121.

Measures requiring that exporting countries comply with, or adopt, certain policies prescribed by the importing country are, in fact, typical of the measures that Article XX *can* justify. They are definitely not *a priori* excluded from the scope of Article XX.

To date, the Appellate Body has yet to rule whether measures that protect, or purport to protect, a societal value or interest outside the territorial jurisdiction of the Member taking the measure, can be justified under Article XX. There is no *explicit* jurisdictional limitation in Article XX. However, the question is whether there is an *implied* jurisdictional limitation, in that Article XX cannot be invoked to protect non-economic values *outside* the territorial jurisdiction of the Member concerned. In *US – Shrimp*, a case involving an import ban on shrimp harvested through methods resulting in the incidental killing of sea turtles, the Appellate Body noted that sea turtles migrate to or traverse waters subject to the jurisdiction of the United States, and subsequently stated:

> We do not pass upon the question of whether there is an implied jurisdictional limitation in Article XX(g), and if so, the nature or extent of that limitation. We note only that in the specific circumstances of the case before us, there is a sufficient nexus between the migratory and endangered marine populations involved and the United States for purposes of Article XX(g).[7]

While the position of the Appellate Body on the use of Article XX of the GATT 1994 for the protection or promotion of a societal value or interest *outside* the territorial jurisdiction of the Member taking the otherwise GATT-inconsistent measure is still undetermined, the Panel in *EC – Tariff Preferences* found that:

> the policy reflected in the Drug Arrangements is not one designed for the purpose of protecting human life or health *in the European Communities* and, therefore, the Drug Arrangements are not a measure for the purpose of protecting human life or health under Article XX(b) of GATT 1994.[8]
>
> [Emphasis added]

This issue of the territorial scope of application of Article XX of the GATT 1994 awaits clarification by the Appellate Body.

Questions and Assignments 7.1

When can a Member invoke Article XX of the GATT 1994? Which societal values are covered by Article XX? Give at least two examples of non-economic, societal values that are not explicitly referred to in Article XX. Does Article XX provide for an exhaustive list of grounds of exception? If so, what are the advantages and the disadvantages of such a closed-list approach? What did the Appellate Body rule in *US – Shrimp* regarding the kinds of measure that may be justified under Article XX? Are measures aimed at protecting societal values outside the territorial jurisdiction of the Member taking the measure, within the scope of application of Article XX?

---

[7] *Ibid.*, para. 133.   [8] Panel Report, *EC – Tariff Preferences*, para. 7.210.

7.2.2. The two-tier test under Article XX of the GATT 1994

Article XX sets out a two-tier test for determining whether a measure, other-wise inconsistent with GATT obligations, can be justified. In *US – Gasoline*, the Appellate Body stated:

> In order that the justifying protection of Article XX may be extended to it, the measure at issue must not only come under one or another of the particular exceptions – paragraphs (a) to (j) – listed under Article XX; it must also satisfy the requirements imposed by the opening clauses of Article XX. The analysis is, in other words, two-tiered: first, provisional justification by reason of characterization of the measure under Article XX(g); second, further appraisal of the same measure under the introductory clauses of Article XX.[9]

Thus, for a GATT-inconsistent measure to be justified under Article XX, it must meet:

- the requirements of one of the exceptions listed in paragraphs (a) to (j) of Article XX; *and*
- the requirements of the introductory clause, commonly referred to as the 'chapeau', of Article XX.

In *US – Shrimp*, the Appellate Body clarified the relationship between these two elements of the Article XX test, and therefore the order in which they must be analysed, as follows:

> The sequence of steps indicated above in the analysis of a claim of justification under Article XX reflects, not inadvertence or random choice, but rather the fundamental struc-ture and logic of Article XX . . . The task of interpreting the chapeau so as to prevent the abuse or misuse of the specific exemptions provided for in Article XX is rendered very difficult, if indeed it remains possible at all, where the interpreter (like the Panel in this case) has not first identified and examined the specific exception threatened with abuse.[10]

In examining whether a measure can be justified under Article XX, one must always examine, first, whether this measure can be provisionally justified under one of the specific exceptions listed in paragraphs (a) to (j) of Article XX and, if so, whether the application of this measure meets the requirements of the chapeau of Article XX. Hence, an analysis under Article XX first focuses on the measure at issue itself and then on the application of that measure. This distinction between the two elements of the Article XX test is well illustrated by the Panel in *Brazil – Retreaded Tyres*:

> [In its analysis under Article XX(b)] [t]he Panel will *not* . . . examine . . . the manner in which the measure is implemented *in practice*, including any elements extraneous to the measure itself that could affect its ability to perform its function . . ., or consider situa-tions in which the ban does *not* apply . . . These elements will, however, be relevant to later parts of the Panel's assessment, especially under the chapeau of Article XX, where the focus will be, by contrast, primarily on the manner in which the measure is applied.[11]
>
> [Emphasis added]

---

[9] Appellate Body Report, *US – Gasoline*, 20. See also Appellate Body Report, *Brazil – Retreaded Tyres*, para. 139.
[10] Appellate Body Report, *US – Shrimp*, paras. 119–20.   [11] Panel Report, *Brazil – Retreaded Tyres*, para. 7.107.

The following paragraphs will first discuss the specific exceptions and their requirements provided for in paragraphs (a) to (j) of Article XX before analysing the requirements of the chapeau of Article XX.

Questions and Assignments 7.2

What are the main elements of the Article XX test? Does the sequence in which these elements of the Article XX test are examined matter?

7.2.3. Specific exceptions under Article XX of the GATT 1994

Article XX sets out, in paragraphs (a) to (j), specific grounds of justification for measures which are otherwise inconsistent with provisions of the GATT 1994. These grounds of justification relate, *inter alia*, to the protection of economic and non-economic societal values such as human, animal or plant life or health, exhaustible natural resources, national treasures of artistic, historic or archaeological value and public morals.[12] Comparing the terms used in the different paragraphs of Article XX, the Appellate Body stated in *US – Gasoline*:

> In enumerating the various categories of governmental acts, laws or regulations which WTO Members may carry out or promulgate in pursuit of differing legitimate state policies or interests outside the realm of trade liberalization, Article XX uses different terms in respect of different categories: 'necessary' – in paragraphs (a), (b) and (d); 'essential' – in paragraph (j); 'relating to' – in paragraphs (c), (e) and (g); 'for the protection of' – in paragraph (f); 'in pursuance of' – in paragraph (h); and 'involving' – in paragraph (i).
>
> It does not seem reasonable to suppose that the WTO Members intended to require, in respect of each and every category, the same kind or degree of connection or relationship between the measure under appraisal and the state interest or policy sought to be promoted or realized.[13]

Thus, the paragraphs of Article XX contain different requirements regarding the relationship between the measure at issue and the societal value pursued. Some measures need to be 'necessary' for the protection or promotion of the societal value they pursue (e.g. the protection of life and health of humans, animals and plants), while for other measures it suffices that they 'relate to' the societal value they pursue (e.g. the conservation of exhaustible natural resources). Therefore the grounds of justification, and the accompanying requirements provided for in Article XX, will be examined separately.

7.2.3.1. Article XX(b): 'measures necessary to protect human, animal or plant life or health'

Article XX(b) concerns measures which are 'necessary to protect human, animal or plant life or health'. It sets out a two-tier test to determine whether a measure

---

[12] As noted above, the list of grounds of justification contained in Article XX of the GATT 1994 is exhaustive. See above, p. 617.   [13] Appellate Body Report, *US – Gasoline*, 16.

is *provisionally* justified under this provision. The Panel in *US – Gasoline* held that a GATT-inconsistent measure is provisionally justified under Article XX(b) if:

- the measure is designed to protect life or health of humans, animals or plants (meaning that the policy objective pursued by the measure is the protection of life or health); and
- the measure is necessary to fulfil that policy objective.[14]

The first element of this test under Article XX(b) is relatively easy to apply and has not given rise to major interpretative problems. In *Thailand – Cigarettes*, for example, the Panel ruled with regard to this element of the test under Article XX(b) that it:

> accepted that smoking constituted a serious risk to human health and that consequently measures designed to reduce the consumption of cigarettes fell within the scope of Article XX(b).[15]

In *EC – Tariff Preferences*, the European Communities sought to justify under Article XX(b) its additional tariff preferences under the Drug Arrangements of the EC Generalized System of Preferences by arguing that:

> narcotic drugs pose a risk to human life and health in the European Communities and that tariff preferences contribute to the protection of human life and health by supporting the measures taken by other countries against the illicit production and trafficking of those substances, thereby reducing their supply to the European Communities.[16]

In its examination of whether the additional tariff preferences of the Drug Arrangements are designed to achieve the stated health objectives, the Panel noted that it needed to consider not only the express provisions of the legislation or measures at issue, but also the design, architecture and structure of this legislation or measures.[17] As already noted above, the Panel in *EC –Tariff Preferences* came to the conclusion that:

> the policy reflected in the Drug Arrangements is not one designed for the purpose of protecting human life or health in the European Communities and, therefore, the Drug Arrangements are not a measure for the purpose of protecting human life or health under Article XX(b) of GATT 1994.[18]

In *Brazil – Retreaded Tyres*, Brazil submitted with regard to its import ban on retreaded tyres that:

> the accumulation of waste tyres creates a risk of mosquito-borne diseases such as dengue and yellow fever . . . because waste tyres create perfect breeding grounds for disease carrying mosquitoes and that these diseases are also spread through interstate transportation of waste tyres for disposal operations . . . [The] accumulation of waste tyres [also] creates a risk of tyre fires and toxic leaching . . .

---

[14] See Panel Report, *US – Gasoline*, para. 6.20. For a more recent application of this test, see Panel Report, *EC – Tariff preferences*, paras. 7.179 and 7.199, and Panel Report, *Brazil – Retreaded Tyres*, paras 7.40–7.41.

[15] GATT Panel Report, *Thailand – Cigarettes*, para. 73.   [16] Panel Report, *EC – Tariff Preferences*, para. 7.180.

[17] See *ibid.*, para. 7.200. In support of this approach, the Panel referred to Appellate Body Report, *Japan – Alcoholic Beverages II*, 29 (relating to Article III:2 of the GATT 1994; see above, p. 366); and Appellate Body Report, *US – Shrimp*, para. 137 (relating to Article XX(g) of the GATT 1994; see below, p. 637).

[18] Panel Report, *EC – Tariff Preferences*, para. 7.210.

> . . . mosquito-borne diseases also pose health risks to animals. Numerous toxic chemi-
> cals and heavy metals contained in pyrolytic oil released from tyre fires harm animal and
> plant life and health, and hazardous substances contained in toxic plumes emitted from
> tyre fires harm not only humans but also animals.[19]

The Panel accepted Brazil's arguments and concluded that:

> Brazil's policy of reducing exposure to the risks to human, animal or plant life or health
> arising from the accumulation of waste tyres falls within the range of policies covered by
> Article XX(b).[20]

As Article XX(b) covers measures designed for the protection of 'human, animal
or plant life or health', it covers public health policy measures as well as environmental policy measures. However, as the Panel noted in *Brazil – Retreaded Tyres*, a
party invoking environmental policy measures under Article XX(b) 'has to establish the existence not just of risks to "the environment" generally, but specifically
of risks to animal or plant life or health'.[21] Not all environmental policy measures
fall within the scope of application of Article XX(b) of the GATT 1994.[22]

The second element of the test under Article XX(b), the 'necessity' requirement, is more problematic than the first element. In *Thailand – Cigarettes*, the
Panel examined whether Thailand's import prohibition of cigarettes – inconsistent with Article XI of the GATT 1947 – was justified under Article XX(b), and
ruled as follows:

> The Panel noted that this provision clearly allowed contracting parties to give priority to
> human health over trade liberalization; however, for a measure to be covered by Article XX(b)
> it had to be 'necessary'.
>
> The Panel concluded . . . that the import restrictions imposed by Thailand could be consid-
> ered to be 'necessary' in terms of Article XX(b) only if there were no alternative measure con-
> sistent with the General Agreement, or less inconsistent with it, which Thailand could
> reasonably be expected to employ to achieve its health policy objectives.[23]

The principal health objectives advanced by Thailand to justify its import restrictions on cigarettes were twofold: first, to ensure the quality of cigarettes so as to
protect the public from harmful ingredients in imported cigarettes; and, secondly, to reduce the consumption of cigarettes in Thailand. Applying its 'necessity' test defined above, the Panel in *Thailand – Cigarettes* therefore examined:

> whether the Thai concerns about the *quality* of cigarettes consumed in Thailand could be
> met with measures consistent, or less inconsistent, with the General Agreement. It noted
> that other countries had introduced strict, non-discriminatory labelling and ingredient dis-
> closure regulations which allowed governments to control, and the public to be informed
> of, the content of cigarettes. A non-discriminatory regulation implemented on a national
> treatment basis in accordance with Article III:4 requiring complete disclosure of ingredi-
> ents, coupled with a ban on unhealthy substances, would be an alternative consistent with
> the General Agreement. The Panel considered that Thailand could reasonably be expected

---

[19] Panel Report, *Brazil – Retreaded Tyres*, paras. 7.53 and 7.84.   [20] *Ibid.*, para. 7.102. This issue was not
appealed.   [21] *Ibid.*, para. 7.46.
[22] Note that Article XX(g) of the GATT 1994 is concerned with measures relating to the conservation of
exhaustible natural resources. See below, p. 634.
[23] GATT Panel Report, *Thailand – Cigarettes*, paras. 73 and 75.

> to take such measures to address the quality-related policy objectives it now pursues through an import ban on all cigarettes whatever their ingredients.[24]

With regard to the second health objective of the import restriction at issue, namely, the reduction of the consumption of cigarettes:

> The Panel then considered whether Thai concerns about the *quantity* of cigarettes consumed in Thailand could be met by measures reasonably available to it and consistent, or less inconsistent, with the General Agreement . . .
> . . . A ban on the advertisement of cigarettes of both domestic and foreign origin would normally meet the requirements of Article III:4 [or] . . . would have to be regarded as unavoidable and therefore necessary within the meaning of Article XX(b) because additional advertising rights would risk stimulating demand for cigarettes.[25]

The Panel in *Thailand – Cigarettes* thus came to the conclusion that there were in fact various measures consistent with the GATT which were reasonably available to Thailand to control the quality and quantity of cigarettes smoked and which, taken together, could achieve the health policy goals pursued by the Thai government. The import restrictions on cigarettes were therefore not 'necessary' within the meaning of Article XX(b).[26]

In short, for the Panel in *Thailand – Cigarettes*, a measure is 'necessary' within the meaning of Article XX(b) only when there exists no alternative measure that is GATT-consistent or less inconsistent, and that a Member could reasonably be expected to employ to achieve the public health objective pursued. It is clear that a Member can only be reasonably expected to employ an alternative measure when that measure is at least *as effective* in achieving the policy objective pursued.

In *US – Gasoline*, the Panel made an important clarification as to the requirement of 'necessity' under Article XX(b): it is not the necessity of the policy objective but the necessity of the disputed measure to *achieve* that objective which is at issue. The Panel stated:

> it was not the necessity of the policy goal that was to be examined, but whether or not it was necessary that imported gasoline be effectively prevented from benefiting from as favourable sales conditions as were afforded by an individual baseline tied to the producer of a product. It was the task of the Panel to address whether these inconsistent measures were necessary to achieve the policy goal under Article XX(b). It was therefore not the task of the Panel to examine the necessity of the environmental objectives of the Gasoline Rule, or of parts of the Rule that the Panel did not specifically find to be inconsistent with the General Agreement.[27]

In this case, the Panel then examined whether measures existed that were 'consistent or less inconsistent' with the GATT 1994 and 'reasonably available to the United States to further its policy objectives of protecting human, animal and plant life or health'.[28]

In *EC – Asbestos*, a dispute between Canada and the European Communities on a French ban on asbestos and asbestos products, Canada argued on appeal that

[24] *Ibid.*, para. 77. [25] *Ibid.*, para. 78. [26] See *ibid.*, para. 81. [27] Panel Report, *US – Gasoline*, para. 6.22.
[28] *Ibid.*, para. 6.25.

the Panel had erred in applying the 'necessity' test under Article XX(b) of the GATT 1994. In addressing Canada's arguments in support of its appeal, the Appellate Body clarified the 'necessity' test under Article XX(b) in three important respects.

First, the Appellate Body noted:

> it is undisputed that WTO Members have the right to determine the level of protection of health that they consider appropriate in a given situation. France has determined, and the Panel accepted,[29] that the chosen level of health protection by France is a 'halt' to the spread of *asbestos-related* health risks. By prohibiting all forms of amphibole asbestos, and by severely restricting the use of chrysotile asbestos, the measure at issue is clearly designed and apt to achieve that level of health protection.[30]

It is therefore for WTO Members to determine the *level* of protection of health or the environment they consider appropriate.[31] Other Members cannot challenge the level of protection chosen; they can only argue that the measure at issue is not 'necessary' to achieve that level of protection.[32]

Secondly, in *EC – Asbestos*, the Appellate Body clarified the meaning of the requirement, formulated in *Thailand – Cigarettes* and *US – Gasoline*, that there is 'no alternative to the measure at issue that the Member could *reasonably* be expected to employ'. Canada asserted before the Appellate Body that the Panel had erred in finding that 'controlled use' of asbestos and asbestos products is not a reasonably available alternative to the import ban on asbestos. According to Canada, an alternative measure is only excluded as a 'reasonably available' alternative if implementation of that measure is 'impossible'. The Appellate Body stated that in determining whether a suggested alternative measure is 'reasonably available', several factors must be taken into account, alongside the difficulty of implementation. It subsequently referred to its earlier findings on the 'necessity' test under Article XX(d) in *Korea – Various Measures on Beef*, finding that the term 'necessary' in Article XX(d) refers to a 'range of degrees of necessity', so it may be assumed that the same is true for Article XX(b).[33] In *EC – Asbestos*, the Appellate Body noted with respect to 'necessary' in Article XX(b):

> We indicated in *Korea € Beef* that one aspect of the 'weighing and balancing process . . . comprehended in the determination of whether a WTO-consistent alternative measure' is reasonably available is the extent to which the alternative measure 'contributes to the realization of the end pursued'. In addition, we observed, in that case, that '[t]he more vital or important [the] common interests or values' pursued, the easier it would be to accept as 'necessary' measures designed to achieve those ends. In this case, the objective pursued by the measure is the preservation of human life and health through the elimination, or reduction, of the well-known, and life-threatening, health risks posed by asbestos fibres. The value pursued is both vital and important in the highest degree.[34]

---

[29] Panel Report, *EC – Asbestos*, para. 8.204.

[30] Appellate Body Report, *EC – Asbestos*, para. 168. This finding is in line with the case law under the *SPS Agreement*: see below, p. 851.

[31] See, for a more recent application, Panel Report, *Brazil – Retreaded Tyres*, para. 7.108.

[32] As France did in *EC – Asbestos*, a WTO Member can choose a zero-risk level. This means that there will be few, if any, measures other than a full ban that will achieve this level of protection.

[33] It was held that there is no reason to interpret the 'necessity' requirement in Article XX(b) differently from that in Article XX(d) of the GATT. See below, p. 632.   [34] Appellate Body Report, *EC – Asbestos*, para. 172.

In deciding whether a measure is necessary, the Appellate Body therefore also considers the *importance* of the societal value pursued by the measure at issue,[35] as well as the *extent* to which the measure at issue will contribute to the protection or promotion of that value.[36] It is clear that the more important the societal value pursued by the measure at issue (e.g. human life and health) and the more this measure contributes to the protection or promotion of this value, the more easily the measure at issue may be considered to be 'necessary'. A third factor in the weighing and balancing process identified by the Appellate Body in *Korea – Various Measures on Beef*, namely the restrictive impact of the measure at issue on international trade, was not explicitly referred to by the Appellate Body in *EC – Asbestos*. However, in later case law on 'necessity' under Article XX(b), and in particular in *Brazil – Retreaded Tyres*, this factor was considered.[37] The less restrictive the impact of the measure at issue is on international trade, the more easily the measure may be considered to be 'necessary'.

Thirdly, instead of the requirement in *Thailand – Cigarettes* that the alternative measure needs to be GATT-consistent or less GATT-inconsistent, the Appellate Body in *EC – Asbestos* put forward another requirement, namely, that the alternative measure must be *less trade-restrictive* than the measure at issue.[38] In summarising the test under Article XX(b), the Appellate Body held in *EC – Asbestos*:

> The . . . question . . . is whether there is an alternative measure that would achieve the same end and that is less restrictive of trade than a prohibition.[39]

Canada, the complainant in *EC – Asbestos*, had asserted that 'controlled use' of asbestos and asbestos products represented a 'reasonably available' measure

---

[35] Note that critics have questioned whether it is appropriate for panels or the Appellate Body to come to conclusions on the relative importance of societal values pursued by Members. For example, is it appropriate for panels or the Appellate Body to find that the pursuit of religious purity or piety is a less compelling objective than the protection of human health? See R. Howse and E. Türk, 'The WTO Impact of Internal Regulations: A Case Study of the *Canada – EC Asbestos* Dispute', in G. A. Bermann and P. C. Mavroidis (eds.), *Trade and Human Health and Safety* (Cambridge University Press, 2006), 116.

[36] In *Brazil – Retreaded Tyres*, the Appellate Body rejected the European Communities' argument that the contribution of the measure at issue to the achievement of its objective must be quantified by a panel. It held instead that both a quantitative and a qualitative evaluation is permissible. According to the Appellate Body, what is required is 'a genuine relationship of ends and means between the objective pursued and the measure at issue. The selection of a methodology to assess a measure's contribution is a function of the nature of the risk, the objective pursued, and the level of protection sought. It ultimately also depends on the nature, quantity, and quality of evidence existing at the time the analysis is made.' Appellate Body Report, *Brazil – Retreaded Tyres*, para. 145. See also *ibid.*, para. 146. Note, however, that the Appellate Body further held that 'when a measure produces restrictive effects on international trade as severe as those resulting from an import ban, it appears to us that it would be difficult for a panel to find that measure necessary unless it is satisfied that the measure is *apt to make a material contribution* to the achievement of its objective.' *Ibid.*, para. 150 (emphasis added). As Brazil had developed and implemented a comprehensive strategy to deal with waste tyres, a *key element* of which was the import ban at issue, the Appellate Body held that the ban was 'likely to bring a material contribution to the achievement of its objective of reducing the exposure to risks arising from the accumulation of waste tyres'. *Ibid.*, para. 155.

[37] See Panel Report, *Brazil – Retreaded Tyres*, para. 7.104, and Appellate Body Report, *Brazil – Retreaded Tyres*, para. 143.

[38] Note that in *Korea – Various Measures on Beef*, the Appellate Body still applied the *Thailand – Cigarettes* requirement that the alternative measure must be GATT-consistent or less inconsistent. See Appellate Body Report, *Korea – Various Measures on Beef*, para. 165.

[39] Appellate Body Report, *EC – Asbestos*, para. 172. A more recent application of this test can be found in the Panel Report *EC – Tariff Preferences*, para. 7.211. However, in *Brazil – Retreaded Tyres*, the Panel reverted to the *Thailand – Cigarettes* requirement and examined whether the alternative measure was WTO-consistent or less inconsistent. See Panel Report, *Brazil – Retreaded Tyres*, para. 7.152 and footnote 1279 thereto. The Appellate Body in this case referred to the need to compare the measure applied with its possible alternatives, which may be 'less trade restrictive' while providing an equivalent contribution to the achievement of the objective pursued. See Appellate Body Report, *Brazil – Retreaded Tyres*, para. 156.

that would serve the same end as the ban on asbestos and asbestos products. The issue for the Appellate Body was, therefore, whether France could reasonably be expected to employ 'controlled use' practices to achieve its chosen level of health protection – a halt in the spread of asbestos-related health risks. The Appellate Body concluded that this was not the case. It reasoned as follows:

> In our view, France could not reasonably be expected to employ *any* alternative measure if that measure would involve a continuation of the very risk that the Decree seeks to 'halt'. Such an alternative measure would, in effect, prevent France from achieving its chosen level of health protection. On the basis of the scientific evidence before it, the Panel found that, in general, the efficacy of 'controlled use' remains to be demonstrated. Moreover, even in cases where 'controlled use' practices are applied 'with greater certainty', the scientific evidence suggests that the level of exposure can, in some circumstances, still be high enough for there to be a 'significant residual risk of developing asbestos-related diseases'. The Panel found too that the efficacy of 'controlled use' is particularly doubtful for the building industry and for DIY enthusiasts, which are the most important users of cement-based products containing chrysotile asbestos. Given these factual findings by the Panel, we believe that 'controlled use' would not allow France to achieve its chosen level of health protection by halting the spread of asbestos-related health risks. 'Controlled use' would, thus, not be an alternative measure that would achieve the end sought by France.[40]

In *Brazil – Retreaded Tyres*, the Appellate Body confirmed that a Member cannot reasonably be expected to employ an alternative measure if that measure does not allow it to achieve its desired level of protection with respect to the policy objective pursued. The Appellate Body also recalled in *Brazil – Retreaded Tyres* its finding in *US – Gambling* that:

> '[a]n alternative measure may be found not to be "reasonably available" . . . where it is merely theoretical in nature, for instance, where the responding Member is not capable of taking it, or where the measure imposes an undue burden on that Member, such as prohibitive costs or substantial technical difficulties'.[41]

It consequently held that in the assessment of whether alternative measures or practices are 'reasonably available', 'the capacity of a country to implement remedial measures that would be particularly costly, or would require advanced technologies', may be relevant.[42]

Note also that the Appellate Body in *EC – Asbestos* stated with regard to the evaluation of the 'necessity' of a measure that:

> In justifying a measure under Article XX(b) of the GATT 1994, a Member may also rely, in good faith, on scientific sources which, at that time, may represent a divergent, but

---

[40] Appellate Body Report, *EC – Asbestos*, para. 174. Similarly, in *Brazil – Retreaded Tyres*, the Appellate Body (referring to its finding in *US – Gambling* on this matter) held that 'in order to qualify as an alternative, a measure proposed by the complaining Member must be not only less trade restrictive than the measure at issue, but should also "preserve for the responding Member its right to achieve its desired level of protection with respect to the objective pursued" '. Appellate Body Report, *Brazil – Retreaded Tyres*, para. 156.

[41] Appellate Body Report, *Brazil – Retreaded Tyres*, para. 156, citing Appellate Body Report, *US – Gambling*, para. 308.

[42] Appellate Body Report, *Brazil – Retreaded Tyres*, para. 171. *In casu* the Appellate Body found that the alternative measures proposed by the European Communities were either already part of the strategy implemented by Brazil to deal with waste tyres, did not achieve the level of protection chosen by Brazil, or were costly and required advanced technologies and know-how not readily available on a large scale. Therefore they could not be regarded as 'reasonably available' alternatives to the import ban. See *ibid.*, paras. 17–175.

> qualified and respected, opinion. A Member is not obliged, in setting health policy, automatically to follow what, at a given time, may constitute a majority scientific opinion. Therefore, a panel need not, necessarily, reach a decision under Article XX(b) of the GATT 1994 on the basis of the 'preponderant' weight of the evidence.[43]

The case law on the issue of 'necessity' is well summarised by the Appellate Body in the recent *Brazil – Retreaded Tyres* case:

> in order to determine whether a measure is 'necessary' within the meaning of Article XX(b) of the GATT 1994, a panel must consider the relevant factors, particularly the importance of the interests or values at stake, the extent of the contribution to the achievement of the measure's objective, and its trade restrictiveness. If this analysis yields a preliminary conclusion that the measure is necessary, this result must be confirmed by comparing the measure with possible alternatives, which may be less trade restrictive while providing an equivalent contribution to the achievement of the objective. This comparison should be carried out in the light of the importance of the interests or values at stake. It is through this process that a panel determines whether a measure is necessary.[44]

The Appellate Body emphasised that the 'weighing and balancing' required by the necessity test is a 'holistic operation that involves putting all the variables of the equation together and evaluating them in relation to each other after having examined them individually, in order to reach an overall judgement.'[45]

On the question of which party bears the burden of proof with regard to the existence of a reasonably available alternative measure, the Appellate Body in *Brazil – Retreaded Tyres* recalled its finding in *US – Gambling* (concerning the 'necessity' requirement under Article XIV(a) of the GATS).[46] Applying the same allocation of the burden of proof as in the latter case, the Appellate Body stated:

> It rests upon the complaining Member to *identify* possible alternatives to the measure at issue that the responding Member could have taken. As the Appellate Body indicated in *US – Gambling*, while the responding Member must show that a measure is necessary, it does not have to 'show, in the first instance, that there are *no* reasonably available alternatives to achieve its objectives.'[47]
>
> [Emphasis added]

Questions and Assignments 7.3

What are the constituent elements of the test under Article XX(b) of the GATT 1994? When is a measure 'necessary' within the meaning of Article XX(b)? What factors are to be taken into account in determining whether there is a 'reasonably available alternative' within the meaning of the case law on Article XX(b)? Must a Member invoking Article XX(b) justify the *level* of protection of public health or the environment it has chosen to pursue? Can a Member consider a measure to be 'necessary' to achieve a health or environmental policy objective when the prevailing view among scientists is that such a measure is *not* necessary? Briefly describe the measures at issue in *Thailand – Cigarettes, EC – Asbestos* and *Brazil –*

---

[43] *Ibid.*, para. 178. This finding follows the case law under the *SPS Agreement*, discussed below, p. 851.
[44] Appellate Body Report, *Brazil – Retreaded Tyres*, para. 178. The Appellate Body referred to its report in *US – Gambling*, para. 307, in this regard.   [45] Appellate Body Report, *Brazil – Retreaded Tyres*, para. 182.
[46] Appellate Body Report, *US – Gambling*, paras. 309–11, discussed below, p. 658.
[47] Appellate Body Report, *Brazil – Retreaded Tyres*, para. 156.

Retreaded Tyres and explain how the Panel or the Appellate Body concluded that these measures were or were not provisionally justified under Article XX(b). Who has the burden of proof to establish that there is or is not an alternative measure that is reasonably available under the 'necessity' requirement of Article XX(b) of the GATT 1994?

7.2.3.2. Article XX(d): 'measures necessary to secure compliance with . . .'

As mentioned above, Article XX(d) concerns and can justify measures:

> necessary to secure compliance with laws or regulations which are not inconsistent with the provisions of this Agreement, including those relating to customs enforcement, the enforcement of monopolies operated under paragraph 4 of Article II and Article XVII, the protection of patents, trade marks and copyrights, and the prevention of deceptive practices.

Article XX(d) sets out a two-tier test for the provisional justification of otherwise GATT-inconsistent measures.[48] In *Korea – Various Measures on Beef*, a dispute concerning the regulation of retail sales of both domestic and imported beef products (the dual retail system) designed to secure compliance with a consumer protection law, the Appellate Body ruled:

> For a measure, otherwise inconsistent with GATT 1994, to be justified provisionally under paragraph (d) of Article XX, two elements must be shown. First, the measure must be one designed to 'secure compliance' with laws or regulations that are not themselves inconsistent with some provision of the GATT 1994. Second, the measure must be 'necessary' to secure such compliance. A Member who invokes Article XX(d) as a justification has the burden of demonstrating that these two requirements are met.[49]

Thus, for a GATT-inconsistent measure to be provisionally justified under Article XX(d):

- the measure must be designed to *secure compliance* with national law, such as customs law or intellectual property law, which, in itself, is not GATT-inconsistent; and
- the measure must be *necessary* to ensure such compliance.[50]

With respect to the first element of the Article XX(d) test, namely, that the measure must be 'designed to secure compliance' with GATT-consistent laws or regulations, note that the Panel in *US – Gasoline* found that:

---

[48] Note that the Panel in *Canada – Wheat Exports and Grain Imports* applied a three-tier test. See below, footnote 50.

[49] Appellate Body Report, *Korea – Various Measures on Beef*, para. 157. See also Panel Report, *US – Gasoline*, para. 6.31.

[50] As mentioned above, the Panel in *Canada – Wheat Exports and Grain Imports* applied a *three*-tier test. According to the Panel, for a GATT-inconsistent measure to be provisionally justified under Article XX(d):
   (a) the measure for which justification is claimed must secure compliance with other laws or regulations;
   (b) those other laws or regulations must not be inconsistent with the provisions of the GATT 1994; and
   (c) the measure for which justification is claimed must be necessary to secure compliance with those other laws or regulations. See Panel Report, *Canada – Wheat Exports and Grain Imports*, para. 6.218.

> maintenance of discrimination between imported and domestic gasoline contrary to Article III:4 under the baseline establishment methods did not 'secure compliance' with the baseline system. These methods were not an enforcement mechanism. They were simply rules for determining the individual baselines. As such, they were not the type of measures with which Article XX(d) was concerned.[51]

Two more recent cases, *Mexico – Taxes on Soft Drinks* and *EC – Trademarks and Geographical Indications*, provide us with further insights into the first element of the Article XX(d) test. In *Mexico – Taxes on Soft Drinks*, the Appellate Body was called upon to clarify the meaning of the phrase 'to secure compliance with laws or regulations'. Mexico had argued before the Panel that the measures at issue in this case were necessary to secure compliance 'by the United States with the United States' obligations under the NAFTA, an international agreement that is a law not inconsistent with the provisions of the GATT 1994'.[52] The Panel, however, found that 'the phrase "to secure compliance" in Article XX(d) does not apply to measures taken by a Member in order to induce another Member to comply with obligations owed to it under a non-WTO treaty'.[53] In considering Mexico's appeal of this Panel finding, the Appellate Body started with an analysis of the terms 'laws or regulations' of Article XX(d).[54] According to the Appellate Body:

> The terms 'laws or regulations' are generally used to refer to domestic laws or regulations. As Mexico and the United States note, previous GATT and WTO disputes in which Article XX(d) has been invoked as a defence have involved domestic measures. Neither disputes that the expression 'laws or regulations' encompasses the rules adopted by a WTO Member's legislative or executive branches of government. We agree with the United States that one does not immediately think about international law when confronted with the term 'laws' in the plural . . . .. In our view, the terms 'laws or regulations' refer to rules that form part of the domestic legal system of a WTO Member. Thus the 'laws or regulations' with which the Member invoking Article XX(d) may seek to secure compliance do not include obligations of *another* WTO Member under an international agreement.[55]

The Appellate Body made it clear that 'laws or regulations' refer to domestic rules, and not the obligations of another WTO Member under an international agreement. This conclusion is strengthened by the illustrative list of 'laws or regulations' in Article XX(d). As the Appellate Body stated:

> This list includes '[laws or regulations] relating to customs enforcement, the enforcement of monopolies operated under paragraph 4 of Article II and Article XVII, the protection of patents, trade marks and copyrights, and the prevention of deceptive practices'. These matters are typically the subject of domestic laws or regulations, even though some of these matters may also be the subject of international agreements. The matters listed as examples in Article XX(d) involve the regulation by a government of activity undertaken by a variety of economic actors . . . as well as by government agencies.[56]

---

[51] Panel Report, *US – Gasoline*, para. 6.33. The Panel referred in a footnote to GATT Panel Report, *EEC – Parts and Components*, paras. 5.12–5.18. See also Panel Report, *Canada – Periodicals*, para. 5.11, where the Panel held that Tariff Code 9958, prohibiting the import of certain periodicals, could not be justified under Article XX(d) as the import prohibition was not necessary to 'secure compliance' with the Canadian Income Tax Act.   [52] Panel Report, *Mexico – Taxes on Soft Drinks*, para. 8.162.   [53] *Ibid.*, para. 8.181.
[54] See Appellate Body Report, *Mexico – Taxes on Soft Drinks*, paras. 68–9.   [55] *Ibid.*, para. 69.
[56] *Ibid.*, para. 70.

The Appellate Body further referred to the context of Article XX(d) and to other provisions of the GATT 1994. It noted that where international laws or agreements are meant to be covered by the relevant GATT rules, explicit reference is made to them.[57] Where international law is a part of domestic law, whether through implementation or through direct effect,[58] the Appellate Body recognised that it falls within the ambit of the terms 'laws or regulations' as used in Article XX(d). However, this is only the case for international obligations of the WTO Member concerned. International obligations of *other* WTO Members, such as *in casu* obligations of the United States under the NAFTA, are *not* covered by the terms 'laws or regulations' of Article XX(d) of the GATT 1994.[59]

The Appellate Body then turned to the terms 'to secure compliance'. According to the Appellate Body, these terms 'speak to the types of measures a WTO Member can seek to justify under Article XX(d)' and 'relate to the design of the measures to be justified'.[60] The Panel had argued that there was uncertainty regarding the effectiveness of the tax measures, and that it was therefore not convinced that these measures were meant 'to secure compliance'. The Appellate Body, however, did not agree with this reasoning:

> In our view, a measure can be said to be designed 'to secure compliance' even if the measure cannot be guaranteed to achieve its result with absolute certainty. Nor do we consider that the 'use of coercion' is a necessary component of a measure designed 'to secure compliance'. Rather, Article XX(d) requires that the design of the measure *contribute* 'to securing] compliance with laws or regulations which are not inconsistent with the provisions of' the GATT 1994.[61]
>
> [Emphasis added]

The fact that the tax measures are designed 'to secure compliance' did not alter the general conclusion of the Appellate Body that Article XX(d) is not applicable. As explained above, international obligations of other WTO Members, such as the United States' obligations under the NAFTA, do not fall within the scope of the terms 'laws or regulations' with which Article XX(d) measures must be designed to secure compliance.

In *EC – Trademarks and Geographical Indications*, the European Communities had invoked the exception of Article XX(d) to justify the otherwise GATT-inconsistent measures at issue in this case, contending that these measures were employed to secure compliance with an EC regulation, namely EC Council Regulation (EEC) No. 2081/92 of 14 July 1992 on the protection of geographical indications and

---

[57] See *ibid.*, para. 71.   [58] See *ibid.*, footnote 148 to para. 69.
[59] The Appellate Body noted in addition that an interpretation of 'laws or regulations' which would comprise international obligations (including WTO obligations) is not in accordance with WTO law for two other reasons. First, allowing such an interpretation of Article XX(d) would lead to a situation in which WTO Members would determine unilaterally whether another Member has acted inconsistently with WTO law. This is inconsistent with the obligations of Members under Article 23 of the DSU. Secondly, if international obligations were encompassed by the terms 'laws or regulations', WTO panels and the Appellate Body would need to assess those international obligations in order to solve the dispute. It is, however, not the function of panels and the Appellate Body to solve non-WTO related disputes. See Appellate Body Report, *Mexico – Taxes on Soft Drinks*, paras. 77 and 78.   [60] *Ibid.*, para. 72.
[61] *Ibid.*, para. 74. See also GATT Panel Report, *EEC – Parts and Components*, paras. 5.14– 5.18, where the Panel held that 'to secure compliance' means 'to enforce obligations under laws and regulations' rather than 'to ensure the attainment of the objectives of the laws and regulations'.

designations of origin for agricultural products and foodstuffs. The Panel noted that the terms 'laws or regulations' in Article XX(d) are qualified by the phrase 'not inconsistent with the provisions of this Agreement'.[62] In other words, the 'laws or regulations' referred to in Article XX(d) have to be GATT-consistent. However, the Panel found EC Council Regulation (EEC) No. 2081/92 to be inconsistent with the GATT 1994,[63] and therefore not to qualify as a 'law or regulation' within the meaning of Article XX(d).[64]

With respect to the second element of the Article XX(d) test, namely, the 'necessity' requirement, the GATT Panel Report in *US – Section 337* stated:

> It was clear to the Panel that a contracting party cannot justify a measure inconsistent with another GATT provision as 'necessary' in terms of Article XX(d) if an alternative measure which it could reasonably be expected to employ and which is not inconsistent with other GATT provisions is available to it. By the same token, in cases where a measure consistent with other GATT provisions is not reasonably available, a contracting party is bound to use, among the measures reasonably available to it, that which entails the least degree of inconsistency with other GATT provisions.[65]

The meaning given to the 'necessity' requirement of Article XX(d) in *US – Section 337* was thus very similar to the meaning given to the 'necessity' requirement of Article XX(b) in *Thailand – Cigarettes*, discussed above.[66] A measure is 'necessary' within the meaning of Article XX(d) only when there exists no alternative measure that is GATT-consistent or less GATT-inconsistent, and that a Member could reasonably be expected to employ to ensure compliance with GATT-consistent laws or regulations.

In *Korea – Various Measures on Beef*, the Appellate Body further clarified the 'necessity' requirement of Article XX(d) of the GATT 1994. The Appellate Body first noted that:

> We believe that, as used in the context of Article XX(d), the reach of the word 'necessary' is not limited to that which is 'indispensable' or 'of absolute necessity' or 'inevitable'. Measures which are indispensable or of absolute necessity or inevitable to secure compliance certainly fulfil the requirements of Article XX(d). But other measures, too, may fall within the ambit of this exception. As used in Article XX(d), the term 'necessary' refers, in our view, to a range of degrees of necessity. At one end of this continuum lies 'necessary' understood as 'indispensable'; at the other end, is 'necessary' taken to mean as 'making a contribution to'. We consider that a 'necessary' measure is, in this continuum, located significantly closer to the pole of 'indispensable' than to the opposite pole of simply 'making a contribution to'.[67]

The Appellate Body subsequently stated:

> It seems to us that a treaty interpreter assessing a measure claimed to be necessary to secure compliance of a WTO-consistent law or regulation may, in appropriate cases, take into account the relative importance of the common interests or values that the law or regulation to be enforced is intended to protect. The more vital or important those common

---

[62] See Panel Report, *EC – Trademarks and Geographical Indications (Australia)*, para. 7.331, and Panel Report, *EC – Trademarks and Geographical Indications (US)*, para. 7.296.   [63] *Ibid.*, para. 7.332, and *ibid.*, para. 7.297.
[64] *Ibid.*, para. 7.332, and *ibid.*, para. 7.297.   [65] GATT Panel Report, *US – Section 337*, para. 5.26.
[66] See above, p. 623.   [67] Appellate Body Report, *Korea – Various Measures on Beef*, para. 161.

interests or values are, the easier it would be to accept as 'necessary' a measure designed as an enforcement instrument.

There are other aspects of the enforcement measure to be considered in evaluating that measure as 'necessary'. One is the extent to which the measure contributes to the realization of the end pursued, the securing of compliance with the law or regulation at issue. The greater the contribution, the more easily a measure might be considered to be 'necessary'. Another aspect is the extent to which the compliance measure produces restrictive effects on international commerce, that is, in respect of a measure inconsistent with Article III:4, restrictive effects *on imported goods*. A measure with a relatively slight impact upon imported products might more easily be considered as 'necessary' than a measure with intense or broader restrictive effects.[68]

The Appellate Body thus came to the following conclusion concerning the 'necessity' requirement of Article XX(d) in *Korea – Various Measures on Beef*:

In sum, determination of whether a measure, which is not 'indispensable', may nevertheless be 'necessary' within the contemplation of Article XX(d), involves in every case a process of weighing and balancing a series of factors which prominently include the contribution made by the compliance measure to the enforcement of the law or regulation at issue, the importance of the common interests or values protected by that law or regulation, and the accompanying impact of the law or regulation on imports or exports.[69]

In brief, an evaluation of whether a measure is 'necessary', as required by the second element of the test under Article XX(d), involves, in every case, the weighing and balancing of factors such as:

- the relative importance of the common interests or values protected (or intended to be protected) by the law or regulation compliance with which is to be secured;
- the extent to which the measure contributes to the securing of compliance with the law or regulation at issue; and
- the extent to which the compliance measure produces restrictive effects on international trade.

As noted by the Appellate Body in *Korea – Various Measures on Beef*, the weighing and balancing of these factors:

is comprehended in the determination of whether a WTO-consistent alternative measure which the Member concerned could 'reasonably be expected to employ' is available, or whether a less WTO-inconsistent measure is 'reasonably available'.[70]

Note that the Panels in *Canada – Wheat Exports and Grain Imports* (2004), *Dominican Republic – Import and Sale of Cigarettes* (2005), and *EC – Trademarks and Geographical Indications* (2005) have applied the 'necessity' requirement of Article XX(d) as interpreted and clarified by the Appellate Body in *Korea – Various Measures on Beef*.[71]

---

[68] *Ibid.*, paras. 162–3. In *ibid.*, para. 165, the Appellate Body cited GATT Panel Report, *US – Section 337*, para. 5.26.   [69] Appellate Body Report, *Korea – Various Measures on Beef*, para. 164.   [70] *Ibid.*, para. 166.
[71] See Panel Report, *Canada – Wheat Exports and Grain Imports*, paras. 6.222–6.248; Panel Report, *Dominican Republic – Import and Sale of Cigarettes*, paras. 7.205–7.209, 7.212–7.215, 7.217–7.232; Panel Report, *EC – Trademarks and Geographical Indications (Australia)*, paras. 7.333–7.341; and Panel Report, *EC – Trademarks and Geographical Indications (US)*, paras. 7.298–7.306 and 7.449–7.462.

On the question of who has the burden of proof to establish that there is, or is not, an alternative measure that is reasonably available,[72] recall that the Appellate Body in *Brazil – Retreaded Tyres* (concerning the 'necessity' requirement under Article XX(b) of the GATT 1994) held that:

> While the responding Member must show that a measure necessary, it does not have to 'show, in first instance, that there are *no* reasonably available alternatives to achieve its objectives'.[73]

According to the Appellate Body in *Brazil – Retreaded Tyres*, it rests upon the complaining Member to identity possible alternative measures.[74]

Questions and Assignments 7.4

What are the constituent elements of the test under Article XX(d) of the GATT 1994? How does one establish whether a measure is 'necessary' within the meaning of Article XX(d)? Explain why the Appellate Body concluded that the measures at issue in *Korea – Various Measures on Beef*, *Mexico – Taxes on Soft Drinks* and *EC – Trademarks and Geographical Indications* were not provisionally justified under Article XX(d).

7.2.3.3. Article XX(g): 'measures relating to the conservation of exhaustible natural resources . . .'

Article XX(g) concerns measures relating to the conservation of exhaustible natural resources. Article XX(g) is fundamentally important because, together with Article XX(b), it permits measures that depart from core GATT rules for environmental protection purposes.

Article XX(g) sets out a three-tier test requiring that a measure:

- relate to the *conservation of exhaustible natural resources*;
- *relate to* the conservation of exhaustible natural resources; and
- be made effective *in conjunction with* restrictions on domestic production or consumption.

With respect to the first element of the test under Article XX(g), namely, that the measure must relate to the 'conservation of exhaustible natural resources', the Appellate Body, in *US – Shrimp*, adopted a broad, 'evolutionary' interpretation of the concept of 'exhaustible natural resources'. In this case, the complainants had taken the position that Article XX(g) was limited to the conservation of 'mineral' or 'non-living' natural resources. Their principal argument was rooted in the notion that 'living' natural resources are 'renewable' and therefore cannot be 'exhaustible' natural resources. The Appellate Body disagreed. It noted:

---

[72] See also above, p. 628 and below, p. 658.
[73] Appellate Body Report, *Brazil – Retreaded Tyres*, para. 156.   [74] See *ibid*.

> We do not believe that 'exhaustible' natural resources and 'renewable' natural resources are mutually exclusive. One lesson that modern biological sciences teach us is that living species, though in principle, capable of reproduction and, in that sense, 'renewable', are in certain circumstances indeed susceptible of depletion, exhaustion and extinction, frequently because of human activities. Living resources are just as 'finite' as petroleum, iron ore and other non-living resources.[75]

The Appellate Body further noted with regard to the appropriate interpretation of the concept of 'exhaustible natural resources':

> The words of Article XX(g), 'exhaustible natural resources', were actually crafted more than 50 years ago. They must be read by a treaty interpreter in the light of contemporary concerns of the community of nations about the protection and conservation of the environment. While Article XX was not modified in the Uruguay Round, the preamble attached to the *WTO Agreement* shows that the signatories to that Agreement were, in 1994, fully aware of the importance and legitimacy of environmental protection as a goal of national and international policy. The preamble of the *WTO Agreement* – which informs not only the GATT 1994, but also the other covered agreements – explicitly acknowledges 'the objective of *sustainable development*'.
>
> . . . From the perspective embodied in the preamble of the *WTO Agreement*, we note that the generic term of 'natural resources' in Article XX(g) is not 'static' in its content or reference but is rather 'by definition, evolutionary'. It is, therefore, pertinent to note that modern international conventions and declarations make frequent references to natural resources as embracing both living and non-living resources.[76]

The Appellate Body thus concluded on the scope of the concept of 'exhaustible natural resources':

> Given the recent acknowledgement by the international community of the importance of concerted bilateral or multilateral action to protect living natural resources, and recalling the explicit recognition by WTO Members of the objective of sustainable development in the preamble of the *WTO Agreement*, we believe it is too late in the day to suppose that Article XX(g) of the GATT 1994 may be read as referring only to the conservation of exhaustible mineral or other non-living natural resources. Moreover, two adopted GATT 1947 panel reports previously found fish to be an 'exhaustible natural resource' within the meaning of Article XX(g). We hold that, in line with the principle of effectiveness in treaty interpretation, measures to conserve exhaustible natural resources, whether *living* or *non-living*, may fall within Article XX(g).[77]

With respect to the second element of the test under Article XX(g), namely, that the measure must be a measure 'relating to' the conservation of exhaustible natural resources, the GATT Panel in *Canada – Herring and Salmon* observed that:

---

[75] Appellate Body Report, *US – Shrimp*, para. 128. In a footnote, the Appellate Body noted that the World Commission on Environment and Development stated: 'The planet's species are under stress. There is growing scientific consensus that species are disappearing at rates never before witnessed on the planet.' World Commission on Environment and Development, *Our Common Future* (Oxford University Press, 1987), 13.   [76] Appellate Body Report, *US – Shrimp*, paras. 129 and 130.

[77] *Ibid.*, para. 131. In a footnote, the Appellate Body also noted that the drafting history does not demonstrate an intent on the part of the framers of the GATT 1947 to *exclude* 'living' natural resources from the scope of application of Article XX(g). The Appellate Body also noted that in the GATT 1947 Panel Reports in *US – Tuna (Canada)*, para. 4.9, and *Canada – Herring and Salmon*, para. 4.4, fish had previously been found to be an 'exhaustible' natural resource.

> Article XX(g) does not state how the trade measures are to be related to the conservation ... This raises the question of whether *any* relationship with conservation ... [is] sufficient for a trade measure to fall under Article XX(g) or whether a *particular* relationship ... [is] required.
>
> ... The Panel noted that some of the subparagraphs of Article XX state that the measure must be 'necessary' or 'essential' to the achievement of the policy purpose set out in the provision (cf. subparagraphs (a), (b), (d) and (j)) while subparagraph (g) refers only to measures 'relating to' the conservation of exhaustible natural resources. This suggests that Article XX(g) does not only cover measures that are necessary or essential for the conservation of exhaustible natural resources but a wider range of measures. However, as the preamble of Article XX indicates, the purpose of including Article XX(g) in the General Agreement was not to widen the scope for measures serving trade policy purposes but merely to ensure that the commitments under the General Agreement do not hinder the pursuit of policies aimed at the conservation of exhaustible natural resources. The Panel concluded for these reasons that, while a trade measure did not have to be necessary or essential to the conservation of an exhaustible natural resource, it had to be *primarily aimed at* the conservation of an exhaustible natural resource to be considered as 'relating to' conservation within the meaning of Article XX(g).[78]
>
> [Emphasis added]

In *US – Gasoline*, the Appellate Body accepted the interpretation of the Panel in *Canada – Herring and Salmon* of the words 'relating to ... the conservation' as meaning 'primarily aimed at the conservation'. The Appellate Body stated in *US – Gasoline*:

> All the participants and the third participants in this appeal accept the propriety and applicability of the view of the *Herring and Salmon* report and the Panel Report that a measure must be 'primarily aimed at' the conservation of exhaustible natural resources in order to fall within the scope of Article XX(g). Accordingly, we see no need to examine this point further, save, perhaps, to note that the phrase 'primarily aimed at' is not itself treaty language and was not designed as a simple litmus test for inclusion or exclusion from Article XX(g).[79]

Applying this test to the baseline establishment rules for the quality of gasoline, the measure at issue in *US – Gasoline*, the Appellate Body held that these rules were 'primarily aimed at' the conservation of clean air, an exhaustible natural resource. The Appellate Body considered that:

> the baseline establishment rules cannot be regarded as merely incidentally or inadvertently aimed at the conservation of clean air in the United States for the purposes of Article XX(g).[80]

According to the Appellate Body, a 'substantial relationship' existed between the baseline establishment rules and the policy objective of preventing further deterioration of the level of air pollution.

The Appellate Body further clarified its understanding of the concept of 'relating to' the conservation of exhaustible natural resources in *US – Shrimp*. In this case, the Appellate Body stated with regard to the measure in dispute,

---

[78] GATT Panel Report, *Canada – Herring and Salmon*, paras. 4.5–4.6.
[79] Appellate Body Report, *US – Gasoline*, 17. In a footnote, the Appellate Body noted that the same interpretation had been applied in two recent unadopted panel reports: GATT Panel Report, *US – Tuna (EEC)* and GATT Panel Report, *US – Taxes on Automobiles*.   [80] Appellate Body Report, *US – Gasoline*, 18.

Section 609 of Public Law 101-162 Relating to the Protection of Sea Turtles in Shrimp Trawl Fishing Operations:

> In its general design and structure . . . Section 609 is not a simple, blanket prohibition of the importation of shrimp imposed without regard to the consequences (or lack thereof) of the mode of harvesting employed upon the incidental capture and mortality of sea turtles. Focusing on the design of the measure here at stake, it appears to us that Section 609, *cum* implementing guidelines, is not disproportionately wide in its scope and reach in relation to the policy objective of protection and conservation of sea turtle species. The means are, in principle, reasonably related to the ends. The means and ends relationship between Section 609 and the legitimate policy of conserving an exhaustible, and, in fact, endangered species, is observably a close and real one.[81]

Thus, according to the Appellate Body in *US – Shrimp*, Article XX(g) requires 'a close and real' relationship between the measure and the policy objective. The means employed, i.e. the measure, must be *reasonably* related to the end pursued, i.e. the conservation of an exhaustible natural resource. A measure may *not* be *disproportionately wide* in its scope or reach in relation to the policy objective pursued.

The third element of the test under Article XX(g), namely, that the measure at issue is 'made effective in conjunction with . . .', has been interpreted by the Appellate Body in *US – Gasoline* as follows:

> the ordinary or natural meaning of 'made effective' when used in connection with a measure . . . may be seen to refer to such measure being 'operative', as 'in force', or as having 'come into effect'. Similarly, the phrase 'in conjunction with' may be read quite plainly as 'together with' or 'jointly with'. Taken together, the [third] clause of Article XX(g) appears to us to refer to governmental measures like the baseline establishment rules being promulgated or brought into effect together with restrictions on domestic production or consumption of natural resources. Put in a slightly different manner, we believe that the clause 'if such measures are made effective in conjunction with restrictions on domestic product or consumption' is appropriately read as a requirement that the measures concerned impose restrictions, not just in respect of imported gasoline but also with respect to domestic gasoline. The clause is a requirement of *even-handedness* in the imposition of restrictions, in the name of conservation, upon the production or consumption of exhaustible natural resources.[82]

Basically, the third element of the Article XX(g) test is a requirement of 'even-handedness' in the imposition of restrictions on imported and domestic products. Article XX(g) does *not* require imported and domestic products to be treated equally: it merely requires that they are treated in an 'even-handed' manner. The Appellate Body in *US – Gasoline* stated in this respect:

> There is, of course, no textual basis for requiring identical treatment of domestic and imported products. Indeed, where there is identity of treatment – constituting real, not merely formal, equality of treatment – it is difficult to see how inconsistency with Article III:4 would have arisen in the first place.[83]

Note that, if the requirement of 'even-handedness' is not met, it is also doubtful whether the measure at issue meets the 'primarily aimed at . . .' requirement of

---

[81] Appellate Body Report, *US – Shrimp*, para. 141.　　[82] Appellate Body Report, *US – Gasoline*, 19.

[83] *Ibid.*, 21.

the second element of the Article XX(g) test.[84] The Appellate Body observed in *US – Gasoline*:

> if *no* restrictions on domestically-produced like products are imposed at all, and all limitations are placed upon imported products *alone*, the measure cannot be accepted as primarily or even substantially designed for implementing conservationist goals. The measure would simply be naked discrimination for protecting locally-produced goods.[85]

Applying the 'even-handedness' requirement to the baseline establishment rules, the measure at issue in *US – Gasoline*, the Appellate Body held as follows:

> In the present appeal, the baseline establishment rules affect both domestic gasoline and imported gasoline, providing for – generally speaking – individual baselines for domestic refiners and blenders and statutory baselines for importers. Thus, restrictions on the consumption or depletion of clean air by regulating the domestic production of 'dirty' gasoline are established jointly with corresponding restrictions with respect to imported gasoline. That imported gasoline has been determined to have been accorded 'less favourable treatment' than the domestic gasoline in terms of Article III:4, is not material for purposes of analysis under Article XX(g).[86]

In *US – Gasoline*, the Appellate Body also stated that it did not believe that the third element of Article XX(g) was intended to establish an empirical 'effects test' for the availability of the Article XX(g) exception. The Appellate Body reasoned as follows:

> In the first place, the problem of determining causation, well-known in both domestic and international law, is always a difficult one. In the second place, in the field of conservation of exhaustible natural resources, a substantial period of time, perhaps years, may have to elapse before the effects attributable to implementation of a given measure may be observable. The legal characterization of such a measure is not reasonably made contingent upon occurrence of subsequent events. We are not, however, suggesting that consideration of the predictable effects of a measure is never relevant. In a particular case, should it become clear that realistically, a specific measure cannot in any possible situation have any positive effect on conservation goals, it would very probably be because that measure was not designed as a conservation regulation to begin with. In other words, it would not have been 'primarily aimed at' conservation of natural resources at all.[87]

In *US – Shrimp*, the Appellate Body confirmed its approach to the third element of the Article XX(g) test and stated as follows:

> We earlier noted that Section 609, enacted in 1989, addresses the mode of harvesting of imported shrimp only. However, two years earlier, in 1987, the United States issued regulations pursuant to the Endangered Species Act requiring all United States shrimp trawl vessels to use approved TEDs [turtle excluder devices], or to restrict the duration of tow-times, in specified areas where there was significant incidental mortality of sea turtles in shrimp trawls. These regulations became fully effective in 1990 and were later modified. They now require United States shrimp trawlers to use approved TEDs 'in areas and at times when there is a likelihood of intercepting sea turtles', with certain limited exceptions. Penalties for violation of the Endangered Species Act, or the regulations issued thereunder, include civil and criminal sanctions. The United States government currently relies on monetary sanctions and civil penalties for enforcement. The government has the

[84] See also GATT Panel Report, *Canada – Herring and Salmon*, para. 4.7.
[85] Appellate Body Report, *US – Gasoline*, 19.   [86] *Ibid.*   [87] *Ibid.*, 19–20.

ability to seize shrimp catch from trawl vessels fishing in United States waters and has done so in cases of egregious violations. We believe that, in principle, Section 609 is an even-handed measure.[88]

In *US – Shrimp* the record reflected that the United States had – through earlier regulations – taken measures applicable to US shrimp trawl vessels to prevent the incidental killing of sea turtles. Because of these regulations imposing 'restrictions on domestic production', the import ban at issue in this case met the 'even-handedness' requirement of the third element of the Article XX(g) test.

Questions and Assignments 7.5

What are the constituent elements of the test under Article XX(g) of the GATT 1994? How has the Appellate Body interpreted the concept of 'exhaustible natural resources'? Pursuant to Article XX(g), what kind of relationship must exist between the measure at issue and the environmental conservation policy objective pursued? When does a Member meet the requirement of Article XX(g) that 'measures are made effective in conjunction with restrictions on domestic production or consumption'? Must a Member impose identical conservation measures on imported and domestic products? Briefly describe the measures at issue in *US – Gasoline* and *US – Shrimp* and explain why the Appellate Body concluded that these measures were provisionally justified under Article XX(g).

7.2.3.4. Other paragraphs of Article XX

Among the other possible exceptions for measures protecting or promoting other societal values and interests provided for in Article XX, note in particular Article XX(a), which concerns measures necessary for the protection of public morals. Just as Members are free to determine, each for themselves, their appropriate level of protection of public health in the context of Article XX(b),[89] they should also be free to determine their public morals. Public morals differ from Member to Member; what is morally acceptable in one Member is not necessarily so in another. To date, there is no WTO case law on Article XX(a). Article XX(a) was referred to in *US – Malt Beverages* and *US – Tuna* but in neither case did the Panel examine the relevance of this provision.[90] In *US – Tuna (Mexico)*, Australia, a third party in this case, suggested that the measure at issue could be justified under Article XX(a) as a measure against inhumane treatment of animals.[91] Arguably, public morals can be invoked as a ground for justification by a Member adopting or maintaining an import ban on products of child labour, on

---

[88] Appellate Body Report, *US – Shrimp*, para. 144.   [89] See above, p. 625.
[90] See Panel Report, *US – Malt Beverages*, paras. 3.126 and 5.70.
[91] See GATT Panel Report, *US – Tuna (Mexico)*, para. 4.4.

alcoholic beverages, on pornographic materials and on blood diamonds.[92] To be provisionally justified, the measure must be 'necessary' to protect the public morals of the Member taking the measure. The interpretation of the term 'necessary' within the meaning of Article XX(b) and (d), as discussed above, is undoubtedly of relevance in the context of Article XX(a).[93] The case law discussed below on Article XIV(a) of the GATS, i.e. the 'public morals' exception under the GATS, is clearly also relevant should panels or the Appellate Body be called upon to interpret Article XX(a) of the GATT 1994.[94] While there is no case law to date on Article XX(a), it is frequently invoked (explicitly or otherwise) by Members to impose import bans or restrictions on a wide array of products. Bangladesh, for example, invokes Article XX(a) to justify an import ban on horror comics, obscene and subversive literature and 'maps, charts and geographical globes which indicate the territory of Bangladesh but do not do so in accordance with the maps published by the Department of Survey, Government of the People's Republic of Bangladesh'.[95] From the Report of the Working Party on the Accession of Saudi Arabia, it appears that this Member, which acceded to the WTO in December 2005, invokes Article XX(a) of the GATT 1994 to ban the importation of the Holy Quran; alcoholic beverages and intoxicants of all kinds, including those containing alcohol in any intoxicating proportion; all types of machines, equipment and tools for gambling or games of chance; live swine, meat, fat, hair, blood, guts, limbs and all other products of swine; dogs, other than hunting dogs, guard dogs or guide dogs for the blind; mummified animals; and all foodstuffs containing animal blood in their manufacturing.[96]

Article XX(e) concerns measures 'relating to' the products of prison labour. On this basis, Members can, for example, ban the importation of goods that have been produced by prisoners. Article XX(e) is currently of little importance, and there is no case law under this paragraph to date. This could change, however, if an evolutionary interpretation of the concept of 'products of prison labour' would allow this concept to include products produced in conditions of slave labour or conditions contrary to the most fundamental labour standards.[97]

Finally, Article XX(f) concerns measures 'imposed for' the protection of national treasures of artistic, historic or archaeological value. It allows Members to adopt or maintain trade-restrictive measures for the protection of national treasures. Note that Article XX(f) does not require that these measures are 'necessary' for, but merely that they are 'imposed for', the protection of national treasures. There is no case law on Article XX(f) to date. If the concept of 'national treasures of artistic value' would be given a broad meaning and include also 'endangered' cultural goods, Article XX(f) may be useful to justify otherwise

[92] 'Blood diamonds' are diamonds of which the sales revenue is used to finance civil war, most notably in Africa.   [93] See above, pp. 621–8, 629–34.
[94] For a discussion of the case law on Article XIV(a) of the GATS (i.e. US – Gambling), see below, pp. 655–9.
[95] See Report by the Secretariat, Trade Policy Review: Bangladesh, WT/TPR/S/168, dated 9 August 2006, Appendix, Table AIII.3.
[96] See Report of the Working Party on the Accession of the Kingdom of Saudi Arabia to the World Trade Organization, WT/ACC/SAU/61, dated 1 November 2005, Annex F, List of Banned Products.
[97] For an example of evolutionary interpretation, see the findings of the Appellate Body on the concept of 'exhaustible natural resources' in US – Shrimp, discussed above, p. 634.

GATT-inconsistent measures for the protection and promotion of cultural identity and/or diversity.

7.2.4. The chapeau of Article XX of the GATT 1994

As discussed above, Article XX sets out a two-tier test for determining whether a measure, otherwise inconsistent with GATT obligations, can be justified. First, a measure must meet the requirements of one of the particular exceptions listed in the paragraphs of Article XX. Secondly, the application of that measure must meet the requirements of the chapeau of Article XX.

The legal requirements imposed by the chapeau of Article XX of the GATT 1994 have been highly relevant in dispute settlement practice. Several of the most controversial decisions by panels and the Appellate Body have turned on these requirements. The chapeau of Article XX, with regard to measures provisionally justified under one of the paragraphs of Article XX, imposes:

> the requirement that such measures are not applied in a manner which would constitute a means of arbitrary or unjustifiable discrimination between countries where the same conditions prevail, or a disguised restriction on international trade.

7.2.4.1. Object and purpose of the chapeau of Article XX

With respect to the object and purpose of the chapeau of Article XX, the Appellate Body ruled in *US – Gasoline*:

> The chapeau by its express terms addresses, not so much the questioned measure or its specific contents as such, but rather the manner in which that measure is applied . . . The chapeau is animated by the principle that while the exceptions of Article XX may be invoked as a matter of legal right, they should not be so applied as to frustrate or defeat the legal obligations of the holder of the right under the substantive rules of the *General Agreement*. If those exceptions are not to be abused or misused, in other words, the measures falling within the particular exceptions must be applied reasonably, with due regard both to the legal duties of the party claiming the exception and the legal rights of the other parties concerned.[98]

Further, in *US – Shrimp*, the Appellate Body stated with regard to the chapeau:

> we consider that it embodies the recognition on the part of WTO Members of the need to maintain a balance of rights and obligations between the right of a Member to invoke one or another of the exceptions of Article XX, specified in paragraphs (a) to (j), on the one hand, and the substantive rights of the other Members under the GATT 1994, on the other hand. Exercise by one Member of its right to invoke an exception, such as Article XX(g), if abused or misused, will, to that extent, erode or render naught the substantive treaty rights in, for example, Article XI: 1, of other Members. Similarly, because the GATT 1994 itself makes available the exceptions of Article XX, in recognition of the legitimate nature of the policies and interests there embodied, the right to invoke one of those exceptions is not to be rendered illusory.[99]

[98] Appellate Body Report, *US – Gasoline*, 20–1. In a footnote, the Appellate Body referred to GATT Panel Report, *US – Spring Assemblies*, para. 56, and to EPCT/C. 11/50, 7.

[99] Appellate Body Report, *US – Shrimp*, para. 156. In a footnote, to the following paragraph, the Appellate Body referred to GATT Panel Report, *US – Section 337*, para. 5.9.

In short, the object and purpose of the chapeau of Article XX is to avoid that provisionally justified measures are *applied* in such a way as would constitute a misuse or an abuse of the exceptions of Article XX.[100] According to the Appellate Body, a balance must be struck between the *right* of a Member to invoke an exception under Article XX and the substantive rights of the other Members under the GATT 1994. The chapeau was inserted at the head of the list of 'General Exceptions' in Article XX to ensure that this balance is struck and to prevent abuse. The Appellate Body held in *US – Shrimp*:

> In our view, the language of the chapeau makes clear that each of the exceptions in paragraphs (a) to (j) of Article XX is a *limited and conditional* exception from the substantive obligations contained in the other provisions of the GATT 1994, that is to say, the ultimate availability of the exception is subject to the compliance by the invoking Member with the requirements of the chapeau.[101]

According to the Appellate Body, the chapeau of Article XX is an expression of the principle of good faith, a general principle of law as well as a general principle of international law, which controls the exercise of rights by States. As the Appellate Body held:

> One application of this general principle, the application widely known as the doctrine of *abus de droit*, prohibits the abusive exercise of a State's rights and enjoins that, whenever the assertion of a right 'impinges on the field covered by [a] treaty obligation, it must be exercised bona fide, that is to say, reasonably'. An abusive exercise by a Member of its own treaty right thus results in a breach of the treaty rights of the other Members, and, as well, a violation of the treaty obligation of the Member so acting.[102]

In light of the above, the Appellate Body came to the following conclusion in *US – Shrimp* with respect to the interpretation and application of the chapeau:

> The task of interpreting and applying the chapeau is, hence, essentially the delicate one of locating and marking out a line of equilibrium between the right of a Member to invoke an exception under Article XX and the rights of the other Members under varying substantive provisions (e.g. Article XI) of the GATT 1994, so that neither of the competing rights will cancel out the other and thereby distort and nullify or impair the balance of rights and obligations constructed by the Members themselves in that Agreement. The location of the line of equilibrium, as expressed in the chapeau, is not fixed and unchanging; the line moves as the kind and the shape of the measures at stake vary and as the facts making up specific cases differ.[103]

In short, the interpretation and application of the chapeau in a particular case is a search for the appropriate *line of equilibrium* between the right of Members to adopt and maintain trade-restrictive legislation and measures that pursue certain legitimate societal values or interests *and* the right of other

---

[100] In *Brazil – Retreaded Tyres*, the Appellate Body emphasised that the 'focus of the chapeau, by its express terms, is on the application of a measure already found to be inconsistent with an obligation of the GATT 1994 but falling within one of the paragraphs of Article XX'. Appellate Body Report, *Brazil – Retreaded Tyres*, para. 215.   [101] Appellate Body Report, *US – Shrimp*, para. 157.

[102] *Ibid.*, para. 158. See also Appellate Body Report, *Brazil – Retreaded Tyres*, paras. 215 and 224.

[103] Appellate Body Report, *US – Shrimp*, para. 159. This was reiterated in Appellate Body Report, *Brazil – Retreaded Tyres*, para. 224.

Members to trade. The search for this line of equilibrium is guided by the requirements set out in the chapeau that the application of the trade-restrictive measure may not constitute:

- either 'arbitrary or unjustifiable discrimination between countries where the same conditions prevail';
- or 'a disguised restriction on international trade'.

The following sections examine these requirements of the chapeau in more detail.

7.2.4.2. 'Arbitrary or unjustifiable discrimination between countries where the same conditions prevail'

For a measure to be justified under Article XX, the application of that measure, pursuant to the chapeau of Article XX, may *not* constitute 'arbitrary or unjustifiable discrimination between countries where the same conditions prevail'. In *US – Gasoline*, the Appellate Body found that the 'discrimination' at issue in the chapeau of Article XX must necessarily be different from the discrimination addressed in other provisions of the GATT 1994, such as Articles I and III. The Appellate Body stated:

> The enterprise of applying Article XX would clearly be an unprofitable one if it involved no more than applying the standard used in finding that the baseline establishment rules were inconsistent with Article III:4. That would also be true if the finding were one of inconsistency with some other substantive rule of the *General Agreement*. The provisions of the chapeau cannot logically refer to the same standard(s) by which a violation of a substantive rule has been determined to have occurred. To proceed down that path would be both to empty the chapeau of its contents and to deprive the exceptions in paragraphs (a) to (j) of meaning. Such recourse would also confuse the question of whether inconsistency with a substantive rule existed, with the further and separate question arising under the chapeau of Article XX as to whether that inconsistency was nevertheless justified.[104]

As the Appellate Body noted, the chapeau of Article XX does not prohibit discrimination *per se*, but rather *arbitrary* and *unjustifiable* discrimination.

Furthermore, the Appellate Body in *US – Gasoline* addressed the meaning of the words 'discrimination *between countries* where the same conditions prevail'. The Appellate Body found that these words refer not only to discrimination *between exporting countries* where the same conditions prevail but also to discrimination *between an importing country and an exporting country* where the same conditions prevail.[105]

In *US – Shrimp*, the Appellate Body found that three elements must exist for 'arbitrary or unjustifiable discrimination' to be established:

> First, the application of the measure must result in *discrimination*. As we stated in *United States – Gasoline*, the nature and quality of this discrimination is different from the discrimination in the treatment of products which was already found to be inconsistent with

---

[104] Appellate Body Report, *US – Gasoline*, 21.   [105] See *ibid*.

one of the substantive obligations of the GATT 1994, such as Articles I, III or XI. Second, the discrimination must be *arbitrary* or *unjustifiable* in character . . . Third, this discrimination must occur *between countries where the same conditions prevail*. In *United States – Gasoline*, we accepted the assumption of the participants in that appeal that such discrimination could occur not only between different exporting Members, but also between exporting Members and the importing Member concerned.[106]

In *US – Shrimp*, the Appellate Body further elaborated on the concept of 'discrimination' and stated:

It may be quite acceptable for a government, in adopting and implementing a domestic policy, to adopt a single standard applicable to all its citizens throughout that country. However, it is not acceptable, in international trade relations, for one WTO Member to use an economic embargo to *require* other Members to adopt essentially the same comprehensive regulatory program, to achieve a certain policy goal, as that in force within that Member's territory, *without* taking into consideration different conditions which may occur in the territories of those other Members.

We believe that discrimination results not only when countries in which the same conditions prevail are differently treated, but also when the application of the measure at issue does not allow for any inquiry into the appropriateness of the regulatory program for the conditions prevailing in those exporting countries.[107]

The Appellate Body then came to the conclusion that the application of the measure at issue constituted '*arbitrary* discrimination' as follows:

Section 609, in its application, imposes a single, rigid and unbending requirement that countries applying for certification . . . adopt a comprehensive regulatory program that is essentially the same as the United States' program, without inquiring into the appropriateness of that program for the conditions prevailing in the exporting countries. Furthermore, there is little or no flexibility in how officials make the determination for certification pursuant to these provisions. In our view, this rigidity and inflexibility also constitute 'arbitrary discrimination' within the meaning of the chapeau.[108]

The Appellate Body thus decided that discrimination may also result when the same measure is applied to countries where different conditions prevail. When a measure is applied without any regard for the difference in conditions between countries and this measure is applied in a rigid and inflexible manner, the application of the measure may constitute 'arbitrary discrimination' within the meaning of the chapeau of Article XX.

To implement the recommendations and rulings in *US – Shrimp*, the United States modified the measure at issue in this case. Malaysia challenged the WTO-consistency of the implementing measure before an Article 21.5 panel. This Panel in *US – Shrimp (Article 21.5 – Malaysia)* concluded that, unlike the original US measure, the implementing measure was justified under Article XX and thus WTO-consistent. In the appeal from this Panel report, the Appellate Body held:

In our view, there is an important difference between conditioning market access on the adoption of essentially the same programme, and conditioning market access on the

---

[106] Appellate Body Report, *US – Shrimp*, para. 150. See also Panel Report, *EC – Tariff Preferences*, paras. 7.225–7.235, and *Brazil – Retreaded Tyres*, paras. 7.226–7.251.
[107] Appellate Body Report, *US – Shrimp*, paras. 164–5.   [108] *Ibid.*, para. 177.

> adoption of a programme *comparable in effectiveness*. Authorizing an importing Member to condition market access on exporting Members putting in place regulatory programmes *comparable in effectiveness* to that of the importing Member gives sufficient latitude to the exporting Member with respect to the programme it may adopt to achieve the level of effectiveness required. It allows the exporting Member to adopt a regulatory programme that is suitable to the specific conditions prevailing in its territory. As we see it, the Panel correctly reasoned and concluded that conditioning market access on the adoption of a programme *comparable in effectiveness*, allows for sufficient flexibility in the application of the measure so as to avoid 'arbitrary or unjustifiable discrimination'.[109]

Note that the Appellate Body thus seems to introduce into the chapeau of Article XX an 'embryonic' and 'soft' requirement on Members to recognise the equivalence of foreign measures comparable in effectiveness.[110] The Appellate Body found in *US – Shrimp (Article 21.5 – Malaysia)* that the revised US measure at issue in the implementation dispute was sufficiently flexible to meet the standards of the chapeau.[111] The Appellate Body added:

> a measure should be designed in such a manner that there is sufficient flexibility to take into account the specific conditions prevailing in *any* exporting Member, including, of course, Malaysia. Yet this is not the same as saying that there must be specific provisions in the measure aimed at addressing specifically the particular conditions prevailing in *every individual* exporting Member. Article XX of the GATT 1994 does not require a Member to anticipate and provide explicitly for the specific conditions prevailing and evolving in *every individual* Member.[112]

In *US – Gasoline*, the Appellate Body concluded that the measure at issue constituted '*unjustifiable* discrimination' for the following reasons:

> We have above located two omissions on the part of the United States: to explore adequately means, including in particular cooperation with the governments of Venezuela and Brazil, of mitigating the administrative problems relied on as justification by the United States for rejecting individual baselines for foreign refiners; and to count the costs for foreign refiners that would result from the imposition of statutory baselines. In our view, these two omissions go well beyond what was necessary for the Panel to determine that a violation of Article III:4 had occurred in the first place. The resulting discrimination must have been foreseen, and was not merely inadvertent or unavoidable. In the light of the foregoing, our conclusion is that the baseline establishment rules in the Gasoline Rule, in their application, constitute 'unjustifiable discrimination'.[113]

Note that the Appellate Body emphasised the *deliberate* nature of the discrimination. Likewise, the Panel in *Argentina – Hides and Leather* found that the application of the measure at issue resulted in unjustifiable discrimination as several alternative measures were available, which rendered the measure *not unavoidable*.[114]

The Appellate Body in *US – Shrimp* also addressed the question of whether the application of the measure at issue constituted an 'unjustifiable discrimination' within the meaning of the chapeau. The Appellate Body noted the following:

---

[109] Appellate Body Report, *US – Shrimp (Article 21.5 – Malaysia)*, para. 144.
[110] See also G. Marceau and J. Trachtmann, 'A Map of the WTO Law of Domestic Regulations of Goods', in G. A. Bermann and P. C. Mavroidis (eds.), *Trade and Human Health and Safety* (Cambridge University Press, 2006), 42.   [111] See Appellate Body Report, *US – Shrimp (Article 21.5 – Malaysia)*, paras. 145–8.
[112] *Ibid.*, para. 149.   [113] Appellate Body Report, *US – Gasoline*, 27.
[114] See Panel Report, *Argentina – Hides and Leather*, paras. 11.324–11.330.

> Another aspect of the application of Section 609 that bears heavily in any appraisal of justifiable or unjustifiable discrimination is the failure of the United States to engage the appellees, as well as other Members exporting shrimp to the United States, in serious, across-the-board negotiations with the objective of concluding bilateral or multilateral agreements for the protection and conservation of sea turtles, before enforcing the import prohibition against the shrimp exports of those other Members.[115]

The Appellate Body made three observations in this respect. First, the Congress of the United States expressly recognised in enacting Section 609 the importance of securing international agreements for the protection and conservation of the sea turtle species. Secondly, the protection and conservation of highly migratory species of sea turtle, i.e. the very policy objective of the measure, demands concerted and cooperative efforts on the part of the many countries whose waters are traversed in the course of recurrent sea turtle migrations. The need for, and the appropriateness of, such efforts have been recognised in the WTO itself as well as in a significant number of other international instruments and declarations.[116] Thirdly, the United States negotiated and concluded *one* regional international agreement for the protection and conservation of sea turtles: the Inter-American Convention.[117] The existence of the Inter-American Convention provided convincing demonstration that an alternative course of action was reasonably open to the United States for securing the legitimate policy goal of its measure, a course of action other than the unilateral and non-consensual procedures of the import prohibition under Section 609. The record did not, however, show that serious efforts were made by the United States to negotiate similar agreements with any other country or group of countries. Finally, the record also did not show that the United States attempted to have recourse to such international mechanisms that exist to achieve cooperative efforts to protect and conserve sea turtles before imposing the import ban.[118] The Appellate Body therefore concluded:

> Clearly, the United States negotiated seriously with some, but not with other Members (including the appellees), that export shrimp to the United States. The effect is plainly discriminatory and, in our view, unjustifiable. The unjustifiable nature of this discrimination emerges clearly when we consider the cumulative effects of the failure of the United States to pursue negotiations for establishing consensual means of protection and conservation of the living marine resources here involved.[119]

The extent to which a Member has to seek a multilateral solution to a problem before it may address the problem by unilateral measures was one of the main issues in *US – Shrimp (Article 21.5 – Malaysia)*. The Appellate Body made it clear that, in order to meet the requirement of the chapeau of Article XX, the Member needs to make serious efforts, in good faith, to negotiate a multilateral

---

[115] Appellate Body Report, *US – Shrimp*, para. 166.
[116] The Appellate Body made reference to the Decision on Trade and Environment, the Rio Declaration on Environment and Development and Agenda 21, and the Convention on the Conservation of Migratory Species of Wild Animals.   [117] See Appellate Body Report, *US – Shrimp*, para. 169.
[118] The United States, for example, did not make any attempt to raise the issue of sea turtle mortality due to shrimp trawling in the CITES Standing Committee as a subject requiring concerted action by States.
[119] Appellate Body Report, *US – Shrimp*, para. 172.

solution before resorting to unilateral measures.[120] Failure to do so may lead to the conclusion that the discrimination is 'unjustifiable'.

Finally, the Appellate Body noted in *US – Shrimp* that the application of the US measures also resulted in other differential treatment among various countries desiring certification: for example, by granting different countries different phasing-in periods to comply with the US requirements.[121] The Appellate Body concluded:

> When the foregoing differences in the means of application of Section 609 to various shrimp exporting countries are considered in their cumulative effect, we find, and so hold, that those differences in treatment constitute 'unjustifiable discrimination' between exporting countries desiring certification in order to gain access to the United States shrimp market within the meaning of the chapeau of Article XX.[122]

In *Brazil – Retreaded Tyres*, the Panel, after examining dictionary definitions, noted the following as regards the term 'unjustifiable':

> in the context of the chapeau of Article XX, these definitions suggest, overall, the need to be able to 'defend' or convincingly explain the rationale for any discrimination in the application of the measure.[123]

The Panel subsequently considered the Appellate Body Reports in *US – Gasoline*, *US – Shrimp* and *US – Shrimp (Article 21.5 – Malaysia)*, all discussed above, and held that these Reports provided useful illustrations on what might render discrimination 'arbitrary' or 'unjustifiable' within the meaning of the chapeau of Article XX.[124] However, the Panel continued:

> We do not assume . . . that exactly the same elements will necessarily be determinative in every situation . . . We recall in this regard the Appellate Body's observation, in its ruling in *US – Shrimp*, that the 'location of the line of equilibrium [between the right of a Member to invoke an exception under Article XX and the rights of the other Members under varying substantive provisions], as expressed in the chapeau, is not fixed and unchanging; the line moves as the kind and the shape of the measures at stake vary and as the facts making up specific cases differ'.[125]

In *Brazil – Retreaded Tyres*, the Panel had determined that discrimination arose in the application of the measure at issue, an import ban on retreaded tyres, from two sources: discrimination arising from the exemption from the import ban of imports of remoulded tyres originating in MERCOSUR countries (the MERCOSUR exemption); and discrimination arising from the importation of used tyres under court injunctions.[126]

With regard to the application of the import ban, in conjunction with imports of remoulded tyres under the MERCOSUR exemption, the Panel found that this application constituted neither arbitrary nor unjustifiable discrimination,[127] as the MERCOSUR exemption was granted to MERCOSUR countries

---

[120] *See* Appellate Body Report, *US – Shrimp (Article 21.5 – Malaysia)*, paras. 115–34.
[121] *See* Appellate Body Report, *US – Shrimp*, paras. 173–5.　　[122] *Ibid.*, para. 176.
[123] Panel Report, *Brazil – Retreaded Tyres*, para. 7.260.　　[124] See *ibid.*, para. 7.261.　　[125] *Ibid.*, para. 7.262.
[126] *See ibid.*, para. 7.251.　　[127] *See ibid.*, para. 7.289.

pursuant to a ruling by the MERCOSUR Tribunal finding an import ban on remoulded tyres inconsistent with MERCOSUR rules.[128] The Panel thus ruled that:

> the discrimination resulting from the MERCOSUR exemption cannot, in our view, be said to be 'capricious' or 'random'. To that extent, the measure at issue is not being applied in a manner that would constitute *arbitrary* discrimination.[129]

The Panel considered that if imports of remoulded tyres under the MERCOSUR exemption were to take place in such amounts that the achievement of the objective of the import ban would be significantly undermined, the application of the import ban, in conjunction with the exemption, would constitute a means of *unjustifiable* discrimination.[130] The Panel found, however, the levels of imports 'not to have been significant'[131] and thus concluded that the operation of the MERCOSUR exemption had not resulted in the measure being applied in a manner that would constitute *unjustifiable* discrimination.[132]

Similarly, with regard to the application of the import ban, in conjunction with imports of used tyres under court injunctions, the Panel found that this application did not constitute *arbitrary* discrimination because the discrimination was not the result of 'capricious' or 'random' action (but the result of court injunctions).[133] However, the Panel concluded that the application of the import ban, in conjunction with imports of used tyres under court injunctions, constituted *unjustifiable* discrimination because the imports of used tyres under court injunctions had taken place 'in significant amounts', undermining Brazil's stated policy objective.[134]

On appeal, the Appellate Body, referring to its analysis of whether the application of a measure results in arbitrary or unjustifiable discrimination in *US – Gasoline*, *US – Shrimp* and *US – Shrimp (Article 21.5 – Malaysia)*, noted that:

> [a]nalyzing whether discrimination is arbitrary or unjustifiable usually involves an analysis that relates primarily to *the cause or the rationale* of the discrimination.[135]
> [Emphasis added]

The Appellate Body thus rejected the Panel's interpretation of the term 'unjustifiable' as it did not depend on the *cause* or *rationale* of the discrimination but, instead, 'focused exclusively on the assessment of the *effects* of the discrimination'.[136] According to the Appellate Body, an abuse of the Article XX exceptions exists, contrary to the purpose of the chapeau, when the reasons given for discrimination 'bear no rational connection to the objective falling within the purview of a paragraph of Article XX, or would go against that objective'.[137]

---

[128] *See ibid.*, para. 7.270.   [129] *Ibid.*, para. 7.281.   [130] *See ibid.*, para. 7.287.   [131] *Ibid.*, para. 7.288.
[132] *See ibid.*, para. 7.289.   [133] *See ibid.*, para. 7.294.   [134] *See ibid.*, para. 7.303.
[135] Appellate Body Report, *Brazil – Retreaded Tyres*, para. 225.
[136] *Ibid.*, para. 229. The Appellate Body noted that the approach of the Panel of focusing exclusively on the quantitative impact of the discrimination had no support in the text of Article XX and appeared inconsistent with the Appellate Body's interpretation of the concept of 'arbitrary or unjustifiable discrimination' in previous cases. See *ibid*. However, the Appellate Body recognised that, depending on the circumstances of the case, the effects of the discrimination may be one relevant factor, *among others*, for determining whether the discrimination is justifiable. See *ibid.*, para. 230.   [137] *Ibid.*, para. 227.

Therefore whether discrimination is 'arbitrary or unjustifiable' should be assessed in the light of the *objective* of the measure.[138] The Appellate Body then had to assess whether the explanation provided by Brazil, namely that it had introduced the MERCOSUR exemption to comply with a ruling issued by a MER-COSUR tribunal, was 'acceptable as a justification for discrimination between MERCOSUR countries and non-MERCOSUR countries in relation to retreaded tyres'.[139] The Appellate Body stated:

> we have difficulty understanding how discrimination might be viewed as complying with the chapeau of Article XX when the alleged rationale for discriminating does not relate to the pursuit of or would go against the objective that was provisionally found to justify a measure under a paragraph of Article XX.
>
> ... the ruling issued by the MERCOSUR arbitral tribunal is not an acceptable rationale for the discrimination, because it bears no relationship to the legitimate objective pursued by the Import Ban that falls within the purview of Article XX(b), and even goes against this objective, to however small a degree. Accordingly, we are of the view that the MERCOSUR exemption has resulted in the Import Ban being applied in a manner that constitutes arbitrary or unjustifiable discrimination.[140]

While the Appellate Body agreed with the Panel that Brazil's decision was not 'capricious' or 'random', since decisions to implement rulings of judicial or quasi-judicial bodies cannot be characterised as such, it noted that 'discrimination can result from a rational decision or behaviour, and still be "arbitrary or unjustifiable", because it is explained by a rationale that bears no relationship to the objective of a measure provisionally justified under one of the paragraphs of Article XX, or goes against that objective'.[141] The Appellate Body made a similar finding with regard to the imports of tyres under court injunctions.[142]

In brief, the application of a provisionally justified measure will constitute 'arbitrary or unjustifiable' discrimination when the discrimination arising in the application of the provisionally justified measure is explained by a rationale that bears no relation to the objective of the measure or even goes against that objective. As the Appellate Body held in *Brazil – Retreaded Tyres*, whether discrimination is arbitrary or unjustifiable depends on the cause or rationale of the discrimination, *not* on the effects of the discrimination (as the Panel had held). The rationale of the discrimination must be assessed in the light of the contribution of the discrimination to achieving the legitimate objective provisionally found to justify the measure at issue.

---

[138] See *ibid.*   [139] *Ibid.*

[140] *Ibid.* paras. 227–8. Note that the Appellate Body stated: 'we observe, like the Panel, that, before the arbitral tribunal established under MERCOSUR, Brazil could have sought to justify the challenged Import Ban on the grounds of human, animal, and plant health under Article 50(d) of the Treaty of Montevideo. Brazil, however, decided not to do so. It is not appropriate for us to second-guess Brazil's decision not to invoke Article 50(d), which serves a function similar to that of Article XX(b) of the GATT 1994. However, Article 50(d) of the Treaty of Montevideo, as well as the fact that Brazil might have raised this defence in the MERCOSUR arbitral proceedings, show, in our view, that the discrimination associated with the MERCOSUR exemption does not necessarily result from a conflict between provisions under MERCOSUR and the GATT 1994.' *Ibid.*, para. 234.   [141] *Ibid.*, para. 232.   [142] See *ibid.*, paras. 246–7.

7.2.4.3. 'Disguised restriction on international trade'

With respect to the requirement that the application of the measure at issue does not constitute a 'disguised restriction on international trade', the Appellate Body stated in *US – Gasoline*:

> 'Arbitrary discrimination', 'unjustifiable discrimination' and 'disguised restriction' on international trade may, accordingly, be read side-by-side; they impart meaning to one another. It is clear to us that 'disguised restriction' includes disguised *discrimination* in international trade. It is equally clear that *concealed or unannounced* restriction or discrimination in international trade does *not* exhaust the meaning of 'disguised restriction'. We consider that 'disguised restriction', whatever else it covers, may properly be read as embracing restrictions amounting to arbitrary or unjustifiable discrimination in international trade taken under the guise of a measure formally within the terms of an exception listed in Article XX.[143]

According to the Appellate Body in *US – Gasoline*:

> the kinds of considerations pertinent in deciding whether the application of a particular measure amounts to 'arbitrary or unjustifiable discrimination', may also be taken into account in determining the presence of a 'disguised restriction' on international trade. The fundamental theme is to be found in the purpose and object of avoiding abuse or illegitimate use of the exceptions to substantive rules available in Article XX.[144]

The Panel in *EC – Asbestos* further clarified the requirement of the chapeau that the application of the measure at issue does not constitute a 'disguised restriction on international trade' as follows:

> a restriction which formally meets the requirements of Article XX(b) will constitute an abuse if such compliance is in fact only a disguise to conceal the pursuit of trade-restrictive objectives. However, as the Appellate Body acknowledged in *Japan – Alcoholic Beverages*, the aim of a measure may not be easily ascertained. Nevertheless, we note that, in the same case, the Appellate Body suggested that the protective application of a measure can most often be discerned from its design, architecture and revealing structure.[145]

The Panel in *US – Shrimp (Article 21.5 – Malaysia)* took the same approach.[146] In short, a measure which is provisionally justified under Article XX will be considered to constitute 'a disguised restriction on international trade' if the design, architecture or structure of the measure at issue reveals that this measure does not pursue the legitimate policy objective on which the provisional justification was based but, in fact, pursues trade-restrictive, i.e. protectionist, objectives. Such a measure cannot be justified under Article XX.

In *Brazil – Retreaded Tyres*, in order to determine whether Brazil's import ban on retreaded tyres was a 'disguised restriction on international trade', the Panel

---

[143] Appellate Body Report, *US – Gasoline*, 23.   [144] *Ibid.*
[145] Panel Report, *EC – Asbestos*, para. 8.236. In a footnote, the Panel noted that '[a]lthough this approach was developed in relation to Article III:4 of the GATT 1994, we see no reason why it should not be applicable in other circumstances where it is necessary to determine whether a measure is being applied for protective purposes'. *Ibid.*, footnote 199.
[146] Panel Report, *US – Shrimp (Article 21.5 – Malaysia)*, paras. 5.138–5.144.

again examined whether imports of used tyres under the MERCOSUR exemption as well as under court injunctions were taking place in significant amounts, so as to undermine the achievement of the objective of the import ban. It found this to be the case with regard to imports under court injunctions but not under the MERCOSUR exemption.[147] These findings were overturned by the Appellate Body, for the same reasons that it overturned the Panel's findings on 'arbitrary or unjustified discrimination'.[148]

Questions and Assignments 7.6

What is the object and purpose of the chapeau of Article XX? When is discrimination 'arbitrary or unjustifiable' within the meaning of Article XX? Which types of discrimination do the words 'discrimination *between countries* where the same conditions prevail' refer to? What is 'a disguised restriction in international trade' within the meaning of the chapeau of Article XX? Briefly describe the measures at issue in *US – Gasoline, US – Shrimp* and *Brazil – Retreaded Tyres* and discuss why the Appellate Body found that these measures did not meet the requirements of the chapeau of Article XX. Why and to what extent must a Member who wishes to invoke Article XX to justify an otherwise GATT-inconsistent measure, seek a multilateral solution to the problem the measure addresses? What does the Appellate Body Report in *Brazil – Retreaded Tyres* add to our understanding of the concepts of arbitrary and unjustifiable discrimination within the meaning of the chapeau of Article XX of the GATT 1994?

7.2.5. Scope for Members to protect other societal values

In two prominent WTO disputes involving the protection of the environment, *US – Gasoline* and *US – Shrimp*, the measures at issue were found to be provisionally justified under Article XX(g) but the application of the measures failed to satisfy the requirements of the chapeau of Article XX. The public perception of the Appellate Body reports in these disputes has been negative and unsympathetic. In particular, there is a widely held view among environmental activists that the WTO undermines necessary environmental legislation. It is noteworthy that the Appellate Body (with great foresight but only with relative success) added a paragraph to the end of both its report in *US – Gasoline* and its report in *US – Shrimp*. Here the Appellate Body explained in straightforward language the scope for Members to enact environmental legislation and the limited nature of its rulings in both cases. In *US – Shrimp*, the Appellate Body concluded with the following observation:

> In reaching these conclusions, we wish to underscore what we have *not* decided in this appeal. We have *not* decided that the protection and preservation of the environment is of

---

[147] See Panel Report, *Brazil – Retreaded Tyres*, paras. 7.354 and 7.355.
[148] See Appellate Body Report, *Brazil – Retreaded Tyres*, paras. 239 and 251.

no significance to the Members of the WTO. Clearly, it is. We have *not* decided that the sovereign nations that are Members of the WTO cannot adopt effective measures to protect endangered species, such as sea turtles. Clearly, they can and should. And we have *not* decided that sovereign states should not act together bilaterally, plurilaterally or multilaterally, either within the WTO or in other international fora, to protect endangered species or to otherwise protect the environment. Clearly, they should and do.

What we *have* decided in this appeal is simply this: although the measure of the United States in dispute in this appeal serves an environmental objective that is recognized as legitimate under paragraph (g) of Article XX of the GATT 1994, this measure has been applied by the United States in a manner which constitutes arbitrary and unjustifiable discrimination between Members of the WTO, contrary to the requirements of the chapeau of Article XX. For all of the specific reasons outlined in this Report, this measure does not qualify for the exemption that Article XX of the GATT 1994 affords to measures which serve certain recognized, legitimate environmental purposes but which, at the same time, are not applied in a manner that constitutes a means of arbitrary or unjustifiable discrimination between countries where the same conditions prevail or a disguised restriction on international trade. As we emphasized in *United States – Gasoline*, WTO Members are free to adopt their own policies aimed at protecting the environment as long as, in so doing, they fulfill their obligations and respect the rights of other Members under the *WTO Agreement*.[149]

Questions and Assignments 7.7

How much freedom does the GATT 1994 leave WTO Members to define and pursue environmental policy objectives? Do you consider the environmentalist criticism of the decisions in *US – Gasoline* and *US – Shrimp* justified?

7.3.   GENERAL EXCEPTIONS UNDER THE GATS

Like the GATT 1994, the GATS also provides for a 'general exceptions' provision allowing Members to deviate, under certain conditions, from obligations and commitments under the GATS. Article XIV of the GATS provides, in relevant part:

Subject to the requirement that such measures are not applied in a manner which would constitute a means of arbitrary or unjustifiable discrimination between countries where like conditions prevail, or a disguised restriction on trade in services, nothing in this Agreement shall be construed to prevent the adoption or enforcement by any Member of measures:

a. necessary to protect public morals or to maintain public order;
b. necessary to protect human, animal or plant life or health;
c. necessary to secure compliance with laws or regulations which are not inconsistent with the provisions of this Agreement including those relating to:
    i.   the prevention of deceptive and fraudulent practices or to deal with the effects of a default on services contracts;

---

[149] Appellate Body Report, *US – Shrimp*, paras. 185 and 186. For a similar statement in *US – Gasoline*, see Appellate Body Report, *US – Gasoline*, 28.

ii. the protection of the privacy of individuals in relation to the processing and dissemination of personal data and the protection of confidentiality of individual records and accounts;

iii. safety;

d. inconsistent with Article XVII, provided that the difference in treatment is aimed at ensuring the equitable or effective imposition or collection of direct taxes in respect of services or service suppliers of other Members;

e. inconsistent with Article II, provided that the difference in treatment is the result of an agreement on the avoidance of double taxation or provisions on the avoidance of double taxation in any other international agreement or arrangement by which the Member is bound.

The similarities between Article XX of the GATT 1994 and Article XIV of the GATS are striking. However, there are also differences. An obvious difference is that some of the justifications in Article XIV of the GATS, such as the maintenance of public order, the protection of safety and privacy, and the equitable and effective imposition or collection of direct taxes, do not appear (at least not explicitly) in Article XX of the GATT 1994. Likewise, other grounds in Article XX of the GATT 1994, such as the protection of national treasures of artistic value, are not included in Article XIV of the GATS. Nevertheless, Article XX of the GATT and its jurisprudence provide us with a basis to interpret Article XIV of the GATS. In the first case that dealt with Article XIV of the GATS, *US – Gambling*, the Appellate Body stated:

> Article XIV of the GATS sets out the general exceptions from obligations under that Agreement in the same manner as does Article XX of the GATT 1994. Both of these provisions affirm the right of Members to pursue objectives identified in the paragraphs of these provisions even if, in doing so, Members act inconsistently with obligations set out in other provisions of the respective agreements, provided that all of the conditions set out therein are satisfied. Similar language is used in both provisions, notably the term 'necessary' and the requirements set out in their respective chapeaux. Accordingly, like the Panel, we find previous decisions under Article XX of the GATT 1994 relevant for our analysis under Article XIV of the GATS.[150]

7.3.1. The two-tier test under Article XIV of the GATS

As with Article XX of the GATT 1994, Article XIV of the GATS sets out a two-tier test for determining whether a measure, otherwise inconsistent with GATS obligations and commitments, can be justified. As the Appellate Body in *US – Gambling* stated:

> Article XIV of the GATS, like Article XX of the GATT 1994, contemplates a 'two-tier analysis' of a measure that a Member seeks to justify under that provision. A panel should first determine whether the challenged measure falls within the scope of one of the paragraphs of Article XIV. This requires that the challenged measure address the particular interest specified in that paragraph and that there be a sufficient nexus between the measure and the interest protected. The required nexus – or 'degree of connection' – between the measure and the interest is specified in the language of the paragraphs themselves, through the use of terms such as 'relating to' and 'necessary to'. Where the

---

[150] Appellate Body Report, *US – Gambling*, para. 291.

> challenged measure has been found to fall within one of the paragraphs of Article XIV, a panel should then consider whether that measure satisfies the requirements of the chapeau of Article XIV.[151]

Thus, to determine whether a measure can be justified under Article XIV of the GATS, it must be examined:

- first, whether this measure can provisionally be justified under one of the specific exceptions under paragraphs (a) to (e) of Article XIV; and, if so
- second, whether the application of this measure meets the requirements of the chapeau of Article XIV.

This section therefore, firstly, discusses the specific exceptions provided for in Article XIV, and, secondly, analyses the requirements of the chapeau of Article XIV.

Questions and Assignments 7.8

What are the main elements of the Article XIV test? Explain why the interpretation of Article XX of the GATT is relevant for the analysis of Article XIV of the GATS. Give some examples of similarities and differences between Article XX of the GATT and Article XIV of the GATS.

7.3.2. Specific exceptions under Article XIV of the GATS

Article XIV of the GATS sets out, in paragraphs (a) to (e), specific grounds of justification for measures which are otherwise inconsistent with provisions of the GATS. These grounds of justification relate, *inter alia*, to:

- the protection of public morals;
- the maintenance of public order;
- the protection of human, animal or plant life or health;
- the prevention of deceptive and fraudulent practices;
- the protection of the privacy of individuals;
- the protection of safety; and
- the equitable or effective imposition or collection of direct taxes.

As the Appellate Body noted in *US – Gambling*, the paragraphs of Article XIV of the GATS contain different requirements regarding the relationship between the measure at issue and the policy objective pursued. For a measure to be provisionally justified under the exceptions listed in paragraphs (a), (b) and (c) of Article XIV, that measure must be *necessary* to achieve the policy objective pursued. No such requirement of necessity exists under paragraphs (d) and (e). To date, there is case law only on the exceptions under paragraphs (a) and (c) of Article XIV.

---

[151] *Ibid.*, para. 292.

7.3.2.1. Article XIV(a): 'measures necessary to protect public morals or to maintain public order'

Article XIV(a) of the GATS deals with measures which are 'necessary to protect public morals or to maintain public order'. Article XIV(a) sets out a two-tier test to determine whether a measure is *provisionally* justified under this provision. The Member invoking Article XIV(a) must establish that:

- the policy objective pursued by the measure at issue is the protection of public morals or the maintenance of public order; and
- the measure is necessary to fulfil that policy objective.

With regard to the first element of this two-tier test, note that the Panel in *US – Gambling* dealt extensively with its interpretation and application. Antigua challenged the GATS-consistency of a number of US federal and state laws, including the Wire Act, the Travel Act and the Illegal Gambling Business Act, which prohibit the remote supply of gambling and betting services, including internet gambling. The United States, *inter alia*, argued that the measures at issue could be justified under Article XIV(a) of the GATS, as necessary to protect public morals and maintain public order. With regard to the meaning of the concepts of 'public morals' and 'public order', the Panel in *US – Gambling* found that it:

> can vary in time and space, depending upon a range of factors, including prevailing social, cultural, ethical and religious values. Further, the Appellate Body has stated on several occasions that Members, in applying similar societal concepts, have the right to determine the level of protection that they consider appropriate. Although these Appellate Body statements were made in the context of Article XX of the GATT 1994, it is our view that such statements are also valid with respect to the protection of public morals and public order under Article [XIV] of the GATS.[152]

According to the Panel:

> Members should be given some scope to define and apply for themselves the concepts of 'public morals' and 'public order' in their respective territories, according to their own systems and scales of values.[153]

To determine the ordinary meanings of 'public morals' and 'public order', the Panel turned to the *Shorter Oxford English Dictionary* and found that the term 'public' is defined therein as: 'Of or pertaining to the people as a whole; belonging to, affecting, or concerning the community or nation'. The Panel thus ruled that a measure that is sought to be justified under Article XIV(a) must be aimed at 'protecting the interests of the people within a community or a nation as a whole'.[154] The term 'morals' is defined in the *Shorter Oxford English Dictionary* as: 'habits of life with regard to right and wrong conduct'. The Panel ruled that the term 'public morals' denotes:

---

[152] Panel Report, *US – Gambling*, para. 6.461.   [153] *Ibid*.   [154] *Ibid*., para. 6.463.

> standards of right and wrong conduct maintained by or on behalf of a community or nation.[155]

Finally, with regard to the term 'order', the Panel in *US – Gambling* noted that the dictionary definition that appears to be relevant in the context of Article XIV(a) reads as follows:

> 'A condition in which the laws regulating the public conduct of members of a community are maintained and observed; the rule of law or constituted authority; absence of violence or violent crimes'.[156]

The Panel subsequently noted that footnote 5 to Article XIV(a) of the GATS states with regard to the 'public order' exception that it:

> may be invoked only where a genuine and sufficiently serious threat is posed to one of the fundamental interests of society.

The Panel in *US – Gambling* thus concluded that the dictionary definition of the term 'order', read together with footnote 5, suggests that 'public order' refers to:

> the preservation of the fundamental interests of a society, as reflected in public policy and law. These fundamental interests can relate, *inter alia*, to standards of law, security and morality.[157]

While 'public morals' and 'public order' are two different concepts, the Panel in *US – Gambling* considered that overlap may nevertheless exist as those concepts 'seek to protect largely similar values'.[158] The Appellate Body left the Panel's interpretation of the concepts of 'public morals' and 'public order', as well as the Panel's application of the first element of the test under Article XIV(a), undisturbed.[159]

The United States had argued that Internet gambling posed threats with regard to organised crime, money laundering and fraud; risks to children; and risks to health due to possible development of an addiction to gambling.[160] The Panel had no difficulty in finding that these concerns fell within the scope of 'public morals' and 'public order' as meant in Article XIV(a) and that the Wire Act, the Travel Act and the Illegal Gambling Business Act, the measures at issue, are measures to protect 'public morals or public order'.[161]

The second element of the test under Article XIV(a) of the GATS concerns the 'necessity' requirement. As both the Panel and the Appellate Body in *US – Gambling* explicitly recognised, the extensive case law on the 'necessity' requirement of Article XX(b) and (d) of the GATT 1994 – discussed at length above – is very relevant for the interpretation and application of the 'necessity' requirement of Article XIV

---

[155] *Ibid.*, para. 6.465.   [156] *Ibid.*, para. 6.466.   [157] *Ibid.*, para. 6.467.   [158] *Ibid.*, para. 6.468.
[159] See Appellate Body Report, *US – Gambling*, paras. 296–9. The Appellate Body merely clarified the function of footnote 5 to Article XIV(a). According to the Appellate Body, this footnote does not require a separate and explicit finding that its standard is met. See Appellate Body Report, *US – Gambling*, para. 298.
[160] See Panel Report, *US – Gambling*, para. 6.479.
[161] See *ibid.*, para. 6.487. The Appellate Body upheld the Panel's findings, but did not discuss them substantively: see Appellate Body Report, para. 299.

of the GATS.[162] On the basis of this GATT case law, the Panel stated that in determining whether a measure is 'necessary' within the meaning of Article XIV(a) of the GATS it must assess the following factors:

> (a) the importance of interests or values that the challenged measure is intended to protect. (With respect to this requirement, the Appellate Body has suggested that, if the value or interest pursued is considered important, it is more likely that the measure is 'necessary'.)
>
> (b) the extent to which the challenged measure contributes to the realization of the end pursued by that measure. (In relation to this requirement, the Appellate Body has suggested that the greater the extent to which the measure contributes to the end pursued, the more likely that the measure is 'necessary'.)
>
> (c) the trade impact of the challenged measure. (With regard to this requirement, the Appellate Body has said that, if the measure has a relatively slight trade impact, the more likely that the measure is 'necessary'. The Appellate Body has also indicated that whether a reasonably available WTO-consistent alternative measure exists must be taken into consideration in applying this requirement.).[163]

With regard to the *first* of these factors to be assessed, the Panel found that the interests and values protected by the Wire Act, the Travel Act and the Illegal Gambling Business Act[164] can be characterised as 'vital and important in the highest degree'.[165] With regard to the *second* factor, the Panel found that all three Acts contribute, at least to some extent, to addressing the concerns pertaining to money laundering, organised crime, fraud, under-age gambling and pathological gambling.[166] With regard to the *third* factor, the Panel noted that:

> a key element of the application of the 'necessity' test of Article XIV in this dispute is whether the United States has explored and exhausted reasonably available WTO-consistent alternatives to the US prohibition on the remote supply of gambling and betting services that would ensure the same level of protection.[167]

However, the Panel found that the United States, in rejecting Antigua's invitation to engage in bilateral or multilateral consultations, failed to pursue a good faith course of action to explore the possibility of finding a reasonably available WTO-consistent alternative.[168] Having assessed each of the three factors, the Panel then 'weighed and balanced' those factors and concluded that the measures at issue were *not* 'necessary' within the meaning of Article XIV(a) of the GATS.[169]

On appeal, the Appellate Body stated that the weighing and balancing process to determine whether a measure is 'necessary' to maintain public order or protect public morals within the meaning of Article XIV(a) of the GATS begins with:

---

[162] See above, pp. 621–34.

[163] Panel Report, *US – Gambling*, para. 6.477. Note that one could debate whether this is a fully correct rendition of the case law on the 'necessity' requirement of Articles XX(b) and XX(d) of the GATT 1994. See above, pp. 621–34.

[164] Namely, to protect society against the threat of money laundering, organised crime, fraud and risks to children (i.e. under-age gambling) and health (i.e. pathological gambling).

[165] Panel Report, *US – Gambling*, para. 6.492. The Panel noted that this characterisation is similar to the characterisation of the protection of human life and health against a life-threatening health risk by the Appellate Body in *EC – Asbestos*. See Appellate Body Report, *EC – Asbestos*, para. 172.

[166] See Panel Report, *US – Gambling*, para. 6.494.   [167] *Ibid.*, para. 6.528.   [168] See *ibid.*, para. 6.531.

[169] See *ibid.*, para. 6.535.

an assessment of the 'relative importance' of the interests or values furthered by the challenged measure. Having ascertained the importance of the particular interests at stake, a panel should then turn to the other factors that are to be 'weighed and balanced'. The Appellate Body has pointed to two factors that, in most cases, will be relevant to a panel's determination of the 'necessity' of a measure, although not necessarily exhaustive of factors that might be considered. One factor is the contribution of the measure to the realization of the ends pursued by it; the other factor is the restrictive impact of the measure on international commerce.[170]

Next, having assessed each of these factors,

[a] comparison between the challenged measure and possible alternatives should then be undertaken, and the results of such comparison should be considered in the light of the importance of the interests at issue. It is on the basis of this 'weighing and balancing' and comparison of measures, taking into account the interests or values at stake, that a panel determines whether a measure is 'necessary' or, alternatively, whether another, WTO-consistent measure is 'reasonably available'.[171]

With respect to the availability and the nature of an 'alternative measure', the Appellate Body noted:

An alternative measure may be found not to be 'reasonably available', however, where it is merely theoretical in nature, for instance, where the responding Member is not capable of taking it, or where the measure imposes an undue burden on that Member, such as prohibitive costs or substantial technical difficulties. Moreover, a 'reasonably available' alternative measure must be a measure that would preserve for the responding Member its right to achieve its desired level of protection with respect to the objective pursued under paragraph (a) of Article XIV.[172]

As to the question of who bears the burden of proof to establish the existence of a reasonably available 'alternative measure', the Appellate Body noted that:

it is not the responding party's burden to show, in the first instance, that there are *no* reasonably available alternatives to achieve its objectives. In particular, a responding party need not identify the universe of less trade-restrictive alternative measures and then show that none of those measures achieves the desired objective. The WTO agreements do not contemplate such an impracticable and, indeed, often impossible burden.

Rather, it is for a responding party to make a *prima facie* case that its measure is 'necessary' by putting forward evidence and arguments that enable a panel to assess the challenged measure in the light of the relevant factors to be 'weighed and balanced' in a given case. The responding party may, in so doing, point out why alternative measures would not achieve the same objectives as the challenged measure, but it is under no obligation to do so in order to establish, in the first instance, that its measure is 'necessary'.

If, however, the complaining party raises a WTO-consistent alternative measure that, in its view, the responding party should have taken, the responding party will be required to demonstrate why its challenged measure nevertheless remains 'necessary' in the light of that alternative or, in other words, why the proposed alternative is not, in fact, 'reasonably available'.[173]

As discussed above, the Panel had concluded that the United States had not established that its measures were 'necessary' because, in rejecting Antigua's

---

[170] Appellate Body Report, *US – Gambling*, para. 306.   [171] *Ibid.*, para. 307.   [172] *Ibid.*, para. 308.
[173] *Ibid.*, paras. 309–11.

invitation to engage in bilateral or multilateral consultations, it had failed to explore and exhaust reasonably available WTO-consistent alternatives to the measures at issue.[174] According to the Appellate Body, the Panel's 'necessity' analysis was flawed because it did *not* focus on an alternative measure that was reasonably available to the United States to achieve the stated objectives.[175] Engaging in consultations with Antigua was not an appropriate alternative for the Panel to consider *because* consultations are 'by definition a process, the results of which are uncertain and therefore not capable of comparison with the measures at issue in this case'.[176]

Having reversed the Panel's conclusion on 'necessity', the Appellate Body then examined for itself whether the measures at issue, the Wire Act, the Travel Act and the Illegal Gambling Business Act, were 'necessary' within the meaning of Article XIV(a) of the GATS.[177] The Appellate Body agreed with the United States that the 'sole basis' for the Panel's conclusion that the measures were not necessary was its finding relating to the requirement of consultations with Antigua.[178] As the Appellate Body had found that the Panel had erred in finding that consultations with Antigua constituted a measure reasonably available to the United States,[179] and as Antigua had raised no other 'alternative measure', the Appellate Body concluded as follows:

> In our opinion, therefore, the record before us reveals no reasonably available alternative measure proposed by Antigua or examined by the Panel that would establish that the three federal statutes are not 'necessary' within the meaning of Article XIV(a). Because the United States made its *prima facie* case of 'necessity', and Antigua failed to identify a reasonably available alternative measure, we conclude that the United States demonstrated that its statutes are 'necessary', and therefore justified, under paragraph (a) of Article XIV.[180]

According to the Appellate Body, the measures at issue in *US – Gambling*, which prohibit the remote supply of gambling and betting services, including Internet gambling, are 'necessary' for the maintenance of public order and the protection of public morals within the meaning of Article XIV of the GATS.

Questions and Assignments 7.9

What are the constituent elements of the test under Article XIV(a) of the GATS? How did the Panel in *US – Gambling* interpret the concepts of 'public morals' and 'public order'? Did the Appellate Body agree with this interpretation? Give some examples of 'public morals'. When is a measure 'necessary' within the meaning of Article XIV(a)? When can an 'alternative measure' be found not to be 'reasonably available'? Does the responding party have to prove that there is no reasonably available alternative measure? Why did the Appellate Body in *US – Gambling*

---

[174] See Panel Report, *US – Gambling*, para. 6.531. For a summary by the Appellate Body of the key findings of the Panel, see Appellate Body Report, *US – Gambling*, para. 315.
[175] See Appellate Body Report, *US – Gambling*, para. 317.   [176] *Ibid.*
[177] See Appellate Body Report, *US – Gambling*, para. 325.
[178] The Appellate Body noted that the Panel had acknowledged that it would have found that the United States had made its *prima facie* case that its measures were 'necessary' if the United States had not refused to accept Antigua's invitation to consult. See *ibid.*, para. 325.   [179] See *ibid.*, para. 317.   [180] *Ibid.*, para. 326.

reverse the Panel's finding on the 'necessity' requirement under Article
XIV(a) of the GATS?

7.3.2.2. Article XIV(c): 'measures necessary to secure compliance with . . .'

As mentioned above, Article XIV(c) concerns and can justify otherwise GATS-
inconsistent measures:

> necessary to secure compliance with laws or regulations which are not inconsistent with
> the provisions of this Agreement including those relating to:
>
> i.   the prevention of deceptive and fraudulent practices or to deal with the effects of a
>   default on services contracts;
> ii. the protection of the privacy of individuals in relation to the processing and dissemi-
>   nation of personal data and the protection of confidentiality of individual records and
>   accounts;
> iii safety.

As held by the Panel in *US–Gambling*, Article XIV(c) of the GATS sets out a three-
tier test to determine whether a measure is *provisionally* justified under Article
XIV(c). The Member invoking Article XIV(c) must establish that:

- the measure at issue is designed to *secure compliance* with national laws or regulations;
- those national laws and regulations are not inconsistent with the *WTO
  Agreement*; and
- the measure at issue is *necessary* to secure compliance with those national
  laws and regulations.[181]

For the interpretation and application of the first two elements of the test
under Article XIV(c) of the GATS, the Panel in *US – Gambling* referred back to the
case law on Article XX(d) of the GATT 1994, discussed above.[182] In view of the similarity of Article XIV(c) of the GATS with Article XX(d) of the GATT 1994, this case
law is, according to the Panel in *US – Gambling*, most relevant. Consequently, the
Panel in *US – Gambling* noted that measures for which justification is sought
must enforce 'obligations' contained in the laws and regulations rather than
'merely ensure attainment of the objectives of those laws and regulations'.[183] In
addition, the Panel stated that a measure does not have to be designed exclusively to secure compliance; it is sufficient that 'securing compliance' is part of
the reason to put the measure into place.[184] Finally, the Panel noted that the list
in Article XIV(c) of possible laws and regulations is not exhaustive.[185]

---

[181] See Panel Report, *US – Gambling*, para. 6.536.
[182] See *ibid.*, paras. 6.536–6.540. With regard to the case law on Article XX(d) of the GATT 1994, see above,
     p. 629.
[183] Panel Report, *US – Gambling*, para. 6.538. See also GATT Panel Report, *EEC – Parts and Components*, paras.
     5.14–5.18.
[184] See Panel Report, *US – Gambling*, para. 6.539. See also Panel Report, *Korea – Various Measures on Beef*, para. 658.
[185] See Panel Report, *US – Gambling*, para. 6.540. Laws and regulations other than those that fall within the
     list may be relied upon in justifying a GATS-inconsistent measure under Article XIV(c) provided that
     those other laws and regulations are WTO-consistent. See *ibid.*

The third element under the Article XIV(c) test concerns the 'necessity' requirement. The analysis required to determine whether a measure is necessary under Article XIV(c) of the GATS is essentially the same as the analysis required under Article XIV(a) of the GATS, discussed above. The Panel in *US – Gambling* applied the same analysis, but in doing so, it quite logically made the same mistake as the Appellate Body had identified in the Panel's Article XIV(a) analysis.[186] The Appellate Body thus also reversed the Panel's conclusion on the 'necessity' requirement under Article XIV(c).[187]

Questions and Assignments 7.10

What are the constituent elements of the test under Article XIV(c) of the GATS? What does the necessity test under Article XIV(c) entail?

7.3.2.3. *Other paragraphs of Article XIV of the GATS*

With regard to the remaining paragraphs of Article XIV of the GATS, a distinction must be drawn between paragraph (b), which requires that the measure be *necessary* to achieve the policy objective pursued, and paragraphs (d) and (e), which do not impose such a 'necessity' requirement.

Paragraph (b) relates to measures 'necessary to protect human, animal or plant life or health'. Hence, for an otherwise GATS-inconsistent measure to be *provisionally* justified under Article XIV(b):

- the policy objective pursued by the measure must be the protection of life or health of humans, animals or plants; and
- the measure must be necessary to fulfil that policy objective.

To date, there has been no case law on the requirements set out by Article XIV(b). However, as regards the 'necessity' test, it may be assumed that the interpretation of the necessity requirement under Article XIV(a) and (c) of the GATS and the extensive case law on the necessity requirement of Article XX(b) and (d) of the GATT 1994 are relevant.[188]

With regard to Article XIV(d) and (e) of the GATS, it must be noted that the scope of these provisions is rather narrow. The grounds of justification set out in these provisions *only* justify inconsistency with the national treatment obligation of Article XVII of the GATS *or* the MFN treatment obligation of Article II of the GATS. With regard to measures relating to direct taxation, Article XIV(d) of

---

[186] The Panel considered that the measures at issue were not 'necessary' because, in failing to engage in consultations with Antigua, the United States failed to explore and exhaust all reasonably available alternative measures. See above, pp. 658–9.

[187] See Appellate Body Report, *US – Gambling*, para. 336. Note that the Appellate Body did not consider it necessary to complete the legal analysis and determine whether the measures at issue were justified under Article XIV(c) since it had already found that the measures were justified under Article XIV(a). See Appellate Body Report, *US – Gambling*, para. 337.   [188] See above, pp. 623, 632.

the GATS allows Members to adopt or enforce measures which are inconsistent with the national treatment obligation of Article XVII:

> provided that the difference in treatment is aimed at ensuring the equitable or effective imposition or collection of direct taxes in respect of services or service suppliers of other Members.[189]

Footnote 6 to Article XIV(d) contains a non-exhaustive list of measures that are aimed at ensuring the equitable or effective imposition or collection of direct taxes. This list includes, for example:

- measures taken by a Member under its taxation system which apply to non-residents in order to ensure the imposition or collection of taxes in the Member's territory; and
- measures taken by a Member under its taxation system which apply to non-residents or residents to prevent the avoidance or evasion of taxes, including compliance measures.

Article XIV(e) of the GATS allows a Member to adopt or enforce measures which are inconsistent with the MFN treatment obligation of Article II:

> provided that the difference in treatment is the result of an agreement on the avoidance of double taxation or provisions on the avoidance of double taxation in any other international agreement or arrangement by which the Member is bound.

Questions and Assignments 7.11

Discuss the measures relating to direct taxes which Members are allowed to take under Article XIV of the GATS.

7.3.3. The chapeau of Article XIV of the GATS

As discussed above, Article XIV of the GATS sets out a two-tier test for determining whether a measure, otherwise inconsistent with GATS obligations, can be justified. Under this test, once it has been established that the measure at issue meets the requirements of one of the particular exceptions of paragraphs (a) to (e), it must be examined whether the measure meets the requirements of the chapeau of Article XIV. The chapeau of Article XIV requires that the *application* of the measure at issue does not constitute:

- either 'arbitrary or unjustifiable discrimination between countries where the same conditions prevail';
- or 'a disguised restriction on trade in services'.

Note that the language of the chapeau of Article XIV of the GATS is quite similar to that of the chapeau of Article XX of the GATT 1994. Therefore, many lessons

---

[189] Article XIV(d) of the GATS.

can be drawn from the extensive case law on the application of the chapeau of Article XX, discussed in detail above.[190] The Panel in *US – Gambling* looked at this case law and concluded:

> To sum up these interpretive principles, the chapeau of Article XX of the GATT 1994 addresses not so much a challenged measure or its specific content, but rather the manner in which that measure is applied, with a view to ensuring that the exceptions of Article XX are not abused. In order to do so, the chapeau of Article XX identifies three standards which may be invoked in relation to the same facts: arbitrary discrimination, unjustifiable discrimination and disguised restriction on trade. In our view, these principles would also be applicable in relation to Article XIV of the GATS.[191]

Moreover, the Panel stated that in determining whether the application of the measures at issue constitutes 'arbitrary and unjustifiable discrimination' or a 'disguised restriction on trade':

> the *absence of consistency* in this regard may lead to a conclusion that the measures in question are applied in a manner that constitutes 'arbitrary and unjustifiable discrimination between countries where like conditions prevail' and/or a 'disguised restriction on trade'.[192]
>
> [Emphasis added]

In the course of its examination of the requirements of the chapeau of Article XIV of the GATS, the Panel found that the United States had not prosecuted certain domestic remote suppliers of gambling services and that the US Interstate Horseracing Act was 'ambiguous' as to whether or not it permitted certain types of remote betting on horse racing within the United States.[193] On the basis of these two findings indicating a lack of consistency in the application of the prohibition on the remote supply of gambling and betting services, the Panel in *US – Gambling* thus concluded that:

> the United States has not demonstrated that it does not apply its prohibition on the remote supply of wagering services for horse racing in a manner that [constitutes] 'arbitrary and unjustifiable discrimination between countries where like conditions prevail' and/or a 'disguised restriction on trade' in accordance with the requirements of the chapeau of Article XIV.[194]

On appeal, the United States argued that the 'consistency' standard applied by the Panel is not adequate for a complete examination under the requirements of the chapeau of Article XIV.[195] The Appellate Body, however,

---

[190] See above, pp. 641–50.
[191] Panel Report, *US – Gambling*, para. 6.581. The Appellate Body confirmed the importance of Article XX of the GATT for interpretation of Article XIV of the GATS in *US – Gambling*, as explained above, p. 653.
[192] *Ibid.*, para. 6.584.
[193] On the failure to prosecute certain domestic remote suppliers of gambling services, see Panel Report, *US – Gambling*, para. 6.588. On the US Interstate Horseracing Act, see Panel Report, *US – Gambling*, para. 6.599.
[194] Panel Report, *US – Gambling*, para. 6.608.
[195] According to the United States, the Panel assessed only whether the United States treats domestic service suppliers differently from foreign service suppliers. The United States considered such an assessment to be inadequate, because the chapeau of Article XIV of the GATS also requires a determination of whether differential treatment, or discrimination, is 'arbitrary' or 'unjustifiable'.

dismissed this argument of the United States and upheld the Panel's 'consistency' standard.[196]

Questions and Assignments 7.12

In what way does the chapeau of Article XIV of the GATS differ from the chapeau of Article XX of the GATT 1994? What is the object and purpose of the chapeau of Article XIV of the GATS?

7.4. SECURITY EXCEPTIONS

In addition to the 'general exceptions' contained in Article XX of the GATT 1994 and Article XIV of the GATS, WTO law also provides for exceptions relating to national and international security. This section discusses, first, the security exception of Article XXI of the GATT 1994 and, then, the security exception of Article XIV *bis* of the GATS.[197]

7.4.1. Article XXI of the GATT 1994

Article XXI of the GATT 1994, entitled 'Security Exceptions', states:

> Nothing in this Agreement shall be construed
>
> a. to require any [Member] to furnish any information the disclosure of which it considers contrary to its essential security interests; or
> b. to prevent any [Member] from taking any action which it considers necessary for the protection of its essential security interests
>   i.   relating to fissionable materials or the materials from which they are derived;
>   ii. relating to the traffic in arms, ammunition and implements of war and to such traffic in other goods and materials as is carried on directly or indirectly for the purpose of supplying a military establishment;
>   iii. taken in time of war or other emergency in international relations; or
> c. to prevent any [Member] from taking any action in pursuance of its obligations under the United Nations Charter for the maintenance of international peace and security.

Unlike Article XX, Article XXI has not played a significant role in the practice of dispute settlement under the GATT 1947 or the WTO to date. Article XXI has been invoked in only a few disputes.[198] Nevertheless, this provision is not

---

[196] Appellate Body Report, *US – Gambling*, paras. 348–51. Note, however, that while the Appellate Body agreed with the Panel's approach to the examination of the chapeau of Article XIV of GATS, it eventually upheld only the Panel's finding of 'inconsistency' with regard to the Interstate Horseracing Act. The Appellate Body reversed the Panel's finding of 'inconsistency' based on the alleged non-prosecution of certain domestic remote suppliers of gambling services (because the three Acts at issue, on their face, do *not* discriminate between United States and foreign suppliers of remote gambling services *and* the evidence of the alleged non-enforcement of the three Acts was 'inconclusive'). See Appellate Body Report, *US – Gambling*, paras. 351–7, 358–66 and 368–9.

[197] Note that the *TRIPS Agreement* contains a similar provision in Article 73.

[198] Article XXI of the GATT was invoked as a defence in *US – Export Restrictions* (1949), *US – Imports of Sugar from Nicaragua* (1984), *US – Trade Measures Affecting Nicaragua* (1986), *EEC – Trade Measures taken against the Socialist Republic of Yugoslavia* (1991) and *US – The Cuban Liberty and Democratic Solidarity Act (Helms–Burton Act)* (1996).

without importance. WTO Members do, on occasion, take trade-restrictive measures, either unilaterally or multilaterally, against other Members as a means to achieve national or international security and peace. Members taking such measures will seek justification for these measures under Article XXI. As will be discussed, there is a significant structural and interpretative difference between Article XX and Article XXI.

7.4.1.1. *Article XXI(a) and (b) of the GATT 1994: national security*

Traditionally, in international relations, national security takes precedence over the benefits of trade. This may be the case in three types of situation. First, States may consider it necessary to restrict trade in order to protect strategic domestic production capabilities from import competition. The judgement as to which production capabilities deserve to be qualified as strategically important differs among countries and is, to a great extent, political. Defined broadly, all industries equipping the military, including for example boot manufacturers, could be viewed as being of strategic importance.

Secondly, States may wish to use trade sanctions, as an instrument of foreign policy, against other States who either violate international law or pursue policies considered to be unacceptable or undesirable.

Thirdly, States may want to prohibit the export of arms or other products of military use to countries with which they do not have friendly relations.

Article XXI of the GATT 1994 is not concerned with *all* of these situations. Note that also other provisions of the GATT 1994 allow Members leeway to preserve national industries of strategic importance. WTO Members can, subject to limitations, provide protection through import tariffs, production subsidies and government procurement practices. In some situations, however, Article XXI can be useful to provide justification for otherwise GATT-inconsistent measures.

Article XXI(a) allows a Member to withhold information, that it would normally be required to supply when 'it considers' disclosure of that information 'contrary to its essential security interests'. This provision has been interpreted broadly by some Members. In this regard, note the following statement by the United States:

> The United States does consider it contrary to its security interest – and to the security interest of other friendly countries – to reveal the names of the commodities that it considers to be most strategic.[199]

Article XXI(b) allows a Member to adopt or maintain certain measures which that Member considers necessary for the protection of its essential security interests. The categories of measure concerned are broadly defined in subparagraphs (i), (ii) and (iii) of Article XXI(b) as:

- measures relating to fissionable materials;

---

[199] GATT/CP.3/38, 9.

- measures relating to trade in arms or in other materials, directly or indirectly, for military use; and
- measures taken in time of war or other emergency in international relations.

Unlike Article XX of the GATT 1994, Article XXI does not have a chapeau to prevent misuse or abuse of the exceptions contained therein.[200]

In view of their wording, and in particular the use of the terms 'action which it *considers* necessary' (emphasis added), the question arises whether the exceptions of Article XXI(b) are 'justiciable', i.e. whether the application of these exceptions can usefully be reviewed by panels and the Appellate Body. Indeed, Article XXI(b) gives a Member very broad discretion to take national security measures which it 'considers necessary for the protection of its essential security interests'. However, it is imperative that a certain degree of 'judicial review' be maintained; otherwise the provision would be prone to abuse without redress.[201] At a minimum, panels and the Appellate Body should conduct an examination as to whether the explanation provided by the Member concerned is reasonable or whether the measure constitutes an apparent abuse.[202]

The exceptions of Article XXI(b) have been invoked in a few GATT disputes and have been discussed on a few other occasions before the establishment of the WTO. For instance, in the discussion on the complaint by Czechoslovakia against export restrictions imposed by the United States, it was stated that:

> every country must be the judge in the last resort on questions relating to its own security. On the other hand, every Contracting Party should be cautious not to take any step which might have the effect of undermining the General Agreement.[203]

In 1982, in the context of the armed conflict between the United Kingdom and Argentina over the Falkland Islands/Islas Malvinas, the European Economic Community and its Member States as well as Canada and Australia applied trade restrictions against imports from Argentina. In a 'reaction' to these actions, the GATT CONTRACTING PARTIES adopted a Ministerial Declaration which stated that:

> the contracting parties undertake, individually and jointly: . . . to abstain from taking restrictive trade measures, for reasons of a non-economic character, *not consistent* with the General Agreement.[204]
>
> [Emphasis added]

At the time, the GATT CONTRACTING PARTIES also adopted the following *Decision Concerning Article XXI of the General Agreement*:

> *Considering* that the exceptions envisaged in Article XXI of the General Agreement constitute an important element for safeguarding the rights of contracting parties when they

---

[200] See above, pp. 641–2.

[201] See the GATT Panel's statement in *US – Trade Measures Affecting Nicaragua*, in *GATT Activities 1986*, 58–9.

[202] See further W. Cann, 'Creating Standards and Accountability for the Use of the WTO Security Exception: Reducing the Role of Power-Base Relations and Establishing a New Balance between Sovereignty and Multilateralism', *Yale Journal of International Law*, 2001, 426.

[203] GATT Panel Report, *US – Restrictions on Exports to Czechoslovakia*, GATT/CP.3/SR.22, Corr.1.

[204] L/5424, adopted on 29 November 1982, 29S/9, 11.

consider that reasons of security are involved; *Noting* that recourse to Article XXI could constitute, in certain circumstances, an element of disruption and uncertainty for international trade and affect benefits accruing to contracting parties under the General Agreement; *Recognizing* that in taking action in terms of the exceptions provided in Article XXI of the General Agreement, contracting parties should take into consideration the interests of third parties which may be affected;That until such time as the CONTRACTING PARTIES may decide to make a formal interpretation of Article XXI it is appropriate to set procedural guidelines for its application;

The CONTRACTING PARTIES *decide* that:

1. Subject to the exception in Article XXI:a, contracting parties should be informed to the fullest extent possible of trade measures taken under Article XXI.
2. When action is taken under Article XXI, all contracting parties affected by such action retain their full rights under the General Agreement.
3. The Council may be requested to give further consideration to this matter in due course.[205]

In 1985, the United States imposed a trade embargo on Nicaragua.[206] The United States was strongly opposed to the communist Sandinistas who were in power in Nicaragua at that time. Nicaragua argued that the trade embargo imposed by the United States was inconsistent with Articles I, II, V, XI and XIII and Part IV of the GATT and could not be justified – as the United States argued – under Article XXI. Nicaragua requested the establishment of a panel. According to the United States, however, Article XXI left it to each Contracting Party to judge what action it considered necessary for the protection of its essential security interests.[207] A Panel was established in this case but the terms of reference of this Panel stated that the Panel could not examine or judge the validity or motivation for the invocation of Article XXI by the United States. In its report, the Panel therefore concluded that:

as it was not authorized to examine the justification for the United States' invocation of [Article XXI], it could find the United States neither to be complying with its obligations under the General Agreement nor to be failing to carry out its obligations under that Agreement.[208]

To date, the exceptions of Article XXI have not been invoked in any case before a WTO panel or the Appellate Body. Note, however, that in *US – Cuban Liberty and Democratic Solidarity Act*, commonly referred to as *US–Helms-Burton Act*, the United States informed the WTO that it would not participate in the panel proceedings since it was of the opinion that the Helms-Burton Act was not within the scope of application of WTO law and, therefore, not within the jurisdiction of the Panel. The Helms-Burton Act permits US nationals to bring legal action in US courts against foreign companies that deal or traffic in US property confiscated by the

---

[205] L/5426, 29S/23.
[206] Note that in 1983 Nicaragua's share of the total US sugar import quota was already substantially reduced. The US stated before the GATT Panel examining this measure that 'it was neither invoking any exceptions under the provisions of the General Agreement nor intending to defend its actions in GATT terms' (para. 3.10). The Panel found that the US had acted inconsistently with Article XIII of the GATT 1947. GATT Panel Report, *US – Imports of Sugar from Nicaragua*.
[207] See *Analytical Index: Guide to GATT Law and Practice* (WTO, 1995), 601, 603 and 604.
[208] GATT Panel Report, *US – Trade Measures Affecting Nicaragua*, L/6053, dated 13 October 1986, para. 5.3. This report was never adopted.

Cuban government. The European Communities contended that this and other measures provided for under the Helms-Burton Act were inconsistent with the obligations of the United States under Articles I, II, V, XI and XII of the GATT 1994.[209] According to the United States, however, this dispute concerned diplomatic and *security issues* and 'was not fundamentally a trade matter' and, therefore, not a WTO matter.[210] Few Members shared this opinion.[211]

Questions and Assignments 7.13

Which measures, otherwise GATT-inconsistent, can be justified under Article XXI(a) and (b) of the GATT 1994? Why is 'judicial review' by panels and the Appellate Body of the invocation by Members of the exceptions of Article XXI(b) problematic? Is such review desirable and, if so, to what extent? Give an example of a measure that could be justified under Article XXI(b) of the GATT 1994.

7.4.1.2. *Article XXI(c) of the GATT 1994: international peace and security*

Article XXI(c) of the GATT 1994 allows WTO Members to take actions in pursuance of their obligations under the United Nations Charter for the maintenance of international peace and security. This means that Members may depart from their GATT obligations in order to implement economic sanctions imposed by the United Nations. Article 41 of the UN Charter empowers the Security Council to impose economic sanctions pursuant to Article 39 of the Charter, once it has determined the existence of any threat to the peace, breach of the peace or act of aggression. Article 41 of the Charter provides:

> The Security Council may decide what measures not involving the use of armed force are to be employed to give effect to its decisions, and it may call upon the Members of the United Nations to apply such measures. These may include complete or partial interruption of economic relations and of rail, sea, air, postal, telegraphic, radio, and other means of communication, and the severance of diplomatic relations.

Such Security Council decisions to apply economic sanctions are binding on UN Members according to Article 25 of the Charter:

> The Members of the United Nations agree to accept and carry out the decisions of the Security Council in accordance with the present Charter.

Hence, Article XXI(c) enables WTO Members to honour their commitments under the UN Charter and gives effect to the rule of conflict contained in Article 103 of the Charter. Article 103 provides:

---

[209] See Request for Consultations, *US – The Cuban Liberty and Democratic Solidarity Act (Helms–Burton Act)*, WT/DS38/1, dated 13 May 1996.
[210] WT/DSB/M/24, dated 16 October 1996, 7. At the request of the European Communities, the Panel proceedings were suspended to allow for further negotiations to reach a mutually agreed solution to this dispute. No such solution has ever been explicitly agreed on but the United States has never applied the most controversial aspects of the Helms–Burton Act.   [211] See WT/DSB/M/24, dated 16 October 1996, 8–9.

> In the event of a conflict between the obligations of the Members of the United Nations under the present Charter and their obligations under any other international agreement, their obligations under the present Charter shall prevail.

At first glance, the issue of 'justiciability' appears to be less problematic for the exception provided in Article XXI(c), given that this provision does not refer to what the Member invoking the exception 'considers' to be necessary. The basis for the departure from GATT obligations must be an obligation under the UN Charter, and a panel can assess the question of whether there is such an obligation.

Questions and Assignments 7.14

Which measures, otherwise GATT-inconsistent, can be justified under Article XXI(c) of the GATT 1994? Give an example of a measure that could be justified under Article XXI(c) of the GATT 1994.

7.4.2. Article XIV *bis* of the GATS

Article XIV *bis* of the GATS, entitled 'Security Exceptions', states, in its first paragraph:

> Nothing in this Agreement shall be construed:
>
> a. to require any Member to furnish any information, the disclosure of which it considers contrary to its essential security interests; or
> b. to prevent any Member from taking any action which it considers necessary for the protection of its essential security interests:
>   i. relating to the supply of services as carried out directly or indirectly for the purpose of provisioning a military establishment;
>   ii. relating to fissionable and fusionable materials or the materials from which they are derived;
>   iii. taken in time of war or other emergency in international relations; or
> c. to prevent any Member from taking any action in pursuance of its obligations under the United Nations Charter for the maintenance of international peace and security.

Article XIV *bis* of the GATS thus allows Members to adopt and enforce measures, in the interest of national or international security, otherwise inconsistent with GATS obligations. The language of this provision is virtually identical to Article XXI of the GATT 1994. Like Article XXI of the GATT 1994, Article XIV *bis* of the GATS is not without importance. On occasion, WTO Members take unilateral or multilateral measures affecting trade in services against other Members, as a means to achieve national or international security and peace. Members taking such measures can seek justification for these measures under Article XIV *bis*.

Note that Article XIV *bis* of the GATS, unlike Article XXI of the GATT 1994, provides for a notification requirement. The second paragraph of Article XIV *bis* states:

> The Council for Trade in Services shall be informed to the fullest extent possible of measures taken under paragraphs 1(b) and (c) and of their termination.

To date, Article XIV *bis* of the GATS, unlike Article XXI of the GATT, has never been invoked in dispute settlement proceedings.

Questions and Assignments 7.15

How does Article XIV *bis* of the GATS differ from Article XXI of the GATT 1994? Give an example of a trade measure of the European Communities or one of the Member States of the European Union that would be justified under Article XIV *bis* of the GATS.

7.5. ECONOMIC EMERGENCY EXCEPTIONS

Apart from the 'general exceptions' and the 'security exceptions', discussed above, WTO law also provides for 'economic emergency exceptions'. These exceptions allow Members to adopt measures, otherwise WTO-inconsistent, in situations where a surge in imports causes, or threatens to cause, serious injury to the domestic industry. The possibility to restrict trade in such situations is a 'safety valve' which has always been, and still is, provided for in most trade agreements, including the *WTO Agreement*. It reflects the political reality that trade liberalisation may be difficult to sustain if and when it creates unexpected and severe economic hardship for certain sectors of a country's economy. The otherwise WTO-inconsistent measures taken in economic emergency situations are referred to as 'safeguard measures'. Safeguard measures temporarily restrict import competition to allow the domestic industry time to adjust to new economic realities. Their application does not depend upon 'unfair' trade actions, as is the case with anti-dumping or countervailing measures.[212] Safeguard measures are applied to 'fair trade', i.e. trade occurring under normal competitive conditions and in accordance with WTO law. The Appellate Body therefore noted in *Argentina – Footwear (EC)*:

> the import restrictions that are imposed on products of exporting Members when a safeguard action is taken must be seen . . . as *extraordinary*. And, when construing the prerequisites for taking such actions, their extraordinary nature must be taken into account.[213]
>
> [Emphasis added]

This section discusses the rules on safeguard measures with respect to trade in goods, provided for in Article XIX of the GATT 1994 and the *Agreement on Safeguards*. It examines the characteristics of safeguard measures, the conditions for the use of safeguard measures and the rules on the procedural requirements

---

[212] See above, pp. 546–54, 585–99.   [213] Appellate Body Report, *Argentina – Footwear (EC)*, para. 94.

that Members must meet when imposing safeguard measures. Note that WTO law also provides for *special* safeguard measures that may be applied on imports of agricultural products.[214] As briefly discussed in this section, the requirements for the use of these special safeguard measures are less stringent than those for the use of the normal safeguard measures.[215]

As discussed above, China's Accession Protocol provides for a specific *transitional* safeguard mechanism that other WTO Members can resort to in order to limit imports of goods from China until December 2013.[216] This specific safeguard mechanism is briefly discussed below.[217]

The GATS does not currently provide for the possibility to take safeguard measures. Article X of the GATS, however, calls for multilateral negotiations on safeguard measures for trade in services.[218] Such negotiations are now conducted in the context of the Doha Development Round.[219]

Since the establishment of the WTO in 1995, 159 initiations of safeguard measure investigations were reported to the WTO. Less than half of these investigations resulted in the actual imposition of safeguard measures.[220] India has been the most frequent user of safeguard measures with a total of fifteen reported initiations since 1995. Jordan follows with twelve initiations, and then Chile and Turkey with eleven initiations each. The United States has also been a prolific user with ten initiations and its 2002 safeguard measures on steel were some of the biggest ever imposed in terms of magnitude.[221] The European communities has initiated only four investigations since 2005. It seems that the European Communities tries to avoid using safeguard measures when possible. An example of an 'unfortunate' and highly publicised measure under the special safeguard regime for Chinese textiles was the measure imposed in 2005 by the European Communities.[222] During the first ten months of 2007, there have been

---

[214] See Article 5 of the *Agreement on Agriculture*. The *Agreement on Textiles and Clothing* provided in its Article 6 for transitional safeguard measures on imports of textile products. However, the *Agreement on Textiles and Clothing* is no longer in force. See above, p. 46.   [215] See below, p. 693.   [216] See above, pp. 112–13.

[217] See below, pp. 694–5.

[218] Pursuant to Article X of the GATS, the results of these negotiations should have entered into effect no later than 1 January 1998. However, this deadline for the negotiations has since repeatedly been extended.

[219] Ministerial Conference, *Doha Ministerial Declaration*, adopted on 14 November 2001, WT/MIN(01)/DEC/1, dated 20 November 2001, para. 15.

[220] To date, eighty-two final safeguard measures have been imposed. This number is based on the notifications of Members under Article 12.1 of the *Agreement on Safeguards* from 1 January 1995 to 31 October 2007. It excludes notifications of measures taken in terms of Article 5 of the *Agreement on Agriculture* or Section 16 of the *Protocol on the Accession of the People's Republic of China*. See www.wto.org/english/news_e/news07_e/safeg_nov07_e.htm, visited on 12 November 2007.

[221] On 5 March 2002, the United States imposed safeguard measures on imports of a range steel products in the form of additional duties ranging from 8, 13, 15 and up to 30 per cent as well as a tariff quota for a three-year period beginning on 20 March 2002. This was the first time a safeguard measure was applied by a major economy against one of the most traded products in the world (it affected as much as 1.31 billion tons of steel trade per year). See Y. S. Lee, 'Test of Multilateralism in International Trade: US Steel Safeguards', *bepress Legal Series* Paper 253, 2004, 4. See also http://ec.europa.eu/trade/issues/sectoral/industry/steel/index_en.htm, visited on 1 December 2007.

[222] This safeguard measure was imposed after consultations between the European Communities and China (as required by para. 242(b) of the Working Party Report on China's Accession to the WTO), which resulted in a Memorandum of Understanding on 10 June 2005 setting import restrictions on ten categories of Chinese textile and clothing products until the end of 2007. This understanding was implemented in *Commission Regulation (EC) No. 1084/2005 of 8 July 2005 amending Annexes II, III and V to Council Regulation (EEC) No. 3030/93 on Common Rules for Imports of Certain Textile Products from Third Countries*, OJ L177. As, due to strategic action by textile exporters and importers, the quota limits were already reached in

only four new investigations initiated.[223] This represents a sharp fall from the thirteen initiations in 2006. New initiations of safeguard investigations peaked at thirty-four in 2002 but have since then stayed relatively low, with fifteen initiations, fourteen initiations, seven initiations, and thirteen initiations in 2003, 2004, 2005 and 2006, respectively.[224]

The number of disputes relating to safeguard measures has been fairly moderate. To date, there have been thirty-five disputes relating to Article XIX of the GATT and the *Agreement on Safeguards*.[225] In only eight of these disputes were panel reports issued, of which six were appealed.[226]

Questions and Assignments 7.16

What is the political rationale behind the 'economic emergency exception'? In your opinion, are safeguard measures applied to fair *or* unfair trade? According to the Appellate Body in *Argentina – Footwear (EC)*, how does the nature of the trade to which safeguard measures are applied affect the interpretation of the requirements for the application of safeguard measures?

7.5.1. Article XIX of the GATT 1994 and the *Agreement on Safeguards*

Article XIX of the GATT 1994 and the provisions of the *Agreement on Safeguards* set out the rules according to which Members may take safeguard measures. Article XIX of the GATT 1994, entitled 'Emergency Action on Imports of Particular Products', provides, in paragraph 1(a):

> If, as a result of unforeseen developments and of the effect of the obligations incurred by a [Member] under this Agreement, including tariff concessions, any product is being imported into the territory of that [Member] in such increased quantities and under such conditions as to cause or threaten serious injury to domestic producers in that territory of like or directly competitive products, the [Member] shall be free . . . to suspend the obligation in whole or in part or to withdraw or modify the concession.

Under Article XIX of the GATT 1947, which was, in all respects, identical to Article XIX of the GATT 1994, some 150 safeguard measures were officially notified to the CONTRACTING PARTIES. However, Contracting Parties often resorted to measures other than safeguard measures, to address situations in which imports caused particular economic hardship. These 'other' measures included voluntary export

Foonote 222 (*cont.*)

August 2005, resulting in large amounts of Chinese textiles being held at EU harbours, agreement was reached to transfer some of the 2006 quota to 2005. This agreement was implemented in *Commission Regulation (EC) No. 1478/2005 of 12 September 2005 amending Annexes V, VI and VII to Council Regulation (EEC) No. 3030/93 on Common Rules for Imports of Certain Textile Products from Third Countries,* OJ L236.

[223] See www.wto.org/english/news_e/news07_e/safeg_nov07_e.htm, visited on 12 November 2007.
[224] See *ibid.*
[225] By October 2007, there had been thirty-five complaints under the *Agreement on Safeguards*: see www.worldtradelaw.net/dsc/database/agreementcount.asp, visited on 9 November 2007.
[226] See www.worldtradelaw.net/dsc/database/safeguards.asp, visited on 9 November 2007.

restraints (VERs), voluntary restraint arrangements (VRAs) and orderly marketing arrangements (OMAs), discussed above.[227] Unlike safeguard measures, these other measures did not require any compensation and could be applied selectively to the main exporting countries.[228] This explained the 'popularity' of VERs, VRAs and OMAs. The *Agreement on Safeguards* was negotiated during the Uruguay Round because of the need to clarify and reinforce the disciplines of Article XIX of the GATT, to re-establish multilateral control over safeguard measures and to eliminate measures, such as VERS, VRAs and OMAS, that escaped such control. The *Agreement on Safeguards* now prohibits these 'other' measures and requires that all safeguard measures comply with Article XIX of the GATT 1994 and the detailed disciplines of the *Agreement on Safeguards* discussed below.

The *Agreement on Safeguards*, which is part of Annex 1A to the *WTO Agreement*, confirms and clarifies the provisions of Article XIX of the GATT 1994 but also provides for new rules. The *Agreement on Safeguards* sets out:

- the substantive requirements that must be met in order to apply a safeguard measure (Articles 2 and 4);
- the (national and international) procedural requirements that must be met by a Member applying a safeguard measure (Articles 3 and 12); and
- the characteristics of, and conditions relating to, a safeguard measure (Articles 5 to 9).

On the relationship between the provisions of the *Agreement on Safeguards* and Article XIX of the GATT 1994, the Appellate Body in *Korea – Dairy* ruled, on the basis of Articles 1 and 11.1(a) of the *Agreement on Safeguards*, that:

> any safeguard measure imposed after the entry into force of the *WTO Agreement* must comply with the provisions of *both* the *Agreement on Safeguards* and Article XIX of the GATT 1994.[229]

As the Appellate Body noted in *Argentina – Footwear (EC)*, nothing in the *WTO Agreement* suggests the intention by the Uruguay Round negotiators to subsume the requirements of Article XIX of the GATT 1994 *within* the *Agreement on Safeguards* and thus render those requirements no longer applicable.[230] This is of particular importance for the requirement that the surge in imports be the result of 'unforeseen developments'. This requirement is included in Article XIX of the GATT 1994 but not in the more detailed *Agreement on Safeguards*. Nevertheless, this requirement is fully applicable. Article XIX of the GATT 1994 and the *Agreement on Safeguards* apply *cumulatively*.[231]

---

[227] See above, pp. 453–5.
[228] For a discussion on the requirement of compensation and the difficulty of applying safeguard measures selectively, see below, pp. 690–2.   [229] Appellate Body Report, *Korea – Dairy*, para. 77.
[230] See Appellate Body Report, *Argentina – Footwear (EC)*, para. 83. The Appellate Body therefore rejected the Panel's finding that those requirements of Article XIX of the GATT 1994 which are not reflected in the *Agreement on Safeguards* were superseded by the requirements of the latter.
[231] Note, however, that this does not prevent a panel or the Appellate Body from exercising judicial economy with respect to a claim of violation of Article XIX where it has found that the measure at issue is inconsistent with the *Agreement on Safeguards*. On the exercise of judicial economy, see above, pp. 251–3.

Questions and Assignments 7.17

Why was the *Agreement on Safeguards* negotiated in the context of the GATT Uruguay Round? Why did GATT Contracting Parties prefer voluntary export restraints (and other similar measures) over safeguard measures? How does the *Agreement on Safeguards* relate to Article XIX of the GATT 1994?

7.5.2. Requirements for the use of safeguard measures

Article 2.1 of the *Agreement on Safeguards* provides:

> A Member may apply a safeguard measure to a product only if that Member has determined, pursuant to the provisions set out below, that such product is being imported into its territory in such increased quantities, absolute or relative to domestic production, and under such conditions as to cause or threaten to cause serious injury to the domestic industry that produces like or directly competitive products.

Article XIX:1(a) of the GATT 1994, which – as explained above – applies together with the *Agreement on Safeguards*, provides for the same requirements for the application of safeguard measures as Article 2.1, but, in addition, requires that the increase in imports occurs:

> as a result of unforeseen developments and of the effect of the obligations incurred by a [Member] under this Agreement.

In short, Members may apply safeguard measures only when three requirements are met. These requirements are:

- the 'increased imports' requirement (including the 'unforeseen developments' requirement);
- the 'serious injury' requirement; and
- the 'causation' requirement.

This section examines each of these requirements.

7.5.2.1. 'Increased imports' requirement

Article 2.1 of the *Agreement on Safeguards* explicitly states that the increase in imports can be:

- an *absolute* increase, i.e. an increase by tonnes or units of the imported products; *or*
- a *relative* increase, i.e. an increase in relation to domestic production.

This, however, leaves the question unanswered as to how much, and over what time span, imports must have increased. In *Argentina – Footwear (EC)*, the Appellate Body further clarified the 'increased imports' requirement for the application of safeguard measures by ruling that:

the increase in imports must have been recent enough, sudden enough, sharp enough, and significant enough, both quantitatively and qualitatively, to cause or threaten to cause 'serious injury'.[232]

In *US – Steel Safeguards*, the Appellate Body reaffirmed this interpretation of the 'increased imports' requirement. According to the Appellate Body, the 'increased imports' requirement demands the presence of the following four elements: recent increase, sudden increase, sharp increase and significant increase. The Appellate Body also held that there is no absolute standard as to *how* sudden, recent and significant the increase in imports must be.[233] This test is not to be applied *in abstracto*, but requires a *concrete* evaluation on a case-by-case basis. The result of the test is not dependent on the proof of mere existence of the conditions, but on the extent and intensity of their manifestations.[234] That was why the Appellate Body held in *US – Steel Safeguards* that a demonstration of '*any* increase' in imports is not sufficient to establish 'increased imports' under the *Agreement on Safeguards*.[235] According to the Appellate Body:

[t]he question whether 'such increased quantities' of imports will suffice as 'increased imports' to justify the application of a safeguard measure is a question that can be answered only in the light of 'such conditions' under which those imports occur. The relevant importance of these elements varies from case to case.[236]

It is clear that, if the increase in imports is not recent, sudden and sharp, there can be no economic *emergency* situation justifying the application of a safeguard measure. Furthermore, the *rate* of the increase (e.g. an increase by 30 per cent) as well as the *amount* of the increase (e.g. an increase by 10,000 units) must be considered.[237] In addition, the import trends during the investigation period must be considered. It does not suffice to compare the level of imports at the start of the investigation period with the imports at the end to conclude that there is an increase in imports within the meaning of the *Agreement on Safeguards*.[238] The analysis of the import trends during the investigation period must also show an increase in imports. However, recall that the increase in imports must be sudden and recent.[239] Therefore, the investigation period should be the *recent past*. Thus, it is not appropriate to examine the import trends over an investigation period of, for example, five years.[240]

Furthermore, while the competent authorities must consider the data for the entire investigation period,[241] the primary emphasis is on the data relating to

---

[232] Appellate Body Report, *Argentina – Footwear (EC)*, para. 131.

[233] See Appellate Body Report, *US – Steel Safeguards*, para. 358. See also Panel Report, *US – Steel Safeguards*, paras. 10.167–10.168. The Panel in *Chile – Price Band System*, para. 7.156, noted that to show a rise in imports was recent, sudden, sharp and significant enough, the competent authority needs to identify a 'discernible upward trend' in import quantities. Also see para. 7.161, to the effect that the increase in imports must be *actual* and that a threat of increased imports is not sufficient under Article 2.1.

[234] For a detailed discussion, see Appellate Body Report, *US – Steel Safeguards*, paras. 352–60.

[235] *Ibid.*, para. 355.   [236] *Ibid.*, para. 351.   [237] Article 4.2 of the *Agreement on Safeguards*.

[238] See Appellate Body Report, *Argentina – Footwear (EC)*, para. 129.   [239] See above.

[240] See Appellate Body Report, *Argentina – Footwear (EC)*, para. 130.

[241] In *US – Lamb*, the Appellate Body noted that: 'in conducting their evaluation under Article 4.2(a), competent authorities cannot rely *exclusively* on data from the most recent past, but must assess that data in the context of the data for the entire investigative period'. Appellate Body Report, *US – Lamb*, para. 138. See also Appellate Body Report, *Argentina – Footwear (EC)*, para. 129. The Panel in *Argentina – Preserved*

Figure 7.1 'Increased imports' requirement: example 1

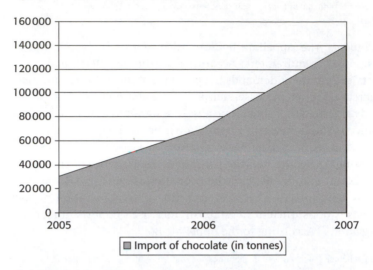

☐ Import of chocolate (in tonnes)

Figure 7.2 'Increased imports' requirement: example 2

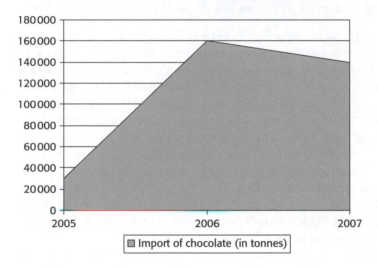

☐ Import of chocolate (in tonnes)

the most recent past within the investigation period. In *US – Steel Safeguards* the Appellate Body held that the United States made a serious error by failing to address the decrease in imports that had occurred at the very end of the investigation period.[242]

Consider the examples in Figures 7.1 and 7.2 of imports of chocolate in Member A during the investigation period 2005–7. In both examples, there is an increase in imports in the investigation period. The rate of increase as well as the amount of

Footnote 241 (*cont.*)
Peaches stated that: 'Indeed, detecting an increase in only part of the period is synonymous with isolating the data for that part from the data corresponding to the entire period.' See Panel Report, *Argentina – Preserved Peaches*, para. 7.67.   [242] Appellate Body Report, *US – Steel Safeguards*, para. 388.

increase is quite significant. In both examples, imports increased from 30,000 tonnes to 140,000 tonnes, representing an increase of more than 460 per cent during the investigation period. However, if one also looks at the import trends, a different picture emerges. Example 1 is a clear case of a recent, sudden and sharp increase in imports within the meaning of the *Agreement on Safeguards*. It is doubtful whether that same conclusion can be reached with respect to example 2.[243]

Pursuant to Article XIX:1 of the GATT 1994, the increase in imports must occur as a result of 'unforeseen developments' and as a result of the effect of obligations incurred under the GATT 1994. According to the Working Party in *US – Fur Felt Hats*, 'unforeseen developments' are:

> developments occurring after the negotiation of the relevant tariff concession which it would not be reasonable to expect that the negotiators of the country making the concession could and should have foreseen at the time when the concession was negotiated.[244]

In that case, in 1951, the Working Party held that the fact that hat styles had changed did not constitute an 'unforeseen development'. However, the degree to which the change in fashion affected the competitive situation could, according to the Working Party, not reasonably be expected to have been foreseen by the United States authorities in 1947.

As noted earlier, despite a challenge to the continuing existence of the 'unforeseen developments' requirement under the renovated multilateral safeguards framework of the WTO, this requirement is still 'alive'.[245]

In 2000, the Appellate Body ruled in *Korea – Dairy* that 'unforeseen developments' means unexpected developments.[246] Note that, before taking a safeguard measure, the Member concerned must demonstrate, as a matter of fact, that the increase in imports is indeed the result of unforeseen, i.e. unexpected, developments.[247] The requirement to demonstrate the causal relationship between the measure taken and an 'unforeseen development' is independent of factual proof of increase in imports. As stated by the Panel in *Argentina – Preserved Peaches*:

> [I]ncrease in imports and the unforeseen developments must be two distinct elements. A statement that the increase in imports, or the way in which they were being imported, was unforeseen, does not constitute a demonstration as a matter of fact of the existence of unforeseen *developments*.[248]
>
> [Emphasis in original]

---

[243] It may also be possible to conclude that there is an increase in imports in example 2, within the meaning of the *Agreement on Safeguards*, if it can be shown that the decline in 2007 was of a temporary and incidental nature.   [244] Working Party Report, *US – Fur Felt Hats*, para. 9.
[245] See discussion in section 7.5.1.   [246] See Appellate Body Report, *Korea – Dairy*, para. 84.
[247] See *ibid.*, para. 85. See also Appellate Body Report, *Argentina – Footwear (EC)*, para. 92.
[248] Panel Report, *Argentina – Preserved Peaches*, para. 7.24. There seems to be a difference of opinion on the link between the 'unforeseen developments' and the 'increase in imports'. The Panel in *Argentina – Preserved Peaches* expressly disagreed with the Appellate Body in *Argentina – Footwear (EC)* that the unforeseen development could itself be the increased quantities of imports. The contradiction appears to pertain to *what* may qualify as an unforeseen development – whether such development ought to be a factor *other than* the increased imports, though *necessarily resulting* in such increased imports, or whether the increased imports could have themselves been unforeseen (para. 7.24.), Note, however, that the Appellate Body itself interpreted the sentence in question, 'the increased quantities of imports should have been "unforeseen" or "unexpected" ' appearing in *Argentina – Footwear (EC)* (para. 131) as 'referring to the fact that the increased imports must, under Article XIX:1(a), *result* from "unforeseen developments" '. Appellate Body, *US – Steel Safeguards*, para. 350.

In *US – Steel Safeguards*, the Appellate Body held that, when an importing Member wishes to apply safeguard measures on imports of several products, it is not sufficient for the competent authority merely to demonstrate that 'unforeseen developments' resulted in increased imports of a *broad category of products* which includes the specific products on which the safeguard measure is applied.[249] According to the Appellate Body, the competent authorities are required to demonstrate that the unforeseen developments have resulted in increased imports for the *specific products* on which the safeguard measures are applied.[250]

Also in *US – Steel Safeguards*, the Appellate Body held that the competent authority of the importing Member imposing a safeguard measure must demonstrate in its published report, *through a reasoned and adequate explanation*, that unforeseen developments resulted in increased imports.[251] The Panel in *US – Steel Safeguards* ruled with respect to the determination of 'unforeseen circumstances':

> The nature of the facts, including their complexity, will dictate the extent to which the relationship between the unforeseen developments and increased imports causing injury needs to be explained. The timing of the explanation [relating to unforeseen developments], its extent and its quality are all factors that can affect whether [that] . . . explanation is reasoned and adequate.[252]

On appeal by the United States, the Appellate Body upheld this finding.[253] The Appellate Body pointed out that, since a panel may not conduct a *de novo* review of the evidence before the competent authority, it is the *explanation* given by the competent authority for its determination alone that enables a panel to determine whether there has been compliance with the substantive requirements for the imposition of a safeguard measure.[254]

Questions and Assignments 7.18

What constitutes 'increased imports' within the meaning of the *Agreement on Safeguards*? Do imports that have increased steadily over a period of five years from 10 per cent to 60 per cent of domestic consumption, while decreasing in absolute terms, meet the 'increased imports' requirement of Article 2.1 of the *Agreement on Safeguards*? In your opinion, what could be 'unforeseen developments' within the meaning of Article XIX:1 of the GATT 1994?

7.5.2.2. *'Serious injury' requirement*

A second main substantive requirement for the application of a safeguard measure on the imports of a product is the existence of serious injury or

---

[249] See Appellate Body Report, *US – Steel Safeguards*, para. 319.   [250] See *ibid*.
[251] See *ibid*., paras. 289–91. See also para. 273. The Panel in *Argentina – Preserved Peaches*, forcefully asserted that '[a] mere phrase in a conclusion, without supporting analysis of the existence of unforeseen developments, is not a substitute for a demonstration of fact'. Panel Report, *Argentina – Preserved Peaches*, para. 7.33.   [252] Panel Report, *US – Steel Safeguards*, para. 10.115.
[253] See Appellate Body Report, *US – Steel Safeguards*, paras. 293–6.   [254] See *ibid*., paras. 298–9 and 301–3.

threat thereof to the domestic industry producing like or directly competitive products.

Article 4.1 of the *Agreement on Safeguards* defines 'serious injury' as 'a significant overall impairment in the position of a domestic industry'.

The Appellate Body has recognised the standard of 'serious injury' to be very high and 'exacting'.[255] It is significantly stricter than the standard of 'material injury' of the *Anti-Dumping Agreement* and the *SCM Agreement*. Since safeguard measures, unlike anti-dumping and countervailing duties, are applied to 'fair' trade, it is not surprising that the threshold for applying these measures is higher.

Article 4.1(c) of the *Agreement on Safeguards* defines a 'domestic industry' as:

> the producers as a whole of the like or directly competitive products operating within the territory of a Member, or those whose collective output of the like or directly competitive products constitutes a major proportion of the total domestic production of those products.

Article 4.1(c) lays down two criteria to define the 'domestic industry' in a particular case. The first criterion relates to the products at issue; the second criterion relates to the number and the representative nature of the producers of these products.

As to the first criterion, note that the domestic industry consists of producers making products that are 'like or directly competitive' to the imported products. Therefore, to determine what the 'domestic industry' is, in a particular case, one must first identify the domestic products which are 'like or directly competitive' to the imported products. The producers of those products will make up the 'domestic industry'. The concepts of 'like products' and 'directly competitive products' are not defined in the *Agreement on Safeguards* and there is little relevant case law, as yet, on the meaning of these concepts as used in the *Agreement on Safeguards*. However, there is a significant body of case law on the meaning of these concepts as used in the GATT 1994.[256] While the Appellate Body has ruled that the concept of 'like products' has different meanings in the different contexts in which it is used, this case law – discussed in detail above – is definitely of relevance here. It follows from this case law that the determination of whether products are 'like products' or 'directly competitive products' is, fundamentally, a determination about the nature and extent of the competitive relationship between these products. The factors that must be considered in determining 'likeness' or 'direct competitiveness' are, among other relevant factors:

- the physical characteristics of the products;
- their end-use;
- consumer habits and preferences regarding the products; and
- the customs classification of the products.[257]

---

[255] Appellate Body Report, *US – Wheat Gluten*, para. 149. [256] See above, pp. 329–31, 351–6, 360–4, 374–82.
[257] See above, pp. 329–82.

In *US – Lamb*, one of the very few safeguard cases in which the issue of 'like products' and 'directly competitive products' was addressed, the Appellate Body held that the fact that products are in a continuous line of production (for example, lambs and lamb meat) does not make these products 'like products'.[258] In general, production structures are – according to the Appellate Body – not relevant in determining whether products are 'like' or 'directly competitive'.[259]

As mentioned above, the second criterion to define the 'domestic industry' in a particular case relates to the number and the representative nature of the producers of the like or directly competitive products. The 'domestic industry' for the purposes of the *Agreement on Safeguards* is:

- the totality of the domestic producers; or
- at least a major proportion thereof.

There is no general explanation of what constitutes 'a major proportion' of the domestic producers. What is required to meet this condition will depend on the specific circumstances of a case and will most likely differ from case to case.[260]

Once the domestic industry has been identified, one can examine whether there has been serious injury to this domestic industry. To this end, Article 4.2(a) of the *Agreement on Safeguards* requires an evaluation of 'all relevant factors of an objective and quantifiable nature having a bearing on the situation of that industry'. These so-called 'injury factors' include:

- the rate and amount of the increase in imports, of the product concerned, in absolute and relative terms;
- the share of the domestic market taken by increased imports; and
- changes in the level of sales, production, productivity, capacity utilisation, profits and losses, and employment.[261]

This list of injury factors is not exhaustive. *All* factors having a bearing on the situation of the domestic industry can and must be examined.[262] The examination of the factors expressly mentioned is, however, a minimum.[263] Domestic authorities do not have an unlimited duty to investigate *all* other possible injury factors. However, if the domestic authority considers a factor, other than a factor raised by one of the interested parties, to be relevant, it must be investigated.[264]

It does not suffice for domestic authorities applying safeguard measures to examine all relevant injury factors. They must also give a reasoned and adequate explanation of how the facts support their conclusion that the domestic industry

---

[258] See Appellate Body Report, *US – Lamb*, para. 90.

[259] See *ibid.*, para. 94. The ruling of the Panel in *Chile – Price Band System* indicates that the correctness of the identification of the domestic industry will be determined in the light of the question whether the competent authority made adequate findings and reasoned conclusions with respect to the issue of likeness or direct competitiveness. See Panel Report, *Chile – Price Band System*, paras. 7.141–7.149.

[260] This issue also arises in the context of anti-dumping measures and countervailing measures: see above, pp. 527–8, 579.   [261] See Article 4.2(a) of the *Agreement on Safeguards*.

[262] See Appellate Body Report, *Argentina – Footwear (EC)*, para. 136; Appellate Body Report, *US – Wheat Gluten*, para. 55; and Appellate Body Report, *US – Lamb*, para. 103. Failure to consider a relevant factor, in full or in part, amounts to a violation of Article 4.2(a) of the *Agreement on Safeguards*.

[263] All principles laid down with regard to Article 4.2(a) now seem to be well established. See Panel Report, *Chile – Price Band System*, paras. 7.166–7.169.   [264] See Appellate Body Report, *US – Wheat Gluten*, paras. 55–6.

is suffering 'serious injury'.[265] To find 'serious injury', it is not necessary that all injury factors show that the domestic industry is under threat.[266] In a situation in which employment and capacity utilisation in an industry are declining but profitability remains positive, it may nevertheless be possible to conclude that 'serious injury' exists.

As noted above, a safeguard measure can be applied not only in case of 'serious injury' but also in case of a 'threat of serious injury'. A 'threat of serious injury' is defined as 'serious injury that is clearly imminent'.[267] The concept of 'clearly imminent' was clarified by the Appellate Body in *US – Lamb*. 'Imminent' implies that the anticipated 'serious injury' must be on the verge of occurring; 'clearly' indicates that there must be a very high degree of likelihood that the threat will materialise in the very near future.[268] In this regard, there is a duty to 'assess' the data from the most recent past against the overall trends of the investigating period in an injury analysis,[269] very similar to the duty in an 'increased imports' determination under Article 2.1.[270]

For the determination of a 'threat of serious injury', Article 4.1(b) of the *Agreement on Safeguards* requires, in addition, that this determination must 'be based on facts and not merely on allegation, conjecture or remote possibility'.[271]

The relationship between 'serious injury' and a 'threat of serious injury' was considered in *US – Line Pipe*. The question was whether a domestic authority could make an alternative finding as to 'serious injury *or* [a] threat of serious injury', without a discrete finding as to which of these was in fact the reason for the imposition of the safeguard measure. Reversing the Panel finding, the Appellate Body held:

> [A]s the right [to impose a safeguard] exists if there is a finding by the competent authorities of a 'threat of serious injury' or – something *beyond* – 'serious injury', then it seems to us that it is irrelevant, *in determining whether the right exists*, if there is 'serious injury' or only 'threat of serious injury'–so long as there is a determination that there is *at least* a 'threat'.[272]
>
> [Emphasis in original]

Questions and Assignments 7.19

How does one define in a particular case the 'domestic industry' within the meaning of Article 4.1(c) of the *Agreement on Safeguards*? Do

---

[265] See Appellate Body Report, *US – Lamb*, para. 103. This is usually referred to as the *substantive* aspect of the examination of the injury factors. See also Panel Report, *Argentina – Preserved Peaches*, paras. 7.102–7.117.

[266] See Appellate Body Report, *US – Lamb*, para. 144.   [267] Article 4.1(b) of the *Agreement on Safeguards*.

[268] See Appellate Body Report, *US – Lamb*, para. 125. Note that an independent fact-based assessment of the 'high degree of likelihood' is necessary and that mere acknowledgment of possibility is not sufficient. See Panel Report, *Argentina – Preserved Peaches*, para. 7.122.

[269] See Appellate Body Report, *US – Lamb*, para. 138.

[270] See Panel Report, *Chile – Price Band System*, footnote 714 to para. 7.153. In fact, the Panel affirmed this duty as applying *mutatis mutandis* to Article 2.1 and Article 4.1(b), read with Article 4.2(a). The Panel ruled in this case that where a pre-existing measure like a Price Band System is in place, already increasing tariffs significantly, it is not proper for a competent authority to argue *a contrario* in a safeguards investigation that the removal/restriction of such a measure would lead to lower net duties on the product, thus causing injury. See *ibid.*, para. 7.172.

[271] As discussed above, the previous injury must be 'clearly imminent'. See above, footnote 268.

[272] Appellate Body Report, *US – Line Pipe*, para. 170.

> producers of cars and producers of light trucks belong to the same 'domestic industry'? Do mills and bakeries belong to the same domestic industry? What is 'serious injury' to the domestic industry? What is a 'threat of serious injury'? How must domestic authorities determine whether there is serious injury or a threat thereof to the domestic industry?

7.5.2.3. 'Causation' requirement

The third and last substantive requirement for the application of a safeguard measure to the imports of a product is the 'causation' requirement. Article 4.2(b) of the *Agreement on Safeguards* provides:

> The determination referred to in subparagraph (a) shall not be made unless this investigation demonstrates, on the basis of objective evidence, the existence of the causal link between increased imports of the product concerned and serious injury or a threat thereof. When factors other than increased imports are causing injury to the domestic industry at the same time, such injury shall not be attributed to increased imports.

The test for establishing causation is twofold:

- a demonstration of the causal link between the 'increased imports' and the 'serious injury' or threat thereof, (the 'causal link' element);[273] and
- an identification of any injury caused by factors other than the increased imports and the non-attribution of this injury to these imports (the 'non-attribution' element).[274]

With respect to the 'causal link' element, the Appellate Body has ruled in *US – Wheat Gluten* that it is not necessary to show that increased imports *alone* must be capable of causing serious injury:

> the need to distinguish between the facts caused by increased imports and the facts caused by other factors does *not* necessarily imply . . . that increased imports *on their own* must be capable of causing serious injury nor that injury caused by other factors must be *excluded* from the determination of serious injury.[275]

With respect to the 'non-attribution' element, the Appellate Body ruled in *US – Lamb*:

> In a situation where *several factors* are causing injury 'at the same time', a final determination about the injurious effects caused by *increased imports* can only be made if the injurious effects caused by all the different causal factors are distinguished and separated.

---

[273] With respect to the phrase in Article 2.1, 'imported . . . under such conditions', the Panel in *US – Wheat Gluten* noted: 'We are of the view that the phrase "under such conditions" does not impose a separate analytical requirement in addition to the analysis of increased imports, serious injury and causation. Rather, this phrase refers to the *substance* of the causation analysis that must be performed under Article 4.2(a) and (b) SA'. Panel Report, *US – Wheat Gluten*, para. 8.108.

[274] See e.g. Appellate Body Report, *US – Line Pipe*, para. 215.

[275] Appellate Body Report, *US – Wheat Gluten*, para. 70. Thereby the Appellate Body reversed the Panel's finding that the imports, *in and of themselves*, must have caused the serious injury. See Panel Report, *US – Wheat Gluten*, paras. 8.90–8.154.

> Otherwise, any conclusion based exclusively on an assessment of only one of the causal factors – increased imports – rests on an uncertain foundation, because it *assumes* that the other causal factors are *not* causing the injury which has been ascribed to increased imports. The non-attribution language in Article 4.2(b) precludes such an assumption and, instead, requires that the competent authorities assess appropriately the injurious effects of the other factors, so that those effects may be disentangled from the injurious effects of the increased imports. In this way, the final determination rests, properly, on the genuine and substantial relationship of cause and effect between increased imports and serious injury.[276]

Domestic authorities therefore have to separate and distinguish the injurious effects of 'other factors' from the injurious effects of the increased imports. They have to give a reasoned and adequate explanation of the nature and the extent of the injurious effects of the other factors, as distinguished from the injurious effects of the increased imports.[277]

Finally, it is clear that when a competent authority's report neither passes the test of 'increased imports' under Article 2.1, nor satisfies the requirement of existence of 'threat of serious injury' under Article 4.2(b), *a fortiori*, no causal link between the two can exist.[278]

Questions and Assignments 7.20

What does the 'causation requirement' of Article 4.2(b) of the *Agreement on Safeguards* entail? If a domestic industry suffers serious injury as a result of a mix of factors, including increased imports and changes in consumer preferences, can a domestic authority still conclude that the 'causation requirement' of Article 4.2(b) of the *Agreement on Safeguards* is met? How must domestic authorities determine whether the 'causation requirement' of Article 4.2(b) of the *Agreement on Safeguards* is met?

7.5.3. Domestic procedures and notification and consultation obligations

The *Agreement on Safeguards* sets out procedural requirements which domestic authorities, wishing to impose safeguard measures, must meet.[279] Most importantly, Article 3 of the *Agreement on Safeguards* requires that a Member apply a safeguard measure only following an investigation by the competent authorities of

---

[276] Appellate Body Report, *US – Lamb*, para. 179.
[277] See Appellate Body Report, *US – Hot-Rolled Steel*, paras. 226 and 230. See also Appellate Body Report, *US – Line Pipe*, para. 213. The mere assertion that injury caused by other factors has not been attributed to increased imports is definitely not sufficient to meet the requirement of Article 4.2(b) of the *Agreement on Safeguards*. As the Appellate Body noted in *US – Steel Safeguards*: 'In order to provide such a reasoned and adequate explanation, the competent authority *must explain how it ensured that it did not attribute* the injurious effects of factors other than included imports . . . to the imports included in the measure.' (Emphasis added.) Appellate Body Report, *US – Steel Safeguards*, para. 452.
[278] See Panel Report, *Chile – Price Band System*, para. 7.176, relying on Appellate Body Report, *Argentina – Footwear (EC)*, para. 145.
[279] These procedural obligations are set out in Articles 3, 6 and 12 of the *Agreement on Safeguards*.

that Member pursuant to procedures previously established and made public.[280] The competent domestic authorities must also publish a report setting forth their findings and reasoned conclusions reached on all pertinent issues of fact and law.[281] Failure to do so results in a formal defect in the safeguard measure. Moreover, if the report of the competent domestic authorities does not address the issues arising under Article 2 (increased imports) and/or Article 4 (serious injury), this failure amounts to a failure to show that the requirements of Articles 2 and 4 were met and results in a finding of violation of Articles 2 and/or 4.

The *Agreement on Safeguards* also provides obligations on Members to notify the WTO Committee on Safeguards of matters relating to safeguard measures and to consult with other Members on such measures. Article 12.1 of the *Agreement on Safeguards* requires 'immediate' notification from Members to the WTO Committee on Safeguards whenever an investigation is initiated, a finding of serious injury or threat of serious injury caused by increased imports is made or where a decision is taken to apply or extend a safeguard measure.[282]

As to when a notification is necessary in the case of 'taking a decision to apply or extend a safeguard measure', the Appellate Body held in *US – Wheat Gluten* that notification needs to be given *only* after a decision has been taken and not when a decision is *proposed to be taken*.[283]

Article 12.2 of the *Agreement on Safeguards* provides that a Member making a finding of serious injury or threat thereof, or taking a decision to apply or extend a safeguard should provide 'all pertinent information' to the WTO Committee on Safeguards. The pertinent information to be provided includes a mandatory minimum list,[284] comprising: evidence of serious injury or threat thereof due to increased imports, precise description of the product involved and the proposed measure, proposed date of introduction, expected duration and a timetable for progressive liberalisation. The 'evidence of serious injury' to be demonstrated is one that would satisfy the requirements of Article 4.2(a), and not merely what the applying Member considers sufficient.[285]

---

[280] See Article 3.1 of the *Agreement on Safeguards*. Note that this investigation must include reasonable public notice to all interested parties and public hearings or other appropriate means by which importers, exporters and other interested parties could present evidence, and their views, *inter alia*, as to whether or not the application of a safeguard measure would be in the public interest. These procedural 'due process rights' of the parties to a safeguard investigation are set out in Article 3.1 of the *Agreement on Safeguards*.

[281] Article 3.1 of the *Agreement on Safeguards*. As to publication of confidential information, see Panel Report, *US – Wheat Gluten*, paras. 8.13–8.26. It is impermissible to adduce evidence of consideration of relevant information in a document that is not made available *publicly*: see Panel Report, *Chile – Price Band System*, para. 7.128.

[282] See Panel Report, *US – Wheat Gluten*, paras. 8.185–8.207. The use of the term 'immediately' indicates a certain degree of urgency of the notification. See Appellate Body Report, *US – Wheat Gluten*, para. 105. The Panel in *Korea – Dairy* noted that the requirement to notify 'immediately' does not mean notifying 'as soon as practically possible'. See Panel Report, *Korea – Dairy*, para. 7.134. The degree of urgency that is required by the duty to notify immediately is assessed on a case-by-case basis. This degree of urgency will depend on administrative difficulties, the character of the information and the need to translate documents (if any). In any case, the time taken for notification should be kept to the bare minimum. See Appellate Body Report, *US – Wheat Gluten* paras. 105–6.

[283] See Appellate Body Report, *US – Wheat Gluten*, paras. 119–25, reversing the Panel's interpretation.

[284] See Appellate Body Report, *Korea – Dairy*, para. 105. Additional information may be requested by the Council for Trade in Goods or the Committee on Safeguards in terms of Article 12.2 of the *Agreement on Safeguards*.

[285] See Appellate Body Report, *Korea – Diary*, para. 108, reversing the Panel's interpretation.

Under Article 12.3 of the *Agreement on Safeguards*, the Member applying or extending a measure shall provide *adequate opportunity* for prior consultations with Members affected by the measure, for the purpose of reviewing the information provided, exchanging views and, most importantly, to facilitate reaching an understanding on levels of concessions to be maintained under Article 8.1. As the Appellate Body explained in *US – Wheat Gluten*, 'adequate opportunity' means that the exporting Member should be provided with sufficient *information* and *time* to allow a *meaningful exchange* on the issues identified.[286] In *US – Line Pipe*, the Appellate Body stated that the final measure applied ought to be one that is substantially the same as the proposed measure covered during the prior consultations:

> [W]here . . . the proposed measure 'differed substantially' from the measure that was later applied, and not as a consequence of 'prior consultations', we fail to see how meaningful 'prior consultations' could have occurred, as required by Article 12.3.[287]

It is to be noted that a violation of Article 12.3 automatically triggers a violation of Article 8.1 of the *Agreement on Safeguards*. As the Appellate Body ruled in *US – Wheat Gluten*:

> In view of this explicit link between Articles 8.1 and 12.3 of the *Agreement on Safeguards*, a Member cannot . . . 'endeavour to maintain' an adequate balance of concessions unless it has, as a first step, provided an adequate opportunity for prior consultations on a proposed measure.[288]

Questions and Assignments 7.21

Discuss the main procedural requirements under the *Agreement on Safeguards* that a Member imposing a safeguard measure must meet.

7.5.4. Characteristics of safeguard measures

Safeguard measures are measures, otherwise inconsistent with Articles II or XI of the GATT 1994, which are justified under the economic emergency exception provided for in Article XIX of the GATT 1994 and the *Agreement on Safeguards*. The purpose of a safeguard measure is to give 'breathing space' to a domestic industry to adapt itself to the new market situation by temporarily restricting imports. Safeguard measures therefore typically take the form of:

- customs duties above the binding (inconsistent with Article II:1 of the GATT 1994); or
- quantitative restrictions (inconsistent with Article XI of the GATT 1994).[289]

---

[286] See Appellate Body Report, *US – Wheat Gluten*, para. 136.
[287] Appellate Body Report, *US – Line Pipe*, para. 104. See also Appellate Body Report, *US – Wheat Gluten*, para. 137.　　[288] Appellate Body Report, *US – Wheat Gluten*, para. 146.
[289] On customs duties above the binding and on quantitative restrictions, see above, pp. 422–4, 444–60.

Safeguard measures can also take other forms, because, unlike anti-dumping measures and countervailing measures, discussed above, safeguard measures are not limited to particular types of measures.[290] This does not mean, however, that safeguard measures are not subject to strict requirements. In general terms, Article 5.1, first sentence, of the *Agreement on Safeguards* provides:

> A Member shall apply safeguard measures only to the extent necessary to prevent or remedy serious injury or to facilitate adjustment . . . Members should choose measures most suitable for the achievement of these objectives.[291]

The *Agreement on Safeguards* sets out specific requirements with respect to:

- the duration of safeguard measures;
- the non-discriminatory application of safeguard measures;
- the extent of safeguard measures;
- the compensation of affected exporting Members; and
- provisional safeguard measures.

7.5.4.1. Duration of safeguard measures

Safeguard measures are, by nature, *temporary* measures. Article 7.1 of the *Agreement on Safeguards* provides that safeguard measures may only be applied:

> for such period of time as may be necessary to prevent or remedy serious injury and to facilitate adjustment.[292]

In fact, the initial period of application of a definitive safeguard measure must not exceed four years.[293] Furthermore, a safeguard measure exceeding one year must be progressively liberalised,[294] and, if the measure exceeds three years, the Member applying the measure must carry out a mid-term review to establish whether the measure still meets the requirements discussed below.[295] Extension of a safeguard measure beyond four years is possible but only if:

- the safeguard measure continues to be necessary to prevent or remedy serious injury to the domestic industry;[296] and
- there is evidence that the domestic industry is adjusting.[297]

---

[290] See above, pp. 546–54, 585–99.
[291] Also Article XIX:1 of the GATT 1994 states that Members 'shall be free' to take safeguard measures 'to the extent and for such time as may be necessary to prevent or remedy such injury'.
[292] Article 7.1, first sentence of the *Agreement on Safeguards*.
[293] See Article 7.1 of the *Agreement on Safeguards*. Pursuant to Article 6, the duration of a provisional safeguard measure, if applied, is included in this maximum period of four years.
[294] See Article 7.4 of the *Agreement on Safeguards*.
[295] See Article 7.3 of the *Agreement on Safeguards*. As a result of the review, the Member must, if appropriate, withdraw the safeguard measure or increase the rate of liberalisation of trade.
[296] Note that when the initial measure is itself not in compliance with Articles 2, 3, 4 or 5 of the *Agreement on Safeguards*, any extension of such measure by definition is tainted by inconsistency as well. See Panel Report, *Chile – Price Band System*, para. 7.198.
[297] See Article 7.2 of the *Agreement on Safeguards*. A safeguard measure that is extended may never be more restrictive than it was at the end of the initial period. See Panel Report, *Argentina – Footwear (EC)*, paras. 8.303–8.304.

In no case, however, may the duration of a safeguard measure exceed eight years.[298] Once the import of a product has been subjected to a safeguard measure, this product cannot be subjected to such a measure again for a period of time equal to the duration of the safeguard measure that was previously applied.[299] In other words, if a Member applies a safeguard measure on imports of trucks for a period of eight years, it cannot apply any safeguard measure on imports of trucks during the eight years following the termination of the first measure. In this way, the *Agreement on Safeguards* prevents a situation where the temporary character of safeguards is circumvented by the repeated application of safeguard measures on the imports of the same product.

Note that Article 9.2 of the *Agreement on Safeguards* allows developing-country Members to apply a safeguard measure for up to ten years, instead of eight. Developing-country Members may also apply a *new* safeguard measure on the same product sooner than developed-country Members.[300]

Questions and Assignments 7.22

For how long may a safeguard measure be applied? Can a safeguard measure be extended? What is the maximum duration of a safeguard measure? How does Article 7.5 of the *Agreement on Safeguards* ensure that the provision on the maximum duration of safeguard measures is not circumvented? In what way do the rules on the duration of safeguard measures applied by developing-country Members differ from the rules on the duration of safeguard measures applied by other Members?

7.5.4.2. Non-discriminatory application of safeguard measures

Article 2.2 of the *Agreement on Safeguards* provides:

> Safeguard measures shall be applied to a product being imported irrespective of its source.

Under the GATT 1947, there was much disagreement as to whether safeguard measures could be applied on a selective basis, i.e. only against certain supplying countries and not against others. The *Agreement on Safeguards* has put an end to that debate by clearly requiring that safeguard measures be applied on an MFN basis, i.e. without discrimination between supplying Members. If the computer industry of Member A suffers serious injury as a result of a sudden surge of imports of laptops from Member B, Member A may be entitled to take a safeguard measure, for example, in the form of a quota on laptops, but this measure will have to apply to the importation of all laptops, whether from Member B or

---

[298] See Article 7.3 of the *Agreement on Safeguards*.
[299] See Article 7.5 of the *Agreement on Safeguards*. However, the minimum period during which a safeguard measure cannot be applied again is two years. An exception to this rule, allowing for the application of safeguard measures of short duration (i.e. a maximum of 150 days), is provided for in Article 7.6 of the *Agreement on Safeguards*. [300] See Article 9.2 of the *Agreement on Safeguards*.

from other exporting countries. The 'selective' application of safeguard measures is, in principle, prohibited.[301]

However, the *Agreement on Safeguards* provides for two exceptions to the prohibition of 'selective' application of safeguard measures. These exceptions are set out in Article 5.2(b) and Article 9.1 of the *Agreement on Safeguards*. Article 5.2(b) allows the selective application of safeguard measures taken in the form of quotas allocated among supplying countries if, apart from other requirements:

> clear demonstration is provided to the Committee [on Safeguards] that . . . imports from certain Members have increased in disproportionate percentage in relation to the total increase of imports of the product.[302]

Article 9.1 of the *Agreement on Safeguards* provides for an exception to the prohibition of selective application for the benefit of developing-country Members. Article 9.1 states:

> Safeguard measures shall not be applied against a product originating in a developing country Member as long as its share of imports of the product concerned in the importing Member does not exceed 3 per cent, provided that developing country Members with less than 3 per cent import share collectively account for not more than 9 per cent of total imports of the product concerned.

The Appellate Body held in *US – Line Pipe* that Article 9.1 does not contain an obligation to provide a specific list of developing-country Members that are included or excluded from the safeguard measure.[303] In *US – Line Pipe*, the United States had set, for each country without any differentiation, a quantitative allocation of 9,000 tonnes for imports free from supplementary duties. These 9,000 tonnes represented 2.7 per cent of its overall imports. The United States argued that since the safeguard measure would reduce the level of imports, it was 'expected' that any country which breached its quota-free import threshold of 9,000 tons would also breach the 3 per cent *de minimis* level set in Article 9.1. The Appellate Body rejected this argument and held that the United States had not taken all reasonable steps to ensure that imports from developing-country Members above the US threshold level but still below the *de minimis* level, would be excluded from the application of the safeguard measure.[304] Therefore, this mechanism was inconsistent with Article 9.1 of the *Agreement on Safeguards*.[305]

Questions and Assignments 7.23

Member A imposes a safeguard measure on the importation of bicycles following a 200 per cent increase in imports from Member B. The

---

[301] The question has arisen whether a Member can exclude products from Members that are its partners in a free trade area or a customs union from the application of a safeguard measure. In *Argentina – Footwear (EC)*, the Appellate Body ruled that, if a WTO Member has imposed a measure after conducting an investigation on imports from *all* sources, it is also required under Article 2.2 of the *Agreement on Safeguards* to apply such a measure to all sources, including partners in a free trade area. See Appellate Body Report, *Argentina – Footwear (EC)*, para. 112. See also below, pp. 699–709.
[302] For the other requirements, see Article 5.2(b) of the *Agreement on Safeguards*.
[303] See Appellate Body Report, *US – Line Pipe*, para. 128.
[304] See Appellate Body Report, *US – Line Pipe*, paras. 120–33.   [305] See *ibid.*, para. 133.

safeguard measure takes the form of a quota to be allocated among the supplying Members. The shares of imports of bicycles are currently as follows: Member B, 70 per cent; Member C, 20 per cent; Member D, 7 per cent; and Members E and F each 1.5 per cent. Note that Members D, E and F are developing-country Members. To which bicycles should the safeguard measure apply – bicycles originating in Member B, C, D, E and/or F? Is your answer different if Member A takes a safeguard measure in the form of an increased customs duty or a tariff quota on bicycles?

7.5.4.3. *Safeguard measures commensurate with the extent of necessity*

As mentioned above, Article 5.1 of the *Agreement on Safeguards* provides that a safeguard shall apply only to the extent necessary to prevent or remedy serious injury and to facilitate adjustment. Article 5.1 also provides that where the safeguard measure takes the form of a quantitative restriction and such a measure reduces the quantity of imports to a level less than the average imports in the last three representative years, a 'clear justification' to that effect is necessary.

A safeguard measure may not seek to address injury caused by factors other than *increased imports*. In *US – Line Pipe*, the Appellate Body held that although the term 'serious injury' has the same meaning in Articles 4.2 and 5 of the *Agreement on Safeguards*,[306] safeguard measures may only be applied to the extent that they address the serious injury (or threat thereof) attributable to *increased imports*.[307]

Explaining the nature of the provision in Article 5.1, the Appellate Body in *Korea – Dairy* held that there is an '*obligation* on a Member applying a safeguard measure to ensure that the measure applied is commensurate with the goals of preventing or remedying serious injury or facilitating adjustment'.[308] This obligation applies regardless of the particular form that a safeguard measure might take.[309] However, the Appellate Body disagreed with the Panel in this case that Members are always required '*to explain* how they considered the facts before them and why they concluded, *at the time of the decision*, that the measure to be applied was necessary to remedy the serious injury and facilitate the adjustment of the industry'.[310] Instead, the Appellate Body held that Article 5.1, second sentence, requires 'clear justification' only for safeguard measures taking the form of a quantitative restriction which reduces the quantity of imports below the average of imports in the last three representative years for which statistics are available.[311]

---

[306] The US had argued that, since the Appellate Body had held in *US – Wheat Gluten* that in the determination of 'serious injury' under Article 4.2 of the *Agreement on Safeguards*, injury caused by factors other than increased imports need not be excluded, safeguard measures may be applied to address the 'entirety' of serious injury. See Appellate Body Report, *US – Line Pipe*, paras. 242–3.

[307] Appellate Body Report, *US – Line Pipe*, paras. 242–62.

[308] Appellate Body Report, *Korea – Dairy*, para. 96. The Panel in *Chile – Price Band System* held that the word 'ensure' means that there must be a 'rational connection' between the measure imposed and the objective of preventing or remedying serious injury or facilitating adjustment. See Panel Report, *Chile – Price Band System*, para. 7.183.   [309] See Appellate Body Report, *Korea – Dairy*, para. 96.

[310] Panel Report, *Korea – Dairy*, para. 7.109.   [311] See Appellate Body Report, *Korea – Dairy*, para. 98.

The Appellate Body reiterated this view in *US – Line Pipe*. It stated:

> Article 5.1 imposes a general substantive obligation, namely, to apply safeguard measures only to the permissible extent, and also a particular procedural obligation, namely, to provide a clear justification in the specific case of quantitative restrictions reducing the volume of imports below the average of imports in the last three representative years. Article 5.1 does not establish a general procedural obligation to demonstrate compliance with Article 5.1, first sentence, at the time a measure is applied.[312]

However, the Appellate Body clarified that this does not imply that in cases not covered by Article 5.1, second sentence, 'the measure may be devoid of justification or that the multilateral verification of the consistency of the measure with the *Agreement on Safeguards* is impeded.'[313] Instead, several obligations in the *Agreement on Safeguards*, including those requiring Members to separate and distinguish the injurious effects of factors other than increased imports (Article 4.2(b)) and to include this detailed analysis in the report of their findings and reasoned conclusions (Articles 3.1 and 4.2(c)), 'should have the incidental effect of providing sufficient "justification" for a measure and . . . should also provide a benchmark against which the permissible extent of the measure should be determined'.[314]

In cases in which the safeguard measure takes the form of a quota allocated among supplying countries, Article 5.2(a) of the *Agreement on Safeguards* provides for rules on the allocation of the share of the quota. These rules are similar to the rules of Article XIII of the GATT 1994, discussed above.[315]

Questions and Assignments 7.24

What is the appropriate extent of a safeguard measure? Is a Member obliged to demonstrate in the context of a safeguard measure investigation that the safeguard measure concerned is 'commensurate with the extent of necessity'?

7.5.4.4. Compensation of affected exporting Members

As discussed above, a safeguard measure is a measure that restricts *fair* trade from other Members.[316] A safeguard measure disturbs the balance of rights and obligations to the detriment of the affected exporting Members. Therefore, the *Agreement on Safeguards* requires that a Member taking a safeguard measure agree with the affected exporting Members on appropriate compensation so as to restore the balance of rights and obligations. Article 8.1 of the *Agreement on Safeguards* provides:

---

[312] Appellate Body Report, *US – Line Pipe*, para. 234.   [313] *Ibid.*, para. 236.   [314] *Ibid.*
[315] See above, pp. 456–8. Note, however, that Members may deviate from these rules as provided for in Article 5.2(b) of the *Agreement on Safeguards*, discussed above, p. 688. Also note that, unlike Article XIII of the GATT 1994, Article 5.1, second sentence, and Article 5.2(a) do not apply to tariff quotas. See Panel Report, *US – Line Pipe*, para. 7.75.   [316] See above, pp. 670–2.

> A Member proposing to apply a safeguard measure or seeking an extension of a safeguard measure shall endeavour to maintain a substantially equivalent level of concessions and other obligations . . . between it and the exporting Members which would be affected by such a measure . . . To achieve this objective, the Members concerned may agree on any adequate means of trade compensation for the adverse effects of the measure on their trade.

The objective of appropriate compensation is to be achieved by following the consultation procedures established under Article 12.3 of the *Agreement on Safeguards*. Where a Member fails to consult affected Members in terms of Article 12.3, there is also a violation of Article 8.1.[317]

If an agreement on compensation is not reached within thirty days, Article 8.2 of the *Agreement on Safeguards* provides that the affected exporting Members are free:

> to suspend . . . the application of substantially equivalent concessions or other obligations under GATT 1994, to the trade of the Member applying the safeguard measure.[318]

However, affected exporting Members cannot always exercise this right of suspension. As set out in Article 8.3 of the *Agreement on Safeguards*, this right of suspension shall not be exercised for the first three years that a safeguard measure is in effect in cases where:

- the safeguard measure has been taken as a result of an absolute increase in imports; and
- the safeguard measure conforms to the provisions of the *Agreement on Safeguards*.

In *US – Steel Safeguards*, the United States arguably did not provide an adequate opportunity for consultations on compensation prior to the imposition of its safeguard measures as it implemented the measures only fifteen days after its notification of the measures.[319] Although this issue was not raised before the Panel, several affected Members, including the European Communities, Japan, China, Switzerland and Norway notified, as required by Article 12.5 of the *Safeguards Agreement*, their intention to suspend concessions to an equivalent amount against the United States.[320] In September 2002, the United States

---

[317] See Appellate Body Reports, *US – Wheat Gluten*, paras. 144–6, and *US – Line Pipe*, paras. 114–19. Both Articles 8.1 and 12.3 make an explicit reference to each other and are thus automatically linked. See also above, p. 685.

[318] The right of suspension of 'substantially equivalent concessions' is conditional upon the notification of the proposed suspension measure to the Council for Trade in Goods and the non-disapproval by this Council. As the Council for Trade in Goods takes decisions by consensus, disapproval is *de facto* excluded.

[319] Y.S. Lee, 'Test of Multilateralism in International Trade: US Steel Safeguards', *bepress Legal Series* Paper 253, 2004, 42.

[320] See G/SG/43 and Suppl.1, G/SG/44 and Suppl.1, G/SG/45, G/SG/46, G/SG/47, all dated May 2002. For example, the European Communities notified the adoption of Council Regulation (EC) No. 1031/2002 of 13 June 2002 establishing additional customs duties on imports of certain products originating in the United States of America, OJ L157/8. The regulation notes that the safeguard measure applied to 'certain flat steel products' was not taken in response to an *absolute increase* in imports and therefore that a part of the Community's concessions corresponding to the safeguard measure that was not taken as a result of an absolute increase of imports and representing an amount of applicable duties of €379 million might be subject to additional duties as from 18 June 2002. However, the Community indicated that it would decide on the application of additional duties in the light of decisions by the United States on

notified a reduction of the range of steel products subject to its safeguard measures.[321] After the adoption of the Panel and Appellate Body reports finding its steel safeguards WTO-inconsistent, the United States withdrew these measures and the threatened suspensions of other Members were not carried out.[322]

Questions and Assignments 7.25

Why must a Member applying a safeguard measure try to reach an agreement on compensation? Do exporting Members, adversely affected by a safeguard measure, have a right to suspend, in 'retaliation', equivalent concessions or other obligations? If so, are there any limitations to this right?

7.5.4.5. Provisional safeguard measures

Article 6 of the *Agreement on Safeguards* allows Members to take provisional safeguard measures in 'critical circumstances'. Critical circumstances are defined as circumstances 'where delay would cause damage which it would be difficult to repair'. In order to take provisional safeguard measures, the competent domestic authorities must make a preliminary determination that there is clear evidence that the increased imports have caused or are threatening to cause serious injury.[323]

Provisional measures may only be applied for a maximum of 200 days and can only take the form of tariff increases.[324] If, after a fully fledged investigation, it is concluded that the conditions for imposing a safeguard measure are not fulfilled, the provisional measure shall lapse and duties collected must be refunded.[325]

Questions and Assignments 7.26

When can a Member take a provisional safeguard measure? Why does Article 6 of the *Agreement on Safeguards* provide that provisional safeguard measures can only take the form of tariff increases?

Footnote 320 (*cont.*)
  economically meaningful product exclusions and on the presentation of an acceptable offer on trade compensation. Similarly, Japan notified the adoption of the Cabinet Order concerning the Suspension of Concessions to Certain Steel Products Originating in the United States of America (Cabinet Order No. 212, proclaimed by publication in the Official Gazette on 17 June 2002) on 14 June 2002, which would become effective on 18 June 2002, upon the expiration of thirty days from the day on which written notice of the suspension was received by the CTG.
[321] G/SG/N/10/USA/6/Suppl.7, G/SG/N/11/USA/5/Suppl.7, dated September 2002.
[322] G/SG/N/10/USA/6/Suppl.8, dated 12 December 2003.
[323] On these requirements for the application of provisional safeguard measures, see above, pp. 672–83.
[324] Extension is not possible and the duration of the provisional safeguard measure will be counted for the purpose of calculating the duration of the definitive safeguard measure (see above, pp. 686–7).
[325] See Article 6 of the *Agreement on Safeguards*.

7.5.5 Other safeguard measures

In addition to the safeguards regime contained in Article XIX of the GATT 1994 and the *Agreement on Safeguards*, the WTO also has other safeguard regimes. This section deals with the special safeguard mechanisms under the *Agreement on Agriculture*, and the Protocol on the Accession of the People's Republic of China.[326]

7.5.5.1. *Special safeguards under the Agreement on Agriculture*

The *Agreement on Agriculture* provides for 'special safeguards' that a Member may take in relation to the products that have been 'tariffied' and that have been designated in that Member's Schedule with the symbol 'SSG'.[327] Under Article 5 of the *Agreement on Agriculture*, a special safeguard can be imposed when the *volume* of imports of an agricultural product during any year *exceeds* a specific trigger level,[328] or, where the *import price* of such product, determined on its c.i.f. import price, falls *below* a trigger price which is equal to the average 1986–8 reference price for the product.[329]

With regard to special safeguards based on *prices*, the Appellate Body held in *EC – Poultry* that the import price to be considered against the trigger price is merely the c.i.f. price and that it does not include ordinary customs duties that became payable on the imports.[330] Under Article 5.1(b), therefore, the price at which 'the product may enter the customs territory of the Member granting the concession, as determined on the basis of the c.i.f. import price' is the c.i.f. import price alone and not the c.i.f. import price *plus* applicable duties.

The method of calculation of these trigger levels and prices is specified in paragraphs 4 and 5 of Article 5, respectively. The amount of additional duty that may be imposed on a product is determined in accordance with these provisions.

The Appellate Body held in *EC – Poultry* that under Article 5.5, the comparison of the c.i.f. price with the trigger price can only be on a *shipment-by-shipment basis*. The practice of the European Communities of determining the import price on the basis of what it fixed as a standard 'representative price' therefore became impermissible.[331] Note that to impose special safeguards, there is no need to demonstrate injury to the domestic industry/agricultural sector. Note also that special safeguard measures can only take the form of additional duties on the products concerned.[332]

---

[326] On the transitional safeguard measures under the *Agreement on Textiles and Clothing*, see above, p. 671, footnote 214.   [327] On 'tariffication', see above, p. 451. 'SSG' stands for 'special safeguards'.

[328] See Article 5.1(a) of the *Agreement on Agriculture*. The trigger level relates to existing market access opportunity as set out in Article 5.4. Note that. as a general rule, safeguards imposed of this kind will terminate by the end of the given year. See Article 5.4 of the *Agreement on Agriculture*.

[329] See *ibid.*, Article 5.1(b) of *Agreement on Agriculture*. According to the footnote to the provision, this will in general be the average c.i.f. per unit value of the product. Subparagraphs (a) and (b) of Article 5.1 cannot be applied concurrently.

[330] See Appellate Body Report, *EC – Poultry*, paras. 144–6. Note that the Panel's interpretation in this regard was reversed.   [331] See *ibid.*, paras. 159–71.

[332] On the relationship between the *Agreement on Agriculture*, on the one hand, and the *Agreement on Safeguards* and the GATT 1994, on the other hand, note Article 5.8 and Article 21.1 of the *Agreement on Agriculture*.

7.5.5.2. *Special safeguards under China's Accession Protocol*

Paragraph 16 of the Protocol on the Accession of the People's Republic of China, commonly referred to as China's Accession Protocol, provides for a *transitional product-specific safeguard mechanism*.[333] Paragraph 16.1 of China's Accession Protocol sets out the general conditions for the application of a special safeguard measure under this mechanism.[334] It states:

> In cases where products of Chinese origin are being imported into the territory of any WTO Member in such increased quantities or under such conditions as to cause or threaten to cause *market disruption* to the domestic producers of like or directly competitive products, the WTO Member so affected may request consultations with China with a view to seeking a mutually satisfactory solution.
>
> [Emphasis added]

As a core condition for application, market disruption is deemed to exist whenever imports of a product, like or directly competitive with a product produced by the domestic industry, are increasing rapidly, either absolutely or relatively, so as to be a significant cause of material injury, or threat of material injury to the domestic industry.[335] Therefore, in contrast to the serious injury requirement for the application of general safeguard measures, only material injury or threat of material injury to the domestic industry is needed to meet the 'market disruption' requirement of paragraph 16.1 of the Protocol. The Protocol further provides that the affected WTO Member shall consider objective factors, including the volume of imports, the effect of imports on prices for like or directly competitive products, and the effect of such imports on the domestic industry producing like or directly competitive products in determining the existence of market disruption. Compared to the relevant provisions of the *Agreement on*

---

[333] It should be noted that many trading partners enacted relevant regulations in order to implement paragraph 16 of the Protocol on the Accession of China. The EU published Council Regulation No 427/2003 on 8 March 2003. See Council Regulation No. 427/2003 on a Transitional Product-Specific Safeguard Mechanism for Imports Originating in the People's Republic of China and Amending Regulation No. 519/94 on Common Rules for Imports from Certain Third Countries. For the United States, the relevant legal basis is Section 421 of the Trade Act of 1974 regulating market disruption investigation and section 422 of Trade Act of the 1974 regulating trade diversion investigation, available at www.usitc.gov/trade_remedy/731_ad_701_cvd/investigations/completed/index.htm, visited on 30 August 2007.

[334] Note that, in addition to the transitional product-specific safeguard mechanism provided for in para. 16 of China's Accession Protocol, an additional safeguards regime, applicable to textiles and clothing, is established in para. 242 of the Report of the Working Party on the Accession of China. Under this provision, if a Member believes that Chinese textiles or clothing imports are, due to market disruption, threatening to impede the orderly development of trade in these products, it may request consultations with China. Upon receipt of the consultations request, China will hold its shipments in the relevant textile categories to a level no greater than 7.5 per cent (or 6 per cent for wool categories) above the amount entered during the first twelve months of the most recent fourteen months preceding the month of the request for consultations. This regime is applicable until 31 December 2008 and is part of the terms and conditions for China's accession (therefore it is considered part of China's Protocol of Accession). Giving effect to this special safeguard regime, the European Union inserted Article 10a into Regulation (EEC) No. 3039/93 by means of Regulation (EC) No. 138/2003 and adopted Council Regulation (EC) No. 2200/2004 of 13 December 2004, amending Council Regulations (EEC) No. 3030/93 and (EC) No 3285/94 as regards common rules for imports of textile products from third countries, OJ L364. In June 2005, the European Commission requested and held consultations with China under these provisions, and a Memorandum of Understanding was agreed to, in terms of which China will limit exports of ten categories of textile and clothing products to the EU to agreed levels until the end of 2007. On the problems that arose in the European Union in the context of the implementation of the agreed quotas as a result of the strategic behaviour of textile importers, see further above, p. 671, footnote 222.

[335] See paragraph 16.4 of China's Accession Protocol.

Safeguards, there are fewer factors to be considered in determining the existence of injury. Moreover, there is no 'non-attribution' element with respect to the causation requirement.

If, in the course of bilateral negotiations, it is agreed that imports of Chinese origin cause market disruption and that action is necessary, China shall, under paragraph 16.2 of the Accession Protocol, take such action as to prevent or remedy the market disruption. If consultations do not lead to an agreement between China and the WTO Member concerned within sixty days of the receipt of a request for consultations, the WTO Member affected shall, under paragraph 16.3 of the Accession Protocol, be free to withdraw concessions or otherwise to limit imports. Rules on special safeguard measure investigations are set out in paragraph 16.5 of the Accession Protocol.[336]

With respect to the duration of the measures, paragraph 16.6 of China's Accession Protocol provides that a WTO Member can apply a measure for such a period of time as may be necessary to prevent or remedy the market disruption. However, it does not stipulate the maximum duration of such a measure. Paragraph 16.6 also grants China the right to suspend the application of substantially equivalent concessions or obligations under the GATT 1994 on the trade of the WTO Member applying the measure. However, China's right of suspension cannot be exercised for the first two years if a measure is taken as a result of a relative increase in imports, and for the first three years if based on an absolute increase in imports.

It is clear that the threshold for the application of special safeguard measures under China's Accession Protocol is lower than that for general safeguard measures under the *Agreement on Safeguards* and that some provisions of paragraph 16 of the Protocol are inconsistent with the disciplines of the *Agreement on Safeguards*. However, these deviations from the general safeguard regime are limited in time. Pursuant to paragraph 16.9 of China's Accession Protocol, the special safeguard mechanism will be terminated at the end of 2013.[337]

7.6. REGIONAL INTEGRATION EXCEPTIONS

In addition to the 'general exceptions', the 'security exceptions' and the 'economic emergency exceptions' discussed above, WTO law also provides for 'regional integration exceptions'. These exceptions allow Members to adopt measures, otherwise WTO-inconsistent, taken in the context of the pursuit of regional economic integration. The regional integration exceptions are set out in Article XXIV of the GATT 1994 and Article V of the GATS. The regional integration exception for trade in goods is elaborated on further in the *Understanding on*

---

[336] Note the trade diversion clause of paragraph 16.8 of China's Accession Protocol, which Members can invoke when action taken either voluntarily by China at the request of other WTO Members or unilaterally by affected Members causes or threatens to cause significant diversions of trade into its market.

[337] See Y.S. Lee, 'The Specific Safeguard Mechanism in the Protocol on China's Accession to the WTO', *Journal of World Intellectual Property*, 2002, 219–231.

the Interpretation of Article XXIV of the GATT 1994 (the *'Understanding on Article XXIV'*), which forms part of the GATT 1994.

Since the early 1990s, there has been a proliferation of regional trade agreements (or RTAs).[338] Currently, over 200 regional trade agreements are in force,[339] and this number is likely to double by 2010.[340] Well-known examples of regional integration efforts are the European Communities, the North American Free Trade Agreement (NAFTA),[341] the ASEAN (Association of Southeast Asian Nations) Free Trade Area (AFTA), the Common Market for Eastern and Southern Africa (COMESA), the Common Market of the South (MERCOSUR),[342] the Common Market of the Caribbean (CARICOM) and the Australia–New Zealand Closer Economic Relations Agreement. In 2007, all but one WTO Members were party to one or more regional trade agreements.[343] A significant part of world trade takes place under the terms of regional trade agreements.

The key characteristic of regional trade agreements is that the parties to such agreements offer each other more favourable treatment in trade matters than they offer other trading partners. To the extent that these other trading partners are WTO Members, such discriminatory treatment is – as discussed in chapter 4 – inconsistent with the MFN treatment obligation, one of the basic principles of WTO law. Yet, both the GATT 1994 and the GATS allow, under certain conditions, regional trade agreements establishing customs unions or free trade areas. As is stated in Article XXIV:4 of the GATT 1994:

> The [Members] recognize the desirability of increasing freedom of trade by the development, through voluntary agreements, of closer integration between the economies of the countries parties to such agreements.

WTO law recognises the advantages of economic integration and trade liberalisation even when these efforts involve only some of its Members. At a regional level, it may be possible to achieve a degree of trade liberalisation which may be out of reach at the global level. It is argued that trade liberalisation will occur more quickly if it is pursued within regional trading blocs. Also, regional trade liberalisation may create significant economic growth within the region concerned which can, in turn, generate more trade with the rest of the world. However, economic studies of customs unions and free trade areas have revealed that the trade-creation effects may often be smaller than the trade-diversion effects as trade between the participants replaces trade between the participants and non-participants. It is not clear whether regional trade agreements *divert* rather than *create* trade. As the Sutherland Report noted:

---

[338] See, for instance, 'Everybody's Doing it', *The Economist*, 26 February 2004.
[339] On 18 July 2007, 205 RTAs notified to the GATT/WTO were in force. See
www.wto.org/english/tratop_e/region_e/summary_e.xls, visited on 14 August 2007.
[340] See Pascal Lamy, *Regional Agreements; the 'pepper' in multilateral 'çurry'*, Speech delivered at the Confederation of Indian Industries, Bangalore, 17 January 2007, available at
www.wto.org/english/news_e/sppl_e/sppl53_e.htm, visited on 10 November 2007.
[341] A free trade agreement between Canada, Mexico and the United States.
[342] A customs union between Argentina, Brazil, Paraguay, Uruguay and Venezuela.
[343] Mongolia was not party to any regional trade agreement. See
www.wto.org/english/tratop_e/region_e/summary_e.xls, visited on 11 November 2007.

> There is . . . real reason to doubt assertions that the pursuit of multiple PTAs will enhance, rather than undermine, the attractiveness of multilateral trade liberalization[344]

The dangers of the current proliferation of regional trade agreements for the multilateral trading system has been widely recognised. Guy de Jonquières noted in 2006 that:

> abandonment of multilateral liberalisation in favour of bilateralism and regionalism could, in the longer term, erode the rules and disciplines underpinning the WTO. As its members' political commitment weakened, so too could their willingness to respect its disputes settlement proceedings, the bedrock of its authority.[345]

However, apart from economic reasons, countries may also have political reasons to pursue deeper economic integration and trade liberalisation with some other countries. The example *par excellence* here is the European Union, which through economic integration of, and trade liberalisation between, its Member States sought to create, and was successful in creating, 'an ever closer union' among the peoples of Europe to avoid the recurrence of war. The establishment of MERCOSUR, a customs union originally between Argentina, Brazil, Paraguay and Uruguay,[346] was motivated by the wish to buttress democracy in these countries. Furthermore, regional trade agreements can also serve to reinforce the participation of their Member countries in the WTO, particularly in the case of the developing countries. A case study on the role of the COMESA and SADC membership of Zambia and Mauritius in supporting and facilitating the participation of these countries in the WTO revealed that:

> [while] RTA Membership had little *direct* impact so far on the preparation and conduct of the WTO negotiations . . . regional groupings can play a much needed role in the WTO preparations through indirect means . . . By raising awareness, by training, by providing a platform for the exchange of views and information, and by stimulating trade capacity building initiatives, COMESA and the SADC have contributed to a better preparation of their member countries on trade issues, which have had positive spillovers on their participation [in] the WTO.[347]

WTO law should not stand in the way of such processes. However, a balance must be struck between the interests of countries pursuing closer economic integration among a select group of countries and the interests of countries excluded from that group. The *Understanding on Article XXIV* states in its preamble:

> the purpose of [regional trade] agreements should be to facilitate trade between the constituent territories and not to raise barriers to the trade of other Members with such territories; . . . in their formation or enlargement the parties to them should to the greatest possible extent avoid creating adverse effects on the trade of other Members.

---

[344] Report by the Consultative Board to the Director-General Supachai Panitchpakdi, *The Future of the WTO: Addressing Institutional Challenges in the New Millennium* (the 'Sutherland Report') (WTO, 2004), para. 85. 'PTA' stands for 'Preferential Trade Agreement'.

[345] G. de Jonquières, 'Gobal Trade: Outlook for Agreements Nears Moment of Truth', *Financial Times*, 24 January 2006.   [346] Note that Venezuela joined MERCOSUR as a full member on 4 July 2006.

[347] S. Bilal and S. Szepesi, 'How Regional Economic Communities can Facilitate Participation in the WTO: the Experience of Mauritius and Zambia', in P. Gallagher, P. Low and A. Stoler (eds.), *Managing the Challenges of WTO Participation: 45 Case Studies* (Cambridge University Press, 2005), 389–90.

WTO rules should ensure that regional trade agreements create trade more than they divert. In the context of the Doha Development Round, Members are negotiating with the aim of further clarifying and improving the current rules applying to regional trade agreements.[348] While negotiations on the clarification and improvement of the substantive rules on regional trade agreements have not been successful to date, Members have been successful in agreeing on a new transparency mechanism.[349] This transparency mechanism provides for early announcement of negotiations towards a regional trade agreement, as well as of newly signed regional trade agreements. It sets out detailed notification requirements for parties to regional trade agreements, which could 'help Members establish a "clearer picture" of the rapidly-growing "spaghetti bowl" of overlapping RTAs'.[350] It also establishes a procedure for the consideration of RTAs, on the basis of a factual presentation by the WTO Secretariat.[351]

While, in times of no or slow progress in multilateral trade liberalisation in the context of the WTO, regional trade liberalisation is often put forward as an alternative, note that such efforts may aggravate the lack of progress at the multilateral level and that they are likely to leave out many of the world's poorest countries.[352] As Jagdish Bhagwati noted:

> Everyone loses out but the poor countries suffer the most because their companies are least prepared to deal with the confusion.[353]

Moreover, Bhagwati observed that:

> where a significant power such as the US or the European Union is involved in an agreement, it almost always sneaks in reverse preferences – and trade-unrelated issues such as patent protection and labour standards – that exact a heavy cost on developing countries.[354]

Nonetheless, the debate on regionalism is gradually shifting away from a discussion on costs and benefits to a discussion on how regional trade agreements can

---

[348] See Ministerial Conference, *Doha Ministerial Declaration*, adopted on 14 November 2001, WT/MIN(01)/DEC/1, dated 20 November 2001, para. 29. For an overview of the issues under negotiation, see *Compendium of Issues Related to Regional Trade Agreements*, Background Note by the Secretariat, TN/RL/W/8/Rev.1, dated 1 August 2002. Also noteworthy is the *Synopsis of Systemic Issues Relating to Regional Trade Agreements*, Note by the Secretariat, WT/REG/W/37, dated 2 March 2000.

[349] General Council, *Transparency Mechanism for Regional Trade Agreements*, Decision adopted on 14 December 2006, WT/L/671, dated 18 December 2006. It must be noted that the new mechanism is implemented on a provisional basis, to be reviewed and replaced by a permanent mechanism as part of the overall results of the Doha Development Round. To date, thirty-one early announcements of RTAs have been made, and eleven RTAs have been considered, under the new mechanism. Committee on Regional Trade Agreements, *Annual Report 2007*, see WT/REG/18, dated 3 December 2007 and WTO Secretariat, 'WTO considers RTAs under new transparency mechanism', available at www.wto.org/english/news_e/news07_e/rta_may07_e.htm, visited on 14 August 2007.

[350] *BRIDGES*, *Weekly Trade News Digest*, 12 July 2006, 6. The Annex to the Decision on the new transparency mechanism contains detailed requirements regarding the data to be submitted by parties to an RTA in their notifications.

[351] The Committee on Regional Trade Agreements must implement the transparency mechanism for RTAs falling under Article XXIV of the GATT 1994 and Article V of the GATS and the Committee on Trade and Development must do so for RTAs falling under paragraph 2(c) of the Enabling Clause. See WT/L/671, para. 18.

[352] See Report by the Consultative Board to the Director-General Supachai Panitchpakdi, *The Future of the WTO: Addressing Institutional Challenges in the New Millennium* (the 'Sutherland Report') (WTO, 2004), paras. 75–87 for a critical view on bilateralism and regionalism.

[353] J. Bhagwati, 'A Costly Pursuit of Free Trade', *Financial Times*, 6 March 2001.   [354] *Ibid.*

serve to reinforce the multilateral trading system. Pascal Lamy, Director-General of the WTO, noted the following:

> I find the debate about whether regionalism is a good or bad thing sterile. This is not the point. We need to look at the manner in which RTAs operate, and what effects they have on trade opening and on the creation of new economic opportunities . . . We often think and talk about how regionalism might be hurting multilateralism, either by bolstering discriminatory interests, or perhaps by fostering an anti-trade-openness posture, if regionalism is seen as a way of building protectionist structures behind enlarged closed markets . . . what I would like to do is turn the question around. I would like to ask what the WTO might do to help avoid a situation in which these negative aspects of regional agreements prevail, and ultimately to promote multilateralization.[355]

This section discusses first the regional integration exception and its limits under the GATT 1994. Then it examines this exception under the GATS.

Questions and Assignments 7.27

Name three regional integration agreements other than those referred to above. From a WTO law perspective, what is the problem with regional integration agreements? Why does WTO law, under certain conditions, allow for regional integration agreements?

7.6.1. Article XXIV of the GATT 1994

The chapeau of Article XXIV:5 of the GATT 1994 provides, in relevant part:

> the provisions of this Agreement shall not prevent . . . the formation of a customs union or of a free-trade area or the adoption of an interim agreement necessary for the formation of a customs union or of a free-trade area.

In examining this provision in *Turkey – Textiles*, the Appellate Body noted:

> We read this to mean that the provisions of the GATT 1994 *shall not make impossible* the formation of a customs union. Thus, the chapeau makes it clear that Article XXIV may, under certain conditions, justify the adoption of a measure which is inconsistent with certain other GATT provisions, and may be invoked as a possible "defence" to a finding of inconsistency.[356]

There are two conditions under which Article XXIV may justify a measure which is otherwise GATT-inconsistent. As the Appellate Body stated in *Turkey – Textiles*:

> First, the party claiming the benefit of this defence must demonstrate that the measure at issue is introduced upon the formation of a customs union that fully meets the requirements of sub-paragraphs 8(a) and 5(a) of Article XXIV. And, second, that party must

---

[355] P. Lamy, 'Proliferation of regional trade agreements "breeding concern" ', Speech of the Director-General at the opening of the 2007 Conference on Multilateralizing Regionalism, Geneva, 10 September 2007, available at www.wto.org/english/news_e/sppl_e/sppl67_e.htm, visited on 10 November 2007.

[356] Appellate Body Report, *Turkey – Textiles*, para. 45.

demonstrate that the formation of that customs union would be prevented if it were not allowed to introduce the measure at issue.[357]

There is therefore a two-tier test to determine whether a measure, otherwise inconsistent with the GATT 1994, is justified under Article XXIV. Such measure is justified:

- if the measure is introduced upon the formation of a customs union, a free trade area or an interim agreement that meets all the requirements set out in WTO law; and
- if the formation of the customs union or free trade area would be prevented, i.e. made impossible, if the introduction of the measure concerned were not allowed.

This section will discuss these conditions, first, with regard to a measure adopted in the context of a customs union, secondly, with regard to a measure adopted in the context of a free trade area, and, finally, with regard to a measure adopted under an interim agreement. This section also discusses, *in fine*, special rules for developing-country Members' regional trade agreements as well as general procedural issues.

Questions and Assignments 7.28

In general terms, what is the test to determine whether a measure which is otherwise inconsistent with the GATT 1994 is justified under Article XXIV?

7.6.1.1. Customs unions

As noted above, a measure which is otherwise GATT-inconsistent is justified under Article XXIV of the GATT 1994:

- if that measure is introduced upon the formation of a customs union that meets the requirements of Article XXIV:8(a) and Article XXIV:5(a); and
- if the formation of that customs union would be made impossible if the introduction of the measure concerned were not allowed.

The Appellate Body noted in *Turkey – Textiles* that it is necessary to establish that both conditions are fulfilled and that it may not always be possible to determine whether the second condition is met 'without *first* determining whether there *is* a customs union'.[358]

A 'customs union' is defined in Article XXIV:8(a) of the GATT 1994 as follows:

A customs union shall be understood to mean the substitution of a single customs territory for two or more customs territories so that

---

[357] *Ibid.*, para. 58. See also Appellate Body Report, *Argentina – Footwear (EC)*, para. 109.
[358] Appellate Body Report, *Turkey – Textiles*, para. 59. Emphasis on 'first' added.

i. duties and other restrictive regulations of commerce (except, where necessary, those permitted under Articles XI, XII, XIII, XIV, XV and XX) are eliminated with respect to *substantially all the trade* between the constituent territories of the union or at least with respect to substantially all the trade in products originating in such territories, and,

ii. ... *substantially the same* duties and other regulations of commerce are applied by each of the members of the union to the trade of territories not included in the union.

[Emphasis added]

To satisfy the definition of a 'customs union', Article XXIV:8(a) establishes:

- a standard for the *internal trade* between constituent members (under (i)); and
- a standard for the *trade* of constituent members *with third countries* (under (ii)).

With respect to the first standard, i.e. the standard for the *internal trade* between the constituent members of a customs union, Article XXIV:8(a) requires that members of a customs union eliminate 'duties and other restrictive regulations of commerce' with respect to 'substantially all the trade' between them. As the Appellate Body noted in *Turkey – Textiles*, the WTO Members have never reached an agreement on the interpretation of the term 'substantially' in this provision.[359] According to the Appellate Body, it is clear that 'substantially all the trade' is not the same as *all* the trade, and also that 'substantially all the trade' is something considerably more than merely *some* of the trade.[360] It should also be noted that members of a customs union may maintain, where necessary, certain restrictive regulations of commerce in their internal trade that are permitted under Articles XI to XV and under Article XX of the GATT 1994.[361] The Appellate Body in *Turkey – Textiles* therefore agreed with the Panel in that case that Article XXIV:8(a)(i), which sets out the standard for the *internal trade*, offers 'some flexibility' to the constituent members of a customs union when liberalising their internal trade. However, the Appellate Body cautioned that the degree of 'flexibility' is limited by the requirement that 'duties and other restrictive regulations of commerce' be 'eliminated'.

In *Argentina – Footwear (EC)*, the question arose whether Article XXIV:8(a)(i) prohibited Argentina, as a member of MERCOSUR, from imposing safeguard measures on other MERCOSUR countries. The Appellate Body considered that Article XXIV:8(a)(i) did not prohibit the imposition of safeguard measures on other MERCOSUR countries. In the light of the specific circumstances of this case, the Appellate Body was even of the opinion that Argentina *should* have applied the safeguard measures also to other MERCOSUR countries. The Appellate Body ruled:

we find that Argentina's investigation, which evaluated whether serious injury or the threat thereof was caused by imports from *all* sources, could only lead to the imposition of safeguard measures on imports from *all* sources. Therefore, we conclude that Argentina's investigation, in this case, cannot serve as a basis for excluding imports from other MERCOSUR member States from the application of the safeguard measures.[362]

---

[359] See *ibid.*, para. 48.   [360] See *ibid.*
[361] See Article XXIV:8(a)(i) of the GATT 1994. For a discussion on Articles XI and XIII, see above, pp. 444–60; Article XII, see below, pp. 715–22; and Article XX, see above, pp. 616–51.
[362] Appellate Body Report, *Argentina – Footwear (EC)*, para. 113.

As the Panel in *Argentina – Footwear (EC)* had already noted, there must be a '*parallelism* between the scope of a safeguard *investigation* and the scope of the *application* of safeguard measures'.[363] The requirement of parallelism was reaffirmed by the Appellate Body in *US – Steel Safeguards*.[364] In that case, the competent authority of the United States considered *all imports* in its injury investigation, but afterwards did not apply the safeguard measures to imports from Canada, Israel, Jordan and Mexico.

As to the question whether Article XXIV:8(a)(i) prohibits a member of a customs union from imposing a safeguard measure, an anti-dumping measure, or a countervailing duty, on imports from other members of the customs union, note that, as discussed above, Article XXIV:8(a)(i) offers 'some flexibility' to the constituent members of a customs union when liberalising their internal trade.

With respect to the second standard, i.e. the standard for the trade of constituent members *with third countries*, Article XXIV:8(a)(ii) of the GATT 1994 requires that the constituent members of a customs union apply 'substantially the same' duties and other regulations of commerce to trade with third countries. The constituent members of a customs union are therefore required to apply a common external trade regime, relating to both duties and other regulations of commerce. As the Appellate Body noted in *Turkey – Textiles*, it is *not* required that each constituent member of a customs union applies the *same* duties and other regulations of commerce as other constituent members with respect to trade with third countries. Article XXIV:8(a)(ii) requires that *substantially the same* duties and other regulations of commerce shall be applied.[365] Also, the phrase 'substantially the same' offers a certain degree of 'flexibility' to the constituent members of a customs union in 'the creation of a common commercial policy'. However, as the Appellate Body cautioned again, this 'flexibility' is limited. Something closely approximating 'sameness' is definitely required.[366]

A customs union under Article XXIV must, however, not only meet the requirements of Article XXIV:8(a). It must also meet the requirement of Article XXIV:5(a). This provision states:

> with respect to a customs union . . . the duties and other regulations of commerce imposed at the institution of any such union . . . in respect of trade with [Members] not parties to such union . . . shall not on the whole be higher or more restrictive than the general incidence of the duties and regulations of commerce applicable in the constituent territories prior to the formation of such union . . . as the case may be.

The precise meaning of the requirement that the duties and other regulations of commerce, applicable after the formation of the customs union, are, *on the whole*, not higher or more restrictive than the *general incidence* of the duties and

---

[363] Panel Report, *Argentina – Footwear*, para. 8.87.
[364] See Appellate Body Report, *US – Steel Safeguards*, paras. 440–4.
[365] See Appellate Body Report, *Turkey – Textiles*, para. 49. The Appellate Body agreed with the Panel in *Turkey – Textiles* that the expression 'substantially the same duties and other regulations of commerce are applied by each of the Members of the [customs] union' would appear to encompass both quantitative and qualitative elements, the quantitative aspect being emphasised more in relation to duties (see Panel Report, *Turkey – Textiles*, para. 9.148).   [366] Appellate Body Report, *Turkey – Textiles*, para. 50.

other regulations of commerce applicable prior to the formation of the customs union, has been controversial. Paragraph 2 of the *Understanding on Article XXIV* has sought to clarify this requirement. With respect to duties, paragraph 2 requires that the evaluation under Article XXIV:5(a) of the *general incidence of the duties* applied before and after the formation of a customs union:

> shall . . . be based upon an overall assessment of weighted average tariff rates and of customs duties collected.[367]

As noted by the Appellate Body in *Turkey – Textiles*, under the GATT 1947, there were different views among the GATT Contracting Parties as to whether one should consider, when applying the test of Article XXIV:5(a), the *bound* rates of duty or the *applied* rates of duty. This issue has been resolved by paragraph 2 of the *Understanding on Article XXIV*, which clearly states that the *applied* rate of duty must be used.[368]

With respect to 'other regulations of commerce', paragraph 2 of the *Understanding on Article XXIV* recognises that it may be difficult to evaluate whether the general incidence of the 'other regulations of commerce' after the formation of the customs union is more restrictive than before the formation. Paragraph 2 recognises, in particular, that the quantification and aggregation of regulations of commerce other than duties may be difficult. Therefore, paragraph 2 of the *Understanding on Article XXIV* provides:

> for the purpose of the overall assessment of the incidence of other regulations of commerce . . . the examination of individual measures, regulations, products covered and trade flows affected may be required.

The test for assessing whether a specific customs union meets the requirements of Article XXIV:5(a) is, in essence, an *economic* test, i.e. a test of the extent of trade restriction before and after the formation of the customs union.[369]

If, in the formation of a customs union, a constituent member must increase a bound duty (because the duty of the customs union is higher than the bound duty applicable before the formation of the customs union), Article XXIV:6 of the GATT 1994 requires that the procedure for modification of schedules, set out in Article XXVIII of the GATT 1994, be applied.[370] This procedure for the withdrawal or modification of previously made tariff concessions must be entered into with a view to achieving mutually satisfactory compensatory adjustment.[371] Article XXIV:6 further stipulates, however, that:

> In providing for compensatory adjustment, due account shall be taken of the compensation already afforded by the reduction brought about in the corresponding duty of the other constituents of the union.

---

[367] This assessment shall be based on import statistics for a previous representative period to be supplied by the customs union, on a tariff-line basis and in values and quantities, broken down by WTO country of origin. The WTO Secretariat shall compute the weighted average tariff rates and customs duties collected in accordance with the methodology used in the assessment of tariff offers in the Uruguay Round. For this purpose, the duties and charges to be taken into consideration shall be the applied rates of duty. See para. 2 of the *Understanding on Article XXIV*.   [368] See Appellate Body Report, *Turkey – Textiles*, para. 53.
[369] See *ibid.*, para. 55.   [370] See above, pp. 426–8.   [371] See *Understanding on Article XXIV*, para. 5.

If the reduction in the corresponding duty of other constituent members of the customs union is not sufficient to provide the necessary compensatory adjustment, the customs union must offer compensation.[372] This compensation may take the form of reductions of duties on other tariff lines. If no agreement on compensatory adjustment can be reached, the customs union shall nevertheless be free to modify or withdraw the concessions at issue; and the affected WTO Members shall then be free to withdraw substantially equivalent concessions in accordance with Article XXVIII.[373]

As noted at the beginning of this section, a measure, otherwise GATT-inconsistent, is justified under Article XXIV of the GATT 1994 when two conditions are fulfilled. The first condition – the measure must be introduced upon the formation of a customs union that meets the requirements of Article XXIV:8(a) and Article XXIV:5(a) – is discussed in detail above. The second condition requires that, without the introduction of the measure concerned, the formation of a customs union would be impossible.

In *Turkey – Textiles*, the measures at issue were quantitative restrictions on textiles and clothing from India. Turkey did not deny that these quantitative restrictions were inconsistent with its obligations under Articles XI and XIII of the GATT 1994 and Article 2.4 of the *Agreement on Textiles and Clothing*. However, according to Turkey, these quantitative restrictions were justified under Article XXIV. Turkey argued that, unless it was allowed to introduce quantitative restrictions on textiles and clothing from India, it would be prevented from forming a customs union with the European Communities.[374] Turkey asserted that, had it not introduced the quantitative restrictions on textiles and clothing products from India that were at issue, the European Communities would have excluded these products from free trade within the EC–Turkey customs union. According to Turkey, the European Communities would have done so in order to prevent the circumvention of the EC's quantitative restrictions on textiles and clothing from India by importing them into the European Communities via Turkey. Turkey's exports of these products accounted for 40 per cent of Turkey's total exports to the European Communities. Therefore, Turkey expressed strong doubts as to whether the requirement of Article XXIV:8(a)(i) that duties and other restrictive regulations of commerce be eliminated with respect to 'substantially all trade' between Turkey and the European Communities could be met if 40 per cent of Turkey's total exports to the European Communities were excluded.[375] The Appellate Body rejected this argument. It ruled:

> We agree with the Panel that had Turkey not adopted the same quantitative restrictions that are applied by the European Communities, this would not have prevented Turkey and the European Communities from meeting the requirements of sub-paragraph 8(a)(i) of Article XXIV, and consequently from forming a customs union. We recall our conclusion

---

[372] Note that the GATT 1994 does not require a WTO Member, benefiting from a reduction of duties upon the formation of a customs union, to provide compensatory adjustment. See *Understanding on Article XXIV*, para. 6.   [373] See *Understanding on Article XXIV*, para. 5; and see above, p. 427.

[374] See Appellate Body Report, *Turkey – Textiles*, para. 61.

[375] For this summary of Turkey's argument, see *ibid.*, para. 61.

that the terms of sub-paragraph 8(a)(i) offer some – though limited – flexibility to the constituent members of a customs union when liberalizing their internal trade. As the Panel observed, there are other alternatives available to Turkey and the European Communities to prevent any possible diversion of trade, while at the same time meeting the requirements of sub-paragraph 8(a)(i). For example, Turkey could adopt rules of origin for textile and clothing products that would allow the European Communities to distinguish between those textile and clothing products originating in Turkey, which would enjoy free access to the European Communities under the terms of the customs union, *and* those textile and clothing products originating in third countries, including India.[376]

Questions and Assignments 7.29

What requirements must a 'customs union', within the meaning of Article XXIV of the GATT 1994, meet? What is the meaning of the concepts of 'substantially all trade' and 'substantially the same' in Article XXIV:8(a)? How does the *Understanding on Article XXIV* clarify the requirements that a 'customs union', within the meaning of Article XXIV, must meet? What did the Panel and the Appellate Body rule in *Turkey – Textiles* with respect to the question of whether the regional trade arrangement between Turkey and the European Communities is, in fact, a 'customs union' which meets the requirements of paragraphs 8(a) and 5(a) of Article XXIV? How did the Appellate Body come to the conclusion in *Turkey – Textiles* that the quantitative restriction at issue in that case could not be justified under Article XXIV of the GATT 1994?

7.6.1.2. Free trade areas

As noted above, a measure which is otherwise GATT-inconsistent is justified under Article XXIV of the GATT 1994:

- if that measure is introduced upon the formation of a free trade area that meets the requirements of Article XXIV:8(b) and Article XXIV:5(b); and
- if the formation of that free trade area would be made impossible if the intro-duction of the measure concerned were not allowed.

A 'free trade area' is defined in Article XXIV:8(b) of the GATT 1994 as follows:

A free-trade area shall be understood to mean a group of two or more customs territories in which the duties and other restrictive regulations of commerce (except, where neces-sary, those permitted under Articles XI, XII, XIII, XIV, XV and XX) are eliminated *on substantially all the trade* between the constituent territories in products originating in such territories.

[Emphasis added]

---

[376] *Ibid.*, para. 62. The Appellate Body also noted that Decision 1/95 of the EC-Turkey Association Council specifically provided for the possibility of applying a system of certificates of origin. Rather than making use of this possibility, Turkey had adopted quantitative restrictions on imports of textiles and clothing from India.

Unlike the definition of a 'customs union', discussed above, the definition of a 'free trade area' establishes only a standard for the *internal trade* between constituent members. There is no standard, i.e. there are no requirements, for the trade of constituent members *with third countries*.

The standard for the *internal trade* between constituent members of a free trade area – namely, the elimination of duties and other restrictive regulations of commerce on substantially all trade between constituent members – is identical to the standard for the internal trade between constituent members of a customs union. The case law discussed and observations made in the previous section on 'customs unions' are therefore also relevant for free trade areas.

A free trade area under Article XXIV, however, must not only meet the requirements of Article XXIV:8(b). It must also meet the requirement of Article XXIV:5(b). This provision states:

> with respect to a free-trade area . . . the duties and other regulations of commerce maintained in each of the constituent territories and applicable at the formation of such free-trade area . . . to the trade of [Members] not included in such area . . . shall not be higher or more restrictive than the corresponding duties and other regulations of commerce existing in the same constituent territories prior to the formation of the free-trade area.

Article XXIV:5(b) therefore requires that the duties and other regulations of commerce applied by a member of a free trade area to trade with third countries *after* the formation of the free trade area must *not be higher or more restrictive* than the duties and other regulations of commerce applied by that member *before* the formation of the free trade area. To establish that this is indeed the case is much less problematic than to establish whether the requirements of Article XXIV:5(a) with respect to customs unions are met.[377]

As noted at the beginning of this section, for a measure, otherwise GATT-inconsistent, to be justified under Article XXIV of the GATT 1994, that measure must be such that, if the introduction of the measure concerned were not allowed, the formation of a free trade area would be made impossible. There is no relevant WTO case law on this point yet.

Questions and Assignments 7.30

What requirements must a 'free-trade area' within the meaning of Article XXIV of the GATT 1994 meet? How does a 'free-trade area' differ from a 'customs union'? When are otherwise GATT-inconsistent measures justified under Article XXIV of the GATT 1994?

7.6.1.3. Interim agreements

Measures which are otherwise GATT-inconsistent may be justified under Article XXIV if they are taken in the context of interim agreements leading to

---

[377] See above, pp. 700–5.

the establishment of customs unions and free trade areas meeting the requirements discussed in the two previous sections.[378] This is a recognition of the fact that customs unions and free trade areas will not, and cannot, be established overnight. Nevertheless, although most customs unions and free trade areas have been – at least in part – implemented in stages, only a few have expressly been notified as 'interim agreements'.[379] The number of interim agreements is much lower than one would expect it to be.

Article XXIV:5(c) of the GATT 1994 requires with respect to interim agreements:

> any interim agreement . . . shall include a plan and schedule for the formation of such a customs union or of such a free-trade area within a reasonable length of time.

Not surprisingly, the vague requirement that the customs union or free trade area be established 'within a reasonable length of time' was quite controversial under the GATT 1947. The *Understanding on Article XXIV* therefore provides that this reasonable period of time should not exceed ten years except in exceptional circumstances.[380] It remains to be seen whether and how this ten-year time limit will be applied.

Questions and Assignments 7.31

Why does Article XXIV provide rules for interim agreements leading to the formation of a customs union or free trade area? When may measures, otherwise GATT-inconsistent, be justified under Article XXIV as measures taken in the context of an interim agreement leading to the establishment of a customs union or a free trade area?

7.6.1.4. *Regional trade agreements and developing-country Members*

The Decision of the GATT Contracting Parties of 28 November 1979 on *Differential and More Favourable Treatment, Reciprocity and Fuller Participation of Developing Countries*, commonly referred to as the 'Enabling Clause',[381] provides, in relevant part:

> 1. Notwithstanding the provisions of Article I of the General Agreement, [Members] may accord differential and more favourable treatment to developing countries, without according such treatment to other [Members].
> 2. The provisions of paragraph 1 apply to the following:
>   . . .
>   c. Regional or global arrangements entered into amongst less-developed [Members] for the mutual reduction or elimination of tariffs and, in accordance with criteria or conditions which may be prescribed by the [Ministerial Conference], for the mutual reduction or elimination of non-tariff measures, on products imported from one another.[382]

---

[378] See above, pp. 700–7.   [379] See WT/REG/W/37, para. 47.   [380] See *Understanding on Article XXIV*, para. 3.
[381] On the Enabling Clause, see also above, p. 412, and below, pp. 726–30.   [382] BISD 26S/203.

The Enabling Clause is now part of the GATT 1994, and is therefore still in force. It allows preferential arrangements among developing-country Members in derogation from the MFN treatment obligation of Article I of the GATT 1994. The conditions that regional trade agreements under the Enabling Clause must meet are less demanding and less specific than those set out in Article XXIV of the GATT. In fact, paragraph 3 of the Enabling Clause 'merely' requires that:

> Any differential and more favourable treatment provided under this clause:
>
> a. shall be designed to facilitate and promote the trade of developing countries and not to raise barriers to or create undue difficulties for the trade of any other [Members].

The regional trade agreements under the Enabling Clause include:

- the Treaty Establishing the Common Market for Eastern and Southern Africa ('COMESA');
- the Treaty Establishing the Common Market of the South ('MERCOSUR'); and
- the Common Effective Preferential Tariffs Scheme for the ASEAN Free Trade Area ('AFTA').

Questions and Assignments 7.32

Does Article XXIV of the GATT 1994 apply to regional trade agreements between developing-country Members? What requirements apply to these agreements?

7.6.1.5. Procedural issues

Customs unions and free trade areas, as well as interim agreements leading to the formation of such a union or area, are reviewed by the WTO to determine their consistency with the GATT 1994. WTO Members deciding to enter into a customs union, free trade area or an interim agreement must notify this intention to the Council for Trade in Goods.[383] Since 1996, such notifications are examined by the Committee on Regional Trade Agreements (CRTA).[384] The CRTA reports to the Council for Trade in Goods, which then makes a recommendation to the Members concerning the GATT-consistency.[385] The examination of the GATT-consistency is, as was stated by the Panel in *Turkey – Textiles*, 'a very complex undertaking' requiring consideration by the CRTA 'from the economic, legal and political perspectives of different Members, of the numerous facets of a

---

[383] See Article XXIV: 7(a) of the GATT 1994. For example, on 27 Septemper 2006, the European Communities notified the Treaty of Accession of Bulgaria and Romania to the European Union. See WT/REG220/N/1, dated 2 October 2006.

[384] On the terms of reference of the CRTA, see WT/L/127. Note that the regional trade agreements falling under the Enabling Clause are examined by the Committee on Trade and Development.

[385] See *Understanding on Article XXIV*, para. 7.

regional trade agreement'.[386] The CRTA has thus far examined forty-six regional trade agreements concering trade in goods but has adopted only one report on the GATT-consistency of a customs union, free trade area or interim agreement.[387] The CRTA has found it very difficult, if not impossible, to reach the required consensus among its Members for the adoption of a report.[388]

It has been suggested that in view of the existence of the political process of reviewing the GATT-consistency of customs unions, free trade areas and interim agreements, WTO dispute settlement panels (and the Appellate Body) would not have jurisdiction to decide on the GATT-consistency of such unions, areas or agreements. In *Turkey – Textiles*, the Appellate Body has effectively rejected this view.[389]

Customs unions and constituents of free trade areas must report periodically (i.e. every two years) to the Council for Trade in Goods.[390] Any significant changes to the agreements establishing customs unions or free trade agreements should be reported as they occur.[391] As noted above, WTO Members agreed in December 2006, in the context of the Doha Development Round negotiations, on a new transparency mechanism for regional trade agreements which provides for more detailed notification requirements and a specific procedure for the consideration of notified RTAs.[392]

Questions and Assignments 7.33

Has the examination of the GATT-consistency of customs unions, free trade areas and interim agreements by the CRTA been 'successful'? In your opinion, should panels have jurisdiction to assess the GATT-consistency of customs unions, free trade areas and interim agreements?

7.6.2. Article V of the GATS

Article V of the GATS, entitled 'Economic Integration', is the counterpart of Article XXIV of the GATT 1994 for trade in services. Article V:1 of the GATS provides:

---

[386] Panel Report, *Turkey – Textiles*, para. 9.52.
[387] *Report on the Czech Republic-Slovak Republic Customs Union*, WT/REG/W/37, 10. See also Committee on Regional Trade Agreements, *Annual Report 2007*, WT/REG/18, dated 3 December 2007. Also, under the GATT 1947, the working groups examining the GATT-consistency of customs unions, free trade areas or interim agreements were unable, in all but a few cases, to come to a conclusion.
[388] On decision-making in the WTO, see above, pp. 138–60.
[389] Appellate Body Report, *Turkey – Textiles*, para. 60. Although the Appellate Body was not called upon to address this issue, it explicitly referred to its conclusions on a 'similar' issue in *India – Quantitative Restrictions*. See below, pp. 719–22. Furthermore, note para. 12 of the *Understanding on Article XXIV* which states: 'The provisions of Articles XXII and XXIII of GATT 1994 as elaborated and applied by the Dispute Settlement Understanding may be invoked with respect to any matters arising from the application of those provisions of Article XXIV relating to customs unions, free-trade areas or interim agreements leading to the formation of a customs union or free-trade area.'
[390] See *Understanding on Article XXIV*, para. 11.
[391] See *ibid*. These reporting requirements are not applicable to regional trade agreements among developing-country Members.
[392] See above, p. 698. Note that the decision provides that it does not prejudge the substance and the timing of the notifications required under Article XXIV of the GATT 1994, Article V of the GATS or the Enabling Clause, nor does it affect Members' rights and obligations under the WTO agreements in any way. General Council, *Transparency Mechanism for Regional Trade Agreements*, Decision adopted on 14 December 2006, WT/L/671, dated 18 December 2006, para. 1.

> This Agreement shall not prevent any of its Members from being a party to or entering into an agreement liberalizing trade in services between or among the parties to such an agreement, provided that such an agreement:
>
> a. has substantial sectoral coverage,[393] and
> b. provides for the absence or elimination of substantially all discrimination, in the sense of Article XVII, between or among the parties, in the sectors covered under subparagraph (a), through:
>   i. elimination of existing discriminatory measures, and/or
>   ii. prohibition of new or more discriminatory measures,
>
> either at the entry into force of that agreement or on the basis of a reasonable time-frame, except for measures permitted under Articles XI, XII, XIV and XIV *bis*.

Article V:4 of the GATS states:

> Any agreement referred to in paragraph 1 shall be designed to facilitate trade between the parties to the agreement and shall not in respect of any member outside the agreement raise the overall level of barriers to trade in services within the respective sectors or subsectors compared to the level applicable prior to such an agreement.

The Panel in *Canada – Autos* noted that:

> Article V provides legal coverage for measures taken pursuant to economic integration agreements, which would otherwise be inconsistent with the MFN obligation in Article II.[394]

It follows from Article V:1 that a measure which is otherwise GATS-inconsistent is justified under Article V:

- if the measure is introduced as part of an agreement liberalising trade in services that meets all the requirements set out in Article V:1(a) (the 'substantial sectoral coverage' requirement), Article V:1(b) (the 'substantially all discrimination' requirement) and Article V:4 (the 'barriers to trade' requirement); and
- if WTO Members would be prevented from entering into such an agreement liberalising trade in services, if the measure concerned were not allowed (see the chapeau of Article V:1).

This section, further, discusses primarily the requirements that an economic integration agreement pursuant to Articles V:1(a), V:1(b) and V:4 of the GATS must meet.

7.6.2.1. 'Substantial sectoral coverage' requirement

Pursuant to Article V:1(a) of the GATS, an economic integration agreement must have 'substantial sectoral coverage' of the trade in services among the parties to the agreement. The footnote to the provision states that 'substantial sectoral coverage' should be 'understood in terms of the number of sectors, volume of trade affected and modes of supply'.[395] The footnote also provides

---

[393] The original footnote 1 in the quote reads: 'This condition is understood in terms of number of sectors, volume of trade affected and modes of supply. In order to meet this condition, agreements should not provide for the *a priori* exclusion of any mode of supply.'   [394] Panel Report, *Canada – Autos*, para. 10.271.
[395] It is not clear whether the parameters to be examined in order to determine conformity between an economic integration agreement and Article V of the GATS are limited to the parameters listed in the footnote, or whether there are other considerations.

that an economic integration agreement may not *a priori* exclude any of the four modes of supply. In particular, no economic integration agreement should *a priori* exclude investment or labour mobility in the sense of modes 3 and 4. Members disagree on whether one or more service sectors can be excluded from an economic integration agreement but the use of the wording 'number of sectors' in the footnote to paragraph 1(a) seems to indicate that not all sectors must be covered under an economic integration agreement to meet the 'substantial sectoral coverage' test. However, it is clear that the number of exclusions must be limited.

As the Panel in *Canada – Autos* stated:

> the purpose of Article V is to allow for ambitious liberalization to take place at a regional level, while at the same time guarding against undermining the MFN obligation by engaging in *minor preferential arrangements*.[396]
>
> [Emphasis added]

7.6.2.2. 'Substantially all discrimination' requirement

Article V:1(b) of the GATS requires that an economic integration agreement should provide for 'the absence or elimination of substantially all discrimination'.[397] As Article V:1(b) does not require the absence or elimination of *all* discrimination, but rather the absence or elimination of *substantially all* discrimination, the question arises as to what extent discriminatory measures should be allowed to exist in an economic integration agreement.[398] The scope of such permissible discriminatory measures is, of course, affected by the scope of the list of exceptions in Article V:1(b). This list explicitly includes exceptions permitted under Articles XI, XII, XIV and XIV *bis* of the GATS, but it is unclear whether this list is exhaustive. The scope of permissible discriminatory measures is also affected by the meaning given to the 'and/or' wording in Article V:1(b) linking provisions (i) and (ii). Some Members are of the opinion that the 'or' allows the parties to an economic integration agreement to choose between provisions (i) and (ii), that is, the elimination of existing discriminatory measures, or, alternatively, the use of a standstill. A party could therefore choose only to eliminate the possibility of adding new measures or of making existing measures more restrictive, rather than also having to eliminate existing measures. Other Members have rejected this interpretation. They argue that, considering that Article V:1(b) aims to deal with 'substantially all discrimination', it would be appropriate to interpret the 'and/or' wording in such a way that both (i) and (ii) are found to be applicable. Thus, it is argued that paragraphs (i) and (ii) are *options* to be judged as appropriate against the circumstances of the sector

---

[396] Panel Report, *Canada – Autos*, para. 10.271.

[397] Note that Article V:2 of the GATS states that the evaluation of an agreement's consistency with Article V:1(b) may also take into account its relationship with 'a wider process of economic integration or trade liberalization' among the parties to the agreement. A 'wider process of economic integration' refers to a process of economic integration involving the elimination of barriers to trade not only in services but also in goods.

[398] Note that Article V:6 of the GATS provides that a third-party service supplier, legally recognised as a juridical person by a party to an economic integration agreement, is entitled to equivalent treatment granted within the economic integration area, provided that it engages in 'substantive business operations' in the territory of the parties to that agreement.

being considered, *not* as *alternatives* to be freely chosen by the parties to the economic integration agreement.[399]

The Panel in *Canada – Autos* noted with respect to the obligation under Article V:1(b):

> Although the requirement of Article V:1(b) is to provide non-discrimination in the sense of Article XVII (National Treatment), we consider that once it is fulfilled it would also ensure non-discrimination between all service suppliers of other parties to the economic integration agreement. It is our view that the object and purpose of this provision is to eliminate all discrimination among services and service suppliers of parties to an economic integration agreement, including discrimination between the suppliers of other parties to an economic integration agreement.[400]

According to the Panel, it would be inconsistent with Article V:1(b) if a party to an economic integration agreement were to extend more favourable treatment to the service suppliers of one party than it does to the service suppliers of another party to that agreement.[401] In other words, the obligation under Article V:1(b) also has an MFN treatment dimension.

The concept of 'a reasonable time-frame' in Article V:1(b) is not defined or clarified in any way in the GATS. On the basis of Article XXIV:5(c) of the GATT 1994 and paragraph 3 of the *Understanding on Article XXIV* concerning the similar concept of 'a reasonable length of time', it would be reasonable to suppose that, in defining the 'reasonable time-frame' of Article V:1(b), a ten-year limit would be used as a general starting-point.

7.6.2.3. 'Barriers to trade' requirement

Article V:4 requires that an economic integration agreement must be designed to facilitate trade between the parties to the agreement and must *not*, in respect of any Member outside the agreement, *raise* the overall level of *barriers* to trade in services within the respective sectors or subsectors compared to the level applicable prior to such an agreement. The absence of detailed data on trade in services and differences in regulatory mechanisms between Members makes it difficult to evaluate the level of barriers in effect before the establishment of an economic integration agreement. A possible approach to the application of this 'barriers to trade' requirement would be to require that an economic integration agreement reduce neither the level, nor the growth, of trade in any sector or subsector below a historical trend.[402]

7.6.2.4. Economic integration agreements and developing-country Members

With regard to economic integration agreements to which developing countries are parties, Article V:3(a) of the GATS provides for flexibility regarding the

---

[399] See Committee on Regional Trade Agreements, *Examination of the North American Free Trade Agreements*, Note on the Meeting of 24 February 1997, WT/REG4/M/4, dated 16 April 1997.
[400] Panel Report, *Canada – Autos*, para. 10.270.   [401] *Ibid.*, para. 10.270.
[402] Changes in the volume of trade could be judged by data on domestic economic activities if data on trade in services is unavailable.

conditions set out in Article V:1, quoted and discussed above. This flexibility is to be granted 'in accordance with the level of development of the countries concerned, both overall and in individual sectors and subsectors'.

Article V:3(b) of the GATS provides that, in the case of an economic integration agreement involving only developing countries, 'more favourable treatment may be granted to juridical persons owned or controlled by natural persons of the parties to such an agreement'.[403]

7.6.2.5. Procedural matters

Article V:7 requires WTO Members that are parties to an economic integration agreement promptly to notify such an agreement (and any enlargement or any significant modification of that agreement) to the Council for Trade in Services.[404] At the request of the Council for Trade in Services, the CRTA will examine such an agreement (or enlargement or modification of that agreement) and report back on its GATS-consistency.[405] The Council for Trade in Services may make such recommendations as it deems appropriate. The regional integration agreements referred to date to the CRTA for an examination of their GATS-consistency include:

- the Treaty of Accession of Austria, Finland and Sweden to the European Union;[406]
- the North American Free Trade Agreement;[407]
- the Australia–New Zealand Closer Economic Relations Trade Agreement;[408]
- the Free Trade Agreement between Chile and Mexico;[409] and
- the Treaty of Accession of the Czech Republic, Estonia, Cyprus, Latvia, Lithuania, Hungary, Malta, Poland, Slovenia and the Slovak Republic to the European Union.[410]

Article V:5 of the GATS requires a party to an economic integration agreement to provide at least ninety days, advance notice of any modification or withdrawal of a specific commitment that would give rise to an inconsistency with the terms and conditions set out in its Schedule. In such situations, that party must initiate the procedure for the modification of schedules and the compensatory adjustment set forth in Article XXI of the GATS.

7.6.2.6. Labour markets integration agreement

Article V *bis* of the GATS entitled 'Labour Markets Integration Agreements', deals with a specific form of economic integration agreement which establishes full integration of labour markets between or among the parties to such an

---

[403] Article V:3(b) applies notwithstanding Article V:6 of the GATS, referred to in p. 711, footnote 398.

[404] See Article V:7(a) of the GATS. Note that Members which are parties to an economic integration agreement which is implemented on the basis of a timeframe shall report periodically to the Council for Trade in Services on its implementation. See Article V:7(b) of the GATS.

[405] Recall that regional trade agreements under the Enabling Clause are examined by the Committee on Trade and Development. Regional trade agreements among developed-country Members will be examined by the CRTA.   [406] See S/C/M/2, paras. 9 and 10.   [407] See S/C/M/3, paras. 27 and 28.

[408] See S/C/M/14, Section E.   [409] See S/C/M/52, Section C.   [410] See S/C/M/73, Section A.

agreement. Such agreements give the nationals of the parties free entry to each other's labour markets. Usually, these agreements also include provisions concerning conditions of pay, other conditions of employment and social benefits.

Article V *bis* provides that the GATS shall not prevent any WTO Member from being a party to such agreement provided that the agreement:

- exempts citizens of parties to the agreement from requirements concerning residency and work permits; and
- is notified to the Council for Trade in Services.

Questions and Assignments 7.34

When is a measure, which is otherwise GATS-inconsistent, justified under Article V of the GATS? Give two examples of economic integration agreements not already mentioned above. When must a party to an economic integration agreement initiate the procedure for the modification of schedules and compensatory adjustment set forth in Article XXI of the GATS? What are labour markets integration agreements?

7.7. BALANCE-OF-PAYMENTS EXCEPTIONS

In addition to the 'general exceptions', the 'security exceptions', the 'economic emergency exceptions' and the 'regional integration exceptions' discussed above, WTO law also provides for 'balance-of-payments exceptions'. The balance-of-payments exceptions are set out in Articles XII and XVIII:B of the GATT 1994 and Article XII of the GATS. The balance-of-payments exception for trade in goods is further elaborated in the *Understanding on Balance of Payments Provisions of the GATT 1994* (the '*Understanding on BoP Provisions*'), which is part of the GATT 1994. These exceptions allow Members to adopt measures, otherwise GATT- or GATS-inconsistent, to safeguard their external financial position and to protect their balance of payments. The outflow of money from a country can indeed be limited, in a fairly easy and effective manner, by imposing trade restrictive measures on imports into the country. In the past, the balance-of-payments exceptions have been quite important. In today's world of floating exchange rates, balance-of-payments problems may be resolved by other means than through trade restrictions. Nevertheless, the balance-of-payments exceptions are still of some importance. Developing-country Members, in particular, continue to use these exceptions. In times of rapid economic development, countries often experience severe pressure on their monetary reserves. However, important users in the 1980s and 1990s of trade restrictions for balance-of-payments purposes, such as India and Nigeria, no longer use such measures.[411]

---

[411] On India, see Report by the Secretariat, *Trade Policy Review: India*, WT/TPR/S/182, dated 18 April 2007, para. 58. On Nigeria, see A. Oyejide, O. Ogunkola and A. Bankole, 'Nigeria: Import Prohibition as a Trade Policy', in: P. Gallagher, P. Low and A. Stoler (eds.), *Managing the Challenges of WTO Participation, 45 Case Studies* (Cambridge University Press, 2005), 444–5.

7.7.1. Articles XII and XVIII:B of the GATT 1994

Article XII of the GATT 1994, entitled 'Restrictions to Safeguard the Balance of Payments', states, in its first paragraph:

> Notwithstanding the provisions of paragraph 1 of Article XI, any [Member], in order to safeguard its external financial position and its balance of payments, may restrict the quantity or value of merchandise permitted to be imported, subject to the provisions of the following paragraphs of this Article.

Article XVIII of the GATT 1994, entitled 'Governmental Assistance to Economic Development', provides in paragraph 4(a) as follows:

> a [Member], the economy of which can only support low standards of living and is in the early stages of development, shall be free to deviate temporarily from the provisions of the other Articles of this Agreement, as provided in Sections A, B and C of this Article.

Section B of Article XVIII, i.e. paragraphs 8 to 12 of Article XVIII, provides for a special balance-of-payments exception for developing-country Members. Article XVIII:9 states, in relevant part:

> In order to safeguard its external financial position and to ensure a level of reserves adequate for the implementation of its programme of economic development, a [Member] coming within the scope of paragraph 4(*a*) of this Article may, subject to the provisions of paragraphs 10 to 12, control the general level of its imports by restricting the quantity or value of merchandise permitted to be imported; *Provided* that . . .

Under Article XII, the purpose of a Member's balance-of-payments (BoP) measure is 'to safeguard its external financial position and its balance of payments'. Under Article XVIII:B, the purpose of a BoP measure taken by a developing-country Member is also 'to safeguard its external financial position' but, in addition, 'to ensure a level of reserves adequate for the implementation of its programme of economic development'. This section examines:

- the nature of measures that may be taken for BoP purposes;
- the requirements for taking such measures; and
- procedural issues related to the taking of such measures.

7.7.1.1. Nature of BoP measures

Articles XII and XVIII:B of the GATT 1994 only allow quantitative restrictions to be used to address balance-of-payments problems. They do not allow for tariff measures.[412] However, it was common practice under the GATT 1947 for Contracting Parties to take balance-of-payments action in the form of tariff or tariff-like measures, such as import surcharges. In 1979 the use of such measures was formally authorised in the *Declaration on Trade Measures Taken for Balance of Payments Purposes* (the '*1979 Declaration*').[413] The 1994 *Understanding on BoP*

---

[412] Note that this rule is inconsistent with the general GATT preference for using tariffs instead of quantitative restrictions. See above, pp. 445–6.

[413] Adopted on 28 November 1979, BISD 26S/205–9. Note that this Declaration is still applicable law.

Provisions goes much further and commits WTO Members to give preference to price-based BoP measures. Paragraph 2 of the *Understanding on BoP Provisions* states:

> Members confirm their commitment to give preference to those measures which have the least disruptive effect on trade. Such measures (referred to in this Understanding as 'price-based measures') shall be understood to include import surcharges, import deposit requirements or other equivalent trade measures with an impact on the price of imported goods. It is understood that, notwithstanding the provisions of Article II, price-based measures taken for balance-of-payments purposes may be applied by a Member in excess of the duties inscribed in the Schedule of that Member . . .

If a Member decides to apply a price-based BoP measure, it must indicate the amount by which the price-based measure exceeds the bound duty clearly and separately.[414]

While under Article XII, quantitative restrictions were initially the only form of BoP measures allowed, paragraph 3 of the *Understanding on BoP Provisions* now provides:

> Members shall seek to avoid the imposition of new quantitative restrictions for balance-of-payments purposes unless, because of a critical balance-of-payments situation, price-based measures cannot arrest a sharp deterioration in the external payments position.

If a Member applies a quantitative restriction as a BoP measure, it must provide justification as to the reasons why price-based measures are not an adequate instrument to deal with the balance-of-payments situation.[415]

Pursuant to the *Understanding on BoP Provisions*, not more than one type of restrictive import measure, taken for balance-of-payments purposes, may be applied on the same product.[416] A combination of price-based measures and quantitative restrictions on the same product is therefore prohibited.

7.7.1.2. *Requirements for the use of BoP measures*

BoP measures, whether in the form of price-based measures or quantitative restrictions, are often inconsistent with the obligations under Articles II or XI of the GATT 1994. Therefore, they can only be applied when strict requirements are met.

First, BoP measures may not exceed what is necessary to address the balance-of-payments problem at hand. Article XII:2 of the GATT 1994 states that BoP measures adopted by a Member:

> shall not exceed those necessary:
>
> i.   to forestall the imminent threat of, or to stop, a serious decline in its monetary reserves, or

---

[414] See para. 2 of the *Understanding on BoP Provisions*. For this purpose, the notification procedure, discussed below, must be followed.

[415] See para. 3 of the *Understanding on BoP Provisions*. Note that Members applying quantitative restrictions as BoP measures must also indicate in successive consultations the progress made in significantly reducing the incidence and restrictive effect of such measures (*ibid*).

[416] See para. 3 of the *Understanding on BoP Provisions*.

> ii. in the case of a [Member] with very low monetary reserves, to achieve a reasonable rate of increase in its reserves.

Article XVIII:9 of the GATT 1994 requires that BoP measures adopted by a developing-country Member:

> shall not exceed those necessary:
>
> a. to forestall the threat of, or to stop, a serious decline in its monetary reserves, or
> b. in the case of a [Member] with inadequate monetary reserves, to achieve a reasonable rate of increase in its reserves.

Note that developing-country Members can adopt BoP measures to forestall a *threat* of a serious decline in monetary reserves, while other Members can only do so to forestall an *imminent threat* of such decline. Also, developing-country Members with *inadequate* monetary reserves may in addition adopt BoP measures to achieve a reasonable rate of *increase* in their reserves while other Members may do so only when they have *very low* monetary reserves. In *India – Quantitative Restrictions*, the Panel distinguished the requirements for taking BoP measures under Article XVIII from the requirements applicable under Article XII, and noted:

> These provisions reflect an acknowledgement of the specific needs of developing countries in relation to measures taken for balance-of-payments purposes.[417]

At its Doha Session in November 2001, the WTO Ministerial Conference explicitly affirmed that Article XVIII is a special and differential treatment provision for developing-country Members and that recourse to it should be *less onerous* than to Article XII.[418]

The determination of what constitutes a serious decline of monetary reserves or an (imminent) threat thereof, or the determination of what constitutes very low or inadequate monetary reserves, is primarily left to the IMF. The WTO consults the IMF on these matters, and Article XV:2 of the GATT 1994 states, in relevant part:

> The [WTO] in reaching [its] final decision in cases involving the criteria set forth in paragraph 2(a) of Article XII or in paragraph 9 of Article XVIII, shall accept the determination of the [IMF] as to what constitutes a serious decline in the [Member's] monetary reserves, a very low level of its monetary reserves or a reasonable rate of increase in its monetary reserves, and as to the financial aspects of other matters covered in consultation in such cases.

Note that in *India – Quantitative Restrictions* the IMF reported that India's reserves as of 21 November 1997 were US$25.1 billion and that an adequate level of reserves at that date would have been US$16 billion. The IMF had also reported that India did not face a serious decline of its monetary reserves or a threat

---

[417] Panel Report, *India – Quantitative Restrictions*, para. 5.155.
[418] See Ministerial Conference, *Ministerial Decision on Implementation-Related Issues and Concerns*, adopted on 14 November 2001, WT/MIN(01)/17, dated 20 November 2001, para. 1.1.

thereof.[419] To a large extent, the Panel's conclusions in this case were based on these IMF findings.

Secondly, paragraph 4 of the *Understanding on BoP Provisions* provides that a BoP measure:

> may only be applied to control the general level of imports and may not exceed what is necessary to address the balance-of-payments situation.

BoP measures must avoid unnecessary damage to the commercial and economic interests of other Members.[420] BoP measures may be discriminatory with respect to products (i.e. apply to some products and not to others), but *not* with respect to countries (i.e. apply to some countries and not to others). Note that the *Understanding on BoP Provisions* requires that Members administer BoP measures in a transparent manner. The authorities of the importing Member must therefore provide adequate justification as to the criteria used to determine which products are subject to the BoP measure.[421]

Thirdly, BoP measures are temporary measures. Members applying BoP measures must announce publicly, as soon as possible, time-schedules for the removal of these measures.[422] Referring to the conditions for their adoption (such as 'a serious decline in monetary reserves' or 'inadequate monetary reserves'), Article XII:2(b) of the GATT 1994 states:

> [Members] applying restrictions under sub-paragraph *(a)* of this paragraph shall progressively relax them as such conditions improve, maintaining them only to the extent that the conditions specified in that sub-paragraph still justify their application. They shall eliminate the restrictions when conditions would no longer justify their institution or maintenance under that sub-paragraph.

As the external financial situation improves, the BoP measures must be relaxed; when the external financial situation has returned to 'normal', the BoP measures must be eliminated.[423] Article XVIII:11 of the GATT 1994 provides for similar obligations with respect to the elimination or relaxation of BoP measures adopted by developing-country Members. However, Article XVIII:11 adds the proviso:

> that no [Member] shall be required to withdraw or modify restrictions on the ground that a change in its development policy would render unnecessary the restrictions which it is applying under this Section.

---

[419] See Panel Report, *India – Quantitative Restrictions*, paras. 5.174 and 5.177.

[420] See Articles XII:3(c)(i) and XVIII:10 of the GATT 1994.

[421] In the case of certain 'essential products', Members may exclude or limit the application of surcharges applied across the board or other measures applied for balance-of-payments purposes. The concept of 'essential products' shall be understood to mean products which meet basic consumption needs or which contribute to the Member's effort to improve its balance-of-payments situation, such as capital goods or inputs needed for production. See Articles XII:3 and XVIII:10 of the GATT 1994; and para. 4 of the *Understanding on BoP Provisions*.   [422] See para. 1 of the *Understanding on BoP Provisions*.

[423] For BoP measures of developing-country Members, however, note that, if the elimination or relaxation of the BoP measures would produce immediately or very quickly the conditions justifying the adoption or intensification of BoP measures, the BoP measures 'may be maintained'. See Note *Ad* Article XVIII; and Appellate Body Report, *India – Quantitative Restrictions*, paras. 117–120.

In *India – Quantitative Restrictions*, the Appellate Body upheld the Panel's finding that India could manage its balance-of-payments situation using macroeconomic policy instruments alone, without maintaining quantitative restrictions. India appealed this finding, arguing that the Panel required India to change its development policy. The Appellate Body, however, ruled:

> we are of the opinion that the use of macroeconomic policy instruments is not related to any particular development policy, but is resorted to by all Members regardless of the type of development policy they pursue.[424]

The Appellate Body clarified the meaning of the proviso of Article XVIII:11 by stating:

> We believe that structural measures are different from macroeconomic instruments with respect to their relationship to development policy. If India were asked to implement agricultural reform or to scale back reservations on certain products for small-scale units as indispensable policy changes in order to overcome its balance-of-payments difficulties, such a requirement would probably have involved a change in India's development policy.[425]

Questions and Assignments 7.35

When is a Member allowed to adopt a BoP measure? What form may such a measure take? With which obligations of the GATT 1994 may a BoP measure be inconsistent: the obligations under Article I, Article II or Article XI? When must a Member eliminate or relax the BoP measures it applies?

7.7.1.3. Procedural issues

BoP measures are reviewed by the WTO to determine their consistency with the GATT 1994. This review is conducted by the Committee on Balance-of-Payments Restrictions (the 'BoP Committee'). The procedures applicable to this review are set out in the *Understanding on BoP Provisions*.[426] A Member shall notify the introduction of, or any changes in the application of a BoP measure to the General Council.[427] A Member applying new restrictions or raising the general level of its existing restrictions must enter into consultation with the BoP Committee within four months of the adoption of such measures.[428] If the Member

---

[424] Appellate Body Report, *India – Quantitative Restrictions*, para. 126. [425] *Ibid.*, para. 128.

[426] As para. 5 of the *Understanding on BoP Provisions* states, the BoP Committee shall follow the procedures for consultations on balance-of-payments restrictions approved on 28 April 1970 (BISD18S/48–53) (the 'full consultation procedures'), subject to the provisions set out in the *Understanding*. Consultations may be held under the 'simplified consultation procedures' approved on 19 December 1972 (BISD 20S/ 47–9) in the case of least-developed-country Members or in the case of developing-country Members in certain situations. See para. 8 of the *Understanding on BoP Provisions*.

[427] See para. 9 of the *Understanding on BoP Provisions*. Every year, each Member shall make available to the WTO Secretariat a consolidated notification on all aspects of the BoP measures applied. *Ibid.*

[428] See para. 6 of the *Understanding on BoP Provisions*. Note that the Member adopting BoP measures may request that a consultation be held under Articles XII:4(a) or XVIII:12(a) of the GATT 1994 as appropriate. *Ibid.* On the course of the consultation process and the role of the WTO Secretariat, see paras. 11 and 12 of the *Understanding on BoP Provisions*.

concerned fails to request a consultation, the Chairman of the BoP Committee shall invite that Member to hold such a consultation. Any Member may request that notifications on BoP measures are reviewed by the BoP Committee.[429] Furthermore, all BoP measures are subject to *periodic* review in the BoP Committee.[430] For instance, Bangladesh has been subject to GATT/WTO consultations since 1973 for the import bans and restrictions it employs on certain products for BoP purposes.[431] The last consultations took place in October 2002 and November 2004. In February 2004, Bangladesh notified the BoP Committee that it had withdrawn restrictions in seven categories, maintaining import restrictions only on four categories of products: chicks, eggs, cartons and common salt.[432] Bangladesh subsequently notified the removal of restrictions on cartons as from July 2005 and common salt as from 31 December 2008.[433] In 2007, Bangladesh submitted a document to the BoP Committee, providing information with regard to its economic situation and pointing out that its last BoP restrictions would be removed by 31 December 2008. However, it stated:

> It is to be mentioned that more than three million people are involved in the production, distribution and marketing of eggs, chicks and salt. They are mainly small poor farmers, women and youth. They totally depend on these items for their livelihood. If the import restrictions on these items are withdrawn, it is apprehended that these poorer sections of the population will suffer enormously. Yet, the Government of Bangladesh is highly committed to maintain its commitments with the WTO. It has therefore decided to withdraw BOP restrictions under GATT Article XVIII:B on the remaining items from 31 December 2008 in consistence with the decision of the Committee on BOPs. It is expected that the next one year and eight months will provide a breathing time to these sections of population to adjust themselves with the new competitive environment.[434]

The BoP Committee reports on its consultations to the General Council. Pursuant to paragraph 13 of the *Understanding on BoP Provisions*, the BoP Committee shall endeavour to include in its conclusions 'proposals for recommendations aimed at promoting the implementation of Articles XII and XVIII:B, the 1979 Declaration and this Understanding'. In those cases in which a time-schedule has been presented for the removal of BoP measures, the General Council may recommend that, in adhering to such a time-schedule, a Member shall be deemed to be in compliance with its GATT 1994 obligations. Whenever the General Council has made specific recommendations, the rights and obligations of Members shall be assessed in the light of such recommendations. In the absence of specific proposals for recommendations by the General Council, the Committee's conclusions should record the different views expressed in the Committee.[435]

---

[429] See para. 10 of the *Understanding on BoP Provisions*.
[430] See para. 7 of the *Understanding on BoP Provisions*, which refers in this respect to Articles XII:4(b) and XVIII:12(b) of the GATT 1994.
[431] See Report by the Secretariat, *Trade Policy Review: Bangladesh*, WT/TPR/S/168, dated 9 August 2006, 55.
[432] See WT/BOP/N/62, dated 18 February 2004.
[433] See WT/BOP/N/63, dated 9 September 2005 and WT/BOP/N/64, dated 20 April 2007.
[434] See WT/BOP/G/14, dated 2 May 2007, para. 16.
[435] Note also the powers given to the Ministerial Conference in Articles XII:4(c), (d) and (f) and XVIII:12(c), (d) and (f) of the GATT 1994. These powers have never been used.

Since its establishment in 1995, the BoP Committee has reviewed many BoP measures notified by Members. In most cases, the Members concerned made commitments to eliminate or relax the BoP measures under review and these commitments satisfied the BoP Committee. In other cases, Members were unable to agree within the BoP Committee on a timeframe for the relaxation and/or elimination of the BoP measures under review.

In *India – Quantitative Restrictions*, India argued that it had the right to maintain BoP measures until the BoP Committee or the General Council ordered it to eliminate or relax these measures. The Panel rejected this argument. It noted that the obligation of Article XVIII:11 to eliminate or relax BoP measures:

> is not conditioned on any BOP Committee or General Council decision. If we were to interpret Article XVIII:11 to be so conditioned, we would be adding terms to Article XVIII:11 that it does not contain.[436]

In *India – Quantitative Restrictions*, India also argued that WTO dispute settlement panels have no authority to examine Members' justifications of BoP measures.[437] India based its position on the second sentence of footnote 1 to the *Understanding on BoP Provisions*, which reads:

> The provisions of Articles XXII and XXIII of GATT 1994 as elaborated and applied by the Dispute Settlement Understanding may be invoked with respect to any matters arising from the application of restrictive import measures taken for balance-of-payments purposes.

India interpreted this footnote to mean that the WTO dispute settlement system may be invoked in respect of matters relating to the specific use or purpose of a BoP measure or to the manner in which a BoP measure is applied in a particular case, but not with respect to the question of the balance-of-payments *justification* of these measures. More generally, India argued for the existence of a 'principle of institutional balance' that requires panels to refrain from reviewing the justification of balance-of-payments restrictions under Article XVIII:B. Such review was entrusted to the BoP Committee and the General Council, political organs of the WTO. Thus panels and the Appellate Body, the 'judicial' organs of the WTO, must refrain from such review. The Appellate Body rejected India's arguments and stated:

> Any doubts that may have existed in the past as to whether the dispute settlement procedures under Article XXIII were available for disputes relating to balance-of-payments restrictions have been removed by the second sentence of footnote 1 to the *BOP Understanding* . . .
>
> . . . in light of footnote 1 to the *BOP Understanding*, a dispute relating to the justification of balance-of-payments restrictions is clearly within the scope of matters to which the dispute settlement provisions of Article XXIII of the GATT 1994, as elaborated and applied by the DSU, are applicable.[438]

The fact that panels are competent to review the justification of BoP measures does *not* make the competence of the BoP Committee and the General Council,

---

[436] Panel Report, *India – Quantitative Restrictions*, para. 5.79.   [437] See also above, p. 719.
[438] Appellate Body Report, *India – Quantitative Restrictions*, paras. 87 and 95.

discussed above, redundant. In *India – Quantitative Restrictions*, the Appellate Body ruled:

> We are cognisant of the competence of the BOP Committee and the General Council with respect to balance-of-payments restrictions under Article XVIII:12 of the GATT 1994 and the *BOP Understanding*. However, we see no conflict between that competence and the competence of panels. Moreover, we are convinced that, in considering the justification of balance-of-payments restrictions, panels should take into account the deliberations and conclusions of the BOP Committee, as did the panel in *Korea€Beef*.[439]

The Appellate Body agreed with the Panel that the BoP Committee and panels have different functions, and that the BoP Committee procedures and the dispute settlement procedures differ in nature, scope, timing and type of outcome.[440]

Questions and Assignments 7.36

What is the role of the BoP Committee? Find out whether South Africa or Brazil currently maintain BoP measures. Can a panel review the balance-of-payments justification of the BoP measure before or during the review of the GATT-consistency of this measure by the BoP Committee?

7.7.2. Article XII of the GATS

Article XII:1 of the GATS, entitled 'Restrictions to Safeguard the Balance of Payments', provides, in its first sentence:

> In the event of serious balance-of-payments and external financial difficulties or threat thereof, a Member may adopt or maintain restrictions on trade in services on which it has undertaken specific commitments, including on payments or transfers for transactions related to such commitments.

Article XII:1, second sentence, of the GATS recognises that particular pressures on the balance of payments of a Member in the process of economic development or economic transition may necessitate the use of restrictions to ensure, *inter alia*, the maintenance of a level of financial reserves adequate for the implementation of its programme of economic development or economic transition.

In situations of *serious* balance-of-payments and external financial difficulties or a threat thereof, Members may adopt or maintain BoP measures which restrict trade in services in a manner which is GATS-inconsistent. However, as is explicitly provided in Article XII:2 of the GATS, these BoP measures shall:

- not discriminate among Members;
- be consistent with the *Articles of Agreement of the IMF*;
- avoid unnecessary damage to the commercial, economic and financial interests of any other Member;

---

[439] *Ibid.*, para. 103   [440] See *ibid.*, paras. 5.90 and 5.114.

- not exceed those necessary to deal with the circumstances described in Article XII:1, quoted above; and
- be temporary and be phased out progressively as the situation specified in Article XII:1 improves.

Any BoP measure restricting trade in services, or any changes thereto, must be promptly notified to the General Council.[441] Members adopting or changing BoP measures must consult with the BoP Committee promptly.[442] As for BoP measures restricting trade in goods, BoP measures restricting trade in services are the subject of periodic consultations. The consultations with the BoP Committee shall address the compliance of BoP measures with the requirements of Article XII:2, in particular the progressive phase-out of restrictions.[443] The IMF also plays a central role with regard to BoP measures restricting trade in services in the consultations on the GATS-consistency of BoP measures.[444]

Questions and Assignments 7.37

When are measures which restrict trade in services, in a manner which is GATS-inconsistent, justified under Article XII of the GATS?

7.8. ECONOMIC DEVELOPMENT EXCEPTIONS

As explicitly stated in the Preamble to the *WTO Agreement*, there is:

> need for positive efforts designed to ensure that developing countries . . . secure a share in the growth in international trade commensurate with the needs of their economic development.

The 'positive efforts' in favour of developing countries currently undertaken by the WTO take many forms. Almost all WTO agreements provide for special and differential treatment provisions for developing-country Members to facilitate their integration into the world trading system and to promote their economic development. These provisions, also referred to as 'S&D treatment' provisions, can be subdivided into six categories:

- provisions aimed at increasing the trade opportunities of developing-country Members;
- provisions under which WTO developed-country Members should safeguard the interests of developing-country Members;[445]

---

[441] See Article XII:4 of the GATS.   [442] See Article XII:5(c) of the GATS.

[443] See Article XII:5(d) of the GATS.

[444] See Article XII:5(e) of the GATS. All findings of statistical and other facts presented by the IMF relating to foreign exchange, monetary reserves and balance of payments shall be accepted and the conclusions of the BoP Committee shall be based on the assessment by the IMF of the balance of payments and the external financial situation of the consulting Member.

[445] Most of these provisions are couched in hortatory language, or at most entail 'best-endeavour' obligation. See, for example, the interpretation of Article 15 of the *Anti-Dumping Agreement*, discussed above, pp. 554–6. See also the interpretation of Article 10.1 of the *SPS Agreement*, discussed below, pp. 882–4.

- flexibility of commitments, of action, and use of policy instruments;
- transitional time periods;
- technical assistance; and
- provisions relating to least-developed-country Members.

A detailed overview of all WTO S&D treatment provisions, agreement-by-agreement, can be found in the 2001 Note by the WTO Secretariat on Implementation of Special and Differential Treatment Provisions in WTO Agreements and Decisions.[446] Some of these S&D treatment provisions have been dealt with, or at least referred to, above. As discussed in chapter 2, the *WTO Agreement* establishes a Committee on Trade and Development, and the WTO provides technical assistance to developing-country Members to allow these Members to exercise fully their rights and obligations under the *WTO Agreement* and to participate effectively in trade negotiations.[447] As discussed in chapter 3, the *Dispute Settlement Understanding* contains special rules for developing-country Members in order to help those countries to overcome the problems they encounter as complainants or respondents in WTO dispute settlement proceedings.[448] As discussed in chapter 5, Article XXXVI:8 of the GATT 1994 and the Enabling Clause provide that, in tariff negotiations with developed-country Members, developing-country Members are expected to 'reciprocate' only to the extent that is consistent with their development, financial and trade needs.[449] Article XXXVII:1 of the GATT 1994 calls upon developed-country Members to give high priority to the reduction and elimination of existing market access barriers, and to refrain from introducing new barriers, on products currently or potentially of export interest to developing-country Members.[450] Chapter 6 discussed special rules that apply to developing countries applying anti-dumping duties or countervailing duties or that grant subsidies.[451] As discussed earlier in this chapter, special, more flexible rules exist for the benefit of developing-country Members taking safeguard measures, forming customs unions or free trade areas or taking BoP measures.[452]

In the last section of this chapter, the focus will be on two S&D treatment provisions that have not been discussed yet, namely:

- the infant-industry-protection exception under Article XVIII of the GATT 1994; and
- the Generalised System of Preferences (GSP) exception under the Enabling Clause.

---

[446] See Committee on Trade and Development, *Implementation of Special and Differential Treatment Provisions in WTO Agreements and Decisions*, Note by the WTO Secretariat, WT/COMTD/W/77/Rev.1, dated 21 September 2001, para. 3. See also the addenda to this Note and, in particular, Addendum 4, WT/COMTD/W/77/Rev.1/Add.4, dated 7 February 2002.   [447] See above, pp. 126–7 and 98–102.
[448] See above, pp. 232–5. These special DSU rules in favour of developing-country Members are found in Article 3.12 (regarding the application of the 1966 Decision), Article 4.10 (regarding consultations), Article 8.10 (regarding the composition of panels), Article 12.10 (regarding consultations and the time to prepare and present arguments), Article 12.11 (regarding the content of panel reports), Article 24 (regarding least-developed countries) and Article 27.2 (assistance from the WTO Secretariat).
[449] See above, pp. 411–12.   [450] See above, p. 408.   [451] See above, pp. 554–6, 604–5.
[452] See above, pp. 687–8, 707–8, 715, 717.

These exceptions allow Members to adopt measures, otherwise WTO-inconsistent, to promote the economic development of developing-country Members.

7.8.1. Infant-industry-protection exception

As discussed in chapter 1, one of the traditional arguments used to justify trade restrictions is the *infant-industry-protection* argument.[453] On the basis of this argument, during the nineteenth century, the infant manufacturing industries of the United States and Germany were protected against import competition. Today, this argument could be of relevance and importance for developing countries.[454] While developing countries may have a potential comparative advantage in certain industries, their 'infant' producers are not yet in a position to compete with the already established producers in developed countries. By means of a customs duty or an import restriction, national producers can be afforded temporary protection, allowing them breathing space to become strong enough to compete with well-established producers.

Article XVIII of the GATT 1994 allows developing-country Members, under specific conditions, to take measures which are otherwise GATT-inconsistent to protect their infant industries against import competition. Article XVIII:2, entitled 'Governmental Assistance to Economic Development', states that, for Members 'the economies of which can only support low standards of living and are in the early stages of development', i.e. developing-country Members:

> it may be necessary . . . in order to implement programmes and policies of economic development designed to raise the general standard of living of their people, to take protective or other measures affecting imports, and that such measures are justified in so far as they facilitate the attainment of the objectives of this Agreement.

Article XVIII:4 explicitly states that developing-country Members:

> shall be free to deviate temporarily from the provisions of the other Articles of this Agreement, as provided in Sections A, B and C of this Article.

Section A of Article XVIII, i.e. Article XVIII:7, of the GATT 1994 is of particular relevance to the infant-industry-protection exception.[455] Pursuant to this provision, if a developing-country Member considers it desirable, in order to promote the establishment of a particular industry, to *modify or withdraw a tariff concession*, it

---

[453] See above, p. 22. Note that the argument for infant-industry protection had already been made by Alexander Hamilton in 1791.

[454] Empirical research, however, has demonstrated that the infant-industry doctrine must be resorted to carefully. See Report by the Consultative Board to the Director-General Supachai Panitchpakdi, *The Future of the WTO: Addressing Institutional Challenges in the New Millennium* (the 'Sutherland Report'), (WTO, 2004), para. 92.

[455] Section B of Article XVIII, i.e. Article XVIII:7 to XVIII:12, of the GATT 1994 provides for a special balance-of-payments exception for developing-country Members, discussed in detail above, pp. 715, 716. Section C of Article XVIII, i.e. Articles XVIII:13 to XVIII:21, of the GATT 1994 allows developing-country Members to grant governmental assistance to 'promote the establishment of a particular industry'.

can do so. Article XVIII:7 therefore allows a developing-country Member to take a measure which is otherwise inconsistent with its obligations under Article II:1 of the GATT 1994. However, the developing-country Member concerned must enter into negotiations with the Members primarily affected by the modification or withdrawal of the tariff concession in order to come to an agreement on compensatory adjustment.[456] If no agreement is reached, it is for the General Council to decide whether the compensatory adjustment offered is adequate. Where the General Council considers the compensation to be adequate, the developing-country Member is then free to modify or withdraw the tariff concession provided that, at the same time, it gives effect to the compensatory adjustment. Should the General Council find the compensation offered to be inadequate, but also that every reasonable effort was made to offer adequate compensation, the developing-country Member may proceed with the modification or withdrawal of the tariff concession.[457] Any other Member affected by the modification or withdrawal is then free to modify or withdraw substantially equivalent concessions with regard to the developing-country Member concerned.[458] Under the GATT 1947, the GATT Council was generous in allowing developing-country Members to modify or withdraw tariff concessions without requiring any compensatory adjustment. As discussed in chapter 1, the contribution of the exception under Article XVIII:7 to the economic development of developing countries has been limited.[459] In fact, the infant-industry-protection exception under Article XVIII:7 has not been invoked by any developing-country Member since the entry into force of the *WTO Agreement* in 1995.[460]

7.8.2. Generalised System of Preferences exception

The 1979 GATT Decision on Differential and More Favourable Treatment, Reciprocity and Fuller Participation of Developing Countries is commonly referred to as the 'Enabling Clause'.[461] The Enabling Clause, which is now an integral part of the GATT 1994,[462] states, in paragraph 1:

> Notwithstanding the provisions of Article I of the General Agreement, [Members] may accord differential and more favourable treatment to developing countries, without according such treatment to other [Members].

---

[456] See Article XVIII:7(a) of the GATT 1994   [457] See Article XVIII:7(b) of the GATT 1994.

[458] See *ibid.*   [459] See above, p. 22.

[460] Committee on Trade and Development, *Implementation of Special and Differential Treatment Provisions in WTO Agreements and Decisions*, Note by the WTO Secretariat, Addendum 4, WT/COMTD/W/77/Rev.1/ Add.4, dated 7 February 2002, 2.

[461] GATT Document L/4903, dated 28 November 1979, BISD 26S/203. The Enabling Clause was adopted by the GATT CONTRACTING PARTIES in the context of the Tokyo Round of Multilateral Trade Negotiations. Note that the Enabling Clause replaced, and expanded, a 1971 *Waiver Decision on the Generalised System of Preferences*, GATT Document L/3545, dated 25 June 1971, BISD 18S/24. This Waiver Decision was in turn adopted to give effect to the *Agreed Conclusions* of the UNCTAD Special Committee on Preferences, adopted in 1970. These *Agreed Conclusions* recognised in para. I:2 that preferential tariff treatment accorded under a generalised scheme of preferences was key for developing countries '(a) to increase their export earnings; (b) to promote their industrialization; and (c) to accelerate their rates of economic growth'.

[462] The Enabling Clause is one of the 'other decisions of the CONTRACTING PARTIES' within the meaning of para. 1(b)(iv) of Annex 1A incorporating the GATT 1994 into the *WTO Agreement*. See Appellate Body Report, *EC – Tariff Preferences*, para. 90 and footnote 192.

7.8.2.1. *Preferential tariff treatment for developing countries under the Enabling Clause*

Paragraph 2(a) of the Enabling Clause provides that the differential and more favourable treatment referred to in paragraph 1 includes:

> Preferential tariff treatment accorded by [developed-country Members] to products originating in developing countries in accordance with the Generalized System of Preferences . . .[463]

As the Appellate Body ruled in *EC – Tariff Preferences*, the Enabling Clause operates as an 'exception' to Article I:1 of the GATT 1994.[464] Paragraph 1 of the Enabling Clause explicitly exempts Members from complying with the obligation contained in Article I:1 for the purposes of providing differential and more favourable treatment to developing countries.[465] The Enabling Clause authorises developed-country Members to grant enhanced market access to products from developing countries extending beyond the access granted to like products from developed countries.[466] The Enabling Clause thus permits Members to provide 'differential and more favourable treatment' to developing countries in spite of the MFN treatment obligation of Article I:1, which normally requires that such treatment be extended to all Members 'immediately and unconditionally'. What is more, WTO Members are *not merely allowed* to deviate from Article I:1 in the pursuit of 'differential and more favourable treatment' for developing countries; they are *encouraged* to do so.[467]

As discussed in chapter 5, most developed-country Members grant preferential tariff treatment to imports from developing countries under their respective Generalised Systems of Preferences (GSP) schemes. The Enabling Clause thus plays a vital role in promoting trade as a means of stimulating economic growth and development.[468]

As with all of the other exceptions discussed in this chapter, before the Enabling Clause can successfully be invoked, certain conditions must be fulfilled. The deviation from the MFN obligation of Article I:1 is allowed only when, and to the extent that, the conditions set out in paragraphs 3 and 4 of the Enabling Clause are met. Paragraph 3 sets out the following substantive conditions:

---

[463] The footnote in the original reads: 'As described in the Decision of the CONTRACTING PARTIES of 25 June 1971, relating to the establishment of "generalized, non-reciprocal and non-discriminatory preferences beneficial to the developing countries" (BISD 18S/24).'

[464] See Appellate Body Report, *EC – Tariff Preferences*, para. 99. On this point, the Appellate Body upheld the finding of the Panel; see Panel Report, *EC – Tariff Preferences*, para. 7.53. The European Communities argued in *EC – Tariff Preferences* that the Enabling Clause, reflecting the fundamental objective of assisting developing-country Members, is not an exception to Article I:1 of the GATT 1994 but exists 'side-by-side and on an equal level' with Article I:1. The Appellate Body disagreed and ruled that: 'characterising the Enabling Clause as an exception, in our view, does not undermine the importance of the Enabling Clause within the overall framework of the covered agreements and as a "positive effort" to enhance economic development of developing-country Members. Nor does it "discourag[e]" developed countries from adopting measures in favour of developing countries under the Enabling Clause.' Appellate Body Report, *EC – Tariff Preferences*, para. 95.   [465] See *ibid.*, para. 90.

[466] See *ibid.*, para. 106.   [467] See *ibid.*, para. 111.

[468] See *ibid.*, para. 106. Note, however, that the Sutherland Report is very critical of the functioning of the GSP in practice. See Report by the Consultative Board to the Director-General Supachai Panitchpakdi, *The Future of the WTO: Addressing Institutional Challenges in the New Millennium* (the 'Sutherland Report') (WTO, 2004), paras. 88–102.

> Any differential and more favourable treatment provided under this clause:
>
> a. shall be designed to facilitate and promote the trade of developing countries and not to raise barriers to or create undue difficulties for the trade of any other [Members];
> b. shall not constitute an impediment to the reduction or elimination of tariffs and other restrictions to trade on a most-favoured-nation basis;
> c. shall in the case of such treatment accorded by [developed-country Members] to developing countries be designed and, if necessary, modified, to respond positively to the development, financial and trade needs of developing countries.

Paragraph 4 sets out the procedural conditions for the introduction, modification and withdrawal of a preferential measure for developing countries. Pursuant to paragraph 4, Members granting preferential tariff treatment to developing countries must notify the WTO and afford adequate opportunity for prompt consultations at the request of any interested Member with respect to any difficulty or matter that may arise.

7.8.2.2. Additional preferential tariff treatment under the Enabling Clause

In *EC – Tariff Preferences*, the question arose as to whether the European Communities could grant *additional* preferential tariff treatment to certain developing countries to the exclusion of others. Council Regulation (EC) No. 2501/2001 of 10 December 2001, the EC's former Generalised System of Preferences Regulation,[469] provided for five preferential tariff 'arrangements', namely:

- the 'General Arrangements';
- special incentive arrangements for the protection of labour rights;
- special incentive arrangements for the protection of the environment;
- special arrangements for least-developed countries; and
- special arrangements to combat drug production and trafficking.

The General Arrangements, which provide for tariff preferences for all developing countries, and the special arrangements for least-developed countries, were, and still are, not problematic. Both arrangements were, and are, justified under the Enabling Clause: the General Arrangements under paragraph 2(a), discussed above; and the special arrangements for least-developed countries under paragraph 2(d). The latter provision states that the Enabling Clause also covers:

> Special treatment of the least developed among the developing countries in the context of any general or specific measures in favour of developing countries.

However, questions as to GATT-consistency arose with regard to the other preferential arrangements, i.e. the special incentive arrangements for the protection of labour rights, the special incentive arrangements for the protection of the environment and the special arrangements to combat drug production and trafficking. Only some developing countries were beneficiaries of these special

---

[469] OJ 2001, L346,1.

arrangements. For example, preferences under the special incentive arrangements for the protection of labour rights and the special incentive arrangements for the protection of the environment were restricted to those countries that were 'determined by the European Communities to comply with certain labour [or] environmental policy standards', respectively. Preferences under the special arrangements to combat drug production and trafficking (the 'Drug Arrangements') were provided only to eleven Latin American countries and Pakistan.[470]

While India, the complainant in *EC – Tariff Preferences*, challenged, in its panel request, the WTO-consistency of the Drug Arrangements as well as the special incentive arrangements for the protection of labour rights and the environment, it later decided to limit its complaint to the Drug Arrangements. Accordingly, the *EC – Tariff Preferences* dispute, and the rulings in this case, only concerned the WTO-consistency of the Drug Arrangements. However, it is clear that the rulings in this case are also of relevance to other special arrangements.

The main substantive issue disputed between India and the European Communities in *EC – Tariff Preferences* was whether the Drug Arrangements were consistent with paragraph 2(a) of the Enabling Clause, and, in particular, the requirement of non-discrimination in footnote 3 thereto, quoted above.[471] With regard to paragraph 2(a) and its footnote, the Panel in *EC – Tariff Preferences* found that:

> the clear intention of the negotiators was to provide GSP equally to all developing countries and to eliminate all differentiation in preferential treatment to developing countries . . .[472]

As the Drug Arrangements do not provide identical tariff preferences to *all* developing countries, the Panel concluded that the Drug Arrangements were inconsistent with paragraph 2(a) of the Enabling Clause and, in particular, the requirement of non-discrimination in footnote 3 thereto.[473] According to the Panel, the term 'non-discriminatory' in footnote 3 requires that identical tariff preferences under GSP schemes be provided to all developing countries without differentiation.[474]

On appeal, the Appellate Body reversed this finding.[475] After a careful examination of the text and context of footnote 3 to paragraph 2(a) of the Enabling Clause, and the object and purpose of the *WTO Agreement* and the Enabling Clause, the Appellate Body came to the conclusion that:

> the term 'non-discriminatory' in footnote 3 does not prohibit developed-country Members from granting different tariffs to products originating in different GSP beneficiaries, provided that such differential tariff treatment meets the remaining conditions in the Enabling Clause. In granting such differential tariff treatment, however, preference-granting

---

[470] See Appellate Body Report, *EC – Tariff Preferences*, para. 3. Preferences under the Drug Arrangements are provided to Bolivia, Colombia, Costa Rica, Ecuador, El Salvador, Guatemala, Honduras, Nicaragua, Pakistan, Panama, Peru and Venezuela.

[471] The requirement of non-discrimination is derived from the words 'non-discriminatory preferences' in footnote 3. See above, p. 727, footnote 463.   [472] Panel Report, *EC – Tariff Preferences*, para. 7.144.

[473] See *ibid.*, para. 7.177.   [474] See *ibid.*, paras. 7.161 and 7.176.

[475] See Appellate Body Report, *EC – Tariff Preferences*, para. 174.

> countries are required, by virtue of the term 'non-discriminatory', to ensure that identical treatment is available to all similarly-situated GSP beneficiaries, that is, to all GSP beneficiaries that have the 'development, financial and trade needs' to which the treatment in question is intended to respond.[476]

In other words, a developed-country Member may grant additional preferential tariff treatment to some, and not to other, developing-country Members, as long as additional preferential tariff treatment is available to all *similarly situated* developing-country Members. *Similarly situated* developing-country Members are all those that have the development, financial and trade needs to which additional preferential tariff treatment is intended to respond.

The determination of whether developing-country Members are similarly situated must be based on objective criteria. With respect to the Drug Arrangements of the European Communities, however, the Appellate Body found in *EC – Tariff Preferences* that these arrangements provided for a *closed* list of twelve identified beneficiaries and contained no criteria or standards to provide a basis for distinguishing developing-country Members which are beneficiaries under the Drug Arrangements from other developing-country Members.[477] The Appellate Body therefore upheld – albeit for different reasons – the Panel's conclusion that the European Communities 'failed to demonstrate that the Drug Arrangements are justified under paragraph 2(a) of the Enabling Clause'.[478]

Questions and Assignments 7.38

Give a brief overview of the different categories of S&D treatment provisions set out in the WTO agreements. Discuss the infant-industry-protection exception under Article XVIII:7 of the GATT 1994. What does the Generalised System of Preferences exception under the Enabling Clause allow Members to do that they would otherwise not be allowed to do? Where in the GATT 1994 can the Enabling Clause be found? Is it appropriate and correct to identify the Enabling Clause as an 'exception' to the basic MFN treatment obligation of the GATT 1994? Does the

---

[476] *Ibid.*, para. 173.   [477] See *ibid.*, paras. 187 and 188.
[478] *Ibid.*, para. 189. On 27 June 2005, the EC adopted Council Regulation (EC) No. 980/2005, replacing Council Regulation (EC) No. 221/2003 and establishing a new scheme of preferential tariff arrangements. The preferential tariff arrangements are reduced from five to three:

- the 'General Arrangements';
- the 'special incentive arrangement for sustainable development and good governance' (GSP+);
- the 'Everything but Arms' (EBA) arrangement.

While the 'General Arrangements' provide tariff preferences for all developing countries, the GSP+ is available only to developing countries that have ratified and implemented a number of international conventions set out in Annex 3 of the Regulation. The GSP+ system replaces the Drug Arrangements (and the special incentive arrangements referred to above) so as to comply with the Appellate Body's ruling in *EC – Tariff Preferences*. It applies to 'vulnerable' countries meeting a set of objective criteria set out in Articles 9 and 10 of the Regulation. Note that the following countries are eligible for GSP+: Bolivia, Colombia, Costa Rica, Ecuador, El Salvador, Georgia, Guatemala, Honduras, Moldova, Mongolia, Nicaragua, Panama, Peru, Sri Lanka and Venezuela. Lastly, the EBA arrangement extends duty-free and quota-free market access to least-developed countries, save for arms and ammunition. The Regulation applies from 1 January 2006 until 31 December 2008, but the GSP+ provisions already applied from 1 July 2005. See WTO Secretariat, *Trade Policy Review Report – European Communities*, WT/TPR/S/177, dated 22 January 2007, 35–6.

Enabling Clause allow developed-country Members to treat certain
developing-country Members more favourably than others?

7.9. SUMMARY

Trade liberalisation and its rules on non-discrimination and market access often
conflict with other important societal values and interests, such as the promotion and protection of public health, consumer safety, the environment, employment, economic development and national security. WTO law provides for rules
to reconcile trade liberalisation with these other important societal values and
interests. These rules take the form of wide-ranging *exceptions* to the basic WTO
disciplines. There are six main categories of these exceptions:

- the 'general exceptions' of Article XX of the GATT 1994 and Article XIV of the
  GATS;
- the 'security exceptions' of Article XXI of the GATT 1994 and Article XIV *bis* of
  the GATS;
- the 'economic emergency exceptions' of Article XIX of the GATT 1994 and the
  Agreement on Safeguards;
- the 'regional integration exceptions' of Article XXIV of the GATT 1994 and
  Article V of the GATS;
- the 'balance-of-payments exceptions' of Articles XII and XVIII:B of the GATT
  1994 and Article XII of the GATS; and
- the 'economic development exceptions'.

These exceptions allow Members, under specific conditions, to adopt and maintain legislation and measures that protect other important societal values and
interests, even though this legislation or these measures are in conflict with substantive disciplines imposed by the GATT 1994 or the GATS. These exceptions
clearly allow Members, under specific conditions, to give *priority* to certain societal values and interests *over* trade liberalisation.

The most important of these exceptions 'reconciling' trade liberalisation
with other societal values and interests are the 'general exceptions' of Article XX
of the GATT 1994 and Article XIV of the GATS.

In determining whether a measure which is otherwise GATT-inconsistent can
be justified under Article XX of the GATT 1994, one must always examine:

- first, whether this measure can *provisionally* be justified under one of the specific exceptions under paragraphs (a) to (j) of Article XX; and, if so,
- secondly, whether the application of this measure meets the requirements of
  the chapeau of Article XX.

Article XX(b) concerns otherwise GATT-inconsistent measures allegedly adopted
or maintained for the protection of public health or the environment. For such a
measure to be provisionally justified under Article XX(b):

- the *policy objective* pursued by the measure must be the protection of the life or health of humans, animals or plants; and
- the measure must be *necessary* to fulfil that policy objective.

A measure is considered 'necessary' if no alternative measure exists that would achieve the same end and is less restrictive to trade than the measure at issue. In deciding whether a measure is necessary, the following factors must be 'weighed and balanced':

- the *importance* of the societal value pursued by the measure at issue,
- the *impact* of the measure at issue on trade, and
- the *extent* to which the measure at issue contributes to the protection or promotion of that value.

It is clear that the more important the societal value pursued by the measure at issue, the more this measure contributes to the protection or promotion of this value, and the less restrictive its impact is on international trade, the more easily the measure may be considered to be necessary. If this analysis yields a preliminary conclusion that the measure is necessary, this result must be confirmed by comparing the measure at issue with possible alteratives, which may be less trade restrictive but provide an equivalent contribution to the achievement of the measure's objective.

Article XX(d) concerns otherwise GATT-inconsistent measures allegedly adopted or maintained to secure compliance with national legislation. For such a measure to be provisionally justified under Article XX(d):

- the measure must be designed to *secure compliance* with national law, such as customs law or intellectual property law, which is in itself not GATT-inconsistent; and
- the measure must be *necessary* to ensure compliance.

The term 'necessary' in Article XX(d) is interpreted in the same way as the term 'necessary' in Article XX(b).

Article XX(g) concerns otherwise GATT-inconsistent measures allegedly adopted or maintained for the conservation of exhaustible natural resources. For such a measure to be provisionally justified under Article XX(g):

- the measure must relate to the '*conservation of exhaustible natural resources*';
- the measure must '*relate to*' the conservation of exhaustible natural resources; and
- the measure must be made effective '*in conjunction with*' restrictions on domestic production or consumption.

The concept of 'exhaustible natural resources' has been interpreted in a broad, evolutionary manner to include not only minerals and other non-living resources, but also living resources and, in particular, endangered species. A measure 'relates to' the conservation of exhaustible natural resources if the measure is 'primarily aimed' at the conservation of these resources. The relationship between the means, i.e. the measure, and the end, i.e. the conservation of exhaustible resources, must be real and close. Finally, the requirement that the measure must be 'made effective in conjunction with restrictions on domestic production or consumption' is, in essence, a requirement of 'even-handedness' in the imposition of restrictions on imported and domestic products.

Measures provisionally justified under one of the exceptions of Article XX(a) to (j) must subsequently meet the requirements of the chapeau of Article XX. The object and purpose of the chapeau is to avoid the possibility that the *application* of the measures provisionally justified could constitute a misuse or abuse of the exceptions of Article XX. The interpretation and application of the chapeau in a particular case is a search for the appropriate *line of equilibrium* between the right of Members to adopt and maintain trade-restrictive measures that pursue certain legitimate societal values *and* the right of other Members to trade. The search for this line of equilibrium is guided by the requirements set out in the chapeau that the *application* of the trade-restrictive measure may not constitute:

- an *arbitrary* or *unjustifiable discrimination* between countries where the same conditions prevail; or
- a *disguised restriction* on international trade.

Discrimination has been found to be 'unjustifiable discrimination' when the discrimination 'was not merely inadvertent or unavoidable'. Unjustifiable discrimination also exists when a Member fails to make serious, good faith efforts to negotiate a multilateral solution before resorting to the unilateral, discriminatory measure for which justification is sought. Discrimination has been found to be 'arbitrary' when a measure is applied without any regard for the difference in conditions between countries and the measure is applied in a rigid and inflexible manner. The Appellate Body has held that whether discrimination is arbitrary or unjustifiable depends on the *cause* or *rationale* of the discrimination, *not* the effects of the discrimination. The rational must be assessed in the light of its contribution to the legitimate objective provisionally found to justify the measure. A measure which is provisionally justified under Article XX will be considered to constitute a 'disguised restriction on international trade' if the design, architecture or the structure of the measure at issue reveals that this measure does not in fact pursue the legitimate policy objectives on which the provisional justification was based but, in fact, pursues trade-restrictive, i.e. protectionist, objectives.

Although Article XX provides for exceptions to basic GATT rules and disciplines, the Appellate Body has not given a narrow interpretation to Article XX. Instead, it has insisted that a balance must be struck between trade liberalisation and the other societal values referred to in Article XX. The Appellate Body has repeatedly emphasised that WTO Members are free to adopt their own policies and measures aimed at protecting or promoting other societal values, such as public health or the environment, as long as, in so doing, they fulfil their obligations, and respect the rights of other Members, under the *WTO Agreement*. Note that, if the conditions discussed above are fulfilled, Article XX can justify inconsistencies with any of the GATT provisions.

As is the case for Article XX of the GATT 1994, Article XIV of the GATS sets out a *two-tier test* for determining whether a measure affecting trade in services, otherwise inconsistent with GATS obligations and commitments, can be justified under that provision. To determine whether a measure can be justified under Article XIV of the GATS, one must always examine:

- first, whether this measure can be provisionally justified under one of the specific exceptions under paragraphs (a) to (e) of Article XIV; and, if so,
- secondly, whether the application of this measure meets the requirements of the chapeau of Article XIV.

The similarities between Article XX of the GATT 1994 and Article XIV of the GATS are striking. However, there are also differences. The specific grounds of justification for measures which are otherwise inconsistent with provisions of the GATS set out in Article XIV(a) to (e) of the GATS include:

- the protection of public morals;
- the protection of public order;
- the protection of human, animal or plant life or health;
- the prevention of deceptive and fraudulent practices;
- the protection of the privacy of individuals; and
- the equitable or effective imposition or collection of direct taxes.

Article XIV(a) of the GATS concerns otherwise GATS-inconsistent measures that are 'necessary to protect public morals or to maintain public order'. To provisionally justify its measure under Article XIV(a), a Member must establish that:

- the policy objective pursued by the measure at issue is the protection of *public morals* or the maintenance of *public order*; and
- the measure is *necessary* to fulfil that policy objective.

Article XIV(c) of the GATS makes provision for otherwise GATS-inconsistent measures adopted to secure compliance with national laws or regulations. For its measure to be provisionally justified under Article XIV(c) of the GATS, a Member must establish that:

- the measure at issue is designed to *secure compliance* with national laws or regulations;
- those national laws and regulations are not inconsistent with the *WTO Agreement*; and
- the measure at issue is *necessary* to secure compliance with those national laws and regulations.

To be provisionally justified under the exceptions listed in paragraphs (a), (b) and (c) of Article XIV, a measure must be *necessary* to achieve the policy objective pursued. As regards the 'necessity' test, the extensive case law on the necessity requirement of Article XX(b) and (d) of the GATT 1994 has been held to be relevant. In particular, the same three factors must be 'weighed and balanced' to determine whether there is a reasonably available alternative measure that is less restrictive to trade. No such requirement of necessity exists under paragraphs (d) and (e) of Article XIV.

Just as with the chapeau of Article XX of the GATT 1994, the chapeau of Article XIV of the GATS requires that the *application* of the measure at issue does not constitute:

- *arbitrary or unjustifiable discrimination* between countries where the same conditions prevail; or
- a *disguised restriction* on trade in services.

In addition to the 'general exceptions' contained in Article XX of the GATT 1994 and Article XIV of the GATS, the GATT 1994 in Article XXI and the GATS in Article XIV bis also provide for exceptions relating to national and international security. WTO Members take, on occasion, either unilaterally or multilaterally, trade-restrictive measures against other Members as a means to achieve national or international security. Members taking such measures seek justification for these measures under Article XXI of the GATT 1994 or Article XIV bis of the GATS. Article XXI(b) of the GATT 1994 allows a Member to adopt or maintain:

- measures relating to fissionable materials;
- measures relating to trade in arms or in other materials, directly or indirectly, for military use; and
- measures taken in time of war or other emergency in international relations,

if and when that Member *considers* such measures to be necessary for the protection of its essential security interests. Article XIV *bis*(b) of the GATS is virtually identical to Article XXI(b) of the GATT 1994. The 'justiciability' of these exceptions is problematic. At a minimum, however, panels should have the authority to conduct an examination as to whether the explanation provided by the Member concerned is reasonable or whether the measure qualifies as apparent abuse. Article XXI(c) of the GATT 1994 and Article XIV *bis*(c) of the GATS are much less problematic in this respect as they allow WTO Members to take trade and economic sanctions in pursuance of their obligations under the UN Charter for the maintenance of international peace and security.

WTO law also provides for 'economic emergency exceptions'. These exceptions, set out primarily in Article XIX of the GATT 1994 and the *Agreement on Safeguards*, allow Members to adopt measures which are otherwise WTO-inconsistent in situations where a surge in imports causes, or threatens to cause, serious injury to the domestic industry. The otherwise WTO-inconsistent measures taken in economic emergency situations are referred to as *safeguard measures*. Safeguard measures temporarily restrict imports to allow the domestic industry concerned time for structural adjustment to new economic realities. Safeguard measures typically take the form of customs duties above the binding or quantitative restrictions. Safeguard measures must be limited in time and applied in a non-discriminatory manner. Moreover, a Member applying a safeguard measure must seek to compensate other Members affected by the measure. Safeguard measures may only be applied when three requirements are met:

- the 'increased imports' requirement;
- the 'serious injury or threat thereof' requirement; and
- the 'causation' requirement.

The required 'increase in imports' must be recent, sudden, sharp and significant. The required 'serious injury' exists when there is a significant overall impairment in the position of a domestic industry. A 'threat of serious injury' exists when serious injury is clearly imminent. The relevant domestic industry is the industry (or at least many of the important domestic producers) producing like or directly competitive products. To determine whether there is, in fact, serious injury or a threat thereof to a domestic industry, all relevant factors of an objective and quantifiable nature having a bearing on the situation of that industry must be considered. The test for establishing 'causation' is twofold:

- a demonstration of the causal link between the 'increased imports' and the 'serious injury or threat thereof' (the 'causal link' sub-requirement); and
- an identification of any injury caused by factors other than the increased imports and the non-attribution of this injury to these imports (the 'non-attribution' sub-requirement).

Besides the 'general exceptions', the 'security exceptions' and the 'economic emergency exceptions', WTO law also provides for 'regional integration exceptions'. These exceptions allow Members to adopt measures which are otherwise WTO-inconsistent taken in the context of the pursuit of regional economic integration. The regional integration exceptions are set out in Article XXIV of the GATT 1994 (elaborated in the *Understanding on Article XXIV*) and Article V of the GATS. WTO law recognises the advantages of economic integration and trade liberalisation even when these efforts involve only some of its Members. A measure which is otherwise inconsistent with the GATT 1994 is justified under Article XXIV of the GATT 1994:

- if the measure is introduced upon the formation of a customs union, a free trade area or an interim agreement that meets all the requirements set out in Article XXIV:8 and Article XIV:5 of the GATT 1994; and
- if the formation of the customs union or free trade area would be prevented, i.e. made impossible, if the introduction of the measure concerned were not allowed.

A measure which is otherwise GATS-inconsistent is justified under Article V of the GATS:

- if the measure is introduced as part of an agreement liberalising trade in services that meets all the requirements set out in Article V:1(a), Article V:1(b) and Article V:4 of the GATS; and
- if WTO Members would be prevented from entering into such an agreement liberalising trade in services if the measure concerned were not allowed.

WTO law also provides for 'balance-of-payments exceptions', set out in Articles XII and XVIII:B of the GATT 1994 (elaborated in the *Understanding on BoP Provisions*) and Article XII of the GATS. These exceptions allow Members to adopt measures, otherwise inconsistent with Articles II and XI of the GATT 1994, to safeguard their external financial position and to protect their balance of payments. BoP measures restricting trade in goods can take the form of quantitative restrictions *or* tariff-like, i.e. price-based, measures (such as import surcharges). The latter type of BoP measure is preferred. Generally speaking, BoP measures adopted by a Member must not exceed those necessary in view of the external financial situation of that Member (in terms of decline of its monetary reserves or the level of its monetary reserves). The requirements for BoP measures restricting trade in goods taken by developing-country Members (see Article XVIII:B) are less stringent than those for BoP measures taken by other Members (see Article XII).

Finally, WTO law provides for 'economic development exceptions' in favour of developing countries. Almost all WTO agreements provide for special and differential treatment provisions for developing-country Members to facilitate their integration in the world trading system and to promote their economic development. These provisions, also referred to as 'S&D treatment' provisions, can be subdivided into six categories:

- provisions aimed at increasing the trade opportunities of developing-country Members;
- provisions under which developed-country Members should safeguard the interests of developing-country Members;
- flexibility of commitments, of action and use of policy instruments;
- transitional time periods;
- technical assistance; and
- provisions relating to least-developed-country Members.

Of these S&D treatment provisions, the Generalised System of Preferences (GSP) exception under the Enabling Clause is of particular importance. The Enabling Clause allows, under certain conditions, developed-country Members to grant preferential tariff treatment to imports from developing countries. This exception therefore allows Members to deviate from the basic MFN treatment obligation of Article I:1 of the GATT 1994 to promote the economic development of developing-country Members. Under specific conditions, the Enabling Clause also allows developed-country Members to grant preferential tariff treatment to some developing countries to the exclusion of others.

The 'general exceptions', 'security exceptions', 'economic emergency exceptions', 'regional integration exceptions', 'balance-of-payments exceptions' and the 'economic development exceptions' in the GATT 1994 and/or the GATS reconcile trade liberalisation with other important societal values and interests. These wide-ranging exceptions will often allow Members, promoting or protecting these other societal values or interests, to adopt otherwise GATT- or GATS-inconsistent measures. These exceptions demonstrate that WTO Members can, when necessary and under certain other conditions, give priority to societal values and interests other than trade liberalisation.

7.10. EXERCISE: TETRA-PACK CONTAINERS AND GLASS PRODUCERS IN DIRE STRAITS

Tetra-pack containers

Since 1997, Newland has prohibited the sale and importation of non-alcoholic beverages (such as milk and fruit juice) in tetra-pack containers. It only allows the sale and importation of non-alcoholic beverages in glass bottles. According to Newland, glass bottles can be recycled more easily and more efficiently than tetra-pack containers. Newland claims that glass bottles are almost 100 per cent recyclable while tetra-pack containers are only 70 per cent recyclable. Newland has some scientific studies in support of this contention on recyclability. Most scientific studies on the 'recyclability' of glass bottles and tetra-pack containers conclude, however, that there is, in practice, little difference between the two types of container.

Before 1997, Richland was the main exporter of non-alcoholic beverages in tetra-pack containers to Newland. It was, therefore, much affected by Newland's prohibition on the sale and importation of non-alcoholic beverages in tetra-pack containers. Ever since Newland became a WTO Member, Richland has been considering whether to challenge the import ban as inconsistent with WTO law. According to Richland, Newland sets an exaggeratedly high level of environmental protection. Richland argues that there is no scientific basis for the import ban. In the alternative, Richland argues that Newland, rather than prohibiting the sale and importation of tetra-pack containers, could pursue its environmental policy objectives by discouraging the use of tetra-pack containers through the imposition of an environmental tax on tetra-pack containers. It should be noted that Newland does not prohibit the use of tetra-pack containers for alcoholic beverages such as wine. Moreover, Richland argues that Newland did not take into consideration that Richland, unlike Newland, has a long tradition of using tetra-pack containers for non-alcoholic beverages. Richland also notes that Newland rejected without much ado Richland's invitation to start multilateral negotiations on a gradual reduction of the use of tetra-pack containers for non-alcoholic beverages.

Richland has requested consultations with Newland on the import ban on non-alcoholic beverages in tetra-pack containers. You are the Legal Advisor to the Permanent Representative of Richland to the WTO. You have been instructed to prepare a legal brief in support of the position of Richland. Limit yourself to the legal issues arising under the GATT 1994.

Glass producers in dire straits

The prohibition of the sale and importation of non-alcoholic beverages in tetra-pack containers was adopted in 1997 under pressure from Newland's environmental NGOs. However, behind the scenes, *TrueBleu* and *Verras*, Newland's manufacturers of glass bottles, had also lobbied hard for the prohibition on the sale and importation of non-alcoholic beverages in tetra-pack containers. While the prohibition initially benefited *TrueBleu* and *Verras*, both companies are now in dire straits. Over the last two years, they saw their combined share of the market in Newland for glass bottles drop from 60 per cent to 30 per cent and they had to lay off almost half of their workforce. Since 2001, the import of glass bottles into Newland has doubled every year. Most of these imports come from Richland, the home of the world's most efficient manufacturers of glass bottles. To prevent further job losses at *TrueBleu* and *Verras* and to give both companies some 'breathing space' to allow them to modernise their production, the Government of Newland decided last month to limit the import of glass bottles from Richland to 1999 levels. It should be noted that the problems of Newland's manufacturers of glass bottles are due not only to import competition but also to the fact that in recent times beer drinkers in Newland seem to prefer their beer in aluminium cans rather than glass bottles.

Richland has requested consultations with Newland on the import restriction of glass bottles. You are a lawyer with the Geneva-based Advisory Centre on WTO Law (ACWL). Newland, a member of the ACWL, has requested the ACWL to advise and assist the Ambassador of Newland to the WTO in the upcoming informal discussions. You have to write a legal brief in support of the position of Newland.

Towards harmonisation of national regulation

Contents

8.1. INTRODUCTION

As discussed in chapters 4 and 5 of this book, tariffs, quotas and discriminatory treatment of imports are subject to effective WTO disciplines.[1] Their importance as barriers to trade has thus gradually decreased. As noted in chapter 5, 'other non-tariff barriers' to trade, such as technical regulations, standards, sanitary and phytosanitary measures, customs formalities and government procurement practices, have, however, gained in importance and have in fact become more problematic to international trade than tariffs and quotas, the 'traditional' barriers to trade. Several WTO agreements, and in particular the GATT 1994, address such 'other non-tariff barriers' to trade.[2] These agreements focus on diminishing the negative trade effects of 'other non-tariff barriers' by increasing their transparency, ensuring their fair and non-discriminatory application and reducing unnecessary procedural delays and complexities.[3]

However, three WTO agreements go further in addressing 'other non-tariff barriers' to trade by, in addition to the usual WTO disciplines, promoting regulatory harmonisation around international standards. These are the *TRIPS Agreement*, the *TBT Agreement* and the *SPS Agreement*. All three of these agreements rely on standards set by other (i.e. non-WTO) international bodies as a *basis* for their harmonisation obligations, thereby making use of the established expertise of these international bodies.[4] However, these three agreements work in different ways with the tool of harmonisation. The *TRIPS Agreement* lays down mandatory minimum standards of intellectual property protection and enforcement, based on pre-existing international conventions. The *SPS Agreement* and the *TBT Agreement* do not lay down minimum standards. Instead, they encourage Members to harmonise measures falling under the scope of application of the *SPS* and *TBT Agreements* around standards set by the relevant international standard-setting bodies. The use of stricter standards is allowed but constrained by rigorous disciplines.

These three agreements can therefore be said to go far beyond the usual trade liberalisation rules and to venture into 'behind-the-border' regulatory areas to a greater extent than other WTO agreements dealing with non-tariff barriers to trade. They entail greater implementation costs and have a larger impact on the regulatory policy objectives of Members. For these reasons, they have generated more controversy and have caused more implementation problems than other WTO agreements. Many Members have been reluctant to engage in negotiations towards new agreements that would harmonise behind-the-border regulatory policies, for example in the areas of competition policy and investment.[5]

This chapter discusses the main disciplines of the *TRIPS Agreement*, i.e. rules on

---

[1] See above, pp. 320–506.
[2] Among other relevant WTO agreements, note the plurilateral *Agreement on Government Procurement*. See above, p. 474.   [3] See above, pp. 461, 466, and 470.
[4] Note, however, that the *TRIPS Agreement* adds to and supplements the protection of intellectual property rights contained in the WIPO conventions. See below, p. 751.
[5] On the difficulty in launching negotiations on the so-called 'Singapore issues', see above, pp. 90–1.

the protection of intellectual property, and the *TBT Agreement* and the *SPS Agreement*, i.e. the rules on technical barriers to trade.[6]

8.2. THE *TRIPS AGREEMENT*

The *Agreement on Trade-Related Aspects of Intellectual Property Rights* (*TRIPS Agreement*) is arguably the most innovative of the WTO agreements. It is the first to establish positive regulatory obligations for Members. While references to intellectual property (IP) rights were included in the GATT 1947,[7] the *TRIPS Agreement*, for the first time, imposes on Members the obligation to ensure a minimum level of protection and enforcement of IP rights in their territories.

Part I of the *TRIPS Agreement* contains general provisions and basic principles that apply to all the IP rights falling within its coverage. Part II is subdivided into eight sections, each dealing with a different area of IP protection. In Part III, the *TRIPS Agreement* sets out the obligations of Members with regard to enforcement of IP rights. The remainder of the *TRIPS Agreement* addresses issues relating to the acquisition and maintenance of IP rights and contains institutional and procedural provisions.

This section aims to provide an overview of the *TRIPS Agreement*, focusing on:

- its origins and objectives;
- its scope of application;
- its basic principles;
- the substantive protection it provides to selected IP rights;
- its rules on enforcement of IP rights;
- its rules on acquisition of IP rights;
- its institutional and procedural provisions; and
- its rules providing for special and differential treatment of developing-country Members.

8.2.1. The origins and objectives of the *TRIPS Agreement*

8.2.1.1 *Origins of the TRIPS Agreement*

Intellectual property, broadly speaking, refers to the legal rights that result from intellectual activity in the artistic, literary, scientific or industrial fields.[8] When this intellectual activity leads to the creation of something new and innovative, many

---

[6] This chapter is largely based on a text written by Denise Prévost, shortened and adapted to fit the format and focus of this book. I am much indebted to her for her contribution to this chapter. I am also indebted to Marielle Matthee for her contribution to the section on the *TBT Agreement*.

[7] Articles XX(d), IX, XII:3(c)(iii) and XVIII:10 of the GATT 1947 refer to intellectual property rights. In addition, other GATT provisions lay down general rules that are also applicable to trade-related aspects of intellectual property rights, for example the national treatment and most-favoured-nation obligations and the prohibition on quantitative restrictions. See Negotiating Group on Trade-Related Aspects of Intellectual Property Rights, including Trade in Counterfeit Goods, *GATT Provisions bearing on Trade-Related Aspects of Intellectual Property Rights*. Note by the Secretariat, MTN.GNG/NG11/W/6, dated 22 May 1987,

countries recognise and protect the right of the author or creator in his/her creation, in order to reward and stimulate creative endeavour. They thus have rules in place for the protection and enforcement of IP rights. IP rights, it should be noted, confer only *negative* rights, i.e. the right to exclude others from the use of the protected subject matter for a particular period of time. They do not confer positive rights, such as the right to produce or market the product embodying the IP right.

Trade and intellectual property protection are closely connected. The achievements in liberalisation of trade through traditional disciplines on trade barriers, discussed in previous chapters of this book, can be greatly undermined if the IP rights related to the traded goods or services are not respected in the export market. The possibility that traded products will be copied or that brand names or service marks will be used by competitors creates a strong disincentive for innovation, investment and trade.

International agreements to harmonise protection in the field of IP law have existed since the late nineteenth century to deal with this problem. However, they were plagued by deficiencies. In particular, they were fragmented in their coverage of IP rights; they lacked effective enforcement standards and systems for the settlement of disputes; and they were often subject to low membership, with non-members being notorious violators of IP rights.

At the start of the Uruguay Round negotiations, some participants noted that:

> trade distortions and impediments were resulting from, among other things: the displacement of exports of legitimate goods by unauthorized copies, or of domestic sales by imports of unauthorized copies; the disincentive effect that inadequate protection of intellectual property rights had on inventors and creators to engage in research and development and in trade and investment; the deliberate use in some instances of intellectual property right protection to discourage imports and encourage local production, often of an inefficient and small-scale nature; and the inhibiting effect on international trade of disparities in the protection accorded under different legislations.[9]

The *TRIPS Agreement* was negotiated to address these problems. The initial resistance of developing countries to the inclusion of negotiations on IP protection in the Uruguay Round was overcome when they realised that they were better off with multilateral disciplines than being subject to bilateral pressure to provide IP protection.[10]

8.2.1.2 Objectives and principles of the TRIPS Agreement

The objectives of the *TRIPS Agreement* clearly reflect the concerns of negotiators, mentioned above. As identified in its Preamble, the main objective of the *TRIPS Agreement* is:

para. 2. On the relationship between the GATT 1994 and the *TRIPS Agreement*, see the General Interpretative Note to Annex 1A of the *WTO Agreement*, discussed above, at p. 47.

[8] See *WIPO Intellectual Property Handbook: Policy, Law and Use* (WIPO, 2004), 3, available at www.wipo.int/about-ip/en/iprm/index.html, visited on 15 November 2007.

[9] Negotiating Group on Trade-Related Aspects of Intellectual Property Rights, including Trade in Counterfeit Goods, *Meeting of 25 March 1987*. Note by the Secretariat, MTN.GNG/NG11/1, dated 10 April 1987, para. 4. Reference was also made to trade problems arising from restrictive business practices linked to intellectual property rights. See *ibid*.

[10] See P. Drahos, 'Developing Countries and International Intellectual Property Standard-Setting', *Journal of World Intellectual Property*, 2002, 774.

> to reduce distortions and impediments to international trade, . . . taking into account the need to promote effective and adequate protection of intellectual property rights, and to ensure that measures and procedures to enforce intellectual property rights do not themselves become barriers to legitimate trade;

This embodies the awareness that the lack of adequate protection of IP rights restricts trade, while at the same time IP protection can be used to prevent importation and protect local producers. The need to balance the competing interests of holders of IP rights on the one hand and the public on the other, by ensuring a minimum level of IP protection while allowing for measures to prevent abuse of IP rights, forms the basic rationale underlying the rights and obligations laid down in the *TRIPS Agreement*.

The different objectives of the *TRIPS Agreement* are sometimes in conflict with each other. As aptly noted by Thomas Cottier:

> Lack of, or insufficient protection [of intellectual property rights] amounts to *de facto* restrictions on market access, as exported products will be replaced by both generic and copied products that free ride on research and development, investment in creative activities and in quality control and product differentiation undertaken elsewhere. On the other hand, lack of appropriate limitations on rights may unduly hamper the flow of goods and services. *The real issue is one of balancing different policy goals.*[11]
>
> [Emphasis added]

The *TRIPS Agreement* represents an effort to achieve this balance. According to Carlos Correa:

> The TRIPS Agreement must be viewed as a means for the realization of public policy objectives via the 'inducement to innovation' *and* the access to the results thereof by those who need them. In other words the objectives of the patent system would not be fulfilled if it only served to induce innovations to the benefit of those who control them.[12]

Article 7 of the *TRIPS Agreement*, entitled 'Objectives', reflects the underlying aim of the *TRIPS Agreement* to ensure a balance between these competing goals. It states:

> The protection and enforcement of intellectual property rights should contribute to the promotion of technological innovation and the transfer and dissemination of technology, to the *mutual advantage* of producers and users of technological knowledge and in a manner conducive to *social and economic welfare*, and to a *balance* of rights and obligations.
>
> [Emphasis added][13]

The objective of creating equilibrium between rewarding creators of IP and protecting the public interest is also present in Article 8 of the *TRIPS Agreement*,

---

[11] T. Cottier, 'The Agreement on Trade-Related Aspects of Intellectual Property Rights', in P. F. J. Macrory, A. E. Appleton and M. G. Plummer (eds.), *The World Trade Organization: Legal, Economic and Political Analysis* (Springer, 2005), 1054.

[12] C. M. Correa, *Trade-Related Aspects of Intellectual Property Rights A Commentary on the TRIPS Agreement* (Oxford University Press, 2007), 94.

[13] While couched in hortatory language ('should' instead of 'shall'), the fact that this provision is in the operative part of the agreement rather than in its preamble 'heightens its status' in informing the interpretation of the *TRIPS Agreement*. See D. Gervais, *The TRIPS Agreement: Drafting History and Analysis* (Sweet and Maxwell, 2003), 116.

entitled 'Principles'. Paragraph 1 of Article 8 allows Members to adopt measures 'necessary to protect public health and nutrition' and to 'promote the public interest in sectors of vital importance to their socio-economic and technological development'. Paragraph 2 of Article 8 permits Members to take appropriate measures to counteract abuse of IP rights by right holders, or anticompetitive practices.[14] While the types of measures that could fall under Article 8 are in some respects similar to those falling under Article XX of the GATT 1994, unlike Article XX, which provides a general exception for measures which are otherwise GATT-inconsistent, the provision in Article 8 is limited by the requirement that measures falling thereunder be *consistent* with the provisions of the *TRIPS Agreement*.[15] Thus, rather than creating an exception from *TRIPS* disciplines for measures serving public policy objectives, Article 8 is best seen as enunciating a fundamental principle of the *TRIPS Agreement*, to be taken into account, with Article 7, when interpreting and applying its remaining provisions.

In *Canada – Pharmaceutical Patents*, the European Communities challenged provisions of Canada's patent law that allowed producers of generic medicines, before the expiry of the patent term, to stockpile generic products and to use patented products to prepare their submissions for marketing authorisation of the generic version. While Canada conceded that these provisions violated Article 28.1 of the *TRIPS Agreement*, which grants exclusive rights to patent holders, it relied on the exception of Article 30 to justify its measures, and argued that the objectives and principles of Articles 7 and 8 of the *TRIPS Agreement* should inform the interpretation of Article 30. The Panel in *Canada – Pharmaceutical Patents* held that:

> Article 30's very existence amounts to a recognition that the definition of patent rights contained in Article 28 would need certain adjustments. On the other hand, the three limiting conditions attached to Article 30 testify strongly that the negotiators of the Agreement did not intend Article 30 to bring about what would be equivalent to a renegotiation of the basic balance of the Agreement. Obviously, the exact scope of Article 30's authority will depend on the specific meaning given to its limiting conditions. The words of those conditions must be examined with particular care on this point. Both the goals and the limitations stated in Articles 7 and 8.1 must obviously be borne in mind when doing so as well as those of other provisions of the TRIPS Agreement which indicate its object and purposes.[16]

In an important further development since *Canada – Pharmaceutical Patents*, the Doha Declaration on the TRIPS Agreement and Public Health reaffirms the right of WTO Members to use, to the full, the provisions in the *TRIPS Agreement*, which provide flexibilities for Members in order to protect public health.[17] It then states:

---

[14] Specifically, Article 8.2 refers to measures needed to prevent 'the resort to practices which unreasonably restrain trade or adversely affect the international transfer of technology'.

[15] See also Panel Report, *EC – Trademarks and Geographical Indications (Australia)*, para. 7.210; and Panel Report, *EC – Trademarks and Geographical Indications (US)*, para. 7.176.

[16] Panel Report, *Canada – Pharmaceutical Patents*, para. 7.26.

[17] See Ministerial Conference, *Doha Declaration on the TRIPS Agreement and Public Health*, adopted on 14 November 2001, WT/MIN(01)/DEC/2, dated 20 November 2001, para. 4. While the legal status of this Declaration is not clear, it may be argued that it is a 'subsequent agreement between the parties regarding the interpretation of the [TRIPS Agreement] to the application of its provisions', thus falling under Article 31.3(a) of the *Vienna Convention on the Law of Treaties* and having to be taken into account together with the 'context' for the interpretation of the *TRIPS Agreement*.

> Accordingly . . ., while maintaining our commitments in the TRIPS Agreement, we recognize that these flexibilities include:
>
> In applying the customary rules of interpretation of public international law, *each provision* of the TRIPS Agreement shall be read in the light of the object and purpose of the Agreement *as expressed, in particular, in its objectives and principles.*[18]
>
> [Emphasis added]

Questions and Assignments 8.1

What is intellectual property (IP)? What is the link between international trade and the protection of IP rights? Is the *TRIPS Agreement* the first international agreement addressing the protection of IP rights? What are the objectives of the *TRIPS Agreement*? What is the role of Articles 7 and 8 of the *TRIPS Agreement*? Compare Article 8 of the *TRIPS Agreement* with Article XX of the GATT 1994. What is the importance of the Doha Declaration on the TRIPS Agreement and Public Health in this context?

8.2.2. Scope of application of the *TRIPS Agreement*

This section on the scope of application of the *TRIPS Agreement* distinguishes between its substantive and temporal scopes of application.

8.2.2.1. Substantive scope of application of the TRIPS Agreement

Article 1.3 of the *TRIPS Agreement* requires Members to accord the treatment provided for in this Agreement to nationals of other Members.[19] Nationals are understood as:

> those natural or legal persons that would meet the criteria for eligibility for protection provided for in the Paris Convention (1967), the Berne Convention (1971), the Rome Convention and the Treaty on Intellectual Property in Respect of Integrated Circuits, were all Members of the WTO members of those conventions.

The *TRIPS Agreement* does not define the concept of IP. Instead it specifies which categories of IP rights are covered by its provisions. Article 1.2 provides:

---

[18] *Ibid.*, para. 5. Note that it has been argued in commentary on the Panel Report in *Canada – Pharmaceutical Patents* that reliance on the principles and objectives of the *TRIPS Agreement* did not have an identifiable influence on the outcome of *TRIPS* disputes. See F. Abbott, 'TRIPS', in *Course on Dispute Settlement in International Trade, Investment and Intellectual Property* (UNCTAD, 2003), 8. See e.g. Panel Report, *Canada – Pharmaceutical Patents*, para. 7.26.

[19] As the *TRIPS Agreement* confers IP protection on the 'nationals' of WTO Members, but separate customs territories (that may be WTO Members) do not confer nationality, a supplementary definition was required of 'nationals' in the case of separate customs territories that are WTO Members. These are defined in footnote 1 to the *TRIPS Agreement* as 'persons, natural or legal, who are domiciled or who have a real and effective industrial or commercial establishment in that customs territory'. Note that, as recognised by the Panel in *EC – Trademarks and Geographical Indications*, the European Communities is not a 'separate customs territory Member' of the WTO and its nationals are therefore not defined by the terms of this footnote. See Panel Report, *EC – Trademarks and Geographical Indications (Australia)*, paras. 7.191–7.205; and Panel Report, *EC – Trademarks and Geographical Indications (US)*, paras. 7.141–7.171.

> For the purposes of this Agreement, the term 'intellectual property' refers to all categories of intellectual property that are the subject of Sections 1 through 7 of Part II.

Thus, clearly the *TRIPS Agreement* does *not* cover every form of IP right. Sections 1 to 7 of Part II of the *TRIPS Agreement* cover:

- Copyright and related rights;
- Trademarks;
- Geographical indications;
- Industrial design;
- Patents;
- Layout-designs of integrated circuits; and
- Protection of undisclosed information.

It should be borne in mind, however, that the categories of IP rights covered by the *TRIPS Agreement* are not always clear cut, and are not limited to those mentioned in the titles of Sections 1 to 7. In *US – Section 211 Appropriations Act*, the Panel was faced with the interpretation of Article 2.1 of the *TRIPS Agreement* in relation to 'trade names', which although not explicitly covered in the *TRIPS Agreement*, are referred to in Article 1(2) of the *Paris Convention*. The Panel was of the view that as Article 1.2 of the *TRIPS Agreement* refers to 'all categories', it indicates that this is an exhaustive list.[20] The Appellate Body disagreed with this analysis. It stated:

> The Panel interpreted the phrase ' "intellectual property" refers to all categories of intellectual property that are the *subject* of Sections 1 through 7 of Part II' (emphasis added) as if that phrase read 'intellectual property means those categories of intellectual property appearing in the *titles* of Sections 1 through 7 of Part II.' To our mind, the Panel's interpretation ignores the plain words of Article 1.2, for it fails to take into account that the phrase 'the subject of Sections 1 through 7 of Part II' deals not only with the categories of intellectual property indicated in each section *title*, but with other *subjects* as well. For example, in Section 5 of Part II, entitled 'Patents', Article 27(3)(b) provides that Members have the option of protecting inventions of plant varieties by *sui generis* rights (such as breeder's rights) instead of through patents. Under the Panel's theory, such *sui generis* rights would not be covered by the *TRIPS Agreement*. The option provided by Article 27(3)(b) would be read out of the *TRIPS Agreement*.[21]

The categories of IP rights covered by the *TRIPS Agreement* are those expressly mentioned in Sections 1 to 7 of Part II *as well as* those in the incorporated conventions that are the 'subject' of these Sections.[22]

The *TRIPS Agreement* does not cover every aspect of IP protection for the covered categories of IP rights. For example, it expressly excludes the issue of exhaustion of IP rights from its coverage.[23] Other aspects of the protection of IP

---

[20] See Panel Report, *US – Section 211 Appropriations Act*, para. 8.26.

[21] Appellate Body Report, *US – Section 211 Appropriations Act*, para. 335.

[22] Note that other forms of IP, as such traditional knowledge, folklore, genetic resources, breeders' rights, domain names and non-original databases are *not* covered by the disciplines of the *TRIPS Agreement*. See C. M. Correa, *Trade-Related Aspects of Intellectual Property Rights: A Commentary on the TRIPS Agreement* (Oxford University Press, 2007), 35.

[23] See below, p. 761. Note that Members are still obliged to respect the non-discrimination principles in respect of exhaustion of rights.

rights that are not mentioned in the *TRIPS Agreement* or in the incorporated provisions of the WIPO conventions are also excluded from the disciplines of the agreement.[24] This issue arose in *US – Section 211 Appropriations Act*, where the European Communities challenged Section 211 of the United States' Omnibus Appropriations Act, which effectively prohibits registration and renewal of trademarks and trade names used in connection with a business or assets that were confiscated without compensation by the Cuban government after the revolution without the consent of the original owner or *bona fide* successor-in-interest. Under this provision, the trademark 'Havana Club' that had been confiscated by the Cuban government without compensation from its Cuban owners could not be registered or enforced. The trademark was later in the hands of a French–Cuban joint venture. The European Communities claimed that Section 211 of the Appropriations Act violated the rules of the *Paris Convention* on trademark registration and was inconsistent with the national treatment and MFN treatment obligations of the *TRIPS Agreement*. The Panel, and later the Appellate Body, held that Articles 15 and 16 of the *TRIPS Agreement*, dealing with the protectable subject matter and the rights conferred with regard to trademarks, do not apply to the issue of 'ownership' of trademarks. As held by the Appellate Body:

> We have concluded already that Section 211(a)(1) is a measure that relates to ownership in that, in certain circumstances, it determines who is *not* the owner of a defined category of trademarks and trade names under United States trademark law. Therefore, Section 211(a)(1) does not in any way concern those issues that are addressed by Article 15.1, such as the inherent distinctiveness of signs, distinctiveness acquired through use and visual perceptibility. Section 211(a)(1) does not in any way prevent or preclude the registration of signs or combinations of signs that meet the requirements of Article 15.1, so long as the application for registration as a trademark is not made by a person who is not the legitimate owner of the sign or combination of signs according to United States law. Therefore, Section 211(a)(1) is not inconsistent with the requirements of Article 15.1 concerning 'protectable subject matter'.[25]

8.2.2.2 *Temporal scope of application of the TRIPS Agreement*

Article 70 of the *TRIPS Agreement* deals with the protection of existing subject matter, i.e. the temporal scope of application of the *TRIPS Agreement*. Article 70.1 specifies certain acts which do *not* give rise to obligations under the *TRIPS Agreement*. It states:

> This Agreement does not give rise to obligations *in respect of acts which occurred* before the date of application of the Agreement for the Member in question.[26]
>
> [Emphasis added]

[24] See e.g. Panel Report, *Indonesia – Autos*, para. 14.275. With regard to these aspects of IP rights, Members do not have to ensure a minimum level of protection, and further do not have to provide non-discriminatory treatment (under the *TRIPS Agreement*).
[25] Appellate Body Report, *US – Section 211 Appropriations Act*, para. 166. Within the limits of the *Paris Convention*, therefore, each Member may make its own determination regarding the ownership of a trademark.   [26] The emphasis was added in this way by the Appellate Body in *Canada – Patent Term*.

In other words, the *TRIPS Agreement* does not apply retroactively to acts that occurred before its 'date of application' for a Member.[27] In contrast, Article 70.2 of the *TRIPS Agreement* provides that the Agreement does create obligations in respect of subject matter that existed at the date of application. It provides, in relevant part:

> Except as otherwise provided for in this Agreement, this Agreement gives rise to obligations *in respect of all subject matter existing* at the date of application of this Agreement for the Member in question, and which is *protected* in that Member on the said date, or which meets or comes subsequently to meet the criteria for protection under the terms of this Agreement . . .[28]
>
>   [Emphasis added]

In *Canada – Patent Term*, Canada relied on Article 70.1 to argue that its (Old) Patent Act, which granted a patent protection term of seventeen years, did not have to comply with the twenty-year term of protection required by Article 33 of the *TRIPS Agreement*. On appeal, the Appellate Body interpreted the phrase 'acts which occurred before the date of application' as encompassing acts of public authorities as well as acts of private or third parties.[29] According to the Appellate Body, where such acts 'occurred' (were done, carried out or completed) before the date of application of the *TRIPS Agreement* for a Member, Article 70.1 provides that no obligation of the *TRIPS Agreement* is to be imposed on that Member in respect of those 'acts'.[30] However, the Appellate Body noted the fundamental importance, in the realm of IP rights, of distinguishing between 'acts' and the 'rights' created by those acts.[31] For example, the grant of a patent is an 'act' conferring various substantive rights such as national treatment, MFN treatment, term of protection, etc. The Appellate Body then identified the key question before it in *Canada – Patent Term* as:

> [I]f patents created by 'acts' of public authorities under the Old Act continue to be in force on the date of application of the *TRIPS Agreement* for Canada (that is, on 1 January 1996), can Article 70.1 operate to exclude those patents from the scope of the *TRIPS Agreement*, on the ground that they were created by 'acts which occurred' before that date?[32]

The Appellate Body answered this question in the negative. It conceded that an 'act' is something that is 'done', and that the use of the phrase 'acts which occurred' suggests that what was done is now complete or ended.[33] However, the Appellate Body pointed out that this 'excludes situations, including existing rights and obligations, that have *not* ended'.[34] The Appellate Body noted that if 'acts which occurred' would be interpreted *to* cover all continuing situations involving patents granted before the date of application of the *TRIPS Agreement,* then:

> Article 70.1 would preclude the application of virtually the whole of the *TRIPS Agreement* to rights conferred by the patents arising from such 'acts'.[35]

---

[27] The 'date of application' refers to the dates at which different transition periods for developed, developing and least-developed countries expire, as discussed below. See below, pp. 802–3.
[28] The emphasis was added in this way by the Appellate Body in *Canada – Patent Term*.   [29] See *ibid.*, 55.
[30] See *ibid.*   [31] *Ibid.*, para. 56.   [32] *Ibid.*, para. 57.   [33] See *ibid.*, para. 58.   [34] *Ibid.*   [35] *Ibid.*, para. 59.

Questions and Assignments 8.2

To whom do the obligations of the *TRIPS Agreement* apply? To whom does the *TRIPS Agreement* give rights? What is the substantive scope of application of the *TRIPS Agreement*? Give two examples of aspects of the protection of IP rights that are not covered by the *TRIPS Agreement*. To what extent does the MFN treatment obligation apply to these aspects? Do the disciplines of the *TRIPS Agreement* apply to a Member with regard to IP rights acquired before the date of application of the *TRIPS Agreement* for the Member concerned?

8.2.3. General provisions and basic principles of the *TRIPS Agreement*

Part I of the *TRIPS Agreement* contains the general provisions and basic disciplines that apply to the covered areas of IP. Article 1.1 of the *TRIPS Agreement* obliges Members to 'give effect' to its provisions. However, it expressly states that Members are 'free to determine the appropriate method' of implementing their obligations under the agreement within their own legal systems and practice.[36] In addition, Article 1.1 provides that Members are free, but not obliged, to implement more extensive protection than that laid down in the *TRIPS Agreement*. This firmly establishes the nature of the *TRIPS Agreement* as laying down a *minimum level* of harmonised IP protection. The flexibility available to Members with regard to *how* they give effect to their *TRIPS* obligations is an important tool in balancing the competing policy goals mentioned above.[37] However, the flexibility available to Members is obviously not without limits. In *India – Patents (US)*, the Appellate Body, in interpreting India's obligation under Article 70.8(a) of the *TRIPS Agreement*,[38] recalled the 'important general rule' contained in Article 1.1 and noted:

> Members, therefore, are free to determine how best to meet their obligations under the *TRIPS Agreement* within the context of their own legal systems. And, as a Member, India is 'free to determine the appropriate method of implementing' its obligations under the *TRIPS Agreement* within the context of its own legal system.[39]

However, in this case the Appellate Body, like the Panel, was not persuaded that the 'administrative instructions' given by India to its patent office to accept

---

[36] Note that in *EC – Trademarks and Geographical Indications (US)*, the United States claimed a violation of Article 1.1 due to the fact that the EC's inspection structure requirements for the protection of geographical indications conditioned protection on the adoption by other Members of structures that the EC unilaterally determines to be equivalent to its own. The Panel disagreed, holding that the evidence before it did not disclose that these inspection structures concerned the systems of protection of *other* WTO Members but rather that they only concerned compliance with the product specifications, which are a feature of the European Communities' system of protection. See Panel Report, *EC – Trademarks and Geographical Indications (US)*, paras. 7.762–7.766.

[37] See, for example, the flexibility in determining the scope of the 'fair use' exception to copyright, discussed below, p. 774.

[38] This obligation entails that Members making use of transitional arrangements under Part VI of the *TRIPS Agreement* to delay providing patent protection must nevertheless provide a 'means' by which patent applications can be filed. These applications are often referred to as 'mailbox applications' and Article 70.8 is called the 'mailbox provision'.   [39] Appellate Body Report, *India – Patents (US)*, para. 59.

'mailbox' applications as required under Article 70.8(a) would prevail over the contradictory mandatory provisions of the Indian Patents Act.[40] Therefore, despite the flexibility provided in Article 1.1, India was held not to have properly implemented its obligations under Article 70.8(a) of the *TRIPS Agreement*.[41]

This section discusses the basic principles laid down in Part I of the *TRIPS Agreement*. More specifically, it addresses:

- the relationship between the *TRIPS Agreement* and WIPO conventions;
- the national treatment obligation;
- the most-favoured-nation treatment obligation; and
- the issue of exhaustion of IP rights.

8.2.3.1. Relationship between the TRIPS Agreement and WIPO conventions

The *TRIPS Agreement* builds upon the standards of IP protection developed in the context of the World Intellectual Property Organization (WIPO) and embodied in its conventions. It does so by incorporating by reference specific provisions of the relevant conventions, namely the *Paris Convention for the Protection of Industrial Property of 1883*, as revised in the Stockholm Act of 1967 (the *Paris Convention (1967)*), the *Berne Convention for the Protection of Literary and Artistic Works of 1886*, as revised in the Paris Act of 1971 (the *Berne Convention (1971)*), the *International Convention for the Protection of Performers, Producers of Phonograms and Broadcasting Organizations of 1961* (the *Rome Convention*) and the *Treaty on Intellectual Property in respect of Integrated Circuits of 1989* (the *IPIC Treaty*). The obligations of the *TRIPS Agreement* must therefore be read together with the relevant WIPO conventions.

However, the *TRIPS Agreement* does more than simply incorporate the provisions of these conventions. Developed-country negotiators of the *TRIPS Agreement* viewed the existing WIPO conventions as 'inadequate to address the needs of their business sectors in the "post-industrial era" or "information age"'.[42] Therefore, the *TRIPS Agreement* supplements and updates the rules of the relevant WIPO conventions, as well as expressly provides new rules in some areas. In addition, and more importantly, it creates an obligation on Members to have a system in place for the enforcement of the protected IP rights and links them to the effective and enforceable dispute settlement system of the WTO.[43]

The relationship between the WIPO conventions and the *TRIPS Agreement* is set out in Article 2 of the *TRIPS Agreement*. Article 2.1 of the *TRIPS Agreement* explicitly obliges Members to comply with Articles 1 to 12 and 19 of the *Paris Convention (1967)* in respect of Parts II, III and IV of the *TRIPS Agreement*. Therefore, even WTO Members that are not contracting parties to the *Paris*

---

[40] See *ibid.*, paras. 69–70.

[41] See *ibid.*, para. 71. See also Panel Report, *Canada – Patent Term*, para. 6.94. There the Panel noted that: 'Article 1.1 gives Members the freedom to determine the appropriate method of implementing [the two requirements at issue], but not to ignore either requirement.' See further below, p. 780.

[42] F. Abbott, 'TRIPS', in *Course on Dispute Settlement in International Trade, Investment and Intellectual Property* (UNCTAD, 2003), 11.

[43] See D. Matthews, *Globalising Intellectual Property Rights: The TRIPs Agreement* (Routledge, 2002), 46. These enforcement obligations are discussed below, p. 794.

Convention (1967) must comply with these provisions thereof.[44] Article 2.2 of the *TRIPS Agreement* provides that nothing in Parts I to IV of the *TRIPS Agreement* shall derogate from Members' obligations under the *Paris Convention*, the *Berne Convention*, the *Rome Convention* or the *IPIC Treaty*. This non-derogation clause does not create new obligations but seeks only to ensure that Members do not apply their *TRIPS* obligations in a manner that results in a violation of their obligations under the mentioned WIPO conventions. In addition, various provisions in Part II of the *TRIPS Agreement* dealing with each of the categories of IP rights incorporate certain provisions of the relevant WIPO conventions. With regard to the *Berne Convention*, the *Paris Convention* and the *IPIC Treaty*, these incorporating provisions oblige all WTO Members to comply with the incorporated articles of the WIPO conventions, making them binding even on those WTO Members that are not contracting parties to the incorporated WIPO convention.[45]

Questions and Assignments 8.3

What kind of 'flexibility' does Article 1.1 of the *TRIPS Agreement* give to Members? Which provisions of WIPO conventions are incorporated by reference in the *TRIPS Agreement*? Does the *TRIPS Agreement* do more than incorporate these provisions? If so, what and why does the *TRIPS Agreement* do more? How does the *TRIPS Agreement* relate to the WIPO conventions referred to therein?

8.2.3.2. *The national treatment obligation*

The non-discrimination obligations of national treatment and MFN treatment, familiar from the discussion of the GATT 1994 and the GATS, apply also in the context of the *TRIPS Agreement*.[46] However, there are some differences in their application in order to take into account the intangible nature of IP rights.

The national treatment obligation of the *TRIPS Agreement* is contained in Article 3 thereof.[47] This obligation requires each Member to accord to nationals of other Members treatment 'no less favourable' than that it accords to its own nationals in respect of IP protection. Footnote 3 to the *TRIPS Agreement* defines 'protection' for purposes of Articles 3 and 4, providing that it:

---

[44] See Appellate Body Report, *US – Section 211 Appropriations Act*, para. 125.

[45] See, for example, Article 9.1 of the *TRIPS Agreement*, which obliges Members to comply with Articles 1 to 21, and the Appendix to the *Berne Convention (1971)* and Article 35 of the *TRIPS Agreement*, which obliges Members to provide protection to layout-designs of integrated circuits in accordance with Articles 2 to 7 (except Article 6(3)), 12 and 16(3) of the *IPIC Treaty*. Note that there is no such provision with regard to the *Rome Convention*, which continues to bind only its Contracting Parties.   [46] See above, pp. 322–95.

[47] In addition, the *TRIPS Agreement* incorporates three national treatment obligations of pre-existing IP conventions, namely Article 2 of the *Paris Convention (1967)* (incorporated by Article 2.1 of the *TRIPS Agreement*); Article 5 of the *Berne Convention (1971)* (incorporated by Article 9.1 of the *TRIPS Agreement*); and Article 5 of the *IPIC Treaty* (incorporated by Article 35 of the *TRIPS Agreement*). See e.g. Panel Report, *EC – Trademarks and Geographical Indications (US)*, footnote 166 to para. 7.131.

shall include matters affecting the availability, acquisition, scope, maintenance and enforcement of intellectual property rights as well as those matters affecting the use of intellectual property rights *specifically addressed in this Agreement.*

[Emphasis added]

In *Indonesia – Autos*, the Panel noted in this respect:

> As is made clear by the footnote to Article 3 of the TRIPS Agreement, the national treatment rule set out in that Article does not apply to use of intellectual property rights generally but only to 'those matters affecting the use of intellectual property rights specifically addressed in this Agreement'.[48]

Therefore the national treatment obligation of the *TRIPS Agreement* is limited in its scope of application to only the IP rights specifically addressed in the *TRIPS Agreement* (including in the incorporated conventions).[49] Unlike the national treatment obligations of the GATT 1994 and the GATS, the national treatment obligation in Article 3 of the *TRIPS Agreement* applies with respect to 'nationals' as defined in Article 1.3, rather than with respect to 'like products' or 'like services or service providers'. This is because IP rights are intangible, and attach to an IP right holder, rather than to the product or service in which they are embodied.

The Appellate Body addressed the national treatment obligation in the *TRIPS Agreement* for the first time in *US – Section 211 Appropriations Act*. In this case, the Appellate Body observed the 'fundamental significance of the obligation of national treatment . . . in the *TRIPS Agreement*'[50] and noted that:

> Indeed, the significance of the national treatment obligation can hardly be overstated. Not only has the national treatment obligation long been a cornerstone of the Paris Convention and other international intellectual property conventions. So, too, has the national treatment obligation long been a cornerstone of the world trading system that is served by the WTO.[51]

The Appellate Body stated that the national treatment obligation is 'a fundamental principle underlying the *TRIPS Agreement*, just as it has been in what is now the GATT 1994'.[52] It agreed with the Panel that as the language of Article 3.1 of the *TRIPS Agreement* is similar to that of Article III:4 of the GATT 1994, the case law on Article III:4 of the GATT 1994 'may be useful in interpreting the national treatment obligation in the *TRIPS Agreement*'.[53]

Applying the national treatment obligation in *US – Section 211 Appropriations Act*, the Appellate Body pointed out that Section 211(a)(2) of the US Appropriations Act, on its face, imposed an 'extra hurdle' on successors-in-interest to the confiscated trademark who were not US nationals that was not faced by successors-in-interest that were US nationals. Namely, non-nationals faced the additional problem that in terms of Section 211(a) of the

---

[48] Panel Report, *Indonesia – Autos*, para. 14.275.
[49] See C. M. Correa, *Trade-Related Aspects of Intellectual Property Rights: A Commentary on the TRIPS Agreement* (Oxford University Press, 2007), 62.
[50] Appellate Body Report, *US – Section 211 Appropriations Act*, para. 240.   [51] *Ibid.*, para. 241.
[52] *Ibid.*, para. 242.   [53] *Ibid.*

Appropriations Act, their trademark would not be recognised, validated or enforced by US courts. Although the chance that in practice foreign nationals would actually have to overcome both 'hurdles' was small, according to the Appellate Body 'even the *possibility* that non-United States successors-in-interest face two hurdles is *inherently less favourable* than the undisputed fact that United States successors-in-interest face only one'.[54] Therefore, the Appellate Body found that the US violated the national treatment obligation in Article 3.1 of the *TRIPS Agreement*.[55]

The Panel in *EC – Trademarks and Geographical Indications* also addressed the national treatment obligation of Article 3.1 of the *TRIPS Agreement*. In that case, the measure at issue was an EC regulation containing two sets of detailed procedures for the registration of geographical indications (GIs) for agricultural products and foodstuffs. The first procedure (Articles 5–7) applied to the names of geographical areas located in the European Communities. The second procedure (Articles 12a and 12b) applied to the names of geographical areas located in third countries outside the European Communities. Further additional conditions (Article 12(1)) applied, requiring that a third country must itself provide reciprocal and equivalent protections for GIs to those offered in the European Communities (known as the 'reciprocity and equivalence conditions').[56] The complainants (the US and Australia) claimed that the EC regulation at issue was inconsistent with the national treatment obligation of Article 3.1 of the *TRIPS Agreement*, because it imposed conditions of reciprocity and equivalence on the availability of protection.[57] The Panel in *EC – Trademarks and Geographical Indications* identified two elements that must be satisfied to establish an inconsistency with the national treatment obligation of Article 3.1 of the *TRIPS Agreement*:

- first, the measure at issue must apply with regard to the protection of intellectual property; and
- second, the nationals of other Members must be accorded 'less favourable' treatment than the Member's own nationals.[58]

Examining the *first* element of this two-tier test, the Panel pointed out that it was undisputed that 'designations of origin' and 'geographical indications', as defined in the EC regulation at issue, fell within the category of 'geographical indications', i.e. the subject of Section 3 of Part II of the *TRIPS Agreement*, and were therefore part of a category of intellectual property within the meaning of the *TRIPS Agreement*.[59] The Panel concluded that:

---

[54] *Ibid.*, para. 265.
[55] See *ibid.*, para. 268. The Appellate Body also found that the United States acted inconsistently with Article 2(1) of the *Paris Convention (1967)*. See *ibid.*
[56] See Panel Report, *EC – Trademarks and Geographical Indications (US)*, para. 7.105; Panel Report, *EC – Trademarks and Geographical Indications (Australia)*, para. 7.90.
[57] See Panel Report, *EC – Trademarks and Geographical Indications (US)*, para. 7.104; Panel Report, *EC – Trademarks and Geographical Indications (Australia)*, para. 7.154. Note that the United States and Australia also claimed that the EC regulation was inconsistent with the national treatment obligation of Article 2(1) of the *Paris Convention (1967)*, as incorporated by Article 2.1 of the *TRIPS Agreement*.
[58] See Panel Report, *EC – Trademarks and Geographical Indications (US)*, para. 7.125; Panel Report, *EC – Trademarks and Geographical Indications (Australia)*, para. 7.175.   [59] See *ibid.*, para. 7.128; *ibid.*, para. 7.178.

this claim concerns the 'protection' of intellectual property, as clarified in footnote 3 to the TRIPS Agreement, within the scope of the national treatment obligation in Article 3 of that Agreement.[60]

Turning to the *second* element of the two-tier test under Article 3.1 of the *TRIPS Agreement*, namely that of 'less favourable treatment' accorded to nationals of other Members, the Panel in *EC – Trademarks and Geographical Indications* noted:

> It is useful to recall that Article 3.1 of the TRIPS Agreement combines elements of national treatment both from pre-existing intellectual property agreements and GATT 1994. Like the pre-existing intellectual property conventions, Article 3.1 applies to 'nationals', not products. Like GATT 1994, Article 3.1 refers to 'no less favourable' treatment, not the advantages or rights that laws now grant or may hereafter grant, but it does not refer to likeness.[61]

The Panel pointed out that not only measures which *on their face* discriminate between the nationals of a Member and foreign nationals are prohibited by Article 3. Also *de facto* discriminatory measures fall foul of this provision. The Panel referred to the case law regarding the concept of 'no less favourable treatment' in Article III:4 of the GATT 1994, which has been interpreted as sufficiently broad to include situations where the application of formally identical legal provisions would in practice accord less favourable treatment.[62] The Panel then held:

> We consider that this reasoning applies with equal force to the no less favourable treatment standard in Article 3.1 of the TRIPS Agreement. In our view, even if the provisions of the Regulation are formally identical in the treatment that they accord to the nationals of other Members and to the European Communities' own nationals, this is not sufficient to demonstrate that there is no violation of Article 3.1 of the TRIPS Agreement.[63]

The Panel recalled that the Panel and Appellate Body in *US – Section 211 Appropriations Act*[64] found that the appropriate standard for 'no less favourable treatment' under Article 3 of the *TRIPS Agreement* is that laid down by the GATT Panel in *US – Section 337* with respect to Article III of the GATT.[65] The Panel in *EC – Trademarks and Geographical Indications* thus proceeded to examine whether the difference in treatment affected the 'effective equality of opportunities' between the nationals of other Members and the European Communities' own nationals with regard to the protection of intellectual property rights, to the detriment of nationals of other Members.[66] The equivalence and reciprocity conditions of the EC regulation at issue were held by the Panel to modify the effective equality of opportunities to obtain protection with respect to intellectual property.[67] Those conditions, according to the Panel, represented a significant 'extra hurdle'[68] in

---

[60] *Ibid.*, para. 7.129; *ibid.*, para. 7.179.　　[61] *Ibid.*, para. 7.131; *ibid.*, para. 7.181.
[62] See *Ibid.*, para. 7.173; *ibid.*, para. 7.207.　　[63] *Ibid.*, para. 7.176; *ibid.*, para. 7.210.
[64] See Panel Report, *US – Section 211 Appropriations Act*, paras. 8.131–8.133; and Appellate Body Report, *US – Section 211 Appropriations Act*, para. 258.　　[65] See GATT Panel Report, *US – Section 337*, para. 5.11.
[66] See Panel Report, *EC – Trademarks and Geographical Indications (US)*, para. 7.134; Panel Report, *EC – Trademarks and Geographical Indications (Australia)*, para. 7.210.　　[67] See *ibid.*, para. 7.139; *ibid.*, para. 7.189.
[68] Here the Panel referred to the approach of the Appellate Body in *US – Section 211 Appropriations Act* to an 'extra hurdle' imposed only on foreign nationals. See Appellate Body Report, *US – Section 211 Appropriations Act*, para. 268.

obtaining GI protection that did not apply to geographical areas located in the European Communities. It accordingly concluded that:

> the equivalence and reciprocity conditions modify the effective equality of opportunities with respect to the availability of protection to persons who wish to obtain GI protection under the Regulation, to the detriment of those who wish to obtain protection in respect of geographical areas located in third countries, including WTO Members. This is less favourable treatment.[69]

As the EC regulation at issue referred to the location of geographical indications, whereas the national treatment obligation in Article 3.1 of the *TRIPS Agreement* refers to treatment accorded to 'nationals', the Panel then had to determine how the less favourable treatment accorded under the EC regulation with respect to the *availability of protection* affects the treatment accorded to the *nationals* of other Members and that accorded to the European Communities' *own nationals* for the purposes of Article 3.1 of the *TRIPS Agreement*.[70] Noting that the fact that the EC regulation, on its face, provided formally identical treatment to the nationals of other Members and to the European Communities' own nationals was not sufficient to demonstrate that there was no violation of Article 3.1 of the *TRIPS Agreement*, the Panel proceeded to examine whether the 'fundamental thrust and effect' of the regulation at issue was such that it affected the 'effective equality of opportunities' with regard to the protection of IP rights. On the question of which nationals to compare, the Panel held that:

> the nationals that are relevant to an examination under Article 3.1 of the TRIPS Agreement should be those who seek opportunities with respect to the same type of intellectual property in comparable situations. On the one hand, this excludes a comparison of opportunities for nationals with respect to different categories of intellectual property, such as GIs and copyright. On the other hand, no reason has been advanced as to why the equality of opportunities should be limited *a priori* to rights with a territorial link to a particular Member.[71]

Therefore the Panel did not need to make a factual assumption that 'every person who wishes to obtain protection for a GI in a particular Member is a national of that Member'.[72] Examining the provisions of the EC regulation at issue, the Panel found that:

> the distinction made by the Regulation on the basis of the location of a GI will operate in practice to discriminate between the group of nationals of other Members who wish to obtain GI protection, and the group of the European Communities' own nationals who wish to obtain GI protection, to the detriment of the nationals of other Members. This will not occur as a random outcome in a particular case but as a feature of the *design and structure of the system*. This design is evident in the Regulation's objective characteristics, in particular, the definitions of 'designation of origin' and 'geographical indication' and the requirements of the product specifications. The structure is evident in the different registration procedures.[73]
>
> [Emphasis added]

---

[69] Panel Report, *EC – Trademarks and Geographical Indications (US)*, para. 7.140; Panel Report, *EC – Trademarks and Geographical Indications (Australia)*, para. 7.190.   [70] See *ibid.*, para. 7.141; *ibid.*, para. 7.191.
[71] *Ibid.*, para. 7.181; *ibid.*, para. 7.217.   [72] *Ibid.*, para. 7.182; *ibid.*, para. 7.218.
[73] *Ibid.*, para. 7.194; *ibid.*, para. 7.230.

The Panel pointed out that the *TRIPS Agreement* itself recognises that discrimination according to residence and establishment will be a 'close substitute for nationality'.[74] In its view, the object and purpose of the *TRIPS Agreement*:

> would be severely undermined if a Member could avoid its obligations by simply according treatment to its own nationals on the basis of close substitute criteria, such as place of production, or establishment, and denying treatment to the nationals of other WTO Members who produce or are established in their own countries.[75]

Therefore, the Panel found a violation of national treatment with respect to the reciprocity and equivalence conditions in the EC Regulation as applicable to the availability of GI protection, as the treatment accorded to the group of nationals of other Members was different from, and less favourable than, that accorded to the European Communities' own nationals.[76]

The national treatment obligation in Article 3.1 of the *TRIPS Agreement* is subject to exceptions. As pointed out by the Panel in *EC – Trademarks and Geographical Indications*:

> The scope of the national treatment obligation in Article 3.1 of the TRIPS Agreement also differs from that of the national treatment obligation in Article III:4 of GATT 1994, as it is subject to certain exceptions in Articles 3.1, 3.2 and 5, one of which is inspired by the language of Article XX of GATT 1994. There is also a series of specific exceptions in the provisions relating to the minimum standards in Part II of the TRIPS Agreement and Part VII contains a provision on security exceptions analogous to Article XXI of GATT 1994, but none on general exceptions.[77]

Article 3.1 subjects the national treatment obligation to the exception already provided for in the *Paris Convention (1967)*, the *Berne Convention (1971)*, the *Rome Convention* or the *IPIC Treaty*.[78] This exception recognises the fact that IP treaties often require reciprocity. Further, the national treatment obligation applies to performers, producers of phonograms and broadcasting organisations only with respect to the rights provided in the *TRIPS Agreement*.[79] This prevents Members that are not parties to the *Rome Convention* from receiving, 'through the back door',[80] the IP protection secured under this convention without undertaking to provide such protection themselves. In addition, Article 5 provides that the national treatment obligation of Article 3 does not apply to procedures for the

---

[74] *Ibid.*, para. 7.198; *ibid.*, para. 7.234. Here the Panel pointed to the criteria set out in footnote 1 to the *TRIPS Agreement* which it stated 'are clearly intended to provide close substitute criteria to determine nationality where criteria to determine nationality as such are not available in a Member's domestic law. These criteria are "domicile" and "real and effective industrial or commercial establishment".'

[75] *Ibid.*, para. 7.199; *ibid.*, para. 7.235.   [76] See *ibid.*, paras. 7.204 and 7.213; *ibid.*, paras. 7.240 and 7.249.

[77] *Ibid.*, para. 7.211; *ibid.*, para. 7.247.

[78] Note that Article 3.1 of the *TRIPS Agreement* provides that in the case of two of these exceptions, those under Article 6 of the *Berne Convention* and Article 16.1(b) of the *Rome Convention*, notification to the Council for TRIPS is required if a Member intends to avail itself of them.

[79] Article 3.2 of the *TRIPS Agreement* provides that the exceptions of Article 3.1 that relate to judicial and administrative procedures apply only to the extent necessary to secure compliance with laws and regulations that are not inconsistent with the *TRIPS Agreement* and where they are not applied in a way that constitutes a disguised restriction on trade. Compare this to Article XX(d) of the GATT 1994, discussed above, p. 629.

[80] C. M. Correa, *Trade-Related Aspects of Intellectual Property Rights: A Commentary on the TRIPS Agreement* (Oxford University Press, 2007), 63.

acquisition of IP rights provided in multilateral agreements negotiated under the auspices of WIPO.[81]

Questions and Assignments 8.4

How does the national treatment obligation of the *TRIPS Agreement* differ from the national treatment obligations of the GATT 1994 and the GATS? Is the case law on the national treatment obligations of the GATT 1994 and the GATS of relevance to the application and interpretation of Article 3.1 of the *TRIPS Agreement?* What are the constituent elements of the national treatment test of Article 3.1 of the *TRIPS Agreement* as identified in *EC – Trademarks and Geographical Indications*? Does Article 3.1 of the *TRIPS Agreement* cover both *de jure* and *de facto* discrimination? How did the Panel in *EC – Trademarks and Geographical Indications* come to the conclusion that the less favourable treatment accorded under the EC regulation with respect to the *availability of protection* constituted less favourable treatment accorded to the *nationals* of other Members? Are there any exceptions to the national treatment obligation of Article 3.1 of the *TRIPS Agreement?*

8.2.3.3. *The most-favoured-nation treatment obligation*

Article 4 of the *TRIPS Agreement* embodies the MFN obligation for purposes of this Agreement. It requires that any advantage, favour, privilege or immunity with regard to IP protection granted by a Member to the nationals of any other country be accorded immediately and unconditionally to the nationals of all other Members. Once again, the definition of 'protection' is that contained in footnote 3 to the *TRIPS Agreement*.[82] Members are arguably obliged to provide MFN treatment only with respect to the protection provided for in the *TRIPS Agreement* (including in the incorporated IP conventions).[83]

Like the national treatment obligation in Article 3 of the *TRIPS Agreement*, and different from the national treatment and MFN treatment obligations of the GATT 1994 and the GATS, the MFN treatment obligation of the *TRIPS Agreement* applies with respect to 'nationals' as defined in Article 1.3, rather than with

---

[81] Note that the Article 5 exception applies also to the MFN obligation of Article 4 of the *TRIPS Agreement*.

[82] This footnote is quoted above, pp. 752–3.

[83] Correa sees footnote 3 as limiting the MFN principle to the rights specifically addressed in the *TRIPS Agreement* and incorporated IP conventions. Therefore, according to Correa, Members that provide higher levels of IP protection, beyond that required by the *TRIPS Agreement*, under bilateral agreements (so-called 'TRIPS-plus' protection) need not extend that same protection to all WTO Members. See C. M. Correa, *Trade-Related Aspects of Intellectual Property Rights: A Commentary on the TRIPS Agreement* (Oxford University Press, 2007), 66–7. See *contra* T. Cottier, 'The Agreement on Trade-Related Aspects of Intellectual Property Rights', in P. F. J. Macrory, A. E. Appleton and M. G. Plummer (eds.), *The World Trade Organization: Legal, Economic and Political Analysis* (Springer, 2005), 1068. Cottier regards the MFN treatment obligation as extending to all IP protection, not only that specifically referred to in the *TRIPS Agreement*. Cottier notes that a consequence of this is that Members that extend TRIPS-plus protection to *certain* countries are obliged by Article 4 to extend such protection to *all* WTO Members. Note that the *TRIPS Agreement* does not contain an exception to the MFN treatment obligation for regional trade agreements, as provided in Article XXIV of the GATT 1994 and Article V of the GATS. See *ibid.*, 1068 and 1069.

respect to 'like products' or 'like services or service providers'. As noted above, this is because IP rights are intangible, and attach to an IP right holder, rather than to the product or service in which they are embodied. Interestingly, none of the existing IP conventions provides for an MFN treatment obligation. Thus the *TRIPS Agreement* introduces such an obligation for the first time with respect to IP protection. In *US – Section 211 Appropriations Act*, the Appellate Body emphasised the importance of extending the MFN obligation, which is key to the multilateral trading system, to the *TRIPS Agreement*. It noted:

> Like the national treatment obligation, the obligation to provide most-favoured-nation treatment has long been one of the cornerstones of the world trading system. For more than fifty years, the obligation to provide most-favoured-nation treatment in Article I of the GATT 1994 has been both central and essential to assuring the success of a global rules-based system for trade in goods. Unlike the national treatment principle, there is no provision in the Paris Convention (1967) that establishes a most-favoured-nation obligation with respect to rights in trademarks or other industrial property. However, the framers of the *TRIPS Agreement* decided to extend the most-favoured-nation obligation to the protection of intellectual property rights covered by that Agreement. As a cornerstone of the world trading system, the most-favoured-nation obligation must be accorded the same significance with respect to intellectual property rights under the *TRIPS Agreement* that it has long been accorded with respect to trade in goods under the GATT. It is, in a word, fundamental.[84]

Like the national treatment obligation, the MFN treatment obligation in Article 4 of the *TRIPS Agreement* is subject to exceptions. Advantages granted by a Member deriving from international agreements on judicial assistance or law enforcement need not be granted to all Members.[85] Further, the advantages granted in the *Rome Convention* and the *Berne Convention (1971)* on condition of reciprocity are excluded from the obligation of MFN treatment.[86] Members are also not obliged to provide on an MFN basis the rights of performers, phonogram producers and broadcasting organisations protected under the *Rome Convention*.[87] The most important exception to the MFN treatment obligation is that contained in Article 4(d) of the *TRIPS Agreement*. It relates to advantages deriving from international agreements 'related to the protection of intellectual property' which predate the entry into force of the *WTO Agreement*.[88] Such advantages do not have to be extended to all WTO Members on an MFN basis, provided that

---

[84] Appellate Body Report, *US – Section 211 Appropriations Act*, para. 297. As the arguments of both parties with regard to the alleged violation of the MFN treatment obligation in this dispute were basically the same as those they used for the claim of violation of the national treatment obligation, discussed above, the Appellate Body held, for the same reasons *mutatis mutandis*, that a violation of Article 4 had been established. See *ibid.*, paras. 305–16. See also above, pp. 753–4.

[85] See Article 4(a) of the *TRIPS Agreement*. Note that the agreements referred to are 'of a general nature and not particularly confined to the protection of intellectual property'.

[86] See Article 4(b) of the *TRIPS Agreement*.

[87] This is in line with the exclusion of the *Rome Convention* from the national treatment obligation in the second sentence of Article 3.1 of the *TRIPS Agreement*. See above, p. 757.

[88] This exemption has been interpreted broadly by Members, and they have made clear in communications in this respect that future acts based on such agreements would also be exempted from the MFN treatment obligation. See the notification of the European Communities and its Member States, IP/N/4/EEC/1, dated 29 January 1996; the notification of the ANDEAN Pact, Bolivia, Colombia, Ecuador, Peru, Venezuela, IP/N/4/BOL/1, IP/N/4/COL/1, IP/N/4/ECU/1, IP/N/4/PER/1, IP/N/4/VEN/1, dated 19 August 1997; and the notification of MERCOSUR, Argentina, Brazil, Paraguay, Uruguay, IP/N/4/ARG/1, IP/N/4/BRA/1, IP/N/4/PRY/1, IP/N/4/URY/1, dated 14 July 1998.

the relevant agreements have been notified to the Council for TRIPS, and they 'do not constitute an arbitrary or unjustifiable discrimination against nationals of other Members'.[89] In addition, Article 5 of the *TRIPS Agreement* provides that the MFN treatment obligation of Article 4 does not apply to procedures for the acquisition of IP rights provided in multilateral agreements negotiated under the auspices of WIPO.[90]

Questions and Assignments 8.5

How does the MFN treatment obligation of the *TRIPS Agreement* differ from the MFN treatment obligations of the GATT 1994 and the GATS? Is the case law on the MFN treatment obligations of the GATT 1994 and the GATS of relevance to the application and interpretation of Article 4 of the *TRIPS Agreement*? Is the MFN treatment obligation a 'novelty' among international rules on IP protection? What is the most important exception to the MFN treatment obligation of Article 4 of the *TRIPS Agreement*?

8.2.3.4. *Exhaustion of IP rights*

Intellectual property rights are embodied in a product (for example, a book, compact disc or medicine). However, they exist independently of the products to which they relate. Theoretically therefore, IP rights can 'follow' products indefinitely, even after they have been legitimately sold, allowing the IP right holder to control their resale. In order to balance the rights of the IP right holder with the interests of the market, the doctrine of exhaustion of rights is applied to determine when the IP right holder's right to control the product in which the IP right is embodied ends. Note that exhaustion applies only to the right to control the *resale* of the product after it has been lawfully put on the market, by means of IP rights.[91] It does not affect the essence of an IP right, namely the right to exclude others from exploiting the IP right without the consent of the right holder (for example, by making pirated copies of a compact disc or copying a patented medicine).[92]

---

[89] Correa notes that this exception seems to imply that parties to agreements related to IP protection (such as free trade agreements with chapters on IP protection) that post-date the entry into force of the *WTO Agreement are* obliged to extend the advantages contained therein to all WTO Members. This would be the case despite the fact that WTO Members that are not parties to these agreements are not obliged to extend reciprocal advantages to such parties, which Correa regards as a 'troublesome implication' of this provision. See C. M. Correa, *Trade-Related Aspects of Intellectual Property Rights: A Commentary on the TRIPS Agreement* (Oxford University Press, 2007), 69.

[90] Note that, as stated above, the Article 5 exception applies also to the national treatment obligation of Article 3 of the *TRIPS Agreement*. See above, pp. 757–8.

[91] See T. Cottier, 'The Agreement on Trade-Related Aspects of Intellectual Property Rights', in P. F. J. Macrory, A. E. Appleton and M. G. Plummer (eds.), *The World Trade Organization: Legal, Economic and Political Analysis* (Springer, 2005), 1069. See, however, C. M. Correa, *Trade-Related Aspects of Intellectual Property Rights: A Commentary on the TRIPS Agreement* (Oxford University Press, 2007), 82 , who argues that Article 6 of the *TRIPS Agreement* refers to 'IP rights' without qualification and states that, therefore, the question arises whether exhaustion may be applied to all exclusive rights or only a subset thereof.

[92] See T. Cottier, 'The Agreement on Trade-Related Aspects of Intellectual Property Rights', in P. F. J. Macrory, A.E. Appleton and M. G. Plummer (eds.), *The World Trade Organization: Legal, Economic and Political Analysis* (Springer, 2005), 1069.

There are three possible approaches to the exhaustion of IP rights:

- *National* exhaustion of rights means that the lawful sale of a product exhausts IP rights to control the resale of the product only on the national market. The IP right holder retains these rights in other countries.
- *Regional* exhaustion of rights means that the lawful sale of a product in a country that is a party to a regional agreement exhausts IP rights to control resale in other parties to the regional agreement.
- *International* exhaustion of rights means that once a product is lawfully sold, whether on the domestic market or on a foreign market, the IP rights to control the resale of the product are exhausted both domestically and internationally.

International exhaustion makes it possible to allow the parallel importation of products that are subject to IP rights. This means that it is legally possible to import and resell a product without the consent of the IP right holder, if that product was put on the market of the exporting country legally. This is of great importance to developing countries, as it enables their importers to buy products that are subject to IP rights, such as patented medicines, wherever they are cheapest and to resell them on their domestic markets. As noted by Correa:

> Parallel imports increase static efficiency, that is the allocation of products at the lowest possible price. Like the availability of compulsory licences, parallel imports provide an important device to discipline markets and to induce suppliers to commercialize their products on reasonable conditions. Parallel imports from compulsory licensees may provide in some instances (particularly after the TRIPS Agreement becomes fully operative in all countries) the only way to get access to low-priced medicines.[93]

As negotiators were deeply divided on the issue of exhaustion, the *TRIPS Agreement* does not mandate a particular approach to the exhaustion of IP rights. In Article 6 of the *TRIPS Agreement*, it expressly provides that nothing in this Agreement, aside from the obligations of national treatment and MFN treatment, shall be used to address the subject of exhaustion of IP rights. Thus Members are free to choose their own approach to this matter. However, they must apply their chosen approach in a non-discriminatory manner since Article 6 specifically subjects this issue to national treatment and MFN treatment obligations in Articles 3 and 4 of the *TRIPS Agreement*.

Due to concerns regarding the interpretation of Article 6 of the *TRIPS Agreement*, the Doha Declaration on the *TRIPS Agreement* and Public Health made clear that:

> The effect of the provisions in the TRIPS Agreement that are relevant to the exhaustion of intellectual property rights is to leave each member free to establish its own regime for such exhaustion without challenge, subject to the MFN and national treatment provisions of Articles 3 and 4.[94]

---

[93] C. M. Correa, 'The TRIPS Agreement and Developing Countries', in P. F. J. Macrory, A. E. Appleton and M. G. Plummer (eds.), *The World Trade Organization: Legal, Economic and Political Analysis* (Springer, 2005), 449.

[94] Doha Ministerial Conference, *Declaration on the TRIPS Agreement and Public Health*, adopted on 14 November 2001, WT/MIN(01)/DEC/2, dated 20 November 2001, para. 5(d).

While this statement does not add anything to the *TRIPS Agreement*, it does clarify that Members cannot be challenged under the *TRIPS Agreement* for allowing for the international exhaustion of IP rights, and therefore permitting parallel importation.[95] Note, however, that currently under the General Council Decision on waiving the obligations of Article 31(f) of the *TRIPS Agreement* Members are required to take reasonable measures to prevent re-exportation of essential medicines imported under the compulsory licence regime provided under the Waiver.

Questions and Assignments 8.6

Explain the concept of 'exhaustion' of IP rights. Why is the issue of exhaustion of IP rights important to international trade? Is the issue of exhaustion regulated by the *TRIPS Agreement*? Do Members have any obligations under the *TRIPS Agreement* with regard to their national rules on the exhaustion of IP rights? What is the relevance of the Doha Declaration on the *TRIPS Agreement* and Public Health for the issue of exhaustion of IP rights?

8.2.4. Substantive protection of intellectual property rights

Part II of the *TRIPS Agreement* contains the mandatory minimum standards of IP protection that Members are obliged to ensure in their territories. These standards concern, more specifically, the availability, scope and use of those IP rights covered by the *TRIPS Agreement*. As noted above, the *TRIPS Agreement* does not cover every category of IP, but only deals with those seven categories specified in Sections 1 to 7 of Part II of the Agreement.[96] As explained by the Panel in *EC – Trademarks and Geographical Indications*:

> Part II of the TRIPS Agreement contains minimum standards concerning the availability, scope and use of intellectual property rights. The first seven Sections of Part II contain standards relating to categories of intellectual property rights. Each Section sets out, as a minimum, the *subject matter* which is eligible for protection, the scope of the *rights conferred* by the relevant category of intellectual property and permitted *exceptions* to those rights.[97]

This section limits itself to an examination of four of these IP rights, namely copyright and related rights, trademarks, geographical indications (or 'GIs') and patents, i.e. the IP rights that have already been the subject of WTO dispute settlement.

---

[95] One of the main incentives for this clarification in the *Doha Declaration on the TRIPS Agreement and Public Health* was the fact that the US and large pharmaceutical firms challenged the South African Ministry of Health's authorisation of parallel importation of medicines under Section 15C of the South African Medicines and Related Substances Control Amendment Act, No. 90 of 1997. The challenge was withdrawn in 2001. See C. M. Correa, *Trade-Related Aspects of Intellectual Property Rights: A Commentary on the TRIPS Agreement* (Oxford University Press, 2007), 87–8.

[96] See the list of categories of IP dealt with in the *TRIPS Agreement*, set out above, p. 747.

[97] Panel Report, *EC – Trademarks and Geographical Indications (US)*, para. 7.598; Panel Report, *EC – Trademarks and Geographical Indications (Australia)*, para. 7.598.

8.2.4.1. *Copyright and related rights*[98]

Section 1 of Part II of the *TRIPS Agreement* deals with copyright and related rights. It incorporates and supplements the relevant provisions of the *Berne Convention*.[99] The coverage of copyright protection under the *TRIPS Agreement* is set out in Article 9.2 as follows:

> Copyright protection shall extend to expressions and not to ideas, procedures, methods of operation or mathematical concepts as such.

Thus copyright protection is only granted to the 'expression' of an idea, not the idea itself because ideas are seen as common goods that should be available to all, whereas the expression thereof may be subject to property rights. Frederick Abbott illustrated the idea–expression dichotomy with the following example:

> the idea of writing a book about wizards and witches probably is as old as book writing itself. Yet in the past several years, an author has earned a great deal of money by writing a popular series of children's books concerning a young man's coming of age in a school for wizards and witches. The author of this series cannot through copyright protection of her books prevent other authors from writing new books about wizards and witches. That would represent an attempt to control the use of an idea. What the author may be able to prevent is the use by others of a particular way of expressing an idea, such as describing specific individuals or the details in a storyline.[100]

Article 9.1 of the *TRIPS Agreement* expressly incorporates Articles 1 to 21 and the Appendix of the *Berne Convention*.[101] In Article 2, the *Berne Convention* contains a non-exhaustive list of 'copyrightable' works which covers 'every production in the literary, scientific and artistic domain'.[102] The copyright provisions of the *Berne Convention* are supplemented by the recognition in the *TRIPS Agreement* of new rights regarding the protection of computer programs and compilations of data and related rights of performers and broadcasters. However, under both the *Berne Convention* and the *TRIPS Agreement* every party is free to determine the *level* of originality or artistic creativity required for the work to be subject to copyright protection.

---

[98] This section draws to a large extent on P. Van den Bossche, *Free Trade and Culture: A Study of Relevant WTO Rules and Constraints on National Cultural Policy Measures* (Boekmanstudies, 2007), 126–34.

[99] Note that the Panel in *US – Article 110(5) Copyright Act* held: 'In the area of copyright, the Berne Convention and the TRIPS Agreement form the overall framework for multilateral protection. Most WTO Members are also parties to the Berne Convention. We recall that it is a general principle of interpretation to adopt the meaning that reconciles the texts of different treaties and avoids a conflict between them. Accordingly, one should avoid interpreting the TRIPS Agreement to mean something different than the Berne Convention except where this is explicitly provided for. This principle is in conformity with the public international law presumption against conflicts, which has been applied by WTO panels and the Appellate Body in a number of cases.' Panel Report, *US – Article 110(5) Copyright Act*, para. 6.66.

[100] F. Abbott, 'TRIPS', in *Course on Dispute Settlement in International Trade, Investment and Intellectual Property* (UNCTAD, 2003), 12–13.

[101] Note, however, that the rights under Article 6 *bis* of the *Berne Convention* have been expressly excluded. These relate to the 'moral rights' of authors, which refer to the inherent and inalienable rights of authors, aside from economic rights, such as the right to prevent distortion or modification of the author's work in a way that would negatively affect his/her reputation or honour. Under the *TRIPS Agreement*, Members are not obliged to extend protection to these 'moral rights'.

[102] Article 2(1) of the *Berne Convention*.

The *Berne Convention* provides that authors of literary and artistic works shall have the exclusive rights to make and authorise the translation[103] and the reproduction of their works in any form, which includes any sound or visual recording.[104] Authors of dramatic, dramatico-musical and musical works enjoy the right to authorise the public performance of their works, as well as any communication to the public thereof, including translations.[105] The broadcasting or the communication to the public, by wire, rebroadcasting, loudspeaker or any other analogous instrument is also regarded as an exclusive right of authors of literary and artistic works.[106] In 1998, the United States requested consultations with Greece because a significant number of television stations in Greece regularly broadcasted copyrighted motion pictures and television programmes without the authorisation of copyright owners and there appeared to be no effective provision or enforcement of remedies against copyright infringement in Greece.[107] The matter was resolved through consultations, as notified to the WTO in 2003.[108] Further, authors of literary works enjoy the exclusive right of authorising the public recitation of their works by any means or process and any communication thereof to the public.[109] In addition, the *Berne Convention* grants authors of literary or artistic works the right to authorise adaptations, arrangements and other alterations of their works,[110] as well as the cinematographic adaptation, the reproduction of these works, the public performance thereof and the communication to the public.[111] The author of a book, for example, would have to be asked before a producer of movies could adapt the story of the book into a screenplay.

With regard to authors of original works of art and original manuscripts, State parties to the *Berne Convention* have the option to grant them the right to an interest in any sale of the work subsequent to the first transfer by the author of the work, referred to as 'droit de suite'.[112] There is, however, no obligation on State parties to grant such a right. In contrast, Article 11 of the *TRIPS Agreement*, dealing with 'rental rights', contains a significant innovation – it requires the recognition of 'rental rights' in some cases. Specifically, Members to the *TRIPS Agreement* are required to permit authors (and their successors) of computer programs and cinematographic works to authorise or to prohibit the commercial rental to the public of originals or copies of their copyright works.[113] However, Article 11 exempts Members from this obligation in respect of cinematographic works unless such rental has led to widespread copying of the copyrighted works which materially impairs the right of reproduction of the author. This means that authors of cinematographic works can only request the right to authorise

---

[103] See Article 8 of the *Berne Convention*.   [104] See Article 9(1) and 9(3) of the *Berne Convention*.
[105] See Article 11 of the *Berne Convention*.   [106] See Article 11 *bis* of the *Berne Convention*.
[107] See Request for Consultations by the United States, *Greece – Enforcement of Intellectual Property Rights for Motion Pictures and Television Programmes*, WT/DS125/1, dated 7 May 1998.
[108] See Notification of Mutually Agreed Solution, *Greece – Enforcement of Intellectual Property Rights for Motion Pictures and Television Programmes*, WT/DS125/2, dated 26 March 2003.
[109] See Article 11 *ter* of the *Berne Convention*.   [110] See Article 12 of the *Berne Convention*.
[111] See Article 14 of the *Berne Convention*.   [112] See Article 14 *ter* of the *Berne Convention*.
[113] Note that this is limited to 'commercial rental' and therefore not-for-profit rentals are not covered by this obligation.

or prohibit the commercial rental of their works if they can prove that otherwise the copying of their work leads to the loss of considerable revenue. In respect of computer programs, this obligation does not apply to rentals where the program itself is not the essential object of the rental. Here one can think of the example of global positioning software included in rental cars.

Under Article 14 of the *TRIPS Agreement*, special rights apply to performers, producers of phonograms and broadcasting organisations. According to Article 14.1, performers have the exclusive right to authorise the fixation, i.e. recording or taping, of their unfixed performances, the reproduction of such fixation and/or the broadcasting/communication to the public of their live performance. For example, a music band performing in a concert has the right to authorise or prohibit the recording of its performance. Furthermore, producers of phonograms enjoy the right to authorise or prohibit the reproduction of their sound recordings.[114] In this respect, note that in 1997, the United States filed a complaint alleging that Ireland did not grant sufficient protection to producers and performers of sound recordings.[115] Ireland eventually amended its copyright law on various points to remedy this lack of protection.[116] According to Article 14.3 of the *TRIPS Agreement*, broadcasting organisations have the right to prohibit the refixation or rebroadcasting of broadcasts.

Copyright protection is usually not granted indefinitely, but is limited to a particular term of protection. According to Article 7.1 of the *Berne Convention*, incorporated by reference in the *TRIPS Agreement*, the minimum term of protection is the life of the author plus fifty years after his/her death. With regard to the duration of the protection of copyright held by a person other than a natural person, Article 12 of the *TRIPS Agreement* provides:

> Whenever the term of protection of a work, other than photographic work or a work of applied art, is calculated on a basis other than the life of a natural person, such term shall be *no less than* 50 years from the end of the calendar year of authorized publication, or, failing such authorized publication within 50 years for the making of the work, 50 years from the end of the calendar year of making.[117]
>
> [Emphasis added]

There are, however, exceptions to this basic rule. In the case of cinematographic works, the minimum term of protection, required by the *Berne Convention*, is fifty years after the work has been made available to the public with the author's consent, or failing such an event, fifty years after the making.[118] The term of protection for performers and producers of phonograms shall last at least fifty years from the end of the year in which the fixation was

---

[114] See Article 14.2 of the *TRIPS Agreement*.
[115] See A. B. Zampetti, 'WTO Rules in the Audio-Visual Sector', *HEEA Hamburg Report 229*, 24.
[116] See Complaints by the United States, *European Communities and Ireland – Measures Affecting the Grant of Copyright and Neighbouring Rights*, WT/DS82/1, WT/DS115/1 and WT/DS82/3, WT/DS 115/3, dated 22 May 1997.
[117] This provision solves the problem that arose under the *Berne Convention* with regard to the term of protection in countries which do not recognise legal persons as 'authors'. It provides for the term of protection where this is calculated 'on a basis other than the life of a natural person'.
[118] See Article 7(2) of the *Berne Convention*.

made or the performance took place.[119] Fewer than fifty years of protection are required for three categories of works. Article 7(4) of the *Berne Convention* specifies that photographic works and works of applied art shall be protected for at least twenty-five years from the making of such a work. Article 14.5, second sentence, of the *TRIPS Agreement* requires that broadcasting organisations be granted a minimum term of protection of twenty years from the year in which the broadcast took place. With regard to the duration of protection for performers and producers of sound recordings, in 1996 the United States and the European Communities filed a complaint against Japan at the WTO. According to the complainants, Japanese law only granted protection to foreign sound recordings produced on or after 1 January 1971, the date on which Japan first provided specialised protection for sound recordings under its copyright law.[120] After consultations, this issue was resolved one year later by amendments to the Japanese copyright law providing for protection to recordings produced between 1946 and 1971.[121]

Both the *Berne Convention* and the *TRIPS Agreement* set out limitations to the strict application of the rules regarding exclusive rights. In other words, both agreements provide for the possibility of using protected works in particular cases without having to obtain the authorisation of the owner of the copyright. There is, however, a difference between the limitations provided in the *Berne Convention* and those provided in the *TRIPS Agreement*. The *Berne Convention* allows for the free use of copyrighted works in special cases. The way in which countries make use of these, in part, optional free uses of works is a matter of cultural preferences and differs from country to country. These exceptions are then included in national law and therefore apply to individuals directly. The relevant provision in the *TRIPS Agreement* is Article 13, which is entitled 'Limitations and Exceptions' and states:

> Members shall confine limitations and exceptions to exclusive rights to certain special cases which do not conflict with a normal exploitation of the work and do not unreasonably prejudice the legitimate interests of the right holder.

Article 13 of the *TRIPS Agreement* constitutes a binding guideline for WTO Members. It lays down the requirements that exceptions and limitations to exclusive rights provided for in national IP law have to meet. The limitations contained in the *Berne Convention* and in the *TRIPS Agreement* will be dealt with in turn.

Pursuant to Article 2.8 of the *Berne Convention*, news of the day or mere items of press information are clearly excluded from copyright protection. The protection of some other categories of works is optional; thus every State party may decide to what extent it wishes to protect works of applied art (Article 2(7)),

---

[119] Article 14.5, first sentence, of the *TRIPS Agreement*.
[120] Complaint by the United States and the European Communities, *Japan – Measures Concerning Sound Recordings*, WT/DS28/1 and WT/DS42/1, dated 14 February 1996 and 4 June 1996.
[121] See Notification of a Mutually-Agreed Solution, *Japan – Measures Concerning Sound Recordings*, WT/DS28/4, dated 5 February 1997.

folklore (Article 15(4)) and political speeches (Article 2*bis* (1)), and to what extent lectures, addresses and other oral works may be reproduced by the press, broadcast and communicated to the public.[122] State parties to the *Berne Convention* also have the possibility to limit the protection of works to their being fixed in some material form.[123] For example, the protection of performances of a theatre play may be dependent on their being fixed in some form. Furthermore, the *Berne Convention* permits the free use of protected works in certain special cases (Article 9(2)); allows quotations and the use of works for teaching purposes (Article 10); permits the reproduction of newspaper or similar articles for the purpose of reporting current events (Article 10 *bis*); and allows ephemeral, i.e. brief and temporary, recordings (Article 11 *bis* (3)). Consequently, if a State party to the *Berne Convention* has permitted the reproduction of articles already published in newspapers or periodicals on current topics, a broadcaster established in that country can use these articles in its broadcastings.

The rationale behind Article 13 of the *TRIPS Agreement*, quoted above, is the search for the 'appropriate balance between the rights of creators and the public interest in access to copyrighted works'.[124] Too many limitations could reduce the economic rewards to right holders; however, certain exceptions are desired in order to advance the public good. While Article 13 undisputedly applies to the newly created rights set out in the *TRIPS Agreement*, the question arises whether it also creates a new exception to the existing rights in the *Berne Convention*. In *US – Section 110(5) Copyright Act*, the European Communities argued that Article 13 of the *TRIPS Agreement* applies only to those rights that were added to the *TRIPS Agreement*, and, therefore, not to those provisions of the *Berne Convention (1971)* that were incorporated into the *TRIPS Agreement* by reference.[125] The scope of application of Article 13 of the *TRIPS Agreement* was addressed by the Panel as follows:

> In our view, neither the express wording nor the context of Article 13 or any other provision of the TRIPS Agreement supports the interpretation that the scope of application of Article 13 is limited to the exclusive rights newly introduced under the TRIPS Agreement.[126]

According to the Panel, Article 13 of the *TRIPS Agreement* sets out three cumulative requirements for limitations and exceptions to exclusive rights. They must:

- be confined to certain special cases;
- not conflict with a normal exploitation of the work; and
- not unreasonably prejudice the legitimate interests of the right holder.[127]

The Panel emphasised from the outset that:

> Article 13 cannot have more than a narrow or limited operation. Its tenor, consistent as it is with the provisions of Article 9(2) of the Berne Convention (1971), discloses that it was

---

[122] See Article 2 *bis* (2) of the *Berne Convention*.   [123] See Article 2.2 of the *Berne Convention*.
[124] UNCTAD–ICTSD, *Resource Book on TRIPS and Development* (Cambridge University Press, 2005), 186.
[125] See Panel Report, *US – Section 110(5) Copyright Act*, para. 6.75.   [126] *Ibid.*, para. 6.80.
[127] See *ibid.*, para. 6.97.

not intended to provide for exceptions or limitations except for those of a limited nature.[128]

With regard to the *first requirement*, the Panel in *US – Section 110(5) Copyright Act* found that the concept of 'certain special cases' prohibits broad exceptions of general application. Limitations under Article 13 'should be clearly defined and should be narrow in scope and reach'.[129] Note that the *Berne Convention* provides for special exceptions that allow the unauthorised use of copyrighted material, as explained above.[130] These exceptions can be invoked and relied upon regardless of Article 13 of the *TRIPS Agreement*.[131]

The *second requirement* of Article 13 concerns the 'conflict with the normal exploitation of the work'. On a case-by-case basis, an exception would have to be analysed as to how a work is in fact exploited as well as whether the nature of the exploitation is permissible or desirable.[132] In *US – Section 110(5) Copyright Act*, the Panel referred in that regard to the empirical and normative component that has to be evaluated. According to the Panel, the commercial use of a work is not necessarily in conflict with the normal exploitation. Such a conflict would exist, however, if the use of a work 'enter[ed] into economic competition with the ways the right holders normally extract economic value from that right'.[133] For example, there might be a conflict if copies of copyrighted works were sold on the market and thus reduced sales opportunities for the copyright holder. If copies of copyrighted work would be used for research only, this would most likely not interfere with the normal use of the copyright by the right holder.

Finally, the *third requirement* of Article 13 requires that an exception shall not 'unreasonably prejudice the legitimate interests of the right holder'. The Panel in *US – Section 110(5) Copyright Act* ruled that 'legitimate interests' constitute both normative *and* legal positivist advantages of the right holder.[134] The normative concern for protecting interests could arguably refer to public policy interests such as free speech objectives, given that it is one of the objectives that underlie the protection of copyright. An 'unreasonable loss' to the copyright owner occurs if a limitation 'has the potential to cause an unreasonable loss of income to the copyright owner'.[135] This is most likely not the case if the exception is limited to teaching or research purposes. A heavily commercial use, however, would probably not pass this test.

In *US – Section 110(5) Copyright Act*, the European Communities complained about the so-called 'business exemption' and 'homestyle exemption' of Section 110(5) of the US Copyright Act. These exemptions permitted the playing of radio and television music in public places such as bars, shops and restaurants, without paying a royalty fee. The United States argued that both exemptions met the conditions of Article 13 of the *TRIPS Agreement*. The Panel found that the

---

[128] *Ibid.*   [129] See *ibid.*, paras. 6.111–6.112.   [130] See above, p. 766.
[131] In *US – Section 110(5) Copyright Act*, the Panel held that 'neither the express wording nor the context of Article 13 or any other provision of the TRIPS Agreement supports the interpretation that the scope of application of Article 13 is limited to the exclusive rights newly introduced under the TRIPS Agreement'. Panel Report, *US – Section 110(5) Copyright Act*, para. 6.80.   [132] See *ibid.*, para. 6.166.
[133] *Ibid.*, para. 6.183.   [134] See *ibid.*, para. 6.224.   [135] *Ibid.*, para. 6.229.

'business' exemption, which allowed the non-payment of royalties if the size of the establishment was limited to a certain square footage, did not comply with the requirements of Article 13. The Panel stated that, in fact, the substantial majority of the eating and drinking establishments were covered by the business exemption and therefore did not constitute a 'certain special case' to which Article 13 of the *TRIPS Agreement* refers.[136] With regard to the 'homestyle' exemption, allowing small restaurants and retail outlets to amplify music broadcasts by the use of 'homestyle' equipment (i.e. equipment of a kind commonly used in private homes) only, the Panel found that the conditions of Article 13 were fulfilled and that this exemption was therefore lawful.[137]

Questions and Assignments 8.7

What is the coverage of copyright protection under the *TRIPS Agreement*? What is the relationship between Article 9 of the *TRIPS Agreement* and Articles 1 to 21 and the Appendix of the *Berne Convention*? Is a Member free to determine the *level* of originality or artistic creativity required for a work to be subject to copyright protection? What do the exclusive rights granted to the copyright owner under the *TRIPS Agreement* refer to? What does the concept of '*droit de suite*' refer to? Which special rules exist for 'rental rights'? Which specific IP rights do performers and broadcasting organisations enjoy? What is the *minimum* or *maximum* period of time for which Members shall give copyright protection under the *TRIPS Agreement*? Do the *TRIPS Agreement* and the *Berne Convention* provide for the possibility of using protected works in particular cases without having to obtain the authorisation of the copyright owner? Discuss the three-tier test for the application of Article 13 of the *TRIPS Agreement*.

8.2.4.2. Trademarks

Section 2 of Part II of the *TRIPS Agreement* deals with trademarks. Trademarks are signs that aim to distinguish goods or services by communicating information about their source. These marks have economic value, as they can build up a reputation (for example, with regard to quality or reliability) and generate goodwill. Section 2 incorporates the rights of trademark owners set out in the *Paris Convention* into the *TRIPS Agreement* and strengthens them.[138]

Article 15.1 of the *TRIPS Agreement* defines the protectable subject matter, i.e. that capable of constituting a trademark and therefore eligible for registration as such, as follows:

> Any sign, or any combination of signs, capable of distinguishing the goods or services of one undertaking from those of other undertakings, *shall be capable of constituting a*

---

[136] See *ibid.*, para. 6.133.   [137] See *ibid.*, para. 6.159.
[138] For example, the protection of well-known trademarks in the *Paris Convention* is expanded.

> *trademark*. Such signs, in particular words including personal names, letters, numerals, figurative elements and combinations of colours as well as any combination of such signs, *shall be eligible for registration as trademarks*. Where signs are not inherently capable of distinguishing the relevant goods or services, Members may make registrability depend on distinctiveness acquired through use. Members may require, as a condition of registration, that signs be visually perceptible.
>
> [Emphasis added]

This provision covers both trademarks for goods and trademarks for services (otherwise known as 'service marks').[139] In principle, *distinctiveness* is required – whether inherent in the sign itself or acquired through use. As held by the Appellate Body in *US – Section 211 Appropriations Act*:

> If such signs are capable of distinguishing the goods or services of one undertaking from those of other undertakings, then they become *eligible for* registration as trademarks. To us, the title of Article 15.1 – 'Protectable Subject Matter' – indicates that Article 15.1 embodies a *definition* of what can constitute a trademark. WTO Members are obliged under Article 15.1 to ensure that those signs or combinations of signs that meet the distinctiveness criteria set forth in Article 15.1 – and are, thus, *capable of constituting a trademark* – are *eligible for registration* as trademarks within their domestic legislation.[140]

In *US – Section 211 Appropriations Act*, the European Communities argued that because Section 211(a)(1) of the US Appropriations Act prohibits registration of trademarks that are 'protectable', it is contrary to Article 15.1 of the *TRIPS Agreement* as this provision obliges Members to register trademarks that meet the requirements of Article 15.1.[141] As emphasised by the Appellate Body in this case, the fact that a sign falls under the definition of Article 15.1 means only that it is capable of registration, not that Members are obliged to register it. The Appellate Body stated:

> [I]n our view, the European Communities sees an obligation in Article 15.1 that is not there. Identifying certain signs that are *capable of* registration and imposing on WTO Members an obligation to make those signs *eligible for* registration in their domestic legislation is not the same as imposing on those Members an obligation to register *automatically* each and every sign or combination of signs that are *capable of* and *eligible for* registration under Article 15.1. This Article describes which trademarks are 'capable of' registration. It does not say that all trademarks that are capable of registration 'shall be registered'. This Article states that such signs or combinations of signs 'shall be *eligible* for registration' as trademarks. It does not say that they 'shall be registered'.[142]

Therefore, according to the Appellate Body, Members are free under Article 15.1 to lay down in their national legislation conditions for the registration of trademarks that do *not* address the definition of either 'protectable subject matter' or what constitutes a trademark.[143] In particular, Article 15.2 provides that Members

---

[139] While the *Paris Convention* obliges parties to protect service marks, it does not require them to provide for the registration of such marks. In this sense the *TRIPS Agreement* increases the protection of the *Paris Convention*.   [140] Appellate Body Report, *US – Section 211 Appropriations Act*, para. 154.

[141] See *ibid.*, para. 149.   [142] *Ibid.*, para.155.

[143] See *ibid.*, para. 156. The Appellate Body further pointed out that Article 6(1) of the *Paris Convention* allows parties to determine the conditions for filing and registration of trademarks in their national legislation. In the Appellate Body's view, Article 15.1 of the *TRIPS Agreement* limits the right of Members to determine

are permitted to deny trademark registration on 'other grounds' provided that they do not derogate from the *Paris Convention (1967)*. Such 'other grounds' are, as noted by the Appellate Body in *US – Section 211 Appropriations Act*, 'grounds *different from* those already mentioned in Article 15.1, such as lack of inherent distinctiveness of signs, lack of distinctiveness acquired through use, or lack of visual perceptibility'.[144] The Appellate Body stated in *US – Section 211 Appropriations Act*:

> The right of Members under Article 15.2 to deny registration of trademarks on grounds other than the failure to meet the distinctiveness requirements set forth in Article 15.1 implies that Members are not obliged to register any and every sign or combination of signs that meet those distinctiveness requirements.[145]

As stated above, Article 15.2 requires that the other grounds for denial of trademark registration 'do not derogate from the provisions of the Paris Convention (1967)'. The question thus arises to what extent, if at all, 'Members are permitted to deny trademark registration on grounds *other than those expressly provided for* in the *TRIPS Agreement* and the Paris Convention (1967).'[146] The Appellate Body in *US – Section 211 Appropriations Act* pointed out in this regard that Article 6(1) of the *Paris Convention (1967)* allows each party to determine conditions for the filing and registration of trademarks in its domestic legislation, provided that this is done consistently with the provisions of the *Paris Convention*.[147] These provisions set out internationally agreed grounds for denying registration,[148] as well as internationally agreed grounds for *not* denying registration.[149] Therefore, implicitly, Members have the right to refuse trademark registration under Article 6(1) of the *Paris Convention (1967)* on grounds other than those explicitly set out in the convention.[150] Thus, the Appellate Body found that:

> 'other grounds' for the denial of registration within the meaning of Article 15.2 of the *TRIPS Agreement* are not limited to grounds expressly provided for in the exceptions contained in the Paris Convention (1967) or the *TRIPS Agreement*.[151]

Therefore, Members are free to define in their own legislation the 'other grounds' for denying trademark registration, provided that they are not among those explicitly prohibited by the *Paris Convention (1967)*.

---

the conditions for filing and registration of trademarks under their domestic legislation pursuant to Article 6(1) *only* as it relates to the distinctiveness requirements enunciated in Article 15.1. See *ibid.*, para. 165.   [144] *Ibid.*, para. 158.

[145] *Ibid.*, para. 159. One of such 'other grounds' mentioned in Article 15.2 is, as pointed out by the Appellate Body in *US – Section 211 Appropriations Act*, made explicit in Article 15.3, first sentence, which permits Members to condition registration of a trademark on use. See *ibid.*, para. 164. See further below, pp. 771–2.

[146] *Ibid.*, para. 174.   [147] See *ibid.*, para. 175.

[148] For example, Article 6 *bis* of the *Paris Convention (1967)* requires the refusal of the registration of a well-known trademark by a third party and Article 6 *ter* covers prohibitions on the registration of State emblems, official hallmarks and emblems of international organisations. Further, Article 6 *quinquies* (B) permits the denial of registration to trademarks that are devoid of distinctive character or have become customary, that are contrary to morality or public order, or infringe rights acquired by third parties.

[149] See Appellate Body Report, *US – Section 211 Appropriations Act*, paras. 175–6. An example of a ground upon which registration may not be refused, mentioned by the Appellate Body, is that contained in Article 6(2) of the *Paris Convention (1967)*, which limits the legislative discretion of parties by providing that an application for registration by a national of a country of the Paris Union may not be refused on the ground that the national has not filed for registration or renewal in its country of origin. See *ibid.*, footnote 111 to para. 176.   [150] See *ibid.*, para. 176.

[151] *Ibid.*, para. 178. See also Panel Report, *US – Section 211 Appropriations Act*, para. 8.108.

A controversial issue in the negotiation of the *TRIPS Agreement* was whether *use* could be required as a condition for the registration of a trademark.[152] Article 15.3 of the *TRIPS Agreement* reflects the compromise reached: Members may make registrability, but not the filing of an application for registration, depend on use.[153] Pursuant to Article 15.4 of the *TRIPS Agreement*, the nature of the goods and services to which a trademark is applied may not be used as a ground to deny registration of the trademark.

In order to promote transparency, Article 15.5 of the *TRIPS Agreement* requires a Member to publish each trademark either before, or promptly after, it is registered. Members must provide an opportunity for petitions to cancel registration and *may* provide an opportunity for the registration of a trademark to be opposed.

Article 16 of the *TRIPS Agreement* sets out the exclusive rights conferred on trademark owners. It provides in paragraph 1 thereof:

> The owner of a registered trademark shall have the exclusive right to prevent all third parties not having the owner's consent from using in the course of trade identical or similar signs for goods or services which are identical or similar to those in respect of which the trademark is registered where such use would result in a likelihood of confusion. In case of the use of an identical sign for identical goods or services, a likelihood of confusion shall be presumed. The rights described above shall not prejudice any existing prior rights, nor shall they affect the possibility of Members making rights available on the basis of use.

Therefore, a Member may decide for itself whether it will not only provide these exclusive rights to owners of registered trademarks, but also confer these rights on the basis of use. It is also up to a Member to determine who the 'owner' of a trademark is. In *US − Section 211 Appropriations Act*, the Appellate Body agreed with the Panel that:

> Article 16.1 does not, in express terms, define how ownership of a registered trademark is to be determined. Article 16.1 confers exclusive rights on the 'owner', but Article 16.1 does not tell us who the 'owner' *is*.[154]

The European Communities' argument that under the *TRIPS Agreement*, the 'undertaking' that uses the trademark to distinguish its goods or services must be regarded as the owner of the trademark was rejected by the Appellate Body as having no basis in the text of the *TRIPS Agreement*.[155] It concluded that:

> neither Article 16.1 of the *TRIPS Agreement*, nor any other provision of either the *TRIPS Agreement* [or] the Paris Convention (1967), determines who owns or who does not own a trademark.[156]

---

[152] In Anglo-American legal systems, trademark rights can be created through use of the trademark without registration, and actual use is traditionally required as a condition for trademark registration. In civil law systems, trademarks are acquired through registration. See C. M. Correa, 'The TRIPS Agreement and Developing Countries', in P. F. J Macrory, A. E. Appleton and M. G. Plummer (eds.), *The World Trade Organization: Legal, Economic and Political Analysis* (Springer, 2005), 181.

[153] In addition, a Member may not refuse to register a trademark *solely* on the ground that the intended use has not taken place within three years of the filing of the application.

[154] Appellate Body Report, *US − Section 211 Appropriations Act*, para. 187.   [155] See *ibid.*, para. 194.

[156] *Ibid.*, para. 195.

A few elements of the rights conferred under Article 16.1 of the *TRIPS Agreement* deserve attention. Note that the exclusive right is limited to the right to use the trademark 'in the course of trade'. Non-commercial use of trademarks is therefore not covered. Also the owner is only granted the right to prevent the use of 'identical or similar signs' for goods or services that are 'identical or similar' to those in respect of which the trademark is registered. There is no definition of how similarity is to be determined, and this is left to Members to determine in their own legal systems. Note further that the exclusive right to prevent use of a trademark is only granted 'where such use would result in a likelihood of confusion'.[157]

In *EC – Trademarks and Geographical Indications*, the complainants alleged a violation of Article 16.1 of the *TRIPS Agreement* by the EC Regulation on the protection of geographical indications ('GIs') and designations of origin for agricultural products and foodstuffs. This regulation allowed for so-called 'coexistence', i.e. a legal regime under which a GI and a trademark can be used concurrently to some extent even though the use of one or both of them would otherwise infringe the rights conferred by the other. The complainants argued that the EC Regulation did not ensure that a trademark owner was able to prevent uses of GIs which would result in a 'likelihood of confusion' with a prior trademark.[158] The Panel examined whether Article 16.1 of the *TRIPS Agreement* requires Members to make available to trademark owners the right to prevent confusing uses of signs, even where the signs are used as GIs. It noted:

> Although each of the Sections in Part II provides for a different category of intellectual property, at times they refer to one another, as certain subject matter may be eligible for protection by more than one category of intellectual property. This is particularly apparent in the case of trademarks and GIs, both of which are, in general terms, forms of distinctive signs. The potential for overlap is expressly confirmed by Articles 22.3 and 23.2, which provide for the refusal or invalidation of the registration of a trademark which contains or consists of a GI.[159]

Examining the text of Article 16.1, the Panel noted that it contains no express or implied limitation with respect to GIs.[160] It held:

> The text of Article 16.1 stipulates that the right for which it provides is an 'exclusive' right. This must signify more than the fact that it is a right to 'exclude' others, since that notion is already captured in the use of the word 'prevent'. Rather, it indicates that this right belongs to the owner of the registered trademark alone, who may exercise it to prevent certain uses by 'all third parties' not having the owner's consent. The last sentence provides for an exception to that right, which is that it shall not prejudice any existing prior rights. Otherwise, the text of Article 16.1 is unqualified.[161]

---

[157] See C. M. Correa, 'The TRIPS Agreement and Developing Countries', in P. F. J Macrory, A. E. Appleton and M. G. Plummer (eds.), *The World Trade Organization: Legal, Economic and Political Analysis* (Springer, 2005), 186. Correa points out that Article 15.1 informs the meaning of 'confusion', i.e. confusion should be understood in relation to the capacity of the trademark to distinguish the similar/identical goods or services of one undertaking from those of another.

[158] See Panel Report, *EC – Trademarks and Geographical Indications (US)*, para. 7.512; Panel Report, *EC – Trademarks and Geographical Indications (Australia)*, para. 7.516.　[159] *Ibid.*, para. 7.599; *ibid.*, para. 7.599.

[160] See *ibid.*, paras. 7.601 and 7.603; *ibid.*, paras. 7.601 and 7.603.　[161] *Ibid.*, para. 7.602; *ibid.*, para. 7.602.

Therefore the trademark owner has the exclusive right to prevent use of the trademark by all third parties, also GI holders, without the owner's consent.

Articles 16.2 and 16.3 of the *TRIPS Agreement* extend the protection of Article 6 *bis* of the *Paris Convention* in respect of 'well-known' trademarks on identical or similar goods to include, respectively:

- 'well-known' trademarks on identical or similar *services*; and
- 'well-known' trademarks on goods or services that are *not similar* to those in respect of which a trademark is registered.

To determine whether a trademark is 'well known', Members must take account of the knowledge of the trademark in the relevant sector of the public, including that resulting from the promotion of the trademark.[162] Note that the knowledge need not be present in the public at large, but it is sufficient if it is present in the 'relevant sector' (for example, software users in the banking sector). However, the level of knowledge required for a mark to be 'well known' is left to Members to determine for themselves within their own legal systems. The extension of protection to 'well known' trademarks on goods or services that are not similar to those in respect of which the trademark is registered is limited to situations where the use of the trademark in relation to those goods or services would 'indicate a connection' between them and the trademark owner and thereby damage the latter's interests.[163] This aims to prevent 'dilution' of a trademark, i.e. where the value of the trademark is diminished by it becoming associated with products that are, for example, of lesser quality.

The possibility to provide exceptions to trademark rights is contained in Article 17 of the *TRIPS Agreement*, which states:

> Members may provide limited exceptions to the rights conferred by a trademark, such as fair use of descriptive terms, provided that such exceptions take account of the legitimate interests of the owner of the trademark and of third parties.

Note that this provision does not create an exception itself – it only allows Members to do so. The possibility to make such exceptions is, however, explicitly subject to two requirements, as identified by the Panel in *EC – Trademarks and Geographical Indications*, namely:

- the exception must be limited; and
- the exception must satisfy the provision that 'such exceptions take account of the legitimate interests of the owner of the trademark and of third parties'.[164]

According to the Panel:

> These elements provide a useful framework for an assessment of the extent to which an exception curtails the right provided for in Article 16.1.[165]

---

[162] See Article 16.2 of the *TRIPS Agreement*.   [163] See Article 16.3 of the *TRIPS Agreement*.
[164] See *ibid.*, para. 7.648; *ibid.*, para. 7.648.   [165] *Ibid.*, para. 7.653; *ibid.*, para. 7.653.

With regard to the first requirement of Article 17 of the *TRIPS Agreement*, the Panel in *EC – Trademarks and Geographical Indications* agreed with the interpretation of the Panel in *Canada – Pharmaceutical Patents*, of the identical term of 'limited exceptions' in Article 30 of the *TRIPS Agreement*, that '[t]he word "exception" by itself connotes a limited derogation, one that does not undercut the body of rules from which it is made'.[166] The Panel in *EC – Trademarks and Geographical Indications* held:

> The addition of the word 'limited' emphasizes that the exception must be narrow and permit only a small diminution of rights. The limited exceptions apply 'to the rights conferred by a trademark'. They do not apply to the set of all trademarks or all trademark owners. Accordingly, the fact that it may affect only few trademarks or few trademark owners is irrelevant to the question whether an exception is limited. The issue is whether the exception to the *rights conferred by a trademark* is narrow.[167]

Finding that only one right, namely the exclusive right to prevent certain uses of a sign provided in Article 16.1, was conferred by the trademark at issue in this dispute, the Panel found it necessary to examine the exception of Article 17 'on an individual "per right" basis'.[168] According to the Panel:

> This is a legal assessment of the extent to which the exception curtails that right. There is no indication in the text of Article 17 that this involves an economic assessment, although economic impact can be taken into account in the proviso. In this regard, we note the absence of any reference to a 'normal exploitation' of the trademark in Article 17, and the absence of any reference in Section 2, to which Article 17 permits exceptions, to rights to exclude legitimate competition. Rather, they confer, *inter alia*, the right to prevent uses that would result in a likelihood of confusion, which can lead to the removal of products from sale where they are marketed using particular signs, but without otherwise restraining the manufacture, sale or importation of competing goods or services.[169]

The Panel held that the EC regulation at issue curtailed the trademark owner's right:

- 'in respect of certain goods but not all goods identical or similar to those in respect of which the trademark is registered';[170]
- 'against certain third parties, but not "all third parties" ';[171] and
- 'in respect of certain signs but not all signs identical or similar to the one protected as a trademark'.[172]

Therefore, the Panel found that the EC regulation at issue created a 'limited exception' within the meaning of Article 17 of the *TRIPS Agreement*.[173]

With regard to the second element of Article 17 of the *TRIPS Agreement*, namely that the limited exceptions must satisfy the proviso that 'such exceptions take account of the legitimate interests of the owner of the trademark and of third parties', the Panel in *EC – Trademarks and Geographical Indications* agreed

---

[166] Panel Report, *Canada – Pharmaceutical Patents*, para. 7.30.
[167] Panel Report, *EC – Trademarks and Geographical Indications (US)*, para. 7.650; Panel Report, *EC – Trademarks and Geographical Indications (Australia)*, para. 7.650.   [168] *Ibid.*, para. 7.651; *ibid.*, para. 7.651.
[169] *Ibid.*, para. 7.651; *ibid.*, para. 7.651.   [170] *Ibid.*, para. 7.655; *ibid.*, para. 7.655.
[171] *Ibid.*, para. 7.656; *ibid.*, para. 7.656.   [172] *Ibid.*, para. 7.657; *ibid.*, para. 7.657.
[173] See *ibid.*, para.7.661; *ibid.*, para. 7.661.

with the interpretation of the Panel in *Canada – Pharmaceutical Patents* of the term 'legitimate interests' of a patent owner and third parties in the context of Article 30 of the *TRIPS Agreement*.[174] The Panel in *Canada – Pharmaceutical Patents* held that the term must be defined as:

> a normative claim calling for protection of interests that are 'justifiable' in the sense that they are supported by relevant public policies or other social norms.[175]

With respect to the 'legitimate interests' of the trademark owner and third parties in the context of Article 17 of the *TRIPS Agreement*, the Panel in *EC – Trademarks and Geographical Indications* held:

> The TRIPS Agreement itself sets out a statement of what all WTO Members consider adequate standards and principles concerning trademark protection. Although it sets out standards for legal rights, it also provides guidance as to WTO Members' shared understandings of the policies and norms relevant to trademarks and, hence, what might be the legitimate interests of trademark owners. The function of trademarks can be understood by reference to Article 15.1 as distinguishing goods and services of undertakings in the course of trade. Every trademark owner has a legitimate interest in preserving the distinctiveness, or capacity to distinguish, of its trademark so that it can perform that function. This includes its interest in using its own trademark in connection with the relevant goods and services of its own and authorized undertakings. Taking account of that legitimate interest will also take account of the trademark owner's interest in the economic value of its mark arising from the reputation that it enjoys and the quality that it denotes.[176]

The Panel found that the EC regulation at issue took account of the trademark owner's rights in preserving the distinctiveness of its trademark in various ways. The Panel emphasised that the proviso to Article 17 requires only that exceptions '*take account*' of the legitimate interests of the owner of the trademark.[177] The Panel subsequently examined whether the EC regulation took account of the legitimate interests of third parties. The Panel identified as relevant third parties consumers and GI users[178] and determined that the interests of these third parties were taken into account in the EC regulation at issue.[179] Therefore, the Panel found the EC regulation at issue to be justified by Article 17 of the *TRIPS Agreement*.[180]

Unlike copyright, trademarks are protected for an unlimited period. Article 18 of the *TRIPS Agreement* provides that trademarks 'shall be renewable indefinitely'. Although Members may require that trademark registrations be renewed, this may not be more often than once every seven years. However, a trademark registration may be cancelled if a Member requires use to maintain a registration, as permitted by Article 19 of the *TRIPS Agreement*. Such a requirement may lead to the

---

[174] *Ibid.*, para. 7.663; *ibid.*, para. 7.663.   [175] Panel Report, *Canada – Pharmaceutical Patents*, para. 7.69.
[176] Panel Report, *EC – Trademarks and Geographical Indications (US)*, para. 7.664; Panel Report, *EC – Trademarks and Geographical Indications (Australia)*, para. 7.664.
[177] There is no reference to 'unreasonabl[e] prejudice' to those interests, unlike the provisos in Articles 13, 26.2 and 30 of the *TRIPS Agreement* and Article 9(2) of the *Berne Convention (1971)* as incorporated by Article 9.1 of the *TRIPS Agreement*, suggesting that a lesser standard of regard for the legitimate interests of the owner of the trademark is required. See *ibid.*, para. 7.671; *ibid.*, para. 7.671.
[178] See *ibid.*, paras. 7.676, 7.680 and 7.681; *ibid.*, paras. 7.675 and 7.679.
[179] See *ibid.*, para. 7.686; *ibid.*, para. 7.684.   [180] See *ibid.*, para. 7.688; *ibid.*, para. 7.686.

cancellation of the trademark registration only after an uninterrupted period of at least three years, and not if the non-use was for valid reasons due to obstacles to such use.[181] Valid reasons are, for example, import restrictions or other government requirements for goods or services protected by the trademark.[182]

Article 20 prohibits unjustifiable encumbrances on trademarks by means of 'special requirements' such as use with another trademark or in a special form or manner that is detrimental to its capability to distinguish the goods or services of one undertaking from those of another. In *Indonesia – Autos*, the United States claimed that the Indonesian National Car Programme violated Article 20 as:

- a foreign company that enters into an arrangement with a Pioneer company would be encumbered in using the trademark that it used elsewhere for the model that was adopted by the National Car Programme; and
- non-Indonesian car companies are encumbered in using their trademarks in Indonesia due to the competitive disadvantage they are placed at because the cars produced under the National Car Programme bearing the Indonesian trademark benefit from tariff, subsidy and other benefits flowing from that programme.[183]

The Panel disagreed, holding in this regard:

> if a foreign company enters into an arrangement with a Pioneer company it does so voluntarily and in the knowledge of any consequent implications for its ability to use any pre-existing trademark. In these circumstances, we do not consider the provisions of the National Car Programme as they relate to trademarks can be construed as 'requirements', in the sense of Article 20.
> . . . Moreover, the United States has not explained to our satisfaction how the ineligibility for benefits accruing under the National Car Programme could constitute 'requirements' imposed on foreign trademark holders, in the sense of Article 20 of the TRIPS Agreement.[184]

Note that it is only 'unjustifiable' encumbrances that are caught by this prohibition. A requirement such as that a mandatory health warning must be displayed prominently on packets of cigarettes, thereby reducing the permissible size of the trademark, could be regarded as justified by its public health function.[185]

Finally, note that under Article 21 of the *TRIPS Agreement*, Members are free to determine conditions on the licensing and assignment of trademarks. The only limitations on this freedom, also contained in Article 21, are:

---

[181] Article 5C(1) of the *Paris Convention (1967)* also allows the cancellation of a trademark for non-use after a reasonable period if the trademark holder does not justify his inaction. However, the reasonable period is not specified. In this regard the *TRIPS Agreement* supplements the *Paris Convention*.

[182] Note that the use of a trademark by someone other than the owner will be recognised as 'use' of the trademark for purposes of maintaining the registration if such use is subject to the control of the trademark owner. See Article 19.2 of the *TRIPS Agreement*.

[183] See Panel Report, *Indonesia – Autos*, paras. 14.277–14.278. Note that these claims were made in the context of a claim of violation of Article 3 of the *TRIPS Agreement*.   [184] *Ibid.*

[185] See C. M. Correa, 'The TRIPS Agreement and Developing Countries', in P. F. J Macrory, A. E. Appleton and M. G. Plummer (eds.), *The World Trade Organization: Legal, Economic and Political Analysis* (Springer, 2005), 200.

- the prohibition on compulsory licensing of trademarks;[186] and
- the requirement that Members allow the transfer of a trademark with or without the transfer of the business to which it belongs.

Questions and Assignments 8.8

What are 'trademarks'? Are Members free under Article 15.1 of the *TRIPS Agreement* to lay down in their national legislation conditions for the registration of trademarks and the grounds for denying such registration? Can a Member refuse to register a trademark that is not used? What, pursuant to the *TRIPS Agreement*, must fall within the exclusive rights conferred on trademark owners? Are there special rules on the protection of 'well-known' trademarks? Can Members limit the rights conferred to trademark owners? Is there a *minimum* or *maximum* period of time for which Members shall give protection to trademarks under the *TRIPS Agreement*? Can Members freely determine the conditions on the licensing and assignment of trademarks under the *TRIPS Agreement*?

8.2.4.3. *Geographical indications*

The quality, characteristics or reputation of a product are sometimes determined by where it comes from, i.e. its geographical origin. Geographical indications (such as 'Champagne', 'Parma' ham, 'Bohemian' crystal, 'Orkney' beef, 'Tequila' and 'Gorgonzola') are place names that are used to identify the products that originate in these places and have the characteristics associated with that place. The provision of protection to geographical indications was a contentious issue in the Uruguay Round negotiations. Section 3 of Part II of the *TRIPS Agreement* reflects the compromise reached.

Geographical indications ('GIs') are defined in Article 22.1 of the *TRIPS Agreement* as:

> indications which identify a good as originating in the territory of a Member, or a region or locality in that territory, where a given quality, reputation or other characteristic of the good is *essentially attributable to its geographical origin.*
>
> [Emphasis added]

In terms of this definition, it is clear that in order to have a GI protected it is not necessary to show that the product coming from that geographical area is *in fact* better or different from a similar product that originates elsewhere. It may also be established that a particular reputation or goodwill has been built in a particular place with regard to that product.[187] The geographical location

---

[186] Correa notes that compulsory licences have rarely been granted in the field of trademarks, so Article 21 is merely preventative of an unlikely future event. See *ibid.*, 202.

[187] It may be harder to prove that a particular reputation is essentially attributable to a geographical location, than that a product characteristic or the product quality are so attributable. It will be up to the Member in which GI protection is sought to determine whether the conditions for acquiring a GI are met, within the limits set by Article 22.1. See C. M. Correa, *Trade-Related Aspects of Intellectual Property Rights: A Commentary on the TRIPS Agreement* (Oxford University Press, 2007), 220.

referred to in the GI could be a country (for example 'Greek' yoghurt), but could also be a region or locality (for example 'Idaho' potatoes or 'Newcastle' brown ale). The 'indication' used is not required to be the place name itself, but may also be a name or symbol that is understood by the public as identifying a specific geographical origin (for example 'Basmati' rice).[188] Note that a geographical indication is *not* the same as an indication of origin, such as 'Made in Taiwan', which only specifies the place where the product was produced, without indicating any associated product attributes. Different from trademarks, which identify the *undertaking* offering the product or service on the market, GIs indicate only the *place* where the product is produced, therefore several undertakings may use the same GI.[189]

The protection of geographical indications that is required under the *TRIPS Agreement* is specified in two provisions:

- Article 22.2 of the *TRIPS Agreement* sets out the standard level of GI protection to be accorded to *all* products. This protection focuses on preventing misuse of GIs so as to mislead the public or constitute unfair competition.
- Article 23 of the *TRIPS Agreement* provides a higher or enhanced level of GI protection for *wines and spirits*. This protection must be provided even if misuse would not mislead the public.

These two levels of protection will now be discussed in more detail.

Pursuant to Article 22.2 of the *TRIPS Agreement*, Members must protect GIs for all products by providing interested parties with the 'legal means' to prevent:

- use of any means in the designation or presentation of the good that misleads the public as to the geographical origin of the good; and
- use that constitutes unfair competition under Article 10 *bis* of the *Paris Convention (1967)*.

The form that these 'legal means' take is left up to the Member involved.[190] Pursuant to Article 22.4 of the *TRIPS Agreement*, the protection against use of a GI that 'misleads the public' is extended to the use of 'homonymous' GIs. This prevents the use of a GI that is literally true as to the origin of the product, but falsely represents to the public that the product originates in another place with the same name. For example, the GI 'Champagne', which indicates a sparking wine originating in the French locality of Champagne, may not be used by producers in the Swiss locality of Champagne, if it is shown that the public would believe that the product originates in French Champagne.

---

[188] For example, 'Ouzo' is associated with Greece and 'Grappa' with Italy, and symbols such as the Eiffel Tower and the Matterhorn are widely associated with France and Switzerland respectively. See *ibid.*, 212, footnotes 12 and 13.

[189] As several undertakings may be producing the relevant product in the identified geographical location, the GI may be combined with a trademark in order to identify a particular producer within the geographical area. See *ibid.*, 210.

[190] Note that Members are obliged, under Article 22.3 of the *TRIPS Agreement*, to refuse or to invalidate trademark registration where the trademark is a GI with respect to goods not originating in the indicated territory, if the use of the GI in the trademark is of such a nature as to mislead the public as to the true place of origin of the product.

To avoid the use of a GI that 'misleads the public', producers may use additions such as 'imitation', 'like' or 'type' (for example, 'Roquefort-type' cheese or 'Delft-style' pottery). It will be up to the authorities in the Member where GI protection is provided to determine if public confusion is effectively avoided in this way.[191]

In *EC – Trademarks and Geographical Indications*, the complainant, the United States, alleged a violation of Article 22.2 of the *TRIPS Agreement* by the EC regulation at issue for three reasons:

- because it did not provide interested parties in other WTO Members which did not satisfy the *equivalence and reciprocity conditions*, the legal means to protect their GIs on a uniform basis throughout the territory of the European Communities;[192]
- because under the procedure for verification and transmission of applications, interested parties in other WTO Members had to depend on their respective governments to intercede on their behalf;[193] and
- because the possibilities for objections to the registration of GIs were limited.

The Panel examined the nature of the obligation contained in Article 22.2 of the *TRIPS Agreement* and held:

> Article 22.2 of the TRIPS Agreement imposes an obligation on Members. The obligation is owed to other Members, as the TRIPS Agreement creates rights and obligations between WTO Members. In this regard, it can be noted that the dispute settlement system of the WTO serves, *inter alia* to preserve the rights and obligations of *Members* under the covered agreements. However, a particularity of the TRIPS Agreement is that the assessment of the conformity of measures with Members' obligations generally requires an assessment of the manner in which they confer rights or protection on private parties.[194]
>
> [Emphasis added]

Thus, in order to establish whether the European Communities had implemented the obligations it owed to other Members under Article 22.2, the Panel had to examine whether it had provided the 'legal means' required by that provision for interested parties who were nationals of other Members.[195] Although the Panel readily found that the EC regulation itself did not provide the required 'legal means' specified in Article 22.2 of the *TRIPS Agreement*,[196] it noted that the complainant had chosen not to address the other measures, outside the EC regulation, by means of which the European Communities submitted that it implemented its obligations (for example, the EC Directives on foodstuffs labelling and misleading advertising and implementing legislation of the EU Member States).[197] Therefore the complainant had not made a *prima facie* case

---

[191] See C. M. Correa, *Trade-Related Aspects of Intellectual Property Rights: A Commentary on the TRIPS Agreement* (Oxford University Press, 2007), 231.
[192] See Panel Report, *EC – Trademarks and Geographical Indications (US)*, para. 7.730.   [193] See *ibid.*, para. 7.731.
[194] *Ibid.*, para. 7.741.   [195] See *ibid.*, para. 7.743.   [196] See *ibid.*, para. 7.745.
[197] See *ibid.*, paras. 7.745–7.747. The Panel pointed out that under Article 1.1 of the *TRIPS Agreement*, the European Communities is free to determine the appropriate method of implementing the provisions of the *TRIPS Agreement* within its own legal system and was therefore not obliged to ensure that the particular regulation at issue implemented Article 22.2 where it had other measures that did so.

that the European Communities had not complied with its obligations under Article 22.2.[198] With regard to the arguments related to the possibilities for objection, the Panel noted that, unlike Article 15.5 of the *TRIPS Agreement* which provides a right for objection to trademark registration, Article 22.2 of the *TRIPS Agreement* does not provide for a right of objection to the registration of a GI.[199] Therefore these claims of inconsistency with Article 22.2 were also declared unfounded.[200]

The enhanced GI protection for wines and spirits provided in Article 23 of the *TRIPS Agreement* entails that Members must provide interested parties with legal means to prevent the use of a GI identifying a wine or a spirit for a wine or a spirit not originating in the place indicated by the GI in question. This is the case even if the use of these GIs would *not* cause the public to be misled or lead to unfair competition. According to Article 23.1 of the *TRIPS Agreement*, a Member must make it possible for the holder of a GI to prevent the use of the GI on the non-originating product even if confusion is prevented by an indication of the true origin of the product, the translation of the GI or the use of terms such as 'like' or 'type' (for example 'Champagne-like' or 'Bordeaux-type') to distinguish products originating outside the place attributed to the GI.[201] Article 23.3 of the *TRIPS Agreement* deals with the use of homonymous GIs for wines (not for spirits) whose use is not misleading under Article 22.4.[202] It provides that both GIs shall be protected and the Member concerned must determine the practical conditions under which the homonymous GIs will be differentiated from each other. Such conditions must ensure that the producers concerned are treated equitably and that consumers are not misled.

Under Article 24.4 of the *TRIPS Agreement*, Members agree to negotiate towards increasing the protection of individual GIs under Article 23. The expansion of coverage of the higher level of protection of Article 23 of the *TRIPS Agreement* beyond GIs for wine and spirits to other products is on the agenda of the Doha Development Round, as part of the implementation issues.[203] However, deep divisions remain between Members on this issue. Some Members advocate the extension of the higher level of protection of Article 23 to other products as a way to differentiate their products more effectively from those of their competitors, and to prevent other Members from 'usurping' their GIs. Others see the protection reflected in Article 22 as sufficient and are concerned that added protection would restrict legitimate marketing practices. They also point out that since a number of Members have received many immigrants who have brought with them their cultural traditions, including names and terms, it would be culturally insensitive for Members, predominantly those from which

---

[198] See *ibid.*, para. 7.751. [199] See *ibid.*, para. 7.754. [200] See *ibid.*, para. 7.757.
[201] With regard to footnote 4 dealing with the enforcement of the protection, see below, pp. 793–8.
[202] For example, 'Rioja' wine is produced in both Spain and Argentina. See D. Gervais, *The TRIPS Agreement: Drafting History and Analysis* (Sweet and Maxwell, 2003), 197, footnote 60.
[203] See Ministerial Conference, *Doha Ministerial Declaration*, WT/MIN(01)/DEC/1, dated 20 November 2001, para. 18.

these people had migrated, to try to claim back terms that had been used for decades without being contested.[204]

Article 23.4 of the *TRIPS Agreement* provides for negotiations in the Council for TRIPS to establish a multilateral system of notification and registration of geographical indications for wines in those Members participating in the system, in order to facilitate the protection of GIs for wines. Although this provision refers only to wines, paragraph 18 of the Doha Ministerial Declaration provides for negotiations on the establishment of a multilateral system of notification and registration of geographical indications for wines and spirits, with a view to completing the work started in the Council for TRIPS on the implementation of Article 23.4.[205] These negotiations were to be completed by the Fifth Session of the Ministerial Conference, i.e. the Cancún Session in 2003, but due to strongly diverging positions of Members, no agreement has been reached on such a system to date. Key issues on which disagreement exist are: what legal effect, if any, registration of a GI in such a 'multilateral register' should be required to be given in Members; to what extent, if at all, this effect should apply to Members that choose not to participate in the system; and whether the administrative and financial costs of implementing such a system for individual governments would outweigh the possible benefits.[206]

In order to prevent the provisions on GI protection in the *TRIPS Agreement* from leading to a reduction in the protection already provided by some Members, Article 24.3 of the *TRIPS Agreement* contains an 'anti-rollback' provision, which states:

> In implementing this Section, a Member shall not diminish the protection of geographical indications that existed in that Member immediately prior to the date of entry into force of the WTO Agreement.

The obligation in Article 24.3 of the *TRIPS Agreement* applies indefinitely and prohibits any reduction in the level of protection for GIs, even if the protection remains above the standards mandated by the *TRIPS Agreement*.[207]

The protection of GIs required by the *TRIPS Agreement* is not unlimited. Permissible exceptions to GIs protection are set out in paragraphs 4 to 9 of Article 24 of the *TRIPS Agreement*. Note, for example, that Article 24.5 of the *TRIPS Agreement* prevents the protection of GIs from prejudicing prior trademark rights that were acquired in good faith. Under this exception, the fact that a trademark is identical with or similar to a GI shall not prejudice the eligibility for or validity of the registration of the trademark if it has been applied for, registered or acquired through use, in good faith, either:

---

[204] On the positions taken by Members in these negotiations, see Trade Negotiations Committee, *Issues Related to the Extension of the Protection of Geographical Indications Provided for in Article 23 of the TRIPS Agreement to Products Other Than Wines and Spirits. Compilation of Issues Raised and Views Expressed. Note by the Secretariat*, TN/C/W/25, WT/GC/W/546, dated 18 May 2005, para. 14.

[205] See Ministerial Conference, *Doha Ministerial Declaration*, WT/MIN(01)/DEC/1, dated 20 November 2001, para. 18.

[206] The WTO Secretariat has made a useful compilation of the proposals and comments received on this issue. See Council for TRIPS, Special Session, *Side-by-Side Presentation of Proposals. Compilation of Points Raised and Views Expressed on the Proposals. Note by the Secretariat*, TN/IP/W/12, dated 4 May 2007.

[207] Note the difference with Article 65 of the *TRIPS Agreement*, discussed below. See below, p. 802.

- before the provisions of Section 3 of Part II became applicable in the Member concerned (i.e. before expiry of the applicable transitional period); or
- before the GI was protected in its country of origin.[208]

An exception to the requirements for GI protection with regard to wines and spirits is contained in Article 24.4 of the *TRIPS Agreement*. It provides that a Member may allow continued and similar use of a geographical indication of another Member for wines or spirits by its nationals or domiciliaries who have used that GI continuously and with regard to the same goods or services in its territory, where the prior continuous use was either:

- for at least ten years preceding 15 April 1994; or
- in good faith preceding that date.

As a final example of an exception to GI protection, consider Article 24.6 of the *TRIPS Agreement*. Pursuant to Article 24.6, a Member is not obliged to provide protection to a GI of another Member that is identical with a term that is customary in common language as the common name for goods or services in its territory. This takes account of the fact that some GIs have become common terms for particular products (for example, champagne).

Note that Members availing themselves of the use of the exceptions provided for in Article 24 of the *TRIPS Agreement* must be willing to enter into negotiations under Article 24.1 about their continued application to individual geographical indications.

Questions and Assignments 8.9

What are 'geographical indications'? Are Members required to give protection to geographical indications under the *TRIPS Agreement*? Is Argentina under Article 22.2 of the *TRIPS Agreement* required to prohibit the marketing in Argentina of a domestically produced cheese identified on the label as a 'Roquefort-type' cheese? Is France allowed to prohibit the marketing of this product in France? Is your answer to the previous two questions the same if the product concerned is a 'Bordeaux-type' wine? Discuss at least three exceptions to GI protection permissible under the *TRIPS Agreement*.

8.2.4.4. Patents

Minimum requirements for patent protection are set out in Section 5 of Part II of the *TRIPS Agreement*. Article 27.1 of the *TRIPS Agreement* defines the patentable subject matter as follows:

---

[208] For an analysis of the scope and nature of Article 24.5 of the *TRIPS Agreement* as well as possible conflicts between the protection of GIs and trademarks, see Panel Report, *EC – Trademarks and Geographical Indications (US)*, paras. 7.604–7.625; Panel Report, *EC – Trademarks and Geographical Indications (Australia)*, paras. 7.604–7.625.

> Subject to the provisions of paragraphs 2 and 3, patents shall be available for any inventions, whether products or processes, in all fields of technology, provided that they are new, involve an inventive step and are capable of industrial application. Subject to paragraph 4 of Article 65, paragraph 8 of Article 70 and paragraph 3 of this Article, patents shall be available and patent rights enjoyable without discrimination as to the place of invention, the field of technology and whether products are imported or locally produced.

Thus, patent protection is extended to any invention in any field, provided three requirements are met:

- the invention is new;
- it involves an inventive step; and
- it is capable of industrial application.[209]

Note, in addition, the non-discrimination obligation in the last sentence of Article 27.1 of the *TRIPS Agreement*, which prohibits discrimination regarding the availability and enjoyment of patent rights based on:

- the place of invention;
- the field of technology; and
- whether products are imported or locally produced.

Discrimination based on the nationality of the patent owner is not mentioned here, as it is addressed in Articles 3 and 4 of the *TRIPS Agreement*. In *Canada – Pharmaceutical Patents*, the European Communities claimed that Canada's regulatory review exception constituted discrimination regarding the enjoyment of patent rights based on the field of technology. The European Communities contended that there was less protection in the field of pharmacology than in other fields of technology. On the evidence before it, the Panel found, however, that the European Communities failed to prove that the adverse effects of the regulatory review exemption were limited to the pharmaceutical industry, or that the objective indications of purpose demonstrated that the purpose was to impose disadvantages on pharmaceutical patents in particular. The Panel in *Canada – Pharmaceutical Patents* thus found no violation of Article 27.1 of the *TRIPS Agreement*.[210]

Articles 27.2 and 27.3 of the *TRIPS Agreement* allow Members to exclude certain inventions from patentability. Article 27.2 provides that:

> Members may exclude from patentability inventions, the prevention within their territory of the commercial exploitation of which is necessary to protect ordre public or morality, including to protect human, animal or plant life or health or to avoid serious prejudice to the environment, provided that such exclusion is not made merely because the exploitation is prohibited by their domestic law.

---

[209] The three criteria for patentability are not defined in the *TRIPS Agreement*. Although these criteria are common to most national patent systems, the meaning of each is subject to different interpretations in different national legal systems.

[210] See Panel Report, *Canada – Pharmaceutical Patents*, para. 7.105. Note that the Panel emphasised in a footnote that it had *not* addressed the question (raised by third parties) 'whether measures that are limited to a particular area of technology – *de jure* or *de facto* – are necessarily "discriminatory" by virtue of that fact alone, or whether under certain circumstances they may be justified as special measures needed to restore equality of treatment to the area of technology in question'. This was unnecessary for the Panel to address on the record before the Panel. *Ibid.*, footnote 439 to para. 7.105.

It is likely that, in line with case law on the concept of public order and public morality under the GATS, this exception will take into account national perceptions that differ across Members. Note that health and the environment are illustrative examples only, as indicated by the word 'including', and that this is therefore not a closed list. The link between the use of the exception and the prevention of commercial exploitation of the invention in the territory of the Member aims to ensure that this exception is not used to deny patent protection to an invention on public order or morality grounds, while the invention itself is in fact exploited commercially in the Member.[211]

Article 27.3 of the *TRIPS Agreement* allows the exclusion from patentability of:

- diagnostic, therapeutic and surgical methods for the treatment of humans or animals;
- plants and animals other than micro-organisms, and essentially biological processes for the production of plants or animals other than non-biological and microbiological processes.[212]

The exclusive rights conferred on patent owners are set out in Article 28 of the *TRIPS Agreement*. Article 28.1 of the *TRIPS Agreement* provides:

> A patent shall confer on its owner the following exclusive rights:
>
> (a) where the subject matter of a patent is a product, to prevent third parties not having the owner's consent from the acts of: making, using, offering for sale, selling, or importing[213] for these purposes that product;
> (b) where the subject matter of a patent is a process, to prevent third parties not having the owner's consent from the act of using the process, and from the acts of: using, offering for sale, selling, or importing for these purposes at least the product obtained directly by that process.

Article 28.2 of the *TRIPS Agreement* additionally gives patent owners the right to assign, or transfer by succession, the patent and to conclude licensing contracts.

Patent applications are usually subject to conditions. In terms of Article 29.1 of the *TRIPS Agreement*, Members must require patent applicants to disclose the invention 'in a manner sufficiently clear and complete' for a person skilled in the art to be able to carry out the invention. Members may also require the applicant to disclose the best way of carrying out the invention known to the inventor. In addition, Members may require the applicant to provide information about his/her foreign applications for or grants of patents.[214]

---

[211] There is a debate, however, as to whether a requirement can be read into this provision that a ban on the commercialisation of the invention be imposed where patentability is excluded under this exception. On its wording, Article 27.2 requires only the *necessity* of such a ban. See C. M. Correa, *Trade-Related Aspects of Intellectual Property Rights: A Commentary on the TRIPS Agreement* (Oxford University Press, 2007), 291.

[212] Note in respect of this exclusion that Members are, however, required to provide for the protection of plant *varieties* either by patents or by an 'effective *sui generis* system', or by any combination thereof. See Article 27.3(b), second sentence, of the *TRIPS Agreement*.

[213] Footnote 6 to the *TRIPS Agreement* notes that '[t]his right, like all other rights conferred under this Agreement in respect of the use, sale, importation or other distribution of goods, is subject to the provisions of Article 6'. Article 6 provides that nothing in the *TRIPS Agreement* shall be used to address the issue of exhaustion of IP rights: see above, p. 761.   [214] See Article 29.2 of the *TRIPS Agreement*.

There are two provisions in the *TRIPS Agreement* allowing for exceptions to the exclusive rights conferred by a patent:

- the 'limited exceptions' provision of Article 30 of the *TRIPS Agreement*; and
- the 'compulsory licences' provision of Article 31 of the *TRIPS Agreement*.

Article 30 of the *TRIPS Agreement* states:

> Members may provide limited exceptions to the exclusive rights conferred by a patent, provided that such exceptions do not unreasonably conflict with the normal exploitation of the patent and do not unreasonably prejudice the legitimate interests of the patent owner, taking account of the legitimate interests of third parties.

In *Canada – Pharmaceutical Patents*, the European Communities challenged the regulatory review and stockpiling exceptions in Canada's patent law. Canada conceded that these provisions were inconsistent with Article 28.1 of the *TRIPS Agreement*, which grants exclusive rights to patent holders.[215] However, it relied on the exception of Article 30 of the *TRIPS Agreement* to justify its measures, and argued that the objectives and principles of Articles 7 and 8 of the *TRIPS Agreement* should inform the interpretation of Article 30. The Panel in *Canada – Pharmaceutical Patents* identified three cumulative requirements that must be met to qualify for an exception under Article 30:

- the exception must be 'limited';
- the exception must not 'unreasonably conflict with a normal exploitation of the patent'; and
- the exception must not 'unreasonably prejudice the legitimate interests of the patent owner, taking account of the legitimate interests of third parties'.[216]

Turning to the first requirement of Article 30 of the *TRIPS Agreement*, namely that the exception be 'limited', the Panel chose a narrow interpretation, holding:

> Although the word itself can have both broad and narrow definitions, . . . the narrower definition is the more appropriate when the word 'limited' is used as part of the phrase 'limited exception'. The word 'exception' by itself connotes a limited derogation, one that does not undercut the body of rules from which it is made. When a treaty uses the term 'limited exception', the word 'limited' must be given a meaning separate from the limitation implicit in the word 'exception' itself. The term 'limited exception' must therefore be read to connote a narrow exception – one which makes only a *small diminution of the rights in question*.[217]
>
> [Emphasis added]

On a literal reading of the text, the Panel focused on the extent to which rights have been curtailed, rather than the extent of the economic impact, to determine whether the exception was 'limited'. The Panel supported this conclusion by referring to the fact that the other two requirements of Article 30 'ask more

---

[215] See Panel Report, *Canada – Pharmaceutical Patents*, para. 7.12.   [216] See *ibid.*, para. 7.20.
[217] *Ibid.*, para. 7.30.

particularly about the economic impact of the exception, and provide two sets of standards by which such impact may be judged'.[218] In examining the extent to which the stockpiling exception curtailed the patent owner's rights to exclude 'making' and 'using' the patented product, the Panel noted that this exception sets no limitation at all on the quantity of the product that could be produced and stockpiled pending expiry of the patent.[219] The Panel thus found that the stockpiling exception constituted a *substantial* curtailment of the exclusive rights to be granted to patent owners under Article 28.1 and was thus not a 'limited' exception.[220] With regard to the regulatory review exception, however, the Panel found that it was a 'limited' exception as required by Article 30. It held:

> It is 'limited' because of the narrow scope of its curtailment of Article 28.1 rights. As long as the exception is confined to conduct needed to comply with the requirements of the regulatory approval process, the extent of the acts unauthorized by the right holder that are permitted by it will be small and narrowly bounded.[221]

With regard to the second requirement of Article 30 of the *TRIPS Agreement*, namely that the exception must not 'unreasonably conflict with a normal exploitation of the patent', the Panel in *Canada – Pharmaceutical Patents* held that 'exploitation' refers to 'the commercial activity by which patent owners employ their exclusive patent rights to extract economic value from their patent'.[222] With regard to the meaning of 'normal', the Panel noted that it 'defines the kind of commercial activity Article 30 seeks to protect' and that it has both an empirical content (what is 'common' within a community) and a normative content (a standard of entitlement).[223] The Panel agreed with Canada that the additional period of market exclusivity arising from using patent rights to prevent submissions for regulatory authorisation could not be seen as 'normal' exploitation.[224] Consequently, the Panel held that the regulatory review exception did not conflict with the 'normal exploitation' of patents, under the second requirement of Article 30.

With regard to the third requirement of Article 30 of the *TRIPS Agreement*, namely that the exception must not 'unreasonably prejudice the legitimate interests of the patent owner, taking account of the legitimate interests of third parties', the Panel noted that similar considerations arose as under the second requirement. The key issue was again the fact that the exception would remove the additional period of *de facto* market exclusivity enjoyed by patent owners if they were permitted to employ their rights to exclude 'making', 'using' and 'selling' the patented product during the term of the patent to prevent potential competitors from preparing and/or applying for regulatory approval during the term of the patent. In the case of the third requirement the issue was:

> whether patent owners could claim a 'legitimate interest' in the economic benefits that could be derived from such an additional period of de facto market exclusivity and, if so, whether the regulatory review exception 'unreasonably prejudiced' that interest.[225]

---

[218] *Ibid.*, paras. 7.31 and 7.49.   [219] See *ibid.*, para. 7.34.   [220] See *ibid.*, para. 7.36.   [221] *Ibid.*, para. 7.45.
[222] *Ibid.*, para. 7.54.   [223] See *ibid.*   [224] See *ibid.*, para. 7.57.   [225] *Ibid.*, para. 7.61.

The European Communities claimed that 'legitimate' should be equated with 'lawful', implying that full respect of the legal interests reflected in Article 28.1 is necessary. The Panel disagreed. It held:

> To make sense of the term 'legitimate interests' in this context, that term must be defined in the way that it is often used in legal discourse – as a normative claim calling for protection of interests that are 'justifiable' in the sense that they are supported by relevant public policies or other social norms.[226]

Therefore the Panel held that the argument of the European Communities, which was based only on the legal rights of the patent owner under Article 28.1, 'without reference to any more particular normative claims of interest' did not show non-compliance with the third requirement of Article 30.[227] The European Communities raised a second argument with regard to the 'legitimate interests' requirement. It pointed out that as patent owners are required to get marketing approval for their innovative products, they suffer delays that prevent them from marketing their products for a large part of the patent term, thereby reducing their period of market exclusivity. They should therefore be entitled to impose the same type of delay in connection with corresponding regulatory requirements upon the market entry of competing products.[228] According to the Panel, the 'primary issue was whether the normative basis of that claim rested on a widely recognized policy norm'.[229] Examining the approaches of various governments to this issue, the Panel noted that governments are still divided in this regard. It then stated:

> Article 30's 'legitimate interests' concept should not be used to decide, through adjudication, a normative policy issue that is still obviously a matter of unresolved political debate.[230]

Consequently, the Panel held that Canada's regulatory review exception fell within the exception under Article 30 of the *TRIPS Agreement* and was thus not inconsistent with Article 28.1 thereof.[231]

Apart from Article 30 of the *TRIPS Agreement*, the other provision in the *TRIPS Agreement* allowing for exceptions to the exclusive rights conferred by a patent is Article 31. Article 31 relates to the exception for 'other use' of a patent without authorisation of the right holder. 'Other use' is defined as use other than that allowed under Article 30.[232] This other use of a patent without authorisation of the right holder is commonly known as *compulsory licensing*, although this term is not used in Article 31. Article 31 refers to the situation where:

> the law of a Member allows for other use of the subject matter of a patent without the authorisation of the right holder, including use by the government or third parties authorised by the government.

Article 31 of the *TRIPS Agreement* contains a detailed list of requirements for the grant of compulsory licences.[233] However, it does not limit the grounds on which

---

[226] *Ibid.*, para. 7.69.   [227] *Ibid.*, para. 7.73.   [228] See *ibid.*, para. 7.74.   [229] *Ibid.*, para. 7.77.
[230] *Ibid.*, para. 7.82.   [231] See *ibid.*, para. 7.84.   [232] See footnote 7 to Article 31 of the *TRIPS Agreement*.
[233] See the conditions set out in paragraphs (a) to (l) of Article 31 of the *TRIPS Agreement*.

compulsory licences may be granted.[234] It only mentions some possible grounds, such as:

- public non-commercial use;[235]
- national emergency;[236]
- remedying of anticompetitive practices;[237] and
- dependent patents (i.e. patents on improvements to an earlier patent-protected invention).[238]

Due to concerns regarding the interpretation of this provision, the *Doha Declaration on TRIPS and Public Health* confirms that:

> Each member has the *right* to grant compulsory licences and the *freedom to determine the grounds* upon which such licences are granted.[239]
>
> [Emphasis added]

However, Article 31 of the *TRIPS Agreement* lays down conditions and limitations for the exercise of the right to grant compulsory licences. Article 31(a) of the *TRIPS Agreement* requires that authorisation of compulsory licences be considered on its individual merits. Therefore compulsory licences cannot be granted with regard to broad categories of patents. Under Article 31(b) of the *TRIPS Agreement*, an attempt must have been made prior to the compulsory licence to get authorisation to use the patent from the patent holder on reasonable commercial terms and conditions. Only if that attempt was unsuccessful within a reasonable period, can the compulsory licence be granted. However, there are three exceptions to this requirement:

- cases of national emergency or other circumstances of extreme urgency;
- cases of public non-commercial use;
- cases where the use is permitted to remedy an anticompetitive practice.[240]

To date, the use of compulsory licences in cases of 'national emergency' has often been related to the need to ensure affordable access to essential medicines to deal with public health crises. Compulsory licences may be used to authorise producers of generic medicines to copy a patented drug, without the consent of the right holder. The Doha Declaration on the *TRIPS Agreement* and Public Health recognises explicitly that as part of the 'flexibilities' provided in the *TRIPS Agreement*:

---

[234] An exception to this is in the case of semiconductor technology which may only be subject to compulsory licence for public non-commercial use and to remedy anticompetitive practices determined as such through a judicial or administrative process. See Article 31(c) of the *TRIPS Agreement*.

[235] See Article 31(b) of the *TRIPS Agreement*.   [236] See *ibid*.   [237] See Article 31(k) of the *TRIPS Agreement*.

[238] See Article 31(i) of the *TRIPS Agreement*.

[239] Ministerial Conference, *Doha Declaration on the TRIPS Agreement and Public Health*, adopted on 14 November 2001, WT/MIN(01)/DEC/2, dated 20 November 2001, para. 5(b).

[240] Note that while the exceptions of national emergency and public non-commercial use are contained in Article 31(b), that of remedying an anticompetitive practice is reflected in Article 31(k) of the *TRIPS Agreement*. In the first case the right holder must be notified as soon as is reasonably practicable, and in the second case as soon as there are demonstrable grounds to know that the patent will be used by or for the government.

> Each member has the right to determine what constitutes a national emergency or other circumstances of extreme urgency, it being understood that public health crises, including those relating to HIV/AIDS, tuberculosis, malaria and other epidemics, can represent a national emergency or other circumstances of extreme urgency.[241]

Epidemics such as HIV/AIDS and malaria can thus constitute a 'national emergency' or situations of 'extreme urgency' within the meaning of Article 31(b) of the *TRIPS Agreement*. The Doha Declaration made it very clear that situations of 'national emergency' or of 'extreme urgency' are not limited to short-term crises. In addition, by giving Members the right to determine for themselves what is an emergency, the burden of proof shifts to the complaining party to show that an emergency does *not* in fact exist. This differs from the situation under the general exceptions of Article XX of the GATT 1994 and Article XIV of the GATS.[242]

Further requirements for granting of compulsory licences, set out in subsequent paragraphs of Article 31 of the *TRIPS Agreement*, are:

- that the scope and duration of the use of the patent shall be limited to the purpose for which it was authorised (paragraph (c));
- that such use shall be non-exclusive (paragraph (d));
- that such use shall be non-assignable except with that part of the enterprise or goodwill which enjoys such use (paragraph (e));
- that any such use shall be authorised predominantly for the supply of the domestic market of the authorising Member (paragraph (f));[243]
- that authorisation of such use is liable to be terminated when the circumstances that led to it cease to exist (paragraph (g));[244]
- that the right holder be paid adequate remuneration in the circumstances of each case (paragraph (h));[245] and
- that the decision to authorise such use and the decision relating to the remuneration be subject to review by a court or other independent higher authority (paragraphs (i) and (j)).[246]

---

[241] Ministerial Conference, *Doha Declaration on the TRIPS Agreement and Public Health*, adopted on 14 November 2001, WT/MIN(01)/DEC/2, dated 20 November 2001, para. 5(c).

[242] See above, pp. 616 and 652. See further on this point, C. M. Correa, 'The TRIPS Agreement and Developing Countries', in P. F. J Macrory, A. E. Appleton and M. G. Plummer (eds.), *The World Trade Organization: Legal, Economic and Political Analysis* (Springer, 2005), 441.

[243] This requirement does not apply in cases of compulsory licences to remedy anticompetitive practices. See Article 31(k) of the *TRIPS Agreement*.

[244] Under this paragraph, the competent authority is required to have the authority to review the continued existence of such circumstances upon motivated request. In cases of compulsory licences to remedy anticompetitive practices, competent authorities may refuse to terminate the authorisation if the anticompetitive practices are likely to recur. See Article 31(k) of the *TRIPS Agreement*.

[245] The economic value of the authorisation must be taken into account in calculating the remuneration, under Article 31(h) of the *TRIPS Agreement*. In cases of compulsory licences to remedy anticompetitive practices, the need to correct such practices may be taken into account in determining the remuneration in terms of Article 31(k) of the *TRIPS Agreement*.

[246] With respect to compulsory licences to permit the exploitation of a dependent patent (a patent that cannot be exploited without infringing another prior patent), three additional conditions apply: (1) the invention in the second patent must involve an important technical advance of considerable economic significance in relation to the first patent; (2) the owner of the first patent must be entitled to a cross-licence on reasonable terms to use the second patent; and (3) the use shall be non-assignable except with the assignment of the second patent. See Article 31(i) of the *TRIPS Agreement*.

An important problem arose in complying with the requirement of Article 31(f) of the *TRIPS Agreement* with regard to the use of compulsory patents to ensure access to essential medicines in developing countries. Article 31(f), as set out above, requires that compulsory licences be provided 'predominantly for the supply of the domestic market'. However, some countries lack sufficient manufacturing capacity in pharmaceuticals to enable them to produce the necessary generic medicines for their domestic market. Article 31(f) prevents other Members from granting compulsory licences to produce generic medicines for export to such developing countries. Before 1 January 2005, during the transition period for implementation of patent protection by developing countries, discussed below, countries could import generic medicines from other developing countries, such as India, that do have such manufacturing capacity. However, this was no longer possible after the end of the transition period and countries with insufficient manufacturing capacity could no longer ensure access to affordable essential medicines, even if they granted compulsory licences. A first step towards resolving this serious problem for many developing-country Members, and in particular, least-developed country Members, was made in the Doha Declaration on the *TRIPS Agreement* and Public Health, which, in paragraph 6, instructed the Council for TRIPS, to 'find an expeditious *solution* to this problem and to report to the General Council before the end of 2002'.[247] A solution was found in 2003. The General Council adopted, on 30 August 2003, a decision whereby the obligations of Article 31(f) were waived in order to allow Members to export medicines produced under compulsory licence to Members with insufficient manufacturing capacity.[248] On 6 December 2005, the General Council took an important further step by adopting the decision to amend the *TRIPS Agreement* in order to resolve the problem with Article 31(f) in a permanent manner.[249] When the amendment takes effect,[250] a new Article 31 *bis* as well as a new Annex will be added to the *TRIPS Agreement*, providing that the obligations of Article 31(f) do not apply with respect to the grant by a Member of a compulsory licence necessary for the production of a pharmaceutical product and its export to an 'eligible' importing Member in accordance with the terms set out in paragraph 2 of the new Annex to the *TRIPS Agreement*.[251]

---

[247] Ministerial Conference, *Doha Declaration on the TRIPS Agreement and Public Health*, adopted on 14 November 2001, WT/MIN(01)/DEC/2, dated 20 November 2001, para. 6 (emphasis added).

[248] On waivers, see above, pp. 114–15. Recall that waivers adopted under Article IX of the *WTO Agreement*, as was the waiver at issue here, are *temporary* in nature. Note that the obligations under Article 31(h) of the *TRIPS Agreement* were also waived in the Decision of the General Council of 30 August 2003.

[249] See General Council, *Amendment of the TRIPS Agreement. Decision of the General Council of 6 December 2005*, WT/L/641, dated 8 December 2005. Note that this is the first and thus far only decision to amend a WTO agreement. See above, p. 144.

[250] To take effect, the amendment must be ratified by two-thirds of WTO Members (about 100 Members). The deadline for ratification was set for 1 December 2007. However, it has since been extended by two years to December 2009, as only eleven Members had ratified by then. On 24 October 2007, the European Parliament endorsed the amendment, paving the way for the twenty-seven Member States of the European Union to ratify the amendment, and on 28 October 2007 the Chinese legislature approved the amendment. On the procedure for the amendment of WTO agreements, see above, pp. 143–4.

[251] Annex 2, paragraph 2 defines an 'eligible' importing Member as any least-developed-country Member; and any other Member that has notified the Council for TRIPS of its intention to use the Article 31 *bis* system as an importer. Note that the notification does *not* need to be approved by any WTO body before the Article 31 *bis* system may be used.

Rwanda and Canada are currently the only Members using the possibility provided under the waiver decision of 30 August 2003. Apotex, a Canadian pharmaceutical firm, exports to Rwanda TriAvir, a generic HIV medicine produced under a compulsory licence granted by Canada.[252] As reported in *BRIDGES Weekly Trade News Digest* in July 2007:

> Following Rwanda's WTO notification, Apotex is believed to be seeking a voluntary licence – permission to manufacture generics in exchange for a negotiated royalty payment – from the two companies [GlaxoSmithKline and Boehringer Ingelheim] that hold the patents related to TriAvir . . . If they cannot come to an agreement within 30 days, Apotex would be eligible to apply to [Canada's] patents commissioner for a compulsory licence and the determination of a royalty to be paid to the patent holders.[253]

As the patent holders, GlaxoSmithKline and Boehringer Ingelheim, could indeed not come to an agreement with Apotex on a voluntary licence, Canada granted Apotex a compulsory licence to produce TriAvir for export to Rwanda.

The duration of patent protection is addressed in Article 33 of the *TRIPS Agreement*. It provides:

> The term of protection available shall not end before the expiration of a period of twenty years counted from the filing date.[254]

Article 33 was at issue in *Canada – Patent Term* involving a challenge by the United States to Canada's patent legislation, which granted patent protection for only seventeen years for patents filed before 1 October 1989. Examining the terms of Article 33, the Appellate Body held:

> In our view, the words used in Article 33 present very little interpretative difficulty. The 'filing date' is the date of filing of the patent application. The term of protection 'shall not end' before twenty years counted from the date of filing of the patent application. The calculation of the period of 'twenty years' is clear and specific. In simple terms, Article 33 defines the earliest date on which the term of protection of a patent may end. This earliest date is determined by a straightforward calculation: it results from taking the date of filing of the patent application and adding twenty years. As the filing date of the patent application and the twenty-year figure are both unambiguous, so too is the resultant earliest end date of the term of patent protection.[255]

The Appellate Body rejected Canada's argument that a twenty-year period was in fact available under its regulatory practices and procedures, as every patent applicant has statutory and other means to delay the procedure so as to extend the period of patent protection to at least twenty years.[256] According to the Appellate Body, not only 'those who are somehow able to meander successfully

---

[252] On 4 October 2007, Canada notified the Council for TRIPS of its granting of a compulsory licence to Apotex. See *Notification under Paragraph 2(c) of the Decision of 30 August 2003 on the Implementation of Paragraph 6 of the Doha Declaration on the TRIPS Agreement and Public Health – Canada*, IP/N/10/CAN/1, dated 8 October 2007. There is a dedicated page on the WTO website for notifications of this kind, available at www.wto.org/english/tratop_e/trips_e/public_health_e.htm, visited on 26 November 2007.

[253] *BRIDGES Weekly Trade News Digest*, 25 July 2007.

[254] Footnote 8 to this provision clarifies that Members that do not have a system of original grant may provide that the term of protection shall be calculated from the filing date in the system of original grant.   [255] Appellate Body Report, *Canada – Patent Term*, para. 85.   [256] See *ibid.*, para. 91.

through a maze of administrative procedures'[257] must have the opportunity to obtain the twenty-year patent term, but this opportunity:

> must be a readily discernible and specific right, and it must be clearly seen as such by the patent applicant when a patent application is filed. The grant of the patent must be sufficient *in itself* to obtain the minimum term mandated by Article 33.[258]

Finally note that Article 32 of the *TRIPS Agreement* requires that any decision to revoke or forfeit a patent must be subject to an opportunity for judicial review.

Questions and Assignments 8.10

Must patents be available for 'any invention in any field' under the *TRIPS Agreement*? Are Members allowed to give patent protection exclusively to inventions made on their territory? What are the exclusive rights of patent holders under the *TRIPS Agreement*? What are the three requirements that must be met for an exception to be allowed under Article 30 of the *TRIPS Agreement*? On what grounds and under which conditions may a Member grant a compulsory licence? Discuss the rules applicable to compulsory licences for the production of essential medicines for export to developing-country Members with insufficient manufacturing capacity. What is the minimum duration of patent protection under the *TRIPS Agreement*?

8.2.5. Enforcement of intellectual property rights

The protection of IP depends not only on substantive norms providing minimum standards of protection, but also on procedural rules effectively enforcing them. One of the problems with the WIPO conventions was the lack of such procedural enforcement obligations. The inclusion of rules on enforcement of IP rights in the *TRIPS Agreement* is a significant innovation by which it supplements the existing WIPO conventions and strengthens the protection of IP rights. The Preamble to the *TRIPS Agreement* reflects the recognition that new rules and disciplines were needed concerning 'the provision of effective and appropriate means for the enforcement of trade-related intellectual property rights, taking into account differences in national legal systems'. These rules on enforcement are contained in Part III of the *TRIPS Agreement*. The broad coverage of Part III was noted by the Appellate Body in *US – Section 211 Appropriations Act*. The Appellate Body held that Part III on 'Enforcement of Intellectual Property Rights':

> applies to all intellectual property rights covered by the *TRIPS Agreement*. According to Article 1.2 of the *TRIPS Agreement*, the term 'intellectual property' refers to 'all

---

[257] *Ibid.*, para. 92.
[258] *Ibid.* The Appellate Body pointed out that the text of Article 33 of the *TRIPS Agreement* does not support the notion of an 'effective' term of protection as distinguished from a 'nominal' term of protection. See *ibid.*, para. 95.

> categories of intellectual property that are the subject of Sections 1 through 7 of Part II' of that Agreement.[259]

Part III of the *TRIPS Agreement* deals with:

- general obligations (Section 1);
- civil and administrative procedures and remedies (Section 2);
- provisional measures (Section 3);
- special requirements related to border measures (Section 4); and
- criminal procedures (Section 5).

The main elements of the obligations set out in each of these Sections are discussed briefly below.

8.2.5.1. *General obligations*

The general obligation with regard to enforcement of IP rights is contained in Article 41 of the *TRIPS Agreement*. Article 41.1 requires Members to ensure that the enforcement procedures specified in Part III are available under their law 'so as to permit effective action' against infringement of IP rights protected in the *TRIPS Agreement*. This is specified as including expeditious remedies to *prevent* infringements and remedies to *deter* further infringements.

Article 41.1 of the *TRIPS Agreement* further requires that the enforcement procedures must be applied in a way that avoids creating barriers to legitimate trade and to provide safeguards against their abuse. Article 48 of the *TRIPS Agreement* supplements this general obligation by providing for compensation of a party that has suffered injury due to abuse of enforcement procedures.

Article 41.2 to 41.4 of the *TRIPS Agreement* sets out normal due process requirements. These paragraphs require that:

- enforcement procedures be fair and equitable, and not unnecessarily costly, complicated or lengthy (Article 41.2);
- decisions on the merits of a case be reasoned and preferably in writing, and be based on evidence on which the parties had an opportunity to be heard (Article 41.3); and
- parties to a proceeding have the opportunity for judicial review of administrative decisions and of at least the legal aspects of judicial decisions (with the exclusion of acquittals in criminal cases) (Article 41.4).

Article 41.5 of the *TRIPS Agreement* clarifies that Part III does not oblige Members to create a separate judicial system for the enforcement of IP rights, or create any obligation regarding the distribution of resources between enforcement of IP rights and other law enforcement. This provision reflects developing-country concerns with respect to the costs of implementation of enforcement procedures for IP rights. It clarifies that the enforcement of IP rights can take

---

[259] Appellate Body Report, *US – Section 211 Appropriations Act*, para. 205.

place through the existing law enforcement system of a country, provided that the required level of enforcement specified in Part III is achieved.

8.2.5.2. *Civil and administrative procedures and remedies*

The usual way of enforcing IP rights is through civil procedures. Article 42 of the *TRIPS Agreement* specifies that Members are required to make available to right holders civil *judicial* procedures for the enforcement of any IP right covered by the *TRIPS Agreement*. This means that *administrative* enforcement procedures are insufficient.[260] Article 42 contains detailed requirements to ensure that civil judicial procedures are 'fair and equitable'.[261] These requirements reflect normal due process rules applicable in civil proceedings.

Article 42 of the *TRIPS Agreement* was at issue before the Appellate Body in *US – Section 211 Appropriations Act*. The European Communities claimed that Sections 211(a)(2) and (b) of the US Appropriations Act violated Article 42 of the *TRIPS Agreement* as they expressly denied the availability of United States courts to enforce the rights targeted by Section 211.[262] The Panel found that Section 211(a)(2) violates Article 42.[263] It noted:

> While Section 211(a)(2) would not appear to prevent a right holder from initiating civil judicial procedures, its wording indicates that the right holder is not entitled to effective procedures as the court is *ab initio* not permitted to recognize its assertion of rights if the conditions of Section 211(a)(2) are met. In other words, the right holder is effectively prevented from having a chance to substantiate its claim, a chance to which a right holder is clearly entitled under Article 42, because effective civil judicial procedures mean procedures with the possibility of an outcome which is not pre-empted *a priori* by legislation.[264]

On appeal, the Appellate Body agreed with the Panel that:

> the ordinary meaning of the term 'make available' suggests that 'right holders' are entitled under Article 42 to have *access* to civil judicial procedures that are effective in bringing about the enforcement of their rights covered by the Agreement.[265]

The Appellate Body also noted that as the term 'civil judicial procedures' is not defined in Article 42 of the *TRIPS Agreement*:

> [t]he *TRIPS Agreement* thus reserves, subject to the procedural minimum standards set out in that Agreement, a degree of discretion to Members on this, taking into account 'differences in national legal systems'.[266]

The Appellate Body then turned to the fourth sentence of Article 42 of the *TRIPS Agreement*, which requires that '[a]ll parties to such procedures shall be duly

---

[260] An exception is made for the enforcement of the enhanced protection for GIs on wine and spirits, which may take place through administrative action rather than judicial proceedings. See footnote 4 to Article 23.1 of the *TRIPS Agreement*.   [261] See *ibid.*, para. 207.   [262] See *ibid.*, para. 208.

[263] With regard to Article 211(b), the Panel held that the European Communities had failed to explain the provisions referred to in the Article and had therefore not proved its case. See Panel Report, *US – Section 211 Appropriations Act*, para. 8.162.   [264] *Ibid.*, para. 8.100.

[265] Appellate Body Report, *US – Section 211 Appropriations Act*, para. 215, referring to para. 8.95 of the Panel Report, *US – Section 211 Appropriations Act*.

[266] Appellate Body Report, *US – Section 211 Appropriations Act*, para. 216.

entitled to substantiate their claims and to present all relevant evidence'. It noted that right holders are entitled thereby to choose how many and which claims to bring, to provide grounds for their claims and to bring all relevant evidence.[267] The Appellate Body stated:

> we understand that the rights which Article 42 obliges Members to make available to right holders are *procedural* in nature. These *procedural* rights guarantee an international minimum standard for nationals of other Members within the meaning of Article 1.3 of the *TRIPS Agreement*.[268]

The Appellate Body then noted that Sections 211(a)(2) and (b) deal with the *substantive* requirements of ownership of trademarks in particular cases.[269] Further, it pointed out that the European Communities agreed with the United States that US Federal Rules of Civil Procedure apply to cases under Section 211 and guarantee 'fair and equitable . . . civil judicial procedures'.[270] Referring to the argument of the European Communities that Sections 211(a)(2) and (b) limit the discretion of the courts by directing the courts to examine certain substantive requirements before, and to the exclusion of, other substantive requirements, the Appellate Body held:

> In our view, a conclusion by a court on the basis of Section 211, after applying the Federal Rules of Civil Procedure and the Federal Rules of Evidence, that an enforcement proceeding has failed to establish ownership – a requirement of substantive law – with the result that it is impossible for the court to rule in favour of that claimant's or that defendant's claim to a trademark right, does not constitute a violation of Article 42. There is nothing in the *procedural* obligations of Article 42 that prevents a Member, in such a situation, from legislating whether or not its courts must examine *each and every* requirement of substantive law at issue before making a ruling.[271]

Consequently, the Appellate Body found that Sections 211(a)(2) and (b) of the Appropriations Act were not, on their face, inconsistent with Article 42.[272]

The other provisions of the *TRIPS Agreement* relating to 'Civil and Administrative Procedures and Remedies' set out the powers that the judicial authorities involved are required to have in enforcement proceedings, such as:

- the authority to require, in specific cases, the production of evidence by a party in whose control the evidence is (Article 43);
- the authority to order a party to desist from an infringement, including to prevent the entry of infringing imports into channels of commerce in their jurisdiction after clearing customs (Article 44); and
- the authority to order the infringer to pay damages and costs in certain cases (Article 45).[273]

---

[267] See *ibid.*, paras. 219–20.   [268] *Ibid.*, para. 221.   [269] See *ibid.*, para. 222.   [270] See *ibid.*, para. 223.
[271] *Ibid.*, para. 226.   [272] See *ibid.*, para. 231.
[273] Other remedies aimed at creating an effective *deterrent* to infringement of IP rights (e.g. by ordering the destruction of infringing goods without compensation) are provided for in Article 46 of the *TRIPS Agreement*.

8.2.5.3. *Provisional measures and border measures*

Article 50 and Articles 51 to 60 of the *TRIPS Agreement* contain rules with regard to provisional measures and border measures respectively. These rules have in common that they aim to prevent infringement of IP rights. Article 50 of the *TRIPS Agreement* requires judicial authorities to have the authority to order 'prompt and effective provisional measures':

> (a) to prevent an infringement of any intellectual property right from occurring, and in particular to prevent the entry into the channels of commerce in their jurisdiction of goods, including imported goods immediately after customs clearance;
>
> (b) to preserve relevant evidence in regard to the alleged infringement.

Article 50 aims to deal with infringements that are taking place or are imminent.[274] It requires judicial authorities to have the authority to adopt provisional measures without hearing the other party (*inaudita altera parte*) where appropriate, in particular:

- where any delay is likely to cause irreparable harm to the right holder, or
- where there is a demonstrable risk of evidence being destroyed.

Article 51 of the *TRIPS Agreement* deals with measures applied *at the border* (i.e. applied to imports) in order to prevent IP infringements. Such measures can be applied when a right holder has valid grounds for suspecting that importation of counterfeit trademark or pirated copyright goods may take place.[275] While Article 50 of the *TRIPS Agreement* aims to prevent the introduction of the infringing product into commerce *after* it has cleared customs, Article 51 of the *TRIPS Agreement* addresses measures applied at the border *before* the release of the infringing product into free circulation by the customs authority. It provides for procedures to apply for the suspension by customs authorities of the release of the goods. While these border measures are required only for counterfeit trademark or pirated copyright goods, they *may* be extended to goods that involve infringements of other IP rights. Articles 52 to 60 of the *TRIPS Agreement* provide rules on the application of these border measures.

8.2.5.4. *Criminal procedures*

Article 61 of the *TRIPS Agreement* deals with criminal procedures and penalties for infringement. It requires criminal procedures and penalties to be provided at least in cases of wilful trademark counterfeiting or copyright piracy on a commercial scale.[276] It requires the remedies of 'imprisonment and/or monetary fines sufficient to provide a deterrent, consistently with the level of penalties

---

[274] See Article 50.3 of the *TRIPS Agreement*. On this point, see C. M. Correa, *Trade-Related Aspects of Intellectual Property Rights: A Commentary on the TRIPS Agreement* (Oxford University Press, 2007), 432.

[275] For a definition of 'counterfeit trademark goods' and 'pirated copyright goods', see footnote 14 to Article 51 of the *TRIPS Agreement*.

[276] Members may, but are not obliged to, extend the application of criminal procedures and penalties to other cases of IP infringement, in particular where they are committed wilfully and on a commercial scale.

applied for crimes of a corresponding gravity'. In appropriate cases, the remedies must also include 'the seizure, forfeiture and destruction of the infringing goods and of any materials and implements the predominant use of which has been in the commission of the offence'.

Questions and Assignments 8.11

Briefly summarise the enforcement efforts which the *TRIPS Agreement* requires Members to undertake. What do the due process requirements set out in Article 41 of the *TRIPS Agreement* entail? Does the *TRIPS Agreement* require Members to establish IP courts to enforce IP rights within their territory? What are 'civil judicial procedures' within the meaning of Article 42 of the *TRIPS Agreement*? What is the difference between measures taken under Article 50 and measures taken under Article 51 of the *TRIPS Agreement*? When does the *TRIPS Agreement* require Members to provide criminal procedures and penalties for infringement of IP rights?

8.2.6. Acquisition and maintenance of intellectual property rights

Part IV of the *TRIPS Agreement* deals with the procedural aspects of acquisition and maintenance of IP rights. For practical reasons, formalities and procedures apply to the acquisition of IP rights (for example, through the registration of a trademark or filing of a patent) and to their maintenance. This is recognised in Article 62.1, which acknowledges that Members may require compliance with reasonable procedures and formalities as a condition for the acquisition or maintenance of the IP rights provided for in the *TRIPS Agreement*, except copyright and undisclosed information.[277]

At the same time as acknowledging the necessity of procedural requirements, the *TRIPS Agreement* reflects an awareness that the effective protection of IP rights can be undermined if these procedural requirements are used to unfairly restrict the access to, and exercise of, these rights. Therefore Article 62 of the *TRIPS Agreement* disciplines the procedures and formalities for the acquisition and maintenance of IP rights.[278]

8.2.7. Institutional and procedural provisions of the *TRIPS Agreement*

Parts V and VII of the *TRIPS Agreement* contain the provisions dealing with institutional and procedural arrangements. These provisions relate to:

---

[277] This is because, under Article 5.2 of the *Berne Convention*, copyrights cannot be subject to these types of formalities, and undisclosed information is by the very nature of the protected subject matter not subject to registration. See C. M. Correa, *Trade-Related Aspects of Intellectual Property Rights: A Commentary on the TRIPS Agreement* (Oxford University Press, 2007), 467.
[278] For example, Article 62.2 obliges Members to prevent unreasonable delays in procedures for the acquisition of IP rights and Article 62.5 requires that decisions on the acquisition or maintenance of IP rights be subject to judical or quasi-judicial review.

- the transparency requirements (Article 63);
- the rules on dispute settlement under the *TRIPS Agreement* (Article 64);
- the tasks of the Council for TRIPS, including with regard to review and amendment of the *TRIPS Agreement* (Articles 68 and 71);
- international cooperation between Members to prevent trade in infringing goods (Article 69); and
- the prohibition on reservations to the provisions of the *TRIPS Agreement* without the consent of other Members (Article 72).

The most important of these provisions are briefly discussed in this section.

8.2.7.1. Transparency

Interestingly, the transparency provisions of the *TRIPS Agreement* are contained in Part V, entitled 'Dispute settlement and prevention'. It appears therefore that transparency with regard to IP protection is regarded as a way of preventing disputes between Members. Article 63 of the *TRIPS Agreement* lays down transparency obligations on Members. Under Article 63.1, Members are required, with regard not only to laws and regulations, but also to judicial decisions and administrative rulings of general application pertaining to the subject matter of the *TRIPS Agreement*, to publish them or, if this is impracticable, to make them publicly available in a manner that enables governments and IP right holders to become acquainted with them.[279] Article 63.2 requires Members to notify the Council for TRIPS of any laws and regulations referred to in Article 63.1, to facilitate the Council's review of the operation of the *TRIPS Agreement*. Members are required, under Article 63.3, to be prepared to supply information of the sort referred to in Article 63.1 or with regard to specific judicial decisions or administrative rulings in response to a written request by another Member. However, Members are not required to disclose confidential information.[280]

In *India – Patents (US)*, the Panel found a violation by India of the transparency obligation in Article 63.1 due to the fact that an administrative ruling regarding the mechanism for the implementation of the 'mailbox' system for patent applications under Article 70.8(a) of the *TRIPS Agreement* had not been published or made publicly available.[281] India's argument that the existence of the mailbox system was recognised in a written answer from the Government to a question in Parliament was rejected by the Panel, which pointed out that such a way of conveying information could not be regarded as a sufficient means of publicity under Article 63.1 of the *TRIPS Agreement*.[282]

---

[279] The subject matter of the TRIPS is defined as 'the availability, scope, acquisition, enforcement and prevention of the abuse of IP rights'. Article 63.1 further requires that agreements between Members or their governmental agencies concerning the subject matter of the *TRIPS Agreement* also be published.
[280] See Article 63.4 of the *TRIPS Agreement*.
[281] This finding was reversed by the Appellate Body on procedural grounds as the terms of reference of the Panel did not include Article 63 of the *TRIPS Agreement*. See Appellate Body Report, *India – Patents (US)*, paras. 85–6.   [282] See Panel Report, *India – Patents (US)*, para. 7.48.

8.2.7.2. Dispute settlement

One of the great achievements of the *TRIPS Agreement* is that it brings disputes regarding IP protection falling within its scope under the effective and enforceable mechanism for dispute settlement contained in the DSU. Article 64.1 of the *TRIPS Agreement* provides that the rules of Articles XXII and XXIII of the GATT 1994, as elaborated and applied by the DSU, apply to the settlement of disputes under that agreement, except as otherwise specifically provided therein. As noted by the Appellate Body in *India – Patents (US)*, the first case ever brought under the *TRIPS Agreement*:

> The *TRIPS Agreement* brings intellectual property within the world trading system for the first time by imposing certain obligations on Members in the area of trade-related intellectual property rights. As one of the covered agreements under the DSU, the *TRIPS Agreement* is subject to the dispute settlement rules and procedures of that Understanding.[283]

To date, twenty-six disputes have been initiated involving complaints under the *TRIPS Agreement*.[284] Of these, nine have resulted in panel reports and three eventually in Appellate Body reports.[285]

The *TRIPS Agreement* contains a specific provision deviating from the normal WTO dispute settlement rules, specifically those dealing with the causes of action. Under normal dispute settlement rules, Members can bring three types of complaints: violation complaints, non-violation complaints and situation complaints.[286] There was strong resistance from developing countries during the Uruguay Round negotiations against inclusion of non-violation and situation complaints as a cause of action under the *TRIPS Agreement*, as they were concerned that this would create the possibility to extend the protection of the *TRIPS Agreement* beyond that specified in its provisions.[287] As noted by Carlos Correa:

> Admitting non-violation complaints might . . . open the door for threatening weak WTO Members with complaints aimed at inducing changes in public policies in a multiplicity of fields, and could embark the WTO dispute settlement bodies in ruling on measures that are within the policy space reserved for Members when adopting the TRIPS Agreement.[288]

For this reason, Article 64.2 of the *TRIPS Agreement* provided that, for a period of five years from the entry into force of the *WTO Agreement*, no non-violation or

---

[283] Appellate Body Report, *India – Patents (US)*, para. 29.
[284] Seventeen of these disputes, or 65 per cent, have been initiated by the United States. See www.worldtradelaw.net/dsc/database/searchcomplaints.asp, visited on 22 November 2007.
[285] See www.worldtradelaw.net/dsc/database/trips.asp, visited on 22 November 2007.
[286] These are discussed above, pp. 182–6.
[287] Abbott notes two specific concerns of developing countries, namely that developed countries would: (1) claim that the TRIPS provisions are intended to provide IP right holders with market access, not just protection of their IP rights; and (2) try to use the non-violation cause of action to 'expand the literal language of the TRIPS Agreement in light of whatever their 'expectations' might have been about its effects'. F. M. Abbott, 'TRIPS in Seattle: The Not-So-Surprising Failure and the Future of the TRIPS Agenda', *Berkeley Journal of International Law*, 2000, 172.
[288] C. M. Correa, *Trade-Related Aspects of Intellectual Property Rights: A Commentary on the TRIPS Agreement* (Oxford University Press, 2007), 489. According to Correa, 'If upheld, non-violation complaints could extraordinarily reduce the room for Members to adopt public policies, clearly to an extent unforeseen by the parties that negotiated the TRIPS Agreement.' *Ibid.*, 488.

situation complaints could be brought under the *TRIPS Agreement*. The moratorium under Article 64.2 of the *TRIPS Agreement* expired on 1 January 2000.[289] Under Article 64.3, the Council for TRIPS was directed to examine and make recommendations to the Ministerial Conference on non-violation and situation complaints. Any decision of the Ministerial Conference to adopt such recommendations or to extend the moratorium must be made by consensus.[290] To date, no agreement could be reached on this issue. However, it has been agreed that Members will not initiate non-violation or situation complaints under the *TRIPS Agreement* until agreement is reached on the extension of the moratorium.[291]

8.2.7.3. *Council for TRIPS*

Article 68 of the *TRIPS Agreement* establishes a Council for TRIPS. As is the case with all political WTO bodies, the Council for TRIPS is composed of representatives of all WTO Members. Pursuant to Article 68, the tasks of the Council for TRIPS are:

- to monitor the operation of the *TRIPS Agreement*, and in particular, Members' compliance with their obligations thereunder;
- to provide the possibility for Members to consult on matters relating to the trade-related aspects of IP rights; and
- to carry out any other responsibilities assigned to it by the Members, and provide any assistance requested by them in the context of dispute settlement procedures.

In carrying out its functions, the Council for TRIPS may consult with or seek information from any source it deems appropriate. Within a year of its first meeting, the Council for TRIPS was required to seek to establish appropriate arrangements for cooperation with WIPO. A cooperation agreement was concluded between the WTO and WIPO in 1995, and came into force on 1 January 1996.[292]

The Council for TRIPS is also required, under Article 71.1 of the *TRIPS Agreement*, to review the implementation of the *TRIPS Agreement* every two years.[293]

Questions and Assignments 8.12

What does the transparency obligation under the *TRIPS Agreement* entail? Are all disputes between Members on rights and obligations under the *TRIPS Agreement* subject to the rules and procedures of the

---

[289] With regard to Article 64.2 of the *TRIPS Agreement*, see Appellate Body Report, *India – Patents (US)*, paras. 36–42.　　[290] See Article 64.3 of the *TRIPS Agreement*.

[291] This agreement was last renewed at the Hong Kong Session of the Ministerial Conference. See Ministerial Conference, *Hong Kong Ministerial Declaration*, WT/MIN(05)/DEC, dated 22 December 2005, para. 45.

[292] See www.wto.org/english/tratop_e/trips_e/wtowip_e.htm, visited on 1 December 2007.

[293] Additional tasks of the Council for TRIPS are, for example, set out in Articles 23.4 and 24.2 of the *TRIPS Agreement* (with regard to GIs) and Article 66.1 of the *TRIPS Agreement* (with regard to the extension of the transitional period for least-developed countries).

DSU? Can Members initiate non-violation complaints under the *TRIPS Agreement*?

8.2.8. Special provisions for developing-country Members

The implementation of the obligations under the *TRIPS Agreement* requires regulatory capacity and an infrastructure for enforcement. This may create problems for developing-country Members in particular. The *TRIPS Agreement* thus provided, and to some extent still provides, for transitional periods for implementation of the obligations, and provides for technical cooperation.

8.2.8.1. Transitional periods

Article 65.1 of the *TRIPS Agreement* provided a *one-year* implementation period for *all* Members from the entry into force of the *WTO Agreement*, except for Articles 2 (on the IP conventions), 3 (on national treatment) and 4 (on MFN treatment), which applied as from 1 January 1995. However, pursuant to Article 65.2 of the *TRIPS Agreement*, developing-country Members, and certain Members with economies in transition,[294] could delay implementation of the provisions of the *TRIPS Agreement* (other than Articles 3, 4 and 5) for a further four years, until 1 January 2000.[295] An additional five-year implementation period was added to this initial period by Article 65.4 of the *TRIPS Agreement* in the area of patent protection for those developing-country Members which did not provide such protection to areas of technology at the time when the *TRIPS Agreement* became applicable to them under Article 65.2 of the *TRIPS Agreement*.[296] These transitional periods have now all come to an end. Only least-developed-country Members still 'benefit' from a transitional period. In view of their 'special needs and requirements', their 'economic financial and administrative constraints', and their need for 'flexibility to create a viable technological base', least-developed-country Members were given, in Article 66 of the *TRIPS Agreement*, a transitional period of eleven years, starting from the date of the entry into force of the *WTO Agreement*. The transitional period was thus due to expire on 1 January 2006. However, the Council for TRIPS is authorised to accord extensions of this period upon a duly-motivated request from a least-developed-country Member.

---

[294] Note that only Members in transition from a centrally planned economy to a free-market economy that are undertaking structural reform of their IP systems and facing 'special problems' in preparing and implementing IP laws can make use of this additional transition period. See Article 65.3 of the *TRIPS Agreement*.

[295] Note that the transitional periods of Article 65 of the *TRIPS Agreement* do not apply to Article 70.8 (known as the 'mailbox' provision). See Panel Report, *India – Patents (US)*, para 7.27. On Members' obligations under the 'mailbox' provision, see Appellate Body Report, *India – Patents (US)*, para. 58.

[296] Note that Article 65.5 of the *TRIPS Agreement* contains an 'anti-rollback' obligation, i.e. an obligation that during the implementation period, no changes could be made to national legislation that resulted in a lesser degree of consistency with the *TRIPS Agreement*. See also on Article 65.5 of the *TRIPS Agreement*, Panel Report, *Indonesia – Autos*, para. 14.282.

The Doha Declaration on the *TRIPS Agreement* and Public Health states, in paragraph 7, that least-developed-country Members will not be obliged, with respect to pharmaceutical products, to implement the obligations of the *TRIPS Agreement* regarding patents and the protection of undisclosed information or to enforce these IP rights until 1 January 2016. The Council for TRIPS was directed to take the necessary action to give effect to this, pursuant to Article 66.1 of the *TRIPS Agreement*. In accordance with this direction, on 27 June 2002 the Council for TRIPS approved a decision extending until 2016 the implementation period for least-developed-country Members with regard to *certain pharmaceutical patents*.[297] In addition, on 8 July 2002, the General Council approved a waiver exempting least-developed countries from the obligation under Article 70.9 of the *TRIPS Agreement* to provide exclusive marketing rights for any new drugs in the period when they do not provide patent protection.[298]

On 29 November 2005, the Council for TRIPS decided to extend the transitional period for least-developed-country Members to give effect to *all* provisions of the *TRIPS Agreement* (except Articles 3, 4 and 5) until 1 July 2013, or until the Member involved graduates from least-developed-country status.

8.2.8.2. *Technical cooperation*

Article 67 of the *TRIPS Agreement* obliges developed-country Members to provide technical and financial assistance to developing- and least-developed-country Members, upon request and on mutually agreed terms and conditions. Such assistance includes helping with the preparation of legislation for the protection and enforcement of IP rights and the prevention of their abuse, as well as support for the establishment and maintenance of the relevant national offices and agencies, including training their staff.[299] To make information on available technical assistance accessible and to facilitate the monitoring of compliance with the obligation of Article 67, developed-country Members have agreed to submit descriptions of their technical and financial cooperation programmes annually. Intergovernmental organisations have also presented, on the invitation of the Council for TRIPS, information on their activities in order to promote transparency.[300]

---

[297] Council for TRIPS, *Extension of the Transition Period under Article 66.1 of the TRIPS Agreement for Least-Developed Country Members for Certain Obligations with Respect to Pharmaceutical Products, Decision of the Council for TRIPS of 27 June 2002*, IP/C/25, dated 1 July 2002. The TRIPS Council noted that it considered para. 7 of the *Doha Declaration on the TRIPS Agreement and Public Health* to be a 'duly motivated request' by least-developed-country Members under Article 66.1 for the extension of their transitional period.

[298] See General Council, *Least-Developed Country Members – Obligations Under Article 70.9 of the TRIPS Agreement with Respect to Pharmaceutical Products. Decision of 8 July 2002*, WT/L/478, dated 12 July 2002.

[299] Cottier notes that there have been substantial efforts in this area in terms of Article 67 by Members and in cooperation with WIPO. See T. Cottier, 'The Agreement on Trade-Related Aspects of Intellectual Property Rights', in P. F. J. Macrory, A. E. Appleton and M. G. Plummer (eds.), *The World Trade Organization: Legal, Economic and Political Analysis* (Springer, 2005), 1079.

[300] See www.wto.org/english/tratop_e/trips_e/intel9_c.htm, visited on 26 November 2007. The information from developed-country Members, intergovernmental organisations and the WTO Secretariat on their technical cooperation activities with regard to the *TRIPS Agreement* is circulated in documents in the IP/C/W/ series.

Developed-country Members are also obliged, under Article 66.2 of the *TRIPS Agreement*, to provide incentives to their enterprises and institutions to promote the transfer of technology to least-developed-country Members so that they can create a 'sound and viable technological base'. However, little has been done in this regard.[301] In order to establish a mechanism for ensuring the monitoring and full implementation of the obligations in Article 66.2, as instructed in the Doha Decision on Implementation-Related Issues and Concerns,[302] the Council for TRIPS adopted a decision on 19 February 2003.[303] In terms of this decision, developed-country Members must submit annual reports on actions taken or planned in pursuance of their commitments under Article 66.2.[304] The Council for TRIPS must review these submissions at its end-of-year meeting each year and Members shall have an opportunity to pose questions, request additional information and 'discuss the effectiveness of the incentives provided in promoting and encouraging technology transfer to least-developed-country Members in order to enable them to create a sound and viable technological base'.[305]

The Decision of the Council for TRIPS of 29 November 2005 also includes commitments on technical assistance for least-developed-country Members to help them prepare to implement the agreement.[306] The Decision requested least-developed-country Members to provide to the Council for TRIPS, preferably by 1 January 2008:

> as much information as possible on their individual priority needs for technical and financial cooperation in order to assist them taking steps necessary to implement the TRIPS Agreement.[307]

Sierra Leone and Uganda are the first two least-developed-country Members to formally make submissions identifying their needs in respect of policy, legislative and administrative reforms. As reported in *BRIDGES Weekly Trade News Digest*:

> Sierra Leone called for financial and logistical assistance to complement its ongoing intellectual property reform programmes, such as funds to hire intellectual property policy analysts in its trade ministry, and to set up a small permanent mission in Geneva to participate in WTO negotiations. Uganda asked for help at setting up a 'National Intellectual Property Policy Forum' through which representatives from government, the private sector, and civil society would produce a draft national policy framework.

[301] See T. Cottier, 'The Agreement on Trade-Related Aspects of Intellectual Property Rights', in P. F. J. Macrory, A. E. Appleton and M. G. Plummer (eds.), *The World Trade Organization: Legal, Economic and Political Analysis* (Springer, 2005), 1079.

[302] See Ministerial Conference, *Doha Decision on Implementation-Related Issues and Concerns*, WT/MIN(01)/17, adopted on 14 November 2001, para. 11.2.

[303] See Council for TRIPS, *Implementation of Article 66.2 of the TRIPS Agreement. Decision of the Council for TRIPS of 19 February 2003*, IP/C/28, dated 20 February 2003.

[304] Members must provide new detailed reports every third year and, in the intervening years, provide updates to their most recent reports. These reports shall be submitted prior to the last Council meeting scheduled for the year in question. See *ibid.*, para. 1.

[305] *Ibid.*, para. 2. Paragraph 3 of this decision sets out the information which must be provided in these annual submissions.

[306] See Council for TRIPS, *Extension of the Transitional Period under Article 66.1 for Least-Developed-Country Members, Decision of the Council for TRIPS of 29 November 2005*. See also WTO News Item, 'Poorest countries given more time to apply intellectual property rules', Press/424, dated 29 November 2005, available at www.wto.org/english/news_e/pres05_e/pr424_e.htm, visited on 26 November 2007.   [307] *Ibid.*, para. 2.

The two papers stress the importance of allowing countries ample time to develop a national strategy on intellectual property. They call for intellectual property to be used as a tool for socio-economic development, through the establishment of a national scientific and technological creative base. Both set out specific activities and timelines for updating the intellectual property legal framework and administration infrastructure, strengthening enforcement and regulation, and using IP to promote innovation, creativity and technology transfer.

Diplomats from Sierra Leone and Uganda are hopeful that other LDCs will follow their lead.[308]

8.3. THE *TBT AGREEMENT*

Television sets, toys, cosmetics, medical equipment, fertilisers, meat and cheese are all subject to requirements relating to their characteristics and/or the manner in which they are produced. The purpose of these requirements may be the protection of life or health, the protection of the environment, the prevention of deceptive practices or to ensure the quality of products. These requirements may be mandatory, set and enforced by governments. More often, however, these requirements are rules laid down by national standardisation bodies which are not mandatory but are nevertheless generally adopted in business transactions in a given country. In both cases, these requirements may constitute formidable barriers to trade, even where they are not applied in a discriminatory manner. The divergence in the regulatory requirements imposed in different countries increases the cost and difficulty of gaining market access for exporters. Television sets and cheese made according to the requirements of country A may be banned from, or difficult to market in, country B when the requirements of country B relating to the characteristics or the manner of production are different. Furthermore, procedures used to verify whether a product meets certain mandatory or voluntary requirements may obstruct trade. Measures of this kind are commonly referred to as 'technical barriers to trade'. The 2005 *World Trade Report*, entitled 'Exploring the Links between Trade, Standards and the WTO', highlights the tension between the legitimate objectives that technical barriers may pursue, and their protectionist effects:

Increased standardization activity reflects, among other factors, demand by consumers for safer and higher quality products, technological innovations, the expansion of global commerce and the increased concern paid by many governments and NGOs to social issues and the environment. Standards have played an important role in fulfilling these needs.

On the other hand, standards can be a means of hidden protection. Even if standards are not protectionist in intent, badly designed and applied standards can have highly discriminatory consequences for trade partners. In a world of reduced tariff protection and multilateral trade rules that limit the ability of governments arbitrarily to increase taxes

---

[308] *BRIDGES Weekly Trade News Digest*, 31 October 2007. See also IP/C/W/499 (for Sierra Leone) and IP/C/W/500 (for Uganda). The needs assessments were facilitated by the International Centre for Trade and Sustainable Development, a Geneva-based organisation.

and quantitative restrictions on trade, it is not surprising that they are sometimes tempted to use other means to restrict imports. This is a perennial issue in international trade relations.[309]

WTO law sets out specific rules on technical barriers to trade in the *Agreement on Technical Barriers to Trade*, commonly referred to as the *TBT Agreement*, and the rules of the *Agreement on the Application of Sanitary and Phytosanitary Measures*, commonly referred to as the *SPS Agreement*. The rules of the *TBT Agreement* apply to the general category of technical barriers to trade, while the rules of the *SPS Agreement* apply to a special category of technical barriers to trade, namely sanitary and phytosanitary measures. Both sets of rules are of great importance to international trade. As discussed in this chapter, these rules go significantly beyond the GATT obligations not to discriminate among or against imported products. They impose certain international disciplines on national regulation regarding products, their characteristics and production. Significantly, they promote the harmonisation of national regulation on the basis of international standards.

The rules of the *SPS Agreement* are addressed in section 8.4 of this chapter. This section addresses the rules of the *TBT Agreement* and discusses:

- the scope of application of the *TBT Agreement*;
- the relationship between the *TBT Agreement* and other WTO agreements, in particular, the *SPS Agreement* and the GATT 1994;
- the substantive provisions of the *TBT Agreement*;
- the institutional and procedural provisions of the *TBT Agreement*; and
- special provisions for developing-country Members.

8.3.1. Scope of application of the *TBT Agreement*

With respect to the scope of application of the *TBT Agreement*, this section distinguishes between the *substantive* scope of application, i.e. the types of measures to which the *TBT Agreement* applies, the *personal* scope of application, i.e. the entities to whom rules of the Agreement apply, and the *temporal* scope of application of the Agreement.

8.3.1.1. *Substantive scope of application*

The rules of the *TBT Agreement* apply to:

- technical regulations;
- standards; and
- conformity assessment procedures.

---

[309] *World Trade Report 2005: Exploring the Links between Trade, Standards and the WTO* (World Trade Organization, 2007), 29. Note that in this excerpt the term 'standard' is used in a broad, non-technical manner and refers to technical barriers to trade in general, rather than to 'standards' as defined in Annex 1 of the *TBT Agreement* and discussed below. See below, p. 807.

As the Appellate Body stated in *EC – Asbestos*, the *TBT Agreement* thus applies to a 'limited class of measures'.[310] The three types of measures to which the *TBT Agreement* applies are defined in Annex 1 of the *TBT Agreement*.

In Annex 1.1, a *technical regulation* is defined as a:

> [d]ocument which lays down product characteristics or their related processes and production methods, including the applicable administrative provisions, with which compliance is mandatory. It may also include or deal exclusively with terminology, symbols, packaging, marking or labelling requirements as they apply to a product, process or production method.

For example, a law requiring that batteries be rechargeable or a law requiring that wine be sold in green glass bottles is a technical regulation within the meaning of the *TBT Agreement*. A law requiring that the production of pharmaceutical products meet certain requirements regarding plant cleanliness is also a technical regulation falling within the scope of application of the *TBT Agreement*.

Annex 1.2 of the *TBT Agreement* defines a *standard* as a:

> [d]ocument approved by a recognised body, that provides, for common and repeated use, rules, guidelines or characteristics for products or related processes and production methods, with which compliance is not mandatory. It may also include or deal exclusively with terminology, symbols, packaging, marking or labelling requirements as they apply to a product, process or production method.

Contrary to technical regulations, standards are of a voluntary nature, meaning that compliance is not mandatory. The voluntary standards set by CENELEC (the European Committee for Electrotechnical Standardisation), such as standards for mobile phones or handheld computers, are clearly standards within the meaning of the *TBT Agreement*. Other examples include standards for sustainable forest management set by the Forest Stewardship Council, standards for socially responsible production and trade set by the Fairtrade Foundation, or the standards for certification of agricultural products set by EurepGAP. While only products complying with the standards would be eligible to be certified by the relevant public or private body or to bear its logo, non-complying products would still be permitted on the market. Companies comply with these voluntary standards for various reasons, ranging from the wish to be responsive to consumer concerns to practical considerations of compatibility of products. However, often companies have no choice but to comply with these voluntary standards as non-adherence would, in practice, exclude their products from the market. It is therefore important that these voluntary standards are also subject to international disciplines under the *TBT Agreement*.

In addition to technical regulations and standards, conformity assessment procedures also fall within the scope of application of the *TBT Agreement*. Conformity assessment procedures are defined in Annex 1.3 of the *TBT Agreement* as:

---

[310] Appellate Body Report, *EC – Asbestos*, para. 80.

> [a]ny procedure used, directly or indirectly, to determine that relevant requirements in technical regulations or standards are fulfilled.

Examples of conformity assessment procedures include procedures for sampling, testing and inspection.

The *TBT Agreement* applies to technical regulations, standards and conformity assessment procedures relating to:

- products (including industrial and agricultural products); and
- processes and production methods (PPMs).[311]

It is the subject of much debate, however, whether the processes and production methods to which the *TBT Agreement* applies, include so-called *non-product related processes and production methods* (NPR-PPMs). This term refers to processes and production methods that do not affect the characteristics of the final product put on the market. An example of a technical regulation on a NPR-PPM is the prohibition of the use of environmentally unfriendly sources of energy in the production of a product. Another example is the prohibition to market beef from cattle fed with genetically modified feed. During the negotiations on the *TBT Agreement* discussion took place on whether this group should be included in the scope of the Agreement. However, as explicitly recorded, the negotiators failed to reach agreement on this issue.[312] The definitions in Annex 1, paragraphs 1 to 3, quoted above, seem to indicate that technical regulations, standards and conformity assessment procedures relating to NPR-PPMs do *not* fall within the scope of application of the *TBT Agreement*.[313] However, note that in the last sentence of the definitions of technical regulations and standards, it is stated that technical regulations and standards also include measures that are concerned with 'terminology, symbols, packaging, marking or labelling requirements *as they apply to a product, process or production method*' (emphasis added). Therefore, while there may be uncertainty and debate about whether technical regulations standards or conformity assessment procedures relating to NPR-PPMs in general fall within the scope of application of the *TBT Agreement*, it is clear that 'labelling requirements' relating to NPR-PPMs are TBT measures within the meaning of Annex 1 to the *TBT Agreement*, and thus fall within the scope of application of the *TBT Agreement*.[314] A good

---

[311] See Article 1.3 and the explanatory note to Annex 1, paragraph 2, of the *TBT Agreement*. Note that the *TBT Agreement* does not apply to technical regulations, standards and conformity assessment procedures that deal with services.

[312] See Committee on Technical Barriers to Trade, *Negotiating History of the Coverage of the Agreement on Technical Barriers to Trade with regard to Labelling Requirements, Voluntary Standards and Processes and Production Methods Unrelated to Product Characteristics*, Note by the Secretariat, G/TBT/W/11, dated 29 August 1995. This disagreement persisted, as is shown by the discussion in the Committee on Trade and Environment in 1996 on voluntary eco-labelling schemes. See Committee on Trade and Environment, *Report (1996) of the Committee on Trade and Environment*, WT/CTE/1, dated 12 November 1996.

[313] Note that the definition in Annex 1.1 states 'product characteristics or their *related* processes and production methods' and that in Annex 1.2 states: 'characteristics for products or *related* processes and production methods' (Emphasis added).

[314] See P. Van den Bossche, N. Schrijver and G. Faber, *Unilateral Measures addressing Non-Trade Concerns. A Study on WTO Consistency, Relevance of other International Agreements, Economic Effectiveness and Impact on Developing Countries of Measures concerning Non-Product-Related Processes and Production Methods* (Ministry of Foreign Affairs of the Netherlands, 2007), available at www.minbuza.nl/binaries/en-pdf/thema-s-en-dossiers/beleidscoherentie/boek-wto.pdf, 143–7, visited on 29 November 2007.

example would be a law requiring that eggs bear a label that in the production process animal welfare requirements were met.[315] To date, however, no NPR-PPM measure has been tested under the *TBT Agreement*. Some uncertainty and debate regarding the scope of the *TBT Agreement* is likely to persist as long as the Appellate Body has not yet ruled on this issue.[316]

While there is no case law yet on standards or conformity assessment procedures under the *TBT Agreement*, in three disputes to date, *EC – Asbestos*, *EC – Sardines* and *EC – Trademarks and Geographical Indications (Australia)*, panels and the Appellate Body have had occasion to examine whether the measures at issue were technical regulations falling within the scope of the *TBT Agreement*.

In *EC – Asbestos*, the measure at issue consisted of, on the one hand, a general ban on asbestos and asbestos-containing products and, on the other hand, some exceptions referring to situations in which asbestos-containing products would be allowed. The Panel concluded that the ban itself was *not* a technical regulation, whereas the exceptions to the ban *were*.[317] On appeal, the Appellate Body reversed the Panel's finding that the ban did not constitute a technical regulation. In addressing this issue, the Appellate Body first firmly rejected the Panel's approach of considering separately the ban and the exceptions to the ban. According to the Appellate Body, the 'proper legal character' of the measure cannot be determined unless the measure is looked at as a whole, including both the prohibitive and the permissive elements that are part of it. The Appellate Body stated:

> Article 1 of the Decree contains broad, general prohibitions on asbestos and products containing asbestos. However, the scope and generality of those prohibitions can only be understood in light of the exceptions to it which, albeit for a limited period, *permit*, *inter alia*, the use of certain products containing asbestos and, principally, products containing chrysotile asbestos fibres. The measure is, therefore, *not* a *total* prohibition on asbestos fibres, because it also includes provisions that *permit*, for a limited duration, the use of asbestos in certain situations. Thus, to characterize the measure simply as a general prohibition, and to examine it as such, overlooks the complexities of the measure, which include both prohibitive and permissive elements.[318]

The Appellate Body then examined whether the measure at issue, considered as a whole, was a technical regulation within the meaning of the *TBT Agreement*. On the basis of the definition of a 'technical regulation' of Annex 1.1, quoted above, the Appellate Body set out a number of considerations for determining whether a measure is a technical regulation. This section discusses these considerations.

First, for a measure to be a 'technical regulation', it must 'lay down' – i.e. set forth, stipulate or provide – 'product characteristics'. With respect to the term 'characteristics', the Appellate Body noted:

> the 'characteristics' of a product include, in our view, any objectively definable 'features', 'qualities', 'attributes', or other 'distinguishing mark' of a product. Such 'characteristics'

---

[315] See *ibid*.   [316] See *ibid*.   [317] See Panel Report, *EC – Asbestos*, paras. 8.71–8.72.
[318] Appellate Body Report, *EC – Asbestos*, para. 64.

> might relate, *inter alia*, to a product's composition, size, shape, colour, texture, hardness, tensile strength, flammability, conductivity, density, or viscosity. In the definition of a 'technical regulation' in Annex 1.1, the *TBT Agreement* itself gives certain examples of 'product characteristics' – 'terminology, symbols, packaging, marking or labelling requirements'. These examples indicate that 'product characteristics' include, not only features and qualities intrinsic to the product itself, but also related 'characteristics', such as the means of identification, the presentation and the appearance of a product.[319]

The Appellate Body also noted that a technical regulation may be confined to laying down *only* one or a few product characteristics.

Second, a 'technical regulation' must regulate the characteristics of products in a binding or compulsory fashion. According to the Appellate Body, it follows that:

> with respect to products, a 'technical regulation' has the effect of *prescribing* or *imposing* one or more 'characteristics' – 'features', 'qualities', 'attributes', or other 'distinguishing mark'.[320]

Product characteristics may be prescribed or imposed with respect to products in either a *positive* or a *negative* form. That is, the regulation may provide, positively, that products *must possess* certain 'characteristics', or the regulation may require, negatively, that products *must not possess* certain 'characteristics'. In both cases, the legal result is the same: the regulation 'lays down' certain binding 'characteristics' for products.[321]

Third, the Appellate Body held that a 'technical regulation' must 'be applicable to an *identifiable* product, or group of products. Otherwise, enforcement of the regulation will be, in practical terms, impossible.'[322] Clearly, identification of the product coverage of a technical regulation is required. The Panel in *EC – Asbestos* interpreted this to mean that a 'technical regulation' must apply to 'given' products which are actually named, identified or specified in the regulation. The Appellate Body disagreed. Nothing in the text of the *TBT Agreement* suggests that the products concerned need be named or otherwise *expressly* identified in a 'technical regulation'. The Appellate Body noted that:

> there may be perfectly sound administrative reasons for formulating a 'technical regulation' in a way that does *not* expressly identify products by name, but simply makes them identifiable – for instance, through the 'characteristic' that is the subject of regulation.[323]

On the basis of the above three considerations, the Appellate Body examined the measure at issue in *EC – Asbestos*, a French decree, noting that the first and second paragraphs of Article 1 of the decree imposed a prohibition on asbestos *fibres*. According to the Appellate Body, the prohibition on these *fibres* did not, *in itself*, prescribe or impose any 'characteristics' on asbestos fibres but simply banned them in their natural state. Accordingly, if this measure consisted *only* of a prohibition on asbestos *fibres*, it might not constitute a 'technical regulation'.[324] The Appellate Body then noted, however:

---

[319] *Ibid.*, para. 67.   [320] *Ibid.*, para. 68.   [321] See *ibid.*, para. 69.   [322] *Ibid.*, para. 70.   [323] *Ibid.*, para. 70.
[324] See *ibid.*, para. 71.

> An integral and essential aspect of the measure is the regulation of '*products containing asbestos fibres*', which are also prohibited by Article 1, paragraphs I and II of the Decree. It is important to note here that, although formulated *negatively* – products containing asbestos are prohibited – the measure, in this respect, effectively prescribes or imposes certain objective features, qualities or 'characteristics' on *all* products. That is, in effect, the measure provides that *all* products must *not* contain asbestos fibres. Although this prohibition against products containing asbestos applies to a large number of products, and although it is, indeed, true that the products to which this prohibition applies cannot be determined from the terms of the measure itself, it seems to us that the products covered by the measure are *identifiable*: all products must be asbestos free; any products containing asbestos are prohibited. We also observe that compliance with the prohibition against products containing asbestos is mandatory and is, indeed, enforceable through criminal sanctions.[325]

The prohibition of all asbestos-containing products is a measure which effectively prescribes – albeit negatively – certain objective characteristics for all products. Furthermore, the Appellate Body noted that Articles 2, 3 and 4 of the decree contain certain exceptions to the prohibitions found in Article 1 of the decree. Any person seeking to avail of these limited exceptions must provide a detailed justification to the authorities, complete with necessary supporting documentation concerning 'the state of scientific and technological progress'.[326] Compliance with these administrative requirements is mandatory. Through the exceptions to the prohibitions, the measure at issue sets out the 'applicable administrative provisions, with which compliance is mandatory' for products with certain objective 'characteristics'.[327] The Appellate Body thus concluded in *EC – Asbestos*:

> Viewing the measure as an integrated whole, we see that it lays down 'characteristics' for all products that might contain asbestos, and we see also that it lays down the 'applicable administrative provisions' for certain products containing chrysotile asbestos fibres which are excluded from the prohibitions in the measure. Accordingly, we find that the measure is a 'document' which 'lays down product characteristics . . . including the applicable administrative provisions, with which compliance is mandatory.' For these reasons, we conclude that the measure constitutes a 'technical regulation' under the *TBT Agreement*.[328]

Confirming its ruling in *EC – Asbestos*,[329] the Appellate Body in *EC – Sardines* established a three-tier test for determining whether a measure is a 'technical regulation' under the *TBT Agreement*:

- the measure must apply to an identifiable product or group of products;
- the measure must lay down product characteristics; and
- compliance with the product characteristics laid down in the measure must be mandatory.[330]

Applying this test in *EC – Sardines* to EC Regulation 2136/89 on common marketing standards for preserved sardines, the Appellate Body further clarified its reasoning in *EC – Asbestos*. With regard to the first element of its three-tier test, the

---

[325] *Ibid.*, para. 72.   [326] *Ibid.*, para. 73.   [327] *Ibid.*, para. 74.   [328] *Ibid.*, para. 75.
[329] See *ibid.*, paras. 66–70.   [330] *See* Appellate Body Report, *EC – Sardines*, para. 176.

Appellate Body held that a measure which does not expressly identify the products to which it applies could still be applicable to identifiable products (as required by the first element of the test).[331] The tool that the Appellate Body used to determine whether, in this case, *Sardinops sagax* was an identifiable product was an examination of the way the EC Regulation was enforced. As the enforcement of the EC Regulation had led to a prohibition against labelling *Sardinops sagax* as 'preserved sardines', this product was considered to be identifiable.[332]

With regard to the second element of the three-tier test, the question arose as to whether a 'naming' rule, such as the rule to name *Sardina pilchardus* 'preserved sardines', laid down product characteristics. The Appellate Body held in this respect that product characteristics include means of identification and that, therefore, the naming rule at issue definitely met the requirement of the second element of the test.[333] As the European Communities did not contest that compliance with the Regulation at issue was mandatory, the Appellate Body found that the third element of the three-tier test was also met, and the measure was therefore a 'technical regulation' for purposes of the *TBT Agreement*.[334]

In *EC – Trademarks and Geographical Indications (Australia)*, the Panel applied this three-tier test in order to assess whether a labelling requirement and inspection structures for the registration of individual geographical indications (GIs) qualified as a technical regulation. First, with regard to the labelling requirement, setting out the condition that the country of origin must be indicated clearly on the product label, the Panel concluded that this requirement was a 'technical regulation' within the meaning of Annex 1.1 of the *TBT Agreement*.[335] Secondly, with regard to the inspection structures, Australia had argued these inspection structures qualified as a 'technical regulation'. The Panel disagreed. Looking at the term 'technical regulation' in its context of Annex 1 of the *TBT Agreement*, the Panel observed that this term 'is one of a suite of definitions that includes "standard" and "conformity assessment procedures" '.[336] The Panel also noted that the terms 'technical regulations' and 'standards' are themselves part of the definition of the term 'conformity assessment procedures'. Looking at this context and the object and purpose of the *TBT Agreement*, the Panel held:

> This definition shows that 'conformity assessment procedures' assess conformity with 'technical regulations' and 'standards'. This suggests that they are not only distinct from one other, but mutually exclusive . . . The object and purpose of the TBT Agreement is, in large part, disclosed by the two main groups of substantive provisions that it contains: one that relates to technical regulations and standards in Articles 2 to 4, and another that

---

[331] *Ibid.*, para. 180.   [332] *Ibid.*, para. 184.   [333] See *ibid.*, paras. 190–1.   [334] See *ibid.*, paras. 194–5.
[335] The Panel in *EC – Trademarks and Geographical Indications (Australia)* noted that '[t]he issue is not whether the content of the label refers to a product characteristic: the label on a product *is* a product characteristic'. Panel Report, *EC – Trademarks and Geographical Indications (Australia)*, para. 7.449. With regard to the third element of the test, namely whether compliance with the labelling requirement was mandatory, the Panel noted that the negative implication that follows from the labelling requirement is that products with a GI identical to a Community protected name that do not satisfy this labelling requirement must *not* use the indications PDO (protected designation of origin), PGI (protected geographical indication) or equivalent national indications and, to the extent that they fall within the protection granted to a prior identical Community protected name, must *not* be marketed in the European Communities using that GI. Consequently, the Panel held that the labelling requirement at issue was a mandatory requirement. *Ibid.*, para. 7.456.   [336] *Ibid.*, para. 7.511.

relates to conformity assessment procedures in Articles 5 to 9. It is also reflected in the preamble, of which the fifth recital, and also the third and fourth recitals, draw this distinction. If the Panel were to embed measures subject to Articles 5 to 9 in the definition of a technical regulation and thereby subject them to the technical regulations provisions in Articles 2 to 4 as well, it would lead to an unreasonable result. In this respect, we note that the explanatory note refers to 'procedures for . . . inspection' as an example of conformity assessment procedures. This suggests that a procedure for inspection is not a technical regulation.[337]

According to the Panel, the inspection structures were 'conformity assessment procedures' and since they were 'conformity assessment procedures', they could not be 'technical regulations' at the same time. The Panel held that the inspection structures concerned could be 'excluded *a priori* from the definition of a 'technical regulation' under the TBT Agreement'.[338]

Questions and Assignments 8.13

What types of measure fall within the scope of application of the *TBT Agreement*? What are the criteria to determine whether a measure is a 'technical regulation' for purposes of the *TBT Agreement*? Explain these criteria. What is the main difference between a technical regulation and a standard for purposes of the *TBT Agreement*? Why can a conformity assessment procedure not be regarded as a technical regulation as defined in the *TBT Agreement*?

8.3.1.2. *Personal scope of application*

Although the *TBT Agreement* is mainly addressed to central government bodies, it explicitly aims to extend its application to 'other bodies' responsible for the establishment of technical regulations, standards, or execution of conformity assessment procedures. These 'other bodies' covered by the *TBT Agreement* primarily consist of local government bodies and non-governmental bodies. Local government bodies are all bodies of government other than central government, such as provinces, *Länder*, cantons or municipalities. They include any organ subject to the 'control of such a government in respect of the activity in question'.[339]

Non-governmental bodies in the context of the *TBT Agreement* are defined as bodies other than central government or local government bodies. The *TBT Agreement* extends its application to those 'other bodies' by imposing, on WTO Members, the obligation:

- to take measures in order to ensure compliance with the *TBT Agreement* by local government bodies and non-governmental bodies; and

---

[337] *Ibid.*, paras. 7.512–7.513.
[338] *Ibid.*, para. 7.514. As Australia had challenged the inspection structures only under Article 2.2 of the *TBT Agreement*, which deals with technical regulations, and had made no claims under the disciplines that cover conformity assessment procedures, the Panel did not need to consider this issue further.
[339] Annex 1.7 of the *TBT Agreement*.

- to refrain from taking measures that could encourage actions by these other bodies that are inconsistent with the provisions of the *TBT Agreement*.

It does so with respect to the obligations related to technical regulations, standards and procedures for assessment of conformity.[340] Note, in particular, the 'Code of Good Practice' in Annex 3 of the *TBT Agreement*. This 'Code of Good Practice' applies to the preparation, adoption and use of standards. Members have to ensure that their central government standardising bodies accept and comply with the 'Code of Good Practice'. In addition, Members have, pursuant to Article 4 of the *TBT Agreement*, the obligation to take such reasonable measures as are available to them to ensure that local and non-governmental standardising bodies also accept and comply with the Code.[341] This provision is of particular importance as private standards have an increasing impact on international trade. In 2006, *BRIDGES* reported the following on the growing importance of private standards as barriers to trade:

> The issue of private standards has . . . come up in the Committee on Technical Barriers to Trade (TBT) . . . [M]any voluntary schemes that would be covered by the TBT Agreement are being imposed by private actors. In this context, the proliferation of eco-labels in developed country market[s] has attracted particular concern from developing country exporters.[342]

8.3.1.3. *Temporal scope of application*

In *EC – Sardines*, the issue arose whether the *TBT Agreement* applies to technical regulations which were already in force on 1 January 1995, i.e. the date on which the *TBT Agreement* entered into force. In deciding this issue, the Panel and Appellate Body referred to Article 28 of the *Vienna Convention on the Law of Treaties*, which states that:

> [u]nless a different intention appears from the treaty or is otherwise established, its provisions do not bind a party in relation to any act or fact which took place or any situation which ceased to exist before the date of entry into force of the treaty with respect to that party.

Applying this basic provision of treaty law, both the Panel and the Appellate Body held that the EC regulation at issue, although adopted prior to 1 January 1995, was still in force and thus could not be considered as a 'situation which has ceased to exist'.[343] Therefore, it can be concluded that the *TBT Agreement* applies to technical regulations which, although adopted prior to 1995, are still in force.

---

[340] See Articles 3, 4, 7 and 8 of the *TBT Agreement*.
[341] As of 31 January 2007, 160 standardising bodies from 114 WTO Member countries had notified their acceptance of the 'Code of Good Practice', among them, eighty-three central governmental standardising bodies, sixty-six nongovernmental standardising bodies, three statutory bodies, two parastatal bodies, three non-governmental regional bodies, one central governmental/nongovernmental body, one central governmental/local governmental body and one autonomous body. See Committee on Technical Barriers to Trade, *List of Standardising Bodies That Have Accepted the Code of Good Practice for the Preparation, Adoption and Application of Standards since 1 January 1995. Note by the Secretariat*, G/TBT/CS/2/Rev.13, dated 2 March 2007 and G/TBT/CS/2/Rev. 13/Corr.1, dated 8 March 2007.
[342] *BRIDGES Weekly Trade News Digest*, 18 October 2006, 6.
[343] See Panel Report, *EC – Sardines*, para. 7.60, and Appellate Body Report, *EC – Sardines*, para. 216.

Questions and Assignments 8.14

What institutions or bodies are covered by the rules of the *TBT Agreement*? Why are the rules of the *TBT Agreement* not limited to central government bodies? What are 'private standards'? Are 'private standards' subject to the disciplines of the *TBT Agreement*? Does the *TBT Agreement* apply to a technical regulation adopted in 1990?

8.3.2. Relationship with other WTO agreements

This section examines first the relationship of the *TBT Agreement* with the *SPS Agreement* and the *Agreement on Government Procurement*, and then its relationship with the GATT 1994.

8.3.2.1. *The SPS Agreement and the Agreement on Government Procurement*

As mentioned above, the scope of application of the *TBT Agreement* is determined by the type of measure. The *TBT Agreement* applies, in principle, to technical regulations, standards and conformity assessment procedures as defined in Annex 1 thereof. However, to avoid overlap with other WTO agreements, the scope of application of the *TBT Agreement* has been limited in favour of two other WTO agreements: the *SPS Agreement* and the *Agreement on Government Procurement*. The applicability of either of these agreements to a measure excludes the applicability of the *TBT Agreement*, even where the measure at issue is found to be in conformity with these agreements.

Pursuant to Article 1.4 of the *TBT Agreement*, purchasing specifications related to the production or consumption of governmental bodies do not fall within the scope of application of the *TBT Agreement* as they are dealt with in the *Agreement on Government Procurement*. Note, however, that the *Agreement on Government Procurement* is a plurilateral agreement; the disciplines set out in this agreement do not apply to most WTO Members.[344]

Pursuant to Article 1.5 of the *TBT Agreement*, sanitary and phytosanitary measures are excluded from the scope of application of the *TBT Agreement*, even if they take the form of technical regulations, standards or conformity assessment procedures. Sanitary and phytosanitary measures are subject to the distinct disciplines of the *SPS Agreement*, discussed later in this chapter.[345] It is the *purpose* of the measure that qualifies it as a sanitary or phytosanitary measure. In *EC – Hormones*, the United States and Canada claimed, *inter alia*, that the measures at issue were inconsistent with the *TBT Agreement*. Referring to Article 1.5 of the *TBT Agreement*, the Panel found, however, that, since these measures were

---

[344] See above, p. 474.
[345] See Article 1.5 of the *TBT Agreement*. For further discussion of the definition of sanitary and phytosanitary measures, see below, pp. 834–7.

SPS measures, the *TBT Agreement* did not apply in the *EC – Hormones* dispute.[346] In a more recent case, *EC – Approval and Marketing of Biotech Products*, the Panel further clarified the relationship between the *SPS Agreement* and the *TBT Agreement* as follows:

> Article 1.5 makes clear that to the extent the requirement at issue qualifies as an SPS measure, the provisions of the *TBT Agreement* would 'not apply', even though the requirement at issue is contained in a law which meets the definition of a technical regulation . . . to the extent the requirement at issue is applied for a purpose not covered by Annex A(1) of the *SPS Agreement*, it can be viewed as embodying a non-SPS measure. By its terms, Article 1.5 is not applicable to non-SPS measures. However, given that the requirement is assumed to be part of a technical regulation, it falls to be assessed under the *TBT Agreement*, to the extent it embodies a non-SPS measure.[347]

The Panel recognised that a single measure can have more than one purpose: one that falls within the definition of an SPS measure *and* one that does not. The Panel held that, assuming that the measure at issue falls within the definition of a technical regulation, to the extent that the measure is applied for a non-SPS purpose, it is a measure to which the disciplines of the *TBT Agreement* apply.

8.3.2.2. The GATT 1994

The relationship between the GATT 1994 and the *TBT Agreement* is of a different nature and is not characterised by mutual exclusivity. The Panel in *EC – Asbestos* held that in a case where both the GATT 1994 and the *TBT Agreement* appear to apply to a given measure, a panel must first examine whether the measure at issue is consistent with the *TBT Agreement* since this agreement deals 'specifically and in detail' with technical barriers to trade.[348] However, should a panel find a measure to be consistent with the *TBT Agreement*, it must still examine whether the measure is also consistent with the GATT 1994.

Note, in general, that the relationship between the GATT 1994 and the other multilateral agreements on trade in goods (including the *TBT Agreement*) is governed by the *General Interpretative Note to Annex 1A* of the *WTO Agreement*.[349] This Note provides that in case of conflict between a provision of the GATT 1994 and a provision of another multilateral agreement on trade in goods, the latter will prevail to the extent of the conflict.

Questions and Assignments 8.15

Can the *SPS Agreement* and the *TBT Agreement* apply to the same measure? Can the *TBT Agreement* and the GATT 1994 apply to the same measure? How would a Panel deal with such a situation?

---

[346] See Panel Report, *EC – Hormones (US)*, para. 8.29, and Panel Report, *EC – Hormones (Canada)*, para. 8.32.

[347] Panel Reports, *EC – Approval and Marketing of Biotech Products*, para. 7.167.

[348] See Panel Report, *EC – Asbestos*, para. 8.16. See on this point more generally, Appellate Body Report, *EC – Bananas III*, para. 204. See also Panel Report, *EC – Sardines*, paras. 7.14–7.19.   [349] See above, p. 47.

8.3.3. Basic substantive provisions of the *TBT Agreement*

The basic substantive provisions of the *TBT Agreement* contain several principles that are also found in the GATT 1994, such as: the most-favoured-nation (MFN) treatment obligation, the national treatment obligation and the obligation to refrain from creating unnecessary obstacles to international trade. In *EC – Asbestos*, the Appellate Body observed that the *TBT Agreement* intends to further the objectives of the GATT 1994. However, it immediately noted that the *TBT Agreement* does so through a specialised legal regime, containing different and additional obligations to those emanating from the GATT 1994.[350] The following sections examine the basic substantive provisions of the *TBT Agreement* relating to the following:

- MFN treatment;
- national treatment;
- the necessity requirement; and
- the use of international standards.

8.3.3.1. *MFN treatment and national treatment obligations*

With respect to technical regulations, Article 2.1 of the *TBT Agreement* provides that:

> Members shall ensure that in respect of technical regulations, products imported from the territory of any Member shall be accorded treatment no less favourable than that accorded to like products of national origin and to like products originating in any other country.

The national treatment obligation and the MFN treatment obligation thus apply to technical regulations.[351] Pursuant to Annex 3.D and Article 5.1.1 of the *TBT Agreement*, these obligations also apply to standards and conformity assessment procedures respectively. Thus, a requirement that tropical wood coming from Brazil be labelled as 'tropical wood', while there is no such requirement for tropical wood from African countries, would constitute a violation of the MFN treatment obligation set out in Article 2.1 of the *TBT Agreement*. Requiring accurate testing for the presence of GMOs in corn imported from the United States, while such verification is not required for corn from Australia, would constitute a violation of the MFN treatment obligation set out in Article 5.1.1 of the *TBT Agreement*. A requirement that imported furniture is fire-resistant, while no such requirement exists for domestically produced furniture, would constitute a violation of the national treatment obligation set out in Article 2.1 of the *TBT Agreement*.

---

[350] See Appellate Body Report, *EC – Asbestos*, para. 80. Therefore, caution needs to be used when transposing the interpretation given to these obligations under the GATT 1994 to the similar provisions in the *TBT Agreement*. The different context, structure and formulation of the provisions of the *TBT Agreement* can result in an interpretation that deviates from previously pronounced interpretations under the GATT 1994.

[351] Note that with regard to technical regulations adopted by local government bodies or non-governmental bodies, Article 3 of the *TBT Agreement* requires Members to take such reasonable measures as may be available to them to ensure compliance by such bodies with the provisions of Article 2.

Note that the Panel in *EC – Trademarks and Geographical Indications (Australia)* rejected Australia's claim of inconsistency with Article 2.1 of the *TBT Agreement* because Australia had not demonstrated that the formal difference made in the measure at issue between domestic and imported products led to any difference in treatment.[352]

As under the GATT 1994, when establishing whether a certain treatment is discriminatory, the determination of 'likeness' of the two products, which are subject to different treatment, is a prerequisite. The concept of 'like products' within the meaning of the relevant provisions of the *TBT Agreement* has not yet been the subject of dispute settlement proceedings.[353] As discussed above, the concept of 'like products' has been clarified in panel and Appellate Body reports relating to Articles I and III of the GATT 1994.[354] This case law is undoubtedly instructive for the interpretation of the concept of 'like products' in the context of the *TBT Agreement*. Remember, however, that the Appellate Body in *Japan – Alcoholic Beverages II* ruled that the concept of 'like products' has different meanings in the different *contexts* in which it is used.[355] In the GATT *context* a finding that products are like and are given discriminatory treatment leads to a finding of inconsistency with Article I or III of the GATT 1994. However, in the GATT context this GATT-inconsistency may subsequently be justified by the general exceptions under Article XX of the GATT.[356] Note that such a 'rule–exception' relationship, which exists between Articles I and III of the GATT 1994, on the one hand, and Article XX of the GATT 1994, on the other hand, is not so clearly replicated in the *context* of the *TBT Agreement*. The relationship between, for example, Articles 2.1 and 2.2 of the *TBT Agreement* remains to be clarified.[357]

Questions and Assignments 8.16

Describe the non-discrimination obligations contained in the *TBT Agreement*. Give some examples (other than those mentioned above) of measures that would constitute a violation of these non-discrimination obligations. How are the non-discrimination obligations under the *TBT Agreement* similar to or different from the non-discrimination obligations under the GATT 1994?

8.3.3.2. Necessity test

Article 2.2 of the *TBT Agreement* provides that, with respect to technical regulations:

---

[352] See *EC – Trademarks and Geographical Indications (Australia)*, paras. 7.473 and 7.475. On the requirements of the national treatment obligation of Article III:4 of the GATT 1994, and in particular, the 'treatment no less favourable' requirement, see above, p. 383.

[353] In *EC – Trademarks and Geographical Indications (Australia)*, the Panel found it unnecessary to rule on this issue in view of its finding that Australia had not made a *prima facie* case of less favourable treatment under Article 2.1. See *ibid.*, para. 7.463.   [354] See above, pp. 329, 351, 374.

[355] See Appellate Body Report, *Japan – Alcoholic Beverages II*, 114.

[356] On the 'general exceptions' under Article XX of the GATT 1994, see above, p. 616.

[357] On Article 2.2 of the *TBT Agreement*, see below, p. 818.

> Members shall ensure that technical regulations are not prepared, adopted or applied with a view to or with the effect of creating unnecessary obstacles to international trade.

With respect to standards and conformity assessment procedures, Annex 3.E and Article 5.1.2 of the *TBT Agreement* provide for the same obligation that such measures shall not be 'prepared, adopted or applied with the view to, or the effect of, creating unnecessary obstacles to trade'.[358]

To ensure that technical regulations do not constitute unnecessary obstacles to trade, Article 2.2 of the *TBT Agreement* further requires that:

> technical regulations shall not be more trade-restrictive than necessary to fulfil a legitimate objective, taking account of the risks non-fulfilment would create.

Article 2.2 enumerates several legitimate objectives that may justify the creation of a trade obstacle in the form of a technical regulation. The list of legitimate policy objectives of Article 2.2 includes:

- national security;
- the prevention of deceptive practices;
- the protection of human health and safety, animal or plant life or health; and
- the protection of the environment.

As indicated by the words '*inter alia*' in the introduction of the list, this is not an exhaustive list of legitimate policy objectives.[359] It will be up to panels and the Appellate Body to assess whether policy objectives other than those listed, such as animal welfare or fair labour practices, are, in a particular case, *legitimate* policy objectives within the meaning of Article 2.2. Note that Article 2.2 does not specify that the policy objectives referred to must be pursued within the territory of the regulating Member. Recall in this respect the discussion on the implicit jurisdictional limitation in Article XX of the GATT 1994.[360]

A technical regulation 'justified' under Article 2.2 as necessary to fulfil a legitimate policy objective will not automatically remain 'justified' in the future. Article 2.3 of the *TBT Agreement* provides that:

> Technical regulations shall not be maintained if the circumstances or objectives giving rise to their adoption no longer exist or if the changed circumstances or objectives can be addressed in a less trade-restrictive manner.

This could be seen as an 'elaboration' of the necessity test of Article 2.2.[361] Members thus continually have to assess the necessity of their technical regulations. They continually have to assess whether their technical regulations are not more trade-restrictive than necessary to fulfil a legitimate policy objective.[362]

---

[358] With respect to conformity assessment procedures, the implementation of this obligation is further specified in Articles 5.2.2, 5.2.3, 5.2.6 and 5.2.7 of the *TBT Agreement*.

[359] Recall that the list of legitimate policy objectives of Article XX of the GATT 1994 is an *exhaustive* list. See above, p. 617.   [360] See above, p. 619.

[361] See A. Appleton, 'The Agreement on Technical Barriers to Trade', in P. F. J Macrory, A. E. Appleton and M. G. Plummer (eds.), *The World Trade Organization: Legal, Economic and Political Analysis* (Springer, 2005), 394.

[362] A similar provision with regard to the evaluation of necessity in changed circumstances relating to conformity assessment procedures can be found in Article 5.2.7. This Article requires that, in cases where

In assessing the necessity of their technical regulations, Members must – as is explicitly stated in Article 2.2 of the *TBT Agreement* – take 'account of the risks non-fulfilment would create'.[363] It is clear that the risks of non-fulfilment of a technical regulation, aimed at meeting consumer preferences or avoiding deceptive practices, will be different from the risks that non-fulfilment of a regulation, aimed at the protection of human health, may entail.[364] Other elements that, according to Article 2.2, may be useful to consider in assessing the necessity of a technical regulation include: available scientific and technical information; related processing technology; and intended end-uses of products. To date, there is no case law on the assessment of necessity under the *TBT Agreement*. However, in line with the case law on the assessment of necessity under Article XX(b) and (d) of the GATT 1994, it is to be expected that the assessment of necessity under the *TBT Agreement* will also involve a process of 'weighing and balancing' the above-mentioned and other factors and elements.[365]

Questions and Assignments 8.17

What does the necessity requirement of Article 2.2 of the *TBT Agreement* entail? How is it likely to be applied? Is consumer protection a legitimate policy objective within the meaning of Article 2.2 of the *TBT Agreement*? Compare Article 2.2 of the *TBT Agreement* with Article XX of the GATT 1994.

8.3.3.3. *Use of international standards*

The harmonisation of national technical regulations and standards around international standards greatly facilitates the conduct of international trade.[366] Harmonisation around international standards diminishes the trade-restrictive effect of technical regulations and standards by minimising the variety of requirements that exporters have to meet on their different export markets, thus making it possible for them to take advantage of economies of scale.

Footnote 362 (*cont.*)
a product's specifications have changed after the determination of its conformity with the relevant technical regulations or standards, the conformity assessment procedure for that product be limited to what is necessary to determine that the product still meets the regulations or standards concerned.

[363] With regard to conformity assessment procedures, Article 5.1.2 states that risks of non-conformity shall be taken into account in the evaluation of necessity. Annex 3.E (standards) does not contain a provision regarding risks to be taken into account.

[364] As the *TBT Agreement* does not explicitly require a quantitative evaluation of risk, one could argue that, in line with the case law on Article XX(b) of the GATT 1994 and on Article 5.1 of the *SPS Agreement* an indication of risks in qualitative terms would suffice to justify a more trade-restrictive measure. See Appellate Body Report, *EC – Asbestos*, para. 167 (discussed above, pp. 624–8); and Appellate Body Report, *EC – Hormones*, para. 186 (discussed below, p. 854). In addition, it is likely that, again in line with this case law, Members may rely on scientific sources which, although diverging from the majority scientific opinion, constitute a qualified and respected opinion. See Appellate Body Report, *EC – Asbestos*, para. 178 (discussed above, pp. 627–8) and Appellate Body Report, *EC – Hormones*, para. 194 (discussed below, p. 857).

[365] See above, pp. 621 and 629.

[366] Also the harmonisation of national conformity assessment procedures around international guides and recommendations for conformity assessment procedures facilitates international trade.

Thus, the *TBT Agreement* requires Members to base their technical regulations on international standards. Article 2.4 of the *TBT Agreement* provides in relevant part:

> Where technical regulations are required and relevant international standards exist or their completion is imminent, Members shall use them, or the relevant parts of them, as a basis for their technical regulations.[367]

However, Article 2.4 further provides that Members do not have to base their technical regulations on international standards when:

> such international standards or relevant parts would be an ineffective or inappropriate means for the fulfilment of the legitimate objectives pursued, for instance because of fundamental climatic or geographical factors or fundamental technological problems.

The Panel and Appellate Body Reports in *EC – Sardines* illustrate the importance, as well as the contentious nature, of the requirement under Article 2.4 of the *TBT Agreement* that a technical regulation be based on an international standard. One of the central issues that arose in this case was whether the international standard 'Codex Stan 94', developed by an international food-standard-setting body, the Codex Alimentarius Commission, constituted a *relevant* international standard for the purposes of Article 2.4. The Panel's examination of this question focused on whether the product coverage of the Codex Stan 94 was similar to that of the EC's technical regulation, the measure at issue. According to the Panel, the examination of relevance with regard to the subject matter entails an analysis of whether the Codex Stan 94 'bears upon, relate[s] to or [is] pertinent to' the EC's technical regulation.[368] The European Communities argued that while the Codex Stan 94 deals with sardines and other sardine-type products, the EC's technical regulation exclusively concerns the product *Sardina pilchardus*.[369] However, the Panel concluded that this argument was not sufficient to reject the relevance of Codex Stan 94 as an international standard as both measures cover the same product (*Sardina pilchardus*) and include similar types of requirements as regards this product, such as those relating to labelling, presentation and packing medium.[370] The Appellate Body upheld the findings of the Panel on this issue.[371]

Another issue that arose in *EC – Sardines* was whether the EC's technical regulation was – as required by Article 2.4 – *based on* the international standard. In line with the case law on the meaning of 'based on' in the *SPS Agreement*, the Panel in *EC – Sardines* concluded that the term 'based on' is not equivalent to the term 'conform to', but imposes the obligation to 'employ or apply' the international standard as 'the principal constituent or fundamental principle for the purpose of enacting the technical regulation'.[372] According to the Appellate

---

[367] In view of this requirement, it is not surprising that Article 2.6 of the *TBT Agreement* requires Members to play a full part, within the limits of their resources, in the preparation of international standards for products for which they either have adopted or expect to adopt technical regulations.
[368] Panel Report, *EC – Sardines*, para. 7.68.   [369] See Appellate Body Report, *EC – Sardines*, para. 230.
[370] Panel Report, *EC – Sardines*, para. 7.69.   [371] See Appellate Body Report, *EC – Sardines*, para. 233.
[372] Panel Report, *EC – Sardines*, para. 7.110. On the meaning of 'based on' in the *SPS Agreement*, see below, pp. 849–50 and 856–7.

Body in *EC – Sardines*, this comes down to an analysis of 'whether there is a contradiction between Codex Stan 94 and the EC regulation'.[373] It would seem that in the absence of a 'contradiction' between the technical regulation and the international standard, the technical regulation can be considered to be 'based on' the international standard.

With regard to the concept of 'international standard', note that the Appellate Body interpreted the Explanatory Note to the definition of the term 'standard' set out in Annex 1.2 of the *TBT Agreement* as not requiring adoption by consensus in the relevant standard-setting organisation.[374] Thus, an international standard not adopted by consensus can still constitute a relevant international standard for the purposes of Article 2.4 of the *TBT Agreement*.[375]

As indicated above, a technical regulation does *not* have to be based on the relevant international standard *when* that standard constitutes an inappropriate or ineffective means to achieve the legitimate objective pursued. In *EC – Sardines*, the Panel and the Appellate Body examined whether this exemption from the obligation to base the technical regulation on the relevant international standard was applicable.

A first step in this examination is whether a 'legitimate objective' is pursued. As discussed above, Article 2.2 of *TBT Agreement* contains a *non-exhaustive* list of legitimate policy objectives. The objectives pursued by the EC's technical regulation at issue in *EC – Sardines* – namely, the protection of market transparency, consumer protection and fair competition – are objectives not included in the list of Article 2.2. However, Peru, the complainant, did not contest the legitimacy of these objectives and the Panel thus refrained from ruling on their legitimacy.[376]

A second step in the examination of the applicability of the Article 2.2 exemption is whether the international standard is an inappropriate or ineffective means to achieve the legitimate objective(s) pursued by the technical regulation. According to the Appellate Body in *EC – Sardines*, it is for the complainant to demonstrate that the international standard in question is both an effective *and* an appropriate means to fulfil the legitimate objective.[377] The difference between effectiveness and appropriateness is that:

---

[373] Appellate Body Report, *EC – Sardines*, para. 249.

[374] See *ibid.*, paras. 222–3. This finding upholds that of the Panel in this case. See Panel Report, *EC – Sardines*, para. 7.90.

[375] Note that the TBT Committee has adopted a decision regarding the principles it considered important in the development of international standards, in which one of the principles laid down is that of consensus. See Committee on Technical Barriers to Trade, *Decisions and Recommendations Adopted by the Committee since 1 January 1995*, Note by the Secretariat, Revision, G/TBT/1/Rev.8, adopted 23 May 2008. However, the Panel in *EC – Sardines* declined to use this decision as an interpretative tool in deciding whether the standard at issue was a relevant standard for purposes of the *TBT Agreement*, finding that it was 'a policy statement of preference and not the controlling provision in interpreting the expression 'relevant international standard' as set out in Article 2.4 of the TBT Agreement'. Panel Report, *EC – Sardines*, para. 7.91.

[376] The Panel, however, referred to the interpretation of the Panel in *Canada – Pharmaceuticals Patents* of the concept of 'legitimate interests' as 'a normative claim for protection of interests that are 'justifiable' in the sense that they are supported by relevant public policies or other social norms'. Panel Report, *EC – Sardines*, para. 7.121.

[377] See Appellate Body Report, *EC – Sardines*, paras. 274–5 and 287. Given the conceptual similarities between Articles 3.1 and 3.3 of the *SPS Agreement*, and Article 2.4 of the *TBT Agreement*, the Appellate Body held that

> [t]he question of effectiveness bears upon the *results* of the means employed, whereas the question of appropriateness relates more to the *nature* of the means employed.[378]

In other words, the international standard 'would be *effective* if it had the capacity to accomplish all . . . objectives [pursued], and it would be *appropriate* if it were suitable for the fulfilment of all . . . objectives [pursued]'.[379]

Note that – as provided for in Article 2.5 of the *TBT Agreement* – a technical regulation which is adopted with a view to achieving a legitimate objective explicitly enumerated in Article 2.2 and is in accordance with a relevant international standard, shall be *presumed* not to create an unnecessary obstacle to trade, as required by Article 2.2 discussed above. This means that in combination with the enumerated legitimate objectives under Article 2.2, international standards have the function of exempting trade-restrictive technical regulations from the necessity requirement of Article 2.2.

With regard to conformity assessment procedures, the *TBT Agreement* introduces similar requirements in Article 5.4. Member countries shall use the relevant guides or recommendations, existent or imminent, as a basis for their conformity assessment procedures, unless the guide or recommendation is an inappropriate means to ensure conformity. Unlike Article 2.4, the criterion of effectiveness of the international guide or recommendation is not mentioned in Article 5.4.

With regard to standards, note that paragraph F of the Code of Good Practice obliges standardising bodies to use as a basis for their standards international standards that exist or whose completion is imminent, unless they would be ineffective or inappropriate.

Questions and Assignments 8.18

Do Members have to base their technical regulations on international standards? When is a technical regulation 'based on' an international standard? Under what circumstances may Members adopt or maintain a technical regulation that is not based on an existing international standard? Is it for the Member, adopting such a regulation, to establish that the existing international standard is 'an ineffective or inappropriate means for the fulfilment of the legitimate objectives pursued'? Is the harmonisation of national technical regulations and national standards around international standards, in your opinion, a useful exercise?

8.3.4. Other substantive provisions

Apart from the basic substantive provisions discussed in the previous section, the *TBT Agreement* also contains a number of other substantive provisions which

---

its findings in *EC – Hormones* regarding the burden of proof under the former provisions were 'equally apposite' for the case at hand. It accordingly found that 'as with Articles 3.1 and 3.3 of the *SPS Agreement*, there is no "general rule–exception" relationship between the first and the second parts of Article 2.4'. *Ibid.*, para. 275.   [378] Panel Report, *EC – Sardines*, para. 7.116.
[379] Appellate Body Report, *EC – Sardines*, para. 288.

deserve to be mentioned. This section briefly examines the substantive provisions of the *TBT Agreement* relating to:

- equivalence and mutual recognition;
- product requirements in terms of performance; and
- transparency and notification.

8.3.4.1. *Equivalence and mutual recognition*

Article 2.7 of the *TBT Agreement* provides:

> Members shall give positive consideration to accepting as equivalent technical regulations of other Members, even if these regulations differ from their own, provided they are satisfied that these regulations adequately fulfil the objectives of their own regulations.

The *TBT Agreement* thus requires WTO Members to *consider* accepting, as equivalent, the technical regulations of other Members. They should, however, accept technical regulations of other Members as equivalent only if the foreign technical regulations *adequately* fulfil the legitimate objectives pursued by their own technical regulations.

With regard to conformity assessment procedures, Article 6.1 of the *TBT Agreement* requires Members to accept the results of such procedures by other Members, even if their conformity assessment procedures differ, as long as they provide an assurance of conformity with the domestic technical regulations or standards. Compliance with international guides and recommendations on conformity assessment procedures shall be taken into consideration when evaluating the adequateness of the competent conformity assessment bodies. Members are encouraged to enter into negotiations for the conclusion of agreements for the mutual recognition of the results of each other's conformity assessment procedures.[380] Article 9 of the *TBT Agreement* encourages the adoption of, and participation in, international and regional systems for conformity assessment. Such systems aim for cooperation between national certification bodies of Members and often take the form of multilateral recognition agreements. Examples of such international or regional systems are the International Accreditation Forum (IAF) and the Worldwide System for Conformity Testing and Certification of Electrical Equipment (IECEE).

8.3.4.2. *Product requirements in terms of performance*

With respect to technical regulations, Article 2.8 of the *TBT Agreement* provides:

> Wherever appropriate, Members shall specify technical regulations based on product requirements in terms of performance rather than design or descriptive characteristics.

The *TBT Agreement* thus prefers Members to adopt technical regulations on the basis of product requirements in terms of performance. With regard to standards,

---

[380] See Article 6.3 of the *TBT Agreement*.

Annex 3.I of the *TBT Agreement* provides for the same preference for standards based on product requirements in terms of performance. Performance-based requirements are typically less prescriptive than requirements based on product characteristics. Note, however, that the obligation of Article 2.8 applies only when 'appropriate'.

8.3.4.3. *Transparency and notification*

When no relevant international standard exists or when a proposed technical regulation is not in accordance with a relevant international standard and the proposed technical regulation may have a significant effect on trade of other Members, Article 2.9 of the *TBT Agreement* requires Members to:

- publish a notice, at an early stage, in such a manner as to enable interested parties in other Members to become acquainted with the proposed technical requirement;
- notify other Members through the WTO Secretariat of the products to be covered by the proposed technical regulation, together with a brief indication of the objective and rationale of the technical regulation; this notification must be done at an early stage of the process, when amendments to the proposed technical regulation can still be made and comments can be taken into account;
- provide other Members, upon their request, with copies of, and information on, the proposed technical regulation, including information on how the proposed technical regulation deviates from relevant international standards; and
- allow a reasonable time for other Members to make comments on the proposed technical regulation, to discuss these comments upon request, and to take the comments and the resulting discussion into account when eventually deciding on the technical regulation.[381]

The TBT Committee has adopted a decision clarifying the concept of 'significant effect on trade' as follows:

> For the purposes of Articles 2.9 and 5.6, the concept of 'significant effect on trade of other Members' may refer to the effect on trade:
>
> (a) of one technical regulation or procedure for assessment of conformity only, or of various technical regulations or procedures for assessment of conformity in combination;
> (b) in a specific product, group of products or products in general; and
> (c) between two or more Members.
>
> When assessing the significance of the effect on trade of technical regulations, the Member concerned should take into consideration such elements as the value or other

---

[381] The TBT Committee recommends that a minimum sixty-day time-limit be set for comments on notifications. The notifying Member is, however, encouraged to set a time-limit beyond sixty days. See Committee on Technical Barriers to Trade, *Decisions and Recommendations Adopted by the Committee since 1 January 1995*, Note by the Secretariat, Revision, G/TBT/1/Rev.8, dated 23 May 2002.

> importance of imports in respect of the importing and/or exporting Members concerned, whether from other Members individually or collectively, the potential growth of such imports, and difficulties for producers in other Members to comply with the proposed technical regulations. The concept of a significant effect on trade of other Members should include both import-enhancing and import-reducing effects on the trade of other Members, as long as such effects are significant.[382]

When a technical regulation is adopted to address an *urgent* problem of safety, health, environmental protection or national security, a Member may set aside the notification (and consultation) requirements set out in Article 2.9 of the *TBT Agreement*. However, in such instances, Members are subject to certain notification (and consultation) obligations *after* the adoption of the technical regulation.[383]

Article 2.11 of the *TBT Agreement* requires that all adopted technical regulations are:

> published promptly or otherwise made available in such a manner as to enable interested parties in other Members to become acquainted with them.

Except when a technical regulation addresses an *urgent* problem as referred to above, technical regulations may not enter into force immediately after publication. Article 2.12 of the *TBT Agreement* provides in relevant part:

> Members shall allow a reasonable interval between the publication of technical regulations and their entry into force in order to allow time for producers in exporting Members . . . to adapt their products or methods of production to the requirements of the importing Member.

Such a reasonable interval between the publication and the entry into force of a technical regulation is particularly important for producers in exporting developing-country Members. In accordance with the Doha Decision on Implementation-Related Issues and Concerns,[384] the TBT Committee adopted a decision in 2002 that the phrase 'reasonable interval', subject to the conditions in Article 2.12, 'shall be understood to mean normally a period of not less than 6 months, except when this would be ineffective in fulfilling the legitimate objectives pursued'.[385]

The *TBT Agreement* contains similar provisions with regard to the notification of standards and conformity assessment requirements.[386] As an additional requirement for standards, the *TBT Agreement* requires standardising bodies to publish, at least every six months, their work programme and report on the progress regarding the preparation and adoption of standards.[387]

Furthermore, Article 10 of the *TBT Agreement* requires each Member to establish an enquiry point which will answer enquiries of other Members and which will provide relevant documentation related to adopted technical regulations,

---

[382] *Ibid.*   [383] See Article 2.10 of the *TBT Agreement*.

[384] See Ministerial Conference, *Doha Decision on Implementation-Related Issues and Concerns. Decision of 14 November 2001*, WT/MIN(01)/17, dated 20 November 2001, para. 5.2.

[385] Committee on Technical Barriers to Trade, *Decisions and Recommendations Adopted by the Committee since 1 January 1995*, Note by the Secretariat, Revision, G/TBT/1/Rev.8, dated 23 May 2002.

[386] See Annex 3.L, M, N and O of the *TBT Agreement* (for standards) and Articles 5.6, 5.7, 5.8 and 5.9 of the *TBT Agreement* (for conformity assessment procedures).   [387] See Annex 3.J of the *TBT Agreement*.

standards and conformity assessment procedures.[388] If a Member reaches an agreement with any other country on issues related to technical regulations, standards or conformity assessment procedures which may have a significant effect on trade, at least one Member party to the agreement is required, under Article 10.7, to notify other Members.[389]

Another provision of the *TBT Agreement* that enhances transparency is Article 15.2, which requires governments to inform other Members about how they are implementing the agreement. Since 1995, 115 Members have submitted at least one statement under this provision.[390]

In order to ensure the uniform and efficient implementation of the transparency obligations in the *TBT Agreement*, the TBT Committee has agreed on guidelines and a recommended format for notifications.[391]

The case of the Colombian labelling regulations on natural rubber condoms challenged by Malaysia offers a good illustration of the relevance of the transparency and notification requirements of the *TBT Agreement* (as well as of the role of the TBT Committee, discussed below).[392] The Colombian Ministry of Social Welfare had proposed a draft regulation for the labelling of natural latex condoms, which required that each condom container provided for certain information such as a warning that natural rubber latex could cause irritation. Colombia had notified this proposed technical regulation to the WTO Secretariat, and thus to all other WTO Members, as required under Article 2.9 of the *TBT Agreement*. A Malaysian condom manufacturer voiced complaints on the proposed regulation, arguing that the regulation contravened Article 2.2 of the *TBT Agreement* due to a lack of scientific proof that natural rubber causes allergies. In addition, the Malaysian manufacturer argued that the draft regulation exceeded the international harmonised standard for the production of natural latex condoms that it already applied and that the draft regulation was thus as such contrary to Article 2.4 of the *TBT Agreement*. Taking up the concerns of its manufacturer, Malaysia submitted an objection to the notified draft regulation to Colombia, and raised the matter for discussion at the following meeting of the TBT Committee. In line with the practice of TBT Committee, the Colombian

[388] A full list of national enquiry points is contained in the following document: Committee on Technical Barriers to Trade, *National Enquiry Points*. Note by the Secretariat, G/TBT/ENQ/30, dated 22 June 2007 (last update).

[389] Such notification must indicate the products covered by the agreement and provide a brief description of the agreement. As of 19 October 2007, fifty-two such notifications were made and circulated by the Secretariat under document series G/TBT/10.7/N/*.

[390] See www.wto.org/english/news_e/news07_e/tbt_9nov07_e.htm, visited on 13 November 2007. The day before the July 2007 meeting of the TBT Committee, a workshop was organised to help those thirty-six Members that have not made statements under Article 15.2 so far. It was well attended and looked at different approaches and experiences, including those developing countries (such as Niger, Paraguay and Botswana) which have submitted statements. After this workshop, six Members submitted a statement under Article 10 of the *TBT Agreement*.

[391] See Committee on Technical Barriers to Trade, *Decisions and Recommendations Adopted by the Committee since 1 January 1995*, Note by the Secretariat, Revision, G/TBT/1/Rev.8, dated 23 May 2002. In 2005, the TBT Committee adopted, on a two-year trial basis, the *Format for the Voluntary Notification of Specific Technical Assistance Needs and Responses*, G/TBT/16, dated 8 November 2005. There have been four notifications thus far, all with regard to technical assistance needs.

[392] See N. Mansor, N. Hasniah Kasim and Y. Sook Lu, 'Malaysia: Labelling Regulations on Natural Rubber Condoms and the WTO TBT Agreement', in P. Gallagher, P. Low and A. L. Stoler (eds.), *Managing the Challenges of WTO Participation* (Cambridge University Press, 2005), 337–48.

government had the opportunity to respond to Malaysia's objection. The Colombian government did not respond officially but it appears that it withdrew the draft regulation as a consequence of Malaysia's action.[393]

Questions and Assignments 8.19

Under what circumstances are Members obliged to consider other Members' technical regulations as equivalent? Should technical regulations be based on product requirements in terms of performance rather than design or descriptive characteristics? When are Members required to notify their proposed technical regulations or conformity assessment procedures? What does the notification obligation entail?

8.3.5. Institutional and procedural provisions of the *TBT Agreement*

In addition to the substantive provisions discussed above, the *TBT Agreement* also contains a number of institutional and procedural provisions. This section deals with the provisions on:

* the TBT Committee; and
* dispute settlement.

8.3.5.1. *TBT Committee*

The *TBT Agreement* established a Committee on Technical Barriers to Trade, commonly referred to as the 'TBT Committee'.[394] This Committee is composed of representatives of all WTO Members and meets when necessary.[395]

In 2007, the TBT Committee held three regular meetings.[396] The function of the TBT Committee is to provide Members with a forum for consultations regarding any matters pertaining to the operation or objectives of the *TBT Agreement*. At the TBT Committee meeting of 5 July 2007, for example, Members discussed approximately thirty different trade concerns, including draft Dutch and Belgian laws on trade in seal products; Chinese pollution control policies for electronic information products; United States requirements for country of origin labelling; draft standards for the composition of cheese in Canada; Thai requirements for the labelling of snack foods; and a regulation of the European Communities dealing with the Registration, Evaluation and Authorisation of Chemicals (REACH).[397]

---

[393] The Malysian condom manufacturer reported that it continued to export condoms using its original packaging and continued to have a controlling market share in Colombia. See *ibid.*
[394] See Article 13.1 of the *TBT Agreement*.
[395] Pursuant to Article 13.1 of the *TBT Agreement*, the TBT Committee has to meet *at least* once a year.
[396] Committee on Technical Barriers to Trade, *Report (2007)*, G/L/843, dated 21 November 2007.
[397] See WTO News Item 'Technical Barriers to Trade', 5 July 2007, available at: www.wto.org/english/news_e/news07_e/tbt_5july07_e.htm, visited on 8 November 2007.

The TBT Committee must also undertake an annual review of the implementation and operation of the *TBT Agreement* (annual review).[398] Moreover, at the end of every three-year period, the TBT Committee undertakes an in-depth review of the operation of the Agreement (triennial review). At that time, the TBT Committee may recommend amendments to the rights and obligations contained in the Agreement if this is considered necessary 'to ensure mutual economic advantage and balance of rights and obligations'.[399] To date, the TBT Committee has undertaken twelve annual reviews and four triennial reviews, the last of which was concluded on 14 November 2006.[400] None of these reviews has resulted in any recommendation for amendment to the *TBT Agreement*.

8.3.5.2. *Dispute settlement*

Consultations and the settlement of disputes with respect to any matter affecting the operation of the *TBT Agreement* shall follow the provisions of Articles XXII and XXIII of the GATT 1994 as elaborated on and applied by the DSU.[401] The *TBT Agreement* contains a few 'special or additional rules and procedures' set out in Articles 14.2, 14.3, 14.4 and Annex 2 of the *TBT Agreement*.[402] These 'special or additional rules and procedures' prevail over the rules and procedures of the DSU to the extent that they differ.[403] Pursuant to Article 14.2 of the *TBT Agreement*, a panel, charged with the settlement of a dispute under the *TBT Agreement*, may establish, at the request of one of the parties to the dispute or at its own initiative, a *technical expert group* to assist the panel in questions of a technical nature.[404] In *EC – Asbestos*, the Panel decided to consult experts on an individual basis, rather than in a technical expert group. The European Communities argued that this was contrary to Article 14.2, which in its view *required* the establishment of a technical expert group in case of scientific or technical matters. The Panel held that the special rules or procedures only prevail over the provisions of the DSU where they cannot be read as complementing each other.[405] Article 14.2 does not exclusively prescribe the establishment of a technical expert group and can thus be read to complement Article 13 of the DSU, which allows a Panel to consult individual experts.[406] The Panel in *EC – Approval and Marketing of Biotech Products*

---

[398] See Article 15.3 of the *TBT Agreement*.   [399] See Article 15.4 of the *TBT Agreement*.

[400] See Committee on Technical Barriers to Trade, *Fourth Triennial Review of the Operation and Implementation of the Agreement on Technical Barriers to Trade under Article 15.4*, G/TBT/19, dated 14 November 2006.

[401] See Article 14.1 of the *TBT Agreement*. For a detailed discussion of the WTO dispute settlement system, see above, pp. 169–316.   [402] See Appendix 2 of the DSU.

[403] See Article 1.2 of the DSU. For a detailed discussion, see above, p. 179.

[404] As stated in Article 14.3, a technical expert group is governed by the procedures set out in Annex 2 of the *TBT Agreement*. The panel in question shall define the composition, terms of reference and working procedures of the expert group it has established. The members of a technical expert group shall be persons of professional standing and of relevant experience and shall not include citizens or government officials of a Member that is party to the dispute.

[405] For a discussion on the relationship between the rules and procedures of the DSU *and* special and additional rules and procedures contained in the covered agreements, see above, p. 179.

[406] See Panel Report, *EC – Asbestos*, paras. 8.10–8.11.

also decided to consult individual experts rather than technical expert groups.[407]

As mentioned above, not only central government bodies but also local government and non-governmental entities may adopt and apply technical regulations, standards and conformity assessment procedures. Articles 3, 4, 7, 8 and 9 of the *TBT Agreement* impose certain obligations on Members with regard to the conduct of these local government and non-governmental entities. Article 14.4 of the *TBT Agreement* provides:

> The dispute settlement provisions set out above can be invoked in cases where a Member considers that another Member has not achieved satisfactory results under Articles 3, 4, 7, 8 and 9 and its trade interests are significantly affected. In this respect, such results shall be equivalent to those as if the body in question were a Member.

Questions and Assignments 8.20

What are the most important functions of the TBT Committee? What special rules are in place to deal with the fact that panels may be faced with difficult technical issues in dispute settlement under the *TBT Agreement*? What is special about Article 14.4 of the *TBT Agreement*?

8.3.6. Special provisions for developing-country Members

As with many other WTO agreements, the *TBT Agreement* takes into account the specific situation of developing-country Members and the problems they may encounter in complying with the obligations of the *TBT Agreement*. This section discusses:

- technical assistance for developing-country Members; and
- provisions for special and differential treatment.

8.3.6.1. *Technical assistance*

Pursuant to Article 11 of the *TBT Agreement*, Members shall, upon request, advise or provide technical assistance to requesting Members, in particular to developing-country Members. The advice and technical assistance referred to in Article 11 primarily concern assistance in establishing institutions or legal frameworks dealing with the preparation of technical regulations and standards and the development of conformity assessment procedures. In addition, requested Members shall assist the requesting Member in achieving the following objectives:

---

[407] Panel Reports, *EC – Approval and Marketing of Biotech Products*, paras. 7.12–7.19. As the complainants had, *inter alia*, claimed a violation of the *TBT Agreement*, the Panel relied also on Article 14 of the *TBT Agreement* for its decision to consult individual experts and international organisations. However, the dispute was finally decided under the *SPS Agreement*.

- participation in international standardisation bodies;
- meeting their technical regulations;
- access to their systems of conformity assessment; and
- becoming a member of, or participating in, international or regional systems for conformity assessment.

In the provision of advice or technical assistance under Article 11, priority must be given to the needs of least-developed-country Members.[408] At its Doha Session, the Ministerial Conference placed emphasis on the need to facilitate effective participation of least-developed-country Members in the development of international standards.[409] To this end, cooperation with the relevant international organisations will continue to address the needs for technical assistance. Furthermore, Members are urged to provide financial and technical assistance to help least-developed-country Members to meet the requirements of any newly introduced TBT measure that may have a significant negative trade effect. In order to give Article 11 operational significance, the TBT Committee adopted a decision whereby technical assistance needs or donor programmes may be communicated to Members through the Secretariat.[410] Further, the TBT Committee decided to keep technical assistance as a standing agenda item for its meetings.

In the Fourth Triennial Review, the TBT Committee emphasised the need to improve transparency regarding the demand and supply of technical assistance.[411] It also noted the importance of enhancing efficiency and effectiveness of technical assistance, for example by the use of good practices, and welcomed the increasing participation of developing countries in international standardising bodies.[412]

8.3.6.2. Special and differential treatment

Although the *TBT Agreement* did not foresee a special transition period for developing-country Members during the first years of the WTO, Article 12.8 of the *TBT Agreement* explicitly recognises the difficulties that developing-country Members may face in implementing their obligations under the *TBT Agreement*. For this purpose, the TBT Committee may grant, upon request, time-limited exceptions, in whole or in part, from such obligations. In addition, pursuant to Article 12.4 of the *TBT Agreement*, developing-country Members do not have to

---

[408] See Article 11.8 of the *TBT Agreement*.
[409] See Ministerial Conference, *Doha Decision on Implementation-Related Issues and Concerns*, WT/MIN(01)/17, dated 20 November 2001, para. 5.3.
[410] Further, it was agreed that, if the requesting or donor Member agreed, the information concerning specific needs and technical assistance programmes would be circulated by the Secretariat to all Members on an informal basis. In addition, the Secretariat would reflect this information in annual reviews of the implementation and operation of the *TBT Agreement* if the Members concerned agreed. See Committee on Technical Barriers to Trade, *Decisions and Recommendations Adopted by the Committee since 1 January 1995*, Note by the Secretariat, Revision, G/TBT/1/Rev.8, dated 23 May 2002.
[411] Committee on Technical Barriers to Trade, *Fourth Triennial Review of the Operation and Implementation of the Agreement on Technical Barriers to Trade under Article 15.4*, G/TBT/19, dated 14 November 2006, 15.
[412] See *ibid.*, 16.

base their technical regulations, standards or conformity assessment procedures on international standards, if the international standards are not appropriate to their development or financial and trade needs, with particular
attention to the preservation of indigenous technology and production methods
and processes compatible with their development needs. Finally, Article 12.6 of
the *TBT Agreement* requires that Members shall take 'such reasonable measures
as available to them' to ensure that the international standardising bodies,
upon the request of developing-country Members, examine the possibility of
developing international standards concerning products of special interest to
developing-country Members.

Questions and Assignments 8.21

Are Members obliged to provide technical assistance to developing-
country Members under the *TBT Agreement*? What forms does technical
assistance take? In what ways does the *TBT Agreement* provide for
special treatment of developing-country Members?

8.4. THE *SPS AGREEMENT*

As mentioned above, within the general category of technical barriers to trade, a
specific category of measures can be identified, namely, sanitary and phytosanitary measures, commonly referred to as 'SPS measures'.[413] SPS measures are
measures aimed at the protection of human, animal or plant life or health from
certain specified risks. The negotiators of the WTO agreements considered that
these measures merited special attention due to their close link to agricultural
trade, a sector of trade notoriously difficult to liberalise. As a result, sanitary and
phytosanitary measures are dealt with in a separate agreement, the *Agreement on
the Application of Sanitary and Phytosanitary Measures*, commonly referred to as the
SPS Agreement.

WTO Members frequently adopt SPS measures to protect humans, plants or
animals in their territories from food-safety risks or risks from pests or diseases.
The *Financial Times* reported in January 2006 on a Japanese import ban on meat
as follows:

> Japan on Friday night reimposed a ban on all US beef imports after discovering a spinal
> cord in meat imported from a US farm at Narita airport, near Tokyo. The ban, which will
> be a huge blow to US meat producers, comes just a month after Japan began to re-import
> US meat following a two-year import prohibition . . . Japan had lifted its ban on condi-
> tion that meat come from cattle under 20 months old and that high-risk material, includ-
> ing spinal chord, be removed . . . The original Japanese ban was imposed in 2003 after
> the discovery of a cow on a farm in Washington state infected with bovine spongiform
> encephalopathy (BSE), or 'mad cow disease', which can be fatal in humans . . . Junichiro

---

[413] See above, p. 816.

Koizumi, Japan's prime minister, said he backed the decision by Shoichi Nakagawa, agriculture minister, to stop all beef imports until the US satisfactorily explained how potentially dangerous material had slipped through its safety checks.[414]

However, developing and developed countries exporting food and agricultural products, as well as international organisations, have observed that in recent years SPS measures are increasingly used as instruments of 'trade protectionism'. W. Barnes reported in the *Financial Times* in April 2006:

Stringent, often excessively strict, hygiene standards are increasingly being used by rich countries to block food imports from developing economies, according to researchers in Thailand, India and Australia . . . The recent bird flu scare was manna for Western safety officials, said a trade negotiator at the Thai commerce ministry. 'The rich food importers are getting better and better at manufacturing safety hazards – real and imagined,' the official said . . . A World Bank study found that trade in cereals and nuts would increase by \$12bn if all 15 importing countries [referring to the then 15 Member States of the European Union] adopted the international Codex standards for aflatoxin contamination, which is produced by a cancer-linked mould, than if they all abided by tougher EU requirements. Some safety measures appear exotic. Australia demands that imported chicken flesh be heated to 70 degrees Celsius for 143 minutes, creating 'poultry soup' according to one exporter.[415]

Similarly, the following report by A. Beattie in the *Financial Times* in July 2007 illustrates well the tension between regulations to address health concerns and trade in food and agricultural products:

The spat between the US and China over contaminated food exports highlights a rapidly spreading battle line in the world economy: the use of product standards to regulate, and some would say stifle, international trade. Such 'non-tariff barriers', particularly food standards, are frequently both more important and harder to eliminate than simple tariffs. Arguments frequently descend into a mire of competing scientific claims about safety and risk in which trade negotiators – let alone ministers and the general public – risk drowning in complexity. And while consumers' patriotic desire to protect domestic farmers or manufacturers requires some degree of altruism, given the higher prices this entails, fears of being poisoned by foreign food appeal directly to their self-interest . . . As the global trade in processed and perishable food grows faster than that for traditional commodities, there appears every likelihood that standards rather than tariffs will be the greater barrier to such goods' unimpeded journey around the world economy.[416]

The rules contained in the *SPS Agreement* reflect an attempt to balance the sometimes conflicting interests of the protection of health against SPS risks and the liberalisation of trade in food and agricultural products.

This section deals with:

- the scope of application of the *SPS Agreement*;
- the relationship between the *SPS Agreement* and other WTO agreements;
- the basic principles of the *SPS Agreement*;
- risk analysis obligations under the *SPS Agreement*;

[414] D. Pilling, 'Japan Re-imposes Ban on US Beef Imports', *Financial Times*, 20 January 2006.
[415] W. Barnes, 'Food Safety Fears "Used as Excuse to Ban Imports" ', *Financial Times*, 6 April 2006.
[416] A. Beattie, 'Food Safety Clash Tells of Trade Battles Ahead', *Financial Times*, 31 July 2007.

- other substantive, institutional and procedural provisions of the *SPS Agreement*; and
- special provisions for developing-country Members.

8.4.1. Scope of application of the *SPS Agreement*

With regard to the scope of application of the *SPS Agreement*, this section distinguishes between:

- the *substantive* scope of application, i.e. the types of measures to which the Agreement applies;
- the *personal* scope of application, i.e. the entities to which the Agreement applies; and
- the *temporal* scope of application of the Agreement.

8.4.1.1. *Substantive scope of application*

The disciplines of the *SPS Agreement* do not cover all measures for the protection of human, plant or animal life or health but, rather, apply to a clearly circumscribed set of measures. The substantive scope of application of the *SPS Agreement* is set out in Article 1.1, which provides in relevant part:

> This Agreement applies to all sanitary and phytosanitary measures which may, directly or indirectly, affect international trade.

For a measure to be subject to the *SPS Agreement*, therefore, it must be:

- a sanitary or phytosanitary measure; and
- a measure that may affect international trade.

A sanitary or phytosanitary measure, or 'SPS measure', is defined in paragraph 1 of Annex A of the *SPS Agreement* as:

> Any measure applied:
>
> (a) to protect animal or plant life or health within the territory of the Member from risks arising from the entry, establishment or spread of pests, diseases, disease-carrying organisms or disease-causing organisms;
> (b) to protect human or animal life or health within the territory of the Member from risks arising from additives, contaminants, toxins or disease-causing organisms in foods, beverages or feedstuffs;
> (c) to protect human life or health within the territory of the Member from risks arising from diseases carried by animals, plants or products thereof, or from the entry, establishment or spread of pests; or
> (d) to prevent or limit other damage within the territory of the Member from the entry, establishment or spread of pests.
>
> Sanitary or phytosanitary measures include all relevant laws, decrees, regulations, requirements and procedures including, *inter alia*, end product criteria; processes and production methods; testing, inspection, certification and approval procedures; quarantine treatments including relevant requirements associated with the transport of animals or plants, or with the materials necessary for their survival during transport; provisions on

> relevant statistical methods, sampling procedures and methods of risk assessment; and packaging and labelling requirements directly related to food safety.

From this definition, it is clear that the question of whether a measure is an 'SPS measure' depends on its *purpose* or *aim*. In broad terms, an 'SPS measure' is one that:

- aims at the protection of human or animal life or health from food-borne risks;
- aims at the protection of human, animal or plant life or health from risks from pests or diseases; or
- aims at the prevention or limitation of other damage from risks from pests.

Note that the definitions in Annex A refer specifically to the protection of human, animal or plant life or health or the prevention of other damage 'within the territory of the Member', thus excluding measures aimed at extraterritorial health protection from the scope of application of the *SPS Agreement*.

In *EC – Approval and Marketing of Biotech Products*, involving a challenge by the United States, Canada and Argentina against the European Communities with respect to measures affecting the approval and marketing of biotech products, the Panel had to determine whether three types of contested measures fell within the definition of an 'SPS measure'. These were: the European Communities' alleged *de facto* moratorium on the approval of biotech products; certain measures of the European Communities affecting the approval of specific biotech products, known as the 'product specific measures'; and the bans in place in six Member States of the European Union on varieties of biotech products that had already been approved at European level, known as the 'safeguard measures'.[417]

The Panel found that there are three elements in the definition of an SPS measure contained in Annex A.1 of the *SPS Agreement*:

- the *purpose* of the measure, as enumerated in sub-paragraphs (a) to (d);
- the *form* of the measure, as described in the second paragraph ('all relevant laws, decrees, [and] regulations'); and
- the *nature* of the measure, also set out in the second paragraph ('requirements and procedures, including . . .').[418]

In applying the first element of the definition, the Panel interpreted the purposes enumerated in sub-paragraphs (a) to (d) of the definition very broadly to cover almost all the objectives of the European approval legislation relevant to this dispute,[419] and the Member States' safeguard measures.[420] Only with regard

---

[417] Nine separate safeguard measures were taken by six Member States, namely Austria, France, Germany, Greece, Italy and Luxembourg. In each case, the relevant scientific committee of the EC found that there was no scientific basis for the use of the safeguard.

[418] See Panel Reports, *EC – Approval and Marketing of Biotech Products*, para. 7.149.

[419] The relevant EC approval procedures are those concerning the deliberate release of biotech products into the environment (Council Directive 90/220/EEC of 23 April 1990 and subsequently Directive 2001/18/EC of the European Parliament and of the Council of 12 March 2001 and repealing Directive 90/220/EC) and those concerning novel foods and novel food ingredients (Regulation (EC) 258/97 of the European Parliament and of the Council of 27 January 1997 concerning novel foods and novel food ingredients).

[420] The Panel examined each of the purposes of the EC approval legislation as well as of each of the nine safeguard measures individually and found that, except for two of the objectives of Regulation 258/97,

to the Regulation on novel foods and novel food ingredients did it find that two of the three purposes of the Regulation were outside the scope of sub-paragraphs (a) to (d).[421] Therefore the Regulation was to that extent held not to be an SPS measure. Interestingly, the Panel disagreed with the European Communities' argument that the *SPS Agreement* was not intended to cover risks to the environment in general. Instead, the Panel interpreted 'other damage' in sub-paragraph (d) to include not only economic damage or damage to property, but also damage to the environment (other than to the life or health of plants or animals) encompassing adverse effects on biodiversity, population dynamics of species or geochemical cycles.[422]

In applying the second element of the definition, the *form* requirement, the Panel recognised its broad ambit, noting the use of the word 'include', and held that, 'the reference to "laws, decrees [and] regulations" should not be taken to prescribe a particular legal form'.[423] It thus found that the *de facto* moratorium, the product-specific measures and the nine safeguard measures all met this requirement.[424]

The Panel then turned to the third element it had read into the definition of an 'SPS measure', namely the *nature* requirement, which it regarded as 'key' to its determination.[425] It relied on this requirement to find that the European Communities' general *de facto* moratorium on biotech approvals did not fall under the definition of an SPS measure. The Panel regarded the general *de facto* moratorium as neither a 'requirement' nor a 'procedure' but rather as the 'application' of approval procedures.[426] As the second paragraph of Annex A.1 does not refer to the 'application' of requirements and procedures, the Panel saw its way clear to conclude that the moratorium was not an SPS measure.[427] Similarly, the

---

Footnote 420 (*cont.*)

they all fell within the scope of subparagraphs (a) to (d) of Annex 1.A. See Panel Reports, *EC – Approval and Marketing of Biotech Products*, paras. 7.189–7.416 (with regard to the approval legislation) and paras. 7.2568–7.2592, 7.2617–7.2652, 7.2669–7.2692, 7.2709–7.2735, 7.2756–7.2765, 7.2781–7.2799, 7.2820–7.2840, 7.2862–7.2875 and 7.2898–7.2908 (with regard to each of the nine safeguard measures).

[421] According to the Panel, to the extent that the Regulation seeks to achieve the first of its three purposes, namely to ensure that novel foods do not present a danger for the consumer, it is applied for the purpose identified in Annex A.1(b) and is an SPS measure. To the extent that it is applied to achieve its second and third purposes, namely to ensure that novel foods do not mislead the consumer, and that they are not nutritionally disadvantageous for the consumer, it is not a measure applied for one of the purposes mentioned in Annex A.1 and is therefore not an SPS measure. See *ibid.*, paras. 7.415–7.416.

[422] See *ibid.*, paras. 7.197–7.211.   [423] *Ibid.*, paras. 7.422–7.423.

[424] The Panel here noted the fact that these measures were all legally binding and attributable to the European Communities or the relevant Member State government. See *ibid.*, para. 7.423 (with regard to the European Communities' approval legislation) and paras. 7.2598, 7.2655, 7.2694, 7.2740, 7.2773, 7.2804, 7.2845, 7.2881 and 7.2913 (with regard to each of the nine safeguard measures).

[425] See *ibid.*, para. 7.1338.

[426] The Panel found that the general moratorium should be characterised as a decision to delay final approval of the decision on specific applications until certain conditions were met. It rejected the argument that the moratorium should be seen as an across-the-board marketing ban on biotech products requiring approval, and thus as a 'requirement'. The Panel correctly noted that the pre-marketing approval system itself imposes a provisional ban on biotech products for which approval is sought, pending the final approval decision, yet the complainants chose not to challenge the pre-marketing approval system. The Panel also disagreed that the moratorium could be seen as itself a 'procedure' by setting out a particular mode or course of action to be followed by the Commission and the group of five EU Member States delaying applications. Instead, the Panel found that the European Communities continued to apply its existing approval procedures, but intentionally did not make full use of these procedures to complete the approval process. Panel Reports, *EC – Approval and Marketing of Biotech Products*, paras. 7.1338–7.1378.   [427] See *ibid.*, para. 7.1382.

Panel regarded the product-specific measures challenged in this dispute as 'the alleged failure by the [EC] to consider particular applications for final approval'.[428] As this was seen by the Panel to be neither a 'procedure' nor a 'requirement' but rather the 'application' of an approval procedure, it did not meet the Panel's 'nature' requirement and therefore did not fall under the definition of Annex A.1.[429] The Member States' safeguard measures, however, were found to meet the third element of the definition. In this regard the Panel recalled that,

> the reference in [Annex A.1] to 'requirements' is broad and unqualified. Hence, both an authorization to market a particular product and a ban on the marketing of a particular product may be considered as 'requirements'. The second example would constitute a negative requirement.[430]

Noting that each safeguard measure prohibited the marketing of the biotech product at issue, the Panel expressed its view that:

> a prohibition on the marketing of a particular product (within a particular territory) may be considered a 'requirement' for the purposes of Annex A(1).[431]

Therefore the nine safeguard measures were found to be 'SPS measures' within the meaning of the definition in Annex A.1 of the *SPS Agreement*.

A further requirement for the application of the *SPS Agreement* according to Article 1.1 is that the measure at issue must be a measure that 'may directly or indirectly affect international trade'. This requirement is easy to fulfil, as any measure that applies to imports can be said to affect international trade. Moreover, as pointed out by the Panel in *EC – Approval and Marketing of Biotech Products*, Article 1.1 only requires that the measure *may* affect international trade. Thus, 'it is not necessary to demonstrate that an SPS measure has an actual effect on trade'.[432] Hygiene requirements for street food vendors are arguably an example of an SPS measure which does not fall within the scope of application of the *SPS Agreement* because it does not – actually or potentially – affect international trade.

When a measure is an SPS measure *and* affects international trade, actually or potentially, that measure falls within the substantive scope of application of the *SPS Agreement*.[433]

---

[428] *Ibid.*, para. 7.1690.
[429] The Panel rejected the argument that the failure to consider particular applications for final approval amounted to a ban, and was thus a 'requirement' under Annex A.1. It also disagreed with the allegation that the EC's failure to consider particular applications for final approval was in itself a 'procedure' as it modified the approval procedure with respect to the biotech product in question. See *ibid.*, paras. 7.1690–7.1697 (with regard to the US claim), paras. 7.1701–7.1704 (with regard to the Canadian claim) and paras. 7.1711–7.1712 (with regard to Argentina's claim).
[430] *Ibid.*, para. 7.2597. This was reiterated with regard to each of the nine safeguard measures.
[431] *Ibid.*, para. 7.2599. Again, this finding was reiterated with regard to each of the nine safeguard measures.
[432] *Ibid.*, para. 7.435.
[433] As the Panel in *EC – Hormones* noted, there are no additional requirements for the applicability of the *SPS Agreement*. Contrary to what the European Communities argued in that case, the *SPS Agreement* contains, in particular, no requirement of a prior violation of a provision of the GATT 1994. See Panel Report, *EC – Hormones (Canada)*, para. 8.39; and Panel Report, *EC – Hormones (US)*, para. 8.36.

8.4.1.2. Personal scope of application

The adoption and implementation of SPS measures may sometimes be in the hands of bodies other than central government such as regulatory agencies, regional bodies and sub-federal governments. The *SPS Agreement* takes this into account by providing, in Article 13, that Members are fully responsible for the implementation of the Agreement and must enact and implement positive measures to ensure the observance of its rules by bodies other than central government bodies. The Panel in *Australia – Salmon (Article 21.5 – Canada)* held that the sanitary measures taken by the government of Tasmania, an Australian state, were subject to the *SPS Agreement* and fell under the responsibility of Australia.[434]

Members must take all reasonable measures available to them to ensure that local and regional government bodies as well as non-governmental bodies in their territories comply with the *SPS Agreement*. Members may not rely on non-governmental bodies to implement their SPS measures unless these bodies comply with the *SPS Agreement*. The obligation enshrined in Article 13 of the *SPS Agreement* is important as private standards have an increasing impact on international trade.[435] While they have the potential to boost international trade, they can also be burdensome for small suppliers:

> Some Members have suggested that governments should take responsibility for the WTO-compatibility of voluntary standards set by companies within their borders. At a meeting of the Committee on Sanitary and Phytosanitary (SPS) Measures from 27–28 June, Egypt, Argentina and several other developing countries said that governments were, in fact, responsible for the standard-setting activities of private sector entities operating within their territory. With this debate, meeting participants continued a two-year-old debate on private sector standards, which started when the small island state of St Vincent and the Grenadines first drew attention to the challenges it faced when trying to access the EU market due to strict standards set by commercial supermarket chains . . . Some developing countries cautioned that the remit of private sector standards was expanding, now touching on issues such as production methods, environmental concerns including 'food miles' (i.e. carbon emissions associated with transport of agricultural products), and labour and fair trade issues. This led to high expenses and further complications for their exporters.[436]

Note that it is still being discussed whether private standards should fall within the scope of the *SPS Agreement*.[437] As of yet, no determination has been made in this respect.[438]

---

[434] See Panel Report, *Australia – Salmon (Article 21.5 – Canada)*, para. 7.13.

[435] See also above, p. 814.

[436] *BRIDGES Weekly Trade News Digest*, 4 July 2007. See also www.wto.org/english/news_e/news07_e/sps_29 june07_e.htm, visited on 29 November 2007.

[437] There have been two years of 'exploratory discussions' on this issue. After reaching an impasse on the question whether the WTO has a role to play in disciplining private standards, at the SPS Committee meeting of 18–19 October 2007 Members agreed that future discussions should address proposals on how to deal with the challenges posed by private sector standards, and should focus on concrete case studies. See *BRIDGES Weekly Trade News Digest*, 31 October 2007.

[438] See Committee on Sanitary and Phytosanitary Measures, *Private Standards and the SPS Agreement*, Note by the Secretariat, G/SPS/GEN/746, dated 24 January 2007, 4. See also www.wto.org/english/news_e/news07_e/sps_28feb_1march07_e.htm, visited on 29 November 2007.

8.4.1.3. *Temporal scope of application*

The question arises whether the *SPS Agreement* is applicable to SPS measures adopted and/or applied before the entry into force of the agreement. This question was raised by the European Communities in *EC – Hormones*, and answered by the Appellate Body as follows:

> If the negotiators had wanted to exempt the very large group of SPS measures in existence on 1 January 1995 from the disciplines of provisions as important as Articles 5.1 and 5.5, it appears reasonable to us to expect that they would have said so explicitly. Articles 5.1 and 5.5 do not distinguish between SPS measures adopted before 1 January 1995 and measures adopted since; the relevant implication is that they are intended to be applicable to both.[439]

Therefore, Members have to review all of their existing SPS measures in the light of the disciplines of the *SPS Agreement*.

Questions and Assignments 8.22

What requirements must be met for the *SPS Agreement* to apply to a specific measure? Would a ban on the use of lead in children's playground equipment be regarded as an SPS measure? Explain your answer. Would an SPS measure adopted by a local regulatory agency be covered by the rules of the *SPS Agreement*? If so, against whom could the complaining Member institute a challenge? Give five examples of 'real-life' SPS measures.

8.4.2. Relationship with other WTO agreements

The *SPS Agreement* is not the only WTO agreement of relevance to measures for the protection of human, animal or plant life or health. The GATT 1994 and the *TBT Agreement* obviously also contain rules applicable to such measures. The position of health measures, under WTO law, is thus determined, within their respective spheres of application, by all three of these agreements. It is therefore necessary to examine the relationship between the *SPS Agreement* and the other relevant WTO agreements.

8.4.2.1. *The TBT Agreement*

The *TBT Agreement*, as discussed earlier in this chapter, applies to technical regulations, standards and conformity assessment procedures in general, including those aiming at the protection of human, animal or plant life or health. Clearly, SPS measures may often take the form of technical regulations, standards or

---

[439] Appellate Body Report, *EC – Hormones*, para. 128. For the issue of the temporal scope of the *TBT Agreement*, see above, p. 814.

conformity assessment procedures. As the rules of the *SPS Agreement* are in some respects stricter than those of the *TBT Agreement*, it could be to the advantage of a complaining Member to challenge a measure under the *SPS Agreement* rather than the *TBT Agreement*. However, this choice is not left to Members. As already discussed above and as explicitly set out in Article 1.5 of the *TBT Agreement*, the *TBT Agreement* does not apply to SPS measures.[440] When a measure is an 'SPS measure', as defined in Annex A.1 of the *SPS Agreement*, the *SPS Agreement* applies to the exclusion of the *TBT Agreement*, even if the measure would otherwise be considered a 'technical regulation, standard or conformity assessment procedure' for purposes of the *TBT Agreement*. The relationship between the *SPS Agreement* and the *TBT Agreement* can thus be described as one of mutual exclusivity.

However, as discussed above,[441] the Panel in *EC – Approval and Marketing of Biotech Products* noted that a single requirement may be imposed for a purpose that falls within the definition of an SPS measure as well as for a purpose not covered by this definition. It held that:

> to the extent the requirement in the consolidated law is applied for one of the purposes enumerated in Annex A(1), it may be properly viewed as a measure which falls to be assessed under the *SPS Agreement*; to the extent it is applied for a purpose which is not covered by Annex A(1), it may be viewed as a separate measure which falls to be assessed under a WTO agreement other than the *SPS Agreement*. It is important to stress, however, that our view is premised on the circumstance that the requirement at issue could be split up into two separate requirements which would be identical to the requirement at issue, and which would have an autonomous raison d'être, *i.e.*, a different purpose which would provide an independent basis for imposing the requirement.[442]

Such a requirement, according to the Panel, would simultaneously embody an SPS measure and a 'non-SPS measure'. As Article 1.5 of the *TBT Agreement* does not apply to non-SPS measures, if the requirement falls within the definition of a 'technical regulation' as defined in Annex 1.1 of the *TBT Agreement*, it would fall to be assessed under the *TBT Agreement* 'to the extent it embodies a non-SPS measure'.[443]

8.4.2.2. The GATT 1994

Contrary to the situation with respect to the *TBT Agreement*, no relationship of mutual exclusivity exists between the *SPS Agreement* and the GATT 1994. It is thus possible for a measure to be caught by the GATT disciplines as well as those of the *SPS Agreement*. Broadly speaking, the GATT 1994 would catch those SPS measures that are discriminatory or constitute quantitative restrictions to imports, in which case the measures would need to be justified under the exception contained in Article XX(b) of the GATT 1994 with respect to health protection measures. Although one of the motives behind the negotiation of the *SPS*

---

[440] See above, pp. 815–16.   [441] See above, p. 816.

[442] Panel Reports, *EC – Approval and Marketing of Biotech Products*, para. 7.165.

[443] *Ibid.*, para. 7.167. Although the Regulation on novel foods was found to be both an SPS measure and a non-SPS measure, the Panel found it unnecessary to decide the claims of Canada and Argentina under the *TBT Agreement* as the product-specific measures and the safeguard measures challenged were all found by the Panel to fall under the *SPS Agreement*. See *ibid.*, paras. 7.2524 and 7.2527 (with regard to the product-specific measures) and paras. 7.3412–7.3413 (with regard to the safeguard measures).

Agreement was the need to clarify and flesh out the Article XX(b) exception, it is important to note that the *SPS Agreement* goes much further than a mere elaboration of Article XX(b) by imposing a new and comprehensive set of rules.[444] However, this new Agreement did not replace the relevant GATT rules. Thus a measure that falls within the definition of an 'SPS measure' under Annex A.1 of the *SPS Agreement* and is therefore subject to the rules of the *SPS Agreement* may, to the extent that it is discriminatory or constitutes a quantitative restriction, also be caught, in principle, by the rules of the GATT.

As noted above, the relationship between the GATT 1994 and the other multilateral agreements on trade in goods (including the *SPS Agreement*) is governed by the *General Interpretative Note* to Annex 1A of the *WTO Agreement*.[445] This provides that in case of conflict between a provision of the GATT 1994 and a provision of another multilateral agreement on trade in goods, the latter will prevail to the extent of the conflict. However, a conflict between the *SPS Agreement* and the GATT 1994 is rather unlikely as the *SPS Agreement* takes on board the existing GATT disciplines relevant to health measures. This is reflected in the fact that Article 2.4 of the *SPS Agreement* contains a presumption of consistency with the relevant provisions of the GATT 1994 for all measures that are in conformity with the *SPS Agreement*. Thus, it would be logical, in a dispute involving an SPS measure, to begin by examining the measure's conformity with the rules of the *SPS Agreement* before examining its compliance with the GATT 1994. This is supported by the finding of the Panel in *EC – Hormones*.[446]

Questions and Assignments 8.23

How would you describe the relationship between the *SPS Agreement* and the *TBT Agreement*? Is it possible that the *SPS Agreement* and the *TBT Agreement* both apply to one and the same measure? If a particular measure falls under both the *SPS Agreement* and the GATT 1994, how should a panel proceed?

8.4.3. Basic principles of the *SPS Agreement*

The basic principles of the *SPS Agreement*, contained in Articles 2 and 3 thereof, reflect the underlying aim of balancing the need to increase market access for food and agricultural products, on the one hand, with the recognition of the sovereign right of governments to take measures to protect human, animal and plant life and health in their territories, on the other.

This section discusses the following basic principles of the *SPS Agreement*:

- the sovereign right of WTO Members to take SPS measures;

---

[444] This was recognised by the Panel in *EC – Hormones*. See Panel Report, *EC – Hormones (Canada)*, para. 8.41; and Panel Report, *EC – Hormones (US)*, para. 8.38.   [445] See above, pp. 47 and 816.
[446] See Panel Report, *EC – Hormones (Canada)*, para. 8.45; Panel Report, *EC – Hormones (US)*, para. 8.42.

- the obligation to take or maintain only SPS measures *necessary* to protect human, animal or plant life or health (the 'necessity requirement');
- the obligation to take or maintain only SPS measures based on scientific principles and on sufficient scientific evidence (the 'scientific disciplines');
- the obligation not to adopt or maintain SPS measures that arbitrarily or unjustifiably discriminate or constitute a disguised restriction on trade; and
- the obligation to base SPS measures on international standards except if there is scientific justification for deviation from those standards (the 'goal of harmonisation').

8.4.3.1. *Right to take SPS measures*

It is significant that the *SPS Agreement*, in Article 2.1, expressly recognises the *right* of Members to take SPS measures necessary for the protection of human, animal or plant life or health. This differs from the position of health measures under GATT rules where discriminatory measures or quantitative restrictions are in principle prohibited; justification for such measures must be found under Article XX(b) of the GATT 1994. This difference has important implications for the burden of proof in dispute settlement proceedings.[447] Under the GATT 1994, a Member imposing a discriminatory health measure or one that constitutes a quantitative restriction bears the burden of proof to show that it complies with the requirements of the Article XX(b) exception. On the contrary, under the *SPS Agreement*, the complaining Member must show that the measure is inconsistent with the rules of the *SPS Agreement*.

The right to take SPS measures is, however, not unlimited but is subject to the disciplines contained in the rest of the *SPS Agreement*. The basic disciplines can be found in Article 2.2 and 2.3, and are elaborated on further in later provisions of the *SPS Agreement*. These provisions take on board the existing GATT rules applicable to health measures *and* introduce new requirements for the use of SPS measures.

Questions and Assignments 8.24

What is the most significant implication of the principle that WTO Members have the right to adopt and maintain SPS measures? How does the treatment of health measures under the *SPS Agreement* differ from that under Article XX(b) of the GATT?

8.4.3.2. *Necessity requirement*

As set forth in Article 2.2 of the *SPS Agreement*, the sovereign right of Members to take SPS measures is, first of all, limited by the requirement that:

---

[447] See above, p. 628.

> any sanitary or phytosanitary measure is applied only to the extent necessary to protect human, animal or plant life and health.

This 'necessity' requirement clearly reflects the familiar 'necessity' requirement contained in Article XX(b) of the GATT 1994, the health policy exception in the GATT 1994.[448] The necessity requirement in Article 2.2 has not yet been subject to interpretation in dispute settlement.[449] As this requirement is made more specific in other provisions of the *SPS Agreement*, Members prefer to challenge SPS measures under these more specific provisions.[450]

Questions and Assignments 8.25

Do you agree that the 'necessity' requirement of Article 2.2 of the *SPS Agreement* reflects the 'necessity' requirement of Article XX(b) of the GATT 1994? Are complainants likely to argue a violation of the 'necessity' requirement of Article 2.2 of the *SPS Agreement*?

8.4.3.3. Scientific disciplines

Article 2.2 of the *SPS Agreement* also introduces new scientific disciplines for the use and maintenance of SPS measures. It requires that:

> any sanitary or phytosanitary measure . . . is based on scientific principles and is not maintained without sufficient scientific evidence, except as provided for in paragraph 7 of Article 5.

These requirements introduce science as the touchstone against which SPS measures will be judged. These scientific requirements are further elaborated on in Article 5.1, which provides that SPS measures must be based on a risk assessment.[451] With regard to these scientific disciplines, the Appellate Body in *EC – Hormones* held:

> The requirements of a risk assessment under Article 5.1, as well as of 'sufficient scientific evidence' under Article 2.2, are essential for the maintenance of the delicate and carefully negotiated balance in the *SPS Agreement* between the shared, but sometimes competing, interests of promoting international trade and of protecting the life and health of human beings.[452]

---

[448] See above, pp. 621–8.

[449] In *Japan – Apples*, the claim of the United States under Article 2.2, in both the original and the compliance disputes, did not address the necessity requirement but was limited to the allegation that the measure was maintained without sufficient scientific evidence. See Panel Report, *Japan – Apples*, para. 8.77, and Panel Report, *Japan – Apples (Article 21.5 – US)*, para. 8.35. The Panel in *EC – Approval and Marketing of Biotech Products* exercised judicial economy with regard to the claims of Canada and Argentina that the EU Member States' safeguard measures violated the necessity requirement of Article 2.2, after having found a violation of Article 5.1. See Panel Reports, *EC – Approval and Marketing of Biotech Products*, para. 7.3394.

[450] An example of such a more specific provision is Article 5.6 of the *SPS Agreement*, which requires, as discussed below, that SPS measures are not more trade-restrictive than required to achieve their policy objective.   [451] See below, pp. 853–7.   [452] Appellate Body Report, *EC – Hormones*, para. 177.

The Panel in *Japan – Apples* was the first to consider the meaning of the term '*scientific*' and the term '*evidence*' in Article 2.2.[453] It held that for evidence to be 'scientific' it must be gathered through scientific methods[454] and it favoured relying on scientifically produced evidence rather than purely circumstantial evidence.[455] With regard to the term 'evidence', the Panel held:

> Negotiators could have used the term 'information', as in Article 5.7, if they considered that any material could be used. By using the term 'scientific evidence', Article 2.2 excludes in essence not only insufficiently substantiated information, but also such things as a non-demonstrated hypothesis.[456]

The Panel noted that it would equally consider both direct and indirect scientific evidence, although their probative value would differ.[457]

The issue of what is meant by '*sufficient* scientific evidence' was addressed for the first time in *Japan – Agricultural Products II*. In that case, the Appellate Body held that it requires a *rational relationship* between the SPS measure and the scientific evidence. The Appellate Body ruled as follows:

> [W]e agree with the Panel that the obligation in Article 2.2 that an SPS measure not be maintained without sufficient scientific evidence requires that there be a rational or objective relationship between the SPS measure and the scientific evidence. Whether there is a rational relationship between an SPS measure and the scientific evidence is to be determined on a case-by-case basis and will depend upon the particular circumstances of the case, including the characteristics of the measure at issue and the quality and quantity of the scientific evidence.[458]

It is thus clear that panels have some discretion in determining whether a 'rational relationship' between the measure and the scientific evidence exists, in the light of the particular circumstances of each case. It would seem that where reputable scientific support for a measure exists, the requirement of 'sufficient scientific evidence' would be met. Moreover, in *EC – Hormones* the Appellate Body noted that in determining whether sufficient scientific evidence exists, panels should:

> bear in mind that responsible, representative governments commonly act from perspectives of prudence and precaution where risks of irreversible, e.g. life-terminating, damage to human health are concerned.[459]

Thus, the more serious the risks to life or health, the less demanding the requirement of 'sufficient scientific evidence'. In *Japan – Apples*, the Panel further elaborated on the 'rational relationship' test by introducing a proportionality criterion into Article 2.2 of the *SPS Agreement*. It found, on the evidence before it, that the risk of transmission of fire blight through the importation of apple fruit was negligible,[460] and contrasted this with the rigorous requirements composing the measure at issue. It found the measure at issue to be clearly

---

[453] See Panel Report, *Japan – Apples*, paras. 8.91–8.98.   [454] *Ibid.*, para. 8.92.
[455] *Ibid.*, para. 8.95, where it quoted a statement to this effect by a panel expert.   [456] *Ibid.*, para. 8.93.
[457] See *ibid.*, para. 8.98.   [458] Appellate Body Report, *Japan – Agricultural Products II*, para. 84.
[459] Appellate Body Report, *EC – Hormones*, para. 124.   [460] See Panel Report, *Japan – Apples*, para. 8.169.

disproportionate to the risk and thus a violation of Article 2.2.[461] The Appellate Body did not take issue with this proportionality test and noted that:

> for the Panel, such 'clear disproportion' implies that a 'rational or objective relationship' does not exist between the measure and the relevant scientific evidence, and, therefore, . . . that the measure is maintained 'without sufficient scientific evidence' within the meaning of Article 2.2 of the SPS Agreement.[462]

Further, in *Japan – Apples*, the Panel found that the scientific evidence, in order to be sufficient, must confirm the existence of a risk.[463] This was reiterated by the Panel in *Japan – Apples (Article 21.5 – US)* as follows:

> In other words, in order for scientific evidence to support a measure sufficiently, it seems logical to us that such scientific evidence must also be sufficient to demonstrate the existence of the risk which the measure is supposed to address. As a result, it seems reasonable to consider the extent of the relationship between the scientific evidence and the risk which this evidence is claimed to establish.[464]

According to the Panel, the new studies submitted by Japan did not provide sufficient scientific evidence to establish, in natural conditions, the risks which Japan tried to support with those studies.[465]

Pursuant to Article 2.2 of the *SPS Agreement*, quoted above, SPS measures must not be maintained without sufficient scientific evidence, *except* as provided for under Article 5.7. This provision, discussed in more detail below, deals with a situation in which there is insufficient scientific evidence. Governments are sometimes faced with situations where they need to act to prevent a possible risk despite insufficient scientific data regarding the existence and likelihood of the risk. Article 2.2 takes account of this fact by expressly referring to Article 5.7, which allows for provisional SPS measures to be taken. The relationship between Articles 2.2 and 5.7 was set out by the Appellate Body in *Japan – Agricultural Products II* as follows:

> [I]t is clear that Article 5.7 of the *SPS Agreement*, to which Article 2.2 explicitly refers, is part of the context of the latter provision and should be considered in the interpretation of the obligation not to maintain an SPS measure without sufficient scientific evidence. Article 5.7 allows Members to adopt provisional SPS measures '[i]n cases where relevant scientific evidence is insufficient' and certain other requirements are fulfilled. Article 5.7 operates as a *qualified* exemption from the obligation under Article 2.2 not to maintain SPS measures without sufficient scientific evidence. An overly broad and flexible interpretation of that obligation would render Article 5.7 meaningless.[466]

The existence of Article 5.7 thus argues against an overly broad and flexible interpretation of the obligation of Article 2.2 that SPS measures should not be maintained without sufficient scientific evidence. In *EC – Approval and Marketing of Biotech Products*, the relationship between Article 5.7 and the scientific obligations contained in Article 2.2 (and Article 5.1) was again at issue. The European

[461] See *ibid.*, para. 8.198. [462] Appellate Body Report, *Japan – Apples*, para. 163.
[463] Panel Report, *Japan – Apples*, para. 8.104. [464] Panel Report, *Japan – Apples (Article 21.5 – US)*, para. 8.45.
[465] *Ibid.*, para. 8.71. [466] Appellate Body Report, *Japan – Agricultural Products II*, para. 80.

Communities argued that 'Article 5.7 is not an exception to Article 2.2 in the sense that it could be invoked as an affirmative defence to a claim of violation under Article 2.2.'[467] Rather, it averred that 'Article 5.7 establishes an autonomous right of the importing Member.'[468] Therefore, in cases where Article 5.7 is applicable, the European Communities argued that the complaining party has to prove that the importing Member has acted inconsistently with this Article. The Panel, relying on the test used by the Appellate Body in *EC – Tariff Preferences*,[469] agreed with the European Communities that Article 5.7 is an autonomous right, and not merely an exception from the scientific obligations under Article 2.2 and Article 5.1.[470] Therefore, a measure falling under Article 5.7 is excluded from the scope of application of these scientific obligations.[471] The Panel explained the practical implications of this characterisation of Article 5.7 as follows:

> In concrete terms, characterizing Article 5.7 as a qualified right rather than an exception means that if a challenged SPS measure was adopted and is maintained consistently with the four cumulative requirements of Article 5.7, the situation is 'as provided for in paragraph 7 of Article 5' (Article 2.2), and the obligation in Article 2.2 not to maintain SPS measures without sufficient scientific evidence is not applicable to the challenged measure. Conversely, if a challenged SPS measure is not consistent with one of the four requirements of Article 5.7, the situation is not 'as provided for in paragraph 7 of Article 5' (Article 2.2), and the relevant obligation in Article 2.2 is applicable to the challenged measure, provided there are no other elements which render Article 2.2 inapplicable.[472]

The Panel pointed out that this has implications for the burden of proof regarding a violation of Article 5.7. In cases where the complainant claims a violation of Article 2.2, it is incumbent on the complainant to prove that the challenged measure is inconsistent with at least one of the four requirements set out in Article 5.7. 'If such non-compliance is demonstrated, then, and only then, does the relevant obligation in Article 2.2 apply to the challenged SPS measure.'[473]

Note that – as mentioned above – the basic scientific disciplines contained in Article 2.2 are further specified in Articles 5.1 and 5.2 of the *SPS Agreement*, which require – as discussed below – that SPS measures be based on a risk assessment, taking into account certain factors.[474]

---

[467] Panel Reports, *EC – Approval and Marketing of Biotech Products*, para. 7.2962.

[468] *Ibid*. The argument of the European Communities was based on an analogy with the relationship between Articles 3.1 and 3.3 of the *SPS Agreement*, as set out by the Appellate Body in *EC – Hormones*, para. 104, discussed further below at pp. 848–52. See *ibid*.

[469] See Panel Reports, *EC – Approval and Marketing of Biotech Products*, para. 7.2985, citing Appellate Body Report, *EC – Tariff Preferences*, para. 88. See also above, p. 211.

[470] See Panel Reports, *EC – Approval and Marketing of Biotech Products*, paras. 7.2969 and 7.2976. While this is contrary to the finding of the Panel in *Japan – Apples*, which held that the burden of proof under Article 5.7 is on the respondent, the Panel in *EC – Approval and Marketing of Biotech Products* understood the Appellate Body in the former case as implicitly expressing its reservations with regard to this allocation of the burden of proof.

[471] See Panel Reports, *EC – Approval and Marketing of Biotech Products*, para. 7.2969.   [472] *Ibid*., para. 7.2974.

[473] *Ibid*., para. 7.2976.

[474] See below, pp. 853–7, and Appellate Body Report, *EC – Hormones*, para. 180. As the Appellate Body noted in *Australia – Salmon*, Article 2.2 is more general than Articles 5.1 and 5.2, and a violation of Article 2.2 can thus exist independently of a violation of Articles 5.1 and 5.2. See Appellate Body Report, *Australia – Salmon*, para. 137.

Questions and Assignments 8.26

What are the 'scientific disciplines' set forth in Article 2.2 of the *SPS Agreement*? When is a measure maintained 'without sufficient scientific evidence'? Are Members ever allowed to maintain SPS measures for which there is insufficient scientific evidence? What is the relationship between Article 2.2 and Article 5.7 of the *SPS Agreement*? What are the implications of this relationship for the burden of proof?

8.4.3.4. *No arbitrary or unjustifiable discrimination or disguised restriction on trade*

A third basic limitation on a Member's right to impose SPS measures can be found in Article 2.3 of the *SPS Agreement*. Article 2.3 reflects the familiar GATT non-discrimination obligations of national treatment and most-favoured-nation treatment and incorporates part of the chapeau of Article XX of the GATT 1994.[475] Article 2.3 provides:

> Members shall ensure that their sanitary and phytosanitary measures do not arbitrarily or unjustifiably discriminate between Members where identical or similar conditions prevail, including between their own territory and that of other Members. Sanitary and phytosanitary measures shall not be applied in a manner which would constitute a disguised restriction on international trade.

Article 2.3 was at issue in *Australia – Salmon (Article 21.5 – Canada)*, where Canada claimed that Australia violated this provision by insisting on import requirements for salmonids from Canada but providing no internal control measures on the movement of dead Australian fish. The Panel identified three cumulative requirements that must be met for a violation of Article 2.3 of the *SPS Agreement* to be established, namely that:

- the measure discriminates between the territories of Members other than the Member imposing the measure, or between the territory of the Member imposing the measure and another Member;
- the discrimination is arbitrary or unjustifiable; and
- identical or similar conditions prevail in the territory of the Members compared.[476]

Further, the Panel in *Australia – Salmon (Article 21.5 – Canada)* noted that discrimination in the sense of the first element of Article 2.3 includes discrimination between different products (in this case salmonids from Canada and other dead fish from Australia).[477] This differs significantly from the GATT non-discrimination

---

[475] See Appellate Body Report, *Australia – Salmon*, para. 251. For a detailed discussion of Articles I and III of the GATT 1994, see above, pp. 322–34 and 344–90; for a discussion of the chapeau of Article XX of the GATT 1994, see above, pp. 641–51.   [476] See Panel Report, *Australia – Salmon (Article 21.5 – Canada)*, para. 7.111.
[477] *Ibid.*, para. 7.112.

rules that apply only to 'like' or 'directly competitive or substitutable' products.[478] The broader scope of Article 2.3 takes into account that dissimilar products may pose the same or similar health risks and should therefore be treated in the same way. For example, different animals may be carriers of foot-and-mouth disease and should thus be subject to the same measures where this risk is present. This broad prohibition on discriminatory treatment is tempered by the other two requirements that must be met before a violation of Article 2.3 exists. Thus, if the different treatment can be justified or if conditions in the Members compared are not similar or identical, Article 2.3 is not violated. In this regard, the Panel in *Australia – Salmon (Article 21.5 – Canada)* was not convinced that 'identical or similar' conditions prevailed in Australia and Canada, as there was a substantial difference in the disease status of these two Members.[479]

The basic discipline in Article 2.3 finds reflection in the more specific prohibition in Article 5.5 on arbitrary or unjustifiable distinctions in the levels of protection chosen by a Member in different situations, where these distinctions lead to discrimination or disguised restrictions on trade.[480] A violation of Article 5.5 will necessarily imply a violation of Article 2.3, but the opposite is not true as Article 2.3 is broader than Article 5.5.[481]

Questions and Assignments 8.27

What are the criteria for a violation of Article 2.3 of the *SPS Agreement*? What significant difference is there between the obligation contained in Article 2.3 and the non-discrimination rules of the GATT 1994?

8.4.3.5. The goal of harmonisation

Due to the different factors that regulators take into account when enacting SPS measures (national consumer preferences, industry interests, geographic and climatic conditions, etc.), there are large differences in SPS measures from one country to another. The resulting wide variety of SPS measures that producers face on their different export markets has a negative impact on market access for their products, as they will have to adjust products to the many different SPS measures.[482] The *SPS Agreement* addresses this problem in Article 3 by encouraging, but not obliging, Members to harmonise their SPS measures around international standards.[483]

The aim of Article 3 of the *SPS Agreement* was expressed as follows by the Appellate Body in *EC – Hormones*:

---

[478] See above, p. 329 (for Article I of the GATT 1994) and pp. 329, 351 and 374 (for Article III of the GATT 1994).
[479] See Panel Report, *Australia – Salmon (Article 21.5 – Canada)*, para. 7.113.   [480] See below, pp. 858–60.
[481] See Appellate Body Report, *Australia – Salmon*, para. 252; and Panel Report, *Australia – Salmon (Article 21.5 – Canada)*, para. 8.160.   [482] See also above, p. 841.
[483] Article 3 refers to 'international standards, guidelines or recommendations'. For reasons of convenience, the term 'international standards' will be used in this chapter to refer to 'international standards, guidelines or recommendations'.

In generalized terms, the object and purpose of Article 3 is to promote the harmonization of the SPS measures of Members on as wide a basis as possible, while recognizing and safeguarding, at the same time, the right and duty of Members to protect the life and health of their people.[484]

Under Article 3 of the *SPS Agreement*, Members have three autonomous options with regard to international harmonised standards, each with its own consequences. Members may choose to:

- *base* their SPS measures on international standards according to Article 3.1;
- *conform* their SPS measures to international standards under Article 3.2; or
- impose SPS measures resulting in a *higher level* of protection than would be achieved by the relevant international standard in terms of Article 3.3.

In *EC – Hormones*, the Appellate Body confirmed that these are equally available options and there is no rule-exception relationship between them.[485] Thus a Member is not penalised for choosing the Article 3.3 alternative. The three options will now be examined in more detail.

The *first* option is set out in Article 3.1 of the *SPS Agreement*. Article 3.1 obliges Members to base their SPS measures on international standards where they exist, except as provided for in Article 3.3.[486] The 'international standards' to which Article 3.1 refers are standards set by international organisations, such as the Codex Alimentarius Commission with respect to food safety, the World Organisation for Animal Health (formerly called the International Office of Epizootics (OIE))[487] for animal health, and the Secretariat of the International Plant Protection Convention with respect to plant health.[488]

Where a relevant international standard exists, Members must – according to Article 3.1 – base their SPS measures thereon. With respect to the meaning of the 'based on' requirement, the Appellate Body made the following observations in *EC – Hormones*:

To read Article 3.1 as requiring Members to harmonize their SPS measures *by conforming those measures with international standards*, guidelines and recommendations, *in the here and now*, is, in effect, to vest such international standards, guidelines and recommendations (which are by the terms of the Codex *recommendatory* in form and nature) with *obligatory* force and effect. The Panel's interpretation of Article 3.1 would, in other words, transform those standards, guidelines and recommendations into binding *norms*. But, as already noted, the *SPS Agreement* itself sets out no indication of any intent on the part of the Members to do so. We cannot lightly assume that sovereign states intended to

---

[484] Appellate Body Report, *EC – Hormones*, para. 177.   [485] See *ibid.*, para. 104.
[486] See above, footnote 483, on the use of the term 'international standards'.
[487] In 2003, at the 71st General Session of the International Committee of the OIE, Members adopted a resolution to use the name 'World Organization for Animal Health' while keeping the historical acronym OIE.
[488] See Annex A, paragraph 3(a), (b) and (c) of the *SPS Agreement*. For matters not covered by the three mentioned organisations, international standards within the meaning of Article 3 of the *SPS Agreement* may also be standards set by other relevant international organisations open for membership to all WTO Members, as identified by the SPS Committee (see Annex A, paragraph 3(d) of the *SPS Agreement*). Pursuant to Article 3.4 of the *SPS Agreement*, Members have an obligation to participate in the work of the Codex Alimentarius Commission and the other organisations to the extent that their resources permit and to promote the development and periodic review of international standards.

> impose upon themselves the more onerous, rather than the less burdensome, obligation by mandating *conformity* or *compliance with* such standards, guidelines and recommendations. To sustain such an assumption and to warrant such a far-reaching interpretation, treaty language far more specific and compelling than that found in Article 3 of the *SPS Agreement* would be necessary.[489]

Thus, the non-binding standards set by the international standard-setting organisations do not become binding through the operation of the *SPS Agreement*. According to the Appellate Body in *EC – Hormones*, a measure that is 'based on' an international standard is one that 'stands' or 'is founded', or 'built' upon or 'supported', by the international standard. An SPS measure which is 'based on' an international standard need not 'conform to' that standard, since not all of the elements of that standard have to be incorporated into the measure.[490]

The consequences of choosing the option under Article 3.1, by 'basing' an SPS measure on an international standard, were set out by the Appellate Body in *EC – Hormones* as follows:

> The Member imposing this measure does not benefit from the presumption of consistency set up in Article 3.2; but, as earlier observed, the Member is not penalized by exemption of a complaining Member from the normal burden of showing a *prima facie* case of inconsistency with Article 3.1 or any other relevant article of the *SPS Agreement* or of the GATT 1994.[491]

The *second* option available to Members under Article 3.2 of the *SPS Agreement* is to 'conform' their SPS measures to the relevant international standard. To 'conform to' is obviously more demanding than to 'base on'. In *EC – Hormones*, the Appellate Body interpreted this requirement as follows:

> Such a measure would embody the international standard completely and, for practical purposes, converts it into a municipal standard.[492]

Article 3.2 provides that SPS measures which 'conform to' international standards are presumed to be consistent with the *SPS Agreement* and the GATT 1994.[493] The implications of this presumption were addressed by the Appellate Body as follows:

> The presumption of consistency with relevant provisions of the *SPS Agreement* that arises under Article 3.2 in respect of measures that conform to international standards may well be an *incentive* for Members so to conform their SPS measures with such standards. It is clear, however, that a decision of a Member not to conform a particular measure with an international standard does not authorize imposition of a special or generalized burden of proof upon that Member, which may, more often than not, amount to a *penalty*.[494]

Clearly, therefore, the burden of proof lies on the complaining party to demonstrate a violation of the *SPS Agreement*, under both the Article 3.1 option and the Article 3.2 option. However, the burden is heavier in the latter case as the

---

[489] Appellate Body Report, *EC – Hormones*, para. 165.   [490] *Ibid.*, para. 163.   [491] *Ibid.*, para. 171.
[492] *Ibid.*, para. 170.
[493] This presumption was held to be rebuttable by the Appellate Body in *EC – Hormones*. See *ibid.*
[494] *Ibid.*, para. 102.

complaining party has to overcome the presumption of consistency in Article 3.2. This provides an incentive for Members to conform their measures to international standards, thereby making their measures less vulnerable to challenges under the *SPS Agreement* and the GATT.

The *third* option that Members may choose, with respect to international standards, is to deviate from the international standard by choosing a measure resulting in a higher level of protection than that achieved by the international standard. This option, provided for in Article 3.3 of the *SPS Agreement*, is important as it reflects the recognition of Members' right to choose the level of protection they deem appropriate in their territories. In respect of this option, the Appellate Body in *EC – Hormones* held, as mentioned above, that:

> [t]his right of a Member to establish its own level of sanitary protection under Article 3.3 of the *SPS Agreement* is an autonomous right and *not* an 'exception' from a 'general obligation' under Article 3.1.[495]

This right to choose measures that deviate from international standards is not an 'absolute or unqualified right', as confirmed by the Appellate Body in *EC – Hormones*.[496] Two *alternative* conditions are laid down in Article 3.3, namely that:

- either there must be a scientific justification for the SPS measure (defined in a footnote as a scientific examination and evaluation in accordance with the rules of the *SPS Agreement*);
- or the measure must be a result of the level of protection chosen by the Member in accordance with Articles 5.1 through 5.8.

The difference between these two conditions is not clear and the Appellate Body noted, in *EC – Hormones*, that 'Article 3.3 is evidently not a model of clarity in drafting and communication.'[497] What is clear, however, is that under both alternative conditions a risk assessment in terms of Article 5.1 is required. In this respect, the Appellate Body in *EC – Hormones* held as follows:

> It is true that situation (a) does not speak of Articles 5.1 through 5.8. Nevertheless, two points need to be noted. First, the last sentence of Article 3.3 requires that 'all measures which result in a [higher] level of . . . protection', that is to say, measures falling within situation (a) as well as those falling within situation (b), be 'not inconsistent with any other provision of [the SPS] Agreement'. 'Any other provision of this Agreement' textually includes Article 5. Secondly, the footnote to Article 3.3, while attached to the end of the first sentence, defines 'scientific justification' as an 'examination and evaluation of available scientific information in conformity with relevant provisions of this Agreement . . .'. This examination and evaluation would appear to partake of the nature of the risk assessment required in Article 5.1 and defined in paragraph 4 of Annex A of the *SPS Agreement*.[498]

Therefore the Appellate Body held that, although the European Communities had established for itself a level of protection higher than that implied in the relevant Codex standards, it was bound to comply with the requirements

---

[495] *Ibid.*, para. 172.   [496] See *ibid.*, para. 173.   [497] *Ibid.*, para. 175.   [498] *Ibid.*

established in Article 5.1.[499] The result of this ruling is that a Member which claims scientific justification for its deviation from the relevant international standard must base its claim on a proper risk assessment in the same way as a Member which claims its deviation is a result of the higher level of protection that it has chosen.

Questions and Assignments 8.28

What three options do Members have with regard to international standards? When is an SPS measure 'based on' an international standard? When does an SPS measure 'conform to' an international standard? Is the right of Members to adopt or maintain measures that deviate from international standards an 'absolute and unqualified right'? Explain. Are they penalised for choosing the option under Article 3.3 of the *SPS Agreement*?

8.4.4. Risk analysis obligations

The national regulatory process by means of which SPS measures are imposed typically involves *risk analysis*. For the purposes of the *SPS Agreement*, two elements of risk analysis are relevant, namely risk assessment and risk management. The term '*risk assessment*' refers to the scientific process of identifying the existence of a risk and establishing the likelihood that the risk may actually materialise according to the measures that could be applied to address the risk. '*Risk management*', by contrast, is the policy-based process of determining the level of protection a country wants to ensure in its territory and choosing the measure that will be used to achieve that level of protection. In risk management decision-making, not only are the scientific results of the risk assessment taken into account but also societal value considerations such as consumer preferences, industry interests, relative costs, etc. The distinction between these two elements of the risk analysis process is not absolute and non-scientific considerations do play some part in risk assessment. However, the distinction is a useful tool in enhancing the understanding of the regulatory process.

The risk assessment/risk management distinction is *implicitly* taken into account in those disciplines of the *SPS Agreement* that relate to the risk analysis process contained in Article 5. Articles 5.1 to 5.3 set strict scientific disciplines for risk assessments on which SPS measures must be based, whereas a Member's choice of an appropriate level of protection – an aspect of risk management – is largely respected by the provisions of Articles 5.4 and 5.5. The choice of a measure to achieve this level of protection – another aspect of risk

---

[499] *Ibid.*, para. 176. With regard to this interpretation of Article 3.3 of the *SPS Agreement*, the Appellate Body noted: 'We are not unaware that this finding tends to suggest that the distinction made in Article 3.3 between two situations may have very limited effects and may, to that extent, be more apparent than real. Its involved and layered language actually leaves us with no choice.' *Ibid.*

management – is subject to trade-related rather than scientific disciplines in Articles 5.3 and 5.6.

As noted by the Appellate Body in *EC – Hormones*, the *SPS Agreement* does not expressly use the term 'risk management'.[500] However, it is undeniable that the *SPS Agreement* deals in different ways with the obligations of Members with regard to risk assessment and their obligations applicable to what is commonly referred to as risk management.

8.4.4.1. Risk assessment

Article 5.1 of the *SPS Agreement* states:

> Members shall ensure that their sanitary or phytosanitary measures are based on an assessment, as appropriate to the circumstances, of the risks to human, animal or plant life or health, taking into account risk assessment techniques developed by the relevant international organizations.

Article 5.1 thus obliges Members to base their SPS measures on a risk assessment as appropriate to the circumstances. As noted by the Panel in *EC – Approval and Marketing of Biotech Products*, to determine if there is a violation of Article 5.1, two distinct issues must be addressed:

(i)   whether there is a 'risk assessment' within the meaning of the *SPS Agreement*; and

(ii) whether the SPS measure at issue is 'based on' this risk assessment.[501]

A 'risk assessment' is defined in paragraph 4 of Annex A of the *SPS Agreement* as follows:

> The evaluation of the likelihood of entry, establishment or spread of a pest or disease within the territory of an importing Member according to the sanitary or phytosanitary measures which might be applied, and of the associated potential biological and economic consequences; *or* the evaluation of the potential for adverse effects on human or animal health arising from the presence of additives, contaminants, toxins or disease-causing organisms in food, beverages or feedstuffs.
>
> [Emphasis added]

There are thus *two* types of risk assessment, each with different requirements. The type of risk assessment required in a given case will depend on the objective of the SPS measure at issue. The first type of risk assessment is applicable to SPS measures aimed at risks from pests or diseases; the second to SPS measures aimed at food-borne risks.[502] The former involves not only an assessment of the risk of entry, establishment or spread of a pest or disease but also an assessment of the risk of the associated potential biological and economic consequences.[503] Such a risk assessment must:

---

[500] See *ibid.*, para. 181.   [501] See Panel Reports, *EC – Approval and Marketing of Biotech Products*, para. 7.3019.
[502] The requirements of the second type are less strict as human health issues are more likely to be at stake in such cases.   [503] See Panel Report, *Australia – Salmon*, para. 8.72.

- *identify the pests or diseases* whose entry, establishment or spread a Member wants to prevent, as well as the *potential biological and economic consequences* associated with the entry, establishment or spread of such pests/diseases;
- *evaluate the likelihood* of entry, establishment or spread of these pests or diseases and the associated biological and economic consequences; and
- evaluate the likelihood of entry, establishment or spread of these pests or diseases *according to the SPS measures that might be applied.*[504]

There are two requirements for the second type of risk assessment, which applies to food-borne risks, namely that the risk assessment must:

- *identify the adverse effects* on human or animal health (if any) arising from the additive, contaminant, toxin or disease-causing organism in food/beverages/ feedstuffs *at issue*; and
- if such adverse health effects exist, evaluate the *potential of occurrence* of these effects.[505]

Note certain important differences between these two types of risk assessment. First, the requirements for the second type of risk assessment do not include an evaluation of associated biological and economic consequences.[506] Second, while the first type of risk assessment requires an evaluation of the 'likelihood' that the risk might materialise, the second type requires only an evaluation of the 'potential' for adverse effects. Neither 'likelihood' nor 'potential' imply that the risk assessed must be quantified (i.e. expressed numerically) or that a certain threshold level of risk be shown.[507] Instead, the risk may be expressed either quantitatively or qualitatively.[508] However, the word 'likelihood' used with regard to the first type of risk assessment was held to imply a higher degree of potentiality than the word 'potential' used with regard to the second type.[509] This difference in wording was emphasised by the Appellate Body in *Australia – Salmon*.[510] The Appellate Body found that:

---

[504] This three-pronged test was set out by the Panel and endorsed by the Appellate Body in *Australia – Salmon*. See Appellate Body Report, *Australia – Salmon*, para. 121. This test was confirmed in Appellate Body Report, *Japan – Agricultural Products II*, para. 113, and used again in Panel Report, *Australia – Salmon (Article 21.5 – Canada)*, para. 7.41.

[505] These requirements are generalised on the basis of the findings of the Panel in *EC – Hormones* (Panel Report, *EC – Hormones (Canada)*, para. 8.101; and Panel Report, *EC – Hormones (US)*, para. 8.98) as modified by the Appellate Body (Appellate Body Report, *EC – Hormones*, paras. 184–6).

[506] These economic factors are the potential damage in terms of loss of production/sales in the event of the entry, establishment or spread of a pest or disease; the costs of control or eradication of the pest or disease; and the relative cost effectiveness of alternative risk-reduction strategies. See also Article 5.3 of the *SPS Agreement* which specifies certain economic factors that Members must take into account in assessing risks to animal or plant life or health (but not to human life or health). The exclusion of risk assessments with regard to human health risks from the provisions of this Article indicates that Members are not obliged to take economic factors into account in making decisions regarding the protection of human health, most likely because the drafters of the *SPS Agreement* did not think it reasonable to require Members to weigh up economic considerations and associated biological risks in such circumstances.

[507] See Appellate Body Report, *EC – Hormones*, para. 186; and Appellate Body Report, *Australia – Salmon*, para. 125.

[508] With regard to the first definition of risk assessment, the Appellate Body agreed with the Panel that the evaluation of likelihood may be expressed quantitatively or qualitatively in Appellate Body Report, *Australia – Salmon*, para. 124. In respect of the second definition, the Appellate Body noted that there is no basis for a quantitative requirement in Appellate Body Report, *EC – Hormones*, para. 186. This was reiterated in Panel Reports, *EC – Approval and Marketing of Biotech Products*, para. 7.3027.

[509] See Appellate Body Report, *EC – Hormones*, para. 184.

[510] Appellate Body Report, *Australia – Salmon*, footnote 69.

> it is not sufficient that a risk assessment [of the first type] conclude that there is a *possibility* of entry, establishment or spread of diseases and associated biological and economic consequences. A proper risk assessment of this type must evaluate the 'likelihood', i.e., the 'probability', of entry, establishment or spread of diseases and associated biological and economic consequences as well as the 'likelihood', i.e., 'probability', of entry, establishment or spread of diseases *according to the SPS measures which might be applied.*[511]

Third, a risk assessment of the first type must evaluate likelihood according to the SPS measures 'which might be applied'. In *Japan – Apples*, the Appellate Body agreed with the Panel that a risk assessment under this definition may not be limited to an examination of the measure already in place but that other possible alternatives must also be evaluated.[512] The Appellate Body emphasised that a risk assessment:

> should not be distorted by preconceived views on the nature and the content of the measure to be taken; nor should it develop into an exercise tailored to and carried out for the purpose of justifying decisions *ex post facto.*[513]

It would appear that the differences between the two types of risk assessment are intended to set less strict requirements for those risk assessments where risks to human health are more likely to be at issue, namely when dealing with food safety issues rather than when the risk relates to animal or plant pests or diseases.

Furthermore, some general observations can be made with respect to the requirements for risk assessments as identified in the case law. First, the Appellate Body has held that a risk assessment must show proof of an actual risk, not just a theoretical uncertainty.[514] Second, the Appellate Body has recognised that a risk assessment may go beyond controlled laboratory conditions and take account of the actual potential for adverse effects in the 'real world where people live and work and die'.[515] Third, the risk assessment must be specific to the particular type of risk at issue in the case and not merely show a general risk of harm.[516] Fourth, Article 5.1 does not oblige Members to carry out their own risk assessments. Instead they may rely on risk assessments carried out by other Members or an international organisation.[517] Fifth, since Article 5.1 is to be read together with Article 2.2, which requires that SPS measures not be 'maintained' without sufficient scientific evidence, the subsequent evolution of the scientific evidence must be assessed as 'this may be an indication that the risk assessment should be reviewed or a new assessment undertaken'.[518]

---

[511] *Ibid.*, para. 123.   [512] See Panel Report, *Japan – Apples*, para. 8.283.
[513] Appellate Body Report, *Japan – Apples*, para. 208.
[514] See Appellate Body Report, *EC – Hormones*, para. 186.   [515] See *ibid.*, para. 187. See also below, p. 856.
[516] See *ibid.*, para. 200. In *Japan – Apples*, the Appellate Body agreed with the Panel that a risk assessment must be specific not only to the harm at issue but also to the agent that causes the harm (in that case the product that transmitted the disease). See Appellate Body Report, *Japan – Apples*, para. 204.
[517] See Appellate Body Report, *EC – Hormones*, para. 190.
[518] Panel Report, *Japan – Apples*, para. 7.12. In a similar vein, in *EC – Approval and Marketing of Biotech Products*, the Panel held that as circumstances may change (for example, new scientific evidence may affect the relevance or validity of a risk assessment on which a measure is based), a panel must determine whether, on the date of its establishment the measure at issue was based on an assessment of risks which was appropriate to the circumstances existing *at that time*. See Panel Reports, *EC – Approval and Marketing of Biotech Products*, paras. 7.3033–7.3034.

Although the *SPS Agreement* does not lay down any methodology of risk assessment to be followed by Members, other than to require them to take account of risk assessment techniques developed by international organisations,[519] it does specify certain factors that Members must take into account in their risk assessments. Article 5.2 of the *SPS Agreement* lists certain scientific and technical factors that Members must consider when assessing risks. These are:

> [A]vailable scientific evidence; relevant processes and production methods; relevant inspection, sampling and testing methods; prevalence of specific diseases or pests; existence of pest- or disease-free areas; relevant ecological and environmental conditions; and quarantine or other treatment.

From this list it is clear that a risk assessment for the purposes of the *SPS Agreement* is *not* purely scientific (in the sense of laboratory science) but includes a consideration of real-world factors that affect risk, such as climatic conditions, control mechanisms, etc. The Appellate Body in *EC – Hormones* rejected the Panel's finding that the risks relating to control and detection of failure to observe good veterinary practices must be excluded from risk assessments as they are non-scientific and thus outside the scope of Article 5.2. The Appellate Body held:

> to the extent that the Panel purports to exclude from the scope of a risk assessment in the sense of Article 5.1, all matters not susceptible of quantitative analysis by the empirical or experimental laboratory methods commonly associated with the physical sciences, we believe that the Panel is in error. Some of the kinds of factors listed in Article 5.2 such as 'relevant processes and production methods' and 'relevant inspection, sampling and testing methods' are not necessarily or wholly susceptible of investigation according to laboratory methods of, for example, biochemistry or pharmacology. Furthermore, there is nothing to indicate that the listing of factors that may be taken into account in a risk assessment of Article 5.2 was intended to be a closed list. It is essential to bear in mind that the risk that is to be evaluated in a risk assessment under Article 5.1 is not only risk ascertainable in a science laboratory operating under strictly controlled conditions, but also risk in human societies as they actually exist, in other words, the actual potential for adverse effects on human health *in the real world where people live and work and die*.[520]
>
> [Emphasis added]

As noted above, Article 5.1 of the *SPS Agreement* requires that SPS measures are 'based on' a risk assessment. The meaning of 'based on' was clarified by the Appellate Body in *EC – Hormones*. The Appellate Body in that case rejected the Panel's finding that the risk assessment must be shown to have been 'taken into account' by the Member in imposing the SPS measure and that the SPS measure must 'conform' to the risk assessment.[521] Instead, the Appellate Body held that for an SPS measure to be 'based on' a risk assessment, there must be a 'rational

---

[519] See Article 5.1 of the *SPS Agreement*. It can be assumed that these organisations are those referred to in the definition of 'international standards, guidelines and recommendations' in Annex A.3, since these are the most relevant for SPS matters.

[520] Appellate Body Report, *EC – Hormones*, para. 187. However, the Appellate Body qualified its finding by noting that it does not imply that risks related to problems of control *always* need to be evaluated in a risk assessment. The necessity to evaluate such risks depends on the circumstances of each case. See *ibid.*, para. 206.   [521] *Ibid.*, paras. 189 and 193.

relationship' between the measure and the risk assessment and the risk assessment must 'reasonably support' the measure.[522]

The Appellate Body also ruled that it is permissible for an SPS measure to be based on a divergent view rather than mainstream scientific opinion. In this respect, the Appellate Body stated in *EC – Hormones*:

> We do not believe that a risk assessment has to come to a monolithic conclusion that coincides with the scientific conclusion or view implicit in the SPS measure. The risk assessment could set out both the prevailing view representing the 'mainstream' of scientific opinion, as well as the opinions of scientists taking a divergent view. Article 5.1 does not require that the risk assessment must necessarily embody only the view of a majority of the relevant scientific community . . . In most cases, responsible and representative governments tend to base their legislative and administrative measures on 'mainstream' scientific opinion. In other cases, equally responsible and representative governments may act in good faith on the basis of what, at a given time, may be a divergent opinion coming from qualified and respected sources. By itself, this does not necessarily signal the absence of a reasonable relationship between the SPS measure and the risk assessment, especially where the risk involved is life-threatening in character and is perceived to constitute a clear and imminent threat to public health and safety. Determination of the presence or absence of that relationship can only be done on a case-to-case basis, after account is taken of all considerations rationally bearing upon the issue of potential adverse health effects.[523]

However, as clarified by the Panel in *EC – Approval and Marketing of Biotech Products*, an SPS measure cannot be said to be based on a 'divergent opinion' in a risk assessment if that risk assessment sets out a single opinion with which the Member concerned disagrees. According to the Panel, to the extent that Members disagree with some or all of the conclusions contained in such an assessment:

> it would in [the Panel's] view be necessary for Members to explain, by reference to the existing assessment, how and why they assess the risks differently, and to provide their revised or supplemental assessment of the risks.[524]

Questions and Assignments 8.29

Explain the distinction between risk assessment and risk management. How is this distinction reflected in the *SPS Agreement*? What are the main differences between the two types of risk assessment defined in Annex A paragraph 4 of the *SPS Agreement*? What do you think is the reason for these differences? When is an SPS measure 'based on' a risk assessment? Can an SPS measure, which is not 'based on' mainstream scientific opinion, be consistent with Article 5.1 of the *SPS Agreement*?

---

[522] *Ibid.*, para. 193. In *EC – Approval and Marketing of Biotech Products*, the Panel held that there existed no apparent rational relationship between the safeguard measures at issue, which imposed a complete prohibition, and the relevant risk assessments, which found no evidence that the biotech products concerned present any greater risk to human health or the environment than their conventional (non-biotech) counterparts. See Panel Reports, *EC – Approval and Marketing of Biotech Products*, paras. 7.3067, 7.3085, 7.3106, 7.3127, 7.3137, 7.3157, 7.3177, 7.3195, 7.3211.

[523] Appellate Body Report, *EC – Hormones*, para. 194.

[524] Panel Reports, *EC – Approval and Marketing of Biotech Products*, para. 7.3062.

Must a WTO Member adopting an SPS measure necessarily conduct a
risk assessment?

8.4.4.2. Risk management

Risk management, as explained above, entails policy decision-making regarding
the level of protection that a country wants to secure in its territory *and* the
measure it will use to achieve this level of protection. These choices are 'based
on' both scientific evidence and societal value judgements. The *SPS Agreement*
gives national regulators substantial latitude in making risk management decisions, but there are certain non-scientific disciplines in place to ensure that the
adverse trade effects of these decisions are limited as much as possible.

Risk management thus entails, in the first place, the decision on the 'appropriate level of protection', defined in paragraph 5 of Annex A of the *SPS Agreement* as:

> The level of protection *deemed appropriate by the Member* establishing a sanitary or phy-
> tosanitary measure to protect human, animal or plant life or health within its territory.
>
> [Emphasis added]

Thus, there is a clear recognition that it is the prerogative of the Member
imposing the SPS measure to choose the level of protection of human, animal
or plant life or health it will ensure in its territory. The *SPS Agreement* does not
oblige Members to lower their level of protection, even where this would be
most trade-efficient. Once the existence of a risk has been established by
means of risk assessment, a Member is free to choose even a zero-risk level of
protection.[525]

Two provisions in the *SPS Agreement* deal with the choice of an appropriate
level of protection. First, Article 5.4 provides that 'Members should . . . take into
account the objective of minimising negative trade effects' when choosing their
level of protection. The word 'should' indicates that this provision is only horta-
tive, containing no binding obligation. Obliging Members to choose the least
trade restrictive level of protection would go against the underlying principle of
the *SPS Agreement* that it is the prerogative of the Member to determine the level
of protection it deems appropriate in its territory.

The second discipline with regard to the appropriate level of protection is
contained in Article 5.5, which provides in relevant part:

> With the objective of achieving consistency in the application of the concept of appropri-
> ate level of sanitary or phytosanitary protection against risks to human life or health, or to
> animal and plant life or health, each Member shall avoid arbitrary or unjustifiable distinc-
> tions in the levels it considers to be appropriate in different situations, if such distinctions
> result in discrimination or a disguised restriction on international trade.

The Article 5.5 discipline consists of two elements, namely:

---

[525] See Appellate Body Report, *Australia – Salmon*, para. 125.

- the *goal* (for the future) of achieving consistency in the application of the 'concept' of appropriate level of sanitary or phytosanitary protection;[526] and
- the *legal obligation* to avoid arbitrary or unjustifiable distinctions in the levels of protection deemed appropriate in different situations, *if* these distinctions lead to discrimination or disguised restrictions on trade.

In *EC – Hormones*, the Appellate Body recognised that countries establish their levels of protection *ad hoc* as risks arise, thus absolute consistency in levels of protection is not realistic, and also not required by Article 5.5.[527]

Three cumulative requirements must be met before a violation of Article 5.5 of the *SPS Agreement* exists:

- the Member has set different levels of protection 'in different situations';
- the levels of protection show 'arbitrary or unjustifiable' differences in their treatment of different situations; and
- these arbitrary or unjustifiable differences lead to 'discrimination or disguised restrictions' on trade.[528]

Clearly not all health risks can be treated the same. Thus, according to the Appellate Body in *EC – Hormones*, the 'different' situations compared in the *first element* of the test under Article 5.5 of the *SPS Agreement* must be *comparable*, that is, they must have some common element or elements.[529] For example, a common element would be the fact that the spread of the same disease is at issue, or that identical biological or economic consequences could result.[530] A difference in the levels of protection applied in the comparable situations must then be shown.[531]

The *second element* of the test under Article 5.5 of the *SPS Agreement* requires that the differences in levels of protection be 'arbitrary or unjustifiable'. To determine whether this requirement is met, panels and the Appellate Body examine whether reasons exist to justify the differences in levels of protection. In the case law so far, they have examined:

- whether different levels of risk are at issue in the different situations compared;[532]
- whether the difficulty of controlling the risk differs in each case;[533] or

---

[526] In *EC – Hormones*, the Appellate Body agreed with the Panel that no legal obligation of consistency in levels of protection exists, but that consistency in levels of protection is only a goal for the future. See Appellate Body Report, *EC – Hormones*, para. 213.   [527] *Ibid.*, para. 213.
[528] See *ibid.*, para. 214, reiterated in Appellate Body Report, *Australia – Salmon*, para. 140.
[529] Appellate Body Report, *EC – Hormones*, para. 217.
[530] See Appellate Body Report, *Australia – Salmon*, para. 146.
[531] Note that the Panel in *Australia – Salmon* held that the chosen level of protection is reflected in the SPS measure imposed, thus ensuring that a difference in the measures applied in the situations being compared would indicate a distinction in the level of protection. Although this particular finding was not appealed (see Appellate Body Report, *Australia – Salmon*, footnote 106), it should be noted that in dealing with Article 5.6, the Appellate Body, in this case, held that nothing in the DSU or the *SPS Agreement* permits a panel or the Appellate Body to imply a Member's appropriate level of protection from the measure it imposes. Only if a Member does not express its chosen level of protection or does so too vaguely, can its level of protection be inferred from the measure it applies. This issue is discussed further in the analysis of Article 5.6 of the *SPS Agreement*. See below, pp. 860–2.
[532] See Appellate Body Report, *Australia – Salmon*, para. 158.
[533] See Appellate Body Report, *EC – Hormones*, paras. 221–5.

- whether the degree of government intervention necessary to achieve the same level of protection differs in each situation.[534]

The *third element* of the test under Article 5.5 of the *SPS Agreement* (according to the Appellate Body in *EC – Hormones*, the most important of the three elements) is the requirement that the arbitrary or unjustifiable distinctions in levels of protection lead to 'discrimination or disguised restrictions on trade'.[535] Whether this requirement is met can be determined by means of three 'warning signals' identified in the case law, which are not conclusive in their own right but taken together and with other factors may support the finding that the third element of the test under Article 5.5 is met.[536] This will depend on the circumstances of each case. The 'warning signals' are:

- the arbitrary character of the differences in the levels of protection (i.e. that the second element of Article 5.5 is met);
- the existence of rather substantial differences in the levels of protection; and
- the absence of scientific justification (based on earlier findings of a violation of Articles 2.2 and 5.1), which indicates that the measure is a disguised restriction on trade.

In June 2000, the SPS Committee drew up guidelines for the implementation of Article 5.5.[537] The guidelines, resulting from a series of consultations in the SPS Committee, reflect the clarifications emerging from the case law on Article 5.5, including the use of the three 'warning signals'.

In addition to the disciplines regarding the choice of an appropriate level of protection, the *SPS Agreement* contains rules regarding the choice of an SPS measure to achieve the chosen level of protection.

The first such rule is Article 5.3 of the *SPS Agreement*, which lists certain economic criteria, such as damage in terms of loss of production or sales that Members must consider in their choice of SPS measures. This rule, however, only applies to SPS measures for the protection of life and health of animals and plants.[538]

The second and much more important rule on the choice of measure is contained in Article 5.6 of the *SPS Agreement*, which provides:

> Without prejudice to paragraph 2 of Article 3, when establishing or maintaining sanitary or phytosanitary measures to achieve the appropriate level of sanitary or phytosanitary protection, Members shall ensure that such measures are not more trade-restrictive than required to achieve their appropriate level of sanitary or phytosanitary protection, taking into account technical and economic feasibility.

In a footnote to Article 5.6, it is stated:

---

[534] See *ibid.*, para. 221.   [535] See *ibid.*, para. 240.
[536] See Panel Report, *Australia – Salmon,* paras. 8.149–8.151, as approved by the Appellate Body. See Appellate Body Report, *Australia – Salmon,* paras. 162, 164 and 166. The first two warning signals were also relied upon in Appellate Body Report, *EC – Hormones,* paras. 215 and 240.
[537] These guidelines are contained in Committee on Sanitary and Phytosanitary Measures, *Guidelines to Further the Practical Implementation of Article 5.5,* G/SPS/15, dated 18 June 2000. They are not binding but are intended to assist officials in the application of Article 5.5.   [538] See also above, p. 854, footnote 506.

> For purposes of paragraph 6 of Article 5, a measure is not more trade-restrictive than required unless there is another measure, reasonably available taking into account technical and economic feasibility, that achieves the appropriate level of sanitary or phytosanitary protection and is significantly less restrictive to trade.

On the basis of this footnote, the Panel in *Australia – Salmon* identified a three-pronged test which was later upheld by the Appellate Body, namely that an SPS measure is more trade restrictive than required *only* if there is an alternative SPS measure which:

- is reasonably available, taking into account technical and economic feasibility;
- achieves the Member's appropriate level of protection; and
- is significantly less trade restrictive than the contested measure.[539]

Since these requirements are cumulative, all three must be met in order to prove a violation of Article 5.6.[540]

To determine whether the *first* element of this test under Article 5.6 of the *SPS Agreement* is met, a panel will look at the facts of the case, including the characteristics of the SPS measure actually applied, as well as the alternative measures considered in the risk assessment, in order to determine which of the latter measures is a feasible alternative.[541]

To determine whether the *second* element of this test is met, it is necessary to establish what the appropriate level of protection is for the importing Member. In *Australia – Salmon*, the Appellate Body rejected the Panel's finding that the appropriate level of protection can be implied from the level of protection that is afforded by the SPS measure imposed. The Appellate Body emphasised that the choice of a level of protection is the prerogative of the Member concerned.[542] Further, it held:

> The 'appropriate level of protection' established by a Member and the 'SPS measure' have to be clearly distinguished. They are not one and the same thing. The first is an *objective*, the second is an *instrument* chosen to attain or implement that objective.
>
> It can be deduced from the provisions of the *SPS Agreement* that the determination by a Member of the 'appropriate level of protection' logically precedes the establishment or decision on maintenance of an 'SPS measure'.[543]

There are, however, cases where Members do not expressly determine their appropriate level of protection, or do so with insufficient clarity so that it becomes impossible to apply Article 5.6 (and Article 5.5). The Appellate Body in *Australia – Salmon* recognised this and thus read an implicit obligation on Members to determine their appropriate levels of protection into paragraph 3 of Annex B and Articles 4.1, 5.4 and 5.6. It held that:

---

[539] See Panel Report, *Australia – Salmon*, para. 95, and Appellate Body Report, *Australia – Salmon*, para. 194.
[540] See Appellate Body Report, *Australia – Salmon*, para. 194, reiterated in Appellate Body Report, *Japan – Agricultural Products II*, para. 95.
[541] See Panel Report, *Australia – Salmon*, para. 8.171, and Panel Report, *Australia – Salmon (Article 21.5 – Canada)*, paras. 7.146–7.149.
[542] Appellate Body Report, *Australia – Salmon*, para. 199. See also above, p. 858, footnote 525.
[543] *Ibid.*, paras. 200–1.

> in cases where a Member does not determine its appropriate level of protection, or does so with insufficient precision, the appropriate level of protection may be established by panels on the basis of the level of protection reflected in the SPS measure actually applied. Otherwise, a Member's failure to comply with the implicit obligation to determine its appropriate level of protection – with sufficient precision – would allow it to escape from its obligations under this Agreement and, in particular, its obligations under Articles 5.5 and 5.6.[544]

Thus, where Members do not comply with their implicit obligation to determine their appropriate level of protection, their appropriate level of protection may be deduced from the SPS measure actually applied.

The *third* element of the test under Article 5.6 of the *SPS Agreement*, namely that the alternative measure is significantly less trade restrictive, was examined by both the original Panel and the Article 21.5 Panel in *Australia – Salmon* and by the Panel in *Japan – Agricultural Products II*.[545] It appears from these cases that the issue relates to whether market access would be substantially improved if an alternative measure were imposed.

Questions and Assignments 8.30

What obligation does Article 5.5 impose on Members? Does it include the obligation to ensure consistency in the level of SPS protection maintained in comparable situations? Discuss the three-tier test under Article 5.5 as established in the case law. Are Members required to adopt and maintain the least-trade-restrictive SPS measure? How does one establish that the SPS measure at issue is more trade-restrictive than required?

8.4.4.3. Provisional measures and the precautionary principle

While the *SPS Agreement* requires that SPS measures are 'based on' science and uses science as the touchstone against which SPS measures will be judged, it is obvious that science does not have clear and unambiguous answers to all regulatory questions. Situations may arise where there is, in fact, insufficient scientific evidence regarding the existence and extent of the relevant risk but where governments consider they need to act promptly and take measures to avoid possible harm. Thus, governments act with precaution without waiting for the collection of sufficient scientific information to assess the risks conclusively. This is commonly referred to as acting in accordance with the 'precautionary principle', or the 'precautionary approach'. Considerable difference of opinion exists between Members regarding the role that precaution plays in the regulatory process. The following excerpt from *The Economist* illustrates this well:

---

[544] *Ibid.*, paras. 205–7.
[545] See Panel Report, *Australia – Salmon*, para. 8.182; Panel Report, *Australia – Salmon (Article 21.5 – Canada)*, paras. 7.150–7.153; Panel Report, *Japan – Agricultural Products II*, paras. 8.79, 8.89, 8.95–8.96 and 8.103–8.104.

Brussels is becoming the world's regulatory capital. The European Union's drive to set standards has many causes – and a protectionist impulse within some governments (e.g., France's) may be one. But though the EU is a big market, with almost half a billion consumers, neither size, nor zeal, nor sneaky protectionism explains why it is usurping America's role as a source of global standards. A better answer lies in transatlantic philosophical differences. The American model turns on cost–benefit analysis, with regulators weighing the effects of new rules on jobs and growth, as well as testing the significance of any risks. Companies enjoy a presumption of innocence for their products: should this prove mistaken, punishment is provided by the market (and a barrage of lawsuits). The European model rests more on the 'precautionary principle', which underpins most environmental and health directives. This calls for pre-emptive action if scientists spot a credible hazard, even before the level of risk can be measured. Such a principle sparks many transatlantic disputes: over genetically modified organisms or climate change, for example.

In Europe corporate innocence is not assumed. Indeed, a vast slab of EU laws evaluating the safety of tens of thousands of chemicals, known as REACH, reverses the burden of proof, asking industry to demonstrate that substances are harmless. Some Eurocrats suggest that the philosophical gap reflects the American constitutional tradition that everything is allowed unless it is forbidden, against the Napoleonic tradition codifying what the state allows and banning everything else.

Yet the more proscriptive European vision may better suit consumer and industry demands for certainty. If you manufacture globally, it is simpler to be bound by the toughest regulatory system in your supply chain. Self-regulation is also a harder sell when it comes to global trade, which involves trusting a long line of unknown participants from far-flung places (talk to parents who buy Chinese-made toys).[546]

However, it is indisputable that precaution is an inherent part of risk regulation, particularly in the area of health and environment.[547] It is thus important to establish to what extent the *SPS Agreement* allows for precautionary measures.

In Article 5.7, the *SPS Agreement* provides for the possibility to take – under certain conditions – provisional SPS measures where scientific evidence is insufficient. Article 5.7 could thus be regarded as a particular formulation of the precautionary principle. It provides:

In cases where relevant scientific evidence is insufficient, a Member may provisionally adopt sanitary or phytosanitary measures on the basis of available pertinent information, including that from the relevant international organizations as well as from sanitary or phytosanitary measures applied by other Members. In such circumstances, Members shall seek to obtain the additional information necessary for a more objective assessment of risk and review the sanitary or phytosanitary measure accordingly within a reasonable period of time.

From this article, four cumulative requirements for provisional measures were identified by the Panel, and confirmed by the Appellate Body, in *Japan – Agricultural Products II*, namely that the measure must:

---

[546] 'Brussels Rules OK. How the European Union is Becoming the World's Chief Regulator', *The Economist*, 20 September 2007.

[547] It is disputed whether precaution should be taken into account in risk assessment or whether it only comes into play in risk management decisions. There is also a difference of opinion as to whether precaution has emerged as a 'principle' in international law, or whether it is a mere 'approach' followed by countries.

- be imposed in respect of a situation where relevant scientific evidence is insufficient;
- be adopted on the basis of available pertinent information;
- not be maintained unless the Member seeks to obtain the additional information necessary for a more objective assessment of risk; and
- be reviewed accordingly within a reasonable period of time.[548]

In *Japan – Apples*, the Panel addressed the *first* requirement. It held that the existence of a situation where 'relevant scientific evidence is insufficient' cannot merely be implied from a finding that the measure is maintained 'without sufficient scientific evidence' under Article 2.2.[549] It held:

> Article 5.7 refers to 'relevant scientific evidence' which implies that the body of material that might be considered includes not only evidence supporting Japan's position, but also evidence supporting other views.[550]

Since a wealth of scientific evidence was submitted in that case by both the parties and the panel experts, the Panel found that it was indisputable that a large amount of relevant scientific evidence was available. It held:

> The current 'situation', where scientific studies as well as practical experience have accumulated for the past 200 years, is clearly not the type of situation Article 5.7 was intended to address. Article 5.7 was obviously designed to be invoked in situations where little, or no, reliable evidence was available on the subject matter at issue.[551]

On appeal, Japan challenged the Panel's finding that Article 5.7 is intended only to address situations where little, or no, reliable evidence was available on the subject matter at issue. According to Japan, such an interpretation would not provide for situations of 'unresolved uncertainty'. According to Japan, Article 5.7 covers not only situations of 'new uncertainty' (where a new risk is identified) but also 'unresolved uncertainty' (where considerable scientific evidence exists on the risk but uncertainty still remains). The Appellate Body, however, upheld the Panel's finding, pointing out that Article 5.7:

> is triggered not by the existence of scientific uncertainty, but rather by the insufficiency of scientific evidence.[552]

Moreover, it noted that the Panel's finding referred to the availability of *reliable* evidence, and thus did not exclude cases:

> where the available evidence is more than minimal in quantity, but has not led to reliable or conclusive results.[553]

In addition, in its discussion of the first element of Article 5.7, the Appellate Body identified a contextual link between the first requirement of Article 5.7

---

[548] See Panel Report, *Japan – Agricultural Products II*, para. 8.54; and Appellate Body Report, *Japan – Agricultural Products II*, para. 89.   [549] Panel Report, *Japan – Apples*, para. 8.215.   [550] *Ibid.*, para. 8.216.
[551] *Ibid.*, para. 8.215.   [552] Appellate Body Report, *Japan – Apples*, para. 184.   [553] *Ibid.*, para. 185.

and the obligation to perform a risk assessment in Article 5.1.[554] Thus, relevant scientific evidence will be insufficient for purposes of Article 5.7 if it:

> does not allow, in qualitative or quantitative terms, the performance of an adequate assessment of risks as required under Article 5.1.[555]

According to the Appellate Body in *Japan – Apples*, the factual findings of the Panel showed that the scientific evidence available *did* permit the performance of a risk assessment under Article 5.1 and the relevant scientific evidence was thus not insufficient within the meaning of Article 5.7. This analysis of the first requirement of Article 5.7 in *Japan – Apples* is groundbreaking. It clarifies the role of Article 5.7, establishing that it is there to address situations where there is a true lack of sufficient scientific evidence regarding the risk at issue, either due to the small amount of evidence on new risks, or due to the fact that accumulated evidence is inconclusive or unreliable. In either case, the insufficiency of the evidence must be such as to make the performance of an adequate risk assessment impossible. Thus Article 5.7 cannot be used to justify measures that are adopted in disregard of reliable scientific evidence.

The first requirement of Article 5.7 of the *SPS Agreement* was again at issue in *EC – Approval and Marketing of Biotech Products*. The European Communities argued that because the safeguard measures imposed by certain of its Member States are by nature provisional, it is by reference to the rules in Article 5.7, not the rules in Article 5.1, that these safeguard measures must be assessed.[556] The Panel examined this argument in the light of the first sentence of Article 5.7. It found:

> The first sentence follows a classic 'if – then' logic: if a certain condition is met (*in casu*, insufficiency of relevant scientific evidence), a particular right is conferred (*in casu*, the right provisionally to adopt an SPS measure based on available pertinent information). Thus, it is clear that Article 5.7 is applicable whenever the relevant condition is met, that is to say, in every case where relevant scientific evidence is insufficient. The provisional adoption of an SPS measure is not a condition for the applicability of Article 5.7. Rather, the provisional adoption of an SPS measure is permitted by the first sentence of Article 5.7.[557]

Therefore, the trigger for applicability of Article 5.7 is the insufficiency of the scientific evidence, not the provisional nature of the measure at issue.[558] In the cases at hand, scientific evidence was not 'insufficient', since enough evidence was available to permit a risk assessment as required under Article 5.1.[559] Thus,

---

[554] The Appellate Body found these contextual elements in the following: first, the concepts of relevance and insufficiency in Article 5.7 imply a relationship between scientific evidence and something else; second, Article 5.1, obliging Members to base their measures on a risk assessment, contains a key discipline under Article 5 and informs the other provisions of Article 5; and third, Article 5.7 itself refers to 'a more objective assessment of risks'. See *ibid.*, para. 179.   [555] *Ibid.*, para. 179.

[556] See Panel Reports, *EC – Approval and Marketing of Biotech Products*, paras. 7.2930–7.2933.

[557] *Ibid.*, para. 7.2939.

[558] Further, the Panel pointed out that the insufficiency of the evidence must be determined by reference to the time the relevant provisional SPS measure was adopted. See *ibid.*, para. 7.3253.

[559] The Panel disagreed with the European Communities that the insufficiency of the scientific evidence must be assessed in relation to the appropriate level of protection of the importing Member, but found that it relates to the sufficiency of the scientific evidence to permit the performance of a risk assessment as defined in Annex A.4. See Panel Reports, *EC – Approval and Marketing of Biotech Products*, para. 7.3239.

this was not the kind of situation where Members are allowed to adopt provisional measures.

There is no guidance in the case law applying the *second* requirement of Article 5.7 of the *SPS Agreement*, namely that provisional measures must be adopted on the basis of available pertinent information. In *Japan – Agricultural Products II*, *Japan – Apples* and *EC – Approval and Marketing of Biotech Products*, the Panels, exercising judicial economy, found it unnecessary to decide on this point.[560] However, in the latter case the Panel did analyse the meaning of the second requirement as part of its examination of the relationship between Articles 5.1 and 5.7 of the *SPS Agreement*.[561] The Panel in *EC – Approval and Marketing of Biotech Products* noted that the reference in the third requirement of Article 5.7 to a *more objective* assessment of risk suggests that provisionally adopted SPS measures must also be based on a risk assessment, namely on a risk assessment that takes into account 'available pertinent information'. Thus, according to the Panel, such a risk assessment:

> would necessarily be different in nature from the kind of risk assessment envisaged in Annex A(4). In other words, any risk assessment which might be required by the first sentence of Article 5.7 would not need to meet the definition of a risk assessment contained in Annex A(4). [562]

The Panel further supported its conclusion by pointing out that if the right conferred by Article 5.7 arises only when scientific evidence is insufficient for an adequate risk assessment under Article 5.1, as defined in Annex A.4, by definition the risk assessment required under the second requirement of Article 5.7 'could not meet the standard set out in Annex A(4)'.[563]

The *third* requirement of Article 5.7 of the *SPS Agreement*, which obliges Members to seek to obtain the additional information necessary for a more objective risk assessment, was clarified by the Appellate Body in *Japan – Agricultural Products II* as follows:

> Neither Article 5.7 nor any other provision of the *SPS Agreement* sets out explicit prerequisites regarding the additional information to be collected or a specific collection procedure. Furthermore, Article 5.7 does not specify what actual results must be achieved; the obligation is to 'seek to obtain' additional information. However, Article 5.7 states that the additional information is to be sought in order to allow the Member to conduct 'a more objective assessment of risk'. Therefore, the information sought must be germane to conducting such a risk assessment, i.e., the evaluation of the likelihood of entry, establishment or spread of, *in casu*, a pest, according to the SPS measures which might be applied. We note that the Panel found that the information collected by Japan does not 'examine the appropriateness' of the SPS measure at issue and does not address the core issue as to whether 'varietal characteristics cause a divergency in quarantine efficacy'. In the light of this finding, we agree with the Panel that Japan did not seek to obtain the additional information necessary for a more objective risk assessment.[564]

---

[560] See Panel Report, *Japan – Agricultural Products II*, para. 8.59; Panel Report, *Japan – Apples*, para. 8.222; and Panel Reports, *EC – Approval and Marketing of Biotech Products*, para. 7.

[561] In particular, in applying the test set out in *EC – Tariff Preferences* to determine if these Articles are in a relationship of exclusion or of exception to each other, the Panel had to examine whether Article 5.7 permits what Article 5.1 does not allow. For this reason, it examined, *inter alia*, the second requirement of Article 5.7.   [562] Panel Reports, *EC – Approval and Marketing of Biotech Products*, para. 7.2992.   [563] *Ibid.*

[564] Appellate Body Report, *Japan – Agricultural Products II*, para. 92.

In *EC – Approval and Marketing of Biotech Products*, the Panel also examined the third requirement of Article 5.7 of the *SPS Agreement*. It noted:

> We understand the phrase 'a more objective assessment of risk', taken as a whole, to refer to a risk assessment which satisfies the definition provided in Annex A(4) – or at least which is closer to satisfying the definition in Annex A(4) than consideration of 'available pertinent information'.[565]

After noting the Appellate Body's finding in *Japan – Apples* that 'relevant scientific evidence' will be 'insufficient' within the meaning of Article 5.7 if the body of available scientific evidence does not allow the performance of a proper risk assessment as required under Article 5.1 and defined in Annex A.4,[566] the Panel in *EC – Approval and Marketing of Biotech Products* pointed out that:

> if a Member may provisionally adopt an SPS measure on the basis of available pertinent information in situations where the scientific evidence is insufficient for an adequate risk assessment, as required by Article 5.1 and as defined in Annex A(4), it makes sense to require, as the second sentence of Article 5.7 does, that that Member seek to obtain 'the additional information necessary' for such a risk assessment. Once a Member has obtained the additional information necessary for a risk assessment which meets the definition of Annex A(4), it will be in a position to comply with its obligation in Article 5.1 to base its SPS measure on a risk assessment which satisfies the definition of Annex A(4).[567]

The *fourth* requirement of Article 5.7 of the *SPS Agreement*, namely to review the provisional SPS measure within a reasonable period of time, is a reflection of the time-limited nature of such measures under the *SPS Agreement*. However, as scientific uncertainty may sometimes persist for extended periods of time, artificially linking the requirement of review to a fixed time-limit was avoided in the *SPS Agreement*. Instead, Article 5.7 refers to a 'reasonable period of time'. Thus, the possibility for a Member to maintain a measure as long as necessary for a scientific assessment to establish the presence or absence of a risk is not compromised. In *Japan – Agricultural Products II*, the Appellate Body interpreted the requirement of review within a reasonable period of time as follows:

> In our view, what constitutes a 'reasonable period of time' has to be established on a case-by-case basis and depends on the specific circumstances of each case, including the difficulty of obtaining the additional information necessary for the review *and* the characteristics of the provisional SPS measure. In the present case, the Panel found that collecting the necessary additional information would be relatively easy. Although the obligation 'to review' the varietal testing requirement has only been in existence since 1 January 1995, we agree with the Panel that Japan has not reviewed its varietal testing requirement 'within a reasonable period of time'.[568]

The maintenance of provisional measures under Article 5.7, therefore, is dependent on the state of scientific knowledge which has a direct impact on the difficulty of obtaining the additional information necessary for review of the measure. This allows some flexibility with respect to the temporary nature of

---

[565] Panel Reports, *EC – Approval and Marketing of Biotech Products*, para. 7.2988.
[566] See Appellate Body Report, *Japan – Apples*, para. 179.
[567] Panel Reports, *EC – Approval and Marketing of Biotech Products*, para. 7.2990.
[568] Appellate Body Report, *Japan – Agricultural Products II*, para. 93.

provisional SPS measures. However, as shown in *Japan – Agricultural Products II*, there are limits to this flexibility.

The question has arisen whether Article 5.7 of the *SPS Agreement* exhausts the relevance of the precautionary principle for purposes of the *SPS Agreement*. In *EC – Hormones*, the European Communities tried to rely on the precautionary principle as a rule of general or customary international law, or at least a general principle of law applicable to the interpretation of the scientific disciplines in the *SPS Agreement*. The Appellate Body expressed doubts as to whether the precautionary principle had developed into a principle of general or customary international law as follows:

> The status of the precautionary principle in international law continues to be the subject of debate among academics, law practitioners, regulators and judges. The precautionary principle is regarded by some as having crystallized into a general principle of customary international *environmental* law. Whether it has been widely accepted by Members as a principle of *general* or *customary international law* appears less than clear. We consider, however, that it is unnecessary, and probably imprudent, for the Appellate Body in this appeal to take a position on this important, but abstract, question. We note that the Panel itself did not make any definitive finding with regard to the status of the precautionary principle in international law and that the precautionary principle, at least outside the field of international environmental law, still awaits authoritative formulation.[569]

According to the Appellate Body, Article 5.7 does not exhaust the relevance of the precautionary principle. This principle is also reflected in the sixth paragraph of the Preamble to the *SPS Agreement* as well as in Article 3.3 of the *SPS Agreement*. Both these provisions deal with the right of Members to set their own level of protection, even if this level is higher than that reflected in international standards. It is doubtful whether these provisions do indeed reflect the precautionary principle, however, since the choice of a particular level of protection, however high, presupposes that a risk has been established by means of a risk assessment. The precautionary principle is relevant only where there is insufficient scientific information for the conduct of a proper risk assessment.

With respect to the relationship between the precautionary principle and the disciplines of the *SPS Agreement*, the Appellate Body held in *EC – Hormones* that the precautionary principle (presumably regardless of its status under international law) cannot override the explicit requirements of Articles 5.1 and 5.2 of the *SPS Agreement*.[570] The effect of this ruling is to limit the applicability of the precautionary principle under the *SPS Agreement* to the situation covered by Article 5.7. The precautionary principle can thus not be relied upon to add flexibility to the scientific disciplines of the *SPS Agreement*. This approach was followed by the Panel in *EC – Approval and Marketing of Biotech Products*. In response to the European Communities' argument that the precautionary principle has 'by now' become a fully fledged principle of international law, the Panel noted:

> It appears to us from the Parties' arguments and other available materials that the legal debate over whether the precautionary principle constitutes a recognized principle of

---

[569] Appellate Body Report, *EC – Hormones*, para. 123.   [570] See *ibid.*, para. 124.

general or customary international law is still ongoing. Notably, there has, to date, been no authoritative decision by an international court or tribunal which recognizes the precautionary principle as a principle of general or customary international law.[571]

While agreeing that the precautionary principle has explicitly or implicitly been incorporated into many international conventions and declarations and has been applied by States at the domestic level, it noted that this is mostly in the field of environmental law. It pointed out that questions remain as to the 'precise definition and content of the precautionary principle'.[572] Moreover, while many authors have expressed the view that the precautionary principle exists as a general principle in international law, at the same time others have expressed scepticism and consider that the precautionary principle has not yet attained this status.[573] Therefore the Panel held:

> Since the legal status of the precautionary principle remains unsettled, like the Appellate Body before us, we consider that prudence suggests that we not attempt to resolve this complex issue, particularly if it is not necessary to do so.[574]

The relationship between Article 5.7 and Article 5.1 of the *SPS Agreement* also deserves examination. It was addressed by the Panel in *EC – Approval and Marketing of Biotech Products*. The European Communities had argued that the safeguard measures imposed by certain of its Member States fell to be assessed under Article 5.7, to the exclusion of Article 5.1, because 'Article 5.7 is not an exception from a general obligation under Article 5.1, but an autonomous right.'[575] As it did when examining the relationship between Article 5.7 and Article 2.2, the Panel applied the test laid down in *EC – Tariff Preferences*.[576] It stated:

> We begin by noting that unlike Article 2.2, Article 5.1 does not explicitly say that its provisions apply 'except as provided for in paragraph 7 of Article 5'. However, Article 5.7 opens with the phrase '[i]n cases where relevant scientific evidence is insufficient'. As mentioned by us before, the Appellate Body opined that ' "relevant scientific evidence" will be "insufficient" within the meaning of Article 5.7 if the body of available scientific evidence does not allow, in quantitative or qualitative terms, the performance of an adequate assessment of risks as required under Article 5.1 and as defined in Annex A to the *SPS Agreement*'. Accordingly, if the right conferred by the first sentence of Article 5.7 only arises in cases where the scientific evidence is insufficient for an adequate risk assessment as defined in Annex A(4), and if, as the Appellate Body suggests, Article 5.1 requires such a risk assessment, then the logical conclusion to be drawn is that the obligation in Article 5.1 to base SPS measures on a risk assessment was not intended to be applicable to measures falling within the scope of Article 5.7. Indeed, '[i]n cases where relevant scientific evidence is insufficient', it is impossible, under the Appellate Body's interpretation of that phrase, for Members to meet the obligation to base their SPS measures on a risk assessment as defined in Annex A(4). We find it unreasonable to assume that Members would accept, even in principle, an obligation with which they cannot comply. In our view, the phrase '[i]n cases where relevant scientific evidence is insufficient' should, therefore, be taken to suggest that the obligation in Article 5.1 is not applicable to measures falling within the scope of Article 5.7.[577]

---

[571] Panel Reports, *EC – Approval and Marketing of Biotech Products*, para. 7.88.   [572] *Ibid.*   [573] See *ibid.*
[574] *Ibid.*, para. 7.89.   [575] *Ibid.*, para. 2.984.   [576] This test is set out above, p. 211, footnote 191.
[577] Panel Reports, *EC – Approval and Marketing of Biotech Products*, para. 7.2995.

Consequently, the relationship between Articles 5.7 and 5.1 can be said to be one of exclusion, rather than exception. As a result, a Member challenging the consistency of an SPS measure with Article 5.1 bears the burden of proof to show that the measure is inconsistent with at least one of the cumulative requirements of Article 5.7.

Questions and Assignments 8.31

How does the *SPS Agreement* provide for situations where scientific evidence is insufficient? What requirements must Members meet in order to be able to take measures in such situations? Does Article 5.7 of the *SPS Agreement* allow Members to take provisional SPS measures in all situations of scientific uncertainty? Can the precautionary principle override the explicit provisions of the *SPS Agreement*? Does Article 5.7 of the *SPS Agreement* exhaust the relevance of the precautionary principle for the *SPS Agreement*? Why can the precautionary principle not be relied on to add flexibility to the scientific disciplines of the *SPS Agreement*?

8.4.5. Other substantive provisions

In addition to the basic substantive provisions discussed in the previous section, the *SPS Agreement* also contains a number of other substantive provisions which deserve to be mentioned. This section briefly examines the substantive provisions of the *SPS Agreement* relating to:

- equivalence;
- adaptation to regional conditions;
- control, inspection and approval procedures; and
- transparency and notification.

8.4.5.1. *Equivalence*

Due to differences between Members with regard to local climatic and geographical conditions, consumer preferences and technical and financial resources, it may sometimes be difficult or even undesirable to harmonise SPS measures. In such cases, the resulting variety of SPS measures can substantially hinder trade. However, the negative impact of divergent measures can be limited by the recognition that it is possible for different measures to achieve the same level of protection (i.e. be equally effective in reducing risk) and thus by allowing imports of products that comply with different, but equally effective, SPS measures. For this reason, Article 4 of the *SPS Agreement* sets out certain obligations for Members with regard to the recognition of equivalence.

Article 4.1 of the *SPS Agreement* obliges Members to accept different SPS measures as equivalent if the exporting Member objectively demonstrates to the importing Member that its measures achieve the latter's appropriate level of protection. For this purpose, the importing Member must, upon request, be given reasonable access to carry out inspections, tests and other relevant procedures. In addition, Article 4.2 obliges Members to enter into consultations, upon request, with the aim of concluding agreements on the recognition of equivalence.

Problems with the implementation of Article 4 of the *SPS Agreement* led the SPS Committee to engage in discussions on equivalence. These discussions resulted in the adoption, in October 2001, of the 'Equivalence Decision'.[578] This decision sets out binding guidelines for any Member requesting the recognition of equivalence and for the importing Member to whom such request is addressed. The decision also formally encourages the three main international standard-setting bodies, namely the Codex Alimentarius Commission, the World Organization for Animal Health and the Secretariat of the International Plant Protection Convention, to elaborate guidelines on equivalence. After the adoption of the Equivalence Decision, the SPS Committee undertook a work programme to clarify and further elaborate certain provisions of that decision. This led to the adoption, in 2004, of a revised version of the Equivalence Decision.[579] In addition, in 2002 recommended procedures for the notification of a determination of the recognition of equivalence were adopted by the SPS Committee.[580] The SPS Committee's Equivalence Decision and the clarifications thereto adopted through the work programme have gone some way towards illuminating and operationalising Article 4 of the *SPS Agreement*. It remains to be seen if this work will bear fruit by promoting the recognition of equivalence.

Questions and Assignments 8.32

When are Members obliged to accept the SPS measures of other Members as equivalent? Compare Article 4 of the *SPS Agreement* with Article 2.7 of the *TBT Agreement*. Find the actual text of the Equivalence Decision and discuss the reasons for its adoption. Can non-compliance with the Equivalence Decision be the basis for a dispute settlement complaint?

8.4.5.2. Adaptation to regional conditions

Although traditionally an importing country applies its SPS measures to an exporting country as a whole, differences in sanitary and phytosanitary

---

[578] See Committee on Sanitary and Phytosanitary Measures, *Decision on the Implementation of Article 4 of the Agreement on the Application of Sanitary and Phytosanitary Measures*, G/SPS/19, dated 24 October 2001.

[579] See Committee on Sanitary and Phytosanitary Measures, *Decision on the Implementation of Article 4 of the Agreement on the Application of Sanitary and Phytosanitary Measures. Revision*, G/SPS/19/Rev.2, dated 23 July 2004.

[580] See Committee on Sanitary and Phytosanitary Measures, *Notification of Determination of the Recognition of Equivalence of Sanitary or Phytosanitary Measures*, G/SPS/7/Rev.2/Add.1, dated 25 July 2002. This notification procedure has only been used once to date, by Panama, to notify its recognition of the equivalence of United States' regulatory systems for meat, poultry and processed products for human or animal consumption (G/SPS/N/EQV/PAN/1, dated 9 August 2007).

conditions *within* exporting countries often exist. In particular, pest and disease prevalence is independent of national boundaries and can differ within a specific country, due to variations in climate, environment, geographic conditions and regulatory systems in place to control or eradicate pests or diseases. The adaptation of SPS measures to the conditions prevailing in the region of origin of the product may thus be highly desirable. Failure to adapt SPS measures to regional conditions is 'unfair' and leads to SPS measures which are excessively trade restrictive.

For this reason, Article 6 of the *SPS Agreement* obliges Members to ensure that their SPS measures are adapted to the SPS *characteristics* of the region of origin and destination of the product. These characteristics must be determined with reference to, *inter alia*:

- the level of pest or disease prevalence;
- the existence of eradication or control programmes; and
- guidelines developed by international organisations.

Article 6.2 of the *SPS Agreement* specifically obliges Members to recognise the concepts of pest-free and disease-free areas and areas of low pest and disease prevalence. It is for the exporting Member to provide the necessary evidence that regions in its territory are pest-free or disease-free or have low pest or disease prevalence. For this purpose, the importing Member is entitled to reasonable access to carry out inspection, testing and other relevant procedures.[581]

The case of an avian influenza outbreak in Chile offers a good example of the use of the provision on adaptation to regional conditions.[582] In May 2002, Chile was confronted with the first-ever outbreak of avian influenza on its territory. In response to this, the European Commission adopted an import ban on Chilean poultry on 23 July 2002. Three months later, when the Chilean government had the disease under control, it requested the Commission to consider the 'regionalisation of the Chilean territory' for the purposes of imports in accordance with Article 6 of the *SPS Agreement*. After the Chilean authorities presented sufficient evidence, the European Commission adopted a decision on 14 October 2002 allowing for the temporary regionalisation of Chile for the purposes of poultry imports and allowed for importation from areas which were designated as disease free.

---

[581] Note that, despite the fact that the IPPC and OIE have both established guidelines for countries seeking to establish or be recognised for pest- or disease-free status, 'exporting countries still suffer from delayed recognition of their pest- or disease-free status by importing countries'. See Committee on Sanitary and Phytosanitary Measures, *Review of the Operation and Implementation of the Agreement on the Application of Sanitary and Phytosanitary Measures*, Report adopted by the SPS Committee on 30 June 2005, G/SPS/36, dated 11 July 2005, paras. 77–80. Informal discussions on how to improve the implementation of Article 6 of the *SPS Agreement* are ongoing in the SPS Committee. To date, no agreement has been reached on whether the SPS Committee should develop clear guidelines in this regard, or whether the responsibility for this issue rests with the OIE and IPPC instead. See *ibid.*, paras. 80–1.

[582] See C. Orozco, 'The SPS Agreement and Crisis Management: The Chile–EU Avian Influenza Experience', in P. Gallagher, P. Low and A. L. Stoler (eds.), *Managing the Challenges of WTO Participation* (Cambridge University Press, 2005), 150–68.

Questions and Assignments 8.33

Must SPS measures be adapted to regional conditions? How is the existence of pest-free or disease-free areas within countries taken into account by the *SPS Agreement*?

8.4.5.3. *Control, inspection and approval procedures*

In order to ensure that their SPS requirements are complied with, countries usually have control, inspection and approval procedures in place. If these procedures are complex, lengthy or costly, they may effectively restrict market access. To avoid this, Article 8 of the *SPS Agreement* obliges Members to comply with the disciplines contained in Annex C as well as other provisions of the *SPS Agreement* in the operation of their control, inspection and approval procedures. The disciplines in Annex C aim to ensure that procedures are not more lengthy and burdensome than is reasonable and necessary and do not discriminate against imports.

In *EC – Approval and Marketing of Biotech Products*, the complainants claimed that the general *de facto* moratorium on the approval of biotech products and the product-specific measures in place in the European Communities were inconsistent with Annex C.1(a), which provides:

> Members shall ensure, with respect to any procedure to check and ensure the fulfilment of sanitary or phytosanitary measures, that:
>
> (a) such procedures are undertaken and completed without undue delay and in no less favourable manner for imported products than for like domestic products;

The Panel found that the European Communities' approval procedures for biotech products were 'procedures to check and ensure the fulfilment of SPS measures' as referred to in Annex C.1. It therefore found Annex C.1(a) applicable to these procedures. Thus, the obligation to ensure that these approval procedures were 'undertaken and completed without undue delay' had to be complied with. The Panel noted that what matters for purposes of this obligation is not the length of the delay, but rather whether there is a legitimate reason or justification for it.[583] The Panel examined and rejected the European Communities' arguments that the delays were justified by the perceived inadequacy of its existing legislation and the prudent and precautionary approach it applied due to the fact that the relevant science was evolving and in a state of flux.[584] The Panel then examined a particular approval procedure to determine if

---

[583] This must be determined on a case-by-case basis. Logically, a Member is only responsible for delays that are attributable to it (thus not for delays caused by the applicant). The Panel considered that Members applying approval procedures must be allowed to take the time reasonably needed to determine with adequate confidence that their SPS requirements are met. See Panel Reports, *EC – Approval and Marketing of Biotech Products*, paras. 7.1496–7.1498.

[584] See *ibid.*, paras. 7.1511–7.1530. While the Panel agreed that limited availability of scientific evidence may mean that deferring decisions might allow for better decisions to be taken, it pointed out that the core obligation of Annex C.1(a) is for Members to come to a substantive decision. This decision need not give 'a

the moratorium had led to undue delay and readily found this to be the case.[585] It therefore found that the general moratorium constituted a violation of the procedural prohibition in Annex C.1(a), first clause, and consequently of Article 8 of the *SPS Agreement*.[586]

Argentina, one of the three complainants in *EC – Approval and Marketing of Biotech Products*, additionally claimed that the product-specific measures were inconsistent with the *second* clause of Annex C.1(a), namely the prohibition on less favourable treatment of imported products. It argued that the European Communities had undertaken approval procedures in a less favourable manner for the biotech products that were the subject of the product-specific measures challenged by Argentina than for 'like' novel non-biotech products. Argentina averred that undue delays had taken place only in the processing of applications concerning biotech products, not in those concerning non-biotech products. According to the Panel, in order to establish a violation of the second clause of Annex C.1(a), it is necessary to establish:

> (i) that imported products have been treated in a 'less favourable manner' than domestic products in respect of the undertaking and completion of approval procedures, and (ii) that the imported products which are alleged to have been treated less favourably are 'like' the domestic products which are alleged to have been treated more favourably.[587]

Turning to the first requirement, the Panel noted that it clearly lays down a national treatment obligation, and it therefore considered it useful to 'look to the jurisprudence on Articles III:1 and III:4 of the GATT 1994 for appropriate interpretative guidance'.[588] Reading Article C.1(a), second clause, in the light of this jurisprudence, it considered that:

> in undertaking and completing its approval procedures, a Member may, in principle, differentiate between products that have been found to be like because this would not, by itself, mean that the relevant approval procedures have been undertaken or completed in less favourable manner for the group of like imported products than for the group of like domestic products. In particular, a mere showing that a Member has undertaken or completed a particular approval procedure in a manner which is unfavourable for a given imported product would not be sufficient to establish a 'less favourable manner' of undertaking or completing approval procedures if the relevant Member's conduct is explained by factors or circumstances unrelated to the foreign origin of the product.[589]

Turning to examine Argentina's arguments, it noted:

Footnote 584 (*cont.*)
    straight yes or no answer to applicants'. Instead, a Member, for example, may reject an application subject to later review, or give a time-limited approval.   [585] See *ibid*., para. 7.1567.
[586] See *ibid*. Similarly, with respect to the product-specific measures challenged in this dispute, the Panel examined the procedures followed with regard to the twenty-seven products specified by the complainants and determined that there had been 'undue delay' in twenty-four of the twenty-seven cases, contrary to Article 8 and Annex C.1(a). The analysis was carried out for a large number of approval procedures (*ibid*., paras. 7.1779–7.2389). The Panel then summarised its conclusions in the form of a table. See *ibid*., para. 7.2391.   [587] *Ibid*., para. 7.2400.
[588] *Ibid*., para. 7.2401. The Panel examined the findings regarding the national treatment obligation in Appellate Body Report, *EC – Asbestos*, para. 100, and Appellate Body Report, *Dominican Republic – Import and Sale of Cigarettes*, para. 96. These findings are discussed above, pp. 383–4 and 387–8.
[589] Panel Reports, *EC – Approval and Marketing of Biotech Products*, para. 7.2408.

> Argentina is not alleging that the manner of processing applications under Regulation 258/97 has differed depending on the origin of the products. In these circumstances, it is not self-evident that the alleged less favourable manner of processing applications concerning the relevant imported biotech products (*e.g.*, imported biotech maize) is explained by the foreign origin of these products rather than, for instance, a perceived difference between biotech products and novel non-biotech products in terms of the required care in their safety assessment, risk for the consumer, etc. Argentina has not adduced argument and evidence sufficient to raise a presumption that the alleged less favourable treatment is explained by the foreign origin of the relevant biotech products.[590]

The Panel thus rejected Argentina's claim of inconsistency with Annex C.1(a), second clause, of the *SPS Agreement*.

Finally, note that according to the Panel in *EC – Approval and Marketing of Biotech Products*, Annex C.1(b) of the *SPS Agreement* contains 'five separate, but related, obligations to be observed by Members in the operation of approval procedures'.[591] These obligations relate to:

> (i) the publication or communication to applicants of the processing period of each procedure;
> (ii) the examination of the completeness of the documentation and the communication to applicants of deficiencies;
> (iii) the transmission of the results of the procedure;
> (iv) the processing of applications which have deficiencies; and
> (v) the provision of information about the stage of a procedure and the provision of an explanation of any delay.[592]

However, the Panel in this case rejected the claims of inconsistency with Article C.1(b) as the complainants had not brought sufficient evidence to show a violation of these obligations.[593]

8.4.5.4. *Transparency and notification*

Lack of transparency with regard to SPS measures may constitute a significant barrier to market access since it increases the cost and difficulty for exporters in determining what requirements their products must comply with on their export markets. This issue is addressed in Article 7 of the *SPS Agreement*, which obliges Members to notify changes in their SPS measures and to provide information on their SPS measures according to Annex B of the *SPS Agreement*. Annex B contains detailed rules ensuring publication of adopted SPS measures and prior notification of proposed SPS measures that differ from international standards, to allow time for comments from other Members. According to the Appellate Body in *Japan – Agricultural Products II*:

> The object and purpose of paragraph 1 of Annex B is 'to enable interested Members to become acquainted with' the sanitary and phytosanitary regulations adopted or maintained by other Members and thus to enhance transparency regarding these measures. In

---

[590] *Ibid.*, para. 7.2411.   [591] *Ibid.*, para. 7.1574.   [592] *Ibid.*

[593] *Ibid.*, paras. 7.1585–7.1602 (with regard to the United States' claim in respect of the general *de facto* moratorium) and paras. 7.2439–7.2472 (with regard to the claims of the United States and Argentina in respect of the product-specific measures).

> our opinion, the scope of application of the publication requirement of paragraph 1 of Annex B should be interpreted in the light of the object and purpose of this provision.[594]

In *Japan – Agricultural Products II*, the Appellate Body upheld the Panel's finding that Japan had violated Annex B.1 and Article 7 of the *SPS Agreement* on the grounds that it was undisputed that Japan's varietal testing requirement was generally applicable and the actual impact of the varietal testing requirement on exporting countries was such that it had 'a character similar to laws, decrees and ordinances', i.e. the instruments with regard to which Annex B.1 explicitly imposes a publication requirement.[595]

In *Japan – Apples*, the United States claimed that Japan had violated Article 7 and Annex B.5 and B.7 of the *SPS Agreement* due to its failure to notify changes that had been made to its fire blight measures since the entry into force of the *SPS Agreement* in 1995. The Panel thus had to determine whether the relevant changes constituted changes which were required to be notified under Article 7 because, *inter alia*, they 'may have a significant effect on trade of other Members' in the context of the chapeau to Annex B.5. The Panel considered:

> that the most important factor in this regard is whether the change affects the conditions of market access for the product concerned, that is, would the exported product (apple fruit from the United States in this case) still be permitted to enter Japan if they complied with the prescription contained in the previous regulations. If this is not the case, then we must consider whether the change could be considered to potentially have a *significant* effect on trade of other Members. In this regard, it would be relevant to consider whether the change has resulted in any increase in production, packaging and sales costs, such as more onerous treatment requirements or more time-consuming administrative formalities.[596]

However, the United States had not presented arguments regarding in what respects the new regulations departed from the previous ones. It had therefore failed to make a *prima facie* case. After examining the changed measures at issue, the Panel came to the following interesting conclusion:

> the MAFF Notification of 1997 may reflect a change in a phytosanitary measure whose content is 'not substantially the same as the content of an international standard'. However, we do not consider that those changes 'may have a significant effect on trade of other Members' and that Japan was required to notify them in accordance with Article 7 and Annex B of the *SPS Agreement*.
>
> . . .
>
> We note that most of the changes in the MAFF Detailed Rules for US Apples do not appear to have resulted in any further change which might have affected the access of US apples to Japan. However, when considering the Detailed Rules that have been translated into English from the Japanese language it is difficult to determine whether a change is strictly editorial or whether a more substantial change has been introduced. We are therefore unable to reach any conclusion as to whether Japan was required to notify the changes in the MAFF Detailed Rules for US Apples introduced in 1997.[597]

---

[594] Appellate Body Report, *Japan – Agricultural Products II*, para. 106.
[595] See *ibid.*, paras. 107–8. Footnote 5 to Annex B.1 refers to 'laws, decrees and ordinances'.
[596] Panel Report, *Japan – Apples*, para. 8.314.   [597] *Ibid.*, paras. 8.324 and 8.326.

In order to promote the implementation of the transparency obligations, the SPS Committee has adopted recommended notification procedures.[598] In addition, it has adopted procedures for the notification of a determination of the recognition of equivalence, of the availability of unofficial translations of notified measures, and of S&D treatment.[599] By 31 August 2007, 8,217 notifications had been circulated.[600] In 2006, 1,157 notifications were submitted, a considerable increase as compared to 2005, when 850 notifications were made.[601] Despite this increase in notifications, however, the failure to notify SPS measures is a frequently raised concern at meetings of the SPS Committee.[602]

Annex B of the *SPS Agreement* also obliges Members to create the necessary infrastructure to carry out their transparency obligations, in the form of the establishment of a National Notification Authority, responsible for the implementation of notification procedures, and an Enquiry Point, responsible for answering all reasonable questions and providing relevant documents upon request.[603]

Finally, note that Article 5.8 of the *SPS Agreement* also contains an important obligation for the promotion of transparency. It obliges Members to provide information, upon request, regarding the reasons for their SPS measures where such measures are not 'based on' international standards or no relevant international standards exist. A Member which has reason to believe that such an SPS measure does or could potentially restrain its exports, may request information under Article 5.8 of the *SPS Agreement* from the Member adopting or maintaining the SPS measure.

---

[598] See Committee on Sanitary and Phytosanitary Measures, *Recommended Procedures for Implementing the Transparency Obligations of the SPS Agreement (Article 7)*, Revision, G/SPS/7/Rev.2, dated 2 April 2002. These recommended procedures are currently again in the process of revision. One proposal in this revision process is to include an encouragement to Members to notify also those SPS measures that are substantially the same as an international standard, if they are expected to have a significant impact on trade. See Committee on Sanitary and Phytosanitary Measures, *Compilation of Proposals regarding the Revision of the 'Recommended Procedures for Implementing the Transparency Obligations of the SPS Agreement (Article 7)'*, Note by the Secretariat, G/SPS/W/215, dated 8 October 2007, para. 7.

[599] See Committee on Sanitary and Phytosanitary Measures, *Notification of Determination of the Recognition of Equivalence of Sanitary or Phytosanitary Measures*, G/SPS/7/Rev.2/Add.1, dated 25 July 2002; Committee on Sanitary and Phytosanitary Measures, *Unofficial Translations*, Note by the Secretariat, G/SPS/GEN/487, dated 23 April 2004; Committee on Sanitary and Phytosanitary Measures, *Procedure to Enhance Transparency of Special and Differential Treatment in favour of Developing Countries, Decision by the Committee of 27 October 2004*, G/SPS/33, dated 2 November 2004 (extended by a decision of the SPS Committee on 1 February 2006).

[600] Committee on Sanitary and Phytosanitary Measures, *Overview regarding the Level of Implementation of the Transparency Provisions of the SPS Agreement*, Note by the Secretariat, G/SPS/GEN/804, dated 11 October 2007, para. 9. This number includes both regular and emergency notifications and corrigenda, addenda and revisions to both. It also includes one notification of equivalence and twelve supplementary notifications of the availability of translations of notified measures.

[601] *Ibid.*, and WTO Secretariat, *Annual Report 2007* (WTO, 2007), 29.

[602] An additional problem with which Members are faced is the formidable task of managing the flow of information by keeping track of all notified SPS measures, National Notification Authorities, Enquiry Points and other SPS-related official documents. To assist Members in this, the *SPS Information Management System* was launched by the WTO on 19 October 2007. It is a comprehensive system that facilitates searching for relevant SPS-related information. It is available at http://spsims.wto.org. See also Committee on Sanitary and Phytosanitary Measures, *Overview regarding the Level of Implementation of the Transparency Provisions of the SPS Agreement*, Note by the Secretariat, G/SPS/GEN/804, dated 11 October 2007, para. 11.

[603] The WTO Secretariat regularly updates and circulates lists of these authorities, under official document numbers G/SPS/NNA/* and G/SPS/ENQ/*. As of 8 October 2007, 131 Members had designated a National Notification Authority and 139 had submitted the contact information of their Enquiry Point. See Committee on Sanitary and Phytosanitary Measures, *Implementation of the Transparency Provisions as of 8 October 2007*, Note by the Secretariat. Revision, G/SPS/GEN/27/Rev.17, dated 9 October 2007.

Questions and Assignments 8.34

What are the key obligations under the *SPS Agreement* with respect to control, inspection and approval procedures? What notification obligations do Members have under the *SPS Agreement*? In your opinion, why are transparency and notification obligations with respect to SPS measures important?

8.4.6. Institutional and procedural provisions of the *SPS Agreement*

In addition to the substantive provisions discussed above, the *SPS Agreement* also contains a number of institutional and procedural provisions. This section deals with the provisions on:

- the SPS Committee; and
- dispute settlement.

8.4.6.1. *SPS Committee*

The Committee on Sanitary and Phytosanitary Measures, commonly referred to as the 'SPS Committee', is established under Article 12.1 of the *SPS Agreement* with a mandate to carry out the functions necessary for the implementation of the *SPS Agreement* and the furtherance of its objectives.[604] The SPS Committee is composed of representatives of all WTO Members and takes decisions by consensus. It meets at least three times a year.[605] In 2007, it held three formal meetings.[606]

The SPS Committee has three main tasks. First, pursuant to Article 12.2 of the *SPS Agreement*, it is a forum for consultations and must encourage and facilitate consultations or negotiations between Members on SPS issues. Often SPS disputes can be resolved through such consultations without resort to dispute settlement. At each meeting of the SPS Committee, Members raise and discuss specific trade concerns with regard to the SPS measures of other Members. By the end of 2006, 245 specific trade concerns had been raised, of which 120 were by developing-country Members and two by least-developed-country Members.[607] Of these, sixty-six trade concerns have been reported resolved and fifteen partially resolved.[608] In 2006 for instance, the SPS Committee discussed 'measures

---

[604] In terms of this mandate, the SPS Committee has, for example, adopted the *Equivalence Decision* referred to above, p. 871. A compilation of the major decisions and documents of the SPS Committee from its inception until the summer of 2006 has been published by the WTO, and is available at www.wto.org/english/tratop_e/sps_e/decisions06_e.pdf, visited on 1 December 2007.

[605] WTO Secretariat, *Annual Report 2007*, 28.

[606] Committee on Sanitary and Phytosanitary Measures, *Report (2007) on the Activities of the Committee on Sanitary and Phytosanitary Measures*, G/L/842, dated 20 November 2007, para. 2.

[607] The WTO Secretariat maintains an annually updated list, summarising specific trade concerns brought to the Committee's attention since 1995. See e.g. Committee on Sanitary and Phytosanitary Measures, *Specific Trade Concerns*, Note by the Secretariat, G/SPS/GEN/204/Rev.7, dated 6 February 2007.

[608] See *ibid.*, 5.

taken in response to avian influenza, bovine spongiform encephalopathy (BSE), foot-and-mouth disease (FMD) and Newcastle disease; and various plant health concerns, including import restrictions on longhorn beetles in wooden handicrafts, tolerance levels for soil content on potato tubers, and import restrictions on Enoki mushrooms'.[609] The SPS Committee thus serves as an important international forum for debate, as illustrated by the following report published in *BRIDGES* in April 2006:

> At a meeting of the WTO Committee on Sanitary and Phytosanitary Measures on 29–30 March [2006], several developing countries expressed concerns that the EU's new draft rules on 'novel foods' – those introduced to the EU market relatively recently – would hinder their ability to export 'small exotic traditional products' based on their rich biodiversity . . . The law, which originally extended to cover genetically modified organisms (GMOs), has been undergoing amendment. The amended regulation is slated to come into force in 2007, but the draft is potentially still subject to modification. At the meeting, Colombia, Ecuador and Peru, along with Paraguay, Costa Rica, Honduras, El Salvador, Chile, Brazil, Mexico, Argentina, Uruguay, Benin and India, contended that biodiversity products which have been available for centuries are safe, and should not be lumped together with GMOs as was the case under the original version of the law. They argued that products based on biological diversity and traditional knowledge should be excluded from the legislation.
>
> The EU responded by saying that the amended regulation was targeted at new technologies and products, not biodiversity products. It added, however, that 'biodiversity products' had in the past included imports which were unsafe for European consumers, leading to a backlash against such products that was not in the interest of exporters. The concerned countries said they would continue to discuss the new draft regulation in Brussels.[610]

Second, pursuant to Article 12.2 of the *SPS Agreement*, the SPS Committee must encourage the use of international standards by Members. In this respect, the SPS Committee is obliged, pursuant to Article 12.3 of the *SPS Agreement*, to maintain close contact with the international standard-setting organisations, and must, pursuant to Article 12.4 of the *SPS Agreement*, develop a procedure for the monitoring of the process of international harmonisation.[611]

Third, pursuant to Article 12.7 of the *SPS Agreement*, the SPS Committee is obliged to undertake a review of the operation and implementation of the *SPS Agreement* three years after its entry into force and as necessary thereafter. Where appropriate, it may propose amendments to the *SPS Agreement* to the Council for Trade in Goods. The first review was completed in 1999 and no amendments were proposed. In the *Decision on Implementation-Related Issues and Concerns*, adopted by the Doha Session of the Ministerial Conference, the SPS Committee is instructed to conduct subsequent reviews at least once every four years.[612] The second review

---

[609] WTO Secretariat, *Annual Report 2007* (WTO, 2007), 29.   [610] *BRIDGES Weekly Trade News Digest*, 5 April 2006.

[611] Such a procedure was developed in 1997 (see G/SPS/11) on a provisional basis, in terms of which the SPS Committee draws up annual reports regarding the use of existing standards, the need for new standards and work on the adoption of such standards. This provisional procedure was revised in October 2004 (see G/SPS/GEN/11/Rev.1) and extended indefinitely in 2006 (see G/SPS/40).

[612] Ministerial Conference, *Doha Decision on Implementation-Related Issues and Concerns*, WT/MIN(01)/17, dated 14 November 2001.

was completed in June 2005, resulting in a report with forty recommendations for further work by the SPS Committee.[613]

8.4.6.2. Dispute settlement

The provisions of Articles XXII and XXIII of the GATT 1994 as elaborated by the DSU apply to consultations and the settlement of disputes under the *SPS Agreement*, except as otherwise provided.[614] The *SPS Agreement* contains only one 'special or additional rule and procedure'.[615] Article 11.2 of the *SPS Agreement* authorises panels to consult experts to help them to deal with the complex issues of scientific fact that arise in SPS disputes.[616] These experts are chosen by the panel in consultation with the parties. Panels may also set up advisory technical expert groups or consult relevant international organisations. They may do so at the request of either party to the dispute or on their own initiative. In all SPS disputes to date, panels have consulted individual experts to help them to understand the complex issues of scientific fact that arose in these disputes.[617]

Questions and Assignments 8.35

What are the main tasks of the SPS Committee? How does the *SPS Agreement* deal with the fact that panels are often faced with complex scientific issues in disputes under the *SPS Agreement*?

8.4.7. Special provisions for developing-country Members

Although the disciplines contained in the *SPS Agreement* apply equally to developed- and developing-country Members, the *SPS Agreement* does reflect a recognition of the special constraints that developing countries face. For this reason, special rules exist to take account of developing-country needs. This section examines the provisions of the *SPS Agreement* concerning:

- technical assistance; and
- special and differential treatment for developing-country Members.[618]

---

[613] Committee on Sanitary and Phytosanitary Measures, *Review of the Operation and Implementation of the Agreement on the Application of Sanitary and Phytosanitary Measures*, G/SPS/36, dated 11 July 2005.
[614] See Article 11 of the *SPS Agreement*.
[615] See Appendix 2 of the DSU. Note that special or additional dispute settlement rules and procedures prevail over the rules and procedures of the DSU to the extent that they differ (see Article 1.2 of the DSU and see above, p. 829).
[616] Note that Article 13 of the DSU generally authorises panels to seek information and technical advice from any individual or body, and to seek information from any source, consult experts or request advisory reports. This provision also applies to disputes under the *SPS Agreement*.
[617] See *EC – Hormones*, *Australia – Salmon*, *Japan – Agricultural Products II* and *Japan – Apples*. For a detailed discussion of the use of experts in WTO dispute settlement, see above, pp. 281–3.
[618] Note that Article 14 of the *SPS Agreement* provided for the possibility for developing- and least-developed-country Members to delay, until 1997 and 2000 respectively, the implementation of their obligations under the *SPS Agreement*.

8.4.7.1. *Technical assistance*

Due to the financial and human resource constraints encountered by developing-country Members, they are often in need of technical assistance in various areas of relevance to the *SPS Agreement*. Technical assistance encompasses not only information to enhance understanding of the disciplines of the *SPS Agreement* and practical training on its operation, but also the provision of soft infrastructure (training of technical and scientific personnel and the development of national regulatory frameworks) and hard infrastructure (laboratories, equipment, veterinary services and the establishment of pest- or disease-free areas).[619]

A case study of the Indonesian shrimp industry offers a good example of the difficulties developing countries face in complying with Western food-safety standards.[620] A 2001 regulation of the European Community required all imported shrimp to be free from natural chloramphenicol, an antibiotic used to exterminate salmonella. Indonesian producers did not have the capacity to switch to the use of synthetic cholarmphenicol as the costs of access to a special instrument capable of distinguishing natural and synthetic chloramphenicol were too high. Abandoning the use of chloramphenicol was not an option either as the EU also requires imported shrimp to be free from salmonella. Thus, producing chloramphenicol-free and salmonella-free shrimp proved almost impossible for Indonesian shrimp producers without technical assistance and trade facilitation from developed countries. The case study therefore makes a strong call to Indonesia's developed trading partners for technical assistance.

Technical assistance is dealt with in Article 9 of the *SPS Agreement*. In terms of Article 9.1, Members 'agree to facilitate' the provision of technical assistance to other Members, especially developing countries, either bilaterally or through international organisations.[621] Such technical assistance may take various forms and may aim, *inter alia*, at helping developing countries to comply with SPS measures on their export markets. Article 9.2 deals with the situation where a Member's SPS measure requires substantial investments from an exporting developing-country Member and obliges the importing Member to 'consider providing' technical assistance to allow the developing country to maintain or increase its market opportunities for the relevant product. These provisions are in the nature of 'best-endeavour' obligations and are thus difficult to enforce.

---

[619] This typology of technical assistance was drawn up by the Secretariat. See Committee on Sanitary and Phytosanitary Measures, *Technical Assistance Typology*, Note by the Secretariat, G/SPS/GEN/206, dated 18 October 2000.

[620] See R. Oktaviani and Erwidodo, 'Indonesia's Shrimp Exports: Meeting the Challenge of Quality Standards', in P. Gallagher, P. Low and A. L. Stoler (eds.), *Managing the Challenges of WTO Participation* (Cambridge University Press, 2005), 253–63.

[621] Currently, the Codex Alimentarius Commission, the World Organization for Animal Health and the International Plant Protection Convention have established trust funds to increase the participation of developing-country Members in their standard-setting activities. Further, they have established or strengthened technical assistance programmes to improve national capacities on SPS matters. In addition, several Members currently provide bilateral technical assistance.

The Doha Ministerial Decision on Implementation-Related Issues and Concerns urges Members to provide technical and financial assistance to least-developed-country Members to help them respond to SPS measures that may affect their trade and to assist them to implement the *SPS Agreement*.[622]

8.4.7.2. *Special and differential treatment*

The *SPS Agreement* provides for special and differential (S&D) treatment of developing-country Members, both by other Members and by the SPS Committee, in order to take account of the difficulties they face in implementing the *SPS Agreement* and complying with SPS measures on their export markets. These provisions aim to give additional flexibility to developing-country Members.

Article 10.1 of the *SPS Agreement* obliges Members to take account of developing-country (and especially least-developed-country) needs in preparing and applying SPS measures. This Article was relied upon for the first time ever by Argentina in *EC – Approval and Marketing of Biotech Products*. Argentina claimed that the general *de facto* moratorium on the approval of biotech products maintained by the European Communities had important implications for Argentina's economic development, due to its strong dependence on agricultural exports and its position as the world's second-largest producer, and leading developing-country producer, of biotech products.[623] It further pointed to its great interest in the integrated European market. Therefore, Argentina argued that the European Communities was obliged, under Article 10.1 of the *SPS Agreement*, to take into account Argentina's special needs in the preparation and application of its SPS measure. Argentina emphasised the mandatory nature of Article 10.1 and claimed that it requires more than mere attention to developing-country problems. Instead, Article 10.1 requires 'positive action', in this case 'preferential market access' for developing-country products or implementation of the Member's obligations in a manner that is 'beneficial, or less detrimental, to the interests of developing country Members'.[624] According to Argentina, the European Communities had failed to comply with this obligation. The Panel interpreted Article 10.1 in keeping with previous case law on S&D treatment provisions in other WTO agreements.[625] It held that the obligation to 'take account' of developing-country needs merely requires Members 'to consider along with other factors before reaching a decision' the needs of developing countries. This obligation, according to the Panel, does not prescribe a particular result to be achieved, and notably does not provide that the importing Member must invariably accord S&D treatment where a measure may lead to a decrease, or slower

---

[622] Ministerial Conference, *Doha Decision on Implementation-Related Issues and Concerns*, WT/MIN(01)/17, dated 14 November 2001, para. 3.6.

[623] Note that, as discussed above, the Panel considered the general moratorium *not* to be an SPS measure but rather the application of an SPS measure. See above, p. 836. The Panel, therefore, could not and did not find Article 10.1 of the *SPS Agreement* applicable to it. However, the Panel regarded Argentina's claim as less than clear and, in light of its status as a developing country, the Panel was willing to consider that Argentina regarded in fact the EC legislation (and not the general moratorium) as the SPS measure at issue. See Panel Reports, *EC – Approval and Marketing of Biotech Products*, para. 7.1611.

[624] *Ibid.*, para. 7.1607.   [625] See above, pp. 554, 802, 830.

increase, in developing-country imports.[626] In fact, it is conceivable, according to the Panel, that the European Communities did take account of Argentina's needs, but at the same time took account of other legitimate interests (such as those of its consumers and environment) and gave priority to the latter.[627] After examining the arguments made by Argentina in this regard, the Panel found that Argentina had not met its burden of proof for purpose of showing a violation of Article 10.1.[628]

Article 10.2 of the *SPS Agreement* encourages, but does not oblige, Members to grant developing countries longer timeframes for compliance with new SPS measures where the appropriate level of protection allows. This extended period was specified as normally not less than six months by the Doha Ministerial Decision on Implementation-Related Issues and Concerns. The Doha Decision further provides that if longer timeframes for compliance are not possible and a Member identifies specific problems with the measure, the importing Member must enter into consultations with a view to reaching a mutually satisfactory solution that continues to achieve its appropriate level of protection.[629]

An obligation to allow a reasonable period between publication of a measure and its entry into force for exporting Members, especially developing countries, to adapt to the new measure, is contained in paragraph 2 of Annex B. An exception is made for urgent circumstances. Once again, the Doha Ministerial Decision on Implementation-Related Issues and Concerns specifies this period as normally not less than six months, but notes that the particular circumstances of the measure and the actions needed for its implementation must be considered.[630]

In order to enable developing-country Members to comply with their obligations under the *SPS Agreement*, Article 10.3 allows the SPS Committee to grant them, upon request, specified, time-limited exemptions from some or all of their obligations, taking account of their financial, trade and development needs. To date, no developing country has requested such an exemption.

Lastly, Article 10.4 of the *SPS Agreement* provides that Members should encourage and facilitate the participation of developing countries in the relevant international organisations. This provision does not contain any binding obligation but is purely hortatory.

---

[626] See Panel Reports, *EC – Approval and Marketing of Biotech Products*, para. 7.1620.
[627] See *ibid.*, para. 7.1621.
[628] The Panel found Argentina's arguments in support of its claim that the EC had failed to take account of its needs as a developing country insufficient. According to the Panel, the absence of reference to developing-country needs in the approval legislation does not demonstrate a failure to take account of those needs in the adoption or application of that legislation. Further, the Panel found the absence of evidence supporting the conclusion that the European Communities took Argentina's needs into account insufficient to indicate that Argentina had met its burden of proof. The Panel noted that Article 10.1 does not require a Member to document how it has complied with this Article. In addition, the Panel stated that Argentina had noted the absence of relevant evidence without specifying what efforts it had made to collect such evidence. While recognising that Argentina may not have ready access to information regarding whether and to what extent the EC took its special needs as a developing country into account, the Panel found no evidence to show that Argentina had approached the EC for such information. The Panel, however, explained that it did not mean to suggest that there is a duty on developing countries to specifically request that their needs as developing countries be considered. See *ibid.*, paras. 7.1623–7.1625.
[629] See Ministerial Conference, *Doha Decision on Implementation-Related Issues and Concerns*, WT/MIN(01)/17, dated 14 November 2001, para. 3.1.   [630] See *ibid.*, para. 3.2.

The Doha *Ministerial Declaration* mandates a review of S&D treatment provisions, in order to make them more precise, effective and operational.[631] The General Council adopted a decision in 2004, referring proposals in this regard to specific WTO bodies and instructing them to complete consideration thereof expeditiously.[632] Five such proposals concerning Articles 9 and 10 of the *SPS Agreement* were referred to the SPS Committee, and formal and informal discussions have taken place. However, the SPS Committee has been unable to develop any clear recommendations for a decision on these proposals.[633]

Questions and Assignments 8.36

What options are available to a developing-country Member which is unable to meet its obligations under the *SPS Agreement*? Can Members be obliged to provide technical assistance to developing countries under the *SPS Agreement*? What forms could technical assistance take? Can a developing country insist on being given a longer time period for compliance with other Members' new SPS measures? Has any change been brought about in this situation by the Doha *Decision on Implementation*?

8.5. SUMMARY

In addressing 'other non-tariff barriers' to trade, there are three WTO agreements that go further than the usual WTO disciplines, by promoting regulatory harmonisation around international standards. These are the *TRIPS Agreement*, the *TBT Agreement* and the *SPS Agreement*. All three of these agreements rely, to varying degrees, on standards set by other (i.e. non-WTO) international bodies as a *basis* for their harmonisation obligations.

The *Agreement on Trade-Related Aspects of Intellectual Property Rights* (*TRIPS Agreement*) reflects the recognition that trade and intellectual property protection are closely connected. The achievements in liberalisation of trade through traditional disciplines on trade barriers can be greatly undermined if the IP rights related to the traded goods or services are not respected in the export

---

[631] Ministerial Conference, *Doha Ministerial Declaration*, WT/MIN(01)/DEC/1, dated 20 November 2001, para. 44.
[632] See General Council, *Doha Work Programme, Decision adopted by the General Council*, WT/L/579, dated 2 August 2004.
[633] See Committee on Sanitary and Phytosanitary Measures, *Report on Proposals for Special and Differential Treatment*, G/SPS/35, dated 7 July 2005, para. 41. The report notes that some Members are concerned that modification of Articles 9 or 10 could change the balance of rights and obligations established by the *SPS Agreement*. However, the Committee agreed to undertake discussions on further work to address the concerns underlying the proposals. The latest report of the Chairman of the SPS Committee to the General Council on the Committee's consideration of the issue of S&D treatment mentions discussions regarding two proposals by Egypt. One aims to revise Article 10.1 to create an obligation of result rather than of conduct. The other addresses improvements to the new transparency mechanism for S&D treatment, discussed above. No agreement was reached on these proposals. See Committee on Sanitary and Phytosanitary Measures, *Special and Differential Treatment. Report by the Chairman to the General Council*, G/SPS/46, dated 29 October 2007.

market. The *TRIPS Agreement* is arguably the most innovative of the WTO agreements. It is the first to establish positive regulatory obligations for Members to ensure a minimum level of protection and enforcement of IP rights in their territories. The need to balance the competing interests of holders of IP rights on the one hand and the public on the other, by ensuring a minimum level of IP protection while allowing for measures to prevent abuse of IP rights, forms the basic rationale underlying the rights and obligations laid down in the *TRIPS Agreement*. The Doha Ministerial Declaration on the *TRIPS Agreement* and Public Health reaffirms the right of WTO Members to use, to the full, the provisions in the *TRIPS Agreement*, providing flexibilities for Members in order to protect public health.

The *TRIPS Agreement* builds upon the standards of IP protection developed in the context of the World Intellectual Property Organization (WIPO) and embodied in its conventions. It does so by incorporating by reference specific provisions of the relevant conventions, namely the *Paris Convention (1967)*, the *Berne Convention (1971)*, the *Rome Convention* and the *IPIC Treaty*. The obligations of the *TRIPS Agreement* must therefore be read together with the relevant WIPO conventions. However, the *TRIPS Agreement* does more than simply incorporate the provisions of these conventions. It supplements and updates the rules of the relevant WIPO conventions, as well as expressly providing new rules in some areas. In addition, and more importantly, it creates an obligation on Members to have a system in place for the enforcement of the protected IP rights and links them to the effective and enforceable dispute settlement system of the WTO.

The *TRIPS Agreement* does *not* cover every form of IP right, but only those expressly mentioned in Sections 1 to 7 of Part II *as well as* those in the incorporated conventions that are the 'subject' of these Sections. These Sections address:

- Copyright and related rights;
- Trademarks;
- Geographical indications;
- Industrial design;
- Patents;
- Layout-designs of integrated circuits; and
- Protection of undisclosed information.

The *TRIPS Agreement* does not apply retroactively to *acts* that occurred before its 'date of application' for a Member. In contrast, the Agreement does create obligations in respect of *subject matter* that existed at the date of application of the Agreement.

The *TRIPS Agreement* obliges Members to 'give effect' to its provisions, but leaves Members 'free to determine the appropriate method' of implementing their obligations under the agreement within their own legal systems and practice. In addition, Members may, but are not obliged to, implement more extensive protection than that laid down in the *TRIPS Agreement*. The *TRIPS Agreement* therefore lays down a *minimum level* of harmonised IP protection.

The non-discrimination obligations of national treatment and MFN treatment apply also in the context of the *TRIPS Agreement*. However, there are some differences in their application compared to the national treatment and MFN treatment obligations of the GATT 1994 and the GATS, in order to take into account the intangible nature of IP rights. These obligations apply only to the IP rights specifically addressed in the *TRIPS Agreement* (including in the incorporated conventions) and apply with respect to 'nationals' as defined in Article 1.3 of the *TRIPS Agreement*, rather than with respect to 'like products' or 'like services or service providers' as is the case in the GATT 1994 and GATS respectively. Both the national treatment and the MFN treatment obligations in the *TRIPS Agreement* are subject to specific exceptions.

The *TRIPS Agreement* does not mandate a particular approach to the exhaustion of IP rights. Members are free to choose their own approach to this matter, provided that they apply their chosen approach in a non-discriminatory manner.

Part II of the *TRIPS Agreement* contains the mandatory minimum standards of IP protection that Members are obliged to ensure in their territories. Sections 1 to 7 of Part II contain standards relating to various categories of intellectual property rights (including copyright, trademarks, geographical indications and patents) and set out, as a minimum, the *subject matter* which is eligible for protection, the scope of the *rights conferred* by the relevant category of intellectual property and permitted *exceptions* to those rights.

The protection of IP depends not only on substantive norms providing minimum standards of protection, but also on procedural rules effectively enforcing them. Part III of the *TRIPS Agreement* therefore contains rules on enforcement of IP rights. This constitutes a significant innovation by which the *TRIPS Agreement* supplements the existing WIPO conventions and strengthens the protection of IP rights. Members are required to ensure that the enforcement procedures specified in Part III are available under their law 'so as to permit effective action' against infringement of IP rights protected in the *TRIPS Agreement*, including by providing expeditious remedies to *prevent* infringements and remedies to *deter* further infringements. In general, Members are required to have civil *judicial* procedures available for the enforcement of any IP right covered by the *TRIPS Agreement*. Criminal procedures and penalties must be provided at least in cases of wilful trademark counterfeiting or copyright piracy on a commercial scale.

Part IV of the *TRIPS Agreement* deals with the procedural aspects of acquisition and maintenance of IP rights. It allows Members to require compliance with procedures and formalities as a condition for the acquisition or maintenance of IP rights (except copyright and undisclosed information), but limits these to what is 'reasonable'.

Part V of the *TRIPS Agreement* sets out rules with regard to transparency and dispute settlement. Members are required to publish not only laws and regulations, but also judicial decisions and administrative rulings of general application pertaining to the subject matter of the *TRIPS Agreement*. If this is impracticable, Members must make them publicly available in a manner that enables governments and IP right holders to become acquainted with them. The WTO dispute settlement rules and procedures, discussed in chapter 3, apply to disputes under the *TRIPS Agreement*. The *TRIPS Agreement* contains one special dispute settlement rule, with regard to the possible causes of action. For a period of five years from the entry into force of the *WTO Agreement*, no non-violation or situation complaints could be brought under the *TRIPS Agreement*. Although this moratorium has expired and no agreement could be reached on whether or not to extend it, it has been agreed that Members would not initiate non-violation or situation complaints under the *TRIPS Agreement* until agreement is reached on the extension of the moratorium.

Members consult on all matters pertaining to the *TRIPS Agreement* in the Council for TRIPS. This Council is composed of all WTO Members. Finally, the *TRIPS Agreement* acknowledges the difficulties developing-country Members may face in implementing their obligations under that Agreement. It thus provided, and to some extent still provides, for transition periods for implementation of the obligations, and provides for technical cooperation.

In modern society, products are often subject to requirements relating to their characteristics and/or the manner in which they are produced. The purpose of these requirements may be the protection of life or health, the protection of the environment, the prevention of deceptive practices or to ensure the quality of products. These requirements may constitute formidable barriers to trade. Moreover, procedures set up to verify whether a product meets certain requirements may obstruct trade.

These barriers to trade are referred to as *technical barriers to trade*. One must distinguish between:

- the general category of technical barriers to trade, for which rules have been set out in the *TBT Agreement*; and
- a special category of technical barriers to trade, namely sanitary and phytosanitary measures, for which rules are provided in the *SPS Agreement*.

The rules of the *TBT Agreement* and the *SPS Agreement* are of great importance to international trade. They go significantly beyond the GATT obligations not to discriminate among or against imported products or not to impose quantitative restrictions, but also lay down certain international disciplines on national regulation regarding products, their characteristics and production. In particular, they encourage harmonisation of regulation around international standards.

The rules of the *TBT Agreement* apply to technical regulations, standards and conformity assessment procedures relating to:

- products (including industrial and agricultural products); and
- *related* processes and production methods (PPMs).

A measure is a 'technical regulation' within the meaning of the *TBT Agreement* if:

- the measure applies to an identifiable product or group of products;

- the measure lays down product characteristics; and
- compliance with the product characteristics laid down in the measure is mandatory.

A standard differs from a technical requirement in that compliance with a standard is not mandatory.

Although the *TBT Agreement* is mainly addressed to central government bodies, it extends its application also to local government bodies and non-governmental bodies by imposing on WTO Members the obligation:

- to take measures in order to ensure compliance with the *TBT Agreement* by local government bodies and non-governmental bodies; and
- to refrain from taking measures that could encourage actions by these other bodies that are inconsistent with the provisions of the *TBT Agreement*.

With regard to the relationship between the *TBT Agreement* and other WTO agreements, note that the applicability of the *SPS Agreement* or the *Agreement on Government Procurement* to a specific measure excludes the applicability of the *TBT Agreement* to that measure. However, the *TBT Agreement* and the GATT 1994 can both be applicable to a specific measure.

The *TBT Agreement* requires that, in respect of TBT measures, Members accord national treatment and MFN treatment to products imported from other Members. The *TBT Agreement* also requires that TBT measures do not create unnecessary obstacles to international trade. To this end, technical regulations, for example, shall not be more trade-restrictive than necessary to fulfil legitimate objectives, such as the protection of human life or health or the protection of the environment. The *TBT Agreement* requires that Members base their technical regulations on international standards, except when these standards would be an ineffective or inappropriate means of fulfilling the legitimate objectives pursued. Furthermore, the *TBT Agreement* requires WTO Members to consider accepting, as equivalent, the technical regulations of other Members if they are satisfied that the foreign technical regulations *adequately* fulfil the legitimate objectives pursued by their own technical regulations. The *TBT Agreement* subjects Members to a number of detailed transparency and notification obligations.

Members consult, regarding any matters pertaining to the operation or objectives of the *TBT Agreement*, in the TBT Committee which is composed of all WTO Members and meets several times a year. The WTO dispute settlement rules and procedures, discussed in chapter 3, apply to disputes concerning the *TBT Agreement*. The *TBT Agreement* contains a few special or additional rules and procedures, primarily with regard to the possibility for panels to consult technical experts. Finally, in recognition of the difficulties developing-country Members may face in implementing the obligations under the *TBT Agreement*, the *TBT Agreement* provides for technical assistance and some S&D treatment for developing-country Members.

The *SPS Agreement* applies to SPS measures that may affect international trade. Whether a measure is an 'SPS measure' depends on its purpose or aim. In broad terms, an 'SPS measure' is a measure that:

- aims at the protection of human or animal life or health from food-borne risks; or
- aims at the protection of human, animal or plant life or health from risks from pests or diseases.

The adoption and implementation of SPS measures is sometimes in the hands of bodies other than central government, such as regulatory agencies, regional bodies and sub-federal governments. The *SPS Agreement* takes this into account by providing that Members are fully responsible for the implementation of the Agreement and must enact and implement positive measures to ensure the observance of its rules by other than central government bodies.

With regard to the relationship between the *SPS Agreement* and other WTO agreements, note that when a measure is an 'SPS measure' as defined in Annex A of the *SPS Agreement*, the *SPS Agreement* applies to the exclusion of the *TBT Agreement*. However, no relationship of mutual exclusivity exists between the *SPS Agreement* and the GATT 1994.

The *SPS Agreement* explicitly acknowledges the sovereign right of WTO Members to take SPS measures. At the same time, however, the *SPS Agreement* subjects Members to a number of obligations regarding their SPS measures. These obligations include:

- the obligation to take or maintain only SPS measures *necessary* to protect human, animal or plant life or health;
- the obligation to take or maintain only SPS measures 'based on' scientific principles and on sufficient scientific evidence;
- the obligation not to adopt or maintain SPS measures that arbitrarily or unjustifiably discriminate or constitute a disguised restriction on trade; and
- the obligation to base SPS measures, on international standards, except if there is scientific justification for deviation from these standards.

The substantive obligations provided for in the *SPS Agreement* also include obligations with respect to risk analysis, i.e. risk assessment and risk management. With regard to risk assessment, the *SPS Agreement* primarily requires that SPS measures are 'based on' the relevant type of risk assessment, i.e. a scientific assessment of the risk to human, animal or plant life or health. With regard to risk management, the *SPS Agreement* primarily requires that Members must:

- avoid arbitrary or unjustifiable distinctions in the levels of protection deemed appropriate in different situations, if these distinctions lead to discrimination or disguised restrictions on trade; and
- ensure that SPS measures are not more trade-restrictive than required to achieve their appropriate level of protection.

Where scientific evidence is insufficient for the conduct of a risk assessment, the *SPS Agreement* allows Members to take – under certain conditions – provisional

SPS measures which are not based on a risk assessment. The *SPS Agreement* thus incorporates the precautionary principle to some extent.

The *SPS Agreement* also provides for substantive provisions relating to the recognition of equivalence of SPS measures of other Members; relating to the obligation of Members to adapt their SPS measures to regional conditions; relating to control, inspection and approval procedures; and relating to transparency and notification obligations regarding SPS measures.

Members consult regarding any matters pertaining to the operation or objectives of the *SPS Agreement* in the SPS Committee. This Committee is composed of all WTO Members and meets several times a year. The WTO dispute settlement rules and procedures, discussed in chapter 3, apply to disputes concerning the *SPS Agreement*. The *SPS Agreement* contains one special or additional dispute settlement rule, providing panels with the possibility to consult scientific experts. Finally, the *SPS Agreement* acknowledges the difficulties developing-country Members may face in implementing the obligations under the *SPS Agreement* and thus provides for technical assistance and some S&D treatment for developing-country Members.

8.6. EXERCISE: TUTTI FRUTTI'S EXPORTS TO UTOPIA

Utopia, a wealthy province of Richland, a WTO Member, has enacted a provincial regulation, requiring that all fruit marketed and sold in Utopia be organically grown and packaged in biodegradable materials made from natural fibres. According to Utopia, all pesticides and fertilisers used in conventional fruit farming have a harmful effect on human health in the long term. In addition, Utopia claims that non-biodegradable packaging is a major source of pollution and constitutes a serious environmental problem in its territory.

Newland, a neighbouring developing-country Member whose main export is fruit, is hard hit by this regulation. Its main export market is Richland, and particularly Utopia, whose health-conscious inhabitants eat a lot of fruit. Due to the high incidence of fruit flies and the inhospitable soil in Newland, its fruit farmers use chemical pesticides and fertilisers in their orchards, but ensure that the residues of these chemicals do not exceed the maximum residue limits set by the Codex Alimentarius Commission. These farmers lack both the technical know-how and the financial resources to switch to organic farming. In addition, while Newland exporters use recyclable packaging for their fruit, biodegradable packaging is too costly for them.

Tutti Frutti, Newland's largest fruit exporter, approaches the Newland government to request that this matter be brought before the WTO dispute settlement system. It claims that the Utopian regulation should have been notified under both the *TBT Agreement* and the *SPS Agreement* and a reasonable adaptation period should have been provided. It also argues that the prohibition on all fertilisers and pesticides exceeds the Codex Alimentarius Commission standards, which instead set maximum residue levels (MRLs) for particular harmful substances in pesticides and fertilisers. It further points out that there is no scientific evidence that pesticide or fertiliser residues below the Codex MRLs have harmful effects on health. The long-term effects of small quantities of these chemicals have never been established. Further, it notes that vegetable imports into Utopia are not required to be organically grown. With regard to Utopia's packaging requirements, Tutti Frutti claims that they are more trade-restrictive than necessary, as simply requiring recyclable packaging would eliminate the risk to the environment.

In order to try to resolve this matter without having to resort to WTO dispute settlement, Newland would like to raise trade concerns with regard to these issues at the next meetings of the TBT Committee and the SPS Committee. It would like to raise and discuss all relevant points of WTO law relating to this emerging dispute. You are the legal advisor to Newland's representative at the TBT Committee and the SPS Committee. You have been asked to brief this representative in preparation of the meetings.

Epilogue

This brings us to the end of our voyage through the law and policy of the World Trade Organization. The first edition of this book included a brief chapter on that 'Challenges for the future'. Due to constraints on the length of this book, that chapter has been dropped in this edition. It would be wrong to conclude from this, however, that the challenges facing the WTO have become less daunting. The opposite is true. First of all there are of course the issues on the agenda of the Doha Development Round, and in particular:

- the liberalisation of trade in agricultural products, in the form of increased market access for agricultural products and the reduction or elimination of agricultural export subsidies and domestic support measures;
- market access for non-agricultural products, including the further reduction or, where appropriate and possible, the elimination of customs duties and tariff escalation as well as non-tariff barriers to trade;
- the further liberalisation of trade in services, including the supply of services through the presence of natural persons (mode 4);
- the clarification and improvement of the WTO rules on dumping and subsidised trade;
- the clarification and improvement of the WTO rules and procedures applying to regional trade agreements;
- the relationship between trade and the protection of the environment, and in particular the relationship between existing WTO rules and specific trade obligations set out in multilateral environmental agreements;
- the extension of protection of intellectual property rights, and in particular the protection of geographical indications; and
- the further integration of developing countries into the WTO system through the improvement of the special and differential treatment provided for developing-country Members in WTO law.

While currently not debated within the WTO, the issue whether the scope of WTO law should be extended in the fields of investment, competition policy, government procurement and the protection of minimum labour standards has arisen in the past and is likely to resurface.

Readers interested in an inspired but realistic perspective on these and other challenges are recommended to read the 2004 Sutherland Report on *The Future of the WTO,* to which I have frequently referred in this book. In addition, readers may want to refer to the academic debate triggered by this report as reflected, for example, in the *Journal of International Economic Law,* the *Journal of World Trade* and the *World Trade Review.*

Index

Countries involved in WTO disputes should be traced through the Table of Cases